D1130545

FATAL DISCORD

ALSO BY MICHAEL MASSING

The Fix

Now They Tell Us: The American Press and Iraq

FATAL DISCORD

ERASMUS, LUTHER,
AND THE
FIGHT FOR THE WESTERN MIND

MICHAEL MASSING

HARPER

An Imprint of HarperCollins*Publishers*

FATAL DISCORD. Copyright © 2018 by Michael Massing. All rights reserved. Printed in the United States of America. No part of this book may be used or reproduced in any manner whatsoever without written permission except in the case of brief quotations embodied in critical articles and reviews. For information, address HarperCollins Publishers, 195 Broadway, New York, NY 10007.

Insert image credits. Page 1: Heritage Image Partnership Ltd/Alamy Stock Photo; page 2 (top): RMN-Grand Palais/Art Resource, NY; page 2 (bottom): akg-images/ Pictures From History; page 3 (top): Artexplorer/Alamy Stock Photo; page 3 (bottom): Ian Dagnal l/Alamy Stock Photo; page 4 (top): Historical Images Archive/ Alamy Stock Photo; page 4 (bottom): akg-images/Fototeca Gilardi; page 5 (top) and page 14: akg-images; page 5 (bottom): Bildarchiv Monheim GmBH/Alamy Stock Photo; page 6 (top): Peter Horree/Alamy Stock Photo; page 6 (bottom): Eye Ubiquitous/Alamy Stock Photo; page 7 (top): The British Museum; page 7 (bottom): Ivy Close Images/Alamy Stock Photo; page 8 (top): akg-images/ euroluftbild.de; page 8 (bottom): Ian D Dagnall/Alamy Stock Photo; page 9 (top): FineArt/Alamy Stock Photo; page 9 (bottom): PRISMA ARCHIVO/Alamy Stock Photo; page 10 (top): classicpaintings/Alamy Stock Photo; page 10 (bottom): Reiner Elsen/Alamy Stock Photo; page 11 (bottom): World History Archive/Alamy Stock Photo; page 12 (top): James L. Amos/Corbis Historical/Getty; page 12 (bottom): Prisma by Dukas Presseagentur GmbH/Alamy Stock Photo; page 13 (top): Novarc Images/Alamy Stock Photo; page 13 (bottom): *The Departure of Erasmus from Basel*, illustration from *The History of Protestantism* by James Aitken Wylie (1808–1890), pub. 1878 (engraving), English School, (19th century)/The Stapleton Collection/ Bridgeman Images; page 15: Classic Image/Alamy Stock Photo.

HarperCollins books may be purchased for educational, business, or sales promotional use. For information, please e-mail the Special Markets Department at SPsales@harpercollins.com.

FIRST EDITION

Designed by William Ruoto

Library of Congress Cataloging-in-Publication Data has been applied for.

ISBN 978-0-06-051760-1

18 19 20 21 22   DIX/LSC   10 9 8 7 6 5 4 3 2 1

To my mother

and

To Ann, Larry, and Judith

for their invaluable help

CONTENTS

PART IV: AGITATION

PART V: RUPTURE

INTRODUCTION

Toward the end of the year 1516, Erasmus of Rotterdam, then living in the Low Countries, received a letter from George Spalatin, the secretary to Frederick the Wise of Saxony. After expressing his esteem for the Dutch humanist, Spalatin explained that he was writing on behalf of an Augustinian priest, whom he did not name. The priest had read Erasmus's recently published annotations on the New Testament—notes on the Latin translation known as the Vulgate—and had two concerns. One related to original sin. Erasmus, the priest believed, had misunderstood Paul's position on this doctrine and urged him to read Augustine's commentary on it, which, he felt, would set him right. He also objected to Erasmus's understanding of "works." Erasmus seemed to feel that Paul, in rejecting the performance of works, was referring only to rites and ceremonies when in fact he meant works of all kinds, including the keeping of the Ten Commandments. The priest wanted to make sure that Erasmus understood this, since, given his great prestige, he might otherwise lead people astray.

The priest was Martin Luther. Thirty-three years old at the time, he was a little-known friar and Bible professor in the eastern German town of Wittenberg. He had just completed a long series of lectures on Paul's Epistle to the Romans, delivered in a weather-beaten hall to a small group of clerics and students. Erasmus, who was about fifty, was Europe's most celebrated scholar. Kings, dukes, and cardinals all vied to bring him to their lands. He was an associate of Pope Leo X, a friend of Henry VIII of England, and a councilor to Charles V, the Holy Roman Emperor. He was also Europe's bestselling author. Thanks to his mastery of the new medium of print, Erasmus was the first person in Europe able to live off the income from his writing, and at the Frankfurt book fair every spring and autumn, his books regularly sold out.

Several times a week, Erasmus received a bundle of letters from around Europe, providing news, offering praise, seeking his opinions. He was unable to respond to them all, and he paid little attention to the complaints of the anonymous priest. The following October, however, Luther would post his Ninety-Five Theses in Wittenberg, challenging the Roman Church's practice of selling indulgences. These certificates, by remitting the penalties imposed on sinners for their transgressions, reduced the amount of time they had to spend in purgatory before being admitted to heaven. To Luther, they seemed to turn repentance into a form of barter, and he proposed his theses as an invitation to debate. No one accepted it, but within weeks his protest appeared in print, and as copies circulated around Germany, he became a household name.

Initially, the Church ignored the impertinent friar, assuming the matter would blow over, but Luther—tenacious, blunt, fearless—spoke out ever more forcefully against what he saw as Rome's laxity, venality, and exploitation of ordinary Christians. And many of those Christians— burdened by tithes and fees and the sanctions imposed for not paying them—rallied to his cause. As opposition surged, Rome finally moved to silence Luther, but the harder it tried to suppress him, the more outspoken he became, until finally he was questioning the authority of the pope himself. No ecclesiast, however lofty, he declared, could tell a Christian how to behave or think. By the summer of 1520, the threat posed by Luther had become so great that Pope Leo X signed a bull threatening to excommunicate him if he did not appear in Rome and recant. Luther responded by burning the bull. Demanding an independent hearing, he finally got one in April 1521, when he was summoned before the Imperial Diet of the German nation, meeting in Worms. Standing before the emperor and a phalanx of imperial and ecclesiastical officials, Luther refused to retract what he had written, declaring that he could not act against his conscience.

This moment, when a lone individual appealing to his conscience stood fast before the highest authorities in the land, is considered by many a milestone in Western history—the moment when the medieval gave way to the modern. Luther's defiance would inspire a broad revolt against

Rome—the Protestant Reformation—that would break the thousand-year hold of the Church on the spiritual life of the West.

It would also push Erasmus off the historical stage. In just a few years, the Dutchman would go from being Europe's most renowned thinker to a largely ignored figure, scorned by both Catholics (for being too critical of the Church) and Protestants (for being too timid). After his death, in 1536, Erasmus was all but forgotten as Europe experienced a century of religious strife. Even today, his works are only sporadically read, and his ideas receive scant attention. They deserve to be revived. For Erasmus was an architect of the Northern Renaissance. While Leonardo, Michelangelo, and Raphael were revolutionizing Western art and culture, Erasmus was helping to transform the continent's intellectual and religious life. In some ways, he represents the path not taken. At a time of rising nationalism, he was a committed internationalist. In an age of persecution and incessant war, he urged tolerance and promoted peace, and he argued that religion should be more about conduct than doctrine. Erasmus was, in short, the leading exponent of Christian humanism, extolling human dignity, modest piety, and brotherhood in a world gripped by zealotry, rancor, and sectarianism.

In his books and essays, Erasmus laid out a program to reform and revitalize European culture. His *Enchiridion Militis Christiani* ("The Handbook of the Christian Soldier") became a manual for Europe's growing middle class as it sought a form of inner spirituality more fulfilling than the performance of formal acts like going to confession or visiting a shrine. The *Praise of Folly*, with its barbed put-downs of pedantic theologians and self-seeking princes, helped puncture the pretensions and excesses of Europe's ruling elite. The *Adages*, a thick compendium of aphorisms culled from ancient Greece and Rome and explained in lively essays, did more than any other work to revive interest in classical culture. Erasmus's treatises on education helped shape Western pedagogy for centuries, and his *Colloquies*—colorful dialogues and sketches based on everyday life—offered sharp observations on the customs and conventions of sixteenth-century Europe.

Above all, Erasmus revolutionized the study of the Bible. At the time, the Vulgate was the source of all teaching and doctrine in the Western Church, its language consecrated by centuries of tradition and decree. Prepared during the waning days of imperial Rome, it was a Latin translation from the original Greek (in the case of the New Testament) and Hebrew (in the case of the Old). And its accuracy was coming under challenge. Many of its words and phrases seemed to diverge from their original meaning, and misspellings and other errors had been introduced by nodding scribes. Intent on correcting it, Erasmus spent years struggling to learn Greek so that he could read old manuscripts of the New Testament in its original tongue. In 1516, after much toil, he came out with his revised edition, which included a Greek text, an emended Latin translation, and annotations explaining the reasoning behind his changes.

Erasmus's new New Testament, offering scholars and exegetes a comprehensive apparatus for reading the Bible anew and arriving at their own interpretations, set off an explosion across Europe. It was to the study of Scripture what Copernicus's *On the Revolutions of the Heavenly Spheres* (first printed in 1543) was to the study of astronomy. Just as the Polish astronomer shattered the idea that the earth was the center of the heavens, so did the Dutch humanist seek to bring Scripture down from heaven to earth. From that point on, the Bible would be seen by many as a document that, though divinely inspired, had been fashioned by human hands and which could be deconstructed and edited in the same manner as a text by Livy or Seneca.

It was this work that prompted Luther to approach Erasmus. At that point, Luther was a great admirer of the Dutchman and eagerly followed his writings. And he shared Erasmus's diagnosis of what ailed the Catholic Church. Later, in fact, Erasmus's conservative critics would accuse him of having "laid the egg that Luther hatched." At an early point, however, Luther went his own way. Where Erasmus was skeptical, temperate, and undogmatic, Luther was ardent, volatile, and uncompromising. At the age of twenty-one, he had entered a monastery in the hope of overcoming a deep spiritual crisis. Convinced of his utter worthlessness before God, he intently searched the Bible for a new way to him. He found it in Paul's epistles. Luther's famous "discovery" of the doctrine of justification by faith alone while reading the Epistle to the Romans would become the foundation of his challenge to Rome and the core of the new Protestant faith.

Erasmus, who had similarly entered a monastery at a young age but left it to see the world, was interested less in faith than in works; a Christian, he held, should in all things seek to imitate Christ. While Erasmus stressed the capabilities of man, Luther exalted the power of God. Where Erasmus sought to reform the Church from within, Luther proposed a more thoroughgoing transformation. Eventually, the widening differences between the two men flared into a bitter competition, with each seeking through tracts and pamphlets to win over Europe to his side. Their rivalry represented the clash of not just two intellectuals but also of two worldviews—the humanist, embracing the common bonds of humanity and the diversity of cultures and viewpoints within it, and the evangelical, stressing God's majesty and Christ's divinity and insisting that all recognize those truths as supreme and incontestable.

These two schools remain with us today. The conflict between Erasmus and Luther marks a key passage in Western thinking—the point at which these two fundamental and often colliding traditions took hold. The struggle between them continues to shape Western society. On one side are Erasmus-like humanists: seekers of concord, promoters of pluralism, believers in the Bible as a fallible document open to multiple interpretations, and advocates of the view that man is a fully autonomous moral agent. On the other are Lutheran-style evangelicals who seek a direct relationship with God, embrace faith in Christ as the only path to salvation, accept the Bible as the Word of God, and consider the Almighty the prime mover of events.

The continuing influence of these two outlooks can be seen in the divergent paths taken by Europe and America. Since World War II, Europe has embraced a creed founded on many of the same principles as Erasmian humanism. The European Union embodies many of Erasmus's core ideals. Luther's ideas, meanwhile, have found their most fertile ground in America. The one-fourth or so of American adults who are evangelical in orientation seem in many ways Luther's offspring.

Traditionally, John Calvin has been considered the Reformation figure who has most shaped American life. His teachings about predestination, grace, salvation, and the elect are widely seen as having strongly influenced early American society, leaving a permanent imprint on the country's spiritual, cultural, and political life. This perspective owes much to Max Weber. In *The Protestant Ethic and the Spirit of Capitalism*, he argued that the Calvinist preoccupation with salvation led early Americans—anxious for signs that they had been saved—to embrace such godly virtues as industriousness, asceticism, and thrift. Becoming engrained in the American way of life, such traits helped nurture the capitalist spirit.

Weber's thesis has given rise to a massive literature both pro and con. Whatever its merits, *The Protestant Ethic* has had the effect of highlighting Calvin's influence in American life. Yet Calvin got many of his ideas from Luther. It was Luther who developed the doctrine of predestination that was so central to Calvinism. It was Luther who developed the revolutionary idea that Christian authority rests not with popes, councils, or tradition but with the Bible. And it was Luther who insisted that all Christians should have the right to read that document on their own. Luther further held that once a Christian has determined the Word of God, he must tirelessly proclaim and promote it, even in the face of scorn, mockery, and persecution.

Later in life, Luther backed away from some of these principles. Enraged by the peasants' uprising of 1525 and their invoking of his writings, he increasingly looked to the princes to ensure both the survival of the Reformation and his own physical safety, and he jettisoned some of the more populist elements of his program. More generally, Luther rejected actions aimed at effecting broad social or political change based on one's religious beliefs. By contrast, Calvin in Geneva sought to remake society in line with his theology—to build a heavenly city on earth. His followers in subsequent generations similarly sought to transform the world according to biblical principles. This was true both in Europe and in America, where the New England Puritans sought to create a biblically based community. Luther eschewed all such activism.

In the Calvinist stress on the community, however, the place of the individual got lost. And it is here that Luther's influence in America seems so fundamental. His insistence on the right of lay Christians to read Scripture on their own; on the critical importance of the individual's faith in Christ; on the need to stand alone and accountable before God; on remaining true to one's spiritual convictions in the face of formidable obstacles—all seem aspects of an evangelical perspective. In their commitment to a highly individualized faith based in Christ and Scripture, America's evangelicals seem—however unconsciously—to be following the path blazed by Luther five centuries ago. Examining his life can help shed light on the origins of modern-day evangelicalism. And studying Erasmus's life can help unlock the origins of modern-day humanism.

The Protestant Reformation is one of history's most well-chronicled events and Luther one of its most written-about figures. Most biographies of Luther, however, focus narrowly on his life and character, his circle of associates, and events in Wittenberg. The broader European setting of Luther's revolt, and how his ideas roused a continent, are often neglected. Most biographies of Erasmus, meanwhile, while offering much useful information and analysis, are aimed at specialized audiences. The most readable of them, by Stefan Zweig, appeared more than eighty years ago. Furthermore, while books about Luther and Erasmus invariably touch on their famous rivalry, few place it at their center. Concentrating on that rivalry offers an opportunity to explore the complex relationship between two great historical movements, the Renaissance and the Reformation.

In what follows, I describe the parallel lives of Erasmus and Luther, their gradual entanglement, and their eventual estrangement. A journalist by trade, I have approached the subject much as I would a newspaper or magazine assignment. Rather than visit a far-off land, I have traveled to a distant century. As with many assignments, the cultural setting often seemed foreign, but I felt I was able to bring a fresh eye to well-trodden terrain (mindful all along of my debt to the many historians who have gone before). Journalism, it is said, is the first draft of history; in writing about the Reformation, I am preparing perhaps the five-hundredth. Throughout, though, I have often felt the same surge of excitement I have had while reporting a good story.

I have tried to convey that excitement. One of the most striking things about the sixteenth century is the passion with which people debated ideas, and this book is as much about the ideas as the people. In researching the lives of Erasmus and Luther, I have undertaken my own journey back to the sources, and I offer sketches of some of the remarkable figures I encountered along the way, including the Apostle Paul, the inspirer of Luther; Augustine, the most influential Catholic thinker; Jerome, the temperamental translator of the Bible; Thomas Aquinas, the indefatigable Scholastic systematizer; Petrarch, the first great humanist; Lorenzo Valla, the disruptive Renaissance iconoclast; Johannes Reuchlin, the embattled champion of Hebraic studies; Erasmus's close friend Thomas More; Luther's collaborator Philipp Melanchthon; the runaway nun Katharina von Bora, whom Luther married; the publishers Aldus Manutius and Johann Froben; the radical reformers Andreas von Karlstadt and Thomas Müntzer; Jan Hus, Luther's Czech forerunner; Huldrych Zwingli, the father of the Swiss Reformation; William Tyndale, the translator of the Bible into English; and John Calvin.

I have also tried to describe what it was like to live in some of Europe's leading cities and towns, from London and Paris to Basel and Rome. The Eternal City's transformation in this period from the shrunken, malodorous wasteland it had become during the Middle Ages into the cultural and historical showcase it is today is one of the subthemes of my book. In my conclusion, I try to trace the modern-day echoes of the rivalry between Erasmus and Luther—between humanism and evangelicalism—and show how that competition continues to shape our world.

PART I

Early Struggles

1

THE NEW EUROPE

For religious tourists wanting to see the cities associated with the rise of the Reformation, the itinerary is well established: Prague, the home of Jan Hus; Zurich and Geneva, the citadels of Huldrych Zwingli and John Calvin; Erfurt, where Luther studied and became a friar; Worms, the site of his stand at the Imperial Diet; and, of course, Wittenberg, the reformer's longtime center of operations. Yet there is another city that, though absent from such tours, played a key part in incubating the ideas that helped set off the great religious upheaval that transformed Europe: Deventer, in the eastern Netherlands.

Today, Deventer seems indistinguishable from thousands of other orderly, prosperous towns that dot the map of Western Europe. In its well-preserved center, pedestrians stroll along cobblestoned streets, peering at shop windows that display elegant prints, fine handicrafts, and high-end housewares. The Brink, the town's long, narrow central plaza, is bordered by cafés and restaurants that in warm months fill with tourists and locals who wash down sandwiches with the local pilsner. Deventer's public squares are graced with tasteful modern sculptures, and every August it holds an open-air book fair that is one of the largest in Europe. Of the four churches that were operating on the eve of the Reformation, one now serves primarily as an arts center and another as an events space—by-products of the ongoing de-Christianization of Europe. The larger of the remaining churches—the vast Grote of Lebuinuskerk—was once affiliated with the Catholic Church and called St. Lebwin's. In 1580, however, it was taken over by Calvinists, who stripped the interior of all altars and statues and whitewashed its walls, and it remains a Protestant sanctuary. The church's lone tower houses a seventeenth-century carillon that serenades the town with everything from Bach to "Havah Nagila."

Across from this church stands a trim three-story building. In the late Middle Ages, the site was home to a renowned Latin school, which, run by St. Lebwin's, attracted students from hundreds of miles around. Among its prominent alumni was Geert Groote, a pious deacon and itinerant preacher who in the late fourteenth century founded the *Devotio Moderna* ("Modern Devotion"), a lay movement that stressed the inner spirit over formal rituals. Another graduate, Thomas à Kempis, summed up Groote's ideas in *The Imitation of Christ*, a manual of piety that urged Christians to withdraw from the world and seek a direct relationship with God. From the moment it appeared, in the early fifteenth century, the *Imitation* found a huge audience. (It remains popular, ranking as the most widely read devotional work after the Bible.) From its base in Deventer and the IJssel valley, the *Devotio Moderna* spread throughout the Netherlands and into western Germany, becoming the most important reform movement in northern Europe.

The spirit of the *Devotio Moderna* pervaded St. Lebwin's. And it left a deep mark on the school's most famous alumnus—Erasmus. Though he would later condemn the school's instruction as barbarous, it was here that, in addition to learning the rudiments of Latin, he absorbed the earnest piety of the *Devotio Moderna*. The building that now rises on the school's site features above its entryway a depiction in colored glass of Erasmus writing on a piece of paper the names of Groote, Kempis, and others associated with the school. Above him are the words *Non Scholae Sed Vitae Discimus*—"We learn not for school but for life"—a saying of Seneca's that reflected Erasmus's own outlook.

In the public mind, Erasmus is associated not with Deventer but with Rotterdam, the city of his birth. In midlife, he would add its name to his own, becoming Erasmus Roterodamus—Erasmus of Rotterdam. Prior to World War II, there was a small house in Nieuw-Kerk Street in central Rotterdam whose facade had an inscription stating that the famous Erasmus had been born there. (The building, along with much of Rotterdam, was obliterated by German bombs on May 14, 1940.) The house was a short walk from the Nieuwe Maas, one of the branches of the Rhine as that river reaches the North Sea. Erasmus would later note with pride that he was born "between the banks of the Rhine." In addition to being a vital commercial artery connecting the North Sea with Central Europe, the Rhine was a flourishing cultural corridor, and Erasmus would spend much of his life traveling along it.

Today, a tall bronze statue of Erasmus stands in a plaza in front of St. Lawrence's church, not far from the site of the house in Nieuw-Kerk Street. Produced in the early seventeenth century in the midst of the Eighty Years' War, it has somehow managed to survive centuries of unrest, war, and indifference. (During World War II, it lay buried in the court-yard of a local art museum.) The statue shows the Dutch humanist in a full-length fur-trimmed mantle and a canon's cap, examining the pages of a thick folio-edition New Testament (no doubt his). A Latin inscription on the pedestal proclaims him "the first man of his age," the "most out-standing citizen of all citizens," and "one who rightly attained an immor-tal name by his eternal writings." The florid tribute, however, is belied by the bleak surroundings. The plaza is secluded and bordered by unsightly storefronts—a reflection, perhaps, of Rotterdam's ambivalence toward its famous son, who left it at an early age and rarely returned.

The statue has an odd feature. On the front, it gives Erasmus's year of birth as 1469; on the back, it says 1467. At various points, Erasmus himself gave each of those years (as well as 1466) as that of his birth (while never wavering on the day: October 28). The confusion reflects the chaotic cir-cumstances of his parents' lives (about which little is known). His father, Gerard, the second-youngest of ten children born to a couple living in the town of Gouda, some twelve miles east of Rotterdam, was well educated, having learned both Latin and Greek. His mother, Margaret, was the daughter of a physician in the North Brabant village of Zevenbergen. She and Gerard became intimate, and she gave birth to a boy named Pieter. Nearly three years later, Margaret again conceived. The couple wanted to marry, but Gerard's parents would not allow it. Gerard—seeking, perhaps, to escape their disapproval—left for Rome, where he supported himself copying manuscripts of classical authors. When Margaret was ready to de-liver, she was taken to Rotterdam, where her mother lived. The boy would be named Erasmus, after one of the Fourteen Holy Helpers. He would later add the name Desiderius, "longed for" in Latin.

Erasmus would never know a normal family life. Not only had he been born out of wedlock; his father at some point became a priest. Europe was full of the children of priests, and the Church considered them nonpersons, barring them from holding certain offices and from receiving various perks except when dispensations were granted. Whether Gerard became a priest before or after Erasmus was born is not clear, but in any case Erasmus would always feel anxiety and shame over his illegitimacy.

He spent his first few years in Rotterdam in the care of his grandmother. When he was around four, his father arranged for him to attend primary school in Gouda. With a population of around 10,000, Gouda was among the largest cities in Holland. It was laced by canals and dominated by the ornately turreted town hall that still stands on its marketplace. Every Thursday, farmers from surrounding villages came to sell the buttery cheese for which Gouda even then was known. It was even more famous for its high-quality beer, which was shipped to Flanders in exchange for grain.

Its school was less distinguished. Erasmus, whose writings on education would change the course of Western pedagogy, drew heavily on his own experiences as a student, and from his first days in Gouda, they were overwhelmingly negative. The main subject was Dutch, and the instruction was unrelievedly monotonous and harsh. The headmaster, Pieter Winckel, was a selfish, narrow-minded man who administered the rod for the slightest infractions. Such severities, together with what Erasmus saw as the coarseness and provincialism of the locals, left him with a lifelong distaste for Gouda. "Greasy of mouth and palate" was his tart description of its residents. In 1478, when Erasmus was ten or so, his mother, wanting more for her son, took him sixty-five miles east to Deventer and its famous Latin school.

In many respects, Deventer remained a medieval town. Its narrow streets echoed with the clang of hammers and shriek of saws, the shouts of vendors and barks of town criers. Opening onto the streets were the workshops of carpenters, tailors, locksmiths, apothecaries, shoemakers, and bakers, each trade with its own quarter. Houses rose helter-skelter along the street, their upper stories protruding over the lower and blocking out the sun. Most were ramshackle wooden structures, the windows covered by oiled paper or pigskin and the roofs made of thatch. Here and there stood the more stately residences of merchants and patricians—multistory timber houses with panes of glass and roofs of tile. Like most medieval towns, Deventer (which had a population of 8,000) was encircled by thick walls mounted by towers, made necessary by the ever-present threat from criminals, marauders, and enemy armies. On a daily basis, however, the main danger to public order came from within. With taverns on every corner and drinking the main pastime, drunkenness was rampant, contributing to the high rates of crime and violence that were endemic features of medieval life.

Walking around Deventer, the young Erasmus would have had to watch his step. Like most medieval towns, it lacked even the most rudimentary sanitation, and streets served as sewers. Butchers slit open cows and pigs in front of their shops, letting the blood run into the gutter; fishmongers dumped fish heads and rotting stock into alleyways; tanners emptied vats of the acrid solutions of urine and dung they used to turn animal hides into leather. Chickens, goats, and pigs all roamed freely, depositing their waste in the street; when it rained, the excrement mixed with offal, carcasses, moldy cheese, and rotting vegetables to form a muddy, putrid mess. Chamber pots were routinely emptied from second-story windows, creating a hazard for passersby. The thatch on roofs was an ideal breeding ground for rats, and lice and fleas were so abundant that not even dukes or bishops could escape them. Despite the presence of bathhouses, people often went weeks without bathing, and underwear was changed perhaps once a fortnight.

Through this foul loam, however, the buds of a new civilization were poking. Deventer was one of many thriving towns in the northern Netherlands. (The Netherlands then comprised not only the modern-day country of that name but also Belgium, parts of northern France, and Luxembourg—an area also known as the Low Countries.) Along with northern Italy, the northern Netherlands was the most highly urbanized region in Europe, with some twenty walled cities of between 5,000 and 15,000 inhabitants. As Erasmus later observed, "No other region can be found containing so many towns in such a small area. Admittedly, they are of modest size, but they have an incredibly attractive appearance." As the French historian Fernand Braudel has observed, towns "are like electric transformers. They increase tension, accelerate the rhythm of exchange and constantly recharge human life." The northern Netherlands was thick with such transformers.

It's remarkable that these catalysts would emerge in such a backwater—a term literally applicable in this case. Most of the northern Netherlands was at or below sea level. From the north and west, the North Sea surged relentlessly in, flooding plains and feeding lakes. The many rivers crisscrossing the region regularly overflowed, inundating farms and pastures. Beginning in the thirteenth century, though, Dutch farmers, seeking to contain the waters, banded together to construct an elaborate system of dams, dikes, floodgates, and drainage canals, with windmills used to pump water from the land. The large tracts thus reclaimed, called polders, were divided up among those who had contributed labor. Unlike the rest of northern Europe, where feudal relations prevailed, this region had a rough social equality, with many independent farmers living in humble homes and working small plots of land. The increase in agricultural productivity freed people to move off the land and into towns, which became marketing centers for farm and dairy products, especially cheese.

These towns, in turn, established commercial ties abroad. And here the water proved a boon, facilitating links to the outside world. In the first half of the fifteenth century, the Dutch developed a fleet of seagoing vessels that enabled them to dominate the bulk-carrying trade as well as the herring grounds of the North Sea. The building of ships, their equipping and manning, the provision of sails and rope—all became thriving industries. The resulting prosperity made funds available for schools, teachers, and books, which in turn facilitated the rise of a dynamic new class of educated urbanites. These burghers—magistrates, merchants, notaries, accountants, teachers, lawyers—were proud, curious, public spirited, and eager for a new design for living. Erasmus would spend much of his life trying to provide it. He would, in effect, become the most articulate spokesman for this new urban class.

In Deventer, the signs of the new Europe were everywhere visible. In 1477, Deventer got its first printing press, and the town quickly became a top publishing center. Its location on the IJssel River gave it ready access to both the Rhine and (via the Zuider Zee) the North Sea, and ships were constantly putting in with wood from Germany, grain from Poland, dried fish from Norway, and wine from the Rhineland. Along with these goods, the ships and their crews brought new ideas and perspectives, adding to the intellectual ferment.

Finally, there was St. Lebwin's. The school had eight grades and two hundred or more students in each, for a total student body of around two thousand. It had one great mission: teaching how to write and speak good Latin—the passport to a better life. Latin was the medium in which commercial contracts were signed, government communiqués issued, university lectures delivered, international affairs transacted, ecclesiastical business carried out. Those proficient in Latin could also participate in the animated intellectual life that was beginning to take root across borders, regions, and nations.

At St. Lebwin's, the curriculum in the lower grades was dominated by the traditional medieval trivium: grammar, rhetoric, and logic. Of these, grammar predominated. Unfortunately, instruction in it remained mired in the old ways, with textbooks that were hopelessly dull and arcane. They included the *Pater Meus*, an exercise book for declensions; the *Tempora*, a similar guide to conjugations; and the *Catholicon*, an etymological dictionary that was so obscure and convoluted that Erasmus would call it "the most barbarous book in the world."

Because printing was still in its infancy, only the instructor had books, and students sat on the floor around him as he dictated a text slowly enough so that each could take down every word; he then translated and commented on that text. Students were forced to memorize the inflections of nouns and verbs reflecting the various cases and moods, and when it came time to recite this information, the school rang "with horrific shrieks of pain," as Erasmus put it. Some of the teachers had such uncouth manners that even their wives could not possibly feel affection for them, and "no useless, disreputable scoundrel" was "disqualified by general opinion from running a school."

The torments inflicted on the students were not limited to parsing and conjugating. Teachers as well as parents beat children savagely for the smallest violations, to the point of blinding, crippling, or even killing them. Schools, Erasmus observed, were like "torture chambers," in which one heard nothing "but the thudding of the stick, the swishing of the rod, howling and moaning, and shouts of brutal abuse." Was it any wonder, then, "that children come to hate learning?" Anyone caught speaking Dutch—even in the school yard—was subject to a fine, and boys were encouraged to inform on one another. The students themselves engaged in ugly hazing rituals in which young men of good families were forced to undergo outrages "fit for executioners, torturers, pimps, thieving Carians, or galley-slaves." Erasmus would later become a strong opponent of corporal punishment in schools, condemning it as not only inhumane but also ineffective.

In this cruel and unforgiving world, Erasmus had to make his own way. And, while trudging through the endless dictations and dreary exercises, he made a key discovery. Like other Latin schools, St. Lebwin's offered readings of classical writers, such as Cicero, Virgil, Horace, and Terence. Meant to serve as technical models, these readings were usually provided in the form of excerpts and abridgments, without much attention to content or style. As he read them, however, Erasmus was struck by how much their Latin differed from that taught in the school's primers. In the centuries since Rome's fall, the language had constantly evolved to meet the practical needs of daily life. While helping to make Latin a living language, these changes had robbed it of much of its elegance and concision. When Erasmus read the poets and playwrights of ancient Rome, he felt transported from his sordid surroundings into a world of harmony and light. As he later wrote, a "kind of secret natural force swept me into liberal studies. My teachers might forbid it; even so, I furtively drank in what I could from such books as I had managed to acquire." He was so taken with Terence that he learned many of his plays by heart. His greatest love, however, was poetry, and he strove to compose odes after Horace and elegies echoing Virgil. A polished aesthete seemed in the making.

At St. Lebwin's, though, Erasmus was exposed to another cultural current that would leave a permanent residue of moral earnestness. Deventer was permeated by the spirit of the *Devotio Moderna*, the movement of Geert Groote and Thomas à Kempis. The town was home to several houses run by the Brethren and Sisters of the Common Life, as the movement's followers were called. They were easy to spot: they wore plain clothes, kept their eyes on the ground, uncomplainingly helped their neighbors, and occasionally uttered short prayers, called ejaculations. The Brethren had close ties to St. Lebwin's, and from them the students picked up the precepts of the *Devotio Moderna*. In the IJssel valley as a whole, communities of bakers and cooks, teachers and tailors inspired by its teachings were trying to lead lives of apostolic simplicity. The movement's rapid spread attested to the growing hunger for more personal forms of piety than those offered by the medieval Church.

As the fifteenth century drew to a close, the Latin Church was completing seven centuries as the dominant institution in northern Europe. Its spires defined the skyline, its bells tolled the hours, its calendar determined the rhythm of work and rest, and its courts had jurisdiction over everything from inheritances and interest rates to blasphemy and adultery. The Church even determined what one could eat: there were almost seventy days during the year when adults were required to fast (i.e., abstain from meat and other animal products like milk and cheese). There were an additional forty or fifty feast days when the faithful were expected to abstain from work and to fast the night before. Through the seven sacraments, the Church ruled over the key passages in a Christian's life, including baptism, confirmation, marriage, and last rites. When not hosting services, churches served as community centers, with parishioners stopping by to close deals, hear the latest news, arrange celebrations—even hold trysts.

Most of all, the Church offered hope and consolation in a treacherous and unforgiving world. Fires and floods, famine and war, epidemics and contagions, brigandage and riots all helped to make daily life a tissue of anxiety and dread. Stark memories remained of the Black Death, the outbreak of plague from 1348 to 1350 that had carried off an estimated 35 million people—one-third of Western Europe's population; entire villages were wiped out in a catastrophe not equaled before or since. The plague remained a constant threat, and dysentery, malaria, influenza, typhoid, diphtheria, and St. Anthony's fire (which blistered, deformed, and killed its victims) were all rampant. As many as one of every three women died in their first childbirth; as many as one of every four children died before the age of one. Desperate to ward off such calamities, the faithful sought whatever protection they could. The Church responded with an array of customs, practices, and institutions that were both broadly popular and, increasingly, loudly criticized.

Veneration of the saints was one such practice. By virtue of their exemplary lives, the saints were believed to be endowed with a special ability to intercede with God through Christ on behalf of the devout. St. Christopher offered protection to travelers. St. Nicholas could help rescue children from danger. St. Barbara offered protection against sudden and violent death at work, and St. George could help one from falling into the hands of the enemy. The Fourteen Holy Helpers stood ready to relieve a variety of debilitating conditions, from plague and epilepsy to headaches and toothaches. And every occupation had its own patron—Crispen for leatherworkers and Cecilia for musicians, Honoratus for bakers and Bernard for candle makers.

Across Europe, shrines to the saints proliferated, and roadways were filled with crowds of pilgrims heading to them. While Jerusalem and Rome were the most hallowed destinations, Santiago de Compostela in northwestern Spain was the most popular. In its magnificent Romanesque cathedral there lay (it was said) the remains of the apostle James. Four roads originating at different points in France passed through the Pyrenees to join the nearly five-hundred-mile *camino* to the town, located just inland from the Atlantic Ocean. Around the cathedral's altar rose piles of abandoned crutches, model ships, and wax replicas of limbs, eyes, and breasts, all bearing witness to the saint's miraculous ability to heal and rescue.

The popularity of a shrine depended on the quality of its relics. These included bones, teeth, strips of flesh, locks of hair, and articles of clothing, all offering physical proximity to the saint's prowess and prestige. Churches boasted slivers of the True Cross, shreds from the tablecloth of the Last Supper, thorns from Christ's crown, patches of his swaddling clothes. After the sack of Constantinople in 1204, the trade in relics soared as the market was flooded with shriveled body parts whose authenticity could not be verified. While St. Elizabeth of Hungary lay in state, in

1231, a crowd of worshippers tore away strips of the linen enveloping her face and cut off her hair, her nails, even her nipples. Fourteen churches in Europe claimed to have the head of John the Baptist.

By far the most venerated figure was Mary. Though receiving only minor mention in the New Testament, the Virgin Mother in the late Middle Ages became the center of a fervent cult that revered her as a source of mercy far more approachable than the righteous Father or the judging Son. All over Europe, chapels and shrines displayed jars and vials of Mary's milk, the viewing of which was said to speed one's wishes to God. Hundreds of churches were consecrated to Mary, ships were named after her, and stories multiplied about her miraculous intervention in the world on behalf of the troubled and bereft.

Meanwhile, the Mass—the centerpiece of Catholic worship—was invested with all sorts of wonder-working powers. People raced from church to church to be present at the Eucharist, when the bread and wine were transubstantiated into the flesh and blood of Christ, for witnessing it was considered a means of accumulating merit in the eyes of God. On their deathbed, many noblemen and merchants—worried about the agonies they might face in the afterlife—left all or part of their possessions to their local church to create an endowment for the saying of Masses on their behalf that could speed their passage through purgatory.

Through such bequests, churches and monasteries grew wealthy. Many cloisters amassed large estates, turning abbots into landlords who saw the laity as tenants to be managed rather than souls to be cured. Even the Franciscans, whose rule stipulated that they go barefoot among the poor and support themselves by begging, became rich and built imposing friaries. Bishops and cardinals behaved like secular princes, maintaining lavish courts and meddling in political affairs. Some monasteries kept large packs of hounds, which were allowed to run wild and which ate the food that should have gone to the poor. At all levels of clerical life, absenteeism grew, concubinage spread, and tales of ignorance multiplied.

The papacy, meanwhile, was in utter turmoil. In 1305, a Frenchman, Clement V, was elected pope. He had his coronation in Lyon, then moved to Avignon in 1309. So began a period of papal exile that came to be known as the Babylonian Captivity. During it, the popes remained sub-servient to the French king, and the Holy See became notorious for its nepotism and simony (the sale of offices). When the Babylonian Captivity finally ended, in 1377, the Church plunged into the Great Schism, during which there was a pope in Rome and an antipope in Avignon, each with his own college of cardinals and profit-seeking curia; at one point, there were not two pontiffs but three. By the time the Church again had one Holy Father, in 1417, its sacred aura had been badly tarnished.

The rampant anticlericalism of the late Middle Ages was reflected in two of its greatest literary works. In Boccaccio's *Decameron* (written in the early 1350s), a group of young Florentines fleeing the plague take refuge in a secluded villa and tell one another stories to pass the time. Clerical lechery and hypocrisy are recurrent themes. In one of the most famous tales, a monk—approached by an innocent young woman saying she wants to get closer to God—offers to show her how to "put the devil back in Hell"; he then deflowers her. (She so enjoys the experience that she repeatedly asks the monk to put the devil back in Hell.) In *The Canterbury Tales* (begun in 1387), thirty or so pilgrims travel from south London to the shrine of St. Thomas à Becket at Canterbury cathedral. Of them all, the Pardoner, a seller of absolution for sins, is by far the most corrupt; he freely acknowledges that the relic bones he sells come from pigs, not departed saints, and that he pockets the proceeds rather than hand them over to the Church. Instead of feeling remorse over such ruses, he takes pride in their ingenuity.

Chaucer's pilgrims capture the paradoxical status of the late medieval Church. On the one hand, they are willing to endure the discomfort of a sixty-mile journey over rough roads to visit a shrine and take advantage of its supposedly miraculous powers—a reflection of the strength of popular piety. On the other, a cleric entrusted with the sacred power of pardon is shown to be given over to greed and deceit. By the late fifteenth century, the Church seemed more mighty—and compromised—than ever. And the voices of dissent were growing louder.

Four such voices—commemorated in the great Reformation monument in Worms—helped prepare the way for that religious transformation.

Erected in 1868, the monument shows a statue of Luther atop a pedestal, with the four forerunners seated below. All four questioned the practices of the medieval Church, driven by their conviction—drawn from reading Scripture—that it had strayed too far from the spirit of the apostolic church. Peter Waldus was a twelfth-century merchant from Lyon who gave away his possessions, donned plain clothes, placed his wife and daughter in a convent, and preached repentance to the urban masses. Around him there formed a band of followers, called Waldensians, whose resolute rejection of devotional practices not mentioned in the Bible led to intense persecution by the Church. (In 1545, hundreds of Waldensians living in villages in southeastern France were massacred on the order of King Francis I.)

John Wyclif was a fourteenth-century Oxford don who, going around barefoot in a long russet gown, attacked the Church for its temporal holdings and urged it to distribute its wealth to the poor. In addition to producing a flood of theological and polemical tracts, he inspired a group of disciples to translate the Vulgate (Latin) Bible into English. After his death, in 1384, his followers, called Lollards (from a Dutch word meaning "mumblers"), met in secret to read the Bible in English and keep alive the principle that Scripture should be the sole foundation of a Christian's life.

Wyclif's greatest disciple, however, was found not in England but in Bohemia. Jan Hus was a professor of theology at the University of Prague who, through reading Wyclif and the Bible, became an outspoken advocate for reform. Excommunicated, he retreated to the countryside, where he turned out a series of tracts in which he condemned the entire framework of the Roman Church, including the papacy, as not sanctioned by Scripture. For such views, Hus was summoned before the Council of Constance in 1414. He was offered a safe-conduct, but upon his arrival it was revoked, and the following year, after refusing repeated demands that he recant, he was burned at the stake.

No less unfortunate was Girolamo Savonarola, a charismatic Dominican friar who drew overflow crowds to the church of San Marco in Florence with fierce denunciations of clerical dissolution and apocalyptic visions of the city transformed into the New Jerusalem. After the exile of the Medici, in 1494, Savonarola became the city's de facto ruler. During carnival season, he organized a "bonfire of the vanities," into which were fed musical instruments, playing cards, risqué paintings, women's toiletries, and other supposed symbols of moral decay. With Florence placed under a papal interdict and Savonarola's lurid prophesies failing to materialize, the population turned against him, and in 1498 he was hanged on the same spot on which the bonfire had burned the previous year.

As all these cases show, Rome demanded full compliance with its authority and was willing to use savage means to enforce it. Yet there was another forerunner of the Reformation who managed to escape persecution and who—though absent from the Worms monument—played a critical part in preparing the way for change.

As a young man, Geert Groote (born in Deventer in 1340) liked the good life. A wandering scholar, he moved from town to town in search of books, conversation, and women. At one point, though, he fell ill and, worried about his fate in the afterlife, felt intense remorse at the many years he had spent gratifying his desires. Recovering, he decided to start afresh. He opened his house to several poor women, burned his large collection of books on magic, and studied the Bible and the Church Fathers, especially Augustine, whose struggles to control his fleshly impulses seemed to mirror Groote's own. Groote spent two years in a Carthusian monastery, fasting regularly and praying into the night. Having found a living faith, however, he wanted to share it with others and so left the cloister.

Embarking on a roving ministry, Groote urged his listeners to disdain worldly honors, shun external observances, and nourish the spirit within. Like Christ, they should endure their trials in humble submission and extend their love for him to their fellow man. While reproving the clergy for their indolence and dissolution, Groote steered clear of doctrine and expressed respect for the pope. His concern was for the inner development of the individual rather than the sacramental power of the Church. The best way to reach God was not through rites like baptism or confession but through an inner kernel of devotion. Inviting young people into his home to study the Bible, he put them to work copying manuscripts while urging them to return to the Gospels.

At the time of Groote's death, in 1384, some of his followers were living in simple piety in the home of the vicar of St. Lebwin's church in Deventer. As word of the community spread, others came to join it. They were attacked by the mendicant friars, who insisted that living in common without taking monastic vows violated Church canons, but for these disciples the whole point was to have a holy life outside the cloister. Like-minded communities began to form throughout the IJssel valley. Under the banner of inner renewal, the *Devotio Moderna* spread westward throughout Holland, southward into Flanders, and eastward into Germany. A parallel network of houses for women also arose. These communities became known as the Brethren and Sisters of the Common Life. Because some members preferred a more structured environment, a monastery founded on the principles of the *Devotio Moderna* was established near Zwolle, not far from Deventer, and by the mid-fifteenth century dozens of branches had arisen throughout northwestern Europe.

From one of these monasteries would emerge Groote's most influential disciple. Thomas à Kempis was in his twenties when, in the early fifteenth century, he entered the monastery of Mount St. Agnes near Zwolle. He would remain for nearly seventy years, copying and composing devotional tracts while wrestling with his longings, urges, and doubts. Over time, he compiled some two thousand homiletic statements (about half of them from the Bible) that offered comfort and inspiration. These became the basis for *The Imitation of Christ*. Influenced by the medieval mystics, Thomas urged readers to achieve union with God by shunning the outside world and cultivating the inner spirit. "The Kingdom of God is within you," he wrote, quoting Christ. "Forsake this wretched world and your soul shall find rest. Learn to despise external things, to devote yourself to those that are within."

Habit and tonsure, he declared, profit a man little; a change of heart and the shackling of the passions make a true monk. Rather than run off to distant shrines and kiss sacred bones, the truly religious stay at home, work hard, and pray intently. They disdain wealth, forswear honors, avoid gossip, shun the company of the powerful, and resist the impulses of the flesh. We should not take pride in our deeds or consider ourselves better than others. And we should spurn all learning that does not deepen our relationship with God. On Judgment Day, "we shall not be asked what we have read, but what we have done"; not how well we have spoken, but how well we have lived. There was but one path to salvation and everlasting life—through the cross. By taking it up, a man can make his own life one of Christlike mortification.

Thomas's vision of internal purification through surrender to God strongly appealed to educated Europeans who felt unfulfilled by rote prayers and sacramental rites. Initially circulating in manuscript form, *The Imitation of Christ* was copied by hand and passed from cloister to cloister. The first printed edition appeared around 1473; nearly fifty more editions appeared by the end of the fifteenth century and another sixty-five during the sixteenth. Thomas More would call the *Imitation* one of the three books everyone should own; Ignatius Loyola, the founder of the Jesuits, read a chapter a day and regularly gave away copies. Translated into hundreds of languages and appearing in more than five thousand editions, the *Imitation* remains the bestselling Christian book after the Bible.

Erasmus would not be among its admirers. He was never one for spiritual contemplation. Nor did he place much value on austerity and self-denial. Most off-putting of all was Thomas's disdain for secular knowledge. "Do not desire the reputation of being learned," Thomas wrote—but Erasmus desired little else. Later in life, he would dismiss the Brethren of the Common Life as small-minded and provincial. Whereas Thomas taught withdrawal from the world, Erasmus yearned to enter and experience it. Yet while he was in Deventer, and without being quite aware of it, he was being imprinted with the movement's ideas about inward religion, simple piety, and imitating Christ, and he would carry them with him as he moved into the outside world.

Toward the end of his stay in Deventer, Erasmus caught an exciting glimpse of that world. In 1484, when he was seventeen or so, St. Lebwin's received a visit from the humanist scholar Rodolphus Agricola. A native of Frisia on the North Sea who had been schooled by the Brethren, Agricola had joined the flow of northerners to Italy in search of Renaissance enlightenment. For ten years he had read the Roman classics, studied Greek, and written books on rhetoric and logic. Returning home, he embarked on a lecture tour promoting the New Learning, as the revival of interest in classical culture was called. Despite his association with the Brethren, Agricola had little sympathy for their piety and asceticism. He was a bohemian who loved food, fame, and conversation. At the same time, he considered himself a devout Christian intent on practicing the spirit of the Gospels, and he sought to harmonize classical ideals and Christian precepts in a creed he called the philosophy of Christ.

Agricola, Erasmus later wrote, "was one of the first to bring a breath of the New Learning from Italy" to the north. Agricola's leading disciple, Alexander Hegius, became the director of St. Lebwin's by 1483, and he immediately began reshaping its curriculum, phasing out the old textbooks and introducing instruction in Greek—something very uncommon in secondary schools at the time. Erasmus would get a taste of that language, but otherwise he was not able to take advantage of these changes, for he was nearing the end of his stay at the school. In his six or seven years there, he had completed courses in logic, physics, metaphysics, and morals and had become so familiar with Horace, Ovid, and Terence that he could recite large sections of their works by heart—a firm educational foundation, despite his later complaints about the school's mediocrity. Most important, Erasmus had been exposed to two parallel but competing currents—the secular ideals of classical culture and the pious values of the *Devotio Moderna*—and he would spend the rest of his life trying to combine them.

In 1483, Deventer was hit by the plague. The outbreak became so severe that magistrates fled the town, friends avoided one another, and some residents took to sleeping in haystacks in the surrounding countryside. Among the hundreds felled was Erasmus's mother, Margaret. His father, Gerard, who had returned from Italy and was now living in Gouda, summoned Erasmus and his brother Pieter there, but he, too, soon died. Now in his late teens, Erasmus was suddenly without parents or prospects. His future lay in the hands of three guardians who had been appointed by his father. As he made his way back to Gouda (probably in the summer of 1484), Erasmus had one overriding wish—to continue his education.

MINER'S SON

On the outskirts of the Saxon town of Eisleben in central Germany rise a series of mammoth slate-colored mounds. Standing along roadsides, behind apartment buildings, and next to shopping malls, they look otherworldly and vaguely sinister, as if they had once served as the altars of an ancient cult. In fact, they are refuse heaps, consisting of discarded rocks from the region's mines, which once formed the backbone of the local economy. Between Eisleben and the Harz Mountains about forty miles to the north, there are hundreds of them. The taller mounds rise about four hundred feet and come to a point, giving the appearance of pyramids. The shorter ones are half as tall and flat on top. These date back to the late Middle Ages, and some were no doubt present during the time of Martin Luther. He was born in Eisleben, in 1483, and the heaps offer important clues about the world in which he was raised.

Like many great historical figures, Luther was fond of citing his lowly origins. Both his father and his grandfather, he liked to say, had peasant backgrounds. This is misleading. While Luther's distant forebears were indeed peasants, his father's parents were not. Rather, they were independent farmers who lived in Möhra, a hamlet of about sixty families in Thuringia in central Germany. Their eldest son, Hans Luder (as the family name was originally spelled), married Margarete Lindemann, who came from a prosperous burgher family in nearby Eisenach. According to the strict inheritance rules of Thuringia, the Luder farm was to pass intact to the youngest son, Heinz. Hans—unhappy at the prospect of working for his younger brother—decided to strike out on his own. The area around Eisleben, about ninety miles to the northeast, was experiencing a mining boom. It had begun around 1470, when the demand for copper in Europe took off (stimulated by a growing market for copper and bronze pots for cooking). Mansfeld, the county in which Eisleben was located, was one of Europe's top producers of both copper and silver, and Hans hoped to take advantage.

Several months after he and Margarete arrived in Eisleben, their first child, Martin, was born, on November 10, 1483, in a house located a short walk from the town's main square. Finding work in Eisleben proved harder than Hans had expected, and after a few months he moved his family to the town of Mansfeld, ten miles to the north. Set amid hills and woods, it had barely 2,000 residents, but among them were the powerful counts of Mansfeld, who controlled the region's mines and whose imposing Gothic castle sat on a bluff overlooking the town. Hans quickly found work, while Margarete (like most women of that era) spent her time keeping house and tending to her children. (In all, the couple had eight children, only five of whom would survive into adulthood.)

Later, Luther, in his Table Talk—a thick compendium of comments taken down at the dinner table by students staying in the Black Cloister in Wittenberg—said that his parents kept him "under very strict supervision, even to the point of making me timid." On one occasion, his mother, discovering that he had stolen a nut, beat him "until the blood flowed." On another, his father "whipped me so severely that I ran away from him, and he was worried that he might not win me back again." By such strict discipline, "they finally forced me into the monastery."

Such comments figure prominently in one of the most famous studies of Luther, Erik Erikson's *Young Man Luther*, published in 1958. Seeking the psychological sources of Luther's revolt against the Catholic Church, Erikson focused on what he described as the identity crisis Martin faced as a result of his strained relations with his "jealously ambitious" father. According to Erikson, Hans's "excessive harshness" and his "angry, and often alcoholic, impulsiveness" bred constant fear in his son. The "suppressed rage" Martin felt toward his father and his desire to escape his father's control eventually drove him to enter the monastery in defiance of Hans's wishes. Over time, Martin transferred the anger he felt toward his father to the Catholic Church as a whole. As Erikson summarized it, "he rebelled: first against his father, to join the monastery; then against the Church, to found his own church."

Erikson's analysis has not fared well with Luther scholars. Most, in fact, are curtly dismissive. They maintain that the known facts about Luther's childhood and his relations with his parents are too slight to support such sweeping conclusions. Erikson himself acknowledged that he took liberties with the record, writing that "a clinician's training permits, and in fact forces, him to recognize major trends even where the facts are not all available." Special scorn has been reserved for his focus on Luther's "anality." Erikson—noting Luther's frequent use of scatological language, his lifelong problems with constipation and urine retention, and the corporal punishment meted out by his parents, probably to the buttocks—wrote that Luther's anal zone became the seat of both sensitive and defiant associations. Luther's fear that his parents and teachers might subject him by dominating this zone and thus gain power over his will "may have provided some of the dynamite in that delayed time bomb of Martin's rebellion," which eventually exploded with such force.

The line from Luther's constipation to his rebellion against Rome seems tenuous. All that aside, Luther's father does seem to have had a strong influence on his outlook. As Luther's later letters attest, he cared a great deal about his father's judgments of his choices in life, and he constantly chafed at Hans's efforts to dictate them. It does not take a great leap to assume that the tense relations between them helped shape Martin's temperament and contribute to his more general distrust of authority.

In the end, though, it was the raw realities of the Mansfeld mining world that would leave the deepest mark. "In his youth," Luther remarked in his Table Talk, "my father was a poor miner." Whether Hans actually descended into the mines is not clear. What is clear is that he quickly worked his way up to become a *Hüttenmeister*—a supervisor of one of the smelters used to heat the ore to separate the copper from the sulfur and bitumen. Enterprising and hardworking, Hans eventually gained an interest in several smelters. He did well enough to be able to buy a two-story stone dwelling at the foot of Mansfeld's central street, on which most of the town's well-to-do lived. Men in his position, though, often went into debt, and while Hans's fortunes steadily improved, they fluctuated along with the market and other variables. The stress and the need to scrimp in the Luther household were no doubt unrelenting.

The gashed landscape itself reflected the ferocity of the mining world.

Shafts had to be dug deep into the earth, leading to tunnels that were dark, poorly ventilated, and barely wide enough for the men to enter single file. In a flash a mine could collapse, fill with water, or catch fire, killing all inside. Miners could be maimed and paralyzed by falling rocks and cracking beams; the poisonous dust clotted their windpipes and corroded their lungs. Avalanches were common, burying miners under tons of rock, and the years of constant strain and cramping left their bodies bent and spirits sapped. The mining fields themselves were an inferno of belching furnaces, smoldering faggots, smoking chimneys, polluted pools of water, wagons filled with charcoal, bellows pumping air into the tunnels, and piles of discarded axles, pump rods, cranks, crowbars, cauldrons, and shovels. Over all hung the smoke from the never-sleeping smelters.

The boom-and-bust cycles of the industry, the large financial outlays it required, the rapid technological changes, the disputes over mine boundaries, the tense relations between owners and workers—all marked the Mansfeld mines as an outpost of early capitalism. This economic system, with all its disruptive and destabilizing effects, was just taking root in Europe, and Hans, rising from miner to smelter master, was an early participant. With his drive, industry, and readiness to take risks, he was an emblematic figure of the emerging new order—the entrepreneur—and to his son he would pass on his robust individualism.

As much as Mansfeld's mines anticipated Europe's future, however, the town's culture remained rooted in its folkloric past. A striking indication appears in *De Re Metallica*, a pioneering treatise on the mining industry by the Saxon scholar and humanist Georgius Agricola that was published in 1556. In an otherwise fastidiously factual account of the extracting, transporting, and refining of minerals, Agricola at one point observes that the mines are home to "pernicious pests" and "fierce murderous demons," which, if detected, often cause the mines to be shut down, for if such fiends could not be expelled, "no one escapes from them."

As a boy, Martin had such beliefs drummed into him. Superstitions were of course common in that period, but their grip was tightened by the great risks and dangers that miners faced. Luther's world abounded in demons, gnomes, evil spirits, and other malevolent agents. In central

Germany, the stock of such sprites was enlarged by the presence of its dark, trackless forests, in which it was easy to get lost and fall prey to wolves, outlaws, or witches. In Mansfeld, Luther was taught that witches lurk on all sides and cast their spells on man, beast, and crops. His mother was tormented by a neighbor who she claimed was a witch, and when one of Martin's brothers died, she blamed the neighbor. From his father he learned of earth spirits who disturbed workmen in the solitude of the tunnels. When crops failed, it was because demons had befouled the air. "We may not doubt that pestilences, fevers, and other grave diseases are the work of demons," Luther would later remark in his Table Talk.

He would also feel the seductive presence of the Devil. In later years, Satan would regularly materialize, shattering Luther's calm with unsettling questions about his faith. It was in the acrid, smoldering world of the Mansfeld mines that the Prince of Darkness first cast his spell. Hell, meanwhile, was no metaphor for Luther but rather a place to which the souls of the damned went to suffer eternal punishment—to burn in an unquenchable fire, forever and ever. Devotional guides gave advice on the various steps that could be taken to avoid hell and its torments, which were tailored to fit the crime, or sin.

Around the same time that Luther was growing up in Germany, Hieronymus Bosch in the Netherlands was painting his *Last Judgment*. Based on the book of Revelation, it shows an apocalyptic landscape in which the damned are subjected to all kinds of unspeakable acts by ghoulish beasts. A man with an arrow through his chest is tied to a pole and carried like a slain deer. Naked men are whipped while turning a mill wheel. Others are depicted being impaled, mutilated, hung from butcher hooks, and ridden like animals. Presiding over the carnage is Christ the Judge, who, seated resplendently on an arc, is flanked by Mary, the apostles, and trumpet-blowing angels.

The image of the judging Christ struck fear in the young Luther. He would later recall the dread he felt as a child on seeing in church a painting of Christ seated on a rainbow, looking down in wrathful disapproval at the wayward world. In many church images, Christ wielded a sword—a symbol of his severity. The sight of a crucifix would terrify Luther with its air of menace and mercilessness. The suffering Christ, his arms splayed in agony on the cross, seemed to demand a much greater sacrifice than any human could bear. The piercing pain and sense of abandonment associated with the crucifixion were chillingly captured by Matthias Grünewald in his famous Isenheim Altarpiece, painted in Alsace in the second decade of the sixteenth century. Christ's emaciated body is taut with the torment caused by the nails driven through his hands and feet; his flesh is covered with sores and punctured by thorns. Nearly every church in northern Europe had an image of the crucifixion featuring nails, thorns, spears, whips, and dripping blood, while tableaux of the saints showed them undergoing ghastly forms of martyrdom.

The violence in these depictions was not far removed from everyday life. Clubbings, slashings, stabbings, assaults, and rapes were routine occurrences in the late Middle Ages. Alcohol-fueled brawls frequently broke out in taverns, and since everyone carried a knife, they often turned fatal. The law itself was pitiless, and penalties were often brutal. Capital punishment was decreed for a score of offenses, ranging from murder and witchcraft to robbery, forgery, and heresy. Wealthy burghers generally got off with a simple beheading. The less fortunate were usually hanged, while heretics and husband-killers were burned. A Salzburg municipal ordinance stipulated that "a forger shall be burned or boiled to death. A perjurer shall have his tongue torn out by the neck. A servant who sleeps with his master's wife, daughter or sister shall be beheaded or hanged." Traitors faced being hanged, drawn, and quartered. This entailed hanging them to the point of losing consciousness, then reviving them, then disemboweling them, then finally beheading them and chopping the body into quarters. Those condemned to be broken on the wheel were tied to a wagon wheel, then beaten with a club or cudgel until nearly every bone in their body was broken. Executions were public entertainments, with families showing up with food and drink to heighten their enjoyment.

Going hand in hand with this savagery was a general obsession with death. A key reason, no doubt, was the Black Death—a three-year crucible of terror during which parents abandoned their children, streets filled with corpses, and towns became morgues. Outbreaks of the plague continued to cause panic and spur flight. An estimated half all Europeans died, usually from disease, before reaching the age of thirty. Because death could occur at any moment, one had to be careful not to die in a state of unrepentant sin and so be consigned to eternal damnation. To convey the full horror of death, preachers and painters emphasized the putrefying corpse—stinking and hideous, with clenched hands, rigid feet, frozen mouth, and bowels swarming with worms. A favorite theme was the Dance of Death, which showed gleeful skeletons cavorting with startled men and women of all classes, grasping them with their bony hands to be dragged off to their fate.

In the Mansfeld mining community, with its acute sense of vulnerability and danger, the embrace of saints, relics, and other religious totems was especially strong. The miners had their own patron saint—Anne, the mother of Mary. Though she is mentioned nowhere in the Bible and remained obscure during Christianity's first millennium, a cult began to form around her in the thirteenth century, especially in central Germany; in Mansfeld, she was second only to Christ in importance. At the Church of St. Peter and Paul in Eisleben, where Luther was baptized, an altarpiece honors St. Anne, and the predella at the bottom shows three shepherds carrying miners' lamps. At a critical moment in his life, Luther would appeal to Anne's intercessionary powers.

The mines of Mansfeld may help explain another of Luther's conspicuous traits—his scatology. His relish for obscenity and toilet language would prove embarrassing to not just contemporary supporters but also generations of Protestants. In his tracts and Table Talk, references to the Word of God and love of Christ appear alongside mentions of farting and belching, asses and excrement. "I have shit in the pants, and you can hang them around your neck and wipe your mouth with it," he said at the table one day. (In many Table Talk editions, such comments are either cleaned up or excised.) Mansfelders, operating in a harsh and unforgiving environment, were known for their crude, blunt language. Luther moreover lived at a time when people were much less squeamish about their bodily functions than they are today—when people defecated on roadsides and emptied chamber pots into the street. The fastidious Erasmus was a rare exception. A son of the emerging middle class, he had modern ideas about hygiene, and throughout his life he would wage a lonely battle against the muck and grime of his age.

In so many ways, the worlds in which Luther and Erasmus grew up set them on divergent courses. Deventer was surrounded by cleared land worked by independent farmers and linked by water to the outside world; Mansfeld was located deep inside densely wooded Germany, on the far edges of Christendom. It was a land with few books, few itinerant humanists, few warming rays from Italy. The only glow came from the charcoal-fired smelters used to separate metals from their ore. Whereas Erasmus would constantly move from country to country and consider himself a citizen of none, Luther would remain rooted in Germany, shaped by its culture and folkways, its coarse language and earthy humor. Whereas Erasmus would decisively turn his back on the Middle Ages as he developed a reform program for Europe, Luther would retain much of the medieval as he blazed his own distinctive path into the modern world.

CANDLELIGHT STUDIES

For a youth who, like Erasmus, had no parents, resources, or connections, there was one common destination: the monastery. It offered safety, sustenance, and a clear path to salvation. Erasmus's principal guardian, Pieter Winckel (the same stern, irascible man who had served as the headmaster of the school in Gouda), strongly supported this course and pressed both Erasmus and his brother Pieter to take it. They refused. Now about sixteen, Erasmus had become so devoted to literature and so intent on seeing the world that the idea of withdrawing from it seemed intolerable. He wanted to attend a university. His father had left a collection of manuscripts that he had copied and which, if sold, could bring a decent sum. In a letter that Erasmus sent to Winckel at the end of 1484—the first of his to have survived—he urged him to put the books on the market. "Time flies by on wingèd feet," he wrote, quoting Ovid, with a flourish that would rankle Winckel.

In a compromise, Winckel arranged for the boys to attend a school run by the Brethren of the Common Life in 's Hertogenbosch (Dutch for "the Duke's Wood"), thirty-five miles southeast of Gouda. The Brethren, he hoped, would persuade them of the merits of monastic life. But just the opposite occurred. Erasmus by this point had a greater command of Latin than his teachers, and the more than two years he spent under their tutelage seemed to him a complete waste of time. One teacher who felt special regard for him, wanting to test him, charged him with an offense of which he was in fact innocent, then flogged him. When the teacher realized his error, he expressed regret, but too late for Erasmus. "This incident," he wrote, "destroyed all love of study within me and flung my young mind into such a deep depression that I nearly wasted away with heart-break." The main purpose of the Brethren, he concluded, was to break the spirit of boys through punishment and threats in order to make them fit for monastic life.

When an outbreak of the plague in 's Hertogenbosch forced Erasmus and his brother to return to Gouda, they found to their dismay that Winckel had arranged for both to enter a monastery near Delft. Erasmus insisted that he was too young to take monastic vows, which, once made, could not be revoked. He would be in a better position to make such a judgment if he were first allowed to spend some years in study. His brother agreed. Winckel flew into a rage. Eager to be rid of his charges, he denounced them as worthless rascals and claimed there was no money left to support them. When that failed to move them, he enlisted a procession of men and women, frocked and unfrocked, to impress on them the benefits of the cloister and the perils of the world. To Erasmus's fury, Pieter quickly gave in, but Erasmus himself held out.

While being thus badgered, however, he ran into an old friend who was living in a nearby monastery and who painted a blissful picture of the serenity and concord of monastic life. The cloister had a well-stocked library and allowed ample time for reading, and to Erasmus it sounded less like a monastery than a "garden of the Muses."

His resistance was further weakened by the conflict then raging in the Dutch lands. It pitted the *Kabeljauws* ("Cods") against the *Hoeks* ("Hooks," a reference to a hooked stick used to catch cod). One side supported the governing House of Burgundy and the other opposed it; the result was an unending series of atrocities and outrages. Crops were burned, villages torched, laborers killed, trade ties disrupted by brigands, and prisoners broken on the wheel. These horrors would make a deep impression on Erasmus, providing the seeds for the antiwar views that would become so central to his reform program. They also made monastic life seem somewhat less repellent, for cloisters were generally spared attack. Facing an increasingly exasperated Winckel and anxious about the depletion of his inheritance, Erasmus finally gave in, and in 1486 or 1487 he entered the monastery of the Canons Regular of St. Augustine at Steyn, about a mile outside Gouda. Now nineteen or so, he was about to get a firsthand look at this hallowed precinct of Christian life.

Because the monastery at Steyn burned down in 1549, little is known of its physical layout, but it no doubt followed the basic plan of the medieval cloister—an abbey church with a long nave for processions, a rectangular courtyard where monks could take the air, a refectory for eating, a dormitory for sleeping, a lavatorium for washing, a guesthouse, an infirmary, servants' quarters, and the necessarium, a latrine usually connected to the dormitory and located over a stream that could carry waste away. Like most monasteries, it would have been largely self-sufficient, with a bakery, barns, pigsties, chicken coops, a stable for horses and donkeys, a cowshed smelling of milk and manure, extensive gardens producing vegetables and medicinal herbs, and granaries that, even in winter, remained comfortably full. For Erasmus, however, the accommodations fell well short of his exacting standards, and he would later describe the monastery as "so much decayed, so unhealthy that it was scarcely fit for keeping cattle, let alone for such a delicate constitution."

Erasmus was fortunate in one respect. The Canons Regular of St. Augustine followed a less severe regimen than that of many other orders. It loosely adhered to the Rule of St. Augustine—guidelines for a cloistered life drawn from the writings of Augustine of Hippo of the late fourth and early fifth centuries. The Augustinian Canons, as they were also known, were not strictly monks who lived a reclusive life but a type of priest who performed services in the outside world. Erasmus was initially a postulant, i.e., on probation; during this period, his desire to become a monk was tested. Fulfilling expectations, he moved on to his novitiate, a period lasting a year and a day that would culminate (if both parties agreed) in the taking of vows. As at all monasteries, the day was built around the canonical hours—seven sessions of prayer, beginning with matins at around two in the morning and ending with compline in the evening. Meals were simple and featured readings from the Bible and Church Fathers. Several hours a day were given over to individual prayers, the study of prescribed religious texts, and contemplation, plus manual chores like gardening, chopping wood, and copying manuscripts. Silence was enjoined, though not nearly as strictly as by more rigorous orders. The values were those of the *Devotio Moderna*: simplicity, modesty, tranquility.

When the delicacy of Erasmus's constitution became clear, special allowances were made for him. On fast days, when the morning meal was postponed until early afternoon and meat and dairy products were proscribed, Erasmus would grow weak and so was permitted to take some food earlier in the day; because he loathed fish (the mere smell of which gave him a severe headache), he was allowed alternatives. Because he had trouble falling asleep and, once awake, had trouble falling back, he was given permission to skip matins. As for chores, Erasmus probably performed most of his in the scriptorium, copying books. The cloister had a decent library, and Erasmus was allowed to linger there.

As the days passed, Erasmus settled into a routine. But then the unexpected happened: he fell in love. The object of his affection was a fellow monk named Servatius Rogerus. Erasmus had only fleeting opportunities to speak with him directly (probably at chapel) and so instead sent him long, tender notes. Remarkably, nine have survived, and they offer a revealing look into Erasmus's state of mind.

Initially, all went well. "If we cannot be together in person, which would of course be the most pleasant thing possible," he wrote, "why should we not come together, if not as often as might be, at least sometimes, by exchanging letters?" Servatius was of the same mind, and a period of bliss followed. After a while, though, Servatius's mood seemed to darken, and Erasmus pressed him to explain why. "You surely know that you are dearer to me than my life itself and that there is no task so difficult or unpleasant that I would not undertake it gladly for your sake."

After some days passed without any word forthcoming, and with Servatius seeming to go out of his way to avoid him, Erasmus began to worry that he himself was the source of his distress. Crushed, he poured forth his anguish: "What is it that makes you so hard-hearted that you not only refuse to love him who loves you so well but do not even regard him with esteem?" His waking hours were an annoyance; his sleep was restless; his food was tasteless. The few days that had passed without his company "seemed longer than an entire year to me; they exhausted me with such pain and racked me with such lamentations that I actually came to the point, in my hatred of life's cruelty, where I more than once begged for death."

When a letter finally arrived affirming Servatius's affection, Erasmus was overjoyed. But the reprieve proved short-lived; Servatius again cooled. From Servatius's overcast look Erasmus could see that his own presence had become a burden to him. Gradually and painfully, Erasmus reconciled himself to Servatius's indifference. Deftly altering course, he recast himself as Servatius's mentor. Erasmus urged him to shake off his sluggishness, strip away his faintheartedness, and throw himself into literary studies. If he did, Erasmus would be there to help. "Do not be ashamed of any solecism you fall into. You will find that my purpose is to correct you, not to sneer at you."

These letters raise obvious questions about Erasmus's sexuality. Some have dismissed them as epistolary exercises of the sort monks of the period commonly engaged in. Erasmus's frequent citations of Horace, Ovid, and Virgil lend support to this idea. Yet something far more fundamental seems at work. The fierceness of Erasmus's devotion, the rapid fluctuations in his mood, the disruption of his sleep, the loss of his appetite—all suggest a deep passion. A. L. Rowse, an Oxford historian who in 1977 published a book titled *Homosexuals in History*, includes Erasmus (along with Leonardo and Michelangelo) in a chapter on the Renaissance. He cites not only Erasmus's letters to Servatius but also the strong attachment Erasmus later formed to a young Englishman whom he tutored in Paris. In the end, the evidence seems too thin to allow firm conclusions. What does seem clear, though, is that the young Erasmus, sequestered in the drab, regimented world of the monastery, craved intimacy and found it with a fellow monk. (Servatius, interestingly, would become the prior of Steyn, and he and Erasmus would remain on cordial terms.)

As the end of his novitiate approached, Erasmus—tiring of the monastery's unvarying routines—felt sure that the cloister was not for him and told his superiors so. They were furious. If he left, they warned, he would be considered an apostate and would never again be able to show his face in Christian company; he would fare even worse in the afterlife. They also enlisted Erasmus's guardians and some of his friends to press him, and in the end Erasmus felt he had no choice but "to accept the halter," as he put it, "much as captives in war offer their hands to the victor to be manacled."

Spurned in love and bored by his monastic rounds, Erasmus found another outlet for his devotion: books. The joys of ancient literature that he had discovered in Deventer and that had sustained him at 's Hertogenbosch became his lifeline at Steyn, and he spent more and more time in its library. Its holdings included not only authorized religious texts but also a number of classical ones, and it was to these that he was most drawn. Because the Church considered many Roman poets and playwrights immoral and blasphemous, Erasmus had to read them on the sly. So, during the day, he read Augustine, Jerome, Origen, Chrysostom, and other early Church Fathers; at night, by candlelight, he consumed Virgil, Horace, Ovid, Cicero, Quintilian, and Terence. With their wit, elegance, reflections on virtue, and insights into human nature, these writers seemed much better company than the taciturn drudges and narrow-minded moralists around him.

Erasmus organized a small reading group of like-minded monks to recite poetry, discuss texts, and share compositions. His closest collaborator was his friend Cornelis Gerard, who was living in a monastery near Leiden. Erasmus's letters to him abound in references to "Apollo's lyre" and "Pan's rustic reed," "your Horace" and "our favorite Virgil." In place of the tearful pleas he had formerly directed at Servatius, he now sent Cornelis stylized professions of chaste love based on their "bond of affection"—a shared devotion to literature. Inspired by Virgil's eclogues, Erasmus wrote a long *Carmen Buccolicum* ("Rural Song") that featured dancing naiads, dryad maidens, Aonian Muses, and a shepherd who from afar falls in love with the goddess-like Gunifolda.

On one occasion, Erasmus sent a friend a play by Terence that he had copied with his own hand. The plays of this Roman writer of the second century B.C.E. feature an unsavory cast of cads, flatterers, shrews, and priapic schemers forever trying to seduce young maidens, and many clerics considered them unfit for Christian minds. In his accompanying letter, Erasmus vigorously defended Terence against "the prattling of those ignorant and indeed malevolent dwarfs" who failed to perceive "how much moral goodness exists in Terence's plays, how much implicit exhortation to shape one's life." Those content to stammer could make do with the standard medieval texts, but anyone wanting to speak clearly had to read Terence, whom "no one but a barbarian has ever failed to love."

The term "barbarian" is a tip-off to Erasmus's membership in a growing fraternity of philosophers, poets, scholars, and clergymen who saw in the gleam of the ancient world an inspiring alternative to the gloom of their own. Erasmus was, in short, feeling the glow of the Renaissance. More than a century after it had first surfaced in Italy, this movement was finally gaining a foothold north of the Alps. Though that label for the period did not come into broad use until the nineteenth century, it captures the sense of rebirth that scholars felt as they rediscovered the classical past. In Italy itself, this renewal was transforming art, architecture, literature, science, and urban design. At no point, however, would it significantly challenge the political or social order. The Roman Church, Italy's dominant institution, would succeed in absorbing and co-opting it. In the north, however, the Renaissance would prove far more unsettling, testing axioms and institutions that had gone unchallenged for centuries. Erasmus would be a bridge as the movement traveled from south to north, and in his hands it would take on a far more disruptive character.

For Erasmus, the Italian Renaissance meant not the frescoes being applied to church walls or the statues going up in town squares but rather the journey that scholars were making *ad fontes*—to the sources. Rummaging about in musty libraries, they were discovering ancient works of literature, poetry, philosophy, rhetoric, and history that had for centuries been lost or forgotten. And they were reading familiar texts anew—not as collections of disaggregated opinions to be worked up into theorems, as with the Scholastics, but as living documents with ideas relevant to the present. The impact was dramatic. For a millennium, Christian thinkers had placed God the Almighty at the center of the universe and cast man as his frail, sinful dependent. Now, with the recovery of Greek and Roman literature, a new appreciation for the individual and his capabilities was taking root. It was promoted by a group of inquisitive and cultivated men who called themselves *umanisti*, or humanists, in recognition of the group to which they most owed their allegiance: humankind. This new human-centered outlook provided the intellectual foundation for the Renaissance. It was, in effect, a revolution in consciousness, and it was set in motion by one man: Francesco Petrarch.

Today, Petrarch is best known for the *Canzoniere*, his cycle of Italian sonnets, but during his own lifetime (1304 to 1374) he was most celebrated for his tireless efforts to revive and spread awareness of the classical past. Petrarch was the first to see the medieval centuries as a distinct period and the first to label it a "Dark Age"—a time when the cultural lights went out across Europe. Seeking an alternative, Petrarch found in antiquity a set of virtues and ideas that seemed to speak to his own day. Introspective, idiosyncratic, and relentlessly self-promoting, he is widely considered the father of Renaissance humanism. Some call him the first modern man. The attitudes and methods Petrarch pioneered would provide the foundation for the intellectual innovations that Erasmus would later use to such effect in the north.

Petrarch's new outlook arose in reaction to the revulsion he felt at the squalor and corruption of his own world. Though born in Arezzo, Tuscany, he spent much of his life in Avignon. His father, a notary, moved there in 1312 in search of work. There was plenty of it, for just three years earlier Pope Clement V had made that city his seat. His reign marked the start of the papacy's Babylonian Captivity, a term Petrarch himself coined. With the pope's arrival, thousands of strangers poured into this Provençal town, seeking employment, adventure, patronage, and pardons. The papal court became a great fiscal machine in which fees were charged for every service and offices were auctioned off to the highest bidder. The pope himself was given to unbridled ostentation, hosting nine-course banquets that featured roebucks and stags eaten off plates of gold and silver—a life of indulgence that contrasted with the fetid conditions in which most residents lived. Avignon was notorious for the terrible odor rising from the great pools of waste that collected in the town. The city, Petrarch declared, was "the most dismal, crowded, and turbulent in existence, a sink overflowing with all the gathered filth of the world," with rank-smelling alleys filled with "obscene pigs and snarling dogs."

As the papal court offered the clearest path to a lucrative career, Petrarch decided to become a cleric. Skilled in Latin and silken in manners, he gained entrée to the salons and boudoirs of the elite. He became a fixture at the palace of Cardinal Giovanni Colonna, a member of a great noble Italian family, who would become his chief patron.

While attending church one day in April 1327, Petrarch caught sight of the beautiful wife of a local nobleman. Her name was Laura, and he was instantly smitten. She did not return his ardor, however, and Petrarch would spend years pouring his frustration and anguish into his poetry. In the 366 poems that make up the *Canzoniere*, he abandoned the courtly conventions of medieval verse for intense emotional expression and obsessive self-analysis. His lyrical style was to become the model for Italian poetry for the next three centuries, earning him a claim to be the first modern poet.

Thwarted in his love for Laura, Petrarch instead cultivated his passion for ancient Rome. As a boy, he had become enamored of Cicero and, through him, of Roman literature. How noble the statesmen of Rome seemed, how pure its poets sounded, when compared with the scheming and cacophony at the papal court. By recovering the cultural heritage of antiquity, Petrarch hoped to nudge his own society onto a new path, and he began amassing a library of ancient poets and philosophers. In this period before the birth of printing, such works were available only in manuscript form and so were difficult to find. When foreign visitors appeared at the Colonna Palace, Petrarch urged them to seek out volumes by Cicero upon their return home. He sent similar appeals to France, Germany, Spain, and Tuscany, thus creating a network of hunters for rare books.

In his readings, Petrarch frequently came upon references to works that had not been seen for centuries. Rumors spread of caches of precious manuscripts languishing in the libraries of monasteries and cathedrals. Copied and recopied over centuries, these books were gathering—and in some cases turning to—dust. Petrarch worried that many crucial texts would be lost forever. "No one can doubt that the loss of the sweet solace of manuscripts is more damnable than commerce with demons," he wrote. Seeing these books as the delicate captives of barbarian jailers, he set out to free them.

It is a paradox of history that medieval monks, who so shunned pagan values, became the main rescuers of pagan texts. With the fall of Rome in the fifth century, the physical infrastructure of knowledge—schools, libraries, scribes—also crumbled. As monasteries began to appear in Italy, in the sixth century, scriptoria were established to make copies of texts, both Christian and classical. The work in these copy centers was often grueling, with scribes fighting boredom, cramps, bad light, and numb fingers, but, thanks to their perseverance, much of the Latin cultural heritage was preserved on parchment and stored on the shelves of ecclesiastical libraries.

Those libraries were notoriously hard to penetrate, however. Books were objects of reverence, and the fear of theft was acute. Monasteries also worried about the subversive content of pagan works and so were reluctant to let them circulate. In the late thirteenth century, however, in the university town of Padua, a group of learned lawyers—believing that a revival of pagan literature could help rescue Christendom—began visiting those libraries in search of lost treasures. The manuscript-hunting movement was thus born. It was not until the early fourteenth century, however, when Petrarch joined in, that the hunt got under way in earnest.

Despite the many hardships that travelers in those days faced—inclement weather, rutted roads, dirty inns, ruthless highwaymen, surly customs officials, the cost of renting horses—Petrarch loved to travel. (Many consider him the first modern tourist.) If, while on the road, he happened to see a monastery in the distance, he would often make a detour, saying to himself, "Who knows if there may not be something there I want."

His first great find came in 1333. Seeking to shake off his longing for Laura, he set out on a northern tour, traveling on the great highway to Paris. Unimpressed with that city, he quickly moved on to the Low Countries, traveling north to Ghent and then to Liège. The ecclesiastical library in that city was known for its valuable collection, and Petrarch made a companion wait while he searched it. He found two orations by Cicero that he had never heard of. One was *Pro Archia*, a speech given in defense of the poet Archias, who had been charged with falsely claiming to be a Roman citizen. Reading it, Petrarch was captivated. Cicero, then at the height of his fame as an orator, spoke in support not just of this one poet but of poets in general. These gifted men, he declared, performed an invaluable service by providing posterity with likenesses of heroic men—not statues or portraits of their physical selves but effigies of their "minds and characters."

To Petrarch, such statements seemed almost subversive. The medieval Church shunned glory and achievement. It prized meekness rather than strength and retreat over activism. Yet here was Cicero saluting poets for publicizing and promoting the deeds of generals and statesmen. Cicero further acknowledged that "ambition is a universal factor in life" and that "the nobler a man is, the more susceptible is he to the sweets of fame." Rather than "disclaim this human weakness," we should "admit it unabashed." This echoed Petrarch's own longing for a life of noble acts and the honors they bring.

One phrase in Cicero's speech in particular stood out: *de studiis humanitatis*—humanist studies. Cicero used the term to refer to all the liberal arts that students needed to realize their full potential as human beings and to participate fully in the life of the community. This suggested a much broader approach to education and culture than that provided by the knotty manuals of the medieval schoolroom or the convoluted exercises of the Scholastic doctors.

Petrarch's joy at discovering these long-lost works was tempered by his sorrow at their condition: mutilated, mildewed, faded, and riddled with errors. In the quiet of his study, he developed a method to correct those errors and produce a text as close to the original as possible. He had an early success with Livy's *History of Rome*. This work was a primary source of information about imperial Rome, but only 35 of its 142 books had survived, and even they were badly mangled. Petrarch had at hand two copies—one from the cathedral in Chartres, the other from the library of the Sorbonne in Paris. Drawing on his knowledge of Latin grammar, classical style, and Roman history, he compared the manuscripts and, where they differed, deduced the superior reading. He also wove together Livy's account of three different decades into a single coherent narrative. The finished version was more complete and accurate than any other version then available. With this work, Petrarch helped inaugurate the discipline of critical textual editing—an essential tool of modern scholarship, and one that Erasmus would apply to radical effect.

In his efforts to revive the Roman heritage, Petrarch decided to visit its seat. After sailing from Marseilles in late December 1336, he was in Rome by March 1337. He was dismayed to see how far the Eternal City had fallen. Its population—around a million at its imperial height—had declined to about 20,000, many of them beggars and prostitutes taking shelter among the broken palaces, collapsed temples, and decapitated columns. With a medieval guidebook in hand, Petrarch wandered amid the ruins, seeking out landmarks of Rome's pagan and Christian past. Passing the moss-covered temples, the hovels around the Pantheon, the goats drinking from marble sarcophagi, he conjured up great moments from the Roman past: here Brutus prepared vengeance for his offended honor; there Cincinnatus plowed when he was summoned to be dictator; here Peter was crucified; there Paul was beheaded. Climbing to the roof of the Baths of Diocletian, Petrarch would gaze out on the shattered city and recall the glittering metropolis that had once been.

Back in Avignon, Petrarch found its hypocrisy and filth more repulsive than ever, so he moved twenty miles to Vaucluse, the site of a famous fountain. There, living in a simple cottage, he became one of history's first literary recluses. His main companions were his books, which, he wrote, were like living persons to him, except that they never bored him and were always obedient to his command. He loved the serenity of the landscape—Petrarch wrote frequently of his fondness for nature—but he detested the hordes of visitors to the fountain.

Still in Rome's thrall, Petrarch pondered how he might promote its glory. He came up with the idea of restoring the ancient tradition of crowning poets with laurel leaves on the Capitoline Hill. And he had the perfect candidate: himself. Now in his midthirties, Petrarch was largely unknown in Rome, but his reputation as a Latinist was spreading, and he worked his connections to arrange such an honor. When in September 1340 a messenger arrived with an invitation from the Roman Senate to come to the city to be crowned poet laureate, Petrarch feigned surprise, but he immediately began preparing for the journey.

The event took place on Easter Day 1341. Petrarch entered the Senatorial Palace on the Capitoline Hill and ascended to the audience chamber on the second floor. There he gave an oration in which he extolled the contributions that poets can make to society. After the laurel crown was placed on his head, he recited a sonnet on the heroes of Rome, then declared himself a Roman citizen. In doing so, Petrarch hoped to send a signal to others that seeking glory was not something to be ashamed of. More generally, he sought to remind the world of the cultural brilliance that Rome had once radiated and could give off again.

Petrarch's oration on the Capitoline Hill is commonly considered the starting point of the literary Renaissance in Italy. But another episode in his life, though less dramatic, would prove even more consequential. In 1345, while visiting the cathedral library in Verona, he discovered a codex of Cicero's letters to his friend Atticus and several other acquaintances. (A codex is a hand-copied manuscript bound together in the form of a book.) These letters had been lost for centuries, but Petrarch knew of them from references in other works. Reading them, he was shocked. Instead of the sage statesman and eloquent orator with whom he was familiar, he encountered the private, everyday Cicero, who offered unguarded comments on political affairs, contemporary figures, his own comings and goings, and his business dealings. Cicero came across as combative, self-glorifying, vacillating, ruthlessly ambitious, and, in not a few cases, unscrupulous.

The more time he spent in Cicero's company, however, the more Petrarch came to admire him. Written in colloquial yet engaging Latin, his letters offered an inside look at his efforts to cope with the chaos engulfing the Roman republic as it slid toward dictatorship. No less engaging were Cicero's observations about daily life—the books he read, the dinner parties he attended, the delight he took in his country villas, and, finally, the grief he felt over the death of his beloved daughter, Tullia. Impressed with Cicero's gift for self-revelation, Petrarch came to see him as not simply a spokesman for the classical past but a real person driven by fears, ambitions, and appetites.

Cicero's letters showed Petrarch how the ordinary occurrences of everyday life could become the stuff of literature, and he began using his own correspondence to offer opinions about people, places, events, and ideas, with a larger audience—and posterity—in mind. In this way, he helped focus new attention on the art of letter writing (which Erasmus would further advance). More generally, Cicero's letters fed Petrarch's absorption with the unique nature of his own sentiments, and in his letters he offered a carefully crafted image of himself. It was an early expression of the individualism that Jacob Burckhardt, in *The Civilization of the Renaissance in Italy*, identified as one of the era's defining traits.

More profoundly, Cicero's writings gave Petrarch a new perspective on man and his place in society. The medieval Church was concerned overwhelmingly with man's relationship to God and how the faithful could through his grace attain salvation. Cicero was more concerned with man's relation to man. All humans, he believed, belong to a universal brotherhood irrespective of state, race, or caste (though Cicero himself owned slaves), and every individual has a spark of the divine. "Just as the horse is designed by nature for running, the ox for plowing, and the dog for running," Cicero wrote in *De finibus*, "so man, as Aristotle observes, is born for two purposes: thought and action." In contrast to the medieval values of hierarchy, obedience, and self-denial, Cicero championed civic engagement and public service. *Studia humanitatis* offered a curriculum through which such values could be imparted.

Because Cicero and other Roman thinkers derived most of their ideas from the Greeks, Petrarch set out to learn their language. Since the division of the Roman Empire in the third century, the knowledge of Greek had gradually faded from the Latin West. Petrarch made only limited progress, however. After one diplomat presented him with a volume of Homer, he recalled in a letter how he would sometimes clasp the work to his breast and sigh, "O great man, how gladly would I hear you speak!"

For all his admiration for pagan literature, Petrarch remained a devout Christian, believing that "on the Gospel alone" could "all true learning" be built. When he was around forty, he experienced a spiritual crisis brought on by his inability to control his physical urges, especially sexual ones. For support and consolation, he turned to Augustine's *Confessions*. Carrying the book around with him, he would consult it in moments of despair. In a famous episode that took place in 1336, Petrarch scaled Mont Ventoux in Provence; on reaching the summit, he opened his copy of the *Confessions* at random and alighted on a passage that admonished men for admiring mountains while losing sight of their own souls. At that moment, he wrote, he began turning from worldly things. In his *Secretum* ("My Secret Book"), Petrarch engaged in an imaginary dialogue with Augustine. Over and over, the African bishop chastises him for pursuing fame and love rather than devoting himself fully to God. Ultimately, the *Secretum* expressed the conflict Petrarch felt between the ideals of medieval withdrawal and those of secular engagement, and he would spend his remaining years trying to reconcile them—to blend Cicero and Christ.

At that he would never quite succeed. As Petrarch's piety increased, so did his prickliness, vanity, and self-absorption. While his physical fires faded, his lust for fame continued to burn, and he never found a way to square his yearning for laurels and applause with his belief in humility and contemplation. Petrarch had pointed the way toward a new vision; it would fall to his successors to define it.

Foremost among them was Giovanni Boccaccio. He and Petrarch first met in 1350, when Petrarch, on his way to Rome to celebrate the Jubilee year, passed through Florence, where Boccaccio lived. Thus began one of the most famous literary friendships in history. Already at work on *The Decameron*, Boccaccio began, under Petrarch's tutelage, to write in Latin. He compiled a sprawling encyclopedia of the pagan gods that would become a standard reference work for five centuries. Catching from Petrarch the book-collecting fever, Boccaccio became a frequent visitor to monastic libraries; at Monte Cassino, he helped recover some long-lost codices of Tacitus. Boccaccio also began studying Greek and, after gaining some fluency, worked with a tutor to make rough Latin translations of the *Iliad* and the *Odyssey*, which he presented to Petrarch as gifts.

Thanks to Boccaccio's influence, Florence became the center of humanist studies in Italy. In 1397, Manuel Chrysoloras, a leading Byzantine classical scholar, arrived to teach Greek, and over the next five years he trained a cadre of students who helped revive the Greek tradition. In the mid-fifteenth century, a modern version of Plato's Academy was established in the city, helping spark a new wave of enthusiasm for Platonic philosophy. Books were venerated like saintly relics, and scholars seeking fame schemed their way into monastic libraries in the hope of finding long-neglected classics. Florence became known as the Athens on the Arno, a city of freedom and refinement in which men of talent and ambition could cultivate literature, the arts, and their careers.

From Florence, the movement spread to Venice, Verona, Milan, and, finally, Rome itself. After the end of the Great Schism in 1417 and the return of the papacy to Rome, humanists were appointed to many key positions, and every bull and brief was given a fine Ciceronian gloss. Then, in 1447, Rome got a humanist pope. As a poor young scholar, Nicholas V had discovered several important manuscripts, and as pontiff he drew on the full resources of his office to expand his collection. At the time of his death, in 1455, it had several thousand volumes; bequeathed to the Church, they became the basis for the Vatican Library.

A century after Petrarch was crowned on the Capitoline Hill, then, his vision of restoring Rome to its traditional place as the center of Western civilization was becoming a reality. Across Italy, humanists congratulated themselves on having banished the Dark Ages and replaced them with an era of eloquence and wisdom; from the north, aspiring scholars came by the thousand to catch a glint of the brilliant blaze. In the end, though, the humanists fell well short of their goal. In their push to recover the past, they became enslaved to it; they did not simply study the ancients but idolized them, and much of their work was mannered and contrived. Rome became an arena for courtly intrigue, libelous attacks, and venomous feuds set off by disagreements over tenses and punctuation. Dependent on ruling elites for jobs and patronage, the humanists for the most part kowtowed to them. Thus wedded to the status quo, they were unable to develop a compelling alternative.

There was one notable exception: Lorenzo Valla. If Petrarch was the founding father of humanism, Valla was its enfant terrible. Of all the Italian humanists, this pioneering philologist would have the strongest influence on Erasmus. Whereas Petrarch was charming and engaging, Valla was combative and obnoxious. During his brief life (1407 to 1457), he had to keep constantly on the move to elude his enemies. Intellectually, however, no other Renaissance figure could match him.

Valla's specialty was grammar. Educated in Greek and Latin by the top schoolmasters of his day, he used his knowledge of syntax and semantics to decipher documents and decode texts. His most famous feat was his debunking of the so-called Donation of Constantine—a hallowed document cited by generations of popes to justify their involvement in temporal affairs. In it, the emperor Constantine, on his deathbed, ceded sweeping powers and properties to Sylvester I (pontiff from 314 to 335), including control of Rome, Italy, and all of the western provinces of the empire, to be held in perpetuity by the Roman See. From the ninth to the fifteenth centuries, the Donation had been generally accepted as genuine.

Valla set out to demolish it. In *On the Falsely Believed and Fictitious Donation of Constantine*, he first pointed out the implausibility of an emperor's signing away such claims, then offered a string of examples of anachronistic language in the document. For instance, it used the word "satraps," even though this term was not applied to higher officials in Rome until the mid-eighth century. "Numbskull, blockhead!" he wrote. "Whoever heard of satraps being mentioned in the councils of the Romans?" On the basis of such blunders, Valla pronounced the Donation a forgery, speculating that it had been drafted in the eighth century to bolster the papacy's claims in its conflict with the Carolingian emperors. (Subsequent research has borne him out.) Valla's literary sleuthing thus helped undermine a central pillar of papal authority.

This was but one of many takedowns Valla carried out. He used grammar to raise questions about the plausibility of the Trinity. He claimed that some of the presumed facts in Livy's *History of Rome* could not possibly be true. He argued that Aristotle's ten categories of classification should be reduced to three. Most audaciously of all, he insisted that the Apostles' Creed was produced not by the apostles but by the fourth-century Council of Nicaea. Infuriated by such apostasies, the Church via the Inquisition launched an investigation into Valla's writings. They were found to be heretical on eight counts. Only the personal intervention of Alfonso I of Aragon, king of Naples, for whom Valla was then working as a royal secretary, kept him from the stake.

Undaunted, Valla—seeing the plum positions being handed out to humanists in Rome—wanted one for himself, and, despite the many headaches he had caused the Church, he managed to secure an appointment as an apostolic secretary to Nicholas V. He was put to work translating Thucydides and Herodotus. On the side, though, Valla prepared what would be his most daring work. Comparing the text of the Latin Vulgate with old Greek and Latin manuscripts of the New Testament, he concluded that the Vulgate was full of solecisms, obscurities, and clumsy translations, and he compiled a series of notes pointing them out and offering alternatives. In short, Valla was using grammar to correct the Bible itself; not even theologians, he maintained, should be exempt from the rules governing tenses and cases. His annotations on the New Testament were so explosive that few copies were put into circulation; most instead sat unexamined in monastic libraries—grenades waiting to go off.

Because of Valla's irreverence and offensiveness, the Church made sure that most of his works remained inaccessible. One exception was *De Elegantiae Linguae Latinae* ("Elegances of the Latin Language"). This mammoth folio of some five hundred pages was the most ambitious new Latin grammar to appear since late antiquity. On the surface, it seemed harmless enough, offering technical observations on the use of some two thousand terms. But Valla was not interested simply in helping people write better Latin; he wanted to spark a cultural revolution. As he explained in his introduction, the Roman conquests, however bloody and cruel, had served the cause of civilization by spreading Latin, "a gateway to every form of knowledge." But, just as ancient Rome had been overrun by the Goths, so had its language been invaded by barbarian usages; he was now seeking to rally a force to drive them out and restore Latin to its original splendor. In the body of the text, Valla, drawing on Cicero, Quintilian, and many others, sought to show how the language had been corrupted and how it could be purified.

The superiority of *De Elegantiae* to medieval grammar manuals was immediately recognized. Despite its great bulk and steep price, it found a huge market, appearing in fifty-nine editions in sixty-five years and remaining a fixture in grammar schools until the start of the nineteenth century. It is now considered a foundational text of modern linguistics.

At Steyn, Erasmus managed to obtain a copy of this work, and it became his intellectual compass. *De Elegantiae* opened his eyes to how sloppy language can obscure meanings and conceal abuses and how a knowledge of usage and idiom could be applied to challenge the claims and presumptions of ruling institutions. When Erasmus pressed the book on his reading group, however, he met great resistance; given the Church's condemnation of Valla, the members were reluctant to read him. Rising to his defense, Erasmus admonished his friend Cornelis Gerard that, in impugning Valla, "you have hurt all educated men."

Valla's great influence on Erasmus's thinking would be apparent in his first major literary undertaking, begun while he was at Steyn. (It would not be published until 1520, after he had become famous.) Titled *Antibarbari* ("Against the Barbarians") and framed as a dialogue, it captured Erasmus's contempt for those philistines who sought to discourage Christians from reading secular literature. Jacob Batt, a real-life town clerk who was a friend of Erasmus's and who here serves as his mouthpiece, derides the narrow-minded tyrants who, acting as society's censors, impose their mediocre standards on everyone else. He expresses special contempt for those who oppose reading the pagans on the grounds that they are licentious or obscene. Pagan writers had helped prepare the world for Christ, he declares, and Christianity had borrowed a great deal from them. In the end, the enemies of the humanities were no different from the Goths who had overrun Rome.

The *Antibarbari* featured some of the humanists' worst flaws—verbosity, arrogance, a love of polemics, and unqualified deference toward the ancients. Batt's inability or unwillingness to imagine content that might genuinely offend pious Christians or be unsuitable for young minds reflected Erasmus's refusal to seriously engage with the issue. But engagement was not his purpose. The humanists were trying to raise a revolt against the monks and metaphysicians who, feeling threatened by the cultural revival under way, wanted to quash it. The *Antibarbari* was meant as a rallying cry in the campaign to discredit them and acclaim the New Learning.

In April 1492—six years after entering the cloister—Erasmus was ordained a priest. He was now a full-fledged cleric, authorized to perform the Mass, hear confession, and perform baptisms. But, as the scornful tone of his dialogue suggests, he had grown impatient with his surroundings. The dreaded bell summoning the monks to matins; the procession of fast days that unsettled his stomach; the monotonous rounds of prayer and chanting; the insularity of his fellow inmates—all were becoming unbearable. Erasmus heard that the bishop of Cambrai to the south was seeking a Latin secretary, and he put himself forward as a candidate. His superiors—convinced that he was no Thomas à Kempis—approved his application. So did the bishop.

Erasmus's departure, in 1493, was kept secret, for monks were not normally allowed to leave the cloister. He did, however, inform Willem Hermans, a fellow monk and good friend, of his plans. Eager to bid him farewell, Hermans positioned himself at a point on the road outside Gouda where Erasmus was due to pass. When the appointed hour came, however, there was no sign of Erasmus. Determined to hide his movements, he had intentionally misled his friend, and the poor fellow was left to wait haplessly on the side of the road.

Seemingly inconsequential at the time, Erasmus's flight from the monastery would in fact prove profoundly significant—a herald of the great monastic exodus to come. In his baggage he had a rough draft of the *Antibarbari*, which he planned to use as a calling card in humanist circles. Now in his midtwenties, Erasmus headed south into the world, eager to make his mark on it.

PENANCE AND DREAD

Throughout his life, Martin Luther experienced crushing bouts of despair. In his letters and his Table Talk, he described the acute anguish he felt during these spells—the sweating and shaking, the panic and fear, the sense of worthlessness and abandonment. These episodes have led to speculation that Luther suffered from depression. That may well have been so, but as Luther described them, these squalls had a strong spiritual dimension. *Anfechtungen*, he called them, meaning a type of existential trial sent by God to test the soul. When they struck, Luther felt gripped by a sort of cosmic angst, in which the Father, the Son, and Mother Church all seemed to conspire against him. Luther's decision to enter the monastery was driven in part by a desire to overcome these attacks, and the inability of the cloister to provide relief helped set off his revolt against the Church. It was in his youth that these dark phases first struck, and so it is there that one must seek their source.

At first glance, Luther's schoolboy days seem to have been unremarkable. The Latin school he attended in Mansfeld had none of the renown of St. Lebwin's in Deventer, but its curriculum was similar. Latin grammar was the main subject, and, as with Erasmus, Martin had its fundamentals pounded into him. In each class a student was assigned the role of *lupus*, or wolf, who was charged with keeping a list of demerits for violations of the school's code; these infractions included cursing and speaking German. (The vernacular was not considered important enough to teach.) Those with the most infractions at the end of each week were whipped, and the students who performed worst in class were forced to wear an *asinus*, a wooden donkey's head.

Luther was once beaten fifteen times for failing to conjugate something he had yet to be taught. Schools in those days, he later wrote, were "a hell and purgatory" in which students "were tormented with cases and tenses" yet "learned less than nothing despite all the flogging, trembling, anguish, and misery." Luther did, however, get to read Aesop's fables, which would become lifelong favorites, as well as selections from such Latin writers as Plautus and Terence, which he enjoyed. And, despite his bitter memories, his lessons in Mansfeld would prove of incalculable benefit. Luther was one of the sixteenth century's greatest writers; from the moment he burst onto the scene with his Ninety-Five Theses, he showed an astounding ability to move, mobilize, and unsettle with his pen. And it was at the little Latin school in Mansfeld that he first began to learn the rudiments of rhetoric.

By his fourteenth year, he had exhausted the school's offerings, and his father, seeing his intelligence and envisioning for him a legal career that could be of use in protecting his own economic interests, arranged for him to attend a secondary school in Magdeburg, located forty miles to the north on the Elbe River. In the spring of 1496 or 1497, Luther, accompanied by an older boy whose father was a business associate of Hans's, left sleepy Mansfeld on his first real foray into the world. On the road he joined a continent restlessly on the move—merchants transporting goods, envoys carrying communiqués, scholars taking up university posts, seasonal workers seeking employment, preachers in search of pulpits, penitents en route to shrines, and students like himself traveling from out-of-the-way towns and hamlets to big-city secondary schools.

With a population of more than 20,000 and a thriving trade in grain, wool, and textiles, Magdeburg was the dominant city between Germany's central mountains and the Baltic Sea. In addition to being the seat of an archbishopric and the site of a great cathedral famous for its many relics, the city was known for its schools. Though details about Luther's time there are scant, the school he attended is believed to have been associated with the Brethren of the Common Life—the same movement of pious laymen that Erasmus had encountered in Deventer. In all, Luther would spend a year there, and from the Brethren he got an early glimpse of a type of inner faith very different from the elaborate ritualism of the Church.

In 1498, Luther transferred from Magdeburg to a school in Eisenach, about a hundred miles to the southwest. Here, he was just ten or so miles from Möhra, the home of his father's family. His mother had relatives there, and Martin stayed with them. Her family members were well-off urban professionals, most of whom had graduated from a university, and they no doubt instilled in Luther the value of education. Eisenach had no more than 3,000 or 4,000 residents, and Luther seemed to prefer its small-town tranquility to Magdeburg's metropolitan bustle. "My beloved city," he would later call it. It was located on the fringes of the Thuringian Forest, a rolling expanse blanketed with pines and firs. Just outside town, on a great bluff, sat the famous Wartburg Castle, an imposing medieval fortress that, though largely abandoned, would play a critical part in Luther's later life.

The house in which Luther lived is today a whitewashed four-story dwelling that includes a museum (the Lutherhaus) offering exhibits of scenes from Luther's life. Just a five-minute walk away, remarkably, is the Bachhaus, a museum dedicated to Johann Sebastian Bach, who was born in Eisenach in 1685 and who spent his first ten years there. Bach was baptized at St. George's, the parish church, a dilapidated structure in the center of town, where several members of his family were organists. The church also ran the Latin school that Luther attended. At both the school and the church, Bach would absorb the language and cadences of Luther's Bible, and he would later put into music Luther's theological vision. This one modest church in this one provincial town, then, helped shape the early lives of two of Germany's most towering figures.

At the school, Luther continued his study of grammar and rhetoric, with some instruction in logic and moral philosophy as well. It was outside the classroom, though, that he got some of his most lasting lessons. Even by late-medieval standards, Eisenach was awash in piety. An estimated one-tenth of its residents were clergymen, and while the town as a whole struggled economically, its churches and cloisters thrived. Later, Luther would call Eisenach a "nest of priests," but at the time he was fully immersed in its reverent ways. The family he stayed with, the Schalbes, were prominent burghers who, while professionally ambitious, were also deeply devout. Heinrich Schalbe, the family head, was a generous backer of the Franciscans, who had a cloister at the foot of the Wartburg. Luther frequently visited the friars and became close to Johannes Braun, a priest who was the vicar of a local religious foundation. Luther served as a choir-boy at St. George's and was a fixture at the vespers service on Sunday.

He was also present for many sermons. Now in his impressionable teen years, Martin would absorb from them the core tenets of the medieval Church, including the complex rituals and doctrines surrounding penance, the centerpiece of the medieval system of piety. This sacrament was the point at which the Church most frequently and intimately touched the lives of the laity—Luther's included. His exposure to it played a key part in setting off his dark moods and, much later, spurring his revolt.

Medieval sermons were very long, typically lasting an hour or more. They seemed even longer, for seating in most churches was limited, and many congregants had to stand. By one estimate, an urban dweller heard as many as eight hundred sermons in a lifetime. Most of them were based on the daily Bible passages fixed by the Church, and preachers often explained a passage word for word, with little context and even less inspiration. Others offered extravagant allegories—a pelican symbolizing Christ's atonement, goats standing in for the bodies of the saints, shoes representing the Gospel incarnate. To hold the congregation's attention, preachers often resorted to irreverent anecdotes, sensational stories, off-color jokes, fables from the animal kingdom, and miraculous episodes from the lives of the saints. As Erasmus would observe in the *Praise of Folly*, whenever a preacher expounds a serious argument, "everybody is asleep or yawning or feeling queasy," but if he embarks on "some old wives' tale," as so often happened, "his audience sits up and takes notice open-mouthed."

The most reliable means of riveting an audience, however, was to summon up the prospect of death and the gruesome agonies awaiting those expiring in a state of unexpiated sin. This was a staple theme of the preaching manuals and sermon collections that flowed from the printing presses in the late fifteenth century. They stressed the need to impress the laity with behaving righteously so as to minimize the suffering they would have to endure in the afterlife. Because of Adam's original sin, it was held, man is by nature depraved and so bound to transgress. Fortunately, the Church in its abounding mercy offered a means for absolving sin: penance.

This sacrament had three parts. First, the penitent had to show contrition—to feel genuine remorse over his transgression. Next, he had to confess—to offer a full accounting of his mortal sins and acknowledge his sorrow for them. If the priest felt that a heartfelt confession had been made, he as Christ's representative pronounced absolution, taking away the individual's sin and making him guiltless before God. Finally, there was satisfaction—the acts the sinner had to perform to compensate for the injury he had done to God. Prescribed by the priest and based on the gravity of the sin, these ranged from the mildly inconvenient or uncomfortable—reciting a number of Hail Marys, giving alms to the poor, fasting—to the seriously afflicting, such as flagellation, nightly vigils, pilgrimages, and the wearing of hair shirts.

The obligation of Christians to confess their sins to a priest is not mentioned in the Bible, but medieval writers, drawing on several ambiguous passages, maintained that such an act was mandated by divine law. In 1215, this requirement was made binding by the papal decree *Omnis utriusque sexus.* At least once a year—preferably at Easter—all adult Christians were expected to confess. To help priests carry out this task, numerous confessor manuals were produced. These listed the different types of sins, weighed their seriousness, and suggested questions to ask. The sins covered the full range of human behavior, from oversleeping and stinginess to intoxication and blasphemy. Sexual activity received special attention. One manual listed sixteen levels of sexual transgression, from chaste kisses at one end to bestiality at the other; masturbation was ranked the twelfth most serious offense—higher even than incest and rape (since ejaculation occurred without the possibility of procreation). The late-medieval French theologian Jean de Gerson prepared an entire volume to guide confessors on masturbation. Not only deeds but also thoughts—especially those involving sins of desire—were considered transgressions, and the penitent had to take note of every wayward impulse, ache, and craving. He also had to relate the "aggravating circumstances" in which each sin occurred so that the priest could determine the state of his heart and the degree of his guilt.

Even when penitents performed the required acts of satisfaction, there remained a residue of sin that had to be expiated before they could be admitted to heaven. This expiation took place in purgatory, a sort of halfway house between heaven and hell. Like private confession, purgatory is not mentioned in the Bible. During Christianity's first millennium, the dead were divided into two groups—the saved and the damned—and were consigned to heaven or hell. But the stark nature of this divide, and the fear of being trapped for all eternity on the wrong side of it, led in the late twelfth century to the conceiving of a physical realm between the two. Unlike hell, to which those guilty of mortal sins such as murder and adultery were condemned and from which there was no escape, purgatory received those who were guilty of lesser sins such as sloth and envy and who had to work off their debt to God before gaining access to paradise.

The main motif of purgatory was fire. (This was based on 1 Corinthians 3:10–15, where Paul fleetingly mentions that every work will be tested by fire.) There were circles of fire, rivers of fire, lakes of fire, fire-breathing monsters, burning walls and moats, and flaming valleys and mountains. These fires burned away the remaining traces of the sins committed on earth, purifying the soul in preparation for its heavenward journey. The length of the stay depended on the gravity of the sins. Usually, the duration was relatively short—a few days or months—but it could seem an eternity because, as Thomas Aquinas observed, "the least pain of Purgatory surpasses the greatest pain in this life."

In Dante's *Purgatorio*, this realm is a mountain in the southern hemisphere with seven terraces, each corresponding to one of the seven deadly sins. The proud carry heavy weights on their backs, becoming permanently stooped. The envious have their eyelids sewn shut with iron wire. The wrathful are enveloped in black smoke, which blinds them. The slothful are forced to run without rest. The punishments on Mount Purgatory are considerably milder than those in the Inferno, and the atmosphere as a whole is more hopeful, for the penitents there can, through great labor, cleanse themselves in preparation for entering Paradiso.

Most medieval preachers, however, stressed punishment over purgation as they sought to jolt their congregants onto the path of virtue. With great ingenuity they conjured up the torments that souls face in purgatory—the fires more scorching than any that burn on earth; the sleepless nights spent chained to red-hot furnaces; the searing brands applied to the flesh; the sadistic attendants inflicting tortures from head to toe, causing more intense pain than that suffered by St. Lawrence when he was martyred on a gridiron. According to the Church, those in purgatory could be aided by the actions of the living, so the laity in their desperation rushed to take advantage of every available means of relief. The wealthy left large bequests to churches to endow the saying of Masses on their behalf for years after their death, in the belief that those Masses would shorten their stay in purgatory. The common man bought indulgences—certificates that remitted the punishment due for sin and so helped reduce the purgatorial sentence, both for themselves after death and for departed loved ones in current anguish.

With sin held to be inevitable and absolution always incomplete, however, a stay in purgatory was all but ensured; the only question was for how long. A stray lustful thought, an impulsively uttered oath, an imperfectly performed fast—all constituted transgressions that added to the purgatorial sentence. The Church's parallel insistence on the existence of free will and the individual's ability to abstain from sin magnified the psychological burden. The medieval system of penance thus turned everyday life into a source of never-ending anxiety. As Pope Gregory I (the Great) observed, it was a characteristic of the pious "to recognize guilt where there is no guilt."

This system gave the Church extraordinary control over the lives of the laity. The main agent was the priest. Only the priest had the power to grant absolution. It was up to him to determine the thoroughness of the confession and the degree of satisfaction required. Only the priest, with the words "I absolve you," could free the penitent from serious sin. That phrase became a sort of incantation, which, when uttered, offered relief from any additional burden to be faced in the afterlife. According to Scholastic theology, the expression of contrition did not produce forgiveness apart from the absolution granted by the priest, so without the sacrament of penance, relief was impossible.

The power this gave priests invited abuse. Many charged a fee for hearing confession. The rite provided them with a license to pry into the most intimate corners of a penitent's life. Many priests lacked the judgment, training, or tact needed to carry out this delicate task. Even more important in the light of future events was the way in which penance turned the personal act of remorse over one's sins into a formalized act that offered salvation as a reward to all who followed the rules, apart from any genuine internal change. Such a system was bound to stir unhappiness among members of the expanding middle class who craved more intimate forms of fulfillment.

Growing up in Mansfeld, young Martin had shuddered at the judgment of Christ, the horrors of hell, the scheming of the Devil. Now, attending sermons in St. George's church in Eisenach, he heard dire warnings about the wages of sin and the excruciating punishments awaiting those who transgressed. No matter how hard he tried to avoid sin, it seemed, he was doomed to stray and be severely punished for his trespasses. This prospect pitched him into a slough of desolation and dread. Whatever psychological disorder Luther may have suffered from, the Church's penitential system contributed strongly to his *Anfechtungen*.

Despite these trials, he managed to complete his studies at St. George's. University was next. Of the existing institutions, Heidelberg seemed too far to the west and Leipzig too far to the east. The University of Erfurt, in Thuringia, was only fifty miles from his parents' home in Mansfeld and so was considered more suitable. In the spring of 1501, at the age of eighteen, Martin set off for that prominent city in central Germany. It would be his springboard into history.

5

BREAKTHROUGH

As he covered the 150 miles from Steyn to Cambrai, in 1493, Erasmus was moving from the insular, Dutch-speaking lands of the northern Netherlands to the more refined, French-speaking lands of the south. Cambrai was a major commercial city whose prosperity rested on the production of woolen cloth and cambric, a fine linen named after the town. The diocese of Cambrai was unusually large, with a thousand or so parishes spread across a large expanse of what is now southern Belgium and northern France; the bishop, Hendrik van Bergen, was as powerful as any count or duke. His main goal was to obtain a cardinal's hat, and in pursuit of it he planned to visit Rome. If he did go, Erasmus as his secretary would probably accompany him.

In the meantime, Erasmus helped Hendrik as he moved from town to town on diocesan business, polishing the Latin of the bishop's letters and orations. He may have also joined Hendrik on his visits to the Burgundian court in Brussels, the most splendid in all of Europe. After six years of monastic seclusion, Erasmus found himself in the glittering company of squires, counselors, envoys, and abbots.

Unfortunately, Hendrik's campaign to become a cardinal stalled, and the trip to Italy was postponed. And, after an initial show of warmth toward his young assistant, the bishop cooled. Disappointed, Erasmus consoled himself with books. Catching the manuscript-hunting fever, he began visiting the libraries of nearby monasteries. In an Augustinian priory in the Sonian Forest outside Brussels, he found a bulky codex containing several works by Augustine, and he took it with him into his cell at night. One of the monks recalled how all there were "amazed and amused that a cleric should prefer one of those large codices to other things, and they could not understand what he found in the saint to delight him so."

Feeling lonely and unappreciated, Erasmus began plotting his escape.

Ever since entering the monastery, he had regretted the interruption of his studies. A hundred miles to the south was Paris, home of Europe's most prestigious university, with its celebrated school of theology. A degree from it would provide an invaluable credential as he sought to make his way in the world of Christian letters. The bishop gave his blessing and a pledge of support, and in 1495 Erasmus set off for Europe's intellectual capital.

With a population of around 100,000, Paris was one of Europe's largest cities, but it remained in many ways medieval, as Erasmus—probably entering from the north—would have immediately sensed while he made his way through its grimy neighborhoods. The streets were so narrow that when a pack mule was unloaded, all traffic came to a halt. Unpaved alleyways led off into congested districts of fishmongers and apothecaries, barbers and blacksmiths, money changers and cabinetmakers. The Right Bank was home to much of the city's commerce, and as Erasmus proceeded south, he would have seen stately trading houses and administrative buildings as well as the sturdy *maisons* of the upper bourgeoisie.

Crossing Pont Notre-Dame, he would have entered the even more packed Left Bank. The main north-south artery, Rue Saint-Jacques, was full of students milling about its bookshops, open-air stalls, and printing houses. (Paris at the time was northern Europe's leading book center.) The street led into the Latin Quarter—a grubby maze of monasteries, churches, inns, taverns, brothels, dance halls, and the buildings and boardinghouses of the University of Paris. Four thousand students from around Europe were enrolled there—a rowdy, polyglot mix of nationalities able to communicate in their shared language, Latin (hence the quarter's name). Most lived and studied in the sixty or so run-down residences known as colleges.

Erasmus's residence, the Collège de Montaigu, sat on Montagne Sainte-Geneviève, the great hill on the Left Bank. (Today, the site is occupied by the austerely classical Bibliothèque Sainte-Geneviève, part of the University of Paris library system; across the street is the Panthéon.) The master of the college, Jan Standonck, had established a special dormitory for poor students, and it was here that Erasmus lived. To his dismay, the conditions were even more severe than they had been at Steyn. Fasts were frequent, and meals often consisted of no more than a single (usually rotten) egg and a third of a pint of cheap wine mixed with water. Because firewood was expensive, there was no heat, and in winter the cold was debilitating. The cubicles on the ground floor had moldy walls and reeked from a nearby latrine. Those unable to keep up with the study schedule were savagely whipped, often to the point of injury. Of the many students in Standonck's charge, Erasmus would later write, he had within a year "caused the deaths of very many capable, gifted, promising youths" and brought others "to blindness, emotional breakdown, or leprosy." The privations Erasmus experienced there would reinforce his aversion to monkish asceticism.

The curriculum was no less punishing. The University of Paris had four faculties—arts, law, medicine, and theology. The doctorate in theology took a minimum of eight years and an average of fifteen to complete. The theology school was also known as the Sorbonne, after Robert de Sorbon, a wealthy theologian who in 1257 had provided the funds for some communal housing for poor students. Even more than Rome, the University of Paris was considered authoritative in matters of doctrine; the pope often looked to its faculty to settle differences and arbitrate disputes. Paris owed its reputation in part to the eminent figures who over the centuries had taught there, including Peter Abelard, the master of the dialectical method; Peter Lombard, the author of the main handbook of medieval theology; and Thomas Aquinas, whose *Summa Theologica* was considered the supreme intellectual achievement of the medieval Church.

These men were central figures in the movement known as Scholasticism. It dominated the faculty at Paris, as at other theology schools. By applying logic to theological questions, the Scholastics sought to demonstrate religious propositions with the same precision and rigor as scientific ones. Students were trained in constructing syllogisms, analyzing theses and the arguments against them, and stating refutations and conclusions. (A sample syllogism: Socrates is a man; all men are mortal; therefore, Socrates is mortal.) A key element of instruction was the disputation. A question posed by the master was defended by a senior student against objections posed by other students; at the end, the master summarized the course of the debate and presented his own solution, answering major objections. At the Sorbonne, these sessions were often uproarious affairs, with egos un-chained and passions unleashed. Sometimes the discussions spilled into the street, where, fueled by alcohol, they exploded into brawls and even riots.

To Erasmus, the whole enterprise seemed pointless. The lectures were filled with jargon, stuffed with arcane metaphysics, and given over to in-tricate classifying and subdividing. Instructors piled up citations from the Bible and the Church Fathers, philosophers and theologians, without any regard to authorship, context, or history. Shivering in the Sorbonne's poorly lit classrooms, fighting off the hunger pangs caused by the meager meals, Erasmus had to endure discussions of matter and form, substance and accident, potentiality and actuality, the three types of distinctions, the four causes, and the nine types of faith.

The questions posed, meanwhile, seemed obscure to the point of par-ody. How long had Christ been in the Virgin's womb? Does God the Father hate the Son? Could God have taken upon himself the likeness of a woman, a devil, an ass, a gourd, a piece of flint? Will we be forbidden to eat and drink after the resurrection? What, Erasmus wondered, did any of this have to do with faith and devotion, repentance and redemption?

Erasmus's encounter with Scholasticism would be of critical historical significance. In the years to come, he would emerge as the movement's fiercest critic, seeking to discredit it by deploying his most lethal weapon, mockery. The theologians at Paris would fight back, mounting a vigorous campaign to harass and marginalize him. They would similarly help lead the opposition to Luther after his rise to prominence. The Sorbonne, in short, was the chief bulwark of Catholic orthodoxy, and its doctors stood in the way of any program aimed at reforming the Church.

Remarkably, the dominant figure in Scholasticism was not a theologian or even a Christian but a pagan philosopher who lived three centuries before Christ: Aristotle. Scholasticism arose out of the response of medieval theo-logians to the rediscovery of Aristotle's lost works. Those works covered the whole range of human knowledge, from logic, ethics, politics, and law to astronomy, biology, physics, and metaphysics. After the collapse of the Roman Empire, most of these works, written in Greek, became inacces-sible to the Latin-speaking West. In the early sixth century, the Roman philosopher and statesman Boethius—fearing they would be permanently lost—set out to translate them into Latin, beginning with the treatises on logic. He managed to complete only six of them, however, before he was arrested in 524 on charges of treason. He was convicted and beaten to death, and with his passing, Aristotle's remaining works faded from Western consciousness.

Even the six treatises Boethius had translated, known collectively as the *Organon*, were neglected as the interest in classical culture waned. Not until the early twelfth century would they again receive close scrutiny. Western Europe at that time was undergoing a mini-renaissance, with a creative outpouring in art, literature, and philosophy, and the *Organon* came to the attention of Christian theologians. They were deeply impressed. Aristotle's system of knowledge, his rules for observing empirical reality, his principles of syllogistic reasoning, and his guide to constructing arguments offered an entirely new approach to understanding the world. In the past, theologians seeking to explain religious truths had had to rely on revelation, but now, with Aristotle to guide them, they could use reason as well.

Leading the way was Peter Abelard. A prickly contrarian and canny showman from Brittany, Abelard would become the greatest of the era's itinerant scholars, moving from town to town, challenging instructors, giving his own sparkling lectures. From the moment he arrived in Paris, in 1100, to study at the famous school run by the cathedral of Notre Dame, he caused a stir with his dynamic classroom manner and questioning of long-accepted axioms. His fame was cemented by his book *Sic et non* ("Yes and No"), which featured 158 theological propositions along with citations pro and con culled from the Bible, the Church Fathers, papal edicts, and conciliar decrees. Abelard hoped to show that even the most basic doctrines remained open to discussion and that vigorous debate and rigorous analysis were the best ways to arrive at the truth.

The most useful tool in that pursuit, he believed, was Aristotelian logic—especially the dialectical method. This entailed stating a proposition, presenting the main objections, rebutting them, and offering a resolution. Applying this formula, Abelard sought to clarify everything from the creation to the resurrection, and he did so with such ingenuity that a cult began to form around him.

The same brilliance that so dazzled his students, however, got him into trouble with one of them. Heloise was the niece of a prominent canon at Notre Dame, who, impressed by Abelard, entrusted her education to him. They quickly fell in love and began exchanging blissful letters. When Heloise became pregnant, Abelard sent her to stay with his sister-in-law in Brittany, where she had a son. Heloise's uncle—both enraged at Abelard for seducing his niece and worried that he was going to abandon her— sent a team of ruffians to Abelard's quarters. While he slept, they bribed their way in and, as Abelard described it, "took cruel vengeance on me of such an appalling barbarity as to shock the whole world; they cut off the parts of my body whereby I had committed the wrong of which they complained." Abelard, in short, was castrated (meaning no doubt the removal of his testicles rather than a more drastic emasculation).

Abelard recounted this episode in his memoir, *The History of My Calamities*—the most lively autobiography since Augustine's *Confessions* seven centuries earlier. True to his craving for attention, it offered titillating details about his affair with Heloise. Ultimately, though, it was Abelard's theological audacity that brought about his downfall. Around 1120, he published a short essay about the Trinity. This core doctrine, which defined the relations between the Father, the Son, and the Holy Spirit, was a treacherous zone that for centuries had caused recrimination, division, and strife. With characteristic panache and the assistance of Aristotelian logic, however, Abelard set out to clarify the relations among the three. Such impertinence infuriated his enemies, especially Bernard of Clairvaux, a pious militant of the Church, and in 1140 Abelard was brought before a French council on charges of heresy. In a proceeding that foreshadowed Luther's appearance at Worms, he was duly condemned, and he spent his remaining two years as a Cluniac monk.

The excitement caused by his work, however, could not be contained, and it was carried on by one of his students, Peter Lombard. An Italian who began teaching in Paris around 1140 and who would later become the city's bishop, he was most known for his *Four Books of Sentences*, in which he proposed hundreds of questions about God, man, salvation, and the sacraments. Going beyond Abelard, he offered not only citations pro and con but also a judgment or conclusion (*sententia*) on each question. Succinctly written and conveniently organized, the *Sentences* would become the chief handbook of Scholasticism, generating more than four thousand commentaries. In his most lasting contribution, Lombard declared that seven acts (baptism, penance, the Mass, and so on) deserved sacramental status—a position that was made official in 1215 at the Fourth Lateran Council.

By the time of Lombard's death, in 1160, theological life in Paris was experiencing another upheaval, thanks to a sensational scholarly discovery. After centuries of fighting, Christian armies had finally succeeded in taking back most of Spain from the Moors. From local scholars, Christian clerics learned of the great libraries that the Moors had established in Toledo, Córdoba, and other centers of Islamic learning. Eager to assimilate the knowledge of conquered lands, the Muslims had arranged for the translation into Arabic of the works of virtually every important Greek writer, Aristotle included, and copies were deposited in these libraries.

When Christian clerics learned of this trove, they at once decided to make it available to the Latin-speaking West. Around 1126, Archbishop Raymond of Toledo set up a translation center and invited top scholars to work at it. A Jewish scholar translated the Arabic texts word for word into Castilian; an archdeacon at the cathedral turned the Castilian into Latin. As word of the project spread, scholars eager to participate arrived from England, France, Germany, and northern Italy. Translation centers soon opened in Sicily, Provence, and other places where Christians, Muslims, and Jews freely mixed. Working with little recognition or remuneration, these scholars played a heroic part in reintroducing to the Latin West the great works of Greek learning.

Gradually, those works began appearing in the libraries of Paris and other centers of Christian study. Those of Aristotle caused the most excitement. Scholars now had access to not only the *Organon* but also the *Metaphysics*, his pioneering inquiry into the nature of being; *De anima*, his famous treatise on the soul; scientific works like the *Physics*, *On the Heavens*, and the *History of Animals*; the *Politics*; the *Nicomachean Ethics*, his pathbreaking study of moral conduct; and the other works of logic that Boethius had not translated. The sudden appearance of these treatises would cause a revolution in Western thinking. They offered a rational, self-contained view of how the universe works—one that at many key points challenged and contradicted reigning Christian beliefs.

The concept of sin, for instance, is absent from Aristotle's writings. As he saw it, man has natural appetites and impulses that sometimes become excessive but which he can control through an exercise of will. Humans are essentially rational beings able to improve themselves morally through education and practice. Aristotle proposed a mechanistic God who is a simple prime mover and does not intervene actively in the world. He rejected the idea that the world was created from nothing, thus ruling out the possibility of a creation story, and he denied the immortality of the soul, doing away with an afterlife toward which man can strive. Rather than renounce worldly pleasures in the quest for eternal bliss, he taught, man should seek contentment in the present by pursuing a golden mean between extremes.

On all these points, Aristotle's views conflicted with the Augustinian notion of fallen man and with the pessimism that had dominated medieval thinking. And, as his writings circulated, they stirred tremendous anxiety. Could Christian theology stand up to the challenge posed by this alternative system of knowledge? In 1210, alarmed Church elders imposed a ban on Aristotle's works on metaphysics and natural philosophy. This simply stimulated interest in them, however. In addition to studying Aristotle, theologians were reading the philosophers of two competing faiths who had already incorporated his teachings—Avicenna and Averroës of the Muslims and Maimonides of the Jews. In 1255, the faculty of arts at Paris, seeing the futility of trying to suppress Aristotle, reversed course and made him required reading. Rather than silence the Greek intruder, the Church would try to absorb him.

That effort would be led by the greatest Scholastic of them all, Thomas Aquinas. In contrast to most medieval theologians, who were loud, impatient, and contentious, Thomas was humble, soft-spoken, and legendarily absentminded. Obese, he became known as "the dumb ox"—dumb in the sense of silent. When it came to intellectual capacity, he was without peer. In a writing career that lasted nearly a quarter century, he would show otherworldly stamina, filling ten thousand double-column folio pages. Over time, his understanding of doctrine would become that of the Roman Church itself. In 1323 he was canonized, and in 1567 he was given the title "Angelic Doctor"; in 1879 Pope Leo XIII issued an encyclical letter ("On the Restoration of Christian Philosophy") that established Thomas's teaching as the foundation for all Catholic study and that urged universities to use it "for the refutation of prevailing errors." Apart from Augustine, no one would do more to shape the Catholic mind.

Born around 1225 into the ruling family of Aquino, a town midway between Rome and Naples, Thomas while in his midteens informed his parents that he wanted to join the Dominican order. Appalled at the idea of their son becoming a penniless friar, they urged him to reconsider. When he refused, his mother sent his two brothers to abduct him, and he was held captive in a family castle. He would not budge, however, and after a year his mother finally relented. Aided by the Dominicans, Thomas immediately set off on the long journey to Paris.

Arriving in 1245, he became both a friar and a master of theology. In fifteen years he produced thirty thick tomes, the greatest of which was the *Summa Theologica*. Thomas was the first Christian theologian to have full access to the new translations of Aristotle's works, and in his own monumental treatise he sought to demonstrate and explain Christian doctrines through the application of Aristotelian logic. The *Summa* examines more than six hundred questions, ranging from the most cosmic, such as whether the existence of God is self-evident, to the most mundane, such as whether the pleasures of touch are greater than those of other senses. Using the dialectical method, Thomas seeks to prove that God is perfect, infinite, immutable, ubiquitous, eternal, and good. He offers precise descriptions of the six days of Creation, the repercussions of the Fall, the nature of original sin, the relation between grace and merit, the place of the soul during the resurrection, and—most eye-catching of all—the properties of angels. In his discussion of angels (which extends over more than sixty pages in most modern-day editions), Thomas seeks to answer such questions as whether an angel can be in several places at once (no), whether one angel can know another (yes), whether angels can know the future (no—only God can), and whether angels are numerous (yes, very). Thomas nowhere addresses the famous question attributed to medieval theology—How many angels can dance on the head of a pin?—but his discussion clearly seems to have inspired it.

Of more lasting consequence were Thomas's comments about man. Like all medieval thinkers, he placed God—all-powerful and all-knowing—at the center of his system. But, influenced by Aristotle's embrace of human capability, he preserved a critical space for man as well. While man is subject to habits and passions that incline him toward sin, Thomas wrote, these can be reined in through the exercise of reason. Though God predestines all, man has free will. "Otherwise, counsels, exhortations, commands, prohibitions, rewards and punishments would be in vain." As Thomas saw it, a person who freely does good works in a state of grace cooperates in achieving his salvation—the type of balanced proposition that typifies his theology. Thanks in part to the *Summa*, the idea that man has a degree of free will would become inscribed in Catholic theology. Centuries later, it would become a flash point between Erasmus and Luther.

In Thomas's own day, his embrace of human capability angered many orthodox churchmen. So did his faith in reason. He was denounced for putting Aristotle ahead of the Gospels, logic before revelation, metaphysics over exegesis. Toward the end of his life, Thomas himself seems to have developed doubts about the merits of his enterprise. Returning to Naples, in 1272, he continued to work on the *Summa*, but on December 6, 1273, while he was celebrating Mass in the presence of a friend, something happened to him, and he could not return to work. When pressed by his friend to do so, Thomas said, "I cannot, because all I have written seems like straw to me."

It is not clear what happened. Thomas may have had a mystical revelation that made his logical exercises seem pointless. Or he may have had a stroke. Three months later, he was dead, his masterwork unfinished. Eager to suppress it, the bishop of Paris in 1277 issued a decree branding as heretical 219 Aristotelian propositions, among them several charged to

Thomas. The opposition to him was especially fierce among the Dominicans' chief rivals, the Franciscans. From among them rose the star of the next generation: John Duns Scotus.

Born around 1266 in the Scottish town of Duns, Scotus would outstrip all other Schoolmen (as the Scholastics were also known) in his love of nuanced distinctions, hence his nickname: the "Subtle Doctor." Teaching at both Oxford and Paris, he wrote a series of highly technical tracts in which he sought to place limits on the range of religious truths that could be demonstrated through logical analysis. Matters like divine power, original sin, and the immortality of the soul, he insisted, could not be proved through theses and countertheses. God is absolutely omnipotent and free to act without limits imposed by human understanding. Scotus wanted to restore the place of revelation in the spiritual life of the believer—to free God from the bounds of human reason and to recognize his unlimited freedom to will whatever does not contradict the essence of his being, which is love.

For all his hostility toward Thomas, however, Scotus shared his affinity for arcane exposition. In terms of opacity, in fact, his equal would not be seen for centuries. His lexicon included terms like *haecceity* (an object's "thisness"), *quiddity* (an object's essence), and *univocity* (a word's having the same meaning when applied to different things). "The quiddity or definition of one extreme is the middle term in demonstration," went a sample passage. Scotus's most famous cause was the doctrine of the Immaculate Conception, which held that Mary was born without original sin. The idea that anyone other than Christ—even his mother—could have come into the world untainted by Adam's transgression caused an uproar, especially among Dominicans. In Paris, the Thomists and Scotists warred over the matter, assailing each other with citations, libels, insults, and slurs. As the categories and theorems multiplied, the rancor and resentment grew. This, in the end, was one of the main consequences of Scholasticism: a proliferation of doctrines, and of violent clashes over them.

The debate over the Immaculate Conception was still raging two centuries later, at the end of the fifteenth century, when Erasmus was at Paris.

(The matter would not be fully resolved until 1854, when the doctrine was declared a dogma of the Catholic Church by Pope Pius IX.) The Scotists dominated the theological faculty, and, thanks to their appetite for obscure speculation and fine distinctions, "Dunsman" would became a synonym for a hairsplitting sophist. (In English, it would come to mean a blockhead incapable of learning, i.e., a dunce.)

Forced to endure lectures about propositions, definitions, conclusions, demonstrations, and other "super-subtle subtleties," Erasmus grew exasperated. "If only you could see your Erasmus sitting agape among those glorified Scotists," he wrote to a fellow student, these "quasi-theologians" whose "brains are the most addled, tongues the most uncultured, wits the dullest, teachings the thorniest, characters the least attractive, lives the most hypocritical, talk the most slanderous, and hearts the blackest on earth."

Lost in all the syllogisms, corollaries, and refutations, Erasmus believed, was the Bible itself. It was no longer read as an account of actual events or the teachings of real men. As he would later write, the apostles "baptized wherever they went, yet nowhere did they teach the formal, material, efficient, and final causes of baptism, nor did they ever mention the delible and indelible marks of the sacraments."

Erasmus managed to suppress his contempt long enough to receive a bachelor's degree in theology (probably in April 1498), but he decided not to continue. Striking out on his own, he moved into a boardinghouse and began spending time with the small but lively circle of Parisian humanists, who congregated at Josse Bade's famous printing house and bookstore on Rue Saint-Jacques. Erasmus also sought to cultivate Paris's leading humanist, Robert Gaguin, an elderly monk, a diplomat, and a prolific author. Soon after arriving in Paris, Erasmus had sent him a letter full of exaggerated praise, with references to the integrity of Scipio and the eloquence of Nestor. Writing back, Gaguin noted his dislike of flatterers and urged Erasmus to leave aside all such pretense in the future.

Erasmus heeded his advice, and the two developed a genuine bond. When Gaguin learned from the printers that an edition of a history of France that he had written had a blank page at the end, he asked Erasmus to fill it. Erasmus happily obliged, but in so doing he relapsed, noting that

Gaguin's histories displayed "the elegance of a Sallust" and "the good taste of a Livy." Clearly, Erasmus could not easily shake the habit of humanist hyperbole, and his addendum to Gaguin's history would attract little notice.

Now around thirty, Erasmus bemoaned his thin résumé. His health, which had been seriously impaired during his time at Montaigu, remained poor in crowded, insalubrious Paris. At one point it rained without stop for nearly three months, causing the Seine to overflow and flood the city center. On top of it all, his funds were dwindling. On arriving in Paris, he had resolved not to waste his time tutoring the wealthy, but he was running out of options, and in the spring of 1497 he took on two brothers from Lübeck who, studying at the University of Paris, wanted to improve their Latin.

They were soon joined by two Englishmen, Thomas Grey and Robert Fisher, who shared a house with Erasmus under the watchful eye of their guardian. Erasmus quickly grew attached to Grey, and the guardian, becoming suspicious, asked him to leave. Erasmus did, but in his anguish he sent a series of notes to the young man filled with lamentations, self-pity, and expressions of love for his "sweetest Thomas." "See how my very real grief makes me burst into floods of tears, though I hoped the injury had healed!" he moaned. He denounced the guardian as an "ungrateful scoundrel" and "abominable monster" with sagging jowls and nostrils "choked with thickets of bristly hair." Erasmus's messages to Grey have the same impassioned quality as those he had earlier sent to Servatius—he even refers to them as "lovers' letters"—and they add to the questions about his sexual leanings.

Tutoring would prove every bit as burdensome as Erasmus had expected, but he found a way to turn it to his advantage. Having endured so much punitive pedagogy over the years, he now had an opportunity to test some alternatives. To teach his students colloquial Latin, he drafted a series of exchanges showing how to greet friends, inquire after their health, and decline an invitation. These would become the basis for his *Colloquies*, the collection of wry dialogues and sketches that would be his most popular work. To show his students how to compose letters, Erasmus prepared a series of examples; he would later expand them into a guide to the epistolary art. He also began work on a manual on how to write well, plus a program for curricular reform—the seeds for Erasmus's later education texts, through which he would help shape the course of European schooling for centuries.

For the moment, though, he continued to founder. In the spring of 1498, he came down with a low-grade but stubborn fever that made him feel he was wasting away. Seeking a break, he traveled to Holland to see friends, but he drank heavily, placing an added strain on his health. On the way back to Paris, Erasmus stopped in Brussels to speak with the bishop of Cambrai and request his continued support, but the bishop was noncommittal. Word began spreading about Erasmus and his intemperate behavior in Holland, prompting his friend Willem Hermans to send him a reproachful letter. Erasmus bristled. "I greatly fear you may suppose that I am wasting my time here in frivolity, feasting, and love affairs," he wrote to Hermans toward the end of 1498. While acknowledging that his concern for his health had caused him "to relax somewhat the rigor" of his former style of life, he chided his friend for his offensive statements. He would however admit that, overwhelmed by troubles, he felt "utterly wretched."

These comments offer tantalizing hints of a man who, entering middle age, was relieving his frustration and despondency with bouts of dissolution. Unfortunately, details remain scant. What does come through is Erasmus's lack of direction and of purpose at this point in his life. That was about to change, however. In the summer of 1499, one of his students, William Blount (also known as Lord Mountjoy), invited Erasmus to join him on a visit to England to see his family. Erasmus quickly accepted. While there, he would have his great intellectual breakthrough.

For those who today cross the English Channel on high-speed trains or fleet ferries, it takes an imaginative leap to grasp how perilous the trip was in Erasmus's day. It took anywhere from three days to three weeks, with as many as seventy-five people packed onto sixty-foot-long skiffs. They had to endure foul food, seasickness, fickle winds, treacherous currents, and sudden storms that could prove fatal. Erasmus's first trip would leave him with a deep dread of the crossing, which was unfortunate, because from the moment he stepped foot in England, he was captivated.

Mountjoy's family had close ties to the court of King Henry VII, and after all the hardships and setbacks he had faced in Paris, Erasmus suddenly found himself moving amid the upper reaches of English society. The Mountjoys had estates in both Greenwich, just east of London, and Hertfordshire, thirty miles north of the capital, and Erasmus divided his time between them. Haggard and gaunt after the years of scraping by in the Latin Quarter, he basked in the regal homes, the fine meals, the clean linen, and even the climate, which seemed positively balmy when compared with waterlogged Paris. He was especially taken with the women—"nymphs of divine appearance," he called them. "When you arrive, you are received with kisses on all sides, and when you take your leave they speed you on your way with kisses." Wherever one turns, "the world is full of kisses." Although Erasmus spoke no English, his wit, polished Latin, breadth of knowledge, and practiced horsemanship won him entrée to the English court, and he became "mannerly" in salutation and "conciliatory" in address.

Erasmus was enjoying the fruits of early Tudor rule. Fourteen years earlier, Henry VII had come to power after the defeat and death of Richard III at the Battle of Bosworth Field—an event that had helped end the thirty-year Wars of the Roses. Henry had (with ruthless efficiency) reestablished order, replenished the royal treasury, and promoted the wool trade, helping initiate a period of unprecedented economic growth that allowed not only the landed gentry and merchants to flourish but also a circle of influential humanists to take root. These men had all attended Oxford; all had visited Italy and brought back the flame of the New Learning to their remote, fogged-in isle. On this visit, Erasmus met several who were to become lifelong friends—Thomas More chief among them.

At twenty-two, More was nearly ten years younger than Erasmus, but the two formed an instant bond based on their shared love of literature and language. More was as adept in Latin as Erasmus was, and the two began bantering and challenging each other in it. Erasmus was from the start struck by More's "sweetness," as he later put it—a reference to his good humor, charming disposition, and ability to get along with just about everyone. He was also impressed by More's looks. (Erasmus, with his aquiline face, prominent nose, and sallow complexion, always fretted about his appearance, and he was reluctant to have his portrait painted.)

Just a few miles from Greenwich was Eltham, the site of a royal residence, and one day in the autumn of 1499 Mountjoy invited Erasmus and More to walk there with him. Beneath the burnished hammerbeam roof of this stately complex, several members of the royal household had gathered. Among them was the eight-year-old Prince Henry, for whom the king had deemed Mountjoy a suitable companion. Henry was not the heir to the throne—his older brother Arthur was—but he was nonetheless being groomed for a life in the public eye, and his tutor, the well-known scholar John Skelton, was exposing him to the best classical writers. More, who had learned from Mountjoy that they were going to meet the prince, had prepared a brief tribute in Latin, which he presented to him. Erasmus, who had been told nothing, was embarrassed at arriving empty-handed, and during dinner Henry sent him a note asking him to compose something for him. Back in Greenwich, Erasmus spent three days sweating over a 150-line poem in Latin, in which he paid tribute to the Apollo-like Henry VII and his royal offspring. In a dedicatory letter, Erasmus—echoing Cicero—observed that, while kings may deserve immortal fame for their glorious deeds, poets alone can confer it with their praise. It was a carefree start to a relationship with a boy who, as England's next sovereign, would so profoundly affect the fortunes of both Erasmus and More, and of the English nation as a whole.

After a summer of dinner parties and country outings, Erasmus was ready to return to Paris, but the royal government, seeking the capture of a fugitive duke wanted for treason, had forbidden anyone to leave the kingdom. Desiring a break from the trammels of courtly life, Erasmus decided to visit Oxford, whose theology faculty was second only to that of Paris in prestige. Mountjoy had initially offered to take him but was detained by other business, and so in October 1499 Erasmus rode alone across the rolling countryside. He had with him a letter of introduction to a religious scholar named John Colet. Colet was causing much excitement at the university with his lectures on the epistles of Paul. On meeting him,

Erasmus felt at once that Colet stood apart from all the other scholars he had met in England—indeed, from the whole world of humanist letters in which he had been moving.

Colet, the son of a wealthy merchant who had served as lord mayor of London, had as a young man joined the flow of aspiring classicists to Italy. While there, he had been drawn to not only the idealism of Plato (who was undergoing a revival) but also the pious teachings of the apostles and the Church Fathers. Like so many others, Colet had learned to read the Bible in Scholastic fashion, as an assemblage of proof-texts for use in theological dispute, but as he studied Scripture in the heartland of Christianity, he became absorbed in the story of Christ's life and death and of Paul's tireless efforts to spread awareness of the sacrifice that the Redeemer had made on behalf of mankind.

Excited at this new way of reading Scripture, Colet on his return to England arranged to lecture at Oxford on Paul's Epistles to the Romans and the Corinthians. In place of the jargon-filled exercises of the Scholastics, his lectures treated Paul as a real human being wrestling with urgent moral, social, and spiritual problems. Colet described the fractious, turbulent world of the eastern Mediterranean in which Paul moved and the fledgling communities of Christian believers that he was attempting to establish. Above all, Colet tried to show how the crises and challenges that Paul faced mirrored those confronting present-day Christians. The Corinthians were prey to lust, envy, wantonness, and gluttony, but, by becoming reborn in Christ, Paul taught, they could embark on a new path.

In his lectures, Colet repeatedly lashed out at the clergy of his own day. Like dogs returning to vomit and sows to their filthy wallowing (images from the Bible), they had abandoned the simplicity and humility commended by Christ to acquire worldly goods and pursue earthly pleasures. Unaccountably, they had lost sight of the exemplary lives of the apostles and other early Christians who had given up so much for their faith.

Colet's lectures were a landmark in the history of Christian scholarship. As if for the first time, those attending awoke to the richness of Scripture and the relevance of Paul's missionary work. Erasmus, too, was impressed. While it is not clear if he actually attended the lectures, he found Colet's approach to the Bible refreshing. On a personal level, Colet had an air of modesty and sobriety that appealed to Erasmus's own earnestness, and the two began taking long walks in the Oxford gardens. Erasmus also became a regular at Colet's table. The fare served there was less plentiful than at the Mountjoys', but the conversation was far more nourishing, with lively discussions of sacred texts.

Colet could be very severe. He always wore black, habitually abstained from dinner, and was censorious about sex, maintaining that it should be engaged in as seldom as possible. Most off-putting to Erasmus was Colet's disdain for pagan literature. The best way to understand Scripture, Colet insisted, was through meditation and prayer, without any resort to the "demonic" wisdom of the pagans. All truth "is contained in the splendid, the plentiful table of Holy Scripture." For all the freshness of his lectures on Paul, Colet remained in many ways a medieval figure.

At one point, he and Erasmus got into an argument over the nature of Christ's agony in the garden of Gethsemane while he awaited arrest. The discussion centered on Christ's words at Mark 14:36: "Father, let this cup pass from me; yet not as I will, but as thou wilt." Colet, drawing on Jerome, maintained that Christ was referring not to his impending death on the cross but to the agony he felt in witnessing the guilt of the Jews in sending him to it. To Erasmus, this seemed obscure and far-fetched. Surely at that moment, he wrote to Colet in explaining his position, Christ was deeply saddened at the prospect of death and viewed it with terror: "at that moment he spoke as a man, for men, to men, and in the words of men, expressing man's fears." Christ wanted his death to be of the most humiliating kind and through it "to set us an example of patience and gentleness which he bade us learn from him."

Erasmus here gave an early sense of the Christ he would come to embrace—a very human savior seeking to inspire others through his gentleness and forbearance. Colet was unpersuaded. While praising Erasmus's argument for its vigor and clarity, he dismissed it as unperceptive. Erasmus in turn chided Colet for refusing to accept what the text plainly seemed to say—that "here is a man, who stands in fear of death." He could not see in Christ's comments anything that had to do with the Jews.

Despite such differences, Colet was sufficiently impressed with Erasmus's learning to urge him to stay on in Oxford, suggesting that he lecture on either the Five Books of Moses or Isaiah. Though flattered, Erasmus felt he was not up to it. "How could I ever be so brazen as to teach what I myself have not learned?" he wrote. "How can I fire the hearts of others when I myself am trembling and shivering all over?"

Erasmus most keenly felt his lack of Greek. This was the language in which the New Testament had originally been written; if he wanted to understand the true essence of Christ's teachings, he felt, he needed to read them in that tongue. Colet did not know Greek, and it showed. Lecturing from the Latin Vulgate, he at one point said that Paul had reproached the Corinthians for priding themselves on "their skill with languages"; a glance at the Greek showed that Paul was actually referring to speaking in tongues.

From Lorenzo Valla, Erasmus had learned how fundamentally the nuances of language can affect the meaning of a text. If this was true for Cicero and Livy, how much more so must it be for Scripture—the foundation of the Christian faith? If classical texts had become corrupted in the course of being transmitted over the centuries, the same was no doubt true of sacred texts. Could not the same critical methods developed by the humanists to repair secular works be applied to Christianity's holy books as well?

The two or three months Erasmus spent in Oxford would prove a turning point in his life. His letters from this period have a depth and sense of resolve absent from his earlier correspondence. Erasmus's conversations with Colet had helped awaken the strain of Christian piety that he had absorbed from the Brethren of the Common Life but which had remained dormant. He now longed to apply to sacred studies the same energy he had previously devoted to classical ones.

As he prepared to leave England, Erasmus exulted over the six months he had spent there. "I have never found a place I like so much," he wrote on December 5, 1499, to his former pupil Robert Fisher, who was now studying law in Italy. England had "such a quantity of intellectual refinement and scholarship, not of the usual pedantic and trivial kind either, but profound and learned and truly classical, in both Latin and Greek, that I have little longing left for Italy, except for the sake of visiting it. When I listen to Colet, it seems to me that I am listening to Plato himself." Eager to get to work on Greek, Erasmus prepared to forsake the spacious manors and kissing damsels of England for the cold, hunger, and crowding of Paris. His real lifework was about to begin.

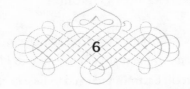

THE VOW IN THE STORM

On the surface, the four years that Luther spent at the University of Erfurt (1501 to 1505) would pass quietly. Unlike Erasmus, he would prove a diligent student; he would register no complaints, pass no sardonic notes. Inside, though, an explosion was building.

Known as "Little Rome" for its many religious institutions, Erfurt had twenty-one parish churches, eleven monastery churches, and four endowed churches, plus a large presence of Augustinians, Benedictines, Carthusians, Dominicans, and Franciscans. The Church's presence was symbolized by two fortresslike sanctuaries that stood side by side on a bluff overlooking the town: St. Mary's, the cathedral, which had Europe's largest free-swinging bell, and St. Severus, whose facade featured three austere towers. Majestic and forbidding, this enclave formed a sort of mini–Holy See.

With a population of 20,000, Erfurt was one of Germany's three or four largest cities. It was also one of the most prosperous, owing to its dominance of the trade in woad, a plant of the mustard family used to make a popular blue dye. Even more than in most towns, however, the wealth was concentrated among a small sliver of merchants and patricians who lived in great comfort while the mass of laborers and seasonal workers struggled in the shabby suburbs. Social unrest ran deep, and in 1509 it would erupt in a "year of madness," which became so violent that part of the university was leveled—an outburst that no doubt contributed to Luther's later antipathy to popular protest. (Erfurt is now ten times as large as it was then, but, thanks to having been largely spared by World War II and neglected by the East German government, it retains strong—and charming—traces of its medieval past.)

The university was located in a warren of streets just off the fish market. The students lived in ten or so *bursae*, or hostels. In each, the day was as regimented as in a monastery. Students had to rise every morning at four and retire every evening at eight. They had to speak Latin at all times and wear monk-like garb. At night they could leave only with special permission, and because of the lack of streetlights and the presence of many hazardous streams, they had to check out lanterns at the rector's office—a procedure that allowed for the close monitoring of their movements. During lectures, no one was allowed to loiter in the streets. New students had to take an oath to obey the college head, to listen patiently to his instructions, and "to refrain from plots and cabals against him." Fights and disruptions were nonetheless frequent, and Luther would later say the city was no better than "a whorehouse and a beer house."

On the Erfurt faculty, humanists were gaining an ever-greater foothold, but the Scholastics remained in charge, and Luther's courses were dominated by them. While the bachelor's program in which he was enrolled did feature readings in Ovid, Terence, Virgil, Plautus, and other classical writers, Luther mostly studied grammar and logic, rhetoric and natural philosophy. He completed the program in the minimum amount of time—three semesters—and on the exam finished thirtieth out of fifty-seven, suggesting that he was a middling student.

The master's program, to which he immediately advanced, offered instruction in the four arts of the quadrivium—music, astronomy, arithmetic, and geometry. More than anything else, though, students were drilled in dialectic. Luther learned to define terms, identify premises, marshal citations, construct syllogisms, offer corollaries, and uncover fallacies in the arguments of adversaries. In all, he participated in fifteen disputations, gaining experience in the cut-and-thrust, attack-and-parry tactics of these high-pressure exercises—skills that would serve him well in later years, when he was frequently called upon to participate in contests of a similar nature but with far higher stakes.

No less than Erasmus, Luther would reject the Scholastics, but for fundamentally different reasons. Whereas Erasmus derided the Scholastic method, with its arid dialectics and speculative flights, Luther would thoroughly absorb it. The work that first brought him to public attention, his protest on indulgences, was, tellingly, framed as theses for debate. For the rest of his life, Luther would seek to prove religious truths by assembling long strings of passages from the Bible, with limited regard to context or setting. As a result, he and his followers would be labeled "the new Scholastics."

When it came to the substance of Scholasticism, however, Luther, after a period of dutiful acceptance, would turn violently against it. In order to construct his own system, he first had to overthrow the old one. His time as a master's student in Erfurt would thus prove a critical way station on his path to a new theology.

While Erasmus in Paris had to contend with the Scotists, Luther in Erfurt had to deal with the Ockhamists. Years later, he would call William of Ockham "the most ingenious" of all the Scholastic doctors and identify himself as a member of his party. Eventually, though, he would reject him along with all the rest. Ockham, who was born around 1285 in a village in Surrey, England, and schooled in a Franciscan convent, was another of the perpetually disgruntled and pugnacious controversialists who periodically threw the medieval Church into turmoil. (He was the model for the learned inspector in Umberto Eco's *The Name of the Rose*.)

Today, Ockham is best known for his "razor"—the principle that the simplest explanation is likely to be the best. Ockham never put it quite so simply; his closest version was, "Whatever can be done with fewer assumptions is done in vain with more." He proposed it in opposition to the Scholastics' fondness for building complex metaphysical systems. Ockham rejected the very idea that universals exist outside the mind. Universal ideas do not exist in reality—only discrete, concrete objects do. There is no such thing as a universal "chairness"—there are only individual chairs, from which we mentally construct the symbolic idea of a chair. This school of thought is known as nominalism, and Ockham is considered one of its founding fathers. In his uncompromising attachment to the real world, he would anticipate the radical empiricism of Hume and Wittgenstein.

Theologically, Ockham was a follower of Scotus and shared his preference for revelation over reason, but he pushed it even further, holding that such basic tenets as the infinity of God and the immortality of the soul cannot be demonstrated by rational means. He thus advanced the separation of logic and metaphysics that Scotus had begun, and he further loosened the grip of Aristotle on Christian theology.

On a more practical level, Ockham's zeal for simplicity brought him into bitter conflict with the pope, in ways that would later bear on Luther's own relations with Rome. While lecturing at Oxford, Ockham wrote a commentary on Peter Lombard's *Sentences*. The former chancellor of Oxford, John Lutterell, was so disturbed by the errors he found in it that he traveled all the way to Avignon to lay them before Pope John XXII. The pope summoned Ockham to defend himself, and in 1324 he made the long journey across France. A panel of theologians determined that some of Ockham's articles were in fact erroneous, but he somehow managed to escape condemnation.

While he was there, however, he became embroiled in a long-simmering feud between the papacy and the Franciscans on the matter of poverty. At the center of it was a group of Franciscan purists, called the Spirituals, who felt that not only their own order but also the Church as a whole had become too attached to worldly goods. Since neither Christ nor the apostles had owned property, they maintained, the Church should follow suit and divest itself of all temporal possessions. Under John XXII, however, the Holy See had become a highly profitable enterprise, and the idea that it should relinquish its holdings horrified him. In the early 1320s, he issued decrees declaring that Christ and the apostles had in fact owned property and so were not practitioners of the type of extreme poverty demanded by the radicals; to maintain otherwise, he held, was heretical.

This drew loud protests from many Franciscans, including their general, Michael of Cesena, whom John ordered to appear in Avignon to be held to account. After arriving, Cesena asked Ockham to examine the pope's statements on poverty. With typical impudence, Ockham concluded not only that the Franciscan position was correct but that John's assertions were themselves heretical. For this, both Ockham and Cesena were thrown into prison. On the night of May 25, 1328, however, they managed to escape, and they took a boat down the Rhone to the southern French coast. There, they boarded a galley that had been sent by Ludwig IV of Bavaria. An implacable foe of the pope, Ludwig had recently been crowned Holy Roman Emperor in Rome. The Franciscans' conflict with the pope made them Ludwig's natural allies, and he enlisted the support of Ockham and Cesena. The galley took the two men to Pisa, where Ludwig eventually joined them, and from there the party proceeded to Munich.

Ockham joined Ludwig's "Munich academy," an informal group of scholars and artists, and from it he turned out a stream of books and pamphlets castigating the pope. He challenged the papacy's right to exercise temporal power and to interfere in the affairs of the empire. The Church, he held, should not be equated with the clergy but rather should encompass the entire community of the faithful. The authority of the Church was inferior to that of Scripture; while popes could err, Scripture could not. Ockham continued to berate the papacy in this vein until his death (perhaps due to the Black Death) around 1348.

Ockham's antipapal polemics provided a rich vein of arguments for future challengers of Roman authority. His preference for the authority of Scripture over that of the papacy, in fact, strikingly anticipated Luther's later views. Whether or not Luther was exposed to these polemics while in Erfurt—given the university's conservatism, "not" seems more likely—Ockham's campaign helped provide a precedent for Luther's future insurgency.

There was, however, one idea derived from Ockham that Luther would emphatically reject. For all his assertions about divine power, Ockham—like Aquinas and other Scholastics—reserved a place for free will. His followers took this a step further. In the *Summa Theologica*, Aquinas had maintained that while man cooperates with God in attaining salvation, it is God who initiates the process, bestowing grace as a special gift, apart from any prior action on the part of the individual. On receiving it, the individual could then work with God in attaining salvation. The Ockhamists, however, pointed to several passages in the Bible that suggested that the individual can play a more active part. At Zechariah 1:3, for instance, the Lord says, "Turn to me, and I will turn to you." On the basis of such injunctions, Ockham's followers maintained that man can through his own efforts initiate the process. They used the phrase *facere quod in se est*—"doing that which is within oneself." By striving to do his best, a person could expect to receive an infusion of divine grace, enabling him to perform works that would make him worthy of eternal life. This would become a central principle of late Scholasticism.

The Ockhamists, then, while agreeing with other Scholastics that salvation could not be attained without grace, diverged in insisting that grace could be set in motion through moral striving on the part of the individual. This innovation offered man more control over his fate; it also saddled him with more responsibility. It thus had the potential to inflame the general anxiety caused by the sacrament of penance. For a sensitive young man like Luther—already terrified at the prospect of suffering in purgatory—studying Ockham caused the clamp of fear to tighten further.

In the end, though, Luther's main complaint was not with Ockham but with the thinker who stood behind him. Aristotle was an inescapable presence at the University of Erfurt. Students spent eight months on the *Nicomachean Ethics*, six on the *Metaphysics*, six on the *Politics*, and one on the *Economics*, while also delving into the *Physics* and *De anima*. "Without Aristotle, no one becomes a doctor of theology," is how a suffragan bishop in Erfurt put it. Of the two professors to whom Luther became closest, one, Jodokus Trutfetter, wrote a series of books on logic that drew heavily on Aristotle; the other, Bartholomäus Arnoldi von Usingen, was the author of a compendium of natural philosophy that was based almost entirely on Aristotle as adapted by Aquinas and others.

Later, while developing his own philosophy, Luther would turn furiously against Aristotle, holding him responsible for much that had gone wrong with Christian theology. The "whole Aristotle is to theology as darkness is to light," he declared in his "Disputation Against Scholastic Theology," issued in 1517 on the eve of the Ninety-Five Theses. Three years later, in his famous address *To the Christian Nobility*, Luther lamented how "this damned, conceited, rascally heathen has deluded and made fools of so many of the best Christians with his misleading writings."

Luther did not want to jettison all of Aristotle. His *Logic*, *Rhetoric*, and *Poetics* all seemed worth retaining. But he wanted to suppress Aristotle's writings on physics, metaphysics, the soul, and ethics, on the grounds that "nothing can be learned from them either about nature or the Spirit." Most of all, he reviled the *Nicomachean Ethics*, calling it "the worst of all books" and charging that it "flatly opposes divine grace and all Christian virtues." Luther's great revolt would spring in part from his fierce reaction to this work.

Named after Aristotle's son Nicomachus, the *Nicomachean Ethics* seeks to describe the nature of virtue and how man can achieve it. For Aristotle, virtue is not a natural attribute, like sight or height; people are not born good or evil. They are, however, born with the capacity for virtue, which should be developed through education and practice, beginning at an early age and continuing over a lifetime. Just as men become builders through the act of building and become musicians by playing instruments, so they become virtuous by doing virtuous deeds. For Aristotle, choice is central. We have it within our power to perform or avoid moral acts. Though he does not actually use the phrase "moral responsibility," that is what he is describing.

Aristotle has little to say about the intense struggles many face in trying to do the right thing in the face of temptation and weakness. Supreme rationalist that he was, he barely mentions longing and lust, craving and compulsion. Unlike the Scholastics, who held that man ultimately has to rely on divine grace in attaining salvation, Aristotle placed the full burden on the individual.

While at Erfurt, Luther dutifully absorbed these teachings. And they added to his disquiet. From the many sermons he had attended, he knew that, owing to original sin, human nature is warped, making transgression inevitable. Was he to be held responsible for his every lapse, as Aristotle seemed to insist? If he could not refrain from losing his temper or using the Lord's name in vain, would God find him unrighteous and hence undeserving of salvation? (Erasmus's works, by contrast, would be permeated by the spirit of the *Nicomachean Ethics*.)

During Luther's time in Erfurt, his *Anfechtungen* intensified. He felt that he was an irredeemable sinner whom the wrathful Christ would surely condemn. During these spells, he felt utterly forlorn, forsaken, without hope. The question pressed in on him: what would happen to him if he died?

All around him, he heard the rattle of death. A close friend was killed in a fight. At one point Erfurt was hit by the plague, and the casualties included a baccalaureate at the university and one of the participants in his master's examination. Luther himself had a bad scare when, while traveling to see his parents, he accidentally cut an artery in his thigh with the student dagger he carried. Lying alone in a field while a friend ran for help, he prayed to Mary to intercede. A doctor who arrived managed to stop the bleeding, but during the night the wound reopened, causing Luther in his panic to again entreat the Virgin. While recovering, he learned to play the lute. He found the resonant tones soothing, but death continued to loom.

Despite it all, Luther in January 1505 completed his master's program, placing second among seventeen students. Years later, he would recall the thrill he felt: "What majesty and splendor there was when one received his master's degree! They brought torches to him and presented them. I think that no earthly joy could be compared with it." He prepared for the next stage of his education: the law. This was in accord with the wishes of his father. In addition to paying Martin's tuition, Hans provided him with the funds to buy a complete edition of the *Corpus Juris Civilis* of Justinian, a mammoth sixth-century code that served as the basis for civil law in Europe. A remunerative career seemed ensured. But Luther's heart was not in it. The law seemed a technical and bloodless field, especially when compared with the great existential matters taken up in theology and philosophy.

On July 2, 1505, Luther was returning to Erfurt on foot from a visit to Mansfeld. In a field outside the village of Stotternheim, about four miles from Erfurt, he was caught in a thunderstorm. As bolts of lightning crashed down around him, he fell to the ground and in his terror cried out, "Saint Anne, help me! I will become a monk!" In this moment of extremity, Luther appealed to the patron saint of miners. Such vows were commonplace in that day, and just as commonly forgotten. But not by Luther. Given the tempest in his soul, the cloister beckoned. In medieval Europe, the monastery was considered the "gate of Paradise"—a place that, sealed off from temptation and distraction, offered its inmates a clear path to salvation. Luther was determined to take it. When he told his friends of his plan, they were aghast. How could this bright and affable young man embarking on such a promising career exchange it for a life of silence and seclusion? Few were aware of the depths of his inner torment.

Of the many orders in Erfurt, Luther chose the Augustinian Hermits. In addition to being less austere than most of the others, they were known for their educational opportunities. Luther arranged to sell his books, including the *Corpus Juris Civilis*, keeping only his volumes of Virgil and Plautus. Two weeks after making his vow, he held a farewell dinner to which he invited several scholars and (according to one account) some "modest and virtuous girls and women"—the last time he would be able to mix in such company. Growing animated, he entertained the group on his lute. On the following day, July 17, Luther, accompanied by several friends, walked to the Augustinian cloister, located on the edge of town. "Today you see me, but never again!" he declared to his tearful companions, then disappeared through the arched gate in the cloister's stone wall.

Erasmus had left an Augustinian monastery to see the world; Luther was now forsaking the world to enter an Augustinian monastery.

Luther first told the story of the vow in the storm many years later, and questions have been raised about whether it occurred just as he said. The episode bears strong parallels to Paul's conversion on the road to Damascus. Could Luther have embellished his account to heighten the similarities? Whatever the reality, his decision to enter a monastery would prove no less momentous for the future of Christianity than Paul's own transformation. The spot where Luther is believed to have made his vow is now marked by a seven-foot-high pillar of reddish stone set in a quiet grove of linden trees. Erected in 1917, on the four-hundredth anniversary of the posting of the Ninety-Five Theses, the pillar bears the inscription:

GEWEIHTE ERDE—WENDEPUNKT DER REFORMATION

[HALLOWED GROUND—STARTING POINT OF THE REFORMATION].

PART II

Discoveries

BACK TO THE FATHERS

The troubles that Erasmus encountered on his return journey from England to France, in January 1500, began in Dover. He had on him money worth about twenty pounds—enough to sustain him for many months. But the British Crown, hungry for revenue, had issued a decree forbidding the export of all gold and silver from the country. Erasmus had been assured by Colet and More that, because he had no English coins and had brought most of the money into the country with him, he would be exempt. They were wrong, and the customs officials confiscated all but a tiny sum. In one swift blow, Erasmus was reduced to penury.

Things got no better on the other side of the Channel. The horse Erasmus rented in Amiens turned out to be lazy and slow. Stopping at an inn, he became so convinced that he was going to be assaulted that he could barely sleep. The next morning, when he went to pay his bill, he spent several hours haggling with the innkeeper over exchange rates. After settling, he decided to abandon his horse and, despite the cold and damp, to make the rest of the journey on foot. On February 2, 1500—six days after leaving Dover—he staggered into Paris, "very tired from traveling and with an empty purse," as he wrote in a long, agitated letter to his friend Jacob Batt.

Erasmus was about to enter his period of greatest hardship. After the genteel comforts of England, he was now sharing a friend's run-down quarters on the Left Bank. A fever he had picked up on the way back from England would linger for months, sapping both his energy and his spirits. Even more distressing was his continued anonymity. Seven years after fleeing the monastery, Erasmus remained a minor figure in the world of letters, and the mortification of it daily ate at him.

He was buoyed, however, by his new enthusiasm for sacred studies. After years of suffering through the sterile exercises of the Scholastics, he longed to read the Gospels and Epistles as the story of Christ's ministry and the efforts by his apostles to spread his message. As he had realized in Oxford, however, the New Testament would give up its secrets only if read in its original language, and so he set out to learn Greek.

It was a daunting enterprise. More than a century had passed since Petrarch and Boccaccio had sought to revive the study of Greek in the Latin West, yet arranging instruction in it remained difficult. Few books had been printed in Greek, and tutors were even scarcer. With the fall of Constantinople to the Turks, in 1453, some Greek-speaking scholars had fled to the West and were offering their services, but most lived in Italy; the few north of the Alps were well beyond Erasmus's means. While at Deventer, he had learned the Greek alphabet and a smattering of vocabulary, and during his brief time at the University of Paris he had picked up a few rudiments more, and with that shaky foundation he set out to teach himself.

The drudgery tormented him. Working late into the night in his chilly quarters, he grappled with the tenses, cases, voices, moods, genders, accents, breathings, and enclitics of ancient Greek. "My readings in Greek all but crush my spirit," he wrote to Batt. As soon as he got some money, the first thing he would do would be "to buy some Greek authors; after that, I shall buy clothes." When another acquaintance asked him to return a volume of Homer that he had borrowed, Erasmus protested that his friend was robbing him of his "only consolation" in his "dreary situation."

During Lent of 1500, the postponement of meals caused Erasmus to grow weak—part of a yearly pattern since he had begun living in France. Urged by a doctor to reduce his workload, he decided to pass the time rereading some of his favorite classical works. Desperate to earn some money, he got the idea of gathering adages from them and collecting them into a book. Erasmus shared the humanist fascination with ancient proverbs. They were used to enliven texts, add levity, fortify an argument, and—not least—display one's learning. Erasmus could hardly write a letter without slipping in a reference to putting one's scythe to the harvest, taking an ox to wrestling school, or playing the sow who teaches Minerva (i.e., trying to instruct someone who is far wiser).

After two months of strolling through the "gardens of the classics" and plucking "flowerets of every hue," as he put it, he had 818 proverbs, about a fifth of them in Greek and the rest in Latin. He found a printer in Paris, and in June 1500 the *Adagiorum Collectanea* ("Collected Adages") appeared. A slender volume of 152 pages, it was Erasmus's first full book in print. There were sayings from Plato, Virgil, Plautus, Terence, Catullus, Horace, Pliny the Elder, and Cicero, each illumined with a few lines of commentary. Some of the entries are appealingly eccentric. *Crambe bis posita mors*—"Twice-cooked cabbage is death"—referred to the practice of serving cabbage at banquets in ancient Greece; when recooked, it induced nausea. The saying came to signify aversion, as with a speech that, sounding fresh the first time around, becomes deadly on successive servings. Other unfamiliar adages include "as quick as asparagus is cooked," "to a pig even marjoram seems sweet," and "adopting the outlook of a polyp" (i.e., changing with the circumstances).

Other sayings are more familiar: "to be afraid of your shadow," "to break the ice," "to teach an old dog new tricks," "to leave no stone unturned," "a dog in the manger," "the tip of the tongue," "the hedgehog and the fox." Are these sayings known to us because of Erasmus's book or because they were already fixed in Western usage? A bit of both, perhaps. One expression fully credited to Erasmus is, "In the land of the blind, the one-eyed man is king." Two other sayings can be traced back to mistakes he made. "Pandora's box" resulted from Erasmus's mistranslation of the Greek word *pithos*, which means a "large jar," as *pyxis*, or "box"; the original saying was "Pandora's jar." And "to call a spade a spade" stems from his belief that the Latin *scapha* signified a tool for digging rather than a dugout boat or washtub.

Unfortunately, the volume did little to ease his financial woes. In those early years of printing, writers usually received no payment or royalties from publishers, only complimentary copies of the book that they could sell. Erasmus promptly sent off copies of the collection to several friends to peddle; hoping to stir interest, he got one friend to give public lectures on it in Paris. Sales lagged, however, and an acquaintance whom Erasmus had sent to England with a hundred copies disappeared. Even more disappointing was the reception by his fellow humanists. Erasmus's commentaries were slight and the book was riddled with printer's errors, and Robert Gaguin, among others, dismissed it as meager and formulaic. Stung, Erasmus immediately began collecting more adages with the intention of producing a new edition.

Thus began an enterprise that would occupy him for the rest of his life. In all, Erasmus would produce ten editions of the *Adages*, each thicker than the last, with commentaries that in some cases swelled into long essays stuffed with anecdotes, gossip, miscellaneous information, and opinions about religion, politics, and literature. The *Adages* would appear in sixty printings during Erasmus's lifetime and another seventy-five in the seventeenth century. The work would be a key means by which Renaissance Europe assimilated knowledge of the ancient world—its agricultural practices, marriage customs, geography, literature, coins, laws, and superstitions, as well as such oddments as the Areopagites of Athens, the frogs of Seriphus, and the bald heads of the Myconians. Its future admirers would include Montaigne. "If anyone had taken me to see Erasmus in old days," he wrote, "I should have expected nothing to fall from his lips but adages and maxims, even in speaking to his servants and the hostess of the inn."

As was so often the case in these early years, however, the acclaim would come only later. Desperate to get something else into print, Erasmus resumed work on his guide to letter writing and his manual of style, but he made little headway. And he had a new worry: he learned that the bishop of Cambrai—annoyed at his remaining in Paris without permission—had sent someone to Paris with the task of "ferreting his way through all the secret places" of Erasmus's life there. On top of it all, the city in the summer of 1500 was hit by the plague. Erasmus fled to Orléans, some sixty miles to the southwest, where he stayed with a friend.

There, he took up the urgent but unappetizing task of finding new patrons. That effort, documented in his letters, shows the humbling lengths to which independent writers had to go before the advent of foundations, fellowships, book advances, and writers' colonies. His quarry was Lady Anna van Borssele, the wealthy daughter of a prominent Dutch nobleman living in a castle in Tournehem, two hundred miles to the north. Erasmus's friend Jacob Batt, who was tutoring her son, informed him of her generosity toward scholars, and Erasmus pressed him to approach her on his behalf. Batt said that he should write to her directly. Erasmus testily replied that he did not have the time and again pushed Batt to help. Batt reluctantly agreed, but when a messenger arrived bearing only a few paltry coins, Erasmus exploded. He sent back detailed instructions on how Batt should approach the lady: he should tell her that "I am positively unable to live in miserable surroundings now that I have a literary reputation, such as it is," and he should explain "how much greater is the glory she can acquire from me, by my literary works, than from the other theologians in her patronage," since "there is everywhere a huge supply of such uneducated divines as these, while such a one as I am is scarcely found in many generations," and so on.

This irked Batt even more. After Erasmus returned to Paris, in early 1501, he took Batt's advice and wrote to Lady Anna directly. "No matter how many thunderbolts Fortune aims at me, I see no reason to abandon literature or lose heart so long as you shine, like an immovable polestar, to guide me on my way," he trilled. Anna must have seen through him, however, for no more coins were forthcoming. Erasmus would have to grovel elsewhere.

He was faring much better in his efforts to learn Greek and read Scripture anew. In March 1501, Erasmus exulted to Antoon van Bergen, an abbot in Saint-Omer, about his "good fortune" in coming upon some Greek books, which he was secretly copying night and day. (Why secretly is not clear; perhaps he had intercepted a bundle intended for someone else.) Despite the "exorbitant fee," he had decided to hire a Greek tutor for several months. Even with his primitive knowledge of Greek, he had come to see the truth of the claim made by many authors "that Latin scholarship, however elaborate, is maimed and reduced by half without Greek." While the Latins "have but a few small streams, a few muddy pools, the Greeks possess crystal-clear springs and rivers that run with gold." This was especially true for sacred texts. He could see what "utter madness" it was to study the mysteries of the faith "unless one is furnished with the equipment of Greek as well," since the Latin translators of the Bible offered such literal versions of Greek idioms that, without a knowledge of that language, no one could grasp their true meaning.

As an example, he offered a phrase from the Latin version of the Psalms: *Et peccatum meum contra me est semper*—"And my sin is ever against me." Many theologians in interpreting this, he wrote, would launch into "a long story about how the flesh wages an endless war with the spirit." But an examination of the Greek word underlying *contra*—*enopion*—showed that the intended sense of the preposition was not "against" but "before," so that the passage would more accurately read, "And my sin is continually before me." In other words, the writer of the psalm meant that his guilt displeased him so much that he never lost consciousness of it but had it always "in his view, as if it were physically present."

This was an important breakthrough for Erasmus. By looking past the Latin to the underlying Greek, he was able to push beyond the convoluted explanations of the subtle doctors to what seemed a more correct reading. That, in turn, pointed toward a more commonsense interpretation of the relationship between guilt and sin than they favored. Such discoveries made Erasmus think that he was on the right track. Through a mastery of Greek grammar, syntax, and vocabulary, he hoped to free the words of the evangelists and the apostles from the dead hand of the sophists; by thus purifying the biblical text, he hoped to revitalize the faith itself.

That undertaking was full of peril, however. For the Latin version of the Bible—known as the Vulgate (from *Vulgata editio*, or common edition)—was considered inviolable by the Church. For more than a thousand years, it had served as the scriptural foundation of Western Christianity. When, after the fall of Rome, missionaries headed into the barbarian hinterland, it was the Vulgate they carried with them. When Abelard, Aquinas, and Scotus formulated their theorems, they did so in its Latin. Many Church doctrines and sacraments, including original sin, penance, marriage, and the Trinity, were based on specific words and phrases in the Vulgate. Its text was thought to have been produced under the guidance of the Holy Spirit, its every word sanctified by God. The very authority of the Church, and the social order it embodied, rested on this document.

Yet a close inspection of the Vulgate raised obvious questions about its hallowed status. For the text was full of spelling mistakes, grammatical errors, and clumsy constructions. Lines were repeated. Homonyms were confused. In some places, words seemed to have been inserted out of nowhere, turning passages into nonsense; in others, key terms were omitted or mangled. At John 5:2, for instance, the Vulgate gave the name of the pool in Jerusalem not as Bethesda (Hebrew for "house of mercy") but Bethsaida (a town in Galilee meaning "house of fishing"). At Acts 28:1, some versions had Paul shipwrecked not at Melita (Malta) but at Mytilene (on the island of Lesbos), Melitus (in ancient Ionia), or Melitene (a city on the Euphrates River). Such variations were not surprising; prior to the advent of printing in the 1450s, the Vulgate had been transcribed exclusively by hand and so had suffered from the same carelessness and wandering attention that had produced errors in secular manuscripts.

That the Vulgate New Testament was a translation from Greek introduced another level of distortion. From his studies, Erasmus knew how hard it is to turn ancient Greek into good Latin. One verb tense in Greek, the optative, has no equivalent in Latin. While Greek uses articles (both definite and indefinite), Latin does not, forcing the translator to resort to various expedients, some more fitting than others. Greek similarly uses the final infinitive (expressing a goal or intention), while Latin does not, and the Greek partiality to participles resulted in a concision of expression not always easily reproduced in Latin. Prepositions pose a particular challenge, since the meaning of each changes with the context. The Greek word *dia*, for instance, could mean "by," "in," "through," "before," or "because of." By mastering Greek, Erasmus hoped to identify and clarify these slips and ambiguities.

It was the prospect of such tampering that so unnerved conservative churchmen. By consulting Greek versions of the Scriptures, Erasmus would be in a position to suggest readings at variance with those sanctioned by Rome and consecrated by centuries of use. The Greek text of the New Testament was itself shunned as the heterodox product of a church (the Greek Orthodox) considered schismatic. Greek was seen as the language of troublemaking theologians like Arius and Origen, of licentious writers like Sappho and Epicurus, of Neoplatonists seeking to overthrow the Scholastic master, Aristotle.

Greek, in short, was seen as an agent of subversion. That, however, only enhanced its appeal for Erasmus. Along with his own studies, he began a more general effort to promote the language, touting the merits of its best authors and urging his friends to learn it. Keeping at it for the rest of his life, Erasmus would through this campaign have a profound impact on Western culture, making the study of Greek seem progressive, avant-garde, fashionable.

Nowadays, Erasmus observed in his letter to Antoon van Bergen, "we are perfectly satisfied with the most elementary rudiments of Latin, no doubt because we are convinced that we can get everything out of Scotus, as a sort of horn of plenty." As for himself, he was determined to pursue his program to learn Greek and read Scripture afresh—"the path to which I am beckoned by St. Jerome and the glorious choir of all those ancient writers."

The reference to Jerome signaled the other great project Erasmus had embarked on in this period—restoring the reputation of that saint. Along with Augustine, Ambrose, and Gregory the Great, Jerome was one of the four great "Doctors" of the Western Church, whose authority was second only to Scripture itself. Of them, Jerome was the most learned, the best trained in languages, the most elegant stylist. During his lifetime (c. 347 to 420), he produced an astonishing array of biblical commentaries, theological tracts, pamphlets, sermons, polemics, prefaces, manuals, and letters—all featuring his distinctive blend of soaring imagery, thunderous proclamation, and acerbic sarcasm. In addition to his command of Latin, Jerome was one of the few Westerners of his day to know Greek. Even more exceptionally, he knew Hebrew and so was a trilinguist—a master of the three main biblical tongues. (He also knew Aramaic and Syriac.) Drawing on this facility, Jerome was the greatest translator of antiquity. He was, in fact, the principal translator of the Bible into Latin. The Vulgate was generally known as "Jerome's Bible," and, despite the many errors that had disfigured it over the centuries, it retained the marks of Jerome's flair for languages, his vast knowledge of the Bible and the Holy Land, and his immersion in classical literature.

As Erasmus waded into the treacherous waters of biblical commentary and translation, he found in Jerome both a precedent and an inspiration.

Just as the eloquent Doctor had used his knowledge of Greek and Hebrew to produce the Bible of the medieval Church, so was Erasmus now studying Greek to recover the true spirit of the text.

Jerome's reputation as a scholar had faded during the Middle Ages, eclipsed by that of his contemporary Augustine, the preeminent theologian of the medieval Church. To the extent that Jerome was honored, it was not for his scholarship but for his piety. As a young man, he had lived as a hermit in the Syrian Desert, sleeping on the ground and wearing rags in an effort to repent for his earlier high living in Rome. In the fourteenth century, as saint veneration surged, Jerome became the center of an ardent cult. The story was told of how one day he had been approached by a lion who seemed in great pain. Examining the lion's paws, Jerome found a thorn stuck in one of them and removed it. Thereafter, the grateful lion never left his side. This became a metaphor for Jerome's success in taming the beast within man. Special healing powers were ascribed to Jerome's relics, and his image began appearing on canvases and church walls, usually as a gaunt, half-clad penitent expiating his sins in the desert.

In the fifteenth century, though, humanists—seeking sanction for their own sacred studies—began reviving Jerome's image as a scholar. He was honored as the patron saint of universities, libraries, and translators. In a resplendent 1475 portrait, Antonello da Messina showed Jerome, draped in a cardinal's red robes, sitting at his desk in rapt contemplation of a large folio volume, his immense and airy study radiating out around him. Standing in the foreground is a peacock, symbolizing paradise; the docile lion has been pushed off into the shadows. The painting is an iconographic representation of the Christian Father as a scholar-saint, joining wisdom and holiness in the pursuit of spiritual enlightenment.

Eager to hasten the recovery of Jerome the scholar and restore his place in the Christian pantheon, Erasmus set out to edit his letters. About 150 had survived, making them one of the four richest caches from ancient times (along with those of Cicero, Seneca, and Pliny the Younger). Jerome's letters offered a remarkable look at the state of the Church in its formative years, when it was taking root in the Roman Empire and its core doctrines and rituals were being debated and defined.

This was the patristic era. Coming after the apostolic age, it was dominated by the Fathers (*patres* in Latin)—sixty-five or so scholars, monks, and theologians, some writing in Latin and others in Greek, who, in the second through the sixth centuries, provided in their tracts, commentaries, and letters the foundation for the Church as it pushed to fill the vacuum left by the collapse of the empire. To Erasmus and other humanists, these men showed how scholarship and devotion could be combined in a program far more enriching than the speculative labors of the Scholastics.

While at Steyn, Erasmus had copied out all of Jerome's letters by hand—quite a feat, since some are the length of small books. Unfortunately, the letters, like almost all of Jerome's works, had become corrupted, mutilated, and "filled with mistakes and monstrosities" through "ignorance of classical antiquity and Greek," as Erasmus wrote. He planned not only to edit the letters but also to elucidate them in a great commentary so that "every reader in his study" would come to recognize the greatness of this Church Father, "the only scholar in the church universal who had a perfect command of all learning both sacred and heathen."

The editing of Jerome's letters, and the broader effort to revive his reputation, would absorb Erasmus for years. The project was in many ways critical to his own career. As the revered translator of the Bible into Latin, Jerome could provide cover for Erasmus's efforts to repair the Vulgate. More generally, his combining of scholarship and piety and his use of classical literature to enhance Christian understanding could serve as a model for Erasmus's own work in scriptural studies.

As models went, however, Jerome was far from ideal. For all his saintly eminence, he was vain, impulsive, combustible, and vindictive. Given to extreme opinions, he spent much of his life pursuing quarrels and vendettas. The same proficiency in language that made him such a skilled translator also made him a master of insult and invective. In this, he was not atypical of the Church Fathers. The patristic era that Erasmus and other humanists so romanticized was one of the most contentious and volatile in the history of the Church. Like Renaissance thinkers in general, Erasmus, in seeking to recover this figure from the past, would have to refashion him to serve his own needs.

That task was especially delicate in light of Jerome's work as a Bible translator. The Vulgate bore the imprint of not only his eloquence and erudition but also his temperament and prejudices. Many of the problems that Erasmus was uncovering in this hallowed text could be traced back to the very man he so enthusiastically embraced.

Jerome got his charge to translate the Bible (or at least part of it) from Pope Damasus I, an imperious and charismatic Iberian who devoted his pontificate (366 to 384) to strengthening the claim of the Roman See to supremacy within Christendom. He restored the catacombs, organized the papal archives, commissioned many new churches, and gave his household the trappings of an imperial court. In addition to thus enhancing the Church's physical presence, Damasus wanted to strengthen its scriptural foundation.

At the time, the Latin Bible used by the Roman Church was in disarray. The New Testament had first been translated from Greek into Latin around the year 200, probably in northern Africa. Other translations followed in Italy, Gaul, and Spain. Each of these regional translations (which together are known as the *Vetus Latina*, or Old Latin edition) quickly developed its own character. As these versions were carried elsewhere, they became mixed with other readings when new copies were made. With each copy, scribal errors were introduced. Because Christians in the third and early fourth centuries had to operate underground, most copyists were amateurs working in secret, causing slips to multiply. What's more, the New Testament was then considered a "living text," with scribes feeling free to improve on it not only grammatically and stylistically but also theologically. Orally transmitted stories, passages from the liturgy, and clauses designed to combat heresy were all incorporated into the biblical text.

After Christians were granted tolerance by Constantine, the New Testament could at last be openly transcribed. But, with Church membership swelling and the demand for texts growing, translations proliferated, each with its own errors and embellishments. The *Vetus Latina* used in Rome was very uneven, with many clumsy and untidy passages.

Around the year 383, Damasus decided he wanted a more reliable text of the Gospels, and he called upon Jerome to prepare it. Then in his midthirties, Jerome had impressed the pope with his forceful character, writing skills, and vast learning. His entire life to that point had seemed one long apprenticeship for the great task now before him. "In Latin, almost from the very cradle, I have spent my time among grammarians and rhetoricians and philosophers," he would later write. Raised in the town of Stridon, in the province of Dalmatia, at the head of the Adriatic Sea, Jerome did so well in grade school that when he was twelve his parents sent him to Rome to study in a school run by Aelius Donatus, the most renowned schoolmaster of that time. Reading Cicero and Terence, Virgil and Sallust, Jerome developed not only a love of classical literature but also an obsession with grammatical precision that he would later use to rip into his adversaries for their poor syntax. He also began to amass a library that would become famous for its size and quality.

During his eight years in Rome, pagans and Christians were competing for the support of the population, and Jerome, like so many others, felt torn. From his letters, it is clear that he sampled the city's pleasures, but he was also drawn to the new faith, with its monotheistic God, redeemer Son, and promise of salvation. Visiting the city's catacombs and seeing the burial sites of the Christian martyrs, he was deeply moved by their sacrifice, and he decided to undergo baptism—a sign of serious commitment in those days.

Considering a career in public affairs, Jerome moved to Trier, a provincial capital in eastern Gaul on the "half-barbarous banks of the Rhine," as he put it. Gradually tiring of professional striving, however, he began studying theology. The ascetic ideals of withdrawal and renunciation—long popular in the East—were catching on in the West, and Jerome felt their pull. After several years in Trier, he returned to Dalmatia to see his family, but he spent much of his time in nearby Aquileia, an episcopal capital with a growing community of devout Christians. Jerome might have settled down there had he not become involved in a violent blowup that blackened his reputation in the community and soured his relations with his family. Though the exact cause of the explosion is not clear, it was no doubt linked to his hair-trigger temper. Forced to leave, he decided (probably in late 372) to head eastward, to Jerusalem.

It was a bold decision, for the Levant at that time was a remote and untamed land and the journey to it long and difficult. This was, however, the birthplace of the faith, and it remained home to its most prominent theologians, its most learned scholars, its most rigorous ascetics. Many were following the path of St. Anthony, the Egyptian hermit who in the late third century had spent years in self-punishing seclusion in the desert and whose exploits had been popularized in a widely circulated hagiography. Jerome wanted to similarly test himself. The Roman roads were so well maintained that he was able to take his library along with him. The trip was nonetheless grueling, and the long trudge in midsummer across the Anatolian plateau left him near collapse. Reaching Antioch, the great Syrian metropolis, Jerome decided to remain there while recuperating. Greek was the main language, and for the first time he began systematically to study it.

During Lent of 374 or thereabouts, Jerome had a dream that would prove one of the most famous in Christian annals. It was his habit, after long bouts of fasting, to refresh himself with some pages from Cicero; after punishing nightlong vigils, he would seek relief in Plautus. When he read the Hebrew prophets, they seemed crude and boorish by comparison. As his commitment to Christianity grew, however, Jerome became uneasy at the pleasure he took in heathen writers. One night, while in the grip of a fever so severe that preparations were being made for his funeral, he felt himself hauled before the judgment seat. "Who art thou," the Judge demanded. "A Christian," Jerome replied. "Thou liest," the Judge said; "thou art a Ciceronian, not a Christian." He ordered Jerome whipped, and as the lashes fell, Jerome begged for mercy. Some bystanders dropped to their knees and urged the Judge to take pity on Jerome and allow him to repent. The beatings stopped, but Jerome was warned that they would resume if he ever again opened the books of the Gentiles. "O Lord," Jerome in his terror swore, "if ever again I possess worldly books or read them, I have denied thee." When Jerome opened his eyes, he found that his shoulders were black and blue, and he ached from the bruises long after he had awakened. From that time on, he would later observe, "I read the books of God with a greater zeal than I had given before to the books of men."

No other passage in patristic literature more vividly captures the tension many early Christians felt between the siren call of the pagans and the austere demands of their faith. "Jerome's Dream" (as it came to be known) would for centuries be invoked by traditionalists seeking to seal the ears of the pious against the lure of the secular. For many years, Jerome kept to his vow. Later, however, he would stray, citing as justification a passage from Deuteronomy in which the Lord granted the Israelites permission to take captive beautiful non-Israelite women for their wives if they shaved the heads of these women and sheared off their eyebrows. By similarly cropping secular wisdom to his needs, Jerome wrote, he had made it his "handmaid." Nonetheless, Jerome's Dream would remain a powerful argument in the hands of those seeking to suppress pagan literature, as Erasmus would later learn.

Determined to cure himself of worldly desires, Jerome decided to follow through on his plan. Not far from Antioch began the Syrian Desert, a menacing wilderness of ravines, cliffs, and gorges that was home to clusters of filthy, emaciated hermits engaged in spectacular acts of self-mortification; some lived atop pillars so as to be closer to heaven. Jerome lived in a cave, slept on the ground, and followed such a meager diet that he, too, turned skeletal. Even in this forbidding setting, however, he was able to continue his studies. Remarkably, he had his library with him and was able to expand it, hiring a team of copyists as well as messengers to ferry his requests for books to be transcribed.

In addition to polishing his Greek, Jerome learned some Syriac and studied Hebrew with a local Jewish convert to Christianity. Having no Hebrew grammar texts to guide him, however, he struggled mightily with the harsh and alien tongue. Even more vexing were his sexual urges. In his heightened rhetorical style, Jerome (in a later letter) would describe his torment: "How often, when I was living in the desert, in the vast solitude which gives to hermits a savage dwelling-place, parched by a burning sun, how often did I fancy myself among the pleasures of Rome!" Sackcloth hanging from his shrunken limbs, scorpions and wild beasts his only companions, Jerome often felt himself "amid bevies of girls. My face was pale and my frame chilled with fasting; yet my mind was burning with desire, and the fires of lust kept bubbling up before me when my flesh was as good as dead. Helpless, I cast myself at the feet of Jesus, I watered them with my tears, I wiped them with my hair; and then I subdued my rebellious body with weeks of abstinence."

Sometimes Jerome would cry aloud and beat his breast all night. Dreading his cell, he would make his way alone into the desert:

> Wherever I saw hollow valleys, craggy mountains, steep cliffs, there I made my oratory, there the house of correction for my unhappy flesh. There also—the Lord Himself is my witness—when I had shed copious tears and had strained my eyes toward heaven, I sometimes felt myself among angelic hosts, and for joy and gladness sang: "Because of the savor of thy good ointments, we will run after thee."

Like many early Christians, Jerome felt that satisfying the demands of the flesh undermined the effort to exalt the spirit. Remorseful over his earlier licentiousness, he began in this period to develop the creed of extreme chastity that would come to dominate his writing and, ultimately, affect his work as a translator.

After two years in the desert, Jerome—tiring of the pounding sun, the empty expanses, the vainglory of the monks, and the raving "frenzy" of the Arians, whose questioning of Christ's divinity was plunging the Church into chaos—decided to rejoin civilization. In 379, he returned to Antioch, then traveled to Constantinople. There, for the first time, he ventured into the field of religious translation, putting into Latin Eusebius's famous *Chronicle*, a valuable but highly sensationalized and error-ridden history of the world from the time of Abraham on. With it, Jerome showed a knack for creating arresting turns of phrase—for endowing even the most prosaic expressions with a sense of majesty and uplift. He also showed his willingness to enhance the text—highlighting his own special interests, adding gossipy details about people, giving free rein to his prejudices. He was very careless as well, dictating in haste to a stenographer, and as a result, the translation was filled with errors.

While in Constantinople, Jerome, who had begun corresponding with Damasus, received from him a request to comment on the sixth chapter of Isaiah. The chapter's central image—of the Lord seated on a throne and attended by two six-winged seraphim—had long befuddled biblical commentators. In his reply, Jerome drew on two biblical techniques he had learned while in Constantinople. One was the use of allegory. This involved finding in every name, body part, historical event, and human activity in the Bible a sign of God's higher purposes and Christ's sacred presence. This approach was frequently criticized for allowing readers to find in Scripture whatever they wanted, but Jerome would master it. He also learned the value of comparing old manuscripts of scriptural texts to determine the correct reading—an approach largely unknown in the West. After examining several Greek and Hebrew versions of Isaiah, Jerome concluded that the two seraphim represented the Old and New Testaments and that Isaiah's description testified to their perfect harmony. When the Hebrew prophet declared that "the whole earth is full of his glory," he was referring to the coming of Christ. The commentary heightened Damasus's esteem for Jerome's learning.

Damasus would soon get to meet him in person. In 382, he convened a synod in Rome to discuss issues of papal succession, and Jerome came to serve as an interpreter and adviser. Though Damasus was more than twice as old as Jerome, the two quickly became close, and when the pope decided to commission a new version of the Gospels, he turned to Jerome.

Sensitive to the pull of tradition, Damasus wanted not an entirely new translation but a revision of the Old Latin Bible based on early manuscripts. Even so, Jerome hesitated, for he knew the uproar that such a venture would surely cause. "Is there a man, learned or unlearned," he wrote, "who will not, when he takes the volume into his hands and perceives that what he reads does not suit his settled tastes, break out immediately into violent language, and call me a forger and a profane person for having the audacity to add anything to the ancient books, or to make any changes or corrections therein?"

But Jerome shared Damasus's concern about the debased state of the New Testament, complaining that "there are almost as many forms of texts as there are copies," and so he signed on. Taking up the Gospels, he sought out early Greek codices that could suggest the text of the originals (which had long since disappeared). If truth was the main goal, he wrote, "why not go back to the original Greek and correct the mistakes introduced by inaccurate translators, and the blundering alterations of confident but ignorant critics, and, further, all that has been inserted or changed by copyists more asleep than awake?" Wary of being attacked, however, Jerome proceeded with caution, restricting himself to smoothing rough phrases, correcting obvious solecisms, and pruning provincialisms. In all, he made changes in some 3,500 places.

In the process, however, he created many new problems. Always in a hurry, Jerome became sloppier as he went on. For instance, he converted finite verbs into participles far more often at the beginning of Matthew than at the end. In translating individual words, Jerome was often inconsistent. He thus translated the Greek word *archiereus* ("high priest") as *princeps sucerdotum* in Matthew, as *summus sacerdos* in Mark, and as *pontifex* in John. He gave *doxazo* ("glorify") sometimes as *glorificare*, sometimes as *magnificare*, and at other times as *honorificare*. So, while Jerome's hand was light, it was also erratic and arbitrary, creating many headaches for future exegetes.

Initially, his revision met with little protest, owing in part to his having the pope's blessing. Incapable of avoiding controversy, however, he soon found himself under fire for his personal conduct. Though now celibate, Jerome craved female company, and he became close to two patrician widows, Marcella and Paula. Marcella's palace, located on the Aventine Hill, was a meeting place for well-to-do Christian women. Eastern-style asceticism, while still relatively rare in Rome, was growing in appeal, especially among aristocratic women who wanted more control of their bodies. Jerome was well known to these women through the letters he had written from the East, and Marcella invited him to discuss the Bible with them. Quickly developing a hold on the group, Jerome impressed on them the importance of prolonged fasting, incessant prayer, and chastity. Mesmerized, Paula took to wearing sackcloth, sleeping on the ground, and forgoing bathing, and, at Jerome's insistence, she pledged her adolescent daughter Eustochium to a life of virginity.

To encourage Eustochium, Jerome wrote her a sixteen-thousand-word letter that was actually a small treatise on the subject of women and chastity. Of all the values for which Christianity stood, he declared, female virginity was by far the greatest. "Assuredly no gold or silver vessel was ever so dear to God as is the temple of a virgin's body." Bodily abstention was not enough, since virginity "may be lost even by a thought. Such are

evil virgins, virgins in the flesh, not in the spirit." To make sure Eustochium did not stray, Jerome issued a series of admonitions: She should
shun contact with not only men but also married women and even widows who had had sexual relations. Her companions should be "women
pale and thin with fasting, and approved by their years and conduct." She
should live in seclusion, abstain from wine, fast daily, pray throughout
the day, and rise two or three times during the night to recite Scripture.
She should further avoid all displays of vanity, keep her face hidden, and
stop up her ears against music. Virginity, Jerome asserted, was superior
even to marriage: "I praise wedlock, I praise marriage, but it is because
they give me virgins."

Widely circulated, Jerome's letter to Eustochium was part of an ardent
campaign he would wage for the rest of his life to promote virginity and
celibacy. Though Jerome was hardly the only Church Father to push these
values—Ambrose and Augustine were his equals in this regard—his polemics would play a central part in implanting them in Western Christendom. And the doctrine of Mary's perpetual virginity, which he insistently
proclaimed, would become a foundation of Western Mariology.

At the time, however, many Romans were repelled by such teachings.
To them, Jerome seemed intent on snatching away their women and girls
and turning them into unwashed recluses. Jerome simultaneously came
under attack from the Roman clergy, whom he had repeatedly charged
with lechery, avarice, and ambition. In the spring of 384, the first protests
were raised against his revision of the Gospels. (In translating the New
Testament, Jerome seems not to have gone beyond those four books.) With
typical vitriol he dismissed his critics as "two-legged asses" who preferred
to drink from the "muddy streamlet" of the Old Latin version rather than
water drawn from the "clear spring" of the Lord's words.

Jerome's situation grew more dire when, in December 384, Damasus,
his main protector, died. Around the same time, Blesilla, Paula's eldest
daughter, died after prolonged fasting. Under Jerome's hectoring, she had
in effect starved herself to death. Widely blamed, he was denounced as
the leader of "the detestable tribe of monks," and rumors spread about his
close ties with Paula. An investigation was launched, and in August 385
Jerome was ordered to leave the city. He decided to head once again to

the East. "Let Rome keep her bustle for herself, the fury of the arena, the madness of the circus, the profligacy of the theater," he wrote. "I thank my God that I am held worthy of the world's hate." Paula decided to join him, even though it meant abandoning her two youngest children, and a few months later she and Eustochium met up with him in the East.

For two years they toured the Holy Land and Egypt. In the Nile valley, they saw thousands of ascetics living in secluded communities, and they decided to set up a monastic community of their own, in Bethlehem. It consisted of three convents, a monastery, and a school. The rules were punishingly strict, with Paula policing the fifty or so girls under her supervision for the slightest signs of sexual stirring; the penalty was invariably prolonged fasting. Though little more than a hamlet at the time, Bethlehem was beginning to attract tourists, and Jerome and Paula set up a lodge to receive them. Carrying their impressions back home, these pilgrims helped spread the monastic ideal in the West.

Despite his many responsibilities as the head of the community, Jerome kept up his studies. He reassembled his library in Bethlehem and began pouring forth a torrent of commentaries, translations, homilies, and histories. To tutor him in Hebrew, he hired a local Jew who—fearing the wrath of his fellow Jews—visited only at night. To deepen his knowledge of biblical sites, Jerome crisscrossed Palestine with an experienced guide, surveying its hills and river valleys, visiting its ruins and historic sites. He prepared a dictionary of biblical place-names, which, despite being full of mistakes, became a popular guidebook for Christian tourists.

All of this was a prelude to Jerome's next great undertaking: translating the Old Testament. Jerome had initially intended to revise the Old Latin version of the Old Testament much as he had the four Gospels; that is, by bringing it more closely into line with the underlying Greek text. That text was the Septuagint, a Greek translation of the Hebrew Bible produced in the third century B.C.E. According to legend, the work was carried out by seventy-two translators (six from each of the twelve tribes) brought from Israel to Egypt by King Ptolemy Philadelphus, who wanted a copy of the Hebrew Scriptures for the library at Alexandria. The translators were taken to an island and set to work in isolation from one another. After months of labor, they all miraculously produced identical

Greek texts. (*Septuagint* means "seventy" in Greek.) From its earliest days, the Roman Church had considered the Septuagint divinely inspired and hence the only authorized text of the Old Testament. Whenever Jerome discussed it with Jews, however, they laughed at the many places where it diverged from the Hebrew. Comparing Greek and Hebrew texts, he reluctantly came to agree. The passages contained in the Hebrew and omitted from the Septuagint were "so numerous," he wrote, "that to reproduce them all would require books without number."

Accordingly, Jerome decided to jettison the Septuagint and work directly from what he called the *Hebraica veritas*, the "Hebrew verity." Actually, the Hebrew Bible, like all ancient documents, had itself become corrupted. Jerome's decision to use it as his foundation text was nonetheless a radical step for a Christian. That he was now working without papal sanction added to the boldness of the project. Begun around 390, it would occupy him for the next fourteen years. Jerome's feel for Hebrew, his familiarity with the history and geography of the Holy Land, and his frequent conversations with Jewish scholars helped him capture the majesty and mystery of this complex work. In a preface to his commentary on Genesis, Jerome scornfully dismissed the legend of the Seventy and—anticipating attacks from traditionalists—preemptively denounced them as "filthy swine who grunt as they trample on pearls."

Those traditionalists were soon heard from—Augustine chief among them. Though some ten years younger than Jerome, the bishop of Hippo had already gained renown as a biblical commentator, and for two decades beginning around 394 or 395, the two men would keep up, across the Mediterranean, a correspondence that offers an exhilarating look at the impassioned debates taking place among the Fathers over Scripture and doctrine. In 403 Augustine wrote to Jerome that, while he had found nothing to object to in his translation of the Gospels, there was much in his version of the Old Testament that disturbed him. Augustine was especially upset by Jerome's decision to base his translation on the suspect Hebrew text rather than on the Septuagint, which had "no mean authority," since it was the one that the apostles themselves had relied on. Augustine told of a bishop in a nearby town who, when reading aloud from Jerome's translation of Jonah, had come upon a word (he did not say which) that differed from the one that was familiar to the worshippers and which "had been chanted for so many generations in the church." There arose "such a tumult in the congregation" that the bishop felt compelled to ask the opinion of some local Jewish residents. From this, Augustine added, "we . . . are led to think that you may be occasionally mistaken."

Jerome testily replied that since Augustine had approved of his revision of the New Testament, he should give him credit for his work on the Old as well, "for I have not followed my own imagination, but have rendered the divine words as I found them, understood by those who speak the Hebrew language." Chiding Augustine for not supplying the offensive word so that he might defend himself, Jerome guessed that it was his translation of the Hebrew *qiqayon* as *hedera* ("ivy") instead of the traditional *cucurbita* ("gourd"). Generations of Christians had grown up with the image of Jonah sitting on the ground, shielded from the sun by a gourd, but Jerome argued that the word in Hebrew signified a kind of shrub that had large leaves like a vine and that stood upright by its own stem. Had he used "gourd," he wrote, he would have said what was not found in the Hebrew, and so he had instead used "ivy."

Jerome here showed the length to which he would go to get a single word right, whatever the consequences. Augustine, attentive to the needs of his congregation, focused on the furor that altering a single word of Scripture could cause. Where Jerome strove for linguistic precision, Augustine deferred to received authority and pastoral concerns. For years these two Fathers would spar over how best to translate and interpret Scripture, personifying in the process two models of Christian scholarship—Jerome being first and foremost a scholar while also a pious Christian, and Augustine being mainly a theologian whose readings were informed by deep scholarship. Their contrasting positions on the proper relationship between faith and learning uncannily foreshadowed the bitter fight that Erasmus and Luther would wage more than a millennium later.

Over time, the virtues of Jerome's translation of the Old Testament would become broadly recognized. It elevated the rough and sometimes coarse words of the Hebrew Scriptures into a form of lyric poetry; its narratives move at a brisk pace; its prophetic passages ring with admonitory thunder. But his translation had serious defects as well. As always, he worked quickly and at times carelessly. He claimed to have translated Proverbs, Ecclesiastes, and the Song of Songs in a mere three days. With his eyesight failing, he often dictated his translations to secretaries—hardly an ideal practice in dealing with sacred texts. As with the Gospels, Jerome indulged his love of variation, rarely using the same word twice, even when the context clearly called for doing so. And, while he was generally faithful to the Hebrew text, he did not hesitate to alter it when he thought clarification was needed.

The most famous example came at Isaiah 7:14. In this passage, the Hebrew prophet assured the Judaean king that the disasters befalling his realm would soon give way to better times, with the Lord himself sending a sign: "A young woman will be with child and will give birth to a son, and will call him Immanuel." The Hebrew word for "young woman"—*alma*—is unambiguous. The Septuagint, however, gives it as *parthenos*—"virgin." This is the version cited at Matthew 1:23. The birth of Jesus, it states, took place "to fulfill what had been spoken by the Lord through the prophet, 'Look, the virgin shall conceive and bear a son, and they shall name him Immanuel.'" This passage became the foundation text for the doctrine of the virgin birth. Had Jerome remained true to his philological principles, he would have translated Isaiah as prophesying that a *puella*—a young woman—would bear a child. But this would have undermined both Matthew and one of Jerome's most fundamental beliefs, and so he translated from the Septuagint and used *virgo*, or "virgin." And thus Isaiah would read in the Vulgate.

Nearly sixty years old when the translation was done, Jerome would spend his remaining years contending with his many physical ailments, his dwindling resources, and the passing of close friends, including his beloved Paula. But he lost none of his zest for theological combat. From his remote outpost in Bethlehem, he became embroiled in a series of poisonous feuds that reflected the boundless bitterness of the era. In 416, a mob, inflamed by one of these controversies, invaded Jerome's monastic compound, attacking its residents, killing a deacon, and setting fire to its buildings; in the chaos, Jerome's precious library was destroyed. He escaped to a nearby tower and, despite his despondency and near blindness, somehow managed to resume his biblical studies. He was working on a commentary on Jeremiah when, in 420, the end finally came.

The image of Jerome toiling away on his biblical commentaries in the face of poor health, financial hardship, and attacks from detractors inspired Erasmus as he pursued his own lonely program to renew Christian culture. Jerome's insistence on using Greek manuscripts to revise the New Testament reassured Erasmus that he was on the right course in his own effort to learn Greek so that he could restore the pure crystalline springs of the Bible.

Yet in his campaign to revive Jerome, there was much that Erasmus had to overlook. Jerome's Dream, for instance. Its categorical rejection of pagan works contradicted Erasmus's own strong belief in their value. Jerome's letter to Eustochium championed the type of monkish severity that Erasmus had experienced, and turned his back on, at Steyn. Jerome's strict orthodoxy, his violent attacks on heresy, his furious fights over small points of doctrine—all were alien to Erasmus's own outlook.

Most challenging of all was Jerome's work as a translator. The Vulgate was his masterwork—his great contribution to Western civilization. How, then, to explain its many errors, inaccuracies, and inconsistencies? There were two mitigating factors Erasmus could cite. One was the widespread belief that Jerome was responsible for only part of the Vulgate. That he had revised the Gospels was clear from the preface he prepared for them. He wrote nothing comparable for the other books of the New Testament, and from this and other evidence, Renaissance-era scholars concluded that Acts, the Epistles, and Revelation had been translated by other, unknown hands. The Old Testament, by contrast, was fully Jerome's work. (This assessment is shared by most modern-day scholars.)

As for those parts that were Jerome's responsibility, humanist scholars could point to the many faults that had crept into the text during centuries of copying. In a document of such length and complexity, scribal blunders were inevitable and numerous. By the end of the eighth century, the Vulgate had become so riddled with errors and interpolations that Charlemagne—wanting a uniform text—asked his court scholar Alcuin to prepare a revision. Alcuin arranged for some well-preserved Latin manuscripts to be sent from England, and, using them as a foundation, he revised the Vulgate. With Charlemagne's backing, this new version quickly became the standard edition. Its quality was very uneven, however. Because Alcuin knew little Greek and almost no Hebrew, his corrections were largely limited to spelling and grammar. What's more, the broad demand for this revised text forced scribes to work at an accelerated pace that led to the undoing of many of his improvements.

The rise of the Scholastics added yet another layer of corruption. In support of their theological positions, they frequently cited passages from the Church Fathers. This gave rise to a new genre—the gloss—which featured blocks of Vulgate text surrounded by patristic citations. Over time, some of these citations were incorporated into the text itself, thus becoming an actual part of the Bible.

In the first third of the thirteenth century, as Paris emerged as the capital of Christian scholarship, the trade in Bibles became concentrated there as well. On Rue Saint-Jacques, a dozen or so scribal workshops sprang up to meet the growing demand for Bibles. A single codex of the Vulgate based on Alcuin's revision was selected as a master copy. This Paris Bible (as it came to be called) became the standard edition of the Church and as such the source of all dogmatic authority. Yet it was a thoroughly compromised version, featuring many patristic passages that had been incorporated from the margins. Roger Bacon, an English Franciscan whose knowledge of Greek was unmatched among medieval scholars, set out to document all of the errors in the Paris Bible; he found too many to count.

Nonetheless, when Gutenberg in the early 1450s decided to print a Bible as his first full book, he used a Paris version as his text. The Gutenberg Bible in turn became the text for the many dozens of Bible editions printed through the end of the fifteenth century. So the printing press, while finally making it possible to produce uniform copies of the Bible, had the perverse effect of locking in all the corruptions and embellishments that had accumulated in it over the centuries.

This, then, was the Latin Bible that Erasmus and other scholars faced at the start of the sixteenth century. By finding his way back to a purer version, Erasmus hoped to rejuvenate the faith. He knew how presumptuous such an undertaking might seem to others. "I am not unaware," he wrote to a friend in the summer of 1501, "that the kind of study I have pursued appears to some men uncongenial, to others interminable or unprofitable, while to others again even impious." This, however, had simply deepened his commitment to it. "If mankind refuses to endorse my purpose, I believe that God will both approve it and aid it. . . . And some day mankind too, or posterity at any rate, will give me its approval."

That letter was sent from Tournehem, near Calais, where Erasmus had gone from Paris to escape another outbreak of the plague. While there, he began writing an essay about the essentials of a truly Christian life. His first major work, it would prove a critical document in the movement to reform the Church, proposing a fresh spiritual vision for the emerging new Europe. Erasmus drafted it at the request of a pious woman in the area whom he had gotten to know. Her husband, a gun-foundry owner from Nuremberg, had become a spendthrift and a philanderer, and she asked Erasmus to write something that might help win him back. Erasmus agreed, and in preparation he began rereading Plato (focusing on Plato's embrace of the ideal over the material), Paul (noting the Apostle's preference for the spirit over the flesh), Origen (the great third-century Eastern Father), and Augustine.

While thus engaged, Erasmus moved to a Benedictine monastery in nearby Saint-Omer. There, he became friendly with Jean Vitrier, the warden of a neighboring Franciscan convent. Vitrier had upset his fellow clerics with his readiness to disregard the rule of his order when it seemed to conflict with true piety. He disliked lengthy confessions, thought it unnecessary to rise during the night to say prayers, and rejected the idea that friars should dress differently from everyone else. During Lent, Erasmus—unable to hold out until the afternoon, when the main meal at the monastery was served—arranged to take a basin of soup. When he asked what Vitrier thought of this, Vitrier offered his support, telling him that "you would be doing wrong if you did not do this, and if for the sake of a morsel of food you had to break off your sacred studies and damage your health." Impressed by Vitrier's gentle spirituality, Erasmus tried to capture it in his essay, which he called *Enchiridion Militis Christiani* ("The Handbook of the Christian Soldier").

Enchiridion in Latin can mean not only a handbook but also a dagger, and Erasmus intended his book to serve as a weapon in achieving a truly devout life. He wanted to offer a simple "design for living" for Christians unable to carry around the *Secunda secundae* (the second part of the second part) of Thomas Aquinas's *Summa Theologica*. On the surface, the *Enchiridion* seems innocuous—even banal—offering advice on how to combat such sins as avarice, ambition, pride, anger, and, most important, lust. To subdue the flesh, Erasmus advised, one should avoid suggestive conversations, drink and eat with moderation, and flee all occasions on which the opportunity to act presents itself. Above all, one should read Scripture. "There is really no attack from the enemy, no temptation so violent, that a sincere resort to Holy Writ will not easily get rid of it."

Not even the most dutiful monk could object to such bromides. It is telling, though, that even here, Erasmus dwelled little on such sacramental acts as making a confession or going to Mass. Rather, he was calling on Christians to rely on their own faculties and resources. Elaborating, he offered a set of general rules for Christian living. The most important was the fifth—a way station in Erasmus's spiritual development. Christians, he wrote, should "seek the invisible." "The entire spiritual life consists of this: That we gradually turn from things whose appearance is deceptive to those that are real"—from "the pleasures of the flesh, the honors of the world that are so transitory, to those that are immutable and everlasting." One may venerate the saints, but such reverence is meaningless unless one heeds "their greatest legacy, the example of their lives." One may celebrate Mass daily, but "if you live as if this were only for your own welfare and have no concern for the difficulties and needs of your neighbor, you are still in the flesh of the sacrament." People hang crosses about themselves and keep parts of the True Cross about their homes, but the true value of the cross "is in profiting from its many examples. You cannot say that a person loves Christ if he does not follow His example."

These passages carry unmistakable echoes of *The Imitation of Christ*. The *Enchiridion* shows how fully Erasmus had absorbed the principles of the *Devotio Moderna* while at Deventer and Steyn. Whereas Thomas à Kempis rejected learning as a snare, however, Erasmus embraced it as central to true spirituality. And while Thomas urged Christians to withdraw from the world so as to draw nearer to God, Erasmus was trying to define Christian piety *in* the world. In a seemingly innocuous passage that would later cause a storm, he declared: *Monachatus non est pietas*—"Monasticism is not piety." Rather, it is "a kind of life that can be useful or useless depending on a person's temperament and disposition."

True piety, Erasmus noted, could not be limited to a personal quest for salvation. It had to be directed outward, toward others: "Just as Christ gave Himself completely for us, so also should we give ourselves to our neighbor." True charity consists not in making visits to churches, nor in the lighting of many candles, nor in the repetition of a number of designated prayers, but rather in "the edification of one's neighbor, the attempt to integrate all men into one body so that all men may become one in Christ, the loving of one's neighbor as one's self." Here, for the first time, Erasmus was describing his "philosophy of Christ"—an ethical code based on the life and teachings of Christ.

From a literary standpoint, the *Enchiridion* lacks the snap of Erasmus's later works. His blithe appeal to willpower and his confident assertion that "there is no beast so ferocious" that it "cannot be tamed by human effort" suggest obliviousness of the dark, impulsive forces careening about the human psyche. Such a buoyant view of human nature would later bring Erasmus into sharp conflict with the brooding, pessimistic Luther.

But it was precisely Erasmus's belief in human capacity and potential that would make the *Enchiridion* stand out. It was not just monks who could achieve Christian holiness—lay Christians could, too. Such a statement posed a radical challenge to the Church's conception of the clergy as a special sanctified caste. Erasmus was moreover arguing that true piety could be achieved not through the offices of the Church but through a genuine change of heart. "I would prefer that you really hate your evil deeds internally rather than enumerate them ten times before a priest," he wrote. In extolling inner transformation over formal ritual, the *Enchiridion* pointed the way toward a new form of spirituality rooted in the individual rather than an institution. This vision would prove immensely popular with Europe's new burghers in their quest for a purer, more personalized faith. The *Enchiridion* would go through more than fifteen printings by 1518 and more than one hundred by the end of the sixteenth century. It would be translated into English in 1518, Czech in 1519, German in 1520, Dutch in 1523, Spanish in 1525, and French and Italian in 1529. In the process, it would help establish Erasmus as the tribune of liberal religious reform in Europe.

All that was in the future, however. When the *Enchiridion* first appeared, in 1503, it quickly sank from view. Europe was not yet ready for it. In the meantime, Erasmus pursued his biblical studies. To this point, he remained unclear about what form his program to purify the Bible might take. That would change, however, as a result of a critical discovery he made while in Louvain. Erasmus had moved to this large, fortified town east of Brussels in 1502 to escape plague-ridden Paris, and he would remain there for the next two years. Louvain had airy squares, impressive churches, a thriving beer industry, and a famous university, and Erasmus at once felt at home. Soon after his arrival, Adrian of Utrecht, a professor of philosophy, persuaded the town magistrates to offer Erasmus a lectureship at the university, but Erasmus—worried about the time such a post would take from his work—turned it down. (Adrian would prove a valuable contact, however; twenty years later, he would become Pope Adrian VI.)

"The study of Greek absorbs me completely," Erasmus wrote to his old friend Willem Hermans, "and I have not wholly wasted my efforts, for I have made such good progress that I am capable of expressing my meaning in Greek with reasonable proficiency." As a test, he tried his hand at translating (from Greek into Latin) Euripides's plays *Hecuba* and *Iphigenia in Aulis*. Unfortunately, he quickly got bogged down in the choruses, which were so obscure "as to need a Delian prophet to unlock." Inspired by Jerome, Erasmus began to study Hebrew but found it too difficult and gave up. "The shortness of life and the limitations of human nature will not allow a man to master too many things at once," he observed.

In his spare time, Erasmus liked to visit the Abbé du Parc, a Premonstratensian abbey located just outside the town walls. It had a well-stocked library, and Erasmus enjoyed examining its manuscripts in search of lost treasures. "The most enjoyable sport," he called it. On a visit in the summer of 1504, he found a codex by Lorenzo Valla with which he was unfamiliar. It was Valla's notes on the New Testament. Reading them,

Erasmus grew excited. Valla pointed out hundreds of places where the Vulgate seemed to render the Greek inaccurately or misleadingly. Some discrepancies were relatively minor; others were not. Of particular consequence was Valla's note at 2 Corinthians 7:10. In this passage, Paul in the Vulgate refers to *poenitentia*, meaning "penance." But, as Valla noted, the Greek word underlying it was μετάνοια (*metanoia*)—a compound of μετά (signifying change—the passing from one state to another) and νοέω (to perceive, to think). The intended sense was repentance, remorse, a change of mind. In other words, Paul seemed to be calling on the faithful not to perform the sacrament of penance, with its three-part act of contrition, confession, and satisfaction (which did not even exist at the time of his epistle), but rather to reflect on their actions and improve themselves. The emphasis was on internal reflection rather than external ritual. In this way, Valla was calling into question the scriptural foundation for the sacrament that was at the heart of the Church's system of piety—a potentially explosive observation in an era when reformers were beginning to question the elaborate ceremonialism of the Church.

Valla did not pursue the theological implications of his findings, however. His notes were brief and for the most part restricted to matters of grammar and semantics. And Erasmus, of course, was well aware of the insights that consulting Greek manuscripts could provide. But Valla's work showed how revolutionary grammar could be when applied systematically to the Bible, and it gave Erasmus the idea of producing his own catalog of scriptural emendations.

Erasmus was eager to share his discovery with the world, and so in early 1505, after moving back to Paris, he arranged to have Valla's manuscript printed. Knowing how detested Valla remained and how much controversy this work was likely to cause, Erasmus sought to head it off in his preface. "I do not really believe," he wrote, "that Theology herself, the queen of all the sciences, will be offended if some share is claimed in her and due deference shown to her by her humble attendant Grammar." Erasmus was being coy. However humble an attendant grammar might seem, she could, when assigned to tidy up sacred texts, turn the whole theological household upside down. And that's precisely what Erasmus had in mind. In his preface to Valla's annotations and his defense of applying grammar to Scripture, we can see a line extending from Jerome through Petrarch and Valla to Erasmus—and the first glimmers of the groundbreaking new field of biblical textual editing.

Erasmus's delight at his discovery is apparent in a letter he sent in late 1504 to John Colet, who was now serving as the dean of St. Paul's cathedral in London. Updating him on his studies in Greek and Scripture, Erasmus noted that he was "now eager, dear Colet, to approach sacred literature full sail, full gallop. I have an extreme distaste for anything that distracts me from it, or even delays me." Henceforth, he added, "I intend to address myself to the Scriptures and to spend all the rest of my life upon them."

Unfortunately, he observed, he had been forced by his financial difficulties to put aside this work and take on some literary commissions—a most unwelcome distraction in light of his "burning zeal for sacred studies." He then mentioned Lord Mountjoy. Given the young Englishman's past generosity, Erasmus was desperately hoping for another display of it. Reluctant to approach Mountjoy directly, however, he clearly wanted Colet to do so on his behalf. The letter had its desired effect. Not long afterward, an invitation from Mountjoy arrived, and by the end of 1505 Erasmus was back in his beloved England.

ANGRY WITH GOD

In passing through the gate of the monastery of the Augustinian Hermits in Erfurt, in July 1505, Martin Luther was trading a life of bright conversation and easy companionship for a regimen of coarse robes and plain food, protracted vigils and exacting confessions. Located on a quiet street on the northern edge of the city, the Black Cloister, as it was called, was a somber assemblage of stone walls, heavy arches, and hushed corridors—all offering a refuge from the commotion and bustle of the dormitories and lecture halls to which Luther was accustomed.

Days after his entry into the monastery, some of his friends showed up at the gate to plead for his return, but he would not appear. In entering the cloister, Luther felt "dead to the world," as he would later put it, but, given his crushing sense of worthlessness and fear of damnation, it was a state he devoutly desired. By strictly adhering to the monastic routine of prayer, study, meditation, and self-denial, he hoped to find a pathway to salvation.

Of the many orders in Erfurt, Luther had selected one that, like the order that Erasmus had joined nearly twenty years earlier, adhered to the Rule of St. Augustine, but the Augustinian Hermits were far stricter. For Luther, there would be no passing of confidential notes, no clandestine readings of proscribed texts, no Renaissance rays brightening his cell, but unbroken periods of solitude in cells and backs stiffened from long sessions of prayers. (Technically, Luther was not a monk but a friar, i.e., a member of a mendicant order. Unlike monks, who were restricted to their cloister, friars could leave it to preach, beg, and minister to urban dwellers. But Luther sometimes referred to himself as living like a monk, and many historians use the term as well.)

Luther was initially assigned a room in the monastery's guesthouse, a two-story building set within the walls of the compound but outside the cloister proper. He would remain there for several weeks as the friars took the measure of his sincerity. He dutifully sent word of his decision to his parents. His father, who had invested heavily in his son's education, was horrified. As Luther later recalled, he "went crazy and acted like a fool" and said he was withdrawing his "favor and goodwill." Luther was deeply wounded, but not even the prospect of being disowned by his family could keep him from his chosen course.

After being deemed a fit candidate, Luther was led to the chapter house and the assembled friars. He prostrated himself before the prior, who then described the challenges that awaited him—the frequent fasting, the interrupted sleep, the mortification of the flesh, the strictly enforced humility and obedience. Luther declared his readiness to bear all. His clothes were removed and replaced by the garb of the Augustinian novice. (He had already been tonsured; i.e., the hair on the top of his head had been shorn, leaving a thin circle around the skull.) His novitiate would last a year and a day, and at any point Luther could decide that the cloistered life was not for him—or the friars could make that determination for him.

From the chapel, Luther was led to his cell, located on the second floor of a wing of the main courtyard. Just ten feet long and eight feet wide, it was bare of all ornamentation save for a crucifix on the wall. It had a table and a chair and a wooden bed frame, plus a rough canvas mattress stuffed with straw, two woolen sheets, a coarse blanket, and a pillow. The cell was unheated (as was the monastery as a whole except for one room). No visitors—not even fellow friars—were allowed in, and a peephole in the door allowed superiors to monitor all activities within.

Luther spent those initial weeks learning the order's regulations, summed up in the Rule of Augustine—a rigorous code that, by prescribing a friar's every gesture, utterance, and act, sought to extinguish all self-love and replace it with the love of God. Luther learned how to control his facial expressions; how, when walking, to keep his head bowed, his eyes on the ground, and his hands in the sleeves of his robe; how, when eating, to sit with his back to the wall; how, when drinking, to grasp the cup with both hands. With silence enjoined during meals and idle conversation in general discouraged, Luther had to learn the hand signals used for everyday communication, such as asking the time of day or requesting the salt at meals. The friars were forbidden to laugh or cause others to laugh, to yield to anger or nurse a grudge, or to show an "inordinate desire" for clean clothes. They were also forbidden to fix their eyes on women (who sometimes came to confess or attend church), for "unchaste hearts reveal themselves by exchanging glances even without any words." Anyone who observed a fellow friar exchanging looks with a woman was required to admonish him and, if the friar persisted, to report him.

Above all, the friars were taught how to pray. They did so at seven fixed points during the day. These were the canonical hours, which since the fourth century had defined the rhythms of monastic life. At one or two in the morning, a bell roused the friars from sleep. After quickly washing and dressing in the dark, they made their way to the chapel—a gloomy Gothic sanctuary with a long, narrow nave. After sprinkling themselves with holy water and kneeling before the high altar, they took their assigned stalls and said matins. When it was over, they went to the chapter house for a reading of a chapter of the Bible. The friars said prime at six, terce at nine, sext at noon (after which they took their first meal of the day), none at three, and vespers between four and six (depending on the season). After a light evening refreshment—usually beer and wine served with gingerbread and salted bread—they said compline. The friars then retired to their cells for reading and contemplation, which continued until the bell rang at around nine, announcing the hour for sleep.

In all, the friars spent four to five hours a day in church, singing their way each week through the Psalter—the Vulgate version of the Old Testament book of Psalms. As soon as they finished, they immediately started over. As the novice master made clear, the friars could not mumble or race through the prayers or recite them mechanically. Every line had to be pronounced clearly and sincerely; every word had to be made alive in the heart, as the Augustinian rule put it. Through constant repetition, the Psalms were meant to take hold of and shape the friar's consciousness, helping create a state of spiritual wakefulness and pious serenity. To ensure attentiveness, friars were instructed to be on the lookout for any brother who while in chapel lost his place, let his concentration wander, or—most serious of all—dozed off.

Such infractions were taken up at the collective confession held every

Friday. Each friar (beginning with the eldest) had to confess his own sins and report those he had seen others commit, including speaking without permission, drinking in an improper manner, failing to return a book to its proper place, being late to chapel, laughing, or cursing. The penalties for such minor trespasses were usually mild—reciting extra prayers or having to eat while seated on the floor. More serious offenses—arguing, lying, gossiping with malicious intent—were punishable by up to three days of fasting.

In addition to these collective sessions, each friar was required at least once a week to make a personal confession. This was the central act in the friar's spiritual life—the penitential process through which he acknowledged his sins, expressed contrition for them, and gained absolution from a priest. Monastic confession was far more demanding than the lay variety. Every wayward act, wanton glance, and unauthorized comment had to be recollected and acknowledged and the proper regret felt and expressed. In anticipation, Luther—grateful for this chance to unburden his conscience—would spend the entire week meticulously examining his conduct and making an inventory of his lapses.

In terms of the challenges he faced, Luther stood out in one key respect. For many friars, the supreme test was their carnal urges. As Luther would later put it, there were "horrible temptations to pollution" in the monastery. "Almost every night the brothers were bothered by them." The pollutions were of two kinds—"nocturnal" (released during sleep) and "shameful" (self-induced). The latter included many "idle men" who were "fattened in luxury" and "incited by drunkenness and sloth to engage in such filth almost the whole day long." At this point, however, Luther himself was not much bothered by sexual desires; only years later would they become insistent.

In these early months in the cloister, his battles were of a different kind. As was common in that period, many of his fellow inmates had become friars not out of religious conviction but in a search for security or at the insistence of their families. And, in the cramped quarters of the monastery, their shortcomings were magnified. Petty jealousy erupted, and fierce rivalries flared. Many friars, eager to stand out, were ostentatious in prayer and flamboyant in fasting. Far more than lust, it was pride, impatience, and anger that tested Luther as a friar and that he would have to control if he were to find spiritual tranquility and everlasting peace.

In the friary, every brother was assigned a task, and the novice master, seeing Luther's puffed-up ways, gave him the most lowly: cleaning the latrines. Luther welcomed the challenge. The same was true of the begging he had to perform. As a mendicant order, the Augustinians had originally engaged in this practice to support themselves, but over the years the friary in Erfurt had, like many others, become wealthy, receiving generous endowments from the well-to-do and amassing large tracts of land. Begging had thus become unnecessary, but it was nonetheless retained as a spur to humility, and Luther had to carry a sack around town, soliciting alms. While doing so, he encountered many former colleagues and professors, but he came away feeling not humiliated but humbled.

As so it went with the monastic routine as a whole. The privations Luther had to endure were undeniably challenging. The jolt from the bell in the middle of the night announcing matins; the hunger that gnawed during the long hours before the first meal; the choking heat and humidity that invaded the cells in midsummer; the long stretches of silence and lack of engagement—all tested his fortitude and commitment. Yet as the weeks passed and summer gave way to fall, Luther gradually settled into the unhurried rhythms of the cloister. As his body adjusted to the hard surfaces of the prayer stalls, as his mind adapted to the confinement of his cell, his soul began to open and expand. Freed from everyday worries and distractions, he was able to concentrate on the one thing that truly mattered—his relationship to God. In his cell at night, he ardently beseeched the Lord, seeking his mercy and grace. During confession, he felt his burdens lighten, and when at the end of each session the priest pronounced the sacred words *Ego te absolvo*—"I absolve you"—he felt a rush of relief and comfort. In the darkness of the cloister church, the resonant chanting of the Psalms had an enthralling effect, and at the conclusion of compline, as Luther stood and bowed in praise of God *per omnia saecula saeculorum*—"through all the ages"—he felt spiritually transported, as if "among the choir of angels."

In September 1506, Luther, having demonstrated his earnestness, was approved to take his vows. At the ceremony, the prior warned him that once he committed himself, he would not be free, for whatever reason, to throw off the yoke of obedience. Acknowledging his readiness to so commit, Luther pledged to "live until death without worldly possessions and in chastity according to the Rule of St. Augustine." He was clad in the habit of the order—a white shirt, a short and a long white tunic, a scapular, and a long white cope with a large collar, over which was placed a block cotta (or mantle) with a cowl. The scapular—a long band of cloth with an opening for the head that was worn front and back over the shoulders—symbolized the yoke of Christ. It was to be worn at all times, and leaving the cell without it was considered a serious offense. The prior raised Luther up and gave him the kiss of peace; his fellow friars then did the same. In taking his vow, Luther was deemed to have returned to the original state of grace, and he could now dedicate himself to attaining salvation. The monastic life, which over the centuries had been refined into a precise instrument for the cure of souls, seemed to be having its intended effect. Like so many others, Luther experienced "how peaceful and quiet Satan was wont to be in the first year" of being a friar, as he later wrote.

It was not long, however, before Satan began to stir. The opening was provided, oddly enough, by Luther's first promotion. His superiors—seeing his abilities—decided that he should become a priest, so that, in addition to tending to his own spiritual needs, he could help others address theirs. In preparation, Luther during the fall and winter of 1506 began receiving instruction in the three key priestly duties—preaching, hearing confession, and celebrating Mass.

The Mass—the central act of Christian worship—was the solemn ceremony through which homage was rendered to God for the great blessings he had provided. It involved an intricately choreographed series of hymns, invocations, readings from Scripture, lighting of candles, and ringing of bells, and to ensure that it was faithfully performed, a vast literature had arisen. Luther's main guide was *Exposition on the Canon of the Mass*, by Gabriel Biel, a Tübingen professor who, by the time of his death, in 1495, was recognized as the leading theologian of his generation. The canon—the most sacred part of the Mass—was the long Eucharistic prayer through which the bread and wine were consecrated and transubstantiated into the body and blood of Christ. In four immense volumes, Biel classified, analyzed, and explained the ceremony's every gesture, vestment, phrase, and procedure. He described how to wear the stole, alb, and maniple; how to fill the chalice and place the host on the paten; how to bow, stretch out the arms, hold the palms together, and kiss the cross. He was especially exhaustive on the spiritual, mental, and physical state in which the priest had to approach the ceremony. All impure thoughts had to be banished during the rite. (According to Biel, a priest could not celebrate Mass if he had had a nocturnal emission the night before. In Erfurt, Luther later observed, such emissions were so frequent that this stipulation had to be suspended on days when many Masses were to be performed.)

Luther considered Biel's exposition the best of books on the subject. "When I read it, my heart bled," he later recalled. Given its many stern warnings, however, it caused much anxiety as well. Omitting the stole or mispronouncing a single syllable was considered worse than committing one of the seven deadly sins. Some priests were so terrified by the words of consecration—*Hoc est corpus meum* ("This is my body")—that they trembled all over on reciting them. The words had to be read without any alien thoughts, and anyone who stammered in pronouncing them was said to have committed a great crime.

On April 3, 1507, Luther, having duly completed his training, was ordained a priest. At the age of twenty-three, he was now authorized to stand as an intermediary between man and God and, by celebrating the Mass and administering the sacraments, to summon Christ before the kneeling congregation. His inaugural Mass was scheduled for May 2. In preparation, he had to confess and receive absolution, and with even greater diligence than usual he strove to uncover and root out any internal blemish that might prevent the Holy Spirit from working through him. To add to his worry, his father was scheduled to attend. In the nearly two years since Martin had entered the friary, he had had little contact with Hans, and he hoped that his father, on seeing his rapid progress, would be reconciled to him. Hans's mining interests had flourished, and he made a grand entrance at the monastery, arriving on horseback with twenty or so associates and relatives and making a contribution to the cloister of twenty guldens.

Taking his place before the altar in the chapel, Martin nervously awaited the start of the ceremony. Initially, all went well. When, however, he reached the canon passage, "To Thee, the eternal, living, and true God," Luther—suddenly overwhelmed by the gravity of the occasion and his proximity to the Almighty—was seized by panic. "With what tongue," he thought to himself,

> shall I address such Majesty, seeing that all men ought to tremble in the presence of even an earthly prince? Who am I, that I should lift up mine eyes or raise my hands to the divine Majesty? The angels surround him. At his nod the earth trembles. And shall I, a miserable little pygmy, say, "I want this, I ask for that?" For I am dust and ashes and full of sin and I am speaking to the living, the eternal and the true God.

Because he lacked genuine faith, Luther later observed, he almost died of anxiety and felt an urge to flee the altar.

The prior admonished Luther to remain, and he somehow managed to make it to the end. Afterward, he joined his father and his guests in the refectory. Seeking a word of reassurance, Luther asked why Hans had been so angry about his decision to become a friar. "Don't you know the Fourth Commandment?" Hans said. "Honor your father and your mother? And here you have left me and your dear mother to look after ourselves in our old age." "But father," Luther replied, "I could do more good by prayers than if I had stayed in the world." He then recalled the voice he had heard calling out to him in the thunderstorm. "God grant it was not an apparition of the Devil," Hans snapped. Luther had long been nagged by the same suspicion, and his father's comment (as he later wrote) "drove roots" into his heart, as if God were speaking through Hans's mouth.

Luther's struggle to win the approval of his father mirrored his exhausting efforts to please the Heavenly Father. The fit that seized him during his first Mass stirred up all his old anxieties about his unworthiness before the Lord. His was very much the God of the Old Testament—the wrathful and merciless judge who had obliterated Sodom and Gomorrah for the wickedness of their people and who at Sinai had ordered the slaughter of all who had worshipped the golden calf.

The recitation of the canonical hours added to his dread. While some of the Psalms offered solace and support, others rang with threats of divine violence and retribution. The references in Psalm 90 to God's consuming anger and wrath so unsettled Luther that he could barely bring himself to say it. A recurrent image in the Psalms is "the pit," into which all whom God has abandoned are cast, and Luther forever worried that he would be among them. He was especially troubled by the phrase *iustitia Dei*—the righteousness of God. Over and over it tolled in the Psalms, reminding him each time of God's exacting standards.

Even confession was becoming a burden. In examining his own conduct, each friar had to determine whether and how often he had violated the many codes of Christian behavior, including but not limited to the Ten Commandments, the seven deadly sins, the twelve articles of faith, the seven corporal works of mercy, the six sins against the Holy Spirit, the four cardinal virtues, and the three theological virtues. The penitent was expected to recall not only each sin but also the circumstances in which it had occurred. He was to reveal with whom and where the sins were committed; when they were committed (if on a Sunday or religious holiday, their gravity increased); why they were committed (if done out of depravity, they were more serious than if done in ignorance or fear); and in what manner they were committed (a willfully committed sin was worse than one spurred by an uncontrollable burst of anger).

For Luther, with his sensitive conscience, the constant self-interrogation proved deeply unsettling. The more he sought to root out his transgressions, the more he became preoccupied with them. Upon leaving confession, he would immediately recall how he had stumbled over a passage in the Psalter or left his cell without his scapular, and he would rush back to confess it. He became notorious in the monastery for the length and frequency of his confessions. Though he constantly confessed, he later recalled, "I could not find peace, but I was constantly crucified by thoughts such as these: 'You have committed this or that sin; you are guilty of envy, impatience, etc. Therefore it is useless for you to enter this holy order, and all your good works are to no avail.'"

In his cell at night, Luther was kept awake by the uninvited mur-murings of his heart. That brother is a fool, this one is a gossip, that other keeps everyone up with his snoring. For all his pious deeds, Luther inwardly feared that he remained the same old Martin—short-tempered, resentful, obstinate, proud. And God, he felt sure, would judge him se-verely for it. When Luther told one of his confessors that, even after being absolved, he continued to feel God's wrath, the priest admonished him: "You are a fool! God is not angry with you, but you are angry with God."

With the specter of divine fury thus looming, the *Anfechtungen* re-turned. Without warning these spells would strike, plunging Luther into a chasm of doubt and desolation. During them, Christ seemed to him a merciless tyrant, willing to save only a select few who by their good deeds and saintly behavior had shown they merited salvation; the rest faced an eternity of suffering and torment, and Luther felt sure he would be among them. These bouts, though abbreviated in length, "were so great and so much like hell that no tongue could adequately express them, no pen could describe them, and one who had not himself experienced them could not believe them." If they had "lasted for half an hour, even for one tenth of an hour," the person undergoing them "would have perished completely and all his bones would have been reduced to ashes. At such a time God seems terribly angry, and with him the whole creation. At such a time, there is no flight, no comfort, within or without, but all things accuse."

Even in his blackest moments, however, Luther was able to perform at a high level, and after being ordained a priest, he began (probably in the summer of 1507) to study for a doctor's degree in theology. The Augus-tinian cloister was known for the quality of its instruction, and several of its friars taught at the University of Erfurt. As in Paris, however, the study of theology did not for the most part mean reading the Bible, for it was considered "the cause of all sedition," as one of his teachers explained.

Instead, Luther spent most of his time with Scotus, Ockham, and Biel. The main text was the *Sentences* of Peter Lombard, and Luther sat through lectures on subjects like the unity of the Godhead, the salvific force of the sacraments, and the formation of corporeal entities. In the process, he received further instruction in late Scholastic notions of sin and salvation—in how man, by doing all that is within him, can receive an infusion of divine grace and in that state perform meritorious acts that are pleasing to God, leading to the reward of eternal life. No matter how hard he tried, however, he felt sure that he was falling short.

In the fall of 1508, he was suddenly jolted from this draining routine. A fledgling university in the small Saxon town of Wittenberg on the Elbe River in eastern Germany needed a lecturer in philosophy, and the Augustinian monastery there was asked to provide one. Luther was chosen, and he promptly set off on the nearly hundred-mile journey. Arriving, he found a remote outpost that was far more provincial and rough-hewn than anything he had yet encountered. During this initial visit to Wittenberg, Luther would remain for a year. (After his return, in 1511, he would become a permanent resident.) To his dismay, he was required to lecture on Aristotle's *Nicomachean Ethics*—a cruel distraction from the scriptural texts he so yearned to study. "I am well, thank God," he complained to a friend, "except that my studies are very severe, especially philosophy," which he would gladly change for theology—the theology that "searches out the meat of the nut, the kernel of the grain, the marrow of the bones."

The kernel of the grain was the Bible itself. In March 1509, Luther received his first theological degree—that of *baccalaureus biblicus*, bachelor of the Bible—but, paradoxically, as his letter suggests, he had little time to read it. In the autumn of 1509, he successfully took the exam to become a *sententiarius* (bachelor of the *Sentences*), which qualified him to lecture on Lombard's sprawling text. Later that fall, Luther was recalled to Erfurt and began delivering his lectures there. A copy of the volume he used has survived, and his marginal comments, jotted down amid the thicket of theses, objections, and corollaries, attest to his dutiful acceptance of reigning Catholic interpretations of grace and salvation, the Trinity and the resurrection.

In his notes, however, there appeared a name that would signal the first faint stirring of revolt: Augustine. On almost every page, Luther cited the bishop of Hippo. On the surface, this would seem unremarkable. Augustine was one of the four Doctors of the Western Church—the one, moreover, most venerated by medieval theologians. Luther's own order proudly bore his name, and whenever Luther prayed at chapel, the saint's image gazed down at him from the stained glass window above the altar. But, as with so many other Fathers, Augustine's teachings were known mainly through passages that had been wrested from their context and obscured through centuries of glossing and syllogizing.

In 1506, however, the Basel printer Johannes Amerbach, after almost two decades of editorial labor, had published the final volume of the first scholarly printed edition of Augustine's collected works, and across Europe theologians, friars, and scholars were excitedly reading it. Of all the Fathers being revived in this period, none would have a more galvanizing effect on Christian thinking than Augustine. The Augustinian renaissance would in fact provide a major spur for the Reformation. (Almost alone among early-sixteenth-century thinkers, Erasmus would withhold his approval.)

Few would be more affected than Luther. Reading Augustine, he found a theology sharply at odds with the one in which he had been trained. Remarkably, a volume of Augustine's writings annotated by Luther in 1509 and 1510 was found in the late nineteenth century in a library in Zwickau, Germany, and his notes on it show the stimulating effect that reading the bishop had on him. Just as Erasmus had embraced Jerome as his guide back to the days of the early Church, so would Luther travel there with Augustine. Until then, Luther later recalled, he had been given only Scotus to read, but after discovering Augustine, he not only read but "devoured" him. The experience would represent the first step on the road to the Ninety-Five Theses.

Among the works by Augustine that Luther read in this period was the *Confessions*. Opening it, he found a text unlike any other he had to that point encountered. In contrast to the convoluted treatises and arid handbooks of the medieval classroom, the *Confessions* was intensely personal. Written at the end of the fourth century, when Augustine was in his early forties, it is generally considered the first memoir, with many spicy details served up along with discussions of evil, grace, and salvation. And there was much in it with which Luther could identify.

Like Luther, Augustine (who was born in 354) grew up in a small inland town—Thagaste, which was located on a dry plateau about sixty miles from the Mediterranean coast in what is now Algeria. Where Mansfeld was an insignificant speck in the Holy Roman Empire, Thagaste was a remote outpost in the Roman province of Numidia. Also like Luther, Augustine had an overbearing parent—in this case his mother, Monica. A pious Christian, she would press her son from his earliest years to embrace Christ. She and Augustine's father, Patricius, a pagan, were members of the Latin-speaking middle class and (like Luther's parents) had just enough resources to send their bright son to a Latin school. Here Augustine would receive the training in Latin grammar and literature he needed to move beyond the provinces and onto the public stage. As he recounts in the *Confessions*, he read the comedies of Terence, memorized sections of the *Aeneid*, and learned to lament the death of Dido. (Augustine also developed a lifelong distaste for Greek—a key factor in Erasmus's low estimation of him.)

At the age of sixteen, Augustine was seized by an impulse that for years would torment him: lust. It plunged him into "the whirlpool of sin." One day at the public baths, the "signs of active virility" came to life in him, causing his father to rejoice at this indication that he would one day have grandchildren. (In the vast archive of patristic literature, this is perhaps the only overt reference to an erection.)

Carnal desire, in turn, was but one aspect of a broader psychological attribute that would come to dominate his theology: the will, in all its unruliness. Augustine lied to his tutor, stole from his parents' larder, and joined a gang. One day, he pilfered some pears from a neighbor's tree. The pears were sickly in appearance and sour, and Augustine quickly threw them away, tasting "nothing in them but my own sin, which I relished and enjoyed." Reflecting on this act many years later, he remained troubled by its senselessness and what it said about his nature: "For the sake of a laugh, a little sport, I was glad to do harm and anxious to damage another. Can anyone unravel this twisted tangle of knots?"

In 371, Augustine went to Carthage to continue his studies. The second city in the Western Empire, Carthage (located in what is now Tunisia) had a well-regarded university, streets lined with bookstores, and a spectacular harbor ringed with colonnades. It was also a "hissing cauldron of lust," as Augustine put it. During the several years he spent there, he took a mistress and had a son with her. He was also seized by a new passion—ambition. Augustine wanted to become a great speaker solely for the fame it would bring him; rising to the top of his class in rhetoric, he became "swollen with conceit."

In the course of his studies, though, he came upon a work that would give him his first push onto a new course: Cicero's *Hortensius*. This tract (only fragments of which have survived) urges the study of philosophy, and as Augustine read it, his heart "began to throb with a bewildering passion for the wisdom of eternal truth." Setting out on a quest for knowledge, he turned first to the Bible, in accordance with the wishes of his mother. (Monica herself would ultimately be canonized and lend her name to a southern California city whose freewheeling ways would no doubt have horrified her.)

As he read the Old Testament, however, Augustine was put off by its coarse language, immoral tales, and many contradictions. Moreover, it did not satisfactorily address a question that had come to preoccupy him: the source of evil. He found a more convincing explanation in the teachings of the Manicheans. This underground sect subscribed to a rationalist but esoteric cosmology: that the universe is home to two great forces—those of Good, represented by light, and those of Evil, represented by darkness—and that the captive particles of the Good are always trying to escape those of the Evil. As abstruse as this philosophy was, Augustine found it persuasive, and he became an ardent follower.

After teaching in Thagaste and Carthage, Augustine in 383 accepted an offer to teach literature and oratory in Rome, and with great anticipation he set out for the imperial metropolis. To his disappointment, however, the students there proved no less undisciplined than those back home, and so, when offered a position as a professor of rhetoric in Milan, he at once took it. His job—essentially that of court orator—brought him into contact with generals, statesmen, and philosophers. A distinguished public career seemed ensured. He quickly became disillusioned, however. Among his main tasks was delivering official panegyrics to the emperor and other officials, and the more lies he told, the more praise he received.

In Milan, Augustine was joined by his mother. Intent on arranging a proper marriage for him, she prevailed on him to banish his mistress.

She also continued to press him to accept Christ. Augustine was, in fact, falling under the spell of Milan's bishop, Ambrose. The sermons by this future Doctor of the Church filled the city's large basilica. Using the allegorical method, Ambrose was able to draw spiritual meanings from the rough language of the Old Testament. When Augustine began rereading it, passages that had once seemed childish and far-fetched now seemed alive with transcendent wisdom. Increasingly, he felt drawn to Christ, but more as a model man than a divine savior.

All the while, Augustine remained attached to worldly pleasures, especially physical ones. No matter how hard he tried to control his cravings, they seemed to control him. He yearned to embrace God, but as long as he remained in the grip of the flesh, he felt unable to do so. Desperate to understand his condition, he began reading the Neoplatonists. Popular in Milan, they offered a glimpse into a universe that existed beyond the world of the senses and that was eternal and immovable. Studying Paul's epistles, Augustine could now see that Christ was not simply a moral exemplar but the Word made flesh, sent by God to deliver mankind from its sins. When he came upon Paul's statement in his Epistle to the Romans that man can escape the malignant forces within him only through God's grace, he felt his heart tremble. More than ever, Augustine longed to commit himself to God, but he continued to feel himself held fast—"not in fetters clamped upon me by another, but by my own will, which had the strength of iron chains."

One day in August 386, Augustine and his friend Alypius, with whom he shared a house outside Milan, received a visit from a fellow African named Ponticianus, a fervent Christian. Ponticianus—seeing a volume of Paul's epistles lying on a table—began recounting the story of the Egyptian monk Anthony and his decision to retreat into the desert to devote himself to God. When Ponticianus described how two young acquaintances of his had, on hearing of Anthony's feats, decided to renounce their old lives and devote themselves to God, Augustine felt overcome by shame. Thirteen years had passed since he had first read the *Hortensius* and embarked on his quest for truth, and though he could now see what it was, the "unclean whispers" of his body kept him from embracing it.

After Ponticianus left, Augustine began pouring out his frustration to

Alypius. Taking the volume of Paul's letters, he went out of the house and into the adjoining garden. His friend followed. Knowing in his heart that he should accept God's will and enter into his covenant, Augustine nonetheless continued to resist. He flung himself down beneath a fig tree and, in agony over his indecision, tore at his hair, beat himself on the head, and burst into tears. Why could he not get his body to obey his will? "How long shall I go on saying, 'tomorrow, tomorrow'? Why not now? Why not make an end of my ugly sins at this moment?"

Suddenly, he heard a child's singsong voice coming from a nearby house. "Take it and read, take it and read," the voice called. Seeing in this a divine command, Augustine opened the volume of Paul's epistles and read the first verse to catch his eye. It was Romans 13:13: "Not in reveling and drunkenness, not in lust and wantonness, not in quarrels and rivalries. Rather, arm yourselves with the Lord Jesus Christ, spend no more thought on nature and nature's appetites." By the time he had reached the end of the verse, Augustine recounted, "it was as though the light of confidence flooded into my heart and all the darkness of doubt was dispelled." At last his mind felt free "from the gnawing anxieties of ambition and gain, from wallowing in filth and scratching the itching sore of lust." From that moment on, he no longer "placed any hope in this world but stood firmly upon the rule of faith." Shortly thereafter, Augustine resigned his position at the court and withdrew with some friends to a country villa in Cassiciacum, on the outskirts of Milan, to spend his days studying and contemplating God. In March 387 he returned to Milan. He then went to Rome, where he remained for a year before returning to Africa.

Augustine's embrace of Christ in the garden strongly echoes the conversion of Paul, who on the road to Damascus was overcome after hearing the voice of Jesus call out to him. Augustine was similarly moved upon reading a verse from Paul's Epistle to the Romans. But it was not until he began writing the *Confessions*, around 397, that he was able to make some sense of what had happened in the garden. By then, he had been in the seaport of Hippo for about six years, first as a priest and then as a bishop. In both capacities, Augustine had spent much time tending to the needs of his congregation, and in the process he had begun to see how similar their own struggles with their vices were to his own. North Africans were notorious swearers of oaths, for instance, and despite their sincere desire to change, they constantly relapsed. In Augustine's case, it was his sexual urges that had defied his control.

Augustine's awareness of the partly unconscious nature of the power that those urges had over him gives the *Confessions* its modern feel. As he pondered his experience, he came to see his sexual longings as part of a more general set of selfish impulses (which he called concupiscence) that took hold of his mind, bound fast his will, and kept him from God. "My sin was this," he wrote, "that I looked for pleasure, beauty, and truth not in him but in myself and other creatures, and the search led me instead to pain, confusion, and error." Only by relinquishing his will and surrendering himself to God had he been able to break the hold of these hidden forces. "There can be no hope for me except in your mercy," he wrote. "Give me the grace to do as you command, and command me to do what you will!"

Augustine, however, was not yet clear on the theological implications of his new thoughts about human will and divine grace. He would spend his remaining thirty-plus years working them out. His thinking would be strongly shaped by the many fierce disputes in which he became involved—none of them more important than the one with Pelagius. Many of Augustine's key doctrines were to emerge from his epic clash with this British ascetic—one that foreshadowed the battle that Erasmus and Luther would wage over the same subject centuries later.

Augustine at first paid little attention to Pelagius, who was far away in Rome. Since his arrival there (sometime in the late fourth century), Pelagius had won an ardent following with his uncompromising calls for Christian austerity. (He moved in the same aristocratic circles that Jerome had a few years earlier.) God, Pelagius maintained, had endowed man with the capacity, based on the dictates of his conscience, to choose between good and evil. Distressed by the wishy-washy form of Christianity many Romans seemed to practice, Pelagius insisted that every Christian was bound to keep all of God's commandments, large and small. When a copy of the *Confessions* reached him in Rome, Pelagius bristled at Augustine's stress on human frailty and dependence. Hearing a bishop recite Augustine's famous line—"Give me the grace to do as you command, and command me to do what you will"—he became so agitated that he almost came to blows with the man.

By then, however, Pelagius, like all of Rome, was preparing for calamity. Since the start of the fifth century, barbarian armies had been steadily advancing down the Italian peninsula. Then, in August 410, the unthinkable occurred: an army of Visigoths under the command of Alaric entered Rome. Over three days they burned, pillaged, and caroused, then withdrew. The shock spread around the Mediterranean. Though Rome had by then been eclipsed by other cities in political importance, it remained the center of the Western world, and its penetration by a foreign army seemed to imperil civilization itself. Refugees poured into northern Africa, bearing tales of toppled monuments and plundered palaces.

Pelagius was among them. Arriving in Hippo in 410, he at once sent word to Augustine, requesting a meeting. Augustine was away, however, and Pelagius soon moved on to Carthage and then Palestine. There, he began extolling free will and man's ability to live free of sin. "It is possible to do anything which one really wants to do," he declared. God, in making man in his own likeness, did not leave him "naked and defenseless" in the face of his desires but provided him with the armaments of reason and wisdom, so that he could choose to act virtuously. Since God holds man accountable for his every transgression, all must strive for "complete moral perfection."

When such statements got back to Augustine, he became furious. Aimed at an ascetic elite, they seemed certain to produce frustration and despair among ordinary Christians. Moreover, Pelagius, in ascribing such capabilities to man, was setting intolerable limits on divine power. The triumph of such views could prove injurious to man's relationship with God—and to Augustine's own reputation. He therefore set out to discredit and undermine Pelagius. He mobilized the bishops of Africa, enlisted the support of powerful figures in Rome, and sent Orosius, a fierce Spanish heretic-hunter, to Palestine to organize opposition to Pelagius among local prelates, including Jerome. Augustine also began turning out vitriolic tracts against him. In the *Anti-Pelagian Writings*, as they came to be called, Augustine's pronouncements on human nature turned ever more bleak and extreme, holding man to be not just sinful and selfish but utterly helpless and depraved. (Jerome, in one of the era's most memorable insults, called Pelagius "a dolt of dolts, with his wits dulled by a surfeit of his native Scotch porridge.")

The battle with Pelagius and his followers would loom over Augustine's late, great masterwork, the *City of God*. He embarked on it in 413, three years after the Visigoths had entered Rome, and he would keep at it for the next fourteen years. In it, Augustine can be seen moving dramatically from the classical into the medieval world. The treatise (which exceeds a thousand pages in most modern editions) proposed a stark vision for a new Christian order to fill the vacuum left by the collapsing Roman Empire; it would have tremendous influence on Luther's own thinking.

The immediate spur for the work was provided by the Roman refugees who, arriving in Africa, blamed Christianity for the city's fall. With its emphasis on morality and embrace of meekness, Christianity, they maintained, had weakened the warrior spirit of the empire and so undermined its ability to defend itself. In the *City of God*, Augustine devoted the first ten of the twenty-two books to a stinging rebuttal. He described the series of wars, assassinations, famines, and floods that had afflicted the empire since long before the coming of Christ and that the entire pantheon of Roman gods had been powerless to prevent. He mocked the gods' petty rivalries, their puerile love affairs, their absurdly fine divisions of labor. Even at the height of its power, Rome had been driven by a lust for domination and a love of praise; in its decline, it showed the fate awaiting those who worship their own gods rather than the one true God.

Having thus dispatched paganism, Augustine spent the remainder of his tract proposing an alternative worldview. He did not do so succinctly. Highly digressive, the *City of God* addresses such disparate matters as the different kinds of demons, the contrast between good and offending angels, the many giants who roamed the earth before the Flood, the perfection of the numbers six and seven, the activities of Gog and Magog as agents of the Devil's persecution, the physical properties bodies will have after they are resurrected, and—most important—the Fall. The fateful events that occurred in the Garden of Eden are at the heart of Augustine's theological vision. Adam and Eve, he maintained, at first lived in a state of tranquil bliss. They knew neither anger nor lust and engaged in sexual intercourse rationally and calmly. But then, in an act of "heinous" disobedience of God's wishes, they ate of the fruit of the tree of knowledge. As punishment, God consigned them to a life of toil and suffering, culminating in death, and fornication became a source of shame. God furthermore saw fit to punish all of their descendants. As Augustine put it, "Death has passed to all mankind through the sin of the first human beings." In life, meanwhile, their progeny were to be enslaved to a malignant mass of needs and desires. By himself, a human being was incapable of doing good.

Although earlier Church Fathers had raised the idea of original sin, Augustine was the first to give it such prominence. He offered a lengthy catalog of the fruits of man's warped nature—quarrels, wars, hatred, treachery, cruelty, promiscuity, adultery, incest, and "unnatural vice in men and women (disgusting acts too filthy to be named)"—all springing "from that root of error and perverted affection which every son of Adam brings with him at his birth."

In the grip of this depravity, man had only one means of attaining salvation: divine grace. Only by surrendering his will to God and receiving God's favor could he hope to overcome the evil impulses to which he had been sentenced for the first sin. God extends that grace without regard to any ostensible merits on the individual's part; it is "undeserved." God, who knows all things before they happen, decides who will be saved and who damned before they are even born. Only a small fraction of humankind will be earmarked for salvation; the rest are doomed to an eternity of torment, apart from any individual merit. This is Augustine's famous doctrine of predestination. Not everyone, he acknowledged, would find such a God palatable; many would surely bridle at the idea of a collective punishment imposed on all mankind for one man's sin. But divine majesty was unbounded and indivisible. Since God created the world and its many marvels, "why should he not have the power to make the bodies of the dead rise again, and the bodies of the damned to suffer torment in everlasting fire?"

The "City of God" of Augustine's title refers to the dwelling place of all those predestined to reign with God for eternity. Those doomed to undergo eternal punishment with the Devil reside in the earthly city. The one is a community of the devout; the other consists of the irreligious. In one, love of God has been given first place; in the other, love of self. According to Augustine, these two cities arose out of two companies of angels, the light and the dark. In this sprawling work completed in his twilight years, Augustine showed that he remained beholden to the Manichean thinking to which he had been so attracted as a young man.

Augustine's vision of original sin, human depravity, predestination, and the condemnation of the mass of mankind apart from any individual merit was in many ways terrifying. Remarkably, though, he would succeed in getting it adopted by the Latin Church. This was due, in part, to his skills as a prosecutor and propagandist. Despite Pelagius's repeated protestations that he was a sincere Christian, Augustine's defaming of him would help make him a pariah and establish "Pelagian" as one of the most damning epithets in the Christian lexicon (as Erasmus would unhappily discover). In 431, at the Council of Ephesus, Pelagian theology, with its belief in free will and individual merit, was condemned and its proponents were branded as heretics within the boundaries of the empire.

But more than Augustine's agitation was at work. With Western civilization under threat from the barbarians and tales of brutality and cruelty mounting, Augustine's dark vision of human nature seemed confirmed by events. In 429, another Germanic tribe, the Vandals, who had occupied Spain, headed south across the strait into Africa. Moving quickly eastward along the coast, they seized major ports while committing mass atrocities. At the time of Augustine's death, on August 28, 430, Hippo itself was under siege. Amid such horrors, Augustine's radical pessimism about human nature improbably became the new orthodoxy.

Yet Pelagianism would not die. In practice, Augustine's denial of human agency proved too chilling to serve the needs of the Church. As missionaries headed into the heathen hinterland, a creed that featured a God who has decided in advance to sentence most of humankind to perdition through no fault of their own was hardly conducive to their work.

With the chaos in North Africa, the debate over sin and salvation shifted to southern Gaul. There, some bishops and monks in the late fifth century began to teach that, though salvation ultimately depends on God's grace, lay Christians could through their own acts help initiate that grace—a position that later came to be known as semi-Pelagian.

Toward the end of the sixth century, Pope Gregory I—one of the four great Doctors of the Western Church—endorsed such an approach. Concerned more with pastoral matters than doctrine, he drew on another aspect of Augustine's work—his support for ecclesiastical authority. In addition to his statements about depravity and human helplessness, Augustine offered the framework for a universal (i.e., catholic) church that would absorb all humanity and that, through administering the sacraments, would provide a pathway to salvation. From this kernel, Gregory developed a new formula: while salvation comes only through divine grace, a Christian, by performing the sacraments of the Church, could set in motion a process to attain that grace.

Gregory's ideas became institutionalized in the sacrament of penance—*poenitentia*. By showing contrition, confessing to a priest, and performing acts of satisfaction, those committing sins could obtain absolution. By the thirteenth century, this system had become entrenched, and preachers discussed salvation in terms that presumed a degree of free will. Augustinian thinking about human frailty and divine omnipotence was further diluted by the late Scholastics. By doing all that is within one, they taught, man can perform meritorious works in a state of grace and thus cooperate with God in attaining salvation—a position not far from that of Pelagius.

From reading those Scholastics, Luther had concluded that, by zealously fulfilling the rule of the Augustinian order, he could attain divine grace. Yet his base impulses and impure thoughts kept intruding, feeding his anxiety about salvation. Now, in reading Augustine himself, Luther found nothing about free will, good works, or doing one's best. Instead, he found stern pronouncements about human wickedness, divine majesty, and undeserved grace. If Augustine was correct, the selfish urges and prideful thoughts that were continually welling up in him represented not simply his own personal failings but ingrained features of human nature. As forbidding as Augustine's theology might seem to others, Luther took great comfort in the idea that his fate was not in his own hands.

In the bishop of Hippo, Luther found not only the rudiments of an alternative theology but also a method for arriving at it. In the *Confessions*, Augustine describes how he found God through reading Scripture. His memoir is laced with biblical citations that serve as signposts on his spiritual journey; his dramatic transformation came via a fortuitous encounter with the Epistle to the Romans. Inspired by Augustine, Luther longed to get at the kernel of the grain, the marrow of the bone. And the opportunity to do so would soon arise.

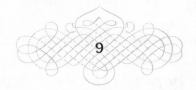

RENAISSANCE TOUR

It was on Erasmus's second visit to England (where he arrived at the end of 1505) that his famous literary friendship with Thomas More would bloom. Now twenty-six, More had recently married Jane Colt, the seventeen-year-old daughter of a country squire, and the couple had moved into a large stone house on Bucklersbury, a busy lane lined with grocers and apothecaries in the heart of the City of London. More was just beginning to attract notice as a lawyer and scholar, and to his house came a steady stream of barristers, merchants, clerics, and scholars to gossip, banter, and debate. Erasmus, who on his earlier visit to England had been impressed by More's geniality, was now fully smitten. "I believe (unless I am deluded by the intensity of the love I bear him) that nature never created a livelier mind, or one quicker, more discerning, or clearer—in short, more perfectly endowed with all the talents—than his; and his intelligence is matched by his power of expression," he wrote to a friend.

In many ways, though, they were an odd couple, with contrasting temperaments and outlooks that, under the pressure of events, would result in a painful separation. Erasmus was the neat one. He liked clean sheets, savory meals, and airy rooms. England would prove a major test in this regard, for the English were widely considered Europe's most slovenly people. The floors of their houses, Erasmus would later write in disgust, "are generally spread with clay and then with rushes from some marsh," which remain in place for as many as twenty years and "under which fester spittle, vomit, dogs' urine and men's, too, dregs of beer and cast-off bits of fish, and other unspeakable kinds of filth," all of which exhale "a sort of miasma." Erasmus cited the fetid state of English houses as a factor in the island's susceptibility to the sweating sickness—a highly contagious and often fatal disease that periodically and pitilessly struck the country beginning in 1485 and which later spread to the Continent. He recommended doing away with the rushes and making sure that rooms were properly ventilated—ideas that showed how advanced he was in matters of hygiene.

More, by contrast, was indifferent to his surroundings. He wore simple clothes, disdained jewelry, shunned drink, and preferred "beef, salt fish, and coarse bread with much yeast to the dishes of which most people are fond," as Erasmus put it. Whereas Erasmus generally avoided the scatology and ribaldry that pervaded the literature of the period, More enthusiastically embraced it. At this time, he was working on his epigrams—short, ironic slivers of Latin verse—whose subjects included vomiting, breaking wind, and wiping snot from the nose. In "Remedies for Ending the Foul Breath Which Results from Certain Foods," he wrote of a man's breath so offensive that *tantum tollere merda potest*—"nothing but shit will remove it." Fascinated by excrement, More had an extensive lexicon for it, including *merda, stercus, lutum,* and *coenum.*

It was in religious sensibility, though, that the gulf between the two men was greatest. Earlier, while pursuing his legal studies, More had lived in the Charterhouse, a cloister of the Carthusian order, whose regimen was far stricter than the Augustinian rule followed by either Erasmus or Luther. More slept on a wooden plank, used a log as a pillow, and wore a hair shirt—an undergarment made of animal hair that was intended to cause pain as a spur to contrition and repentance. He found monastic life so congenial that he seriously considered taking vows. He ultimately decided against it because he wanted to marry, but he would always wonder if he had made the right decision, and he continued to wear a hair shirt. More believed in life after death, said his prayers at fixed hours, and always found time to attend Mass despite his busy schedule. In his correspondence, Erasmus rarely mentions saying prayers and only sporadically refers to attending Mass.

Amid such contrasts, the two were bound together by their shared love of classical literature. One writer in particular fascinated them: Lucian. Erasmus and More got hold of several of his works and jointly set out to translate them. Born in the second century in Samosata, in what is now southeastern Turkey, Lucian wrote in Greek, and after the fall of Rome, as knowledge of that language disappeared from the West, familiarity with his works faded as well. In the early fifteenth century, however, some of his manuscripts had resurfaced, and with translations into Latin quickly following, Lucian became the most popular author of the Renaissance, helping to reintroduce irony into the Latin West after a millennium of mirthlessness.

An irreverent misanthrope, Lucian was trained as a rhetorician but grew bored at home and so took to the road, traveling through Greece, Italy, and Gaul and performing improvised monologues along the way. He eventually worked them up into a series of declamations, panegyrics, essays, and dialogues—mordant entertainments featuring a wayward cast of misers and toadies, spongers and swindlers. Lucian parodied Homer, ridiculed the gullibility of the common man, and wrote about battles between the planets and voyages to the sun and the moon. (Some consider him the father of science fiction.) In his *Dialogues of the Gods*, Zeus, Hera, Apollo, and other members of the Greek pantheon chortle over the absurd acts and ludicrous powers ascribed to them by credulous humans.

Lucian, Erasmus wrote, "satirizes everything with inexpressible skill and grace, ridicules everything, and submits everything to the chastisement of his superb wit," and "quite rightly, too, for what is more detestable or intolerable than rascality which publicly masquerades as virtue?" Like Erasmus, Lucian was a moralist—most of his dialogues had lessons to teach—but he showed that those lessons could be most effectively conveyed when presented in comic garb. A Lucianic mix of scorn and social criticism would show up in many of Erasmus's works, such as the *Praise of Folly* and the *Colloquies*. His project of translating Lucian, undertaken jointly with More, would help open a new era of humanist letters in England.

Erasmus dedicated his translations to various prelates and burghers in the hope that they would express their appreciation monetarily. This would become a common practice for him. Since publishers in those days rarely paid advances or royalties, he hoped through his dedications to reel in patrons. One day in January 1506, his friend William Grocyn took him in a boat across the Thames to meet William Warham, the archbishop of Canterbury, at his palace at Lambeth on London's south bank. Erasmus brought with him a copy of the translation of Euripides's *Hecuba* that he had begun in Louvain, and he presented it to Warham. Warham offered in return a bag of coins. Opening it on the way back, Erasmus was disappointed to see how meager the sum was.

A man of great learning, Warham would later become one of Erasmus's chief backers, but as the spring of 1506 arrived, Erasmus's financial situation was growing bleak. Just when things seemed darkest, however, there came a thunderbolt. Giovanni Battista Boerio, a wealthy Italian who was serving as a physician to King Henry VII, wanted to send his two sons, Giovanni and Bernardo, to Italy to receive a proper humanist education, and he asked if Erasmus would accompany them and supervise their studies. Erasmus jumped at the opportunity. Ever since his school days at Deventer, he had dreamed of joining the tide of scholars heading south across the Alps to see the Renaissance up close. Now he was going to get the chance.

In June 1506, Erasmus, along with the two Boerio boys and their tutor, Clyfton (who would handle the actual instruction), set off. Their destination was Bologna, home to Italy's most prestigious university. The city was more than seven hundred miles away, and just getting there would require an epic display of stamina. The crossing from Dover to Calais alone took four nights "at the mercy of wind and wave," as Erasmus put it, during which he caught a bad cold that left his head throbbing. The group stopped in Paris so that Erasmus could arrange the publication of his translations of Lucian and Euripides, then headed south toward the French Alps. As they rode through the seven-thousand-foot pass at Mont Cenis, Erasmus composed a highly stylized elegy, "On the Troubles of Old Age" (he was then turning forty), in which he wistfully bade farewell to "spurious pleasures" and "delightful Muses" and resolved to devote his remaining years to Christ. Descending to Turin, the group remained for two weeks so that Erasmus could obtain a doctorate in theology. (The university—an early version of a diploma mill—granted degrees through a sitting for orals.)

Heading east toward Milan, the party had to proceed cautiously, for the region was aflame with war. Battalions were camped on roadsides, bands of pikemen were marching through valleys, horses were pulling wagons piled high with armaments. The fighting had wound on since 1494, when France sent a 27,000-man army across the Alps in a bid to control northern Italy. The conflict had drawn in Italy's five main powers—the republics of Florence and Venice, the duchy of Milan, the kingdom of Naples, and the Papal States—as well as contingents from Spain, Switzerland, and the Holy Roman Empire, turning northern Italy into the cockpit of European politics. The Italian wars (which would continue until the mid-1550s) featured a new, more lethal generation of firearms, and though Erasmus had lived through the civil war in the northern Netherlands, he was unprepared for the butchery and devastation he saw in Italy. It was a shocking introduction to the cradle of Western civilization.

On finally reaching Bologna, the travelers found to their dismay that the city was preparing for an attack—by the pope. Two months earlier, Julius II had left Rome at the head of an army of two thousand infantry and four hundred cavalry. His goal was to reclaim the Papal States—a thick girdle of territory across Italy's midsection. Awarded to the papacy in the mid-eighth century by Pepin the Short, these states had gradually slipped from its control. Bologna, the richest city in them, was ruled by Giovanni II Bentivoglio, a petty despot who had rejected the pope's demands for a show of fealty. Julius had responded with a bull excommunicating him and offering a plenary indulgence to anyone who killed him. When that proved unavailing, the pope decided on military action. After taking Perugia, he drove his army north along rugged mountain roads through rainstorms and mudslides.

Amid this discord, the university had closed, so Erasmus and his charges again mounted their horses and headed southwest across the mountains to Florence. There, Leonardo, Michelangelo, and Raphael were all at work, but Erasmus, preferring good letters to fine arts, spent his time translating Lucian. Eventually, word arrived that Bentivoglio had fled Bologna. With the prospect of war receding, Erasmus and his pupils headed back to the city, and they were present on the unseasonably warm day in November 1506 when Julius and his forces triumphantly entered it. Crowds lining the streets cheered as phalanxes of infantry and horsemen marched in, followed by four papal standard-bearers, ten white papal steeds with golden bridles, officials of the court, clergymen with lighted candles, the papal choir accompanying the sacred host, rows of cardinals, and, finally, the pope himself, borne on his portable throne.

It was a formative moment for Erasmus. For the first time, he was laying eyes on a pope, and he was at the head of an occupying army. Erasmus let out a "mighty groan," as he would later write. Julius was "waging war, conquering, leading triumphal processions; in fact, playing Julius to the life." The comparison of Julius II to Julius Caesar was one that Erasmus (and many others) would frequently make: the vicar of Christ as the warrior-pope. As he traveled around the countryside, Erasmus could see the effects that maintaining a papal army had on the people. Peasants whose entire fortune consisted of a yoke of oxen and who could barely support their families had to pay a ducat per ox in tithes and taxes. (The ducat was an international coin containing three and a half grams of gold; the annual salary of a teacher was twenty-five or thirty ducats, while a skilled craftsman made about fifty.)

Erasmus remained in Bologna for about a year, supervising the studies of Giovanni and Bernardo. They were turning out to be considerably less clever and well behaved than he had at first thought, and he resented the time they were taking from his own projects—studying Greek, revising his translations of Euripides, and gathering more adages. The tedium of tutoring, together with the punishing summer heat, helped make Erasmus's year in Bologna his most unhappy yet. In October 1507, as his supervisory duties were coming to an end, he sent a letter to Aldus Manutius, the head of a famous printing house in Venice, asking if he would be interested in reprinting his Euripides translations. (The edition published in Paris had been badly botched.) Aldus was indeed interested, and the new edition appeared in December 1507. Pleased with the result, Erasmus wrote to him again to propose a far more ambitious undertaking—a new edition of the *Adages*. Aldus again expressed interest. Given the scale of the project, Erasmus wanted to oversee it in person, and so, after wrapping up his affairs with his lackluster pupils, he headed to Venice.

Arriving in early January 1508, Erasmus found himself in Europe's richest, grandest, most cosmopolitan city. Along the Grand Canal, gondolas glided past sumptuous palazzi with red-tiled roofs and colonnaded facades of marble and porphyry. Venice's lagoons were filled with boats bringing spices, oils, and foodstuffs from the Black Sea, the Levant, India, and beyond. Traders congregated on the Rialto, the decrepit wooden bridge over the Grand Canal that was the commercial heart of the city. Leading from it to the Piazza San Marco was the Merceria, a narrow, twisting lane lined with stalls offering fine fabrics, jewelry, leather goods, glassware, and books. There were dozens of bookstalls there, tempting passersby with the latest textbooks, treatises, manuals, and romances.

Venice at the start of the sixteenth century was Europe's leading book center. The city's dozens of printing houses turned out about one-sixth of all the volumes produced on the Continent. Of them, the Aldine Press was king. Scholars from England to Hungary avidly sought out its compact editions of Latin and Greek classics. Every day, visitors arrived at Aldus's office to get copies of recent editions, give opinions on textual questions, and offer manuscripts for publication. Aldus became so fed up with the interruptions that he posted a sign above his doorway: "Whoever you are, Aldus asks again and again to say whatever it is you want of him in a few words and then be on your way, unless like Hercules you have come to take the world on your shoulders and give weary Atlas a rest. There will always be something for you to do."

Aldus did not consider Erasmus's visit an interruption. Informed that the Dutch writer was waiting to see him, he eagerly came out to greet him. Erasmus's arrival at the offices of Europe's leading printer would prove a key moment in the intellectual history of the West. He was in effect stepping into the heart of the printing revolution that was just beginning to transform European society; during his months in Venice, Erasmus would help transform print.

The print shop in those days served as a sort of international house, offering itinerant men of letters a social club, message center, and cultural hub. The Aldine house was renowned for the quality of its scholarship; its trademark—a dolphin wrapped around an anchor—served as a symbol of good learning. (Today, it is the insignia of Doubleday publishers.) Aldus was most known for his books in Greek, set in a font designed by a craftsman he had commissioned, which gave him an important edge over the competition. Over the years, he had amassed a library of valuable Greek manuscripts. Like all such volumes, they were full of slips and blunders that needed to be weeded and pruned. At the time, Venice had the largest Western community of Greek-speakers (many of them driven there by the Turkish capture of Constantinople), and Aldus hired the cream. In addition to housing and feeding them, he invited them to join the informal academy he had established to preserve and promote Greek literature. With the help of his typefaces and his academy, Aldus brought out the first print editions of such Greek giants as Thucydides, Sophocles, Aristophanes, Xenophon, Plato, and Aristotle. Thanks in part to his labors, many Greek treatises, plays, and chronicles that had for centuries been buried in private collections and monastic libraries now began to circulate widely in the West.

They were part of a much larger cascade of material tumbling from the printing presses. During the first half century of printing, their products were mainly religious books: the Bible (by far the most popular item), breviaries, missals, Psalters, catechisms, lives of the saints, and various manuals for parish priests. Gradually there appeared more secular texts: dictionaries, grammars, and encyclopedias; textbooks on arithmetic, anatomy, and astrology; and how-to guides on everything from breeding plants to playing an instrument. Latin authors who had been dead for more than a millennium suddenly became bestsellers. Works by Virgil, Horace, Terence, and Seneca went through dozens of printings. Most popular of all was Cicero, with 316 editions of his works appearing before the start of the sixteenth century.

Even amid this outpouring, however, printers did not fully grasp the power of the new medium. Before 1500, printers sought to make their books resemble medieval manuscripts as closely as possible. Most of these *incunabula*, as the early editions were called (after the Latin word for "cradle"), were bulky folios consisting of pages formed by folding once over the large sheets of paper that were standard at that time. In the late fifteenth century, printers began bringing out more compact quarto editions, made from sheets folded twice over. Aldus, who liked to innovate, issued many octavo editions, in which the sheets were folded three times to produce volumes that were roughly the size of modern mass-market paperbacks. For this, he has been called the father of the pocketbook revolution, helping to free books from libraries and lecture halls. He also helped popularize a typeface in which the letters all slanted to the right; winning immediate acclaim across Europe, it became known as italics, after its country of origin.

All of these changes had affected the physical properties of the book. No one had yet figured out how to exploit the potential of print from a literary standpoint. Erasmus in Venice would begin to do so. Soon after his arrival, Aldus invited him to join his academy and gave him full access to his manuscripts. When Erasmus was finally ready to begin writing, Aldus installed him in a corner of the shop. It had several presses, each operated by a three- or four-man crew. Amid the clank of the machines, the chatter of the workmen, and the rich aroma of printers' ink, Erasmus worked from morning until well past dusk, filling page after page. (He did so despite suffering an attack of the stone—the first outbreak of a condition that would torment him for the rest of his life.) Aldus sat in the corner opposite him, reading over each printed page after Erasmus had finished with it. When Erasmus asked him why, Aldus replied, "I'm learning." He expressed amazement that Erasmus could write so quickly amid the din of the shop, but the restless, itinerant Dutchman had learned to compose in the most chaotic of settings.

In another concession, Aldus imposed no word count on his author; thus freed, Erasmus added adage after adage. The total surpassed first one thousand, then two thousand, then three, and still he kept going. As in the first edition, many of the entries were brisk and businesslike, but here and there Erasmus began to improvise, adding anecdotes, asides, opinions, and personal reflections. Gradually, a new literary form emerged.

The process can be seen unfolding in his entry on *Herculei labores* ("the labors of Hercules"). Focusing on the second of Hercules's twelve labors—his battle with the hydra of Lerna—Erasmus began in conventional humanist fashion, piling up references to Cicero, Homer, Horace, Josephus, Pindar, and Ovid. Hercules, Erasmus wrote, in slaying this multiheaded sea monster, performed a great service for mankind—one that could inspire modern-day princes. In administering their realms, they should devote themselves solely to the public good and consider what they can do for others, regardless of the cost to themselves.

Then, in an unexpected leap, Erasmus cited a group who, even more than princes, deserved to have their labors called Herculean—those dedicated "to restoring the monuments of ancient and true literature." In performing the thankless task of preparing old manuscripts for publication, they cut themselves off from life's ordinary pleasures, neglect their daily affairs, pay little heed to their appearances or health. Despite such sacrifices, they encounter much disdain; in return for their long nights of toil, they earn "a few snorts of contempt" from men unworthy to hold their chamber pots.

Erasmus—suddenly sounding a personal note—wearily mentioned the "immense labors and infinite difficulties" that this collection had cost him. He described the long and tedious hours he had spent rummaging through ancient works to puzzle out the meaning of obscure customs and the many texts he had had to consult to root out corruptions and determine the correct reading. He noted the many complaints he was sure he would get from readers who felt that his collection had been rushed into print and should have received greater care and diligence. And, he admitted, such complaints would not be without merit. Because of his many other projects, he had not been able to devote as much time as he would have liked to this one, and so he would not take offense if a better, more diligent scholar came along, corrected his work, and carried off the prize, as long as it was to the benefit of readers.

Offering this aside was a sly move on Erasmus's part. Like his hero Jerome, he was often careless and slapdash in his work; by acknowledging this up front, he could perhaps deflect criticism. Whatever his aim, Erasmus's decision to mention his own scholarly faults in an entry in a book of adages was a bold and original step. His discussion as a whole—discursive, disarming, self-referential—was unlike anything he had previously written. In fact, it was unlike anything that had yet appeared in print. Ruminating on the labors of Hercules in the chaos of Aldus's workshop, Erasmus was giving birth to the modern personal essay.

After nearly nine months of Herculean labor, the volume was done. The final tally came to 3,260 adages, hence the collection's name—*Adagiorum Chiliades* ("Thousands of Adages"). As Erasmus had warned, it contained many errors, but few readers seemed to care. The volume was immediately recognized as a literary landmark, and it brought Erasmus his first real taste of celebrity.

His work in Venice completed, Erasmus in the autumn of 1508 traveled to Padua, home to another Italian university. To help meet expenses, he agreed to tutor Alexander Stewart, an illegitimate son of Scotland's King James IV. Unlike the Boerio brothers, Alexander had an inquisitive mind and a gentle nature, and Erasmus quickly took to him. The threat of war remained ever present, however, and when it got too close to Padua, they moved to Ferrara. When Ferrara, too, became imperiled, they traveled to Siena, where Alexander took some courses in law.

There, Erasmus was only 125 miles from Rome. Leaving Italy without seeing the capital of Latin culture was unthinkable, and so in late February or early March 1509 he mounted his horse and headed south, probably along the Via Francigena, an ancient pilgrimage route stretching from France to Rome. With tremendous expectation Erasmus passed through the old Aurelian Wall—only to find a reeking, overgrown wasteland. Vast tracts of the city had been abandoned and had reverted to scrubland and pasture. The Roman Forum, where Cicero had once declaimed before the Senate, was now a cow pasture, called the Campo Vaccino; the Capitoline Hill, once the seat of the imperial government, was known as Monte Caprino, or Goat Hill. Most of Rome's 40,000 people lived in the lowlying area within the bend of the Tiber, in ramshackle huts set on dark, narrow alleyways filled with slop and debris. On all sides lay the vestiges of Rome's former glory—collapsed temples, shattered palaces, stumps of columns, and triumphal arches lying in heaps of stones, their inscriptions defaced and covered in moss.

"Rome is not Rome," Erasmus would recall years later. "It has nothing but ruins and rubble, the scars and signs of the disasters that befell long ago." Those disasters included fires, earthquakes, floods, and famines; invasions by Goths, Lombards, Normans, and Saracen pirates; bitter feuding between Rome's noble families; strife between bands loyal to popes and antipopes; periodic insurrections; persistent gang warfare; and pervasive criminality. Rome had little manufacturing or commerce. Its economy instead relied heavily on the luxury trades and service industries.

The city was a great diplomatic center, with all of the Italian states keeping ambassadors or agents there. To help them stay in touch with their governments, Rome had an elaborate courier service, able to reach Florence or Naples in three or four days, Milan or Genoa in a week, Paris or Brussels in three weeks, and London in not quite four—all helping to make the city a vital marketplace of information.

Rome's greatest asset was the Holy See, home to the Vatican Palace (the pope's residence) and St. Peter's Basilica, still the central shrine of the Latin Church nearly twelve centuries after it was built. The basilica, along with the city's other great sanctuaries—St. John Lateran, St. Paul Outside-the-Walls, Santa Maria Maggiore, and San Lorenzo—drew pilgrims from around the Continent, and a network of inns, hostels, and taverns had sprung up to serve them. Representatives of kingdoms, principalities, dioceses, monastic orders, and trading houses from across Europe were all there to pursue their business at the Roman Curia—a labyrinth of offices, bureaus, and tribunals located on the Vatican Hill.

Even more than in the time of Lorenzo Valla, humanists dominated the Curia. With their facility in Latin, skill in writing, and knowledge of history and religion, they were ideally suited to handle the flood of paperwork and correspondence generated by the pope and his court. From the initial gift of Nicholas V, the Vatican Library had grown into the single richest book collection in Europe. It, in turn, was but one of many valuable book repositories in the city, and humanists from across the Continent came to consult them.

While in Rome, Erasmus naturally fell in with this group. The acclaim that greeted his new edition of the *Adages* helped him gain access to the upper reaches of Roman society. As a northerner, however, he remained to the Italians a barbarian. His status as an outsider among the Roman elite provided an ideal position from which to observe this remarkable moment in the city's history, when it was simultaneously reaching the height of Renaissance refinement and undergoing the institutional decay that would help bring on the Reformation. During his stay, Erasmus, who would do so much to weaken Rome's prestige, gathered the raw material for his gibes.

He gained entrée, for instance, to the exclusive world of the cardinals. About thirty of them lived in the city, and they could frequently be seen proceeding purple-robed through town, trailed by stately entourages and mules in gold-laced caparisons. Erasmus secured as his main patron Raffaele Riario. As the apostolic chamberlain (the Vatican's chief financial officer), Riario was the second most powerful figure in Rome after Pope Julius II, who was his cousin. He lived in the Cancelleria, a massive three-story palace near the Campo de' Fiore that had a severe classical facade made of stone blocks stripped from the Colosseum. (It still stands, the finest Renaissance palace in the city.) Riario built it with fourteen thousand ducats he won in a night of gambling with the son of Pope Innocent VIII, and he stocked it with priceless vases, statues, and sarcophagi scavenged from ancient monuments. Through Riario, Erasmus became acquainted with members of Julius's personal entourage, including Cardinal Giovanni de' Medici, who was the son of Lorenzo the Magnificent and who would become Pope Leo X. "In Rome," Erasmus would later boast, "there was not one cardinal who did not welcome me as a brother."

One day, Erasmus went with some friends to the Vatican Palace to see a bullfight. Such spectacles had recently been introduced for the amusement of the clerical elite. Erasmus was unimpressed. "I myself never enjoyed those bloody games and remnants of ancient paganism," he wrote years later. His one moment of diversion came between the rounds of slaughter, when a masked man leaped before the crowd and, bearing a sword in one hand and a cloak in the other, impersonated a matador in terrified retreat from a bull. "The drollness of this man seized me more strongly than the rest of the show."

To Erasmus, Rome seemed just that—a show. The exaggerated pomp, the empty grandiosity, the gassy oratory—all repelled him. Bishops clashed with protonotaries over who (according to the rules of protocol) should be seated nearest the pope. The heads of monastic orders vied for influence with the directors of the secular clergy, and the Dominicans feuded endlessly with the Franciscans. Illegitimacy and concubinage were rampant, and the city had as many as a thousand prostitutes. The prostitution, in turn, fed the spread of a terrible new scourge, syphilis. The wine trade was one of the largest businesses in town, thanks to the enormous quantities consumed in salons and banquet halls. Most of the senior clerics in Rome had abandoned their dioceses, preferring the pageants and processions of Rome to the toil and tedium of their home parishes. Among the priests who actually performed sacerdotal duties, mockery was routine, and the Mass was pronounced in an impious and derisive manner. Erasmus would later recall hearing people in Rome "raving against Christ and his disciples in atrocious blasphemies."

Even more off-putting was the state of Roman rhetoric. When it came to writing and speaking Latin, Rome's humanists all sought to imitate one figure: Cicero. They strained to reproduce his vocabulary, his figures of speech, and his sentence structure while ignoring his noble sentiments and judgments. Years later, Erasmus would mock these "Ciceronian apes" in a withering satire, *The Ciceronian*. "For seven whole years now," a member of the sect declares, "I have touched no books but Ciceronian ones, abstaining from all the rest as religiously as a Carthusian from meat." Erasmus described a sermon he heard delivered on Good Friday before a large crowd that included the pope along with many cardinals and bishops. The preacher (a celebrated Latinist) spent most of his time evoking not the crucifixion of Christ but the exploits of Julius II (or "Jupiter Optimus Maximus," as he called Julius, after the supreme deity of ancient Rome). "What," Erasmus wondered, "had all this to do with Julius as the high priest of the Christian religion, the Vicar of Christ and successor of Peter and Paul?"

In his six years as pope, Julius had established himself as the most forceful pontiff since the return of the papacy from Avignon. Tall and thin, with a long white beard and pressed mouth, he was known for his vanity, imperiousness, and truculence. Julius carried a cane that he used to beat subordinates who displeased him and kept at hand a bell to interrupt visitors who bored him—behavior that had earned him the label *il pontefice terribile*. As a cardinal, he had fathered three daughters and (apparently) contracted syphilis from one of his many mistresses. He loved fine Greek and Corsican wines, collected rare silks and velvets, retained both a French and an Italian tailor, and had not one but three jewel-encrusted tiaras. An avid hunter, he arranged for falcons and eagles to be brought from Pisa and Anatolia and horses from Ferrara and Milan.

His hunting, in turn, kept him sharp for his military ventures. At the age of sixty-six, Julius still relished leading troops into battle. After his successful campaign against Bologna, he had returned to Rome in a lavish triumphal march modeled on those of the Roman emperors. He immediately began planning a new offensive against Venice, which had seized papal lands in the Romagna. To reinforce his army, Julius hired two hundred Swiss mercenaries—the origin of the famous Swiss Guard.

With the College of Cardinals debating the pope's plans to go to war with Venice, Raffaele Riario, in the name of the pope, asked Erasmus to compose two orations, one opposing such a campaign, the other supporting it. Fond of Venice, Erasmus put much more effort into the former, but to his dismay the latter carried the day. The constant military preparations in Rome and the drain they placed on the city's finances increased Erasmus's antipathy toward Julius in particular and war in general.

As part of his program to reestablish Roman hegemony, Julius wanted to restore the city to its former splendor, and so he mounted an ambitious urban improvement campaign. During Erasmus's stay, the city was one giant construction site. Streets and piazzas were being torn up, scaffolding was everywhere, and the whole area west of the Forum was filled with limekilns producing mortar and concrete for use in construction. It was under Julius that Rome as we know it today began to take shape. In undertaking these efforts, however, the pope set in motion forces that would help precipitate the greatest crisis in the Church's history.

Julius's skill at military strategy was matched by his taste in art. Thanks to his patronage, Rome would become a magnet for painters, musicians, poets, philosophers, and Greek scholars. As his chief architect, he enlisted Donato Bramante. A brash iconoclast from Milan, Bramante became a sort of minister for urban renewal at the papal court. Under his direction, plazas were modernized, streets were straightened, and a new mint was built.

Julius's main focus of activity, however, was the Vatican. When he became pope, the Vatican Palace—the residence of the pope and his household—was an undistinguished jumble of offices, chapels, ceremonial rooms, and living quarters dating from many different decades. At Julius's urging, Bramante drew up plans to transform its exterior by adding a two-story facade and new galleries. He also designed a new facade for the Belvedere—the papal villa that sat on a hill a thousand feet from the Vatican Palace—and created an enormous courtyard in the space between the two buildings. The lower part (near the palace) became an arena for the staging of classical plays, bullfights, and tournaments; the upper part (near the Belvedere) became a magnificent garden with running streams, laurel and orange trees, and sculptures from Julius's personal collection, including the Apollo Belvedere.

To decorate the rooms of the Vatican Palace, Julius brought Raphael from Florence. At twenty-six, this charming prodigy was largely untested, but Julius, sensing his genius, assigned him to fresco the walls of the Stanza della Segnatura, or Signature Room, which served as a papal study. Beginning in the autumn of 1508 and continuing for the next four and a half years, Raphael created four murals that, in their sweep and clarity, rank among the finest works of the Renaissance. One of them, *The School of Athens*, showed dozens of ancient Greek philosophers, mathematicians, and scientists gathered under the vaulted ceiling of a massive basilica. Here, in the inner sanctum of the Vatican, Raphael offered complementary visions of celestial revelation and worldly reason—a harmonization of Christian and classical ideals that was the essence of Renaissance Rome.

In addition to commissioning such artistic wonders, Julius wanted to create a grand monument to himself, and it was here that the seeds of future calamity were sown. Julius envisioned a tomb on a scale larger than that of any previous pope. To design it, he wanted someone with similarly outsize talent. He had long admired the Pietà that had been installed in St. Peter's a few years earlier, and in the spring of 1505 he called its creator, Michelangelo, from Florence. Thus began one of the most famous patron-artist relationships in history. Michelangelo (who had just turned thirty) proposed a monument that was truly colossal. It was to have three tiers with more than forty larger-than-life statues—some in the form of prisoners (representing the Papal States recaptured by Julius), others personifying the arts and sciences, and still others representing those whom Julius considered his forebears, including Moses, who would be the centerpiece. Topping it all would be a sarcophagus containing the pope's remains. Pleased with the design, Julius gave Michelangelo two thousand ducats to purchase the marble for the tomb, and in April the artist left for Carrara, the famous quarry in northern Italy.

As to where the tomb should be placed, there was only one real possibility: St. Peter's. Constantine's basilica, as it was called (after the emperor who had commissioned it), had since the fourth century stood on the spot where (it was believed) Peter had been crucified and buried, and it remained Christianity's greatest temple. The interior was so vast that, as a fourteenth-century visitor remarked, anyone who lost a companion in it might need a full day to find him. Over the centuries, however, the church had become crammed with chapels, altars, tabernacles, statues, crucifixes, and candelabras, and as cavernous as it was, it was clear that the funerary chapel as envisioned by Julius would not fit.

The most obvious solution would have been to scale down the project. But Julius—captivated by Michelangelo's plan—had a more radical idea. As was universally acknowledged, St. Peter's was in urgent need of repair. A millennium's worth of earthquakes, sieges, sacks, and shuffling pilgrims had caused the structure to become dangerously unstable, with cracks lacing the exterior and the south wall listing out perilously from its base. When Julius consulted Bramante and other architects, however, it became clear that the cost of renovating the shrine would be prohibitive. So, with typical bravado, he decided that rather than renovate the basilica, he would tear it down and build a new one in its place.

To develop a plan, he again turned to Bramante. The architect produced a design for an enormous structure that would take the form of a symmetrical Greek cross, with a giant dome erected over the point of intersection. Julius approved. The old basilica would be demolished piecemeal so that it could continue to serve as a house of worship even as the new one went up around it. Work crews were hired, marble was ordered from Carrara, and a special quarry was leased in Tivoli, north of the city, to supply blocks of travertine, a spongy form of limestone that was the building block of Renaissance Rome.

At dawn on April 18, 1506, at the edge of a twenty-five-foot trench cut into the ground near the basilica, hundreds of dignitaries gathered, including more than thirty cardinals; the Florentine ambassador, Niccolò

Machiavelli; and Bramante. Arriving in his papal sedan, Julius was deposited at the edge of the ditch. Wearing one of his gem-studded tiaras, he descended unsteadily on a rope ladder. An urn holding a dozen gilded medallions symbolizing the twelve apostles was lowered to him, and he placed it near the spot where the marble foundation stone for the new St. Peter's was to be laid. With that, a momentous new era in the history of the Roman Church had begun.

The wrecking crews immediately set to work. Under Bramante's direction, men with pickaxes began hacking away at the walls of the basilica. Priceless statues were carted off, mosaics were removed, altars were dismantled. Even the great pillars that were such a central feature of the basilica were broken up and carried away. The outcry was great, but Bramante would not budge; for such vandalism, he would become known as *il Ruinante*, the destroyer. As the demolition proceeded, Julius continued to officiate over Masses in the basilica, oblivious to the billowing dust, chilly gusts, and occasional cloudbursts that made the attending cardinals long for the warmth of their palaces.

The construction of the new St. Peter's, coming on top of Julius's many other projects, placed an enormous strain on papal finances. In its first year alone, the project consumed 12,500 ducats; in the next, 27,200. Similar expenditures were expected for years to come. Where to get such sums?

The Church was Europe's wealthiest institution. It owned huge tracts of land in Rome and in the surrounding Campagna. It also controlled the production of two key commodities: salt and alum (an essential mineral in the dying process). The pilgrims who flocked to the city further filled the papal treasury. When Julius became pope, however, he found the coffers nearly empty, as a result of the profligacy of a licentious predecessor, Alexander VI. An astute financial manager, Julius set about refilling them. His drive to regain control of the Papal States stemmed in part from financial considerations. The Church levied customs on all goods passing through those lands as well as taxes on the production of all wine, grain, livestock, and timber; with Bologna and other cities back in the papal fold, these proceeds again began flowing to Rome.

Julius also moved to increase the revenue from the Roman Curia. It was here that clerical appointments were made, legal cases heard, dispensations granted, matters of conscience settled. At every step, taxes and fees had to be paid and tips and favors offered. Especially lucrative was the Vatican's control of offices. Over time, the papacy usurped from bishops and cathedral chapters the power to fill more and more positions. Through the practice of "papal months," for instance, the pope claimed the authority to fill any office that fell vacant during six months scattered throughout the year. In return, the appointee normally had to turn over to the papacy the first year's revenues from the office (a sum known as an annate).

Eventually, all offices at the Curia were put on sale, with a printed list of prices. An array of devious practices arose to promote favored candidates. Through *resignatio in favorem*, for instance, an incumbent could resign his office in favor of a designated replacement (in return for a fee, of course). Especially coveted were benefices—pastoral positions that offered a guaranteed income without any accompanying duties. The chase for benefices became notorious across Europe.

The hub of all this horse-trading was the Datary. Located in a handsome building near St. Peter's, it was responsible for the issuing, registering, and dating (hence the name) of all papal appointments. The Datary became a site of pervasive scheming, lobbying, and spying. By Julius's time, it along with the rest of the Curia employed hundreds of lawyers, judges, canonists, notaries, scribes, record keepers, fee collectors, document sealers, and money changers. The Curia was a place where atonement could be granted, vows abrogated, crimes forgiven, fasts alleviated, interdicts lifted, sins pardoned, marriages annulled, and indulgences and dispensations extended—all for a price. Of the papacy's total income, about a half came from the fees and taxes collected by the Curia.

Even that sum, however, was insufficient to finance the building of the new St. Peter's. Seeking an additional source of revenue, Julius consulted his favorite banker, Agostino Chigi. A shrewd and domineering Sienese, Chigi ran the largest of Rome's banking houses—a position that would eventually help him become the city's richest man. Chigi had a genius for concocting revenue-generating schemes, and when approached by Julius, he came up with a creative one: a special indulgence dedicated to the rebuilding of the basilica. Purchasers would be guaranteed a reduction in the amount of time they (or their deceased relatives) had to spend in purgatory. Those selling the indulgences would be allowed to keep half the proceeds; the remainder would go to Rome.

Impressed with Chigi's proposal, Julius had a bull drawn up authorizing the indulgence. Aware of how it might add to Rome's reputation for greed, however, he delayed issuing it. Only in the final days of his papacy, in 1513, with St. Peter's continuing to devour funds, would Julius finally grant approval. This indulgence would ultimately provide the resources needed to keep the project going—but at an unimaginably steep price.

As Erasmus would later write of his time in Rome, there were many things about the city that he loved—"the bright lights, the noble setting of the most famous city in the world, the delightful freedom, the many richly furnished libraries, the sweet society of all those great scholars, all the literary conversations, all the monuments of antiquity, and not least so many leading lights of the world gathered together in one place." But there was just as much that he loathed. The banquets and bullfights, the opulent processions and bloated orations, the humanists with their empty eloquence, "the swill of men who make a living from the trafficking of the place"—all seemed to mock the efforts of the early Christians to create in Rome a see worthy of their savior. The new basilica going up seemed to embody the faith at its most materialistic and grandiose. The Church, Erasmus believed, needed spiritual renewal, not another lavish monument in which to perform lifeless rituals.

In the end, Erasmus's stay in Italy would have a radicalizing effect on him, transforming the fussy aesthete who had entered the country three years earlier into a searing critic of papal, curial, and ecclesiastical excesses.

Erasmus might nonetheless have remained in Rome had it not been for a dramatic far-off event. On April 21, 1509, King Henry VII of England died. Because his elder son, Arthur, had predeceased him, the crown was to pass to Arthur's seventeen-year-old brother, Henry. Sometime in June, Erasmus received an urgent letter from Lord Mountjoy. He was quite sure,

Mountjoy wrote, that at the moment when Erasmus heard that young Henry had succeeded his father, "every particle of gloom left your heart," given his friendship with the prince and his firsthand knowledge of his "exceptional and almost more than human talents."

> And if you knew how courageously and wisely he is now acting, and what a passion he has for justice and honesty, and how warmly he is attached to men of letters, then I should go so far as to swear upon my own head that with or without wings you would fly to us here to look at the new and lucky star. Oh, Erasmus, if you could only see how happily excited everyone is here, and how all are congratulating themselves on their prince's greatness, and how they pray above all for his long life, you would be bound to weep for joy! Heaven smiles, earth rejoices; all is milk and honey and nectar.

To speed Erasmus's return, Mountjoy had enclosed ten pounds to help cover his expenses—half from him and half from William Warham, the archbishop of Canterbury, who, he added, "promises you a benefice if you should return to England."

Erasmus needed little convincing. Under the leadership of Henry VIII, England seemed poised to become an Eden for scholars—a place where the value of letters would be fully recognized and men of talent amply rewarded.

As he made preparations for his return, Erasmus was invited to meet with Cardinal Grimani of San Marco (Venice), one of Rome's great eminences, at his huge palace. In the course of a pleasant two-hour conversation, the cardinal showed Erasmus around his magnificent eight-thousand-volume library. At the end, he invited him to remain in Rome as his guest. "If I had known that man earlier," Erasmus later wrote, "I should never have left a city where I had met with a welcome so much above my deserts. But my departure was so far fixed that I could not honorably remain at Rome."

In mid-July 1509, Erasmus left on the nine-hundred-mile return journey to England. He traveled first to Bologna and then on to the Alps, crossing via the Splügen Pass to Constance. During the long days on horseback, he thought of the English friends he would see, Thomas More chief among them. He mused on how closely More's name resembled the Greek word *moria*, or "folly," and this in turn put him in mind of his friend's playfulness and wit. With the vanity and shallowness of Rome still fresh, Erasmus began to conceive of a Lucian-like work that would offer a lacerating look at folly and its place in human affairs.

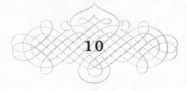

SELF-RIGHTEOUS JEWS

In late 1510, Martin Luther, while absorbed in lecturing on the *Sentences*, reading Augustine, and performing his rounds of prayer and penance, found his daily routine disrupted by a grave disturbance in his order. A movement was under way to unite the order's two wings—the Observants, who followed a strict regimen, and the Conventuals, who were more lenient. Johann von Staupitz, the vicar-general of the Observants, wanted to merge both into one body with himself as its head. He planned to have all the monasteries follow the more rigorous approach, but seven Observant cloisters—certain that such a union would result in the dilution of their own devotion—objected. The loudest protests came from the monasteries in Erfurt and Nuremberg. Two emissaries were chosen to travel to Rome and seek a stay of the merger. One of them was Luther, and in November 1510 the twenty-seven-year-old friar set off for the Eternal City on what would be his life's longest journey.

It is 850 miles from Erfurt to Rome, and Luther and his traveling companion covered them in the only way allowed for a mendicant friar—on foot. They were on the road for about six weeks, staying in the many Augustinian convents that dotted the route. As stipulated by the order's rule, they walked one behind the other, their eyes downcast, their hands tucked into the sleeves of their habits. Like Erasmus, Luther was largely oblivious to the visual splendors around him, though he would later remark on the great bulk of the cathedral in Ulm and the wonderful clock that tolled the hours in Nuremberg. The Alpine passes were treacherous at that time of year, with steep, gloomy trails slick with ice and snow; at the Septimer Pass in Switzerland, which had frequent avalanches, crosses marked the spots where ill-fated travelers had met their ends. One can imagine the two men trudging along in the flimsy footwear required of friars, stoically planting their staffs along windswept ridges framed by mist-shrouded peaks.

Entering Lombardy, Luther was impressed by the fertility of the land, and in Florence he admired the spotless hospitals and foundling homes. He marveled at the skill of Italian tailors, the way people sang and hummed as they went along, and the casual manner in which men relieved themselves on the street, like "dogs." It was only as he neared Rome and first caught sight of the venerated city—probably from the Monte Mario, where so many pilgrims first beheld it—that Luther's emotions rose. "Hail, sacred Rome," he intoned, "sanctified in truth by the holy martyrs with whose blood thou wast drenched."

The friars probably entered the city by the Porta del Popolo, then made their way to the Augustinian monastery of Santa Maria del Popolo, where they stayed. After settling in, they visited the church of Sant'Agostino, near what is now Piazza Navona, where the procurator of their order resided; it was to him that they presented their petition. When it became clear that the matter was not going to be quickly resolved, Luther decided to take advantage of the city's many devotional offerings. Whereas the well-connected Erasmus had earlier mixed with cardinals and curialists, the lowly Luther would experience the Rome of pilgrims and penitents.

While in Rome, pilgrims were encouraged to make a one-day tour of the city's seven great churches. It was not an undertaking for the faint-hearted. Pilgrims were expected to observe a fast throughout the day, breaking it with Communion at the final stop, St. Peter's. The distances to be covered were great and the paths through the city rough and often dangerous, with marauders and pickpockets lying in wait, but those who persevered found sacred treasures like nothing anywhere else. At St. Paul Outside-the-Walls, located about a mile beyond the city's southern wall, the riches included a column beside which Paul was said to have preached and the chain by which he was attached to the soldier assigned to guard him while he was in prison in Rome. On display at Santa Croce were the rope used to drag Jesus during the Passion and the vinegar-soaked sponge offered to him while he was on the cross.

Most prized of all were the relics at St. John Lateran, which included the heads of Peter and Paul encased in splendid golden reliquaries. On Luther's visit, the crush of spectators was so great that he could not get close enough to see them. In the adjoining Lateran Palace, however, he was able to mount the famous Scala Sancta—the sacred staircase that the scourged Jesus had climbed to Pontius Pilate's residence in Jerusalem (and which had supposedly been preserved and moved intact to Rome). Pilgrims who ascended the twenty-eight steps and said a *Pater Noster* at each received nine years' indulgence per step. When Luther reached the top, however, he found himself wondering, "Who knows whether it is true?"

It was one of several unsettling moments the young friar had while in Rome. Like many northern visitors, he was shocked by the ignorance and irreverence of the Italian priests. At one point he saw them race through seven Masses in an hour. *"Passa, passa!"*—"Move along, move along!"— they hissed as Luther plodded his way through one. Performing the Eucharist, they mocked the act of transubstantiation: "Bread thou art and bread thou wilt remain, and wine thou art and wine thou wilt remain." As Luther later recalled, "I was a serious and pious young monk who was pained by such words." One of his chief aims in Rome was to make a full confession of all the sins he had committed since his youth, but when he did so he was surprised by the ineptitude of his confessor. Luther saw the lavish palaces of the cardinals, heard gossip about the dissolute conduct of the clergy, and encountered the prostitutes who swarmed the city. On his visits to the Curia to pursue his monastery's appeal, he passed the pay counters set up to receive the fees for dispensations and indulgences and saw the crowds clamoring for offices and benefices.

He also saw St. Peter's, the last stop on the church tour. Much of the old basilica still stood as the new structure went up around it. All that Luther would later remember of this building that would figure so prominently in his life were some of its relics, including the rope that Judas had supposedly used to hang himself. As a humble friar, he would have had no access to the *stanze* in the Vatican Palace where Raphael was executing his brilliant frescoes, nor to the Sistine Chapel, where Michelangelo (commissioned by Julius) was applying his paints to the ceiling. He expressed admiration for the Pantheon, with its great bulk and the oculus in its dome, but for the most part Rome's ancient monuments seemed to him nothing more than testaments to the transitoriness of secular realms. Luther's great preoccupation during his stay was the state of his soul, and he raced around the city like a "madman full of religious zeal." He was impressed by the catacombs and was so overwhelmed by the altars to faith in the city that he felt sorry his parents were still alive, "for I should have liked to free them from purgatory with my masses and other excellent works and prayers."

After about four weeks, it became clear that no action was going to be taken on the Augustinians' petition—Rome was too absorbed in its own affairs to care much about an intramural dispute in far-off Germany—and so, at the end of January or the beginning of February 1511, he and his companion set off for home. "Like a fool, I carried onions to Rome and brought back garlic," Luther would say, using a German expression for a fruitless transaction. But that was many years later. In contrast to Erasmus's experience, Luther's visit to Rome left no overt signs of disaffection. It did, however, lace his faith in the Church with some imperceptible cracks, which, when subjected to intense pressure, would perilously widen.

After returning to Germany, Luther would never again leave it. As he settled back into his routine in Erfurt, however, he learned that his services were required elsewhere. The University of Wittenberg needed someone to teach theology, and the Augustinian cloister in Erfurt had been asked to supply a candidate. Johann von Staupitz, who in addition to his administrative duties for the Augustinian order was serving as the dean of theology at Wittenberg, felt that Luther would be ideal, and so in the summer of 1511 the young friar returned to the remote settlement on the Elbe.

With a population of barely 2,000, Wittenberg seemed more a village than a town. In contrast to the rich grain fields and thick woods that surrounded Erfurt, Wittenberg was set on a stubby plain with soil so sandy that Luther would later remark that a villainous people must have once lived there and left a curse on the land. The main street, which extended barely three thousand feet from east to west, was lined by squat half-timbered cottages with walls of mud and roofs of hay and straw. Anchoring the street's western end was the castle of Frederick III, the ruler of Electoral Saxony. A hulking Gothic fortress, it served as the prince's residence on his occasional visits to the town. Adjoining it was the Schlosskirche, or Castle Church (also known as All Saints'), whose north door served as a sort of community bulletin board for the posting of notices and proclamations. A few hundred yards to the east, the street opened onto the marketplace, where local craftsmen and neighboring farmers displayed their goods. On the square's northern edge was the town hall, and a short walk to the east was St. Mary's, the town church, whose twin square stone towers stood stolid watch over Wittenberg and which would become known as the mother church of the Reformation.

At the street's eastern end was the Augustinian monastery. It was much smaller than the one in Erfurt, in both size and enrollment (with thirty to forty friars). Nearby was a chapel made of wood and featuring a rough-hewn pulpit. From the upper windows of the monastery, it was possible to see the Elbe winding its sluggish way through the Saxon flatlands.

With trade at a modest volume, the local economy depended on such petty occupations as shoemaking, tailoring, butchering, and brewing. Of the town's 356 taxpaying households, 172 had the right to brew beer, and to judge from Luther's many complaints about public drunkenness, they seem to have set the social tone. There were three public baths and an apothecary, which sold not only drugs but also spices, wax, paint, and paper. There was also a *Frauenhaus*, or brothel, which only single men were allowed to patronize.

On arriving in Wittenberg, Luther felt he was on the "very borderland of civilization." Yet from this outpost he would help set in motion one of Europe's great revolutions. In this respect, the Reformation would stand out. Most of the great intellectual and cultural breakthroughs of the age occurred in thriving cities. Aquinas drafted the *Summa Theologica* in Paris, Dante wrote *The Divine Comedy* in Florence, Petrarch gave birth to humanism in Avignon. Luther, by contrast, would conceive his new theology in a rough-edged frontier town. But Wittenberg's remoteness would actually prove an asset, for it had no intellectual establishment with vested interests or orthodoxies to defend. The university had been founded just nine years earlier, and on its faculty Thomists, Scotists, nominalists, and humanists all vied for supremacy.

What's more, the provincial air of Wittenberg was deceptive, for it was the capital of Electoral Saxony, and Frederick was determined to make it an intellectual and cultural showcase, both to boost his own prestige and to eclipse that of his cousin George, the ruler of neighboring Ducal Saxony. The division of Saxony went back to 1485, when the territory was split between two brothers. While Ducal Saxony got its most prominent city, Leipzig, Electoral Saxony got a vote to elect the Holy Roman Emperor (hence its name). There were only seven such votes, and Frederick's control of one of them gave him much more political influence than the location and resources of his principality by themselves would have made possible.

In the coming battle over Luther and his theology, Frederick would play a pivotal—and enigmatic—part. Until his death, in 1525, he would stand forthrightly behind the reformer, defending him in the face of great risk; had he not, Luther would probably not have survived. Yet the elector to the end remained a stalwart Catholic, devoted to medieval forms of piety. In 1493, at the age of thirty, he had made a pilgrimage to the Holy Land, during which he had acquired many relics, including a thumb of St. Anne's that he found in Rhodes. By the time of Luther's arrival in Wittenberg, Frederick's collection had grown into one of the largest such holdings in Germany—a sprawling assortment of the fingers, limbs, heads, garments, and crosses of prophets, apostles, saints, and martyrs, which were housed in the Castle Church in Wittenberg and exhibited on certain holidays. Thanks to this cache, Wittenberg was one of the most important pilgrimage sites in all of Germany.

While highly traditional on religious matters, however, Frederick was forward-looking on cultural ones. At his favorite castle, in Lochau, about thirty miles southeast of Wittenberg, he had had written on a wall of his bedroom: "You have inherited a Sparta, it is your task to beautify it." Throughout his realm, Frederick was building churches and expanding castles, and to adorn them he was bringing to Saxony some of Europe's most practiced woodcarvers, stonecutters, bronze casters, and chandelier makers. On a visit to Nuremberg in 1496, Frederick met Albrecht Dürer, who was then a largely unknown twenty-five-year-old; sensing his talent, Frederick became the first to commission paintings from him, and a Dürer altarpiece would grace the Castle Church in Wittenberg.

In political affairs, Frederick was very canny. Of all the German princes, he stood out for his caution, honesty, and concern for the welfare of his people, hence his nickname: the Wise. Frederick was shy and would never marry, nor would he ever meet Luther face-to-face. Portraits show him to be a man of prodigious girth, with small eyes set in a fleshy face and a curly beard falling onto a coat with a fur collar. When it came to making decisions, Frederick was so deliberate as to madden some of his advisers. He was especially averse to sending troops into battle. Not once during his nearly forty-year reign did he become involved in a war, despite constant tensions with the more bellicose Duke George—over mines, highways, and, eventually, Luther. Tournaments, archery, and hunting provided all the soldierly outlets Frederick needed, and the resulting peace freed up resources for his various artistic and cultural projects. His main sources of revenue were the rich veins of silver in the Erzgebirge Mountains on Saxony's border with Bohemia. Even their bounty, however, was not sufficient to underwrite his many ventures, and he made up the difference with taxes that created much hardship for his subjects.

Of all his projects, none would occupy Frederick more than the University of Wittenberg, which he founded in 1502. By investing heavily in it, he hoped it would eventually surpass the much older and more celebrated university in Leipzig. When Luther arrived in Wittenberg, the school (like the town as a whole) was undergoing a construction boom, and his stay would take place against the backdrop of constant hammering, sawing, troweling, and the rumbling of wagons dropping off loads of stone and wood. In addition to improving the university's physical plant, Frederick was keen on attracting top talent to it, and along with Luther there arrived two other friar-professors, bringing the total to nearly two dozen. Most of the several hundred students came from within a hundred-mile radius, but thanks to Luther the university would become so famous that nearly a century later Shakespeare would make it Hamlet's alma mater.

To further enhance the university, the elector created a library on the second floor of his castle. It would eventually hold more than three thousand volumes, including not only Bible commentaries, Latin classics, patristic texts, grammars, and legal tomes but also the works of such acclaimed humanists as Ficino, Pico, Valla, and Erasmus, whom Frederick would come to admire greatly. Overseeing the library was George Spalatin, an energetic and conscientious priest who would serve as Frederick's secretary, confessor, and chief liaison with Luther. A dedicated humanist, Spalatin regularly studied the catalogs of Europe's top presses for new editions, and in 1512 he wrote to Aldus in Venice, requesting a complete set of his works. With its diverse holdings, Frederick's library would provide a key resource to Luther as he pursued his theological studies.

Despite its small size, Wittenberg had a printer, Johann Rhau-Grunenberg, whose presses after 1512 would be located close by the Augustinian cloister, giving Luther ready access. Even more central to Wittenberg's cultural life was the painter and businessman Lucas Cranach the Elder. Arriving in Wittenberg in 1505 at Frederick's invitation, Cranach would remain for the next forty-five years; he would be elected burgomaster (mayor) three times. He would also come to own the town's apothecary plus several imposing buildings, including one on the main square that housed his enormous and prolific workshop-residence. Embodying the entrepreneurial spirit of the new Europe, Cranach was to become an early and unwavering supporter of Luther, and his portraits of the reformer would help fix Luther's image in history.

For all these cultural sprouts, however, Wittenberg at the time of Luther's arrival remained a coarse and grubby place, its streets full of dung and offal, scavenging pigs and foraging dogs. Christoph Scheurl, a Nuremberg native who taught in Wittenberg from 1507 to 1512 and who would become a good friend of Luther's, described its citizens as drunken, crude, and quarrelsome, and he would frequently complain of feeling lonely and cut off from the world. Luther himself, however, had no such qualms. Once settled, he threw himself into his work as an instructor of theology, giving lectures on key Scholastic texts. He also continued to perform the Mass and, as best he could, to carry out his devotional rounds—going to confession, holding vigils, praying the hours.

As before, however, the *Anfechtungen*, those debilitating spells of anxiety and dread, continued to occur. No matter how hard he tried, his every devotional act seemed tainted by selfishness. The more sinful he felt, the severer the austerities he imposed. Unlike Erasmus, who detested fast days, Luther welcomed them, convinced that the sharper his hunger, the more God would approve. In the depths of winter, when frigid gusts bore down from the great Eurasian plain, he welcomed the numbness that spread through his limbs. His confessions steadily lengthened, reaching two, three, even six hours in some cases. Once, upon leaving his confessor, he rushed back to disclose some sin he had momentarily forgotten. "God bids us hope in His mercy," the exasperated priest declared—"Go in peace!"

Yet no matter how emphatically the priest pronounced him absolved, Luther felt his pride and selfishness return. Deep down, he could see that his efforts to please God stemmed not from a genuine desire to do good but from a striving for the reward of eternal life. "My conscience," he later recalled, "could never achieve certainty but was always in doubt and said: 'You have not done this correctly. You were not contrite enough. You omitted this in your confession.' Therefore the longer I tried to heal my uncertain, weak, and troubled conscience with human traditions, the more uncertain, weak, and troubled I continually made it." The thought that God in his righteousness would consign humans to whatever fate he pleased, however seemingly unjust, caused him to feel utterly cast away.

Amid these spiritual torments, Luther would to his good fortune find in Wittenberg someone able to understand what he was going through. Johann von Staupitz, the Augustinian prelate who had arranged for Luther's transfer to Wittenberg, would become for him not only a spiritual adviser but also a paternal figure offering moral guidance. Years later, after the two had a painful falling-out, Luther would fully acknowledge his debt to Staupitz, observing that if he did not want to be "a damned ungrateful papal ass," he had to recognize him "as primarily my father in this doctrine."

A plump, balding Saxon nobleman known for his brilliant sermons, Staupitz in his personal relations could be very reserved—a trait that Luther at times found exasperating—but his long experience in counseling monks had made him astute in diagnosing what ailed them. When Martin came to him bemoaning his trespasses, Staupitz tried to shake some sense into him. Murder, adultery, theft—these were real sins. The faults troubling Luther—stumbling over a liturgical passage, growing impatient with a fellow monk—were *Humpelwerk* and *Puppensünden*, weak excuses and play sins. "If Christ is to help you," Staupitz said, "you must keep a list of real honest-to-goodness sins and not go hobbling around nursing toy ones, imagining you commit a sin every time you fart!" (This was Luther's colorful phrasing of Staupitz's statement, which was no doubt more demure.)

Seeing Luther's terror before the righteous God, Staupitz tried to expose him to a different image of the Almighty—that of a benevolent father who cares for his children and desires their love in return. He spoke of God's compassionate readiness to confer his grace on man and of the sanctified path that the sacraments offered to attain it. Penance— *poenitentia*—required not just the performance of outward acts of confession and satisfaction but also a process of internal renewal and repentance; the change had to occur not just in one's conduct but also in one's heart. These words, Luther later wrote, quoting from the Psalms, "pierced me like the sharp arrow of the Mighty."

Seeing Luther's distress, Staupitz came up with a plan to jostle him out of it. In September 1511, he asked Luther to meet him in a garden located just outside the cloister. They sat under a pear tree (of which Luther would become very fond). Because of his many administrative responsibilities, Staupitz said, he was no longer able to carry out his duties as a Bible lecturer. He wanted Luther to study for a doctorate in theology and, upon earning it, to take over the Bible chair at the university and lecture on the Scriptures, as well as preach in the monastery. Terrified at such a prospect, Luther poured forth fifteen objections. His chief excuse, he later explained, was that he did not have the stamina for such an undertaking and in any case did not expect to live long. Well, Staupitz dryly replied, "our God has a large empire and can use learned doctors in heaven."

In the end, the opportunity to read the Bible won Luther over. At long last, he would have a chance to get at the marrow of the bone. Along with his promotion, he was assigned an office in the towerlike upper story of the building that connected the monastery's dormitory to its brewery. Small but heated, the office for the first time offered Luther a space in which he could work undisturbed (and unfrozen), and it was from this "poor little room" that he "stormed the papacy," as he later put it.

After completing the required courses, Luther, in a ceremony held in the Castle Church in October 1512, became a doctor of theology. He was presented with a copy of the Bible, a golden doctor's ring, and a biretta—the signature beret of doctors—which he would proudly wear as a sign of his achievement. In addition to his obligations as a friar, Luther now had to tend to such academic duties as supervising doctoral candidates and presiding over disputations. He also began preaching at the town church, winning praise for his performance, and he was appointed subprior of the Wittenberg monastery, a position that gave him considerable influence over its operations.

Above all, Luther would begin lecturing on the Bible—a task he would keep at for the rest of his life. In later years, after he became famous, his lectures would draw up to four hundred people. When he began, his audience rarely topped twenty. Yet none of his lecture series would be more consequential than the first two. Delivered from 1513 to 1516, they would be Luther's road to Damascus—his pathway to a new faith. Remarkably, his notes for both sets of lectures have survived, allowing us to peer into Luther's mind as he developed the ideas that would set in motion the Reformation.

The subject of the first series was the Psalms. This was a natural choice, given the central place these hymns had in Christian theology and liturgy. They were fixtures not only of the canonical hours but also of Masses, baptisms, and funerals—indeed, of Christian devotion in general. With fierce urgency they expressed the whole range of human emotions, from incapacitating fear and murderous hatred to serene contentment and exuberant thanksgiving to God. Some of the most memorable lines in the New Testament come from the Psalms. Christ's famous cry on the cross as related in Matthew and Mark—"My God, my God, why have you forsaken me?"—is taken verbatim from the first line of Psalm 22.

For Luther, the Psalms had special power. A "beloved book" that gives off "such a fine and precious fragrance," he later called it. The Psalms, he added, depict fear and hope more vividly than any painter could and with greater eloquence than one could find even in Cicero. Luther, like Jesus, often felt forsaken by God and, in studying these verses, he hoped to find the way back to him. "The Psalter," he observed, "is properly a garden of nuts, outwardly somewhat hard at first but having a sweet kernel within."

Cracking open those nuts would take work, however, for the Psalms were a notoriously difficult text. In both the Jewish and the Christian traditions, they were attributed to the warrior-king David. As later analyses have shown, however, they were probably composed by many different hands over a period of five or more centuries, beginning during or before the tenth century B.C.E. The air of peril and disquiet in them reflected the turmoil of that period, with its pervasive court intrigue, frequent mutinies, and never-ending threat of invasion. Probably used in worship services at the time of the first Temple, the Psalms contain many technical terms related to ancient Israelite liturgy and rituals. Because ancient Hebrew used no vowels, words were frequently mangled in translation, and centuries' worth of scribal errors had added to the confusion.

Luther asked Johann Rhau-Grunenberg, the Wittenberg printer, to produce an edition of the Vulgate text of the Psalms with wide margins and generous spaces between the lines so that he could insert his own comments. He was, in a sense, wiping the scriptural slate clean of all the glosses and marginalia that had accumulated over the centuries. By examining the text free of such encumbrances, Luther hoped to grasp its meaning anew.

His lectures were due to begin in August 1513, and in anticipation he began collecting commentaries and other scholarly aids. He had an edition of the *Postillae perpetuae in universam S. Scripturam* by Nicholas of Lyra, the most widely read book of medieval exegesis. Called "the second Jerome," Lyra knew Hebrew and frequently quoted Rashi, the great twelfth-century Jewish exegete, but, like almost all medieval theologians, he read the Old Testament from start to finish as a testament about Christ, and Luther would echo him. Today, Lyra is known mainly for a droll couplet describing his place in Reformation history: *Si Lyra non lyrasset, Lutherus non cantasset*—"If Lyra had not played his lyre, Luther would not have sung."

But Luther would venture far beyond such traditional approaches. For years he had been avidly following the exciting new developments in the field of sacred philology. He knew of the many searching questions being raised about the Vulgate and of the critical methods being used to address them. As he prepared his lectures on the Psalms, he eagerly sought out the stimulating new works issuing from the humanist presses.

One was the *Quincuplex Psalterium*. Appearing in 1509, it offered the Psalter in five Latin translations: the Old Latin version, three Latin translations by Jerome, and a synthesis of all four versions by its editor, Jacques Lefèvre d'Étaples, France's leading humanist. Of the five versions of the *Quincuplex*, the one that caused the greatest stir was the *Psalterium Iuxta Hebraeos*, Jerome's translation of the Psalms directly from the Hebrew. It was considered far more accurate than his two other versions, both of which were revisions of the Old Latin text. Precisely because it was based on the Hebrew rather than on the authorized Greek Septuagint, however, the Church had rejected this translation, and for centuries it had languished in monastic scriptoria. Now, however, Jerome's Hebrew Psalter was readily available, and Luther kept it by his side as he worked his way through these verses.

Even Jerome's Psalter was a translation, however, and Luther, in his resolve to unlock the meaning of the text, wanted to be able to consult the Hebrew directly. Doing so meant venturing into the burgeoning new field of Hebraic studies. Parallel to the resurgence of interest in Greek as a means of restoring the New Testament, there had arisen a new interest in Hebrew as an aid to understanding the Old. Learning Hebrew, though, was even more difficult than learning Greek. Most Hebrew presses were in Italy, and the wars in the north of that country had kept most of their volumes from crossing the Alps; as a result, Hebrew Bibles and grammars were hard to come by.

So were instructors. The only people qualified to teach Hebrew were Jews. Once a fixture in communities across Western Europe, however, the Jews had—through inquisition, expulsion, dispossession, and pogrom—been steadily forced out. England had expelled its Jews in 1290 and France had done the same in 1306 (and again in 1394). In 1492, Spain, after waging a fierce campaign to coerce its Jews to convert, had expelled all those who had refused. By the start of the sixteenth century, most of Germany had become *judenrein*, free of Jews. Even in the few places where they remained, Jews were often reluctant to teach Hebrew to Christians for fear that the knowledge would be used against them. The Talmud actually prohibited Jews from teaching the Torah to Gentiles (though this was sometimes disregarded because the work could be quite lucrative).

In the end, though, the main barrier to learning Hebrew came from other Christians. While Greek was reviled for being the language of schismatics, those schismatics were at least Christian. Hebrew was the language of the accursed children of Israel, who had killed Christ and who continued to reject him. Hebrew was seen as an agent of contagion, infecting wavering Christians with doubt and skepticism. Jews were suspected of aiding and abetting heretics; some Christian dissenters actually did seek refuge with them. Any Christian who studied Hebrew was thus considered contaminated.

In 1506, however, there had appeared *De Rudimentis Hebraicis* ("The Rudiments of Hebrew"). Prepared by the renowned German humanist Johannes Reuchlin, this bulky 625-page folio was a milestone in the field of sacred studies. Offering both a grammar and a lexicon of biblical Hebrew, it enabled Christians for the first time to study the Hebrew Bible on their own. Luther was among those taking advantage of it. In 1508, while in Erfurt, he had obtained a copy of the book, and by the time he began preparing his notes on the Psalms, he had fully absorbed it. As Luther sought to puzzle out the meaning of these hymns, he could now look beyond the Vulgate to the underlying Hebrew (though his knowledge of that language remained limited).

While Luther in his study was preparing his notes on the Psalms (beginning in the early summer of 1513), he would be deeply affected by a fierce controversy taking place outside it, with Reuchlin at its heart. A campaign was under way to confiscate and destroy all Jewish books (except for the Hebrew Bible) in the Holy Roman Empire, and a battle had broken out among Christian theologians and scholars as to whether this was justified. The fight was being waged largely through bitter broadsides turned out by the printing presses. The battle over Jewish books marked the first great clash over free expression in the age of print. It pitted the forces of tradition and orthodoxy against the proponents of humanist studies and the use of languages to understand Scripture. Luther in Wittenberg was closely following this conflict, and it would provide a critical backdrop to his lectures on the Psalms.

Today, Luther is known as one of history's most violent haters of Jews. In his later years, he would produce some of the most vitriolic anti-Jewish tracts ever written. Historians have pored over his earlier writings to see when such sentiments first surfaced. It is surprising how many have neglected his lecture notes on the Psalms. As they show, Luther's hatred for the Jews was present from a very early point. They also show that this hatred, far from occupying some remote recess of his mind, was in fact central to his theological development. It is thus impossible to understand the genesis of Luther's new gospel without taking into account the pervasive anti-Jewish sentiment of the period, as shown most vividly by the unhappy experience of Johannes Reuchlin.

Almost single-handedly, Johannes Reuchlin helped usher in the new era of Hebraic studies in Christian Europe. At a time when scholars saw Hebrew as alien and subversive, and few wanted anything to do with it, Reuchlin extolled it as holding the key to ancient truths. Hebrew, he declared, is simple, pure, sacred, concise, and eternal. It was the language that man used to communicate with the angels and that had been spoken on earth before the chaos of Babel. When reading it, Reuchlin wrote, he seemed to see God himself speaking. "We Latin people drink from the morass, the Greeks drink from the brooks, the Jews drink from the wells." Eager to draw from those wells, Reuchlin managed, through a combination of perseverance, luck, and expenditure, to learn Hebrew, and he would prove equally adept at infecting others with his enthusiasm.

Reuchlin's intoxication with Hebrew was all the more striking in that he was a pillar of Christian society. Born in the Black Forest town of Pforzheim, Württemberg, in 1455, he was judicious in temperament, cautious in judgment, and regal in bearing (he was said to look like a Roman senator). An esteemed jurist and a skilled diplomat, he spent much of his career in the courts of the powerful, helping to mediate dynastic disputes and resolve territorial conflicts. In matters of faith, he was completely devoted to the Church, believing that it offered the one true path to salvation. After the outbreak of the Reformation, when so many of his colleagues went over to it, Reuchlin remained loyal to Rome. But it was his very devotion to Christianity that had led him to Hebrew and that would sustain him in his effort to learn it at a time when it was nearly impossible for Christians to do so.

In addition to Hebrew, Reuchlin knew Latin and Greek, making him one of the first Europeans since Jerome to master all three biblical tongues. Well before Erasmus became captivated by biblical studies, Reuchlin was proclaiming the revelations to be had by applying philology to Scripture, and his work with the Hebrew Bible would help prepare the way for both Erasmus's later revision of the New Testament and Luther's translation of the Old Testament into German.

Like most of Germany, Württemberg had few Jews. In the mid-1480s, Reuchlin managed to find a learned Jew named Calman to teach him the *aleph bet*, but beyond that he was unable to go. A turning point came in 1490, while he was visiting Italy and met Giovanni Pico della Mirandola, the great Renaissance prodigy. A devoted reader of the Kabbalah, a set of Jewish mystical teachings, Pico was the first of many Christians to claim that it was really about Christ and that only they (and not the Jews) could mine its wisdom. Reuchlin was captivated. For all his forward-looking interest in languages, he remained at heart a man of the Middle Ages, with an intense interest in magic and the occult, and in the Kabbalah he felt he had stumbled upon the fountainhead of all philosophical and religious knowledge. The Kabbalah's mathematical rules made it possible, he believed, to prove all kinds of metaphysical propositions, including such key Christian doctrines as the Incarnation, the Trinity, and the messiahship of Jesus.

In 1494, Reuchlin came out with his first Hebraic work, *The Miracle-Working Word*. Using kabbalistic arithmology, he tried to show that, by adding the Hebrew letter *shin* (signifying *logos*) to YHWH (Yahweh)— the unpronounceable tetragrammaton of God—one got YHSWH, or Yehoshua (the Hebrew name of Jesus). This was the miracle-working word—the divine talisman that, as used in the New Testament, helped cure the sick, raise the dead, and make the floodwaters recede. As this shows, Reuchlin was interested in Hebrew mainly for its ability to bare Christian truths. According to a Christian character in *The Miracle-*

Working Word, God rejected the Jews because they had "perverted and obscured the secrets of salvation" and had persecuted Christians "with eternal hatred." For all his love of Hebrew, Reuchlin at this point remained a captive of anti-Jewish stereotypes.

By now, Reuchlin yearned to read the Hebrew Bible itself, but his knowledge of Hebrew remained too limited. In 1498, however, he again visited Italy, and while in Rome he was directed to Obadiah Sforno. Though only twenty-three, this future rabbi and physician already stood out for his brilliance. Jews, Sforno believed, should teach Hebrew to Christians to promote understanding between the two faiths, and he agreed to give Reuchlin lessons. They were very expensive, causing Reuchlin to grumble throughout, but by the end of his two years in Rome he finally had a firm grasp of the language.

On his return to Germany, Reuchlin—appointed to a high judicial post in Stuttgart—spent his every spare moment with the Hebrew texts he had brought back from Italy. Marveling at the spiritual truths he was drawing from the wells of the Jews, he wanted to help other pious Christians drink from them, too, and so he set out to produce a manual for Latin-speakers. On his estate outside Stuttgart, Reuchlin prepared a rudimentary guide to Hebrew. In 1506, the work was done. "I have erected a monument more lasting than bronze," Reuchlin declared, echoing Horace's *Odes*. In addition to a guide to Hebrew grammar and pronunciations, *The Rudiments of Hebrew* offered of a massive lexicon of biblical Hebrew, from *av* ("father") to *tisha* ("nine"). Throughout, he was critical of Jerome and sought to correct the Vulgate (thus helping prepare the way for Erasmus's philological work on the New Testament). The volume's appearance marked the true start of Hebraic studies in Europe. A print run of 1,500 copies was prepared. Sales lagged, however. The book was expensive, and since Hebrew texts remained rare in Germany, students had few opportunities to use it. Hundreds of copies were stashed away in a warehouse. Reuchlin seemed destined to join the ranks of authors who, after expending great effort on a beloved subject, see their work sink from view.

In the end, though, obscurity would no doubt have been preferable to the type of fame Reuchlin would achieve—the product of a storm so fierce that Luther, hunched over the Psalms in his study in Wittenberg, would feel its force. The first suggestion of trouble came in 1509, when Reuchlin received a visit from a Jewish convert to Christianity named Johannes Pfefferkorn. Like many such converts in that period, Pfefferkorn turned violently against his former coreligionists, and in 1507 he began bringing out a series of venomous anti-Jewish pamphlets in Latin and German with titles like *Mirror of the Jews*, *The Enemy of the Jews*, and *How the Blind Jews Observe Their Easter*. The Jews, Pfefferkorn wrote, were "criminal dogs" who took unending delight in cursing Christ, mocking Mary, and sucking the blood of hardworking Christians through their usurious practices as moneylenders. He urged the authorities to drive them from their lands. If, however, the Jews were to remain, they should be compelled to attend Christian sermons and their children forced to undergo baptism. They should be set to work cleaning the streets, sweeping chimneys, emptying cesspools, and removing dog manure. Through the Talmud and similar writings, Pfefferkorn charged, the rabbis had perverted Jewish law, and he called for the seizure of all Jewish books except the Bible from libraries, homes, and synagogues. If the Jews were deprived of their books, he believed, they would abandon their false beliefs and accept Christian ones.

Had he been operating on his own, Pfefferkorn would probably not have gotten very far, but in 1509 he had gone to work for the Dominican priory in Cologne. Along with the Franciscans, the Dominicans led the anti-Jewish agitation in Europe. The prior at Cologne, Jacob van Hoogstraten, hated Jews and humanists in equal measure. As Germany's inquisitor-general, he could tap into a powerful network of militant prosecutors stretching from Cologne to Louvain, Paris to Rome. With Hoogstraten's help, Pfefferkorn was able to arrange a meeting with Maximilian I, the Holy Roman Emperor, who was then in Padua waging war against Venice. Because the Jews were a lucrative source of tax revenue, Maximilian was initially reluctant to move against them, but Pfefferkorn was able to win him over, and in August 1509 the emperor signed a mandate granting Pfefferkorn the authority to confiscate and examine any and all Jewish books in the empire. All volumes that were found to be "in contradiction to the books and laws of Moses and the prophets" or that ridiculed or offended the Christian faith were to be seized, though the process was to be carried out with the knowledge of the local city council and in the presence of the clergy.

As his first arena of operations, Pfefferkorn chose Frankfurt, home to Germany's most thriving Jewish community. On the way there, he stopped in Stuttgart. Given Reuchlin's great prestige as the author of *The Rudiments of Hebrew*, Pfefferkorn hoped to get his blessing for the imperial mandate. Their conversation was amicable, and though Reuchlin remained noncommittal, Pfefferkorn left convinced that they shared the goal of ending the practice of Judaism in Germany.

He traveled on to Frankfurt. On September 28, 1509, Pfefferkorn, flanked by three priests and two magistrates, entered its synagogue, considered the most distinguished in the empire. One hundred sixty-eight books were seized. But the Jews resisted, and they sent envoys to plead their case before both Uriel, the archbishop of Mainz, and Maximilian. In November 1509, the emperor issued a new mandate that called for the creation of a review panel led by the archbishop to examine the Jewish texts for objectionable material. It was to include four universities, one of which was Cologne, and three experts, two of whom were Hoogstraten and Reuchlin. The mandate, though, also authorized the further confiscation of books, and in the following months the seizures continued in Frankfurt and other communities. The Frankfurt city council, however, came out in opposition to the seizures, arguing that the Jews should be allowed to keep their books because they were beneficial to Christianity and, furthermore, that they had a right to them so that they could practice their faith. The council was motivated in part by fears that its Jewish tax base would be eroded. In addition, Jewish booksellers sold many volumes at the Frankfurt book fair, and the council was reluctant to see this trade disrupted. Nonetheless, by April 1510, nearly 1,500 volumes had been confiscated.

Gradually, those commissioned to review the books issued their opinions. All four universities and two of the three individuals supported the confiscations. Not just the Talmud but all Jewish books, they argued, should be impounded and subjected to strict review, and they expressed confidence that the books would be found so full of errors and blasphemies as to merit destruction. Hoogstraten's opinion, titled *The Consultation Against the Filthy Jewish Books*, held that all Jewish books except the Bible and commentaries on it should be burned and that if the Jews refused to recant the falsehoods in them, they should be burned, too.

There was one dissenter: Reuchlin. In a forty-plus-page analysis of Hebrew literature, he absolved all Jewish books of the charges of slandering Jesus, Mary, and the Christian faith, with the exception of two minor volumes that, he said, the Jews themselves had shunned. He devoted the longest section of his assessment to the Talmud, trying to show that it had religious value and so should not be suppressed or burned. Many Jewish biblical commentaries, he wrote, were indispensable to Christian study, and it was a disgrace for theologians to misrepresent what was in the Hebrew Scriptures out of a lack of knowledge of the language. He recommended that the emperor direct schools of higher learning in Germany to hire two instructors in Hebrew for a ten-year term. If such a course of action were followed, he wrote, "I have no doubt but that in a very few years our students will be so conversant in the Hebrew language that they will be ready and able by means of logical and friendly discourse to gently lead the Jews into our camp."

As that last comment shows, Reuchlin remained convinced that Christianity was the one true faith and that Judaism was inherently inferior to it; he never developed a principle of true tolerance toward the Jews. Nonetheless, his opinion represented an extraordinary moment in the history of medieval Christianity—one of the first times a Christian of such standing had defended the Jewish religious tradition and supported extending the rights of free worship and scholarship to the Jews. Reuchlin's proposal to require German universities to hire instructors would in fact be carried out. By the 1530s universities across Germany and Switzerland would have chairs in Hebrew studies, helping to establish those countries as leaders in Old Testament scholarship—a distinction they hold to this day.

Reuchlin did not issue his opinion publicly; rather, he sent it under seal to the archbishop of Mainz for forwarding to Maximilian. Pfefferkorn quickly got hold of it, however, and when he and his Dominican backers read it, they were furious. Fearing that Reuchlin's opinion would prove decisive with the emperor, Pfefferkorn sought to preempt him with another noxious pamphlet. Titled *Handspiegel* ("Magnifying Glass"), it questioned how much Hebrew Reuchlin really knew, assailed him for spending so much time with the Jews, and insinuated that he had been bribed by them. Stepping up his attack on the Jews themselves, Pfefferkorn cast them as murderous enemies of Christians and raised the deadly charges of blood libel (the killing of Christians and the use of their blood in Jewish rituals) and host desecration (vandalizing the bread of Communion).

At the 1511 spring fair in Frankfurt, *Handspiegel* was the fastest-selling item. Indignant, Reuchlin struck back with a sharp tract of his own, which he completed in time for the autumn fair. Titled *Augenspiegel* ("Eye Glasses"), it described what he said were more than thirty falsehoods and misrepresentations in Pfefferkorn's text. Reuchlin denied that he had taken a penny from the Jews and decried the underhanded way in which Pfefferkorn had come into possession of his opinion. The Jews in the empire, he wrote, should be regarded not as serfs or slaves, as was traditional, but as *concives*, or fellow citizens, whose property deserved protection from seizure. But Reuchlin—wary of provoking the powerful theologians who stood behind Pfefferkorn—kept his tone temperate, and he sent conciliatory letters to several members of the Cologne faculty, affirming his full devotion to the Church.

They were not appeased. Prodded by Hoogstraten, the university lodged charges of heresy against Reuchlin, citing forty-three statements in *Augenspiegel* and claiming that it was "impermissibly favorable to Jews." When Reuchlin saw them, he snapped. In his fierce *Defense of Johannes Reuchlin Against the Cologne Slanderers*, he denounced Pfefferkorn as an "ignorant butcher" and a "Jew sprinkled with water" who had written "a slanderous book" stitched together "out of the machinations of those pseudo-scholars and published under the name of the traitor." The Cologne professors were not true theologians but "the vilest scoundrels, wickedest babblers, and lowlife slanderers." All they were trying to do was extort money from the Jews. As to their anger over his calling the Jews fellow citizens, Reuchlin reaffirmed his position: "I want them to rage even more in anger, and I hope their guts burst, because I am saying that the Jews are our brothers."

Rage they would. The *Defense* would prove a serious misstep for Reuchlin. In assailing not just Pfefferkorn but also the powerful interests backing him, he stirred the whole clamorous hive of orthodox doctricians, and they wasted no time in striking back. In August 1513, the Cologne faculty formally condemned *Augenspiegel* for its slanderous statements "savoring of heresy" and for its defense of the Jews, and Hoogstraten proposed to a commission of Dominican judges that they find Reuchlin's tract full of heresies and errors. In an ominous development, he ordered Reuchlin to appear before an inquisitorial court in Mainz to account for his statements. Reuchlin in turn sent a letter in Hebrew to the Jewish physician of Pope Leo X (who had replaced Julius II in March 1513), urging him to appeal to the pontiff on his behalf. Leo proceeded to instruct the bishop of Speyer to judge the points at issue between Reuchlin and Hoogstraten.

During the Middle Ages, such controversies had been fought out on parchment within the walls of universities; now they were being waged in low-cost, highly readable, crudely illustrated pamphlets. It was an early demonstration of the power of the printing press to inform, provoke, and incite. With pro- and anti-Reuchlin factions forming in every town, the strife was widening the gulf between those committed to the traditional ways of interpreting the Bible and those embracing the new critical methods, in the first boisterous sign of Europe's coming crack-up.

In March 1514, the commission appointed by the bishop of Speyer to investigate the matter issued its judgment, acquitting Reuchlin of all charges. Outraged, Hoogstraten left for Rome to lodge an appeal at the papal court; he would spend the next five years pursuing the case. Certain that more contention lay ahead, Reuchlin sought to use the commission's decision to enlist additional allies. High on his list was Erasmus. In a letter to the Dutch scholar, who was then in England, Reuchlin revealed just how beleaguered he felt. His opinion on Jewish books had been attacked by the Cologne theologians "not in a manner suited to learned doctors but with violent tirades and insults directed at myself in the fashion of quite irresponsible buffoons." When he wrote a defense of his actions, those same professors sought to burn his opinion in the city of Mainz "by order of the inquisitor of the Preaching Friars," i.e., Hoogstraten; the preachers "swarmed to the spot like summer flies." Reuchlin was now sending along the favorable ruling from the Speyer court so that Erasmus could press his case with his English friends and thus restore his reputation "in opposition to the burners of books."

Given Erasmus's outspoken support for free inquiry and independent scholarship along with Reuchlin's pioneering work in biblical studies, his backing for Reuchlin would have seemed ensured, but he shrank from offering a public endorsement. All the name-calling and foul language provoked by the affair made him uncomfortable. If he came to Reuchlin's aid, he might face similar abuse. With charges of blasphemy in the air, his very physical safety could be imperiled.

But there was a deeper reason for Erasmus's reticence. While he felt bound to Reuchlin by their shared affection for sacred studies, he did not share Reuchlin's passion for Hebrew. The language seemed to him crude and immature, and he disliked the Kabbalah, the Talmud—even the Five Books of Moses. As he would later write, he would rather "see the entire Old Testament done away with than to see the peace of Christendom torn to ribbons for the sake of the Jewish Scriptures." Erasmus's disdain for Jewish texts extended to the Jews themselves, as he made clear in a biting letter written years later to his friend Wolfgang Capito (who would become a leading Hebraic scholar):

I see them as a nation full of the most tedious fabrications, who spread a kind of fog over everything, Talmud, Kabbalah, Tetragrammaton, Gates of Light, words, words, words. I would rather have Christ mixed up with Scotus than with that rubbish of theirs. Italy is full of Jews, in Spain there are hardly any Christians. . . . If only the church of Christians did not attach so much importance to the Old Testament! It is a thing of shadows, given us for a time, and now it is almost preferred to the literature of Christianity.

Erasmus's letters contained much abuse of this sort. Sometimes it took the form of disgust with Pfefferkorn, who he insisted remained a Jew intent on inciting Christians. "I wish he were an entire Jew—better still if the removal of his foreskin had been followed by the loss of his tongue and both hands," he wrote. To Reuchlin himself, Erasmus wrote, "This half-Jew Christian by himself has done more harm to Christendom than the whole cesspool of Jewry. . . . Let us, my dear Reuchlin, forget these monsters, let us take our joy in Christ and pursue honorable studies." "If it is Christian to detest the Jews," Erasmus remarked elsewhere, "on this count we are all good Christians, and to spare."

Erasmus's rancor toward the Jews had little to do with their actual conduct; his writings contain few references to the moneylending or debt-holding that caused such resentment of them. Even the Jews' rejection of Christ did not overly concern him. What he most objected to in the Jews was their Judaism. The Jewish faith, he believed, exemplified the mechanical, legalistic forms of worship that he so disliked in his own. With their rigid rules governing every aspect of diet and dress, prayer and the Sabbath, the Jews had infected Christians with a similarly obsessive concern for externalized displays of worship. Exactly how this contamination had taken place, Erasmus did not say. Nor did he stop to consider how much his own embryonic philosophy of Christ owed to the Golden Rule and other Jewish precepts. Instead, "Judaizing" became for him a convenient epithet to be applied to all those outbreaks of arid devotion that he felt were undermining the Christian faith. The rebirth of Hebraic studies, he feared, would further entrench this Judaic strain—"the most pernicious plague and bitterest enemy that one can find to the teaching of Christ."

To find so liberal-minded a thinker as Erasmus expressing such intolerance might seem surprising, but Christian humanists were not immune to the swelling anti-Jewish sentiment in Europe. In fact, they were among its leading purveyors. The quest for new, more heartfelt forms of devotion then sweeping Western Europe was accompanied by a revulsion toward all those who stood outside the faith—heretics, apostates, infidels, and Jews. Reuchlin's own interest in Hebrew was driven mainly by a desire to reveal Christian truths, and it was only over time, as he immersed himself in Hebrew studies, that he came to develop greater respect for the Jews.

So, even as Hebraic studies were flourishing among Christian scholars, the Jews themselves were being purged from Western Europe. Accusations of host desecration and blood libel proliferated, leading to executions and expulsions. The Jews were forced to leave Heilbronn in 1475, Tübingen in 1477, Esslingen in 1490, Mecklenburg in 1492, Magdeburg in 1493, Reutlingen in 1495, Württemberg and Würzburg in 1498, Nuremberg and Ulm in 1499, Nördlingen in 1507, and the state of Brandenburg in 1510. The banishment from Brandenburg was accompanied by the execution of thirty-eight Jews on charges of host desecration; the event took place in Knoblauch, just fifty miles north of Wittenberg. The highways of Germany filled with the wagons of Jewish families traveling eastward toward the one Christian country still willing to accept them—Poland, which was just beginning to assume its place as the center of Ashkenazi Jewry.

Many of those wagons passed through Saxony, and Luther may have seen them. He knew few actual Jews, however. Jews had been expelled from Erfurt in 1456 and from Wittenberg in 1304. In commemoration of their expulsion from the latter, there had been carved on an exterior wall of the town church a *Judensau*, or Jewish swine—a popular motif in German-speaking lands. It showed a sow with young piglets, with several Jews beneath it sucking its teats and a rabbi behind it peering into its hindquarters. (It is still there.)

In the absence of any contact with Jews, Luther's attitudes toward them were shaped by his theological and intellectual milieu, which was then dominated by the Reuchlin affair. In 1514, while it was at its height, George Spalatin sought Luther's opinion of a book attacking Reuchlin by Ortwin Gratius, a Cologne professor who had joined the campaign against Jewish books. In his letter, Luther called Ortwin a "dog" and a "ravenous wolf in sheep's clothing" who had made "ridiculous arguments" and distorted the words and meanings "of the definitely innocent Reuchlin." He expressed satisfaction that the matter had been referred to the Apostolic See. "Since Rome has the most learned people among the cardinals," he wrote, "Reuchlin's case will at least be considered more favorably there than those jealous people in Cologne—those beginners in grammar!—would ever allow." He signed off: "Farewell and pray for me, and let us pray for our Reuchlin." It is striking to see Luther fully embrace Reuchlin while Erasmus would not.

But Luther shared Erasmus's disgust with the Jews, as would become apparent in the summer of 1513, when he prepared his notes for his lectures on the Psalms. As was the custom in medieval exegesis, those notes took two forms: brief glosses, entered between the lines and in the margins, and longer scholia, recorded on separate sheets of paper. It was mainly in the scholia that Luther worked out his theological ideas. Placing a piece of paper before him in his cluttered, book-crammed study, he pondered the first Psalm. Just six verses long, it describes in simple but lyrical terms the contrast between those who take delight in the law of the Lord and those who ignore it. With his raven quill, Luther wrote in his small, neat hand: "The first psalm speaks literally concerning Christ thus."

With that brief notation, Luther was placing himself squarely in the medieval tradition of reading the Old Testament as fundamentally about Christ.

He then addressed the psalm's first verse: "Blessed is the man who has not walked in the counsel of the ungodly, nor stood in the way of sinners, nor sat in the chair of pestilence." The "man," Luther wrote, refers to "the only Man" from whom fullness is received. Christ "did not consent to the designs of the Jews, who afterwards crucified Him." The sinners referred to in the verse were the Jews. They had fashioned an idol for themselves in their hearts and refused glory to God. "This is what the Jews did against Christ then and are still doing until now."

The "chair of pestilence," meanwhile, referred to "that death-dealing doctrine by which the Jews corrupted, stained, and killed themselves and their own against Christ." For the Jews to deny that it was a sin to have crucified Christ was worse than doing the actual crucifying. "Oh, what a horrible example that wrath is for us! Cursed be every pride that imitates that error to the present day!"

As Luther made his way through the first psalm, his rage steadily grew. The Jews, he wrote, meditate on vanities and false frenzies according to their own ideas about Scripture. They pierce the truth "with their extremely hard iron lies," they "scourge, stone, and kill the prophets and scribes in the same way as did their fathers." Sucking the living spirit from the Bible, they inspire heretics, who "seek to approve their own empty opinion by the authority of Scripture, Judaizing with Jewish treachery."

Most of the crimes Luther attributed to the Jews in these opening pages were staples of late-medieval polemic. As he neared the end of that first psalm, however, he noted another pernicious feature that others had overlooked. The psalm's final verse mentions the "way of the ungodly." According to Luther, this was another clear reference to the Jews. They set up their own righteousness before God. By praying, fasting, and performing other such works, they believed they could become righteous in his eyes, but in every instance they were motivated by glory, worldly gain, or some other selfish end. This belief was sheer hypocrisy and deceit.

This Jewish self-righteousness seemed to run counter to what Augustine had taught in the *Confessions*. The bishop of Hippo, Luther observed in his notes, "did not set up his own righteousness nor justify himself or attribute anything to himself." He did not make an idol for himself in his heart but "gave the glory to God in the fullest sense." To avoid the sinful ways of the Jews, it was similarly necessary "not to attribute anything to oneself, but rather to establish and be subject to the righteousness of God."

As he concluded his notes on this first psalm, Luther came up with an arresting paradox: It is not those who perform righteous deeds who win God's grace, for God does not care about our deeds. Rather, it is the person who "is displeased with himself and hates his deeds" who will rise again. We cannot obtain divine favor unless our own righteousness falls and utterly perishes. The "more we judge and abhor and detest ourselves, the more abundantly God's grace flows into us."

This idea excited Luther. Since entering the monastery, he had resolutely followed the late Scholastics' exhortation to do all that is within one so as to elicit God's grace, thus opening a path to eternal life. Through the long, punishing sessions of confession and fasting, through the never-ending rounds of prayer and supplication, he had desperately sought reassurance about his everlasting fate. Instead, he had been overwhelmed by a sense of unworthiness. Now, in reading these ancient Hebrew verses, he was beginning to see why. *No* man can please God through his actions; by his very nature, he can only fall short. The Jews persisted in thinking that they could become righteous before God through their own acts—by trusting to their own power. As a result, they had been condemned to perish. Only by recognizing that one is an incurable sinner and incapable of doing good in God's eyes is it possible to begin the process of receiving his grace.

Eagerly pursuing the implications of this idea, Luther filled page after page with observations about human inadequacy and divine grace, Jewish self-righteousness and Augustinian humility. In all, Luther prepared full commentaries on roughly one hundred psalms; only a handful of them were free of anti-Jewish polemic. Summing up his disgust with the Jews, he wrote that they "look for an exclusively human deliverance and do not yet see their own destruction." Paraphrasing Augustine, Luther noted that "the sum total of all human knowledge is this: A man must know that by himself he is nothing." Luther's detestation of Jewish striving had combined with his embrace of Augustinian surrender to produce the foundation for a new spiritual vision, centered not in human agency but in divine grace.

This was a momentous shift. For centuries, the Scholastics had promoted the idea that man, by making use of his reason and free will, could do works that were pleasing to God. Luther was taking a decisive step away from this position. He was in effect reviving in its pure, concentrated form Augustine's pessimism about man's ability to please God through his own powers, before that outlook was watered down by medieval pontiffs and semi-Pelagian theologians.

In the process, he was also moving away from the humanists, Erasmus included. Erasmus's philosophy of Christ was based on the idea that man can choose to do good. A true Christian shows his faith by imitating Christ and demonstrating a similar sense of compassion, sacrifice, and mercy. Luther's own experiences had led him to a very different place. With all his might he had tried to behave in a Christlike fashion, only to fall back into his old ways. Only by acknowledging the futility of such efforts and recognizing man's inability to do good of his own accord was it possible to take the first tentative steps toward salvation. In Luther's rambling notes on this ancient Hebrew text, there appeared the seeds of his future conflict with Erasmus.

Luther delivered his first lecture on the Psalms at six in the morning on August 16, 1513, in the Grosse Hörsaal, or large lecture hall, in the Augustinian cloister. His audience consisted mostly of his superiors and peers from his order, with perhaps a few university faculty members mixed in. One can imagine the twenty-nine-year-old friar seated on a chair before a raised lectern, his face worn from his austerities and crushing workload but lit up by the revelations he was drawing from the well of Scripture. Following the custom of the day, he probably dictated his notes so that the students could take them down verbatim. One student has left a description of Luther as "a man of middle stature" whose voice "combined sharpness and softness: it was soft in tone; sharp in the enunciation of syllables, words, and sentences." He spoke "at an even pace, without hesitation and very clearly."

Luther may have spoken clearly, but following him must have required extraordinary concentration, at least to judge from his notes. For hundreds of pages they went on, offering abstruse digressions, multiple subdivisions, strings of citations, and billowing allegories. "Earrings" were said to pierce ears like the "proof-texts of divine scripture," while "goats" were the "bodies of the saints in perpetual penitence imposed for sins." The "frog" mentioned in Psalm 78 conjured up for Luther the "wordiness and long-windedness" of the Jews, while "curdled mountains" suggested the ways in which the Jews had "been curdled into the hardest kinds of cheese and have been made utterly inedible." Amid such flights, Luther's theological innovations must have been hard to detect.

Reaching Psalm 85, Luther hit upon another paradox: it was not because Christ did righteous deeds that he was righteous; rather, it was because he was righteous that he did righteous deeds. The same was true of man. A person cannot be righteous simply because he behaves in an upright fashion. He must first become righteous; virtuous deeds will then follow. Luther was here turning Aristotle on his head. In the *Nicomachean Ethics*, the Greek philosopher had proposed that man becomes good by doing good deeds; it is through his moral conduct that he shows he is a moral person. For Luther, one must first become a righteous person; righteous deeds will then follow. In these rough notes on the Psalms, one can see the foundations of Western Christianity beginning to shift.

But how to make one's heart righteous? On this point, Luther was not yet clear. As he staggered toward the end of his lectures, he seemed to founder. Coming upon the final verse of Psalm 119—"I have gone astray like a sheep that is lost"—he suggested that the faithful are like lambs who in their meekness and vulnerability need a shepherd to watch over them, "for truly we are all thus going astray." After finally completing his lectures, around Easter of 1515, Luther immediately began work on the next set. In them, he would finally find his way, guided by the figure whom many consider the true founder of the Christian faith.

A BLUEPRINT FOR EUROPE

Arriving in London in the summer of 1509 after the long, grueling trip back from Rome, Erasmus stayed with Thomas More in his house on Bucklersbury Lane. The place was more chaotic than ever. Thomas and his wife, Jane, now had a son and three daughters, plus a large staff of servants, including tutors to instruct the children and a professional fool with a license to poke fun at everyone. A lover of animals, More kept a menagerie that included a fox, a ferret, a weasel, and a pet monkey, plus birds of every feather. While forbidding card games and ball playing, More liked to lead his children in songs, religious devotions, and educational exercises, including one in which they learned the Greek alphabet by shooting at a target painted with its letters. All in all, the More household breathed happiness, as Erasmus later put it.

Adding to the cheer was the excitement sweeping England at the accession of Henry VIII. In the final years of the reign of his dour, penny-pinching father, England had become a place of fear and insecurity. The country was blanketed with informers, the wealthy were hit with subpoenas and fines, and even minor offenses were harshly punished. Now the kingdom was to be ruled by a handsome and vigorous prince who, just two months shy of his eighteenth birthday, radiated virtue and optimism. On June 11, 1509, Henry married Catherine of Aragon, the twenty-three-year-old widow of his brother Arthur. Catherine was six years older than Henry, and even though the match was made more out of political expediency than for love, the decision was loudly applauded. On June 23, the day before the coronation, the couple proceeded through streets festooned with gold cloth and lined with priests in rich copes. The coronation itself—one of the most lavish in English history—was followed by days of feasting, jousting, and dancing. England, Thomas More exulted in a royal panegyric, was entering a "golden age."

The humanists in particular rejoiced. Henry was widely read in the classics, fluent in Latin and French, and practiced in the flute and recorder. Of a pious bent, he had diligently studied Scripture and could recite long passages by heart. Taken with all things Italian, he introduced to his court Renaissance fashions in furniture, decoration, and dress. He arranged for the purchase of rare manuscripts, brought sculptors and painters from Florence and Naples, and lured woodwind and brass players from Flanders and Germany. Standing about six-foot-three, with broad shoulders and muscular calves, Henry had a pinkish complexion, glowing auburn hair, and a face so fine "that it would become a pretty woman," as a visiting Venetian put it. He was also a skilled archer and wrestler as well as a practiced horseman who could remain in the saddle for hours at a time. A master of stagecraft, Henry had commoners admitted to the grounds of his palaces to attend tournaments or watch him as he walked to chapel.

To some, these lavish displays suggested a troubling profligacy, but most accepted them as the harmless indulgences of a youthful enthusiasm. Erasmus was certainly convinced that he had made the right decision in returning to England. After his arrival, he was forced to remain indoors at More's house because of an attack of the stone. He decided to use the time to set down some of the thoughts about folly he had had while on his return journey from Rome. Amid the shouts of More's children and the squawks of his birds, he began drafting what would be his most famous work.

The *Praise of Folly* (*Moriae Encomium* in Latin) begins as a Lucianic lark—a rollicking declamation by Folly, a flippant, garrulous woman who crows over how intolerable life would be without her ministrations. Human existence is so dull and burdensome, so full of disappointment and frustration, she declares, that only through the bestowing of her gifts of illusion and self-deception can it be made tolerable. Love, for instance, would be inconceivable without her diligent efforts to conceal the blemishes and bulges of the beloved. "The fellow who kisses the mole on his mistress' neck, the lover who is delighted with the growth on his dove's nose, the father who calls his son's crossed eyes gleaming—what, I ask, can this be but pure folly?" Old men are dirty, stooped, wrinkled, and bald, yet they so desire to appear young again that one dyes his hoary hair, another cloaks his head in a toupee, a third uses false teeth. Old women, "so like corpses that they seem to have returned from the dead," painstakingly make up their faces, pluck out hairs from the strangest places, are hardly able to pull themselves away from the mirror. "What divorces or even worse things would come about," Folly chirps, "if the domestic life of man and wife were not upheld and nourished by flattery, joking, compromise, ignorance, and duplicity—all satellites of mine?"

Not only the lustful and lovesick but also the learned and lauded benefit from her services, she says. Doctors use flattery to sell their medications. Poets soothe fools' ears with inane quips and silly stories. Merchants lie, perjure themselves, steal, and cheat, yet they consider themselves important "because they have gold rings on their fingers." Hunters swear that they experience great joy whenever they hear the sound of the horns and the baying of the hounds, for "what could be more enjoyable than the butchering of animals?" Folly claims as her constituents logicians ready to fight with any man "over a lock of goat's wool," scholars prepared to go to war with anyone who makes a conjunction of a word that is properly an adverb, and book authors who add, alter, cross something out, reinsert it, recopy their work, show it to friends, and hold on to it for nine years, yet still are not wholly satisfied with it.

So irresistible are her wiles, Folly says, that whole nations succumb to them: the British take pride in their good looks, the Scots boast of their gentility, the French brag of their courtesy, the Italians preen over their eloquence, the Germans proclaim over their great size. "Why should I go on?" Folly cackles. "I think you see how much pleasure is brought to all men, individually and collectively, by self-love."

To this point, the *Praise of Folly* is all lightness and charm, a deft send-up of human foibles and pretensions. Midway through, though, the tone suddenly changes as the subject of religion rounds into view. The bantering Folly quickly fades, and it is the angry voice of the author we now hear. All the fury and scorn that had been building in Erasmus at the shallowness and materialism of the Church come rushing out in a scathing tirade. First up are the theologians. Thomists, Nominalists, Realists, Albertists, Ockhamists, and Scotists all refer to one another with illustrious titles like Renowned Doctor, Subtle Doctor, Very Subtle Doctor, Seraphic Doctor, Invincible Doctor. Reeking of self-regard, they seek to dazzle their uneducated listeners through the use of syllogisms, conclusions, corollaries, concessions, quiddities, and implicit and explicit propositions. Among the urgent questions they ponder: Did divine generation take place at a particular time? Are there several sonships in Christ? Through what channels has original sin come down to us through the generations? How do accidents subsist in the Eucharist without their substance?

Next it is the monks' turn. These "magnificent creatures," who regard illiteracy as a "high state of sanctity," set "an apostolic example for us by their filthiness, their ignorance, their bawdiness, and their insolence." They insist "that everything be done in fastidious detail, as if employing the orderliness of mathematics, a small mistake in which would be a great crime." They declare that just so many knots must be on each shoe; that just so much lace is allowed on each habit; that the girdle must be of just the right material and width; that the hood must be of a certain shape and capacity. One professes a knowledge of more than a hundred hymns, another takes glory in the fact that he has lived parasitically in the same spot for more than fifty-five years, yet another thinks he can use grammar and the relations between letters to prove the existence of the Trinity.

Erasmus reproaches bishops for being too busy feeding themselves to think about caring for their sheep, cardinals for failing to understand that they are the stewards rather than the lords of spiritual affairs, and, finally and most fiercely, the popes. If the supreme pontiffs were to recall that they are Christ's representatives on earth, they would give up their wealth, honors, powers won by victories, dispensations and indulgences, and horses, mules, and carts, and offer instead vigils, fasts, prayers, and sermons. If they did, "a great many copyists, notaries, lobbyists, promoters, secretaries, muleteers, grooms, bankers, and pimps" would be out of jobs. "In other words, that large group of men that burdens—I beg your pardon, I mean to say adorns—the Holy Roman See would be done away with and would have to, as a result, resort to begging as a means of making a living."

Erasmus offers a caustic inventory of the pious dullards of his day— buffoons who calculate the amount of time to be spent in purgatory "down to the year, month, day, and hour, as if it were a container that could be measured accurately with a mathematical formula"; who draw exact pictures of every part of hell, as if they had spent many years in that region; who, in planning their funerals, prescribe the precise number of candles, mourners, singers, and hired pallbearers, as if they were organizing a public show or banquet; and who, stretching Scripture as if it were a sheepskin, deem it a lesser crime to cut the throats of a thousand men than to sew a stitch on a poor man's shoe on the Sabbath.

Just as Erasmus's indignation seems ready to boil over, his tone shifts once again, and in his final pages he returns to the theme of folly, only this time with admiration and awe, for the folly he now wishes to consider is that of Christ, the exemplar of meekness and modesty. Jesus could have mounted a lion without danger but instead chose a donkey; the Holy Spirit could have descended from heaven as an eagle or a hawk but instead took the form of a dove. In his kindness and tolerance, Christ delighted the most in children, women, and fishermen. The apostles he chose were weak and stupid. He called their attention to lilies, mustard seeds, and sparrows—things foolish, lacking in sense, without art. Who could act more foolishly than those "whom the ardor of religion has totally consumed?" They throw away their wealth, neglect injuries, permit themselves to be deceived, fail to discriminate between friend and foe, and give themselves over to hunger, vigils, tears, and labors. Those who in this way gain a foretaste of the invisible world "suffer from something akin to madness." They speak in a manner "that is not quite coherent," their facial expressions "change from joy to sorrow," they "weep and laugh and, in short, are outside themselves."

Embracing the invisible, of course, was a familiar theme with Erasmus. Here, though, he elevates his spiritual vision to another, more transcendent level, striking a note of mysticism that is rare in this most rationalist of writers. This sudden leap into the realm of the ecstatic, coming so unexpectedly after the barbed thrusts at the Church, which itself follows so abruptly on the frolicsome opening, makes the book seem strangely disjointed. Of Erasmus's many works, the *Praise of Folly* is one of the few that have remained continuously in print, yet, for modern readers, its oddly shifting voices, flood of classical references, and frequent allusions to controversies long past give it a dated feel.

In Erasmus's own day, however, the work would strike with explosive force, owing mainly to its pitiless attack on the Church. The substance of Erasmus's indictment was hardly unprecedented. John Wyclif, William of Ockham, and Jan Hus had all produced tracts challenging the authority of popes and the avarice of bishops, but they had used a dense, didactic idiom with limited reach. The *Praise of Folly* was something new—a slashing polemic meant to provoke and rouse. Its lighthearted tone helped conceal just how subversive its message really was. The Church, which had survived schism and rebellion and withstood armies and invaders, would now face a new, more insidious foe: Erasmian ridicule.

What's more, Erasmus, in disseminating his message, would have the help of a powerful new agent—the printing press. The *Praise of Folly* would be Erasmus's first bestselling work, with more than twenty thousand copies in print by 1522 and more than thirty Latin editions appearing during his lifetime. Over time, it would be translated into French, German, Italian, English, Dutch, Swedish, Danish, and Russian. With its leveling assault on the traditions and prerogatives of the old order, Erasmus was helping clear a path for the Reformation.

That would not happen all at once, however. Although Erasmus would later boast (in typical humanist fashion) that he had spent a mere seven days on the *Praise of Folly*, it no doubt took months of work. Where he spent them, however, is not clear, for over the next two years he disappears from the historical record. No letters from this period survive, nor are there any traces of his whereabouts. It seems likely that he remained in London, though probably not at More's house, since the constant commotion there was not conducive to writing.

As to what Erasmus was doing during these "two lost years," as they have been called, it is not hard to surmise. Erasmus was about to enter a critical period of his career. In a few short years, he would issue a small library of essays, commentaries, reference works, and exegetical texts that together would constitute his reform program for Europe. The *Praise of*

Folly was a work of demolition, seeking to clear away the medieval debris of hierarchy, superstition, and convention. Now came the task of construction—of preparing a blueprint for a new order—and during these months when he was out of view, Erasmus was no doubt doing the necessary research, analysis, and drafting.

In drawing up his program, Erasmus would be strongly influenced by his surroundings. While in London, he spent most of his time in the City, a square mile into which were crammed some 50,000 people. As much as anywhere else in Europe, this crowded patch was feeling the impact of the new economic system that was beginning to transform society: capitalism. It was most visible in the buzz of activity on the wharves of the Thames. There, wagonloads of cloth were being bundled into containers for shipment across the Channel and North Sea to Antwerp, Bruges, and other ports. Through most of the fifteenth century, England had been content to send its wool—the finest in Europe—to the Continent to supply the looms of Flanders and Tuscany, but English entrepreneurs, seeking a greater share of the profits, began manufacturing cloth at home and exporting it. Of the more than sixty guilds and fraternities in the City, none was more powerful than the Mercers, who controlled the cloth trade and whose expansionist energies were helping establish England as Europe's top producer.

The signs of new wealth were everywhere. Large stone houses were going up amid London's drab timbered houses and grimy workshops. New schools were rising, streets were being paved, and water conduits were being laid down. The windows of luxury-good shops displayed vases, clocks, globes, necklaces, mirrors, and musical instruments. On the Strand alone stood fifty-two goldsmith shops, "so rich and full of silver vessels" as could not be found in Milan, Rome, Florence, and Venice together, marveled the Venetian ambassador.

Along with the splendor, however, came deepening misery. In the countryside, landowners craving more land for their sheep ruthlessly evicted peasants from their plots and enclosed the commons that small farmers had long used to graze cattle and collect firewood. In hundreds of villages, the local economy collapsed, leading to the formation of armies of the dispossessed, who wandered the land with their families in search of food and work. "Sheep ate men" was the shorthand description of the agrarian revolution taking place, making England a country where one man could earn fifty thousand pounds a year while countless children went hungry.

Many of the landless ended up in London. The city was overrun with beggars, vagrants, and vagabonds. Theft was rampant, and even the sight of the bodies of thieves hanging from gibbets produced little deterrence. London was notoriously violent, noisy, and damp, with chill mists rising off the river. It was also filthy. Though there were public privies, most people simply relieved themselves on the street, and dunghills rose on many corners. The stench could be detected up to twenty-five miles away, and infection and disease were rampant. In 1508, London was hit by a major outbreak of the sweating sickness, which carried off hundreds, many within twenty-four hours of being stricken.

The binding agent in this heaving, tumultuous world was the Church. In most villages, the parish church was not only the largest building but also the center of all social and cultural life. The tintinnabulation of church bells was so constant in England that it became known as "the ringing isle." Through gifts and bequests, the Church at the start of the sixteenth century owned one-fifth to one-third of all land in England. Countrywide, there were some eight hundred monasteries and convents, many of them thick with hangers-on known as "abbey lubbers." London alone had more than a hundred parish churches, plus many great religious houses, including the Black Friars, Grey Friars, Augustinian Friars, White Friars, Crutched Friars, Carthusians, and Bonhommes.

Towering over them all was St. Paul's. Sitting on the same spot as today's cathedral, Old St. Paul's (which was destroyed in the Great Fire of 1666) was, at nearly six hundred feet long, one of Europe's longest sanctuaries; its nearly five-hundred-foot steeple was visible for miles around. Inside, the church was dark and grimy, with massive pillars and heavy stone bays, but from early morning till late evening it hummed with activity. People promenaded up and down its nave in search of news and gossip; merchants gathered to close deals and settle exchange rates; pilgrims came to worship at the altars of saints. The place was so big that children played ball games in the aisles—an activity that church officials tried repeatedly (and unsuccessfully) to suppress. Every day some forty Masses were performed there, most of them by chantry priests praying for the souls of the departed. The churchyard outside was home to the country's largest book mart, and the hubbub from it added to the din within.

With its hulk and bustle, St. Paul's symbolized the integration of Church and society in England. At no time did ecclesiastical power seem greater than at the start of the reign of Henry VIII. Backed by wealth and tradition, the sacraments and the hierarchy, the Church seemed an impregnable rampart of the social order. While in London, however, Erasmus would begin chipping away at it.

During his stay, St. Paul's was his main sanctuary. His friend John Colet, its dean for five years now, had emerged as London's most outspoken prelate. When he preached, crowds of courtiers, merchants, artisans, and laborers came to be instructed and inspired. Dressed in black robes rather than the purple ones favored by most senior clerics, Colet urged repentance and devotion to Christ and inveighed against the vanity and worldliness that he said had captured so much of the English clergy.

St. Paul's had an excellent library, and Colet gave Erasmus access to two early manuscripts of the Vulgate. Erasmus was also able to consult some codices of the Greek New Testament. These documents were central to one of his main projects in this period—revising the Vulgate. Since his discovery of Lorenzo Valla's annotations on the New Testament, Erasmus had been taking notes on the Latin Bible, marking down passages that seemed garbled, ungrammatical, or unclear. While in Rome, he had had a chance to examine some important manuscripts at the Vatican Library, but he now began to undertake a more systematic collation, cross-checking Greek and Latin manuscripts with printed editions of the Vulgate to detect corruptions and deduce the correct reading.

Erasmus was also making headway with another key part of his reform program—education. Here, too, Colet's influence was pivotal. On becoming dean of St. Paul's, Colet had decided that its grammar school (which was four centuries old) was too rigid and old-fashioned to produce the type of upstanding Christian he felt England needed. On the death of his father, in 1505, he inherited a substantial estate, and he decided to use part of it to build a new school with a more modern curriculum that could produce a new generation of virtuous Christians. Soon a stately stone structure was going up in St. Paul's churchyard. Colet asked Erasmus to teach at the school. He politely declined. When Colet followed with a request for help in preparing instructional texts, he at once agreed. Textbooks were a prime vehicle for weaning young people from the Scholastic emphasis on logic and dialectic and instead instilling humanist values and ideals. Years earlier, while tutoring in Paris, Erasmus had begun work on several such texts; now, stirred by Colet's interest, he resumed work on them.

One was *De Copia* ("Foundations of the Abundant Style"), a manual on how to write well. The book was founded on one central premise: that tautology—repeating a word or phrase—is "an ugly and offensive fault." Suggesting ways to add variety and color to speech, Erasmus offered sections on the use of synonyms, metaphors, archaic words, foreign words, poetic words, indecent words, new words, periphrasis, catachresis, allegory, onomatopoeia, metonymy, synecdoche, hyperbole, meiosis, and more. Mixed in with the grammatical instruction were sermons and admonitions seeking to convey Erasmus's ideas for reform. As a practical exercise, he urged teachers to assign students a sentence and ask them to express it in as many different ways as possible. As an example, he gave, "Your letter pleased me mightily," along with more than 140 variants. Some samples: "As a result of your letter, I was suffused by an unfamiliar gladness." "Nectar I would not prefer to a message from you." "The charm of your letter put shackles of delight on my soul." With another example—"Always, as long as I live, I shall remember you"—Erasmus offered two hundred versions, some stretched to the point of parody. "So long as we shall sojourn in this world," went one, "never shall oblivion of your grace assail me."

Decades later, François Rabelais, in *Gargantua and Pantagruel*, would in fact lampoon Erasmus and other champions of the so-called abundant style, offering sentences padded with pointless variations, overripe metaphors, and pompous turns of phrase. *De Copia* would nonetheless become the most popular writer's manual of the Renaissance, appearing in 85 editions during Erasmus's lifetime and more than 150 editions by the end of the sixteenth century. It would be frequently excerpted, pirated, glossed, epitomized, and expanded—and adopted by virtually every school in England.

Considerably shorter but no less influential was *De Ratione Studii* ("On the Method of Study"), a proposal for a new humanist curriculum. Of the many subjects to which students should be exposed, Erasmus wrote, one stands out: languages. Of languages, only two really mattered: Latin and Greek. In a statement that would become famous, Erasmus declared that "almost everything worth learning is set forth in these two languages." As for vernacular tongues, the use of which was spreading across Europe, Erasmus dismissed them as vulgar, i.e., common.

As to how the classical languages should be taught, Erasmus proposed an alternative to the stultifying drills of the medieval classroom. After gaining a few rudiments of grammar, students from an early age should read and study the best authors: among the Greeks, Lucian first of all, followed by Demosthenes, Herodotus, Aristophanes, Homer, and Euripides; among the Latins, Terence foremost, followed by Virgil, Horace, Cicero, Caesar, and Sallust. Erasmus was here helping to define the Western canon. Remarkably, in light of his commitment to teaching Christian values, his reading list contains not a single religious work. Nor does it include any contemporary writers, save for Valla, "the extremely elegant arbiter of elegant Latin." Erasmus does cite other subjects students should learn, among them geography, agriculture, architecture, cooking, mineralogy, mythology, and history, but he mentions these only in passing and even then suggests that they should be taught mainly through readings in the classics. For Erasmus, history was to be learned through Tacitus, science through Pliny, geography via Ptolemy. And those subjects were to be learned through a series of demanding exercises in which students were to practice and master every classical rhetorical device, every part of speech, and a half-dozen kinds of meter.

De Ratione Studii and *De Copia* (both of which appeared in 1512) would become the basis for all instruction at St. Paul's, helping make it the first school in England to adopt a humanist curriculum. From there, the Erasmian program would spread to Eton, Winchester, and other top schools. The focus was overwhelmingly on Latin—its grammar, usage, style, and literature—with Greek added at the more advanced schools. All instruction was in these languages. The authors read were for the most part those proposed by Erasmus, and the methods used to teach them were largely those he recommended. Mathematics, the sciences, philosophy, and the English language were neglected and in many cases scorned. By the end of the sixteenth century, the entire framework of English schooling would be built on Erasmian principles. In fact, the humanist curriculum he prescribed would form the foundation for all education in Europe until the latter part of the nineteenth century. (In a well-known study, *William Shakspere's Small Latine & Lesse Greeke*, T. W. Baldwin argues that Shakespeare got his fundamental knowledge of rhetoric, literary construction, and literary criticism from the Erasmian curriculum. "Without Erasmus," Baldwin writes, "we might have had the John Milton of popular concept, but not William Shakspere.")

The staying power of the Erasmian approach was remarkable. In 1837, a headmaster at St. Paul's was recorded as informing a parent that "we teach nothing but the classics, nothing but Latin and Greek. If you want your son to learn anything else, you must have him taught at home, and for this purpose we give three half-holidays a week." Leonard Woolf (the husband of Virginia), who attended St. Paul's from 1894 to 1899, observed in his autobiography *Sowing* (published in 1960) that he got "irrational pleasure" from knowing that he had attended a school that was more than four centuries old and connected to Erasmus. Nonetheless, he felt despair at the headmaster's narrow and fanatical vision for the school, which was to provide students with "the severest and most classical of classical educations." Students in their final two years "did nothing but Latin and Greek." Use of the mind, intellectual curiosity, interest in work, and the enjoyment of books were all "violently condemned and persecuted."

It is striking that Erasmus, who so prized wit, irony, irreverence, and wordplay, would propose an educational program that would prove so stultifying. One result was that the program failed to produce the type of cultivated, conscientious citizen that was its goal. Even the Latin so beloved by Erasmus suffered, for the version taught at St. Paul's and other schools was not the practical idiom of the medieval classroom but a fossilized version of the classical tongue. By the seventeenth century, Latin would become entombed and Shakespeare, Jonson, Donne, and Hobbes would all write in English.

From a social standpoint, the most striking feature of Erasmus's education program was its elitism. The urgent task of preparing ordinary citizens for a useful and upright life did not interest him. Rather, he sought to train a specialized caste—an aristocracy of culture and taste—that could lead the rest of society into an era of humanist enlightenment. Knowledge of the classics became a ruthlessly clear marker of class. Erasmus's neglect of the education of the common man and his lack of interest in universal education help explain why his reform program as a whole failed to develop a broad social base, in contrast to the more populist educational programs offered by Luther and other reformers.

When Erasmus finally reappears on the historical stage, it is in the form of a letter sent from Dover in April 1511 informing a friend that he was headed to Paris to arrange for the printing of the *Praise of Folly*. Sensing the uproar the tract might cause, he sought to hide his intentions by giving it to a relatively unknown printer, Gilles de Gourmont. (Unfortunately, the printing was badly mangled.) After wrapping up his editorial duties, in June 1511, Erasmus returned to London. He initially stayed with More, but Thomas had a new wife, Alice Middleton (Jane had died a short time earlier), and she took an immediate disliking to Erasmus, due to both his inability to speak English (he relied almost exclusively on Latin) and what she saw as his mooching, so he moved a short distance away to stay with his friend William Grocyn, the rector at St. Lawrence Jewry, a large church in central London.

There, Erasmus resumed his efforts to obtain some of the milk and honey that had lured him back from Italy. Still enjoying a claim on Henry's affections from their long-ago encounter at Eltham Palace, Erasmus occasionally got in to see the king and was always received cordially. His strongest supporter at the royal court, though, was Catherine, who had been schooled in good letters at the direction of her mother, Isabella of Spain, and who as queen became a generous patron of the New Learning. She tried to enlist Erasmus's services as a tutor, but he demurred. Meanwhile, William Warham, the archbishop of Canterbury, sought to arrange a benefice for him, but nothing was immediately forthcoming, so Erasmus had to continue imposing on friends.

Then, in the summer of 1511, he received an offer from John Fisher, who was the bishop of Rochester and chancellor of the University of Cambridge, to lecture on Greek at Cambridge. Given his bleak financial situation, Erasmus had no choice but to accept. As his departure date neared, he came down with the sweating sickness, becoming so ill that rumors of his death spread on the Continent. By mid-August, however, he had recovered enough to make the seventy-mile journey to Cambridge, riding on a lame horse through nonstop rain and with little food. Though home to a university that was more than two centuries old, Cambridge remained a backwater of 2,000 residents. Erasmus lived in a room at the top of the southwest tower in the old courtyard of Queen's College (known to this day as the Erasmus Room). It was just steps from the River Cam, whose banks on mild days offered a prospect for pleasant walks, but there were few of them during the nearly three years Erasmus was in Cambridge. England (like much of Europe) was in the grip of a Little Ice Age that would continue into the nineteenth century, and the weather was persistently gray, cold, and damp, with thick fogs rolling in off the surrounding marshes. Achy and frail in the best of times, Erasmus was almost constantly sick; after one long stretch of rain in winter, he had such a sore throat that he could communicate only "by nods and gestures."

Alone for much of the time, he sought to stay in touch with the world through his letters. Shorn of the literary flourishes in much of his correspondence, they show the everyday Erasmus. He expresses concern about finding reliable messengers, laments the lack of good copyists, discusses the care of his horses, tries to arrange places to stay on his periodic visits to London, and complains about the quality of the wine. Writing to Henry VIII's Latin secretary Andrea Ammonio, his main correspondent in this period, Erasmus pleads, "If you are in a position to arrange for a small cask of Greek wine, the best obtainable, to be sent to me here, you would have done what will make your friend perfectly happy. But quite dry wine please." After an outbreak of the plague, Erasmus wrote to Colet that "everyone is running away from Cambridge in all directions; I myself have already withdrawn to the country, but perhaps the want of wine will drive me back to Cambridge!" Even when the plague abated and Cambridge was full, he lamented, the town "is a lonely place for me." Amid the damp and gray, he pined for Rome. "I cannot without anguish recall the climate, the green places, the colonnades, and the honeyed talk with scholars—the light of the world, the positions, the prospects."

He was faring little better with his lectures. John Fisher had arranged for his position to help promote humanistic studies at the university. Erasmus's subject was the Greek grammar of Chrysoloras, the Byzantine scholar whose lectures in Florence beginning in 1397 had marked the start of the recovery of Greek in the West. His grammar, printed in Venice in 1475, was popular in Italy, and Erasmus was now trying to introduce it in this soggy cow pasture. But attendance was sparse. The faculty remained in the grip of the Scholastics, who continued to regard Greek with suspicion, and at every turn Erasmus found himself doing battle with the Scotists—"the most unbeatable and most successfully complacent class of men there is." His pay was so meager that it did not even cover his basic living expenses, and so, to his humiliation, he had to continue to pester his friends. "I often curse these miserable literary pursuits of mine that produce so little."

Yet in those pursuits he was making good progress. In some ways, the solitude was a blessing, for it allowed Erasmus to work undisturbed in his tower at Queen's. In Cambridge, he found several important manuscripts for use in his revision of the New Testament. One, a codex in the Franciscan library, was of fairly recent vintage, having been copied around 1468 by a Greek scribe from Constantinople in the employ of the archbishop of York, but it was part of an important family of manuscripts that went back to the third century, and it provided Erasmus with a solid basis for assessing the accuracy of the Vulgate. (The manuscript is now known as the Leicester Codex, after its current home, the Leicestershire Record Office.)

Cambridge was also rich in Jerome manuscripts, and Erasmus took the opportunity to resume his work on the learned Church Father. He was so excited at the prospect of editing Jerome's letters, he wrote, that he felt "inspired by some god." But the work was difficult and draining. The manuscripts had been "half eaten away and mutilated by worm and beetle" and were written in the heavy Gothic script favored by medieval copyists, forcing him to "go back to school" to decipher them. Almost every page was corrupted by scribal errors. "One man copies not what he reads but what he thinks he understands; another supposes everything he does not understand to be corrupted, and changes the text as he thinks best, following no guide but his imagination." A third catches an error but while trying to emend it with a conjecture "introduces two mistakes in place of one, and while trying to cure a slight wound inflicts one that is incurable." Sustaining Erasmus through all the tedium was his ongoing belief that Jerome's letters offered a model of how literature and languages could serve as handmaidens to faith and piety.

While working to restore the spirit of the early Church, Erasmus was also retrieving treasures from the storehouse of ancient learning. Two pagan writers in particular seemed rich in insight. One was Seneca the Younger. Erasmus had some reservations about Seneca's style, finding it at times too vehement and prone to a tiresome loquacity, but in the letters and essays, he noted, Seneca "calls the mind away to heavenly things," preaching the path of honor "with such fervor that it was quite clear he practiced all he preached."

On that last point, Erasmus was overlooking the great gulf between Seneca's high-minded ideals and his often sordid conduct. Despite counseling modesty and self-sufficiency, he amassed a huge fortune, threw extravagant banquets, charged usurious interest rates, and condoned the murderous excesses of Nero, whom he served as an adviser and speechwriter. Even in his own day, Seneca was attacked as a hypocrite, an adulterer, a flatterer. Erasmus nonetheless felt that his appeals to brotherhood and his advice on how to maintain a sense of equanimity amid the clamor of daily life reinforced the teachings of the Gospels.

Unfortunately, Seneca's works had become badly garbled. Gaining access to two ancient manuscripts of them, Erasmus painstakingly sought to root out errors. He would later boast that he had slain more than four thousand of them (though, working as always in haste, he gave birth to many others).

Erasmus also took up Plutarch. Of all the ancients, few had more influence on European thought than this Greek essayist and moralist of the first century C.E. His most famous work, *Parallel Lives*—biographical sketches of Greek and Roman generals and statesmen—was an early attempt to show how character shapes history. Erasmus, though, preferred his *Moralia*, genial (if overlong) musings on practical ethical and social problems. Seventy-eight of these treatises, dialogues, and lectures had survived, and as their titles show, Plutarch had many of the same concerns as Erasmus: "On Being a Busybody"; "On Praising Oneself Inoffensively"; "On Complaining"; "On Brotherly Love"; "On the Eating of Flesh"; "How to Profit by One's Enemies." Whereas Socrates "brought philosophy down from heaven to earth," Erasmus observed, "Plutarch brought it into the privacy of the home and into the study and the bedroom of the individual." Given how applicable his moral lessons were to ordinary life, "it is hard to understand why this author's moral treatises are not constantly in people's hands and not studied by the young."

While in Cambridge, Erasmus translated several of those treatises into Latin, including his favorite, "How to Distinguish a Flatterer from a Friend." In it, Plutarch discusses how to identify not obvious sycophants and toadies but more cunning operators who seek to ingratiate themselves with the powerful and prominent by showering them with praise and working subtly to gain their trust. True friends, Plutarch asserts, are those who deal with us straightforwardly and speak plainly to us about our faults. Erasmus believed that Plutarch's observations deserved to be widely circulated, especially among kings and princes, whose exalted status made it hard for them to distinguish true friends from false.

Erasmus dedicated the translation to Henry VIII. As he explained, he was doing so to show Henry, "of all kings the most illustrious," the continued "loyalty and devotion which I expressed to you long ago when you were a boy full of promise." The irony of his praising Henry while sending him an essay about the perils of flatterers was surely not lost on Erasmus. His relations with Henry would always be complex. Throughout his life, he would seek to cultivate good ties to the king, who was in a position to provide not only financial support but also physical security in an age when independent thinking could prove fatal. But Henry's actions would become increasingly distasteful to Erasmus, making it hard for him to produce the effusive displays the king demanded. Henry's stinginess toward Erasmus no doubt reflected his own suspicion that, for all his flattery, the Dutch scholar was not a true friend.

It was during Erasmus's time in Cambridge, in fact, that his disillusionment with Henry began to set in, over a matter that would figure prominently in his reform program: war. Across Europe, armies were mobilizing and populations being roused into fits of nationalist fury. As usual, Italy was the great vortex, but even in England the mood was darkening, as was apparent in Erasmus's letters. In October 1511, he wrote to Andrea Ammonio of his longing to hear "how things are in Italy and what the most invincible Julius is up to." Ammonio informed him that the pope, having successfully reclaimed the Papal States with the help of the French, had recently turned against them and, together with Venice and Ferdinand of Aragon, had formed a Holy League with the goal of driving them from Italian soil. The Venetians had ambushed the French and destroyed more than five hundred of their horses. The Spanish king seemed on the verge of war with France, "and the English will not, it is guessed, stay idly looking on," Ammonio observed.

"What you tell me of Italian affairs is anything but happy news to me," Erasmus replied, "not because I love the French king but because I hate war." With every day bringing news of "the most trivial of raids" taking years to end, "what will be the prospect if such an extensive war breaks out?" In November, Ammonio wrote that the French were once again "in the ascendant" in Italy.

In pressing his campaign against France, Julius hoped to enlist England, and as a sign of his esteem, he sent Henry a Golden Rose. Until this point, Henry, who was barely twenty years old, had shown little interest in state affairs. He liked to linger at his palace in Greenwich with its two-hundred-acre park, where he could hunt and hawk. His nights were given over to elaborate banquets, frilly balls, high-stakes card games, and barely concealed womanizing. Shuttling between his palaces at Greenwich, Eltham, Westminster, and the Tower, Henry glided along the Thames in a magnificent state barge; when visiting his country estates, he insisted on bringing along much of the royal court, at staggering expense.

Such domestic pleasures, however, failed to satisfy him. As a youth,

Henry had been dazzled by the tales of King Arthur and his court and stirred by the accounts of Henry V's great victory at Agincourt in 1415; he now craved similar glory. Eager to establish England as a world power on a par with France and Spain, he exhorted his male subjects to practice archery rather than play at tennis or bowling. He drew close to Thomas Wolsey, a member of the privy council on whom he was coming increasingly to rely. At Wolsey's urging, Henry on November 13, 1511, joined the Holy League. Four days later, he signed a separate agreement with Ferdinand of Aragon—Catherine's father—to come to the Church's defense against France and to force the French to return Bologna to papal control. The prospect of going to war with France thrilled Henry, for the opportunity it would offer both to show off his knightly skills and to resume the Hundred Years' War and thereby recover the lands lost by his predecessors. In November 1512, Henry summoned Parliament and announced that the royal army was preparing to invade France and that when the campaign began, he would lead it.

War fever surged, and Erasmus was dismayed at the sudden change that came over the island. The price of everything soared, he had trouble posting his letters, and he "nearly perished" from a bout of the stone that he attributed to "some horrible flat stuff" he had to drink as a result of shrinking wine supplies. "I cannot tell you how grieved I am to see our fellow-countrymen gradually slipping into the present conflict," he wrote to his friend Pieter Gillis. He was especially disturbed at the failure of his fellow clerics to speak out. "Ah, those tongueless theologians, those mute bishops, who look on such dire human disasters and say nothing."

There was an exception. From his pulpit at St. Paul's, John Colet had continued to reproach his fellow clergymen for neglecting their pastoral duties. In early February 1512, in what is considered the most important pre-Reformation sermon in England, Colet chastised the English clergy for "four evils"—devilish pride, carnal concupiscence, worldly covetousness, and secular living. "What eagerness and hunger after honor and dignity are found in these days among ecclesiastical persons!" The Church needed a thoroughgoing reformation. Simony should be banned, curates should be required to reside at their churches, and the clergy in general should rededicate themselves to "humility, sobriety, charity, spiritual occupations." Colet's words bit so deeply that the bishop of London accused him of heresy.

He would not back off, however. On March 27, 1513 (Good Friday), Colet was to preach before the king and his top retainers at Greenwich. It was a critical moment. A fleet of ships was being readied to carry the royal army to France and along with it twelve giant cannons, each bearing the likeness of one of the twelve apostles. Colet boldly denounced the zeal with which Christians were preparing to slaughter one another. Antagonists claimed to be fighting in the name of Christ when in fact they were marching under the banner of the Devil. It was Christ the peacemaker whom Christians should imitate, not Alexander the Great or Julius Caesar. Angered by Colet's audacity, Henry summoned him to a private meeting to explain himself. Colet was somehow able to mollify the king, and at the end of their hour-long conversation, Henry drank a cup of wine with him and sent him off with an embrace.

In June 1513, the 25,000-man English army departed from Dover aboard three hundred ships bound for Calais, which sat in a narrow sleeve of territory controlled by England. Henry himself soon followed, accompanied by Wolsey, heralds, trumpeters, and hundreds of other members of his household, plus two bishops and assorted nobles. After three weeks of planning and pageantry, a large force of infantry, cavalry, and artillery set off for the small French town of Thérouanne, some thirty miles away. On arriving, the soldiers immediately laid siege to it; they were soon joined by a small contingent led by Maximilian, the Holy Roman Emperor. On August 16, French cavalry arrived to relieve the besieged town, but, encountering English fire, they quickly turned and galloped off, thus giving the skirmish its name: the Battle of the Spurs. Within a week, Thérouanne fell, and Henry and Maximilian triumphantly entered the town; Maximilian ordered it razed (except for the church), and what was not leveled was burned by looters. The allied army then proceeded fifty miles east to Tournai, a scenic town on the Scheldt River; after battering its walls with the holy cannons, the English succeeded in starving the town into submission, and on September 24 Henry entered it in triumph. Unlike Thérouanne, the town was preserved as an English garrison, and Henry presided over three weeks of feasts and tournaments.

While he was thus occupied, King James IV of Scotland, who was allied with France, took advantage of Henry's absence to invade England from the north. It proved a disastrous decision. The English counter-attacked, and on September 9, 1513, on the field of Flodden, some ten thousand Scots died, among them James and his young son Alexander—the same Alexander whom Erasmus had tutored in Italy. In late October, Henry arrived back in Dover to thunderous acclaim. Thus buoyed, he immediately began planning another expedition against France for the following summer.

Erasmus had fond memories of Alexander, and his senseless death fed his grief and anger at this display of Christian bloodletting and the great hardship the fighting was inflicting on the English people. "We are shut in by the plague and beset by highway robberies, instead of wine we drink vinegar and worse than vinegar, and our coffers are emptying, but 'hurrah for victory!'—that is what we sing, being the world-conquerors we are," he wrote to Andrea Ammonio in December 1513.

Two months later, Erasmus left Cambridge. Back in London, he poured his fury into a long, impassioned letter to his friend Antoon van Bergen, an abbot and a diplomat at the Burgundian court in the Netherlands. Aimed at a wide audience, it was Erasmus's first major statement on war. "I can see vast disturbances in the making, and what their outcome will be is not clear; may God in his mercy vouchsafe to quiet the storm that now afflicts Christendom." He wondered what it was "that drives the whole human race, not merely Christians, to such a pitch of frenzy that they will undergo such effort, expense, and danger for the sake of mutual destruction." Whereas animals fight only for food or in defense of their young, human wars "are generally caused by ambition, anger, lust, or some such disease of the mind." Christians are named after Christ, who preached and practiced only gentleness. How, then, could anything in the world "be so important as to impel us to war, a thing so deadly and so grim that even when it is waged with perfect justification, no man who is truly good approves it?"

He went on: "But, you will say, the rights of princes must be upheld." Yet many princes first make up their minds as to what they want, then find a specious pretext to justify their actions. With so many treaties signed and abrogated, no one lacks a reason to go to war. If a rival refuses to accept arbitration, a true Christian prince should reflect on how much it will cost to defend his rights; if the misery, slaughter, and bereavement likely to result are excessive, as is usually the case, he should refrain from pressing his claim.

This was a radical statement. At a time when war was viewed as an ineradicable feature of European life, Erasmus was fiercely denouncing it. At a time when princes leading troops into battle were invariably hailed as protectors of the nation, Erasmus was calling them enemies of the people. And he did not hesitate to name the man he held most responsible for this "hurricane of wars": Julius. (Julius had died in March 1513, making it safer for Erasmus to cite him.)

At this time, Erasmus was preparing a new edition of the *Adages*. Pleased with the reception of the long essays in the Aldine edition, he decided to expand on several more entries in this one, hoping to use the printing press to arouse the public. One was *Dulce bellum inexpertis*— "War is sweet to those who have not experienced it." In earlier editions, he had dispatched this saying in a few lines; now, building on his letter to Antoon van Bergen, he prepared an indictment of war that would prove a landmark in European political thought.

His main target was the doctrine of just war, which was central to Christian thinking on the subject. The doctrine's main architect was Augustine. War, he maintained, could be considered just if it met three criteria: if it was waged by a legitimate authority, if it was fought for a cause considered just, and if it was carried out with righteous intention. During the Middle Ages, the doctrine had been refined by Thomas Aquinas, who argued in the *Summa Theologica* that a war can be considered just if those attacked "deserve it on account of some fault" and if the attacking party has "a rightful intention," intending "the advancement of good" and "the avoidance of evil." In practice, this standard was not hard to meet, and by the early sixteenth century the Church was declaring virtually every military action just. Religion and war had become so entwined that swords were engraved with scenes from the Passion and saints were entreated by generals as they prepared for battle.

Erasmus scorned such thinking: "Two armies advance on each other and both carry the standard of the cross." That heavenly banner "represents the ineffable union of all Christians," but under it men "rush to mutual slaughter, and of this wicked deed we make Christ the witness and author." In fact, Christ "forbade anyone to resist evil." If one weighs the advantages and disadvantages and finds that an unjust peace is preferable by far to a just war, "why should you prefer a throw of the dice with Mars?" If the cost seems to outweigh the profit, "is it not better to give way a little on your rights than to trade such countless ills for so small an advantage?"

Erasmus's hatred of war ran so deep that he questioned its value even when it was waged against the Turks. At the time, Christian Europe lived in dread of the Ottomans and their huge army. After the fall of Constantinople in 1453, the Turks had seized control of much of eastern Europe and some of the territories held by Venice, and Vienna was widely thought to be next. Hardly anyone questioned the need to fight them—except Erasmus. The Muslims, he maintained, were best subdued not through the deployment of armies or the weapons of war but by showing "the sure marks of Christians: a blameless life, the desire to do good even to our enemies, an unshakable tolerance of all injuries, a scorn for money, a disregard for glory, a life held cheap."

Such a stance approached outright pacifism, which rejects even self-defense as unjustified. Realizing that he might be accused of naïveté, Erasmus toward the end of his essay offered a brief qualification, noting that he would not entirely condemn fighting the Turks "if they attack us of their own accord." More generally, he observed, if there is no way to avoid war—if "you have left nothing untried and no stone unturned in your search for peace, then the best expedient will be to ensure that, being an evil thing, it is the exclusive responsibility of evil people, and is concluded with a minimum of bloodshed."

When the new edition of the *Adages* eventually appeared, *Dulce bellum inexpertis* would be the longest entry. Few princes would pay it much heed; Erasmus's opposition to war was too emphatic and categorical. Many men of letters would, however. During Erasmus's lifetime, the essay would be issued many times as a stand-alone pamphlet. With it and his letter to

Antoon van Bergen, Erasmus was introducing a new pacifist strain into Western European thought.

More generally, *Dulce bellum inexpertis* reflected the new radical streak that ran through the revised *Adages*. In *A mortuo tributum exigere* ("To exact tribute from the dead"), Erasmus denounced both secular and ecclesiastical authorities for exploiting citizens through an endless series of fees, tolls, and other exactions. In *Spartam nactus es, hanc orna* ("Sparta is your portion; do your best for her"), he urged princes to resist the temptation to seek glory abroad when so much demanded their attention at home. In the sharply antimonarchical *Scarabaeus aquilam quaerit* ("A dung-beetle hunting an eagle"), he drew parallels between rulers and eagles: both are born to fight and to plunder, to cram themselves with the entrails of innocents, to drink blood, and to seek forever to enlarge their realms.

Erasmus's loathing of tyrants would find its fullest expression in the volume's most unusual entry, *Sileni Alcibiadis*—"The Sileni of Alcibiades." Sileni, he explained, were carved wooden figures in ancient Greece that, appearing worthless and crude on the outside, revealed a deity when opened. This is often the case with things of true value: seemingly vulgar and insignificant on the surface, they contain great treasures within. An example was Socrates. With his peasant face and snub nose, he could be taken for a country bumpkin, but, peering within, one finds "a divine being rather than a man, a great and lofty spirit worthy of a true philosopher." The ultimate Silenus, however, was Christ. His parents were of lowly station, his home was humble, he was poor and had few disciples, but on taking a closer look, "what a treasure you will find, in that cheap setting what a pearl, in that lowliness what grandeur, in that poverty what riches, in that weakness what unimaginable valor, in that disgrace what glory, in all those labors what refreshment, and in that bitter death, in short, a never-failing spring of immortality!"

Alas, Erasmus observed, in his own day it was more common to find inside-out Sileni, especially in the form of princes who flaunt honorific titles, resplendent belts, and bejeweled rings but who on closer examination turn out to be despots who deride peace, oppress men of goodwill, despoil the Church, live by robbery and sacrilege, and sow seeds of discord. The Silenus would become for Erasmus a symbol of the simple piety that he hoped to reclaim from the pomp and ostentation of the medieval Church.

By the summer of 1514, Erasmus had made enough progress on the various parts of his reform program to want to see them into print. Only one publisher seemed up to the task—Johann Froben in Basel. Froben was to northern Europe what Aldus was to Italy—the most prestigious and skilled printer of scholarly books. In addition to having an ample supply of Greek type, Froben had for years been preparing a multivolume edition of Jerome's writings, and Erasmus hoped to join his own work on the great Doctor with that of Froben's.

Financially, Erasmus was finally on firmer ground. William Warham had arranged an appointment for him as the rector of a parish in Kent. Erasmus had no intention of filling it, however, and in one of the financial maneuvers common in that era, he was able to convert it into an annual pension. Thus provisioned, he was ready to quit England. The "golden era" that had brought him back from Rome in 1509 had proved cruelly illusory. After sending ahead his heavy luggage to the home of his friend Pieter Gillis in Antwerp, Erasmus went in July 1514 to Dover for the crossing to Calais. For once, the weather was clement and the sea calm. As he boarded his boat, however, the seamen transferred the portmanteau holding his papers to another vessel. All the work that he had completed over the past five years was suddenly out of his hands. And so, despite the clear skies and favorable breezes, Erasmus spent the entire crossing worrying that all his labor had been lost.

THE GATE TO PARADISE

After completing his lectures on the Psalms, Luther was busier than ever. In the spring of 1515, he was elected district vicar of the Augustinian order for the states of Meissen and Thuringia. Now, in addition to supervising the activities of his own monastery, he had to oversee those of ten others. He began receiving reports about idleness, gossiping, insubordination, and lavish meals served to unauthorized visitors, and he grappled with how to respond. Being district vicar, he complained, was like being the prior of eleven monasteries.

When the preacher of the St. Mary's town church fell ill, Luther was asked to fill in, and he did so well that the town council invited him to preach there on a regular basis. The simple, austere sanctuary was a ten-minute walk from the Augustinian cloister, and soon Luther was making it three or four times a week—a pace he would maintain for the rest of his life. The church provided both a podium for his ideas and a window into the needs and concerns of ordinary Christians. Unlike Erasmus, who shunned pastoral work, Luther would get a firsthand look at lay people's struggles with sin and temptation and at the frequency with which they lapsed back into old habits despite heartfelt efforts at reform.

Luther could certainly identify with them. At the Black Cloister, he continued to experience periods of panic and doubt. Struggling to perform meritorious acts that would please God, he felt overwhelmed by his unfitness. Because of his new responsibilities, he frequently neglected his devotional duties, and he would sometimes go two or three weeks without saying the hours. In a frantic effort to catch up, he would sequester himself in his study for one, two, even three days without food or drink while diligently making his way through the Psalter. "This made my head split," Luther later recalled, "and as a consequence I couldn't close my eyes for five nights, lay sick unto death, and went out of my senses." Had he kept at it, he felt sure, the physical and emotional toll would have killed him.

It was amid such spiritual trials that Luther began to prepare for his next set of lectures, on Paul's Epistle to the Romans. The lectures were due to start around Easter of 1515, and in anticipation Luther asked Johann Rhau-Grunenberg to print a text based on a Vulgate edition published by Johann Froben in 1509. With the usual wide margins and generous spacing between lines, it came to twenty-eight leaves of text. In his tower study, Luther began to fill the margins with notes as well as to prepare longer scholia on separate sheets of paper.

He quickly got bogged down. The epistle seemed obscure and severe. Luther was especially troubled by a phrase at 1:17: *iustitia enim Dei in eo revelatur* ("in it the righteousness of God is revealed"). In a famous autobiographical fragment written in 1545, the year before his death, Luther noted that he despised this passage, for it seemed to say that God in his righteousness punishes the unrighteous sinner. Though he had lived as a monk "without reproach," he felt that he was a sinner "with an extremely disturbed conscience" and that God was not placated by his acts of satisfaction. "I did not love, yes, I hated the righteous God who punishes sinners." It was not enough that "miserable sinners, eternally lost through original sin," were crushed by the law of the Decalogue; God had to add to the pain by "threatening us with his righteousness and his wrath!" With a fierce and troubled conscience, he "beat importunately" upon that phrase, "most ardently desiring to know what St. Paul wanted."

After meditating on these words day and night, Luther at last examined the overall passage in which they occurred: "In it [the gospel] the righteousness of God is revealed, as it is written, 'He who through faith is righteous shall live.'" Suddenly, he began to understand that "the righteousness of God is that by which the righteous lives by a gift of God, namely by faith." He could now see that "the righteousness of God is revealed by the gospel, namely, the passive righteousness with which merciful God justifies us by faith." "Here," Luther recalled, "I felt that I was altogether born again and had entered paradise itself through open gates." As much as he had previously hated the phrase "righteousness of God," he now loved it. "That place in Paul was for me truly the gate to paradise.

Later I read Augustine's *On the Spirit and the Letter*, where contrary to hope I found that he, too, interpreted God's righteousness in a similar way, as the righteousness with which God clothes us when he justifies us."

Luther's Reformation discovery, as this moment is known, is one of the great moments in Protestant history. It was his own "road to Damascus" experience, when, breaking the fetters of medieval theology, he found his way toward a new creed.

Yet the episode is cloaked in confusion and controversy. Luther's concept of the "passive righteousness with which merciful God justifies us by faith" is opaque, and scholars for centuries have struggled to make sense of it. They have wrestled with his chronology as well. Luther says that his breakthrough occurred while he was preparing his second set of lectures on the Psalms. He delivered these in 1519—four years after he began lecturing on Romans and two years after he posted the Ninety-Five Theses. If accurate, this account would mean that Luther did not have his intellectual breakthrough until well after he issued his great protest against indulgences. Luther's reference to *On the Spirit and the Letter* adds to the difficulties, for he had read and absorbed that work by 1515, as he was preparing his lectures on Romans.

These discrepancies have led Reformation scholars to search for a holy grail: the exact point in Luther's writings where his great epiphany occurred. Some have placed the event as early as 1509, when he was writing his glosses on the *Sentences*. Others have located it in 1513 and 1514, during his first lectures on the Psalms, or in 1515 and 1516, when he was lecturing on Romans. Still others have pointed to 1518 and 1519 as the key period, and one prominent scholar argues that the breakthrough did not occur until Luther was preparing *On the Babylonian Captivity*, in 1520.

In the end, Luther's account, written so many years after the fact, has proved too unreliable to provide much guidance. If it is set aside and only contemporary documents are considered, the mystery can be readily cleared up, thanks to a remarkable scholarly find made at the start of the twentieth century.

Until then, it had been assumed that Luther's notes for his 1515 lectures on Romans had been lost for good. In the 1890s, however, the Vatican Library was opened to scholars, and in 1899 Johannes Ficker, a professor of church history at the University of Strasbourg, asked a former student then in Rome to see if the library had some exegetical works by Luther's associate Philipp Melanchthon. The student found catalogs listing manuscripts by not only Melanchthon but also Luther. Among the latter was a copy of Luther's notes for his lectures on Romans that had been transcribed by an assistant. Intrigued, Ficker began a search for the original. It soon turned up, in the Royal Library of Berlin (now the Berlin State Library). As it happened, the manuscript of Luther's handwritten notes (along with some other texts) had been sold by his grandsons in the late sixteenth century to the margrave of Brandenburg. It eventually ended up in the library in Berlin. Nobody, however, had paid it much attention. In 1846, as part of a special exhibition on the three-hundredth anniversary of Luther's death, the document was placed on prominent display, but, again, no one showed much interest. After the exhibition ended, the manuscript was put in a showcase in the large entrance hall leading to the reading room, and there it sat, unnoticed. As word of Ficker's interest spread, its existence was called to his attention. After protracted negotiations with a German professor of church history who claimed the right to publish the document, Ficker finally gained access to it, and in 1908 he issued a preliminary edition. (A fully edited and annotated edition did not appear until 1938.)

The discovery of Luther's handwritten notes on Romans had an electrifying effect on Reformation research, helping to spark a renaissance in Luther studies, especially of his early theological development. It did not, however, resolve the controversy over when Luther's breakthrough occurred, for when scholars examined his notes at 1:17, they found that these were brief and perfunctory and devoid of any sense of discovery. And so the debate continued.

Yet a close reading of Luther's notes shows that he did have a breakthrough while preparing his lectures on Romans. It did not occur at 1:17, however. Rather, the key moment came at a later point in the epistle, where Luther suddenly grasped the idea that would offer him a pathway out of his struggles. That idea would become the core of Luther's new gospel—and the foundation for Reformation theology as a whole. From that point on, Paul would become the central figure in Luther's intellectual life, displacing Augustine. Luther's encounter with Romans in 1515 would thus alter the course of Christian history.

Romans is one of thirteen Pauline epistles in the New Testament. (Of them, seven are considered indisputably his and the rest the work of his followers.) Written twenty to thirty years after the death of Christ, in the mid-50s, they are the earliest surviving Christian documents and are considered the most reliable sources of information about the birth of the Church. (Another important source, the Acts of the Apostles, was written about forty years after Paul's letters and is thought to be considerably less dependable.) Paul's epistles were usually dictated in haste to a stenographer and carried by messenger over the great Roman road system. They contain some of the most memorable lines in Western literature: "I put away childish things." "The love of money is the root of all evil." "Eat, drink, and be merry, for tomorrow we die." "Where, O death, is thy sting?" "I have become all things to all men, that I might save some of them." "For now we see through a glass, darkly." The ideas and doctrines outlined in these letters provided the theological foundation for the new Christian faith. Had it not been for Paul, in fact, Christianity would probably never have emerged as a separate religion but would have been absorbed back into Judaism. His efforts were so critical to the birth of the faith that, though not one of the original twelve apostles, he came to be known as *the* Apostle.

Of all Paul's epistles, none has had more impact than Romans. "The most profound work in existence," Samuel Taylor Coleridge called it. Augustine's famous conversion in the garden was triggered by his chance encounter with Romans 13:13. John Calvin, in founding the Reformed church in the mid-sixteenth century; John Wesley, in establishing Methodism in the mid-eighteenth century; and Karl Barth, the Swiss theologian who founded a neo-orthodox school of Protestantism in the twentieth century, were all profoundly influenced by Romans.

Luther's theology would be heavily indebted to this epistle as well. In it, he found Paul wrestling with many of the same problems he himself faced—foremost among them the place of the law. To what extent was it binding on those following Christ? In Paul's case, the law in question was the Jewish law, i.e., the Torah—the intricate set of commands and prohibitions governing everything from the worship of God and the care of the poor to the washing of hands and the butchering of animals. Most of Christ's early followers were Jews who, while accepting Jesus as the Messiah sent by God to lead the people of Israel, considered adherence to the Mosaic code essential. These followers were concentrated in Jerusalem and included the twelve apostles, led by Peter, Jesus's top disciple. Also prominent was the brother of Jesus, James, known as the Just. The members of this Jerusalem church (as it came to be called) kept the dietary laws, refrained from working on the Sabbath, made the prescribed animal sacrifices, and followed the intricate devotional rituals of the Holy Temple.

Paul, though, had a very different background and would follow a very different course. On the one hand, he was like them a Jew. Born around the same time as Jesus, he went by the Hebrew name Saul. Raised in a strict Jewish family, he became a member of the Pharisees, who were distinguished by their scrupulous adherence to the Torah; he was, as he put it in one of his letters, "zealous" for the faith.

But Paul was raised not in Palestine but in the Diaspora. Of the several million Jews in the Roman Empire, more lived outside Palestine than in it. Paul was born in Tarsus, the capital of the Roman province of Cilicia, in what is now southeastern Turkey. It was famous as a port, a trading emporium, and a center of Hellenistic culture to which professors in Rome liked to retire. Most people in Tarsus spoke Koine, the everyday Greek of the marketplace, and Paul's knowledge of it gave him entrée to the vast region that had been conquered by Alexander the Great. He was also a Roman citizen—a status that bestowed important legal protections. To support himself, he worked as a tent maker—a profitable enterprise in a world where people were constantly on the move.

As a young man, Paul opposed the Jewish followers of Christ with such vehemence that he participated in violent persecution of them. Around the year 33, he traveled to Damascus on a mission to suppress the Jewish Christians living there. While on the road to that city, however, he saw a brilliant flash of light in the sky and, falling to the ground, heard a voice cry out, "Saul, Saul, why do you persecute me?" "Tell me, Lord, who you are," he asked. "I am Jesus," came the reply, "whom you are persecuting." The voice instructed him to get up and continue on to Damascus, where he would be told what to do. Unable to see, Saul was led by his traveling companions into the city.

There, he went three days without eating or drinking. Helped by a local disciple of Christ named Ananias, he recovered his sight and was baptized. The chronology of Paul's life in the following years has many gaps and inconsistences, but it is believed that he spent the next two or three years in "Arabia," the parched region east of Jordan and southeast of Damascus, preaching Christ to the Gentiles. Unlike the Jewish Christians in Jerusalem, many of whom had known Christ, Paul had almost certainly never met him; whereas they cultivated memories of his life, Paul fastened on the circumstances of his death. (His letters contain only a few references to the real-life Jesus.) For Paul, the crucifixion was a redemptive act carried out on behalf of all mankind. Christ, he believed, was not simply the Messiah of the Jews—a political leader come to save the people of Israel—but the Son of God, who, through his atoning death, had come to rescue humanity from its selfishness and sin and deliver it to salvation. Paul was further convinced that Christ's Second Coming was imminent—a conviction that lent urgency to his preaching, since only those who accepted Christ as Lord would be saved.

When Paul preached Christ to the Gentiles, however, there immediately arose the matter of the Jewish law. Was obeying it mandatory even for those who were not Jewish? Paul believed not. Since salvation could come only through faith in Christ, adherence to the Mosaic code was unnecessary.

The members of the Jerusalem church remained attached to that code, however. Because of these differences, Paul decided to go to Jerusalem to give an account of his work. He spent fifteen days with Peter. Of the other apostles he saw only James—an indication, perhaps, of the discontent his preaching was causing. The meeting went off without incident, however, and Paul returned to Syria and Cilicia to resume his ministry.

While in Tarsus, he was visited by Barnabas, a Jewish Christian whom the Jerusalem church had sent to Syria to report on the proselytizing of Greeks in the region. Barnabas brought Paul to Antioch, the great Syrian metropolis, and together they proclaimed the new gospel among the Gentiles. It was in Antioch that the followers of Christ were first called Christians.

This period lasted perhaps fourteen years, and little is known about it. At some point, though, Paul and Barnabas, eager to spread their message, embarked on a great missionary tour. In all, Paul would make three such journeys, preaching his new gospel in communities stretching in a grand arc from the Levant across Asia Minor to Macedonia and Greece down to the Peloponnesus. Following the Roman road system, he trudged up to twenty miles a day, joining crowds of officials, merchants, artisans, athletes, letter carriers, runaway slaves, and itinerant philosophers; by some estimates, he covered nearly ten thousand miles in all. Throughout, he showed remarkable stamina and fortitude, which he described in a famous passage:

> Five times I have received from the Jews the forty lashes minus one. Three times I was beaten with rods. Once I received a stoning. Three times I was shipwrecked; for a night and a day I was adrift at sea; on frequent journeys, in danger from rivers, danger from bandits, danger from my own people, danger from Gentiles, danger in the city, danger in the wilderness, danger at sea, danger from false brothers and sisters; in toil and hardship, through many a sleepless night, hungry and thirsty, often without food, cold and naked.

For the sake of Christ, he wrote, "I have suffered the loss of all things."

Paul's endurance seems all the more remarkable in light of his many infirmities. He was frail of body and halting in speech. In the popular image that has come down to us, he was stooped, balding, bearded, and bowlegged. He suffered from what he called a thorn in the flesh, sent by Satan to torment him and keep him from becoming "too elated." (Paul never said what the thorn was; speculation has centered on epilepsy, malaria, headaches, stammering, and eye problems.) Regarding his personality, Paul in his letters comes across as abrasive, contentious, boastful, and bullying, yet he also suffered debilitating bouts of doubt and self-loathing. "Wretched man that I am!" he moaned in one letter, lamenting his inability to understand his own actions. "I do not do the good I want, but the evil I do not want is what I do."

On his initial journey, which lasted two years, Paul (accompanied by Barnabas) went first to Cyprus, then sailed from there to Asia Minor. Landing at Perga on the Mediterranean coast, they headed north through the immense, fir-covered Taurus Mountains into Anatolia, which had many vibrant towns and a well-educated populace. They met with a mixed reception. Most Jews, on hearing Paul proclaim Christ the Lord whom God had raised from the dead, reacted with fury. In Lystra, a group of them stoned him and dragged him to the edge of town, leaving him for dead. The Gentiles were more receptive. In a world afflicted by war, hunger, disease, and madness, they felt drawn to the idea of a transcendent redeemer who, sacrificing himself for them, made salvation possible.

But questions about the Jewish law kept intruding, with circumcision the main flash point. In Roman times, this procedure was performed with a metal knife used to cut away the outer part of the foreskin. In addition to causing considerable pain, it carried a high risk of infection. Paul adamantly opposed requiring Gentiles to undergo it. The Jerusalem church, however, remained committed to circumcision, as to the Jewish law in general.

After their return to Antioch, Paul and Barnabas, hoping to resolve the matter, went to Jerusalem. They brought with them Titus, an uncircumcised Gentile, as a sort of test case. This time Paul met with all of the Jerusalem leaders in a gathering that would become known as the apostolic assembly or council—a critical moment in the development of the early Church. Paul laid before them the work he had done with the Gentiles. A group of "false believers" (as Paul called them) opposed him, but the "pillars" of the Church—James, Peter, and the apostle John—rose to his defense. In the end, Titus was not forced to undergo circumcision—a victory for Paul—and the Jerusalem leaders gave him and Barnabas "the right hand of fellowship." From then on, Paul wrote, it was agreed "that we should go to the Gentiles and they to the circumcised," i.e., the Jews. Paul agreed to collect money on his travels for the poor in Jerusalem.

By lifting the requirement of circumcision and other legal strictures, Paul opened the way to a vastly increased audience. New tensions arose, however. Peter, while visiting Antioch, took meals with some Gentile Christians. The Jewish dietary laws forbade such fellowship, and Peter's action was taken as a signal that Jewish Christians need not follow them. But he came under intense criticism from a group aligned with James, and, quickly changing course, he gave up eating with Gentiles. Furious, Paul accused Peter of hypocrisy and broke with the Jerusalem church. From then on, he and the communities he founded would be on their own.

And there would be many of them. On his second missionary journey, begun around the autumn of 49, Paul (accompanied by Silas) traveled from Antioch to Tarsus, then, turning north, passed through the Taurus Mountains into Anatolia. After visiting the communities of converts he had made on his earlier journey, Paul continued on to Galatia, a Roman province in central Asia Minor, where he won over more Gentiles. Traveling westward across Anatolia, he and Silas reached the town of Troas on the northwestern coast of Asia Minor. Joined by Luke, they took a coastal boat across the mouth of the Dardanelles to the Aegean island of Samothrace and from there continued on to Neapolis on the coast of Macedonia.

Paul's arrival in this hillside town was a pivotal event in the history of the West—the moment when the new Christian gospel first arrived in Europe, a continent it would eventually capture. Proceeding to Philippi nine miles away, Paul baptized a cloth merchant named Lydia, making her the first Christian convert in Europe. After Paul performed an exorcism on a half-witted girl who was credited with the gift of divination, he was denounced by her guardian, then dragged into the marketplace and attacked by a mob. He was flogged, then thrown into prison along with Silas. Both, however, managed to escape.

Proceeding south to the larger town of Thessalonica, Paul on three successive Sabbaths preached his gospel in a local synagogue, winning over a number of Gentiles and some Jews, but a mob stirred up by his teachings forced him to leave, and he moved on to Athens. Here, in the intellectual capital of the empire, he preached about the crucifixion, the final days, and the resurrection, but he encountered much scorn and so hurried on to Corinth.

Located on the narrow neck of land that connects the Greek mainland to the Peloponnesus, with ports to both the east (serving the Aegean Sea) and the west (serving the Ionian), Corinth was known for its rowdiness, with a district of taverns, brothels, and gaming halls that catered to visiting merchants and sailors. It also had many entrepreneurs and artisans who had come from around the empire in search of a better life. Paul quickly won over Aquila and Priscilla, a Jewish Christian couple who had left Rome as part of a general expulsion ordered by Claudius, and with their help he cultivated Corinth's parvenus. He would remain for eighteen months, working as a tent maker by day and preaching and performing baptisms by night.

Once Corinth's converts seemed able to stand on their own, Paul sailed for Asia Minor and from there made his way back to Antioch. Now in his fifties, he could have been expected to relax after all the hardship and hostility he had faced, but he could think only of all the lands that had yet to be evangelized. Ephesus in particular beckoned. A great Hellenistic port and administrative center on the western coast of Asia Minor, it sat in one of the most densely populated regions of the Roman Empire, and Paul left for it (probably in the summer of 53) on his third great missionary journey. After passing through Galatia to check on the converts he had made there, he arrived in Ephesus (located about fifty miles south of modern-day Izmir, Turkey). For three months he preached in a local synagogue, but after several members of the congregation turned against him, he moved with his disciples to a nearby lecture hall. As word of his message about the crucified Christ spread, Paul made many converts in nearby towns, and, even more than Palestine, western Asia Minor would serve as the seedbed of Christianity.

But Ephesus was home to the giant temple of Artemis, and the local silversmiths and shopkeepers who sold charms and figurines there felt threatened by Paul's presence. He was thrown into prison. During the several months he remained there, he received disturbing reports from Galatia. The region had been visited by rival missionaries who had convinced a number of his Gentile converts that their salvation depended on the acceptance of not only Christ as Savior but also circumcision and the Jewish law in general. Incensed, Paul sent the Galatians an angry epistle. "I am astonished that you are so quickly deserting the one who called you in the grace of God and are turning to a different gospel," he declared. If anyone proclaimed to them a gospel contrary to the one he had preached, "let that one be accursed!" He went on to describe his gospel with blunt fury:

> We ourselves are Jews by birth and not Gentile sinners, yet we know that a person is justified not by the works of the law but through faith in Jesus Christ. And we have come to believe in Christ Jesus, so that we might be justified by faith in Christ, and not by doing the works of the law, because no one will be justified by the works of the law.

Justification was the process by which a person became just, or righteous, in God's eyes, thus becoming worthy of salvation. Works of the law were the ordinances and commandments of the Torah. Such works, Paul insisted, had no value in attaining salvation; only faith in Christ mattered. All who relied on the works of the law were "under a curse." The law had served as a source of discipline prior to the coming of Christ, but now that he had arrived, it was no longer necessary, "for in Christ Jesus you are all children of God through faith."

Here, in the second and third chapters of Galatians, Paul was making a definitive break with Judaism, rejecting not just circumcision and the dietary laws but the Torah as a whole as unnecessary for salvation. He was in effect replacing the old covenant between God and Israel with a new covenant in which justification comes through faith in Christ. The law was "a yoke of slavery," and all who sought to be justified by it had cut themselves off from Christ. As for his rivals, Paul expressed his hope that they "would castrate themselves!"

Being freed from the law did not mean giving in to self-indulgence, Paul warned the Galatians. Rather, they should love one another. "For the whole law is summed up in a single commandment, 'You shall love your neighbor as yourself.'" That commandment came from Leviticus 19:18; that is, from the same Jewish law that Paul was so adamantly rejecting. Obeying it meant shunning fornication, strife, jealousy, anger, and drunkenness and embracing joy, peace, generosity, gentleness, and self-control. Such acts of love were essential, Paul maintained, but they could not make one just in God's eyes; only faith in Christ could.

With its bold rejection of the law and its grand proclamation of faith, the Epistle to the Galatians has been called the Magna Carta of Christian liberty. With its insistence that the Five Books of Moses had been superseded by faith in Christ, however, it would drive a shattering wedge between Jews and Christians.

Paul's dismissal of the law also raised urgent practical concerns. If performing works of the law could not lead to salvation, what would make people behave morally? In fact, Paul soon learned that the converts he had won in Corinth—convinced that their faith was all that mattered—were engaging in all sorts of licentious behavior, including quarreling, drunkenness, bringing lawsuits against one another, and committing sexual acts of a kind found not even among the pagans.

Hurriedly drafting an epistle to the Corinthians, Paul expressed his disgust: "Do not be deceived! Fornicators, idolaters, adulterers, male prostitutes, sodomites, thieves, the greedy, drunkards, revilers, robbers—none of these will inherit the kingdom of God." He expressed his wish that all were like himself, i.e., celibate, but that since this was not possible for most, he added, "it is better to marry than to be aflame with passion." Paul condemned divorce and deemed it "shameful" for women to speak in church. "If there is anything they desire to know, let them ask their husbands at home." (These statements would later be used to justify a subordinate status for women in the Roman Church.) Paul expanded on the call for love he had directed at the Galatians. "If I speak in the tongues of mortals and of angels, but do not have love, I am a noisy gong or a clanging cymbal," he wrote, introducing what would become known as his love hymn. "And if I have prophetic powers, and understand all mysteries and all knowledge, and if I have all faith, so as to remove mountains, but do not have love, I am nothing."

After being freed from prison, Paul—receiving continuing reports of dissolute behavior in Corinth—decided to pay that city another visit. He would spend three months there, exhorting its converts to show their faith in Christ by behaving virtuously. In his spare time, he began planning a new journey, to Spain, where he hoped to open a western front in his evangelization campaign. On the way, he intended to stop in Rome. To introduce himself to its fledgling Christian community, he prepared a letter for them. Given Rome's importance as the imperial capital, Paul decided to offer a broad overview of his thinking. And so, in this seaport of sailors, merchants, and prostitutes, the wandering tent maker in the year 55 or 57 composed an epistle that, more than any other Christian document, would provide the theological foundation for the new faith—and a lifeline for Martin Luther.

The Epistle to the Romans is not only one of the most important religious documents ever written but also one of the most obscure. That is due, in part, to the harried circumstances in which it was drafted. Paul almost certainly had no intention of composing a formal doctrinal treatise; rather, he dictated the letter in haste, with little revising or polishing. That helps explain its dangling clauses, mixed-up word order, and sudden transitions. At bottom, though, the document's complexity reflected Paul's ongoing struggle to balance the competing claims of law and faith, deeds and beliefs.

The difficulties begin at the very outset. After greeting the followers of Christ in Rome and expressing his eagerness to carry the gospel to them, Paul at 1:16–17 offers a clear statement of his core principle: God offers salvation "to everyone who has faith, to the Jew first and also to the Greek," for in the gospel the righteousness of God is revealed "through faith for faith; as it is written, 'The one who is righteous will live by faith.'" This is the passage mentioned by Luther in his 1545 autobiographical fragment. (The quote is from the Old Testament book of Habakkuk, a minor Hebrew prophet.) Paul goes on to denounce the ungodly and their sins, including covetousness, murder, gossip, and the indulging of "degrading passions."

In chapter 2, however, Paul—abruptly shifting course—warns that God will repay each according to his deeds. Those who "by patiently doing good" seek glory and honor will be rewarded with "eternal life," while those "who are self-seeking" and shun truth will receive "wrath and fury." It is not "the hearers of the law who are righteous in God's sight, but the doers of the law who will be justified." These passages seem to run directly counter to Paul's insistence just a few lines earlier that one cannot be justified by doing works of the law. And by the end of the chapter he has returned to his earlier position, chiding those who, relying on the law, boast of their adherence to it and of their relation to God.

The inconsistency in these first two chapters has perplexed scholars down to this day. In chapter 3, however, Paul forcefully and unequivocally restates his position on the primacy of faith: since all have sinned and fallen short, they are made just by the gift of divine grace, through the redemption worked by Christ, "effective through faith." A person "is justified by faith apart from works prescribed by the law." In these key verses (3:21–28), Paul describes his views about the redemptive power of faith—and the futility of works—more emphatically than at any other point in his writings.

He goes on to offer an audacious retelling of the history of sin and salvation. Sin, Paul observes in chapter 5, came into the world through the transgression of Adam, and through that sin came death; since all have sinned, death spread to all. As developed by Augustine, this passage would become the scriptural foundation for the doctrine of original sin. While many have died through this one man's trespass, Paul continues, many more would receive the free gift of grace conferred by God through Christ, leading to eternal life. The catastrophe caused by Adam's disobedience was thus overcome by the miracle of Christ's death and resurrection.

Though God sent his Son in fleshly form to redeem mankind from its sin, not everyone will be saved. At 8:29–30, Paul sets out his views on predestination: God foreknows and predestines those whom he will justify. Those whom he predestined "he also called; and those whom he called he also justified; and those whom he justified he also glorified." From these brief passages would spring all the bitter controversies that for centuries would rage over the doctrine of predestination.

In another momentous passage (chapters 9–11), Paul describes the respective parts played by Jews and Christians in God's plan for the world. Though God had made a covenant with the children of Israel through Abraham, they never attained righteousness, because their efforts were based on deeds rather than faith. Gentiles, who did not strive for righteousness, had attained it, through their faith in Christ. Because the Jews had stumbled, salvation would come to the Gentiles. But God had not completely rejected Israel. A remnant of it would be saved, but by grace rather than works. Those who "do not persist in unbelief" will be grafted in with those who will be saved. These passages would add to the Jews' fury against Paul.

In the last section of his letter, Paul turned from theological speculation to practical admonition: People should love one another, hate what is evil, hold fast to what is good. They should rejoice in hope, be patient in suffering, extend hospitality to strangers. "Bless those who persecute you" and "weep with those who weep. Live in harmony with one another; do not be haughty, but associate with the lowly; do not claim to be wiser than you are." If your enemies are hungry, you should feed them; if they are thirsty, you should give them drink. "Owe no one anything, except to love one another; for the one who loves another has fulfilled the law."

As these passages show, Paul considered moral conduct essential; he just did not think it could lead to salvation. Good works were important but secondary; they were the product of justification, not the cause. Paul's downgrading of works would extend into the political sphere as well. In chapter 13, he issued his famous injunction (which would be so critical to Luther) to "let every person be subject to the governing authorities," for they have been "instituted by God." Since faith was all, political resistance was irrelevant.

Paul's intense focus on faith would set him apart from not just the Jews but also the Jewish Christians in Jerusalem. Sometime after Paul wrote Romans, James the Just (or, more probably, a follower writing in his name) prepared a letter that reads like a direct rebuttal of it. Whoever keeps the whole law "but fails in one point," he wrote, "has become accountable for all of it." A person "is justified by works and not by faith alone."

What good is it, my brothers and sisters, if you say you have faith but do not have works? Can faith save you? If a brother or sister is naked and lacks daily food, and one of you says to them, "go in peace, keep warm and eat your fill," and yet you do not supply their bodily needs, what is the good of that? So faith by itself, if it has no works, is dead.

Offering his own practical rules for piety, James urged his readers to act humbly, avoid gossip, shun selfish ambition, love one's neighbor as oneself, and help the less fortunate. The rich who keep back the wages of their workers should tremble for the miseries that will befall them. "Religion that is pure and undefiled before God, the Father, is this: to care for orphans and widows in their distress, and to keep oneself unstained by the world."

"Orphans and widows" has become a sort of shorthand for the type of ethics-based spirituality at the core of James's teaching. For him, faith, while important, could not on its own lead to salvation; it had to be backed up by conduct.

To a degree, the difference between the Pauline and Jamesian approaches was one of emphasis. For Paul, works performed without faith could degenerate into a grudging compliance with the law, undertaken out of fear of punishment or expectation of reward. For James, faith not backed by works could become mere lip service, an exercise in hypocrisy and sanctimony. Still, their theologies represented two distinct visions of piety—the one based in faith in the risen Christ, the other in the doing of Christlike works; the one stressing belief, the other conduct. Between them, they defined two strands within Christianity that would remain present and in competition over the ages and that would periodically erupt into open conflict—including in the early sixteenth century.

Initially, the Pauline strand seemed destined to fade away, parallel to Paul's own tragic end. Before leaving for Rome, he decided to travel to Jerusalem to deliver the contributions to the poor that he had collected on his missions. On his arrival, around 58, he clashed with both Jews and Jewish Christians. At the urging of some of the latter, he agreed to undergo a seven-day purification ritual in the Holy Temple. As it was nearing its end, he was recognized by some Jews from Asia Minor, who, angry over his rejection of the Jewish law, attacked him and dragged him from the Temple. Only the intervention of a group of Roman soldiers saved him from being beaten to death. After he was arrested and ordered flogged by a Roman tribune, Paul declared that he was a Roman citizen, and he was moved to a prison in Caesarea on the Mediterranean coast. After two years, an effort was finally made to bring him to trial, but Paul—asserting his rights as a citizen—requested a proceeding in Rome.

His appeal granted, he was put on a ship bound for the coast of Asia Minor. There, he was transferred to an Alexandrian vessel heading for Italy. Encountering rough waters, the ship was driven out to sea off Crete, and those on board drifted for fourteen days without food. As it approached an island, the ship ran aground on a reef. At Paul's urging, everyone jumped into the water; clinging to driftwood, all managed to make it ashore. The island turned out to be Malta. After three months there, Paul was put on another ship, which took him to Puteoli, near what is now Naples, and from there he walked to Rome. He had finally made it to the imperial capital, but as a prisoner rather than a proselytizer.

Paul's fate in Rome is unclear. According to Acts, he was kept under house arrest for two years but allowed to teach all who came to see him. According to Christian tradition, he and Peter were in Rome at the same time and both were swept up in the persecution of Christians ordered by Nero after the fire that engulfed Rome in the year 64. The two are said to have been executed on the same day in that year or a short time afterward—Peter crucified in the city and Paul beheaded on the Ostian Road, a short distance outside it.

Meanwhile, the Jews in Palestine were revolting against Rome. Their uprising (lasting from 66 to 70) was put down with singular brutality. The Holy Temple was destroyed, Jerusalem was devastated, and the Jews were forced to scatter. The Jerusalem church collapsed, but in the resulting vacuum the Gentile churches that Paul had helped organize in the Diaspora flourished. Paul's gospel, with its promise of spiritual transformation and eternal life, took hold in the crowded cities and towns of the Mediterranean. The small colony of Christians in Rome to whom Paul had written from Corinth grew into a powerful force that would eventually challenge and displace the empire itself. By the year 200, Paul's letters had been incorporated into the New Testament canon. Thanks in large part to the Apostle's drive and vision, Christianity captured Europe, and the cross became its supreme symbol.

But Paul's faith-centered interpretation was only one current in the New Testament. Another was offered by the Gospels of Matthew, Mark, and Luke, which contained the Sermon on the Mount and the parables and which highlighted Jesus's works of kindness, compassion, and mercy. (The Gospel of John, with its stress on the crucifixion and resurrection, has more in common with Paul's letters.) James's epistle itself was eventually included in the New Testament, reflecting a desire by the Church Fathers to acknowledge the importance of works and the law. As the Church faced the practical task of encouraging ethical conduct among the laity, it inclined more and more in a Jamesian direction. That emphasis grew during the Middle Ages, with Scholastic theologians (influenced by Aristotle) asserting the importance of doing all that is within one. By the late fifteenth century, good works had come to be seen as a crucial part of saving faith.

Paul himself receded in importance. His letters seemed to deal with ancient disputes over arcane differences with little relevance to contemporary concerns. In the *Sentences*, Peter Lombard cited Augustine far more often than he did Paul. Few churches were named after him, and painters and sculptors neglected him as a subject.

Yet as the movement *ad fontes* gained force, interest in Paul revived as well. As the earliest surviving Christian documents, his epistles provided a valuable resource to those hoping to recover the spirit of the early Church. At Oxford, John Colet drew large crowds with his lectures aimed at bringing Paul and his world to life. Erasmus in the *Enchiridion* urged readers to make themselves "completely familiar" with the Apostle and "keep him in your heart at all times." And, in 1512, Jacques Lefèvre d'Étaples came out with a Latin translation of Paul's epistles, with a commentary stating that man can be saved not by good works but by faith in God and the conferring of his grace.

Luther had a copy of Lefèvre's translation and commentary as he prepared for his lectures on Romans, in the weeks prior to Easter 1515. From his notes, it is clear that he had not advanced much beyond the understanding he had arrived at during his lectures on the Psalms. "The sum and substance of this letter," his scholia begin, "is: to pull down, to pluck up, and to destroy all wisdom and righteousness of the flesh," no matter "how heartily and sincerely they may be practiced." He scoffs at those Jews and Gentiles who are inwardly pleased with themselves and "praise themselves in their hearts as righteous and good men." As Luther makes his way through chapters 1 and 2, his discussion grows ever more dense and tangled. He ponders the four stages of perdition, the threefold way in which God is proved truthful, and the two ways in which the phrase "separated unto the gospel of God" can be understood.

When he reaches 3:19–20, however, something remarkable happens. This is the point at which Paul begins his long and forceful discussion of the distinction between the law and faith. Perking up, Luther observes that Paul, in distinguishing between these two categories, also distinguishes between the works associated with them. By works of the law, Paul means those acts that the law compels through the fear of punishment or the promise of reward. By works of faith, Paul means those acts done in a spirit of liberty and love of God. The works of the law cannot contribute anything toward making a person righteous; on the contrary, they are a hindrance because they keep one from seeing oneself as unrighteous.

Luther goes on to offer a parable: Suppose a layman outwardly performs all the functions of a priest. He celebrates Mass, pronounces absolution, and administers the sacraments. Outwardly, these acts seem like those of a real priest; the layman, in fact, may even perform them more skillfully than a priest would. But because the layman has not been ordained, he actually enacts nothing but "merely puts on a play and deceives himself and his friends." So it is with works performed according to the law. A man cannot become justified by such deeds. Rather, he can become justified only "by something else, namely, by faith in Christ."

Faith in Christ: this phrase, which had appeared fleetingly in Luther's commentary on the Psalms, suddenly grabs hold of him. There's a quickening in his notes as he begins to explore the theological implications of Paul's idea that only faith in Christ can justify a man before God. He who seeks to become righteous by the law may do finer and more splendid works than a man who is justified by faith, but he is not really justified and in fact may be even more hindered in becoming righteous in God's eyes. He who does have faith, by contrast, can become just apart from performing such acts.

From the Psalms, Luther had concluded that one could not become just in God's eyes by doing good works. Now, in reading Paul, he can finally see how one *could* become just: through faith. Here, in his notes on the last section of the third chapter of Paul's Epistle to the Romans, Luther begins to formulate the idea that would become the heart of his new gospel: man is justified by faith alone.

Seizing on this revelation, Luther excitedly explores its implications. Faith, he declares, cannot be selective—it is either a "whole faith" or "no faith at all." A man who denies Christ in one aspect denies him in all aspects. That is the way of heretics. Invoking this or that feature of Christ, they insist that their own understanding surpasses that of all believers. Similarly, the Jews believe in much that the Church does, but because they deny Christ, "they perish in their faithlessness." There are others who, recognizing their unrighteousness, think that they can become righteous through prayer, suffering, and confession, without faith in Christ. But this is impossible, for righteousness is given only through such faith. "So it has been determined, so it pleases God, and so it will be."

As for those who do believe, Luther explains, they will always retain some inclination toward evil. Because of our nature, we will always be prone to lust, boastfulness, and pride. Those who realize this are "the new people, the believing people, the spiritual people." With a sigh of the heart and the toil of the body, they seek and pray to be made just in God's eyes, "ever and ever again until the hour of death."

As Luther relates this, it is clear that he considers himself one of these new people. His comments seem to flow from someone who, feeling the lifting of a great burden, experiences a swelling of the heart—who feels born anew. Luther's very language lightens. He describes the "thousand tricks" by which the Devil pursues us. Some he leads astray by tempting them into obvious sins. Others, who consider themselves righteous, he causes to become complacent, so that they give up longing for betterment. Still others he seduces into "fanaticism and ascetic sectarianism," so that they seek to do good works "with a feverish zeal" that fills them with pride and drives them to despise others.

Finally—and here Luther seems to be speaking of himself—there are those whom the Devil urges on "to the foolish enterprise of trying to become pure and sinless saints." He keeps them in terror before God's judgment and exhausts their conscience "almost to the point of despair." Because these people strive so fervently to be righteous, it is not easy to tempt them into straying. Instead, the Devil initially helps them in their effort to become righteous, and so they prematurely conclude that they have rid themselves of all selfish striving. Then, when they discover that they cannot accomplish this, "he makes them sad, dejected, despondent, desperate, and utterly upset in their conscience." For this group, there is nothing left but for them to set their hope on the mercy of God and pray fervently that they may be freed from their sins.

Man, Luther observed, "is like a convalescent: if he is in too much of a hurry to get well, he runs the chance of suffering a serious relapse; therefore, he must let himself be cured little by little and must bear it for a while that he is feeble. It is enough that our sin displeases us, even though it does not entirely disappear. Christ bears all sins, if only they displease us, for then they are no longer our sins but his, and his righteousness is ours in turn."

After all the years of fumbling in the darkness of the monastery, Luther in the third chapter of Romans had finally found the idea that would set him free from its oppressive demands. Paul's denunciation of the law, issued in the heat of battle over whether Gentiles had to uphold the Mosaic code, seemed to Luther to apply to the rules of his order and, more generally, to the many regulations and prohibitions stipulated by the medieval Church. With the Apostle's guidance, Luther was now finding his own pathway to Christ. The gate to paradise was swinging open.

Buoyed by his new awareness of the importance of faith over works, Luther—moving into the fourth chapter of Romans—angrily turns on those who he can now see had led him astray: the Scholastic theologians. Outrageously, they had taught that original sin, like actual sin, can be entirely removed through good works, "as if sins were something that could be moved in the flick of an eyelash, as darkness is by light." But the tinder of sin—concupiscence—always remains, and no one can escape it. "Fool that I was," Luther cries, "I could not understand, in light of this, in what way I should regard myself as a sinner like others," inasmuch as "I had contritely made confession of my sins" and thus thought that those sins had been removed. It was "sheer madness to say that a man can love God above everything by his own powers." "O you fools, you pig-theologians!" he erupted, breaking into German. "Hui! Go to work, please! Be men! Try with all your powers to eliminate these covetings that are in you! Give proof of what you say," that it is possible to love God with all one's strength and "without grace!"

As he proceeds, Luther offers a weary lament: "I have been in the grind of these studies for, lo, these many years and am worn out by it, and, on the basis of long experience, I have come to be persuaded that it is a vain study doomed to perdition." His language sharpening, he calls the subtle doctors foolish perverters whose teachings are full of "utter stupidity." His favorite term for them is *iustitiarii*, which literally means "justifiers" but which for Luther connotes something like "works-mongers"—those who seek to accumulate merits in the ledger books of salvation. (Remarkably, the Jews, whom Luther had so violently assailed in his scholia on the Psalms, are largely absent from his notes on Romans. Now that he has identified the Scholastics as the main source of his misery, the Jews no longer need serve as scapegoats. The medieval theologians were the true Judaizers!)

As Luther makes clear, he did not take works to refer only to rituals and ceremonies. Paul, he wrote, rejected not only those parts of Scripture that deal with rites but "every teaching that prescribes what constitutes the good life whether it is to be found in the Gospel or in Moses." This included even the Ten Commandments. Extrapolating from Paul, Luther was rejecting the saving power of not just formal devotions like the veneration of saints and the worship of relics but the entire moral code, and he fumed at those "who have turned the gospel into a law rather than interpret it as grace, and who set Christ before us as a Moses."

On reaching the eighth chapter of Romans, Luther welcomed Paul's comments on predestination. While many find this teaching "bitter and hard," he noted, God has chosen it "to show that he saves us not by our merits but by sheer election and his immutable will" and thus "renders vain the efforts of so many grasping and very fierce adversaries." For Luther, the doctrine of predestination, by making clear the futility of trying to earn one's way to salvation, offered great comfort.

Luther was fully aware of the radical nature of these ideas—so much so that he seems to have omitted many of them from his actual lectures. The notebooks of several of those who attended have survived, and in them few of his more controversial statements appear. Not until four centuries later, when his notes finally surfaced, did these passages come to light. When they did, they showed how dramatically Luther was moving away from the reigning axioms of his day.

They also showed the gulf opening up between him and Erasmus. For the Dutch humanist, being a pious Christian meant above all heeding the teachings of Jesus as set forth in the Gospels. The works Erasmus rejected were formal ceremonies—lighting candles, making vows, chanting psalms without understanding them, celebrating the Mass without embracing its spirit. Works of an ethical nature, however, remained at the core of his teaching. While accepting Paul's teaching about the importance of faith, he felt that faith unaccompanied by works of charity and compassion or by a spirit of brotherhood and forbearance was stillborn.

To Luther, the performance of such acts, if not arising from faith, was not just useless but dangerous—a self-seeking expression that imparted a false sense of security. Erasmus based his spiritual vision on imitating the living Jesus; Luther, on faith in the crucified Christ. The same divide that had opened up between Paul and James in the middle of the first century was suddenly reappearing in the visions of these two Augustinian clerics.

As Luther began preparing his notes on the ninth chapter of Romans, there arrived from Basel a pathbreaking new edition of the New Testament—one that would both enrich his understanding of Paul and make clear his differences with Erasmus.

13

ANNUS MIRABILIS

Erasmus's crossing of the Channel for once went smoothly, and on the other shore he was reunited with his precious cargo. On July 7, 1514, he arrived in Hammes, near Calais, which was home to an English garrison then under the command of his friend Lord Mountjoy. From there he rode on toward Ghent. On the way, his horse, seeing some bright linen sheets spread on the ground, suddenly lurched, causing Erasmus to wrench his back. He was in such pain that he vowed he would write a commentary on Paul's Epistle to the Romans if he was able to make it to Ghent. He did make it, and he spent several days there recuperating. He then rode on to Louvain and Liège and, finally, the Rhine. While traveling up the river, Erasmus was astonished at what he found. In the towns along its banks, there had formed vibrant societies of scholars and poets dedicated to the New Learning. Putting in at these towns, Erasmus discovered that, while he had been toiling away in seclusion in England, he had become a celebrity among German humanists. The lively erudition of the *Adages*, the quiet piety of the *Enchiridion*, the clever sallies of the *Praise of Folly*—all had captivated these devotees of classical literature, and they celebrated Erasmus's appearance almost like a national holiday, as one participant put it.

In Strasbourg, the well-known printer Matthias Schürer had published new editions of several of Erasmus's works, including *De Copia*, to which he had appended a prefatory address hailing Erasmus as a hero of German letters. Magistrates, councilmen, vicars, and Jacob Wimpfeling, the town's leading literary figure, all came out to toast him. In Sélestat—a flourishing humanist center in Alsace—Erasmus was presented with three flagons of fine wine. In these cultured Rhenish centers, there was emerging an Erasmian movement made up of aspiring men of letters seeking a new design for living and looking to the itinerant scholar to provide it.

The acclaim continued in Basel. Arriving in August 1514, Erasmus at once felt at home in this tidy town, with its winding streets, stately homes, airy gardens, and mild climate. Located at the point where the Rhine bends majestically northward on its journey to the North Sea, Basel (with a population of about 6,000) was a commercial crossroads between Italy, Germany, and France and a gateway for river traffic all the way to the Low Countries. It was dominated by its cathedral, known as the Münster, a towering hulk of red sandstone that stood on a bluff overlooking the river. As a member of the Swiss Confederation, Basel was subject to no king or pope and so had an air of openness and tolerance. It had the oldest university in Switzerland, monastic libraries full of rare manuscripts, and paper mills powered by the streams that coursed through the town.

Thanks to such assets, Basel had become one of Europe's top printing centers. It had more than fifty printing houses, the most prominent of which was the house of Froben. It had been founded around 1475 by Johannes Amerbach with the aim of producing scholarly editions of the four Doctors of the Church; when he died, in 1513, Johann Froben assumed control along with Amerbach's three sons. Erasmus's arrival in Basel would mark the start of a partnership between Europe's greatest scholar and its most prestigious printer north of the Alps, with historic results.

A few days into his stay, Erasmus was welcomed at a banquet attended by leading figures at the university. "I seem to myself to be living in some delightful precinct of the Muses," he wrote, "to say nothing of so many good scholars, and scholars of no ordinary kind. They all know Latin, they all know Greek, most of them know Hebrew too; one is an expert historian, another an experienced theologian; one is skilled in mathematics, one a keen antiquary, another a jurist." There was only one irritant: the reeking stoves that warmed the houses—to suffocating excess, in Erasmus's view. Such "hothouses," as he called them, were common throughout Germany, and whenever he encountered one, his mood turned as foul as the air. Basel would nonetheless become the closest thing Erasmus had to a permanent home.

Like Aldus in Venice, Froben installed Erasmus right there in his shop. Along with the university, it was the main intellectual center in Basel, and at all hours scholars, poets, and linguists could be found mixing with pressmen, correctors, and colporteurs. In the weeks leading up to the spring and autumn book fairs in Frankfurt, carts would pull up to collect printed volumes and take them to the Rhine for transport to that city on the Main River, two hundred miles away.

Amid this commotion, Erasmus began the monumental task of preparing for the printers the great bundle of works that together offered his blueprint for a new Europe. First up was the new edition of the *Adages*. It would contain more than 3,400 entries, including the long essays denouncing despots and condemning war. Also being readied were revised editions of the *Praise of Folly, De Copia*, and the *Enchiridion*; a book on the use of similes; the critical edition of Seneca; translations of Plutarch and Lucian; and the Jerome.

Froben's edition of Jerome—the first collected edition of the works of the scholar-saint—was to fill nine volumes. Erasmus took charge of the first four, consisting of his letters, several polemical and apologetic tracts, and some works falsely ascribed to him. These volumes represented the culmination of the great project Erasmus had embarked on in 1500 to restore the reputation of the Church Father. "I believe that the writing of his books cost Jerome less than I spent in the restoring of them, and their birth meant fewer nightly vigils for him than their rebirth for me," Erasmus wrote in his dedicatory letter. He was referring to the hundreds of blunders he had removed, the Greek and Hebrew words he had corrected, and the spurious interpolations he had identified and excised, along with the extensive notes he had prepared explaining his editorial decisions.

To further enhance the hallowed scholar's stature, Erasmus prepared a "Life of Jerome"—a rare foray for him into the fields of history and biography. In it, he sought to shear away the many miracles and fables that had become attached to Jerome over the centuries and instead call attention to the true marvels of his life—his mastery of languages and literature and his outstanding work as a translator and interpreter of the Bible. "Who ever drew Sacred Scripture from the sources themselves as he did?" Erasmus asked. Who drank more deeply? Who had a more thorough knowledge of the philosophy of Christ, or expressed it more forcefully in his writings or his life? As such passages suggest, Erasmus's sketch was in its own way hagiographic, seeking to replace the cult of the desert hermit with the model of the pious scholar. He thus hoped to use Jerome as both a justification and a shield as he proceeded with his own project to use scholarship to restore the true spirit of the Holy Scriptures.

Even as he was editing Jerome, in fact, Erasmus was preparing his material on the New Testament—the cornerstone of his program to renew Christianity. He had with him hundreds of notes that he had written on scraps of paper during his years of studying Greek and Latin manuscripts and comparing them with the Vulgate. He may also have had the outlines of a revised translation of the Vulgate. Yet, on his arrival in Basel, Erasmus was not yet clear on what shape his new New Testament was to take; only over a period of months would the details fall into place as he consulted and negotiated with the house of Froben.

To that point, no edition of the Greek New Testament had been published. The first house to bring one out would earn a place in history, not to mention a hefty profit. In the university town of Alcalá near Madrid, a group of scholars had for years been preparing a six-volume edition of the Bible, called the Complutensian Polyglot (after Complutum, Alcalá's Latin name). Its first four volumes offered the Old Testament in parallel Hebrew, Aramaic, Greek, and Latin versions; the fifth offered the New Testament in parallel Greek and Latin (Vulgate) texts. (The sixth volume contained instructional aids.) The printing of the Greek New Testament was completed in January 1514, but the project's director, Francisco Jiménez de Cisneros, a cardinal who headed the Spanish Inquisition, wanted the pope's approval before placing it on the market, and that approval had not yet come. (It would in fact not arrive until 1520, and the edition would not be officially published until 1522.)

Eager to be the first on the market, Froben urged Erasmus to prepare a Greek text for inclusion in his edition. The pioneering nature of the project appealed to Erasmus, as did the opportunity it would give readers to check his notes on the Vulgate against the Greek, and so he agreed. To produce such an edition, however, he needed manuscripts on which to base it. The library of the Dominican chapter in Basel, he learned, had a half-dozen codices containing various parts of the Greek New Testament. Cardinal Ivan Stojković of Ragusa in Dalmatia had brought them to the city while attending the Council of Basel in 1431. On his death twelve years later, he left the manuscripts to the Dominicans. Examining them for accuracy, Erasmus hoped to find one that, with a quick edit, could serve as a base text for the printers. Unfortunately, none of the manuscripts contained Revelation, the final book of the New Testament. A codex that did have it had been borrowed by Johannes Reuchlin. Erasmus wrote to him to ask to borrow it, and Reuchlin promptly sent it off.

Over the summer of 1514, Erasmus seems to have worked on both his annotations and his new translation of the Vulgate. On September 21, in a letter to Jacob Wimpfeling in Strasbourg, he for the first time described in full the shape of his New Testament: "My *Adagia* has now begun to be printed. There remains the New Testament translated by me, with the Greek facing, and notes on it by me." Erasmus's decision to publish a new Latin translation would be an even bolder step than printing the Greek New Testament, for it would suggest changes in a text long regarded as sacred and immutable. In 1512, however, the French humanist Jacques Lefèvre d'Étaples had come out with a new Latin translation of the Pauline Epistles, setting a precedent. Erasmus now prepared to offer a new translation of the entire New Testament—not a complete top-to-bottom translation but rather a revision of the Vulgate to make it clearer and more graceful. Froben was eager to publish it, but Erasmus—perhaps holding out for the best possible deal—was not yet ready to commit.

At this key moment in his publishing career, Erasmus in March 1515 decided to make a sudden trip to England. The reason is not clear; most likely, he wanted to inspect some manuscripts for his work on Jerome and the New Testament as well as to renew contacts with friends and potential patrons. He sent ahead to England a box containing materials on Jerome that he was working on. To keep the Froben presses busy while he was gone, he left behind a number of manuscripts to be printed, including his edition of Seneca, his translations of Plutarch and Lucian, and the first volumes of the Jerome edition.

While en route, Erasmus received a letter from Beatus Rhenanus, an assistant to Froben, with an urgent plea: "Froben is asking if he may have your New Testament and says he will give you as much for it as you could get anywhere else," it stated. Rhenanus further noted that only 600 of the

1,800 copies of the new edition of the *Praise of Folly* printed by Froben remained, so a second printing was being readied. Rhenanus also observed that the Seneca was making progress but warned that the manuscript was full of errors.

After a Channel crossing that was difficult but rapid, Erasmus met with some of his English friends, including Archbishop William Warham, who provided some support, and Cardinal Wolsey—by now the real power in Henry's government. A month or so into his stay, however, Erasmus grew nervous about the handling of his manuscripts by the printers and so decided to return to Basel. Passing through Bruges and then continuing on to Antwerp, he found waiting for him an ominous letter from Martin Dorp, a twenty-nine-year-old lecturer in philosophy at the University of Louvain, whom Erasmus knew from his visits there. The letter offered the first sign of the backlash that was building over Erasmus's work. After offering the obligatory expressions of respect, Dorp noted that Erasmus's books had turned many people against him, including some of his most enthusiastic supporters. The main source of complaint was the *Praise of Folly*. In the old days, Dorp observed, "everyone admired you, they all read you eagerly, and now, lo and behold, this wretched Folly . . . had upset everything. Your style, your fancy, and your wit they like; your mockery they do not like at all, not even those of them who are bred in the humanities."

Dorp had also heard about Erasmus's plan to revise the Scriptures. What sort of business was this, he asked, "to correct the Latin copies by means of the Greek"? The Vulgate "contains no admixture of falsehood or mistake." It was not reasonable that the whole Church, in using this edition, "should for all these centuries have been wrong." Nor was it probable that all the Holy Fathers and all the saintly men who had relied on it "should have been deceived." That the Vulgate's Latin could have been more elegant was widely acknowledged, but if anyone were to show him that a sentence in the Latin varied from that in a Greek manuscript, "at that point I bid the Greeks goodbye and cleave to the Latins, for I cannot persuade myself that the Greek manuscripts are less corrupted than the Latin ones." Even if Erasmus simply pointed out places where the Greek manuscripts differed from the Latin, many people would develop doubts about the text. In light of all this, he beseeched Erasmus to limit his project and emend "only those passages in the New Testament where you can retain the sense and substitute something that gives the meaning more fully."

Reading Dorp's letter, Erasmus felt sure that it was written at the behest of powerful members of the Louvain faculty. Those men could make his life very difficult, and so, though still queasy from the Channel crossing, he prepared a strongly worded (and long-winded) reply. He could hardly believe the "peevish pedantry" of those who took offense at a "single humorous piece" like the *Folly*. His aim was no different from the one he had pursued in the *Enchiridion*—to offer "guidance and not satire; to help, not to hurt; to show men how to become better and not to stand in their way." Rather than try to mollify the aggrieved theologians, Erasmus heaped even more scorn on them. Such men, he observed, "poke fun at Greek and Hebrew and even Latin, and, though as stupid as pigs and not equipped with the common feelings of humankind, they suppose themselves to hold the citadel of all wisdom." Erasmus seemed unmindful of the anger such taunts might cause.

He was no less unyielding on the subject of Scripture. Noting the many points at which old Greek and Latin manuscripts diverged from the Vulgate, Erasmus wondered how Dorp could cling so tightly to the latter. He was even more mystified by Dorp's suggestion that Greek manuscripts could not be trusted. The same people who considered Greek exegetes renegades had turned the pagan Aristotle into an unassailable authority. What the theologians really feared in the use of Greek codices was the challenge these posed to their authority. Whenever they misquoted Scripture, they would now have the truer version drawn from the Greek and Hebrew thrown in their teeth. Surely there was no danger that someone would suddenly "abandon Christ" if he happened to hear that in the sacred books a drowsy scribe had corrupted something or that some unknown translator had made a poor rendering. When his revision finally appeared, Erasmus predicted, Dorp would offer his congratulations on the great advance in scholarship it represented.

In this exchange, Dorp and Erasmus were reenacting the great debate over Scripture that Augustine and Jerome had had more than a millennium earlier. Did any individual, however learned, have the right to alter a biblical text that had for centuries been used and authorized by the Church? Were the words of Scripture sacrosanct, even in translation? Which should take precedence in interpreting the Bible, the weight of tradition or the expertise of scholars? In their ardor and urgency, the letters between Dorp and Erasmus echoed the epochal controversies of the past—and anticipated the deep rumblings ahead.

Erasmus's arrival back in Basel in July 1515 would mark the start of the annus mirabilis of his career, when, in a frenzied push, he would bring to completion the many projects he had been laboring on for the past fifteen years, with the revised New Testament towering over everything else. His conversations with Colet at Oxford; his discovery of Valla's annotations in the monastery outside Louvain; his intensive study of pagan and patristic literature; his exhausting efforts to master Greek; his careful inspection of old manuscripts—all had led him to this critical moment, when he was going to apply the tools of syntax and semantics to restore Christianity's most sacred text and thereby revitalize a continent sunk in violence, malice, and greed.

Erasmus wanted to have the New Testament ready for the Frankfurt fair the following spring—a goal that, given the scale of the project, would keep him tethered to Froben's shop for the next six months. The conditions were far from ideal. In the printing of Scripture, precision and meticulousness are essential, for every word is invested with meaning, and even the smallest mistake can set off tremors. But Erasmus had before him a jumble of old manuscripts, rough drafts, and scribbled notes that he had to organize even as the printers around him were setting type, mixing ink, and operating the presses.

The first order of business was the Greek text. Among the manuscripts in the Dominican collection, Erasmus had found one that was complete (except for Revelation) and neatly copied, but—suspecting that it had been corrected against the Vulgate—he rejected it in favor of other manuscripts that seemed older and more authentic. Unfortunately, these texts were filled with spelling mistakes and scribal blunders, so Erasmus had to compare them with other manuscripts to determine the most likely reading. When he arrived at it, he jotted it down between the lines and in the margins. Where the Greek was unclear or lacked words that were in the Vulgate, Erasmus translated from the Latin back into Greek—an egregious violation of the rules of critical editing. Given the time pressure he was under, however, he felt he had no choice, and in any case the Greek text was of secondary concern to him.

Far more important was the revised Latin translation, for many more people would read it. Erasmus had by now come to an agreement with Froben to print it. The New Latin text was to appear in parallel columns with the Greek. Erasmus sought to alter the Vulgate in the hundreds of places where it seemed most obviously defective. Where there were textual corruptions, he restored the original; where he found obscure or ambiguous passages, he offered clarifications; where the translation seemed ungrammatical, he proposed an alternative that seemed more faithful to the Greek. Along the way, Erasmus tried to better capture the plain, colloquial way in which he believed the apostles spoke. As he observed, "they had learned Greek not from the speeches of Demosthenes, but from popular speech." At the same time, Erasmus felt that the power of the Bible derived in part from its rhetorical force, and at certain places he modified the Latin to make it more elegant and thus heighten its impact. This willingness to tamper with Holy Writ for stylistic reasons would infuriate many traditionalists.

Central to Erasmus's New Testament were his annotations. These were his primary vehicle for communicating the mass of ideas and opinions about Scripture that he had developed during his long immersion in sacred studies. Many of the notes were narrowly technical in nature, pointing out places where the Vulgate's cases, tenses, and prepositions strayed from the Greek. Like Valla, he criticized the Vulgate for its lack of consistency in translation. He noted, for instance, that in the first chapter of John, the Vulgate gave the Greek word *phōs* ("light") as *lumen* in verse 7 but as *lux* in verse 8. Such variation, he argued, should be avoided—not because the translation was necessarily wrong but because it could lead readers into needless speculation about the shades of meaning intended.

Seeking to draw a contrast with the stuffiness of traditional commentators, Erasmus salted his annotations with ironic asides, disdainful interjections, and caustic judgments. And at many key points, he ventured far beyond the philological, using grammar to challenge interpretations that had reigned for centuries and hardened into dogma. In his preface to the edition of Valla's annotations that he had had printed in 1505, Erasmus had written that Theology should not be offended if her humble attendant Grammar offers to help with small details; his own annotations would show the explosive impact such tidying up could have. A good example occurred at Ephesians 5:32. Here, in the Vulgate, Paul refers to the sexual union of a man and his wife as a *sacramentum*—"sacrament." Partly on the basis of this passage, the Church had declared marriage one of the seven sacraments. In the Greek manuscripts, though, the word was given as *mysterion*—"mystery"—and so Erasmus in his own Latin translation decided to use *mysterium*. In his annotation, he briefly observed that marriage could not be considered a sacrament on the basis of this passage. With this tweak, Erasmus was raising questions about the sacramental status of a central institution.

He was even bolder at Romans 5:12. In the Vulgate, this passage read: "Wherefore as by one man sin entered the world and by sin death: and so death passed upon all men, in whom all have sinned." Augustine had maintained that the "one man" in question was Adam, and that it was he "in whom all have sinned." In other words, all men were doomed to sin because of Adam's original sin. Thus interpreted, this passage had become the foundation for the doctrine of original sin. In examining the Greek, however, Erasmus saw that the underlying term for the Latin *in quo* ("in whom") was ἐφ' ᾧ (*eph'ho*) and from the context he concluded that it was being used in the sense of "inasmuch as" or "since" we have all sinned. In other words, Erasmus explained, Paul meant to say not that man is doomed to sin because of Adam's original transgression but rather that death is a companion to sin and, inasmuch as all sin, death comes to all. Through this grammatical adjustment, Erasmus was challenging a central tenet of the faith.

With another subtle change, he struck at the cult of the Virgin Mary. At Luke 1:28 in the Vulgate, the angel Gabriel greets Mary, *Ave gratia plena*—"Hail, full of grace." Most medieval exegetes had interpreted *gratia plena* to mean that Mary was full of God's grace (as defined by medieval theologians) and so free of sin. But the underlying Greek word was κεχαριτωμένη (*kecharitomene*), and Erasmus, citing Homer and other authorities, observed that this was more commonly used in the sense of "beloved," as with a person held in affection. A better rendering, he felt, was *Ave gratiosa* ("Greetings, beloved one"), and he changed it to this in his translation. In so doing, Erasmus was casting doubt on the doctrine that Mary had remained free of sin through God's extraordinary grace. Going further, he noted that *kecharitomene* has a loving, amorous connotation. Without realizing it, Erasmus was opening himself to the charge that he was implying an improper relationship between Mary and the angel and so showing a lack of respect for her.

Even more controversial would be his handling of 1 John 5:7. In the Vulgate, this verse read, "And there are three that give testimony in heaven: the Father, the Word, and the Holy Spirit. And these three are one." Known as the *comma Johanneum* ("phrase of John"), this verse was the scriptural foundation for the doctrine of the Trinity. Yet none of the Greek manuscripts examined by Erasmus had it. Instead, they simply said, "There are three that bear witness: the Spirit, the water, and the blood, and these three are one." Jerome had conjectured that the *comma* had been inserted into the text by Latin scribes after the Council of Nicaea in 325 to refute the Arians. This early-fourth-century movement, which held that the Son, though the first creature, was neither equal to nor coeternal with the Father, had set off one of the most wrenching of all Christian disputes. In Erasmus's day, Arianism remained a heretical offense, and Church theologians relied on this passage to rebut it; omitting it would open Erasmus to charges of anti-Trinitarianism. Nonetheless, he decided to follow through on his scholarly instincts and drop it from his revised translation, explaining in his annotations that the words were missing from the Greek codices.

In the end, the most dramatic consequence would result from what was seemingly one of his most modest changes. It came at Matthew 3:2. Here, the Vulgate has John the Baptist saying, *Poenitentiam agite: appropinquavit enim regnum caelorum*—"Do penance: for the kingdom of heaven is at hand." From Valla, Erasmus had learned that the Vulgate's use of *poenitentia* in 2 Corinthians was a misleading rendering of the underlying Greek word μετάνοια (*metanoia*), meaning repentance or a change of mind. From his inspection of Greek manuscripts, Erasmus could see that, at Matthew 3:2 as well, the Greek word underlying *poenitentiam agite* was *metanoein*, the verb corresponding to the noun *metanoia*. In other words, John the Baptist was calling on people not to perform the sacrament of penance but to feel repentant within. Erasmus thus decided to change *poenitentiam agite* to *poeniteat vos*, meaning "repent," so that the passage read, "Repent: for the kingdom of heaven is at hand." As he explained in his annotation, "Our people think that *poenitentiam agite* means to wash away one's sins with some prescribed penalty," yet "*metanoia* is derived from *metanoein*, that is, to come to one's sense afterwards—when someone who sinned, finally, after the fact, recognizes his error." As small as this adjustment might seem, it put a powerful weapon in the hands of those beginning to question the sacrament of penance and the clergy's control over contrition and absolution.

Here, as throughout his notes, Erasmus sought to cast the New Testament as a summons to virtuous living rather than a collection of disconnected citations. At Luke 6:20, for example, where Jesus says, "Blessed are the poor," Erasmus wrote: "Christ's words are what make us true Christians, not the subtle arguments of Scotists and Ockhamists, nor the insipid, meaningless institutions of men." In a note to 1 Timothy 1:6, he warned that we must take care not to turn *theologia* into *mataiologia*—a word used by Paul to mean "idle talk" and which Erasmus took to signify "endless fighting about frivolous claptrap. Let us rather be concerned with those things that transform us into Christians and make us worthy of heaven. How important is it to argue in how many ways sin can be interpreted, whether it is only a privation or leaves a blot on the soul? Let the theologians rather effect that all men fear and hate sin."

Erasmus did not shrink from calling out theologians by name. Augustine, he wrote, "was undeniably a saint and a man of integrity endowed with a keen mind, but immensely credulous and, moreover, lacking the equipment of languages." On this last point, Augustine "was so inferior to Jerome that it would be impudent to compare one man with the other." Erasmus was even sharper toward Aquinas, deriding him for, among other things, working in haste, offering contrived explanations, obscuring the simple meaning of texts so as to support Church doctrines, suggesting ill-informed etymologies, and knowing only one language, "and not even that one fully." Again, he seemed heedless of the offense such comments might give.

As Erasmus neared the end of the project, he faced a delicate problem. In the Greek codex he had received from Reuchlin, the text of Revelation was embedded in a commentary by Andreas of Caesarea, a sixth-century exegete. The two texts were so closely entwined that it was hard to tell what was Scripture and what commentary, and the typesetter had so much trouble deciphering them that he introduced many errors. In about fifty places, moreover, the Greek text was so unclear that Erasmus had to translate from the Latin back into Greek. Finally, the codex lacked its final leaf and along with it the last six verses of Revelation. Since he could hardly issue a Bible without them, he decided to translate the verses from the Latin of the Vulgate into Greek—a mortal sin in sacred studies.

Through January and February 1516, two presses were devoted full-time to the project, with a ternion (twelve pages) produced every day. Erasmus kept expanding and revising his notes even "among the clanging of the presses," as his assistant Beatus Rhenanus put it. (As Erasmus would later admit, the New Testament was "rushed into print rather than published.") To help him, he had two assistants—Nicholas Gerbel, a doctor in canon law who was hired as a corrector, and Johannes Oecolampadius, who had studied under Reuchlin in Stuttgart and who knew not only Latin and Greek but also Hebrew. One of Oecolampadius's tasks was checking the New Testament quotations that were taken from the Septuagint against the original Hebrew of the Old Testament. Neither man was up to the job, however. As for the printers, they treated Erasmus's corrected manuscript as if it were any ordinary copy rather than a sacred text, and so many errors got through that Erasmus was obliged to take upon himself the revision of the final proofs.

This was an imperfect solution, however, for Erasmus hated proof-reading and was not very good at it. What's more, while racing to finish the New Testament, he had to deal with several other projects, including completing a treatise on governance that he planned to dedicate to Prince Charles of Burgundy, to whose advisory council he had recently been appointed. Throughout, Erasmus was interrupted by visitors, among them a messenger from Duke Ernst of Bavaria who conveyed the duke's readiness to pay him two hundred gold pieces a year if he would accept a chair at the University of Ingolstadt. (Erasmus graciously declined.)

On top of it all, Erasmus decided to prepare a series of prefaces for the New Testament, including an essay on exegetical methodology, an *Apologia* defending the revised Latin translation, a preface to the annotations, and, finally, a *Paraclesis* (Greek for "exhortation" or "summons"). In the last of these, Erasmus offered, more than in any other work, the clearest distillation of his religious ideals. Platonists, Pythagoreans, Stoics, and Epicureans all fully appreciate the doctrines of their sects, he wrote; why, then, were Christians so ignorant of the philosophy of Christ? While treasuring his sacraments, they paid little heed to his doctrines, "which offer the most certain happiness to all." He disagreed with those who objected to having the Bible translated into vernacular languages so that it could be read by the uneducated, "as if the strength of the Christian religion consisted in men's ignorance of it." Kings might want their mysteries kept concealed, but Christ wished his to be "published as openly as possible."

Then, in one of his most lyrical passages, Erasmus declared:

I would that even the lowliest women read the Gospels and the Pauline Epistles. And I would that they were translated into all the languages so that they could be read and understood not only by Scots and Irish but also by Turks and Saracens. . . . Would that, as a result, the farmer sing some portion of them at the plow, the weaver hum some parts of them to the movement of his shuttle, the traveler lighten the weariness of the journey with stories of this kind! Let all the conversations of every Christian be drawn from this source.

Christianity, Erasmus noted, is most truly taught not by trained theologians but by those who show by their very lives that riches should be disdained, that a wrong should not be avenged, that good should be wished for those deserving ill, and that death should be desired by the devout, "since it is nothing other than a passage to immortality." Anyone who, inspired by Christ, preaches to, inculcates, and exhorts men with such teachings "is indeed truly a theologian, even if he should be a common laborer or weaver."

At bottom, the *Paraclesis* was a radical call for broadening access to Scripture. Its central ideas—that the New Testament offers the truest expression of Christ's teachings; that the Bible is the common property of all Christians and so should be translated into all the languages; that the humblest laborer who embraces the way of Christ could be more pious than a priest or professor—would all be taken up by the reformers, especially Luther, who would give them a far more populist, and provocative, twist. In light of its future impact, the *Paraclesis* may have been the single most important thing Erasmus ever wrote.

Finally, on March 1, 1516, the New Testament was done. It was a handsomely produced folio of about a thousand pages. On some 550 of them, the Greek text and the revised Latin translation appeared in parallel columns; another 300 or so were filled with the annotations; the rest were given over to the prefaces and other introductory material. Erasmus decided to title the work *Novum Instrumentum* rather than *Novum Testamentum*, arguing that whereas a *testamentum* is a will or covenant that might or might not be written down, an *instrumentum* is a written document that establishes the terms of a pact or agreement and hence is a more accurate description of the Christian Scriptures. (Loudly criticized for tinkering with so hallowed a name, Erasmus would restore *testamentum* in later editions.) The volume opened with a three-page dedication to Pope Leo X. The total press run came to 1,200 copies.

The new edition of the New Testament was a milestone in biblical scholarship—indeed, in Western thought. For the first time, scholars had access to a printed edition of the New Testament in the language in which it had originally been written. Erasmus's text would become the foundation for all Western scholarship on the Greek New Testament for the next three centuries. In addition, his revised translation of the Vulgate offered alternative readings of many phrases that had been sanctified by centuries of use. Most pioneering of all were the annotations. In them, Erasmus argued for a new way of reading the Bible—for seeing it not as an infallible, divinely given text but as a literary document whose meaning could best be unlocked through a knowledge of grammar, philology, history, and classical culture. Erasmus thus sought to move the Bible from the realm of the God-given to that of the man-made. In this way, he hoped that the text would be read not as a collection of miracles, prophecies, and supernatural acts but as the story of a transcendent being whose simplicity, humility, and compassion could encourage readers to change their ways and follow a more pious path.

As copies began circulating, the magnitude of Erasmus's achievement was immediately recognized. "You have protected your name against all the assaults of time and completed a task as acceptable to almighty God as it is necessary and useful to all Christ's faithful," wrote Willibald Pirckheimer, Nuremberg's leading intellectual. "Well done, well done indeed. You have achieved a result that has been denied to all men this side of a thousand years." Gerardus Listrius, who in Basel had worked on the new edition of Erasmus's *Adages* and *Praise of Folly* and who was now the rector of a school in Zwolle, near Deventer, wrote that "all scholars and true Christians here are devoted to you." The *Novum Instrumentum* "is read eagerly here in Greek even by the aged." Many people, he added, "have been won over and inspired by what you write, and are now devoted to the study of Scripture and the Christian way of life," leaving behind the husks of the pagan authors.

Particularly sweet to Erasmus was the tribute he received from John Colet, who had provided the initial inspiration for the project. Copies of the New Testament, he wrote, were being "eagerly bought" and "everywhere read." Expressing regret at never having learned Greek, Colet said that he now intended to begin studying it despite his advanced age (he was nearing fifty). He also marveled at the fecundity of Erasmus's mind: "You conceive so much, have so much in gestation, and bring forth some perfectly finished offspring every day, especially as you have no certain abode and lack the support of any fixed, substantial endowment." Now, he added, he looked forward to getting a copy of the *Institutio Principis Christiani* ("The Education of a Christian Prince").

That was the title that Erasmus had given to the tract on governance that he had somehow managed to complete even while working on the New Testament. It was still in the presses when, in May 1516, he decided to leave Basel for the Low Countries. He wanted to pay his respects to Prince Charles and see what kind of stipend might be attached to his new position as councilor. He received a rousing send-off. "The number of horses that escorted my departure; the emotion with which they bade me farewell!" he wrote to Thomas More. The New Testament, he added, "wins approval even from the people I thought most likely to malign it; the leading theologians are delighted with it. My *Enchiridion* is universally welcome; the bishop of Basel carries it around with him everywhere—I have seen all the margins marked in his own hand."

By May 30, 1516, Erasmus was in Antwerp, where he stayed with his friend Pieter Gillis. To his delight, he found the Jerome on sale there. He took a break from writing so that he could tend to his desperate financial state. Andrea Ammonio in London was coordinating his efforts to obtain a papal dispensation that would allow him to hold one or more benefices despite his illegitimate birth and to wear only a symbolic version of his Augustinian habit (which he had abandoned many years earlier). In August Erasmus made a quick visit to England to consult with him. By the start of October he was in Brussels, where he took a small room near the Burgundian court and became absorbed in its affairs while exploring his prospects for promotion.

While in Brussels, Erasmus received from Thomas More a manuscript that he had recently completed about a fictional New World island. It was titled *Nusquama*—a play on the Latin for "no place." More asked for Erasmus's assistance in getting it published and in arranging "glowing testimonials," i.e., blurbs. Happy to oblige, Erasmus helped see it through the press of Dirk Martens in Louvain, and it would come out in late 1516 under the new title More had given it: *Utopia* ("No place" in Greek).

Interestingly, *Utopia* appeared around the same time that *The Education of a Christian Prince* was coming off the press in Basel. Not long before, Niccolò Machiavelli in Italy had completed *The Prince*. This was thus a formative moment in the history of political thought, when three distinct currents—utopian, Machiavellian, and Erasmian—made their debuts. Comparing Erasmus's work with the other two can help point up the distinctive nature of his own political program.

A Christian prince should have one main object, Erasmus wrote—to serve the public good. "Only those who dedicate themselves to the state, and not the state to themselves, deserve the title 'prince,'" he declared, and in his tract he offered guidance as to how to accomplish this. Central to his program was education. Because the progress of any state depends so heavily on the quality of its schools, the prince, Erasmus argued, should give them his utmost care, with special attention paid to girls. Taxation should be kept low so as not to oppress the people, but to the extent that it is necessary, the burden should fall most heavily on those most able to afford it. Since gross disparities of income can create so many problems, measures should be taken "to prevent the wealth of the many from being allocated to the few." The penalties for crimes should be kept light and aimed more at curing the disease than killing the patient. The state should establish public institutions to look after the sick and elderly and should boost the economy by improving its infrastructure—enhancing cities, constructing bridges, erecting public buildings, draining plague spots, diverting rivers whose courses are destructive, and ensuring that abandoned fields are tilled so as to increase the food supply.

In his own life, meanwhile, the prince should be a model of economy and moderation. Rather than undertake costly tours abroad, he should stay at home and tend to the welfare of his people. When he considers enlarging his retinue or making a brilliant marriage for his granddaughter or sister, he should keep in mind the many thousands of families that will go hungry and be forced into debt as a result of such a diversion of resources. Above all, the prince should avoid war—the greatest source of human misery. Even more forcefully than he had in *Dulce bellum inexpertis*, Erasmus questioned whether any war can be considered just. Any prince who succeeds in ending "this long-standing and terrible mania among Christians for war" and establishes peace and harmony "will have performed a far more dazzling deed than if he had subdued all Africa by arms."

Like Erasmus, Machiavelli had witnessed both the violent struggles for power in northern Italy and the bellicose actions of the Renaissance popes, but from them he had drawn very different conclusions. "A man who strives after goodness in his acts," he observed in *The Prince*, "is sure to come to ruin, since there are so many men who are not good." A prince, in pursuing his objectives, should feel free to show ruthlessness and deceit.

Ideally, a prince would be both loved and feared, but since that is rarely possible, he should strive to be feared (while avoiding being hated). Because war offers the most effective path to power, "a prince must have no other objective, no other thought, nor take up any profession but that of war, its methods and its discipline, for that is the only art expected of a ruler." As models of effective cruelty, Machiavelli held up Alexander the Great, Hannibal, Cesare Borgia, Ferdinand of Aragon (for despoiling the Marranos and driving them from his kingdom)—and Julius II. Unlike Erasmus, who condemned the pope's assault on Bologna, Machiavelli extolled it. With "characteristic fierceness and haste," he wrote, Julius had been able to accomplish what no other pope, exercising "all possible prudence," could have achieved. Julius's actions inspired one of Machiavelli's most oft-quoted aphorisms: "It is better to be impetuous than to be cautious, for fortune is a woman, and in order to be mastered she must be beaten and bullied."

Whereas Machiavelli in writing *The Prince* was grounded in hardheaded realism, Thomas More offered a beguiling alternative to reality. Appalled by the cruelty, injustice, and chaos of England, he conjured up in *Utopia* a society that is clean, egalitarian, and orderly. Everyone lives in one of fifty-four splendid towns all organized on the same plan, with modest houses set on tidy streets, and all meals taken communally. Everyone farms and works at a trade but for only six hours a day; since everyone works, this is all that is needed to provide the essentials. There are no wine taverns, alehouses, brothels, or secret meeting places allowing opportunities for seduction. There is no private property—everything is owned by the state. In fact, there is no privacy of any kind, for everyone is watched all the time. The Utopians disapprove of cosmetics, see no value in gems, use silver and gold to make chamber pots, and have no tailors or dressmakers, since everyone wears the same comfortable homemade clothes. They also have slaves, who consist mostly of convicts and condemned criminals from other countries; the slaves work in chain gangs and do all the butchering of animals so as to spare the locals such unpleasantness. In short, all of the basic needs of Utopia's citizens are met, though at a considerable cost in terms of freedom and privacy.

The world More created in *Utopia* was so imaginative and entertaining that it gave rise to an entire new genre of literature, including such works as Tommaso Campanella's *The City of the Sun*, Francis Bacon's *New Atlantis*, and Aldous Huxley's *Brave New World*. *The Prince* is no less original; never before had anyone so dared to dissociate political action from moral considerations. By comparison, *The Education of a Christian Prince* is prosaic and workmanlike. Unlike More and Machiavelli, Erasmus had no actual political experience and so relied heavily on Plato, Aristotle, and other classical thinkers. The main measure he proposed for ensuring enlightened rule—providing the future prince with a good humanist education—seems entirely inadequate. Preachy and plodding, *The Education of a Christian Prince* reads like a manual for good governance.

Yet its humdrum quality was precisely what made it distinctive. Whereas "utopian" came to suggest the unattainable and "Machiavellian" the amoral, "Erasmian" would come to mean practical, commonsense reform. At a time when Europe was beset by political rivalries, princely despotism, stark social inequities, and recurrent wars, Erasmus was urging its rulers to construct a more humane order based on the principle that the state should serve the people and the powerful should protect the weak—in short, to organize society along the lines of the Gospels. That, in the end, was the central idea underlying the sweeping reform program he had been working on for so many years.

And, remarkably, that program was catching on. The books, essays, and editions of Erasmus that were issuing from the presses were being bought, read, and avidly discussed in Germany and France, England and the Netherlands. The *Enchiridion*, with its vision of heartfelt piety practiced outside the monastery, would appear in fifteen editions over the next three years, emerging as the most influential humanist work north of the Alps. Jerome's letters were calling new attention to the vitality of the early Church, the *Adages* were advertising the wisdom of classical culture, and the *Praise of Folly* was everywhere causing chortles at the expense of the mighty. In courts and at universities, aspiring men of letters were studying Greek, reading Seneca and Plutarch, and asking whether any war could be considered just. Above all, the *Novum Instrumentum* was encouraging

Christians to approach the Bible as a guide to virtuous living rather than a trove of Scholastic propositions.

A new era of enlightenment seemed to be dawning, with Erasmus at its center. Not since Petrarch had an intellectual figure so dominated public discourse as Erasmus did in that enchanted spring of 1516. People wrote to him in the hope of receiving a response that they could show their friends, while young scholars made visits to him as if to the shrine of a saint. "Everywhere in all Christendom your fame is spreading," wrote John Watson, a rector with whom he had become friends while in Cambridge. "By the unanimous verdict of all scholars, you are voted the best scholar of them all, and the most learned in both Greek and Latin." "The devotees of literature flock round you from the whole of Germany," wrote Johann Witz, the master of the famous town school in Sélestat, who signed off, "Greetings to Beatus Rhenanus and all the Erasmians."

Of course, those Erasmians represented a small sliver of society. It was the educated, Latin-speaking elite, dominated by Christian humanists, who most thrilled to the new Erasmian gospel. The kings and princes who actually wielded power were far more inclined to follow Machiavelli, and few of the weavers and plowmen mentioned in the *Paraclesis* knew enough Latin to read it.

Among religious scholars, meanwhile, the backlash to Erasmus's work that had been predicted by Martin Dorp was beginning to appear. From England, Thomas More wrote to warn that some people there had formed a conspiracy to read all that Erasmus had written, in search of errors. "I do beg and beseech you to lose no time in going through and correcting everything," he wrote, for "these men are very sharp, and they have decided to keep a keen look-out for any such opportunity, and seize it greedily and gladly." He urged Erasmus to mobilize all his resources "to deal with so great a danger."

From Basel, Wolfgang Capito—a professor of the Old Testament who had helped Erasmus with his New Testament—similarly pressed him to prepare a careful revision of that work so as to rebut "charges of inconsistency." Given the many places at which Erasmus's Latin translation failed to agree with his notes, he should go over it and "bring the whole into agreement with that skillful pen of yours." And he should do so quickly, for his enemies were seeking opportunities to cause him trouble and denounce him as "a public enemy of Christianity." By June 1516, Erasmus was already at work on a new edition.

In short, the haste with which Erasmus had prepared his New Testament was beginning to catch up with him. As readers were discovering, his new Latin translation was very uneven—lightly revised in some places, completely reworded in others, left untouched elsewhere. The Greek text was even more flawed, with hundreds of editing, spelling, and typographical errors. At many points, the Greek version differed for no apparent reason from the manuscripts on which it was based, thus offering readings with no foundation in the textual tradition. On top of it all, the codices on which Erasmus relied most heavily for his Greek text were relatively late copies now known to be highly undependable. (Other codices of the New Testament that he examined in Basel but rejected as untrustworthy are now recognized as being far more reliable.) Finally, there were hundreds of printer's errors.

In Erasmus's defense, he was working at the dawn of modern biblical scholarship. Not until the late nineteenth and early twentieth centuries would the science of critical editing advance to the point where it could pinpoint the dates of manuscripts with great accuracy, and it seems unfair to hold Erasmus to that standard. But the errors resulting from his own carelessness would have lasting consequences. Because his Greek New Testament was the first to appear in print and because it bore his prestigious name, it would be reprinted many times. In 1633, an edition of it was brought out in Leiden by Abraham and Bonaventura Elzevir; its preface stated, *Textum ergo habes, nunc ab omnibus receptum*—"Here you have the text now received by all." Because of that phrase, their edition came to be known as the *Textus Receptus*, or "received text." This edition became so revered as to achieve divinely ordained status, and it would become the foundation for all Protestant biblical scholarship until the nineteenth century. In other words, the Greek text that Erasmus had prepared on the basis of very flawed codices and which had been printed with such haste and so little copyediting as to become riddled with errors would for three centuries serve as the primary text for scriptural study in the West. It would also provide the basis for the many vernacular editions of the Bible produced over the next century, including the King James Bible of 1611, which would incorporate many of the errors in Erasmus's Greek text. One renowned nineteenth-century biblical scholar called the text "the most faulty book I know."

For all Erasmus's shortcomings as an editor, however, it was his theological observations that would ultimately cause him the most trouble. A foretaste came in a letter from George Spalatin, the secretary to Prince Frederick of Saxony. Spalatin assured Erasmus of his friendly intentions: "We are devoted to you, all of us who have signed on as students of a new and better learning. The output of your gifted mind is held in such high esteem among us that nothing is more eagerly sought for in the fairs or more quickly sold out at the booksellers." Prince Frederick had in his ducal library every book of Erasmus's that Spalatin had been able to find.

Now, however, he was writing on behalf of an Augustinian priest, who, having studied Erasmus's work on the New Testament, had two concerns. One was Erasmus's assertion that Paul in Romans was not speaking about original sin. The priest suggested that Erasmus read Augustine's writings against the Pelagians, which, he felt sure, would help him "not only understand the Apostle correctly but also pay much greater reverence to St. Augustine."

The priest also objected to Erasmus's interpretation of Paul's comments about works. This referred not "merely to ceremonies," as Erasmus suggested, but to "the keeping of the whole Ten Commandments." According to the priest, "we do not become just by performing just actions," but "we become just first and then act justly. For the person must first be changed, and then his works." Because Erasmus carried such worldwide authority, the priest was afraid that he would "encourage people to rush to the defense of the dead, that is, the literal interpretation, which has filled the work of almost everyone since Augustine."

Whether because of his crushing workload or the critical tone of the letter, Erasmus never replied. Soon, however, he would be hearing much more about the Augustinian priest.

14

A FRIAR'S CRY

Sometime during the summer of 1516, while Luther was still lecturing on the Epistle to the Romans, Erasmus's *Novum Instrumentum* arrived in Wittenberg. As he examined its comments on cases and tenses, syntax and vocabulary, Luther immediately saw the great help that this text could provide in grasping Paul's meaning, and Erasmus quickly replaced all other commentators (except Augustine) as his main guide. Luther's first explicit acknowledgment of the Dutchman's contribution came at Romans 9:19. Struggling with the voice of the Latin *queritur* ("find fault"), Luther wrote: "Some, like Laurentius Valla, take this phrase to be passive. Stapulensis understands it as referring to a person; but Erasmus says that all Greek interpreters take it as a deponent, and he agrees with them." From that point on, Erasmus's name would regularly show up in Luther's lecture notes.

So would Erasmian-style complaints about clerical excesses and princely abuses. These began to appear in Luther's notes on the twelfth chapter of Romans, where Paul moves from theological conjecture to practical instruction. Prompted by the Apostle's admonitions, Luther started to work out the real-world implications of his new ideas. Throughout, there are echoes of Erasmus's salvos against the ecclesiastical and secular authorities. In these pages, one can see Luther's rebellion against the Church unfold in real time, along with evidence of the great impact that Erasmian ideas were having on him.

At 12:8, for instance, where Paul urges people to give "with simplicity," Luther lamented how in his day most people gave with the expectation of getting something in return. In the Gospels, he noted, Luke calls on those holding a feast to invite the poor, maimed, and blind. "If only this were observed, how many monstrous evils would the church then be spared today!" Luther was especially critical of the foundations and endowments that were supported by those wishing to have priests say Masses or sing hymns in their names. Such vainglory had turned the worship of God into a "market place." Luther singled out the All Saints' Foundation at the Castle Church in Wittenberg, whose main activity was saying Masses for the souls of the dead. Those giving to it were seeking less to honor God than to blow their own horn in the presence of others. Such practices, he predicted, would bring "great misery" to the Roman Church.

Luther's growing defiance was most apparent in his comments on Paul's famous dictum at 13:1: "Let everyone be subject to the governing authorities." Over the ages, this passage had been taken as a command to obey princes and accept the prevailing order, but it now triggered in Luther a fierce denunciation of "spiritual rulers." Nothing more annoys these "extravagant spendthrifts" than efforts to curtail their privileges and properties. A cleric may be guilty of pride and wantonness, may be given to greed and ingratitude, but as long as he protects the Church's rights and liberties, he is deemed a good Christian. "No wonder that laymen hate the clerics!"

Aware of the sharpness of his tone, Luther was nonetheless unapologetic: "I must perform my duty as a teacher who holds this office by apostolic authority" to "speak up whenever I see that something is done that is not right, even in higher places." And, as he proceeded, he became more and more outspoken. Spurred by Paul's warning not to judge others by what they eat, Luther inveighed against clerical regulations. In contrast to the law of Moses, he declared, Christian law does not set aside special days for fasting nor single out certain types of food as acceptable. In an extraordinary outburst, he called for all fast days and holidays to be abolished, for the entire book of decretals (legal letters issued by the pope) to be purged, and for the pomp of prayer services to be sharply cut back. No priest (unless he wants to) should be required to go without a wife, have a tonsure, or wear a special habit. Rather, it should be left up to each individual to do as much or as little as his conscience and sense of responsibility to God allows.

All of these statements carry distinct Erasmian overtones. Yet, even as Luther was echoing his criticisms of the Church, he was becoming aware of his and Erasmus's theological differences. Reading Erasmus's comments on Romans 5, for instance, Luther was concerned about his failure to state clearly that Paul was speaking of original sin. At the time, he was reading Augustine's *Anti-Pelagian Writings*, in which the bishop of Hippo attacked Pelagius for his belief in free will and in the perfectibility of humankind. If Erasmus were more familiar with these writings, Luther felt sure, he would show greater respect for this doctrine. Erasmus similarly seemed to misapprehend Paul's position on the law. While rejecting ceremonies and statutes, Erasmus seemed to accept the binding nature of ethical codes like the Decalogue. As Luther read Paul, however, it seemed clear to him that the Apostle was rejecting adherence to the law in all its forms. In light of Erasmus's tremendous prestige, Luther considered it his duty to alert him to these misreadings lest he lead others astray.

Given his own anonymity, Luther felt that if he approached Erasmus directly, he would be brushed aside, so he instead decided to go through Spalatin, who, as an adviser to Elector Frederick, would be likely to get a fuller hearing. In his letter to Spalatin (dated October 19, 1516—about six weeks after the end of his lectures on Romans), Luther put his complaints about Erasmus far more bluntly than Spalatin would put them to Erasmus. Spalatin might call him rash "for bringing such famous men under the whip of Aristarch," he wrote, but he was acting "out of concern for theology and the salvation of the brethren." Aristarch was a critic in ancient Greece famous for his sharpness. Luther no doubt learned about him from Erasmus's *Adages*—a borrowing that showed how indebted he was to the celebrated scholar, even while he rushed to set him right.

In his outbursts against the clergy, Luther was drawing on firsthand knowledge. In the spring of 1516, in his capacity as district vicar, he visited several monasteries under his supervision. At most of them, the conditions were deplorable. Guesthouses were being used as resort houses, gluttony was rampant, insubordination was on the rise. The situation was especially serious at his old cloister in Erfurt. After returning to Wittenberg, he wrote to its director, Johann Lang, to urge him to keep a daily log of the amount of beer, wine, bread, and meat consumed in the guesthouse, so that he would be able to see "whether the monastery is a monastery rather than a tavern or hotel." He also recommended that Lang keep an account of "the comings and goings of mendicant friars and their hangers-on" so that he could tell "those restless and insatiable people" who are so proud of their good works "how profusely they imbibe."

At Lang's request, Luther agreed to take in several malingering monks from Erfurt. But the situation did not improve, and Lang asked him to accept several more. Luther said he could not. "I have enough useless friars around here," he wrote on October 26, 1516. The population at the Black Cloister was up to forty-one, and the supplies were barely sufficient for them. Luther complained about the growing demands on his time. "I nearly need two copyists or secretaries. All day long I do almost nothing else than write letters." He was, he noted, a reader during mealtimes, a supervisor of novices, a lecturer on the Bible, a preacher at both the monastery and the town church, the overseer of eleven monasteries, the mediator of a dispute over the control of a parish church in nearby Torgau, and the caretaker of a fishpond from which the Wittenberg friary collected rent. On top of it all, he was preparing for the printers his lecture notes on the Psalms. Thus occupied, he hardly had time to say the hours or celebrate Mass. "Besides all this there are my own struggles with the flesh, the world, and the devil. See what a lazy man I am!"

The day after he wrote to Lang, Luther was due to begin his next set of lectures, on Paul's Epistle to the Galatians. He was worried that the class would be unable to meet, however, for Wittenberg had been hit by the plague. Every day, it claimed two or three people; among them was the son of a craftsman who lived across the street from the Augustinian cloister. Panicked, students were fleeing the city, and Johann von Staupitz, the Augustinian vicar-general, advised Luther to do the same. He refused. "My place is here, due to obedience," he wrote to Lang. "It is not that I am not afraid of death (I am not the Apostle Paul but only a lecturer on the Apostle Paul!), but I hope the Lord will rescue me from my fears." Those fears were setting off new bouts of the *Anfechtungen.* "My life daily approaches nearer hell," he wrote to another friend, "for I become worse and more miserable all the time."

But Luther was about to face a more immediate challenge. With the approach of All Saints' Day (November 1) 1516, Wittenberg (notwithstanding the plague) began to fill with pilgrims come to see Frederick's relics collection, which was placed on display every year at that time. On the evening before, Luther was scheduled to give a sermon, and he would have to decide whether to say anything about the relics. There were more than nineteen thousand of them, including a twig from Moses's burning bush, four hairs of the Virgin Mary, five particles of her milk, a piece of Jesus's swaddling clothes, two pieces of hay from the manger, five pieces of the table from the Last Supper, and eight thorns from Jesus's crown. A catalog prepared by Lucas Cranach of Frederick's collection offered sketches of some of the ornate reliquaries in which these items were displayed—boxes adorned with garlands and fruits, horns bearing images of wild animals, goblets showing scenes from the crucifixion, cylinders held aloft by singing cherubim.

Associated with each relic was an indulgence. Indulgences remitted the penalties associated with sin and so reduced the time the sinner had to spend in purgatory. The Castle Church was one of many churches in Europe authorized by the pope to offer an indulgence once or twice a year to all believers present at a display of relics. To each relic was assigned a specific number of days or years by which the penitent's time in purgatory was reduced. Added together, the relics in Frederick's collection could bring about a reduction of precisely 1,902,202 years and 270 days in purgatory.

Those obtaining indulgences were expected to make a financial contribution to the Church as a form of good work. By the early sixteenth century, indulgences had become a key source of income for the building of bridges, dikes, schools, and hospitals. Many of the great cathedrals of Europe were underwritten in part by the money raised through indulgences. In Saxony, the income from them was supporting the rebuilding of a bridge across the Elbe at Torgau. Indulgences also helped sustain the operations of the Castle Church and the University of Wittenberg. Luther's own welfare was thus bound up with the revenue generated by these dispensations.

But there was much about them that troubled him. Technically, indulgences did not actually take away or forgive sin; rather, they remitted (commuted) the temporal punishment due to sin after the guilt for it had been forgiven following a penitent's show of contrition and the performance of acts of satisfaction. In reality, however, such fine points often got lost, and many purchasers acted as if they had been forgiven for their sins and so no longer had to worry about showing contrition or giving satisfaction. Indulgences also gave believers a sense of reassurance about their fate in the afterlife; a letter of indulgence thus came to be considered a sort of "get out of purgatory" note. That the transaction entailed a financial contribution raised further concerns, for this made it seem that the offender was being given time off not for good behavior but for bribing the judge.

In studying Romans, Luther had come to see that man is by nature sinful and unable through any amount of good works to overcome such weakness. Indulgences, by reassuring people about their spiritual state in both this life and the next, ran the risk of making them neglect true penitence. And so, in his sermon on All Hallows' Eve, Luther decided to speak out. With the rows of sacred items on display in the Castle Church and with crowds of worshippers eager to benefit from them, he issued a stern warning: No one who receives an indulgence can know if the remission of his sins is complete. Only those who engage in heartfelt contrition and confession can receive such remission, and even then no one can be sure he has adequately performed such acts. Indulgences are dangerous because they lull believers into a state of spiritual complacency. What's more, if the pope did have the power to deliver souls from purgatory, as he claimed, he would be cruel not to release all of them, even without indulgences.

This was dangerous territory. Luther was criticizing not only the pope but also, implicitly, Frederick. There were no repercussions, however. The sale of indulgences continued, and the elector took satisfaction in the young professor's growing reputation, as shown by his promise to send Luther the cloth for a new cowl.

But the question of indulgences would not go away. In early 1517, word reached Wittenberg of a new indulgence being offered in the region. It was being preached by a Dominican friar named Johann Tetzel on behalf of the pope. It was a much-coveted plenary indulgence, offering the remission of all temporal punishment due to one's sins over a lifetime and thus eliminating the need for any additional expiation in purgatory. The indulgence was not available in Wittenberg itself, for Frederick—wanting no competition for his own offerings—had barred Tetzel from his territory, but local residents were excitedly discussing the generous benefits being offered.

A seller of indulgences since 1504, Tetzel had over time perfected the art of marketing them. Weeks before he was due to appear in a town, an advance team would come to spread the word. When Tetzel himself appeared, priests, magistrates, and other town notables would come out to greet him. Songs were chanted, flags were raised, candles were lit. As church bells rang, the bull declaring the indulgence was borne aloft on a velvet cushion and cloth of gold; inside the church, a red cross was erected and the pope's banner attached to it. Then Tetzel, a large man with a booming voice and theatrical flair, launched into his appeal: How many mortal sins are committed in a day, a week, a year, a lifetime? They are infinite, and for them an infinite penalty in the fires of purgatory must be paid. By obtaining an indulgence, however, sinners could, for once in a lifetime, gain full remission of those penalties. Such remissions could be used to relieve not only the future torments of the living but also the current agonies of the dead.

Tetzel expertly preyed on the guilt of his listeners:

> Don't you hear the voices of your wailing dead parents and others who say, "Have mercy upon me, have mercy upon me, because we are in severe punishment and pain. From this you could redeem us with a small alms and yet you do not want to do so. . . . You let us lie in flames so that we only slowly come to the promised glory."

Tetzel would then approach the indulgence chest and write out a certificate for some departed relative, and as the coins clinked in the box, he would proclaim, "Now I am sure of his salvation; now I need pray for him no longer." (Or, as the more popular version had it, "As soon as the coin in the coffer rings, the soul from purgatory springs.")

In Wittenberg, Luther was hearing from his parishioners all sorts of wild statements attributed to Tetzel—that he had saved more souls through his indulgences than St. Peter had with his sermons; that his indulgences remitted the penalties for not only past sins but future ones as well; that even if someone had slept with the Virgin Mary, the pope had the power to grant him forgiveness, as long as a contribution was made. Appalled by these reports, Luther decided to preach against them. His sermon, delivered on February 24, 1517, offered one of the first statements of his "theology of the cross," as it came to be called. All those who seek peace of conscience through their own actions, he declared, accomplish nothing other than to increase the restlessness of their souls. It was this zeal to perform meritorious works as a means of winning divine grace that had fed the hunger for indulgences. Indulgences caused people to fear and flee the penalty associated with sin but not to dread sin itself. Only through gentleness and lowliness could the soul find true repose, and only through punishment and suffering could those qualities be attained. Christ did not say, "Do this or that," but rather, "Come to me, get away from yourselves, and carry your cross after me." Alarmed at the crisis he saw gathering, Luther closed with a dramatic cry:

Oh, the dangers of our time! Oh, you snoring priests! Oh, darkness deeper than Egyptian! How secure we are in the midst of all our evils!

Luther's plea had little effect. The Wittenbergers, terrified at the prospect of dying suddenly in a state of unexpiated sin, wanted not trials and suffering but relief and reassurance. In March and April 1517, Tetzel appeared in the towns of Jüterbog and Zerbst in Brandenburg, which were just beyond the border of Electoral Saxony and barely twenty miles from Wittenberg, and townsmen were hurrying there to sample his wares. When hearing confession, Luther was startled to find many of his parishioners refusing to promise to refrain from adultery, usury, and other vices. When he withheld absolution on the grounds that they were not showing true contrition, they produced their indulgence letters, which, they said, offered all the absolution they needed. When Luther refused to honor them, they hurried back to Tetzel to complain. Furious, the Dominican announced that he had orders to burn as a heretic anyone who dared interfere with the indulgence trade, which had been authorized by the pope himself.

The indulgence being preached by Tetzel had a particular feature that would prove especially controversial. The coins clinking in the collection boxes were earmarked for a specific end: St. Peter's in Rome. As stated in the papal bull authorizing the indulgence, the proceeds from it were to underwrite the construction of the new basilica. In his preaching, Tetzel stressed that those purchasing the indulgence would benefit not just their own souls and the souls of the deceased but all Christendom by helping to raise a glorious new sanctuary in the Holy See. In addition to the usual spiritual questions associated with indulgences, then, this one introduced the volatile element of the relations between Germany and Rome and of the large sums being siphoned off from the one to the other.

In Rome, the construction of the new St. Peter's was progressing, but fitfully. The death of Julius II, in February 1513, had removed the prime mover behind the project. His successor, Leo X, lacked not only his sense of commitment to it but also his fire and resolve. That was by design. The cardinals, tired of the irascibility and severity of the warrior-pope, wanted someone more agreeable and temperate. And so it happened that the man chosen to head the Church during what would prove to be its greatest crisis was a pudgy, pampered epicurean. The son of Lorenzo de' Medici, Giovanni (his given name) had the taste and cultivation of his father without the dash and drive. Almost from the cradle he had been groomed for the papacy. His education was entrusted to such giants of the Florentine Renaissance as Angelo Poliziano and Marsilio Ficino. He was made a priest at the age of seven, an abbot at eleven, and a cardinal at thirteen. When elected pope, Leo was, at thirty-seven, one of the youngest pontiffs ever. His goal was to make Rome not only Europe's holiest city but also its most urbane, and under him the Roman Renaissance would reach its apex—and begin its decline.

Leo brought his family's priceless library from Florence and opened it to scholars. He lured from Venice the great Hellenist Marcus Musurus along with ten men of virtuous disposition to teach Greek and establish a Greek printing press. He appointed two celebrated humanists, Jacopo

Sadoleto and Pietro Bembo, as his secretaries, both of whom were known for their pure Ciceronian Latin. A passionate lover of music, Leo kept an instrument in his room on which to improvise, brought celebrated performers from around Europe, and bestowed on a Spaniard whose voice he especially liked the archbishopric of Bari. He had an ear for poetry as well and showered patronage on the crowds of Roman *rimatori* who turned out *sonetti* and *canzoni* in the style of Petrarch and odes and eclogues echoing Horace and Virgil. Leo was particularly fond of the *improvisatori*—quick-witted versifiers able to compose clever poems on the spot on themes suggested by the pontiff and his dinner mates. Leo's reputation as a champion of learning was burnished by his friendship with Erasmus, who paid effusive tribute to him in his dedication to the New Testament.

But Leo had a reputation for self-indulgence as well. "Let us enjoy the papacy, since God has given it to us," he is reported to have said upon his accession, and though the line is probably apocryphal, it captures his unflagging pursuit of pleasure. His inaugural procession was the most opulent spectacle in Rome since the days of the emperors, with Leo riding on a white Arab stallion through streets decorated with triumphal arches, shielded from the sun by a baldacchino of embroidered silk borne by eight Roman patricians. As pope, he lost some eight thousand ducats a month at cards; distributed purses of gold to guests who sang with him; and kept a menagerie that included lions, civet cats, apes, and a snow-white elephant named Hanno, who was a gift from the king of Portugal and became the talk of Rome. The papal household, which under Julius II had numbered fewer than two hundred, ballooned to nearly seven hundred under Leo. An avid hunter, he devoted a month every autumn to the chase. Too ungainly and nearsighted to participate, he would instead follow the hunt from a makeshift stand; when a boar was snared in a net, Leo would move in and, bearing a spear in one hand and a magnifying glass in the other, deliver the coup de grâce, to the applause of his retinue.

Carcasses of exotic animals arrived by the cartload in Rome, where they were prepared by an army of cooks for the pontifical table; peacock tongues and lampreys cooked in a Cretan wine sauce were particular favorites. Entertainment was provided by not only musical ensembles but also an array of dwarfs, jesters, and buffoons, the most famous of whom was Fra Mariano Fetti, a ribald Dominican friar known for his coarse manners and ability to consume up to forty eggs at a sitting. For all his refined sensibilities, Leo loved vulgarity. He also enjoyed theatrical pieces, the more indecent and farcical the better. When it came to saying Mass and performing other divine offices, Leo was conscientious, but if the ceremonies went on too long, he became uncomfortable, perspiring profusely under his heavy robes.

St. Peter's posed a special challenge. As a cardinal, Leo had suffered through the Masses that Julius had presided over in the increasingly exposed basilica, braving the frigid gusts of winter and the broiling sheen of summer. When he became pope, he refused to perform his first Easter Mass in the basilica, owing to the inclement conditions, and used the Sistine Chapel instead. Leo instructed Bramante to build a temporary shelter over the altar so that he could carry out his officiating duties in comfort.

Then, a year into Leo's pontificate, in 1514, Bramante died. During the nine years when he had been in charge, the four great piers designed to support the massive dome had been completed and joined to soaring coffered vaults, and the floor plan was marked out by huge Corinthian pilasters. Work had also begun on the corner chapels. Overall, though, the new basilica remained little more than a skeleton, and Bramante left no instructions for how to proceed. What's more, major structural concerns had begun to emerge: the foundations of the new basilica were shifting, cracks had appeared in the piers, weeds were sprouting in the aisles.

To take Bramante's place as lead architect, Leo selected his favorite artist, Raphael. Leo loved the frescoes Raphael had applied to the walls of the *stanze* of the Vatican and shared his easygoing sensuality. Raphael for his part exulted in being named head of "the greatest building project ever seen" (as he described it in a letter to his uncle), and every day he had an audience with the pope, at which St. Peter's was a prominent subject. But Raphael was at heart a painter, with little architectural experience. (His famous portrait of Leo, now hanging in the Uffizi, captures the pope's plump refinement.) Two other architects were assigned to help him with the basilica, but the project became mired in rivalries, backstabbing, bitter disputes over its basic shape, and continual alterations in plans. Bramante had designed the basilica as a Greek cross, with four equal arms; Raphael changed it to a Latin cross, with a long nave added to the central area, but this added to concerns about the project's cost.

And that cost was skyrocketing. Leo had to make huge outlays just to keep the work crews intact while those in charge pursued other projects. Money was squandered, expenses were inflated, and few cost controls were imposed. For the outer walls, Leo insisted on ordering the most expensive travertine. In his first year alone, he budgeted sixty thousand ducats for St. Peter's, more than twice the already immense sums allocated by Julius.

Upon his death, Julius had left a large surplus in the Vatican treasury, but within two years Leo had frittered it all away. To try to keep the Holy See afloat, he resorted to all sorts of revenue-generating schemes. He created new cardinalates and charged thousands of ducats for each. He announced hundreds of new offices and put them up for sale (bringing the total number at the Vatican to around 1,200). He borrowed heavily from the banking houses of Rome, which, seeing his need, charged exorbitant interest rates. Finally, he expanded the offering of indulgences. These came in many varieties. There were confessional letters that freed the penitent from having to confess to a local priest. There were dispensations that allowed the substitution of other good works for vows that had been made in haste and were difficult to keep. There were the ever-popular "butter letters," which permitted the consumption of eggs, milk, and cheese during fast days. There were even indulgences that sanctioned the possession of illegally acquired goods if the rightful owners had died or could not be found.

The pope's authority to issue indulgences derived from an inventive doctrine developed by Scholastic theologians. Christ, the Virgin Mary, and the saints, they maintained, had performed so many meritorious acts beyond the satisfactions required of them that there had accumulated in heaven a treasury of surplus merits, which could be used to make up for the debts contracted by others. Under the authority of the 1343 *Extravagante Unigenitus*, the pope could draw on this treasury and allocate its merits to individual sinners to remit the temporal penalties they had incurred for their sins. In 1476, Sixtus IV, in a highly controversial move, declared that indulgences could remit the sins of not only the living but also the souls of the deceased in purgatory. With Christians desperate to alleviate the suffering of their departed loved ones, the clamor for indulgences grew.

To add to their allure, the Vatican in the fifteenth century began issuing indulgence letters. Adorned with a papal signature and seal and leaving a space for the name of the purchaser, they provided penitents with tangible evidence of their commuted sentences. With the rise of printing, the letters were run off in large quantities. In Rome, a special bureau was set up to prepare marketing plans for each indulgence, and preachers were deployed across the Alps with the precision of a military operation. The financial aspects were managed by the Fuggers, Europe's richest family. Based in Augsburg, they had branches in many European cities, including Rome, and as the indulgence trade grew, they converted their office in that city into a full-time indulgence agency. The indulgence collection boxes were secured with iron bands, and they could be opened only in the presence of a company agent—a safeguard aimed at preventing embezzlement, which was common. Over time, indulgences became a central part of the Vatican's finances, and by the accession of Julius II they were accounting for up to half the revenues of the Datary.

As was the custom, Leo on becoming pope announced the revocation of all the indulgences that had been proclaimed by his predecessor, with one exception—the St. Peter's indulgence. This he would expand. As stipulated in the authorizing bull (dated March 31, 1515), the indulgence was to be sold for eight years in the church provinces of Mainz and Magdeburg and the state of Brandenburg (as well as in parts of France and the low countries). Those obtaining it did not have to make confession or visit churches and altars but had only to purchase the indulgence letter; those obtaining indulgences on behalf of the departed did not have to be contrite of heart, since the granting of the indulgence depended on the state of grace of the soul at the time of death. All vows except monastic ones could be commuted through the indulgence, and dispensations were available for almost all types of offenses, including adultery.

In issuing this bull, Leo paid little heed to the resentment that was building in Germany at the growing financial encroachments of Rome. Chancery dues, consecration fees, new tithes, annates (the payment to the

Curia of the first year's income of new benefices)—all placed a great burden on the German people. Unlike England, France, the Low Countries,
and Spain, the Holy Roman Empire lacked a strong central government,
so papal tax collectors were able to operate at will. The anger over Rome's
usurpations was feeding a new sense of German nationalism rooted in a
hatred of all things Italian. It found expression in the long list of grievances submitted at the imperial diets (assemblies) held every two or three
years. These *gravamina* (as they were called) were filled with complaints
about the insistent demands for money by the Curia and the excesses connected with them. In these lists, indulgences always received prominent
mention as instruments through which ordinary people were misled and
bilked of their savings.

The St. Peter's indulgence had one feature so potentially inflammatory that great efforts were made to conceal it. In 1514, a vacancy had
opened in the archbishopric of Mainz. This was the most powerful ecclesiastical post in Germany, in part because it controlled one of the seven
votes to elect the Holy Roman Emperor. Among those hungrily eyeing it
was Prince Joachim of Brandenburg, a leading member of the House of
Hohenzollern—one of the great German families. (It would rule Prussia
for four centuries.) Seeing the decisive political advantage that this position could bring, Joachim put forward his brother Albrecht.

Albrecht was not a model candidate. He was fond of food and women
and had only a rudimentary knowledge of theology. That, however, was
no bar to holding ecclesiastical office, and in 1513 he had been named
both archbishop of Magdeburg and the administrator of the diocese of
Halberstadt. Canon law prohibited him from holding yet another position, and at twenty-four he was well short of the minimum age for the
Mainz post. For him to fill it, then, a special papal dispensation would
be needed. The pope was happy to provide it—for a price. On top of the
standard fee for the office, the Vatican imposed a hefty special levy, bringing the total to more than twenty thousand ducats.

Even for a family as wealthy as the Hohenzollerns, this was an enormous sum, and to figure out how to raise it, they turned to the Fuggers.
Drawing on their long experience in the indulgence trade, the Fuggers
came up with a creative arrangement: they would advance the family the

entire fee, and to help repay it, the pope would grant Albrecht jurisdiction over the St. Peter's indulgence. After expenses were deducted, half the remainder would go to the Fuggers to repay the loan and the other half to Rome to support the rebuilding of St. Peter's. In other words, a significant portion of the money being handed over by hardworking Germans in their effort to avoid the torments of purgatory was to go to support the ecclesiastical ambitions of the callow scion of a princely family. Because of various delays, the preaching of the indulgence would not begin until early 1517, when Johann Tetzel set out on his sales tour of eastern Germany.

As Tetzel peddled the indulgence, Luther was completing his lectures on the Epistle to the Galatians. In this document, Paul emphatically asserts his belief that works without faith cannot lead to salvation, and Luther echoed his vehemence. Without Christ's resurrection, he wrote, no one can rise, "no matter how many good works he does." Grace comes not from works but from faith in Christ. Throughout, Luther relied heavily on Erasmus's annotations. The humanist's grammatical observations proved invaluable in unlocking the meaning of Paul's statements. Luther's notes were filled with phrases like "I follow Erasmus," "as Erasmus says," and "that excellent man" Erasmus.

Yet the more Luther read Erasmus, the more disenchanted he became. "I am reading our Erasmus but daily I dislike him more and more," he wrote to Johann Lang on March 1, 1517. While pleased that Erasmus was constantly "exposing and condemning the monks and priests for their deep-rooted and sleepy ignorance," he regretted that "he does not advance the cause of Christ and the grace of God sufficiently," for "human things weigh more with him than the divine." He went on:

> I see that not everyone is a truly wise Christian just because he knows Greek and Hebrew. St. Jerome with his five languages cannot be compared with Augustine, who knew only one language. Erasmus, however, is of an absolutely different opinion on this. But the discernment of one who attributes weight to man's will is different from that of him who knows of nothing else but grace.

Luther added that he wanted to keep his opinion of Erasmus secret so that he would not "strengthen the conspiracy of his enemies." Nonetheless, his early judgment that Erasmus favored the human over the divine would prove unshakable. So would Luther's preference for Augustine over Jerome. It is remarkable to see Erasmus and Luther reenacting the debate that those two great Doctors had conducted more than a millennium earlier.

At the university, meanwhile, Luther was progressing in his campaign to overthrow the Scholastics and institute a curriculum reflecting the gospel of grace. "Our theology and St. Augustine are progressing well and with God's help rule our university," he wrote in May 1517. Aristotle "is gradually falling from his throne, and his final doom is only a matter of time." That summer, when Luther began lecturing on the Epistle to the Hebrews, so many students signed up that the meeting time was moved from the early morning to noon—the hour reserved for the most popular classes. He also won over Andreas von Karlstadt, the dean of the Wittenberg faculty. Initially, Karlstadt, a committed Thomist, had strenuously opposed any changes in the curriculum, but at Luther's urging he had bought an edition of Augustine's works, and as he read through it he experienced an emotional crisis that left him convinced that Luther's ideas about the misapprehensions of the Scholastics and the supreme importance of faith and grace were correct.

In September, Luther was scheduled to preside over a doctoral disputation, and, seeking to deliver a fatal blow to the old school, he prepared ninety-seven theses against Scholastic theology. In them, he attacked Scotus, Ockham, and Biel for spreading false ideas about free will and good works and doing all that one can. We are not masters of our will but its servants, he declared. No one can become righteous without the grace of God; all who seek salvation through works are condemned. Toward Aristotle, Luther was unsparing. "It is an error to say that no man can become a theologian without Aristotle," he wrote. Indeed, "no one can become a theologian unless he becomes one without Aristotle." Aristotle "is to theology as darkness is to light." More than three centuries after the rediscovery of Aristotle's works, the philosopher's grip on Western theology was loosening, and Luther's theses would serve as a sort of epitaph.

In the late summer or early autumn of 1517, Luther saw a copy of a booklet that, bearing the seal of the archbishop of Mainz, contained the instructions for the St. Peter's indulgence. Until then, Luther had assumed that the many outlandish claims made by Tetzel had been the product of his own hucksterism and zeal, but the pamphlet showed that they were authorized by not only Albrecht but the pope himself. It was the pope who had granted the complete remission of all sins and had done away with all the accompanying pain of purgatory. And it was the pope who had decreed that, even without confession or contrition, one could obtain the complete remission of all sins for those souls in purgatory.

The pamphlet even had a fee schedule for the purchase of the indulgence: twenty-five guilders for kings, queens, archbishops, and bishops; ten guilders for counts, barons, abbots, and other higher prelates; six guilders for lesser prelates and nobles; three florins for well-off citizens and merchants; and a half florin for citizens of lesser means. (For those with no means, prayer was deemed sufficient.) Finally, preachers were urged to give the benefits attached to the indulgence "the widest publicity, since through the same, help will surely come to departed souls, and the construction of the church of St. Peter will be abundantly promoted at the same time."

To Luther, it was all becoming clear: to support the construction of a sumptuous new temple in Rome, the pope and his agents were gulling the German people into believing that, by handing over their hard-earned cash for these certificates, they could gain remission of their sins without having to feel any regret or repentance. On his visit to Rome years earlier, Luther had seen the collection boxes at the Datary but paid them little attention. Now, reading the instructions for the St. Peter's indulgence, he could see how greedy and grasping the Holy See had become.

Luther's dismay grew as a result of an important discovery he made while reading Erasmus's annotations. He learned that the word *poenitentia*, used in the Vulgate (in the form *poenitentiam agite*) at Matthew 3:2 (by John the Baptist) and at 4:17 (by Christ himself), was actually based on the Greek *metanoia*. The New Testament was urging people not to do penance but to recognize their misdeeds and undergo a change of disposition. This seemed to echo what Johann von Staupitz had told him years earlier—that penance is genuine only if it begins with a love for God and if the performing of the sacrament is seen as the starting point rather than the end point of the process of coming to terms with one's transgressions. Luther was overcome by this revelation. After all the years he had spent struggling to attain absolution for his sins through contrition, confession, and satisfaction, he now saw that the Church's whole system of penance lacked any basis in Scripture. The philological adjustment that Lorenzo Valla had proposed in his notes on the New Testament and that Erasmus had found in the monastic library outside Louvain and later incorporated into his own annotations had thus helped open the eyes of this tormented friar in remote Wittenberg as to how far Church theologians were leading the faithful astray.

This awakening bore directly on the issue of indulgences. The relief granted by these dispensations did not require any genuine change of attitude; they were said to be effective without regard to any feeling of regret or contrition. What's more, they were given in exchange for money, turning the critical act of penitence into a financial transaction—one being used, moreover, to build an opulent structure in Rome.

With the approach of All Saints' Day (November 1), Wittenberg again began to fill with pilgrims come to see the relics at the Castle Church and obtain an indulgence. After his performance on the previous All Hallows' Eve, Luther was not asked to preach on this one. But, in the face of so grave an abuse, he felt he could not remain silent. He decided to convey his objections in the time-honored form of a set of theses for disputation, with other scholars invited to debate them.

Sitting down to draft what would become his most famous document, Luther began with the recent discovery he had made about penance in his reading of Erasmus's annotations:

> When our Lord and Master Jesus Christ said, "*Poenitentiam agite*, &c," he willed the entire life of believers to be one of repentance.

This word cannot be understood as referring to the sacrament of penance, that is, confession and satisfaction, as administered by the clergy.

At this point, Luther was not yet ready to jettison all external expressions of penitence, so in his third thesis he offered a clarification: penitence does not mean "solely inner repentance," which "is worthless unless it produces various outward mortifications of the flesh."

From that point on, though, Luther offered few qualifications. Instead, he mounted a fierce attack on the whole theological infrastructure of indulgences. The pope, he stated, does not have the power to remit any penalties beyond those imposed at his own discretion or by canon law. Moreover, this power could be applied only to the living and not to the dead, for papal decrees cease to apply at death. Nor was there divine authority for preaching that the soul flies out of purgatory immediately upon the depositing of the coins in the indulgence chest. "When money clinks in the money chest," he wrote, "greed and avarice increase."

Furthermore, Luther observed, it was not consistent with Christian doctrine to preach that those who buy such letters have no need to repent of their sins. Any Christian who is truly repentant enjoys full remission from both the penalty and the guilt attached to sin without obtaining such letters. Christians should be taught that one who passes a person in need in order to give money for an indulgence gains no benefit but only incurs God's wrath. They should also be taught that if the pope knew of the exactions of the indulgence preachers, "he would rather that the basilica of St. Peter were burned to ashes than be built up with the skin, flesh, and bones of his sheep." If the need arose, the pope should be willing to sell St. Peter's and give the proceeds along with his own money to those from whom the pardon merchants extract money.

With each succeeding thesis, Luther grew increasingly cheeky. Whereas in the past the Gospels were used to fish for men of wealth, now indulgences were used to fish for the wealth of men. If the pope could indeed free souls from purgatory, why did he not liberate everyone for the sake of love? Since the pope's income was greater than that of the wealthiest of men, why did he not build St. Peter's with his own money, rather than with that of indigent believers? These questions were serious matters of conscience, and to suppress them by force rather than refute them with reason was "to expose the church and the pope to the ridicule of their enemies, and to make Christian people unhappy."

In his final four theses, Luther—growing emotional after his long spiritual odyssey—offered a ringing peroration:

> Away then with all those prophets who say to the people of Christ, "Peace, peace," and there is no peace.
> Blessed be all those prophets who say to the people of Christ, "Cross, cross," and there is no cross.
> Christians should be diligent in following Christ, their head, through penalties, deaths, and hell,
> And thus be confident of entering heaven through many tribulations rather than through the false security of peace.

By the end, Luther had ninety-five theses. As much as he had tried to keep to a conventional academic format, his long-simmering rage, together with his naturally combative style, had produced a polemic that was witty, biting, and defiant.

Shortly before All Saints' Day, he gave a draft of his theses to Johann Rhau-Grunenberg to be printed as a folio sheet. Titled *Disputation on the Power and Efficacy of Indulgences*, the page declared at the top that "out of love and zeal for the truth and the desire to bring it to light, the following theses will be publicly discussed at Wittenberg under the chairmanship of the reverend father Martin Luther." Around noon on October 31, 1517, Luther set out with an assistant from the Augustinian cloister for the Castle Church, document in hand. As he walked along the rutted, muck-filled main street, he was no doubt greeted by students and parishioners; on reaching the marketplace, he would have encountered visitors come to Wittenberg to view Frederick's relics and obtain indulgences. Reaching the Castle Church, he passed through the covered gateway and crossed the wooden walkway that led to the north door of the church. On it, he posted the Ninety-Five Theses. (In recent years, scholars have raised questions about whether Luther actually affixed the theses to the door of the church or simply distributed—"posted"—them.)

That same day, Luther sent a copy of the theses to Archbishop Albrecht of Mainz, along with a letter explaining his actions. He decried the "gross misunderstanding" that the indulgence preachers had spread among common people: that through these letters they were assured of their salvation and that souls "escape from purgatory as soon as they have placed a contribution into the chest." For all those souls, the archbishop bore the heaviest responsibility. "What a horror, what a danger for a bishop to permit the loud noise of indulgences among his people, while the gospel is silenced, and to be more concerned with the sale of indulgences than with the gospel!" The archbishop should immediately withdraw his booklet of instructions and command the preachers to change their message. "If this is not done," he warned, "someone may rise and, by means of publications, silence those preachers and refute the little book. This would be the greatest danger for Your Most Illustrious Highness. I certainly shudder at this possibility, yet I am afraid it will happen if things are not quickly remedied."

In mid-November 1517, Luther's letter reached Albrecht at his residence in Aschaffenburg, east of Mainz. The archbishop—who had his own relics collection, featuring 8,933 items offering a total of 39,245,120 years and 220 days of relief from purgatory—was furious at Luther's insolence, and he sent the theses to the theological faculty of the University of Mainz for assessment. (It would take no action.) In December, Albrecht forwarded the document to Rome, thus setting in motion the Vatican's actions against Luther. Johann Tetzel, meanwhile, threatened to have Luther burned and his ashes scattered on the waters.

That is what had happened a century earlier to Jan Hus after he had lodged a similar protest. Luther, however, was living in a new age—the age of print. On November 11, 1517, he began sending around copies of the theses, and over the following weeks they were printed as single-sheet broadsides in Leipzig and Nuremberg. In December, they appeared in Basel in booklet form, and soon they were translated into German. By the start of 1518, the Ninety-Five Theses had appeared in towns and villages throughout Germany, "as if the angels themselves had been their messengers," as one contemporary put it. "It is a mystery to me," Luther himself would observe a few months later, "how my theses, more so than my other writings," were "spread to so many places. They were meant exclusively for our academic circle here." Had he anticipated how popular they would become, he added, "I would certainly have done my share to make them more understandable."

But they were in fact understood. For years, the German people had been waiting for someone to put into sharp, concise language the anger and resentment they had been feeling toward Rome. Now an obscure friar in remote Saxony had done so. The friar was obscure no longer, however, and everyone wondered what would happen next.

PART III

Rumblings

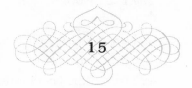

FOR THE WANT OF GREEK TYPE

After months of restlessly moving around the Low Countries, Erasmus in the summer of 1517 decided to settle in Louvain. Located just twenty miles east of Brussels, the city offered easy access to the Burgundian court, where Erasmus continued to have business. From earlier visits, he fondly recalled its mild climate, its printers and libraries, its scholarly bustle. Louvain's university—the only one in the Netherlands—was a stronghold of Scholastic theology. (The University of Louvain remains the largest university in Belgium, though in the late 1960s, after protests and riots, it split into two campuses, with one speaking Flemish and the other French; both remain affiliated with the Catholic Church.) Louvain was also home to the Golden Torch, the print shop of Dirk Martens, who played an important part in disseminating humanist texts (including those of Erasmus) in the Low Countries. Louvain's marketplace was dominated by St. Peter's church, an immense medieval pile featuring seven radiating chapels, waterspouts shaped like gargoyles, elongated arched windows, and a steeply slanted slate roof. Opposite it stood the three-story town hall—a florid mass of stone filigrees, octagonal turrets, and canopied niches that radiated bourgeois pride and was considered the finest civic building in Brabant.

Aside from its university, Louvain was most known for its beer, and the presence of so many taverns along with three thousand students made for a rowdy drinking culture. In his letters, Erasmus frequently complained about the many boisterous parties he had to attend. (Stella Artois got its start in Louvain, and today the town is the headquarters of Anheuser-Busch InBev, the world's largest beer company.)

Of far greater concern to Erasmus were the many conservatives on the Louvain theology faculty. Along with their brethren in Cologne, they had ardently sided with the prosecutors of Johannes Reuchlin. Among the faculty members was Martin Dorp, who had earlier chastised Erasmus for both the astringency of the *Praise of Folly* and his irreverence in seeking to correct the New Testament. Many of the Louvain theologians were still smarting from Erasmus's jeers at the subtle doctors. Dorp had eventually come around, however, and Erasmus's growing celebrity had helped quell the more general carping against him.

He was allotted a spacious room in an upper story of the College of the Lily, one of the university's four colleges. He had a large table on which to place his papers, a couch on which to rest, and a garden in which to receive friends and visitors. And there were many of them, for few scholars could pass through Louvain without seeking an audience with the prince of learning. Nearly every day, a courier brought tributes from dukes, bishops, and professors in Germany, France, Italy, and Spain. Paschasius Berselius, a Benedictine from Liège, wrote to Erasmus about the excitement he felt upon opening a letter from him: "It ravished my heart, my bowels turned to water, my mind failed. Never have I felt so sweetly the bewitching magic of affection." All the while, Erasmus was pestered for copy. "We are daily expecting a great parcel of work from you," Beatus Rhenanus wrote from Basel, "and as soon as it arrives, everything else shall be put on one side, and the house of Froben will print nothing that is not Erasmus."

Erasmus at this moment of peak celebrity is captured in a portrait by Quentin Massys (or Metsys). In the thriving towns of Flanders, a new form of intimate portraiture was emerging as prosperous burghers sought to commemorate their success and individuality, and Massys was one of its masters. He showed Erasmus at his desk, applying his reed pen to a folio-size notebook. Lying on the shelf behind him are his revised New Testament, the *Praise of Folly*, and his editions of Lucian and Jerome. Erasmus's fur-lined black robe and matching black biretta—set against the nut-brown wood of the wall and shelves behind him—exude medieval sobriety. His face, taut and unlined, has the sallow hue of a man who spends too much time indoors. The one bright surface is the luminous page on which he is writing—the text as beacon, lighting the world with its wisdom and insight.

The text in this case (identifiable from the lines written on the page) is Erasmus's paraphrase of the Epistle to the Romans, which he had prepared in Antwerp before moving to Louvain. Erasmus's aim was to put the epistle into a colloquial Latin that educated readers could comprehend. Though Paul was the "one infallible oracle of Christ," he explained, many had been discouraged from reading him by the strangeness of his language. His Greek had such an admixture of Hebrew idiom in it that even Greek speakers had trouble understanding him; Erasmus wanted to strip away the Hebraisms and give Paul a "Roman dress." Appearing in the autumn of 1517, the paraphrase would prove so successful that Erasmus decided to move on to Paul's other epistles. He would ultimately produce paraphrases on nearly the entire New Testament—another part of his project to make Scripture more accessible to laypeople (or at least those who could read Latin).

While in Louvain, Erasmus was preoccupied with another key part of his reform program: peace. Not long after settling there, he completed what would be his longest statement on the subject. *Querela Pacis* ("A Complaint of Peace") features the character of Peace, who issues an ardent appeal for international concord. Erasmus—building on the arguments he had made in *Dulce bellum inexpertis* and *The Education of a Christian Prince*—denounces with even greater indignation the frenzy with which Christians attack and slaughter one another. "What land has not been soaked in Christian blood, what river or sea not stained with human gore?" Peace asks. Neither theologians nor monks, bishops nor cardinals, are ashamed to be the instigators and leaders of the very thing that Christ found so abhorrent. "What has a miter to do with a helmet, a crozier with a sword, the Gospel with a shield?"

Toward the end of the essay, Erasmus decries the nationalist animosities that had set Christian against Christian:

The English are hostile to the French, for no other reason than that they are French. The Scots are disliked by the British, solely for being Scots. Germans don't agree with French, Spaniards don't agree with either. What perversity—for the mere name of a place to divide people when there is so much which could bring them together! . . . How can something so trivial weigh more with people than so many natural ties, and so many bonds in Christ?

He dismissed geographic barriers as similarly artificial. The Rhine separates the French from the Germans, but it should not divide Christian from Christian. The Pyrenees form a physical barrier between the Spanish and the French, but they should not destroy the communion of the Church.

In the ninth century, Charlemagne had advanced the idea of a Christian Europe under the rule of a single sovereign. In the thirteenth, Dante had articulated the ideal of a common humanity governed by a universal monarch, with peace as a precondition. Now, in *Querela Pacis*, Erasmus was making the case for a pan-European identity rooted in the concept of a common Christian brotherhood. First published in December 1517, the essay would appear in more than twenty editions over the next twenty years as well as in numerous translations, helping to confirm Erasmus's position as the leading proponent of European union.

The book that would earn him the most notice, however, did not even bear his name. *Julius Exclusus e Coelis* ("Julius Excluded from Heaven"), published anonymously at the start of 1517, was a piercing satire featuring Pope Julius II appearing before the doors of heaven, only to find them locked. Pounding away, he demands that they be opened. St. Peter appears and, speaking through a window, asks who is making such a racket. Julius indicates his magnificent tiara and bejeweled robe, which is stamped with the letters "P.M." (for "Pontifex Maximus"). "I suppose they stand for 'Pestis Maxima' ['Supreme Plague']," Peter says. Seeing Julius's fierce eyes and the bloody weapons clattering under his garment, he refuses to open the doors.

There follows a long and heated exchange between Julius, who insists on being admitted, and Peter, who resolutely refuses. Julius boasts of the many measures he had taken as pope to enlarge the papal treasury, including adding to the papal lands through the use of arms and inventing a system in which bishoprics could be bought without prompting charges of simony. Peter, unimpressed, notes that he had been instructed by Christ to open the doors not to those carrying "bulls heavy with lead" but to "those who have clothed the naked, fed the hungry, given drink to the thirsty, visited the prisoner, and taken in the stranger." Back and forth they go, with Julius crowing about all the wealth and prestige he had brought to the Holy See and Peter castigating him for becoming a captive of money and power. "You won't open up, then?" Julius asks. "The last person I'd let in is a pestilent fellow like you," says Peter.

The publication of so sharp a lampoon of so recently departed a pope (Julius had died in 1513) was unheard of, and as it circulated around Europe, it set off an uproar—and intense speculation about its author. Most suspected Erasmus. "How I have enjoyed the *Julius*!" Guy Morillon, a member of the Burgundian court in Brussels, exulted to him about the dialogue's enthusiastic reception there. "I paid it the tribute of a continuous chuckle; how delightfully and amusingly, and in a word, Erasmically, he argues with Peter is easier to understand than to explain."

Erasmus himself, however, angrily disclaimed all responsibility for the work. An "egregious absurdity," he insisted, noting that he did not have a mind so irreligious as to poke fun at the Holy Father. Yet Erasmus never categorically denied writing the piece. And, while its authorship has never been conclusively demonstrated, the case for his involvement is overwhelming. The most telling piece of evidence is a letter that Thomas More sent him in December 1516, noting that he had in his possession some notebooks that Thomas Lupset, Erasmus's secretary during his stay in Cambridge, had given to him to be forwarded to Erasmus. Among them was the draft of a dialogue titled *Julius Genius* that was in Erasmus's own hand. This seems an unmistakable reference to *Julius Exclusus*. ("Genius" is a minor character in the dialogue.) Erasmus had probably written it while in Cambridge, soon after the death of Julius.

He had good cause to conceal his involvement, though. At the time, he was continuing to work to persuade the Holy See to grant him dispensations allowing him to hold more than one benefice and absolving him of all penalties associated with putting aside his religious habit. The appearance of such a satire in his name could have derailed that effort. But the manuscript seems to have fallen into the hands of someone who did want it published, and as it spread across the continent, it delivered a major blow to papal prestige.

Erasmus had another reason to hide his connection to *Julius Exclusus*: his relations with the Louvain theologians. Given their devotion to Rome, any more mockery of the Church could upset the provisional peace between them. Already, Erasmus had embarked on a project with the potential to provoke. While traveling around the Low Countries, he had interested a wealthy friend, Jérôme de Busleyden, the archdeacon of Cambrai, in the idea of backing a new college to teach the three biblical languages. Soon after Erasmus's arrival in Louvain, Busleyden died, but in his will he left a sum to endow the salaries for three professors and scholarships for eight students. Taking over the project, Erasmus began laying the foundation for the Collegium Trilingue ("College of Three Tongues"), as it came to be called. Through it, he hoped to train a new generation of scholars who, proficient in Latin, Greek, and Hebrew, could carry on his program to restore Scripture and revitalize the faith.

From the start, however, the college faced strong resistance. Its very premise—that a knowledge of languages was critical to the study of Scripture—seemed to threaten the authority of the Vulgate and the time-honored methods of interpreting it. Suspicions grew as Erasmus recruited its faculty. The leading candidate to fill the Hebrew chair was Matthaeus Adrianus. Born in Spain in 1475 to a Jewish family, he had converted to Christianity and, after studying medicine in Italy, become a physician. In 1512, in Tübingen, Adrianus had met Johannes Reuchlin, who suggested that he teach Hebrew. Erasmus, introduced to him in Brussels, was impressed with his knowledge of the language, and after much prodding Adrianus agreed to take the position in Louvain. His connection to Reuchlin unsettled the Louvain theologians, but for the time being they remained silent.

Erasmus took advantage of the calm to proceed with his new edition of the New Testament. During his travels around the Low Countries, he had been able to inspect several old manuscripts—a codex of the Gospels from a monastery outside Zwolle in the Netherlands; a Greek manuscript from the Augustinian cloister at Corsendonck in Flanders; a third lent by his friend Cuthbert Tunstall—that would prove of great help in his expanding of the annotations and translating of the New Testament. Instead of the partial revision of the Vulgate he had offered in the first edition, Erasmus now planned a completely new translation—a far riskier enterprise.

While he was thus absorbed, the first attack on his first edition arrived.

It came, surprisingly enough, from a fellow humanist, Jacques Lefèvre d'Étaples (also known as Jacobus Faber Stapulensis, the Latinized version of his name). Lefèvre's *Quincuplex Psalterium* and his commentary on Paul's epistles had established him as a pioneer in the new critical methods, and Erasmus had become friendly with him in Paris. When Lefèvre read Erasmus's annotations, however, he was startled by the one on Hebrews 2:7. This verse—one of the most controversial in the New Testament—states that God made Jesus "a little lower than the angels," so that in suffering death, "he might taste death for everyone." The idea that Christ could be lower than the angels, even when appearing in human form, seemed to diminish his divinity, and for centuries exegetes had objected. Lefèvre, in his commentary on Paul, had echoed them. Citing Psalm 8, on which this passage was based, he argued that the text should in fact state that Christ was made a little lower than God, not the angels. In this way, Christ's exalted status would be preserved.

Erasmus strongly disagreed. In his view, Jesus's humanity was the very point of the passage. Ever since his debate with John Colet in Oxford nearly twenty years earlier, he had held fast to the idea that Christ could feel fear and humiliation like ordinary humans. It was precisely the pain and suffering Christ had endured that made his sacrifice and fortitude so inspiring. Erasmus was so committed to this reading that in his annotation on the passage, he had criticized Lefèvre by name for suggesting that it be changed.

Lefèvre was deeply offended, and in a revision of his commentary on Paul that he was preparing, he struck back. To maintain that Christ, even while on the cross, was inferior to the angels, he said, was to deny the unity of the Trinity—a position that was "impious and most unworthy of Christ and God."

Now it was Erasmus's turn to bristle. Convinced that Lefèvre was charging him with blasphemy, Erasmus drafted a detailed defense in which he maintained that to speak of Christ's humiliation is not to scorn him. We honor his cross with reverence; his mocking is our glory. After cataloging what he saw as Lefèvre's many errors of scholarship, Erasmus became cruelly personal: "If only you had refrained altogether from this field of translation and making annotations. It was, as I said before, not your métier. You were capable of greater things. This task, however humble it might be, demanded a knowledge of the two tongues. I need not say what capacities you have in this respect: your writings bear public witness to it."

As soon as his *Apologia ad Fabrum* came off the press, in August 1517, Erasmus sent copies around to friends. Many were troubled by the severity of his comments about Lefèvre; others rued the intramural nature of the dispute, which they felt could only hearten the conservatives. Lefèvre himself—clearly stung by Erasmus's criticism—refused to respond. Taking his silence as an admission of defeat, Erasmus for months boasted of his victory—conduct that struck many of his friends as distinctly un-Christlike.

Just as the clash with Lefèvre was subsiding, another broke out with Johann Eck. A professor of theology at the University of Ingolstadt in southern Germany, Eck was celebrated for both his debating skills and his knowledge of Church tradition and canon law. In early 1518 he sent Erasmus a barbed letter outlining many objections to his annotations. One concerned Erasmus's contention that the authors of the Gospels, in misquoting the Old Testament, had relied on faulty memory. "Listen, dear Erasmus," he wrote, "do you suppose any Christian will patiently endure to be told that the evangelists in their Gospels made mistakes? If the authority of the Holy Scriptures at this point is shaky, can any passage be free from the suspicion of error?" He similarly admonished Erasmus for asserting that the Greek of the evangelists was less than perfect. It was not from Greek teachers that they had learned the language but from the Holy Spirit.

Most disturbing of all in Eck's eyes was Erasmus's preference for Jerome over Augustine. "There is no shortcoming in you which your supporters so much regret as your failure to have read Augustine," he wrote. "Cease therefore, dear Erasmus, to darken by your criticisms a leading light of the church. . . . Admit rather that Augustine was a great scholar, steep yourself in his works and turn his pages with all diligence, and you will regard as quite shameless the man who dares prefer any of the Fathers to Augustine as a scholar."

Erasmus would make no such admission. In a caustic reply, he maintained that the authority of Scripture is not imperiled if an evangelist by a slip of memory had mistakenly substituted one name for another. Nowhere is it said that the apostles spoke Greek by some miracle. Origen and other Greek commentators found many difficulties in Paul's uncouth style. As for Augustine, Erasmus noted, he was the first author he had read, and he had continued to reread Augustine as the need arose, but when he began reading Jerome, he was quickly persuaded of his superiority. Jerome was born in a town very close to Italy and educated in Rome under the best scholars of the day; Augustine was born in Africa, "a barbarous region where literary studies were at an amazingly low ebb." Jerome imbibed the philosophy of Christ with his mother's milk; Augustine was nearly thirty when he finally got around to reading Paul and was immediately distracted by his duties as a bishop. By his own admission, Augustine knew little or no Greek, whereas there was no book in the whole library of Greek literature that Jerome had not mastered. The only reason Augustine was ranked above Jerome and Ambrose in the academic fraternity was that he was more frequently quoted by those authors who ruled it.

At the time, Erasmus was preparing a new collection of his letters for publication, and he planned to include his exchange with Eck in it. In this way, he hoped to further his program to restore both the Bible and Jerome's reputation.

In the end, the greatest challenge to Erasmus's New Testament would come from a most unlikely source. Edward Lee was a cleric of Kentish origins in his midthirties who, after attending Oxford and Cambridge, had come to Louvain to improve his Greek. There he had met Erasmus, who spoke of his plan to revise his first edition of the New Testament and who encouraged Lee to suggest changes. Lee was flattered by the attention, and a friendship developed. As Erasmus progressed with his revision, he showed parts of it to Lee. At one point, Lee disclosed that he had made some notes on Erasmus's annotations, and he shared some of them with him. Lee's comments were not always as supportive as Erasmus would have liked, and Erasmus was occasionally sharp in his replies. Lee began hearing that at social gatherings Erasmus's friends were insulting him, telling jokes at his expense, and mocking him for daring to challenge the great Achilles of scholarship. Hurt, Lee stopped sharing his notes. He continued to compile them, however, and Erasmus, fearing the industry and ambition of the young scholar, became openly hostile toward him.

Erasmus had good cause for concern. After beginning with modest comments on technical points of grammar, Lee had begun to develop more serious objections. He was deeply troubled, for instance, by Erasmus's decision to omit the *comma Johanneum* at 1 John 5:7, with its reference to the Father, the Word, and the Holy Spirit. In doing so, Lee believed, Erasmus was removing the main scriptural foundation for the Trinity, thus threatening to revive the Arian heresy that had thrown the Church into such turmoil more than a millennium earlier. Similarly, Lee (like Luther) feared that Erasmus's questioning of Romans 5:12 as a scriptural foundation for the doctrine of original sin would encourage a revival of Pelagianism, with its heretical insistence on human perfectibility.

More generally, Lee had begun to develop doubts about the central premises of Erasmus's enterprise—that the Vulgate had serious flaws and that they could be repaired through a knowledge of syntax and semantics. Far from restoring the Scriptures to their original purity, Erasmus seemed to be defacing a sacred text. The Latin translator of the Bible had been guided by the Holy Spirit, and whatever faults there might appear to be in the Vulgate, they actually served a divine purpose. Were Erasmus's judgments to replace the sanctioned readings of the Fathers, popes, and councils? In Lee's rough notes on Erasmus's New Testament, one can detect the first signs of the great counterrevolution just beginning to take shape against the application of the new humanist methods to the Bible.

When his schedule allowed, Erasmus planned to make a preemptive strike against Lee. For the moment, however, he remained absorbed in his annotations. As the spring of 1518 approached, he felt that he had made enough progress to seek out a printer. He hoped to find one close to Louvain so that he would not have to travel far, but none, it turned out, had Greek type. Froben, of course, did, but Erasmus shrank from the prospect of making another trip to Basel. The thought of the dirty German inns with their reeking stoves made him queasy. In addition, Basel had recently been hit by the plague, and several prominent scholars had succumbed. On top of it all, a group of discharged soldiers known as the Black Band was plundering towns in the Rhineland, and there were many tales of travelers being murdered. Nonetheless, Erasmus felt he had no choice. "How I wish, my dear Bade, you had a good supply of Greek type!" he wrote to the printer Josse Bade in Paris. "As it is, I am obliged to go to Basel, at the risk of my life, for the New Testament cannot be published unless I am there in person."

Erasmus could, however, take comfort in his cordial relations with the Louvain faculty. "They thank me openly for my Jerome, there are no complaints for my New Testament," he wrote to a friend in the Burgundian court; "in fact the leaders of the faculty heartily approve. Not a dog barks, except a few friars of some sort at Cologne, I hear, and Bruges, but in the distance and behind my back." On all sides he was being congratulated on his conquest of Lefèvre, and his paraphrase of Romans was winning broad praise. Soon, he felt sure, everyone would be speaking in two or three tongues rather than one and drawing Scripture from the clearest springs.

There remained the practical matter of getting to Basel. Erasmus needed both money and a horse, and to solicit them he sent a courier with letters to his friends in England. Since 1495, the export of horses from that country had been restricted by law, but he felt sure that one of his correspondents could find a way around it.

One of those letters went to Thomas More. Erasmus informed his friend that the Froben press was preparing to bring out a new, corrected edition of *Utopia*. He also noted that he was sending along three works: a treatise in praise of liberal education (by the British envoy Richard Pace); a proposal from the pope for a crusade against the Turks; and "the Conclusions on Papal pardons." This last was undoubtedly Luther's Ninety-Five Theses. That Erasmus did not mention Luther's name suggests that he was not yet familiar with it. That would soon change.

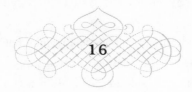
A DRUNKEN GERMAN

Winters in Wittenberg were always bleak. Raw winds swept in off the Central European plains, piercing mantles and penetrating walls. The variety of available foods shrank, making meals even more monotonous than usual. With the sun setting around four in the afternoon, families were trapped in their homes for long periods with little to distract them, and the itinerant preachers and peddlers who visited in warmer months appeared only rarely, deepening the town's sense of isolation.

For Luther, the winter of 1517–1518 was especially difficult. Several times a week, he trudged through the sleet and slush to the town church to mount its pulpit and exhort his huddled congregants. In early 1518, he began a second course of lectures on the Psalms, and, standing before the rows of note-taking students, he again bore into these opaque verses in search of Christ's redemptive presence. Despite his growing frustration with the devotional offices of his order, Luther continued to perform them, rising early in his frigid cell to say matins and holding vigils late into the icy night. To show his resoluteness, Luther went long periods without food or sleep, and the physical toll was mounting. "My poor worn body is exhausted by constant hardships—fasting, abstinence, austerity in labor and clothing," he wearily observed to Johann von Staupitz. The new cowl that Frederick had promised him a year earlier had not yet arrived, and Luther had to write to the elector to remind him of his pledge.

Most trying of all was the response to the Ninety-Five Theses. There wasn't any. After the initial flurry of excitement, the authorities had taken no action, and no one had come forward to accept his invitation to debate. Luther was beset by doubts about what he had written. Some of the theses should perhaps have been omitted, while others seemed in need of more explanation. At night in his study, he began to provide it, taking up the theses one by one and seeking support for them not in Aquinas or Scotus or any other human source but in Scripture. As his watchword, he took Paul's admonition at 1 Thessalonians 5:21: "Test everything; hold fast to what is good."

In his loneliness, books became his lifeline. With great interest Luther was following the tracts and translations that were flowing from the humanist presses. Wolfgang Capito, the Basel scholar who had helped Erasmus with his New Testament and who now began corresponding with Luther, sent reports on the latest productions of the house of Froben. On the basis of these reports, Luther recommended to his friend Johann Lang a list of titles to buy at the upcoming Frankfurt fair: the newest edition of Erasmus's *Adages*, his *Querela Pacis*, the dialogues of Lucian, More's *Utopia*, and Capito's own *Institutiones Hebraicae* (a guide to Hebrew grammar). Luther was especially eager to get a copy of Erasmus's *Apologia* against Lefèvre. Having closely followed their exchange, he expressed regret "that such a conflict should have broken out between these great princes of learning." Erasmus, he observed, "is certainly by far the superior of the two" but "also more violent, though he makes a great effort to preserve friendship."

Luther was also reading *Julius Exclusus*, with delight. The dialogue (he wrote to Spalatin) "is so merry, so learned, so ingenious (that is, so Erasmian), that it makes the reader laugh and joke at the vices and miseries of Christ's church, for which rather every Christian ought to pray and weep." Luther was so captivated that he thought of translating the work into German, but he dropped the idea when he realized that he could not do justice to the style. Luther signed his letter "Eleutherius," Greek for "free"—a sign of both his growing ease in that language and his sense of spiritual emancipation.

Eleutherius's letters in this period contain unmistakable Erasmian echoes. In a message to Spalatin at the end of 1517, for instance, he noted how few saints were honored for offering charity, patience, humility, faith, hope, and other spiritual goods. St. Lawrence was worshipped to ward off fire, Sebastian to prevent the plague, and Valentine to control epilepsy; otherwise, these men "would be little esteemed." This passage seems to have been directly inspired by the *Enchiridion* and its stress on inner piety over formal worship. In his study of Scripture, meanwhile, Luther remained indebted to Erasmus's annotations and the insight they offered on difficult passages.

Where Erasmus's theological insights were concerned, however, Luther was dismissive. Whenever he addressed opponents of the New Learning, he wrote, "I always give Erasmus the highest praise and defend him as much as I can," but "if I have to speak as a theologian rather than a philologian, there are many things in Erasmus which seem to me completely incongruous with a knowledge of Christ." One cannot enter into the meaning of Scripture simply through study or innate intelligence, he added; one must instead rely on prayer and the infusion of the Spirit. Erasmus extolled Jerome, but, to understand Christ and grace, Augustine and Ambrose were superior guides.

Finally, in late January or early February 1518, Luther heard the first rumbles of discontent over the Ninety-Five Theses. They came at a Dominican conclave taking place in Frankfurt an der Oder, about a hundred miles to the east. The Dominicans were bitter rivals of the Augustinians, and their hostility had deepened as a result of Luther's attack on indulgences. It had so eaten into the profits of Johann Tetzel that he had given up selling them. At the meeting, Tetzel defended a set of 106 "anti-theses" on indulgences that attacked Luther's theses at several points. Rallying to Tetzel's defense, Dominican preachers began denouncing Luther from the pulpit, calling him a heretic and predicting that within a month he would be burned at the stake. Tetzel's anti-theses were printed up and carried by booksellers to cities and towns across Germany.

One of those peddlers turned up in Wittenberg. Appearing in the marketplace, he was confronted by a group of students, who, harassing and jostling him, demanded to know how he dared bring such wares into their town. Some bought up copies of the anti-theses; others seized them from his bag. Townspeople were invited to assemble in the marketplace at two o'clock in the afternoon, and at that hour hundreds of copies of the anti-theses were burned. Luther—sure he would be blamed for the act—disapproved.

The Dominicans' campaign was encouraging others, and by mid-February the Ninety-Five Theses were being "overwhelmed with abuse," as Luther put it. Indulgences were "nothing but a snare for souls," but in exposing them as a fraud, he had entered a "dangerous labyrinth of disputation" in which "six hundred Minotaurs" were arrayed against him. "The false preachers of indulgences are thundering against me in wonderful style."

Luther was especially disturbed by the tirade directed at him by Johann Eck—the same Ingolstadt professor who had reproved Erasmus for his New Testament annotations. Earlier, Eck and Luther had had an amicable exchange of letters, leading Luther to consider him a friend, but when Eck read the Ninety-Five Theses, he became so agitated that he immediately wrote down his objections. His manuscript—titled *Obelisks*, after the critical marks used to signify offensive passages in texts—denounced Luther for daring to question so sacred an institution as indulgences. Eck called him a heretic, presumptuous, insubordinate, unlearned, softheaded, a despiser of the pope, and most serious of all, a Bohemian—a term that linked Luther's ideas to those of Jan Hus, whose challenge to indulgences and other Catholic institutions had brought him to the stake a century earlier. Just as Hus had doomed himself by promoting Bible readings unsanctioned by Rome, Eck wrote, so was Luther circulating his own teachings rather than those of the Church.

Eck had not intended to make his comments public, but Luther's friend Wenceslas Link in Nuremberg had obtained a copy and sent it to him. Luther was shocked to see himself treated so severely by someone whom he had considered an ally. Eck's book "is nothing less than the malice and envy of a maniac," he wrote. Luther quickly prepared a counterattack. Titled *Asterisks*, after the marks used to highlight important passages in a text, it was six times as long as *Obelisks* and no less vituperative. Eck, he wrote, is an example of Scholastic sterility who stinks "of his goat Aristotle." His statement that the free will rules in the soul like a king in his kingdom really means like the madam in her brothel, "for the will alone is always a whore and has all the qualities of a whore." *Asterisks* offered an early taste of Luther's talent for invective. But his ferocity was a response to Eck's own vehemence. Rather than engage with the substantive issues raised by indulgences, Eck had immediately turned the matter into a test of ecclesiastical authority—a far graver concern.

Until now, the dispute over indulgences had been confined to the cloister and the university. Seeking a wider audience, Luther decided for the first time to set down his ideas in German. The *Sermon on Indulgences and Grace* was designed to give the laity a succinct summary of the urgent issues at stake. In it, Luther rejected indulgences even more sharply than he had in his theses. It was, he wrote, much better to give alms to those in need than to waste them on such empty contrivances as indulgences, and if he was called a heretic for saying so, he did not care, for only those who did not truly understand the Bible would use such a label.

Printed by Johann Rhau-Grunenberg in March 1518, the *Sermon on Indulgences and Grace* was a crudely produced pamphlet of twelve pages. Copies—packed in wooden kegs and transported by horseback and cart—went quickly, and other printers began bringing out their own editions. More than twenty would appear by the end of 1520; with an edition in those days averaging about a thousand copies, this was an extraordinary number for such a sober work. The *Sermon on Indulgences and Grace* was an example of a new product of the printing industry— the *Flugschrift*, or short pamphlet—and its success suggested the large market that existed for such works. In some ways, the publication of the sermon was as historically significant as the posting of the Ninety-Five Theses, marking the moment when Luther discovered the power of writing in the vernacular.

As Luther's views spread, so did the anger against him. "I know perfectly well that my name is in bad odor with many," he wrote at the end of March 1518. Even many good men had found fault with him "for condemning rosaries, tonsures, chanting psalms and other prayers, in short, all 'good works.'" His preference for the Bible over the Scholastic doctors had excited great hatred among the theologians, who "are almost insane with their zeal," but "with God's help I care nothing for their scarecrows." If Scotus and Biel had the right to dissent from Aquinas, and if the Thomists had the right to contradict everybody else, why should he not be entitled to do the same?

Amid this growing rage, Luther received a summons from Johann von Staupitz, the head of his order, to appear at the next chapter meeting of the Augustinians, to be held in Heidelberg in late April 1518. Staupitz—

wanting to give his protégé an opportunity to show off his skills as a theologian—instructed him to prepare a set of theses for disputation. To minimize controversy, though, he advised him to avoid the subject of indulgences and instead concentrate on his new ideas about faith and grace, works and free will. At long last, Luther was going to get a chance to discuss his views publicly—if, that is, he made it to Heidelberg safely. For the first time since posting his theses, he would be leaving the environs of Wittenberg. Heidelberg was in the Rhineland, about 250 miles away, and getting there would pose great danger.

"Everybody advises me not to go to Heidelberg," Luther wrote to Johann Lang in Erfurt. "But I shall fulfill my vow of obedience and go thither on foot." The elector had taken him under his protection and would not "suffer them to drag me to Rome." Frederick provided a safe-conduct letter as well as introductions to officials in the territories through which Luther was to pass. (The elector also came through with the long-promised cowl.) As an added precaution, Luther traveled incognito, and a careful route with designated stops was mapped out to reduce the threat of abduction or attack.

Apprehensive and resigned, Luther—accompanied by a fellow friar named Leonhard Beier—left Wittenberg on foot on April 11, 1518. From the moment the two men crossed the bridge out of Wittenberg and into the springtime countryside, however, all went well. They traveled south to Leipzig, then passed through the wooded valleys and rolling hills of Thuringia to the village of Judenbach. There they were received by a Saxon councilor, who treated them to a fine dinner. Midway through the journey, Luther reported to Spalatin that he was "terribly fatigued" from walking but that no vehicles were available. Proceeding through groves of pines and firs and over the hill to Coburg, they turned west into the Mainz valley. Stopping in the episcopal seat of Würzburg, they were entertained in the Marienberg castle, a fortress that overlooked the town. Luther was cheered to find that the Augustinian delegation from Erfurt, including Johann Lang, was present, and for the remaining seventy miles to Heidelberg, he and Beier were able to travel in the delegation's wagon.

In Heidelberg, Luther was to his surprise received as a guest of honor. Home to Germany's oldest university, the town was ruled by Count

Palatine Wolfgang. He invited Luther, Lang, and Staupitz (who had arrived in the city) to a grand dinner and showed them the Heidelberg castle, which, rising on a spur above the city, offered a view across the Neckar River to the fertile plain of the Rhine. They also got to see the treasures of the castle church, which included a splinter of the True Cross. Luther stayed in the Augustinian convent, where on April 25, 1518, in the large hall, the chapter meeting began.

Luther had prepared twenty-eight theological and twelve philosophical theses, and he presided while Leonhard Beier defended them. In the audience were Augustinian officials and doctors from around Germany, along with some students and members of other orders eager to see the controversial friar. For the first time, they heard the bracing new theology that Luther had developed from his intensive readings of the Psalms and Romans. His theses stressed the weakness of man and the omnipotence of God, the inutility of works and the centrality of faith. The person who believes "that he can obtain grace by doing what is in him" simply increases his sin, according to one thesis. It is not through works and glory that God's grace can be found but through suffering and the cross.

Physically, Luther made a strong impression. Overwork and undernourishment had left him with chiseled cheekbones that stood out in his large tonsured head, and his dark eyes radiated evangelical intensity. He quoted effortlessly from the Bible, engaged in easy repartee, and spoke with earnest conviction. Some found his views shocking. "If the peasants would hear this, they would certainly stone you to death," a university doctor declared at one point. Most of those in attendance, however, were favorably impressed. The count palatine wrote to Frederick that Luther had performed so well that he had won "no small praise for your Grace's university and was greatly lauded by many learned persons."

Among those persons was Martin Bucer, a twenty-six-year-old Dominican from Alsace then studying in Heidelberg. "Although our chief men refuted him with all their might, their wiles were not able to make him move an inch from his propositions," he wrote to Beatus Rhenanus in Basel. Luther's "sweetness in answering is remarkable, his patience in listening is incomparable, in his explanations you would recognize the acumen of Paul, not of Scotus; his answers so brief, so wise, and drawn from the Holy Scriptures, easily made all his hearers his admirers." On the day after the disputation, Bucer dined with Luther, and the meal was "rich with doctrine rather than with dainties." Luther, he added, "agrees with Erasmus in all things, but with this difference in his favor, that what Erasmus only insinuates he teaches openly and freely."

Bucer's remark shows how natural it was for observers at this point to link the ideas of the two men. Luther, in his sharp condemnations of clerical excesses, his praise for internal piety over formal ceremony, and his preference for the Scriptures over the *Sentences*, did seem to echo Erasmus. Luther's more radical notions about human depravity and help-lessness were not immediately apparent. Bucer's esteem for Luther was especially telling, for he represented a new generation of humanists who in the future would face choosing between schools led by the two men. For many young reformers, the friar's spiritual magnetism would prove hard to resist.

Older traditionalists, however, were largely immune. Luther's attack on Scholastic methods and ideas, including his disdain for the notion that man can cooperate with God in seeking salvation, seemed to senior Augustinians a repudiation of their entire system. The depth of their dis-approval became apparent to Luther on his return to Wittenberg. A group of Nurembergers gave him a ride to Würzburg, where he transferred to the wagon of some brethren from Erfurt, with whom he continued to that city. For part of the journey his companion was Bartholomäus Arnoldi von Usingen, one of his old Erfurt professors. Luther tried hard to win him over to his new concepts but succeeded only in confounding him. In Erfurt, Luther met with another former professor, Jodokus Trutfetter, who, far from being persuaded, angrily reproached him for his defection.

To the Erfurters, his ideas were "twice-deadly cabbage," Luther wrote to Spalatin after arriving back in Wittenberg, on May 15, 1518, lifting a phrase from Erasmus's *Adages*. But he was greatly encouraged by the enthusiasm of the young. Just as Christ, rejected by the Jews, went over to the Gentiles, so he hoped that his "true theology," dismissed "by those opinionated old men, would pass over to the younger generation." Expressing his overall satisfaction with his trip, Luther observed that he "had gone out on foot" but "returned in a wagon." Even the food and drink had agreed with him, so that "some think I look stronger and fatter now."

At the meeting in Heidelberg, Staupitz had arranged for Luther to be relieved of his position as district vicar. His aim was to lighten Luther's workload, but the move represented the first formal loosening of Luther's ties to the Church. Freed from his administrative duties, Luther had more time to devote to preaching, lecturing, and writing, and he used it to further explore his new ideas. On the Sunday following his return, he was scheduled to preach at the town church, and as his subject he chose excommunication, or the ban. At the time, rumors were afoot that Luther himself might be excommunicated, causing great anxiety in the town, but rather than sidestep the issue, he decided to confront it head-on.

Like indulgences, the Church's use of excommunication had produced growing resentment. Once a solemn punishment reserved for heretics and reprobates, it was now being routinely used to enforce the collection of payments and dues, not only from senior clerics unable to meet the levies on their offices but also from ordinary Christians falling behind in their tithes. Further, the original punishment of excluding the banned individual from the community of believers by denying him the sacraments had been extended to include a prohibition on all commercial dealings with the offender. Not only the felonious individual but also all of his relatives were subject to the ban. Crowds of excommunicants, forced from their homes, were reduced to begging. Those who died while excommunicated had to be interred without the rites of the Church and so were exposed to an eternity of torment. By the early sixteenth century, the Church was punishing not only individuals but whole communities it judged to have interfered with its prerogatives. Town councils that tried to impose limits on the commercial activities of monasteries, for instance, frequently found themselves subject to an interdict, with all Church rites and observances prohibited within the town.

In his sermon, Luther inveighed against these practices. The ban, he declared, could affect only the external aspects of the relationship between a Christian and the Church, such as participation in the sacraments. It could not affect his inner relationship with God, which depended on faith, hope, and charity and which no human agent—not even the pope—could disturb. Unfortunately, the authority over such instruments was too often placed in the hands of the Pilates and Herods of the world, who used them to extract sums from the defenseless while the "big Johns" went untouched despite being fornicators, slanderers, and usurers. An unjust ban should be endured but its importance shattered, just as one could pop a pig's bladder filled with peas that rattled (a popular children's toy).

Just days after his return from Heidelberg, Luther was again defying the Church. As it happened, the Dominicans had spies in the town church (a practice that would become commonplace), and from their notes they produced a set of theses on the ban that was even more provocative than Luther's actual statements. Published and circulated under his name, this counterfeit document caused such a stir that Luther felt compelled to reconstruct and publish his sermon. Appearing in August 1518 under the title *Sermon on the Virtue of Excommunication*, it would go through a dozen printings in less than two years.

As this episode shows, the criticism of Luther, far from making him reconsider his views, was hardening them. "The more they threaten," he declared, "the bolder I am." This was certainly apparent in his *Explanations of the Ninety-Five Theses*, which he completed at the end of May 1518 after months of labor. At seventy thousand words, the tract was baggy, rambling, convoluted, and laced with scriptural quotes—features that would become common in Luther's longer theological works. But the *Explanations* was a critical text of his formative years, showing how his ideas about the supreme power of faith and grace were pushing him into conflict with the Church. Luther treated Leo X with respect, calling him "a very good pope" whose "integrity and learning are a delight to all upright persons," but, he noted, he did not much care what pleased or displeased Leo, for "he is a human being just like the rest of us." There were many popes who had not only erred but also committed terrible deeds. A good example was Julius II and the "horrible murders" for which he was responsible. Rome was a "veritable Babylon," an "infernal abyss" of simony, lust, pageantry, murder, and other abominations. The "extortion" to which poor people were subjected through indulgences to help build the new St. Peter's had to cease. Luther expressed his hope that the trials confronting the Church would lead to a "future reformation"—one of his earliest uses of the term that would become so associated with his name.

On completing the *Explanations*, Luther sent a copy to Johann von Staupitz, who had played such a key part in his intellectual development. In the accompanying letter—one of the most revealing he ever wrote—he explained how he had reached this critical point in his career, offering an emotional account that extended back to his early struggles with the term *poenitentia* ("penance"). He thanked Staupitz for having helped him understand that *poenitentia* is not the end of the process of penitence but its beginning. He also acknowledged the contribution of "the most learned men who teach us Greek and Hebrew with such great devotion" and who had pointed out that the Greek word underlying *poenitentia* was *metanoia* (a change in disposition)—a clear reference to Erasmus and his annotations. Thus aided, Luther had seen the spuriousness of the doctrine behind indulgences. He asked Staupitz to forward his treatise to Rome along with a dedicatory letter to Leo X.

In that letter, Luther earnestly tried to make the pope see why he had acted as he had. He described how the preachers of indulgences had with their wild claims threatened to make a mockery of ecclesiastical authority and how he had felt compelled to issue warnings about the scandal they were causing. For this, he had been called a heretic, an apostate, a traitor, and a "hundred other calumnious epithets," and though his ears were horrified, his conscience was at peace. He was now casting himself at the feet of the blessed father. If the pope approved or disapproved of him, raised him or slew him, he would recognize his words as those of Christ. "If I have deserved death, I shall not refuse to die," Luther wrote, convinced that if Leo understood the fullness of his faith, he would recognize the sincerity of his pleas for reform.

For Leo, however, the dyspeptic grumblings of a frustrated friar in far-off Saxony were of little concern. Five years into his pontificate, the Medici pope was close to realizing his goal of making Rome the center of world culture. "All men who have any gifts in the literary way," Cardinal Riario exulted to Erasmus, "flock to this city from every quarter as though it were a theater." At the newly reorganized University of Rome, eighty-eight lecturers gave courses on everything from philosophy and theology to medicine and math, while at the Vatican Library scholars pored over newly acquired rare manuscripts. In the villas of the Quirinal, on the slopes of the Capitoline, in sheltered salons along the Tiber, humanists served up epigrams and elegies praising Pallas's spear and Orpheus's lyre, the scrolls of Clio and Calliope's writing tablet, thus helping to inaugurate a new Augustan age.

All the while, self-indulgence and pleasure-seeking were reaching new heights in the Vatican, and warnings about the possible consequences were multiplying. The most insistent came during the Fifth Lateran Council. Convened in 1512 by Julius II and continuing until March 1517, this conclave had produced a graphic picture of the cupidity and venality that had infected all aspects of Church life. To fight it, a series of remedial bulls and degrees were adopted. Simony, nepotism, and the holding of multiple benefices were all to be ended. Cardinals were admonished to live sober, chaste, and godly lives, and all preachers were to be vetted and discouraged from issuing false prophecies or claiming a personal mission from God. In a famous closing address, the scholar-orator Gianfrancesco Pico della Mirandola (the nephew of the great humanist) inveighed against the materialism, cynicism, selfishness, and general delinquency that had captured the Holy See. "If Leo leaves crime any longer unpunished," he warned, "if he refuses to heal the wounds, it is to be feared that God Himself will no longer apply a slow remedy, but will cut off and destroy the diseased members with fire and sword."

On the very eve of Luther's protest, then, the pope was put on notice of the gathering crisis. He paid little heed, however. Enacting the proposed reforms would have put an end to the easy living to which so many ecclesiasts had become accustomed. The modest measures that were introduced, meanwhile, faced intense resistance from the Curia, and the Holy See remained a cauldron of scheming and intrigue. Shortly after the council's conclusion, Leo shocked Rome by announcing that he had uncovered a conspiracy in the College of Cardinals to poison him.

The plot was just the latest in a series of insurrections led by cardinals against the papacy, and in July 1517 Leo, seeking to put an end to them, named thirty-one new cardinals—a number without precedent in Vatican annals. While some of those named were duly qualified, being pious, learned, and wise, others had far more experience as courtiers than as clerics and were chosen primarily for their connections or wealth. The price tags for the new positions ran as high as thirty thousand ducats, which seemed a bargain in light of the many lucrative benefices and other preferments made possible by a cardinal's hat.

Leo was in desperate need of such sums, for the papal cupboard was nearly bare. On becoming pope, he had declared his intention of avoiding the military adventurism of Julius, but in 1517 he had become involved in a financially ruinous war with the duke of Urbino, a small but culturally rich duchy east of Florence. The campaign was meant to be short but dragged on for eight months, and by the time it was over, in September 1517, it had consumed 800,000 ducats—a sum nearly equal to the annual revenues of the city of Venice.

But Leo refused to retrench. He continued to mount elaborate hunting expeditions, to throw grand banquets featuring the flesh of exotic animals, to distribute bags of coins to favored poets and orators. And no sooner was the conflict with Urbino over than he decided to embark on another costly enterprise—a crusade against the Turks. At the time, all of Western Europe lived in fear of the Ottoman threat. Under the leadership of Sultan Selim I, the 100,000-man Ottoman army had for the past several years marched through the East, pacifying Persia, conquering Syria, occupying Gaza, and gaining control of Jerusalem, beginning a period of Ottoman rule over that city that would last until 1917. Racing across the Sinai into Egypt, the Ottomans in January 1517 toppled the Mamlūk sultanate. With the heart of the Arab world now under his control, Selim declared himself caliph. His conquest of the Levant marked the arrival of the Ottomans as a world power, and it made conflict between the Islamic East and the Christian West appear inevitable.

It certainly seemed that way to Leo. Convinced that the Turks intended to attack Rhodes and then Hungary, he considered it his sacred duty as the head of Western Christendom to rally its princes and peoples against them. Rather than wait to be attacked, Leo wanted to launch a preemptive strike against the infidels on their own turf, and to carry it out he planned to raise a huge force consisting of Swiss infantry, Venetian battalions, and ships from Spain, Portugal, and England, all of which he intended to deploy in a grand campaign to conquer and occupy Istanbul.

The projected cost of such an expedition was 800,000 ducats—the same amount Leo had squandered on the war against Urbino. To raise it, he proposed a special tax to be imposed on Christian Europe. To help get this tax approved, he named four cardinals to serve as legates to the Continent's four great powers: France, England, Spain, and the Holy Roman Empire. The first three headed north in mid-April 1518. The fourth, Cardinal Farnese, who was assigned to the empire, was ill and unable to travel; to take his place, Leo chose Cardinal Tommaso Cajetan, one of the thirty-one new cardinals named the previous summer. Cajetan accepted the post, and on May 5, 1518, he set off on the long journey to Augsburg, where the Imperial Diet—the empire's parliament—was meeting.

Engaged in so many projects, Leo took his eye off a major one: St. Peter's. Raphael remained in charge of the basilica but managed to accomplish little aside from raising one or two small columns and continuing the construction of Bramante's vaulting. The many demands on Raphael's time were partly responsible, but so was the drying up of funds for the project. The flow from the St. Peter's indulgence, once so steady, had shriveled as a result of Luther's opposition.

Years later, Luther recalled having heard that Leo, on first learning of the Ninety-Five Theses, dismissed them as the work of a drunken German who would feel differently when he sobered up. (The remark has never been verified.) After receiving a copy of the theses from the archbishop of Mainz, the pope did take one measure, directing Gabriele della Volta, the vicar-general of the Augustinian Hermits, to take the necessary steps to silence the refractory friar. Volta had relayed that demand to Johann von Staupitz. Staupitz's response, however, had been to invite Luther to Heidelberg, and Luther himself had delivered his sermon against the ban.

The Dominicans would not let the matter rest. In May 1518, they held their annual chapter meeting at Santa Maria sopra Minerva, their seat in Rome. A delegate from Germany described the confusion and havoc the friar was causing there. Johann Tetzel's trade had been seriously disrupted, and respect for the Church had declined. Luther had denounced the ban, impugned Aristotle, and questioned the authority of Aquinas. Urgent action was needed.

To get it, the Dominicans appealed to the Curia. The Curia, in turn, asked Sylvester Prierias, the master of the Sacred Palace, to examine Luther's theses. The Holy See's chief censor, Prierias was responsible for examining texts for heretical content, and he found plenty in Luther's propositions. In a mere three days (or so he claimed), he completed a long-winded dialogue in which Luther's theses were roundly attacked. Concerning Luther's appeal to Scripture, Prierias declared that the authority of the Church was superior to that of the Bible and that the pope's judgment is "the oracle of God." He thus established the ground on which Rome would from the start oppose Luther—that of papal supremacy and the obligation of all Christians to acknowledge it. Filling his pamphlet with abuse, Prierias called Luther a "leper and a loathsome fellow," a "false libeler and calumniator," and a "dog and a son of a bitch, born to snap and bite at the sky with his canine mouth."

The *Dialogue Against the Presumptuous Conclusions of Martin Luther* was printed in Rome in June 1518. The Curia simultaneously drew up an official summons demanding that Luther appear in person in Rome within sixty days of its receipt to give an account of his heretical assertions and his contempt for papal authority. A courier bearing both documents was sent north to Cardinal Cajetan in Augsburg. Another was dispatched to Wittenberg to deliver the documents to Luther.

The start of summer in Wittenberg brought swarms of flies, mosquitoes rising off the Elbe, the stench of moldering garbage, and a new series of attacks on Luther. From Erfurt, his old professor Trutfetter sent a wrathful letter. Count Albrecht of Mansfeld wrote to Johann Lang, the district vicar of the Augustinian order, to warn him not to let Luther leave Wittenberg, for snares were being set for him. Most disturbing of all was the treacherous act Luther experienced while visiting Dresden in late July 1518. He had gone there at the request of Duke George, Frederick's cousin, who wanted to hear him preach. Afterward, Luther was invited to what was billed as a friendly drinking party, but lying in wait for him was a Leipzig Thomist, and a fierce argument broke out over Aquinas and Aristotle. Stationed behind the door were some eavesdropping Dominicans who took notes, and a highly distorted account of the exchange was sent to Rome. For months thereafter, the clerics of Ducal Saxony ridiculed Luther as proud and unlearned and gleefully spread word that he had been badly bloodied in debate.

Then, on August 7, the package from Rome arrived. When Luther saw the words "Master of the Sacred Palace" in the title of Prierias's work, he felt a shudder of anxiety. Here was the first concrete sign that the Ninety-Five Theses had finally come to the pope's attention. As he read the pamphlet, however, his fear turned to contempt. It seemed, he wrote, a "wild, entangled jungle" (a play on Sylvester, Prierias's first name, which is Latin for "jungle"). In just two days (or so he claimed), Luther drafted a blistering response, chiding Prierias for his failure to back up his arguments with Scripture and spewing even more vitriol than Prierias had aimed at him. Even more striking than the invective, however, was Luther's flat assertion that both popes and councils can err and that Scripture is the one true authority. The manuscript was so long that Rhau-Grunenberg was unable to handle it, so Luther sent it to the better-equipped house of Melchior Lotther in Leipzig.

Unlike Prierias's muddle, however, the summons to Rome left Luther shaken. There was only one way to read it, he believed—as an invitation to execution. He could now see how foolish he had been to place his trust in the pope. Rome would be satisfied with nothing less than a full recantation. Offering one, however, would mean repudiating his conscience, and to that death seemed preferable. Unnerved by Rome's fury, Luther confided his worries to Spalatin, who together with Frederick was in Augsburg for the Imperial Diet. "I now need your help more than ever, dear Spalatin," his letter began. He urged him to ask Frederick to intercede with Emperor Maximilian so that his case could be tried before German judges rather than in Rome, where "those murderous Dominicans" were determined to destroy him.

But Maximilian, who at fifty-nine was in declining health and focused on his successor, had little interest in ecclesiastical reform, and after reading the forged copy of Luther's sermon on the ban, he had concluded that he posed a grave threat to public order. Around the same time that Luther was writing to Spalatin, Maximilian was writing to Leo, pressing him to move at once against the rebellious cleric. Noting the damage that the Reuchlin affair had inflicted on the Church, Maximilian said that if the author of these pernicious doctrines were not silenced, he would soon win over not only the unlettered multitudes but also the princes.

Two weeks later, when Maximilian's letter arrived in Rome, Leo finally grasped the gravity of the situation. Jacopo Sadoleto, the papal secretary, hurriedly drew up a *breve*, or brief, for Cardinal Cajetan in Augsburg, directing him to compel the "reprobate Augustinian" to appear before him; Cajetan was also to demand that Luther recant. If Luther did so, Cajetan was authorized to receive him back into the bosom of the Church. If he did not recant or failed to appear, Cajetan was to declare Luther and his adherents "heretics, excommunicated, anathematized, and cursed" and to warn all princes, cities, and corporations who assisted him that they would be subject to the interdict.

On the same day that the *breve* was sent to Cajetan, Leo drafted a stern note to Frederick. From the Dominicans and other sources, the pope had learned that the elector was protecting Luther, and the time had come for Frederick to confront him. "Beloved son," he began with the requisite paternalism, "it has come to our ears from all quarters that a certain son of iniquity," Martin Luther, "sinfully vaunts himself in the Church of God" and that, relying on the elector's protection, he feared the rebuke of no one. To escape suspicion, Frederick should render all due assistance in delivering the said Martin into the custody of the Holy See.

As a devout Christian, Frederick was reluctant to disobey the pope, but he was pleased with the attention that Luther was bringing to his university, and he admired Luther's conviction. While intent on rooting out heresy, he was reluctant to see so pious a man condemned without a hearing. Frederick thus faced a painful choice—to either defy the Holy Father or hand over a sincere, God-fearing subject to almost certain death. On his decision hung Luther's fate.

After learning of the pope's instructions to Cajetan, Luther in late August 1518 sent a messenger to Augsburg to inquire after Frederick's intentions. When the messenger failed to return, Luther anxiously implored

Spalatin for news. Whatever it was, he declared, "I fear nothing." Even if he were to become hateful to emperors and princes, he knew in both his heart and his conscience that all he had came from God. As hard as it would be to escape condemnation without Frederick's help, he would rather suffer it than bring odium upon the elector. He would never be a heretic, but nor would he be "captive to the doctrines of men."

With that, he awaited word from Augsburg.

UNBRIDLED

In the end, Thomas More was able to find a horse for Erasmus, and he sent it along with a rider to Louvain. And Henry VIII sent a gift of sixty angel-nobles—enough cash to finance his trip. Erasmus gathered together his personal effects along with his many manuscripts and at the start of May 1518 left for Basel.

To his great relief, the route to the Rhine was free of robbers, and in Cologne he quickly found a boat to take him upriver. As he sailed along the great waterway, passing castles and crags, Erasmus prepared a fierce attack on Edward Lee. Framed as a letter to Maarten Lips, an Augustinian canon friendly with both men, Erasmus did not mention the English gadfly by name, but his target was clear. He derided the man's barbarous Latin, his clumsy syllogisms, his softheaded fantasies. He took special exception to Lee's central assertion—that the Vulgate had been prepared under the inspiration of the Holy Spirit and so was immune from criticism. Should the Church stick with a version of its sacred text that was known to be faulty? Erasmus ridiculed the idea that the Church cannot err and that a private person without authorization cannot make a new translation or revise an old one. Did he have to wait for a synod to be called before he could correct a corrupted text? "The business in hand calls not for a miter or a red hat, but for a skill in tongues."

Arriving in Basel on May 13, 1518, Erasmus was delighted to find himself back in this humanist haven, with its clean streets, quiet libraries, soaring cathedral, and clement weather. To accommodate him, Froben had a room outfitted with a fireplace rather than a stove. While thus able to avoid the usual reek, Erasmus quickly succumbed to the strange pestilence that was sweeping the city, and for more than a month he suffered from headaches, diarrhea, and abdominal pains.

He could not afford to take time off, however. Erasmus's first order of business was the annotations. In all, he had notes on more than six hundred passages. Wolfgang Capito, in his earlier warning to Erasmus, had urged him to "put a bridle of self-restraint" on his "abundant eloquence" and refrain from saying anything too controversial about the rules governing food, prayers, and penance. But Erasmus would not listen. In the first edition, he had begun the task of clearing away the thickets of sophistic speculation that had overgrown the text. He now wanted to complete the job—to use his knowledge of Greek and grammar to lay bare the true apostolic spirit within. Whereas in the earlier edition he had stuck mostly to points of grammar, he now ventured more deeply into matters of theology. In the process, he became more forthright. Of the five New Testament editions Erasmus would produce, the second would be the most provocative.

At Matthew 11:30, for example, where Christ declares, "My yoke is easy, and my burden is light," Erasmus offered a lengthy catalog of the many unnecessary demands he felt the clergy had imposed on the faithful. On matters of dress and diet, vows and feast days, the Church had encumbered the simple philosophy of Christ with a mass of man-made regulations. The duties of the priesthood had grown so complex that it was easier to learn the complete philosophy of Aristotle than to master them. "Let us drive out the heavenly yoke of men so that we may be truly under the light yoke of Christ," Erasmus declared. "Evangelical love commands less and achieves more."

He was even bolder at Matthew 16:18. Here, Christ says to his chief disciple, "You are Peter, and on this rock I will build my church." Since Peter's name in Greek (*Petros*) means "rock," the Church had long maintained that Christ in this passage was designating Peter the titular head of his church; the popes, as the bishops of Rome, were considered his successors. But Erasmus (following Origen and other Fathers) argued that Christ, in using "rock," was referring not to Peter but to the confession of faith in Christ himself, and that it was on this that he wanted his church built. "Rocky Peter represented the solid faith of the church," Erasmus wrote, thus challenging the scriptural foundation of the papacy.

At Matthew 23, where Jesus rebukes the Pharisees and scribes for creating heavy burdens and laying them on men's shoulders, Erasmus condemned the proliferating shrines and relics venerated by so many Christians. What, he asked, would Jerome say if he could see the Virgin's milk exhibited for money, or so many splinters of the True Cross displayed that one could build a large ship with them? "Here we have the hood of St. Francis, there Our Lady's petticoat or St. Anne's comb, or St. Thomas of Canterbury's shoes," presented not "as innocent aids to religion, but as the substance of religion itself—and all through the avarice of priests and the hypocrisy of monks playing on the credulity of the people."

At several points, Erasmus disputed the Church's rules on sexuality. He called ecclesiastical celibacy too heavy a burden for most to bear, further questioned the sacramental status of marriage, and challenged the Church's unshakable opposition to divorce. At the time, marriage was considered indissoluble and divorce was not recognized; only by obtaining an annulment—a cumbersome and difficult process—could a marriage be undone. In his note on 1 Corinthians 7:36–39, Erasmus acknowledged that Jesus had unequivocally condemned divorce, but, he asked, why was this one stricture so rigidly enforced while so many others had been eased? Given the high rates of unhappy marriages, a radical cure was needed, and divorce seemed to offer it.

Erasmus's refusal to put a bridle on his eloquence was nowhere more apparent than in his note on 1 Timothy 1:6. Using as a springboard Paul's chastisement of those who engage in "idle talk," Erasmus let loose a furious barrage at the Scholastics, listing some fifty highly obscure questions of the sort debated by them. Can God teach evil? Can he communicate the power of creating to the creature? Did the number of divine persons pertain to substance or to relation? Can God restore lost virginity? "Entire lives are wasted on these speculations, and men quarrel and curse and come to blows about them," Erasmus wrote, not considering how the theologians of Louvain and Cologne might react.

Throughout, Erasmus offered many opinionated asides. He censured the quarreling spirit of the monastic orders, the sloth of mendicant friars, theologians puffed up with learning, clerics enamored of war, crusaders seeking converts at the point of a sword, and church services filled with blaring trumpets and yelping choirs. He embraced humility, brotherhood, charity, wise princes, and pacifist priests. At every point, he sought to stress the human qualities of Christ and the value of inner spirituality over external show.

As Erasmus was completing his annotations, Froben was preparing a new edition of the *Enchiridion*. When this manual of piety first appeared fifteen years earlier, it had quickly sunk from view, but the times had caught up with it, and booksellers were having trouble keeping it in stock. To help freshen the edition, Erasmus agreed to add a preface. Framed as a letter to his friend Paul Volz, a Benedictine abbot in Alsace, it would offer the clearest distillation of the Erasmian creed.

The theologians, Erasmus wrote, had issued a flood of tracts addressing every conceivable question in the smallest detail, but who had the time to read them all? There were almost as many commentaries on the *Sentences* as there were theologians. Christian nations were preparing to fight the Turks, but even if they triumphed, how many of the vanquished would be won over if presented with the tomes of Ockham, Scotus, or Biel, with their discussions of instances, formalities, quiddities, and relativities? None of these volumes addressed what is truly essential—how to lead a good life modeled on the example of Christ. Because the Gospels and Epistles are difficult to understand, a group of saintly and learned men should be assigned the task of producing a brief but scholarly summary of "the whole philosophy of Christ," with simple words that could make people understand that Christ's yoke is easy and not harsh. Could anyone deny that the current generation was the most corrupt ever? When before had so much importance been attached to ceremonies? When had iniquity so abounded, or charity waxed so cold? While he had no wish to scold the Franciscans or Benedictines for being devoted to their rules, he did object "that some of them think their rule more important than the Gospel."

In the original edition of the *Enchiridion*, Erasmus had declared, *Monachatus non est pietas*—"Monasticism is not piety"—and this was continuing to rankle monks and mendicants, but he now pressed the point even more forcefully. In the Church's early days, he noted, members of monastic communities had no aim other than to join with friends for a life based on the Gospels. They shunned riches and avoided honors, worked with their hands, and ruled not through violent language and whippings but by inspiration and example. Then, with the passage of time, wealth grew, ceremonies multiplied, and genuine piety cooled. Whereas monastic life was once "a refuge from the world," many monks now devoted themselves to worldly business and exercised "a kind of despotism in human affairs," yet because of their dress or the name they bore, they claimed so much sanctity for themselves that they considered others hardly Christian. Whether monk or layman, all must strive toward one goal—Christ and his teaching in all its purity. All should aid one another in achieving that goal, without envying those who have hurried ahead or disdaining those who have lagged behind. And when each has done what he can, he should behave not like the Pharisee of the Gospels, who boasts before God of his fasting and other good works, but like the servant who does what he knows he should do and speaks of it to no one.

Erasmus's description of early monasticism was highly romanticized. Some of the early hermits nearly killed themselves with spectacular feats of fasting and flagellation. But the idealization served his goal of censuring current monastic excesses and trying to restore a simplified version of the faith, shorn of ornate ritual and abstruse doctrine. The new edition of the *Enchiridion* would thus heighten Erasmus's unpopularity in the abbeys of Europe, but outside them it would achieve extraordinary acclaim as a manifesto of Christian humanism, promoting the idea that to be a pious Christian, one must not only have faith in Christ but also imitate his charity, modesty, and compassion.

For alert readers, there was one passage in this manifesto that stood out. Modern-day Philistines, it stated, had gained strength by preaching not divine but rather human things, which "tend not to Christ's glory but to the profit of those who traffic in indulgences, in compositions, in dispensations, and suchlike merchandise." This traffic was all the more perilous because those engaging in it "give their greed a facade of great names, eminent princes, the supreme pontiff, even Christ himself." This was an unmistakable reference to Luther's Ninety-Five Theses.

While Erasmus was in Basel, everyone was talking about the German friar. At the 1518 fall fair in Frankfurt, Froben had obtained several of his works in Latin, and back in Basel his staff could see how explosive they were. With Luther's views only vaguely known outside Germany, a lucrative market beckoned. Working in secret, Wolfgang Capito (who was helping Erasmus with his New Testament), together with Johannes Oecolampadius, Beatus Rhenanus, and several other scholars, began preparing a collected edition of his works. (In the absence of copyright laws, they did not need Luther's permission.) In a brief preface, Capito captured the excitement Luther was stirring among humanists: "Here you have the theological works of the Reverend Father Martin Luther, whom many consider a Daniel" sent by Christ "to correct abuses and restore the evangelic and Pauline divinity to theologians who have forgotten the ancient commentaries and occupy themselves with the merest logical and verbal trifles." The "conscience of the laity is now awakened," and it should "resist the tutelage of professional theologians." The fact that Capito did not give his name, and that the volume bore no colophon or place of publication, reflected the risks involved in publishing Luther.

A thick quarto of 488 pages, the anthology appeared in October 1518 with the title *Ad Leonem X* ("To Leo X"). In addition to the Ninety-Five Theses and Luther's long explanation of them, it included his sermons on penance, indulgences, and the ban, plus his replies to Prierias and Eck. (On the title page, the typesetters mischievously changed Prierias's identification from *magister palatii*, "master of the palace," to *magirus palatii*, "cook of the palace.") Copies were carted to the Rhine for transport to the towns along its banks, and colporteurs set off with them for France, Switzerland, and Italy. For the first time, Luther's defiant statements about the Church and its practices were made available to Latin-speaking Christians across Europe.

At the same time that Froben was preparing the Luther collection and Erasmus's New Testament, he was also readying a new edition of More's *Utopia*—testimony to his house's dominant position in European publishing. But Erasmus would not be around to witness this historic moment. Eager to return to Louvain, he arranged for his *famulus* (secretary) to remain behind to help oversee the proofreading of the annotations. He also sent letters to several high-ranking friends in Rome requesting their help in gaining the pope's blessing for the new edition.

Erasmus left Basel in early September 1518. It would take him eighteen days to reach Louvain, and his detailed account of his journey—written after his arrival in the form of a letter to Beatus Rhenanus—was meant to be read by his friends and the interested public. Offering a colorful look at the rigors of travel in that age, the letter was an early example of the tell-all travelogue, in which no mishap is too small or intimate to relate. Erasmus described the stench of the horses, the belching stoves, the noise of packed parlors in grimy inns, and the terrible meal he had in the town of Breisach ("dirty pease porridge, lumps of meat, sausage réchauffé more than once—it was simply revolting"). He recounted how, in the town of Boppard, he was recognized and pointed out to the customs officer, Christoph Eschenfelder. Excited, the man insisted on escorting Erasmus to his house. There, on his desk, lay a number of Erasmian volumes. Erasmus expressed delight at finding "a customs officer devoted to the Muses." A ship's crew, however, became angry at the delay, and so the officer sent over to them several flagons of red wine. Thus lubricated, the shipman's wife nearly killed the cook-maid with her large basting spoon.

Leaving the town of Bedburg, Erasmus got caught in a powerful rainstorm, which caused his carriage to shake so badly on the rocky pavement that by the time he reached Aachen he was weak with exhaustion. There, he ate some stockfish, some of it still raw. Retiring to the inn, he became so ill that he had to put his finger down his throat.

Arriving in Louvain, Erasmus felt sure that his rooms would be too cold to inhabit, so he stayed with his friend, the printer Dirk Martens. Over the next four weeks, while convalescing there, he hurriedly finished his translation of the New Testament. His goal was to produce a Latin text that would speak to the educated Christians of his day while remaining true to the original. As he explained, the "countrified and simple style" in which the New Testament was originally written was appropriate for those early days, but now it was necessary to "have it in neater dress, provided it be simple still." Erasmus was thus embracing the principle—radical at the time—that translations of the Bible should be tailored to the needs of each age.

Given the Vulgate's sacred status, however, every change was fraught with risk. Erasmus was nonetheless determined to follow the call of his muse, grammar. A good example came at Matthew 6:12—a passage

from the Lord's Prayer. *Dimitte nobis debita nostra*, stated the Vulgate—
"forgive us our debts." From his examination of Greek manuscripts, Erasmus had concluded that it would be more accurate to say *Remitte nobis
debita nostra*—"remit our debts." And so it would read in his translation.
Though relatively minor, the change would open him to the charge that
he was altering the Lord's Prayer. At Matthew 3:2, he decided to translate
poenitentiam agite not as *poeniteat vos*, as he did in the first edition, but as
resipiscite, meaning "come to your senses," which he felt more accurately
reflected the sense of the underlying Greek term, *metanoia*.

Even more daring was the one-word alteration he made at the start of
the Gospel of John. In the Vulgate, this read *In principio erat verbum*—
"In the beginning was the Word." For centuries, this phrase had rung out
from pulpits, been invoked in sermons, become etched in the minds of
churchgoers. But Erasmus felt that *verbum* did not accurately reflect the
underlying Greek word, *logos*. *Sermo* seemed more apt. Whereas *verbum*
connotes a single word, *sermo* means an ongoing discourse, conversation,
or speech, which is what John seemed to have in mind. In the first edition,
Erasmus had declined to make such a change for fear of the protests it
would raise, but he now decided to act on his philological principles and
translate the passage as *In principio erat sermo*. Scholars, he felt sure, would
understand.

Beyond such specific changes, Erasmus prepared a fifty-page introductory essay, titled *Ratio Verae Theologiae* ("True Theological Method"),
which he hoped would nudge students of the Bible onto a new course.
Rather than look to Scripture as a source of doctrine and divine messages,
he argued, exegetes should regard it as literature—as a text to be deconstructed, emended, repaired, and expounded. Pointing to Origen and Jerome as models, Erasmus maintained that the Bible scholar must first of
all learn the three biblical tongues. He should familiarize himself with the
distinctive features of the language of Scripture—its tropes and allegories,
idioms and enigmas. He should be conversant with history, customs, law,
philosophy, dialectic, myth, astronomy, geography, music, architecture,
animals, and plants. Above all, he should take the text on its own terms,
as an account of real people living at a particular time, so that he might
not only read and follow the story but *see* it, "for it is wonderful how much

light—how much *life*, so to speak—is thrown by this method" onto what by traditional methods seems a "dry and lifeless" text. Approached in this way, the Bible could once again become a living document, and Jesus could emerge as a truly exemplary teacher with qualities found in neither Moses nor Socrates nor any other man.

The *Ratio Verae Theologiae* was at bottom an assault on Scholastic exegetes, seeking to replace them with a new cadre of scholars armed not with syllogisms and corollaries but with grammar and vocabulary. It was in many ways an elitist program, demanding so many qualities in a Bible scholar as to disqualify all but a handful of specialists. Nonetheless, the essay would stir so much interest that it would be printed separately and appear in more than a dozen freestanding editions. With it, Erasmus was laying the foundation for a new approach to the Bible that would lead to the higher criticism of the eighteenth and nineteenth centuries.

Anticipating the protests that he felt sure would come, Erasmus drafted another preface with the impish title "Summary Arguments Against Certain Contentious and Boorish People." To those who would maintain that he was not a qualified theologian, he wrote, "I have played the role of grammarian. If they despise the grammarian, let them take note that the emperor does not despise the services of his barber or secretary." Throughout, he had never willingly departed "even a finger's breadth from the judgment of the church. . . . I have written annotations, not laws, and I have proposed some things for discussion, not to be immediately construed as findings."

By October 15, 1518, Erasmus had moved back into the College of the Lily. Struggling to catch up with his correspondence, he complained that ten secretaries would not be enough to answer it all. He was constantly interrupted by visitors, including "several tedious Spaniards" who pestered him for an interview, which he refused to grant. Two young humanists traveled all the way from Erfurt just to meet him; still recovering from his illness, Erasmus was brusque with them. Remorseful, he sent cordial notes to both men as well as to several of their colleagues. Encouraged, students from Erfurt began making pilgrimages to Louvain just to see him—part of the growing cult of the Dutch humanist as a hero of German letters.

By October 22, Erasmus had completed his new translation. In a concession to his critics, he replaced his original title (*Novum Instrumentum*) with the more traditional *Novum Testamentum*. To carry the manuscript to Basel, he enlisted a young Dutchman who seemed trustworthy.

While wrapping up his work on the New Testament, Erasmus found time to sample some of Luther's works, and he shared his impressions with his friend Johann Lang (the same Augustinian prior who was friendly with Luther): "Eleutherius, I hear, is approved of by all the leading people, but they say that his writings are not what they were." His "Conclusions" (the Ninety-Five Theses) "satisfied everyone, except for a few on purgatory." He had seen Prierias's attack on Luther and considered it "very ill-judged," and he wondered what had gotten into Eck's head "that he should take up the cudgels against Eleutherius." At this early point, Erasmus's opinion of Luther was very favorable.

Two days later, he sent Wolfgang Capito an update on events in Louvain. Matthaeus Adrianus was proving an adept instructor of Hebrew. The *Julius Exclusus* was enjoying wide circulation. Erasmus's copy of Prierias's tract had been stolen from his bag. And, he noted in passing, "Someone writes to me that Martin Luther is in danger."

ONTO THE WORLD STAGE

"It seems to me that the world is exasperated against truth," Johann von Staupitz, Luther's former mentor, wrote to him in September 1518 from Salzburg, where he was then living; "with so great hatred was Christ once crucified, and today I see nothing waiting for you but the cross." Luther had few defenders, Staupitz went on, and even they were in hiding for fear of what might happen to them. "I should like you to leave Wittenberg and come to me, that we may live and die together."

Staupitz's letter starkly captured the sharp increase in danger to Luther in the wake of the pope's condemnation of him. Though moved by Staupitz's offer, Luther had no intention of submitting to Rome's censure. If summoned to the diet in Augsburg, he would travel there and defend himself, whatever the risk.

While waiting for replies from Frederick and Spalatin, Luther was heartened by an important development at the university: the arrival of the new professor of Greek. Along with the chair in Hebrew, this position was central to Luther's efforts to remake the curriculum, away from the arid exercises of the Aristotelians toward the enlightened methods of the humanists. The elector Frederick was taking such a personal interest in the university's fortunes that he had personally led the search. His first choice was Johannes Reuchlin. Still living in Stuttgart, the eminent Hebraist had continued his exploration of Jewish texts despite the continued attacks by the Cologne inquisitors, but—now in his early sixties—he was too worn out from his struggles to suddenly uproot himself and move to Wittenberg.

Instead, he recommended his relative, Philipp Schwartzerd. Though he was just twenty-one, Reuchlin told the elector, he was second only to Erasmus in his command of Greek. His father, an armorer, had died while Philipp was still very young, and the boy had been raised by Reuchlin's sister. Reuchlin himself had supervised his studies. By the time Philipp left the Latin school in Pforzheim, at the age of twelve, he was skilled in both Latin and Greek. By fifteen he had a bachelor's degree from Heidelberg, and by seventeen he had a master's degree from Tübingen. He began lecturing on the classics, and word of his precocity quickly spread. At Reuchlin's suggestion, he classicized his surname to Melanchthon ("black earth" in Greek), thus signaling his membership in the humanist fraternity. In 1516, he composed a paean to Erasmus in Greek, calling him the "Greatest of Men."

Frederick was persuaded, Philipp accepted, and on August 25, 1518, he arrived in Wittenberg. Having heard so much about the *Wunderkind*, Luther hurried to meet him. He was taken aback. Philipp was elfin in appearance and retiring in manner. He had exaggeratedly large eyes, making him seem naive, and he spoke with a slight lisp. Four days later, though, he gave his inaugural address. Speaking before a large crowd at the Castle Church, Melanchthon offered a grand overview of the state of education in the West from ancient times forward. After Rome's fall, he declared, the study of Greek and Roman literature had all but disappeared. Across the West, Aristotle was forgotten, Greek was ignored, and many precious works were lost. With the rise of Scholasticism, fields like medicine, law, and theology had all gone into eclipse. True piety had also suffered as ceremonies and pilgrimages had replaced heartfelt forms of devotion. There was but one way to reverse the decline: by returning to the sources. Through the study of Hebrew, Greek, and Latin, both classical and Christian culture could be renewed. Through reading Scripture in the biblical tongues, it would again be possible to savor the teachings of Christ and be filled with the nectar of divine wisdom; the old Adam could be sloughed off and a new man established in his place.

All of this was pronounced in a Latin so flawless and elegant as to seem delivered from the floor of the Roman Senate, and Luther along with everyone else was captivated. Melanchthon's address was "extremely learned and absolutely faultless," he reported to Spalatin, adding that "we have quickly abandoned the opinion we formed from his small stature and homeliness, and now rejoice and wonder at his real worth. . . . While Philipp is alive, I desire no other Greek teacher." Luther did have two concerns—that Melanchthon's constitution would prove too delicate for the rough ways of Saxony, and that his salary was so meager that he would be lured away by another institution.

Luther need not have worried. Melanchthon's pay was soon raised, and he would remain in Wittenberg until his death forty-two years later. Quickly falling under Luther's spell, he became his closest disciple. "Never was there a greater man on the face of the earth," he later wrote; "I would rather die than sever myself from that man." Yet Luther could be quite callous toward him. When Melanchthon in moments of crisis seemed in danger of buckling, Luther would often cruelly taunt him for his weakness and timidity. But he was dazzled by Melanchthon's command of classical languages and literature, and the soft-spoken scholar was to provide Luther with essential help in his Bible studies. Melanchthon would also take the lead in redesigning the Wittenberg curriculum. Some of his most lasting contributions, in fact, would come in the field of education. A pedagogue at heart, Melanchthon, with input from Luther and others, would establish in Germany the first comprehensive public school system since the fall of Rome—an achievement that would earn him the title *Praeceptor Germaniae*, "Teacher of Germany."

Throughout, however, Melanchthon would remain attracted to humanist values like moderation, pluralism, and free will, and he would maintain warm relations with Erasmus. Such leanings were to bring him into frequent conflict with the more absolutist Luther. Yet Melanchthon was to prove more adept than Luther himself at articulating his doctrines, and in light of the close partnership that would develop between them, and of the part Melanchthon was to play in the unfolding of the Reformation, his arrival in Wittenberg marked a critical moment in Protestant history.

In early September 1518, Luther finally heard from Spalatin: he was to appear before the Imperial Diet in Augsburg. With the election of a new emperor expected soon, Rome needed Frederick's support, and so it had acceded to his demand that Luther be granted a hearing on German soil. He was to appear before Cardinal Cajetan, the pope's legate. Augsburg was in Bavaria, three hundred miles to the southwest, and the trip there would be far more perilous than the one he had made to Heidelberg the previous spring. As before, he was to cover the distance on foot, and he would again be accompanied by Leonhard Beier. Frederick sent Luther letters of introduction and twenty guilders to cover his expenses.

This time, there would be no happy encounters. While making his way southwest toward Erfurt, Luther wondered if he was seeing the hills and valleys of his beloved Thuringia for the last time. "Now I must die," he told himself. "What a disgrace I shall be to my parents!" After traveling to a similar encounter a century earlier, Jan Hus had been burned at the stake. Unlike Hus, Luther did not even have a safe-conduct. Trying to imagine what it would be like to be exposed to the flames, he had to admit that his flesh shrank from the prospect. He wondered if his critics had been right. "Are you alone wise and all the ages in error?" he asked himself. The friars in the Augustinian cloisters where he stayed were full of dire warnings. "They will burn you," the prior at Weimar told him, urging him to turn back.

In Weimar, he was startled to find Frederick's party there on its way back from Augsburg, where the diet had just ended. Asked to preach before the elector, Luther offered the usual denunciation of clerical corruption. (In keeping with Frederick's policy, Luther did not speak with him.) In Nuremberg, his friend Wenceslas Link (who would join him for the rest of the journey) was shocked at his shabby appearance and found a new cowl for him so that he would not look derelict in Augsburg. As he approached that city, Luther developed a severe stomach disorder, no doubt brought on by nervousness, and he almost fainted by the wayside. He became so impaired that a wagon had to be found to carry him the final three miles into the city, where he arrived on October 7, 1518.

With a population of 50,000, Augsburg was among the largest cities in the Holy Roman Empire and one of Europe's great trading and financial centers. Its streets were lined with stalls selling satins from Italy, spices from India, silks from China. With the diet having already ended, most of the delegates were leaving, but their staffs remained behind to wrap up its business. Cajetan was staying at the Fugger Palace, where the diet had taken place and where most of the top dignitaries had stayed. Because the Augustinians had no abbey in Augsburg, Luther went to the Carmelite cloister, which had agreed to put him up.

The danger to Luther seemed so great that the two lawyers assigned by Frederick to advise him urged him not to appear before Cajetan until the imperial staff had granted him a safe-conduct to pass through Augsburg's streets. While the bargaining over it continued, Luther was visited by one of Cajetan's Italian courtiers, the smooth and worldly Urban de Serralonga. Luther's business in Augsburg could be summed up in one word, he said: recant. But, Luther asked, could he not defend his position, or at least be instructed on it? No, Serralonga replied; this was not a game of running in a ring. To Luther, the Italian seemed unctuous and high-handed—an inauspicious sign for his meeting with Cajetan. He sent a letter to Melanchthon, encouraging him to "teach the young the things that are right." He grimly added: "If it please the Lord, I am going to be sacrificed for you and for them. I prefer to perish rather than to recant" and "thus become the occasion for the ruin of the noblest studies."

After three days, the safe-conduct arrived, and on October 12, 1518, Luther, accompanied by Link and several friars, set out for the Fugger Palace to meet Cajetan. A massive four-story building with arches along the ground floor, the palace was the most sumptuous modern residence north of the Alps. It had its own chapel, a stable, running water (which dazzled visitors), fireplaces in almost every room, and windows made with Venetian glass.

Its opulence was testament to the extraordinary wealth of the Fuggers. Of the handful of great merchant-banker families that dominated Augsburg's economy, the Fuggers were the most successful, and Jakob, the family patriarch, was on his way to becoming Europe's richest man. Brilliant at turning political connections into economic gain, he had developed a close partnership with the Hapsburgs, helping to underwrite Emperor Maximilian's dynastic marriages and military adventures; in return for these loans, the Fuggers had gained lucrative concessions in the copper and silver mines of Tirol, Hungary, Silesia, and Thuringia. The Fuggers' other great client was the Church. As the pope's financial representatives in Germany, they oversaw the buying of benefices and bishoprics and managed the indulgence trade, including the great St. Peter's indulgence that had helped spark Luther's revolt. The palace to which Luther was headed, then, had been made possible in part by the sale of indulgences.

Cajetan could not wait to leave it. In the five months since his departure from Rome, everything had seemed to go wrong. Because of repeated border delays, his journey north had taken two full months. Once installed in the Fugger Palace, the cardinal had demanded that his rooms be lined with purple satin, and he ate from silver plates while screened off by an ornate curtain. Delicate and refined, Cajetan found the bread too coarse, the wine too acidic, the German people too large and crude. As the diet dragged on into the fall, he shivered in his quarters, and not a day went by that he did not long for Rome, his warm study, and the time to devote himself to his great love, Thomas Aquinas.

Respected for his integrity and erudition but resented for his arrogance, Cajetan had taken the name Tommaso in homage to the Angelic Doctor, and he had spent years working on a massive commentary on the *Summa Theologica*. Vigorously defending Thomas against the attacks of the Scotists, he had helped revive interest in Thomism, which had gone into decline. He had also debated—and held his ground against— such intellectual giants as the philosopher Pietro Pomponazzi and the humanist polymath Giovanni Pico della Mirandola. Though an insider at the Curia, Cajetan was a strong supporter of reform, and at the recently concluded Council of the Lateran he had spoken out against clerical pluralism and profligacy. At the same time, he was an unyielding defender of hierarchical authority, and in Rome he was most esteemed for his treatise *On the Power of the Pope*. It was in gratitude for this defense of papal rule that Leo had the previous year awarded him a red hat.

During the diet, Cajetan had done his best to persuade the Germans to support the new crusade against the Turks. In resonant Latin, he had declared that the time had come for a holy war that once and for all would subdue the Mohammedans, the greatest threat to Christendom, and that it was the diet's duty to approve the special tax that the pope had proclaimed for this sacred purpose. The reception had been chilly. Over the years, such calls to battle had become as routine as the change in seasons, and the proposed levy seemed yet another Roman ploy for extracting German cash. Augsburg was flooded with anonymous pamphlets reviling the pope as a "hound of hell" who could be appeased only by rivers of gold. The diet submitted a *gravamina* of grievances against the Church that, in its passion and detail, would become a rallying point for German nationalists. These "sons of Nimrod," it declared (referring to a hunter in the Bible), "grab cloisters, abbeys, prebends, canonaries, and parish churches, and they leave these churches without pastors, the people without shepherds." Annates and indulgences had increased, and in the ecclesiastical courts bribes had become routine. German money, "in violation of nature, flies over the Alps. The pastors given to us are shepherds only in name. They care for nothing, but fleece and batten on the sins of the people. Endowed Masses are neglected, the pious founders cry for vengeance. Let the Holy Pope Leo stop these abuses."

As Rome's emissary, Cajetan bore the brunt of this anti-Italian sentiment. Ulrich von Hutten, a firebrand poet and fierce German nationalist who had attended the diet and had good sources inside the Fugger Palace, wrote a withering satire that cast the cardinal as a supercilious dilettante who had threatened to excommunicate the sun if it failed to provide more warmth. Apart from such taunts, Cajetan found the diet a maddening muddle in which the proceedings seemed squeezed in between extended bouts of drinking and feasting. The princes, dukes, and bishops in attendance spent much of their time pursuing petty feuds, and each nobleman seemed to have a personal complaint against the Hapsburgs that he insisted on pressing during the conclave.

Adding to the sense of disorder was the painful spectacle of Maximilian's physical decline. At fifty-nine, he seemed unlikely to survive much longer, and the jockeying over his successor had unceremoniously begun. The emperor was intent on installing his grandson Charles—the same Charles for whom Erasmus was a councilor and who had already been crowned king of Aragon and Castile. Charles's election would ensure the Hapsburgs' continued control of the Holy Roman Empire and through it hegemony over Western Europe. But Charles was not yet nineteen and seemed green even for that age. The other main aspirant, the twenty-four-year-old Francis I of France, was a self-styled Renaissance prince who lusted for power as much as for women and who, if crowned emperor, would become Europe's dominant sovereign. With so much at stake, the competition between Charles and Francis had set off a sordid contest of bribery and blandishments, horse-trading and double-dealing.

Disgusted, Cajetan was counting the days down to his departure. But then he received the *breve* directing him to interview Luther and demand his revocation. After three months of contending with the unruly Goths, Cajetan was annoyed to have to deal with an obstreperous friar. The cardinal was nonetheless determined to treat Luther in a fatherly manner and gently guide him to the required revocation.

Cajetan was by far the most eminent cleric Luther had yet to meet, and upon entering the cardinal's quarters he was for the first time stepping onto the world stage. A small man about to turn fifty, Cajetan was attended by several Italian curates and diplomats. For all of Luther's notoriety, the worldly Cajetan found him distinctly unimposing. A *fratellino*, he would later call him—a little friar—whose dark, piercing eyes suggested to him a mind filled with fanatical fantasies.

In a show of obeisance, Luther prostrated himself before the cardinal. Only after Cajetan had ordered him three times to rise did Luther do so. Addressing him as "dear son," Cajetan complimented him on his scholarship and his activities as a teacher and lecturer in Wittenberg. Once the pleasantries were over, the cardinal told Luther what was required of him—that he come to his senses and retract his errors, that he promise to refrain from committing such errors in the future, and that he avoid any activity that might disturb the Church. As he listened, Luther grew agitated, and when the cardinal finished he said that such demands could have been conveyed to him while he was still in Wittenberg and spared him the difficult journey to Augsburg. Furthermore, he said, if he were to retract anything, he would first have to be shown where he had erred.

The papal *breve* had instructed Cajetan not to engage Luther in debate, but the learned cardinal could not resist. Luther, he said, had erred on two key points. The first was in his fifty-eighth thesis, where he had maintained that the merits of Christ and the saints were not the treasures of the Church and that those merits are always working grace in the inner man, with or without the pope's say-so. This, Cajetan declared, contradicted the *Ex-*

travagante Unigenitus, issued by Pope Clement VI in 1343, which plainly stated that the Church, through Christ's suffering and sacrifice, had acquired an infinite treasure in heaven. Through the power of the keys, this treasure had been placed at the disposal of Peter and his successors to offer the faithful relief from temporal penalties (in part, through the issuing of indulgences). Luther had also erred in teaching that faith was essential to the sacrament of penance. This contradicted both Scripture and the teachings of the Church, for it placed the sinner in a position of such uncertainty that he could never be sure of the sacrament's efficacy.

Cajetan stated all this with the assurance of a senior prelate accustomed to making pronouncements without fear of being challenged. But it was not just his tone that upset Luther. Cajetan said nothing about indulgences—the central issue at hand. Instead, he had dredged up a papal decree so minor that it had not even been included in the *Corpus Juris Canonici*, the main body of canon law, but instead had been relegated to an appendix of decretals known as *Extravagantes* (meaning they had "wandered" outside canon law). Cajetan no doubt assumed that Luther would be unfamiliar with the decree, but during his long months of study, he had in fact come across it, and he felt it was completely unsupported by Scripture.

Bristling at Cajetan's manner and bursting with scriptural citations, Luther made clear that he found the cardinal's assertions unsatisfactory and wanted an opportunity to reply. But Cajetan would not allow it. He had specifically shown Luther where he had erred according to Church law, and there was nothing for him to do but acknowledge his mistake. But Luther, while not wanting to disobey the Church, demanded to be heard. Here, in his first encounter with a senior cleric, the essential contours of the conflict emerged, pitting a hierarchical institution that, resting on centuries of tradition, demanded absolute obedience against a solitary individual who, answering to the dictates of his conscience, insisted on his right to speak.

After that tense first session, Luther returned for a second day of interrogation. This time he was accompanied by Staupitz, who had come from Salzburg to be with him and whose presence provided much comfort. But the climate did not improve. Cajetan grew increasingly frustrated with the obstinate, Bible-quoting friar, and Luther became impatient with Cajetan's habit, when confronted with citations he could not rebut, of retreating into grand assertions of papal authority. As the talk turned to the sacrament of penance and the place of grace in it, the exasperated cardinal pleaded with Luther not to persist in his obduracy. With the discussion deadlocked, Luther asked Cajetan for permission to prepare a written statement, and the cardinal reluctantly granted it.

Back in his chamber, Luther wrote to his colleague Andreas von Karlstadt in Wittenberg that Cajetan was "a puzzle-headed, obscure, senseless theologian," as fit to deal with his case "as an ass to play the harp." By now, however, Luther had become aware of the many supporters he had in Augsburg, among them some of its leading citizens, and, thus buoyed, he wrote out his statement. Prone to rashness in speech, he would always be in greater command when writing. In fifty-six paragraphs filled with Bible passages, he explained how he was familiar with *Unigenitus* but had disregarded it because it seemed so contrary to the spirit of Scripture, which made clear that the merits of Christ could not be dispensed through men. "I did not possess," he wrote, "the extraordinary indiscretion so as to discard so many important clear proofs of Scripture on account of a single ambiguous and obscure decretal of a pope who is a mere human being." The words of the Bible are to be preferred to papal decrees and other human statements, "for the pope is not above, but under the word of God." Citing the many places in which he said the Bible proved his theses, Luther asked that Cajetan deal leniently with him and show how he might understand these doctrines differently. "As long as these Scripture passages stand," he wrote, "I cannot do otherwise, for I know that I must obey God rather than men. . . . I do not want to be compelled to affirm something contrary to my conscience, for I believe without the slightest doubt that this is the meaning of Scripture."

In declaring that Scripture took precedence over papal pronouncements, Luther was articulating a principle that would become one of his guiding ideas: *sola scriptura*—Scripture alone.

The next day, Luther, accompanied by the two lawyers provided by Frederick, presented his statement to the cardinal. Cajetan disdainfully flung it back at him. He again demanded that Luther recant and admonished him in a long speech filled with quotations from Aquinas. Luther repeatedly tried to interrupt, but each time the cardinal silenced him and continued his harangue. In his frustration, Luther began to shout. "If it can be shown that the *Extravagante Unigenitus* teaches that Christ's merits are the treasury of indulgences, then I will recant." At this, the Italian courtiers snickered, and Cajetan, barely able to contain his glee, took hold of the great tome of canon law and, quickly seeking out the section in question, read aloud the passage that stated that Christ had by his merits acquired the treasury.

Luther quickly objected. The passage stated that Christ "has acquired" the treasury of merit, he said. If he has acquired the treasury *by* his merits, then the merits themselves are not the treasury; rather, the treasury is that which the merits earned, namely the keys of the Church. Therefore his thesis was correct. Perplexed, Cajetan tried to move on, but Luther would not let him. "Most Reverend Father," he said, "you should not believe that we Germans are ignorant even in philology. There is a difference between 'there is' a treasury and 'to acquire' a treasury."

At this outburst, Cajetan was understandably puzzled. Feeling cornered, Luther had retreated into a trivial point of grammar. Cajetan had in fact accurately summarized the sense of the decretal. But Luther had in a way been driven to his statement by Cajetan's refusal to engage in a genuine discussion of the issues involved. Each man stood resolute in the certainty of his own correctness. As the strain between them grew, Cajetan, seeing Luther make a move to leave, shouted, "Go, and do not return to me again unless you want to recant."

Luther did leave. In one last bid to bring him around, Cajetan summoned Staupitz and implored him to use his influence to make Luther recant. Staupitz said that he had no such sway. Back at their quarters, Luther and Staupitz awaited further word from Cajetan, but none came. With each passing hour, their alarm grew. Augsburg was swept by rumors that the legate planned to have both men arrested. Staupitz—aware that Luther might have to act without the prior approval of his superiors—released him from his monastic vows. Staupitz further urged Luther to write Cajetan a conciliatory letter apologizing for having spoken irreverently in the heat of argument and asking to be forgiven. Finally, he imparted a valedictory word of advice that Luther would never forget: "Remember, Friar, you began this in the name of our Lord Jesus Christ."

Along with Wenceslas Link, Staupitz quickly left Augsburg without informing Cajetan. Because of both his departure and his releasing of Luther's vows, Luther felt that Staupitz had abandoned him. Left to face the cardinal alone, he somehow summoned the fortitude to draft the conciliatory letter. He also wrote a farewell note in which he stated that he feared any possible punishment far less than he did any errors he might make concerning faith. First one and then two days passed without any word from Cajetan, increasing Luther's fear that the cardinal was preparing to seize him. On the night of October 20, 1518, in one of the many heart-pounding episodes that marked this phase of his career, Luther was suddenly wakened by an attendant. With the walls and gates of the city under close watch, he was led by some sympathetic citizens to a small gate that was opened for him. There, a groom waited with two horses. The situation was so urgent that Luther did not have time to dress properly, and without spurs or stirrups he mounted one of the horses and with the groom rode off.

The horse was unmanageable and the ride wild and uncomfortable, but for eight straight hours he rode, and when he finally stopped, in Monheim, nearly forty miles to the north, he was so exhausted that he sank into the straw in the stable and fell asleep. The next day he rode on to Nuremberg, where, received by friends, he finally felt safe. While there, he saw for the first time the *breve* in which Leo had directed Cajetan to arrest him. He was shocked to see how serious the danger to him had been. Continuing on, Luther lost his way between Leipzig and Wittenberg, but finally, on the afternoon of October 31, 1518—the first anniversary of the posting of the Ninety-Five Theses—he was back at the Black Cloister.

"I have come to-day to Wittenberg safe, by God's grace," he wrote with relief to Spalatin that evening, adding that he was "so full of joy and peace that I wonder that many strong men regard my trial as severe." Of the *breve* he wrote that he could not believe that such a "monster" could have come from Leo, but that if the Curia had in fact produced it, "I will teach them their impudent rashness and wicked ignorance." Luther had kept a record of the proceedings in Augsburg, and, deciding to bring his case before the bar of public opinion, he prepared a forceful account in which he assailed the cardinal, papal bulls, and the Church's haughty refusal to engage him in a discussion of Scripture. "You are not a bad Christian because you do or do not know about the *Extravagante*," he wrote, but "you are a heretic" if "you deny faith in Christ's word." Dismissing the *Extravagante* as false and erroneous, Luther declared, "I solemnly revoke it in this writing and pronounce it damned." That, he added, "is my revocation." Reiterating that no man is saved by indulgences, Luther wrote, "I do not care whether this statement is contrary to an *Extravagante* or an *Intravagante*. The truth of Scripture comes first."

Along with his *Acta Augustana* (as he titled his account), Luther included both the written statement he had submitted to Cajetan and the text of the papal *breve*, so that all the world could see "the clever tricks they used." He denounced the "suave sycophants" who had composed the *breve* against him and who in Rome's name "strive to erect a Babylon for us." He sent the finished text to Rhau-Grunenberg to be printed.

The printing was delayed, however, as Frederick dealt with the fallout from Luther's meeting with the cardinal. Incensed by Luther's unannounced departure, Cajetan had sent the elector an angry letter expressing his indignation at Luther's bad faith and his failure to appreciate the cardinal's fatherly interest in his case. Citing the many heretical assertions in Luther's writings, Cajetan exhorted the elector to hand him over to Rome or, short of that, to banish him from his lands.

Luther—distressed at putting the elector in such a position—made clear his readiness to depart from Wittenberg. Since he daily expected condemnation from Rome, he wrote to Spalatin, he was "setting things in order and arranging everything so that if it comes I am prepared and girded to go, as Abraham, not knowing where, yet most sure of my way, because God is everywhere." He thought of seeking refuge in France, despite the obvious risks such a course would entail.

In the last week of November 1518, Luther prepared his parishioners in Wittenberg for the possibility of his departure. There was much weeping and protest, and Luther urged them not to panic in the face of Rome's threats. On November 28, a letter arrived from the electoral court informing Luther that he should leave Wittenberg at once. Three days later,

Luther held a farewell dinner with his colleagues at the Black Cloister, during which he planned to slip away into the night. Before the meal was over, however, there arrived another letter from the electoral court asking him to delay his departure.

Finally, on December 7, Frederick sent Cajetan his response. Despite the many charges made about Luther's being a heretic, he wrote, he had not yet been judged one by an impartial panel. Until he was so examined, it would be appropriate neither to surrender nor to expel him. It was a critical moment: Frederick—forced to choose between the authority of the Church and his conscience as a Christian—had settled on the latter. He was no doubt motivated in part by a sense of fairness toward Luther and of pride in his university, but he may also have wanted to send the pope a message about Rome's imperious policies toward the German people.

With the elector having spoken, Rhau-Grunenberg began printing the *Acta Augustana*. Because of Wittenberg's remoteness, information about what had occurred in Augsburg had remained scarce, and as the folio sheets came off the press, they were snapped up by townspeople eager for details about the dramatic encounter between the cardinal and the *fratellino*.

UNCOMMITTED

Having failed to silence Luther through admonition and persuasion, Rome would now try intimidation and coercion. Its main agent was Karl von Miltitz, a twenty-eight-year-old Saxon nobleman who had spent the past half-dozen years in Rome, working his way up the curial ladder to become papal chamberlain. Along the way, he had impressed Vatican officials with his knowledge of Saxon affairs, and it was hoped that he could apply it to secure Luther's capitulation. Among the tools provided to him was the papal Golden Rose, which was the highest distinction the pope could confer and which Frederick had long coveted. By dangling this consecrated ornament before the elector, it was hoped, Miltitz could persuade him to hand over his stiff-necked subject.

Miltitz first went to Augsburg, where many German officials remained after the close of the diet, but soon after arriving, in late November 1518, he realized that he could accomplish little there. With Frederick having returned to Altenburg, Saxony, he decided to seek him out. Leaving the Golden Rose in the safekeeping of the Fuggers, he embarked on the three-hundred-mile journey across Germany. Along the way, Miltitz gossiped about the Curia and boasted of his determination to arrest Luther. Word soon reached Luther, who realized that he could be killed at any moment. He remained defiant, however, writing to Spalatin that "the more they rage and seek my life, the less am I afraid."

As Miltitz traveled through the wintry German landscape, however, something unexpected happened. The whole region was aroused over Luther. In the inns where he stayed, Miltitz made a point of talking with other guests, and all seemed to have an opinion about the friar—usually highly favorable. Mention of Rome, by contrast, was met with anger and disgust.

By the time Miltitz reached Altenburg, on December 28, 1518, he had concluded that threats would not work and so decided to use cajolery. Meeting with Frederick, he argued that the elector's duties as a faithful Catholic demanded that he deliver Luther into the pope's custody. Until he did so, Miltitz made clear, the Golden Rose would not be his. But Frederick held to his conviction that Luther should not be condemned until he first received a hearing before an impartial panel.

In the face of Frederick's intransigence, Miltitz decided he might have better luck with Luther himself, and he persuaded the prince to send for him. Despite all the negative things he had heard about Miltitz, Luther decided to go. They met in the first week in January in Spalatin's quarters at Frederick's castle. To his surprise, Miltitz was full of compliments, telling Luther that he was surprised to find that he was not the wrinkled old doctor he had expected but an energetic and engaging young man. The reason for his cordiality became clear when Miltitz described the meetings he had had on his travels through Germany. Of every five people he spoke with, he said, only two or three favored Rome. Luther, by contrast, had so much support that even if Miltitz had 25,000 Swiss soldiers at his command, he would not risk taking him out of Germany.

Over two days, Luther and Miltitz sparred over indulgences, papal authority, and other disputed matters. To show his reasonableness, Miltitz blamed the whole affair on Johann Tetzel and his outlandish claims and said that he had summoned the Dominican to Altenburg to be reprimanded. (By this point, Tetzel had become so despised for his trafficking in indulgences that he had taken refuge in a Dominican monastery in Leipzig, refusing to leave for fear he would be assaulted.) Miltitz tried to impress on Luther the unrest he was causing and the responsibility he would bear if violence broke out. Luther—feeling vulnerable in the face of Rome's unrelenting pursuit—expressed regret at how far the crisis had advanced. At Miltitz's urging, he agreed to remain silent about indulgences and related matters as long as his enemies did the same. He also agreed to write a conciliatory letter to the pope. On the point that Rome deemed most critical, however—recantation—Luther held firm. Until he was shown where he had erred, he said, he would revoke nothing. In the end, the two agreed to refer the matter to the bishop of either Salzburg or Trier for arbitration. At a final dinner at the castle, the nuncio, growing emotional, embraced Luther and gave him a tearful kiss—a "kiss of Judas," Luther would later call it. He had no illusions about Miltitz's intentions.

In his letter to Leo, Luther affirmed his deep respect for Rome but reiterated his refusal to recant; to do otherwise, he maintained, would further defile the Church. His refusal meant in effect that Miltitz's mission had failed. In a stunning act of duplicity, the envoy withheld Luther's letter and instead sent the pope his own report. A complete misrepresentation, it stated that Luther had repented of his views but had been unwilling to do so before Cajetan for fear of being severely reprimanded. On receiving the report, Leo was filled with joy, and he drafted a warm letter to Luther. "With paternal love," he wrote, he happily accepted his explanations. His gratitude was so great that he wished to hear the recantation in person, so Luther, on receiving his letter, should immediately prepare to travel to Rome.

When Leo's letter arrived at the electoral court, Frederick wisely decided not to deliver it, for he knew that Luther would reject the pope's demand out of hand and thus further incense Rome. The whole Miltitz affair, with its bumbling and bluster, captured Rome's ineptness as it sought to stifle the dissident Augustinian.

It was not just inside Germany that Luther's fame was growing. In February 1519, Johann Froben sent him a report on the sales of *Ad Leonem X*, the collection of his works published the previous autumn: "We have sent six hundred copies to France and Spain; they are sold at Paris, and are even read and approved by the doctors of the Sorbonne." A bookseller from Pavia had taken a parcel of his books to Italy "to distribute them among all the cities. Nor does he do it so much for gain as to aid piety." *Ad Leonem X* had also been exported to Brabant and England. "We have sold out all your books except ten copies, and never remember to have sold any more quickly." (Within ten days, Froben added, he expected to bring out a new edition of Erasmus's New Testament, "much enlarged.")

Froben's letter hints at the excitement that *Ad Leonem X* was causing as it circulated throughout Western Europe. For the first time, burghers and magistrates were able to read in a single volume the friar's views on indulgences, penance, excommunication, and clerical abuses, and the effect was electrifying. "Switzerland and the Rhine country as far as the ocean are solid for Luther, and his friends in these regions are both powerful and learned," Wolfgang Capito informed him in February 1519. A lawyer in Basel, writing to a friend in Metz who had asked him to buy some volumes by Luther for him, noted that he had scoured the whole city without finding any, "as they were all sold long ago." Huldrych Zwingli, a reformist priest who was then rising to prominence in Zurich, ordered several hundred copies for colporteurs to distribute on horseback among the laity. In England, agents of Thomas Wolsey, Henry VIII's top adviser, found copies concealed in bales of cotton.

In Wittenberg, couriers arrived with letters from sympathetic clerics in Constance, Ulm, Augsburg, Strasbourg, Breslau, and Paris. At the Black Cloister, dignitaries and students stopped by with letters of introduction, hoping for a meeting with Luther. Applications to the university surged. "Our town can hardly hold them, due to the lack of lodging facilities," Luther observed. Melanchthon's lectures, despite beginning at six in the morning, regularly drew four hundred people, and Luther's classes were nearly as packed.

Luther took advantage of the university's growing prestige to press his program to overhaul its curriculum. Courses on Aristotelian physics and logic were dropped in favor of such humanist favorites as Pliny, Quintilian, and Ovid's *Metamorphoses*. "In this way," Luther wrote to Spalatin, "the subtle hair-splitting finally may perish altogether and genuine philosophy, theology, and all the arts may be drawn from their true sources." "The best studies," Spalatin observed in turn, "are so successfully taught at Wittenberg that you would call it another Athens."

Luther himself was sounding increasingly Athenian. Captivated by Greek, he bought a volume of Homer, and in his letters Greek terms appeared with growing frequency. With Melanchthon's help, he was preparing for publication his notes for the lectures he had given on Paul's Epistle to the Galatians in the winter of 1516 and 1517, and from start to finish he relied heavily on grammar and Greek; he cited Jerome nearly twice as often as he did Augustine and quoted Erasmus almost as much. In his very first sentence, Luther paid tribute to the Dutch scholar: "Now that the whole Christian world knows Greek, and the *Annotations* of that most eminent theologian Erasmus are in everyone's hands and are diligently used, there is no need to point out what the word 'apostle' means—except to those for whom I am writing, not Erasmus." In a letter to two colleagues, Luther expressed regret at not having yet received the paraphrase of Galatians that he had heard was being prepared by Erasmus, "that theologian too great even to envy."

When it came to theological truths, however, Luther remained clear-eyed about their differences. In his notes on Galatians, Luther returned over and over to his key themes of human futility and divine grace, the inutility of works and the saving power of faith. As he starkly put it, "Free will collapses, good works collapse, the righteousness of the Law collapses. . . . Only faith and the invoking of God's completely pure mercy remain." This ran directly counter to Erasmus's belief in human agency and the ability of men and women to use their reason and willpower to show modesty, forbearance, and other Christlike traits.

Nonetheless, Luther was heartened by Erasmus's evident support for some of his key ideas. Wolfgang Capito had written to him about Erasmus's admiration for the Ninety-Five Theses, and Luther himself had seen Erasmus's jab (in his new preface to the *Enchiridion*) at those who profit from indulgences. Given the intense pressure he was under, a few words of support from the great Latin laureate could provide a critical lifeline, and so in late March 1519 Luther decided to write to him directly. Eager to impress, he traded his usual bluntness for the copious style of the humanists.

Given all that he and Erasmus had in common, Luther wrote, it was strange that they had not yet become acquainted. In a sense, though, he felt that he already did know Erasmus, for "where is there someone whose heart Erasmus does not occupy, whom Erasmus does not teach, over whom Erasmus does not hold sway?" Of course, Luther went on, it was presumptuous for him to approach so great a man with "unwashed hands" (a phrase from the *Adages*) and without a proper introduction. But, having been encouraged by Wolfgang Capito and by Erasmus's preface to the *Enchiridion*, he felt compelled to acknowledge Erasmus's outstanding spirit, which had so enriched his own. The hearts of all his readers glowed with gratitude and love for him, and Luther counted himself among them.

Since his own name was now becoming known, he continued, some might misinterpret the silence from the Dutchman. "As a result, my Erasmus, amiable man, if it seems acceptable to you, acknowledge also this little brother in Christ. He is certainly most devoted to you and has the greatest affection for you."

The clumsiness of Luther's language shows how hard it was for him to show such deference—and how strongly he craved Erasmus's support. Justus Jonas, a young Erfurt humanist then visiting Wittenberg, was about to leave for Louvain in the hope of seeing Erasmus, and he agreed to take the letter to him.

Louvain itself, however, was in an uproar, and Luther was the cause. With the arrival of the Froben collection, the theologians there were finally able to read the friar's views in concentrated form, and they were aghast. Luther's rejection of indulgences, his disparagement of penance, his opposition to the ban, his challenge to papal authority—all seemed not only erroneous but heretical. Given the clear danger the book posed to impressionable minds, the religious authorities immediately sought (with limited success) to ban it. In addition, several professors were selected to read through the volume and extract passages that seemed offensive. An assembly was convened, and over several sessions agreement was reached on those articles that seemed to deserve censure.

On a matter of such gravity, however, the Louvain theologians were reluctant to act on their own, and for a second opinion they turned to their colleagues at the university in Cologne. The Dominicans on its faculty had special authority in matters of doctrine. Jacob van Hoogstraten, the inquisitor who had so relentlessly pursued Johannes Reuchlin, had studied at Louvain and had close ties to many of its professors. On February 22, 1519, a bachelor of theology left Louvain for Cologne with a list of suspect passages from the Froben edition.

It was at the very institution to which Erasmus was attached, then, that the formal proceedings against Luther began. The impact on Erasmus's own situation was immediate and dramatic. The Louvain doctors at that moment were especially sensitive because the controversy over Reuchlin had taken a decisive turn against them. In 1517, there had appeared an expanded edition of the *Letters of Obscure Men*, a scathing satire of the Scholastic doctors. The first edition, which had appeared two years earlier, depicted Hoogstraten, Johannes Pfefferkorn, and the Cologne theologians as vulgar pedants who mangled Latin, chased women, drank prodigiously, and engaged in endless quarrels over absurd theological propositions. (One friar mulls whether Jews who convert to Christianity grow back their foreskins.) The new edition was even more caustic, and it frequently alluded to Erasmus as a supporter of the humanist cause. (Erasmus strongly disapproved.) In 1519, support for Reuchlin in Europe was soaring while the Cologne faculty had become a laughingstock. All of which had embittered the conservatives toward Erasmus. Now, in Luther's writings, they saw the fruit of Erasmus's own teachings; some were convinced that Erasmus had helped him.

The first volley against Erasmus came from Jan Briart, the vice-chancellor of the university. Speaking at a graduation ceremony in February 1519, he declared that it was impious to praise marriage at the expense of celibacy. Though he mentioned no one by name, it was clear to whom he was referring. A short time earlier, a Louvain printer—hungry for material by Erasmus—had published his *Encomium Matrimonii*, a paean to marriage that Erasmus had written more than twenty years earlier. In praising marriage, Erasmus had not exactly advocated carnal bliss; his ideal Christian marriage was chaste almost to the point of celibacy. But he had called the single state "a barren way of life hardly becoming to a man" and held up wedlock as superior—an insupportable position to conservatives like Briart. When Erasmus pointed out to him that he had actually written the tract two decades earlier, the vice-chancellor withdrew his comments.

It was too late, however. As if on cue, all the anger and resentment that had been building up at Erasmus and his mockery of monks, criticism of the Vulgate, and broadsides against Julius suddenly exploded. From the pulpit and lectern, friars and theologians inveighed against Erasmus, the New Learning, and the whole idea of reform.

Erasmus's standing was further weakened by the progress being made by the College of Three Tongues. In the spring of 1519, a large building was purchased in the city's fish market to house the institute. Given Erasmus's aversion to fish, the location was hardly ideal, but the prospect of a permanent home for his prized college outweighed any potential blow to his gastrointestinal system. The Louvain theologians, on the other hand, were unhappy with this outpost of Greek and grammar, seeing it as a Trojan horse aimed at undermining their own authority. Jacobus Latomus, an outspoken defender of orthodoxy who since 1517 had loudly criticized Erasmus, published two dialogues deriding pseudo-theologians who sought to make a knowledge of rhetoric, literature, and languages necessary for divine studies; though he, too, avoided mentioning Erasmus by name, his target was no less obvious.

Edward Lee, meanwhile, was continuing to comb Erasmus's New Testament for errors. On his return from Basel, Erasmus had learned that the Englishman now had more than two hundred notes. Lee refused to let him see them, and with rumors spreading of their tartness, Erasmus in a fit of pique challenged Lee to go public with them. Lee had initially had no such intention, but with Erasmus's goading he prepared to do just that.

The attacks against Erasmus seemed so broad and coordinated that he suspected an actual conspiracy at work, directed at not just him but the whole movement to promote good literature. The university of Louvain, he lamented to a colleague, "the peaceful home of literary studies, has been racked by extraordinary turmoil, the like of which I have never seen in all my life." The clerical clans "have made a division of labor among themselves, some of them talking nonsense at the dinner-table or in the council-chamber, others ranting to the ignorant mob which is so easily imposed upon; some arguing in the lecture-room, some dropping their poison in the ears of princes."

Amid all this contention, Erasmus heard from Basel that Froben wanted to publish more Luther. The prospect alarmed him. From the passages in *Ad Leonem X* that he had read, he could see that, while it contained clear echoes of his own work, the language was much stronger, the tone far sharper. Any further airing of Luther's views could provoke a crackdown that might well undermine his own more gradual efforts at reform. And so Erasmus implored his publisher to refrain from printing any more of Luther.

This put Froben in a difficult spot. Erasmus was his premier writer and the main source of his reputation as Europe's leading publisher. But the Luther collection had sold faster than anything of Erasmus's, and the market for this fresh new voice seemed huge. Capito, who had been the main force behind the volume, was especially eager to follow it with more, and when he learned of Erasmus's cease-and-desist order to Froben, he urged Erasmus to reconsider: "Do not, I beg you, exaggerate this business of Martin into a public issue. You know how much your vote matters. I really mean this." While there was much in Luther's work that he himself did not like, Capito noted, it was important that his reputation not suffer. "This will encourage the rest of the younger generation to risk something in the cause of liberty in Christ." In Germany, there were many distinguished people who wished Erasmus and Luther equally well, while Luther and his party were devoted to Erasmus. Luther's enemies desired nothing more than to see Erasmus break with him. And so, Capito pleaded, "Do not let Louvain prove an obstacle."

But Erasmus had seen the inquisitors destroy Reuchlin's reputation and knew they could do the same to him. And so he held firm: if Froben did not give up Luther, he would give up Froben.

The threat worked. Apart from a few minor texts, Froben would publish no more Luther. It would prove a fateful decision—for Froben, not Luther. With so many presses now in operation, Froben's withdrawal simply left the field open to others, and new editions of *Ad Leonem X* soon appeared in Strasbourg, Antwerp, Vienna, and beyond. More generally, the printing industry as a whole was about to undergo a dramatic transformation, leaving Froben—and Erasmus—behind.

To that point, that industry had been dominated by large folios of interest mainly to theologians, clerics, schools, and scholars. Froben's reputation rested on his skill in producing serious books of the highest quality, both in appearance and in content, of which Erasmus's New Testament was the supreme example. Erasmus no doubt had Froben in mind when, in a preamble he prepared in early 1519 for a new edition of Livy's *History*, he paid tribute to printing as an "almost superhuman art" that had made formerly rare works available at very reasonable prices. If Ptolemy Philadelphus had earned such lasting renown from the library he had founded at Alexandria, "what recompense do we not owe to those who daily offer us whole libraries, a whole world so to say of books, in every language and every branch of literature?" But, Erasmus went on, he wished that printers would confine themselves to producing books on subjects that truly deserved it—to restoring the great works of antiquity rather than "adding modern works to the pile."

Erasmus, in short, remained wedded to the great scholarly mission of printing's early decades—the recovery and dissemination of classical and patristic texts. By the end of the second decade of the sixteenth century, however, the hunger for such works was waning and an appetite was growing for texts that were shorter, cheaper, and more topical. This new generation of texts was aimed at a broader, less rarefied audience. And here Luther would lead the way. Around this time he began to write at the furious clip (twenty to thirty titles a year) that he would maintain for many years to come. In 1519 alone he would produce thirteen homiletic pieces (apart from other, more polemical works), most of them written in German and appearing in pamphlet form. They were often intensely practical, with titles like *A Brief Instruction on How Confession Should Be Made* and *A Short Way to Understand and Say the Lord's Prayer for Young Children*. The ten-page *Meditation on Christ's Passion*, which described the mental state with which Christians should approach Easter, appeared in more than a dozen editions in its first year alone. Through such shorter works, Luther was able to reach the weavers and plowmen whom Erasmus had cited in the *Paraclesis*.

The flow of texts from Luther's pen was so great that rumors spread that he was not working alone, but alone he did work, in his small room over the passageway between the cloister and the brewery, writing late into the night in his neat, compact hand. Messengers from the print shop would wait at his door for copy, then rush it off to be set and printed, then return the next day for more. The writing came effortlessly. "I have a swift hand and a quick memory," Luther observed. "When I write, it just flows out; I do not have to press and squeeze." (He also rarely rewrote, which helps explain the disorganized nature of many of his works.) Somehow, this farmer's grandson who had grown up among belching smelters and had spent so much of his adult life in classrooms and monastic cells had managed to develop a forceful, penetrating style that could simultaneously rouse and console, incite and entertain.

Luther's literary power derived not just from his wide vocabulary and rich imagery but also from the sound and cadence of his sentences. He enjoyed onomatopoeia, wordplay, and puns on opponents' names, and he could pass quickly from soaring invocations of divine majesty to vulgar phrases rooted in the Saxon soil. "Here is the beast in its stable, said the devil as he shoved a fly up his mother's backside" was a typical jeer. When it came to coarseness and invective, Luther had few equals.

The pamphlets turned out by him were part of a great flood that was upending Europe's religious and social life. Usually eight or sixteen pages long, these *Flugschriften* used little paper and so were cheap, and they were highly effective at transmitting new ideas to a broad audience. In addition to homilies and sermons that offered spiritual solace and moral advice, the fly sheets included satires, dialogues, polemics, and manifestos seeking to promote an opinion, vilify an opponent, or decry an abuse. Common, too, were one-page broadsheets featuring a crude illustration along with a few inflammatory lines of text. Together, these ephemera were helping create a mass public opinion that had never previously existed and that was thoroughly antipapal and anti-Italian.

As printing grew less elitist, traditional publishing centers like Basel, Antwerp, and Paris were challenged by scrappy upstarts. Leading the way was Wittenberg. Despite its modest size and remote location, it would in a few short years become one of Europe's top book producers, with six hundred titles (most of them pamphlets) appearing from 1518 to 1523. Works published first in Wittenberg would often appear in unauthorized editions elsewhere—a subversion of the normal hierarchies of the book trade.

Overall, in the first decade after the posting of the Ninety-Five Theses, an estimated six million to seven million pamphlets would be printed, the vast majority of them supporting Luther and his cause. Luther himself accounted for about a quarter of them. As his sales rose, those of Erasmus declined, and before long the ardent friar would eclipse the cultivated scholar as Europe's bestselling author. Froben's fortunes receded accordingly.

Had he wanted, Luther could have gotten rich off his writing, but he never asked for compensation of any kind, and this made him a favorite of publishers. The warmth was rarely reciprocated. In Luther's view, most printing houses were driven by one thing only—greed—and he fumed over the low standards of accuracy that had become the norm in Germany as houses sought to undercut and pirate one another. Nonetheless, those printers, by taking financial as well as political risks to bring controversial works before the public, were instrumental in spreading dissident ideas. Thanks to the printing press, a lonely friar on a far edge of Germany was able to challenge the vicar of Christ in Rome. Printing, Luther declared, was "an unquenchable flame"—the "last and highest gift of God for the Gospel."

Despite his ultimatum to Froben regarding Luther, Erasmus remained favorably disposed toward his fellow Augustinian. For all their differences in theology and temperament, both seemed to be working toward the same goal—revitalizing the Church and replacing its calcified rites and ceremonies with more heartfelt forms of repentance and reflection. It was time to offer some support. Two years earlier, Erasmus had sent Frederick the Wise a new edition of Suetonius's *Lives of the Caesars* along with a dedicatory preface. He had never heard back. On the pretext of checking to see if he had received it, Erasmus in mid-April 1519 decided to write to the elector again and while he was at it to set down his thoughts on Luther. (The letter from Luther had not yet arrived.) Since the letter was intended for Frederick's eyes only, Erasmus felt he could be frank.

After saluting the elector for his support of liberal studies, Erasmus warned that those studies would continue to flourish only if sovereigns used their authority to defend them against the "enemies of the Muses," who were agitating to restore the reign of ignorance. Luther was among their chief targets. Though he had read only snatches of Luther's work, Erasmus observed, all who knew him spoke highly of his life. He was free of any suggestion of greed or ambition, and his integrity was approved by all. His detractors were thus unjustified in raging so fiercely against his character. Their agitation was all the more objectionable in that Luther had simply proposed points for discussion. No one had sought to correct or disprove him; instead, cries of "Heresy!" and "Antichrist!" had rung from pulpits and lecture halls. Luther's adversaries in the Church seemed to thirst more for human blood than the salvation of souls.

The accusation of heresy, Erasmus added, should not be too readily cast at men who lead a life worthy of Christ. Those who insist on hurling such charges should themselves behave in a Christian manner, showing mildness in finding fault and charity in offering correction. Why did the theologians prefer to conquer rather than cure, to suppress a man rather than put him right? Christ, who alone of all men was free from error, did not break the bruised reed nor quench the smoking flax. (This image, from Isaiah by way of Matthew, was a favorite of Erasmus's.) As a wise ruler dedicated to protecting the Christian faith, Frederick should not allow an innocent man "to be delivered under the pretext of religion into the hands of the irreligious."

Erasmus's letter shows how solidly he supported Luther at this point. In the current climate, however, he was not willing to say so publicly. Rather, he hoped to prod a powerful prince into using his influence to defend Luther and the broader cause of reform. But the fact that the most celebrated literary figure in Europe had written in support of Luther ensured that his letter would not remain private for long. As soon as it arrived at the electoral court, Spalatin began circulating it. A copy quickly reached Wittenberg and Luther. "The letter of Erasmus pleases me and our friends very much," Luther wrote. Soon afterward, Spalatin translated it into German, and before long the letter was known all over Germany, becoming a powerful piece of propaganda for the reform movement.

Erasmus was mortified. He had placed in the hands of his enemies a ready-made weapon that they could use against him. From now on, he realized, he would have to be far more circumspect.

As the climate in Louvain darkened, Erasmus could take some comfort from one of the high points of his career: the arrival in Louvain (shortly before May 1, 1519) of the second edition of his New Testament. Physically, the *Novum Testamentum* was a true monument: two thick folios totaling more than 1,250 pages, with one containing his new Latin translation (with the Greek alongside) and the other his annotations. In all, about two thousand copies were printed—a remarkable number for so complex and scholarly a work. Prominently displayed at the front was a letter from Leo X endorsing the project. Erasmus hoped that the pope's imprimatur, along with the greatly expanded and revised text, would help quiet the squalls of obloquy raised by his first edition.

Around the same time as the *Novum Testamentum* arrived in Louvain, Luther's letter reached Erasmus. Erasmus's reply, written at the end of May 1519, reflected his new caution. "No words of mine could describe the storm raised here by your books," he wrote. Many suspected that those books had been written with Erasmus's assistance and that he was "a standard-bearer of this new movement." The Louvain theologians were using Luther's work as a pretext for suppressing not only humane studies but also Erasmus's own work. "In the whole business their weapons are clamor, audacity, subterfuge, misinterpretation, innuendo; if I had not seen it with my own eyes—felt it, rather—I would never have believed theologians could be such maniacs." This "poisonous virus," starting in a small circle, had spread to a larger number, creating a contagion of "epidemic paranoia." Erasmus had assured them that Luther was quite unknown to him—that he had not yet read his books and so could not form an opinion of them. He had also urged his critics not to place before the public a distorted account of the affair, "especially since all with one voice speak highly of the author's manner of life."

As for himself, he remained "uncommitted, so far as I can, in hopes of being able to do more for the revival of good literature." One could accomplish more through courtesy and moderation than through tumult and insult. "That was how Christ brought the world under his sway; that was how Paul did away with the Jewish law." Things that are so widely accepted that they cannot be torn from men's minds all at once should be met with close-reasoned argument "rather than bare assertion." In closing, Erasmus observed that he had dipped into Luther's commentary on the Psalms (which had recently been published) and been impressed. It would, he hoped, prove "of great service."

That final grace note, however, could not conceal the letter's chilliness.

Far from providing the lifeline Luther had sought, Erasmus was urging him to be more reasonable and careful. Having already heard many such pleas, Luther was annoyed to get yet another. Even more exasperating was Erasmus's determination to sit on the sidelines in the great contest that loomed ahead. From that moment, Luther's personal disillusionment with the acclaimed humanist set in.

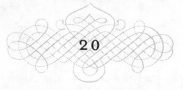

THE GREAT DEBATE

Luther had little time to sulk, however, for he faced a far more pressing matter: a rendezvous in Leipzig with Johann Eck, the Ingolstadt professor who had attacked his Ninety-Five Theses (and Erasmus's annotations). The Leipzig disputation would be a pivotal event in Luther's life, accelerating his theological development, hastening his break with Rome, and deepening the divisions within Christendom.

Ironically, Luther was not even on the original program. Eck was instead due to debate Andreas von Karlstadt, the dean of the Wittenberg faculty. A restless and headstrong theologian who seemed unable to avoid controversy, Karlstadt would become a major figure in the Reformation— and a source of endless exasperation for Luther. When Eck attacked Luther in his *Obelisks*, Karlstadt decided, without informing Luther (who was away in Heidelberg), to defend him with his own set of 405 theses.

Inflamed, Eck challenged Karlstadt to a public disputation. Karlstadt accepted, and Leipzig was agreed on as the site. Seeking permission, they approached Duke George, in whose territory Leipzig sat, and he expressed his willingness to host the event. The duke was unhappy with the growing prominence of the University of Wittenberg and the prestige it was bringing to his cousin Frederick, and he hoped that the debate would deliver a blow to the upstarts. Wary of widening the conflict and offending Frederick, Leipzig's theologians resisted, but George eventually prevailed, and the disputation was scheduled for June 27, 1519.

Eck had no real interest in debating Karlstadt, however; Luther was the real prize. Though nearly as prolific a writer as Luther, Eck had an arid and didactic style that won him little notice, but as a debater, he had few equals. Eck had won acclaim for his performance in earlier disputations at which he had vigorously defended the right of Christians to charge interest on loans despite biblical strictures on usury. A victory over

Luther would further boost his reputation while earning the gratitude of the Holy See.

As the negotiations over the shape of the disputation continued, Eck and Karlstadt issued dueling theses and countertheses. In his, Eck sought to draw out Luther on a subject on which he seemed highly vulnerable: the primacy of the Roman Church. In his *Explanations of the Ninety-Five Theses*, Luther had asserted that the superiority of Rome over all other churches had not been proclaimed until the pontificate of Sylvester I (314 to 335). This contradicted Rome's insistence that its authority extended back to Christ as affirmed in the New Testament. Pouncing on Luther's assertion, Eck reiterated Roman supremacy. Duly provoked, Luther, issuing his own set of theses, went even further than he had in the *Explanations*, arguing that the claims by the Roman Church to be superior to all others rested on "the very feeble decrees of the Roman pontiffs" and were contradicted by Scripture. This position was so radical that Luther's own colleagues in Wittenberg shrank from discussing it.

Eager to take on "that little glory-hungry beast," as he called Eck, Luther sought Duke George's permission to participate in the debate. The duke was willing, but the Leipzig theologians—reluctant to provide a forum to a man censured by Rome—again resisted. Luther was nonetheless determined to debate, and in the weeks leading up to the event he methodically worked his way through the canon law, the decretals, conciliar resolutions, and patristic commentaries. With the help of Erasmus's annotations, he scrutinized the New Testament passages on which papal authority rested, including Matthew 16:18 ("Thou art Peter") and John 21:15–17 ("Feed my sheep"). In a massive tract on papal power that he somehow managed to complete in this period, Luther contended that the papacy is a human institution similar to a political government and could claim no special sacred status, since it has no foundation in Scripture.

Late at night, he was visited by disturbing thoughts. The pope, he wrote to Spalatin, might be the "Antichrist himself," so terribly had the truth been "corrupted and crucified" by him in the decretals. "I am extremely distressed that under the semblance of laws and the Christian name, the people of Christ should be so deluded." A figure from the book of Revelation, the Antichrist was an enemy of Christ's who—inspired and controlled by Satan—was to visit unprecedented calamities on earth in the period before Christ's return. Luther now believed that he might be sitting on the papal throne itself.

As the start of the disputation approached, Wittenberg was afire with anticipation. Leipzig was a hated rival, and the event was being treated like an intramural championship match. A few days before the scheduled start, two carts pulled up to the Black Cloister. Karlstadt filled one with his books and then climbed in, while into the other stepped Luther, Melanchthon, and a group of theologians and lawyers. Joining them were two hundred students, many armed with spears, daggers, and halberds. Amid shouts and cheers, the Wittenbergers set off on the forty-five-mile journey to Leipzig, ready for battle.

For showmanship, drama, and sheer weirdness, few events in early modern Europe could match the Leipzig disputation. Lasting seventeen days, it was attended by princes, counts, councilors, priests, professors, citizens both privileged and common, and theologians both orthodox and reformist. In addition to the detailed records kept by several secretaries, more than thirty other eyewitnesses produced reports, making the disputation one of the most richly documented events of the period. It would be followed by a flood of pamphlets and letters, which, with more acrimony than accuracy, sought to shape public perceptions of the outcome and which would heighten tensions within Christendom. This sober academic affair thus held the seeds of world conflict.

The unruly tenor of the proceedings was set on June 24, 1519, when the two wagons bearing the Wittenberg principals, along with the bands of boisterous students, rolled into town. When the procession reached Grimma, Leipzig's main artery, a wheel of the lead wagon broke, pitching Karlstadt ignobly into the mud. He and Luther then rode on to Hay Street, where the printer Melchior Lotther had prepared quarters for them.

Eck, who had arrived a short time earlier with a single servant, stayed in lodgings provided by the city. Several days were spent wrangling over judges, secretaries, and the structure of the event. The participants, it was agreed, would use the German method of debate, with each side presenting for a half hour without interruption. The most pressing matter—Luther's participation—remained unresolved. Interest in the event nonetheless ran so high that it was moved from the university, which did not have a chamber large enough, to a spacious hall in the Pleissenburg, Duke George's imposing castle. To help keep the peace, an armed detachment every morning marched with fife and drum to station itself at the castle's gate.

On the opening day of the disputation, June 27, 1519, a magnificent Mass was held at six in the morning at St. Thomas's church, followed by a grand procession to the castle. Petrus Mosellanus, a professor of poetics, delivered an address in rolling Ciceronian periods on the art and method of debate, in which he invoked some of the great theological clashes of the past—between Peter and Paul, Jerome and Augustine, Gregory and Basil, Erasmus and Lefèvre. A promising young humanist and acquaintance of Erasmus's, Mosellanus praised Erasmus's Christian spirit, but he was so nervous and spoke in so low a voice that hardly anyone could hear him, and when after two hours he finally finished there was a sigh of relief. After a musical ensemble performed the hymn "Come, Holy Spirit" three times, the assembly adjourned for a lavish meal at which the usual copious amounts of wine were consumed. At a trumpet's blare, everyone returned to the hall, and finally, at two o'clock in the afternoon, the disputation got under way.

Eck and Karlstadt each took a place at a *Katheder*, the elevated chair used by university lecturers. The subject: how much free will does man have in attaining salvation? From the start, it was a mismatch. Eck, tall and solidly built, had (as one observer put it) the meaty face of a butcher and the lungs of a town crier. Known for his quick wit, overbearing manner, and prodigious memory, he could quote with equal facility from the Bible and the Church Fathers, the *Sentences* and the decretals. Eck's chief asset was his win-at-any-cost mentality. He would create diversions, twist his opponents' arguments, even adopt their positions as his own when it suited him. Earlier, he had shown humanist learnings, but as his critical comments on Erasmus's New Testament suggested, he had become an increasingly vocal defender of both Rome and the hierarchical order it represented, and in Leipzig he hoped to put down the Wittenberg insurgency.

Karlstadt was short and sun-darkened and ponderous in presentation. He relied heavily on his books, which were piled so high at his *Katheder* that he sometimes seemed to disappear behind them. He read from them very deliberately so that the secretaries could record his every word. He was excitable and quick to anger but also so hesitant and long-winded that he often sent the audience into a stupor and caused some Leipzig professors to doze off. Eck grew so impatient that at one point he proposed adopting the Italian style of debating, by which everything was allowed except the use of books, and the judges agreed. Enraged at their decision, the Wittenberg students gathered with drawn daggers in front of Eck's quarters, leading the town council to station thirty-four armed guards in the area. The Leipzig students were just as rowdy, and the brawling in the taverns grew so violent that some innkeepers posted guards with halberds. Every morning, Eck, refreshed by a horseback ride in the surrounding countryside, entered the hall clutching his whip, and with orotund flair he presented his intricate arguments while belittling the bantam-size Karlstadt and driving him into fits of befuddlement. Eck, observed one eyewitness, regularly attacked "with nine or ten arguments by which he does not seek to establish the truth but only his own honor."

But Karlstadt doggedly pressed his position. Sharing Luther's attachment to Paul and Augustine, he vociferously argued that man cannot of his own accord, and least of all through his works, do anything good except through an infusion of divine grace; all depends on God. Eck, hewing to the traditional Scholastic position, maintained that man can through his own efforts elicit God's grace. For a full week they went back and forth on this and related points, Eck theatrically invoking Thomas and Lombard and a host of papal pronouncements on behalf of discretionary action, and Karlstadt haltingly appealing to Romans and Galatians and Augustine's *On the Spirit and the Letter* to prove the ineradicability of human sinfulness. As profound and cosmic as the questions were, the debate itself was unbearably tedious and repetitious.

Throughout it all, Luther sat in the upper chamber, watching along with everyone else. All those present had come to see him, not Karlstadt, and they wondered when they would get the chance. Finally, the way for his participation was cleared, and shortly before seven o'clock on the morning of July 4, 1519, the Wittenberg friar entered the arena. The atmosphere among the friars, officials, professors, and students in the hall turned electric as two of Germany's leading theologians prepared to face off. (In a sad coincidence, Johann Tetzel on that same day died in the Dominican monastery a few hundred yards away.) All eyes were on the man who had spoken out so boldly against indulgences, who had so defiantly confronted Cajetan, who was being so relentlessly pursued by the Holy See. They saw a friar of medium height, whose body, though thickset, was worn so thin by his studies and rigors that one could "almost count his bones," as an eyewitness put it. (According to some accounts, Luther carried a bouquet of pink flowers, which he sniffed from time to time.) Looking solemn in a black cowl over a white habit, Luther recognized the moment as a crucial test, placing him in full public view against a forceful spokesman for the Western Church.

He and Eck began right in on the great issue dividing them—the authority of the pope. Eck vigorously pressed his position that the Roman Church was superior to all others, and to buttress his claim he self-assuredly cited Christ's key admonitions on the subject, including "Thou art Peter" and "Feed my sheep." Invoking Jerome, Dionysius the Areopagite, Cyprian, and various decretals, the wily professor maintained that Peter, following Christ's instruction, had been the first bishop of Rome and that the popes as his successors had continued to fill that supreme seat of Christendom. The papacy was thus of incontestably divine origin.

"I impugn these decretals," Luther declared. While affirming his respect for the power of both the pope and the Church, he asserted that the office had been established not by Scripture but by men. Citing Luke, Colossians, and Augustine's *De Trinitate*, Luther argued that the true head of the Church was not any man but Christ himself. Referring to the underlying Greek text of Matthew, he maintained that "the rock" was not Peter but Christ's confession of faith, and that while Peter might have enjoyed special status, Christ had commissioned all of the apostles to carry his message. For a thousand years Greek Christians had not lived under the sway of the pope; did that mean they were all condemned? The earliest Fathers themselves had no pope to direct them; only with the reign of Sylvester I had the papacy come into being. Drawing on his recent study of ecclesiastical history, Luther tried to show how the principle of papal primacy had developed over time, especially through the decrees issued by Rome throughout the previous four centuries.

During that first day's discussion, both men showed off their vast knowledge of the Bible, the Fathers, and Church law, as well as their dexterity in deploying it. But the two seemed to belong to different eras. Eck the traditionalist took as indisputable the established teachings of the Church and sought to demonstrate them by drawing on the accepted body of patristic commentary and canon law. Luther the insurgent used his knowledge of languages and history to scrape away the successive layers of accrued interpretation of the Bible to get at its underlying meaning.

Eck felt he needed an advantage, and on the morning of the second day, before a crowd still buzzing over the previous day's exchanges, he found it. Luther, he alleged, in claiming that Peter was not the head of the Holy Church and that the papacy was not of divine origin, was echoing the views of John Wyclif and Jan Hus. This was an explosive charge, for Wyclif and Hus, along with Arius and Pelagius in earlier centuries, were considered arch-heretics, and to be linked to them in so prominent a setting was very dangerous. Vigorously protesting, Luther said that he had never approved of schismatics like the Hussites; even if the Bohemians had had divine right on their side, they should not have caused such a breach in the Church. Seeing how flustered Luther had become, Eck pressed the point, demanding to know how his position differed from that of the Bohemians. Luther continued to assert his innocence.

At this point, the conclave broke for lunch, and Luther (apparently) took the opportunity to review the proceedings of the Council of Constance and the thirty articles of Hus's that had been condemned there. Among them was one holding that "there is only one holy universal church, which is one with the total number predestined to salvation." Others maintained that Peter was never the head of the Church and that to attain salvation it was not necessary to believe that the Roman Church is superior to all others. These statements were in line with Luther's own readings of the Bible. When the session resumed at two o'clock, he repeated his disapproval of the Bohemian schism but added that it was "certain that many of the articles of Jan Hus and the Bohemians are plainly most Christian and evangelical" and that the universal Church could not condemn them.

There was a moment of stunned silence. "The plague take him!" Duke George bellowed, and pandemonium broke out. After order was restored, Luther explained that whether the condemned articles were those of Wyclif or Hus, he did not care. Basil the Great, Gregory of Nazianzus, and many Greek bishops had all been saved even though they had not believed it was necessary for salvation to regard the Roman Church as superior to all others. But the damage had been done, and Eck rejoiced at how readily Luther had taken his bait.

The Hussite upheaval had faded from memory in much of Europe, but not in Saxony, and least of all in Leipzig. Located just 60 miles from the border with Bohemia and 120 miles from Prague, Hus's center of activity, the city considered Bohemia a source of contagion that at any moment could infect institutions on the German side of the border. After Hus's execution, Bohemia had been engulfed in war, and in Saxony there remained deserted villages that had been burned by Bohemian armies. The University of Leipzig itself had been founded out of the Bohemian chaos. To Duke George and other leading Saxons, then, the Hussite heresy testified to the violence that could result when dissent was allowed to grow unchecked.

At that point, however, neither Duke George nor Luther had much idea who Hus actually was, or of the story behind his rebellion. In many key respects, Hus's revolt anticipated that of Luther. Some, in fact, consider him the first Protestant.

Jan Hus was named after the market village of Husinec in southern Bohemia where he was raised. In the early 1390s, he enrolled in the University of Prague, which, with five thousand to seven thousand students, was the most dynamic in Central Europe. After earning a bachelor's degree in 1393 and a master's degree in 1396, he began studying for a doctorate in theology. At the time, the views of John Wyclif were circulating in Prague. In 1382, the Czech princess Anne had married the English king Richard II, and some Czech students had gone to Oxford to study. There they were exposed to Wyclif's ideas. On their return to Prague, they brought back some of his writings, and Hus, on reading them, was deeply affected, especially by his teaching that Scripture should be considered the supreme Christian authority.

Around 1400 Hus was ordained a priest, and in 1402 he was appointed preacher at the Bethlehem chapel. The chapel had been founded a decade earlier to offer sermons in Czech and to push for ecclesiastical reform. From its pulpit, Hus inveighed against dissolute priests who spent their time gambling, dancing, and drinking. The Church had amassed enormous wealth in Bohemia, and Hus, condemning its greed and materialism, fed a surging sense of national identity. "Bohemia for the Bohemians" was the rallying cry. Such sentiments took root in opposition to not just Rome but also Germany. For decades, Bohemia had been overrun by Germans. Miners, merchants, and artisans had all come seeking their fortune, and as they advanced, they stirred intense resentment among the locals, especially at the university. With only two German universities (Heidelberg and Erfurt) then in operation, Prague was a popular place of study, and German professors occupied many key posts. Though making up only a fifth of the student body, the Czechs demanded more control, and in 1409 the university's constitution was amended to provide it. Outraged, some 1,500 German students and instructors left, and a new university was established in Leipzig.

In 1412, after antipope John XXIII declared a crusade against the excommunicated king of Naples and proclaimed a new indulgence for those joining it, Hus preached in opposition to it and to the more general idea of raising money to spill Christian blood. He was loudly supported by the Czech people, and papal agents were jeered at and harassed.

After Hus resisted an order by the local archbishop to stop preaching, he was excommunicated. When he persisted, all of Prague was placed under an interdict. To help relieve the city, Hus left it, taking shelter in rural castles opened to him by sympathetic lords, and over the next two years he produced a flood of tracts. One of them, *De Ecclesia* ("On the Church"), would be the most influential work on the structure of the Church written in the period between Augustine and Luther. In it, Hus, borrowing liberally from Wyclif, condemned the entire ecclesiastical framework, including the papacy, which, he insisted, had no foundation in Scripture. The Church was ruled not by the pope or by cardinals but by Christ, who was its rock. A pope who lived contrary to Christ was, like any other perverted person, to be called Antichrist. Hus also supported offering the laity wine as well as bread during Communion—a violation of a centuries-old Church stricture.

As popular as these ideas were in Bohemia, they were reviled in Rome, and in 1414 Hus was summoned to account for them at the Council of Constance. Convened to address both ecclesiastical reform and the papal schism that had opened up in 1378, the council would be one of the most important Catholic assemblies to take place during the Middle Ages. Provided a safe-conduct by the emperor-elect Sigismund, Hus in October 1414, accompanied by thirty men on horseback, left on the four-hundred-mile journey to Constance, a town picturesquely set on the western shore of the Alpine lake of the same name. On his arrival, Hus was at first treated civilly, but within a month a special commission ruled that a pledge with a heretic such as he need not be respected, and in violation of the safe-conduct he was thrown into a dungeon in the Dominican monastery on an island in the lake. Hus's cell was close by the latrines, and the unsanitary conditions caused him to become gravely ill. In January 1415, he was transferred to another, slightly less wretched cell, but in March 1415 he was taken in chains by boat to the castle of the bishop of Constance, located on the Rhine outside the city's walls. Confined on the top floor of a tower, Hus was free to walk about in fetters during the day, but at night he had his hands manacled to the wall near his bed.

Finally, on June 8, 1415, after more than two months of such harsh confinement, he was summoned to a formal hearing. He was presented with some three dozen articles, most of them from *De Ecclesia*, that were deemed offensive and scandalous to the Church. Ordered to abjure them, Hus said he would do so only for those articles whose renunciation would not offend God or his conscience based on Scripture. The council countered that Scripture had to be interpreted not by the free judgment of individuals but by the authorized agents of the Church, and it insisted that Hus retract all of the articles without reservation. Citing his conscience, he refused.

He was transferred to a tower adjoining the Franciscan friary. Despite suffering from hemorrhages, the stone, vomiting, headaches, and tooth-aches, Hus over the next month managed to write a series of warm letters to his friends, signing off with phrases like "bound in prison in chains" and "expecting a dreadful death." Till the last moment, attempts were made to change his mind, without success. Finally, on July 6, 1415, after eight months of punishing confinement, he was summoned to the Con-stance cathedral, where the council was meeting. There, thirty of his ar-ticles were condemned as scandalous, erroneous, rash, unacceptable, and, in some cases, notoriously heretical, and *De Ecclesia* and all of his other books were ordered burned. Hus protested that not a single error had been pointed out to him, but he was ordered to keep silent.

With virtually the whole population of Constance gathered in the streets, Hus was led to a meadow outside the city, where his place of exe-cution had been prepared. His outer clothes were removed, his hands were tied behind his back, and his neck was chained to the stake. Two bundles of faggots were mixed with straw and piled around him up to his chin. Given a final opportunity to recant, Hus said that he was ready to die, and he sang hymns as he was roasted alive. To ensure that nothing remained that could become a relic, his skull was smashed, his heart was burned through, and his garments were fed to the flames.

But Hus's example and teachings would prove much harder to extin-guish. When a courier arrived in Prague with the news of his execution, protests erupted. Five hundred leading Czech citizens signed a document proclaiming Hus an upright Christian, denouncing his execution as an in-sult to the country, and committing themselves to fight to the last drop of blood to defend the doctrines of Christ against those of man. Even while Hus was in prison, priests had begun administering Communion in both wine and bread, and the Eucharistic chalice became the symbol of revolt against Rome. There emerged two factions—the Utraquists, who favored gradual reform, and the Taborites, who supported an apocalyptic form of biblical purity. In 1419, an inflamed mob led by an insurrectionary preacher invaded the town hall and threw thirteen Catholic loyalists from an upper window to their deaths, in the "First Defenestration of Prague." The following year, the Utraquists and Taborites agreed on a common program, the "Four Articles of Prague," which advocated Communion in both kinds, clerical rectitude, preaching based solely on God's Word, and a return to apostolic poverty.

To neither Rome nor the emperor was any of this acceptable, and in 1420 the Holy See declared a crusade against the Bohemian heretics. Sigismund, accompanied by several German princes, arrived before Prague at the head of a vast army drawn from around Europe. Almost overnight a large Hussite army formed, and the crusaders were violently repulsed. No fewer than four subsequent crusades were mounted against the Bohemians, each of which was bloodily beaten back. Marching through Bohemia and Moravia, Hussite armies torched monasteries, slaughtered monks, and compelled the population to swear allegiance to the Four Articles. It was the first widespread destruction of monasteries and church art by Christians in the Latin West. The German settlers in Bohemia, who enjoyed great wealth and remained loyal to Rome, became a prime target, and many fled into Saxony and other parts of Germany. The Bohemians mounted "beautiful rides" across the border into Austria, Silesia, and Saxony, spreading terror with battle cries like "Warriors we of God" and "Kill, kill, kill, kill them, every man!" Bearing banners embroidered with the chalice, they fought and plundered their way up to the very walls of Leipzig.

Eventually, the two Hussite factions fell on each other. Fifteen years of brutal warfare followed, forcing thousands to flee, reducing the peasants to serfdom, and leaving Prague in ruins. Peace finally came in 1436, and Rome was forced to tolerate an independent Hussite church. It was based on two key principles—Communion in both kinds and the use of the Czech language in worship. While the Hussites remained bitterly divided among themselves, Bohemia became the first region in Western Europe to slip from papal control—the ultimate consequence of the Church's decision to execute Jan Hus.

Rome, however, managed to keep the insurrection from spilling over Bohemia's borders. All the neighboring lands remained in the Church's orbit. Hus's influence itself did not spread much beyond his homeland. Prior to the invention of printing, his works remained largely unavailable, and his ideas were little known.

* * *

Luther had not read any of Hus's works. The same was true of most of those in the audience at Leipzig. All they knew of Hus were the atrocities, anarchy, and devastation associated with his name. So when Luther was accused of Hussite sympathies, he vehemently objected. After the spectators in the hall had settled down, Eck—pressing his advantage—declared that the "reverend father" was confusing the holy Greeks with heretics and calling the pestilential errors of the Hussites most Christian.

"I protest both to you and this gathering that you speak falsely and impudently about me," Luther declared. Eck—swelling up like an adder, as Luther later put it—piled up patristic and Scholastic citations in an effort to show that Luther, in declaring certain Hussite articles most Christian and evangelical, had spoken against the sacred and honorable Council of Constance and in defense of the Hussite tenet that the Roman Church was not superior to all others. "This is a most impudent lie!" Luther shouted. The argument grew so heated and the crowd so unruly that the presiding judge had to admonish the participants to refrain from accusations and abuse.

During that session and the next several ones, the matter of papal primacy predominated, with attention focused on Matthew 16:18. Eck asserted that it offered clear scriptural sanction for the papacy as the rock of the Church, while Luther invoked the patristic current that interpreted the rock as the confession of faith in Christ. Who, Eck asked, was better able to construe the sense of a biblical passage—the long line of venerated pontiffs and great councils, or Luther himself? Was a simple layman armed with Scripture to be believed above all those venerated authorities? At one point Luther, feeling the audience slipping away, asked to clarify his position in German. Insisting on his innocence of the Hussite heresy, he said that he questioned not the power of the papacy but only its divine origins, and he challenged Eck to prove that a council cannot err.

"I will tell you, reverend father," Eck said, "if you say that a council, properly convoked, can err and has erred, you are for me a heathen and a publican."

Feeling beset and isolated, Luther nonetheless refused to back down. He would hold fast to his beliefs, he said, even if doing so meant shattering the millennial unity of Christendom. His tenacity made a deep impression on those present, sometimes favorably, sometimes less so. Petrus Mosellanus, the humanist who had given the opening address, would afterward praise Luther for his vigor, clear voice, affability, and knowledge of the Bible, but many, he noted, felt that "in answering he is more imprudent and cutting than is safe for a reformer of the Church, or than is decorous for a theologian."

In all, the debate over papal authority lasted five days, with Luther and Eck contending, objecting, and declaiming and the audience gasping, tittering, and cheering as blows were alternately landed and parried. In an interlude of comic relief, Luther and Eck debated whether Duke George's one-eyed court fool should have a wife. Luther said yes, Eck said no, and the fool, taking offense at the latter, subsequently made grimaces whenever Eck entered. Eck retaliated by mimicking the fool, who let loose a volley of profanity, to the delight of the crowd.

Finally, on the sixth day of their encounter, the disputants moved on to the subject of indulgences. Remarkably, on this matter, which had sparked the whole controversy, Eck agreed with almost everything Luther had to say. The same was true of penance, purgatory, and the power of priests to grant absolution. Eck treated these matters as little more than footnotes, which in many ways they were. The real issue was not the acceptability of any particular doctrine but rather who had the authority to define it. In his concluding remarks, Eck declared that "the impatient monk is more scurrilous than becomes the gravity of a theologian. He prefers the authority of Scripture to the Fathers and sets himself up as a second Delphic oracle who alone has any understanding of the Scriptures superior to that of any Father." By this point, Luther had become so disgusted with Eck's quibbling and guile that he waived his right to a final reply.

Eck, remarkably, still had enough stamina left to resume his ponderous debate with Karlstadt over free will and grace. After two days, however, Duke George, needing the hall to entertain some dignitaries arriving for a hunting expedition, ordered the meeting adjourned, and so, nearly three weeks after it had begun, and to the relief of all concerned, one of the most consequential debates in European history had come to an end.

*   *   *

In Leipzig, Eck was immediately proclaimed the victor. For eleven days he remained in the city, feted and toasted at dinners. Duke George invited him to a private dinner, and the town council gave him a coat and a jacket of camel and goat hair. Luther received only a token flagon of wine. On his way back to Wittenberg, he fumed over the insults he had suffered at the hands of the Leipzigers and the ploys Eck had used to outmaneuver him. "I have experienced hatred before, but never more shameless or more impudent," Luther wrote to Spalatin. Instead of promoting harmony between the peoples of Wittenberg and Leipzig, as he had hoped, the debate had deepened the discord. Luther was especially upset at the hostility shown him by Duke George, who from that time on would be an unshakable adversary.

Aside from the bitter personal taste left by the disputation, the encounter would bring about a turning point in Luther's own thinking. Prior to Leipzig, he had continued to consider himself a faithful member of the Roman Church. For all its moral failings and clerical excesses, it remained the institutional embodiment of the Christian community, commanding the love and loyalty of all pious men and women. In arguing that the supreme authority in the Church was not the pope but God's Word, however, Luther had been labeled a heretic, and the more he saw how that term was used, the less horrifying it seemed. Eck's unrelenting campaign to marginalize Luther and declare that the Church had no place for someone with his views made it in fact seem the case.

This idea would take deeper root during the polemical war that erupted in the debate's aftermath. To serve as judges, the contestants had agreed on the universities of Paris and Erfurt, and transcripts were sent to both, but while their verdicts were awaited, pamphlets began pouring forth from the presses, and the tractate combat that had occurred during the Reuchlin affair resumed with new vigor. Everyone who could write, it seemed, felt an urge to weigh in, with one half denouncing Luther as a renegade and pariah intent on dividing Christendom and the other hailing him as a prophet or apostle seeking to sweep the moneylenders from the temple. Eck was the target of a satire titled *The Planed-Down Eck*, which mordantly described a series of painful medical procedures performed on him to smooth his rough edges. Word also spread that

Erasmus had said that Eck's name lacked a letter and should be *Jeck* (Dutch for "fool").

As usual, the criticism and contention served as a goad to Luther, and in the six months after Leipzig, in an astonishing burst of productivity, he turned out sixteen works, several of which sought to explain and expand on the positions he had taken there. Not all were cannon shots, however. When the elector Frederick became so ill that his end seemed near, Spalatin urged Luther to prepare some words of solace. The result was a little book about how Christians do not die alone, for Christ embraces death and pain on their behalf and through his resurrection bestows on them everlasting glory. Though the book was intended for Frederick's personal use, it so impressed Spalatin that he insisted it be published, and it was, under the title *Tesseradecas Consolatoria*, or "Fourteen Consolations." (Frederick recovered.) With Rhau-Grunenberg's shop increasingly overwhelmed, Luther convinced Melchior Lotther in Leipzig to send his son to Wittenberg to set up an operation there, and in the latter part of 1519 he did, offering a trilingual capacity using type from the house of Froben. Before long, Wittenberg would surpass Leipzig as a center of book production.

Physically, Luther remained very vulnerable. From Rome to Cologne, Louvain to Leipzig, he was inspiring angry opposition, and it would have been easy for an assassin to slip into Wittenberg and kill him. In one chilling episode, he was approached by a stranger who shook his hand, and Luther invited him to the monastery. "Dear Doctor," the man said, "it surprises me that you so readily shake hands with strangers; are you not afraid of being shot? I am alone with you." "If you killed me," Luther replied, "you would die, too." "In that case," the man said, "the pope would make me a saint and you a heretic." At that point, Luther called for the monastery servant, and the man quickly left town.

The ever-present threat of violence deepened the feelings of despair and worthlessness to which Luther was so prone. His sense of abandonment was apparent in a sorrowful letter he sent to Johann von Staupitz in October 1519. Since the encounter with Cajetan a year earlier, Luther had heard very little from his former mentor, who was far away in Salzburg, and he now felt bereft, "as a weaned child for his mother." "I hate my wretched life," he wrote. "I fear death; I am empty of faith and full of qualities which, Christ knows, I should prefer much to do without, were it not to serve him thereby." The previous night, he continued, "I had a dream about you. I dreamed that you were leaving me while I wept bitterly, but you waved to me and told me to cease weeping, for you would come back to me, which indeed has happened this very day. But now farewell, and pray for me in my wretchedness."

As for Eck, he would not rest. After the debate, he had sent the Vatican a detailed report, casting Luther as an enemy of papal supremacy and warning the pope not to delay action any longer. When no such action came, Eck decided to deliver a report in person, and in early 1520 he embarked on the long journey to Rome.

THE VIPER STRIKES

In the spring and early summer of 1519, Erasmus—still recovering from his labors on the second edition of the New Testament—limited himself to lighter, less taxing projects. While continuing to paraphrase Paul, he prepared new editions of two ancient figures, Cicero and Cyprian. To Erasmus, Cicero's public-spiritedness and exhortations to do good to all men without expectation of reward seemed a tonic in an age as selfish as Erasmus's own. "What justice, what purity, what sincerity, what truth in his rules for living!" he exulted in his preface. Cyprian, the bishop of Carthage who died a martyr in 258, seemed to breathe such "apostolic energy" in his letters and pastoral writings as to eclipse even Jerome. In his continuing journey back to the sources, Erasmus was characteristically mining both the pagan and the patristic traditions for timeless wisdom.

He was also tending to his ever-widening circle of correspondents. They now included Jan Šlechta, an educated nobleman in Bohemia who had sought Erasmus's acquaintance and through whom Erasmus was trying to spread his ideas in Central Europe. In one letter, Erasmus suggested a principle that would become a pillar of his creed—that "a few truths are enough"; that is, that the central tenets of the faith should be kept to a minimum so as to avoid unnecessary division and strife.

In Louvain, however, there was nothing but division and strife. As Erasmus's revised New Testament circulated and the theologians there had a chance to study it, they were outraged. Far from moderating the most offensive passages in his first edition, Erasmus had sharpened them. On ceremonies and rituals, divorce and confession, clerical privilege and papal authority, he had shown even greater disdain for the accepted way of doing things, and the outcry was fierce. In sermons and lectures, Erasmus was charged with showing insufficient respect for Mary, with writing the sacrament of penance out of the Gospels, with altering the Lord's Prayer and the Magnificat. The similarities between his and Luther's views seemed unmistakable. The divines "have got it into their heads that I am the champion and mainstay of Luther's ideas," Erasmus wrote on July 1, 1519. That summer, the faculty began an investigation into Erasmus's writings, with several bachelors of theology assigned the task of studying them for errors and uncovering similarities with the works of Luther.

With the recriminations in Louvain mounting, a meeting was convened between Erasmus and the theologians. On September 13, 1519, an accord was reached in which the theologians agreed to do everything possible to restore Erasmus's good name and Erasmus promised to urge his friends and acquaintances to stop libeling them. The deal was sealed with one of those rowdy banquets that Erasmus so detested, and an uneasy calm set in.

Then, in early autumn, Jacob van Hoogstraten arrived. The sight on Louvain's streets of the glowering inquisitor in his black mantle sent a shudder through all who had experienced even the slightest doubts about Church dogma. Hoogstraten's remorseless pursuit of Johannes Reuchlin over the past decade had shown his ability to destroy the careers of those he judged insufficiently orthodox. And he was still at it. In April 1519, Hoogstraten had issued *Destructio Cabalae*, a vitriolic attack on Reuchlin's latest treatise on the Kabbalah in which Hoogstraten repeatedly denounced the Hebraist as a "purveyor of cabalistic perfidy."

In that same publication, Hoogstraten had also criticized Erasmus (without naming him) for his annotation on Matthew 19:8, in which he had urged the Church to adopt a more flexible policy on divorce. In response, Erasmus had sent Hoogstraten a long letter in which he both defended his position and chastised the Dominican for treating Reuchlin so severely over so many years. "How I wish you had spent that effort, that expense, those valuable years in preaching the gospel of Christ!" he admonished Hoogstraten. Heresy "is a hateful word," and for that reason one should use it as sparingly as possible.

Hoogstraten had not replied, but before leaving Cologne he had obtained a copy of the letter Erasmus had sent to Luther, and he had brought it with him to Louvain. His main business, though, concerned the Wittenberg friar. On August 30, 1519, the Cologne faculty, examining the

Froben collection of Luther's works, had issued articles of condemnation on eight points, including Luther's position on good works, his method of interpreting Scripture, his misrepresentation of the sacrament of penance, his denial of the treasury of the Church, and his rejection of papal supremacy. According to the faculty, the book was so full of errors that it deserved to be not only suppressed but also burned together with its supporters, and the author himself should be summoned to a public recantation.

On October 12, Hoogstraten presented these findings to the Louvain faculty. Since the universities of both Paris and Erfurt had failed to pass judgment on the wayward friar, he said, it was up to Cologne and Louvain to defend the faith. The Louvain doctors—having been the first to discern the dangers posed by the Froben edition—needed little convincing. With the Cologne findings as a guide, they held a series of assemblies aimed at determining the passages that were so erroneous and impious as to deserve official sanction.

In his meetings with the Louvain theologians, Hoogstraten had also implicated Erasmus, brandishing his letter to Luther as evidence. Its various hedges and reservations, he said, could not hide the humanist's clear sympathies with the Wittenberg professor. At once, the theologians' pact with Erasmus broke down, and he was subjected to a new round of abuse.

Desperate to suppress it, Erasmus decided to appeal to Germany's highest-ranking prelate. Despite his opposition to Luther and the Ninety-Five Theses, Archbishop Albrecht of Mainz remained a devotee of good letters. Matthias Grünewald was a painter at his court, Albrecht Dürer was a regular correspondent, and Lucas Cranach had painted him as Jerome. Erasmus hoped to persuade Archbishop Albrecht to use his authority to halt the conservative onslaught. Though he had done little more than dip into Luther's writings, Erasmus observed, the friar seemed a man of high character. If he was innocent of the charges directed at him, it would be tragic to see him overwhelmed by some villainous faction. If he was wrong, it would be far better to set him right than to destroy him. Unfortunately, certain divines had sought neither to correct nor to instruct him but rather to "traduce him with their crazy clamor," condemning as heretical things in his books that, when found in the writings of Bernard and Augustine, were considered orthodox and even pious. Luther's real offense was that he took the profits out of indulgences; that he did not think much of the mendicant orders; that he did not give man-made subtleties the same respect he showed the Gospels. All of these positions were of course "insufferable heresies," he sardonically observed.

Most insidious of all, Erasmus went on, was the determined effort under way to use Luther to undermine the great strides being made in literature and languages. "What can liberal studies have in common with a question of religious faith?" Whatever the outcome of the Luther affair, the New Learning had to be preserved. And whatever actions the universities might take against Luther, they should carry no risk for him, Erasmus, since he had always been careful not to write anything that conflicted with the teachings of Christ. "I shall never knowingly be either a teacher of error or a promoter of strife, for I will suffer anything rather than rouse sedition."

In this letter, Erasmus laid out the position he would cleave to over the next several years—signaling his support for Luther without actually endorsing him. In this way, he hoped to remain above the fray and preserve his independence. In the current climate, however, even such temperate remarks could prove damaging if made public, and so he needed a dependable courier.

As it happened, Ulrich von Hutten, who had recently joined Albrecht's court, was passing through Louvain. The impetuous knight-poet had met Erasmus in 1514 and become a fervent admirer, calling him the "German Socrates." But Hutten was in the forefront of a younger generation of German humanists with more militant leanings. After studying at several German universities, he had traveled to Italy to study law, but, repelled by the arrogance and avarice he found there, he had returned to Germany determined to rouse his fellow countrymen. Like many of his peers, Hutten had rallied to the defense of Johannes Reuchlin in his battle with the Scholastics, and he was responsible for many of the more abusive entries in the expanded edition of the *Letters of Obscure Men* that had appeared in 1517. Not long afterward, Hutten had published a German edition of Lorenzo Valla's treatise exposing the Donation of Constantine as a forgery, hoping in this way to undermine the papacy's claims to temporal power. Whereas Erasmus, in revisiting the past, sought inspiration for a united

Christendom, younger humanists like Hutten sought the foundations for a German national identity, and after the Leipzig disputation he had thrown his support behind Luther as the leading exponent of the German cause.

To Erasmus, however, Hutten seemed a loyal acolyte, and so he decided to entrust his letter to him. It would prove a serious misstep. Once he was out of Erasmus's sight, Hutten broke the seal of the letter and read it. Immediately seeing its propaganda value, he took it to a printer. When the original reached Albrecht, it was torn and soiled with printers' ink, and the archbishop was furious. Before long, unauthorized editions were appearing throughout Germany. Incensed, Erasmus suspected Hutten of treachery, and their relationship would take a dark and ultimately tragic turn.

On the morning of November 7, 1519, the Louvain theology faculty met in the chapter house of the cathedral. With great solemnity, they adopted fifteen articles of condemnation against Luther. They dealt with indulgences, confession, purgatory, good works, original sin, the Eucharist, and the merits of the saints. Luther, the articles stated, had made many other stupid and false assertions, all harmful to the congregation of believers and the teachings of salvation; the volume containing his works should be committed to the flames and its author summoned to recant his errors. Not a single dissenting vote was cast.

A copy of the judgment was immediately sent to Adrian of Utrecht. This renowned Louvain professor (and future Pope Adrian VI) was now in Spain, serving as the bishop of Tortosa. An endorsement by him would lend weight to the authority of the judgment against Luther, and publication was held off pending its arrival.

Toward Erasmus, however, the theologians felt no such inhibition. The faculty's condemnation of Luther served as a sort of tocsin for campus conservatives, summoning them to battle against the enemies of the faith. Erasmus was considered chief among them. "Gangs of conspirators," he complained, were defaming him everywhere:

at drinking-parties, in markets, in committees, in druggists' shops, in carriages, at the barber's, in the brothels, in public and private classrooms, in university lectures and in sermons, in confidential conversations, in the privacy of the confessional, in bookshops, in the taverns of the poor, in the courts of the rich and in kings' palaces, among superstitious old men and blockheads rich as Midas, to the ignorant public, and to foolish women.

There was no place these assailants could not penetrate, no lie they would not tell, to make him "into an object of general hatred." The ringleaders were the Dominicans and the Carmelites—beggar bullies, he called them—whose ultimate goal was nothing less than the destruction of the humanities.

In his desperation, Erasmus appealed to Leo X. "The battle grows more barbarous, with monstrous abuse on either side, and poisoned pamphlets are the weapons," he wrote to the pope. "Curse answers curse, and discord ripens into madness." Erasmus urged Leo to impose a ban on all contention of this kind so that those lacking proficiency in languages "would cease to cackle like geese at humane studies." Everyone "should actively pursue his calling without denigrating those of other men."

Even had Leo wanted to impose such a ban, however, he lacked the means to enforce it. What's more, Erasmus himself would have trouble adhering to his own standard, as became clear in his dealings with Edward Lee. Throughout the summer and autumn of 1519, the determined Englishman had continued to compile his notes on Erasmus's New Testament, to Erasmus's growing alarm. Since 1514, when he had received the letter from Martin Dorp warning him not to tamper with the Vulgate, Erasmus had faced efforts by conservatives to block his attempts to restore the New Testament, but Lee's notes posed the most serious threat yet. Though at this point Erasmus did not know exactly what was in them, he suspected that Lee was working closely with the mendicant orders to impugn him. His fear swelling into paranoia, his self-regard feeding a morbid touchiness, he was prepared to use every available means to foil his challenger.

There were two printers in Antwerp who had Greek type, and Lee, hoping to enlist one of them, went there. Erasmus followed. One of the printers agreed to take on Lee's project, and he began setting it in type, only suddenly to renege. A servant of Erasmus's was seen entering the printing house—part of a plot, Lee believed, to sabotage the printing. When Lee asked the printer to unlock the type and distribute it back into the cases, he refused—no doubt (Lee believed) so that he could show the copy to Erasmus. The other printer, when approached, was initially eager to take on the job, but within an hour he, too, reconsidered. When Lee left Antwerp for Louvain, Erasmus followed his coach part of the way to make sure that he did not return to Antwerp without his knowledge.

Eventually, Lee managed to find a willing printer in Paris, and when Erasmus saw the finished product, he exploded. "The English viper has burst out at last!" he declared to Wolfgang Capito. "Before us stands Edward Lee, an eternal blot on that isle so highly thought of." The whole world had expected a work of scholarship, but "here before us is a book running over, raving mad I would say, with brawling and fishwives' abuse. . . . No harlot was ever so brazen, no pimp a more abandoned liar." This "three-half-penny booby is as pleased with himself as if the world were likely to believe this to be a human being speaking."

Using his amateurish knowledge of Greek, Lee (Erasmus believed) had twisted Erasmus's words, distorted his message, and incited hatred against him. At the start of his volume Lee had placed a tendentious table of contents that listed Erasmus's alleged offenses, including changing the readings of the Church, adding or omitting things of his own initiative, thinking about marriage in a non-Catholic manner, disparaging Augustine, favoring the Arians, championing the Pelagians, ridiculing the language of the translator, and bringing to life all heresies.

Many of Lee's notes dealt with Erasmus's scholarship, challenging his changes in the tenses, cases, articles, conjunctions, and word order of the Vulgate. Some notes, though, were darkly accusatory. At Luke 1:28, for instance, he lambasted Erasmus for giving a lascivious cast to the angel Gabriel's greeting to Mary ("Hail, beloved one"), making him sound like a suitor. "It seems to me that one ought to speak more reverently and chastely about so sacred a matter and so sublime a message." Lee also expressed dismay at Erasmus's preference for Jerome over Augustine and his criticism of the latter for his imperfect knowledge of Greek. He reproved

Erasmus for maintaining that the New Testament does not support the sacramental status of marriage, for asserting that private auricular confession was not practiced in ancient times, and for implying (in his comments on Romans 5) that the idea of original sin has no scriptural foundation but rather "is an invention of the theologians." Erasmus was thus depriving the Church "of a weapon to slay the heretics," i.e., the Pelagians, with their insistence on man's moral perfectibility.

Erasmus's greatest offense in Lee's eyes, however, was his decision to omit 1 John 5:7, the *comma Johanneum*, with its reference to the Father, the Word, and the Holy Spirit. Had Erasmus more thoroughly checked old manuscripts, Lee maintained, he would not have made such an egregious error. "Such great negligence comes close to impiety in such sacred and venerable teachings and in a passage so necessary to the faith." With the exclusion of this passage, "we will fall once again on Arian times and an endlessly lamentable discord in the holy church." If Arianism again reared its head, he asked, "will not every kind of upheaval, every kind of faction, quarrel, and tempest arise?" More generally, Lee warned of the long-term damage that Erasmus's *Novum Testamentum* could inflict on the faith: "Let the church be mindful and take measures at the outset, lest what began as smoke turn into fire." In Erasmus's biblical notes, then, Lee saw a threat to the very survival of the Church.

In Lee's work, in turn, Erasmus saw nothing but insult, abuse, and poison, and he began orchestrating a campaign to discredit him. "My friends," he instructed one of them, Justus Jonas,

are to write letters highly critical of Lee, but taking care to praise English scholars and the great men in England who support them, and bearing down on Lee and no one else; and him they are to laugh at as a foolish, boastful, deceitful little man, rather than attack him seriously. I should like to see many letters of this kind put together, so that he may be overwhelmed all the deeper. I should like them to be collected from the learned writers and sent me by safe hand, and I will revise them myself and see to their publication. Great variety is desirable.

The letters soon began arriving. "I pray he may enjoy the long and lingering death which he deserves," the eminent humanist Willibald Pirckheimer wrote from Nuremberg. From Basel, Bonifacius Amerbach declared that "out of his native darkness crawls this worm, to gnaw at the splendid harvest which is ours without having won respect himself in any field of study. . . . Numbskulls of this type dare write books in this learned age of ours, and dare to write them against Erasmus!" Another letter, addressed to Lee himself, bluntly concluded, "Go hang yourself!" More than two dozen such letters along with some insulting verses were brought out as a collection by Froben in the summer of 1520. Two schoolmasters assigned their students the task of vilifying Lee, and a copy of Lee's book at a Franciscan library was smeared with excrement. When a vituperative attack on Lee arrived from Ghent, a friend of Erasmus had it printed and posted in more than ten places, including the doors of churches. One libelous poster was affixed to the door of Lee's own dwelling, making him fear for his life.

"If a clandestine attack is made on me, Erasmus is undoubtedly the person responsible," he wrote to the Dutchman, putting him on notice. He called attention to the glaring gap between Erasmus's ugly tactics and his lofty appeals to Christian brotherhood. "Where now is that Christian bosom of yours that breathes nothing but endless charity and reticence and all that is friendly and straightforward?" While acknowledging his own occasional intemperance in the dispute, Lee sarcastically alluded to the famous "modesty" Erasmus had shown in his letters to his friends, in which he had called Lee "in one place a venomous little serpent, in another a monster rather than a man, in another a past master of innuendo!" He added: "Slanders, slanders, slanders—it is your favorite word." With the threats against him turning ever more violent, Lee decided to flee Louvain for England.

Erasmus, meanwhile, began preparing a detailed—and scornful—rebuttal of Lee's notes. He mocked Lee's scholarship, questioned his motives, dismissed him as a pedant, and accused him of hallucinating. "Good God!" he wrote about his comments on Gabriel's greeting. "Does Lee now teach the art of courtship? . . . He shudders at the word 'suitor,' he recoils from the word 'loving,' from the word 'groomsman,' crying out that I used these words in a frivolous manner, as if I had had in mind something unchaste." Erasmus was especially emphatic in defending his omission of the *comma Johanneum*. Having examined more than seven Greek manuscripts and finding the passage in none of them, "I did the only thing possible and indicated what was lacking in the Greek texts." If he had come across one manuscript that had the reading found in the Vulgate, he would have added it. "Let Lee produce a Greek manuscript that has what is lacking in my edition and let him prove that I had access to this manuscript . . . then he may accuse me of negligence in sacred doctrines." From Oxford to Rome, word of Erasmus's challenge quickly spread, and the search for such a manuscript was on.

Erasmus was equally dismissive of Lee's prediction that his New Testament would set off tempests and conflagrations: "I beseech you, what is it that will bring us such a flood of evils, so many schisms, so many heresies, so many upheavals, so many tempests, so many shipwrecks? . . . It is now more than three years since the New Testament as edited by me has been in people's hands. Has any upheaval arisen from it?" On the contrary, "Many say that they made considerable progress on account of my labor."

In terms of scholarship, Lee's notes were pedantic and pedestrian, but when it came to the threat posed by Erasmus's work, he would prove clear-eyed. Erasmus's decision to omit the *comma Johanneum* from his New Testament would help inspire the rise of an anti-Trinitarian movement that, spreading during the Reformation, would eventually lead to the founding of Unitarianism, centered in the belief that God exists in one person only. As for Lee's broader fears about a great conflagration, the spread of Luther's ideas seemed to be providing the spark.

Lee's voice was soon joined by others. Henry Standish, a Franciscan graduate of Oxford who was a popular preacher at the court of Henry VIII and a mentor of Lee's, was so enraged by Erasmus's decision to use *sermo* rather than *verbum* at the start of the Gospel of John that he made it the subject of a fiery sermon delivered at St. Paul's churchyard in London. For more than a thousand years, he declared, the whole Church had read "*In principio erat verbum*," but now "a little Greek somebody will teach us that we ought to read 'In principio erat sermo.' " Unless all new translations were immediately suppressed, he warned, the Christian faith would face utter destruction, and he appealed to the magistrates and citizens who were present to rally around the Church in its hour of trial.

In a hastily written defense, Erasmus sarcastically noted that John in his Gospel had written not *verbum* but *logos*, and he wondered why Jerome had chosen to translate it that way, since *sermo* seemed to far better capture the idea of a speech or continuous narration, which was clearly John's meaning. Despite Erasmus's strenuous efforts to justify his choice, *sermo* would become a rallying cry for his opponents.

In early 1520, the statement on Luther that the Louvain faculty had sought from Adrian of Utrecht finally arrived from Spain. It was unsparing. "I am greatly surprised that one who errs so manifestly and obstinately and who scatters his opinions broadcast is allowed to err with impunity and with impunity to draw others into his pernicious errors," he wrote. Those errors were "such crude and palpable heresies on their face that not even a pupil of theology of the first grade ought to have been caught by them." The Louvain faculty deserved praise for resisting the "pestiferous dogmas" of this insolent man.

With Adrian's imprimatur, the Louvain theologians were now ready to proceed. They sent the articles condemned by the two faculties to Dirk Martens, the Louvain printer, to be typeset. Appearing on February 20, 1520, the *Condemnation of Luther by Cologne and Louvain* marked the first formal censure of the German reformer. Together with Lee's attack on Erasmus, this document moved Louvain into the forefront of the opposition to the reform movement. "The university here has developed incurable insanity," Erasmus observed to Justus Jonas on April 20.

In fact, the events in these months in Louvain were the first steps on the road to the Council of Trent, the historic conclave of the mid-sixteenth century that would help set in motion the great Catholic pushback against Protestantism and which would set the course of the Roman Church for the next four hundred years.

22

THUNDERCLAPS

From across Europe, theologically curious and spiritually hungry Christians were steadily making their way to a new pilgrimage site—not a chapel featuring a vial of the Virgin's milk or a shrine boasting a sliver of the True Cross, but Wittenberg. Alsatians and Walloons, Tiroleans and Czechs, Steiermarkians from central Austria, and even Scotsmen, having read Luther in the Froben collection and other editions, were heading to this small outpost on the Elbe to hear the newly restored gospel. Not only younger aspirants seeking theology degrees but also older men dissatisfied with the tired ritualism that had tinctured the faith crowded the lecture halls to hear Luther, Melanchthon, and other heralds of renewal, helping to vault Wittenberg into the top ranks of German universities.

"I left Italy a few days ago, for two reasons," John Hess, a young theologian from Nuremberg, wrote to a colleague in late 1519: "first, on account of my health, and secondly, to hear Martin." In Italy, he explained, he had met many lovers of Luther who, after reading an account of the Leipzig debate, had, like him, been smitten. The Nuremberg humanist Willibald Pirckheimer declared that "all ages will remember that the Wittenbergers were the first to see the truth, the first to open their eyes after so many centuries, and to begin to separate the degenerate from the Christian philosophy."

"If God help me," Albrecht Dürer wrote to George Spalatin, "I will go to Dr. Martin Luther and make his likeness in copper for a lasting memorial of the Christian man who has helped me out of great anguish. I beg your Honor if Dr. Luther writes anything more in German, please to send it to me at my expense." The Nuremberg master never would get a chance to meet Luther, but, as his comment to Spalatin suggested, he had recently undergone a deep emotional crisis, and his study of Lutheran doctrines had helped him overcome it. Luther's teaching that man is justified by faith would work such a powerful effect on Dürer that he would abandon secular subjects for religious ones and give up his former exuberant style for an intensely austere one.

The influx of visitors and students threatened to overwhelm the town. "Everything is very expensive, the supplies brought in are insufficient, nor is anything administered properly in this most confused and careless city," Luther complained to Spalatin in the spring of 1520. Owing to the shortage of housing, the university was having trouble finding quarters for the prospective new professor of Hebrew: Matthaeus Adrianus. This was the same Adrianus who had been teaching Hebrew in Louvain. He had fallen out with the conservatives in Louvain over a speech he had given praising the three biblical tongues. He had also gone deeply into debt and was being pursued by several creditors, and over the summer he had fled the city. Not long afterward, he had shown up in Wittenberg and applied for a similar position. Luther was eager to have him, but it was unclear if the university could meet his demands on salary or housing. Eventually, both the money and a dwelling were found, and Adrianus in the spring of 1520 began offering instruction in Hebrew.

Meanwhile, Philipp Melanchthon's early-morning lectures on Matthew were packed, leading Luther to observe that "this little Greek beats me even in theology." Still worried that Philipp might be lured away by another university, Luther pressed Spalatin to persuade Frederick to raise his salary. He also became concerned for Melanchthon's health. The frail young man was working himself so hard that he seemed headed for a physical breakdown, and Luther, intent on seeing him better cared for, urged him to find a wife. (Melanchthon said he was not interested.)

As Luther's reputation as a critic of clerical excesses grew, laypeople with grievances against the Church began seeking him out. When a Wittenberg widow who had willed her house to the clerics at the Castle Church decided she wanted to keep it for her family, Luther agreed to serve as a mediator. (The case became so convoluted and time-consuming that he would end up ruing his involvement.) When the city council of Kemberg drafted a petition to Frederick complaining of oppressive taxes, Luther took up their case, writing to Spalatin that "the people there are absolutely sucked dry by this extreme usury." The situation was daily growing worse because of the priests and religious fraternities that were "supported by these sacrilegious taxes and ungodly plunderings." Spalatin would "serve God" if he could make some headway with Frederick.

To his dismay, Luther was also sought out as a marriage counselor. Husbands and wives approached him with complaints about impotence and neglect, infidelity and infertility; young men and women hoping to marry sought his help in navigating the intricacies of canon law. As best he could, the celibate Luther grappled with the many impediments that Rome had placed in the way of marriage. In 1519, he had published a sermon in which he had called physical desire a "wicked lust of the flesh" in need of strict control, but, faced with the messy realities of human desire, he began to rethink such reflexive censure.

That questioning, in turn, was part of a broader transformation taking place in Luther's mind. To this point, the many ideas that had welled up in him since the posting of the Ninety-Five Theses—about indulgences and works, confession and salvation, the papacy and the priesthood—had remained inchoate. They would now begin to cohere. After all the reading and preaching he had done, and after the many exhausting controversies in which he had participated, Luther in the early months of 1520 would have a series of intellectual and theological breakthroughs, culminating in a series of works that together would convulse Europe, rouse the German people, and shake the Roman Church.

The initial trigger for this transformation was the publication of a treatise on the Eucharist that Luther prepared in late 1519. In it, he advocated giving the laity not only the bread but also the cup during Communion. No less than the grain in the bread, he wrote, the grapes in the wine symbolized union with Christ, and to withhold the cup from communicants was to deny them this instrument of divine fellowship.

To Duke George, this position smacked of the Bohemian heresy, and he angrily protested to both his cousin Frederick and the bishop of Meissen, whose diocese bordered Bohemia. Priests in that town began spreading word that it would not be a sin if Luther were murdered, and the bishop ordered the posting of a note prohibiting the circulation of the text. Luther dashed off a fierce reply. Spalatin—worried that the controversy would harm relations between Frederick and George—instructed Luther not to publish his response, but by the time his message arrived, it was already in print.

Spalatin was furious, at both Luther's disobedience and his provocative language. Luther was unapologetic. While acknowledging that he had shown more vehemence than was perhaps prudent, he cited Scripture in his defense. "Was [Christ] scurrilous when he called the Jews a perverse and adulterous generation, offspring of vipers, hypocrites, and children of the devil?" Paul spoke of dogs, vain babblers, and seducers, and in Acts 13 he raged against a false prophet so fiercely as to seem deranged. Those who know the truth "cannot be patient against the obstinate and unconquered enemies of the truth." No one should think that the cause of the gospel "can be advanced without tumult, offense, and sedition. You will not make a pen from a sword, nor peace of war. The Word of God is a sword, it is war and ruin and offense and perdition and poison."

Luther was here invoking Matthew 10:34, where Jesus declares, "Do not think I have come to bring peace to the earth. I have not come to bring peace but a sword, for I have come to set a man against his father, and a daughter against her mother, and a daughter-in-law against her mother-in-law, and one's foes will be members of one's own household." This is one of several such militant passages in the New Testament, which provide a bellicose counterpoint to its irenic statements about turning the other cheek and loving one's enemy. In the New Testament, there appear two very different Christs—one the prince of peace, the other the bearer of the sword. Whereas Erasmus embraced the former, Luther in this period began identifying with the latter.

He also began to speak of himself as a divine messenger. "God so carries me on that I cannot fear their rash and untaught hatred," he wrote of his adversaries. God "acts through me, since I am certain that none of these things have been sought by me, but that they were drawn from me, one and all, by a fury not my own." From this point on, the language of war, the sword, and divine mission would permeate Luther's work. His conviction that he acted on God's behalf would help him stand firm in the face of the greatest peril. It would also make him fiercely opposed to compromise, no matter how grave the consequences.

Luther's new resoluteness is captured in a 1520 woodcut by Lucas

Cranach—the first of his many portraits of the reformer (and one that would become an icon of the new movement). It shows a tonsured monk with a large, powerful head, cheekbones protruding from a gaunt face, lips pursed in determination, eyes enraptured. In contrast to images of Erasmus, which show a man ever aware of life's ironies, Cranach's Luther radiates the fearlessness and steadfastness of one called to preach God's Word.

As a result of Luther's support for the chalice, rumors began to spread that he had Bohemian origins. They became so insistent that in mid-January 1520 he felt compelled to send Spalatin a formal denial, corroborated by details about his birth and youth. Prodded by the controversy, Luther finally decided to read Jan Hus. At the Leipzig disputation, he had been approached by a member of the Hussite church in Bohemia, and when he had expressed interest in Hus's work, the man promised to send him a sample. A copy of *De Ecclesia* arrived in October 1519, but Luther's workload had kept him from reading it. When he finally got around to it, he was startled by what he found. Hus's insistence that the Church was headed not by the pope but by Christ and that God's Word ruled over the palsied doctrines of man prefigured Luther's own views. And Paul and Augustine seemed to foreshadow Hus. "In short we are all Hussites and did not know it," he wrote to Spalatin in mid-February 1520. That such a teacher of evangelical truth had been condemned and burned was shocking, yet no one was allowed to say so. After having so insistently denied any association with Hus at Leipzig, Luther now fully endorsed him, despite the somber realization that in doing so he could meet a similar end.

Luther got a similar surprise from reading Lorenzo Valla. With the publication of Ulrich von Hutten's German edition of Valla's debunking of the Donation of Constantine, this work was for the first time circulating widely in Germany, and Luther was incensed to find that the pope's claims to his temporal possessions rested on a fraudulent document. "I have at hand . . . Lorenzo Valla's proof (edited by Hutten) that the Donation of Constantine is a forgery," he wrote to Spalatin in February 1520. "Good Heavens! what darkness and wickedness is at Rome! You wonder at the judgment of God, that such unauthentic, crass, impudent lies not only lived but prevailed for so many centuries and were incorporated into the Canon Law . . . as articles of faith." Whereas prior to the Leipzig debate

Luther had wondered whether the pope was the Antichrist, he now felt sure about it.

While he was reading Hus and Valla, there arrived in Wittenberg a much less welcome text: the Cologne-Louvain condemnation of his writings. Two of Europe's leading universities had joined forces to denounce him. On examining the document, Luther could see at once that it was the work of the same "doctrinal asses" who had persecuted Reuchlin. In a blistering counterattack, he marveled at the mediocrity of their effort. Swollen with self-regard, these sophists had not even bothered to substantiate their charges against him; in their puffed-up view, simply asserting that he had erred was enough. Until these divine doctors could disprove his statements by Scripture, Luther wrote in one of many richly abusive passages, he would pay no more attention to them than to the rantings of a drunken man.

To show the eminent company he was in, Luther offered a roll call of scholars who had been condemned by universities, only later to be praised by them: Pico della Mirandola, Valla, Reuchlin, Lefèvre, and Erasmus. Attacked by the obscurantists of Cologne and Louvain, Luther was aligning himself with the pantheon of freethinkers who had helped spread the New Learning. (He could not, however, resist taking a swipe at Erasmus and what he saw as his equivocation, calling him a "he-goat with his horns caught in a thornbush.")

While fending off the doctrinal asses of Cologne and Louvain, Luther faced a problem of a far more stubborn nature. Many readers who were otherwise drawn to his ideas balked at his insistence that good works are futile. Were Christians not to perform such works? Would not Luther's position encourage license and immorality? Hearing much confusion over the matter, Spalatin reminded Luther of an earlier pledge to prepare a sermon on it, and in March 1520 he began to do so. The *Treatise on Good Works* showed that Luther had not softened the teachings he had taken from Paul. "Apart from faith all works are dead, no matter how wonderful they look or what splendid names they have," he flatly declared. A heathen, a Jew, a Turk, and a sinner might all do good works, but only a Christian enlightened and strengthened by grace could firmly trust that he pleased God. Just as a husband and wife who love one another need not constantly provide proof, so those with faith in Christ did not have to perform virtuous acts to win God's favor.

Luther spent two months on this treatise, filling it with a great jumble of opinions and ideas. There should be fewer saints' days, for they encourage idleness and gluttony. Pregnant women should not fast if in so doing they would endanger the child they were carrying. Unchastity was a serious and rabid vice, from which a man must flee to prayer. Nothing came from Rome except the shameless selling of spiritual wares—indulgences, parishes, bishoprics, and benefices. On and on Luther went, producing a tract so dense and prolix that, despite brisk sales, it failed to settle the question at hand—the place of good works.

With the approach of the summer of 1520, however, Luther's thinking was jolted into clarity by a dramatic moment in German history: the coming of a new emperor. On June 28, 1519, in the gloom of the Frankfurt cathedral, the seven electors of the Holy Roman Empire, after a shameless display of influence peddling and deal making, had finally arrived at their decision: Charles (the fifth of that name). In the end, the wealth of the Fuggers had proved decisive. Rallying their syndicate, they had laid out on Charles's behalf an astonishing 543,000 florins in bribes, indemnities, and pensions—nearly double the amount that Francis I, his chief rival, was able to muster.

The messiness of the means, however, could not dampen the excitement at the result. Few European sovereigns had such royal bloodlines as Charles. His grandfather on his father's side was the emperor Maximilian I, the head of the house of Hapsburg. His grandparents on his mother's side were Ferdinand of Aragon and Isabella of Castile. At the death of his father, Philip the Handsome, in 1506, Charles had become the duke of Burgundy. In 1515, at the age of fifteen, he had become the ruler of the Netherlands. In 1516, on the death of Ferdinand, he had become king of Aragon and Castile as well as of Naples, Sicily, and Sardinia. With the death of Maximilian in 1519, he inherited the Hapsburgs' Austrian territories, which included parts of Hungary, Bohemia, and Moravia. Now Charles was about to add the jumble of German states, principalities, and episcopates to his empire. At the time of his election, he was in Spain, presiding over a week of celebrations with processions and masquerades. He at once began preparing to head north to claim his crown.

Not yet twenty, Charles seemed young, noble, and idealistic. His very name evoked Charlemagne, his Carolingian predecessor. The coronation was to take place in Aachen, where Charlemagne had been crowned and which had served as his capital. "Sire," his chancellor Mercurino Gattinara wrote to him shortly after his election, "God has been very merciful to you: he has raised you above all the Kings and princes of Christendom to a power such as no sovereign has enjoyed since your ancestor Charles the Great. He has set you on the way towards a world monarchy, towards the uniting of Christendom under a single shepherd." World monarchy seemed a stretch, but from the Rhine to the Oder there spread the hope that the German people at last had a ruler who could unite their fractious lands.

Because of resistance to his rule in Spain, Charles was not able to leave until May 1520. He was expected to spend the summer in the Low Countries before traveling to Aachen for the coronation in late October. In anticipation, both pro-German and anti-Roman sentiment surged. The mood was captured by the ever-incendiary Hutten in his *Roman Trinity*: "Three things are sold in Rome: Christ, the priest, and women. Three things are hateful to Rome: a general council, the reformation of the church, and the opening of German eyes. Three ills I pray for Rome: pestilence, famine, and war. This is my trinity."

Luther was swept up in the jubilation. His own personal conflict with the papacy was now merging with the more general opposition to Roman rule. With his growing mastery of political theater, he set out to seize the moment. "I have the intention of publishing a broadside to Charles and the whole German nobility against the tyranny and wickedness of the Roman court," he informed Spalatin in early June 1520. Over the next six months, Luther would produce three extraordinary texts—three thunderclaps. He had no army, no party, no movement, just a pen and the printing press, but with them he would mount a headlong assault on a world order that had been in place for centuries. Luther's Reformatory tracts, as they are known, would shock the German people into a new awareness and permanently alter the contours of political debate in Europe.

Working at his usual frenetic pace, Luther in a mere two weeks produced the first of these works, *To the Christian Nobility of the German Nation Concerning the Reform of the Christian Estate.* "The time for silence is past, and the time to speak has come," he declared, paraphrasing Ecclesiastes. He was appealing to the ruling classes to reform Christendom because the clergy themselves had become indifferent. With a prophet's wrath, Luther accused the Romanists of cleverly building three walls behind which they practiced their "knavery and wickedness." What was now needed was a trumpet that, as at Jericho, could bring those walls tumbling down.

The first wall was the Romanists' assertion that popes, bishops, priests, monks, and nuns make up a special religious class superior to secular society. In fact, "all Christians are truly of the spiritual estate, and there is no difference among them except that of office." As Paul said (in 1 Corinthians),

> we are all one body, yet every member has its own work by which it serves the others. This is because we all have one baptism, one gospel, one faith, and are all Christians alike; for baptism, gospel, and faith alone make us spiritual and a Christian people.

Luther continued: "Because we are all priests of equal standing, no one must push himself forward and take it upon himself, without our consent and election, to do that for which we all have equal authority." Priests, bishops, and popes all have their own particular work to do, as do cobblers, smiths, and peasants, "yet they are all alike consecrated priests and bishops." It was "intolerable" that canon law attached such importance to the freedom and property of the clergy, "as though the laity were not also as spiritual and as good Christians as they, or did not also belong to the church."

In both concept and language, these passages echoed Erasmus's *Paraclesis*, with its idea that even the most humble layman can be more pious than a theologian. In adapting this proposition, though, Luther characteristically gave it a sharper, more populist edge, rejecting the entire idea of a hierarchical Christian society led by a specialized caste. Luther was here articulating a world-altering concept that would become central to his gospel: the priesthood of all believers (a phrase that he himself, however, did not use).

The second wall behind which the Romanists acted was their insistence that they alone had the authority to interpret Scripture. "Since these Romanists think the Holy Spirit never leaves them, no matter how ignorant and wicked they are, they become bold and decree only what they want." Their claim "that only the pope may interpret Scripture is an outrageous fancied fable." The keys were given not to Peter alone "but to the whole community." Since we are all priests and all have one faith and gospel, "why should we not also have the power to test and judge what is right or wrong in matters of faith?" Since God spoke through Balaam's ass against a prophet, "why should he not be able to speak through a righteous man against the pope?"

The final wall was the Romanists' insistence that no one but the pope can summon a council. There was no scriptural basis for such a contention, Luther wrote. When the pope himself offends Christendom, the temporal authorities are in the best position to convene such a gathering. If a fire breaks out in a city, would it not be unnatural for everyone to stand by and let it burn on because no one has the authority of the mayor? Would it not instead be the duty of every citizen to arouse and summon the rest? Clearly, a fire had broken out in Christendom, and faithful Christians had to join together to extinguish it. "Let us awake, dear Germans, and fear God more than man, lest we suffer the same fate of all the poor souls who are so lamentably lost through the shameless, devilish rule of the Romanists."

After offering this sweeping indictment of Roman oppression, Luther provided a detailed catalog of the Church's abusive practices. Drawing on his own trip to Rome ten years earlier; on his readings of official Church documents; on the list of grievances submitted at recent diets; and on an interview with an attorney from Hamburg who had recently passed through Wittenberg on his way back from Rome, where he had had business with the Curia, Luther wrote with the drive and tenacity of an investigative journalist to expose Rome's inner workings. First, there was the "worldly and ostentatious style" in which the vicar of Christ lived, which no king or emperor could match. While the pontiff wore a triple crown, even the mightiest monarch wore but one. Italy had become "almost a wilderness," its bishoprics despoiled, its cities decayed, its people ruined, the revenues of its churches siphoned away by Rome. "And why? Because the cardinals must have the income! No Turk could have devastated Italy and suppressed the worship of God so effectively!"

Having sucked Italy dry, the Romanists were now turning to Germany. The "drunken Germans" were not supposed to realize what the Romanists were up to until there was not a bishopric, monastery, benefice, or red cent left. "How is it that we Germans must put up with such robbery and extortion of our goods at the hands of the pope?" If 99 percent of the Curia were abolished, it would still be large enough to dispense its duties. "Today, however, there is such a swarm of parasites in that place called Rome that not even Babylon saw the likes of it." With hundreds of thousands of guldens a year flowing from Germany to Rome, "we ought to marvel that we have anything left to eat!"

Luther went on to describe the many insidious devices Rome used to exploit the German people: the annates, those first-year payments that Rome demanded for senior Christian offices; the right to name the holder of a benefice when an opening occurred during six months of the year; the practice of "mental reservation," by which the pope reserved the right to take a benefice and award it to another; and so on. The "Holy Roman See of Avarice" treated benefices "more shamefully than the heathen soldiers treated Christ's clothes at the foot of the cross."

Most noxious of all was the Datary, in whose splendid building near St. Peter's vows were dissolved, monks granted permission to leave their orders, and bastards legitimized—all for a price. In this "brothel of all imaginable brothels," the possession of property acquired by theft and robbery was legalized. It was the duty of good Christians to protect their faith from such confiscations. If it was right to hang thieves and behead robbers, why should the Roman avarice go unpunished? "He is the worst thief and robber that has ever been or could ever come into the world, and all in the holy name of Christ and St. Peter!"

To remedy those abuses, Luther proposed a twenty-seven-point reform program. Annates should be abolished. Benefices and other ecclesiastical preferments should be kept out of Rome's hands. The pope should support his household out of his own pocket. No emperor or anyone else should ever again kiss the pope's feet. The Vatican should give up its claim to Bologna, Vicenza, Ravenna, "and other lands which the pope has seized by force and possesses without right." All Masses and vigils for the dead should be abolished. So should canon law, the decretals, the interdict, church bulls, festivals, canonizations of saints, and butter letters. The common people "think that eating butter is a greater sin than lying, swearing, or even living unchastely." Mendicants should, with few exceptions, be relieved of preaching and hearing confession, and all begging should be abolished and every city required to look after its own poor. The chapels in forests and the churches in fields that had become pilgrimage sites "must be leveled." The Roman Church must admit that Jan Hus had been burned at Constance in violation of the safe-conduct that had been granted him and that the pope and his advisers were to blame for all the misery and death resulting from this grave injustice. Heretics should be overcome "with books, not with fire, as the ancient fathers did." Priests should not be compelled to live without wives but should instead be permitted to marry. "The pope has strangled so many wretched souls with this devilish rope that he has long deserved to be driven out of this world."

While he was at it, Luther called for a thorough overhaul of the university curriculum, beginning with the purging of Aristotle. "It grieves me to the quick that this damned, conceited, rascally heathen has deluded and made fools of so many of the best Christians with his misleading writings." Since the universities were responsible for training Christian youth, the Bible should be taught in place of the *Sentences* and the number of theology books reduced and only the best ones published. By the age of nine or ten, every Christian boy should know the entire Gospel, and every town should have a school for girls so that they, too, could read the Bible in Latin or German. Luther urged a crackdown on extravagant dress, demanded restrictions on the spice trade, and called for controls on the Fuggers and other firms that had amassed great fortunes. He even urged the government to combat excessive eating and drinking, which, he maintained, had given Germans "a bad reputation in foreign lands."

Toward the end of his tract, Luther issued an emotional call to action:

"We have paid tragically and far too dearly for such an empire with incalculable bloodshed, with the suppression of our liberty, the hazarding and theft of all our possessions, especially of our churches and benefices, and with the suffering of unspeakable deception and insult." It was time for the pope to free the German lands "from his intolerable taxing and fleecing: let him give us back our liberty, our rights, our body and soul; and let the empire be what an empire should be, so that the pope's words and pretensions might be fulfilled."

With its merciless ridicule, flaring anger, and damning detail, *To the Christian Nobility of the German Nation* was perhaps the most devastating attack ever leveled at the Roman Church. As Luther himself acknowledged, he had spoken severely and suggested much that would be considered impossible, but, he added, "I would rather have the wrath of the world upon me than the wrath of God. The world can do no more to me than take my life."

When his manuscript was done, on June 23, 1520, Luther sent it to Melchior Lotther, who, immediately grasping its sensational nature, arranged for a print run of four thousand copies—four times the usual number. Within a week a second, enlarged edition was being prepared. Editions soon followed in Leipzig, Strasbourg, and Basel. While many expressed shock that someone had written so violently against the pope, the tract roused not only the ruling class to which it was addressed but also the German masses who most felt Rome's bite.

"Good heavens! what wise liberty is in it!" Martin Bucer, the young cleric who had been so impressed with Luther at the Heidelberg disputation, wrote to Spalatin. "I seem to myself to have found a man undoubtedly acting out the spirit of Christ." John Kotter, an organist and composer in Freiburg, marveled to Bonifacius Amerbach in Basel: "I have never read nor heard the like; all men wonder at it; some think the devil speaks out of him, some the Holy Ghost." The book "shows all the wickedness that goes on at Rome. It can't stand. There must be a reformation. Charles must begin it."

While Luther was inveighing against Rome, Rome was mobilizing against Luther. In the months leading up to the imperial election, the Vatican—

absorbed in the political jockeying—had taken its eye off Luther. Not until early February 1520 did Pope Leo X finally get around to appointing a commission (under the direction of Cardinal Cajetan) to consider the charges that should be brought against Luther, and even then the case stalled.

Then Johann Eck arrived. On meeting the pope, Eck kissed his feet, and Leo kissed Eck in return. ("Let them lick, lap, spit on, and bite each other thus," Luther sneered on hearing this.) Eck showed Vatican officials his notes from the Leipzig debate as well as the Louvain-Cologne condemnation, with its forceful repudiation of Luther's doctrines. He also described the radicalization taking place in Germany and the growing animosity toward Rome. To dramatic effect he conveyed the nationalist fervor of the humanists, especially the inflammatory bombast of Hutten. The Italians found Eck's boasting and boorishness irritating, but his success at Leipzig and his firsthand knowledge of developments in Germany bolstered his credibility, and at his prodding a new commission was empaneled, with the pope himself presiding.

Relying heavily on the Louvain-Cologne judgment, this body drew up a bull condemning dozens of Luther's articles. On May 2, 1520, Eck carried a draft to Magliana, the papal hunting villa, where Leo was enjoying an early-spring outing. Located some five miles west of Rome, the compound included a *palazzetto*, a chapel, stables, and an arsenal. A rabbit warren and apiary had been built with the aim of creating a rural paradise amid the plentiful game fields of the Roman Campagna. Leo was spending more time here as he devoted himself to the pleasures of the hunt, and he regularly invited scholars, poets, and artists to come and provide entertainment after the excitement of the day's chase.

Here, amid the shrieks of birds and the grunts of boars, and with two cardinals and a Spanish scholar present, Leo approved the articles. A preface was drafted that reflected the surroundings. It began, *Exsurge Domine*—"Arise O Lord"—a phrase by which the document would become known. "Foxes have arisen that want to devastate thy vineyard, where thou hast worked the wine-press. . . . A roaring sow of the woods has undertaken to destroy the vineyard, a wild beast wants to devour it." From Magliana, the bull was carried back to Rome for discussion by a consistory, or ecclesiastical council. Between May 25 and June 1 it met four times, in sessions lasting from six to eight hours each—a measure of the contentiousness of the issue. One key point of debate was whether Luther's articles should be condemned uniformly or distinctions made between those deemed heretical and those considered simply scandalous or offensive to pious ears. With reports reaching Rome that some princes were drifting into Luther's camp, it was decided that quick action was needed, and a blanket condemnation was adopted as the most expedient course.

In the end, the bull listed forty-one points on which Luther had erred. A number cited Luther's pronouncements on penance, including his assertion that the practices associated with it (contrition, confession, satisfaction) lacked any foundation in Scripture. Others dealt with his views on indulgences, including his position that they were of no use for the dead or dying. Also included were his demand for allowing Communion in both kinds, his contention that in every good work the righteous man sins, and his teaching that Christians should not fear but cherish excommunications. Luther was admonished as well for his statements supporting Hus and rejecting the pontiff's claim to be the vicar of Christ. In a measure of the length to which the Church was willing to go to extinguish dissent, the bull censured Luther for maintaining that the burning of heretics went against the Holy Spirit. The final error cited was Luther's opposition to mendicancy.

A section was added setting out sanctions and demands. The errors found in Luther's writings were to be condemned, rejected, and denounced for all times, and no Christian under any circumstance was "to read, speak, preach, laud, consider, publish or defend such writings, sermons, or broadsides or anything contained therein." Rather, such writings were to be publicly burned. "Dear God," the bull stated with stentorian sorrow, "what have we failed to do, what have we avoided, what paternal love did we not exercise, to call him back from his errors? . . . We reminded him through our writings that he should desist from his error or else, with safe-conduct and the necessary provisions, to come to us and talk with us." Had he done so, "we would have clearly instructed and taught him that the holy popes, our predecessors, whom he chides without all reason, never erred in their statutes and regulations, which he boldly destroys." For more than a year, however, he had remained disobedient, and so now, with Rome's love having failed to move him, perhaps the "terror of the pain of punishment" would.

Within sixty days of the bull's publication, Luther was to inform the Church of his recantation by submitting a sealed document or, better yet, by personally traveling to Rome and offering assurances of his sincere obedience. If, however, he and his supporters failed to comply with these provisions, they were to be condemned as "barren vines which are not in Christ," and Luther's preaching was to be rejected as "an offensive doctrine contrary to the Christian faith," to "the damage and shame of the entire Christian Church."

Remarkably, it seems not to have occurred to anyone in Rome to provide an actual rebuttal of Luther's teachings, explaining how in fact they contradicted those of the Church. The one concession made was the sixty-day waiting period. While some prelates favored excommunicating Luther outright, others hoped that the threat of sanction would be sufficient to bring him (or Frederick) to his senses. Dated June 15, 1520, the bull was posted the following week both at St. Peter's Basilica and in the Campo de' Fiori, and copies of Luther's works were burned in the Piazza Navona. In Germany, the bull would take effect only after being publicly posted in certain designated towns.

Two emissaries were assigned that task. One was Eck, who was to post the bull throughout Saxony and other parts of eastern Germany as well as to make sure it reached Luther himself. To carry the bull to western Germany and the Low Countries, the Church designated Jerome Aleander. An accomplished humanist, Aleander had taught at the Sorbonne and worked for the prince-bishop of Liège before coming to Rome in 1516 on a diplomatic mission. Showing his political acumen, he had served as secretary to the powerful Cardinal Giulio de' Medici, then become the Vatican librarian. Though much less accomplished a theologian than Eck, Aleander was a far more adept diplomat, and with his many contacts in the Low Countries, he seemed well positioned to deal with Charles V, whose help in executing the bull would be essential.

Saint Jerome in His Study, by Antonello da Messina (1470s), showing the Church Father (and translator of the Vulgate) as Renaissance humanists saw him—the saintly Christian scholar.

ABOVE: *View of the Campo Vaccino*, by Cornelis van Poelenburgh (1620), showing the cow pasture that the Roman Forum had become in the Middle Ages.

BELOW: The execution of Jan Hus, in 1415 at the Council of Constance, in a fifteenth-century print by Diebold Schilling the Elder.

The everyday Erasmus, as shown by Quentin Massys (or Metsys) in Antwerp in 1517.

The iconic Erasmus, as painted by Hans Holbein the Younger in Basel in 1523.

OLD ST. PAUL'S FROM THE SOUTH-WEST, SHOWING THE CHURCH OF ST. GREGORY AND THE CHAPTER HOUSE.
(Compiled by F. Watkins from drawings by E. B. Ferrey.)

ABOVE: Old St. Paul's Cathedral in London—the center of Erasmus's activities in London while his friend John Colet was its dean. It was destroyed in the Great Fire of 1666.

BELOW: Opening page of the Gospel according to Matthew, from Erasmus's 1516 *Novum Instrumentum*.

ABOVE: Woodcut from Georgius Agricola's *De Re Metallica*, showing the disorder of the German mine fields in the sixteenth century.

BELOW: Some of the mining refuse heaps that still dot the landscape around Eisleben and Mansfeld where Luther grew up.

ABOVE: Martin Luther and Katharina von Bora, by Lucas Cranach the Elder (around 1529).

BELOW: A view of Wittenberg, showing St. Mary's Church, where Luther did most of his preaching, and a statue of the reformer in the marketplace.

ABOVE: An image of Luther with dove and halo, by Hans Baldung Grien (1520) after an engraving by Lucas Cranach the Elder. It became popular around the time of the Diet of Worms.

BELOW: *Martin Luther at Worms*, by Anton von Werner (1877), a heroic portrayal of the reformer as he stood unyielding before Charles V, the Holy Roman Emperor.

The Wartburg Castle, where Luther hid after his act of defiance at Worms, overlooking the town of Eisenach.

Luther as Junker Jörg, by Lucas Cranach the Elder (1522), showing him as he appeared during his time in the Wartburg.

Portrait of Leo X and Two Cardinals, by Raphael (1518). The cardinal on the left is Giulio de' Medici, Leo's cousin, who became Pope Clement VII.

Equestrian Portrait of Charles V, by Titian (1548), showing the emperor after his victory in April 1547 over a Protestant army at the Battle of Mühlberg. His triumph proved short-lived.

Phillip Melanchthon, by Albrecht Dürer (1526).

1526.
VIVENTIS·POTVIT·DVRERIVS·ORA·PHILIPPI
MENTEM·NON·POTVIT·PINGERE·DOCTA
MANVS

Statue of Huldrych Zwingli outside the Wasserkirche in Zurich, showing him with a Bible in one hand and a sword in the other.

ABOVE: Woodcut from Luther's *Against the Roman Papacy, an Institution of the Devil,* by Lucas Cranach the Elder (1545), showing the execution of the pope and cardinals.

ELOW: Reading of the Augsburg Confession at the Diet of Augsburg on June 25, 1530—the first time the Lutheran creed received an official hearing.

ABOVE: Luther with other reformers (detail from a copy after *Raising of Lazarus*, by Lucas Cranach the Younger). Among them, strikingly, is Erasmus (fourth from the right). Also shown are Georg Spalatin (behind Luther's right shoulder), Johannes Bugenhagen (behind his left shoulder), Justus Jonas (to Erasmus's left), and Philipp Melanchthon (far right).

BELOW: The Reformation monument in Worms, showing Martin Luther on a pedestal and, seated below him, four forerunners: Peter Waldus, John Wyclif, Jan Hus, and Girolamo Savonarola. On the sides are statues representing Frederick the Wise, Augsburg, Johannes Reuchlin, Speyer, Philipp Melanchthon, Magdeburg, and Philip of Hesse. Erasmus is conspicuously absent.

ABOVE: The Lutherhaus in Wittenberg, where Luther lived as a friar and which became his home after his marriage to Katharina von Bora; today it houses the world's largest museum devoted to the Reformation.

BELOW: *The Departure of Erasmus from Basel* (in 1529), from *The History of Protestantism*, by James Aitken Wylie (1878).

God as Creator, from Luther's 1534 Bible, from the workshop of Lucas Cranach the Elder.

The execution of William Tyndale at Vilvorde Castle in Belgium in 1536. Tyndale was persecuted by both Thomas More for his translation of the Bible into English and by Charles V for his Lutheran beliefs. (From John Foxe's *Book of Martyrs*, published in 1563.)

A defaced image of Erasmus from a copy of Sebastian Münster's *Cosmographia Universalis* (published in Basel in 1550)—a graphic example of the fierce campaign to expunge Erasmus's legacy.

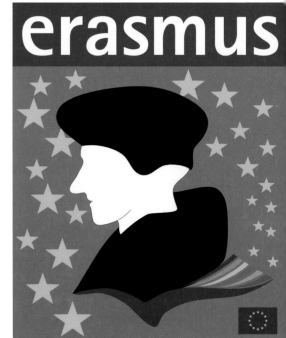

The logo of the Erasmus Program, which enables students in member countries of the European Union to study at universities in other member countries.

On July 17 and 18, 1520, *Exsurge Domine* was placed in the hands of the two envoys. Soon afterward, they set off on their long journeys northward, with Eck bound for the eastern Alpine passes en route to Saxony and Aleander headed to the western passes on the way to the Rhineland. Given the growing rebellion against Rome in the north, each undertook the mission at the risk of his life.

23

BONFIRES

Like so many others, Erasmus was looking forward to Charles's arrival in the north, but with far more modest expectations. As a councilor to Charles and a frequent visitor to the Burgundian court, he knew a great deal about the young man's upbringing and temperament. Charles had grown up without the presence of either his father (Philip the Handsome, who had died in 1506, when Charles was six) or his mother (Joanna the Mad, the daughter of Ferdinand and Isabella, who had been declared mentally ill and confined to Tordesillas Castle in Spain). His religious and moral training was entrusted to Adrian of Utrecht, who had steeped him in an austere brand of Catholic piety. Drawn to tales of knightly chivalry, Charles had developed a love of honor and ceremony, which was magnified by his exposure to the pomp and protocols of the Burgundian court. Erasmus in 1516 had dedicated *The Education of a Christian Prince* to the then-teenage Charles, explaining that he had done so so that those raised to rule great empires might learn the principles of government from his example. With Charles now about to rule such an empire, Erasmus hoped to have the chance to recall him to that ideal.

Charles's court included many Flemish followers of Erasmus, and from them he had received regular reports about Charles's time in Spain and the tremendous trials he had faced there. From the moment of his arrival, in 1517, Charles had been seen as a foreign occupier. A native speaker of French, he knew no Spanish, and—distrustful of anyone outside his immediate circle—had relied heavily on his Burgundian advisers. Greedy and haughty, they had shamelessly taken the most powerful and lucrative positions for themselves. The Spaniards were especially furious at the bestowing of the archbishopric of Toledo on the young and inexperienced William de Croy. Monks had begun preaching against the opulence of the royal court and the large sums being sent out of the country. Amid this growing discontent, Charles was repeatedly forced to delay his departure for Germany and the coronation in Aachen.

Nonetheless determined to leave, Charles in the spring of 1520 went with his court to La Coruña, on Spain's northwestern coast, where a fleet was being readied. He appointed Adrian of Utrecht, the bishop of Tortosa (who in 1517 had been named a cardinal by Leo X), as regent. In need of cash to finance both his journey and his anticipated projects as emperor, Charles convened two sessions of the Castilian Cortes to demand more revenue. Enraged, the communities of Castile (known as Comuneros) formed a league with an eye to setting up a revolutionary government and dethroning Charles and installing his mother, Joanna. For weeks, Charles and his fleet were bottled up in port by a strong northeaster, and during that time the Revolt of the Comuneros broke out. Charles was so eager to head north, however, that when the winds finally shifted, he set off on May 20, leaving Adrian in charge of putting down the revolt.

Charles's initial destination was England. The previous autumn, he had received an invitation from Thomas Wolsey to stop there on his way to the Continent to see Henry VIII. Charles had readily accepted. Visiting England would allow him for the first time to meet his aunt, Catherine of Aragon, who was Henry's queen. It would also give him a chance to win Henry's support against the French king Francis I. Ever since he had lost the imperial crown to Charles, Francis—bellicose by nature and feeling encircled by Charles's lands—was expected to attack him, and Charles saw in England an effective counterweight.

From Wolsey's standpoint, the invitation to Charles was part of a grand new geopolitical plan. After initially overseeing Henry's military adventures in France, the calculating cardinal had improbably turned peacemaker. Through his diplomacy, England and France—Europe's two oldest enemies—had in October 1518 signed a peace treaty in London. The pact was opened up to other powers, and twenty had eventually signed on, including the Holy Roman Empire, the Netherlands, Spain, and the papacy. A prime motive was the need for unity in the face of the Ottomans, but beyond that, Wolsey—influenced by Erasmus, Colet, More, and other Christian humanists—hoped to build on the Treaty of London to create a perpetual peace among the nations of Christendom.

Henry—ready to don the mantle of a man of peace—approved. To solidify the English-French rapprochement, Wolsey had organized a summit between Henry and Francis to take place in June 1520 near Calais. Wolsey had conceived of a meeting beforehand between Henry and Charles as a means of giving Henry added leverage.

On May 26, 1520, after six days at sea, Charles and his fleet were in the English Channel. Wolsey sailed out to meet him, then accompanied him to Dover. Henry rode down at once to see him. The next day, the two monarchs went to Canterbury, where Charles was magnificently received and for the first time presented to Catherine. Henry and Charles spent three days together, with much of the time given over to banqueting and jousting. The subdued Charles seemed uncomfortable in Henry's pleasure-loving world. Only on the afternoon of May 29, 1520, was any serious business transacted, mostly concerning trade. Their time together went well enough, however, for them to agree to meet again on the Continent after Henry's summit with Francis. That evening Henry and Charles left Canterbury together. Five miles outside the city they parted ways, with Henry continuing on to Dover for the Channel crossing to Calais and his rendezvous with Francis, and Charles heading to Sandwich for the trip to Flushing and Brussels.

In the weeks prior to Henry and Francis's summit, Erasmus had received a note from William Warham, his longtime friend and patron, encouraging him to attend. Eager to see his English friends, Erasmus had intended to go, but as the date approached, he came down with a debilitating fever that left him feeling depressed and dissatisfied with himself, and so he decided to forgo the event.

He would miss one of the great pageants of the era, at which two powerful monarchs—both vain, handsome, and athletic—sought to outdo each other in bunting rather than battle. The prevalence of gold cloth in the pavilions and costumes gave the summit its name, the Field of Cloth of Gold. On June 7, 1520, Henry and Francis met on horseback at a spot marked by a spear in the ground. There followed a fortnight of banqueting and dancing, jousts and tilts. Despite the good cheer, however, no formal accord was reached. The main accomplishment was to establish a climate of trust that, it was hoped, would convince the two monarchs that it was better to break bread than exchange fire. The climate would not last long, however, for after the summit Henry traveled to Calais, and two weeks later, on July 10, 1520, he rode the fifteen miles to the town of Gravelines to meet Charles V. Francis was not informed of the meeting and would have been furious had he known of it.

After remaining in Gravelines for forty-eight hours, Henry and Charles rode to Calais, to another palace the English had had built specially for the occasion. There, in a splendid circular hall, Charles for two days was lavishly entertained. In all, the two men remained together for four days. Throughout, Charles implored Henry for a promise of English support in the event that Francis attacked him, but Henry remained noncommittal.

For Charles and Henry's meetings, Erasmus *was* present, in his capacity as a councilor to Charles. He was able to see his old friend Thomas More, who was traveling with Henry's court. He tried to meet with Wolsey, but the cardinal was so busy that he barely had time to shake Erasmus's hand. Erasmus did, however, get in to see Henry. It had been years since their last meeting, and Erasmus hoped to rekindle the king's affections. As Erasmus had anticipated, Henry asked him about Edward Lee (who had many friends in the English court), but the king was more interested in another figure: Martin Luther. In England no less than on the Continent, the outspoken friar was gaining adherents, and Henry asked Erasmus what he thought of him. Henry's views on the subject remained unclear, and Erasmus—wary of antagonizing him—disingenuously claimed that Luther was too good a scholar for someone with as little learning as himself to be able to form an opinion of him.

After the meetings were over, Henry returned to England, where— rewarding himself for all the tiresome summitry—he spent the rest of the summer hunting. Charles went to Bruges, where he spent the last week of July 1520. Erasmus (it is believed) accompanied his court, thus gaining an opportunity to size up the man who was about to become Europe's most powerful ruler.

At twenty, Charles still seemed barely more than a boy. He had a pallid complexion and a thin face framed by lank hair. Because of an adenoidal condition, he had to breathe through his mouth, giving an impression of intellectual sluggishness. He also had a strongly protruding jaw, a prominent trait of the Hapsburg line that resulted from generations of inbreeding (and which came to be known as the Hapsburg jaw). Charles had difficulty chewing food properly and suffered from lifelong indigestion. This was a special burden in light of his love of food and drink, and his gourmandizing would exact a heavy toll on his health. No less than as a child, he remained committed to courtly ceremony. He devoted much of his time to hunting, processions, and jousting, often appearing in the lists in the raiment of the Burgundian nobility. Perpetually dour, Charles seemed unable to enjoy himself, except when collecting timepieces (a lifelong hobby) or listening to music, especially the polyphonic motets and chansons of Josquin des Prez, the leading composer of the day. On top of it all, he had little aptitude for languages. Despite his three years in Spain, he was barely conversant in Spanish, and he knew almost no German—a serious liability for a man about to become *Kaiser* of the German people. (Tradition has attributed to Charles a famous quote: "I speak Spanish to God, Italian to women, French to men, and German to my horse.")

On paper, Charles was the most powerful man in the world. Spanish grandees, Flemish weavers, Austrian miners, Swabian peasants, and Sicilian herdsmen were all his subjects. His lands were home to Europe's richest silver and copper mines as well as its greatest financial centers (Antwerp, Augsburg, and Seville). His domain now extended across the Atlantic to the Americas, where Cortés was carrying out his conquest of Mexico. During Charles's reign as emperor, the whole orientation of European politics would shift from its long-standing north-south axis to an east-west one, with Spain the center of his kingdom. The iconic image of Charles is the portrait he commissioned from Titian in 1548, after the battle of Mühlberg, where he won a smashing victory over Protestant armies. The painting (now hanging in the Prado) shows him in full armor on a richly caparisoned horse, riding with heroic resolve through a brooding Saxon landscape.

In fact, Charles at the time was hobbled by gout, and his victory would prove short-lived; with opposition forces mobilizing against him, he was eventually forced to flee over the Brenner Pass in the Alps to Innsbruck—a humiliating experience that left him so broken that in 1555 he abdicated his throne. Throughout his reign, in fact, his power was more illusory than real. His dominions were scattered far and wide, making communication across them difficult, with letters requiring weeks to travel from one end of his empire to the other. The patchwork nature of his lands made administering them a nightmare. Apart from his bodyguards and grooms, he had no real military to speak of, and none of the European princes, dukes, and burghers who ostensibly owed him allegiance recognized him as overlord. Even with the precious metals that were beginning to arrive from the Americas, his extravagant outlays would keep him in perpetual debt, especially to the Fuggers, whose colossal bribes had made his election possible.

Charles's paramount trait was his unwavering sense of duty—to his Catholic faith, the house of Hapsburg, and the hierarchical principles on which medieval society was based. From his Spanish grandparents, he had inherited the idea of the Church as a universal and absolutist institution that could not tolerate the tainting presence of Jews or Muslims, and his years in Spain had reinforced his distaste for rebels, mutineers, and heretics. It was, he believed, his solemn responsibility to preserve the spiritual and temporal unity of Christendom, at whatever cost. And that cost would prove high. During his long rule, Charles would be almost constantly at war—with the French, Turks, Italians, and Lutherans—helping to ensure that the perpetual peace envisioned by Erasmus and promoted by Wolsey would be very short-lived.

Back in Louvain, Erasmus faced the seething animosity of the mendicants and dialecticians. "The potbellies and their shameless scurrilities under the cloak of religion—these now rule the roost," he observed. Even as he continued to fend off Edward Lee, there arose in Spain "a second Lee," as he put it. Diego López de Zúñiga—or Stunica, his Latin name—would in fact prove a far more formidable foe than the captious Englishman. A master of Latin, Greek, and Hebrew, Stunica had been a member of the team that produced the Complutensian Polyglot Bible in Alcalá. Detecting inconsistencies and mistakes on virtually every page of Erasmus's New Testament, he had come out with his own set of annotations defending the Vulgate against the Dutchman. Stunica was so determined to blacken Erasmus's name that in early 1521 he made the long journey from Spain to

Rome so that he could lobby the Holy See in person. Wearily acknowledging the Spaniard's exegetical skills, Erasmus quickly drafted a defense. He also reluctantly concluded that he would have to produce yet another edition of his New Testament. With the second edition selling well, Froben endorsed the idea, and Erasmus again embarked on the grueling task of checking and collating, editing and explaining.

As he proceeded, there arrived in Louvain a copy of Luther's response to the Cologne-Louvain condemnation. While cheered to see Luther's rude treatment of the "doctrinal asses" who had made his own life so miserable, Erasmus was horrified to find himself favorably mentioned along with Pico, Reuchlin, and Lefèvre. To Erasmus's enemies, this seemed to confirm his part in inspiring Luther's ideas. If Luther referred to him in this way again, the damage could be incalculable, so in early August 1520 Erasmus decided to send the Augustinian friar another letter. His tone was friendly. After recounting the many attacks on liberal studies in Louvain, he described his meeting with Henry VIII and the king's wish that Luther "had written some things with more prudence and moderation." "That wish is shared, my dear Luther, by those who wish you well." If the current agitation was not curbed, it would surely spark a great upheaval. Nonetheless, he observed, "I shall not oppose your policy, for fear that, if it is inspired by the spirit of Christ, I may be opposing Christ. But this at least I would beg you: not to bring my name or my friends' names into what you write in an unpleasant way, as you did in your answer to the condemnations at Louvain and Cologne," for doing so "harms me and does your cause no good."

Luther quickly replied. Though his letter has not survived, he described its gist to Lazarus Spengler, the town clerk of Nuremberg. An early convert to Luther's cause, Spengler had written to Luther to say that he had heard rumors of a rift between him and Erasmus and wanted to know if they were true. Luther assured him they were not, adding that it had never occurred to him "to harbor annoyance or dislike of Erasmus." He had written to Erasmus and promised not to speak of him or any of his friends anymore. "If God will, Erasmus and I will remain at one." It was true, though, he noted, that he and Melanchthon sometimes discussed "how near or far Erasmus is from the way," i.e., the new gospel. Erasmus's insistence on keeping himself at a safe distance from Wittenberg continued to rankle.

With the approach of autumn, however, Erasmus faced a more immediate threat: Jerome Aleander. Erasmus had followed the envoy's northward journey with great trepidation. The two were well acquainted, having first met in 1509, when Erasmus was preparing the *Adages* at Aldus's workshop in Venice and Aleander was working as a proofreader and checker. At the time, Aleander had seemed full of humanist promise. With Erasmus's encouragement, he had traveled to Paris and secured a position at the Sorbonne. His lectures there were wildly popular; one of them, on Plutarch, drew 1,500 people on a scorching July day. In 1513, Aleander became the first Italian named as the school's rector in two centuries. The pay was poor, however, so he had taken a position with the powerful prince-bishop of Liège. Hoping for a cardinal's hat, the bishop had sent Aleander to Rome to try to arrange it. There, Aleander's administrative and political skills were quickly recognized, making him seem a natural choice to execute the bull against Luther in the Low Countries and the Rhineland.

Before most others, Aleander had grasped the gravity of the threat posed by Luther. The best way to silence him, he felt, was by subjecting him to the same punishment Savonarola had received two decades earlier: execution. Though officially subordinate to Marino Caracciolo, the papal nuncio to the Holy Roman Empire, Aleander would become Rome's main agent in the north, and his candid dispatches to Cardinal Giulio de' Medici at the Vatican would leave a vivid record of the Church's campaign against Luther.

After repeated delays, Aleander arrived in Cologne in September 1520. In addition to being one of Germany's largest cities, Cologne was among its most conservative, and on September 22 Aleander was quickly able to arrange publication of *Exsurge Domine*. A copy soon reached Louvain, and when Erasmus saw it, he was appalled. Neither the language nor the proposed penalty seemed to reflect the peaceful spirit of Leo, much less that of the Gospels. Worse, the bull made no effort to refute Luther. The forty-one citations against him were listed without explanation, as if their heretical content were self-evident. While Luther may have been too intemperate in his writings, Rome seemed too imperious in its response, and Erasmus began spreading rumors that the document was a forgery.

From Cologne, Aleander went to Antwerp, where Charles V and his court were staying, and on September 28 he had an audience with the emperor. It was a critical moment in the Luther affair, in which the pope's most able emissary met Europe's most august sovereign. They took an immediate liking to each other. Both spoke French. Both had unqualified respect for Rome and its authority. Like Aleander, Charles saw Luther as an agent of contagion that had to be culled before it infected the whole flock, and to Aleander's great satisfaction he declared his willingness to lay down his life to defend the Church. He also expressed his readiness to enforce *Exsurge Domine* in the Low Countries with every instrument at his command. With Aleander's encouragement, Charles ordered the drafting of an imperial mandate that, on the basis of the bull, ordered the public burning of all Lutheran and other seditious books.

As soon as the mandate was issued, Aleander sought to have it carried out in Antwerp. No less than in Germany, however, Luther's views had taken root in the Low Countries, and notwithstanding the emperor's presence in the city, legal objections were raised to the book burning, and it did not take place.

Louvain seemed to offer better prospects. At the end of September 1520, Charles went there from Antwerp, and Aleander accompanied him. With the Louvain faculty having already condemned Luther, Aleander anticipated few obstacles, but he faced a volley of questions about the bull's authenticity. Suspecting that Erasmus was behind them, Aleander requested a meeting with him. Erasmus—deeply mistrustful of Aleander—refused. The nuncio nonetheless proceeded with his plan, and on October 8, 1520—the day Charles was scheduled to leave Louvain—more than eighty of Luther's books were arranged in a pile in the marketplace along with a number of pamphlets sympathetic to him. High-ranking representatives of the imperial court and foreign governments were present. As the public executioner prepared to ignite the pile, some students added to it several Scholastic tomes, plus a medieval handbook for preachers titled *Sleep Well*.

Louvain thus became the site of the first burning of Luther's books in northern Europe. A decade earlier, the defenders of the faith had sought to stamp out the threat posed by Hebrew studies by confiscating Hebrew texts. Now they were trying to extinguish Luther's ideas by incinerating his books. And Erasmus immediately felt the impact. The day after the burning, Nicholaas Baechem, a Carmelite theologian, was giving a sermon in the Louvain cathedral when Erasmus entered. Baechem immediately began denouncing him as a fervent defender of Luther and insinuating that the source of the contagion was Erasmus's revised New Testament. Catcalls and murmurs of protest came from the audience. Five days later, Baechem nonetheless returned to the theme, warning that both Erasmus and Luther would "come to the stake one day, unless they desist."

In a letter to the university rector, Erasmus protested Baechem's remarks, arguing that it was outrageous for Luther to be suppressed by public uproar before his errors were pointed out to him and his views refuted from Scripture. At Erasmus's insistence, the rector convened a meeting between him and Baechem. Accusations soon began flying, with Erasmus protesting Baechem's use of the pulpit to incite people against him and Baechem pointing to a passage by Erasmus suggesting that he drank too much. As long as Erasmus refused to write against Luther, Baechem declared, he would consider him a member of Luther's party. If that were the standard, Erasmus countered, Baechem himself should be so branded, for he had not written against Luther either. As the charges mounted, the rector cut the session short, saying that it was unworthy of two theologians and that they should instead be directing their ire at Luther—the main problem.

Given the zeal fanned by Aleander and his bonfires, Erasmus decided to take his own countermeasures. In the following days, a fly sheet titled *Acts of the University of Louvain Against Luther* began circulating, and though it had no byline, its style and content marked it as almost certainly by Erasmus. The whole affair against Luther, it stated, had sprung from the hatred of languages and of literature set off by the Reuchlin affair. Luther's books had been burned, Hoogstraten had resumed his job as inquisitor, and Baechem had preached in a "savage and idiotic style." The papal bull printed in Louvain contained many clauses that seemed more in the language of the friars than that of the Roman Curia, arousing suspicions of forgery. With Aleander's presence in Louvain, "the tyranny of blockheads and maniacs is seething to its height." The nuncio was accused of an uncontrollable temper, boundless conceit, insatiable greed, and unrestrained lust. Most damning of all, he was said to be a Jew by birth who had "snatched up his pen with the aim of celebrating his master Moses and darkening the glory of Christ, which is just beginning to blossom again at the present time as superstition and the futile but deadly old rites of mankind lose their force." As evidence for this charge, the document cited general gossip, Aleander's knowledge of Hebrew, and his facial features (he had a prominent nose). Just as Pfefferkorn in Cologne had thrown the Christian world into confusion, "now Aleander, the blood-brother of Judas, is outdoing even his ancestors and is set on betraying the future of the gospel for only three pieces of silver."

As this bit of scurrility shows, Erasmus seemed perfectly willing to put aside his scruples about poisonous pamphlets when such writings served his own purpose. And this instance would prove effective. The charges against Aleander, especially the one about his Jewish origins, would stick to him as he pursued his mission of publicizing the bull and organizing book burnings.

From Louvain, Aleander went to nearby Liège, where he organized another bonfire, which went off without incident. He then traveled east to Aachen, on Germany's border with the Low Countries, for the coronation. On October 22, 1520, Charles entered the town astride a spirited horse (which he controlled with a practiced hand) and with a procession of horsemen, counts, lords, and foot soldiers. At the city gates he was met by the electors of the empire, who kissed his hand while he sat bareheaded in the saddle. The next day, in the great cathedral where Charlemagne had been crowned, Charles pledged to defend the Church, preserve the faith, protect the poor, and rule justly. He was anointed with holy oil and, as trumpets blared and drums rolled, the imperial crown was placed on his head. Once the ceremonies were over, Charles and his party traveled forty miles east to Cologne, arriving on October 28. Aleander went along.

Erasmus was in Cologne, too. Though invited to the coronation, he had apparently decided not to go, in part because the plague had broken out in Aachen. With many German princes staying in Cologne, Erasmus hoped to make one last bid to avert the upheaval he saw looming. In line with his frequent calls for arbitration as an alternative to war, he wanted to see if common ground could be found between the contending parties. Together with a Dominican prior named Johannes Faber, he produced the *Consilium*, a proposal (published anonymously) to submit the Luther matter to a panel of learned and upright men. This was needed to make sure that the dispute was "neither overwhelmed by the billows nor driven to the shallow shore"—that it avoided Scylla while not being sucked into Charybdis. Erasmus, in short, hoped to rally the moderate middle—those who, whether sympathetic to Luther or not, supported resolving the matter without bloodshed.

But that middle was fast shrinking. Between the theologians and friars who despised Luther and the new faithful who exalted him, there were a few holdouts who, while loyal to the Church, shrank from seeing its will imposed by force. Among them was the elector Frederick. He, too, was in Cologne, staying at an inn on the Square of the Three Kings. On October 31, in the sacristy of Cologne's great Gothic cathedral, the stolid Saxon prince met the young, untested emperor. Frederick stated his long-standing belief that no German should be condemned without first receiving a fair hearing. Through an interpreter, Charles said that the matter would be addressed at the first Imperial Diet under his rule, scheduled to start in Worms in January 1521. The language barrier prevented any meaningful exchange, but each showed the exaggerated courtesy demanded by the occasion.

Aleander, too, wanted to meet Frederick, but the prince would not see him. Persisting, Aleander and the nuncio Caracciolo interrupted Frederick while he was attending Mass at a Franciscan monastery and handed him a papal brief demanding that Luther be extradited to Rome and his books burned. The nuncios pressed for an immediate reply, but Frederick demurred.

He first wanted to hear Erasmus's opinion, and the next day he invited him to his quarters. It was no doubt a thrilling moment for Frederick, who greatly admired the Dutchman and had all of his books. Erasmus for his part appreciated the prince's commitment to liberal studies and support for the University of Wittenberg. Erasmus—probably wearing his usual black fur-lined mantle and black cap, from under which his gray hair curled—faced the aging statesman while warming his hands before a fire. Frederick—large and heavy-jowled, with a long curly beard and the deliberate movements of a gout sufferer—asked him to speak in his native Dutch (which was close to German), but Erasmus said he preferred Latin. The prince understood Latin but, uncomfortable speaking it, posed his questions through Spalatin.

Frederick asked if Erasmus felt that Luther had erred. This was a question Erasmus had long sought to avoid, and he paused to collect his thoughts. The many years he had spent gathering proverbs had given him a knack for speaking epigrammatically, and after a few minutes of reflection he gave a response worthy of the *Adages*: "Luther has erred in two points—in attacking the crown of the pope and the bellies of the monks."

The ice thus broken, Erasmus described his concerns about the dangers that the Luther affair posed to humane studies. If Luther was quashed, the whole movement to renew Scripture through scholarship would also collapse. The punishment stipulated in the bull against Luther had stirred tremendous indignation, Erasmus said, and, aside from Cologne and Louvain, no university had been willing to censure him. He expressed approval of Luther's offer to submit to a panel of impartial experts and described some of the steps by which such a policy might be carried out.

Frederick was pleased to find Erasmus's position more or less coinciding with his own, and the humanist agreed to accompany Spalatin to the house of a local count to draft a proposal. There, Erasmus set down twenty-two axioms, criticizing the bull as too severe and calling for the issue to be settled "through the sane advice of unbiased and discreet persons." Given the delicacy of the issue, Erasmus asked Spalatin to return his notes. Spalatin did—but not before making a copy. Not long afterward, in another act of duplicity, Spalatin turned it over to a printer, and in February 1521 Erasmus's axioms would be published in both Leipzig and Wittenberg. To his fury, his bon mot about the pope's crown and monks' bellies flew around Germany.

The more immediate impact, however, was on Frederick. Erasmus's positive remarks about Luther reinforced the elector's own sense that the friar was being treated unfairly. The day after their meeting, Frederick rejected the nuncios' request. He urged them to abandon their aggressive course and instead arrange for Luther to be examined before reasonable and pious judges with the assurance of a safe-conduct. This was a bitter blow to Aleander and Rome: the Saxon elector was in effect rejecting the terms of the papal bull. From now on, the nuncios would have to direct their pleas to the emperor.

Erasmus, meanwhile, agreed to meet with Aleander. The atmosphere was tense. Aleander was fully informed of Erasmus's meeting with Frederick and his advice to him to resist the bull. He had also heard from many sources of Erasmus's efforts to defame him, including calling him a Jew. Erasmus for his part saw Aleander as the prime mover behind Rome's destructive course.

Determined to keep the conversation light so as not to give Erasmus any more fodder against the bull, Aleander recalled the earlier, friendlier times between them. But Erasmus, unable to suppress his anger, complained that he had heard that Aleander had tarnished his name with the princes and was preparing to condemn his and Reuchlin's books. Aleander replied that he had no such intention and that in any case he did not think Erasmus had written anything contrary to the Church's interests. "In short," Aleander later wrote, "I dissembled ably and invented some obliging lies, as in the interest of the faith and of my commission I could not do other." Aleander did, however, express his sorrow over discovering that Erasmus was the source of the opinion that the bull was a forgery. Seeing Erasmus's discomfort, he quickly changed the subject, exhorting Erasmus to direct his writings toward the edification of the Church rather than, like Luther, to its destruction. At the end of five or six hours, the two parted with kisses and avowals of friendship that each knew to be insincere.

Shortly afterward, preparations were made for a burning of Luther's books in Cologne. They were set ablaze before representatives of the local archbishop. Unlike the burning in Louvain, however, this event was staged without publicity, for even in this orthodox stronghold public opinion was turning decisively against the bull. The humanists of Cologne wrote mocking dialogues about Aleander and posted insulting songs on the doors of the university.

Eager to escape Germany and its reeking stoves, Erasmus left Cologne on November 15, 1520, to return to Louvain. The leg to Aachen went smoothly, but west of that town he encountered a maelstrom of wind, rain, and flooding. "Even in the hills we narrowly escaped shipwreck," he wrote, "for we had to take to the water on horseback." With great difficulty his horse swam to shore. Despite the waterlogged conditions, Erasmus insisted on continuing on rather than return in humiliated defeat to his host in Aachen—another striking instance of the physical fortitude of this fastidious man of letters.

While Erasmus returned to Louvain, Charles traveled south to Worms to prepare for the Imperial Diet. Aleander left with him but made a detour to Mainz. As Germany's most powerful ecclesiastical seat, it seemed an ideal place to make an example of Luther's books, and a bonfire was scheduled for November 28, 1520. On that day, his books were piled high in the marketplace, and as the hangman standing on the platform prepared to ignite them, he asked whether the man whose volumes stood before him had been legitimately condemned. "No!" the crowd bellowed. The hangman then leaped down, saying he would not execute judgment against anyone who had not been convicted by due process. The burning was rescheduled for the next day, and in the interim Aleander pressed Archbishop Albrecht to make sure the pope's command was carried out. Throughout the night, however, the archbishop was visited by noblemen who, sympathetic to Luther, advised him against it.

Aleander urged the archbishop to proceed, and in the end a few books were put to the torch by a grave digger who was pressed into service. Only a gaggle of women bringing their geese to market witnessed the event. Reviled as a Jew and a traitor, Aleander was pelted with stones and managed to escape only through the intervention of a sympathetic abbot. Mainz was flooded with defamatory posters, and Ulrich von Hutten commemorated the event in a "Lament over the Lutheran Conflagration in Mainz":

O God, Luther's books they burn.
Thy godly truth is slain in turn.
Pardon in advance is sold,
And heaven marketed for gold.
The German people is bled white
And is not asked to be contrite.
To Martin Luther wrong is done—
O God, be thou our champion.
My good for him I will not spare,
My life, my blood for him will I dare.

The pro-Rome party, meanwhile, was mounting its own furious propaganda campaign, as Erasmus discovered on his return to Louvain. A Dominican lecturing at the university spent several weeks inveighing against the *Praise of Folly*, and two other friars sent Erasmus a pamphlet angrily censuring his use of *sermo* in place of *verbum*. Such agitation, Erasmus believed, had one end—to provoke him into publicly denouncing Luther. "The theologians think that nothing but my pen can polish off Luther and are silently bringing pressure on me to attack him in print," he wrote. "Heaven forbid that I should be so mad!"

Thus buffeted, Erasmus sought refuge with the one institution that seemed able to provide him sanctuary. For all its flaws and shortcomings, the Roman Church remained the institutional embodiment of Christ's spirit and mission, and, unlike Luther, Erasmus could not imagine leaving it. Worried that he had come under suspicion in Rome, he prepared a long, emotional defense of his actions for Cardinal Lorenzo Campeggio. The most esteemed papal diplomat of his generation, Campeggio was Erasmus's highest-ranking friend in the Church, and during the coming upheaval Erasmus would often use him as a conduit to the pope and the Curia.

The letter, dated December 6, 1520, offered Erasmus's most complete statement yet of his position on the most explosive issue of the day. Given the scrutiny he was under, his comments were surprisingly favorable. Though he had not read more than a dozen pages through of Luther's works, he wrote, he had detected in what he had read "rare natural

gifts and a nature finely adapted to expound the mysteries of Scripture."
The world "thirsts for the pure living water drawn from the conduits of
evangelists and apostles," and Luther seemed to have "both the natural
endowments and the necessary zeal." But he had also stumbled on things
in Luther that were "rude and harsh" and which "did not properly reflect
the gentle spirit of the Gospel," and he had written to warn him to follow
Christ's example and not attack the pope or condemn the universities or
monastic orders out of hand.

But then a terrifying bull had been published under the pope's authority, and Luther's books were burned—actions that "could hardly be
done in a more spiteful way." The sole result of the clamor had been to
make Luther's books more famous and to drive more people to read them.
Whatever Luther's sins, it would "be more civilized to cure him than to
snuff him out." In the days of Augustine, heretics were listened to "even
with respect," and the penalty for a convicted heretic who persisted in his
error was no more than expulsion from the community of the faithful.
"Nowadays no proscription is more brutal than an accusation of heresy,"
yet no word comes more easily to the lips of those seeking to enforce orthodoxy. Everyone knows that the pope has the means to either destroy or
terrify whomever he pleases, but he should move slowly in exercising his
authority on such an issue. "If we wish to be told the truth, everyone must
be free to utter his opinion, and even the man who gives bad advice must
be forgiven, provided he was doing his best."

As for himself, Erasmus went on, "I am not impious enough to dissent
from the Catholic Church, I am not ungrateful enough to dissent from
Leo, of whose support and exceptional kindness to me I have personal
experience." He added: "I have never knowingly been nor will I be a leader
in error; I have no intention to be a captain or coadjutor in civil strife. Let
others court martyrdom; it is an honor of which I find myself unworthy."
He "always was and always will be a zealous supporter above all else of the
see of Rome, to which I know myself indebted on so many grounds, and
shall count any of its enemies my personal enemy."

Erasmus's rejection of martyrdom would be cited repeatedly as evidence of his pusillanimity and would do serious damage to his reputation. But it reflected his resolute opposition to fanaticism. In an age when

people were preparing to kill and be killed in the name of God, he refused to participate. And his resistance to the growing demands that he denounce Luther took some backbone. At the same time, Erasmus was unequivocally embracing an institution of which he had been bitterly critical. And, for the rest of his life, he would remain loyal to the Roman Church. No doubt he felt a genuine attachment to that institution. At its best, it embodied the values on which European civilization was built, and Erasmus's reform program was aimed at correcting the abuses that were undermining its authority. Yet the passions unleashed by Luther were becoming so dark and menacing as to make Erasmus fear for his life, and declaring his unstinting loyalty to Rome seemed the one path available to ensure his own survival.

24

FAITH AND FURY

In Wittenberg, as in university towns across Europe, the students were a rowdy and volatile lot. Living far from home in overcrowded conditions; dealing with cold, hunger, and unforgiving workloads; and finding their sole release in alcohol, they posed a perennial threat to public order. In the early months of 1520, the students in Wittenberg began protesting the fact that the apprentices at Lucas Cranach's workshop were allowed to carry weapons while they were not, and in July their unhappiness boiled over into a riot. After clashing with the city militia, they assembled in the churchyard of the Franciscan monastery with the intention of forcing their way into Frederick's castle. The citizens blocked them, however, and the electoral army was called in to keep order.

Luther was furious, for he felt that the students' actions would tarnish the university's image. To his further dismay, the rector and a number of faculty members sided with the students against the town council; when the university senate voted to allow the students to carry weapons, Luther walked out. From the pulpit of the parish church, he denounced the rioters with such vehemence that he was physically threatened; if he preached like that again, one student shouted, someone would hit him on the head with a stone. "Good heavens! How much hatred I won for myself," Luther reported to Spalatin. His reaction gave an early sign of his inclination when faced with civil unrest to side with the forces of order and authority—an attitude that would fatefully resurface when the peasants rose up a few years later.

Adding to Luther's unease were the reports he was receiving of Johann Eck's northward progress. "I almost wish that that notorious raging bull against my teaching would come from Rome," he wrote. That the Church had chosen such a bitter foe of his to deliver the document, he believed, showed its determination to crush him. Frederick, too, was coming under intense pressure to act. In July 1520, he received a letter from Cardinal Riario in Rome imploring him to force Luther to recant. "You can if you will," he wrote. "With just one little pebble the puny David killed the mighty Goliath." Frederick had the letter forwarded to Luther, who read it with "great and silent grief."

"The world presses me down and gnaws me piecemeal," he wrote, complaining of the "many ravenous wolves" who surrounded him. From friends came pleas to temper his language. Johann Lang (who a few months earlier had replaced Staupitz as vicar-general of the Augustinian Observants) was so disturbed by the ferocity of *To the Christian Nobility* that he implored Luther to recall it. "Almost all condemn my stinging tone," Luther wrote to a friend, adding that he had no intention of moderating it, "for I realize that those things which in our age are treated quietly will soon be forgotten, and nobody will care about them." Who could not see that the prophets attacked the sins of the people "with the greatest violence"?

Already, the prophet of Wittenberg was preparing another blast. At the end of *To the Christian Nobility*, he had noted that he was composing "another little song about Rome," to be pitched "in the highest key." This would be the second of his great Reformatory tracts. Whereas *To the Christian Nobility* had been written in German for the lay public, the new work would be written in Latin for the educated elite. That it was not to be an abstruse treatise, however, was apparent from its title: *The Babylonian Captivity of the Church*. Just as the Jews had been carried off from Jerusalem into exile, Luther suggested, so had Europe's Christians been led astray from Scripture and subjected to Roman tyranny.

With *The Babylonian Captivity*, Luther was moving from reform to revolution. Audacious and at times apocalyptic, it offered a fierce assault on the stronghold of Catholic piety—the seven sacraments. These were the primary source of clerical authority and power, and Luther would now take a hammer to them. *The Babylonian Captivity* would serve in effect as the charter document of Protestantism, helping to define its theology, prescribe its rituals, describe the status of its clergy, and outline its positions on marriage and sex.

The sacraments had always had a glaring vulnerability—their relatively recent vintage. They had not been fully defined until the mid-thirteenth century (by Peter Lombard) and their number had not been officially set at seven until 1439 (at the Council of Florence). Applying the principle that Scripture should be the sole authority, Luther would now test the sacraments against the text of the New Testament—and find most of them wanting.

First up was the Mass, or the Lord's Supper. This was the sacrament that had given Luther the most trouble during his early years as a priest. The intricate system of regulations, obligations, and admonitions prescribed by Gabriel Biel and other late Scholastics had brought on fits of terror. In his study of Scripture, however, Luther could find no textual basis for any of it, and he now denounced the way this most holy sacrament had been turned "into mere merchandise, a market, and a profit-making business," on which priests and monks depended for their livelihood—a reference to Masses for the dead and the rich endowments provided for them.

The main cause of these abuses, Luther maintained, was the specious doctrine that the Lord's Supper was "a good work and a sacrifice"—a re-enactment of Christ's redemptive death at Calvary. Defined in this way, it had become a rite that a churchgoer could count as a meritorious work along with fasts, vigils, and pilgrimages to shorten his stay in purgatory. Rather than approach the Mass as passive onlookers, Christians should actively participate in it, seeing it not as a commemoration of Christ's death but as a divine promise of forgiveness for sin to those who have faith in Christ. Luther favored retaining the Lord's Supper as a sacrament, but only if it was performed with the same simplicity and lack of ceremonial pomp that marked Christ's celebration of the Last Supper.

This emphasis on simplicity in the Mass led Luther to continue the task of chipping away at the authority of the priesthood that he had begun in *To the Christian Nobility*. By investing the Mass with so much mystery and miraculous power, he wrote, the Church had greatly enlarged the role of priests as intermediaries between the Christian and God. The physical distance separating the priest at the altar from the laymen in the pews; the withholding of the cup from worshippers during Communion; the whispering of the words of consecration by the priest, "as if they were too sacred to be delivered to the common people"—all such practices were aimed at sealing the rite off from the unclean laity and making it the preserve of a specialized caste. When the priest raises the sign of the sacrament, he should pronounce, "in a loud and clear voice," the words of consecration, and he should do so "in the language of the people," so that faith "may be the more effectively awakened."

To further encourage lay participation, Luther endorsed offering the wine as well as the bread during Communion. The proscription against this had arisen out of a fear that the laity in their carelessness might spill some of the blood of the Lord. Despite the risk, Luther felt that the cup should be made available to all believers, since Jesus at the Last Supper was explicit about this, saying as he offered the cup to his disciples, "Drink of it, all of you." Luther was here veering close to the Bohemian heresy, but what a year earlier had seemed so forbidding now seemed the only defensible course. "Rise up then, you popish flatterers, one and all!" he flared:

> Get busy and defend yourselves against the charges of impiety, tyranny, and lèse-majesté against the gospel, and of the crime of slandering your brethren. You decry as heretics those who refuse to contravene such plain and powerful words of Scripture in order to acknowledge the mere dreams of your brains!

It was not the Bohemians or the Greeks who were heretics and schismatics, for they based their stand on the Gospels, but Rome, which vaunted its own figments against the clear Word of God.

This idea, in turn, led Luther to arraign another key sacrament: priestly ordination. Since the New Testament contains not a single word about this practice, he wrote, it should be eliminated as an invention of the Church and the pope. By manipulating Scripture, the Church had sought "to set up a seed bed of implacable discord" between clergy and laity. The clergy not only exalt themselves above lay Christians but "regard them almost as dogs." The sacrament of the Eucharist "does not belong to the priests, but to all men. The priests are not lords but servants in duty bound to administer both kinds to those who desire them, as often as they desire them." "We are all equally priests," Luther declared; "that is to say, we have the same power in respect to the Word and the sacraments."

Luther was here seeking to transform the priesthood from a divinely ordained elite to a ministry defined by service and duty. From these rudiments would arise the idea of the clergy as a trained and salaried class, taking its place alongside other professions that were emerging in early modern Europe.

Luther similarly dismissed as unsupported by Scripture the sacramental status of confirmation, extreme unction (the ministering to the dying), and, most consequentially, marriage. Drawing on his work as a pastor and sometime marriage counselor, Luther offered a series of startling pronouncements about matrimony and sexuality. His starting point was Erasmus's observation in his annotations that the term *sacramentum* as used by the Vulgate to describe the status of marriage was actually given in the Greek as *mysterion*, or "mystery." Clearly, Luther wrote, there was no scriptural warrant whatsoever for regarding marriage as a sacrament. In declaring it one, the "Roman despots" were asserting oppressive control over what is a human institution, dissolving and compelling marriages as they pleased. The Church's impediments to marriage (eighteen in all, according to Luther) were imposed for the sole end of "filthy lucre," derived from the countless dispensations sought by those desperate to circumvent the Church's "shameful laws." "The Romanists of our day have through them become merchants. What is it they sell? Vulvas and penises."

According to Luther, the only circumstances justifying the annulment of a contracted marriage were impotence, ignorance of a previously contracted marriage, and a vow of chastity. In one of his wildest flights, he argued that if a woman's husband is impotent, she should be allowed to have intercourse with another man. Such an arrangement should be kept secret and the husband compelled to raise the offspring as his own. If he refused, the woman should be allowed to contract a marriage with another man and flee to a distant place.

On one key issue, though, Luther held fast: divorce. He considered it so repellent that even bigamy seemed preferable. Following Christ's position in the New Testament, Luther maintained that "unchastity" (adultery) was the only justifiable grounds for divorce. Apart from this one area, though, Luther was breaking decisively with the traditional Catholic attitude dating back to Augustine, Jerome, and Ambrose that considered sex shameful and physical passion as something to be feared. Luther went so far as to warn parents against committing their children to the monastic life, since its vow of perpetual chastity was so difficult for so many to keep. Luther had come to see sexuality as a natural part of the human condition as created by God—an attitude that would profoundly affect Protestant thinking on the subject.

As for baptism and penance, Luther held that Scripture justified retaining them as sacraments, but even here he denounced what he saw as the unnecessary burdens imposed by the Church. While the New Testament passages on baptism provided sanction for that rite, its true value had been obscured by the many extraneous requirements stipulated at the expense of faith. It was not these external rites but the quickening of the spirit associated with baptism that made it sacred.

Luther similarly rushed to "unmask the tyranny that is rampant" in the sacrament of penance and the rite of confession at its heart. While he acknowledged that the practice of private confession could not be proved from Scripture, he was convinced from his own experience of its value and so supported retaining it, but it had become a workshop "of greed and power." The Romanists had required such stringent satisfactions as to "torture poor consciences to death": one runs to Rome, another to Chartreuse; one scourges himself with rods, another mortifies his body with fasts and vigils. "For these monstrous things we are indebted to you, O Roman See, and to your murderous laws and ceremonies, with which you have corrupted all mankind." As a result, the true value of penance—the experience of genuine contrition for one's sins—had been seriously eroded.

Luther was here drawing on Erasmus's observation that the Vulgate's use of *poenitentia* ("penance") did not accurately capture the meaning of the underlying Greek term, *metanoia* ("to change one's mind"). Erasmus's philological insight thus became in Luther's hands the basis for a dramatic recasting of this key sacrament. By the time Luther was finished wielding his hammer, he had reduced the seven sacraments to two-plus—the Lord's Supper, baptism, and a greatly reduced version of penance.

Luther was not simply redefining the sacraments, however; in *The Babylonian Captivity*, he was unleashing a frontal attack on the authority and hierarchy of the Church. "Neither pope nor bishop nor any other man has the right to impose a single syllable of law upon a Christian man without his consent," he proclaimed, reflecting his radical Paulism. He added: "I lift my voice simply on behalf of liberty and conscience, and I confidently cry: No law, whether of man or of angels, may rightfully be imposed upon Christians without their consent, for we are free of all laws." Luther was thus arguing for a dramatic democratizing of the Church, with the power of the pope and prelates to rule over the laity sharply cut back.

With *The Babylonian Captivity*, Luther was breaking irrevocably with Rome. He was also distancing himself from Church moderates who until then had supported his program to curb Roman excesses and reanimate the faith. With a single blow, he had rent the curtain in the temple. Could the temple survive?

Even as *The Babylonian Captivity* was being prepared by the printers, Johann Eck was arriving in Germany. At first, all had gone smoothly for the Ingolstadt professor. On September 21, 1520, in the town of Meissen, seventy miles southeast of Wittenberg, he had arranged for the bull against Luther to be affixed to the doors of the cathedral. In the following days it was posted in Merseburg, sixty miles to the southwest, and in Brandenburg, forty miles to the northeast, giving the impression of a noose tightening around Wittenberg and Luther.

Then, on September 29, Eck reached Leipzig. A little more than a year earlier, he had been proclaimed the victor here in his disputation with Luther, but the atmosphere had changed dramatically. In the streets students shouted ribald songs after him and posted lampoons around town. Eck felt so threatened that he fled into the Dominican monastery, but even there he was assailed by angry letters, and the university refused to publish the bull.

Eck eventually managed to make it out of Leipzig, but since he dared not show his face in Wittenberg, he gave the bull to a Leipzig militiaman to take there; the militiaman handed it off to a resident of that town. Eck, meanwhile, headed for Erfurt. There, he was accosted by armed students who grabbed copies of the bull. Calling it a "bubble" (a play on the Latin word for "bull"), they tore it into bits and threw them into the river to see if they would float. In Torgau, the document was torn down and be-smeared. Finally, on October 10, the bull reached Peter Burkhard, the Wittenberg rector, and then, on October 11, Luther himself.

"At last that Roman bull brought by Eck has arrived," Luther an-nounced to Spalatin. Its demand that he recant without a hearing did not surprise him—this was how the Roman tyranny worked. What did shock him was the document's slipshod quality—its chaotic piling up of articles; its haughty refusal to explain how his propositions erred; its failure to distinguish among those that were heretical, offensive, scandalous, and impious. With the bull's arrival in Wittenberg, the sixty-day countdown to Luther's excommunication began, but he was characteristically defiant. "I despise it and am now attacking it as impious and fraudulent, Eckian to the core." He was referring to a tract that he was drafting in Latin in which he dismissed the bull as nothing but wasted paper and stated that it would be better to be killed a thousand times than to retract a single article of his own. Just as Rome's ecclesiasts had excommunicated him for blasphemous heresy, he wrote, "so I excommunicate them according to the holy truth of God."

Luther did not have much time to dwell on the matter, however, for he was expected in the town of Lichtenberg, eighty miles to the south, for another meeting with Karl von Miltitz. Since their last encounter, in Jan-uary 1519, the papal envoy had continued to ply his makeshift diplomacy, with little to show for it. Even at this late date, he remained convinced that the whole affair could be settled if Luther sent a personal appeal to the pope. Luther was dubious. In 1518, he had sent such a petition to Cardinal Cajetan. After his first meeting with Miltitz, he had written a conciliatory letter to Leo, which Miltitz had not even sent. In August 1520, at Freder-ick's behest, Luther had drafted an appeal to Charles V, requesting both protection and a fair hearing. Now Miltitz was urging him to approach the pope yet again. With the issuing of *Exsurge Domine*, such a gesture seemed pointless, but Luther, prodded by Frederick, agreed to meet.

The journey to Lichtenberg, undertaken in mid-October, posed great danger. Ulrich von Hutten had gone into hiding amid reports that the Romanists had hired a team to take him bound to Rome or even kill him.

Luther was even more desirable prey. On the trip he was accompanied by Melanchthon, a fellow friar, a nobleman, and four horsemen. Miltitz arrived with four horsemen of his own. In their meeting, which took place in a local cloister, Luther agreed to write a respectful letter to Leo offering his side of the affair and making it clear that he had never intended to attack the pope personally. He told Miltitz that he had an essay on Christian freedom in the works and would frame the letter as a dedication to it.

Back in Wittenberg, he immediately began work on the essay. The idea for it had arisen out of the continuing controversy over his position on works. Matthaeus Adrianus, the converted Jew who had been hired to fill the Hebrew chair, had turned violently against Luther over his teaching that good works avail nothing, and in sermons he was attacking him personally. Others shared Adrianus's anger, and Luther now sought to explain himself.

The Freedom of a Christian would be the third of his great 1520 tracts. In contrast to the bite of *To the Christian Nobility* and the rage of *The Babylonian Captivity*, Luther would now strike a serene, meditative tone. He sought to describe the deep personal transformation that faith can work in the Christian heart. His goal was to develop a foundation for good behavior free of the narrow calculus of self-interest that, he felt, tainted so much human activity.

Luther opened with a pair of paradoxical propositions that would become famous:

> A Christian is a perfectly free lord of all, subject to none.
> A Christian is a perfectly dutiful servant of all, subject to all.

Though these statements might seem contradictory, Luther wrote, they actually complement each other. Taking up the first, he offered his most lyrical tribute yet to the emancipating power of faith. The one thing on which a Christian life depends is the Word of God, and that Word becomes effective only through faith. Since faith alone justifies, and faith can rule only in the inner man, it is clear that man cannot be saved through any external works like dress, food, prayer, or meditation. Every Christian must thus lay aside all confidence in works and concentrate on his faith. "Every Christian is by faith so exalted above all things that, by virtue of a spiritual power, he is lord of all things without exception, so that nothing can do him any harm." For those who lack faith, by contrast, all things turn out badly, for they wickedly seek to turn everything to their own glory rather than to God's. Luther restated his idea that all Christians are priests and that to insist otherwise had produced a tyranny based on the "unbearable bondage" of human works and laws.

Taking up his second proposition, Luther wrote that because faith accomplishes all, some maintain that good works are not necessary. "I answer: not so, you wicked men, not so." Good works do not make a good man, but a good man does good works out of a spontaneous love for God. To illustrate the point, he took an image from Aristotle and turned it on its head. In the *Nicomachean Ethics*, the Greek philosopher argued that men become good or bad builders through building well or badly. The same was true of virtue, Aristotle wrote: we become just or unjust through our acts toward others. Luther rejected this. A good or bad house does not make a good or bad builder, but a good or bad builder makes a good or bad house. The work does not make the workman; the workman makes the work. So it is with the works of man. They are good if done by men of faith and wicked if done in unbelief, for faith alone justifies and saves the person.

Finally, Luther discussed the obligations a faithful Christian has toward others. A Christian should serve others in such a way as to seek advantage not for himself but only for his neighbor. Paul commanded us to give to the needy; he urged the stronger member to serve the weaker. The truly Christian life is one in which faith becomes active through love—through works undertaken freely without hope of reward. A Christian should not distinguish between friend and enemy or anticipate thankfulness or unthankfulness but freely and willingly give of himself and all that he has. By that standard, few monasteries, altars, or other church institutions were truly Christian, for their sole end was profit.

The Freedom of a Christian showed how consistent Luther's core ideas about faith and works had remained since his lectures on the Psalms and

Romans, but in this essay they had ripened into a resonant vision of piety made active in the world through faith. The image of the good builder constructing a good house would become well known.

As with many analogies, however, holes could be poked in it. While it no doubt takes a good builder to make a good house, a builder becomes good in part through the experience of building houses; in the end, he is judged not by his knowledge of architecture but by the quality of the houses he builds.

This image offered a measure of Luther's distance from not only Aristotle but also the Christian humanists. At many points, *The Freedom of a Christian* echoes the *Enchiridion*. Both are concerned with the inner person. Both hold that ceremonies, rites, and other external acts do not constitute true piety; one's internal spirituality is what matters. For Erasmus, however, faith is only one measure of a Christian's life; one's conduct—the quality of the house one builds—is no less vital. Luther's theology was also far more exclusivist than Erasmus's. In the latter's view, virtuous Gentiles like Socrates and Cicero outdid many Christians in exemplifying Christian values. To Luther, however, such figures, lacking faith in Christ, could not be truly moral actors; only faithful Christians could. For all their surface similarities, the *Enchiridion* and *The Freedom of a Christian* capture the sharply divergent worldviews of these two devotedly Christian thinkers.

Reflective, sincere, and concise, *The Freedom of a Christian* is perhaps Luther's most accessible work. That he wrote it while facing possible martyrdom makes its temperate tone all the more remarkable. In his own day, however, it would not succeed in putting the controversy over good works to rest. Readers would pay far more heed to the first than to the second of his opening propositions; works—for both him and them—would always remain secondary to faith. Even so, Luther's idea of the Christian inspired by his faith to apply the gospel in all realms of life would prove a world-changing concept.

If in *The Freedom of a Christian* Luther was at his most earnest, in his letter to Leo X he was at his most mocking. Forced to entreat the pope yet again, he sought to hide his exasperation under a cloak of deference. The result was a rhetorical tour de force—a disdainful put-down masquerading as a reverential tribute.

"Living among the monsters of this age with whom I am now for the third year waging war, I am compelled occasionally to look up to you, Leo, most blessed father, and to think of you," Luther began, immediately placing himself on a first-name basis with the pontiff. He was now writing because it had come to his attention that he stood accused of great indiscretion in his writings, "in which, it is said, I have not spared even your person." While to his knowledge he had spoken only good and honorable words about the pope whenever he had thought of him, he was sorry if he had ever done otherwise, for Leo's reputation and the fame of his blameless life were far too well known "to be assailed by anyone, no matter how great he is."

To be sure, he had "sharply attacked ungodly doctrines" and snapped at his opponents, and of this he did not repent, for he was following in the tradition of Christ, who in his zeal called his opponents a brood of vipers, and of Paul, who branded his adversaries as dogs and deceivers. What is the good of salt if it does not bite? While never thinking ill of Leo personally, he "truly despised" his see and the Roman Curia, which, as no one could deny, was "more corrupt than any Babylon or Sodom ever was" and which, as far as he could tell, was "characterized by a completely depraved, hopeless, and notorious godlessness." The Roman Church, once the holiest of all, "has become the most licentious den of thieves, the most shameless of all brothels, the kingdom of sin, death, and hell." In this den sat Leo, a "lamb in the midst of wolves," a "Daniel in the midst of lions."

Moved by his affection for him, Luther continued, "I have always been sorry, most excellent Leo, that you were made pope in these times, for you are worthy of being pope in better days." The Curia deserved to have not devout men like him but "Satan himself as pope, for he now actually rules in that Babylon more than you do." It was in the hope of saving Leo from his prison that he had made such a strong and stinging attack on it. And, while he was willing to remain silent if his opponents did the same, recant he never would.

In closing, Luther acknowledged that he was perhaps being presumptuous in seeking to instruct so exalted a personage, but, seeing His

Blessedness facing dangers on all sides, he felt that he was in need of even the slightest help from the least of his brothers. As a token of his goodwill, he was sending along a little treatise (*The Freedom of a Christian*). Though small in size, "it contains the whole of Christian life in a brief form, provided you grasp its meaning. I am a poor man and have no other gift to offer, and you do not need to be enriched by any but a spiritual gift."

There is no indication that Leo ever read Luther's letter. Many others did, however. The *Open Letter to Leo X* was immediately printed in Wittenberg and Augsburg. It, along with Luther's three 1520 tracts, set off tremors across Europe, and printers were forced to work overtime to meet the demand. "No one's books are bought more eagerly," Henricus Glareanus, a school instructor in Paris and a friend of Erasmus's, wrote to Huldrych Zwingli in Zurich. At the most recent fair in Frankfurt, he noted, one bookseller sold 1,400 copies of Luther's works. *The Babylonian Captivity* caused such commotion that in some places the authorities were already seeking to ban it.

Luther was unmoved. "I care nothing if my work *The Babylonian Captivity* is prohibited," he wrote in late October 1520. "What does it matter if all my books are prohibited? I will write nothing against those who use force against us. It is enough for me to have taught the truth against those stupid babblers, and to have defended it against the learned who alone are able to hurt." And "what if they kill me? I am not worthy to suffer aught in so blessed a cause." As for the papal bull, it had in no way frightened him; he intended "to preach, lecture, and write in spite of it."

And preach, lecture, and write he did. In this period, Luther stepped up his already prodigious work pace. On November 4, 1520—not long after completing *The Freedom of a Christian*—he finished *Against the Execrable Bull*, his attack, in Latin, on Leo's decree. Later in the month he produced a separate, substantially reworked version in German, *Against the Bull of the Antichrist*. In addition, he began preparing a long exposition on the Magnificat—the humble hymn of the Virgin Mary sung at vespers—as well as a series of postils—homilies on the New Testament—for use by preachers during Advent.

All the while, Luther was delivering daily sermons, giving lectures on the Psalms, and tending to his ever-expanding correspondence. He was helped out by his decision to abandon the canonical hours. He had so regularly fallen behind in saying them, and had so damaged his health in his effort to catch up, that he had finally given them up altogether—another way station on his flight from monasticism. He did, however, continue to wear the Augustinian habit and live in the Black Cloister.

With the approach of December 10, 1520, and the end of the sixty-day grace period stipulated in the bull, Luther had to decide how to respond. With his flair for the dramatic, he settled on an act that would rank among the boldest of his career. On the morning of December 10, Melanchthon posted a notice at the town church calling on all "pious and zealous youth" to assemble at nine o'clock at the chapel of the Holy Cross, which lay just outside the town's eastern walls. At a spot near the Elbe where cattle were butchered, about one hundred students, bundled against the cold, gathered together with Luther, Melanchthon, and other faculty members. Some wood was arranged in a pile and lit by a master of arts. To the flames were fed volumes containing the canon law, the papal decretals, and the *Extravagantes*; a manual for father confessors; and works by Johann Eck and other adversaries of Luther.

As the books were consumed, Luther, trembling and praying, stepped forward and, barely noticed by anyone, added a printed copy of the bull to the flames. Invoking Psalm 21, he said softly, "Because thou hast brought down the truth of God, he also brings thee down unto this fire today, Amen." The students lingered by the flames, singing the *Te Deum Laudamus* and other hymns.

Back in his study, Luther wrote a note to Spalatin informing him of his act. In some ways, burning the canon law and the decretals was even more daring than destroying the bull, for they provided the legal foundation for all ecclesiastical power.

The students, however, treated the event as a lark. In town, they commandeered a farm wagon, in the front of which rode four boys in formal dress who, representing the vanquished "Synagogue" (a symbol of ceremony-addled Rome), chanted dirgelike fragments in Hebrew. Behind them, a flag-bearer brandished a four-foot-long version of the bull, waving it like a plundered standard. As the wagon made its way through the streets, it was heralded by the discordant blasts of a trumpet. As bewildered townspeople looked on, the wagon gradually filled with the tracts of papists, sophists, and enemies of the new gospel. From houses and sheds, shingles were taken to serve as kindling, and the students, returning to the site of the earlier pyre, read mockingly from the bull, sang more dirges, and fed the newly collected books to the flames.

Hearing of this buffoonery, Luther became furious, and at his next day's lecture on the Psalms, he admonished the students about the serious business that lay ahead. Burning the decretals was child's play compared with what was now required—burning the papacy itself, together with its false teachings and cruel policies. Those who failed to oppose with their full hearts the ridiculous rule of the pope would not be saved. It would be far better to live in a desert than to continue suffering in this kingdom of the Antichrist.

"Everything is tending towards a tremendous revolution, of which the outcome is uncertain," Wolfgang Capito wrote to Luther from Mainz in December 1520. Capito had moved there from Basel to take a position with Archbishop Albrecht. From friends, he had heard of the many threats being directed at Luther. While the people stood unanimously behind him, Capito went on, his enemies were protected "by strong bulwarks, castles and moats" and had access to money, arms, and manpower. Expressing concern over the uncompromising course Luther had chosen, Capito, quoting from Paul, called on him to "consider our weakness, that we need milk rather than strong meat," and not to test the devotion of the people "by asking too much of them."

Luther brushed aside such counsels. Seething at the hatred he felt on all sides, he dashed off a pamphlet explaining (as its title put it) *Why the Books of the Pope and His Disciples Were Burned by Doctor Martin Luther.* Mimicking the form of the bull, Luther listed thirty errors that he had found in canon law, the most important of which was the teaching that no one could judge the pope, whereas the pope could judge everyone else. Through this article, Luther argued, all misfortune had entered the world. Not once had the pope sought to refute him through Scripture or reason. "If they are allowed to burn my articles, in which there is more gospel and more of the true substance of Holy Scripture" than "in all the pope's books, then I am justified much more in burning their unchristian law books in which there is nothing good."

As the news of Luther's burning of the bull spread around Christendom, it was greeted with wonder and disbelief. When word reached Rome, the Curia at once began preparing a new bull to formally excommunicate him. Issued on January 3, 1521, *Decet Romanum Pontificem* ("It Pleases the Roman Pontiff") was immediately sent north by messenger to Jerome Aleander, who was now in Worms.

There, final preparations were being made for the new Imperial Diet, scheduled to begin on January 6, 1521. It would be the first diet presided over by the new emperor. With German nationalist fervor rising, with rage at Rome surging, with Luther's books stirring excitement and indignation from the Rhine to the Oder, with all looking to the young Charles to lead the cause of reform, the diet was shaping up as the most historic gathering in Western Europe since the Council of Constance of 1414. Just as Jan Hus's fate had been decided at that assembly, so would Martin Luther's be determined at Worms.

WILL HE COME?

The Reichstag, as the Imperial Diet was called, was the main deliberative body of the Holy Roman Empire. Worms hosted it more than one hundred times between the eighth and sixteenth centuries, earning it the title "Mother of Diets." The town would prove unequal to this one, however. In the weeks prior to its start, the roads into Worms were clogged with the retinues of arriving princes, bishops, and knights. William, duke of Bavaria, came with five hundred horses, and Philip, margrave of Baden, brought six hundred. Just ferrying them across the wintry Rhine (Worms sat on its western bank) required military-like prowess. With so much at stake, the diet attracted Spanish noblemen, Italian diplomats, French and English envoys, and officials from Savoy, Venice, Denmark, Poland, and Hungary, all ready to carry word of its proceedings to the far corners of Europe.

Worms had a population of 7,000, but the influx from the diet would nearly double it. Food was expensive, firewood was scarce, and lodgings were overcrowded. In the inns, knights slept five or six to a room, and a dozen grooms were forced to make do with a single bundle of straw. The emperor himself, staying in the bishop's palace that adjoined the cathedral, had to share a room with Chièvres, his aging counselor, who in any case wanted to keep watch over him.

The crush, in turn, fed the unrest in town. For the past two decades, Worms and its environs had simmered with discontent. In the countryside, peasants had periodically risen up against their feudal overlords, demanding relief from oppressive levies, while town residents constantly feuded with the bishop. As an imperial free city, Worms answered directly to the emperor rather than the Church, yet the clergy retained many privileges, and the citizenry had had to endure many an interdict. Looming over the town was the Dom, or cathedral, a great sandstone monument that, with four Romanesque towers, two domes, and a choir at each end, projected a sense of ecclesiastical might. Anticlerical sentiment ran deep.

So did support for Luther. Like other Rhenish towns, Worms had been flooded with his books, and everyone who had read them, or had heard them read, felt that something momentous was afoot. A popular broadsheet carried an image of Luther's powerful, gaunt head (taken from an engraving by Cranach), sometimes with a dove above, sometimes with a halo. "The people buy these pictures, kiss them, and carry them even in the palace," Jerome Aleander wrote in one of his dispatches to Rome.

Arriving in Worms at the end of November 1520, the papal nuncio was struck by the insurrectionary air in its streets. Former students whom he encountered fled as if from an outlaw, while ordinary citizens accosted him to praise Luther. To his surprise, many priests and monks from orders other than Luther's own seemed ready to defend him to the death. Even more disturbing to Aleander were the widespread rumors that Ulrich von Hutten and his cohort were plotting to murder him. Hutten had taken up residence in the Ebernburg, the fortress of the knight-adventurer Franz von Sickingen, which was located a day's journey to the north and controlled the Rhine valley. "Do you think you can intimidate us by burning books?" Hutten declared. "The question will not be settled by the pen but by the sword." "I feel less safe in this city than on the Campagna," Aleander noted, referring to the bandit-infested region outside Rome.

Knowing how crowded Worms would be, the nuncio had reserved rooms well in advance, but when he went to claim them, he was turned away. He fared no better elsewhere. Despite his willingness to pay more than anyone else, Aleander had to settle for a grim garret in a poor man's house. "I suffer unaccustomed hardship," he lamented. "On the icy bank of the Rhine, I, who have been accustomed to a comfortable heated room from September to May, lack a fire."

Despite the chilly climate, the diet offered Aleander an opportunity to mobilize the German ruling class against the wayward sheep who was leading the flock astray. The key to silencing Luther clearly lay with the emperor. Aleander had been greatly heartened by the imperial edict that Charles had issued against Luther in September 1520, ordering the burning of his books. "The Emperor is a man of the best disposition, such as has hardly appeared for a thousand years," Aleander reported to Rome; "were it not for him, our business would be very much complicated by private passions."

Aleander was thus aghast to find that, two days before his arrival in Worms, the emperor had sent a friendly letter to Frederick the Wise (who was in Saxony for the Christmas season). Playfully addressing the elector as "dear uncle," Charles noted his desire to "put down this movement" from which so much disorder was feared, and to that end he asked the elector to bring Luther with him to the diet to be examined by a learned panel. Until then, Charles added, he hoped that Frederick would direct Luther not to write anything against the pope or the Roman See.

How, Aleander wondered, could Charles have made such a concession? The pope alone was authorized to judge matters of heresy, and since he had already spoken, any hearing granted to Luther would be an intolerable affront to his office. It was the principle of papal supremacy that above all else had to be preserved; there thus could be no examination or debate.

Charles's commitment to that principle was incontestable. But, as he prepared for the diet, Luther was only one of his many preoccupations. Since his departure from Spain, the Comunero uprising had quickly spread, with the rebels seizing control of Valladolid, Toledo, and other key cities. To the east, Sultan Selim's son and successor, Suleiman I the Magnificent, was threatening to march on Belgrade. If he succeeded in capturing it, Hungary could soon follow. More immediately, Charles was intent on traveling to Rome to be crowned emperor by the pope—an act that would confer formal recognition on his imperial claims. But getting his large court there would require a huge outlay. It would also require passing through northern Italy and confronting the French, who controlled Milan. Charles thus needed to form an army, which meant hiring German *Landsknechts* and Swiss mercenaries.

The funding for that would have to come from the German princes, but they in return wanted their own concerns addressed. Fed up with the chaos, violence, and inefficiency of the German political system, they longed for a functioning state that could enforce order, adjudicate disputes, and regulate commerce. They also wanted protection from Rome and a resolution of the lists of grievances that had been regularly submitted—and ignored—at previous diets.

Gaining the cooperation of the Germans would also require addressing the matter of Luther. The delegates were divided between those moved by Luther's call on the ruling class to defend the interests of the German people and those troubled by the unrest he was causing, and as preparations for the diet proceeded, it was unclear where the balance of sentiment lay.

Luther's greatest asset was Frederick. Earlier, at his meeting with Charles in Cologne, the elector had impressed on the emperor the importance of the idea that no German should be banned without cause or hearing. To achieve his own goals, Charles needed Frederick's support, and so on November 28, 1520, he had sent him the letter asking him to bring Luther to Worms.

Aleander, however, felt that Luther's presence, in addition to showing disrespect for the pope, could lead to many unforeseen consequences, and so from the moment of his arrival in Worms, he worked to keep Luther from appearing there. He had received a boost from the appearance of *The Babylonian Captivity*. Its fierce assault on the Mass, its radical redefinition of penance, and its insistence that all Christians are priests had made clear that Luther was a "heretic a thousand times worse than Arius," the fourth-century sower of doubts about the Trinity.

In mid-December, Aleander got in to see the emperor. Assuring the nuncio that he would act as a truly Christian prince, Charles invited him to address the Imperial Council, the empire's executive arm. In his speech, Aleander sought to expose "the grossest errors of this rascal," as he reported to Rome. He called *The Babylonian Captivity* blasphemous for denying all distinctions among Christians and for disdaining obedience to the spiritual authorities. The nuncio produced documents showing that, as far back as the reign of Charlemagne, the Germans had referred to the pope as *Papa Romanae et Universalis Ecclesiae Pontifex* ("the Roman Pope and Pontiff of the Universal Church"). Impressed, Charles on December 17 sent Frederick a letter withdrawing his earlier request to bring Luther to the diet and imploring him instead to press the friar to recant and submit to Rome's judgment. Frederick, he wrote, should bring Luther not to Worms but to Frankfurt or some other nearby place and await further instruction.

On January 5, 1521, Frederick and his advisers arrived in Worms, taking rooms at the Swan tavern. The town was so crowded that the elector had trouble finding quarters for his brother, the co-regent of Saxony. The streets swarmed with princes and bishops with their entourages; *Landsknechts* with their swords; and Spanish, Italian, and Dutch merchants come to sell their wares. Every day Spanish grandees galloped through the marketplace, causing the crowd to scatter. Knights and grooms relieved themselves at every corner, creating breeding pools of contagion. There were fights over food and lodgings and wild scenes in the taverns, with knives frequently drawn. Even at church, nobles contended over seating, with some leaving in a huff rather than accept a place they considered beneath their rank.

Owing to all the jockeying, the diet's opening session was delayed until January 27, 1521. When it finally did convene, the question of Luther— the one thing for which the diet would be remembered—was not even on the agenda. The major items were establishing an efficient administration, reorganizing the judicial system, strengthening law enforcement, reforming the tax code, and addressing the latest list of German grievances, which now numbered more than one hundred. Charles's proposed journey to Italy also needed to be addressed. With the emperor planning to leave Germany at the diet's close, establishing a structure to govern in his absence was considered essential.

The Reichstag consisted of three estates—electors, princes, and representatives of cities—with each making decisions by majority vote and plenary sessions held to ratify actions. The princes' chamber, with forty-five ecclesiastical lords and twenty-seven lay eminences, carried the most weight. Most sessions took place in the town hall, a stately civic monument located a short walk from the cathedral. To accommodate the emperor, a glittering throne was erected in the main meeting hall.

Inside the hall, Luther's name was rarely mentioned; outside, it dominated all conversation. The secretary of the Venetian ambassador noted the rousing effect that Luther's burning of the canon law was having on the German population. He had learned that Luther "has twenty thousand comrades of like mind." A woodcut by Hans Holbein the Younger showed Luther as the German Hercules, holding in his mouth a cord at the end of which dangles a strangled pope. In his left hand Luther clutches Hoogstraten, whom he is about to bludgeon with a spiked club; lying bloodied on the ground are Aristotle, Aquinas, Lyra, Ockham, Lombard, and Scotus, in a tableau crackling with the violence that seemed about to erupt on the street.

At every point, Aleander found his position undermined. The contents of his dispatches to Rome were promptly leaked, then recirculated with rumor and innuendo. And he felt he knew who was responsible: Erasmus. The Dutchman, he believed, had spies in Rome who kept him informed of Aleander's every move. The nuncio found this particularly disturbing in light of how close the two men had once been. "I shared lodging and bed with him at Venice once for six months, and he considered it not beneath his dignity to hear my daily lectures on Plutarch's *Ethics* according to the Greek text," he complained to Cardinal Giulio de' Medici; Aleander urged him to make sure the pope did not place more trust in Erasmus than in him.

Earlier, Aleander had surmised that Erasmus was the real author of Luther's books, but he had since concluded otherwise. Even so, he considered Erasmus "the greatest corner-stone of this heresy," who had helped prepare the way for Luther through his promotion of Greek, his revision of the New Testament, his rejection of ceremonies, and his disdain for the dialecticians. In fact, Aleander believed, Erasmus's ironic style and moderate tone had done more than Luther's fulminations to undermine ecclesiastical authority. Intent on fighting back, Aleander circulated an epigram that was just then gaining currency: "Erasmus laid the egg that Luther hatched."

Erasmus had originally planned to attend the diet, in part so that he could refute such allegations. In Louvain, he heard many variations on them. "Luther is pestilential, but Erasmus more so, for Luther sucked all his poison from Erasmus' teats," went one. A widely circulated broadsheet, titled *Die göttliche Mühle* ("The Godly Mill"), featured a drawing of Christ pouring the wheat of the Gospels into a mill, Erasmus bagging the flour, and Luther kneading the dough into books, which are being rejected by a pope, a cardinal, and a bishop. Above, a bird crying "ban" prepares to attack Luther but is repelled by a faithful peasant wielding a flail.

Being yoked to Luther became especially dangerous after the appearance of *The Babylonian Captivity*. Until then, Erasmus had approved of much of the substance of Luther's writings, objecting mainly to their vehement tone, but Luther's willingness to tamper with the sacraments shocked him. "His *De captivitate Babylonica* alienates many people," he observed, "and he is proposing something more frightful every day. I do not see what he is hoping for in setting this on foot, unless perhaps he is relying on the Bohemians." Paying Luther back for comparing him to a he-goat whose horns are caught in a thornbush, Erasmus wrote that Luther was like "the he-goat who has got himself into a pit without stopping to think how he is to get out."

While the diet would have given Erasmus an opportunity to defend himself, he would also have come under intense pressure to speak out against Luther. He was especially wary of Aleander—"a maniac, a wicked stupid man," he called him. (Erasmus was also worried about a reported outbreak of the plague in Worms.) To add to the pressure, the pope himself was now demanding action. The previous September, Erasmus had written to Leo X to affirm his allegiance to the Church; in passing, he noted that he had not read enough of Luther to judge him. In his reply, the pope dismissed that claim as unpersuasive. "Never was the time more opportune or the cause more just for setting your erudition and your powers of mind against the impious," the pontiff wrote, "nor is anyone better suited than yourself—such is our high opinion of your learning—for this praiseworthy task," i.e., writing against Luther. While he admired Erasmus's expression of goodwill toward the Holy See, the pope observed, it required a demonstration.

If he complied with Leo's request, Erasmus would enjoy all the favors Rome could provide. He would also gain a respite from the attacks of the sophists and potbellies. But if he denounced Luther, the enemies of the Muses would be emboldened. The Vulgate would go unchallenged, Greek and Hebrew would be neglected, Scotus and Aquinas would again reign in the universities. And, no doubt, Luther's own supporters would begin to assail him.

What Erasmus wanted above all else was to be left alone. "I would rather be a spectator of the play than one of the actors," he wrote to Johannes Reuchlin (who had come out vehemently against Luther). Feeling the years slipping away, Erasmus wanted to devote his remaining time to promoting the philosophy of Christ. By this point, he was absorbed in preparing the third edition of his New Testament. And so, pleading ill health, Erasmus decided to skip the diet. He instead wrote a series of letters to several key counselors and prelates in Worms, describing the middle course he hoped to steer at this decisive moment in European affairs. The pope's supporters "have no ideas except to eat Luther alive, and it is not my business whether they prefer him boiled or roast," he callously observed in one of them. But, he added, as dangerous as Luther's teachings might seem, the Church also had to resist the ignorant clamor of his enemies. While determined to stay clear of Luther, Erasmus could not approve of men such as these. To the Church alone he would remain true: "Christ I recognize. Luther I know not."

With the approach of Lent in mid-February 1521, Erasmus—dreading the prospect of another forty-day period of postponed meals and servings of smelly fish—left for Antwerp and the house of his friend Pieter Gillis. Just entering its golden age, this metropolis on the Scheldt was as open and cosmopolitan as any in Europe. Every day, dozens of ships bearing Indian spices, German copper, and English cloth put in there, fortifying its place as the center of the world economy. The arts thrived, the luxury-goods trade boomed, printing houses proliferated, and humanists came to breathe freely. Many of them met regularly at the Gillis dinner table. Among the guests during Erasmus's stay was Albrecht Dürer, who was using Antwerp as a base for his travels around the Netherlands (and who greatly admired Erasmus).

Even here, though, Erasmus could not escape the commotion over Luther. Antwerp's printers were doing a brisk trade in Luther's books. Local Marranos (Spaniards and Portuguese of Jewish extraction) had his works translated and printed in Spanish, and German merchants were eagerly promoting his ideas. Prominent citizens like Cornelius Grapheus, the town clerk, and Jacob Probst, the prior of the Augustinian friars, were moving into Luther's camp. Here as elsewhere, Luther's teachings about the personal transformation that faith can work in the heart, and about the radical change needed in society as a whole, were kindling the people. By comparison, Erasmus's appeals to reason, free will, and moral virtue seemed chilly, piecemeal, and uninspiring.

In Wittenberg, meanwhile, Luther was desperately trying to find out what was going on in Worms. Despite its emergence as Europe's most dynamic theological center, the town remained geographically remote, with couriers needing a week or more to cover the distance from the Rhineland. Spalatin was Luther's main source of information about the diet, and the friar's spirits rose and fell according to the reports he received. Luther was disappointed to learn that the emperor's close advisers all seemed opposed to him, but he was heartened by the news that Charles might summon him to Worms. When Spalatin asked how he would respond to such a directive, Luther assured him that he would go, even if it seemed likely that force would be used against him. "No one's danger, no one's safety can be considered here," he wrote. He would prefer to perish at the hands of the Romanists alone than to have Charles's administration stained early by bloodshed, as Sigismund's had been with Hus's.

Luther's fearlessness was inspiring others. "Rumor constantly tells us how little you are frightened by the threat of tyrants, how bravely you despise death, how much you wish to endure a thousand dangers for Christ's sake," the Erfurt humanist Crotus Rubianus wrote to him. Crotus reported hearing a canon speculate that it would not be hard for someone to kidnap Luther and deliver him to the pope. He warned Luther to be watchful, like Argus.

In the first weeks of 1521, cartloads of Luther's books were burned in the Saxon towns of Merseburg and Meissen. Confessors in several locales were demanding that penitents hand over any volumes by Luther in their possession and denying them absolution if they refused. To help guide them, Luther quickly drafted a pamphlet offering an actual script they could follow when questioned. "Let nothing on earth," he wrote, "even if it were an angel from heaven, be so great as to drive you against your conscience and away from the teaching you recognize and regard as God's."

Johann von Staupitz, Luther's old mentor, was coming under intense pressure to renounce Luther's teachings. In 1520, he had resigned his office as vicar-general of the Augustinian Observants and accepted an invitation from Cardinal Lang in Salzburg to serve as court preacher. There, Staupitz hoped to live out his remaining days in peace, but Lang, pressed hard by Rome, ordered him to appear before witnesses to testify that Luther's opinions were heretical. Staupitz in fact differed with Luther on many points but had resisted saying so publicly. As the threats against him mounted, however, he agreed to sign an equivocal statement against Luther and submit it to the pope. "Martin has begun a hard task and acts with great courage, divinely inspired," Staupitz wrote dolefully to Wenceslas Link on January 4, 1521. "I stammer and am a child needing milk."

When he heard of Staupitz's action, Luther was furious. "If Christ loves you, he will make you revoke that declaration," he wrote. Staupitz "should have stood up for Christ and contradicted the pope's impiety." This was "not the time to tremble but to cry aloud, while our Lord Jesus is being condemned, burned, and blasphemed." As much as Staupitz exhorted him to humility, Luther urged Staupitz to pride: "You are too yielding, I am too stiff-necked." Staupitz's submission, he wrote, showed that he was a different man from the one who had taught him about grace and the cross. Toward weaker colleagues unwilling to follow him into martyrdom, Luther was unforgiving.

Despite the threats pressing in on him, Luther maintained his extraordinary work pace, and—producing letter after letter, sermon after sermon, book after book—he kept four presses busy, as a Wittenberg student marveled. In addition to his two earlier denunciations of the bull against him, Luther composed two more: one in Latin and one in German. The latter (which as usual was more truculent than the former) showed his growing messianism: "God did not choose many eminent and great bishops for his work. St. Augustine was bishop in one little unimportant city, but did he not accomplish more than all the Roman popes with all their fellow-bishops?" Even if he were not a prophet, "I am sure that the Word of God is with me and not with them, for I have the Scriptures on my side and they have only their doctrine. This gives me courage, so that the more they despise and persecute me, the less I fear them."

Luther's zest for combat was most apparent in his polemical skirmishes with Hieronymus Emser, a Dresden-based humanist and secretary for Duke George who, after the Leipzig debate, raised questions about Luther's orthodoxy. The two men began exchanging tracts filled with wild abuse, with Emser playing off Luther's reputation as a "raging bull" and Luther calling Emser a goat. (The coat of arms of Emser's family featured a shield and a helmet adorned with a goat.) *Answer to the Hyperchristian, Hyperspiritual, and Hyperlearned Book by Goat Emser in Leipzig* went the title of one of Luther's attacks. Far from regretting such rancor, Luther felt it confirmed the righteousness of his mission. The preaching of the gospel, he wrote, "must and should cause quarreling, disunity, dissension, and disturbance. Such was the condition of Christianity at the time of the apostles and martyrs, and that was its best time. The discord, dissension, and disturbance produced by God's word are blessed events. With them begins a true faith and struggles against false faith."

Around this time, Luther began referring to his teachings as *evangelische*, or "evangelical," an adjective he adapted from *evangelium*, Latin for "gospel." Luther was thus asserting a connection between his own spiritual message and the good tidings spread by Christ and the apostles, in contrast to the tired doctrines proffered by Rome. (To this day, the Lutheran church in Germany is known as the Evangelische Kirche im Deutschland.)

At the end of January 1521, Joachim I, the elector of Brandenburg, stopped in Wittenberg on his way from Berlin to Worms so that he could meet Luther. On February 3, Luther dined with Duke Bogislav of Pomerania, who was also on his way to the diet. From Worms itself, however, no word about his fate came.

With the approach of Lent and the prayer and fasting it demanded, Luther's sense of frustration and inadequacy grew. To add to it, the lectures he was giving on the Psalms were not going well. Though far more conversant in Hebrew than he had been during his earlier lectures on the Psalms, he was getting even more bogged down in them. His notes were so long that the printers were bringing them out ten psalms at a time. Examining the page proofs for the second volume, Luther felt disgust at their "verbosity, lack of order, and chaotic arrangement." At that moment, he was working on Psalm 22, and its opening line—"My father, why hast thou abandoned me?"—seemed a chilling premonition of what might befall him at Worms.

In Worms itself, there was little fasting or contemplation. Many of the delegates saw the diet as an opportunity to drink, wench, and tourney, and even during Lent they gorged on mutton, boar, pigeons, eggs, and cheese. The guards of princes confiscated wood for fuel, and fights broke out over food as supplies dwindled. "There is racing and jousting almost every day," Prince Frederick complained to his brother; "otherwise everything makes very slow progress."

From the opening session, the delegates intently studied Charles V— and were disappointed. His inability to understand the High German in which the diet was conducted made him seem stiff and remote. Most matters of substance were referred to a commission, from which decisions never seemed to emerge. "The court is so utterly parlous and wretched that no one who has not seen it would believe it," an Austrian wrote home. "The emperor is a child; he takes no action on his own but is under the thumb of some Netherlanders who concede to us Germans neither honor nor any good quality."

Charles's top priority was the planned expedition to Rome, and the discussion of its financing and execution consumed many sessions. When it came to the delegates' demands for curbing Rome's usurpations, however, he appeared indifferent. He was far more receptive to Aleander's appeals to act against Luther. With the envoy's help, Charles had an edict drafted that banned Luther and his books. When it was submitted to the diet, though, the delegates summarily rejected it. No countryman of theirs, they declared, should face such a judgment without first receiving a hearing.

They were strongly influenced by the growing ferment on the streets, which was fed by the *Flugschriften* pouring into Worms. The town had recently gotten its first printing press, which was turning out inflammatory dialogues and lampoons. Many of the pamphlets celebrated *Karsthans*—an idealized, upright man of the soil with an instinctive grasp of the Gospels. Passed from hand to hand, these ephemera gave voice to popular complaints about tithes and the endless fees demanded by parish priests. The mood was captured by a pamphlet showing side-by-side images of Luther holding a book and Hutten clutching a sword. "To the Champions of Christian Freedom," it declared.

Luther's own books were being brought into Worms from the spring fair in Frankfurt, taking place not forty miles away. By this time, half a million copies of his works were in circulation in the empire, and their sheer profusion seemed to attest to an urgent desire for change among the German people. "The whole of Germany is in full revolt," Aleander reported to Rome. "Nine-tenths raise the war cry 'Luther,' while the watchword of the other tenth who are indifferent to Luther is 'Death to the Roman Curia.'" Nothing else was bought in Worms "except Luther's books, even in the imperial court." He himself, Aleander added, had been made an object of such hatred by the burning of Luther's books that it was at great peril that he remained in Germany:

> You won't believe me until (May God prevent it!) I am stoned or torn to pieces by these people, who, if they meet me on the street, always put their hands to their swords or grind their teeth, and, with a German curse, threaten me with death. . . . Mindful of what may happen, I now commend my soul to God's mercy, and ask from his Holiness full absolution.

Despite the growing agitation against the Church, Aleander refused to modify his position in any way. "Heretics," he wrote, in words that could serve as an epigram for the age, "must be punished with an iron rod and with fire, and if they persist in their contumacy, their bodies must be destroyed that their souls may be saved."

For his determination, Aleander was rewarded with an invitation to address the diet on February 13, 1521. It was his last chance to win over the delegates to the urgent need to silence Luther. Battling a fever, he worked through the night on his speech. Lasting three hours, it made a more forceful case against Luther than the bull of excommunication itself had. Through Luther, Aleander declared, Jan Hus had been summoned back to life. Like all heretics, he appealed to the Holy Scriptures while rejecting those parts that did not support him. He challenged the pope's authority and declared that Germans should wash their hands in the blood of papists. Aleander concluded by demanding the adoption of an edict that would proclaim Luther a Hussite and proscribe his writings and order them burned.

Two days later an imperial edict to that effect was submitted to the diet. It caused a storm. The normally restrained Frederick almost came to blows with the margrave of Brandenburg, and the usually taciturn elector of the Palatinate bellowed like a bull against the proposed decree. If Luther were condemned without a hearing, the estates declared in their reply, the people would rise up in the streets.

After many raucous sessions, a compromise was worked out: Luther would be called to Worms, but only so that he could recant. No debate or discussion would be allowed. Remarkably, though, the summons that was drafted made no mention of recantation. It simply stated that Luther's presence was requested "to obtain information about certain doctrines and certain books which formerly originated with you"; he was to be granted a safe-conduct lasting twenty-one days from the time it reached him. Curiously, the letter addressed him as "Honorable, dear, and pious Sir!"—no way to summon a heretic, the horrified Aleander thought. Though completed on March 6, 1521, the document was not signed by the emperor until a week or so later. In the meantime, Charles went ahead and—without the diet's consent—ordered the earlier edict banning Luther and his writings posted throughout the empire.

The summons was entrusted to the imperial herald, Kaspar Sturm. On March 16, Sturm—bearing a square yellow banner emblazoned with the black two-headed eagle that symbolized imperial power—set off on horseback on the long ride across Germany to Wittenberg. In the streets, taverns, and pews of Worms, one subject reigned: Would Luther come?

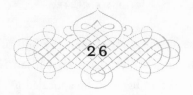

JUDGMENT AT WORMS

In Wittenberg, arrangements were under way for Holy Week, and at the town church Luther prepared his congregation for this period of solemn reflection before Easter. His routine, however, was shattered by the arrival of yet another furious broadside, this one from Ambrosius Catharinus, a Dominican canon lawyer in Italy. Catharinus attacked Luther for his godless and pestilential views, with special fury aimed at his doctrine of Scripture alone. Because the Bible is not always clear, he declared, it requires the Church to provide the proper interpretation, and he called on Luther to repent.

"Good Heavens! what an inept, stupid Thomist!" Luther jeered to Spalatin in early March 1521. "He almost kills us, first with laughing, then with boredom. I will answer him briefly and thus move the Italian beast's bile." For Luther, writing short was much harder than writing long, and as his word count mounted, so did his rage. The *Answer to the Book of Our Esteemed Master Ambrosius* would be Luther's most sulfurous tract yet, with page after page of vitriol directed at Catharinus, the pope, and the synagogue of Satan, i.e., the Church. Dilating at length on the books of Daniel and Revelation, he declared that the Roman Antichrist and his apologists would perish in a maelstrom of fire, hail, and blood. Only the faithful remnant would survive the calamity that God planned to visit on a world sunk in sin. This new apocalyptic note in Luther's writings no doubt reflected the threat of annihilation he now faced. In the coming years, he would repeatedly return to it, thus implanting in Protestant thinking a preoccupation with the onset of the last days—a tendency that would feed fanaticism and set off periodic violent eruptions.

Lucas Cranach (with Luther's help) designed a series of woodcuts that reflected the virulence of the anti-Roman feeling in Wittenberg. They contrasted the merciful ministry of Christ with the depraved practices of the Antichrist, i.e., the pope. One pair showed Christ washing the feet of his disciples and the pope's feet being kissed; another juxtaposed Christ's crown of thorns with the papal tiara. This would become the famous *Passional Christi und Antichristi*, a potent visual tool for spreading the gospel—and hatred of Rome—among the unlettered.

About March 26, 1521—five days or so before Easter—there was a commotion at the town gates. Kaspar Sturm, the imperial herald, had arrived after a breakneck journey across Germany. Directed to the Augustinian cloister, he delivered to Luther the letter from the emperor, requesting his presence in Worms, and the twenty-one-day safe-conduct. Luther was greatly relieved to see that the summons made no mention of recantation; at last, it seemed, he was going to get the hearing he had so long sought. The town fathers procured from Christian Döring, a local goldsmith who also ran a carriage business, a partly covered wagon and horse to carry Luther and those who would accompany him: the theologian Nikolaus von Amsdorf, the Augustinian friar Johann Petzensteiner, and a young Pomeranian nobleman named Peter von Suaven.

As he prepared to leave Wittenberg, Luther felt sure he was going to his death. Though he had a safe-conduct, the fate of Jan Hus showed how easily it could be disregarded. "My dear brother," he said to Melanchthon, "if I do not come back, if my enemies put me to death, you will go on teaching and standing fast in the truth; if you live, my death will matter little."

On April 2, 1521, the little "Saxon cart" (as Luther called it) crossed the Elbe and headed south. Leading the way was the herald Sturm, who, bearing the imperial coat of arms, was to make sure Luther arrived safely. As they proceeded through the springtime countryside, something extraordinary happened. In towns and villages along the way, ordinary people came out to greet the intrepid friar who had been excommunicated by Rome and who was now on his way to face the emperor. Sturm (who, it turned out, was fiercely anticlerical) encouraged such displays, and as the wagon continued on, Germans young and old, educated and illiterate, fell in line behind it, following in reverent silence to the next town, where a new group appeared. In the inns where Luther and his party stayed, crowds pressed in to wish him well. By the time he reached Naumburg, a picturesque town in the Saale valley, the trip had taken on the feel of a triumphal march.

As the party approached Weimar, however, there was a more ominous moment. An acquaintance from Wittenberg returning from the Rhineland informed Luther of the publication of the imperial edict that had been issued at Worms. Soon, Luther saw the document itself, staring down at him from town gates. Reading that his works were to be banned, confiscated, and destroyed, he became furious. Had his writings been condemned even before he was to have the chance to defend them? Many friends and advisers urged him not to continue, but when asked by the herald if he wished to do so, Luther, trembling, said that he did.

As Erfurt neared, his anxiety grew. Theologians devoted to the old ways remained strong at his former cloister and university, and he worried about the reception he would receive. Several miles from the city, however, a party of forty men on horseback rode out to greet him and escort him into town. In the city itself, thousands poured into the streets in the hope of getting a glimpse of him. During his stay, Luther was honored as a distinguished son of the university and of the Augustinian Hermits, and a humanist poet regaled him with four elegies celebrating his achievements.

Arriving on Saturday evening, the party decided to spend Sunday in Erfurt, and Luther was asked to preach at the cloister church. The place was so packed that the balcony at one point creaked ominously, causing a nervous stir, but Luther put everyone at ease by saying it was only the Devil trying to stop him. In this same church, Luther had once spent many lonely hours struggling to recite the Psalter with sufficient ardor to please God; he now sought to convey the liberating vision of the faith-based gospel he had developed in the years since. Good works undertaken for one's own salvation have no merit, he declared. Priests and monks pray the canonical hours, say Mass, and pray the rosary, yet in their hearts they feel such great envy that if they could choke their neighbor and get away with it, they would. No doubt many in the audience would reject such assertions, Luther said, but, he added, "I will tell the truth, I must tell the truth, even though it cost me my neck twenty times over." He left with his neck intact. The new prophet was much honored in his old home—a sign of how profoundly public opinion in Germany was shifting his way.

Luther's progress across Germany was being carefully followed in Worms, and the closer he got to the city, the tenser the mood there became. A messenger from Spalatin came to warn him not to continue, but he had no intention of turning back. "I am coming, my Spalatin, although Satan has done everything to hinder me," he wrote on April 14, 1521. Despite getting sick during the journey, and despite the odious mandate issued by Charles, he observed, "Christ lives, and we shall enter Worms in spite of all the gates of hell and the power in the air. . . . So prepare the lodging."

On the morning of April 16, as Luther and his party approached Worms, a great crowd, some on horseback and some on foot, went out more than two miles to meet him and escort him into town. The mood there was highly charged. The most talked-about man in Europe, the fearless reformer who had given voice to the anti-Roman rage rising in the land, was approaching St. Martin's gate. At ten in the morning, the watchman in the cathedral spire, catching sight of the party, let loose a trumpet blast, and within minutes thousands of people had filled the narrow streets by the gate. The first to enter Worms was the herald, followed by the two-wheeled cart bearing Luther and his three companions. At the sight of the insurgent friar in his cowl and tunic, a surge of excitement passed through the crowd. Immediately after the cart came Justus Jonas, along with the group of nobles and knights who had gone out to meet Luther—some one hundred horsemen in all. The procession rode along the Grosse Kämmererstrasse, which was lined with excited onlookers, until it reached the side street on which the Hostel of the Knights of St. John stood. Because he was under the ban, Luther could not stay at the Augustinian cloister and so instead was to lodge at the hostel, sharing a room with two Saxon officials. As he stepped out of the cart, a priest embraced him and touched his gown three times, as if venerating the relic of a saint. "God will be with me," Luther said as he surveyed the crowd.

After dining with Spalatin and a dozen or so friends, Luther was overwhelmed with visits from counts, barons, knights, and others come to pay their respects and offer encouragement. Philip of Hesse, a young landgrave who would became a key figure in the Reformation, asked Luther about his startling statement in *The Babylonian Captivity* that a woman whose husband was impotent could take another. Luther declined to discuss the matter. He was suffering from indigestion and needed time to prepare for his appearance.

On the day after Luther's arrival, Ulrich von Pappenheim, the imperial marshal, came by at midday to inform him that he was to appear at four o'clock that afternoon before his imperial majesty, the princes, and the rest of the estates. The interrogator was to be Johann von der Eck, the general secretary of the archbishop of Trier (and not the same Eck who had confronted Luther at Leipzig). This was not a good sign, for Eck had presided over the burning of Luther's books in Trier. His selection had been arranged by Aleander, who, remarkably, did not plan to attend the session; since the Holy See had already excommunicated Luther, he did not want by his presence to confer legitimacy on the proceedings. Eck, however, was staying in the same house as Aleander, and the nuncio carefully prepared him for the encounter. The key was to make sure that Luther did not give a speech but simply responded to specific questions. The session was to take place not at the diet's regular site in the town hall but at the bishop's palace next to the cathedral. Aleander, who for weeks had been collecting Luther's books, sent them over there.

As the appointed hour approached, Pappenheim along with Sturm escorted Luther to the bishop's palace. To avoid the crowds that lined the main route (and to prevent a possible attack), Luther was led out through the garden to the adjoining house and through some back streets to a side door of the palace. But his presence could not be kept secret. From every window faces looked down, and many had climbed onto rooftops in the hope of seeing him. When Luther reached the palace, the guards had to use force to keep the crowd from entering along with him. An uproar broke out at the main entrance when it became clear that he was entering by a side door.

Accompanied by Jerome Schurff, a Wittenberg lawyer, and his friends Amsdorf and Jonas, Luther entered the small upper room that had been chosen for the meeting and to his astonishment found himself standing before Charles V, the man on whom he had for so long focused his hopes and anxieties. Next to the emperor were his brother Frederick, the arch-

duke of Austria; four cardinals; and assorted nobles, knights, town officials, and ambassadors ready to send reports back to their sovereigns. The
room was so crowded that officers with pikes and halberds stood by to
maintain control. It was one of the great moments in European history:
the *Kaiser*—heir to a long line of Catholic sovereigns; scion of the house of
Hapsburg; the lord of Austria, Burgundy, the Low Countries, Spain, Naples, the German lands of the Holy Roman Empire, and a vast new empire
taking shape across the Atlantic, who, attired in the rich robes of state,
embodied the unity of Christendom's temporal and spiritual realms—
facing the stiff-necked friar who, raised amid sooty mines and belching
smelters, stood in his threadbare habit, his tonsure freshly shaved, his face
hollowed by sleepless study, his head and shoulders stooped, and his knees
bent in a show of monkish obeisance. Stone benches had been placed
against the walls the length of the room, but most of the crowd stood, and
all strained for their first look at the Augustinian rebel from the eastern
edge of the empire who had caused such a furor in Christendom.

Their first impression was not favorable. With his haggard look and
shabby garb, Luther seemed lacking in dignity; gawking at the dignitaries, he had the air of a bumpkin. Charles was struck by his eyes: dark and
impenetrable, they seemed aglow with fanaticism. "That fellow will never
make a heretic of me," he said (according to Aleander). Luther, in fact,
felt disoriented. He had never before been in such exalted company, and
his proximity to the emperor unnerved him. Despite all his brashness and
defiance, he remained at heart a provincial.

After Luther was warned by Pappenheim not to say anything without
being asked, Eck, a tall man with a strong voice, informed him that his
imperial majesty had summoned him for two reasons: first, to ascertain if
all the books published under his name and piled before him were in fact
his, and second, to see if he wished to retract anything in them. At that
moment, Jerome Schurff, who acted as Luther's lawyer during the trial,
declared that the titles of the works should be read aloud. They were. There
were twenty-two in all, including *To the Christian Nobility*, *The Babylonian
Captivity*, *The Freedom of a Christian*, the *Treatise on Good Works*, *Why the
Books of the Pope and His Disciples Were Burned*, and a copy of the Froben
edition that had first carried Luther's views around Europe.

Luther—wondering how all the volumes had been gathered together—spoke in a voice so low and halting that it was hard for many in the hall to hear him. Yes, he said, he had written all of the books. As to whether he would retract them, Luther—rather than boom out an answer, as most had expected—continued in the same tentative way. Because the question involved matters of faith and salvation, and because it concerned the divine Word, which all are bound to revere, "it would be rash and at the same time dangerous for me to put forth anything without proper consideration." For that reason, he hoped that the emperor would grant him more time to think about the question so that he could satisfactorily answer it "without violence to the divine Word and danger to my own soul."

A ripple of dismay passed through the assembly. More time? Hadn't Luther had months to prepare for this moment? Luther's whole manner caused surprise. He seemed anything but the outspoken prophet who had raged so defiantly at the Roman Antichrist. The supporters of the papacy who were present felt a sense of relief at the hesitant figure before them. In requesting a pause, they suspected, he was simply trying to forestall the solemn judgment that inevitably awaited him. But Luther's desire for more time seems to have been genuine. The demand that he disown all his books had caught him flat-footed. As he later explained, "I thought His Imperial Majesty would have assembled one or fifty scholars and overcome this monk in a straightforward manner." Instead, they had simply said, "Are these your books?" and "Do you want to renounce them or not?"

After some consultation among the princes over Luther's request, Eck again addressed him. Although he had had much time to consider these matters and so did not deserve more, his imperial majesty, in his "innate clemency," had decided to grant him one more day to formulate his response. Luther was to report back with it at the same hour the next day, on the condition that he present his opinion orally and not in writing.

Luther was escorted back to his quarters along the same route by which he had come. Again, the flow of visitors did not cease. Several noblemen assured him that he need not worry about his life, for the people were so fervently behind him that they would rise up if anything happened to him. During a few spare moments, he jotted down some notes for the next day's session. At the urging of one visitor, Luther wrote a brief letter to the man's brother, Johannes Cuspinian, a prominent humanist in Vienna, in which he reported that he had just appeared before the emperor and members of the diet and had been asked whether he would renounce his books. With Christ's help, he stated, "I shall not in all eternity recant the least particle."

In Worms, however, rumors had spread that Luther was in fact going to recant, and when he appeared at the palace the next afternoon, the crowd on the street was even larger. Because of the intense interest, a larger hall was reserved for the session, and Luther had to wait in it amid the packed bodies for more than an hour while the delegates finished the day's business in another room. By the time the assembly was seated, it was nearly dark outside and torches had been lit high on the walls to provide illumination. The space was so crammed with electors, princes, prelates, and envoys that hardly anyone but the emperor could sit, and Luther had to push his way to the front through the sweaty crowd.

Once he got there, Eck told him that his time was up and the moment had come for him to answer: "Do you wish to defend all your acknowledged books, or to retract some?" Luther now showed no hesitation. Speaking in German, he asked to be pardoned if, through his inexperience, he had not addressed the assembled princes with their proper titles or had committed an offense against court etiquette, for he was a man "accustomed not to courts but to the cells of monks." After reconfirming that the books in question were in fact his, Luther took up the matter of whether he stood by them. His books were not all of the same kind. In some he had discussed religious faith and morals "simply and evangelically," so that "even my enemies are compelled to admit that these are useful, harmless, and clearly worthy to be read by Christians." In disavowing them, he would be condemning truths on which both his friends and his enemies could agree.

In a second group were books in which he had attacked the papacy and papists who by their doctrines and wicked examples had "laid waste the Christian world." This was apparent in the innumerable complaints from the faithful, whose consciences had been "most miserably entangled, tortured, and torn to pieces" by the decrees and doctrines of the pope and his see. Much property, especially in Germany, had been devoured by this "unbelievable tyranny." If he were to retract these writings, he would have done nothing but add strength to that tyranny. "Good God! What a cover for wickedness and tyranny I should have then become."

Finally, he had produced a third class of books against private individuals "who strive to preserve the Roman tyranny and to destroy the godliness taught by me." Luther acknowledged that in these books he had been more violent than was perhaps appropriate for a man of his profession, but he was not a saint, and it was not his manner of living that was at issue but "the teaching of Christ." If he were to retract these words, the godlessness that had so oppressed the people would rage even more fiercely.

With the light in the hall fading and the room growing uncomfortably close, Luther went on. When Jesus was questioned about his teaching before Annas, the father-in-law of the high priest Caiaphas, he had asked to be told where he had spoken awry. If Christ himself, who knew he could not err, did not refuse to hear testimony against his teaching, "how much more ought I, who am the lowest scum and able to do nothing except err, desire and expect that somebody should want to offer testimony against my teaching!" He was therefore asking of those present, either high or low, to "expose my errors, overthrowing them by the writings of the prophets and the evangelists." He added that once he had been thus instructed, "I shall be quite ready to renounce every error, and I shall be the first to cast my books into the fire." The excitement and dissension raised by his teaching of God's Word were for him "the most joyful aspect of all in these matters," since Christ had come to bring not peace but a sword and to set sons against fathers.

Luther noted his concern that the reign of the young and noble Charles would get off to an unhappy start—that he would suffer the same fate as the pharaoh in Egypt, the king of Babylon, and the kings of Israel, who, seeking to pacify and strengthen their kingdoms, destroyed themselves. "With these words I commend myself to your most serene majesty and to your lordships, humbly asking that I not be allowed through the agitation of my enemies, without cause, to be made hateful to you."

In all, Luther spoke for about fifteen minutes. With the heat from the torches and the tightly packed bodies, he was sweating heavily, but he was asked to repeat his remarks in Latin, and he somehow found the strength to do so. When he had finished, there was much confusion. His threefold classification of his works was perplexing. His comparison of Charles to the pharaoh was provocative. And his embrace of the sword over peace sounded like an incitement to violence.

After some consultation among the emperor and the princes about how to proceed, Eck stepped forward. Contrasting the moderation shown by the emperor with Luther's presumptuousness, he assailed the friar for his specious threefold division of his books. The plain truth was that the works Luther had written after the papal decree against him were far more offensive than his earlier ones, since in them he had held Jan Hus's heresies—long since rejected—to be Catholic truths and had questioned the authority and prestige of councils. His assertion that some of his books contained teachings that were sound and acceptable to all was specious, for heretical books going back to the Arians had been burned despite containing much that was godly and Catholic. In fact, Eck said, "no doctrine is more effective in deceiving than that which mixes a few false teachings with many that are true."

Furthermore, in saying that he was prepared to accept instruction about the Holy Scriptures from anyone high or low, Luther was doing what heretics always do—insisting on their own readings. Many of the teachings he claimed as his own were in fact similar to the heresies of the Beghards and Waldensians, of Wyclif and Hus, and of many others also long since rejected by the synods. Was it proper to dredge up and drag into dispute matters that the Catholic Church had already settled—"matters which have turned upon the usages, rites, and observances, which our fathers held with absolute faith" and for which "they would rather have endured a thousand deaths than to have fallen away from in any way at all? Do you want us to stray from the path which our fathers faithfully trod?"

Eck—forcefully summarizing the heart of the matter as viewed by the Church—urged Luther not to claim that he was the one and only man who had a genuine understanding of Holy Scriptures, superior to the judgment of so many holy doctors who had toiled night and day to reveal their true meaning. "Do not regard yourself as wiser than all others. Do not cast doubt upon the most holy, orthodox faith which Christ, the perfect lawgiver, instituted; which the apostles spread through the whole world; which the miracles made clear; which the martyrs confirmed with their red blood." In light of all this, it was futile for Luther to expect a debate on the points he had raised. Rather, he should answer sincerely and candidly, and not in an ambiguous or "horned" (sophistical) manner, "whether or not you wish to recall and retract your books and the errors contained in them."

"Since then your serene majesty and your lordships seek a simple answer," Luther replied in the deepening gloom, "I will give it in this manner, neither horned nor toothed."

Unless I am convinced by the testimony of the Scriptures or by clear reason—for I do not trust either in the pope or in councils alone, since it is well known that they have often erred and contradicted themselves—I am bound by the Scriptures I have quoted, and my conscience is captive to the Word of God. I cannot and I will not retract anything, since it is neither safe nor right to go against conscience. May God help me! Amen.

According to some accounts, Luther ended with the phrase, "Here I stand—I cannot do otherwise," but those words do not appear in any of the accounts recorded on the spot; rather, they seem to have been inserted in the earliest printed editions by supporters seeking to highlight the heroic nature of his stand.

Exasperated, Eck again implored Luther to lay aside his conscience, which was in error, and to recant. He especially challenged Luther's contention that councils can err. Luther shouted back that they did err and that he could prove it. By now, the torches had burned down to their sockets, throwing the hall into nearly total darkness, and the air in the overcrowded space had turned unbearably foul. After a long day of wrangling and standing, the assembled dignitaries were eager to break for the nighttime meal and the usual carousing. The emperor—agitated and angry and saying that he had had enough of such talk—rose to his feet, and the crowd surged toward the exits, marveling at the remarkable act of defiance they had just witnessed. Was Luther going to get away with it?

As he passed out of the hall and onto the street, some Spanish courtiers jeered at him: *Al fuego, al fuego*—"To the fire, to the fire." Luther's supporters worried that he would be seized on the spot, but amid the churning multitude such a move would have surely caused a riot. Seeing that he was not going to be taken, Luther thrust forth his arms like a knight who in a tourney has landed a strategic blow and shouted, "I am through! I am through!" A great throng escorted him noisily through the streets to his quarters, where he drank much malmsey wine while receiving a stream of congratulants.

Luther's performance at the Diet of Worms has long been considered one of history's transformative moments. Just as the birth of modern France is often traced back to May 5, 1789 (the day on which the Estates General convened), the dawn of modern Germany is often dated to Luther's appearance in Worms. Many go further, seeing in Luther's unflinching stand in the bishop's palace the start of the modern era, rooted in an individual's assertion of an inalienable right to his conscience against the unassailable strength of church and state. Standing before the mightiest powers in the land—before an emperor whose domain extended from Mexico to Vienna; before princes who had ordered his books burned; before cardinals who represented the consecrated authority of the Roman See—a lone friar, in a clear and steady voice, had resolutely stood by his convictions. (Luther's performance, wrote Thomas Carlyle, was "the greatest moment in the Modern History of Men." English Puritanism, England and all its Parliaments, the Americas, the French Revolution, Europe and its work: "the germ of it all lay there: had Luther in that moment done other, it had all been otherwise.")

This view is vividly captured in a picture of the occasion by the German painter Anton von Werner. It shows a black-robed Luther standing upright in the center of a spotless, brightly lit hall, facing the emperor, who is seated on a throne-like chair. The assembled notables in their richly embroidered robes lean intently forward as the friar, his right hand on his heart, fearlessly proclaims his position. But this painting (now hanging in the Staatsgalerie in Stuttgart) was not executed until 1877, and, because no visual records of the event survived, it was drawn entirely from Werner's imagination. It seems a highly idealized version, purged of all late-medieval grime, gloom, and disorder. The dramatic after-the-fact addendum to Luther's climactic statement at the diet represents a similar embellishment. "Here I stand—I cannot do otherwise" has become a central motif of the Luther story and a watchword of the Protestant tradition, yet Luther almost surely never uttered it. As one historian has noted, it is the most memorable thing Luther never said.

Moreover, Luther was basing his appeal to his conscience not on the general right of individuals to express their opinions but rather on a sense of certainty about his own readings of Scripture. It was the Word of God he was defending, not any human opinion. Luther's ideas about freedom of conscience were thus founded on a perception of divine endorsement. This differed fundamentally from a general principle of free expression of the sort that Erasmus and other humanists espoused, based on the idea that people could draw different meanings from the Bible and discuss them civilly. Feeling answerable only to God, Luther rejected the opinions of all who disagreed with him. He thus eschewed any modern conception of religious or intellectual tolerance.

All that aside, Luther's performance was by any measure extraordinary. Facing the imminent prospect of execution at the joint behest of the Holy Roman Empire and the Roman Catholic Church, he stood resolute behind the views that he had developed during his long, solitary struggle with the Psalms and Paul. From the moment he had posted the Ninety-Five Theses, the conflict between Luther and Rome had essentially been one of authority—of who has the right to interpret the Bible and define the tenets of the faith. In Rome's view, only the Church, represented by popes and councils and drawing on centuries of carefully sifted commentary, had that authority. Luther, drawing on his idea that every Christian is a priest, insisted on his right as a faithful Christian to read the Bible and determine its meaning for himself.

Luther, of course, was not the first Christian to so contend. Peter Abelard had inflamed the ecclesiastical authorities in Paris and Rome with the heterodox opinions he developed by applying the dialectical method. Peter Waldus, John Wyclif, Jan Hus, and Girolamo Savonarola had all claimed the right to interpret Scripture on their own. Slightly more than a century earlier, Hus had stood before Emperor Sigismund and the Council of Constance and refused to recant positions similar to those that Luther defended at Worms.

In each of these cases, however, the Church had succeeded in suppressing the dissenter and the movement he had inspired. Hus's immolation had sparked a bloody uprising that had raged for decades, but the pope and emperor had, through a series of crusades, prevented it from spreading. Now those same authorities were trying to silence Luther and his supporters. If Aleander had had his way, the heretic would have been seized and executed on the spot or bound and delivered to Rome. Many years later, Charles himself, when authorizing the burning of some heretics in Spain, observed, "I did wrong in not killing Luther at the time. I was under no obligation to keep my word," for he had sinned against a greater power than himself—he had sinned against God. "I did not kill him, and as a result this mistake of mine assumed gigantic proportions. I could have prevented this."

In so maintaining, however, Charles was overlooking some fundamental realities. By the time Luther had appeared at Worms, he had a large popular movement behind him. His support came not only from Christians seeking a new form of transcendent piety but also from Germans longing for liberation from Roman tyranny. Luther's religious rebellion was being carried forward by the surging sense of German nationalism. "The movement is now quite independent of Luther," observed Aleander, who went on to quote Hutten: "If Luther were put to death a thousand times, a hundred new Luthers would rise up." That nationalist sentiment, in turn, was being stirred and amplified by the printing press. In addition to enabling Luther to gain a large following for his views, printing also created the sense of an unstoppable tide of opinion in his favor. It was no coincidence that the diet was taking place in the Rhineland, not far from Mainz, the birthplace of printing, and Frankfurt, the site of Europe's largest book fair. Without the tracts, sermons, pamphlets, and broadsides cascading from the presses, Luther might well have suffered the same fate as Hus.

His ordeal was far from over, however. As he was raising glasses with his supporters, the exasperated emperor drafted an edict to muzzle him. It was one of the few statements that Charles, in his thirty-seven-year reign, would write in his own hand. On the next morning (April 19, 1521), he had it read to a group of electors and top princes. Solemnly invoking his venerable forebears, Charles declared that, just as they had steadfastly defended the Catholic faith, he was now determined to do the same. "It is certain that a single monk must err if he stands against the opinion of all Christians. Otherwise Christendom itself would have erred for more than a thousand years. Therefore I am determined to set my kingdoms and dominions, my friends, my body, my life, my soul upon it." The friar was to be allowed to return to his home in accord with the safe-conduct, but "without preaching or admonishing the people with his bad doctrine." After the lapse of the safe-conduct, the emperor declared, he was determined to proceed against Luther "as against a notorious heretic." He implored the members of the estates to join him in that action.

With this statement, Charles established himself as the supreme defender of the old order—and as an implacable opponent of Luther. The German estates were not pleased. On hearing Charles's words, they turned "pale as death," as Aleander put it. As eager as many of them were to see Luther crushed, they knew that any attempt to enforce such a decree in the face of his fervent support could touch off violent disturbances.

In fact, on the night of April 20—the same day the edict was read— Worms was hit by a new wave of fly sheets. Some backed the Church. "Luther! Pope and Kaiser have condemned you," went one. "Now Frederick will not keep your safe-conduct, for in your madness you have merely brought up again the old heresies and presented nothing new." Others came stridently to Luther's defense. Posted to the door of the bishop's palace where Charles was staying was a placard declaring, "Woe to the land whose king is a child!" Another, affixed to the doors of the cathedral, warned that four hundred nobles and a thousand foot soldiers stood ready to avenge any action taken against Luther. It swore violent opposition to the Romanists and especially to the archbishop of Mainz. At the bottom appeared the words *Bundschuh, Bundschuh, Bundschuh.* In the streets that night, the same words were eerily shouted.

No phrase could have more chilled the princes and prelates in Worms. The *Bundschuh,* the sturdy leather shoe used by peasants, was the symbol of social revolt—the German equivalent of a pitchfork. For twenty years it had appeared on the banners of those challenging the established order in the name of economic justice and religious brotherhood. The leaders of these insurrections held that there could be no deliverance from exploitation until the property of counts was seized, the power of the Church was broken, and priests were driven from the land. In support, they cited Scripture. Though most of these revolts had been ruthlessly suppressed, discontent continued to simmer, and memories of the Hussite wars, with their heavy toll in blood and property, remained vivid. The appearance of the *Bundschuh* seemed a call to war.

Adding to the alarm was the knowledge that, a day's journey from Worms, Franz von Sickingen sat in the Ebernburg castle with a strike force far larger than what anyone in the town—even Charles—could marshal. With the volatile Hutten at Sickingen's side, there were worries that his men would swoop into Worms and carry out a massacre. "The Emperor has not so much as four crippled soldiers with him, whereas Sickingen is better supplied with troops than any German prince," Aleander wrote. The people of Worms "desire nothing more than the stamping out of the clergy." With the threat of religious war looming, Archbishop Albrecht of Mainz, for one, became so panicked that he immediately sought out the emperor to express his fears. Charles ridiculed him, but the archbishop prepared to leave Worms at the first opportunity.

In a meeting with the emperor in his quarters, the princes requested that, rather than condemn Luther outright, he appoint a panel of learned men to find a way to get him to admit at least some of his errors. As reluctant as he was to see the affair prolonged, Charles remained beholden to the estates in financial and military matters, and so he gave them three days to get Luther to acknowledge that he had erred. On April 22, 1521, a commission was appointed under the direction of Richard of Greiffenklau, the archbishop of Trier, whom Frederick had long proposed as an arbiter. Most of its members were moderate Catholics. At six o'clock on the morning of April 24, Luther, accompanied by a handful of aides and friends, appeared at Greiffenklau's quarters.

Having already endured a high-profile public scourging, Luther was now to undergo an intense private examination in a series of hearings. If he persisted in his dissent, he was told, civil disorders and anarchy could result. Already, the common people were using *The Freedom of a Christian* to throw off the yoke of the law and behave licentiously. If he wanted to avert further strife, Luther should offer some acknowledgment of the Church's age-old authority to prescribe doctrine and define rites. To bolster their case, the interlocutors cited many passages from the Bible, but for each Luther countered with one of his own.

As the conversations dragged on, the commissioners proposed one compromise after another, informing Luther that he need make only some small concessions while referring the other matters at issue to a council. When these remonstrations failed to budge him, the archbishop of Trier, in a final private conference, made one last appeal, holding out the prospect of a rich priory near one of his castles. In effect, he was trying to bribe Luther. The nuncios tersely captured his response: "He declined all that." They let slip the real goal of these negotiations: the archbishop hoped to get him "to take back even a small part of his errors, which would have turned the whole people against him."

Luther no doubt understood this. Even the most modest concession on his part could have undermined his position as a fearless reformer and provoked a furious backlash. In the end, though, Luther was moved by a deeper concern. As he would put it in a letter a few days later, the pope was no judge of matters concerning the Word of God and his faith. A Christian must examine and judge such matters himself, for Scripture and faith are the property of every man in the community. Once again, Luther was asserting the supreme right of the individual Christian to interpret God's Word. This, however, was something that the Church could not concede.

Luther found the archbishop kind and gracious but unpersuasive. "Thus we parted": with those simple words, Luther signaled his final break with the Church. After the archbishop left, an official from the emperor arrived to say that Luther should depart, and he handed him a new twenty-one-day safe-conduct. During that period, he was not to preach. After it expired, he was told, the emperor would act against him as he deserved.

Having now been in Worms for ten days, Luther was desperate to leave despite the great danger he would face in returning to Wittenberg. Already, it was believed, Aleander and Caracciolo were plotting against him. As Luther prepared to go, however, he was informed that Frederick had devised an alternative plan, by which he would be transported not to Wittenberg but into hiding. The exact details were withheld, but the knowledge brightened Luther's mood, and he spent his last night in Worms drinking more malmsey wine and bidding good-bye to his supporters. The next morning, April 26, 1521, the German Hercules toasted some slices of bread to fortify him for his trip. Between nine and ten o'clock, he and his party rumbled off in two carriages from his lodgings toward one of the city's gates. No one knew exactly where Luther was going, but as he passed through the gate, a rift opened in Western Christendom.

Outside, Luther was met by a troop of horsemen (probably sent by Sickingen at Hutten's request). They rapidly covered the fifteen miles north to Oppenheim. There they were joined by the imperial herald, who was to accompany them back to Wittenberg. On reaching Frankfurt two days later, Luther wrote to Lucas Cranach that he had submitted to being "imprisoned" and hidden away, "though as yet I do not know where." Though he would prefer to die at the hands of tyrants, he had acceded to the counsel of good men. It was necessary to suffer and keep silent for a while, he added, "but Easter Sunday will also come to us"—a reference to martyrdom.

Later that day or the next, at the village of Friedberg, north of Frankfurt, Luther—making one last effort to get through to the young emperor—completed the draft of a letter to him that he had been working on. Intensely emotional and free of the usual polemics, it expressed both his deep respect for Charles and his resolute attachment to Scripture. He was willing to obey his imperial majesty in life or death, glory or shame, gain or loss—in all matters, in fact, except those involving the Word of God. Offering once again to submit his books and doctrines to impartial judges and thanking the emperor for observing the safe-conduct while he was in Worms, Luther made one final plea: "I beg your Sacred Majesty by Christ, not to allow me to be crushed by my enemies, nor to suffer violence and be condemned, since I have so often offered to do what a Christian and an obedient subject ought."

Luther persuaded the imperial herald to carry the letter back to Worms and deliver it to the emperor. This was, in fact, a ploy to get him out of the way. The original copy of this letter has survived, bearing a note in Spalatin's hand: "This letter was never given to the Emperor, because in all this host of nobles there was not one who would give it to him." (In 1911, J. P. Morgan bought the letter for $25,500 and presented it to Wilhelm II, the last German emperor.)

Luther and his party traveled northeast toward Thuringia. At Hersfeld, home to a famous Benedictine abbey, the chancellor and treasurer came out a mile to greet them. The abbot provided a fine meal and allowed Luther to sleep in his private guest room. He also urged Luther to preach, and, despite Luther's reluctance to violate the ban on preaching, he did so, at five in the morning. When the party departed for Eisenach, the abbot accompanied it as far as the forest. As Luther neared the town where he had been a schoolboy, a delegation came out to meet him on foot, and again he preached, though the parish priest, frightened by the risk, testified before a notary that he had protested. The next day, the party split up, with Schurff and Jonas heading on to Erfurt and from there to Wittenberg, and Luther, together with Amsdorf and the student Petzensteiner, climbing up the Thuringian ridge to the village of Möhra, where his father had grown up and where his uncle still lived.

On the morning of May 4, 1521, in Möhra, Luther preached in the open air. He dined in a garden near the priest's house and preached again, this time to peasant and miner families, many of them his relatives. The next day, the party headed northeast toward Erfurt in the direction of the Altenstein Castle, on the southwestern slope of the Thuringian Forest not far from Eisenach. Passing through rolling grain fields, the group in the late afternoon arrived at a bridle crossing set deep in a grove of fir and pine trees. Suddenly a troop of armed horsemen flashing weapons appeared out of the woods. Panicking, Petzensteiner vaulted out of the cart and ran off. "Do not become excited," Luther whispered to Amsdorf. "We are among friends." Pointing his crossbow, the leader of the group demanded to know who was being transported. When Luther identified himself, the man ordered him to surrender. With curses and feigned roughness, Luther was snatched from the cart, but not before he was able to grab two of his most precious possessions—a Hebrew Bible and a Greek New Testament (no doubt a version of Erasmus's edition). Amsdorf and the driver were sent on their way. To an accompaniment of curses, Luther was placed in a harness and forced to run alongside the horsemen as they headed into the forest. (The spot of the abduction is today marked by an obelisk twenty-five feet high, the forest still thick around it.)

After a short distance, Luther was blindfolded and put on a horse. For several hours he was led northward through the woods on a zigzag route designed to elude possible pursuers. Finally, at about eleven in the evening and some fifteen miles from the point where he had been seized, he was led up a steep ridge and across a lowered drawbridge into a fortress. From the parapets, courtyards, and columns, he could see at once where he was—the Wartburg, the medieval castle outside Eisenach, which he knew from his school days in that town. The captain of the castle, Hans von Berlepsch, led him up a ladder to two small rooms. After taking some food, Luther—drained from the ordeal he had endured over the past month—fell asleep, his whereabouts a source of mystery and speculation across Europe.

PART IV

Agitation

THE MARTYR'S CROWN

The news of Luther's disappearance caused astonishment and alarm across Europe. His "abduction" had been pulled off so flawlessly that few knew where he was or even if he was alive. One report had him fleeing to Denmark to seek the protection of its king, Christian II. Another had him going to Bohemia to take shelter with the Hussites. Luther was also reported to have been seized by a robber-knight and his body discovered in a mine, run through with a sword—a deed widely attributed to the papal nuncios. Aleander himself believed that Luther had taken refuge in the Ebernburg castle with a plan to "raise a rebellion," as he reported to Rome.

The distress many felt at Luther's disappearance was captured by Albrecht Dürer in his diary. "I know not whether he yet lives or is murdered, but in any case he has suffered for the Christian truth," he wrote on May 17, 1521. He called on all pious Christians to join him in weeping over "this God-illumined man and beg Him to send us another enlightened one." Dürer had a particular candidate in mind:

> O Erasmus of Rotterdam, where are thou? See what the unjust tyranny of earthly power, the power of darkness, can do. Hear, thou Knight of Christ! Ride forth by the side of the Lord Christ; defend the truth, gain the martyr's crown! As it is, thou are but an old man. I have heard thee say that thou hast given thyself but a couple more years of active service; spend them, I pray, to the profit of the gospel and the true Christian faith, and believe me, the gates of Hell, the See of Rome, as Christ has said, will not prevail against thee.

Even with Luther's swift rise, Erasmus clearly remained a beacon to reform-minded Europeans. At this critical moment in the revolt against Rome, they looked to him for some dramatic gesture. Erasmus had no intention of obliging, however. For one thing, he had heard that Luther "perhaps is in safe keeping," as he wrote to Ludwig Baer, a theologian in Basel, ten days after his disappearance—a testament to Erasmus's unrivaled network of sources. He felt, moreover, that Luther had partly brought his troubles on himself and in the process emboldened the enemies of the humanities, putting "into the hands of certain raging madmen" the weapon they had long sought to destroy good letters. While in Cologne, Erasmus had tried to find a solution to the crisis, but then "lo and behold," Luther had burned the decretals, published *The Babylonian Captivity*, and issued his "over-emphatic assertions" against the bull, thus making "the evil to all appearance incurable."

After returning to Louvain from Antwerp in the spring of 1521, Erasmus was assailed with ever greater bitterness by the monks and mendicants. He was widely alleged to have written *The Lamentations of Peter*, an anonymous dialogue in which the authors of the New Testament complain that no one reads their books anymore; Erasmus in fact had nothing to do with it. "There is not a drinking-party without passionate arguments about Luther, and then the disputation deviates onto Erasmus," he wrote. He became so exasperated with one critic, the Dominican Vincentius Theoderici, that he drafted a ten-thousand-word open letter of admonishment. "Ever since you moved to Louvain," he fumed, "you have never ceased to deliver wild attacks on my reputation at every opportunity."

Erasmus was especially disturbed to learn that throughout Luther's stay in Worms, Justus Jonas had been by his side. Of all the younger German humanists, Jonas had long seemed among the most promising. With Ulrich von Hutten having already declared himself for Luther and Philipp Melanchthon working closely with him in Wittenberg, Erasmus feared that the next generation of humanists was moving into Luther's camp. Hoping to reverse the trend, Erasmus in mid-May 1521 wrote a long appeal to Jonas that was in fact aimed at these younger reformers in general.

Its central message: Luther was too rash and reckless. "I wonder very much, dear Jonas, what god has stirred up Luther's heart to make him write with such freedom of invective against the Roman pontiff, against all the universities, against philosophy, and against the mendicant orders." From the small selection of his writings that he had read, he could tell that Luther had set forth his ideas in language that was bound to offend. Rather than husband the truth, he had "in a savage torrent of invective" poured it out "all at once, making everything public and giving even cobblers a share in what is normally handled by scholars as mysteries reserved for the initiated."

It would be far wiser, he went on, to follow the example of Christ, who said one thing to the multitudes and another to his disciples; of Paul, who declared that he wanted to become all things to all men, that he might gain all for Christ; and of Augustine, who, in arguing with the Donatists and the Manicheans, mixed in charity with his indignation. Skilled physicians do not at the very start administer their ultimate remedies; they first prepare the patient's body with less powerful drugs, then adjust the dose so as to cure and not overwhelm. By contrast, Luther through his impulsiveness had caused great strife, and as a result, Erasmus lamented, "my own work has lost a great part of the effect I hoped for." Above all else, it was necessary to avoid the discord that would "be disastrous to every man of good will." What was required was "a sort of holy cunning," by which the treasure of the Bible could be gradually revealed and the standards of public morality restored.

No less than Luther, Erasmus was being selective in his citations. While Christ had indeed spoken gently to the multitudes, he had also declared that he came with a sword; Paul, in addition to wanting to be all things to all men, had battered his opponents with coarse epithets. In Luther's view, the truth had to be proclaimed without qualification, whatever the consequences; in Erasmus's, it had to be doled out sparingly so as to avoid tumult. At this moment of growing ferment, when the German people seethed with resentment and anger and hungered for change, Erasmus's temperate pleas for understanding and brotherhood seemed pale compared with the drama and excitement of Luther's thunderous blasts against the established order.

More than anything else, Erasmus wanted to be left in peace so that he could continue working on his blueprint for a new Europe. In the spring of 1521, he was occupied with revising the Latin translation for the third edition of his New Testament. Among the major questions he faced was what to do about the *comma Johanneum*—the passage at 1 John 5:7 about the Father, the Word, and the Holy Spirit that he had omitted from his first two editions. In his dispute with Edward Lee, he had written that if he had found this passage in even a single Greek manuscript, he would have retained it in the text. Not long afterward, a Greek codex was duly discovered in England that did contain it. Erasmus suspected that the manuscript had been corrected against the Vulgate—that a scribe had inserted the clause into the codex so that it would conform to the authorized Latin text. Because he remained under attack for dropping the passage, however, he decided to restore it. He was doing so, he explained, not for reasons of scholarship but to ensure that there was "no cause for making malicious accusations." He raised questions about the integrity of the *Codex Britannicus*, as he called it, and described the vast scriptural and patristic evidence against the passage, including its absence from the Greek codices he had examined.

Erasmus's suspicions have been borne out by modern scholars. Among the thousands of Greek New Testament manuscripts examined since Erasmus's time, only a handful are known to contain the verse, and it appears in no manuscript of the Vulgate prior to the ninth century. In the huge literature this subject has generated, there has been much debate (ultimately inconclusive) about whether the manuscript was actually produced for the express purpose of refuting Erasmus. (The manuscript in question has been identified as the *Codex Montfortianus*, named after one of its owners, and is housed in the library of Trinity College in Dublin.) Whichever the case, Erasmus's scholarly instincts were correct, but because of the explosive environment in which he was working, he felt compelled to make this concession.

In one area at least—the financial—Erasmus now felt secure. In addition to the substantial annuity payments he was getting from England and the stipend he was drawing as a councilor of Charles V, he was receiving a steady flow of gifts from wealthy admirers—gold and silver cups and plates, rings, furs, silks, and wine, plus considerable cash—often in response to works he had strategically dedicated to them. As a result, Erasmus now felt like "a regular grandee," as he put it, "keeping as I do two horses who are better cared for than their own master and two servants better turned out than he is."

As always, however, Erasmus's health remained a concern. With the first hot spell of the year, he came down with a severe fever. His digestion got so bad that his doctors prescribed a series of "pills and enemas, powders, ointments, baths, poultices." The prospect of spending another summer in Louvain, with its rotting garbage and festering animosities, seemed unbearable, so when Pieter Wichmans, a friend and canon, invited him to visit his house in Anderlecht, an airy village two miles from Brussels, he gratefully accepted. After sending off his new Latin translation to Basel at the end of May 1521, Erasmus headed there.

Set amid farms and meadows, Wichmans's house was spacious and bright, with wood-beamed ceilings and glazed windows. Within days of his arrival, Erasmus's fever had lifted, his stomach had settled, and he seemed "to grow young again," as he exulted. (Today, Anderlecht is a busy suburb of Brussels, and the house—restored to its former splendor—is a museum dedicated to Erasmus.) Here, amid the chatter of songbirds, Erasmus worked on his New Testament annotations.

He also took on a new project—an edition of the works of Augustine. Froben had first raised the idea back in 1517 as a natural follow-up to the edition of Jerome, but Erasmus had declined. Given Augustine's preeminent place among the Church Fathers, he had assumed that his writings had been faithfully preserved, but then he decided to test the idea by comparing some passages from printed editions against old manuscripts, and to his surprise he found that they were full of "monstrous corruptions." Erasmus thus agreed to serve as the project's editor. Seeking out early manuscripts of Augustine's works, he sent letters to his contacts at monastic and cathedral libraries, asking them to check their collections. Because of the scale of the project, Erasmus decided to farm out parts of it to trusted scholars. To edit and annotate the immense *City of God*, he enlisted his friend Juan Luis Vives, a young convert from Judaism who had fled Spain to escape the Inquisition and who was now living and teaching in the Low Countries. (Vives would go on to become one of the most acclaimed humanists of the sixteenth century.)

While in Anderlecht, Erasmus learned that in England the impression had spread that he was firmly backing Luther. Desperate to dispel it, he hurriedly drafted a letter to his friend Richard Pace, now serving as the dean of St. Paul's. He complained of the many "poisoned pamphlets" that were being aimed at him and of the continuing efforts to prove that Luther had taken things from his books, "as though he had not taken more out of the Pauline Epistles!" While much of Luther's teaching was admirable, Erasmus observed, it had been undercut by "intolerable defects." And even if Luther's writings had been uniformly beneficial, he admitted,

> mine was never the spirit to risk my life for the truth. Not everyone has the strength needed for martyrdom. I fear that, if strife were to break out, I shall behave like Peter. When popes and emperors make the right decisions I follow, which is godly; if they decide wrongly, I tolerate them, which is safe.

For many years—centuries, in fact—Erasmus would be loudly condemned for this passage. At a time when Luther had dramatically shown that he was ready to die for his beliefs, Erasmus was emphatically stating that he was not. Whereas Luther identified with Christ and his willingness to embrace the terrible fate that he knew awaited him, Erasmus saw himself in the frail disciple who, facing arrest as an accomplice of Jesus, thrice denied knowing him. In an era marked by epic demonstrations of faith, Erasmus was frankly acknowledging that he was no hero.

While Erasmus was enjoying the fresh air of Anderlecht, the delegates in fetid Worms were rushing to complete the diet's business. After months of feuding, debating, gorging, and drinking, all were desperate to leave. As the temperature rose, the smell from the piles of waste and pools of urine became overpowering, and a contagion struck that claimed first dozens and then hundreds of lives. Worms was also hit by a new round of high-pitched pamphlets that predicted the end of the world, celebrated *Karsthans*, and demanded an end to Roman tyranny. A priest from the imperial court, encountering a man with eighty copies of *The Babylonian Captivity*, seized and ripped up several of them and would have destroyed the rest had not another bookseller intervened and forced the assailant to seek refuge in the palace. Any day, Ulrich von Hutten and his band were expected to descend on Worms from the Ebernburg castle and carry out a slaughter.

Four days after Luther's departure, the emperor informed the estates that he planned to proceed against him. Furious at having let the apostate slip away, Charles wanted to deploy the empire's full resources against him and his books, and he sent instructions to Aleander to draft a decree to that effect. Delighted at the emperor's resolve, the papal nuncio stayed up all night preparing it.

In its sweep and fury, the Edict of Worms would mark the start of a new era in the Church's war on dissent. The errors, heresies, and false doctrines "of a certain Martin Luther," it declared, had spread such "contagious confusion" that, if not ended, could lead to "the corrupting of all faithful nations and to their falling into abominable schisms." Luther had sought to destroy all civil and ecclesiastical institutions and thereby incited people to "rebel against their superiors" and "start killing, stealing, and burning." He, in short, seemed "not a man but a demon in the appearance of a man, clothed in religious habit to be better able to deceive mankind." He was thus to be considered "an estranged member, rotten and cut off from the body of our Holy Mother Church." No one was to receive, defend, sustain, or favor him. Rather, he was to be "apprehended and punished as a notorious heretic" and delivered to the authorities. Those who helped him in any manner were to be prosecuted and all their goods and belongings confiscated.

Furthermore, no one was "to dare buy, sell, keep, read, write, or have somebody write, print or have printed, or affirm or defend the books, writings, or opinions of the said Martin Luther." All of his books were to be "universally prohibited and forbidden" and burned. Books written by his disciples or imitators of his false doctrines were likewise to be incinerated. But it was not just Lutheran books that were the problem. Every day, new books "full of evil doctrine and bad examples" were being written and published, as were pictures and illustrations that through various tricks sought to capture Christian souls and cause them to doubt their faith. In order "to kill this mortal pestilence," no one was to compose, write, print, sell, buy, or have printed "such pernicious articles" against the Catholic Church. Anything written against the pope, the prelates of the Church, the secular princes, and the leading schools and their faculties was to be similarly condemned. To further ensure that the art of printing was put to good ends, no book dealer or printer or anybody else was to mention the Holy Scriptures or their interpretation without having first received the consent of the local city clerk and the theology faculty of the university.

The Edict of Worms was in effect a declaration of war on the printing press and the forces it had unleashed. The edict committed the full powers of church and state to enforce orthodoxy, extinguish heresy, and restrict free expression. The edict would lead to the creation of an apparatus of intellectual control and censorship, crowned by the establishment in 1559 of the Index of Prohibited Books, which banned not only individual titles but also the entire works of some 550 writers—Erasmus included. Not until 1966 would the index be discontinued. The Edict of Worms, then, inaugurated a period of four hundred years during which the Church resolutely sought to seal off the Christian mind from all material it considered immoral, erroneous, or seditious.

Aleander felt such rapture at the edict's adoption that in his report to Rome he quoted from Ovid's *Art of Love*. And he quickly moved to enforce the decree. On May 29, 1521, three days after its signing, a great pyre of Lutheran books was erected in front of the bishop's palace in Worms, then set ablaze. Bonfires were also organized in Ghent and Antwerp.

While the Vatican and its allies rejoiced over the edict, others had a sense of foreboding. "Here you have, as some imagine, the end of this tragedy, but I am persuaded it is not the end, but the beginning," wrote Alfonso de Valdés, the emperor's secretary and a friend of Erasmus's. The minds of the German people "are greatly exasperated against the Roman See" and so did not attach great importance to the emperor's edicts. Already, he noted, Luther's books were being sold with impunity at every street corner. "From this you will easily guess what will happen when the emperor leaves."

In his eagerness to depart from Worms, Charles would leave a key matter unaddressed. One of the diet's main aims had been to strengthen the *Reichsregiment*, the council that was to govern the empire in the *Kaiser's* absence, but it was denied any real executive power, and Germany was left as splintered and disorganized as ever. Charles would not step foot in Germany for another nine years—a gift to the reformers.

The emperor was already preoccupied with Francis I. The great confrontation long expected between Western Europe's two most powerful men had finally erupted, in northern Italy. In late January 1521, the French lost Alessandria—a strategic fortress midway between Milan and Genoa—and in the early summer imperial troops entered Milan, forcing the French to withdraw. Determined to strike back, Francis opened fronts on his southern and northern borders with lands ruled by Charles, sending a surrogate force across the Pyrenees to attack the Spanish kingdom of Navarre and a detachment across the Meuse (Maas) River to plunder Flanders. Counterattacking, an imperial force under the command of Henry of Nassau burned and looted its way through a broad swath of northeastern France before laying siege to the great cathedral city of Tournai; the nearby towns of Ardres and Mouzon were razed. (In Spain, meanwhile, the Comunero insurgents were being butchered and their rebellion was put down.)

In this geopolitical skirmishing, England remained the great prize. Seeking to build on the Field of Cloth of Gold summit of the previous summer, Thomas Wolsey had organized another meeting between the English and the French, to take place in Calais on August 2, 1521. Francis desperately wanted Henry VIII's support in his conflict with Charles, but the long-standing animosity between England and France persisted, and England retained ties to Charles through Catherine, his aunt. Charles, meanwhile, felt that because his lands had been attacked by France, he was entitled to England's help under the Treaty of London signed three years earlier. Even while the talks between England and France were taking place in Calais, Charles invited Wolsey to see him in Bruges. Wolsey—telling the French that he wanted to persuade Charles to enter into peace talks with France—suspended the negotiations in Calais and traveled the seventy miles to Bruges. In that picturesque, canal-crossed Flemish port, the shape of world politics would be determined.

Erasmus was fully apprised of these developments, for during his stay in Anderlecht he frequently rode into Brussels to see people at the imperial court. Wolsey, he learned, would be accompanied to Bruges by several of his English friends, including Lord Mountjoy, Cuthbert Tunstall, and Thomas More, and Erasmus decided to go in order to catch "many hares in one field," as he put it (quoting from the *Adages*). He stayed with his friend Marcus Laurinus, the dean of St. Donation's cathedral, whose house on Golden-Hand Street served as a sort of hostel for humanists, thanks to both his hospitality and his well-stocked wine cellar. The St. Donation's library itself was well provisioned with manuscripts, and Laurinus arranged for Erasmus to examine four old Latin codices of the New Testament, which would prove of great help in the revising of his annotations.

Erasmus was present when, on August 15, 1521, Charles rode out to see Wolsey. This time the cardinal was able to meet with him. Erasmus also saw a good deal of More. Recently promoted to undertreasurer of the exchequer, More described the tiresome negotiations he was conducting with Hanse merchants. Among the English, though, one topic eclipsed all others: Luther. In England, the friar's views were spreading with unsettling speed, and Wolsey had ordered a crackdown on his writings. On May 12, 1521, a bonfire had been scheduled to take place in the churchyard of St. Paul's cathedral. After Wolsey and Bishop John Fisher delivered fierce tirades against Luther, books by him and other dissidents were fed to the flames, to the cheers of thousands. Two days later, Wolsey issued a mandate banning the importation of Luther's books into England and ordering a search for materials written or edited by him.

As Erasmus heard in Bruges, however, the main blow against Luther had been delivered by Henry VIII himself. Months earlier, Wolsey had sent the king a copy of *The Babylonian Captivity* and suggested that he write against it. Taking up the challenge, Henry had produced the *Assertio Septem Sacramentorum* ("Defense of the Seven Sacraments"). The tract was thick, sober, and studded with citations, and, given Henry's well-known distaste for desk work, rumors had spread that he was not its real author; More, Fisher, and Edward Lee were all said to have had a hand in it. To his dismay, Erasmus was also suspected of having contributed. Examining a copy in Calais, however, he was convinced the book was a product of (again citing the *Adages*) the king's "own bow and spear."

Years later, as Henry's relations with Rome (and Catherine) deteriorated, he would in fact come to wish that he had not written the book, for in the course of accusing Luther, he offered a full-throated defense of the Roman Church. Though plodding, the *Assertio* set out a line of argument against Luther that in the future would be frequently used against him. Over the centuries, Henry maintained, the Church had sifted out the truth of the Christian faith in ways that no mere reading of Scripture could achieve. He mocked Luther's claim to have suddenly discovered the truth about the sacraments after a millennium of darkness. Noting Luther's assertion that the Mass is not a sacrifice, the king wondered how it was that so many Holy Fathers had studied the matter for so many centuries, yet none had been able to perceive what Luther "brags so clearly to see himself!" Citing the Epistle of James, Henry also condemned Luther's all-consuming devotion to faith, on the grounds that it would discourage people from doing good works.

Most offensive of all to Henry was Luther's attack on the sacramental status of marriage. In a section of his book he would later come deeply to regret, the king argued that matrimony was the "first of all Sacraments," instituted by God, given by Christ, and handed down by the apostles "to be honored to the end of the world." As the New Testament made clear, marriage was "an indissolvable bond"; those whom God has joined together in wedlock can never be sundered, except in cases of fornication. For many pages Henry went on in this vein, rhapsodizing about the sacred nature of marriage and railing against the "impertinent calumnies" of Luther, who, based on abstruse Greek parsings, claimed that it was not a sacrament but simply a mystery.

The *Assertio* was rich in such vituperation. Luther, Henry wrote, was a venomous serpent, a "detestable trumpeter of pride, calumnies and schisms," a "hellish wolf" belching out "foul inveighings." He urged his readers not to listen to the insults spewed against the vicar of Christ by "this one little monk." Though weak in strength, Luther was in temper "more harmful than all Turks, all Saracens, all infidels anywhere," and it was up to Christian sovereigns to defend and guard the Holy Roman Church by not only force of arms but also their wits.

Henry dedicated his book to Leo X, and as soon as it was printed he arranged for twenty-eight copies to be sent to Rome, including one bound in gold cloth for the pope. (Today the pope's copy is in the Vatican Library, as are Henry's love letters to Anne Boleyn.) After reading the first few pages, Leo expressed his deep satisfaction, and soon afterward he issued a bull declaring Henry *Fidei Defensor*—"Defender of the Faith"—a title the king would proudly flourish. The *Assertio*, which offered the remarkable spectacle of a sitting sovereign assailing a private individual in print, would become a bestseller, appearing in around twenty editions and translations in the sixteenth century.

In Bruges, there was no copy to spare for Erasmus, but Wolsey promised to send one from England. "I greatly long to read it," Erasmus wrote to Richard Pace with sugary overstatement, "for I have no doubt that it is worthy of that very gifted mind, which shows such extraordinary powers, whatever the topic on which it is exercised."

Erasmus hoped that such praise would placate his English friends. It wouldn't. Now that Henry had entered the arena against Luther, they expected Erasmus to do the same. He was similarly pressed by Jean Glapion, an ardent Franciscan who had recently been named Charles's confessor and who informed Erasmus that it was his duty as a councilor of Charles's to publicly denounce this traducer of true piety.

From Rome, too, the pressure was building. After returning from Bruges to Anderlecht, Erasmus received a letter from Paolo Bombace, an old friend now at the papal court. While reassuring him of Leo's continued support, Bombace said that if Erasmus truly wanted to show his loyalty to the Holy See, he had to write against Luther: "All the other labors which you have undertaken hitherto with your nightly vigils and all your writing have been absolutely barren when compared with what this piece of work would be."

Erasmus, then, was being pushed by the pope, the emperor, and the English king to declare himself against Luther. At the same time, however, Luther's followers were growing increasingly vicious. From Wolfgang Capito, Erasmus received a chilling report on the mood in Wittenberg following Worms. Now working for Albrecht of Mainz, Capito had gone there in the hope of arranging an accommodation between Luther and the archbishop on the subject of relics and indulgences. "Luther's party are crazier and more insolent and more self-assertive in everything," he wrote; "they fix their teeth in anyone, no matter whom, and abuse everyone to his face with barbarous impertinence, such is their public contempt for all brains except their own." Erasmus was one of their principal targets:

"There is no declaration in which they do not criticize you when they are by themselves, and in public they set you up as the leader of their party in the most preposterous fashion. I freely confess, they have made me very angry, passionately devoted as I am to your reputation."

Amid such ill will, Erasmus increasingly feared for his physical safety. Writing to Pierre Barbier, an assistant to Cardinal Adrian of Utrecht, he said that unless the pope could guarantee protection, any declaration of opposition to Luther he might make could prove fatal. He would rather be exposed to the lances of the Swiss than "cut to pieces" by the "sharp-pointed pens" of the Lutheran pamphleteers. He complained that Luther's supporters were dinning into his ears the words of Matthew 10:34: "I have not come to bring peace, but a sword." While some changes in the Christian religion seemed warranted, Erasmus noted, "I can approve no reforms pursued with this sort of uproar." In his effort to stay on good terms with both sides, Erasmus was incurring the wrath of each.

By the end of the summer of 1521, it had become clear to Erasmus that the golden age of peace he had once so hopefully heralded was dead. At Bruges, Charles and Wolsey signed a secret treaty under which Henry was to invade France in May 1523. Leo X—hoping to expel the French from northern Italy and regain lost papal lands—signed his own pact with Charles. Under it, Charles promised to protect the pope against his enemies and ensure the rule of the Medici in Tuscany; Leo, binding himself in perpetuity to the emperor, promised to formally invest him with the crown of Naples. On top of it all, the Ottomans, under their new sultan, Suleiman I the Magnificent, were laying siege to Belgrade. Guarded by a garrison of only seven hundred men, the city fell in late August 1521. The victory—the first of Suleiman's famous military career—opened the way for the Turks to march north along the Danube toward Hungary.

"The whole Christian world, as though it were cut into two halves, is committed to a disastrous war," Erasmus wrote. Charles and Francis, "devotedly intent on mutual destruction," were threatening to "drag the world down to destruction with them." With imperial troops ravaging France and Christian armies warring in Italy, Erasmus wanted to make a show of solidarity with his fellow humanists across national lines. He chose as his vehicle a letter to Guillaume Budé. One of France's leading intellectuals, Budé had made a name for himself with *De Asse*, a dense five-book treatise that sought to estimate the value of every coin and weight of ancient Rome. He was equally well known, however, for his correspondence with Erasmus. For the last five years, the two men had exchanged long, stylized epistles in which they had tried to outdo each other in metaphors, witticisms, epigrams, wordplay, classical allusions, and citations in Greek. They bickered over the aptness of a phrase, argued over perceived slights, and drove each other into fits of neurotic irritation. Throughout it all, though, they remained bound by their shared commitment to humanist ideals and their conviction that good literature can produce good character.

While Erasmus was in Bruges with his English friends, Budé was in Calais with the French party, and in writing to him, Erasmus declared, he was trying to make sure that "these upheavals between monarchs do not disrupt the bonds drawn by the Muses." To further thicken those ties, he offered a tribute to another humanist, Thomas More. During their talks at Bruges, More had told Erasmus of the great strides that his three daughters were making in their literary studies, and Erasmus now praised him for it. At an earlier time, Erasmus acknowledged, he had believed that education had little to offer women and girls, but More's description of his daughters' progress had made him reconsider. They were proving adept at the exercises their father prepared for them, including writing letters in Latin and explaining the sermons they heard in church. They enjoyed reading Livy and could understand authors of that caliber without help from anyone. While he did not object to those who taught their daughters only the domestic arts, Erasmus wrote, "nothing so occupies a girl's whole heart as the love of reading." What's more, a woman must have intelligence if she is to keep her household, mold her children's character, "and meet her husband's needs in every way."

In this letter, Erasmus was for the first time moving beyond the suffocating paternalism of the humanist world; having long shared in the era's boundless condescension toward women, he was with More's help arriving at a new understanding. He praised his friend as a "model literary man" who combined "real wisdom with such charm of character" while also rendering great services to his country. He was truly *omnium hora-rum homo*—a man for all hours (a phrase plucked from the *Adages*). By praising the Englishman More to the Frenchman Budé, the Dutchman Erasmus was trying to keep alive the international sodality of scholars amid rising nationalist and religious tensions.

In mid-October 1521, as the slate skies of autumn gathered, Erasmus returned from serene Anderlecht to boisterous Louvain. With his annotations now ready to be set, he wanted as always to see them through the presses in person. So, despite his advancing years, growing frailty, and loathing of German stoves, he decided to undertake another long journey to Basel. As the day of his departure approached, a Dominican friar at the cathedral preached against him for a full hour. "He seemed to be not so much speaking from a sacred pulpit as thumping a tub," Erasmus wearily observed. From time to time the man dropped in Luther's name to make it seem that Luther and Erasmus were in cahoots. What most riled the friar, however, was Erasmus's intention to edit the works of Augustine, of whom, he charged, he "understood nothing."

Such ravings reinforced Erasmus's desire to leave. He gathered together his manuscripts and personal effects and saddled his horse for the grueling 450-mile journey. Departing on October 28, 1521 (his birthday), Erasmus planned to stay in Basel as long as it took to print his annotations, then travel back to Louvain. In fact, he never would return.

OUTLAW

At the Wartburg, it took Luther some time to adjust to his new surroundings. Geographically, the fortress was not all that remote—Eisenach was only a mile away—but it sat atop a steep ridge that rose out of the Thuringian Forest and was not easily breached. Its centerpiece was a twelfth-century palace that featured a great banquet hall, a chapel decorated with murals, and two hundred columns topped by intricately carved capitals. For generations, the Wartburg was home to the powerful landgraves of Thuringia. The wife of one of them, Elizabeth of Hungary, won renown for her humility and care for the poor; she was canonized just four years after her death (she had died in 1231, at the age of twenty-four). The fortress was also the site of the legendary thirteenth-century contest of the minstrels that Wagner used as the setting for his opera *Tannhäuser*.

At the time of Luther's arrival, the place was largely abandoned. For most of his stay, the only other residents were the warden, an armed guard, and two pages of noble stock who brought him food and drink twice a day. He was assigned a spartan wood-paneled room that had once served as a bailiff's lodge. It had a stove, a bed, a wood desk, a stump that served as a stool, and a small window that offered a view over hills and hollows. At night the narrow stairway to his room was raised on its chain and locked so as to prevent possible intruders. Luther was given lay clothes in place of his habit and ordered to let his hair and beard grow so that he would look like a knight. He had been declared *vogelfrei*—outlawed—meaning that anyone was free to kill or capture him on sight, and so he had to remain indoors for a week while he turned into "Junker Jörg," his new identity. A portrait by Lucas Cranach painted months later shows him with long curly hair, a drooping mustache, and an unruly beard.

After more than three years of nonstop lecturing, preaching, writing, and contending, during which he was almost always the center of attention, Luther now found himself alone and "a strange prisoner," as he wrote. The chilly nights and whipping winds added to his sense of isolation. Bats whirred about the place, and ravens and screech owls produced a constant racket. The pages often brought him walnuts, and one night Luther heard what sounded like the nuts being thrown up at the ceiling from a bag on the table—an act he attributed to the Devil. Later, he would write of the "many evil and astute demons" who amused him during his stay, "but in a disturbing way." Much later, a legend arose that Luther at one point threw his inkpot at the Devil, and for many years a dark blotch was carefully maintained on a wall of the *Lutherstube* (Luther's room), but it attracted so much unwelcome attention that it was eventually removed. In any case, the poltergeists he heard were no doubt the creaks and rattles of an aging building straining under the elements.

Luther's one regular link to the outside world was the bundle of letters brought once or twice a week by special couriers supplied by Frederick and overseen by Spalatin. In his replies, Luther had to be careful so that his location would not leak out, and for many weeks it was known only to a small circle in Wittenberg and at the electoral court. Once Luther was no longer recognizable, the chains of his captivity were relaxed somewhat, and he was allowed to roam the woods and pick strawberries. Occasionally he went out on horseback, riding with a groom at his side. He was instructed on how to behave like a nobleman, including constantly gesturing and stroking one's beard and keeping a hand on one's sword, but he could not resist picking up and thumbing through every book he saw. This drew a rebuke from the groom, who said that that was not the way an aristocrat behaved.

The first letter arrived on May 12, 1521. Posted by Spalatin from Worms, it described the harsh imperial edict being drafted. Chilled, Luther at once sent a note to Melanchthon, ruing that his enemies would "now search the whole world for my little books." Luther, though, had a more immediate source of distress. "The Lord has struck me in the rear end with terrible pain," he complained to Melanchthon; "my excrement is so hard that I have to strain with such force to expel it that I sweat, and the longer I wait, the harder it gets. Yesterday on the fourth day I was able to go once, and then I couldn't sleep all night, and still I have no relief." To his friend Nikolaus von Amsdorf, Luther in his agony groaned in German, *"Mein arss ist vos worden"*—"My ass is sore." Brought on by his unvarying diet and lack of exercise, this constipation would torment him for months. (The translation of these passages in the collected English edition of Luther's works is almost comically bowdlerized, with Luther's frank descriptions replaced by references to "elimination" and "painful constipation.")

In that letter to Melanchthon, Luther gave his location as "in the land of the birds." Other letters were signed "from the wilderness," "from the mountain," "where I am," "Patmos" (the parched isle where according to tradition the apostle John wrote the book of Revelation), and "in the land of the birds that sing sweetly in the branches and praise God with all their power night and day"—a lyrical description of his sense of exile. An added hardship was his lack of books. "I am sitting here all day, drunk with leisure," he wrote to Spalatin on May 14. "I am reading the Bible in Greek and Hebrew." He urged Spalatin to send him the manuscripts he had been working on before leaving for Worms, including his commentary on the Psalter, his *Postils* (a book of homilies), and his exposition of the Magnificat. He planned to write a sermon on confession as well.

Eager for news about Wittenberg, Luther peppered Melanchthon with questions about what was going on there. He also sought to reassure his fretful disciple, who had written of his anxiety over Luther's absence: "I cannot believe what you write, that you are going astray without a shepherd. This would be the saddest and bitterest of news." Even if he were to perish, the gospel would not suffer, for Melanchthon was already surpassing him, as the prophet Elisha had replaced Elijah (as recorded in 2 Kings). News of the outside world was hard to come by, "since I am a hermit, an anchorite, and truly a monk, though neither shaved nor cowled. You would see a knight and hardly recognize me." His life in seclusion meant nothing, but he admitted that he "would rather burn among glowing coals than rot here alone half alive." As far as he was concerned, "all is well, except that the troubles of my soul have not yet ceased, and the former weakness of the spirit and faith persists."

As that last remark suggests, Luther's *Anfechtungen* had returned. Sequestered in this wind-battered, bat-ridden redoubt; hunted by emperor and pope; and cut off from his lively circle of friends in Wittenberg, he was once again experiencing the bouts of doubt and worthlessness that had so often beset him during his long years of torment in the monastery. Forced inward, Luther brooded obsessively on the defiant course he had taken and the disorder it had caused. How was it that he, one lone man, had dared come forward to declare the pope the Antichrist, the bishops apostates, and the universities brothels? Was he alone wise? What if he was mistaken and had led so many into such error that they would be eternally damned?

As he so often did in times of crisis, Luther sought solace in the Psalms. With their cries of anguish and desolation, these ancient hymns offered reassurance that he was not alone. To help pass the time, he began writing expositions on some of those with special resonance, among them Psalm 36 (37 in modern editions). "For evildoers," it stated, "shall be cut off: but they that wait upon the Lord, they shall inherit the land" and "delight in abundance of peace." Dedicating his commentary to "the poor little flock of Christ in Wittenberg," Luther wrote that the psalm "almost precisely fits our needs," for in "an especially loving and motherly way it quiets the rising anger against the slanderers and the arrogant."

Writing helped Luther ward off his loneliness, and during his stay he would produce a large trove of tracts, homilies, polemics, and expositions. His letters from the Wartburg offer an intimate look at both his intellectual development and the physical and emotional trials he faced during his roughly three hundred days there. (Samuel Taylor Coleridge, a great admirer of Luther's letters, singled out the Wartburg letters for praise.)

Luther's Wartburg sojourn would in fact prove a blessing of sorts, offering a break from the crushing demands and nagging distractions of Wittenberg. For long uninterrupted stretches he could explore the truths he had drawn from Scripture and think through their implications for Christian doctrine and devotion. With his decisive break from the Church at Worms, rebellion now had to give way to reform—to redefining the sacraments and the liturgy, the cloister and the priesthood, schools and parishes. In his writings at the Wartburg, Luther would begin the process of creating a new church.

By the start of June 1521, his manuscripts had begun arriving, and he was able to borrow books on the periodic walks he took down to the Franciscan friary in Eisenach. As the days lengthened and the forest bloomed, Luther resumed work on the devotional writings that his trip to Worms had interrupted. For the *Postils*, he decided to switch from Latin to German so that he could reach a larger audience. Unable to preach himself, he wanted to provide homilies on the Gospels and Epistles that pastors could use in their own sermons.

Continuing work on the Magnificat, Luther rhapsodized about Mary, holding her up as a poor, lowly thing who could serve as a model of Christian humbleness. In a startling aside about the Jews, Luther wrote that Christians should not "treat the Jews in so unkindly a spirit, for there are future Christians among them." If "we led Christian lives, and led them with kindness to Christ, there would be the proper response." After his earlier condemnations of the Jews, Luther was entering a period of moderation and forbearance toward them, brought on by his belief that, with the true gospel at last revealed, they would surely see the light and accept Christ as their savior.

While engaged in these devotional works, Luther received frequent reminders of the hatred he was stirring. Nearly two years after the Leipzig disputation, the University of Paris (to cite one example) finally handed down its verdict, declaring 104 passages from Luther's writings heretical. Luther, the faculty stated, deserved not just the ban but also imprisonment and an ordeal by fire. This judgment from Western Europe's most prestigious university would mark the start of a determined campaign to extinguish Luther's thought in France. Responding with a profane blast, Luther denounced the "Parisian street whore" who had been "bold enough to open her legs and uncover her nakedness before the whole world. . . . What schools! What faculties! What theologians! What bilge! What rubbish!"

While at the Wartburg, Luther saw something by Erasmus that criticized him for his vehement language, and Luther expressed his scorn to Spalatin: "He thinks that everything should be discussed civilly and with a certain kindliness and courtesy." Erasmus's books had accomplished nothing precisely because they refrained "from chiding and biting and giving offense." When popes and bishops are admonished in a civil manner, they think they are being flattered and so keep to their abusive ways, "as though they possessed a sort of right to be uncorrected and incorrigible." Reflecting back on his performance at Worms, Luther regretted that he had yielded to the advice of Spalatin and others to hold his spirit in check. "They would hear another story if I stood before them again."

As he completed his manuscripts, Luther sent them off to Wittenberg to be printed. When the published editions returned, he took pleasure in the testimony they offered of his refusal to be silenced. With the arrival of July and the clamminess of summer, however, Luther's industry flagged, owing in part to his worsening constipation. The constant force he placed on his bowels had opened a lesion in his anus, and the application of even the slightest pressure to the exposed membrane sent spasms of pain through his body. Some medications supplied by Spalatin brought a measure of relief, but the wound from the previous rupture kept reopening, causing renewed misery. "It is impossible that I endure this evil any longer," he wrote to Melanchthon on July 13, 1521; "it is easier to endure ten big wounds than this small sign of a lesion." If things did not improve, he would go to Erfurt "and not incognito" to consult a doctor or surgeon. (Luther's presence in the Wartburg had by then become widely rumored.)

In that same letter, Luther noted the emergence of a new source of disquiet. "I sit here like a fool and hardened in leisure, pray little, do not sigh for the church of God, yet burn in a big fire in my untamed body." Rather than be ardent in spirit, he was "ardent in the flesh, in lust, laziness, leisure, and sleepiness." For eight days he had not studied or written anything, in part because of the "temptations of the flesh," and he asked his friends in Wittenberg to pray for him, "since in this seclusion I am drowning in sins."

As a young friar, Luther had witnessed with disgust the nocturnal pollutions of his fellow Augustinians. Now, immured in his own personal hermitage, deprived of companionship, suffering intense bouts of boredom, he seemed for the first time to experience the torments of lust. (Some scholars, however, read these passages as stylized expressions of self-abasement in a long monastic tradition.)

It was around this time that Luther made one of his most controversial statements. "Be a sinner and sin boldly," he exhorted Melanchthon. Luther's enemies would pounce on this, charging him with encouraging license. But they omitted what followed, which was that we must "believe and rejoice in Christ even more boldly." However much we as fallible humans are fated to sin, he wrote, "no sin will separate us from the Lamb, even though we commit fornication and murder a thousand times a day." Because humans are forever relapsing back into sin, Luther seemed to be saying, faith in Christ is the only way to overcome our weakness. His adversaries were not interested in such nuances, however.

Adding to Luther's summertime dejection, ironically, was the positive news coming out of Wittenberg. The university was thriving. Melanchthon was lecturing on Corinthians and Amsdorf on Hebrews, and Justus Jonas (unswayed by Erasmus's appeal) had moved to Wittenberg and was about to begin his own lectures. "You are now well supplied and you manage without me," Luther wrote to Melanchthon. "I do not see why you miss me so much or why my work should be necessary for you. You seem to be able to think for yourself since the affairs at Wittenberg progress more favorably in my absence than in my presence." Since he was obviously not needed in Wittenberg, Luther testily observed, he would consider taking a position in either Erfurt or Cologne if one opened up.

By the end of July, the arrival of some powerful new laxatives from Spalatin had helped relieve the pressure on his bowels, and Luther's spirits lifted. In early August he felt well enough to go on a hunting expedition—his first ever. Luther did not enjoy the experience. At one point, he tried to save a rabbit by hiding it in the sleeve of his coat, but the dogs quickly discovered the terrified animal and, biting through the cloak, tore it to pieces. Luther could not resist allegorizing the incident: the dogs were like the pope and Satan, who in their rage destroyed even the souls that had been saved, despite Luther's best efforts to protect them.

Not long after that episode, a courier arrived with the printed copy of his commentary on confession. The sermon originally planned by Luther had swelled into a forty-leaf booklet. The title was *On Confession: Whether the Pope Has the Power to Require It*, and the answer, unsurprisingly, was no. Since 1215, when the Fourth Lateran Council issued the canon *Omnis utriusque sexus*, annual confession had been mandatory for all Christians.

Luther rejected this as a human invention. The papal command, he wrote, should be regarded no more highly than "the poop in front of you on the street." Luther did endorse voluntary confession, since from his own experience he knew the consolation it could provide, but he urged abandonment of the sophistic practices that had arisen around it. According to Luther, a Christian who sincerely confesses to Christ in his room pleases God more than one who punctiliously confesses his sins to a priest. True repentance was a matter of the heart.

That last statement reflected the continuing importance for Luther of the distinction between *poenitentia* and *metanoia* that Erasmus had pointed out in his annotations. And Luther's rejection of the papal mandate on confession showed the influence of Erasmus's notes on the subject, in which he argued that the practice of priestly confession has no foundation in Scripture but is of human origin.

By midsummer 1521, Luther was dealing with a serious development in Wittenberg, heralded by the arrival of two sets of theses by Andreas von Karlstadt. He was emerging as an important figure in Wittenberg and had put forth his theses as a basis for moving the reform forward. One set, on the Lord's Supper, argued for offering the wine as well as the bread during Communion. Luther himself had embraced this practice in *The Babylonian Captivity*, and Karlstadt's presentation in general seemed to him persuasive. In a striking modification, however, Karlstadt insisted that offering Communion in only one kind was a sin. Examining the relevant passages in the New Testament, Luther could not see how he had arrived at such a conclusion.

The second set of theses, on clerical celibacy, was even more troubling. In them, Karlstadt proposed abolishing this requirement for not only priests but also monks. Of the former Luther fully approved, for Scripture seemed to offer no basis for it. To abolish celibacy for monks, however, would be far more drastic. Though convinced that this vow had inflicted great damage, he did not think it could simply be abandoned. Celibacy was so central to monasticism, in fact, that it was hard to see how the institution could survive without it.

Moreover, the Bible was anything but clear on the matter, and Karlstadt's interpretations of the key passages in Paul seemed sloppy. Given the many souls that had been destroyed by this vow, Luther would have liked nothing more than to do away with it, but he worried that "a great crowd of celibates" would decide to marry on the basis of unreliable readings of Scripture and then afterward feel "continued anguish of conscience" over what they had done. "Aren't we running for an uncertain goal?" he wrote to Melanchthon. "Aren't we beating the air? Why don't we slow down in our race?" To Spalatin a few days later, Luther was even sharper: "Good Lord, will our people at Wittenberg give wives even to the monks? They will not push a wife on me!" Since the Wittenbergers were being closely watched by the outside world, any misstep would be immediately seized upon by their adversaries. "Therefore we need to use the greater care that our word may be without reproach."

Around this same time, Luther became concerned about the preaching situation in Wittenberg. In his view, there was only one person truly qualified to take his place: Melanchthon. Because the young professor was neither ordained nor tonsured, he could not be given a pulpit, but there was nothing to stop him from preaching in a lecture hall or another such space. Because Melanchthon had repeatedly made clear his own reluctance to preach, Luther enlisted Spalatin, urging him to work with the city council and the congregation at the town church to draft him. "Since he is rich in the Word above others, you can see that it is our duty to call him," Luther wrote. He took satisfaction in the strides being made in the modest Hippo on the Elbe: "I am glad that Wittenberg is flourishing, and especially that it is flourishing when I am away, that the wicked may see it and be grieved. . . . May Christ perfect that which He has begun!"

In Wittenberg, the Reformation was indeed moving ahead without Luther. In the wake of his bold performance at Worms, a new era seemed to have arrived. Students walked around town with Bibles under their arms, hailing one another as "brothers at one in Christ." The arrival of Justus Jonas from Erfurt seemed to confirm Wittenberg's status as a center of innovation and renewal, and as he settled in, he wrote to a friend of the "unbelievable wealth of spiritual interests" in the little town.

Along with the exhilaration, however, came apprehension. Wittenberg was a small, defenseless town bordered by enemies. Duke George to the south and Elector Joachim of Brandenburg to the north were both fiercely opposed to Luther and ready to use force against his movement if the opportunity arose. The Edict of Worms had categorically banned any activity in support of Luther or his ideas, and the threat of action by imperial or ecclesiastical agents loomed. And at this moment of supreme danger, the man who had set the whole process in motion was marooned in a distant fortress, leaving a vacuum in leadership.

The most obvious candidate to fill it was Melanchthon, Luther's top disciple, but as always he preferred lecturing on the classics to contending over doctrine. Instead, Karlstadt stepped forward. As he had shown in Leipzig, he could be plodding and erratic in debate, but he was also strong-willed and single-minded. Far more impatient than Luther, he took the Bible far more literally, and he was eager to see its precepts applied at once in the earthly realm.

During the spring of 1521, Karlstadt had been away from Wittenberg. King Christian II of Denmark, an admirer of both Luther and Erasmus, was eager to introduce evangelical reforms in his kingdom, and with Luther himself unavailable, he had turned to Karlstadt. Traveling to Copenhagen, Karlstadt had helped draft a program to curb the power of bishops and encourage priests to marry. But a fierce backlash caused the king to reconsider, and after six largely fruitless weeks, Karlstadt returned to Wittenberg. Though not authorized to take Luther's place at the town church, he began preaching there, using its pulpit to promote his vision of a purified Christianity stripped of the obscure doctrines of Rome.

Clerical celibacy was one such doctrine. This issue pushed its way to the fore because of events on the ground. Three priests in and around Saxony—taking to heart Luther's assault on celibacy in *To the Christian Nobility*—had decided to marry. To the Church, priestly marriage was a grave offense punishable by removal from office and imprisonment, and two of the priests were immediately jailed. The third, Bartholomew Bernhardi, was a former student of Luther's and a rector at the University of Wittenberg who was now serving as provost in the town of Kemberg. Archbishop Albrecht of Mainz demanded that he appear before a diocesan court and urged Frederick to hand him over. But Melanchthon wrote a defense of Bernhardi's position and Karlstadt and others campaigned on his behalf, and he was not surrendered. The other priests, however, languished in prison, and one would ultimately die miserably in a Dresden dungeon.

With the dam thus breaking, Karlstadt prepared a set of theses on clerical celibacy, proposing the abolition of this requirement for both priests and monks. On June 21, 1521, a disputation on them was held, but, amid the prevailing uncertainty, no decision was taken.

There was even more hesitancy over the Mass. Unlike celibacy, this institution touched the lives of every churchgoing Christian. The sanctity and awe in which the sacrament had for centuries been held meant that even modest changes could lead to serious resistance. Giving the cup to the laity remained closely associated with the Hussites and Bohemian radicalism. The clergy at the Castle Church, meanwhile, were devoted to the traditional Mass, including the private Masses said on behalf of souls in purgatory. Some twenty-five priests were assigned to these private Masses, which were underwritten by lucrative endowments, and the income was used to support not only the Castle Church but also the university and some of its students. Eliminating them would thus have important financial repercussions.

But Luther had denounced such Masses as an abomination, and over the summer he had declared his intention never to say another one again. Furthermore, the Mass as traditionally celebrated reinforced the privileged status of the priesthood. If all Christians were priests, as the new gospel insisted, then the Mass had to be radically altered. In the theses he drafted on the subject, Karlstadt sought to prepare the ground for such a change. On July 19, a second disputation was held, but again, no conclusions were reached.

At the Black Cloister, however, a radical new force was emerging. Gabriel Zwilling, a small one-eyed friar who was among the first Augustinians in Wittenberg to embrace Luther's doctrines, was drawing large crowds to its chapel with fiery sermons. Zwilling denounced his fellow monks as lazy and sinful and condemned private Masses as idolatrous acts designed to fatten the purses of the priests who said them. He also rejected the prescribed times for sleeping, rising, eating, drinking, and speaking, which so defined daily life at the cloister. A student from Silesia who attended the sermons wrote home that God had raised up in Wittenberg "a second prophet" who preached the gospel with such sincerity and candor that he seemed a "second Martin."

Among Zwilling's most devoted followers was Melanchthon. The highly impressionable scholar would not miss one of his sermons, and under Zwilling's influence it was he, rather than Karlstadt, who decided to press ahead. During these months, Melanchthon met regularly with a group of students in his home, and on Michaelmas, September 29, 1521, he went with them to the town church. During the service, a layman rather than a priest officiated, and the host, rather than being held aloft and then placed on the tongue of each communicant, as was customary, was handed to each in turn, who then put the wafer on his or her tongue—an act long considered a deadly sin. In addition, the wine was offered to all present, and the words of consecration, rather than being read quietly by a priest and inaudibly to the congregation, were proclaimed for all to hear.

However modest, this impromptu service represented a pivotal moment in the history of the Western Church. A Mass had been held without a priest, the words of consecration had been pronounced audibly, and Communion had been offered in both kinds. By thus worshipping, those in attendance were announcing a break not only with centuries of sacred tradition but also with Rome's authority to define the liturgy.

With this barrier now breached, the first acts of popular resistance occurred. On October 5, a group of mendicants from St. Anthony's cloister in Lichtenberg arrived in Wittenberg. They belonged to a society of ecclesiastical beggars whose members traveled from city to city and who in normal times were grudgingly tolerated by the local population. This time, however, several students (who had to compete with the friars for contributions) angrily accosted them, hurling insults while pelting them with stones and clumps of dirt.

Meanwhile, the Augustinian friars stopped saying the canonical hours. They also celebrated Mass as a communal meal in which both the bread and the wine were passed from friar to friar. When the prior, Conrad Helt, forbade this, the Masses on October 13 were discontinued altogether. In place of the rite, Zwilling preached for two hours, attacking the legitimacy of monastic life and calling on all friars to abandon the cloister. After dinner, he spoke for another hour on the abuse of the Mass. All who heard him in the packed chapel "were astonished," as one of those present put it.

On October 17, 1521, the Mass was the subject of another disputation. While it was broadly agreed that the laity should be offered the cup, sharp disagreements broke out over whether private Masses should continue. Karlstadt—unable to find clear scriptural sanction for their abolition and worried about the tumult that could result—argued for delay. The suddenly emboldened Melanchthon disagreed. There had already been enough talk, he said—it was time to act.

With the differences over the Mass threatening to throw the town into turmoil, a commission was appointed to seek reconciliation; Karlstadt, Melanchthon, and representatives of the Castle Church were among its members. It was agreed that, in general, all abuses in the Mass should cease. The sacrament should no longer be regarded as a sacrifice or good work, and the wine as well as the bread should be administered to the laity. In a concession to Karlstadt, private Masses would be allowed to continue for a while longer so that traditionalists could be won over. On October 20, a report summarizing these points was sent to Frederick.

As always, the elector's position was ambiguous and his motives were unclear. At tremendous risk to both his personal authority and his political fortunes, he was sheltering a man wanted by both the pope and the emperor, and he was facing tremendous pressure to hand Luther over. He would not do so, however; Luther, he felt, had been treated unfairly at the diet, and the Edict of Worms seemed unconstitutional. At the same time, he remained devoted to the Church's traditions and rites. Now presented with proposals for dramatic change in Wittenberg, he resisted. The Mass had been a fixture of Western worship for centuries. Was it to be changed unilaterally by a group of small-town professors? As for private Masses, they helped finance the maintenance of churches and monasteries. The elector wanted the town to move more slowly, and the matter was referred to the faculty and the clergy at the Castle Church for further deliberation.

But the insurgency was proving unstoppable. With the approach of

All Saints' Day (November 1), Wittenberg again filled with pilgrims come to see the relics at the Castle Church and obtain indulgences. Four years after the posting of the Ninety-Five Theses, this practice persisted. As the new provost at the church, Justus Jonas was assigned to preach. This onetime acolyte of Erasmus denounced the relics as rubbish and sought to prove from Scripture that both indulgences and Masses for the dead were spurious. He also condemned penances and pardons as diabolical inventions and called for true penitence in their place. To dramatize the point, Jonas grabbed the money box for indulgences and threw it to the ground, scattering its contents.

At the Black Cloister, meanwhile, Gabriel Zwilling's sermons were growing fiercer by the week. One Sunday he was so ill that he could barely stand, but he insisted on preaching. Monastic life, he declared, was so unholy and hypocritical that no amount of change could save it; whoever helped a friar or nun leave a cloister would deliver a soul from the claws of the Devil. According to one witness, "The preacher's doctrine relative to false faith, obedience, poverty, and chastity was so edifying that many persons shed tears from devotion." Setting an example, Zwilling became the first friar to leave the cloister. By the middle of November, half of the Wittenberg Augustinians (about fifteen) had cast off their cowls.

Helt, the prior, wrote to the elector to complain that some of the departing friars had joined forces with local citizens and students to stir up trouble against those who remained faithful. He himself was reluctant to appear on the street for fear of being attacked. On the Mass and monasticism, Communion and vows, Christian contended with Christian, and no one seemed in charge. "What a mess we are in," Spalatin lamented, "with everybody doing something else!"

Hearing of the ferment in Wittenberg, Luther felt his own absence more acutely than ever. In a letter to Melanchthon, he raised the possibility of a secret meeting to discuss the issues at hand, but the risk remained too great. Instead, he sought to shape events with his pen. With his health fully restored—"at last my behind and my bowels have reconciled themselves to me," he informed Spalatin in early October 1521—he resumed his furious work pace. In the deepening chill of autumn, he composed two sensational tracts that were in effect follow-ups to his three great works of 1520. Together they would help propel the reform forward—and add to the unrest building in Germany.

The first, *The Misuse of the Mass*, reflected the mounting anger Luther felt toward that sacrament. It was, he wrote, an instrument of greed, deceit, and exploitation. To assert that performing Masses in private could reduce a departed soul's time in purgatory was to slander Christ; to regard the Mass as a sacrifice or good work that could be applied to salvation was to insult God. Such doctrines had been invented to enlarge the power and profits of priests. Bishoprics, monasteries, churches, and all other priestly institutions were based and built on holding Masses; "that is, on the most abominable idolatry on earth, on shameful lies, on the perverted, godless misuse of the sacrament, and a disbelief worse than that of the heathen." The priests had persuaded the whole world that the words of consecration should be kept secret and entrusted to no one but themselves when in fact they should be known to all Christians.

As these passages suggest, Luther's real target was the clergy, and his wrath toward them was becoming volcanic. All their money and property, he declared, "are used for nothing but vain pomp, harlotry, and gluttony." Priests were hypocrites, blasphemers, heathens, and Jews—"an unbelieving people of perdition, for whom the wrath of God is reserved eternally." The monks were "a new sea-monster concocted, created, and compiled by the devil himself out of all the components of treachery." It would "be much better to be a devil and a murderer than a priest or monk." Soon these enemies of God would "be eradicated with their prince and creator, the pope, by the coming of our Savior."

In the entire New Testament, Luther stated, the word "priest" is not mentioned "by so much as a single letter." It refers to no priesthood that is tonsured and set apart from the laity; this was simply "an addition of the devil." The writings of the Fathers and the saints did contain many such references, but whereas the Fathers and saints could err in their writings and sin in their lives, the "Scriptures cannot err, and whoever believes them cannot sin in his life." The real priesthood "is a spiritual priesthood, held in common by all Christians, through which we are all priests with

Christ. That is, we are children of Christ, the high priest; we need no priest or mediator other than Christ." Luther was here reaffirming his rejection of the hierarchy and his conviction that all believers are priests.

In place of the abomination currently performed in church, he wrote, the Mass should follow the simple example set by Christ at the Last Supper. If the people of Wittenberg adopted this approach, Christians elsewhere would surely follow. Allowing himself a moment of pride, Luther wondered how it was that God had "willed the awakening of his Word in this forgotten corner of the world." To "us of all people it has been given to see the pure and original face of the gospel." Since the people of Wittenberg had now become "zealots of the Spirit," it was their duty to "spread it out and let others see it," though without strife and with understanding for those weak in faith.

On November 11, 1521, Luther sent *The Misuse of the Mass* to Spalatin, accompanied by a letter in which he announced his next project: "I have decided to attack monastic vows and to free the young people from that hell of celibacy, totally unclean and condemned as it is through its burning and pollution." Through further study, Luther had overcome his earlier doubts about abolishing the vow of celibacy for monks. In fact, he had concluded that not only the vow but the entire institution of monasticism was a human invention and hence counterfeit. With his fellow Augustinians already fleeing the cloister, Luther wanted to persuade others to follow. In a mere ten days, he completed the sixty-thousand-word *Judgment of Martin Luther on Monastic Vows*. It would help empty the monasteries of Germany.

By its very nature, Luther wrote, monastic life, with its tonsures and garb, bellowing and muttering, bowing and scraping, mocked God. If an unbeliever were suddenly to find himself amid these men and hear them not preaching or praying but rather sounding like "pipe organs," each set in a neat row with his neighbors, would he not be justified in thinking they had all gone mad? Do these men really believe that God finds delight in hearing a lot of dumb pipes blowing off into thin air?

In entering the cloister, monks sought to live not in want but in plenty. They were attracted by the granaries of the cloisters and the promise of not having to work with their hands. Monasteries thus turned men into "idlers, who, like locusts, caterpillars, and beetles, devour everyone else's substance." Preoccupied with their own welfare, they showed scant concern for that of others. If a monk sees someone who is hungry, thirsty, naked, or homeless, he is forbidden to leave the monastery to help. Even if a neighbor is dying, he is kept from offering comfort. What harm would come to the monastic system if a monk was allowed to leave the cloister to visit the sick or look after his parents? True obedience consists not in taking a vow to an abbot or a rule but in loving one's parents and serving one's neighbors. Monks love only their own kind.

Of monasticism's many faults, it was the vow of celibacy that Luther found most offensive. "Almost everything about it is befouled," he wrote, "if not by unclean seminal emissions, then by the continual searing of lust which never dies out." For all but a rare few, keeping it is impossible. If an incontinent person is compelled to be continent, "how many uncleannesses, how many fornications, how many adulteries and other evils will you provoke?" Going on at length about lust, Luther wrote that the "inward and intrinsic tyrant in our members" is no more within our power to control than the "ill will of an external tyrant." A man under the influence of sexual desire is like a person impaired by a severe illness, except that the tyranny of the flesh is more violent and harsh than any physical ailment. For this vow more than any other, there were compelling reasons for the Church to grant dispensations, yet it was precisely here that dispensations were most stubbornly withheld.

For these monstrous abuses, Luther held one person responsible: Jerome. More than anyone else, he fumed, this Father had warped Christianity by implanting in it the ideals of celibacy and asceticism. Of his letter to Eustochium, Luther wrote: "How I wish that this praise of virginity had never been spoken, especially by such an authoritative person." On this matter, the words of Jerome had come to have more weight than those of the New Testament itself, which, Luther wrote, contained no passage where God commanded celibacy. Since this vow had nothing to do with faith, celibacy should be regarded as a matter of free choice.

In the millennium since Jerome had beaten his breast in the Syrian Desert over the dancing girls of Rome, no one had so bluntly challenged his exaltation of virginity as Luther did in *On Monastic Vows*. A piercing protest against the whole ecclesiastical regimen of sexual denial, this tract would lay the foundation for Protestants' rejection of celibacy and support for clerical marriage.

Throughout this work, Erasmus's influence is palpable. Luther's fierce put-downs of the monastic orders echo Erasmus's droll send-ups of the pot-bellied and sandal-shod. A clear line can be drawn from Erasmus's modest observation in the *Enchiridion, Monachatus non est pietas*—"Monasticism is not piety"—to Luther's tirades against the entire institution. But Luther's assault was characteristically more furious. "I want the whole idea of the monastery rooted out, wiped out, and abolished," he roared in one passage. God should treat the monasteries like Sodom and Gomorrah, "so that not even their members should be left." Isolated in his hilltop fortress, Luther seemed heedless of the inciting effect such pronouncements could have at a time of rising anticlericalism.

Luther dedicated *On Monastic Vows* to his father, Hans. In an emotional prefatory letter, he sought to repair their strained relations. Nearly sixteen years had passed since he had become a monk, and had he known of his father's unwavering disapproval, Luther wrote, he would never have followed through, but he now urged Hans to see how much good had come of his decision. It was God's will that he personally experience the impieties of monastic life so that no one could accuse him of condemning something of which he was ignorant. He could now show with authority how mad the papists were in holding up continence and virginity as values above all others. In any case, his ultimate allegiance was not to his earthly father but to Christ. He is "my immediate bishop, abbot, prior, lord, father, and teacher; I know no other. Thus I hope that he has taken from you one son in order that he may begin to help the sons of many others through me."

Even as he was attacking monasticism and the Mass, Luther opened a third front. At the beginning of September 1521, Archbishop Albrecht of Mainz—in dire need of funds to maintain his court—published a papal bull promising an indulgence to those visiting his relics collection at the cathedral in Halle, where he resided. The collection's nearly nine thousand items included a container of the mud from which God created Adam, branches from the burning bush, manna from Sinai, and wine from the wedding at Cana. As was the custom, visitors were expected to make a contribution in return for the indulgence. This was the same type of abuse that had driven Luther to write his Ninety-Five Theses, and when word reached the Wartburg that the archbishop was again at it, Luther prepared a stinging protest, denouncing not only Albrecht's "idol" (the relics) but also his "brothel" (a reference to the harlots that he was widely believed to keep). *Against the Idol at Halle*, Luther called it, and when it was done he sent it off to Spalatin to be published.

Anticipating this development, Albrecht had sent Wolfgang Capito to Wittenberg in late September to meet with Melanchthon and others to try to forestall it. The mission was a success: the Saxon court decided to withhold the publication of Luther's tract against Albrecht. When informed by Spalatin of this decision, Luther erupted. "I have hardly ever read a letter that displeased me more than your last one. . . . Your idea of not disturbing the public peace is beautiful, but will you allow the eternal peace of God to be disturbed by the wicked and sacrilegious actions of that son of perdition? Not so Spalatin! Not so Elector!"

Refusing to be deterred, Luther decided to write to Albrecht directly. Twice before, he noted, he had admonished Albrecht for selling indulgences but had not publicly accused him. Disregarding his concerns, the archbishop had now erected at Halle an idol that "robs poor simple Christians of their money and their souls." He implored the archbishop to take the display down. If he did not, Luther would be forced to reveal to the world that the notorious indulgence sale of 1517 had been instigated not by Johann Tetzel, as was generally believed, but by Albrecht himself. He urged Albrecht to recall the "horrible fire" that had been set off by that initial spark. "The whole world was then surely of the opinion that one poor friar was too unimportant to receive the pope's attention and was undertaking an impossible task." But matters had now reached the point where the pope himself could barely contain the blaze. Luther further demanded that Albrecht stop persecuting priests who were marrying. He expected a "definite and speedy reply" to his letter in fourteen days; if it did not come, he would release his book. From his aerie, the solitary friar was presenting Germany's most powerful prelate with an ultimatum.

Luther was worried, however, that the electoral court would not post

his letter to Albrecht. He was also concerned about the status of his manuscripts on the Mass and monastic vows. Weeks after sending them off
to Wittenberg, he had heard nothing back. Had they, too, been held up?
After six months of being cooped up in the Wartburg, Luther longed to
see Melanchthon, Amsdorf, Jonas, and other friends. In another of the
daring acts that marked this phase of his career, he decided to make a secret visit to Wittenberg. Wearing the gray cloak and red beret of a knight,
Luther on December 2, 1521, mounted a horse and, accompanied by a servant, rode down from the Wartburg and headed east toward Wittenberg.

WAS NOWHERE SAFE?

Shortly after leaving Louvain for Basel, Erasmus had a stroke of luck. In the town of Tienen twelve miles to the east, he came upon a detachment of German soldiers who had just been discharged from the imperial army. Traveling in the same direction, they let him join them. Grateful for their protection and finding them far more disciplined than the usual bands, Erasmus would remain with them for the next two hundred miles. On one leg they rode for nine straight hours without stopping to eat because the road, winding through mountains and hills, was vulnerable to attack. Leaving the soldiers at Speyer, Erasmus continued on through Alsace. There, the main hazards were the foul-smelling stoves and the literary societies that insisted on detaining him with their receptions and toasts.

Finally, after nearly three weeks on horseback, Erasmus on November 15, 1521, rode wearily into Basel. The strain of the journey made his return to this oasis of scholars, printers, and proofreaders all the sweeter. Johann Froben had prepared a room for him in the building that housed his own shop and living quarters, with an open fireplace instead of a stove. No sooner was Erasmus installed, though, than he came down with a "pestilent rheum," brought on in part by the growing chill in his rooms. In his letters, he frequently remarked on what seemed his dwindling years, and this lent added urgency to his work as he rushed to complete the remaining elements of his reform program. They included his annotations on the New Testament, his editions of Cyprian and Augustine, a new collection of his letters, and his scriptural paraphrases.

Erasmus had initially planned to limit his paraphrases to the Epistles; the Gospels, with their many discrepancies and obscurities, seemed too daunting. But the paraphrases of the Epistles were proving so popular— "thumbed everywhere, even by laymen," he noted—that he was being urged to move on to the Gospels, and so he took up Matthew. As he proceeded, he saw how mistaken he had been to resist. While the Epistles offered the theology of Christ, the Gospels offered his life. The Sermon on the Mount as recorded in Matthew was central to Erasmus's philosophy of Christ, and in his paraphrase he was able to expand and elaborate on it. "Since the evangelists wrote down the gospel to be read by all," Erasmus observed in his preface, "I do not see why all should not read it, and I have treated it in such a way that even illiterates can understand it."

While Erasmus was thus promoting Christian comity, his own work was causing ever more strife. In Rome, Stunica (Diego López Zúñiga) was continuing to agitate against him. The Spanish scholar had completed a manuscript, called *Erasmi Roterodami Blasphemiae et Impietates*, that offered quotations and excerpts from Erasmus's works along with lengthy comments seeking to show how closely his positions paralleled those of Luther. Stunica was reading from it at dinner parties and making the rounds of bookshops to press "his slanderous views," as a friend reported from Rome. According to another correspondent, Stunica was intent on exposing ten thousand errors in Erasmus's New Testament and to that end had mobilized a force of learned Italians to "make a sortie and bear down headlong on your writings." Stunica had boasted that he was going to keep at it until Erasmus felt compelled to travel to Rome and recant. If he refused, he would be made to "burn in a coat of pitch" (a reference to the *tunica molesta*, or shirt of pain, made of pitch and set on fire to torture criminals).

While Catholic critics like Stunica were denouncing Erasmus as a covert Lutheran, Luther's followers were deriding him as a Roman apologist. One of them, while studying Erasmus's works for impieties, found an egregious example in the ninth chapter of his paraphrase of Romans (written in 1517). There, Erasmus had remarked that some part of salvation "depends on our own will and effort, although this part is very minor when compared to the free kindness of God." This attribution to man of even a tiny bit of control over his actions infuriated the Lutherans. "Luther's party in their public utterance tear me to pieces as a Pelagian, because they think I give more weight than they do to free will," Erasmus wrote in frustration to his friend Willibald Pirckheimer in Nuremberg in early 1522. Six years earlier, Luther had charged Erasmus with this offense in his initial letter to Spalatin. Now the discovery of a fleeting remark about free will in one of his paraphrases was stirring an angry round of accusations. "All Luther's party hate me passionately and pile slanders on me," Erasmus wrote to Jean de Carondelet, an official at the imperial court, but, he added, "I shall never prove false either to the faith of Christ or to the glory of the emperor."

Even as Erasmus was affirming his loyalty to the ruling powers, however, he was preparing a new volume that would rank among his most irreverent—and popular—works. It came about almost by accident. More than twenty years earlier, while working as a tutor in Paris, Erasmus had scribbled down some *formulae*, or patterns of polite conversation, to teach his students colloquial Latin. He had lent them to a fellow tutor, who never returned them. Somehow, they had ended up at the house of Froben, and in 1518 the Basel publisher brought them out as an eighty-page octavo.

Remarkably, the publishing house had not bothered to ask Erasmus's permission, and when the Dutchman saw the volume—and the many errors in it—he exploded. But then he learned how favorably the book had been received, with reprints quickly appearing in Paris and Antwerp. Erasmus at once produced a corrected version, which was published in Louvain in March 1519 under the title *Formulas of Familiar Conversations, by Erasmus of Rotterdam, useful not only for polishing a boy's speech but for building his character.* It sold even more briskly, with at least thirty reprints appearing by 1522.

In Basel, Erasmus began preparing a greatly enlarged edition, with the conversational sketches converted into fully realized dialogues. The first full edition of the *Colloquies* (as he called them) was published by Froben in March 1522. Erasmus would continue working on them for most of his remaining years, producing some sixty in all. In the eighteen years from their initial appearance until Erasmus's death, about a hundred editions would appear. The *Colloquies* would bring both lasting acclaim and bitter controversy. They would be censured by monks, denounced by inquisitors, condemned by universities (especially the University of Paris), and listed in the Index of Prohibited Books, where they would remain until the end of the nineteenth century. Luther would repeatedly attack the

Colloquies, declaring in his Table Talk that in his will he would forbid his sons to read them. Yet Melanchthon's 1527 manual for German schools prescribed them for intermediate students, and for the next three centuries they would remain a standard text in schools across Europe.

The *Colloquies* offered Erasmus an ideal vehicle for promoting his reform program. Under the cover of a lively textbook, he could smuggle his ideas into the minds of readers; since those ideas were expressed by characters, he could deny they were his own. Drawing on a lifetime of restless travels and diverse encounters, Erasmus offered a rich tableau of emblematic figures of early-sixteenth-century Europe—court preachers who claim in sermons that war is just, holy, and right; baseborn women who slather on the cosmetics of fine ladies; prostitutes who profit more from mendicants than from merchants; horse dealers expert at cheating their customers; knights who consider it a matter of principle to relieve travelers of their money; mercenaries ready for a trifling sum to cut a man's throat; and priests who gossip about what they hear in confession—all described with Lucianic wit and driven by an underlying concern for moral and social improvement.

In "Inns," for instance, Erasmus offers a contrast between the French and German variety that both instructs and entertains. In French inns, guests are warmly welcomed by comely women with delightful manners. The fare served is sumptuous, and in the rooms housekeepers cheerfully offer to wash one's clothes. In German inns, there's no one to greet guests, and eighty or ninety people are forced to use the same overheated public room. "One combs his hair, another wipes the sweat off, another cleans his rawhide boots or leggings, another belches garlic." At dinner, the tablecloth seems to have been taken from a boat sail, and there's a wait of an hour or more for the meal to begin. The cheese is full of worms and mold and the wine is sharp and pungent and served in such quantities that after a while there's a deafening uproar, with the Germans singing, shouting, dancing, and stomping. In the rooms, the linen has not been washed for six months.

Erasmus's account was no doubt exaggerated for effect, and there are contrary reports from the period. But the contrast he draws gives him an opportunity to make a broader point about the importance of cleanliness. "Nothing seems to me more dangerous than for so many persons to breathe the same warm air," a character remarks. Quite apart "from the belching of garlic, the breaking of wind, the stinking breaths, many persons suffer from hidden diseases, and every disease is contagious."

Elsewhere in the *Colloquies*, Erasmus proposes various preventive measures, such as changing the sheets in inns for each new guest and keeping people from drinking from the same cup—more evidence of his advanced views on matters of hygiene.

Many of the *Colloquies* deal with marriage, courtship, and women. Erasmus champions marriage over virginity but also acknowledges the many problems experienced by couples, not least in bed. Though both parties usually bear responsibility, he writes, it is up to the wives to make their husbands happy—a highly paternalistic position. In "A Marriage in Name Only, or The Unequal Match," however, Erasmus is critical of arranged marriages, in this case of a charming young woman forced by her parents to marry a syphilitic older man. And, in "The Abbot and the Learned Lady," he celebrates female erudition. The learned lady is Magdalia, whose love of books in Greek and Latin draws the disdain of the abbot, Atronius. He says that he is bored by serious study and discourages the monks in his charge from reading lest they become less tractable and talk back "by quoting from decrees and decretals, from Peter and Paul." The proper equipment for women, he says, is "distaff and spindle"; it is not necessary for them to know Latin, since it does little to protect their chastity. "You think it unsuitable for me to know Latin in order to converse daily with authors so numerous, so eloquent, so learned, so wise?" Magdalia asks. "Books," Atronius sniffs, "ruin women's wits— which are none too plentiful anyway." "If you're not careful," she warns, women will "preside in the theological schools, preach in the churches, and wear your miters."

A major theme of the *Colloquies* is the distinction between true and false piety. In "The Shipwreck," a seafarer recalls a harrowing episode in which passengers aboard a storm-tossed ship make outlandish vows about the thanks they will give if they reach shore alive. An Englishman pledges heaps of gold to the Virgin of Walsingham. Another passenger says he will go to St. James at Compostela barefoot, bareheaded, and begging his bread. A third promises to dedicate to St. Christopher a wax taper as tall as himself in the tallest church in Paris. Amid them all, a woman calmly suckling her baby prays in silence. As the boat goes down, she is the first to make it to shore while most of the rest perish—a testament to the power of earnest devotion. (This colloquy would become one of the most popular satires of the sixteenth century.)

Of all the colloquies, the most Erasmian in spirit is "The Godly Feast." A rebuke to all the raucous dinner parties Erasmus had to attend, it is set in a placid garden featuring an orchard, a fountain, three loggias, and an aviary with birds so tame that at dinnertime they fly through the window and eat from the hands of the guests. Eusebius, the host, says that he emphatically disagrees "with those who think a dinner party isn't enjoyable unless it overflows with silly bawdy stories and rings with dirty songs. True gaiety comes from a clean, sincere conscience." Over servings of lettuce, eggs, partridges, a shoulder of mutton, and a capon from the host's own coop, the guests discuss passages from the Bible. The conversation is unfailingly courteous and high-minded. Along with the Gospels and Epistles, the guests cite Cicero and Plutarch. (It is in this colloquy that Erasmus offers his famous appeal, "St Socrates, pray for us!") The diners contrast the empty nature of Judaic rites and ceremonies with true spiritual depth. They also note the importance of remembering the poor amid such plenty. Eusebius laments the existence of so many richly adorned monasteries and churches at a time when "so many of Christ's living temples are in danger of starvation, shiver in their nakedness, and are tormented by want of the necessities of life." As the meal winds down, he urges his guests to relax while he travels to a nearby village to comfort a friend who is critically ill.

Hovering over this serene sketch is the memory of John Colet. Though the fare served at this feast is far ampler than that offered by the English dean, the earnest discussion of Scripture over supper seems to have been inspired by the many meals Erasmus attended at St. Paul's in London. With its air of uplift and concord, "The Godly Feast" lacks the bite of many other colloquies, but it captures Erasmus's love of refined conversation and his belief that Scripture is open to varying interpretations that can be discussed with civility and respect.

The art of dining is a recurrent theme in the *Colloquies*. This reflected more than Erasmus's epicureanism. In the great religious upheaval then under way, food was becoming a major point of contention. Paul and other early Christians had rejected the elaborate dietary regulations of the Jews, yet the rules of the medieval Church had become no less intricate. Palm Sunday was celebrated with bacchanalian revels, but, as a butcher in the colloquy "A Fish Diet" remarks, anyone who so much as tastes an egg is thrown into jail. Clothing and many other areas of Christian life had become subject to similar regulation, provoking bitter quarrels and hateful slanders. If such strife could be avoided, the butcher adds, "we could live in greater peace, not bothering about ceremonies but straining only after those things that Christ taught."

Many reform-minded Christians agreed—especially in Switzerland. Whereas in Germany celibacy and the Mass had risen to the fore, in Switzerland food and fasting were emerging as the main catalysts. And a rebellion was gathering. Beginning in nearby Zurich, it would quickly spread to other Swiss cities, including Basel, where it would engulf the life of Erasmus. Initially developing parallel to the Lutheran Reformation, the Swiss Reformation (as it came to be known) would become its bitter rival. Over time, these two reformations would divide into separate branches of Protestantism: the Lutheran and the Calvinist (or Reformed). And the starting point for it all was a sausage.

On Ash Wednesday 1522, a dozen or so men, including bakers, vinedressers, and printers, gathered in the parlor of the home of Christoph Froschauer, a printer in Zurich, for a simple evening meal. The maid prepared two pork sausages as well as some eggs. The sausages and eggs were cut into pieces, then passed around and eaten—a clear violation of the Lenten fast. It would no doubt have been excused had it been explained as an accident or admitted to be sinful and absolution sought. The printers were rushing to complete a volume of Paul's epistles in time for the spring fair in Frankfurt, and Froschauer maintained that they needed the sustenance to keep up their stamina—the type of loophole the authorities routinely recognized.

But one of those present, Huldrych Zwingli, had no interest in loopholes. A thirty-eight-year-old canon at the Grossmünster, Zurich's largest and wealthiest church, Zwingli did not himself partake, but he believed that those who did were fully entitled to as pious Christians. A powerful preacher, Zwingli had excited his congregation with sharp attacks on indulgences, the veneration of saints, and the worship of Mary—none of which, he said, was sanctioned by the Bible. Christians should heed the divine words of Scripture over the fallible laws of man—even those issued by a pope or council.

The sausage eaten at Froschauer's house was intended to test those rules. In its time of day, number of participants, and manner of distribution, the meal was consciously meant to evoke the Last Supper, and two weeks later Zwingli defended it in a sermon. While each person could choose on his own to fast and abstain from particular foods, he declared, the Church was not justified in proclaiming this a universal and unchanging law, since there was nothing to that effect in the New Testament. "How dare a man add to the testament, to the covenant of God, as though he would better it?"

Thus encouraged, other Zurich citizens also began testing the fasting regulations. From these modest actions would spring the Swiss Reformation. Zwingli would be its father. He was one of the most learned—and least likable—men of the sixteenth century. A statue of him standing outside the Wasserkirche (Water church) in Zurich shows him holding a Bible in one hand and a sword in the other—an apt image of his militant attachment to the Word of God. At an early age, he would lose his life in religious warfare. What he left unfinished in Zurich, John Calvin would complete in Geneva.

That Zwingli became such a militant reformer is all the more striking in that he began as an Erasmian. As a young man, he was so taken with the Dutch humanist that in the spring of 1515 or 1516 he traveled to Basel to meet him. At the time, Zwingli was serving as a parish priest in Glarus, a rural market town eighty miles from Basel. There, he had turned the second story of his parish house into a library. It eventually contained some three hundred volumes—an extraordinarily large collection for a parish priest. Intent on reading the Greek Fathers, he dedicated himself to learning their language. And he devoured Erasmus, including the *Enchiridion*, the *Adages*, *De Copia*, the *Praise of Folly*, the Jerome, and his writings on war, which made a special impression. Twice during his years in Glarus, Zwingli served as a chaplain to Swiss mercenaries fighting in northern Italy, and he was present in September 1515 when, at the battle of Marignano, more than ten thousand Swiss were slaughtered. In addition to witnessing the bloodshed, Zwingli had to deliver the news to the families of the fallen. From this experience he emerged an Erasmian-style pacifist steadfastly opposed to the mercenary trade.

In his meeting with Erasmus, Zwingli told him that he read his books every night before going to sleep. Erasmus was gracious in return, and back in Glarus Zwingli wrote him an effusive thank-you note, saying that he had made a name for himself simply by boasting that he had seen Erasmus, "the man who has done so much for liberal studies and the mysteries of Holy Scripture." Writing back, Erasmus warmly but patronizingly advised Zwingli to practice his pen from time to time: "This is the best way to learn to express yourself. I perceive Minerva has given you the gift, if you would but exercise it."

When Erasmus's revised New Testament appeared, Zwingli was among the first to obtain a copy, and it changed his entire outlook. Reading the Gospels and Epistles in their original language, he felt as if he were gaining direct access to God's words, untainted by errors in translation or transcription. Moved by Paul's missionary work, he copied out his letters in Greek. The simple piety of the first Christians seemed greatly at odds with the ornate ritualism of the Swiss clergy. Reading Erasmus's explanation of the distinction between *poenitentia* and *metanoia*, he could see that Christ was calling on the faithful to repent rather than perform rote acts of penance. More generally, Zwingli absorbed Erasmus's philosophy of Christ, with its embrace of interior spirituality and its summons to moral improvement.

In the spring of 1516, Zwingli relocated to Einsiedeln, the site of a famous shrine to the Black Virgin that attracted pilgrims from many miles around. It, too, was a backwater, however, and two years later, when a position for a people's priest at the Grossmünster in Zurich opened up, he made his interest known. Zwingli's candidacy was damaged by rumors that he had seduced the virgin daughter of a prominent Einsiedeln citizen. In a letter of self-defense, Zwingli admitted having had relations with the woman, but seeking to shift the blame, he said that she was no virgin and that in any case it was she who had seduced him. That satisfied the search committee, and in December 1518 he got the post. A flourishing trade center on the banks of the Limmat River, Zurich was Switzerland's most powerful city. Like most of the cantons and communes of the Swiss Confederation, it had a long history of self-rule and enjoyed considerable independence from both emperor and pope. In this regard Switzerland contrasted sharply with the princely territories of the Holy Roman Empire, with their absolutist rulers. The reform movement spawned by Zwingli would reflect this, incorporating a tradition of civic participation and communal purpose. It would also feature an Erasmian impulse toward moral improvement. Overall, the Swiss Reformation would have a far more activist spirit than its Lutheran counterpart, apparent in its relentless push to reorganize society along scriptural lines.

In his very first sermon, delivered on January 1, 1519, Zwingli showed his independence. Rather than preach from the text prescribed by the Church, he decided to start at the beginning with the Gospel of Matthew; rather than dilate on Scholastic propositions, he described the life of Christ and the lessons it offered to ordinary Christians. He also stressed the need to hear the pure, unadulterated Word of God and to lead a simplified life of repentance, faith, and love based on it. Many came to listen and were moved.

Over the next three years, however, Zwingli would undergo a dramatic change. The precipitating event was a devastating outbreak of the plague in August 1519. Among the 1,500 people carried off was Zwingli's brother, Andreas. Most of those who could leave the city did, but Zwingli stayed on to perform his pastoral duties, and he became so ill that he nearly died. While convalescing, he wrote a poem, "The Song of Pestilence," that captured his troubled emotional state:

> Help, Lord God, help
> in this trouble!
> I think Death is at the door.
> Stand before me, Christ;
> For thou hast overcome him! . . .

Do what thou wilt;
I am completely thine;
Thy vessel I am.

In the face of death, Erasmian-style exhortations to virtue seemed unavailing; seeking spiritual transformation, Zwingli found redemption in
the reborn Christ.

Around this same time, Zwingli began reading Luther. With increasing frequency, the Augustinian friar's name appeared in his correspondence. He also arranged for colporteurs to carry Luther's tracts to cities,
villages, and churches across Switzerland. Later, after bitterly falling out
with the German reformer, Zwingli would insist that he had arrived at his
views completely independently of him—that he had read Augustine and
Paul on his own and through them had developed a radical pessimism
about man's ability to attain redemption apart from God's grace. But the
themes he now began to expound—the depravity of humankind, the inutility of works, the importance of faith, the authority of Scripture—so
closely resembled Luther's as to invite skepticism about that claim. Whatever his actual pathway, Zwingli joined the ranks of Erasmians moving
toward an insistently faith-based creed.

Assuming the mantle of a prophet, Zwingli from the pulpit inveighed
against superstition, ceremony, and clerical corruption. Though some
of the canons at the Grossmünster objected, most were inspired by his
ardor, and when a vacancy among them opened, Zwingli was named to
fill it. This was in late April 1521, after Luther had made his bold stand
at Worms. Electrified by the news, crowds packed the cathedral to hear
Zwingli extol faith and grace, deride ostentatious displays of devotion,
and call on the pious to take Christ into their hearts.

Then, at the start of Lent in 1522, the sausages were eaten at Froschauer's house. An investigation was launched, and the maid admitted that
she had prepared the meal at her master's bidding. No arrests were made,
but Zwingli decided to draft a pamphlet explaining his views. Titled *On
the Choice and Freedom of Food*, it condemned the laws on fasting. The
ordinances demanding abstention from milk, butter, cheese, and eggs
were of relatively recent origin, he wrote; if it was sinful to consume these

products on fast days, why had it taken the Church fourteen centuries to discover this? Christ's principle that the Sabbath was made for man and not man for the Sabbath should be applied to fasting as well. "In a word, if you will fast, do so; if you do not wish to eat meat, eat it not; but leave Christians a free choice in the matter."

Bishop Hugo of Constance, whose diocese included Zurich, made clear that he would tolerate no such choice, and the town council admonished all citizens to abstain from eating meat on fast days without good cause or permission until the issue could be resolved. No one, it stated, "should become involved in quarrel and strife or employ offensive and inept words against one another concerning the eating of meat, preaching, or similar matters." Everyone, it said, should "be peaceful and calm."

Zurich was anything but, however. The sausage incident would be for Switzerland what Luther's Ninety-Five Theses were for Germany—the trigger for revolt against Rome. Zurich's example quickly spread to other cities—Basel included. On April 13, 1522 (Palm Sunday), several junior clergymen met for dinner at the Klybeck castle, a merchant's residence. A suckling pig was served along with much oratory attesting to the historic nature of the occasion. When word of this Lenten violation spread, there was an "astonishing uproar," as Erasmus wrote, and both the town council and the bishop of Basel (Christoph von Utenheim) issued mandates against all such violations of custom and law.

Summoned before the bishop, the organizers of the event defended themselves in part by citing Erasmus's example. Because of his poor digestion and loathing of fish, Erasmus had sometimes eaten chicken during Lent. But he had always been discreet about it, and he had had a papal dispensation for straying. As much as he detested the proliferation of ecclesiastical ordinances, especially about food, Erasmus was dead set against any public flouting of them. He wanted change, but only if it was orderly and authorized by the Church.

It was to be neither. Though the bishop (who was reform-minded) decided not to punish the defiant diners, the host, a doctor named Sigismund Steinschneider, thought it prudent to leave Basel. At the parish church of St. Alban's, Wilhelm Reublin, a university-trained theologian and priest (and future Anabaptist leader) who had also participated, was attracting up to four thousand people with sermons attacking vigils, Masses for the dead, and the bishop of Basel himself.

Intent on clarifying his position, Erasmus drafted a long open letter to the bishop. *De Esu Carnium* ("On Eating Meat"), as it was titled, dealt not only with the dietary laws but also with saints' days and priestly celibacy and the whole teeming catalog of ecclesiastical regulations. Written on the eve of the Reformation, it offered Erasmus's fullest statement on the best way forward.

On matters of food, he wrote, the New Testament was clear. Christ taught that each was free to eat what he wished, and Paul said that he did not want anyone to be judged on matters of food and drink. Why, then, should eating pork on Fridays be considered as grave an offense as parricide? As for the holy days on which work is prohibited, the New Testament stipulates none of them, so why had they been allowed to proliferate? While each saint must have his day, must men refrain from working on it? Should a farmer let his crop rot rather than take advantage of a good harvest day because it is dedicated to some saint? Surely it would be better to let a man work and support his family.

Similarly, priestly celibacy had not been instituted by Christ but was of fairly recent origin. Long ago, Erasmus observed, the Church abolished nightly vigils at the shrines of the martyrs, even though this had been a custom for centuries. The hours for fasting, which used to extend to noon, had been significantly shortened. Why, then, in the case of priestly celibacy, should the Church cling so tightly to human regulation when there were so many persuasive reasons to change it? Since so few priests were actually chaste, it would be better to allow them to marry and provide their children with a liberal education. In thus arguing, Erasmus noted, he did not intend to defend those priests who had recently married without papal authorization. (In fact, he strongly opposed them.) Rather, he wanted the Church to consider the advantage that would result from adapting an old institution to present usefulness. The people were not there for the bishops—the bishops were there to minister to the people.

Erasmus, in short, was making the case for gradual reform from the top. What was most needed, he believed, was enlightened leadership by the Church. But what if such leadership was not forthcoming? Erasmus did not say. *De Esu Carnium* was nonetheless a great success, appearing in eight editions in 1522 and 1523. It was also much criticized; Erasmus would later call it one of his three most disliked works, along with the *Praise of Folly* and the *Colloquies*. The Catholics hated it because of Erasmus's blithe dismissal of customs and regulations that were an essential part of Church tradition. The reformers reviled it because they took Erasmus's call for caution as a rebuke to their own headlong push for change.

The whole climate in Basel was rapidly changing. The strife set off by the pork-eating incident at Klybeck castle was now seeping into every corner of civic life. Preachers dueled in the pulpits, and laymen contended over whether to fast or not. Erasmus had come to this broad-minded city to escape the turmoil in Louvain, but with the Reformation now gaining a foothold there and agitation rising on all sides, he began to wonder how long he would be able to remain.

30

SATAN FALLS UPON THE FLOCK

On December 4, 1521, Luther rode into a very tense Wittenberg. On the previous morning, a gang of students and townsmen with knives hidden under their coats had gathered at the town church and prevented some priests from entering. Other priests had managed to get in, but when they began celebrating Mass, the agitators snatched their missals and drove them from the altar. They also threw stones at some parishioners who were chanting the Magnificat. The next day, a group of students smashed the door of the Franciscan friary and disrupted the services with hoots and heckling. The town council had to deploy a guard to protect the cloister, and Frederick the Wise angrily demanded that the perpetrators be detained and a full investigation carried out.

On arriving, Luther went straight to the home of his friend Nikolaus von Amsdorf, where Philipp Melanchthon was also staying. Seeing this strange Junker with a flowing beard, red beret, and sword at his side, they wondered who it could be. Upon recognizing him, they were shocked and delighted. Luther wanted to go to the Augustinian cloister but was advised not to, so as not to give away his presence. "Everything . . . pleases me very much," he informed Spalatin on December 5. Surprisingly, he made no mention of the recent disorders. Apparently, he considered them insignificant when measured against the great strides the reform was making.

He was, however, upset to find that no one knew anything about his manuscripts. "There is nothing that would disturb me more at this moment," he wrote to Spalatin, than to know that the manuscripts had reached him "and you were holding them back, since I have dealt in these little books with themes that require the greatest possible haste." In fact, Spalatin was worried about the violence of Luther's language and so had withheld them from the printers. In the face of Luther's fury, however, he quickly capitulated and sent off the tracts on the Mass and monastic vows. He continued to hold back the pamphlet against Albrecht's relics, however, worried about the damage it could do to the elector's relations with the archbishop. At Luther's insistence, though, Spalatin agreed to post his letter to Albrecht, in which he demanded that he take down the "idol" at Halle.

While in Wittenberg, Luther had time to sit for a portrait by Lucas Cranach—the one surviving image of him as Junker Jörg. It's easy to see why his friends failed to recognize him. With his filled-out face and full head of hair, Luther looked nothing like the gaunt friar they had seen leave Wittenberg for Worms eight months earlier. The one constant was his eyes: dark and intense, they gazed off into the distance, as if fixed on matters far beyond the earthly realm.

There was, however, one practical matter that absorbed Luther's attention during his stay. Melanchthon and other friends pressed him to take on a project that they considered of the utmost importance: a translation of the Bible into German. For the gospel to spread, they said, there was needed a text that spoke to the people in their own tongue, and Luther seemed the ideal person to provide it.

Not that there was any lack of German Bibles. Prior to 1521, some eighteen editions had appeared. Most, though, were ornate and expensive. The best-known was a 1475 edition printed in Augsburg, but it (like most others) had been translated from the Vulgate and reproduced its formal, legalistic language. None of the existing translations had taken full advantage of the wondrous new editing tools that had recently been developed to help repair and restore ancient texts.

The Church, for its part, strongly discouraged the production of vernacular Bibles, insisting on the Vulgate as the sole authorized text. But a new era of vernacular translations was dawning, as proclaimed by Erasmus in his *Paraclesis*, where he had called for the Gospels and Epistles to be "translated into all languages" so that the farmer could sing a portion of them at the plow and the weaver hum parts of them at his shuttle. Around this time, Luther, in a clear echo of Erasmus, wrote, "I wish every town would have its interpreter, and that this book alone, in all languages, would live in the hands, eyes, ears, and hearts of all people."

During the early part of his stay at the Wartburg, Luther had tried translating some passages from the New Testament into German and been pleased with the results. Given his insistence on Scripture as the sole Christian authority, a reliable version of the Bible seemed essential, and so he agreed that, once back in the Wartburg, he would attempt a full translation.

With rumors spreading of his presence in Wittenberg, Luther decided after just a few days to leave. On his trip back to the Wartburg, he saw many signs of unrest in the countryside. Priests were marrying, monks were throwing off their cowls, and itinerant preachers were inveighing against the privileges of the hierarchy and the transgressions of the clergy. Roused by such statements, the common man was stirring. Among the inciting pamphlets Luther saw was one titled *Karsthans*, which depicted the simple farmer as an upright Christian ready to use a flail or cudgel against the pope. Already, in Erfurt, the homes of some clergymen had been attacked after it was announced that three canons who had participated in the reception for Luther during his trip to Worms were to be excommunicated. There was even talk of murdering priests.

In the aftermath of Worms, Luther had been heartened by the arousal of the populace, but now, after seeing the explosive forces gathering, he decided to issue a warning. *A Sincere Admonition to All Christians to Guard Against Insurrection and Rebellion*, written shortly after his return to the Wartburg, was Luther's first full statement on the subject of political action, and it gave an early sign of the political conservative lurking within the religious rebel. Though he was pleased to see the papists cowering before the wrath of the people, Luther wrote, "no insurrection is ever right, no matter how right the cause it seeks to promote," for an insurrection "always results in more damage than improvement" and harms the innocent more than the guilty. When *Herr Omnes* ("Mr. Everyman") breaks loose, "he cannot tell the wicked from the upright," making injustice inevitable. Only the princes and other ruling parties should have the authority to wield the sword to set things right. "I am and always will be on the side of those against whom insurrection is directed, no matter how unjust their cause," Luther flatly declared. "I am opposed to those who rise in insurrection, no matter how just their cause, because there can be no insurrection without hurting the innocent and shedding their blood."

This was not to rule out all efforts aimed at bringing about change. Through writing and speaking, Luther observed, the people could spread word of the malevolence and deceit of the pope and his agents. Using violence against the pontiff would only strengthen him; exposing him to the light of truth would surely weaken him. Luther pointed to his own work as a model: "Have I not, with the mouth alone, without a single stroke of the sword, done more harm to the pope, bishops, priests, and monks than all the emperors, kings, and princes with all their power ever did before?" People should likewise get busy and teach, write, and preach that man-made laws are empty, that no one should enter the priesthood or a monastery, and that no money should be given for bulls, candles, or churches. If this were done, in two years' time the pope and bishops and "all the swarming vermin of the papal regime" would "vanish like smoke." Of his followers, Luther asked only one thing—that they not use his name; "let them call themselves Christian, not Lutherans."

By that point, the word *lutherisch*, used as both an adjective and the label of a movement, was in wide circulation. Luther's objections to it reflected more than modesty; he worried that any violent acts carried out in his name would discredit him and his followers. Better to use the pamphlet and the sermon than the flail or the hoe. In a striking demonstration of the power of his own word, Luther received a personal note from Albrecht of Mainz in which he agreed to take down his relics display. "My dear doctor," the archbishop abjectly wrote, "I have received your letter and will see to it that the thing that so moves you be done away, and I will act, God willing, as becomes a pious, spiritual, and Christian prince." Unarmed, isolated, and hidden from the world, Luther had with his pen alone subdued German's top prelate. Few of those stirred by his writings, however, had pens.

After sending the *Admonition* off to the printers, Luther threw himself into what would be the most enduring product of his stay in the Wartburg and one of the greatest feats of his entire career: translating the Bible into German. Luther decided to begin not with the Old Testament, which posed too many challenges, but with the shorter and more manageable New. Even there, though, the obstacles were formidable. "I shall translate the Bible, although I have here shouldered a burden beyond my power," he wrote to Amsdorf. "Now I realize what it means to translate, and why no one has previously undertaken it who would disclose his name." (Most of the previous German translations had appeared anonymously.)

When it came to putting the Gospels and Epistles into German, there was first of all the question of which German. Like the German lands as a whole, the German language was highly fragmented. There were two main variants: High German, spoken in the mountainous south, and Low German, spoken in the flat north. Within each group there were so many dialects that, as Luther observed, "people thirty miles apart can hardly understand each other. The Austrians and Bavarians do not understand the Thuringians and Saxons." This Babel posed a special problem for the chanceries of the various German states, which had to communicate with one another. Over time, their scribes found ways to reconcile the various dialects so that their diplomatic messages could be broadly understood. Because of Saxony's central location, the language developed by its scribes (known as *Kanzleideutsch*, or chancellery German) was the most widely used, and so Luther took it as his starting point.

But this German was dry and bureaucratic, with convoluted syntax and Latinate vocabulary. Luther wanted a Bible that would speak to Germans of all regions and walks of life, from the magistrate at his bench to the carpenter at his lathe, and so he needed to develop a new, more accessible idiom. To that end, he could draw on the rich lexicon he had accumulated on his long treks around Germany and from his encounters with the many layers of German society. As a friar and a theologian, Luther had mastered the most intricate concepts of the faith, and as a pastor and a preacher he had had to find ways to convey them to the laity.

He took the Vulgate as his starting point. This was not only the official Bible of the Church but also the one that he had grown up with and whose phrasing and rhythms were inscribed on his mind. But the grand style used by Jerome and other Latin translators was far removed from the type of *Volksbuch*, or people's book, he had in mind.

To help create it, Luther had a number of reference works at hand. They included medieval fixtures like the *Glossa Ordinaria* and the commentaries of Lyra, plus several Greek and Latin lexicons as well as Reuchlin's *Ru-*

diments of Hebrew. Luther probably also had the 1475 Augsburg German Bible. Most important of all, he had the 1519 edition of Erasmus's New Testament or a reprint of it. Throughout, Luther would rely heavily on the Greek text provided by Erasmus. Even after his many years of studying that language, however, his proficiency in it remained shaky, and so Erasmus's Latin translation and annotations would prove of even greater benefit. A comparison of his finished product with Erasmus's translation and notes shows the great guidance they provided as Luther struggled to capture the sense and meaning of the biblical text.

He quickly developed a procedure. First, he would make a quick literal translation of the Vulgate Latin, using roughly the same word order. Then he would come up with synonyms for each word. Examining each phrase, he would consider the overall sound of the sentence, seeking a cadence that would make the words register and linger.

At Matthew 5:16, for instance, where Jesus exhorts his flock to let their light shine before the people, Luther came up with the euphonious *lasset euer Licht leuchten vor den Leuten.* At Mark 14:33, where Christ grows troubled and distressed, Luther offered *zu zittern und zu zagen.* Among the many idioms he introduced were *Perlen vor die Säue werfen* ("throwing pearls before swine") and *ein Buch versiegelt mit sieben Siegeln* ("a book sealed with seven seals"). Whenever possible, Luther replaced alien Latin terms with familiar German ones. The Greek coin the *drachma* became the German *Groschen*; the centurion referred to at Luke 23:47 became a *Hauptmann* (a German captain). Where the Vulgate referred to *dux* ("ruler"), Luther offered *Herzog* (German for "duke"), and for *Dominus* ("Lord") he gave *Herr* (German for "noble" or "master"). In producing a Bible for the German people, Luther was Germanizing the Bible.

Ultimately, however, he wanted a Bible that was not only rhetorically appealing but also theologically correct. Where, for instance, the Vulgate gave the Greek term *ekklesia* as *ecclesia*, or "church," Luther instead used *Gemeinde*, meaning "community" or "congregation." This reflected his view that the Christian community consists not of the institutional Church but of the body of all believers.

Erasmus's influence is apparent at Matthew 3:2, where John the Baptist admonishes those gathered at the Jordan River. Had Luther followed the Vulgate, he would have translated *Poenitentiam agite*—"Do penance"—as *tut Busse*, as it was given in most German versions. Instead, he offered *Bessert euch*—"Improve thyself"—a clear reflection of Erasmus's comments on the Greek *metanoia*. In this way, the grammatical emendation proposed by Lorenzo Valla and adapted by Erasmus would enter the new Bible being prepared by Luther for the German people, with repentance cast as an internal act rather than a rite administered by a priest.

Luther similarly followed Erasmus at Luke 1:28. Here, the Vulgate had the Archangel Gabriel greet Mary with *Ave gratia plena*—"Hail Mary, full of grace." Erasmus had proposed *Ave gratiosa*—"Hail Mary, favored one." Echoing him, Luther gave this as *Gegrüsset seist du, Holdselige*—"Greetings to you, gracious one." This reading appealed to Luther both because he disapproved of the cult of the Virgin and because he felt the Vulgate's phrasing was too remote from the way a German would actually greet a young woman. Later, when he (like Erasmus) was accused of downgrading Mary's divine status, Luther would reply with characteristic scorn: "When does a German speak like that, 'You are full of grace'? He would have to think of a keg 'full of' beer or a purse 'full of' money." He had instead used "gracious one" "so that a German can at least think his way through to what the angel meant by this greeting."

As much as Luther depended on Erasmus, though, his translation in the end was to bear his own unique stamp. He wanted a New Testament that fully conveyed his belief in the supreme place of faith in Christ. This was especially apparent in Romans, which remained for him the centerpiece of the Bible. In the key section 3:19–30, he sharpened the sense in almost every passage. He was especially bold at 3:28. In the Vulgate, this read, "Man is justified by faith, without the works of the law." When Luther put this in German, however, it seemed to lack the emphasis Paul had intended. To provide it, he added the word *allein*—"alone"—so that the passage read, "Man is justified by faith *alone*, without the works of the law."

Even allowing for the liberties translators invariably take, this was an audacious leap, giving the verse a finality the original lacked, and Luther would later be loudly denounced for it. He would prepare a defense that captured his approach to Scripture. The "papal asses" and "shameless nincompoops" who made such a "tremendous fuss" over this word, he wrote, knew "even less than the miller's beast" how much "skill, energy, sense, and brains are required in a good translator." He knew very well that "alone" appears in neither the Greek nor the Latin text, but its addition conveyed the true sense of the passage and so was needed to make the translation "clear and vigorous." "We do not have to inquire of the literal Latin how we are to speak German, as these asses do," he declared in a famous remark:

> Rather we must inquire about this of the mother in the home, the children on the street, the common man in the marketplace. We must be guided by their language, the way they speak, and do our translating accordingly. That way they will understand it and recognize that we are speaking German to them.

Luther nonetheless acknowledged that, by adding *allein*, he was not simply following the rules of language. In this passage, he wrote, Paul was dealing "with the main point of Christian doctrine, namely that we are justified by faith in Christ without any works of the law," and so the passage urgently required and demanded the addition of the word. Why, then, "this raging and raving, this making of heretics and burning at the stake, when the matter itself at its very core is so clear and proves that faith alone lays hold of Christ's death and resurrection, without any works, and that his death and resurrection are our life and our righteousness?" Therefore, *allein* "will stay in my New Testament, and though all the papal asses go stark raving mad they shall not take it from me."

And stay it did. Luther, who wanted to make the Word of God the sole foundation of Christianity, felt no hesitation in adding a word to make it conform more closely to his own theology.

By early February 1522, Luther had completed about half the New Testament, and he sent the manuscript to Spalatin for forwarding to Melanchthon. Overwhelmed by questions, he longed to consult his younger colleague, whose knowledge of Greek far surpassed his own. His desire to return to Wittenberg was further sharpened by the reports he was receiving of the chaos that had gripped the town since his visit.

*   *   *

After completing an investigation into the unrest of December 3–4, 1521, the electoral authorities had decided to arrest the instigators, but this had sparked an even louder protest, with a mob gathering at the town offices to demand the release of the detainees. With the growing commotion in Wittenberg, Andreas von Karlstadt moved to take charge. Throwing off his earlier caution, he began inveighing against the traditional Mass at both the Castle Church, where he was authorized to preach, and the town church, where he was not. At both, he attracted large crowds. Encouraged, he announced that on New Year's Day he would celebrate a simple Mass at the Castle Church, during which Communion would be offered in both kinds. Alarmed, Frederick directed Christian Beyer, his representative in Wittenberg, to make sure that no such act occurred before the matter was officially resolved, but Karlstadt, intent on evading the elector's wishes, moved the event up to Christmas Day, announcing it at the last possible moment.

With Wittenberg's new notoriety, fervent spirits from around Germany were pouring into it, and on Christmas Eve 1521 groups of boisterous students and freelance agitators roamed the streets. Some swept into the parish church while services were in progress. They smashed the lamps, harassed the priests, and sang ribald songs like "My Maid Has Lost Her Shoe." They then marched to the Castle Church—a bastion of Roman ways—where, as a traditional Mass was being performed, they shouted down the priests while throwing lead balls (probably bullets) at them.

On Christmas Day, the "whole town" (as one observer put it), packed the Castle Church. In this chilly Gothic sanctuary, Karlstadt, dressed in a plain black robe rather than the usual vestments, mounted the pulpit and told the congregation that they need not have fasted or performed confession to take Communion; all that was required was faith and a heartfelt sense of contrition. As the crowd looked breathlessly on, Karlstadt read the Mass in an abbreviated form, leaving out the passages about sacrifice to which Luther had so objected. At the consecration, Karlstadt—omitting the elevation of the host—passed from Latin into German. For the first time in their lives, those present heard in their own language the words

"This is the cup of my blood of the new and eternal testament, spirit and secret of the faith, shed for you to the remission of sins." Each congregant was then invited to commune in both kinds. A hush descended as Christians high and low proceeded to the altar. Instead of receiving the host on the tongue, as was the custom, each was handed a wafer to place on his or her tongue; each was also given the chalice from which to drink. One communicant, on being handed a wafer, trembled so violently that he dropped it. Karlstadt told him to pick it up, but the man was so terrified at the sight of the Lord's body lying desecrated on the floor that he refused to touch it.

This Christmas Day Communion at the Castle Church marked the first time that Luther's new theology had significantly affected the public worship of ordinary Christians. By drinking from the cup and taking the bread in their own hands, laypeople were committing an act of sacramental defiance. Few were troubled; on the contrary, a wave of jubilation swept through the town as the priesthood of all believers seemed to spring to life.

Karlstadt decided to follow this daring act with another. On December 26, 1521, he, together with two wagons full of people, including Melanchthon and Jonas, traveled to the village of Segrehna, seven miles from Wittenberg, to celebrate his engagement (at the age of thirty-five) to Anna von Mochau, the fifteen-year-old daughter of an impoverished nobleman. The wedding was scheduled for January 19, 1522, and Karlstadt, eager to publicize his rejection of clerical celibacy, invited university officials, town councilors, and other prominent citizens. By this act, Karlstadt wrote, he hoped "that many poor, miserable, and lost clerics who now lie in the devil's prison and dungeon might without doubt be counseled and helped by a good model and example." Shortly afterward, Jonas, too, became engaged.

The discord in Wittenberg deepened with the arrival on December 27, 1521, of three wild-eyed men from the town of Zwickau, eighty miles to the south. One, Marcus Thomae Stübner, was a former Wittenberg student; the other two, Nicholas Storch and Thomas Drechsel, were uneducated weavers. Brooding and gaunt, they seemed to have stepped out of the pages of Isaiah or Jeremiah. All had a remarkable command of the

Bible, but, they said, the text alone was not enough. True understanding of Scripture required revelations by the Holy Spirit, which they claimed to get directly from God through dreams and visions. Claiming powers of clairvoyance, they foretold an imminent invasion by the Turks, to be followed by the destruction of all priests and the swift arrival of the godly kingdom. Appearing at baptisms, feasts, and taverns, the Zwickau Prophets (as they came to be called) transfixed the Wittenbergers with their otherworldly aura. Storch in particular, with his long gray robe, wide-brimmed hat, and spiritual charisma, caused a stir as he moved about town.

No one was more affected than Melanchthon. Once a teacher of Stübner's, he now fell under his spell. "Melanchthon continually clings to his side, listens to him, wonders at him, and venerates him," a Swiss student in Wittenberg wrote. "He is deeply disturbed at not being able to satisfy that man in any way." Melanchthon was especially troubled by the prophets' opposition to infant baptism. Only those old enough to affirm their belief in Christ should be allowed to receive this sacrament, they maintained, citing in support Mark 16:16—"he who believes and is baptized will be saved." Infant baptism had been a fixture of the Church since the third century, and even most reformers highly esteemed it, but try as he might, Melanchthon could not refute them. Feeling helpless, he sent an urgent message to Frederick. "They preach strange things about themselves," he wrote, "saying that they are sent by the clear voice of God to teach, that they have familiar conversations with God, that they see the future." It "appears that there are in them certain spirits, concerning which no one save Luther can easily judge."

When Luther at the Wartburg heard of Melanchthon's distress, he became impatient. The Zwickau Prophets seemed to him nothing more than *Schwärmer*—fanatics who, like buzzing insects, could be easily batted aside. "I do not approve of your timidity," he wrote to Melanchthon in mid-January 1522, sending along instructions on how to question the men. He did, however, share Melanchthon's concern about the prophet's opposition to infant baptism. As much as he valued this sacrament, he knew that it lacked a firm biblical foundation. "I have always expected

Satan to touch this sore," he wrote, noting his concern that the issue could lead to a "grievous schism."

In this, Luther would prove prescient. The Zwickau Prophets represented the emergence of a radical and highly combustible current within the reform movement. With Luther having declared Scripture the one true authority and proclaimed every man a priest, people were taking him at his word, feeding a subjectivism that invited sectarianism, fanaticism, and anarchy.

Zwickau was a cradle of this new spirit. Located near the border with Bohemia, it was a showcase of the disruptive forces being set loose by the rise of capitalism. One of the richest cities in Saxony, Zwickau had eight churches and a well-regarded Latin school that drew students from many miles around. Textiles had long been its main source of wealth, but in the late fifteenth century its economy was transformed by a boom in iron and silver mining in the nearby Erzgebirge Mountains. While greatly enriching the town's manufacturers and merchants, the flow of new money had caused a rise in prices, a drop in purchasing power, and a loss of jobs, especially among the *Tuchknappen*, or journeymen clothiers. In the *Paraclesis*, Erasmus had extolled weavers as ideal readers of the Gospels, but in Zwickau as elsewhere they made up a nascent industrial proletariat with militant leanings. Working at looms in large sheds, they traded tales of exploitation and made common cause against their wealthy employers. Because of its proximity to Bohemia, Zwickau was awash in Hussite ideas, which gave the economic discontent a sharp anticlerical edge.

Among those whipping up the citizenry was a preacher who, in his short, violent life, would exert great influence on both the course of the Reformation and Luther's own career: Thomas Müntzer. Friedrich Engels, in *The Peasant War in Germany*, would describe Müntzer as a prototypical communist, and future Marxist historians would hail him as a forerunner of Lenin. Raised in the same mining region as Luther, Müntzer in 1517 had gone to Wittenberg to study, and two years later he had met Luther at the Leipzig disputation. Luther was impressed, and when he was asked to recommend a temporary replacement for an Erasmian preacher at St. Mary's church in Zwickau who was on leave, he suggested Müntzer.

Taking over the pulpit in May 1520, Müntzer immediately began agitating against the local Franciscans, accusing them of living off the alms of the faithful. Church officials tried to silence him but failed as the town council unanimously took his side.

When in October 1520 the Erasmian preacher reclaimed his pulpit, Müntzer quickly gained another at St. Catherine's—the church of Zwickau's weavers. Stirred by the weavers, Müntzer roused them in turn. Demanding the expulsion of Catholic priests, he spoke of slaughter and bloodshed in the name of the divine Word. Around Christmas 1520, a pastor whom Müntzer had violently denounced from the pulpit was almost killed by members of the congregation. Warned by the town council to show restraint, Müntzer instead continued to incite, and on Shrove Tuesday 1521 the windows of his house were shattered. When a local priest was derided in a fly sheet as a drunken libertine who went with harlots, the councillors were convinced that Müntzer was behind it and voted on April 16 to expel him. A crowd of weavers from St. Catherine's rallied in his support, and the council, fearing trouble, detained more than fifty of them. Seeing the hopelessness of his position, Müntzer under cover of darkness slipped out of Zwickau, heading to Bohemia in search of new Christians to mobilize while awaiting an opportunity to return to Germany.

The weavers were released the next day. With Müntzer gone, Nicholas Storch, the leader of St. Catherine's weavers, stepped to the fore. Selecting twelve apostles and seventy-two disciples from among the congregation, he formed a sort of underground cell aimed at overthrowing the oligarchs who ruled the town and improving the lot of the workingman. Fearing an uprising, the town council summoned Storch and his colleagues Stübner and Drechsel to account for their activities. Due to appear on December 16, 1521, they, too, decided to flee, heading north to Wittenberg.

There, the breakdown in authority provided an opening for their radical Bible readings, and a sort of scriptural primitivism set in. Book learning was shunned as elitist, revelation was extolled over exegesis, and civil institutions were condemned as instruments of oppression. The local school was turned into a food pantry, and enrollment at the university plunged as worried parents withdrew their children.

Amid this ferment, senior Augustinian friars began arriving in Wittenberg from around Germany for their order's general chapter meeting, scheduled to begin on January 6, 1522. With more and more monks leaving the cloister, the most urgent matter was the validity of monastic vows. With Luther's opposition by now well known, the friars in a historic step agreed that all who wanted to leave the monastery should be free to do so. Those who wanted to remain had to give up mendicancy and saying private Masses and instead devote themselves to preaching, physical labor, and helping the poor and sick. Emboldened, Gabriel Zwilling on January 10, 1522, led a group of friars in destroying all but one of the side altars of the cloister church and making a bonfire of the paintings, statues, crucifixes, and other sacred items removed from them.

Caught up in the fervor, Karlstadt moved to solidify his control. The simplified Mass that he had performed on Christmas Day had proved very popular, and it was reenacted on New Year's Day, on the following Sunday, and on Epiphany. At each Mass more than a thousand people— many times the usual number—took Communion. The practice of receiving the sacrament in both kinds spread to Eilenburg, Lochau, and other nearby communities. And Karlstadt was already preparing his next great leap. In his return to the sources, he was traveling beyond the New Testament to the Old. Reading in Genesis of how God had driven Adam from the Garden of Eden to till the ground by the sweat of his brow, he urged his students to leave the lecture hall and return to the land. Poor laborers, he said, prayed more sincerely than monks, and craftsmen were better able to understand the Bible than bishops.

In his sermons, Karlstadt spoke of biblical passages like Exodus 20:3— "You shall have no other gods before me." While most reformers rejected the worship of saints and relics, Karlstadt argued that all material images, including works of art and even crucifixes, should be banned from houses of worship as useless. "God hates and despises images," he declared, adding that "churches in which images are placed and honored might readily be considered brothels." He similarly called for the elimination of all musical instruments, organ playing, and communal hymn singing. "Better one heart-felt prayer than a thousand cantatas of the Psalms," he wrote. Karlstadt also stressed the need to help the poor and hungry and to put beggars to work.

Along with Melanchthon and Jonas, Karlstadt pressed the town council to officially adopt the main elements of the reform. Fearing further unrest, the council obliged. The *Praiseworthy Order of the Princely Town of Wittenberg*, issued in late January 1522, approved the Mass (based on Luther's ideas) that Karlstadt had introduced, with Communion offered in both kinds and the words of consecration in German. It also called for the placement of all ecclesiastical revenues into a "common chest" that would be controlled by both laymen and clerics and which would be used to pay the clergy, maintain buildings, and meet the needs of the city's sick and poor. Loans would be extended to indigent craftsmen and scholarships awarded to poor students. Begging was to be abolished and all those refusing to work were to be expelled. Prostitution was to be prohibited and all brothels were to be closed. Finally, a date was to be set on which all religious images would be removed from the churches.

The *Praiseworthy Order* and its provisions for a common chest would be among the most important measures of the early Reformation. Inspiring a wave of similar ordinances, it would over time help transform municipal governance in Germany, with the state taking responsibility for social services that had long been the preserve of the Church.

Even so, the pace of change remained too slow for some. The town council announced a date for the orderly removal of images, but groups of impatient citizens carried out a *Bildersturm*, or iconoclastic riot, taking down images in the Castle Church and other sanctuaries. They were stopped before they could get too far, but the outburst showed the powerful emotions being released. In the eighth century, the dispute over icons had helped precipitate the split between Eastern and Western Christianity; now, in remote Wittenberg, the issue was again flaring.

By this point, Frederick had had enough. Divisions in the town were widening, the clergy at the Castle Church feared being attacked, and the university had all but ceased to operate. The Wittenberg disturbances were giving all of Electoral Saxony a bad name. Frederick's cousin Duke George in particular was incensed. Ever since the Leipzig disputation, he had warned of the chaos that would result if Luther was allowed to spread his Bohemian views. On February 10, 1522, George sent a fierce directive to all officials in his duchy, decrying the outrages Luther was provoking. The monks of his order had left their monasteries, laid off their habits, and let their tonsures grow. They wandered from place to place, preaching against the holy Mass and teaching the people to receive the sacrament in both kinds, even though those who had previously tried to introduce such practices had been deemed "contumacious heretics." The duke ordered his officials to seize and imprison any renegade monk in worldly dress or any priest caught trying to seduce his subjects with Luther's "forbidden and unchristian doctrine." Rumors spread that George was preparing to send an armed force into Electoral Saxony to occupy it and annex it to his own lands.

Seeking to prevent such actions, the electoral court on February 13, 1522, issued an order annulling the January ordinance. The university and the clergy were to introduce no further changes, and images were to be left in place until further notice. Private Masses were to be retained, and the traditional celebration of the Eucharist was to be reinstated. Frederick's agent in Wittenberg sent a stern message to Melanchthon, directing him to silence Zwilling, and another to Karlstadt, urging him to stop preaching or at least moderate his public pronouncements.

Zwilling had in fact already left Wittenberg for Eilenburg, some thirty miles to the south, where he preached with such ardor that stones were thrown through the windows of the local parsonage. Karlstadt promised not to preach again (a vow that would prove temporary). But the disorder continued. Some priests said the words of consecration in Latin, others in German. Some communicants took the wafer in hand, others had it placed on the tongue. Half the population seemed eager for even more radical change, while the other half clung ever more tightly to the old ways. Overall, a doctrinaire and intolerant spirit reigned.

Only one person seemed capable of ending it. Bringing Luther back to Wittenberg would pose its own problems, since he remained under the imperial and papal bans, but the town council saw no other way, and so on February 20, 1522, without consulting Frederick, it sent Luther an urgent message requesting his speedy return to Wittenberg.

*   *   *

When the message arrived, Luther felt it had come from God. From what he had heard, the Wittenbergers seemed to have taken leave of their senses. He was especially annoyed to learn that Karlstadt had been preaching at the town church in *his* pulpit. Indifferent to the prospect of arrest or attack, Luther on February 22, 1522, sent Frederick a brief note, declaring, "God willing, I shall soon be there."

When he learned of this, the elector rushed a letter to John Oswald, his official in Eisenach, directing him to order Luther to remain at the Wartburg. If the pope and emperor proceeded against the reformer and he was forced to answer for it, Frederick wrote, it would cause him "the greatest embarrassment." With a new diet about to open in Nuremberg, Luther should remain in hiding until its direction became clear. On receiving the letter, Oswald immediately went to the Wartburg to deliver it, but Luther would not be moved. After ten months of being cooped up with bats and birds, he longed to see his friends in Wittenberg (and to consult Melanchthon on his New Testament translation, which he had completed). And so, on March 1, 1522, he mounted his horse and left the Wartburg for good.

On March 3, Luther stopped for the night at the Black Bear Inn in Jena. The hostel's public room was warmed by a large German stove and lit by candles, and Luther, sitting at a table with a book and glass of beer, fell into conversation with two students from Switzerland, who were soaked after riding through a rainstorm. With his knightly attire and a hand resting on the hilt of his sword, Luther was not recognized. One of the students, John Kessler, would later write an account of the encounter, which, though no doubt embellished, offers a remarkable glimpse of the reformer at this pivotal moment in his career. The students said they were headed to Wittenberg and asked their tablemate if Luther was there. "I have authentic information that he is not at Wittenberg, but that he will soon return there," he replied.

"If God grant us life we will not rest until we see and hear that man," Kessler said. "For it is on account of him that we are going there. We have heard that he wishes to overturn the priesthood and the Mass, and as our parents have brought us up to be priests, we want to hear what he can tell us and on what authority he acts." Informed that they had been studying in Basel, Luther asked if Erasmus was still there. He was, the students said, but what he did there he kept secret. "What do they think of Luther in Switzerland?" Luther asked. Opinion was divided, Kessler said. Some could not praise him enough for having revealed the truth, while others, especially the clergy, condemned him as "an intolerable heretic."

The other student, whose name was Spengler, picked up Luther's book. To his shock, it was a Hebrew Psalter—not the usual fare for a knight. When Spengler said he would give much to learn Hebrew, Luther said, "You must work hard to learn it. I also am learning it, and practice some every day."

Two merchants then entered, and after they removed their cloaks, one put a book on the table. Luther asked what he was reading. "Doctor Luther's sermons, just out," he said; "have you not seen them?" No, Luther said, but he soon would. He then asked the two men to join him at the table and offered to treat them to supper. A friendly conversation ensued. "Luther must be either an angel from heaven or a devil from hell," one of the merchants said, adding that he would give ten guldens "to have the chance to confess to him; I believe he could give me good counsel for my conscience." After the merchants went out to feed their horses, Luther asked the host to bring him some wine, which he said he preferred to beer. Bidding the students good night, he told them that when they got to Wittenberg, they should remember him to Jerome Schurff.

"Whom shall we remember, sir?" Kessler asked.

"Say only that he that will soon come sends his greetings," Luther said.

On March 5, 1522, Luther was in Borna, south of Leipzig, and there he took a moment to write to Frederick and explain why he had decided to defy his wishes and return to Wittenberg. "I have received the gospel not from men, but from heaven only, through our Lord Jesus Christ," he wrote. He did not intend to ask for the elector's protection. "Indeed I think I shall protect your Eternal Grace more than you are able to protect me," since "he who believes the most can protect the most, and since I have the impression that your Eternal Grace is still quite weak in faith, I can by no means regard your Eternal Grace as the man to protect and save me." Luther excused Frederick from all responsibility should he be captured or put to death, and he asked the elector to put up no resistance if the emperor moved to seize or execute him. It did not occur to Luther to thank Frederick for all he had done to protect him over the previous ten months.

As Luther entered the hostile territory of Duke George, a party of horsemen joined him, and they stayed with him the rest of the way. On March 6, Luther was back in Wittenberg. Elijah had returned.

This time, he decided to stay at the Black Cloister. Before he could settle in, however, the lawyer Jerome Schurff arrived with an urgent message from Frederick asking Luther to fully release him from responsibility if anything should happen to him. Readily obliging, Luther drafted a statement affirming that he had returned without the elector's permission. During his absence, he wrote, Satan had fallen upon his flock in Wittenberg and done things that could not be stopped through his writing but which had to be dealt with in person. He feared that there would be a "real rebellion" in the German territories and that those attempting "to put out the light by force" were only embittering people's hearts and thereby "stimulating them to revolt." With the gospel thus in need, all human commands and concerns had to be laid aside. Christ, the lord of souls, "has sent me and for this he has raised me up. I cannot abandon them."

After Schurff left, Luther received many visitors, who told him of all that had occurred in the three months since his last visit. The local school had closed, the university was near collapse, the cloister was half empty, images and statues had been defaced and shattered, mob violence had broken out. Luther's joy at being back in Wittenberg was overridden by the urgency of the situation and the need to address it.

March 9 was Invocavit Sunday (the first Sunday of Lent), and Luther announced that he would preach at the town church. Word quickly spread. The great champion of evangelical freedom, just returned from his hideout, was going to deliver his first public words since his courageous stand at Worms. Merchants and priests, professors and students, housewives and farmers, excitedly prepared to hear what Europe's most famous citizen had to say.

THE POPE OF WITTENBERG

Aside from the weight he had put on at the Wartburg, Luther looked very much like the friar his congregants remembered from a year earlier. He had shaved off his beard, had his hair cut to restore his tonsure, and exchanged his knightly attire for his black Augustinian habit, which, despite its usual frayed state, conveyed the Lenten gravity of the occasion. Looking down from the pulpit at the careworn Christians in their woolen coats and muddy boots, Luther knew how critical this moment was. He needed to find the right words to banish the atmosphere of carnival and excess that had engulfed the town and recall his parishioners to the meaning of true piety.

"The summons of death comes to us all, and no one can die for another," he declared with the solemnity of a judge handing down a sentence. To be ready for death, everyone must know and be provisioned with the primary things that concern a Christian. God sent his only begotten Son so that all might believe in him and be freed from sin. Yet faith by itself was not enough; there must also be love. "And here, dear friends, have you not grievously failed? I see no signs of love among you."

What was most needed, Luther said, was patience. People should not insist that everyone immediately adopt the correct way; Christians should instead consider the needs of their brothers, for not all were equally strong in their faith. Just as a mother feeds her child first milk, then eggs, and then soft food, so should people of faith bear with their brothers until their faith, too, grows strong.

Only after offering these general reflections did Luther address the situation at hand. Had he been present in Wittenberg, he said, "I would not have gone as far as you have." The cause was good but the haste too great. All those who had had a part in abolishing the Mass had erred. The Mass did eventually have to go, but it had been attacked in too aggressive a manner, without regard for those who found such a sudden change unsettling. Showing a trace of pique, Luther said that he could have been consulted about these matters but had not received the slightest communication. Now that he was back, though, he wanted everyone to show love for one another. Otherwise, "our work will not endure."

Luther's performance had a powerful effect. A student who was present reported that, despite the somberness of Luther's words, his voice was "sweet and sonorous." He came across as "kind, gentle and cheerful," and "whatever he does, teaches, and says is most pious." Everyone who hears him once "desires to hear him again and again, such tenacious hooks does he fix in the minds of his auditors."

Those who wanted to hear him again in fact got the chance, for on each of the next seven days Luther returned to the pulpit. Though attendance no doubt fell off as the workweek began, people from outlying communities, hearing of the reformer's presence, showed up at the church. The Invocavit sermons, as they came to be known, would be Luther's most famous feat of preaching. His message was straightforward: change had to come, but only gradually and calmly. The hearts of the people had to be won over with words and kindness; resorting to force and command would produce "a mere mockery." As in his *Sincere Admonition* a few months earlier, Luther cited his own restraint: "Had I desired to foment trouble, I could have brought great bloodshed upon Germany; indeed, I could have started such a game that even the emperor would not have been safe." But that would have been "mere fool's play." He had opposed indulgences and papists, but never with force. "I simply taught, preached, and wrote God's Word." While he drank Wittenberg beer with his friends Melanchthon and Amsdorf, he folksily observed, "the Word so greatly weakened the papacy that no prince or emperor ever inflicted such losses upon it."

Luther denounced the destruction of altars, the burning of images, and the resort to coercion in general. If a monk wanted to leave the cloister, it should be his choice—it should not be forced on him. In the rush for reform, people had grown so angry that they were ready to kill one another. No one had given to the poor or extended a helping hand to others; everyone had instead sought his own advantage. If acts of compulsion did not stop, he said, "I will go without urging; and I dare say that none of my enemies, though they have caused me much sorrow, have wounded me as you have."

Luther had skillfully gauged the mood of the people. They were chastened by his words and soothed by his presence, and Wittenberg quickly settled down. "There is great gladness and rejoicing here," Jerome Schurff reported to Frederick on March 15, 1522, "both among the learned and the unlearned, over Doctor Martin's return and over the sermons with which, by God's help, he is daily pointing us poor deluded men back again to the way of truth." It "is plain as day that the Spirit of God is in him and works through him. . . . Even Gabriel has confessed that he has erred and gone too far."

"Gabriel" was Gabriel Zwilling. Back in Wittenberg from Eilenburg, he saw the swift change in the town's mood and, giving up the stage, retired to a village twelve miles from Wittenberg. Pleased by his submission, Luther remained on good terms with him.

Not so with Karlstadt. Long exasperated by his mercurial colleague, Luther considered him the principal instigator of the Wittenberg disturbances. What's more, Karlstadt had preached in the pulpit at the town church—Luther's pulpit—without the proper authority. Karlstadt was promptly banned from preaching, and in a private meeting Luther warned him not to publish anything against him. Karlstadt nonetheless wrote a sharply worded tract that, while not mentioning Luther, vigorously defended his actions while also reaffirming his trust in the common man. For this he was called before a university committee and censured. Karlstadt was allowed to resume teaching, and after the summer of 1522 he became dean of the theology faculty, but—humiliated at being so rudely treated and convinced he had been made a scapegoat—he awaited an opportunity to strike back.

In the congregation for the last two of Luther's sermons was Wolfgang Capito. Still in the service of Archbishop Albrecht of Mainz, Capito had come to Wittenberg to seek a reconciliation with Luther. Two months earlier, while still at the Wartburg, Luther had sent him a letter upbraiding him for supporting the archbishop on the sale of indulgences and the persecution of priests who married. Luther had also reproached Capito for urging him to moderate his language. The truth, he declared, had to be spoken "unshackled, pure, and clear." Despite his close friendship with Erasmus, Capito had long admired Luther and was deeply unsettled by his criticism. Seeing the effect Luther had on his congregation and impressed by his go-slow approach, Capito was even more captivated. Meeting with him afterward, he succeeded in convincing Luther of his good intentions. Disillusioned with his life as a courtier, Capito on his return began considering a new path. Another Erasmian was drifting into the Lutheran camp.

Never before had the force of Luther's presence and personality been more on display. To further help Wittenberg regain its footing, he declared a moratorium on change. The traditional Mass was for the time being reinstated. At Easter, Communion was celebrated in one kind, in Latin, and with the usual rituals (although a reformed service was held for those who wanted it). Order was restored at the university and enrollment began to rise again. Luther resumed living in the emptying Augustinian monastery. Within its walls, he occasionally wore lay clothing, but in public he continued to appear in his cowl so as to project a sense of normalcy.

Luther's putting a brake on change was understandable in light of the violence that had broken out. Had the rapid pace of reform continued, the destruction of property that had occurred might well have led to the loss of life. Yet the reforms had been very popular, filling the churches and giving the laity a sense of participation in rites that had previously been reserved for the priesthood. Not only Karlstadt and Zwilling but also Melanchthon, Jonas, and many other prominent citizens, including the town council itself, had supported the changes. Luther now quashed all that. Reform—of not only rites and doctrine but also education, welfare, and social life in general—was to be instituted gradually and directed by Luther working closely with the authorities.

As a result of Luther's opposition to compulsion, Wittenberg would never develop the type of absolutist regime that Calvin was to impose in Geneva, with conduct closely monitored and morals strictly regulated. At the same time, Luther's fear of the mob and distrust of spontaneous action would result in a turning away from the principles of popular participation and communal purpose that were to arise elsewhere as the Reformation spread. In the Lutheran church, reform was to be more an individual than a collective affair; each Christian would have to find his or her own pathway to God.

Luther's caution, however, reflected not just his conservative instincts but also the grave danger he faced. Though both the papal bull and the imperial edict had proved difficult to enforce, Luther remained an outlaw. In late March 1522, a new diet opened in Nuremberg, and as the news spread that Luther was back in Wittenberg, there was much indignation. "I must warn your Grace," Duke George wrote to his cousin Frederick, "that I have recently seen a letter in which it is said that Martin is in Wittenberg and is preaching publicly, though he is under the ban of the Pope and the Empire. Your Grace must beware that this does not become a cause of offense to God and the world, for, however sweetly he may speak, he still has a scorpion's tail."

The seriousness of the situation was driven home by the arrival in Wittenberg that spring of Jacob Probst. Probst had been serving as the prior of the Augustinian friary in Antwerp. A stronghold of Lutheran beliefs, it had become the central target of a ruthless campaign against dissent in the Low Countries. In contrast to Germany, where Charles V had little authority, in this region he had a great deal, and he was determined to crush the reform movement before it took root. Impressed with the success of the Spanish Inquisition in stamping out heresy, the emperor had ordered the establishment of a similar apparatus in the Low Countries. The Netherlands Inquisition would become the most active such operation north of the Alps. Probst (who had studied in Wittenberg) was among the first seized. Taken in Antwerp, he was transferred to Brussels and brutally interrogated; after recanting, he was spared. Sent to the Augustinian monastery in Ypres, he soon repudiated his recantation and was rearrested. Execution seemed certain, but a fellow monk helped him escape, and he fled to Wittenberg.

Soon, other Lutherans in the Low Countries were being detained, and it seemed only a matter of time before the movement had its first martyrs. "The whole Rhine is bloody," Luther wrote, recalling the fate of Jan

Hus. By shedding innocent blood, the princes were hastening their own destruction. "They are planning to burn me, too, at the stake, but I am constantly provoking Satan and his scales all the more."

Despite such peril, Luther refused to restrain his pen. He mocked Duke George as a *Wasserblase* ("water bubble" or "bladder") "who defies heaven with his lofty paunch" and who, denying the gospel, "is destroying many souls." If the princes continued to listen to the "dull-witted" duke, there would be an uprising that would "destroy the princes and rulers of all Germany." Luther's letter quickly became public, driving Duke George into a froth. Frederick as usual took no action, but even had he wanted to act, he would have been constrained by the aroused state of the population.

In addition to these outside threats, Luther had to contend with realities on the ground. Essentially, the Roman Church had disappeared from Wittenberg, and Luther was now its pope. A new order had to be built, and a hundred questions pressed in. With priestly ordination abandoned, who would preach and minister to the people? Who would train pastors, and how would they be paid? What should the order of the church service be? Should it be conducted in Latin or German? Should Communion be in both kinds or just one? Should confession be retained, and if so, in what form?

Luther was overwhelmed with requests for assistance and counsel. The town of Leisnig wrote for advice in setting up a common chest like the one in Wittenberg. The residents of Kemberg asked for help in getting the badly rutted road to Wittenberg paved. When a fisherman was caught poaching in Frederick's waters and ordered to pay a fine of six hundred pieces of silver, Luther pleaded with the elector to instead impose a brief jail sentence or, alternatively, to require the man to live on bread and water for eight days, "so that people may see that the purpose is to reform and not destroy the man." With runaway monks and fugitive priests arriving in Wittenberg, Luther put many up in the vacated cells at the Black Cloister, even though he suspected they were acting "for the sake of the belly and of carnal liberty."

Most taxing of all was the issue of marriage. With ecclesiastical authority over this institution collapsing, Luther was besieged by couples and families contending over engagements and vows, abandonment and betrayal. "How I dread preaching on the estate of marriage!" he declared in the opening sentence of a pamphlet on that subject that he would write later in the year. Nonetheless, he celebrated the new freedom people were enjoying in this area. "Away with this foolishness," he wrote. "Take as your spouse whomsoever you please, whether it be godparent, godchild, or the daughter or sister of a sponsor, and disregard these artificial money-seeking impediments" imposed by the Church. After centuries of strict clerical controls on marriage, people were leaving unsuitable partners and fleeing lifeless unions, and they looked to the abstinent Augustinian to guide them.

In dealing with all these matters, Luther had a small circle on which to rely. Jerome Schurff offered legal advice and Nikolaus von Amsdorf helped in rebutting polemical attacks. Justus Jonas, in addition to teaching canon law at the university, held the strategic post of provost at the Castle Church. Most of the two dozen or so clerics there continued to say Masses for the dead; in the coming months, Jonas would work closely with Luther in figuring out how to deal with them.

A recent addition was Johannes Bugenhagen. A tall, tough-minded native of Pomerania on the southern shores of the Baltic, Bugenhagen had (like Jonas) begun as a humanist committed to Erasmian-style moral improvement. On reading *The Babylonian Captivity*, he had initially felt shock at Luther's audacity and considered him the greatest heretic, but, on examining it more closely, he had come to believe that, in a world groping in blindness, this man "alone sees the truth." In the spring of 1521, Bugenhagen moved to Wittenberg and began lecturing on the Psalms, to great acclaim, and Luther, on his return from the Wartburg, was likewise impressed. "Next to Philipp he is the best professor of theology in the world," he wrote to Spalatin. Bugenhagen was also adept at dealing with the laity, and in the autumn of 1523 Luther would arrange for his appointment as pastor at the town church. Bugenhagen would eventually become Luther's father confessor, replacing Johann von Staupitz as the person to whom he would turn when his spiritual burdens became too great.

But Bugenhagen most excelled where Luther most fell short—in organizational skills. After the disturbances of 1522, he would be instrumental in rebuilding the church in Wittenberg, and from 1525 on he would frequently be away in northern cities, helping to set up reform churches. The rapid success of the Reformation in northern Germany and Scandinavia was due in part to Bugenhagen's organizing work, which earned him the description "Reformer of the North."

Finally, and most important, there was Melanchthon. As always, his relations with Luther remained close—and strained. Melanchthon's bumbling performance during the Wittenberg disturbances had shaken his mentor's confidence in him. Nonetheless, the two would frequently collaborate after Luther's return, especially on the translation of the New Testament. The manuscript Luther had completed at the Wartburg in a mere eleven weeks was rushed and unpolished, and in revising it he relied heavily on Melanchthon's knowledge of Greek and Latin. He also enlisted Spalatin. Spalatin had translated several of Luther's works into German, but Luther now urged him "to give us simple terms" rather than those used at court, "for this book must be adorned with simplicity." As an initial assignment, he asked Spalatin to provide the names and colors of the gems mentioned in Revelation 21, or "better yet, get them from the court, or wherever else you can, and let us have the opportunity to see them."

Luther hoped to have the translation ready for the autumn fair in Leipzig, due to begin on September 29, 1522. Having lost faith in the ability of Johann Rhau-Grunenberg, he entrusted the job to Melchior Lotther. The substantial capital needed for this project was supplied by Christian Döring, the local goldsmith and innkeeper who had provided the carriage for Luther's journey to Worms; the large quantities of paper required were supplied by Lucas Cranach, who owned a paper mill. The typesetting began in early May. Word of the printing was limited to Luther's closest friends for fear that the sheets would be stolen and printed elsewhere.

When he was not revising and writing, Luther was often preaching. (For the time being he was not allowed to lecture at the university lest this be seen as a deliberate flouting of the imperial edict.) Congregants frequently took notes on his sermons, and, after reconstructing them, offered them to printers, who were eager to bring them out. "Everywhere people are thirsting for the gospel," Luther exulted to Spalatin. "From all sides they are asking us for preachers." Congregations, tiring of hearing priests exalt the Virgin and the saints, hungered for men fluent in the new gospel of faith and grace, and pulpit wars broke out between Romanist and Lutheran preachers.

To both promote his ideas and help calm the masses, Luther decided to go on a preaching tour, leaving Wittenberg sometime after Easter 1522. Because his journey took him through the territory of Duke George, he traveled in secular clothing, and at least once he had to ride on horse-back at night, but no move was made against him. Over two weeks he would preach eleven times, and everywhere the reception was rapturous. In Zwickau, the site of the restless weavers, the turnout far exceeded the capacity of the cathedral, so Luther had to preach a second time from a window in the town hall and a third time at the castle. At every stop, he urged patience. The old Roman rites had to go and new ones had to be cre-ated in their place, but only gradually, so that the weak and resistant could be brought along. A Christian could be justified only by faith, but this did not mean that works of love were unimportant. Again and again, Luther affirmed that all believers are priests, but he warned that no one should act on this idea on his own except to comfort others in a brotherly spirit.

Through such preaching, Luther helped restore the peace in most places. One exception was Altenburg, located south of Leipzig. Earlier, its town council had dismissed the Catholic preacher, and Luther, asked to recommend a replacement, had suggested Gabriel Zwilling. In a letter informing the former firebrand of the appointment, Luther urged him to be moderate and to give up the broad-brimmed hat he had taken to wearing. In a trial sermon, Zwilling impressed the congregation, which pushed for his appointment, but old-guard clerics, still loyal to Rome, insisted on reserving the right to name the preacher. On his visit, Lu-ther pressed Zwilling's case, but the issue remained deadlocked. Eventu-ally, Frederick—unwilling to overlook Zwilling's part in the Wittenberg disturbances—rejected his candidacy. As a compromise, the electoral court proposed Wenceslas Link, who had recently resigned as head of the German Augustinians. He accepted the post and assumed it in the sum-mer of 1522, temporarily defusing the situation.

But the issue would not go away. In communities large and small, congregations were demanding the right to name their pastors—part of the popular surge across Saxony and beyond as people responded to Luther's call to Christians to read and interpret the Bible for themselves.

Back in Wittenberg, Luther saw a new collection of letters by Erasmus. Titled *Epistolae ad Diversos*, it had gone on sale at the 1522 spring fair in Frankfurt, and scholars and clerics across Europe were eagerly reading it to see what the famous scholar had to say on the great controversies of the day. Luther found much to dislike. Along with Erasmus's pokes at pedantic philosophers and narrow-minded friars were ardent expressions of loyalty to Rome and large helpings of scorn for the reformers. The volume contained Erasmus's statement "Christ I recognize, Luther I know not," as well as his remarkable admission that he had pressed Froben to stop publishing Luther. In a letter to William Warham, the archbishop of Canterbury, Erasmus wrote of his plan to read through the writings of both Luther and Luther's opponents with the goal of "doing all I can to support the dignity of the Roman pontiff and the peace of Christendom."

For months, rumors had been circulating that Erasmus was preparing to attack Luther, and this seemed to confirm them. To Spalatin, Luther complained that it was better to have an open enemy like Eck than a covert one like Erasmus who posed as a friend—an odd statement, given Erasmus's repeated statements that he was no friend of Luther's. Deciding to make a preemptive strike, Luther in late May 1522 drafted a letter to an anonymous addressee in which he derided Erasmus, singling out his failure to understand the true nature of predestination. "Erasmus is not to be feared either in this or in almost any other important subject that pertains to Christian doctrine." If he "casts the die, he will see that Christ fears neither the gates of hell nor the power of the air. I know what is in this man just as I know the plots of Satan; but I expect him to reveal more clearly from day to day what grudge he nurses against me." Luther's letter was promptly leaked and brought to Erasmus's attention.

Adding to Luther's animus toward the Dutch scholar was the appearance that summer of a German edition of the *Assertio Septem Sacramentorum*, Henry VIII's attack on *The Babylonian Captivity*. Luther knew of Erasmus's close ties to Henry and was convinced the two were working together against him. Frederick urged Luther to ignore Henry's work, and, given the king's stature as Western Europe's third most powerful sovereign (after Charles and Francis), that would have seemed wise. But Henry's air of royal entitlement irritated Luther, and after the appearance of a German translation by the goat Emser, he worried that the book might persuade some unsuspecting souls of the legitimacy of the sacraments. He thus decided to prepare a rebuttal, and in it he would repay Henry's invective with an even stronger dose of his own.

"Since with malice aforethought this damnable and rotten worm has lied against my king in heaven," Luther wrote, "it is right for me to bespatter this English monarch with his own filth and trample his blasphemous crown under feet." For three years these "mad giants" had tilted against him, yet they had still not managed to grasp what the fight was all about. Over and over he had tried to make clear the superiority of Scripture over man-made doctrines, but whenever he declared "Gospel! Gospel! Gospel!" they could only respond, "Fathers! Fathers! Custom! Custom! Decretals! Decretals!"

Seething, Luther asserted his right as a God-fearing Christian to interpret the Bible for himself: "Here I stand, here I sit, here I glory, here I triumph, here I contemn Papists, Thomists, Henricians, sophists," and all others "led astray by the saying of holy men or customs."

> The word of God is above all things. The divine majesty so weighs with me that I care nothing if a thousand Augustines, a thousand Cyprians, a thousand Henrician churches were against me. God cannot err and deceive; Augustine and Cyprian, like all the elect, both could err and have erred.

In a further jab, Luther speculated that the king's book had been written not by Henry but by Edward Lee or "one of those sniveling, driveling sophists bred by the Thomist swine." Whichever "miserable scribbler" did write it had "demonstrated with poisonous words how well he can manage to soil a lot of paper, a truly loyal deed!" Two months after counseling moderation in his Invocavit sermons, Luther was again hurling thunderbolts.

Appearing in German on August 1, 1522, *Against Henry, King of the English* set off a furor exceeded only by that of *The Babylonian Captivity*. In an era of unbounded reverence for monarchs as divinely appointed, people were astounded to see one handled so roughly by a plebeian. Duke George sent a copy to the imperial government in Nuremberg along with a request that Luther be tried for rebellion against royal authority. Luther was unperturbed. Seeking to justify his harsh language, he cited (as was his wont) the examples of Christ, Peter, and Paul, who had called the Jews vipers, murderers, dogs, and children of the Devil. He had written his own books "without any severity, in a friendly and gentle tone," only to face slanders and lies in return. (One wonders which of his books he considered gentle.) Despite the demands that he restrain his language, Luther stated, "I will not and ought not to stop it. My work is not that of one who can take a middle course, and yield this or give up that, as I have done hitherto, fool that I was."

Henry himself was irate over Luther's attack. Ever since being designated a defender of the faith by the pope, he had proudly flaunted that title, and he was not about to let Luther get away with tarnishing it. When a stern protest to Frederick failed to bring redress, Henry turned to his own court. There, planning began for a campaign to avenge the king's honor—a project that would draw in Bishop John Fisher, Thomas More, and, eventually, Erasmus.

As the days of summer dwindled and the Leipzig fair drew near, Luther raced to complete his translation of the New Testament. At Melchior Lotther's shop, three presses were thrown into the fray. For the book of Revelation, Lucas Cranach's workshop prepared twenty-one full-page illustrations bristling with apocalyptic fury. In one, the menacing beast mentioned in Revelation 13 was given a crown that unmistakably resembled the papal tiara. To further clarify the meaning of the text, Luther prepared a series of marginal notes offering linguistic explanations, barbs directed at papists, and theological glosses stressing the supreme importance of faith.

Luther also wrote prefaces for several books of the New Testament, plus one introducing the volume as a whole, in which he grandly described its purpose: "To free the ordinary man from his false though familiar notions, to lead him into the straight road, and to give him some instruction." There was but one gospel, Luther declared—that of the eternal kingdom of Christ, who by his own death and resurrection conquered sin, death, and hell on behalf of all who have faith in him. He warned against making "Christ into a Moses" and the gospel "into a book of law or doctrine." The gospel demands of us no works to make us holy. On the contrary, it condemns works and demands only faith in Christ. If a Christian has faith, though, all his efforts "are directed towards the benefit of his neighbor." If good works and love "do not blossom forth, it is not genuine faith."

To reinforce this point, Luther ranked the books of the New Testament by their importance. The "best and noblest" were those describing not the works and miracles of Christ but faith in Christ, who conquers death and gives life. Of the four Gospels, Luther dismissed Matthew, Mark, and Luke as being primarily about the former; John, being mainly about the latter, was "far superior to the other three, and much to be preferred." Luther similarly endorsed the first Epistle of John, the Epistles of Paul (especially Romans, Galatians, and Ephesians), and the first Epistle of Peter, which together teach "everything you need to know for your salvation." By contrast, the Epistle of James, with its statement that faith without works is dead, "contains nothing evangelical" and so is "an epistle full of straw."

These were audacious statements. In assembling the scriptural canon, the early Fathers had sought to weave together the two main strands of the Christian tradition: Jesus the teacher of virtue and Christ the agent of redemption; the Sermon on the Mount and the cross on Calvary; the value of works and the importance of faith. But Luther in his introduction was insisting that only one of those strands truly mattered—that of the crucified Christ, who, rising from the dead, offered the promise of everlasting peace to all who have faith in him. The real-life Jesus was secondary. In so arguing, Luther was in effect trying to redefine the New Testament canon.

Erasmus, of course, had his own scriptural preferences, esteeming in particular those books that featured Jesus the wise teacher and moral exemplar. In his annotations, he sought to highlight the presence of the human Jesus over the divine Christ. Nowhere, however, did he offer a ranking of books or dismiss those he disagreed with, as Luther did.

As the final pages of the New Testament were being printed, Luther prepared a preface to the Epistle to the Romans. Given the central place this book occupied in his theology, it was fitting that he would leave this task for last. Romans is "the most important document in the New Testament, the gospel in its purest expression," he wrote. A Christian should seek not only to learn it by heart "but also to meditate on it day by day. It is the soul's daily bread and can never be read too often, or studied too much." More than anything else he wrote, Luther's preface to Romans could be considered the Gospel according to Martin, and for centuries it would be an effective recruiting tool.

Around September 25, 1522, after five months of editing, revising, polishing, and printing, the translation was done. Its cover bore the simple inscription *Das Newe Testament Deutzsch*. The sensitivity of the project is indicated by the fact that Luther's name nowhere appeared. Nor did the year. Only the place of publication, Wittenberg, was given. A folio of 222 leaves, the book was very bulky. It was also expensive, selling for about one guilder—the equivalent of two months' salary for a schoolmaster or the price of a calf. The price would have been considerably higher had Luther demanded a fee, but, as usual, he requested no compensation of any kind.

Anticipating strong sales, Lotther printed some three thousand copies. Many were carried by wagon to Frankfurt; others were transported to surrounding communities. Within weeks, all copies of the September Testament (as it was called, after its month of publication) were gone and a new edition was planned. Pleased with the opportunity to correct the errors in the first edition, Luther plunged into the revision. Even while thus engaged, he began translating the Old Testament, and by early November 1522 he was already up to Leviticus.

The following month, the December Testament (as the revised edition was called) was in the bookstores, and it, too, quickly sold out. More editions were planned, and pirated versions soon began appearing. Since the invention of the printing press seven decades earlier, no other German text had sold in such numbers. In its eloquence and majesty, Luther's translation won favor with scholars and theologians; in its earthiness and euphony, it appealed to millers and blacksmiths. Even the unlettered would feel its pull as they heard it read in churches, taverns, and town squares. Exercising such broad appeal, Luther's translation helped forge a common basis of communication and identity across regional and class lines. That the text was the Holy Scriptures gave Luther's words the appearance of divine sanction, further searing them into the German mind.

Luther "created the German language," Heine would later observe. Goethe called his Bible a mirror of the world and said that through it the Germans first became a people. According to Herder, it was Luther's Bible, along with his hymns, that "awoke and liberated the German language, a sleeping giant." Nietzsche, in *Beyond Good and Evil*, called it the "best German book." Among Germans, Luther alone "knew what a syllable weighs, or a word, and how a sentence strikes, leaps, plunges, runs, runs out; he alone had a conscience in his ears." Compared with this "masterpiece of German prose," Nietzsche added, almost everything else was "mere 'literature.'" Just as the King James Version would help create a national culture for the English people, so would Luther's Bible help do for the Germans.

Even Johannes Cochlaeus, an ardent Catholic polemicist and a zealous critic of Luther, had to acknowledge the popularity of his New Testament. It spread so widely, he wrote, "that even tailors and shoemakers, yea, even women and ignorant persons who had accepted this new Lutheran gospel, and could read a little German, studied it with the greatest avidity as the fountain of all truth. Some committed it to memory and carried it about in their bosom." Within months, such people "deemed themselves so learned that they were not ashamed to dispute about faith and the gospel," not only with Catholic laymen "but even with priests and monks and doctors of divinity."

With his notion that all believers are priests, Luther had asserted the right of every Christian to read the Bible for himself. Now those priests could hear Christ and the apostles speak in their own tongue, and the conditions in ancient Palestine seemed to bear remarkable similarities to those in their own lives. Arriving in market towns and hamlets, read by farmers at their plows and weavers at their shuttles, the Luther Bible fed the discontent and unrest that were rising in the land.

THE NEW GOSPEL SPREADS

Basel was among the cities in which Luther's Bible was first reprinted. Not by Froben, however. Following Erasmus's demands, he continued to steer clear of the reformer. Other houses, though, were eager to publish him. Leading the way was Adam Petri. Soon after the September Testament appeared in Wittenberg, Petri obtained a copy, and by the end of 1522 he had brought out an elegant edition. Within four months, he would print two more, putting nine thousand copies in circulation—a measure of the extraordinary demand for this work. Over the course of the next decade, Petri would print nearly a hundred works by Luther—part of a great flood of evangelical literature that would help make Basel (along with Strasbourg) a top distributor of Reformation books outside Wittenberg.

Erasmus could feel the change. After the appearance of Luther's New Testament, he would later complain, the whole book trade came to be dominated by him. The publishing history of the *Enchiridion* illustrates the shift. Some eight editions appeared in 1522 and another eleven in 1523; in 1524, however, only two came out, followed by three in 1525 and just one in 1526. The Erasmian appeal to reason, willpower, and moral improvement could not compete with Lutheran texts extolling faith in Christ and salvation by divine grace.

Erasmus refused to adapt. A true son of the Renaissance, he continued to devote himself to the recovery of lost knowledge. In addition to preparing a sixth edition of the *Adages* and a fourth edition of his own New Testament, he was absorbed in editing Augustine. From Louvain, Juan Luis Vives sent the remaining chapters of his annotated *City of God*. Because of the great significance of this work, Erasmus and Froben decided to bring it out as a stand-alone volume. Unfortunately, Vives's notes were almost as long as the mammoth text itself, and getting them ready for the printers required meticulous attention. Seeking a break from such labors, Erasmus in the afternoon would repair to Froben's garden to read Chrysostom, Seneca, and other sources of ancient wisdom.

The pressure on him to come out against Luther, meanwhile, continued to build. In the summer of 1522, he received a letter from Duke George of Saxony that expressed his delight in the drubbing that Henry VIII had given to Luther and that noted the widespread belief that Erasmus had had a hand in it. Whatever the actual extent of his involvement, the duke went on, Erasmus's duty was now clear: "It would do much good in this regard if you, who brilliantly surpass all other men as a scholar and a fluent speaker and writer, were to descend into the arena." "Arise, most learned Erasmus," George added, "and for the love of Christ Jesus turn all the force of your great natural gifts to meet this challenge" and "silence this man" who had raged with such "profane presumption" against holy things.

Erasmus in his reply politely declined the duke's request, citing his poor health and the many pamphlets that had already been aimed, with little effect, at the heterodox friar. In addition, Erasmus remained wary of what Luther's supporters would do to him if he did deploy his pen as the duke urged. In Basel itself, the evangelicals were growing in both number and assertiveness. Already maligned for the go-slow approach he had advocated in his tract on eating meat, Erasmus was under heightened suspicion for his growing differences with Zwingli. In the summer of 1522, Zwingli had sent Erasmus a warm letter inviting him to move to Zurich and become a citizen. Erasmus sent back a friendly demurral that would become famous as a catchphrase of internationalism: "I am most grateful to you and your city for your kindly thought. My own wish is to be a citizen of the world, to be a fellow-citizen to all men." Erasmus closed on a note of cautious encouragement: "Fight on, dear Zwingli, not only with courage but with prudence, too."

Zwingli would fight on, but with more courage than prudence (at least from Erasmus's standpoint). After the sausage-eating episode, he and his fellow reformers in Zurich grew increasingly impatient. In church, agitators regularly interrupted sermons, demanding that priests preach the true Word of God—a tactic Zwingli himself engaged in.

Over the summer in Zurich, the issue of fasting gradually gave way to that of clerical celibacy. This vow was so routinely violated in Switzerland that the country had, more or less, a married clergy; priests, in fact, were allowed to keep concubines if they paid the bishop of Constance an annual fee. At the start of the year, Zwingli himself had gotten married, to a widow of about his own age, but had kept the marriage secret. Tiring of such hypocrisy, he and ten other priests sent the bishop a petition urging him (as the title put it) *To Allow Priests to Marry, or at Least Wink at Their Marriages*. Because clerical celibacy had no foundation in Scripture, they argued, it should be abolished. The staunchly conservative bishop refused.

Charges of heresy flew. In his defense, Zwingli wrote *Apologeticus Archeteles*, his first full statement of belief. Ironic and indignant, it attacked Church traditions and doctrines as human inventions that were by their nature fallible. Scripture, by contrast, was divine and inerrant. While the bishop was on the side of human law, the reformers were on the side of Christ.

Zwingli immediately sent a copy of the tract to Erasmus, who was taken aback by its militant tone. In the little of the pamphlet that he had read, he wrote back, "there was much on which I wanted to see you put right." If Zwingli published anything more in the future, Erasmus warned, "it is a serious task, and you must take it seriously. Do not forget the modesty and the prudence demanded by the gospel. Consult scholarly friends before you issue anything to the public. I fear that defense of yours may land you in great peril, and even do harm to the church."

As news of the widening rift between the two men spread, Basel's evangelicals all sided with Zwingli. In its strife and dissension, the city was beginning to feel uncomfortably like Louvain, with scriptural absolutists replacing subtle doctors as the main source of discord.

The climate would grow chillier still with the arrival of Johannes Oecolampadius. Seven years earlier, when Erasmus was preparing his first edition of the New Testament, Oecolampadius had worked closely with him, helping to check Greek and Hebrew quotations, and though he had made many mistakes, Erasmus had graciously overlooked them. At the time, Oecolampadius was a dedicated humanist, with an impressive command of the biblical tongues, a lively interest in Jerome, and a commitment to a program of moderate reform. His very name suggested his humanist leanings: Oecolampadius means "shining light" in Greek—a classicized version of his German surname, Husschin or Hussgen.

But Erasmus had not seen him for years, and in the meantime he had undergone a dramatic transformation. After receiving a doctorate in theology from the University of Basel, Oecolampadius in 1518 had taken a position as a preacher at the cathedral in Augsburg. While there, he had felt drawn to Luther's teachings. He resigned his position and entered a Brigittine monastery in Altomünster, near Munich, to reflect. There he produced two tracts on Christian doctrines and practices that showed he was moving away from traditional teachings. Forced to leave the cloister, he took a position as chaplain to the knight Franz von Sickingen at the Ebernburg castle near Mainz. The work proved unfulfilling, however, so when Andreas Cratander, a publisher in Basel for whom he had previously worked, offered him a position as a proofreader, he quickly accepted.

Meeting him soon after his arrival in Basel, in mid-November 1522, Erasmus was struck by how much he had aged. With his long gray beard, deeply wrinkled face, and emaciated frame, he seemed a patriarch out of the Bible. But the change in his theological outlook was even more pronounced. Whereas before Oecolampadius had treated the Bible as a text in need of editing, he now spoke of it as the binding Word of God. Whereas once he had recognized the dignity of man and his ability to do good works, he now fastened on human sinfulness and divine omnipotence.

Oecolampadius planned to spend his spare time translating and editing the Church Fathers. Scholarly in temperament and retiring in manner, he felt more comfortable poring over manuscripts than rallying congregations. But it was precisely his gravity and thoughtfulness, along with his deep learning, that appealed to Basel's reformers. To this point, they had been without a leader, but in Oecolampadius they now felt they had one. He soon began corresponding with Zwingli, and a bond between them quickly developed. The following spring he began lecturing at the university, and not long afterward he would begin preaching at St. Martin's, Basel's oldest parish church, which, located in the heart of the business district, offered an ideal podium for spreading his views. After Zwingli, Oecolampadius would become Switzerland's most prominent reformer (until the coming of Calvin).

Feeling increasingly vulnerable, Erasmus decided to appeal to the highest authority, the pope, for protection. The support Erasmus had long received from Leo X had proved effective in silencing his conservative critics. In November 1521, however, Leo had caught a fever while at his hunting lodge outside Rome, and within a week he was dead. His successor was none other than Adrian of Utrecht, Erasmus's fellow countryman and longtime friend.

The election of Adrian VI had shocked the world—Adrian included. At sixty-two, he was already in his twilight years, and as a non-Italian he was almost completely unknown in Rome. (He would be the last non-Italian pope until John Paul II in 1978.) In 1516, he had accompanied Charles to Spain, where he became the bishop of Tortosa (and, in 1517, a cardinal). Like the other high-ranking Netherlanders in Spain, Adrian had been very unpopular, and he became even more so after his ruthless suppression of the Comunero Revolt. While in Spain, Adrian had established himself as a fierce opponent of Luther and of heresy in general, and he was known for his blameless living. With Rome under attack for its corruption and profligacy, his reputation for rectitude held great appeal, and so in January 1522 the College of Cardinals chose him to guide the Church through this critical passage in its history.

Erasmus's ties to Adrian went back to 1502, when Adrian had tried to arrange a lectureship for him in Louvain. Ever since, he had been well disposed toward Erasmus, defending him against the Louvain theologians and welcoming his New Testament. But Adrian had sided with the Dominicans against Reuchlin and endorsed the Louvain-Cologne condemnation of Luther, and Erasmus worried that Stunica and other detractors in Rome would succeed in turning the new pope against him.

Over the summer of 1522, Erasmus had been working on an edition of a commentary on the Psalms by Arnobius the Younger, a Latin Father of the fifth century, and in an effort to secure Adrian's support, he decided to dedicate it to him. In his cover letter, Erasmus with the usual flattery noted that the current "tempest in human affairs absolutely demanded a man like you at the helm." If any hostile reports about him reached the pope's ears, Erasmus went on, he hoped that Adrian would either dismiss them or at least keep an open mind and wait to hear Erasmus's defense, for in religious matters he had always shown "the spirit proper to an orthodox Christian, and so I shall do to the day of my death."

With Rome some six hundred miles away, Erasmus could expect a reply around mid-September. But September came and went without any word from Rome. October and November similarly passed. Erasmus heard rumors that the pope was displeased with the Arnobius and had pronounced him a heretic and condemned his books. With Christmas approaching and still no reply forthcoming, he decided to send Adrian another appeal. "Most blessed Father," he wrote, "I send you for the second time, by the public courier of Basel, a token of my devotion to you." If His Holiness needed proof of his loyalty, he should propose whatever task he might, and unless Erasmus's obedience was prompt and cheerful, "do not count the name of Erasmus among your servants."

In fact, Adrian had gotten Erasmus's first letter. From the moment of his election, however, his life had been one long tribulation. Shattered by the violence of the Comunero uprising, he now faced the challenge of making the long and dangerous journey to Rome. Because of the fighting between France and Spain, he was unable to travel overland and so had to go by sea. The waters off southern France were so infested with Turkish pirates that a fifty-ship flotilla was thought necessary. Not until August 5, 1522, were Adrian and his armada finally ready to sail. Forced to hug the coast for safety, they did not arrive in Ostia (the port of Rome) until late August. There, Adrian mounted a mule to travel through the mud and heat of the Campagna while his guards looked out for the bands of robbers that roamed the area. As he entered Rome, he was greeted by a gang of naked children who were whipping one another raw. The city had recently been hit by the plague, and most of its curates and aristocrats had fled.

Those who remained had awaited Adrian's arrival with great trepidation. The Dutchman's reputation as a pious bookworm and his reported love of austerity had sown panic among the adventurers, epicures, and aesthetes who packed Rome. His physical appearance seemed to bear out their fears. With his puckered face and tight-fitting cap, Adrian radiated monkish self-denial. He understood no Italian and spoke Latin with a guttural accent that seemed to confirm his barbarian origins. To Adrian, meanwhile, Rome seemed a sinkhole of beggars, buffoons, delinquents, and assassins. Murders took place in the city almost daily, and the right of sanctuary offered by churches and religious houses made it hard to apprehend the perpetrators.

Because of the plague, Adrian was urged to hold his coronation in St. Paul Outside-the-Walls, but he insisted on using St. Peter's. The half-finished basilica remained a jumble of stunted columns, marble heaps, and weather-beaten scaffolding. Adrian kept the ceremony simple, with little of the lavish display that had become a staple of Renaissance Rome. It was a signal of how he intended to rule. To stop the spread of Lutheran doctrines, he believed, the Augean stables had to be cleaned. At long last, Rome had a pope genuinely committed to reform.

In his inaugural speech, delivered on September 1, 1522, Adrian described his top two priorities: mobilizing Christian princes to confront the Turks and purging the Roman Curia. To show his seriousness, he launched a frontal assault on the cardinals, reproaching them for their luxurious living and urging them to limit themselves to an annual income of six thousand ducats. He prohibited them from wearing beards (which were said to make them look like criminals) and barred members of their households from carrying weapons. Moving against absenteeism and pluralism, the pope declared that no one should hold more than one clerical office, and he took steps to end favoritism in the awarding of benefices. Taking aim at the rot at the Datary, he sought to abolish the elaborate schedule of fees for bulls and dispensations. He also set out to restore the integrity of the papal courts; as an example, a clerk who had given false evidence in a case was arrested and deprived of all of his benefices.

Seeking to lead by personal example, Adrian dispensed with the swollen staffs maintained by Julius and Leo and relied on an elderly Flemish woman to do his cooking and washing. He liked to eat alone and preferred simple fare to the exotic meats and rich sauces favored by his predecessors. A strict observer of the canonical hours, he turned in early so that he could attend matins, and after returning to bed he was up again by daybreak to say Mass. He moved into a small study in the Vatican, where he spent many hours trying to complete a Scholastic treatise on which he had long labored. Absorbed in his studies, Adrian was difficult to see, and his brusque manner of speaking alienated many in the capital of eloquence.

The outcry was fierce. "Everyone trembles," wrote the Venetian ambassador. Rome "has again become what it once was," and all the cardinals "have put off their beards." The whole city "is beside itself with fear and terror, owing to the things done by the Pope in the space of eight days." Adrian himself lived in constant fear of being poisoned, and one officer whose livelihood was threatened tried to stab him.

The main obstacles to Adrian's program, though, were the bureaucrats at the Curia. Experts in obstruction and delay, they resisted his every order. In satires, gossip, and dinner-table talk, Adrian was reviled as a miser, a recluse, a Goth. Naive and inexperienced, he had no idea of how to fight back; Rome, he thought, could be transformed into a virtuous place simply through the issuance of a few decrees.

Still, he soldiered on. By the beginning of October 1522, the plague was claiming as many as thirty-five people a day, and all but one cardinal fled the city, but the Dutch pope with stoic conviction remained at his post. And Rome faced an even graver threat: the Turks. After overrunning Belgrade, in August 1521, the Ottomans took aim at Rhodes. Ruled by the Knights of St. John, that island was the last bastion of Christendom in the eastern Mediterranean and a major obstacle to Muslim expansion there. Determined to take it, Suleiman amassed a fleet of four hundred ships along with a ten-thousand-man army and the provisions for a long siege. On June 26, 1522, it began. Though hopelessly outnumbered, the island's defenders bravely held out while awaiting reinforcements. They never came, and in December the knights were forced to surrender. When Adrian heard the news, he burst into tears. Reports spread that the Ottomans planned to invade Italy from the Adriatic and push across the peninsula to Rome. At every opportunity, Adrian proclaimed the need for a crusade against the infidels, and he levied new taxes and tithes with the aim of raising a force of fifty thousand men.

While confronting the Muslims, Adrian was also preparing to repel that other great threat to Western Christendom: Luther. The pope considered him a second Muhammad who was seducing innocent Christians into the arms of false gods. The schism opened up by him had to be closed for collective action to be taken against the Turks; urgent measures were needed to cull the scrofulous sheep from the flock.

An opportunity to achieve that was presented by the new Imperial Diet, due to begin in Nuremberg on November 17, 1522. Adrian hoped to convince the German estates to fully enforce the Edict of Worms and prohibit Luther's writings from circulating. The pope planned to couple that plea with a promise to address the abuses in Rome that had so angered the Germans. He chose Francesco Chieregati, a seasoned Italian diplomat whom he had met in Spain, as his envoy to the assembly.

In addition to enlisting the German princes, Adrian hoped to sway the German people. The letter from Erasmus, with its plea for the pope's blessing, provided an opening. Given the great prestige the prince of letters continued to enjoy among moderate Germans, a penetrating attack by him could help discredit Luther. To prepare his request, Adrian called on two secretaries, one of whom, remarkably, was Jerome Aleander, Erasmus's old adversary, who was now back in Rome. Their successive drafts seemed alternately too warm and too cool, and Adrian's repeated requests for new ones partly explained his delay in replying.

The final version was friendly but insistent. Addressing Erasmus as "Beloved Son," Adrian observed that his letters had caused him delight, both because they came from a man of such outstanding learning and because they gave evidence of his "exceptional devotion" to the Catholic faith. As for Erasmus's fear that malicious gossip would taint him in the pope's eyes, he should put his mind to rest. At the same time, the affection the pope felt for him and the concern he had for his reputation had impelled him to urge Erasmus to attack the "new heresies" with the literary skill with which providence had so uniquely endowed him. Through this sacred undertaking, Erasmus could most effectively silence the suspicions that had arisen concerning his attitude toward Luther. He must hold back no longer. "Can you then refuse to sharpen the weapon of your pen against the madness of these men?" By them "the whole church of Christ is thrown into confusion, and countless souls are involved together with them in the guilt of eternal damnation."

As a sweetener, Adrian invited Erasmus to visit Rome once the plague had lifted. If he did come, Adrian would see to it that he had access to many valuable books in the city as well as conversations with many learned men. On December 1, 1522, the letter was signed and sent north. Adrian was now joining the long list of powerful figures demanding that Erasmus take a public stand against Luther. The pope awaited a response, even as he followed the proceedings of the new diet.

Nuremberg was one of about sixty-five imperial free cities in the Holy Roman Empire. These cities answered to neither a prince nor a bishop but to the emperor, and in practice they enjoyed considerable autonomy. In the religious competition ahead, they would be key battlegrounds, and few more so than Nuremberg. With a population of 40,000, it was the de facto capital of the empire. Both the Imperial Governing Council and the Imperial Chamber Court were located there, and between 1522 and 1524 the city would host three diets.

Nuremberg was also the center of the German Renaissance. It was home to Albrecht Dürer, Germany's most famous artist; to a booming printing industry; and to craftsmen whose skill and ingenuity were admired across the continent. At fairs held three times a year, Nuremberg's market square filled with stalls offering ornate candelabras, exquisite timepieces, precise scientific instruments, guns of every caliber, bells of all sizes, the sturdiest tools, the finest musical instruments, and the most secure locks in Europe.

Nuremberg was known as well for its effective governance. Like most imperial cities, it was ruled by a small elite, with a council dominated by several dozen patrician families whose main interest was maintaining social and economic stability. Strict controls were placed on every aspect of civic life. Sumptuary laws regulated the length of men's jackets, the cut of women's bodices, the types of cakes that could be served at weddings, and the number of candles that could be lit at funerals. A battalion of inspectors policed every aspect of economic life, from the baking of bread and the labeling of wine to the freshness of meat and the purchase of raw materials. In Nuremberg (in contrast to most other cities), pigs were not allowed to forage freely in the streets; once a day they could be driven to the Pegnitz River, which flowed through town, and their droppings had to be scooped up at once and thrown into its turgid waters. Inns had to close at sunset, and when the curfew bell rang two hours later, anyone found outdoors without a valid reason was detained.

Yet even in this highly regimented setting, Luther's ideas were spreading. Their main conduit was the Sodalitas Staupitziana, a circle of reform-minded clergy, scholars, and civic leaders named after Johann von Staupitz, Luther's early mentor. As vicar-general of the Augustinian Observants, Staupitz had frequently passed through Nuremberg on his visitations, and he sometimes stayed over to preach at the Augustinian church. His pronouncements on the sinfulness of man and the need for divine grace made a deep impression, and a group of leading citizens began meeting at the Augustinian friary. They included Dürer; Willibald Pirckheimer, Nuremberg's leading humanist; and Lazarus Spengler, the secretary of the town council. Through the Augustinian prior, Wenceslas Link, the Sodalitas members learned of Luther's pathbreaking lectures on the Bible even before he had issued the Ninety-Five Theses. Reading that justification comes through faith alone, these men felt freed from the uncertainty and anxiety associated with penance and works; reading and interpreting the Bible on their own, they felt empowered to confront the priesthood and its authority.

In 1522, one member of the sodality, Andreas Osiander, who taught Hebrew at the Augustinian monastery, was appointed preacher at St. Lorenz, one of the city's two parish churches. His powerful sermons about the importance of faith over works and of God's Word over man-made laws attracted large crowds. In three other Nuremberg churches as well, reform-minded preachers gained control of pulpits. Churchgoers began disrupting the sermons of more traditional preachers, and fast days were flagrantly violated by craftsmen and journeymen.

The Meistersinger were another vehicle for spreading Luther's ideas. Nuremberg had about two hundred of these master singers, who, joining poetry to music, followed an elaborate code of rules developed over centuries. They performed in public three times a year but met more frequently in the church of the convent of St. Catherine's for highly structured singing contests, with a judge ready to sanction any singer who strayed even minutely from the rules.

When Luther's teachings began circulating in Nuremberg, the Meistersinger quickly incorporated them into their songs. The most nimble was Hans Sachs. Educated at a Latin school and trained as a shoemaker, Sachs worked at that trade for years before discovering a knack for putting words to melodies and communicating ideas through music. On discovering Luther, around 1520, he began celebrating Luther's gospel in catchy poems and songs. Astonishingly prolific, Sachs over his lifetime would produce more than four thousand master songs, two hundred or more dramas, and some two thousand didactic poems in rhyming couplets, plus assorted dialogues, tales, and fables, many of them heralding the new gospel. (Sachs is the central character in Wagner's *Die Meistersinger von Nürnberg*.)

As the delegates in November 1522 began arriving in Nuremberg for the opening of the diet, then, songs about the new gospel could literally be heard in the street. In brazen disregard of the Edict of Worms, Luther's books were openly on sale, and the city was awash in *Flugschriften* denouncing papal tyranny and priestly greed. Anticlerical sentiment ran so deep that when the nuncio Chieregati arrived, the town council denied him permission for the usual ceremonial entry on a white charger caparisoned in purple.

During the initial weeks of the conclave, Chieregati stayed in the background, waiting for his moment. Not until December 10 did he address the matter of Luther in any detail. He noted the rise in disorder caused by Luther's doctrines, the urgent need to enforce the Edict of Worms, and the pope's intention of rectifying curial abuses. The delegates replied that they could take no decision on such matters until they had the pope's proposals in writing.

Throughout the proceedings, Chieregati had kept in close touch with Rome, and toward the end of December he received from Adrian a brief outlining his reform proposals. Drawing on it, the nuncio on January 3, 1523, gave a speech that would become famous in Reformation annals. With resonant solemnity he described the great grief with which the Vatican was afflicted because of the prospering of the Lutheran sect, and he emphasized the pope's eager desire that a speedy end be put to this plague lest Germany become another Bohemia. The German people should be moved by the infamy that Luther was bringing upon their nation. It was time for the princes and clergy of the empire to order a halt to the grievous insults that the Lutherans were directing at God and to enforce at once the apostolic sentence and imperial edict.

To the delegates, all of this sounded familiar. But then Chieregati began speaking of the ills in Rome in a new key. He referred to the "many abominations" that in recent years had arisen in the Holy See. The disease had spread from the head to the members, from supreme pontiffs to low-ranking clerics. Under the new pope, however, the Vatican would spare no effort to ensure that the Roman Curia, from which the evil emanated, was speedily reformed. At the same time, Chieregati cautioned, no one should be surprised if not all these wrongs were corrected at once, for the disease had taken such deep root that the cure could proceed only slowly. As for the complaints that the Holy See had disregarded the lists of grievances submitted in the past, he said, the new pope could not be held responsible for what had gone before. Adrian was resolved to abstain from such abuses during the whole of his pontificate, and he had requested a list of benefices that had gone "to actors and stable-boys rather than to learned men" so that when vacancies occurred, worthy candidates could be named to fill them.

Had Chieregati stopped there, he might have carried the day. But, reflecting the Holy See's unbounded regard for its own authority, he added several warnings. Given how Luther had seduced the German nation from the way shown by the Savior and how his teachings had encouraged disobedience and license, the delegates had "to quench this fire" and by all possible means recall Luther and other instigators of error to the right path. If, God forbid, they would not listen, then "the rod of severity and punishment" would be used according to the laws of the empire and the imperial edict. "God knows our willingness to forgive, but if it should be proved that the evil has penetrated so far that gentle means of healing are of no avail, then we must have recourse to a method of severity in order to safeguard the members as yet untainted by disease."

Then, in a grave miscalculation, Chieregati demanded not only that the imperial edict be enforced but that the city's four evangelical preachers be arrested. They were to be thrown into chains and sent to Rome to be punished. Chieregati further accused their leader, the Hebrew scholar Osiander, of being a Jew (which he was not).

The delegates listened in disbelief. Arresting the four preachers, they knew, would likely touch off disturbances. Indeed, as word of Chieregati's demands spread through Nuremberg, protesters filled its streets, and the police had to be called out. The charged atmosphere was captured in a letter from Willibald Pirckheimer to his friend Erasmus in Basel. Pirckheimer shared Erasmus's reservations about Luther's faith-based spirituality, but he was appalled by what he called Chieregati's "brazen falsehoods" and "outrageous actions," which "very nearly caused serious rioting." The legate had become so unpopular that he could not show his face in public without embarrassment. No one "pays him the slightest respect, and he is the laughingstock and butt of the whole population."

In the end, the estates of the diet rejected Chieregati's demands. Since there were errors and abuses on all sides, they said, the pope should convene a general council of the Church to address them. The reformist preachers were not arrested but instead summoned to the Rathaus and urged to moderate their language and avoid controversial subjects. Penalties were prescribed for all who ate meat on fast days, and booksellers and printers were warned not to produce or sell Lutheran books. Such books, however, remained openly on sale. The Luther affair, Chieregati wrote to an Italian marquis, had taken such root among the people "that a thousand men would not suffice to eradicate it," and he himself had been "subjected to threats, outrages, defamatory libels, and all such insults as can possibly be borne."

The same ferment that was present in Nuremberg was occurring in many other parts of Germany—especially its cities. There, literacy rates were higher than in smaller communities. (As much as 30 percent of the population could read in large cities, compared with 5 to 10 percent outside them.) The cities were also more open to new ideas, and the printing houses there helped disseminate them. Many cities, moreover, were characterized by glaring social and economic inequities, which created resentment among artisans and laborers toward the ruling elite, and this resentment in turn offered fertile ground for populist doctrines. Luther's rejection of the division between the clergy and the laity and his insistence that all believers are priests became the basis for challenging the status quo and demanding social justice.

As in Nuremberg, sermons became a key means of spreading Lutheran ideas, and the demand for reformist preachers became a signpost of the Reformation. Everywhere, though, that demand faced strong resistance from the old order. In Strasbourg, for instance, a forceful preacher named Matthäus Zell was attracting large crowds to the cathedral with his expositions of the Gospels. When the small chapel assigned to him proved inadequate, he sought to move to the great stone pulpit that dominated the nave, but the canons, refusing permission, kept the door to it locked. To accommodate him, some carpenters who lived nearby built a portable wooden pulpit that was carried into the church for each sermon, then carted home by a group of burghers. From these contested beginnings, the new creed would spread with such speed that within two years Strasbourg would challenge Wittenberg and Zurich for intellectual leadership of the movement.

From such large population centers, preachers fanned out to smaller ones. Most were itinerants who, dismissed from their posts for spreading seditious ideas, carried their Luther Bibles and preaching manuals with them as they sought new positions. From pulpits in modest parish churches and on village greens under the lime trees, these renegade preachers proclaimed the new gospel, giving biblical sanction to longstanding grievances against both clerical and oligarchic despotism. With its declaration that a Christian is a free man, subject to none, and that no law could be imposed on him without his consent, the Lutheran creed was working a dramatic change in the German consciousness.

Adrian's letter to Erasmus arrived in Basel in mid-January 1523. On seeing the pope's expression of support for him, Erasmus felt greatly relieved. He would call the letter his *Breve aureum* ("golden brief") and frequently flourish it before opponents. He was less pleased with Adrian's request that he write against Luther. If he complied, he knew, he would be seen as the pope's lackey, with predictable consequences for his reputation and safety.

In his reply, Erasmus noted that the religious discord had reached such a stage that no scholar, least of all himself, could quell it by pen and ink. "My popularity, if I had any, has either cooled off so far that it scarcely exists, or has quite evaporated, or has even turned into hatred." Erasmus ruefully recalled a time when he had received hundreds of letters proclaiming him "the greatest of the great, prince of the world of literature, bright star of Germany, luminary of learning, champion of humane studies, bulwark of a more genuine theology." Now, on the rare occasions when he was mentioned at all, it was to be slandered by madmen, and not just in Germany. He could hardly name all the regions in which "the minds of ordinary people have been penetrated by support of Luther and hatred of the papacy." Day and night he toiled "for the good of all men at my own costs and charges," yet he received "no recompense except to be torn in pieces by both sides."

Erasmus offered a list of reasons for declining the pope's invitation to visit Rome—the prospect of traveling over the snow-covered Alps, the dirty inns with their foul-smelling stoves and acidic wines, his poor health. (For months, Erasmus had been tormented by attacks of the stone—"my own executioner," he called it.) Finally, Erasmus warned the pope against dealing with the matter of Luther by force. The growth had spread too far to be curable by the knife. Whatever course was taken, he feared, the whole business would "end in appalling bloodshed."

TRUE CHRISTIAN WARFARE

As the Lutheran movement spread and the clamor over it grew, the man at the center of it all was living in a small room in the Augustinian monastery in Wittenberg, sleeping on a straw mattress with a rough blanket to cover him. By now, almost all of the friars had fled the Black Cloister; the prior himself was eager to leave but had agreed to remain to help Luther run the place. Luther's one regular source of income was the modest stipend he received for preaching at the town church. Seeing his writing as a spiritual office, he continued to decline all compensation for it, leaving it to his publishers to reap the profits—which were considerable. Lucas Cranach would earn a fortune off Luther's Bible, and between 1523 and 1525 three other printers would set up shop in the city.

So, while many of those around him thrived, Luther lived in near poverty. At one point he complained to Spalatin that the prior of the monastery had no money to pay the tax collector for the supplies of malt it used to brew beer. But Frederick was unmoved. While granting Luther the right to live and operate openly in Wittenberg, he remained stingy toward him. However unchristian such a policy might seem, it reflected the intense pressure the elector was under. The final statement adopted at the Diet of Nuremberg in early 1523 directed him to make sure that Luther did not speak or write publicly, and Adrian VI sent him a stern letter reproving him for letting a heretic live openly in his territory. Henry VIII—still fuming over Luther's attack—wrote to Frederick and other Saxon princes to ask how the Germans could continue to "bear such disgrace from a good-for-nothing friar." He urged the elector to restrain the Lutherans, "without bloodshed if possible, but, if not, by any means."

Most indignant of all was Duke George. His secret service, which was adept at intercepting letters, had gotten hold of the one in which Luther had referred to him as a water bladder. Furious, the duke sent Luther an angry note, demanding to know if he had in fact used such ugly language and wanting to be informed of his position "so that we may know how to act as our honor shall demand." In his reply, Luther—incensed at George's continued plotting against him—referred to him as "your Disgrace" and declared that he would not "tremble for a mere bladder, God willing."

Unable to get at Luther physically, Duke George took aim at his books, especially his translation of the New Testament. On November 7, 1522, the duke issued a decree prohibiting its sale or use in his territory and demanding that everyone in possession of a copy surrender it (for reimbursement). Luther began receiving anxious inquiries as to whether people should comply. He was torn. On the one hand, Paul at Romans 13 had declared that everyone should be subject to the governing authorities; by that standard, all copies should be handed over. Such a course, how-ever, would run counter to Luther's convictions about remaining true to one's conscience. At Worms, he had rejected the emperor's demand that he retract what was in his books. Should faithful Christians now meekly hand over theirs?

To address such questions, Luther produced *Temporal Authority: To What Extent It Should Be Obeyed*. In it, he set forth the core political prin-ciple that would guide him through the coming tumult and which would become inscribed in German Lutheranism. It was inspired by Augustine. In the *City of God*, the bishop of Hippo proposed the idea of the two cities, heavenly and earthly. Adapting it, Luther proposed the existence of two kingdoms. In the heavenly kingdom there dwell the true believers in Christ. Here, princely authority does not apply. Matters of faith and belief, which belong to this realm, must remain the province of personal conscience. The earthly kingdom, by contrast, is home to the unrigh-teous, with all the attendant sin and disorder. Here princely power does apply, and even faithful Christians must submit to it. "The soul is not under the authority of Caesar," Luther wrote; one's life and property are.

So, if a prince commands his subjects to believe this or that or de-mands that they hand over certain books, they should refuse, for in such cases the prince is overreaching and commanding that which he has no right to. As for the "tyrants" who demand that the German New Testa-ment be turned over, their subjects "should not turn in a single page, not even a letter, on pain of losing their salvation." These tyrants, he wrote with typical ferocity, act "as murderers of Christ." Heresy "can never be restrained by force." It is a spiritual matter, "where you cannot hack to pieces with iron, consume with fire, or drown in water." Here, God's Word alone prevails. Although the Jews and heretics were burned, none of them "has been or will be convinced or converted thereby."

Luther, in short, was trying to distinguish between internal belief and external action. Christians had to uphold the former without resorting to the latter. Faith was critical—acts in the real world were not. Luther's political position thus mirrored his theological preference for faith over works.

In the last section of *Temporal Authority*, Luther warned the princes about the fire that was building. Common men and women were at last beginning to think for themselves, and dissatisfaction with princely rule was rising. Unless the princes began to govern more justly, they might feel the fury of the mob. "Men will not, men cannot, men refuse to endure your tyranny and wantonness much longer." The world was no longer what it once was, when princes hunted down and drove the people like so much game. If they continued to brandish the sword in this way, they should beware lest someone come and compel them to sheathe it—"and not in God's name!"

But what if the princes did not change their ways? What recourse would *Herr Omnes* then have? Was there any point at which faithful Christians could justifiably act on their beliefs and actively resist a despot? This was one of the critical political questions of the sixteenth century. For Luther, the growing agitation in the countryside was reinforcing his distrust of spontaneous popular action, and in *Temporal Authority* he was again trying to make clear that his galvanizing religious ideas were not to be applied in the secular sphere.

Yet he continued to feed the unrest. Around the same time that he wrote *Temporal Authority*, Luther became involved in a dispute in Leisnig, a small town seventy miles from Wittenberg, over the appointment of a new pastor. With much of the population embracing the new gospel, the local congregation wanted a pastor who could preach it. But the abbot of a nearby Cistercian monastery, who had the right of patronage over the town, opposed them. Luther was asked to visit. He did, on September 25,

1522, and he discussed with local parishioners their desire to name their own priest and to establish a common chest like the one in Wittenberg. The efforts to reach a compromise failed, however, and a delegation from the town visited Wittenberg to ask Luther to provide a scriptural basis for the congregation's right to appoint its own pastor.

He agreed. The result—*That a Christian Assembly or Congregation Has the Right and Power to Judge All Teaching and to Call, Appoint, and Dismiss Teachers, Established and Proven by Scripture*—was another soaring manifesto aimed at democratizing the faith. Luther's starting point was his idea that all believers are priests. Christ, he wrote, takes the right and power to judge teachings from bishops, scholars, and councils and gives them to all Christians equally. "Spiritual tyrants" who teach things contrary to God's Word should be "chased away as wolves, thieves, and murderers." If a Christian congregation is in possession of the Gospel, it has not only the right but the duty to expose and rescind the authority that bishops and abbots seek to impose. Even if there were decent bishops who wanted to appoint decent preachers, "they still could not and should not do so without the will, the election, and the call of the congregation."

For centuries, the Church's hierarchy had reserved the right to name all clergy, from popes to parish priests. Luther now wanted to transfer that authority to the congregation. In place of ordination from above, he wanted nomination from below. Luther was here advancing the radical principle of congregationalism—local control of church affairs. Centuries later, it would become a prominent strain in American Protestantism. More immediately, *That a Christian Assembly* would further rouse *Herr Omnes.*

A revealing snapshot of Luther on the cusp of the dramatic events that were about to transform his life is offered by Johannes Dantiscus, the ambassador of the Polish king to the court of Charles V. Returning to Poland in the spring of 1523 after three years in Spain, Dantiscus decided to stop in Wittenberg to see the renowned reformer. As he neared the town, he found the surrounding fields flooded by the swollen Elbe and the farmers cursing Luther; because people had eaten meat during Lent, they believed, God was visiting his wrath on the countryside. The ambassador had to leave his horses at the bank of the river and cross it in a boat over to the town. There he met several young men learned in Latin, Greek, and Hebrew, foremost among them Melanchthon, who entertained him throughout his three-day stay. The envoy told Melanchthon of his desire to see Luther, for, as he wrote, "whoever sees Rome without the pope, or Wittenberg without Luther, has really seen nothing."

With Wittenberg full of refugees, runaways, tourists, and spies, Luther was reluctant to meet strangers, and those wanting an audience had to find someone to intercede. Melanchthon agreed to do so for Dantiscus and, after supper, he took him to the Black Cloister, where Luther was gathered with some of the few remaining friars. With their hair grown out, they all looked like peasants, except for Luther, who had the air of a courtier. During almost four hours of conversation over wine and beer, Luther struck Dantiscus as intelligent, learned, and eloquent, but, aside from some biting and disdainful comments about the pope, the emperor, and several princes, "he revealed nothing new." Like many others, Dantiscus was struck by Luther's eyes, which, he wrote, "are piercing and twinkle almost uncannily, the way one sometimes sees in a person possessed." His manner of speaking was passionate and "loaded with banter and taunts." Overall, Luther seemed to be a "good guy," though full of pride and arrogance and given to unbridled "scolding, contradicting, and mocking." Melanchthon seemed far more companionable; of all of Germany's learned men, the ambassador wrote, "this chap I like best."

At the time, Melanchthon was helping Luther with his translation of the Five Books of Moses. In translating the Old Testament, Luther would take even more liberties than he had with the New. Like all Christians, he had been taught to read the Hebrew Scriptures as foreshadowing the coming of Christ, and throughout his translation he gave Hebrew terms Christian shades of meaning. Luther translated "life" as "eternal life," "Deliverer of Israel" as "the Savior," and *chesed* as *Gnade*, "grace." A term frequently appearing in the Hebrew Bible, *chesed* was taken by most Jewish exegetes to mean "loving-kindness," "steadfast love," or "faithful love," which, when applied to God, connoted his covenanted love for the Jewish people. In translating it as "grace," Luther was evoking the divine favor that God bestows on man through his faith in Christ.

In his preface to his translation, Luther explained that to understand the Old Testament, the reader must at all times set Christ before him, "for he is the man to whom it all applies, every bit of it." The Hebrew language had so declined "that even the Jews know little enough about it," and Jewish scholars did not understand their own Scriptures. As a result, "we Christians are the ones who must do the work, for we have the understanding of Christ without which even the knowledge of the language is nothing." In his Table Talk, Luther said that his aim was "to make Moses speak so that you would never know he was a Jew." In fact, he made Moses and virtually everyone else in the Hebrew Bible speak like a Christian. Luther, in short, was Christianizing the Old Testament.

Because of the length of the Old Testament, Luther decided to publish it in parts to keep it affordable. The printing of the Five Books of Moses, begun in December 1522, would continue until the middle of 1523. In the meantime, Luther began translating the historical books of the Old Testament, beginning with Joshua.

That same spring, Luther produced his first work expressly about the Jews. It was prompted by a rumor circulating at the diet in Nuremberg that he had claimed that Mary was not a virgin but had conceived Christ with Joseph and then gone on to have more children. This was a serious charge, and to rebut it, Luther wrote *That Jesus Christ Was Born a Jew*. In typical neo-Scholastic fashion, he laced the tract with biblical citations, many interpreted so arbitrarily as to seem completely divorced from the text. What was most striking about the volume, though, was Luther's temperate attitude toward the Jews. He denounced the popes, bishops, sophists, and other "crude asses' heads" who had treated them "as if they were dogs rather than human beings." By forbidding the Jews to labor and do business with Christians, they had forced them into usury. Had he himself been a Jew and seen such "dolts and blockheads" teaching the Christian faith, he would rather "have become a hog than a Christian." The Jews should be dealt with not according to papal law but according to the law of Christian love. "We must receive them cordially, and permit them to trade and work with us, that they may have occasion and opportunity to associate with us, hear our Christian teachings, and witness our Christian life."

Luther was not urging tolerance of the Jews, however. Rather, he was stating his belief that if they were treated kindly and instructed carefully from Scripture, "many of them will become genuine Christians." He summarized his position in a letter to Bernard, formerly Rabbi Jacob Gipher, who had converted to Christianity and married Karlstadt's maid and to whom Luther sent *That Jesus Was Born a Jew* as a present. The Jews, he wrote, had until then received "not a single spark of light or warmth" from the clergy or the universities, so it was no surprise that they had become alienated. Now that "the golden light of the Gospel is rising and shining, there is hope that many of the Jews will be converted in earnest and be drawn completely to Christ."

Luther would cling to his expectation of Jewish conversion until his final years, when—seeing it fail to materialize—he would turn on the Jews with redoubled fury.

While absorbed in these weighty theological issues, Luther faced a practical challenge that would lead to a radical change in his personal life. Shortly before Easter 1523, he heard that a group of nuns at a convent in Nimbschen, near Grimma, fifty miles from Wittenberg, wanted to leave. Most of them were the daughters of impoverished nobles who had deposited them there after concluding that they were unlikely to find husbands. The convent had a policy of strict seclusion. Relatives who came to visit were allowed to speak only through latticed windows for a few minutes. Silence was the rule, friendships between nuns were forbidden, and even dogs were barred from the premises.

Yet even here Luther's ideas had penetrated, and twelve nuns, inspired by his denunciation of monastic vows, decided to leave. But their families, when contacted, refused to provide assistance. Helping a nun leave a convent was a serious offense, punishable by death, and Duke George, in whose territory the convent sat, kept vigilant watch.

Hearing of their predicament, Luther sent a message to Leonhard Koppe, a member of the town council in nearby Torgau. Koppe had the contract for delivering supplies to the convent, including herring, which he usually transported in barrels in a covered wagon. Thus prodded, Koppe on Easter eve pulled up to the cloister with the wagon and hurriedly bundled the nuns into it. In a state of great anxiety, they headed north across Ducal Saxony, watching out for George's agents. Only upon reaching Torgau, thirty miles away and safely inside Electoral Saxony, did they begin to calm down. Two days later, all the nuns save three (who were taken in by relatives) were in Wittenberg. "Nine fugitive nuns, a wretched crowd, have been brought me by honest citizens of Torgau," Luther wrote to Spalatin on April 10. They were in "miserable condition," having neither shoes nor clothes. Their prospects were equally dismal, for a nun who left a convent was considered disreputable, and, having spent most of their time in prayer, they did not even know how to keep house.

Luther immediately took responsibility for them. With little to spare from his own meager salary and not wanting to burden the city or his order, he urged Spalatin to find some money from his rich courtiers to help support the women until their kinsmen or others could provide for them. Eventually, Luther managed to find places for all but three: two sisters, Ave and Margaret von Schönfeld, and Katharina von Bora.

Katharina's case would prove the most challenging. She had been born into a noble family of declining means in a village near Leipzig. When she was five, her mother died, and she was placed in a Benedictine convent to be educated. Five years later, she was transferred to the cloister at Nimbschen. Now twenty-four, Katharina was unworldly but strong-willed, outspoken, and competent. Later portraits by Cranach show her with a round face and high forehead, eyes set wide apart, and a tight mouth; they do not capture her high spirits. Fearing that she might become a permanent burden, Luther set out to find her a husband. "The monks and nuns who have left their cloisters steal many of my hours," he complained to Johannes Oecolampadius in June 1523.

Over the previous months, Luther had received several letters from Oecolampadius, but only now was he getting around to answering them. He had heard of the excitement Oecolampadius was causing in Basel and of the success he was having with a series of lectures on Isaiah. Luther had also heard of Erasmus's displeasure with those lectures, and in his letter he advised Oecolampadius to ignore it. He belittled Erasmus's judgment on spiritual matters and complained of the "pricks" that the humanist, without openly declaring himself a foe, had given him. Erasmus, Luther wrote, had accomplished what he had been called forth to do: "he has brought us from godless studies to a knowledge of the languages; perhaps he will die with Moses in the plains of Moab, for he does not go forward to the better studies—those that pertain to godliness." He wished that Erasmus

> would stop commenting on the Holy Scriptures and writing his *Paraphrases*, for he is not equal to this task; he takes up the time of his readers to no purpose, and delays them in their study of the Scriptures. He has done enough in showing us the evil; to show us the good and to lead us into the promised land, he is, I see, unable.

Luther was referring to Deuteronomy 32, where Moses, standing atop Mount Nebo on the plains of Moab, looks out over the land that God had promised Abraham, Isaac, and Jacob and which he would not be allowed to enter. After Moses's death, Joshua takes his place and leads the Israelites into Canaan—a role in which Luther clearly saw himself.

Oecolampadius's lectures on Isaiah had indeed caused a stir in Basel. Delivered around Easter 1523 to the theological faculty at the university, they drew up to four hundred people, including not just students and professors but also burghers, craftsmen, and laborers. Like all Christian interpreters of the Old Testament in this era, Oecolampadius read Isaiah as being wholly about Christ, but he used his knowledge of Hebrew and of the Septuagint to bring alive the prophet and his time and to describe the moral guidance Isaiah could offer to believing Christians; he also mixed in German with his Latin, making his presentations more accessible. His Sunday sermons at St. Martin's church were attracting large crowds as well. Oecolampadius's moral fervor seemed all the more inspiring for being delivered in a soft-spoken, nontheatrical manner. Soon other preachers were echoing him, and Basel became increasingly divided between a growing faction demanding far-reaching change and the town elders, who, consisting mostly of merchants and the senior clergy, wanted to keep the peace and maintain the status quo.

Erasmus was startled by Oecolampadius's growing ardor and popularity. What, he wondered, had happened to the retiring corrector and fact-checker he had known just a few years back? In Zurich, too, the reformers were becoming more insistent. In late 1522, Zwingli issued a bitter tirade against Rome, dismissing not only Pope Adrian's proposals to the diet in Nuremberg but also all claims of papal authority. Although he did not attach his name to the work, Erasmus, on seeing it, could tell at once from whose pen it had sprung. "Another piece of nonsense, utter rubbish, has appeared about the pope," he wrote to Zwingli. If "all of Luther's party are like this, I wash my hands of the whole lot of them. I never saw anything more mad than this foolish stuff."

The Church's own zeal in cracking down on its critics, meanwhile, was apparent in the brutal treatment of Sigismund Steinschneider, the surgeon at whose home in Basel the luncheon of roasted pig had taken place the previous Lent. In addition to this offense, Steinschneider had made some remarks about the sacraments and the Virgin Mary that were considered blasphemous. He had then made the mistake of traveling into territory near Freiburg that was under the control of Archduke Ferdinand (the brother of Emperor Charles V), a remorseless pursuer of heretics. Steinschneider was arrested and condemned to death. Before being dispatched, he was forced to undergo horrific tortures. First, his flesh was torn from his back by red-hot tongs. Then his four limbs together with his hips and shoulders were slowly and excruciatingly amputated. His throat was cut and his tongue pulled out through the incision. Finally, the central part of his body except for the heart was burned. By inflicting such harsh punishment on one man, Erasmus lamented, "it was thought large numbers could be cured."

In the face of such cruelty, he decided to issue a stern protest. In early 1523, he and Froben were preparing a new edition of the works of St. Hilary. This fourth-century bishop of Poitiers had helped lead the fight against the Arian heresy and its questioning of Christ's divinity. Reading of the internal battles that tore the Church apart back then, Erasmus was struck by the parallels to his own day, and in his preface he sought to highlight the malignant effects of theological disputation. The essay would be an important text in the history of religious toleration.

"Once," he wrote, "faith was more a matter of a way of life than of a profession of articles." Then came the wicked teachings of the heretics, and in response theologians had formulated more and more definitions, until finally faith came to reside more "in the written word than in the soul." In fighting the Arians, orthodox churchmen devised all kinds of abstract propositions about the nature of God, the creation of the Son, and the relation of both to the Holy Spirit. What did it serve the Church to pronounce on such abstract and ultimately unknowable matters? As doctrines multiplied, sincerity faded; as controversy boiled over, charity grew cold. Hilary viciously attacked the Arians, yet among them there were probably many pious Christians.

Christendom was now being similarly racked by sophistical conflict over obscure questions. "What arrogance, what contentions, what tumult, what discord in the world do we see gush forth from this kind of absurd learning!" Erasmus declared. Meanwhile, the really important things were neglected. "Unless I pardon my brother's sins against me, God will not pardon my transgressions against him. Unless I have a pure heart, I shall not see God." With all his energy, man must strive to purge his soul of malice, envy, avarice, and lust and replace them with charity, patience, kindness, and other fruits of the Spirit. The "sum and substance of our religion," Erasmus offered, "is peace and concord."

As unobjectionable as that last sentiment might seem, it caused a tremendous furor. In 1526, the Sorbonne would censure it along with many other passages from the essay. The Lutherans were no less condemnatory. In that zealous era, the assertion that Christianity was at its core about peace and that godliness of conduct should count for more than purity of doctrine inflamed militants on both sides.

With the chasm between those sides widening, Erasmus was coming under renewed pressure to declare himself. The main source was England. Henry VIII remained intent on striking back at Luther. More than personal honor was at stake. In increasing numbers, Luther's books were invading the island and spreading his subversive doctrines. The hellish wolf had to be silenced. To carry out that task, the king turned to the one man in his kingdom who seemed endowed with the necessary eloquence, knowledge, and conviction: Thomas More.

Now a close adviser to Henry, More was undergoing a dramatic change in outlook as a result of the growing turmoil on the Continent. In *Utopia*, he had made religious tolerance a key principle, with everyone on the island "free to practice what religion he liked, and to try and convert other people to his own faith"—provided that he did it "quietly and politely, by rational argument"; the penalty for "being too aggressive in religious controversy" was either exile or slavery. To More, the Lutherans seemed too aggressive. With Luther calling every Christian a priest and with weavers and miners interpreting the Bible for themselves, the social fabric seemed in danger of unraveling. Seeking an anchor, More found it in the Church. The free-spirited humanist who had translated Lucian with Erasmus and bantered about human folly was turning into a tenacious defender of the established order as embodied in the hierarchy, traditions, and customs of the eternal Church of Rome.

Accepting Henry's request to respond to Luther, More took aim at his doctrine of *sola scriptura*. Luther extolled the authority of the Bible, but without the Church to interpret it, More declared, it was a lifeless book full of contradictions and obscurities. All heretics from the time of Arius on were able to cite Scripture to justify their pernicious doctrines, and Luther was no exception. The Church was the embodiment of divine wisdom, the guardian of true doctrine, the hallowed arbiter of Holy Scripture. The Bible was the servant of the Church, not its master.

Along with such solemn invocations of ecclesiastical sanctity, More served up large helpings of vulgarity and invective. Luther was a "mad friarlet and privy-minded rascal with his ragings and ravings, with his filth and dung, shitting and beshitted." He was an ape, an arse, a drunkard, a liar, a *cacodemon* ("shit-devil") who farted anathema and celebrated Mass *super foricam* ("on the toilet"). This "worthless heretical buffoon" should "swallow down his filth and lick up the dung with which he has so fondly defiled his tongue and pen."

Even in a century given to scatology, More's *Responsio ad Lutherum* stood out for its foulness. More himself seems to have been embarrassed by it, for he brought it out under a pseudonym (William Ross). Even so, it clearly came from someone close to the king and so lost much of its bite. A shaft from Erasmus would penetrate much deeper. From his friends in England, Erasmus had heard that Henry had somehow gotten the idea that he had helped Luther prepare his attack on the king. This was doubly exasperating, since others suspected that Erasmus had helped Henry prepare his *Assertio* against Luther. At great expense, Erasmus sent a servant to England to deliver to the king, Thomas Wolsey, and other notables letters that emphatically denied any such involvement and reaffirmed his unbounded devotion.

A reply came in June 1523 in the form of a letter from his friend Cuthbert Tunstall, now the bishop of London. The king, Tunstall reported, was happy to hear Erasmus confirm his loyalty. It was not enough, however. Duty demanded that he challenge Luther directly and openly. Never before had a man who was as well equipped in theology as Erasmus and who had witnessed the rise of a pernicious heresy during his lifetime failed to attack it. Here, in confronting heresy, Tunstall wrote, was "true Christian warfare."

> I adjure you, by all the toils that Christ endured in his mortal body, by the blood which he shed in death to redeem the world, and by the glory which you look for in the heavens when your course in this life is run: I beg and beseech you, dear Erasmus, or rather it is the church that begs and beseeches you, to grapple after all this time with the hydra-headed monster. Courage is all, and the world is confident that you will win.

Given Tunstall's position, this entreaty could be seen as coming directly from Henry. Erasmus nonetheless continued to resist. As much as he admired Tunstall's devotion to the Church, he replied, he felt that he had to proceed with caution, for he had seen many who in their zeal to pull up the tares had uprooted the wheat as well and who in their pursuit of heretics actually threatened piety and concord. As late as August 29, 1523, Erasmus was informing Willibald Pirckheimer in Nuremberg that "the princes all urge me to attack Luther. But I shall write nothing."

What finally pushed Erasmus over the edge was a calamitous encounter—or rather non-encounter—with his old acquaintance Ulrich von Hutten. In late November 1522, the volatile knight-laureate had arrived in Basel—homeless, penniless, and terminally ill with syphilis. His frantic and unsuccessful efforts to provoke a war against the Romanists had alienated much of Germany. Forced to leave it, he had headed to Basel, home to some of his few remaining friends. He quickly fell in with the circle of reformers around Oecolampadius, who did their best to bolster his spirits.

It was Erasmus, though, whom he most wanted to see. Though the two had drifted apart over the years, Erasmus remained for him the great lodestar of learning, and in his extremity he hoped to rekindle some of their old affection. His feelings were not reciprocated. Erasmus had never forgiven Hutten for leaking his letter to Albrecht of Mainz back in 1519, and he was tired of Hutten's reckless efforts to push him into declaring his support for Luther. More important, Erasmus feared that meeting such a notorious champion of the Lutheran cause would be seized upon by his orthodox opponents as evidence of his own sympathies for it. Also, the very prospect of the unkempt, pox-ridden Hutten invading his premises repelled the fastidious Erasmus. As a pretext for not receiving him, Erasmus sent word that, given the chilliness of his stoveless rooms, it would be unwise for Hutten in his feverish state to visit them. It was a transparent excuse but one that he hoped Hutten would understand.

He wouldn't. Physically ravaged by his disease, pursued by the agents of the pope, banished from his homeland, and intently seeking the support of an old mentor, Hutten felt spurned as if a vagrant. Furious, he began denouncing Erasmus to all who would listen as an unprincipled egotist who reflexively backed winners over losers. He also mocked Erasmus's friends and wrote a fierce satire of a Basel doctor who had proposed some preposterous cures for Hutten's condition. Exasperated, the magistracy of Basel asked him to leave. In mid-January 1523, he did, moving to the nearby village of Mühlhausen and taking up residence in the local Augustinian monastery.

While there, Hutten saw a copy of a long letter that Erasmus had sent to his friend Marcus Laurinus in Bruges and which had been published by Froben. The letter was one of the occasional set pieces Erasmus produced to keep his fellow humanists informed of his thoughts and activities. In it he criticized the Lutherans with unusual acerbity, condemning "their arrogant air and their excessive virulence." He denounced Luther's book against Henry as needlessly abusive and praised the king as "a prince compared with whom there is hardly another alive today more richly endowed with every kingly virtue or further removed from tyranny or more popular with his own people." Boasting of his own stature, Erasmus referred to all the complimentary letters he had received from eminent men and the esteem in which he was held by Europe's three leading monarchs (Charles, Francis, and Henry). As to Hutten's request to visit him, Erasmus said that, had Hutten appeared, he would not have refused to receive him "as an old friend" whose "wonderfully fertile and lively mind" he found attractive "even now," but that Hutten had reconsidered because of the lack of a stove in his rooms.

The baldness of this falsehood infuriated Hutten. So did Erasmus's fawning toward the powerful and hostility toward Luther. In Hutten's mind, Erasmus's dismissal of him personally merged with his rejection of the Reformation as a whole, and he decided to strike back. Redirecting the disdain he had previously aimed at Rome, he composed 272 numbered paragraphs furiously attacking the character, conduct, and opinions of Erasmus.

"Would you have us believe that, after frequently standing in the Main Square for three hours at a time conversing with friends, I was really unable to leave my unheated quarters during the more than 50 days I spent in Basel—whether for reasons of health or whatever other trifling matters—and thus could not have come to pay a visit or two?" Hutten fumed. "I am not at all certain which angers me more, your craftiness or the fact that you have dealt with me so discourteously." Not long before, Erasmus had castigated Rome with his vengeful pen "as a cesspool of depravity and crime." Now this same Erasmus had entered into an unholy alliance with the Roman Church, holding it up as the universal Church itself. Was this due to his lust for fame? His weakness of character? His envy of Luther and his much greater popularity? No, Hutten wrote, the real source of Erasmus's sycophancy, he now realized, was "a certain cowardice inherent in your character," a "timidity which causes you at the slightest provocation to fear the worst and thus to despair." When Reuchlin was in desperate need of his support in his battle with the doctors of Cologne, Erasmus refused to provide it. When the German princes banded together against the Lutherans, Erasmus in his anxiety sought in every possible way to curry favor with the princes. While he thus might succeed in preserving his life, he risked losing something far more precious—his reputation.

Hutten excoriated Erasmus for his assertion that one need not always tell the truth: "This sacrilegious utterance of yours ought to be shoved down your throat," for "what can be more godless and contrary to the teaching of Christ than to assert that the truth does not always have to be told, for the sake of which He wanted us to die?" Did Christ not predict "that because of Him and His word there would be hatred and dissensions, war and slaughter?" Erasmus faced two choices—either to stand firm on the side of Luther or to change sides and state his reasons for joining the enemy. If he refused to commit, he would find himself stranded in no-man's-land and regarded as a traitor by both parties. In a violent crescendo, Hutten declared that "we must fight this out to the very end and engage in hand-to-hand combat so that all can see what a perverse thing you have done and with what a violated, nay utterly prostituted conscience you have undertaken it."

As Hutten was drafting his attack, Erasmus heard of it and at once wrote to him to demand that he desist. By May 1523, however, Hutten's manuscript was in circulation and had been seen by many in Basel, Erasmus included. Hutten, meanwhile, was causing such commotion in Mühlhausen that some of its residents were threatening to storm the monastery where he was staying and seize him. Fleeing in the middle of the night, Hutten went to Zurich, where Zwingli offered him asylum and arranged for him to stay on the island of Ufenau in Lake Zurich in the care of a local pastor. Erasmus wrote to the Zurich town council to demand that it restrain his pen.

By then, however, Hutten's *Expostulatio cum Erasmo Roterodamo* was in print, and Erasmus immediately put aside the biblical paraphrase on which he was working to respond. It took him six full days to read Hutten's "false accusations" and wipe off "the muck he threw on me," he stated in his rebuttal, explaining its title: *Spongia Adversus Aspergines Hutteni* ("The Sponge Against the Aspersions of Hutten"). Defending his decision not to receive Hutten, Erasmus said that he had in fact been informed by an acquaintance that Hutten could not spend time in a room without a stove, but he also acknowledged his worry that word of a meeting with Hutten would quickly reach the pope in Rome and the emperor in Spain. He rejected Hutten's claim that he had an insatiable thirst for glory and fame. The kings of both France and England had written to him in their own hand, yet he had refrained from boasting about this. Nor had he mentioned the personal letters he had received from Emperor Charles and Archduke Ferdinand. "Had Hutten received such letters, imagine how puffed up his cheeks would be! He indeed writes to emperors, cardinals, and papal nuncios, but who among them has answered him?"

In his growing self-absorption, Erasmus could not see how incriminating this was. In the end, though, it was his comments about Luther that would cause the most offense. He charged the German reformer with heaping abuse on Erasmus's books, souring nearly all of his friendships, and causing irreparable harm to the cause of good letters. Erasmus had been unable to persuade himself "that the Spirit of Christ" dwells "in a heart from which such bitterness gushes forth."

Erasmus intended the *Spongia* to be provocative, but its offensiveness would be compounded by a misfortune of timing. On August 29, 1523, as Froben was racing to complete the printing, Hutten died. When the work appeared a few days later, Erasmus seemed to be beating a dead man, and Hutten's friends and supporters, rallying to his posthumous defense, pelted Erasmus with insults.

The first indication that Erasmus had decided to move off his cherished middle ground came in a letter he sent to Henry VIII in early September 1523 along with a copy of his newly completed paraphrase of Luke. Erasmus expressed his hope that the king would look favorably on the book and recognize Erasmus as one who had prayed for his prosperity and happiness. He added: "I have something on the stocks against the new doctrines but would not dare publish it unless I have left Germany first, for fear I prove a casualty before I enter the arena."

Exactly what he had on the stocks, Erasmus did not say. But word that he planned to write against the new gospel quickly spread, and on hearing it the Lutherans flew into "a perfect fury," as Erasmus reported to an official in Rome. If he were to proceed, he went on, he worried that his very life would be in danger.

Then Erasmus heard of Luther's own reaction to the rumor that he planned to write against him. Luther gave it in a letter to Conradus Pellicanus, a professor of theology and Hebrew at the University of Basel, who immediately shared it with Erasmus. Luther expressed his wish that Hutten "had not expostulated" and "still more that Erasmus had not wiped his expostulation out. If that is wiping out with a sponge, what, pray, is malediction and abuse?" Luther noted with dismay the "incredible boasts" Erasmus had made about his reputation and the way he raved against the vices of his friends. If Erasmus were to raise his pen against *him*, Luther observed, it would cause him no injury, for he had the Lord on his side. Erasmus was so far from a knowledge of things "that I will easily endure whatever names he chooses to call me so long as he lets my cause alone." When he was praised, Luther said, he grieved; when he was maligned, he felt joy. "If Erasmus wonders at this, I am not at all surprised. Let him learn Christ and say farewell to human wisdom. May the Lord illuminate him and make Erasmus a different man." In closing, Luther noted that he had no hard feelings for Erasmus, only pity, and he asked Pellicanus to greet Erasmus for him. If Erasmus would not allow it, he would quite willingly give up any wish for continued friendly relations with him.

For Erasmus, Luther's letter was the deciding blow. "Luther passionately abuses the *Spongia*," he wrote on November 21, 1523, to Johannes Fabri, a senior cleric in Constance. "He also said in a letter to Oecolampadius that I am like Moses and must be buried in the wilderness and that too much weight should not be given to Erasmus in spiritual matters. This sort of thing means war." Listing his various projects, Erasmus mentioned a paraphrase of Mark, a commentary on the Lord's Prayer, and a preface to a commentary on Ovid's *Nux*. And, if his strength held out, "I shall add a book on free will."

Free will: this was the subject on which Erasmus had decided to take on Luther. On the surface, it seemed an odd choice. Given all the other pressing matters at hand—the power of the pope, the authority of Scripture, the support for faith over works, the rejection of the sacraments, the abrogation of the Mass—free will seemed abstract and philosophical. But that was part of its appeal. Erasmus agreed with many of Luther's practical ideas for reform, objecting mainly to the vehemence with which he stated them. The subject of free will, though, went to the heart of Erasmus's differences with him. Luther had raised it back in 1516, when he wrote to Spalatin to urge Erasmus to read Augustine's writings against the Pelagians so that he could better understand the doctrine of original sin and man's inability to choose to do good. The initial charge that Erasmus was a Pelagian who attributed too much freedom to man had since grown into a mighty chorus.

In writing in support of free will, Erasmus hoped to salvage a place for the principles of human dignity and autonomy amid the great evangelical tide that was sweeping Europe. Those principles were at the core of the humanist movement as it had developed from Petrarch's time on, and Erasmus, in defending himself, was hoping to keep the flame of the Renaissance alive.

Examining Luther's writings, Erasmus found the clearest description of his position in the thirty-sixth article of the pamphlet he had written in 1520 against the bull threatening to excommunicate him. Among the bull's articles was one condemning Luther's denial of free will. In his defense, Luther provided a blizzard of biblical citations supporting his claim that our lives are "never for a single moment under our control." Instead, he maintained, "all things occur by absolute necessity." No subject needed to be handled more carefully than free will, Luther observed, yet the notion had become so fixed in men's hearts that "I do not see anyone who is fit to understand it or even to dispute with me about it."

Erasmus considered himself so fit. Through the end of autumn and into the winter of 1523, he prepared himself for combat. He reread Origen's *On First Principles*, Jerome's *Hebrew Questions on Genesis*, and Augustine's anti-Pelagian tracts. He studied Thomas Aquinas on first and second causes and Scotus on prevenient, sanctifying, and persevering grace. He read a treatise on free will by Lorenzo Valla and a refutation of Luther's theology by John Fisher, the bishop of Rochester. Most of all, he studied the Bible. As much as he disliked the practice of mustering citations in support of this or that proposition, he knew that if he failed to engage in it, the evangelists would dismiss him. If he presented his argument in a temperate and evenhanded manner, Erasmus felt sure, even the most committed Lutherans would not object.

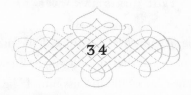

A SHOWER OF STONES

While Erasmus was struggling with free will, Luther was wrestling with Job. After finishing his translation of the second group of Old Testament books, he had moved on to the third, consisting of the prophetic and poetic books. These included the Psalms, Proverbs, Ecclesiastes, and the Song of Solomon, but it was Job that gave him the most trouble, "on account of the grandeur of his sublime style," as he wrote to Spalatin in early 1524. Sometimes Luther got so bogged down in the text that, even with the help of Melanchthon and others, he could translate no more than three lines in four days.

The runaway nuns posed a challenge of a different sort. The sisters Ave and Margaret von Schönfeld and Katharina von Bora remained under his care and in need of husbands. To Luther's relief, Katharina became attached to Jerome Baumgärtner, the scion of a prominent patrician family in Nuremberg who was studying in Wittenberg. He returned her feelings, and the two decided to marry. First, though, Baumgärtner wanted the blessing of his parents, and he left for Nuremberg to get it. Very soon, Luther hoped, Katharina would be off his hands. In the meantime, her presence in Wittenberg was feeding rumors about wild goings-on between priests and harlots.

At the town church, meanwhile, Luther began introducing changes in the service. In addition to requiring Communion in both kinds, he downgraded the importance of the Mass and instead made the sermon the centerpiece of the service. Both on Sundays (after the Eucharist) and on weekdays, the Word of God was to be preached. Luther compared the pulpit to a milking stool: the preacher daily had to pull hard and keep the milk flowing to the people so that they could be patiently and persistently instructed. Thanks to Luther, the sermon would become a fixture of Protestant worship, and churches would be built to make it easier to hear (for instance, by adding galleries). Even today, in urban America, anyone wandering into a Protestant church can hear a sermon at most weekday services.

No less enduring a change was the introduction of hymns. Seeking to encourage lay participation in the worship service, Luther wrote to Spalatin of his intention to "compose for the common people German psalms, that is spiritual songs," so that the Word of God could be spread in musical form. At the start of 1524, the first Reformation hymnal, containing four hymns by Luther, was produced by a Nuremberg printer, and a larger collection appeared in Wittenberg later in the year. From the start, Luther's hymns were very popular. While the Swiss reformers, led first by Zwingli and then Calvin, would shun musical instruments and most song, congregational singing would become a fixture of Lutheran churches. Luther's most famous hymn, "A Mighty Fortress Is Our God," a paraphrase of Psalm 48 that he wrote around 1528, would become the battle hymn of the Reformation. With these first halting steps began the great tradition of Protestant church music, leading two centuries later to the cantatas, chorales, and oratorios of Bach.

With Luther fully in charge, Wittenberg remained calm in the face of these changes. Things were different in the countryside. From Wittenberg south to the border with Bohemia and west to Erfurt and Thuringia, monks and nuns were leaving their cloisters, priests and deacons were marrying, and sacred images were being violently destroyed. In *Temporal Authority*, Luther had insisted on keeping the heavenly and earthly realms distinct, but radical pastors who considered them inseparable were pressing for a sweeping transformation of society from below, based on both the Bible and Luther's own writings.

The loudest rumblings were in the Saale valley, about a hundred miles west of Wittenberg. In the small town of Orlamünde, Luther's colleague and rival Andreas von Karlstadt had resurfaced with a radical program that was stirring *Herr Omnes*. Karlstadt had formulated it in Wittenberg while under the ban Luther had had imposed on him. While dutifully carrying out his responsibilities as professor at the university and archdeacon at the Castle Church, Karlstadt had fumed at the humiliation he had suffered. Immersing himself in the writings of such late-medieval mystics as Johannes Tauler and Thomas à Kempis, he was captivated by the idea of *Gelassenheit*—purging all selfish desires and worldly ambitions and abandoning oneself to God. Poring over the Bible, Karlstadt was struck by Jesus's injunction at Matthew 23 not to be called rabbi or instructor. His whole career, he could now see, had been one long striving after glory. On February 3, 1523, he announced that he would no longer participate in the granting of academic degrees. Acknowledging that he had formerly studied in order to write persuasively and prevail in disputes, he said that it was wrong to read Scripture simply to know it better than others.

Calling himself "a new layman," Karlstadt put aside his academic dress and donned the felt hat and gray cloak of the peasants, which seemed more in keeping with Christ's example than satin, silk, or velvet. He urged his neighbors to call him not "Herr Doktor" or "Herr Pfarrer" ("Mr. Priest") but "Brother Andreas," and he sat down with them to drink beer. He confessed guilt for having lived off the labor of poor peasants without giving anything in return. Hearing that Orlamünde was seeking a new pastor, he put himself forward as a candidate. His authority to fill the post was unclear, but the congregation was eager to have him, and Karlstadt (along with his young wife) took up residence there in the summer of 1523.

Not wanting to burden the congregation, Karlstadt planned to earn a living from his own labor, but the vicarage was in serious decline. The house and fence had deteriorated, the vineyard had withered, the fields had been overfarmed. None of this, though, could diminish his joy at being away from Wittenberg and out from under Luther's thumb. Whereas Luther was proceeding slowly, Karlstadt was intent on instituting changes all at once, even if they caused people to "become angry, howl, and curse." Far more of a biblical literalist than Luther, Karlstadt conceived of a parish living in true conformity with the Scriptures, including not just the New Testament but also the Old, and in this out-of-the-way town he would introduce many of the doctrines and practices that would become fixtures of the radical Reformation.

As in Wittenberg, Karlstadt insisted that all graven images be removed from churches. Music, too, he deemed an unwholesome distraction from true communion with God and so ordered it banned. Since the Israelites celebrated the Sabbath on Saturday, he insisted that his parishioners rest on that day as well. Infant baptism, fasting, and auricular confession were all rejected as unsupported by Scripture. As for the Mass, Karlstadt instituted the changes he had pioneered in Wittenberg, including offering Communion in both kinds and allowing congregants to take the host in their own hands.

Initially, the outside world took little note of these developments, but in late 1523 Karlstadt got access to a printing press in nearby Jena, and he began turning out a series of provocative pamphlets. One, published in December 1523, sought to explain, as the title put it, *Reasons Why Andreas Karlstadt Remained Silent for a Time.* (It was not cowardice, as some had alleged, but the fact that he had not heard God's call.) Karlstadt also explored *Whether Anyone Might Be Saved Without the Intercession of Mary* (the answer was yes) and described *The Abominable and Idolatrous Misuse of the Most Reverend Sacrament of Jesus Christ.* This last was one of several tracts that Karlstadt was to produce in the coming months about the true meaning of the Eucharist—a body of work that would open deep and lasting fissures among the reformers.

When he learned that Karlstadt was again publishing, Luther exploded. "I have read Karlstadt's monstrosities with grief," he wrote to Spalatin on March 14, 1524. The man "is consumed with an unconquerable desire for name and fame." Those who like Karlstadt seek to impose the Law of Moses "are to be despised." In another letter, Luther complained that Karlstadt was attacking him even more vehemently than he was the papists, and he implored the electoral court to force Karlstadt to either stop publishing or submit his writings in advance to censors selected by the princes.

Had Karlstadt been the only enthusiast at work in the area, Luther might have felt less apprehension, but some fifty miles to the north of Orlamünde, in the small market town of Allstedt, another zealous reformer had reappeared: Thomas Müntzer. The events that would make Müntzer a revolutionary hero to Friedrich Engels and other German Marxists—and evil incarnate to Luther—now began to unfold. From Zwickau, Müntzer had gone to Bohemia, where he had picked up the apocalyptic fervor of the radical Hussites. In "The Prague Manifesto," he had luridly prophesized that the "donkey-fart" doctors of theology and other false prophets would soon find themselves in the "fiery lake," to be tormented for eternity by the Antichrist.

Such bloodcurdling pronouncements proved too much even for the Bohemians, and Müntzer was forced to leave. He returned to Germany and eventually landed a position at St. John's church in Allstedt, a town of about 600 people. Seeking to revive the spirit of Zwickau, Müntzer in his sermons railed against both the overfed clergy and the plundering tyrants who would soon be cast down from their seats, and he hailed the oppressed multitudes who in the final days would forcefully inherit what was rightfully theirs.

To further attract congregants, Müntzer introduced what is believed to have been the first worship service entirely in German. The catchy tunes proved popular, and from one Sunday to the next the crowds at his church grew. (Müntzer also found time to get married, to an unfrocked nun of noble birth, who soon bore him a son.) Eager like Karlstadt to spread his ideas, Müntzer had a printing press set up in Allstedt, and at the start of 1524 he produced two feverish pamphlets that, without naming names, made clear the scorn he felt for Luther and the doctrine of justification by faith, which he considered too soft. Men, he wrote, come to faith not through the "honey-sweet Christ" of resurrection and redemption but through the "bitter Christ" of the cross, who can be found only by long, heartfelt suffering. The Church had been grievously harmed by generations of overeducated biblicists who peddled a false faith oblivious to the despair and madness required to achieve true piety.

Such ravings, Luther believed, could end only in violence, and he pressed Frederick to silence Müntzer, but the elector held back. As long as Müntzer's incitements remained verbal, he seemed to feel little need to act. On March 24, 1524, however, an agitated crowd gathered at a chapel outside Allstedt. It housed a picture of the Virgin Mary that was said to work miracles and which made it a popular pilgrimage site. It was thus both a blatant example of medieval superstition and an idolatrous image of the type forbidden by the Ten Commandments. The chapel was set on fire and quickly burned to the ground. Müntzer was present but made no effort to intervene, and he later refused to dissociate himself from the event.

The incident confirmed Luther's fears about the incendiary nature of

Müntzer's preaching. The "murderous spirit of Allstedt," as Luther called him, seemed an agent of Satan, and with one chapel having already gone up in flames, monasteries and churches seemed certain to follow. Luther felt sure that Müntzer's goal was to overturn the civil government and install himself in its place and that to help bring this about he would approach Karlstadt. Luther remained on the lookout for any sign of collusion between the two men, convinced that if they did join forces, central Germany would erupt.

It was not just violence that Luther feared. Wherever the new gospel took root, anti-intellectualism seemed to follow. Academic learning, scholarship, and education were all coming in for contempt. Since the evangelical creed was a religion of the heart, it was said, why bother with books and learning? With the priesthood and the monastery fading as career paths, parents preferred to have their children learn a trade rather than attend school. Schools in any case were being closed as the monasteries and cathedrals that traditionally ran them were attacked. In Erfurt, radical former monks were disparaging higher education, and Eoban Hess, a leading humanist at the university, wrote to Luther of his concern that as the new gospel spread, it was making the German people more barbarous. In Wittenberg, enrollment at the university plunged as parents, questioning the value of higher education and worried about the growing disorder, kept their sons at home.

Luther, who knew how critical the study of languages had been to the formation of the new gospel, set out to reverse the tide. *To the Councilmen of All Cities in Germany That They Establish and Maintain Christian Schools* was another manifesto of his that would leave a permanent mark on German society. In all the German lands, he declared, "schools are everywhere being left to go to wrack and ruin." Such neglect was a "despicable trick of the devil," for it was of vital concern both to Christ and to the world at large that young people be educated. With such large sums lavished on guns, roads, bridges, and dams to ensure peace and prosperity, why shouldn't more be devoted to educating the young? A city's greatest strength lay not in the vast treasures it had amassed or in the magnificent buildings it had erected but in the many able, honorable, and wise citizens it was able to produce. Both boys and girls should attend liberal arts schools for one or two hours a day, spending the rest of their time working at home and learning a trade.

Luther denounced the growing neglect of languages and of the liberal arts in general. The revival of ancient tongues had brought forth so much light and accomplished such great things that the whole world stood amazed. If languages were again allowed to wither, the gospel itself would perish. Luther especially lamented the neglect of the study of history. Because Germany lacked its own chronicles, other nations knew little of the German people, who as a result had to put up with the reputation of being beasts "who know only how to fight, gorge, and guzzle." Germany was now enjoying a jubilee—a bounty of learned men, adept in languages and the arts—and it was essential that something be put away for the future. "O my beloved Germans," Luther proclaimed in a famous passage, "buy while the market is at your door; gather in the harvest while there is sunshine and fair weather; make use of God's grace and word while it is there!"

In this tribute to books and languages, Erasmus's spirit can be felt throughout. Luther seems to have drawn heavily on the *Paraclesis*, *De Ratione Studii*, and other texts in which Erasmus promoted the virtues of learning, both pagan and Christian. Where the two diverged was over the place of education in society. With Erasmus, the focus was always on the elite—with establishing schools where able youths could be drilled in the essentials of Latin and Greek. Grammar and rhetoric were the principal subjects, and eloquence was the chief end. Luther, by contrast, wanted schooling for all—in Latin where appropriate, in the vernacular where not. Erasmus wanted to train a literary priesthood that could preserve and promote good letters; Luther wanted to create a priesthood of all believers. In a way, Luther was building on—and popularizing— Erasmus's ideas about education. With *To the Councilmen of All Cities*, the first step was taken toward the provision of universal public education in Germany, including education for girls; in the quarter century after its appearance, new schools would be established in most German cities and towns.

Not long after completing this tract, Luther heard reports that Eras-

mus was preparing to attack him. Since posting the Ninety-Five Theses more than six years earlier, Luther had faced a formidable array of
assailants, from Prierias, Cajetan, and Eck to Leo X, Adrian VI, and
Henry VIII, but an attack from Erasmus would be of a different order.
With his mastery of Latin, command of Scripture, and still considerable
prestige, the Dutch scholar seemed in a position to cause Luther lasting
harm. Nearly four years had elapsed since the last direct communication
between the two men. Now, in the spring of 1524, Luther decided to put
Erasmus on notice.

"I have now been silent long enough, good friend Erasmus, and though
I expected that you as the older and more eminent of us would break the
silence first, after waiting in vain for so long, I am I think obliged by
charity itself to make the first move," Luther wrote, in the same arch tone
he had used to such devastating effect in his famous letter to Leo X. He
did not wish to complain about the great distance Erasmus had kept from
him, since it had left him free to attack Luther's real enemies, the papists.
Nor had he taken it amiss when Erasmus, to secure the goodwill of those
same papists, had attacked Luther and criticized him with some bitterness,
for he could see that the Lord had not given him the courage or even the
common sense to join with him in openly confronting such monsters.
Moreover, no one could deny that Erasmus, using the special gifts granted
him by God, had opened the way to genuine study of the Bible, for which
the whole world owed him thanks.

But, Luther went on, there was one thing that caused him concern—
the possibility that Erasmus might decide to attack Luther's own opinions
in writing, in which case he would be compelled to oppose him directly.
Thus far, he had restrained others who had wanted to attack Erasmus, and
he actually sympathized with him as the target of so much hatred from
so many quarters. Luther had curbed his own pen and would continue
to do so unless Erasmus came out into the open. Feelings on both sides
were running high, and he wished that those of his friends who were now
so fiercely assailing Erasmus would cease and allow him in his old age to
"peacefully fall asleep in the Lord." They would certainly do so if they recognized Erasmus's weakness and saw how the profound issues at stake had
long since exceeded his abilities. Since Erasmus lacked both the courage

and the capacity to accept the teachings of the new gospel, he should leave them alone and mind his own business.

In closing, Luther urged Erasmus "to be no more than a spectator of this trouble." If Erasmus did not publish an attack on him, he would refrain from going after Erasmus. "There has been enough baring of teeth; we must now make sure that we do not destroy each other, a prospect all the more pitiable as it is most certain that neither party seriously wishes to see religion suffer."

With Erasmus perhaps having already begun to write against him, Luther needed to get his letter to him quickly. As it happened, Melanchthon had been granted his first leave of absence since arriving in Wittenberg six years earlier and planned to use it to visit his hometown, Bretten, in the Rhineland; Basel was about 135 miles to the south. Melanchthon would be accompanied by Joachim Camerarius, a young graduate of the University of Wittenberg with humanist leanings who, eager to meet Erasmus, agreed to take the letter to him. In mid-April 1524, the two men left on horseback on the long journey across Germany.

As Luther's warning was making its way toward him, Erasmus in Basel was feeling the fury of his followers. Since his attack on Hutten, he had been assailed in fly sheets and threatened in letters. "You have dragged in the dirt the reputation of an honorable and distinguished man, Ulrich von Hutten, with a flood of accusations which are false, libelous, and fraudulent," wrote Otto Brunfels, a pastor in the Rhineland who had once greatly admired Erasmus but who had recently thrown his support to Luther. The Germans, who had first learned to write under Erasmus's leadership, "should now by squadrons and battalions sharpen their swords against their pestilent instructor." Erasmus had only one recourse—to repent. If he refused, Brunfels warned, he and his allies would do their utmost "to cast out of the camp the false prophet who prophesies in Baal."

With such libels mounting, Erasmus perceived a conspiracy of evangelicals intent on publishing falsehoods and lies about him. He had a new term for these men: "new gospellers." They went around proclaiming the Word of God while violating every principle of the Christian spirit. "I no longer judge Christians by the doctrines we profess in words," he wrote.

"I judge them by their lives. Wherever ambition and the love of riches and pride and anger and revenge and passion to hurt others are supreme, there I fear that the faith of the gospel is not to be found."

Despite the growing virulence of the Lutherans, Erasmus continued to prepare his attack on Luther. Actually, he did not want to make it seem like an attack. Given Luther's volcanic temper, Erasmus was reluctant to unduly provoke him. And, having rebuked Luther for using immoderate language, Erasmus wanted to avoid it himself. Seeking the right tone, he was influenced by a project he had recently completed, a new edition of Cicero's *Tusculanae quaestiones* ("Tusculan Questions"). Cicero had written it at Tusculum, his country estate outside Rome, while struggling to cope with the death of his daughter Tullia. Framed as a dialogue at his villa, the work impressed Erasmus with its combination of learning and equanimity, and he wanted to make his own book similarly high-minded. With it, he hoped to show how it was possible to debate matters like free will in civil terms, without resorting to the venom and vitriol that seemed so antithetical to Christ's spirit.

That intent was apparent in the title Erasmus chose: *The Freedom of the Will: A Diatribe or Discourse* (in Latin, *De Libero Arbitrio*). By "diatribe," Erasmus meant not a tirade in the modern sense but a discussion or inquiry in the classical sense. Before laying out his argument, he decided to offer a long preamble making clear his constructive aim. This was in many ways the most distinctive and original part of the book. It was "far from a crime," he observed, to take issue with a teaching of Luther's, especially if one engaged in a "temperate debate" aimed at eliciting the truth. He would discuss free will "without abuse," avoiding the "angry repartee" in which the truth was so often obscured. Surely Luther would not take it amiss if someone disagreed with him on a point or two. Moreover, he intended to approach the matter with an open mind and even a "slight bias" in Luther's favor. "I will act as a disputant, not as judge; as inquirer, not as dogmatist."

In fact, Erasmus noted, he was a reluctant disputant. Free will was one of many abstract matters in the Bible whose meaning, though often discussed, remained elusive and about which he would consider himself a skeptic if the Church allowed it. On the precepts of a good life, by contrast, the Scriptures are "absolutely clear." Here, the Word of God "need not be sought by scaling the heights of heaven or brought back from across the sea, but is close at hand, in our mouths and in our hearts." These principles should be learned by all; the rest should be left to God. How many squabbles had broken out over the distinction between the persons in the Trinity, the coinherence of the divine and the human in Christ, the distinction between filiation and procession? What confusion had been stirred by the strife over the conception of Christ by the Virgin Mary? Other matters, while perhaps worthy of debate, were best left unpublicized.

After setting out this statement of principles, Erasmus undertook the (as he saw it) thankless but necessary task of amassing scriptural passages to back his position. In support of free will, he found more than two dozen in the Old Testament alone. Ecclesiasticus 15, for instance, stated that "God created man from the beginning, and left him in the hand of his own counsel." In the story of Cain and Abel, God offered a reward for choosing the right path and threatened punishment for those pursuing the opposite. At Deuteronomy 30, the Lord said to Moses, "I have placed before you the way of life and the way of death. Choose what is good, and walk in it." (This is Erasmus's paraphrase.) What, Erasmus asked, could be clearer? God shows us what is good and what is bad; "the freedom to choose he leaves to man." Nearly the whole of Scripture speaks of conversion, endeavor, and striving to improve, all of which would be meaningless if doing good or evil were considered a matter of necessity rather than choice. In the New Testament, Matthew was especially rich in passages supporting free will. At 7:20, for instance, the Lord says, "By their fruits you shall know them," with "fruits" clearly meaning "works."

Turning to those passages that seemed to deny free will, Erasmus maintained that most were not persuasive. For deniers of free will, a favorite example was the pharaoh in Exodus, who repeatedly declared his intention to let the Israelites go, only to have God harden his heart; the pharaoh's will was thus captive to God's. But, Erasmus argued, God acted in this way because the pharaoh had of his own accord persisted in his godlessness. Even the verses in the Pauline Epistles that seemed to undermine the notion of free will could be seen as simply suggesting the need for divine grace and human will to work together. As many scriptural references as there are to God's help, Erasmus wrote, there are "just as many proofs" of the existence of free will and "they are innumerable," so if the issue was to be decided by the number of scriptural proofs, "the victory is mine."

Moving with relief beyond such Scripture-mongering, Erasmus in the final section of his treatise addressed the fundamental issue of the relationship between God and man. The idea (advanced by Luther) that man should claim no credit for his good deeds but ascribe them all to God's grace was worthy insofar as it deflated human arrogance. But when people maintained that human nature is so worthless that all human works, even those of godly men, are sins, Erasmus wrote, he grew exceedingly uneasy. He went on to state some of the classic objections to the idea of predestination. A God who foreordained great benefits for some but condemned others to eternal torment without their having done anything to deserve it seemed extraordinarily cruel. To try to justify such a God, Luther's adherents had vastly exaggerated the place of original sin, claiming that Adam's and Eve's delinquency had left man so corrupted that he deserved divine punishment. But this, too, made God seem unfair, since he was willing to vent his wrath on the whole of mankind for someone else's sin.

Erasmus took up the biblical image most favored by opponents of free will—that of the potter and his clay, from Jeremiah 18. Just as clay in the potter's hand is to be shaped as he wills, so is man in God's hand. In its place, Erasmus proposed another image—that of a young child learning to walk. When his father shows him an apple from some distance away, the boy wants to run toward it, but because his limbs are weak, his father puts out his hand to guide him. Thus supported, the boy is able to reach the apple, which the father gladly gives him as a reward for his effort. The child could not have stood up if his father had not supported him; he could not have walked if his father had not helped him; he could not have reached the apple if his father had not placed it in his hands. Though the child is completely in his father's debt and so has no reason to glory in his own powers, he has still done something on his own. So it is with God the Father and his children. If he works in us simply as the potter shapes his clay, what blame can be imputed to us if we err?

In the end, Erasmus argued, some space must be allotted to free will to allow the ungodly to be deservedly condemned, to clear God of the accusation of cruelty and injustice, and to spur us on to moral endeavor. Maintaining its existence did not, however, invalidate Luther's godly and Christian assertions that we should remove our trust in our own merits and deeds and place all in God and his promises. Concluding, Erasmus said that he was playing the part not of a judge but of a disputant. Though an old man, he would not be ashamed or reluctant to learn from the young, should there be anyone who could teach him "with evangelical mildness."

The God whom Erasmus conjures up in *The Freedom of the Will* is caring, wise, reasonable, and, above all, just. In many ways, he seems a Christian humanist. Erasmus's God has no divine inscrutability, no hint of a capacity for acting in ways that humans might find incomprehensible or unfair. Some might consider such a deity banal. Erasmus's real concern, though, was not with God but with man. Facing a movement intent on denying any human dignity or autonomy, he was fighting to keep the divine spark alive. Without it, his whole philosophy of Christ, based as it was in the notion that men and women can choose to imitate him, would collapse.

In February 1524, Erasmus sent a copy of his tract to his friend Ludwig Baer, a professor of theology in Basel, inviting his comments. "I send you the first draft of a trifling piece about the freedom of the will," he wrote, seeking to downplay its importance. "On this I have wasted five days"— obviously an understatement—"and very tedious days they were." Not long afterward, he sent a copy to Henry VIII. "If your Majesty, and other learned men, approve this sample of my work," he wrote, "I shall finish it and arrange for its printing elsewhere, for here, in my opinion, there is no printer who dares print anything in which a single word reflects [badly] on Luther, while against the pope one may write what one likes."

While waiting to hear back from the king, Erasmus tended to various other projects, including a paraphrase of the Acts of the Apostles. Erasmus would dedicate this work to the new pope: Clement VII. Adrian VI had died on September 14, 1523, after barely twenty months in office. Clement, a Medici and a cousin of Leo X, had supported Adrian's reform efforts and was expected to continue them. More important, from Erasmus's standpoint, Clement was a longtime admirer. In return for Erasmus's dedication, he sent him two hundred florins. (These payments were a not-insignificant side benefit of Erasmus's loyalty to the Church.) As long as Clement ruled in Rome, Erasmus's Catholic critics there would have to remain silent.

Then, in early May 1524, Joachim Camerarius arrived with Luther's letter. Erasmus, whose relations with Melanchthon remained cordial, took an immediate liking to this young friend of his but had little time to spare for him. Aside from various ailments he was battling, he was trying to fend off a nosy Polish nobleman who was pressing him on his views about Luther. With Camerarius preparing to return to Wittenberg, though, Erasmus hurriedly drafted a reply to Luther that he could take back with him.

Though striving for an even tone, he could not hide his irritation at Luther's taunts. "I do not concede that your passion for the purity of the gospel is more sincere than my own," he wrote. What Luther described as weakness and ignorance "is partly conscience and partly conviction." He had done much more for the cause of the gospel than many of those who so loudly used that word. "I see many desperate and disloyal men taking advantage of the present situation. I see humane letters and good learning tumbling into ruin. I see old friendships broken, and I fear a bloody conflict is about to break out." To that point he had not attacked Luther in writing, even though he could have won the applause of princes by doing so, for he realized that he would have inflicted injury on the gospel. Why should Luther be upset if someone wanted to argue with him in the hope of deepening his understanding? Perhaps Erasmus's opposition would do more for the gospel than all the support Luther had received from the many "dullards" who were making Erasmus's own life so miserable. Such people "are driving me into the opposite camp—even if pressure from the princes were not pushing me in the same direction."

In his letter, Luther had criticized Erasmus for writing so uncharitably about Hutten in his *Spongia*. Erasmus now mentioned all the disreputable things about Hutten that he had left out—his taste for extravagance, women, and dice; his debts, highway robberies, and extortions from monks; the many false charges he had leveled at Erasmus. Hutten and his kind "are not human beings at all, but raging demons. Do you honestly think the gospel will be restored by perverted creatures like these? Are men like this to be the pillars of a renascent church?"

Erasmus did not mention his work on free will, perhaps because he had not yet decided to publish it. After he sent Camerarius on his way, though, he continued to polish it, and on May 13, 1524, he informed Oecolampadius that it was done. On July 21, he wrote to Pirckheimer in Nuremberg that, in light of the many rumors circulating about the book, "I think it best to publish, so that they cannot suspect it to be worse than it is. For I treat the topic with such moderation that I know Luther himself will not take offense." His fear that no one in Basel would publish his tract turned out to be unfounded—Froben took it on—and on August 31 Erasmus reported that *De Libero Arbitrio* was in the press. He had initially planned to dedicate the book to Thomas Wolsey, but he reconsidered when he realized that he would be accused of writing to please him; in the end, he dedicated it to no one.

For years, Erasmus had resisted the demands from Rome and London, popes and kings, that he confront Luther. Having finally given in, he now wanted to make sure that the work got the widest possible circulation. As soon as it came off the press (as a compact octavo), he sent off copies to various friends and patrons. One went to Gian Matteo Giberti, a prominent figure at the Datary in Rome. Two went to Saxony—one to Duke George, the other to Melanchthon. Several went to England, including one to Henry VIII. "The die is cast," he wrote to the king. "A short book on freedom of the will has seen the light of day—a desperate step, believe me, in the present state of Germany. I await a shower of stones."

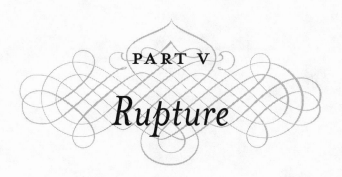

PART V

Rupture

THE GOSPEL OF DISCONTENT

Within weeks of the publication of *The Freedom of the Will*, the tributes began to pour in. From Rome, Gian Matteo Giberti wrote to Erasmus to say that the treatise's style, religious feeling, and wisdom ensured it "the warmest of welcomes." He had shown a copy to Pope Clement VII, who was so appreciative that he would soon provide Erasmus with "the resources and dignity" he so richly deserved. Duke George of Saxony wrote to say that the book had given him "great pleasure" and that he was sure it would make "a lasting contribution to the glory and advancement of Christendom." From England Juan Luis Vives reported that Henry VIII, after reading several pages between church services, had shown signs of being very pleased and that Queen Catherine had likewise expressed her admiration and gratitude. "My book on the freedom of the will," Erasmus exulted in mid-October 1524, "has already produced a change of heart in many people who had been wholly committed to the Lutheran view."

But it was the reaction from Wittenberg that mattered most, and it soon came in the form of a letter from Melanchthon. Erasmus's book, he wrote, had "had a very mild reception here." His moderate attitude "gave great satisfaction, though you do slip in a barbed remark now and again." Luther "is not so irascible that he can swallow nothing. And so he promises to use equal moderation in his reply." Given Luther's goodwill toward Erasmus, Melanchthon observed, it was Erasmus's duty "to make sure that this discussion is not embittered by any greater ill will on your side." In closing, he noted that Luther "sends you his respectful greetings."

Reading this, Erasmus felt tremendous relief. After all the months of anxiety and dread over how Luther and his supporters would respond, he could finally relax.

Unfortunately, Melanchthon had been misinformed. At the time that he wrote to Erasmus, Luther had not actually read *De Libero Arbitrio*.

When he finally got around to sampling it, he felt absolute loathing. Despite the critical importance of the subject, Erasmus had brought nothing new to it. Instead, he had rehashed all the old arguments to which Luther had already responded. Luther was most exasperated by Erasmus's trademark slipperiness. It was the book's very eloquence and polish, unaccompanied by any real substance, that made it so detestable in his eyes. "It is annoying to have to reply to such an educated man about so uneducated a book," Luther wrote to Spalatin on November 1, 1524. But reply he must, since otherwise tongues would wag, saying that he had been bested, and some might use Erasmus's spurious arguments to impugn the evangelical cause. On November 17, Luther informed his friend Nicholas Hausmann that he would answer Erasmus "not for his own sake, but for the sake of those who abuse his authority for their own glorying against Christ."

He would not do so right away, however. In fact, it would take Luther more than a year to get around to the task. For he was about to enter his life's most difficult passage. To this point, his main opponents had been popes and archbishops, princes and dialecticians. To them would now be added a new array of foes, including rebellious peasants, rivals within his own movement, and, finally, the humanists, led by Erasmus. These new conflicts would fundamentally alter Luther's public stature as well as his personal life. More generally, 1525 would be a watershed year for the Reformation as Germany was swept by the largest popular uprising in Europe prior to the French Revolution—an upheaval prompted, in part, by Luther's own writings.

In the Saale valley, the climate was turning explosive. In Allstedt, Thomas Müntzer was loudly proclaiming the advent of the final days. To Luther's dismay, the Saxon princes remained passive. In the second week of July 1524, Elector Frederick and his brother Duke John, passing through Allstedt on their way to Weimar, actually invited Müntzer to preach. Seizing the opportunity, Müntzer took as his portion the second chapter of the book of Daniel—a favorite text of the apocalyptically minded, in which Daniel, interpreting the dreams of Nebuchadnezzar, foretells the downfall of earthly kingdoms and the coming of God's reign. With righteous ferocity, Müntzer urged the princes to take up the sword and purge Christendom of the wicked imposters in its midst. "Do not permit evildoers to live any longer, for a godless person has no right to life when he hinders the pious," he declared. He denounced "Brother Fattened-swine" and "Brother Soft-life"—clear allusions to Luther—who, in rejecting the visions of the prophets, had become an enemy of the gospel and had to be put away. If the rulers refused to wield the sword against impious priests and monks, it would be taken from them; if they worked in opposition to the gospel, they themselves would be "strangled without any mercy."

Müntzer was essentially calling for a religious war and warning the Saxon princes that, if they refused to lead it, they would become its victims. Despite this provocation, Frederick and John continued on to Weimar. Müntzer, meanwhile, set about preparing for that war. On July 24, after another harangue, members of his congregation marched to the Allstedt town hall and enlisted in a Christian league aimed at revolutionary transformation and defending the gospel against the godless.

Infuriated by the princes' inaction, Luther prepared an open *Letter to the Princes of Saxony Concerning the Rebellious Spirit*. The "Satan of Allstedt," he wrote, clearly intended to arm the masses and spur them to topple the government and become "lords of the world." He called on Frederick and John to fulfill their duty as stipulated in Romans 13 to use the sword to prevent mischief and forestall rebellion. If they failed to act, they would surely feel the mob's wrath.

In the meantime, Müntzer—seeking to expand his movement—sent appeals to several nearby communities, including Orlamünde. He urged its citizens to forge an alliance with the people of Allstedt to defend the gospel, with force if necessary. But Karlstadt, who was still in charge there, remained unalterably opposed to the use of violence, and in the reply he helped draft, the Orlamünders—citing Christ's order to Peter to sheath his sword when the guards came to arrest him—rejected Müntzer's plea. "If you want to be armed against your enemies," they advised, "dress yourself in the strong, steel-like, and unconquerable armor of faith." This letter was soon printed in Wittenberg, where Luther saw it. He nonetheless remained convinced that Karlstadt planned to join Müntzer in an unholy alliance.

Under Luther's prodding, the princes finally summoned Müntzer and several Allstedt officials to Weimar for questioning. Müntzer denied that he had preached anything contrary to Scripture or that he had exhorted the people to overthrow the godless. He also denounced Luther's letter as shameful and dishonest. The Saxon authorities allowed him to return to Allstedt, but he soon received a message from them ordering him to close his printing press, disband the Christian league, and refrain from seditious preaching. Furious, Müntzer appealed to Frederick to reconsider. As the days passed and no answer came, Müntzer became convinced that he was going to be arrested, and so on the night of August 7, 1524, he slipped over the town wall and disappeared into the countryside.

Karlstadt remained active, however, and with the growing disorder in the Saale valley, Prince John Frederick (Duke John's son and Elector Frederick's nephew) sent Luther a message urging him to go there in person. Just as Paul had ministered to his far-flung congregations, the prince wrote, he hoped that Luther could find a way to calm the *Schwärmer*, the buzzing activists. Luther agreed, and in mid-August 1524 he set off into the aroused countryside. On August 21, he arrived in Jena, fifteen miles north of Orlamünde. Preaching for an hour and a half to a packed house, he inveighed against the spirit of Allstedt and other sword-wielding radicals who destroyed images, discarded baptism, and besmirched the Eucharist. Such a spirit could only produce rebellion and murder. Luther mentioned no one by name, but the references to Müntzer and Karlstadt were unmistakable.

Sitting in the back of the church was Karlstadt himself, trying without success to hide under a broad-brimmed hat. Furious at being linked to Müntzer, whose violent appeals he had emphatically rejected, he sent a sharp note to Luther, requesting a meeting. That afternoon the two met at the Black Bear Inn—the same hostel at which Luther had stopped on his return from the Wartburg two years earlier. Crowding in were Saxon officials and vigilant farmers eager to witness the historic encounter. A firsthand account captured the intense animosity between the two men as they sat across from each other at a table. Karlstadt objected to Luther's associating him with "the spirit of Allstedt." "I protest publicly before all these brethren assembled together that I have nothing to do with the spirit in the rebellion!" Karlstadt went on to accuse Luther of having written, printed, and preached against him while trying to prevent him from preaching and publishing in return. From the start, he added, Luther had always criticized him harshly rather than try to instruct him in a brotherly fashion. When Luther referred to his smashing of images in Wittenberg, Karlstadt said that he had not engaged in such actions alone but been helped by some of Luther's close associates.

"I know well," Luther said, growing impatient, "that you always go about in a grandiose fashion, boast grandly, and want only yourself to be exalted and noticed." "If I did that," Karlstadt replied, "you should instruct me. But I see clearly who boasts most highly and seeks the greatest honor." Remarkably, the two began wrangling over the Leipzig disputation. Luther complained that Karlstadt in his pride had insisted on going before him at the debate. "Finally, I granted you the honor and allowed it to happen." "Oh, Mr. Doctor, how can you say that?" Karlstadt protested, taken aback. When the dispute began, he (accurately) observed, Luther had not yet been cleared to participate.

If Karlstadt had something to say against him, Luther said, he should put it in writing, "publicly and not secretly." Accusing Karlstadt of standing "among the new prophets," he took a gulden from his pocket and said he would give it to Karlstadt if he would agree to write against him. "Give it to me," Karlstadt said, "for I certainly accept the challenge." "Take it and attack me boldly now," Luther said, handing him the coin. "Attack me sharply!"

"Dear brothers," Karlstadt declared, taking the coin and putting it in his purse, "this is a pledge, a sign, that I have authority to write against Dr. Luther." The two men shook hands and drank a toast to the challenge. "The bolder you attack me, the better I will like it," Luther said. A great division among the reformers was opening up.

While in Jena, Luther received a letter from the citizens of Orlamünde requesting a meeting. It accused him of calling them heretical without foundation and of being unduly lenient on the subject of images. He agreed to meet. On the way there he stopped in the town of Kahla to preach. The pastor there was a supporter of Karlstadt, and Luther, while mounting the pulpit, had to climb over the pieces of a broken crucifix. Though disturbed by the sight, he did not mention it in his sermon, offering instead a more general appeal for patience in the matter of images.

In Orlamünde, Karlstadt tried to join the conversation, but Luther barred him. Taking to heart Luther's idea of the priesthood of all believers, the Orlamünders had become confident exegetes, and a fierce argument broke out over images. "Where in Scripture can you prove that images should be abolished?" Luther asked. When they offered the obvious answer—the Ten Commandments—Luther maintained that the only thing they proscribed was the worshipping of images, not the images themselves. "How can a crucifix on the wall harm me when I do not venerate it?" he asked. The townsmen rejected this as hairsplitting. Growing hostile, they said that the soul needs to be emancipated from all external influences, for it becomes distracted "when it allows itself, bedecked and entwined, to be entertained by forbidden images." Luther slumped into his chair and buried his face in his hands. When accused by another townsman of probably being among the damned, Luther broke off the exchange.

As he prepared to leave town, Luther was warned to "get out in the name of a thousand devils" lest he find his neck broken. Stones were thrown at him, and bells were rung in good riddance. "We who have heard the living voice of God beside the river Saale," Karlstadt told his congregation, "do not need to be taught by any monkish scribe." The encounter left Luther deeply shaken; he was losing control of the forces on the ground.

On his way back to Wittenberg, he stopped in Weimar to brief the princes. Alarmed at his report, the electoral court on September 18 ordered Karlstadt to leave Electoral Saxony. Karlstadt was incensed at being driven out by Luther "unheard and unconvicted," as he later put it. Leaving Orlamünde (and his pregnant wife), he took with him a collection of manuscripts that he had been writing in response to Luther's challenge and headed for the German southwest, where an even bigger storm was brewing.

Meanwhile, Müntzer had resurfaced in Mühlhausen, an imperial free city fifty miles west of Allstedt. With a population of around 8,500, it was not only much larger than Allstedt but also far more volatile, owing to the presence of many craftsmen and weavers frustrated with the strict rule of the town's oligarchs. Already, the townsmen were being roused by a former monk turned activist named Heinrich Pfeiffer, and Müntzer now joined him in stirring them up. In late September, Mühlhausen was swept by a religious storm. For a full week marchers filled the streets, attacking clerical properties and destroying altarpieces; in the suburbs, a village went up in flames. A revolutionary program was drawn up, centered on the demand for a new council to govern in line with God's Word.

In between preaching and agitating, Müntzer prepared several bitter broadsides, including a tirade against Luther titled *A Highly Provoked Defense and Answer to the Spiritless, Soft-Living Flesh at Wittenberg, Who Has Most Lamentably Befouled Pitiable Christianity in a Perverted Way by His Theft of Holy Scripture*. Müntzer called Luther "Doctor Lügner" ("liar"), a "malicious black raven," and a "shameless monk" who claimed to be persecuted while enjoying "his good Malvasian wine" and "whores' banquets." Deriding Luther for his cozy relations with the princes and for ignoring the needs of the poor, Müntzer ended with a gruesome taunt: "Sleep softly, dear flesh! I would rather smell you roasted in your own stubbornness by the wrath of God in a pot over the fire. There, cooked in your own juice, the devil should devour you. Your flesh is like that of an ass. It will be a long time cooking and will make a tough dish for your mealymouthed friends."

The apocalypse sought by Müntzer would be delayed, however. The Mühlhausen town council, somehow managing to regain control of the city, voted to expel both him and Pfeiffer. By the end of September 1524, both were gone. Taking his manuscripts with him, Müntzer, like Karlstadt, headed for the seething southwest.

For the past half century, the Upper Rhine valley had been shaken by popular uprisings. This was the land of the *Bundschuh*—the peasants' crude leather shoe that symbolized economic and social protest. But the eruptions had for the most part remained highly localized and so had been easily—and ruthlessly—suppressed. In the early 1520s, however, the discontent had begun to spread. To the west, peasants were stirring in Alsace, especially in the rich agricultural plain between the Rhine and the foothills of the Vosges Mountains. To the east, tensions were rising in the Black Forest, a region of crystalline lakes, wild vales, and rounded summits covered with fir trees; in the rolling countryside along the northern shore of Lake Constance; and in Upper Swabia, a land of heathery hills and undulating terraces. By the fall of 1524, this southwestern corner of Germany was in a state of incipient revolt.

The main cause was capitalism. With the rise of a money economy, the speculation in land had boomed, and more and more of it was falling into fewer and fewer hands. In their lust for profit, landlords usurped many of the traditional rights to which small farmers had been entitled under feudalism. Common lands, on which peasants had for centuries fattened their cattle and pigs, were enclosed. Forests, an important source of firewood, thatch, and nuts, were declared off-limits. Streams and ponds were reserved for the rich, and any commoner caught fishing in them faced severe penalties, including even execution. At any time, a peasant could be pressed into service to build roads, dredge ponds, or repair bridges—all without compensation. To ensure a reliable pool of labor, strict controls were placed on movement, including restrictions on whom peasants could marry (since marriage often resulted in the moving of one spouse to the village of the other). If the game owned by a lord wandered onto a peasant's plot and trampled his crops, he could not touch it.

Taxes and fees, meanwhile, were being raised to the breaking point. There was a "great" tithe to be paid from the corn crop, a "living" tithe to be paid from among newborn livestock, and the dreaded heriot, claimed by the lord when the head of a household died. The heriot usually required handing over the family's best cow or horse, and it could mean ruin. Resistance was often fierce, and to ensure compliance with this and other rules, lords gradually took over the administration of justice from village courts. Some landowners formed their own police forces to intimidate and arrest recalcitrant peasants; offenders could disappear into jails or dungeons for years with little chance of appeal. In all, dues could consume up to 40 percent of a peasant's income, with an additional 10 percent taken by the tithe.

In a word, serfdom, which had faded from most of Western Europe, was making a comeback in this region, with the rural population bound anew to the soil. Peasants—living amid fertile fields, abundant game, and teeming waterways—were unable to partake in the bounty. In addition, a steady increase in population had forced a continual subdivision of the land, leading to the shrinkage of plots and the creation of a landless proletariat. With harvests failing every two or three years, hunger was endemic.

The sense of injustice was driven home by the itinerant preachers who were crisscrossing the region, proclaiming the social gospel. Arriving in a town or village, they would call for establishing the kingdom of God on earth and organizing society along scriptural lines. Their ranks included poor priests, impoverished knights, fugitive monks, wandering scholars, out-of-work mercenaries, and struggling journeymen, who, speaking the simple language of the people, inveighed against ignorant priests and overfed friars and who, quoting from Luther's German Bible, declared that the poor would inherit the earth, that the last would be first, and that the apostles had held all things in common.

These preachers also cited Luther's own pronouncements. In *To the Christian Nobility*, he had called on the ruling class to rise up and throw off the yoke of Rome. In *The Babylonian Captivity*, he had declared that no pope or bishop has the right to impose a single syllable of the law on laypeople without their consent. In *The Freedom of a Christian*, he had written that a Christian is a free lord, subject to none. Luther's doctrine of the priesthood of all believers was encouraging the laity to read the Bible on their own, and his assertion of the right of every congregation to choose its own pastor was being invoked by parishioners across Germany.

Luther's personal example was no less influential. His defiance of the emperor and the pope, his scorn for the bull of excommunication, and his burning of the canon law were all encouraging others to press their own rights. Luther, of course, had strongly insisted on keeping the earthly and heavenly kingdoms distinct and on not using the Bible to justify worldly demands, but in the hothouse environment of the German southwest, it was Luther's statements that Christ came with a sword and that the gospel causes tumult that were seized upon and echoed.

Luther's denunciations of clerical excesses had special resonance in this region, for monasteries and abbeys were among the largest and most oppressive landholders. In addition to imposing high rents, tight restrictions on movement, and constant demands for labor, they used canon law to protect and extend their privileges. The notorious abbey at Kempten in Upper Swabia, for instance, had over the past thirty years been aggressively expanding its territory, with more than 1,200 peasants forced into bondage; the prince-abbot in charge was loathed for his brutal and systematic harassment of his tenants. So, when Luther in his *On Monastic Vows* denounced monks as "locusts, caterpillars, and beetles that consume everyone else's sustenance," and when he called on God to treat monasteries "like Sodom and Gomorrah, so that not even their members should be left," he seemed to many peasants to be addressing their own miserable circumstances.

Further inciting the masses were the pamphlets and broadsheets that were flooding the countryside. For centuries, the peasant had been an object of scorn, cruel jokes, and crude stereotypes. "Peasants and pigs are one and the same," went one saying. "Don't grieve for a peasant or a Jew," went another. Now, however, the tillers of the soil were being hailed as pious, quick-witted defenders of the gospel. Cartoonists celebrated both the "evangelical peasant" and *Karsthans*—"Hans with a hoe"—who, upright and wise, spoke the truth in a simple and direct manner, in contrast to the forked statements of obfuscating priests and syllogizing theologians. One drawing showed Luther surrounded by peasants as he preached the Word of God; another showed him greasing a *Bundschuh*.

By far the most popular pamphlet was "The Wittenberg Nightingale," a long didactic poem by Hans Sachs, the Nuremberg cobbler-poet. Issued in 1523, it put into rhyming couplets the rising expectations in the countryside. "Awake, awake!" went its famous opening. "Day draws near! In the green woods I hear the delightful nightingale singing; its sound resonates through hill and valley." The poem celebrated the simplicity of Luther's teachings on faith and Scripture as opposed to the lifeless doctrines and ornate rituals of Rome. In an allegorical attack on the Church, it described how the lion (Leo X) and his helpmates (asses, wolves, snakes) were leading the sheep (ordinary Christians) astray, and it offered a summary of the key events of the Reformation up to the Edict of Worms. As it appeared in the villages and hamlets of the German southwest, "The Wittenberg Nightingale" heightened the sense that a new era of freedom and justice was arriving.

The southwest was also inflamed by events in neighboring Switzerland. Through years of struggle, the Swiss cantons had freed themselves from the control of the Hapsburg dynasty and established a republican confederation. In Zurich, Zwingli was moving ahead with his campaign to build a godly society. In his *Sixty-Seven Articles*, he stressed the right of the community to recall secular authorities who failed to rule in a Christian fashion—a republican principle foreign to Luther. In a series of disputations held in Zurich in 1523 and 1524, Zwingli and his followers challenged the legitimacy of both the Mass and images. After months of pressure, the town council, following Zwingli's recommendations, authorized the removal of images. On June 15, 1524, groups of carpenters, stonemasons, and locksmiths descended on Zurich's churches and methodically removed all pictures and statues, stripped bare all altars, tore down saintly images, and painted over frescoes. With that, the city confirmed its full acceptance of the Reformation.

Zurich's example was being closely followed in Waldshut, a town twenty-five miles to the north on the north bank of the Rhine. It was small, with only 1,000 or so residents, but one of them was Balthasar Hubmaier, a forceful preacher and friend of Zwingli (and future leader of the radical Reformation) who rejected the rules on fasting, encouraged the withholding of rents, and railed against images with such force that bands of citizens barged into Waldshut's churches and destroyed pictures and crucifixes. Such acts infuriated Archduke Ferdinand. The brother of Charles V, Ferdinand ruled the Hapsburgs' Austrian duchies, in whose territory Waldshut sat, and he worried that if the reform there succeeded, other localities would follow, so his government demanded that its citizens hand over their preacher. They refused, and in mid-May 1524 Waldshut's streets filled with raucous protesters demonstrating their support for Hubmaier. With so many Austrian troops fighting in northern Italy, Ferdinand was unable to marshal a force large enough to subdue the town, and so, to the astonishment of farmers and laborers throughout southern Germany, tiny Waldshut remained in defiance of the mighty Hapsburgs.

One of the first major peasant outbreaks occurred fifteen miles to the north of Waldshut, on the estate of Count Sigismund of Lupfen in the district of Stühlingen, on the outskirts of the Black Forest. On June 24, 1524, the count's wife, who enjoyed spinning yarn, demanded that some of the tenants take time off from tending their hay to gather empty snail shells that she could use as spools. It was the type of flagrant abuse that the count's peasants had long had to endure, but this time they refused. The count agreed to talk, and a meeting was scheduled for the neighboring town of Tiengen. The farmers were in a militant mood, however, and in the days leading up to the session they decided to organize militarily. They chose Hans Müller as their head, a skilled orator and former mercenary from a nearby village, who proceeded to form a band of several hundred peasants. Armed with flails, scythes, and other farm implements, they marched to Tiengen. No settlement could be reached, and on July 24 the parties agreed to a thirty-day moratorium.

Seeking broader support, Müller led a contingent of some six hundred peasants to Waldshut. He also sent agents through the hills and vales of the Black Forest, and in early October he led his band on a daring march through the region. At each village, the bells were rung to summon local residents. Wherever the band alighted, an eyewitness reported, "they had their grievances read out and heard, stating that they wished to do no harm to anyone; they paid for whatever they ate and drank and admonished the peasants to help them gain justice." After a discussion, those assembled would vote on whether to join the militia. By mid-October 1524, several thousand men had enlisted under Müller's banner. That same month, organizers began moving eastward into the lands around Lake Constance. As winter approached, thirty thousand peasants were under arms in southwestern Germany, many of them refusing to pay dues or provide services and committed to fighting to the death to better their lot.

Erasmus was not far from the action. The Black Forest began just to the north of Basel, and Waldshut was only forty miles up the Rhine. In a

December 1524 letter to Heinrich Stromer, who was a physician and a member of the Leipzig town council, Erasmus took weary note of the iconoclastic outbursts occurring in the region: in Zurich, "they have thrown all the saints out of their temples; in Waldshut even out of the glass windows of private houses." In Basel, the saints remained in place, but the evangelical party was advancing, with Oecolampadius preaching against Erasmus's diatribe on free will and its pervasive Pelagianism.

On top of it all, Erasmus reported, "Karlstadt has been here." In his travels around southwestern Germany, the irrepressible exegete had come to Basel in late October 1524. Given his reputation for troublemaking, any house that agreed to publish his tracts would take on great risk, but the potential readership was great, too, and two Basel printers, Thomas Wolff and Johann Bebel, signed on. The printers tried to conceal their names, but once the pamphlets came out, they were quickly identified and thrown into prison. Karlstadt, Erasmus observed, "teaches that the true body of the Lord is not present in the Eucharist. This no one can tolerate." The matter "will stir great trouble for us, as though we had not more than enough already."

That would prove an understatement. Karlstadt's tracts would create a great commotion among the reformers, leading to years of acrimonious debate and the opening of deep rifts. Their main subject was what happens to the bread and wine during consecration. The reigning interpretation, which was based on centuries of Eucharistic theology and had been made official at the Fourth Lateran Council of 1215, held that the bread and the wine on the altar are transformed into the body and the blood of Christ. Their outward appearance (called "accidents") remains the same but their substance is fundamentally transformed, hence the doctrine's name: transubstantiation. The awe and even terror with which the Eucharist was beheld reflected the belief that Christ becomes physically present in the sacrament, and questioning it was considered heretical.

To many reformers, however, ascribing such importance to the physical elements of the Eucharist seemed a case of superstition and idolatry. No matter what the inner disposition of the individual, partaking in the sacrament was seen as conferring all sorts of spiritual and material benefits, as if an act of magic were being performed. By contrast, the evangelicals, with their stress on the penitent's faith in Christ, wanted to make the Eucharist an instrument for deepening it.

That was Karlstadt's aim. Rejecting the doctrine of transubstantiation as the profane creation of subtle doctors, he argued that the Eucharist should be seen as a symbol or commemoration of Christ's sacrifice on behalf of humankind. Rather than focus on the bread and wine becoming the flesh and blood of Christ, Christians should concentrate on how Christ had made the ultimate sacrifice so that man in his sinfulness could be redeemed.

To help make his case, Karlstadt relied on grammar, applying it to such key passages as Matthew 26. There, Jesus takes the bread and, after blessing it, breaks it into pieces and distributes it to his disciples, saying, "Take, eat; this is my body." To generations of Catholic theologians, the meaning was clear: by "this," Jesus was referring to the bread; in the reenactment of the ceremony, the bread becomes his body. But Karlstadt, examining the underlying Greek, saw that *touto* ("this") is neuter; therefore, it could not refer to *artos* ("bread"), which is masculine. Instead, he insisted, the word referred to *soma*, or "body," which is also neuter. In other words, Christ, in saying "This is my body," must have been pointing not to the bread but to his actual body. In this way, he was directing his followers to focus on the bodily sacrifice he was about to make; the elements were simply symbols to help them recall it. "He who partakes of the Lord's Supper unworthily is guilty as were the murderers of Christ," Karlstadt declared.

In so arguing, Karlstadt was challenging not only the Roman Church but also Luther. While violently attacking many aspects of the Catholic Mass, Luther had continued to believe that the consecrated elements do become the body and blood of Christ. (In a twist, however, he argued that the body and blood of Christ are *in* the bread and the wine without actually becoming them, just as there is fire in a red-hot piece of metal without the metal's actually changing its nature.)

Seeking support for his position, Karlstadt in November 1524 went to Strasbourg. The city was alive with religious excitement. With its reputation for open-mindedness, it had attracted reformers, refugees, and freethinkers from both French- and German-speaking lands, which it straddled. In its taverns and beer halls, carpenters and wagoners loudly debated the new gospel, while its presses turned out crude fly sheets inveighing against both Romanists and evangelists. At the cathedral, Matthias Zell continued to draw large crowds with his powerful descriptions of the personal transformation that faith and grace can work in the soul, in contrast to the burdensome laws of Moses and the stultifying rituals of Rome.

Also now in Strasbourg was Wolfgang Capito. He had arrived in the spring of 1523 after extricating himself from the court of Archbishop Albrecht of Mainz. Taking a position as the provost at St. Thomas's church, he had planned to withdraw from public life and devote himself to study, but he quickly found that this was impossible in the city's charged atmosphere. In a tense confrontation, Zell accused him of being a self-seeking humanist interested mainly in making a name for himself. After a period of painful introspection, Capito concluded that Zell was right, and by October 1524 he had openly embraced Scripture as the sole authority and faith as the one true path to salvation. Another Erasmian humanist had joined the evangelical camp.

The emerging power in the city, though, was Martin Bucer. Ever since 1518, when he had seen Luther in action in Heidelberg, Bucer had been drawn to his ideas. After several unhappy years as a Dominican friar and a priest, he had come to Strasbourg in May 1523 without a job or direction. His reputation as a godly man spread, however, and with Zell's help he would eventually gain a pulpit at St. Aurelia's, the church of the gardeners. Bucer's sermons on the power of the Gospel and its ability to transform the lives of even the damned and unregenerate would help establish him as the city's spiritual leader.

Given Strasbourg's growing influence among the reformers, Karlstadt saw winning its approval as pivotal to his cause. Though he remained only a few days, he as usual caused an uproar. At every opportunity he assailed Luther, complaining that he had forced him and his wife (along with their newborn child) into exile. He inveighed against infant baptism as unsupported by the Bible, denounced images as forbidden by Moses, and promoted his new interpretation of the Eucharist. While put off by Karlstadt's boorishness, the Strasbourgers were impressed by his knowledge of

Greek and the insights it had given him into the Bible. Try as they might, they could not rebut him, and so seven of the city's preachers, led by Bucer, Capito, and Zell, decided to approach Luther. In a November 23, 1524, letter, they asked for his assessment of Karlstadt's views on both the Eucharist and infant baptism. Wary of Luther's temper, they urged him to reply "without stomach," i.e., calmly. To the Strasbourgers, the internal divisions opening up among the reformers seemed an even graver threat than that from the papists, and they hoped that Luther could help point a way out.

The letter, along with several of Karlstadt's tracts, was given to a deacon in Zell's church, who promptly rode off with it toward Saxony.

UPRISING

In Wittenberg, the presence of the three remaining Nimbschen nuns was continuing to spur gossip and speculation. Luther had, in fact, grown so close to them that he jokingly referred to them as his wives. He was especially taken with Ave von Schönfeld. She was also interested in him, but, tiring of waiting for him to make a move, she instead married a pharmacist's assistant. Her sister Margaret likewise became betrothed. That left Katharina von Bora. Jerome Baumgärtner, the man to whom she had become engaged, found on his return to Nuremberg that his parents were adamantly opposed to his marrying a penniless runaway nun. When she heard the news, Katharina was heartbroken. As a substitute, she said she would take Luther himself.

Now forty-one, Luther was under growing pressure to marry. Having so loudly denounced celibacy, he could punctuate the point through his own example. But he was less taken with Katharina than she was with him, considering her too proud and prickly, and in any case he lacked the means to support a family. He was so impoverished that when a former member of his order got married in Magdeburg, he was unable to send a wedding gift.

But he had another, graver reason for not marrying, as he explained to Spalatin in late November 1524. Spalatin had told Luther that he was thinking of resigning his position as chaplain at the electoral court, for he was physically and emotionally drained. His efforts to spread the new gospel had foundered, and some courtiers had poked fun at his preaching style and even his small stature. None of that was a reason to give up, Luther wrote, especially in light of Frederick's declining health. "If it should happen that you were to retire, and he were to die soon afterwards, you would never cease to regret that you had not held on till the time of his death." The only valid reason for resigning would be if Spalatin wanted to marry and so felt he could no longer serve as chaplain. Luther noted his own reluctance to wed. "Not that I lack the feelings of a man (for I am neither wood nor stone), but my mind is averse to marriage because I daily expect the death decreed to a heretic."

With great sorrow, Luther was following the persecution of his followers in the Low Countries. On July 1, 1523, two young friars from the Augustinian cloister in Antwerp had been burned as Lutheran heretics—the first martyrs of the new gospel. In the Austrian town of Rattenberg, a monk who admired Luther was savagely tortured on the orders of Archduke Ferdinand, and in Vienna a merchant named Caspar Tauber had been beheaded after refusing to recant his Lutheran opinions. In Buda, Hungary, a bookseller who had distributed Luther's New Testament and other writings was lashed to a post and his books were piled around him; the books were set on fire, and he was consumed along with them. He "suffered bravely for the Lord," Luther observed.

It was in this grim state of mind that he received the letter from the Strasbourg theologians. When he saw the seriousness with which those learned men were taking Karlstadt's rantings, he became alarmed. His friend Nicholas Gerbel, a lawyer in Strasbourg, informed him of the malicious things Karlstadt had said about him, including the charge that Luther was behind the banishment of him and his family from Saxony. Not even the Catholics had attacked him so sharply, Gerbel wrote. On top of it all, Karlstadt's ideas about images, baptism, and the Lord's Supper were gaining support among the lower classes.

Dismayed, Luther hurriedly drafted an open letter *To the Christians at Strasbourg in Opposition to the Fanatic Spirit*, warning them against Karlstadt's "loose, lame, empty talk." Luther denied that he bore any responsibility for Karlstadt's expulsion from Saxony but acknowledged that he was "glad that he is out of our land, and I wish he were not among you." Christ "finds not only Caiaphas among his enemies, but also Judas among his friends." The "fanaticism" of Karlstadt and the other "new prophets" could lead only to dissension, sects, and errors.

After examining Karlstadt's tracts, Luther decided to prepare a fuller rebuttal. In it, he would ignore the pastors' request that he write without stomach. He was simply incapable of doing so, especially when he felt under attack. *Against the Heavenly Prophets in the Matter of Images and Sacraments*, as Luther called it, grew so long that it would have to be published in two parts. In both, he attacked Karlstadt with a ferocity that even for Luther stood out.

"Karlstadt has deserted us and on top of that has become our worst enemy," he declared. Everyone should know "that he has a perverted spirit that thinks only of murdering the conscience with laws, sin, and works." Luther twitted Karlstadt for wearing the gray garb and felt hat of the peasants and insisting on being called "Brother Andreas"—acts for which he hoped to be "praised as a remarkable Christian." This Satan and his helpers had to be stopped; otherwise, disorder would spread and the masses would be driven to kill all of the wicked. Karlstadt claimed he did not want to kill, but Luther did not believe him, for Karlstadt carried a "murderous weapon"—"the false interpretation of the law of Moses."

Luther mocked Karlstadt for taking the Bible so literally. It was not necessary to do or refrain from all that Christ had done or refrained from. Otherwise, we would "have to walk on the sea, and do all the miracles that he had done"; we "would have to refrain from marriage, abandon temporal authority, forsake field and plow." Karlstadt's assertion that the Ten Commandments prohibit all graven images was similarly misguided. If people wanted to do away with them, they should be allowed to; if they wanted to keep them, that, too, should be permitted. What was unacceptable was doing away with them "in a Karlstadtian manner" (i.e., through the use of force). Such an approach could only make the masses "mad and foolish" and "accustom them to revolution" and other forms of violence.

In offering such judgments, Luther came across as a scriptural pluralist open to differing interpretations of the text. When he turned to the matter of the Eucharist, however, he became a strict constructionist, insisting that the relevant passages allowed for only one reading—that the consecrated bread and the wine are the body and blood of Christ. For page after page Luther mocked Karlstadt's analysis of "This is my body," gleefully referring to his "dear *touto*," his "hopeless *touto*," his *touto tauta* (an onomatopoeic nonsense phrase). How could one take seriously a spirit willing to risk so priceless a truth on the basis of such small technical points? "The ass's head wants to master Greek, and knows neither German nor

Latin, let alone Greek and Hebrew." Karlstadt latched on to small words and smeared them over "with his spittle" while not taking into account other texts that contradict him, "so that he is up-ended with four limbs in the air."

Erasmus, in promoting the use of grammar to understand the Bible, had hoped that such a method, by exposing the true meaning of the text, would help reduce the level of theological strife. In the hands of Luther and Karlstadt, though, grammar was giving rise to a new scholasticism, with cases and tenses replacing syllogisms and corollaries as the main weapons. The vehemence of Luther's response reflected his growing awareness that Scripture—newly proclaimed as the sole Christian authority—could give rise to interpretations different from his own.

Luther's abusiveness would backfire. *Against the Heavenly Prophets* "displeases almost everyone in Zurich, Basel, and here," Gerbel wrote from Strasbourg. Almost all defended Karlstadt and esteemed Zwingli. Gerbel rued the fact that the Eucharist—that supreme symbol of love—was giving rise to such hatred, wrath, and recrimination.

Against the Heavenly Prophets would help feed the sacramentarian controversy, as it came to be called, in which leading reformers would for years violently assail one another over what happens to the bread and wine during Communion. The tract would widen the divide between Luther and Wittenberg, on the one hand, and the reformers in the south (Strasbourg, Zurich, and Basel), on the other. It would also mark the start of the decline of Luther's prestige within the Reformation.

Having dispensed with the challenge from Karlstadt, Luther wearily acknowledged another that demanded his attention. "I owe a book on the freedom of the will," he wrote to Nicholas Hausmann on March 26, 1525. A few days later, Melanchthon informed Joachim Camerarius that Luther had finally begun working on his response to Erasmus and would shortly be done with it. Once again, though, Melanchthon was misinformed. For Luther's life was about to be overtaken by a far more epic development—the outbreak of the Peasants' War.

Over the winter, the agitation in the German southwest had spread from the Black Forest and the Lake Constance region into Upper Swabia. This region—bound by the Danube to the north and the Algäu Alps to the south (and today part of southwestern Bavaria)—was an agrarian Eden, with bountiful orchards, fertile meadows, extensive pastureland, and productive dairy farms. To its peasants, however, it was a suffocating hell, ruled by an array of powerful lords (aristocratic and ecclesiastical) exercising untrammeled control over them. But a revolt was brewing, with those peasants organizing themselves into three large *Haufen*, or military bands.

The most important of them, the Baltringen *Haufen*, arose out of a meeting of aggrieved farmers held on Christmas Eve 1524 at an inn in the village of Baltringen. They began meeting every Thursday, and when carnival arrived, they used the traditional eating and drinking as a cover to move from village to village in search of recruits. By mid-February 1525, nearly ten thousand had signed up. As their leader they chose Ulrich Schmid, a blacksmith of Lutheran sympathies. A canvass of villages about local conditions produced several hundred depositions (like the *cahiers* of the French Revolution), and from them the most common complaints were extracted. Leading the list was serfdom, followed by high rents and dues, the punitive death tax, and the limits placed on access to the forests.

The Baltringen peasants submitted their grievances to the Swabian League, an association of princes, barons, and cities created in 1488 to enforce imperial decrees and put down internal revolts. From its base in Ulm (Upper Swabia's largest city), the league informed the peasants that they should pursue their complaints through the imperial courts. Because the peasants considered those courts biased in favor of the lords, however, Schmid proposed using divine law instead. But who would define such a law? the league mockingly asked. Would God come down from heaven to hold court on the case? Schmid said he would seek out a priest to help define the contents of that law.

He went to Memmingen, the center of unrest in Upper Swabia. There, he was directed to Sebastian Lotzer, a journeyman furrier who was an avid Lutheran. Lotzer had no formal theological training, but—taking to heart the idea of the priesthood of all believers—he had closely studied Luther's German New Testament, and he could frequently be found in the street, debating questions of faith. "Whoever has two coats," he declared, "let him sell one and buy a New Testament. Then you can learn the living words of God yourselves and will understand whenever they try to mistreat you."

Lotzer initially declined Schmid's plea for help, maintaining that he was a simple artisan inexperienced in public affairs, but under further prodding he gave in, and within days he had drawn up a summary of the peasants' grievances. A local evangelical preacher named Christopher Schappeler added a preamble and sixty or so supportive biblical citations to be placed in the margins. The Twelve Articles, as they were called, would become the main manifesto of the peasant uprising. Some consider it the first written set of human rights in Europe, and Memmingen today calls itself *Stadt der Menschenrechte*—City of Human Rights.

The document shows how deeply both the Bible and Luther's ideas about Christian freedom had penetrated the countryside. The preamble, in language at once modest and solemn, offered "a Christian justification for the disobedience, indeed, the rebellions, of all the peasants." In the Gospels, Christ's words and life "teach nothing but love, peace, patience, and concord." If God chose to hear the peasants' plea that they be allowed to live according to his word, who would dare deny him? Just as he had heard the cries of the children of Israel and delivered them from the pharaoh, so would he now save his own children.

The first article—drawn directly from Luther—was a "humble plea" for each community to have the right to elect and appoint its own pastor. This pastor should preach "the holy Gospel to us purely and clearly," without any human additions. According to the Scriptures, man can come to God only through true faith and be saved only through his mercy. "That is why we need such a guide and pastor; and thus our demand is grounded in Scripture." The second article expressed a willingness to pay the tithe on grain, but only to support such a pastor and the needy poor. The small tithe should not be paid, for God "created cattle for the free use of man."

But it was the third article that was the document's centerpiece. The lords' custom of treating the peasants as if they were their serfs, it stated, was "pitiable," for "Christ has redeemed and bought us all by the shedding of his precious blood—the shepherd just as the highest, no one excepted. Therefore it is demonstrated by Scripture that we are free and wish to be free." After making such a bold assertion, the manifesto hastened to show its reasonableness: "Not that we wish to be completely free and have no authority, for God does not teach us that." Rather, "we should humble ourselves before everyone." But no doubt the princes "as true and genuine Christians" would "gladly release us from serfdom, or else show us from the Gospel that we are serfs."

This was an extraordinary statement: the peasants of Upper Swabia were, on the basis of Christian teachings, demanding the abolition of serfdom. The document's remaining articles addressed more specific grievances—the walling off of waterways, the high price of wood, the increase in labor services, and the onerous death taxes that robbed widows and orphans of their goods. In concluding, the manifesto noted that if one or more of its articles could be shown from Scripture not to be in accord with God's Word, it would be abandoned. If, on the other hand, the Bible revealed other grievances as offensive to God, they would be added. Such comments showed the temperate character of the Twelve Articles. Rather than seek the overthrow of the social order, they recognized the existence of different ranks and classes.

Even so, the Twelve Articles packed an explosive punch. If implemented, they would have done away with serfdom and the many restrictions imposed on rights and movement. By granting communities the right to choose their own pastors, they would have eliminated a key source of Church patronage and control. And, by casting their demands in the language of the Bible, the articles sought to give them divine sanction.

In the first week of March 1525, representatives of the three Upper Swabian bands met in the hall of the haberdashers' guild in Memmingen to discuss the articles. After several days of debate, they were duly adopted. The bands also agreed to join together in a Christian Union of Upper Swabia. In submitting the Twelve Articles to the Swabian League, they offered a list of individuals who, as proven expositors of divine law, could serve as arbiters. At the top was Martin Luther. Others included Melanchthon, Zwingli, Bugenhagen, Andreas Osiander of Nuremberg, and Matthias Zell of Strasbourg. Luther's premier position showed the great prestige he continued to enjoy among the people.

Within two months, the Twelve Articles were reprinted two dozen times in cities from Strasbourg to Zwickau, putting as many as 25,000 copies in circulation. Couriers, agitators, preachers, and tradesmen carried them west into the highlands of the Black Forest, south over the Alps into the Tirol, and north beyond Ulm into the duchy of Franconia.

When the Twelve Articles arrived in a village, tocsins were rung, summoning farmers and laborers to meet under a tree, in a field, or at an inn. Grievances were aired and discussed and, finally, a decision was taken on whether to sign up. In this way, the movement quickly spread. To broaden their base, the peasants sent emissaries into the towns. Though many town dwellers remained hostile to rural residents, they disliked the clergy even more, and the biblical language of the Twelve Articles served as a bridge between them. Pressed from within, the towns agreed to provide men or supply firearms and provisions. The insurgency thus came to include not only peasants but also artisans, millers, clerks, butchers, cobblers, smiths, and shopkeepers. It attracted many marginal figures as well, including the urban proletariat, day laborers, beggars, and criminals.

While waiting to hear back from the Swabian League, the peasant bands grew restless. Their disgust with the Church and its exploitive practices, having built up over so many years, proved difficult to contain. An early outburst occurred on March 20, 1525, when a contingent gathered before the abbey of Ottobeuren, eight miles from Memmingen. In the villages that surrounded it there lived several thousand serfs who had been pauperized by the death duties imposed by the cloister. Finding the abbey poorly defended, the peasants quickly overran it. Making for its pantries, they rummaged through its stocks; barging into its cellar, they guzzled its wine. In the abbey itself, they smashed the windows, desecrated the church, drove off the cattle, and burned every piece of paper they could find. Other monasteries quickly followed.

Castles, too, were seized, pillaged, and burned. The peasants met little resistance. In the face of their fury, the nobility—lacking both manpower and willpower—seemed paralyzed. According to the Bavarian chancellor, the lords were like "old women" in their hesitation to fight the peasants. "They fear for their houses and no one will do anything until troops are assembled, which will take some time." The peasants' revolt, which had been undertaken "to repress the princes and the nobility," had "its ultimate source in Lutheran teaching, for the peasants relate the majority of their demands to the Word of God, the Gospel, and brotherly love." Given the authorities' "ineffable faintheartedness," the main challenge was to bring them "to a more manly resolve: that would be the end of the peasantry."

One person who had such resolve was Truchsess (Lord High Steward) George von Waldburg. The commander of the army of the Swabian League, he would be a decisive figure in the coming contest. During two decades of military service, he had gained a reputation for both ruthlessness and efficiency, and even as the peasants were deliberating in Memmingen, he was preparing to confront them. With many German soldiers off fighting in northern Italy and others engaged in putting down an uprising by a local duke, Waldburg found recruitment more difficult than usual, but by the end of March 1525 he had assembled a force of 7,000 foot soldiers and 1,500 horsemen.

The first major encounter was at Leipheim, located on the Danube near Ulm. The town had been recently captured by a band of several thousand rebels, and in early April Waldburg laid siege to it. The peasants, frightened and undisciplined, quickly surrendered. What began as an orderly retreat by the rebels quickly turned into a savage rout as Waldburg's troops mercilessly pursued and slaughtered them. As many as a thousand were killed or drowned in the Danube; the rest were captured.

The slaughter had a deeply demoralizing effect on the Baltringen *Haufen*. After a series of minor skirmishes, it submitted to the league and dissolved itself. Buoyed by this victory, Waldburg marched south to confront the Lake Constance band. On April 15, he came near it at the town of Weingarten. With twelve thousand foot soldiers, including some former mercenaries, this regiment had more experience than most of the other bands. In addition, the terrain was ill suited to the deployment of the league's horses, and the rebels had a number of cannons. Feeling overmatched, Waldburg decided to negotiate rather than fight, and on April 17 a peace treaty was signed.

Waldburg would be fiercely criticized by some nobles for refusing to fight the peasants, but he had astutely read the situation. In return for a promise to arbitrate their grievances, the peasants agreed to surrender the castles and cloisters they had seized, disband their army, and resume rent payments. In effect, the largest of the Upper Swabian armies gave up fighting in return for minor concessions. With Upper Swabia thus pacified, Waldburg began preparing for future battles.

There would be many of them, for peasant bands throughout the southwest were on the move. In the spring of 1525, Hans Müller led a campaign through the Black Forest aimed at gaining by force the concessions that the rebels in the winter had failed to win by negotiation. Traveling around the region in a brilliant red cloak and cap, he was accompanied by a herald who at each stop summoned the villagers to hear the Twelve Articles read aloud. Those who refused to join the evangelical brotherhood (as it was called) were subject to a secular ban, by which they were to be denied all social and economic intercourse and access to all forests and pastures. Müller's army swelled, and over the spring it seized one castle after another, including that of the count of Lupfen, where the infamous snail-shell episode had occurred the previous summer.

By early May, Müller's sights were set on Freiburg. Situated at the strategic point where the Black Forest passes meet the plain of the Rhine valley, it was the best-defended town in the region. Six bands totaling more than ten thousand peasants, many bearing swords and pikes, bore down on it, and refugees from the surrounding region streamed in. "Everything here is in a state of depression and disquietude for fear of an attack," wrote Ulrich Zasius, a prominent jurist and friend of Erasmus, "and not an hour goes by in which we do not dread some catastrophe. Luther, the destroyer of peace, the most pernicious of two-legged creatures, has thrown the whole of Germany into such a state of frenzy that we have come to consider it peace and security if we are not slaughtered at every moment."

Meanwhile, the rebellion was spilling westward across the Rhine into Alsace. In this region of vineyards, wheat fields, and cow pastures, the Church was a major landholder, and peasant indebtedness was a serious problem. The arrival of the Twelve Articles, with their demand for social justice in God's name, had an electrifying effect, and on April 16 several hundred peasants took over the Benedictine abbey at nearby Altorf, plundering its stores. Heading north, they did the same to the abbey at Marmoutier. Marching along a spur of the Vosges Mountains, they reached the town of Saverne, where the bishop of Strasbourg resided. After occupying it, the peasants ransacked its clerical properties. Captured priests were forced to confess their adherence to false teachings and to promise thereafter to preach only the pure gospel. Also targeted were the Jews, some of whom worked in the countryside as moneylenders and so were considered enemies of the poor. By the start of May 1525, the various Alsatian bands had coalesced into a united contingent of twenty thousand, causing panic among the propertied.

The movement was also pushing north from Upper Swabia into Franconia. In this highly fragmented region crisscrossed by the Main, Neckar, and Tauber Rivers, serfdom was less prevalent than in either Upper Swabia or the Black Forest, but the Franconian nobility—moving heavily into sheep farming—were aggressively expanding their estates and in the process grabbing much common land. The resulting shortage had produced a large population of immiserated day laborers. Taxation was onerous and mounting, with monasteries among the heaviest leviers. In Nuremberg, Franconia's largest city, thousands were taking Communion in both kinds, and Dominican friars were being angrily accosted in the streets. From March 3 to March 14 a disputation was held on the religious question; Andreas Osiander carried the day, and the city officially declared for the reform. Churches were ordered to stop celebrating the Roman Mass and instead follow the evangelical service that had been introduced in the city's two great parish churches. The dissolution of the monasteries would soon begin. Nuremberg thus became the first large imperial city in Germany to join the Reformation. The old patriciate remained in charge, however, and it made sure to seal the city off from the agitation in the countryside.

In its absence, Franconia's next largest town, Rothenburg, became the center of revolt. Perched picturesquely on the Tauber River, it was known for the roseate hue given off by its red-tiled roofs, but by early 1525 its mood had darkened as evangelical pastors inveighed against the fatted clergy and pampered oligarchs who ruled its affairs. Adding to the unrest was the presence of Andreas von Karlstadt. After his brief stay in Strasbourg, he had slipped into Rothenburg in late 1524. By now a wanted man, he hid in the home of a former burgomaster. Eventually discovered, he was expelled by the town council, but in February 1525, amid the growing ferment, he managed to return, and at Easter he preached on the Eucharist, to the approval of the urban poor. At the end of March, the ex-burgomaster provoked an iconoclastic campaign, marked by the destruction of images, the driving of the priests from the cathedral, and the leveling of a chapel devoted to the Virgin Mary.

The unrest quickly spread into the nearby Tauber valley, attracting especially the vinedressers, who tended the vines that supported the wine industry and whose fortunes fluctuated with the vagaries of the weather and the swings of the market. In western Franconia another regiment formed, drawing peasants from villages nestled in both the Neckar valley and the Odenwald, a low mountain range. Commanding this force was George Metzler, one of the many innkeepers who became rebel leaders. Under the standard of a *Bundschuh* attached to a pole, he quickly organized a force of two thousand men, who began traveling around the region, encouraging (and in many cases compelling) farmers and laborers to commit themselves to the Twelve Articles. The Neckar-Odenwald district was dotted with castles and abbeys, and in the name of divine justice and Christian liberty, thousands of peasants armed with swords and farm implements assaulted these strongholds of the late-medieval order.

For all their wantonness, the peasants' violence was directed mostly at property; the taking of life was rare. A notorious exception occurred at Weinsberg, a small town in central Franconia that was home to a castle occupied by Ludwig von Helfenstein, a count much hated for his cruelties. On April 16, 1525—Easter Sunday—while many leading citizens were at church, two peasant bands descended on the town. Within minutes, forty people lay dead, and the count, together with his wife and two-year-old son and a number of noblemen and knights, was taken prisoner. They were placed in the charge of Jäcklein Rohrbach, a peasant leader and ruffian known for his frequent run-ins with the law. Metzler ordered Rohrbach not to kill the prisoners, but the next morning, as other commanders slept off a night of heavy drinking, Rohrbach led the count and thirteen other noblemen to a meadow, where they were sentenced to death. Shortly before sunrise, the peasants formed a double row of spears. The countess, hysterical, begged for her husband's life, but Rohrbach ordered two men to hold her up and make her watch. Entering the gauntlet, the count was speared, stabbed, and slashed by the peasants, who while striking angrily recalled the brutal acts he had inflicted on them. Horribly mutilated, he quickly fell. In half an hour, the other prisoners were similarly dispatched. The countess was stripped and dressed in the rags of a beggar and thrown onto a dung cart and driven away. She would spend the rest of her days in a convent.

When the sun rose and it became clear what had happened, there was an outcry among the more moderate rebels, who expelled Rohrbach and his group. As word of the atrocity spread, it caused deep disgust; no other incident, in fact, would do more damage to the peasants' cause. In the short run, though, the massacre sowed terror among the Franconian nobility, and whatever modest resistance they had put up crumbled; during the first part of April 1525 alone, more than one hundred castles were seized or burned. During a three-day rampage through the bishopric of Bamberg, the peasants sacked and destroyed some seventy castles, monasteries, and religious foundations. In Mainz, Archbishop Albrecht fled at the first sign of trouble, and when the bishop ruling in his place failed in an effort to raise the territorial militia, the archbishopric was forced to endorse the Twelve Articles and pay a huge ransom. The most powerful ecclesiastical territory in Germany had fallen into rebel hands.

By this point, nearly all of Franconia had joined the revolt. The one major holdout was Würzburg. Located on the Main River, it was the seat of the most important bishopric in Germany after Mainz. The Franconian bands now headed toward it. Along the way they burned down all of the bishop's castles and plundered thirty-one cloisters. In early May, they arrived before the walls of Würzburg to negotiate its surrender. In the end, it was the threat by the peasant armies to tear up the vineyards around the town that convinced its council, on May 8, 1525, to open its gates. As the rebels streamed in, 250 or so members of the Würzburg garrison, together with many nobles and clerics, retreated into the Marienberg, the great fortress that was perched on a spur overlooking the town. Preparations for a long siege began. If the peasants succeeded in capturing the fortress, their control of Franconia would be complete.

*   *   *

From Franconia, the rebellion swept northward into Hesse and Thuringia—and closer to Luther. By early April, copies of the Twelve Articles had reached Fulda. Located on the western fringe of the Thuringian Forest, the town was home to a famous Benedictine monastery with extensive landholdings, and radical preachers were rousing the locals against its powerful prince-abbot. The town was quickly overrun. The rebellion then spread eastward into the valley of the Werra River, and soon some eighteen thousand men were marching through the forest.

The center of the Thuringian revolt was Mühlhausen, where Thomas Müntzer and Heinrich Pfeiffer had been active the previous summer. In December 1524, Pfeiffer returned to the city and resumed his organizing. Müntzer arrived in early 1525. He had not had much success in the southwest—his calls for holy war did not much resonate with the practical-minded peasants—but their rebellion had convinced him that the final days were at hand, and on hearing of Pfeiffer's return to Mühlhausen, he, too, had headed back there to lead the great apocalyptic struggle.

Müntzer was installed as the pastor of St. Mary's, the city's largest church, and from its pulpit he called for a final reckoning. In mid-March 1525, a group of his supporters, after being incited by him, marched through town, invaded a convent, drove out the remaining sisters, smashed everything in sight, and forced several council members to flee. Pfeiffer and Müntzer then inaugurated a new "eternal council" that was to serve in perpetuity. At St. Mary's, Müntzer's feverish sermons were followed by revolutionary anthems with words drawn from the Old Testament, and a banner was made from coarse silk showing a rainbow on a white background. The council began mobilizing the people of Mühlhausen for action against its clerical and feudal overlords.

Seeking allies, Müntzer sent sympathetic preachers south into the Thuringian Forest and north into the Harz Mountains. In the mining districts around Mansfeld—Luther's hometown—the miners were stirring amid the general unrest, and Müntzer hoped to win them over. "The time has come, the evil-doers are running like scared dogs!" he thundered in an appeal sent to his former parishioners in Allstedt. "Alert the brothers, so that they may be at peace, and testify to their conversion. It is absolutely critical—absolutely necessary!" They were to show no pity and pay no attention to the cries of the godless: "Alert the villages and towns and especially the mineworkers and other good fellows who will be of use. We cannot slumber any longer. . . . Go to it, go to it, while the fire is hot! Don't let your sword get cold! Hammer away ding-dong on the anvils of Nimrod."

By mid-April 1525, much of central Germany seemed on the verge of falling to the peasants.

Luther at that point had little sense of the scale or intensity of the uprising, but that would change as a result of a request from Count Albrecht of Mansfeld. Inspired by Luther's tract on the need to establish Christian schools, the count asked him to set one up in Eisleben, and Luther agreed to do so. On April 16, 1525, he, along with Melanchthon and Johann Agricola, a friend and former student, left Wittenberg. Without knowing it, they were heading into the heart of the Thuringian rebellion.

Luther took with him a copy of the Twelve Articles. Because the peasants had proposed him as an arbiter of their demands, he felt he had to reply. On the way to Eisleben, he stopped in Mansfeld and, in the garden of the home of Johann Duhren, a town councilor, he hurriedly prepared his response. The *Admonition to Peace: A Reply to the Twelve Articles of the Peasants in Swabia* was the first of three pamphlets Luther would produce on the peasant revolt. In his three Reformatory tracts of 1520, he had proposed a bold program to transform society; he would now try to tamp down the expectations they had helped create.

Written in a frenzy, the *Admonition* reads like two separate tracts stitched together. In the first, Luther addressed the ruling class, and he was unsparing: "We have no one on earth to thank for this disastrous rebellion, except you princes and lords, and especially you blind bishops and mad priests and monks, whose hearts are hardened, even to the present day." As temporal rulers, "you do nothing but cheat and rob the people so that you may lead a life of luxury and extravagance." The poor could bear it no longer, and unless the princes and prelates mended their ways, God would undoubtedly visit his wrath on them. Many of the peasants' articles were fair and just, and had he been writing them, he would have added others. Luther endorsed the peasants' demands for the right to choose their own pastors and called their claims about economic exploitation no less just.

Luther then turned to the demands of the peasants, and his tone abruptly and bizarrely shifted. In calling themselves a Christian association, the peasants were taking God's name in vain in violation of the Second Commandment. That their rulers were wicked and unjust did not excuse disorder and rebellion. As Paul taught at Romans 13, those in authority have been instituted by God, and it is they alone who have the right to bear the sword and punish wickedness. Although the rulers erred when they suppressed the gospel and oppressed the peasants in temporal affairs, the peasants were guilty of a much greater wrong when they suppressed God's sword and trod it underfoot. While the rulers take the peasants' property from them, the peasants take from the rulers their authority, without which they would have nothing. The peasants were therefore even greater robbers than the rulers. If authority and government disappeared from the world, the result would be nothing but murder and bloodshed.

For Luther, the peasants were blurring the lines between the two kingdoms—a crime far greater than any the princes had committed. The very idea of the peasants taking action to right wrongs enraged him. It was Christ's desire that we not resist evil or injustice but yield and suffer. Romans, Corinthians, Matthew—all teach that Christians should suffer wrongs committed against them and love their prosecutors and enemies. From such passages,

> even a child can understand that the Christian law tells us not to strive against injustice, not to grasp the sword, not to protect ourselves, not to avenge ourselves, but to give up life and property, and let whoever takes it have it. We have all we need in our Lord, who will not leave us, as he promised. Suffering! suffering! Cross! cross! This and nothing else is the Christian law!

In the past, of course, Luther had frequently written of how Christ came with a sword. Now, however, with the peasants actively resisting injustice in Christ's name, he was furiously demanding that they bear the cross. They had to stop calling themselves Christians and claiming that Christian law was on their side. "As long as there is a heartbeat in my body, I shall do all I can to take that name away from you." The composer of the Twelve Articles was himself neither godly nor honest but a "lying preacher and false prophet" whose citations "smeared on the margin do not help you at all." If the peasants were true Christians, they would strive to achieve their goals by patiently praying to God instead of seeking to compel the rulers to comply through force and violence.

Taking up the individual articles, Luther was no less dismissive. Concerning the right of communities to choose their own pastors, he was of course the originator of this idea, and earlier in the *Admonition* he had said that the peasants were just in proposing it, but now, in a startling shift, he maintained that the peasants should first humbly ask their rulers to provide a pastor to their liking. If he refused, the peasants could choose their own pastor and support him out of their own resources. If, however, the rulers would not tolerate the pastor they chose, the pastor should flee to another city. Whoever does otherwise "is a robber and brawler." Similarly, the peasants, in calling for the tithe to be used to support the pastor and for the remainder to be distributed to the poor, were engaging in "nothing but theft and highway robbery."

Even on the matter of serfdom, Luther was unyielding. When the peasants asserted that no one was to be the serf of anyone else, on the grounds that Christ makes all free, they were turning Christian freedom into a material matter. "Did not Abraham and other patriarchs and prophets have slaves?" This article therefore absolutely contradicted the gospel. "It proposes robbery, for it suggests that every man should take his body away from his lord, even though his body is the lord's property." A slave can be a Christian and have Christian freedom, in the same way that a prisoner or a sick man is a Christian, yet not free. This article "would make all men equal, and turn the spiritual kingdom of Christ into a worldly, external kingdom; and that is impossible. A worldly kingdom cannot exist without an inequality of persons, some being free, some imprisoned, some lords, some subjects, etc."

By this point, Luther was being charged on all sides with having helped spark the uprising. Vehemently objecting, he noted that he had always opposed rebellion and forcefully exhorted the people "to obey and respect" even "wild and dictatorial tyrants." The rebellion came not from him but from "the murder-prophets" (i.e., Müntzer and Karlstadt), whom he alone had fought.

Many disputed this judgment. "It is not the case," a Saxon official observed at the time, "that Müntzer is a captain or in command of the troop, as is alleged. He is simply the Mühlhauseners' preacher. There are many other preachers in the troop, who preach the Gospel according to Luther's interpretation." By inflating Müntzer's part in causing the revolt, Luther was seeking to diminish his own.

Overall, Luther devoted three times as much space to attacking the peasants as he did to the princes. In doing so, he was clearly reacting to the growing anarchy and violence in the land. In his 1522 tract admonishing all Christians to guard against rebellion, he had warned *Herr Omnes* not to use the Bible to justify demands for political and social betterment. Mr. Everyman was not listening. In his fury, Luther was rejecting not only violent actions but actions of any kind undertaken by the poor and oppressed to improve their lot. No matter how just and equitable the peasants' demands, he maintained, their efforts to act on them ran counter to Christian law. As faithful Christians, they had but one available path: acceptance and acquiescence.

When the tract was done, Luther sent it off to Wittenberg to be printed. After completing his business in Eisleben, he continued on through northern and central Thuringia to see his parents, friends, and relatives. He found the whole land south of the Harz Mountains in a state of insurrection. On May 1, 1525, he was in Wallhausen, less than a day's journey from Allstedt, and he preached against the "false prophets." On the following day, he was in Nordhausen, which was thirty miles from Mühlhausen and where a group of radicals was demanding the installation of an eternal council like Müntzer's. In his sermon, Luther cited the crucified Christ as the model for Christians facing injustice; theirs was to suffer and endure. The congregation was in no mood for such instruction. Luther was interrupted by hecklers, and bells were rung so that he could not be heard. He would later recall feeling that his life was in danger.

By then, it seemed only a matter of time before all of central Germany fell to the peasants. Seeing the gravity of the situation, Philip of Hesse, the young landgrave, sent two urgent appeals in late April 1525 to Duke George of Saxony. The peasants "are forming bands and have already seized many important towns and markets," he warned. They "have been heard to say" that "they want to punish all princes, counts, lords, and nobles at their pleasure." He implored the duke to send him five hundred well-armed horses. "If we do not counter such wanton people with seriousness and boldness, then it is a sure and fearful certainty that your grace and all authority must expect the next slap in the face."

Duke John was similarly trying to rally his brother Frederick. He estimated that there were 35,000 troops in the field. "It's wild around here," he wrote from Weimar. "Everyone is in shock. God grant us his divine grace. We probably had it coming to us."

Frederick was in no position to act on such reports, however, for at that moment he lay gravely ill in his castle in Lochau. Even apart from his failing health, however, the elector was reluctant to intervene. Almost alone among the princes, he believed that the peasants had good reason to rebel and that the uprising might be an act of divine retribution for all the years of mistreatment they had suffered. "In many ways," he wrote to Duke John, "the poor are being burdened by us temporal and spiritual rulers." If God willed it, "the common man will rule." If he did not, things would rapidly change. "Let us pray God to forgive our sin." Frederick held out the hope that the conflict could be resolved through negotiations, and Duke John even considered resigning if that would help.

On his way back to Wittenberg, Luther decided to stop in Weimar to speak with Duke John. Arriving on May 3, he found the electoral court in a state of panic. The duke asked him if he should consent to the demands of the Twelve Articles. Not a single one, Luther insisted. Continuing on to Mansfeld, he met with his friend John Rühel, who was now serving as a counselor to Count Albrecht of Mansfeld. From him, Luther heard how Albrecht and his fellow count Ernst were still struggling with how to respond to the revolt. After leaving Mansfeld, Luther sent Rühel a letter urging him to stiffen Albrecht's resolve. Even if there were thousands more peasants, they would still be "robbers and murderers" who in their insolence and wickedness had taken the sword without God's authority. The peasants' revolt showed that the Devil was angry with him and wanted him dead. If he managed to make it home safely, he would prepare for martyrdom and await the arrival of the murderers and robbers. "I would rather lose my neck a hundred times than approve of and justify the peasants' actions."

Luther then dropped a bombshell: If he did survive, he would marry Katharina von Bora. He would do so "to spite the devil," i.e., the peasants, who, he felt sure, wanted him dead.

On May 5, 1525, Frederick died. The man who had been Luther's chief protector and without whom he would have surely ended up in a dungeon or at the stake was gone, and Luther hurried home so that he could preach at his funeral. He also had the idea for a new tract in which he would urge the princes of Germany to strike at the peasants, and strike them hard.

THE MURDERING HORDES

"It is not safe for me to stay here any longer," Erasmus wrote from Basel to Jean Lalemand, an influential member of Charles V's court, on February 24, 1525. As he explained, he lived "within a cluster of regions where the Lutheran faction is especially influential, Zurich being on one side and Strasbourg on the other." Even Wolfgang Capito, his longtime friend and former assistant, had turned against him. Having joined the evangelicals, Capito was now sending accusatory messages from Strasbourg. "You are set in the theater of the world whether you will or no, and you must be seen to be either a clear friend of the truth or a dissembler—such are the times now," Capito wrote. Feeling increasingly at risk, Erasmus around Easter made plans to leave Basel. But then the Peasants' War broke out, making the roads unsafe, and so, as he wearily observed, "I am stuck in this place, between Scylla and Charybdis."

From around the region he received reports of the chaos and fear the uprising was causing. The Benedictine cloister in Alsace where his friend Paul Volz was the abbot had been taken over by peasants, who had destroyed much of its furnishings, including its library and archives, and Volz had lost not only his residence but also many unpublished manuscripts. "My neighbors and even those who claim to be my protectors have stripped me of everything," he wrote to Erasmus. "I have nothing left except the clothes that cover me and a pocket edition of the New Testament." Volz had sought refuge in Strasbourg, but the Austrian authorities who governed the region, suspecting him of Lutheran sympathies, had denied him any assistance, and so he hoped Erasmus could recommend someone who might be able to help.

To Erasmus's relief, Basel itself was untouched by the uprising. In early May 1525, the peasants had marched on the city with demands similar to those of the Twelve Articles. Basel had refused to open its gates but promised concessions, and the peasants were persuaded to return to their villages. Neighboring districts were provided with charters of liberty, and within a month or so peace was restored.

Though physically safe, however, Erasmus faced a bitter new round of attacks from his conservative critics as a result of the rebellion. In the past, their main charge had been his part in inspiring Luther. Now he was also being charged with having incited the peasants. The center of complaint was the University of Paris. Prior to 1525, Erasmus had largely escaped attack by the Sorbonne theologians, owing to the protection of King Francis I, who was an admirer of humanists in general and Erasmus in particular. But in February 1525 Francis had been captured by Charles V at the battle of Pavia, and for months he had been held prisoner in a grim tower in Madrid. His absence left Erasmus exposed. For years the doctors in Paris had bristled at the application of the new critical methods to the Bible and at the resulting erosion in the authority of the Vulgate. The turmoil and sectarianism in Germany showed the disorder that could result, and the theology faculty was determined to keep France free of Lutheranism and of the humanist methods that had incubated it.

In early 1525, Pierre Cousturier, a former Sorbonne theologian turned Carthusian monk, came out with *De Tralatione Bibliae*, a fierce indictment of the application of grammar and languages to theological studies. "Mere rhetoricians" were not qualified to discuss matters of doctrine, he sniffed. The Vulgate was not only authentic but perfect, since it had been produced under the guidance of the Holy Spirit, and any effort to change the biblical text on stylistic grounds was irreverent. Cousturier did not mention Erasmus by name, but it was clear from his argument that it was Erasmus, along with Jacques Lefèvre d'Étaples, the dean of French humanists, to whom he was referring. Lefèvre felt so threatened by these attacks that he left French territory for Strasbourg. Erasmus, though not on French soil, nonetheless feared the Sorbonne's reach.

His anxiety grew when, in the spring of 1525, he learned that he was being investigated by Noël Béda. For the past two decades, Béda had served as the head of the Collège de Montaigu, the same punitive institution whose rotten eggs, moldy walls, reeking latrines, and harsh discipline

Erasmus had endured as a young man. In 1520, Béda had persuaded his fellow theologians to revive the long-dormant office of syndic, and he quickly turned it into an agency for rooting out heresy. Working through it, he would become the main watchdog of orthodoxy on the Paris faculty, carrying out his duties with a zeal that unsettled even some of his fellow doctors.

Much of his ardor would be directed at Erasmus. In May 1525, Béda sent him a long and menacing letter informing him that three of his works (including the *Encomium Matrimonii*) had been condemned by the theology faculty. The works had been translated into French by an energetic but impulsive scholar named Louis de Berquin, who had inserted provocative material from other texts. Béda also complained about Erasmus's paraphrases of the New Testament. For months he had scoured them for passages that strayed from orthodoxy, and he had found dozens. "You have treated many matters in a manner which is dangerous and likely to cause grave scandal to Christ's people," he warned. Béda was especially disturbed by Erasmus's support for translating the Scriptures into the vernacular. "You have been busy propagating this view with great frequency and persistence, not noticing the spiritual dangers and disastrous disturbances which the church has suffered time and again as a consequence; for this reason she banned the practice on more than one occasion." And, he went on, "you will know better than I if the translation of the Scriptures into the German tongue has increased piety among peasant men and women in that country."

Béda was raising many of the same points that Martin Dorp and Edward Lee had made years earlier. Now, with Germany being overrun by Bible-quoting peasants, those charges carried added weight. Erasmus refused to bend, however. In a lengthy rejoinder to Béda that showed him at his eloquent best and blustery worst, he insisted that when he had first set out to revise the New Testament, nothing was further from his mind than displacing the Vulgate. (He had, of course, been trying to do just that.) Nor, he insisted, had he ever encouraged anyone to translate the Scriptures into the vernacular. (In the *Paraclesis*, he had explicitly done so.) He dismissed those who wasted their time on the "labyrinthine intricacies" and "sophistical hairsplitting" of Aristotle or Scotus and mocked those who took refuge in the doctrines of the Schoolmen, "clinging to them as to a holy anchor."

As for the peasant revolt, Erasmus rejected any suggestion that vernacular Bibles had contributed to it. "A few radical preachers were partly to blame," he wrote to Béda, "but much greater responsibility rests with certain scandalmongers who were born to make trouble." Erasmus was more specific in a letter to Willibald Pirckheimer, identifying as the main culprits of the revolt neither the peasants nor the princes but the monks. In the face of the "tyranny of these evil men," the world "cannot endure these scheming hordes of provocateurs much longer." While the looting of the monasteries by the peasants was undoubtedly "a monstrous crime," they had been provoked by the monks' depravity, since "no laws could reform them, and they are blind to their own shortcomings."

As these passages suggest, Erasmus felt considerable sympathy for the peasants and their cause (if not their conduct). Far from wanting to keep the heavenly and earthly kingdoms distinct, as Luther did, he believed that the spiritual had to shape the secular. Manifestos like the Twelve Articles echoed his own philosophy of Christ, envisioning a more just society founded on the principles of the New Testament.

By May 1525, the peasant armies seemed unstoppable. From Alsace in the west to Bavaria in the east, from the Swiss border in the south to the Thuringian Forest in the north, castles, cloisters, towns, and villages were falling to the ragtag bands with little or no resistance.

And the revolt continued to spread. By early June, the peasants had swarmed into Salzburg, Austria. Its archbishop, Matthäus Lang—despised for his arrogance, pride, and fierce allegiance to Rome—was forced to retreat into the Hohensalzburg, a mammoth castle that sat on the bluff that dominated the city. The fighting around Innsbruck, meanwhile, grew so intense that Archduke Ferdinand, who lived there, would not venture beyond its walls. In the towns and valleys of the Inn and Etsch Rivers, the scale of the unrest made it dangerous to walk the streets, and robbing and plundering were so rife that "not a few pious men" were tempted to join in, as a witness put it.

More and more, the insurgency was taking on the air of an anticlerical crusade. In Alsace, convents were a popular target, for they were lightly guarded and thus easily overrun. Many precious works of medieval art were destroyed, and books and manuscripts were used to light fires. The Alsatian rebels considered themselves so well versed in the Bible that they ordered abbots and priests to attend a public disputation at their headquarters, with severe penalties for those who refused. Only Strasbourg and a few other Alsatian towns managed to hold out, and local lords, aware of their help-lessness, appealed to Duke Antoine in neighboring Lorraine to intervene.

In the Black Forest, Freiburg, after an eight-day siege, fell on May 23. Several days later, the peasants surged into Breisach, a fortress town on the east bank of the Rhine. These two victories marked the triumphant culmination of Hans Müller's three-month campaign across the Black Forest. The peasants now faced the challenge of converting their military victories into political gains in order to address the economic and social demands that had been aired after the initial refusal to collect snail shells for the countess of Lupfen.

That was the task facing the movement as a whole. After occupying so many towns and seizing so much territory, the peasants needed to develop a practical program to implement the reforms outlined in the Twelve Arti-cles and other petitions. But they seemed incapable of doing so. They were hampered by their political inexperience, by a shortage of skilled leaders, and, most of all, by a lack of discipline.

Wine in particular was proving the peasants' undoing. Much more expensive (and potent) than beer or ale, it had long been an upper-class luxury. Even during Communion, wine in the Catholic service was re-stricted to the priest; religious doctrine thus reinforced social privilege. In a special affront, landlords sometimes forced tenants to cart bulky barrels of wine that they could never hope to taste. Now, with wine cellars in manor houses and monasteries beckoning, the peasants guzzled away.

The result, in many cases, was bedlam. The peasants' occupation of Würzburg, for example, seemed on the surface a great victory, securing control of a powerful episcopal seat. But the soldiers, noblemen, and clerics in the Marienberg fortress continued to resist, and while the preparations to storm it went on, pandemonium set in. The peasants, joined by the urban poor, looted wine from the city's many ecclesiastical foundations. The rebels, wrote the local bishop's historian, "were always drunk, created much disorder in word and deed, and would be ruled by no one in the afternoons and, if they were drunk, in the mornings as well." In an effort to deter wrongdoers, three gallows were erected in the town, but the rebels took no notice, saying that "they would hang the monks, priests, and all their servants from them." According to an episcopal secretary, it was not clear whether the conflict should be called a peasants' war or a wine war.

The peasants' unruliness was causing terror among the well off and well educated—Karlstadt included. On May 10, 1525, Rothenburg (where he continued to live) swore allegiance to the peasant cause. A resolution was enacted for the seizure of ecclesiastical goods, with wine and corn stocks to be divided among the citizens. Many drank themselves senseless, and even young children could be seen staggering in the streets. In the surrounding countryside, meanwhile, the peasants were storming castles and convents. Karlstadt, who despite his inflammatory sermons remained opposed to violence, felt it was his duty to go out among the peasants to try to calm them.

On May 15, he was escorted by a supporter to a rebel camp near the front. As soon as he was outside the town gates, however, he got into an altercation with a peasant mercenary, and only the swift intervention of a young councilor kept him from being stabbed. In the camp, Karlstadt wrote an open letter to the peasants, urging them to show mercy and warning that those who engaged in violence would feel God's wrath. The peasants were furious at being thus rebuked, and Karlstadt—barely managing to escape—was forced to return alone to Rothenburg across the turbulent countryside. At one point, he approached an inn where a number of armed peasants were gathered, and when they discovered that he was not a peasant but a scholar, they tried to take everything he had; Karlstadt was barely able to talk them out of it.

In Rothenburg, Karlstadt found the place in utter turmoil. One peasant threatened to knife him; another tried to run him down. Concluding that it was no longer safe to remain, he, together with his wife and child, traveled fifty miles north to the town of Karlstadt, where he had grown up and where his mother now took them in. Even there, however, it was dangerous, and Karlstadt, after giving a sermon, was aggressively accosted in the market square. "I was among the peasants as a hare among ferocious dogs," he wrote, adding that they "would have choked me to death on several occasions had not God protected me."

The lords, too, were after Karlstadt, regarding him as an architect of the revolt. Desperate to find a haven, he looked to Saxony. For months he had been in touch with the electoral court, seeking a safe-conduct so that he could return, and with Franconia in ferment, his pleas grew more urgent. The court in turn sounded out Luther on the idea. Given his conviction that Karlstadt had helped instigate the revolt, he was firmly opposed. For the moment, though, the matter was left unresolved, for the peasants were marching uncontested through the Thuringian countryside, threatening the survival of the Reformation—and of Luther himself.

After arriving back in Wittenberg on May 6, 1525, Luther had to wait several days for the body of Frederick to arrive. In the meantime, a new edition of his *Admonition to Peace* was being prepared, and Luther decided to add a section on the growing disorder. It would eventually be published as a stand-alone tract whose title—*Against the Robbing and Murdering Hordes of Peasants*—would add to its infamy. The peasants, Luther wrote, "are robbing and raging like mad dogs." As their actions showed, the statements made in the Twelve Articles "were nothing but lies presented under the name of the gospel." The peasants' rebellion and plundering were not like murder, which produced individual victims, but like "a great fire" that "attacks and devastates a whole land," producing widows and orphans. "Therefore," he declared, in words that would become notorious,

> let everyone who can smite, slay, and stab, secretly or openly, remembering that nothing can be more poisonous, hurtful, or devilish than a rebel. It is just as when one must kill a mad dog; if you do not strike him, he will strike you, and a whole land with you.

For princes who might recoil from slaying the peasants, Luther advised them on how they could proceed with a clear conscience. If a ruler is a Christian and a believer in the new gospel, he must first offer the "mad peasants" an opportunity to come to terms, even though they did not deserve it. If no settlement could be reached, the ruler should then fulfill his duty under Romans 13 and "swiftly take to the sword." If he is in a position to punish them but does not do so, because of a reluctance to kill or shed blood, he himself "becomes guilty of all the murder and evil that these people commit." There could be "no place for patience or mercy. This is the time of the sword, not the day of grace." The rulers should feel assured that killing the peasants was a just cause, for they were simply carrying out the duties of their office, and the peasants in any case deserved death many times over. Anyone killed while fighting on the side of the rulers "may be a true martyr in the eyes of God." Anyone who perished on the side of the peasants was "an eternal firebrand of hell." A "pious Christian ought to suffer a hundred deaths rather than give a hairsbreadth of consent to the peasants' cause." Luther then repeated his central message: "Let whoever can stab, smite, slay. If you die in doing it, good for you! A more blessed death can never be yours."

"Stab, smite, slay" would become a lurid catchphrase for Luther's position on the Peasants' War. He was, in effect, calling for mass slaughter and using the Epistle to the Romans to justify it.

By its language alone, *Against the Robbing and Murdering Hordes of Peasants* would have caused shock, but the outcry over it was magnified by a sudden change of fortunes on the ground. Philip of Hesse, tired of waiting for his fellow princes to act, decided to proceed on his own. Young, brash, and dynamic, he was convinced that the peasant bands, despite their size, were hollow. On April 29, 1525, with just 350 horsemen and 1,400 footmen, he attacked the troop at Hersfeld, in Hesse, and, as he had expected, it quickly folded. On May 3, he marched on Fulda, and the peasants again scattered. By the time he reached Eisenach, the rebellion in southwestern Thuringia as a whole was fizzling.

Philip then headed toward the major center of resistance, Frankenhausen. At the end of April, the citizens of this town on the border between Thuringia and Saxony had staged a popular revolt against its overlords, the counts of Schwarzburg, and six thousand to seven thousand peasants and townsmen from Allstedt, Mansfeld, and other communities converged on it to form a unified army. Hoping to push north and open a new front among the miners, this army sent an urgent appeal for reinforcements to Thomas Müntzer and the Mühlhausen band he had formed.

Müntzer pledged his full support. But, as was so often the case with the peasants, the prospect of plunder intervened. During one expedition, the Mühlhausen force met a party of insurgents from Eichsfeld, thirty miles to the west, who wanted it to travel there and help them resist a counteroffensive by the lords. As if to publicize their cause, the Eichsfelders brought with them eight or nine wagons filled with cured meats, household goods, and other items taken from local convents. Eager for a share, the Mühlhauseners promptly set off in that direction and spent a week pillaging and burning, with scores of castles and cloisters plundered and their inmates forced to flee.

This would prove a fateful moment in the Thuringian revolt, for it tied the Mühlhausen army down in the west just as the princes were preparing to move against Frankenhausen. Finally answering Philip's pleas, Duke George of Saxony and Duke Henry of Brunswick sent detachments of men and horses to join the Hessian forces at Frankenhausen. Also responding was Duke John, Frederick's successor as elector of Saxony. Convinced that his brother had been too lenient toward the peasants, he now dispatched a Saxon brigade to the front.

When Müntzer finally did set out for Frankenhausen, he was accompanied by only three hundred men—another sign of his limited support. Arriving at the Frankenhausen camp, he immediately took charge and with typical bravado sent taunting messages to the counts of Mansfeld, the main lords in the area. To Albrecht, who sympathized with Luther, he was especially crude:

In your Lutheran gruel and Wittenbergian soup, have you not been able to find what Ezek. 37 prophesies? Besides, have you not been able to taste in your Martinian peasant shit how the same prophet goes on to say in chapter 39 that God makes all the birds under heaven devour the flesh of princes and all the dumb animals guzzle the blood of the big shots?

Despite such provocations, another count, Ernst, sent three emissaries, including a priest, to the nearby town of Artern to negotiate with the peasants. The men were immediately captured, bound, and led into a field; a debate then broke out as to whether they should be executed. No decision could be reached, and the three were transferred to Frankenhausen. Müntzer called an assembly in the square by the gate, and, speaking before several thousand men, he asked whether anyone had charges to lay against the three. The prisoners were then interrogated while being subjected to gruesome tortures; finally, with Müntzer's assent, they were beheaded.

Soon afterward, the Frankenhausen band took up a position on the flat summit of a hill outside town and arranged their wagons and cannons in a sort of laager. Overnight the men waited, anxious and in prayer. In the morning, they saw to their horror that what had seemed a position of strength actually left them highly exposed. The Saxon forces had joined the Hessian and Brunswick cavalry to form a formidable army of between six thousand and eight thousand infantrymen and two thousand cavalry. The peasants had roughly the same number of men, but most were inexperienced, and they had but one or two pieces of artillery and a few horses. Desperate, they sent a message to the nobles saying that they wished harm to no one—they wanted only divine justice—and appealing for mercy.

The reply quickly came: if the peasants turned over the false prophet Müntzer and his top accomplices, they would receive favorable treatment. Müntzer, seeking to rouse the camp to reject the offer, began preaching with the usual messianic conviction, citing the examples of Gideon and David, who with small forces had prevailed over much larger ones. On his third day of preaching, an atmospheric halo formed a ring around the sun. Müntzer claimed it was a rainbow like the emblem on the flag of his "eternal council" and urged the peasant-soldiers to show courage and fight. Taking the halo to be a sign of God's blessing, they decided not to surrender Müntzer. On the following day (May 15), the soldiers began singing the hymn "Come, Holy Spirit." What came instead was a salvo from the princes' cannons. The princes' foot soldiers and horses then attacked the nearest of the rebel troops.

Panicking, the peasants broke ranks and fled, and the wagon stockade was quickly penetrated. The peasants raced toward Frankenhausen, but the princes' forces gave chase and cut them down by the hundreds. Most managed to make it into the town, where they desperately sought shelter in its houses and churches, but the princes' troops stormed in and, in an orgy of stabbing and smiting, killed everyone they could find. Within hours, five thousand lay dead. The princes suffered no more than half a dozen casualties. Not satisfied, they ordered three hundred prisoners brought into the square before the Rathaus to be beheaded. The women begged for mercy for their husbands and brothers. They were told that if they killed two captured priests (seen as the true source of the trouble) with their own hands, their men would be spared. Given clubs, the women proceeded to beat the priests so savagely that, according to one eyewitness, "their heads were like unto a rotten cabbage, and the brains did cling unto the clubs." The men were freed.

Müntzer, on whose head a high price had been set, managed to reach Frankenhausen, where he entered a deserted house near the city gate. Hoping to avoid being recognized, he took off some of his clothes and lay down on a bed. Shortly afterward, the servant of a knight entered the house and discovered him. Müntzer pretended to be ill with fever, but when the servant searched his knapsack, he found letters from Count Albrecht. He at once informed his masters, and Müntzer was seized and brought before the princes. He was then taken to Count Ernst's castle at Heldrungen to be tortured and interrogated.

Meanwhile, the princes marched their armies from Frankenhausen to Mühlhausen. Before such a mighty force, the population cowered behind the city's walls. On May 21 or 22, 1525, as those walls were being breached, Heinrich Pfeiffer, who had remained in the city, escaped along with three hundred followers, hoping to join the insurgents in Franconia. A detachment was sent in pursuit, and Pfeiffer was captured near Eisenach. Three days later, Mühlhausen opened its gates to the princes' troops. The citizens were forced to surrender their arms, and the "eternal council" that had been installed by Müntzer and Pfeiffer was deposed and the old council reinstated. Executions of the burgomaster and others quickly followed. Mühlhausen's main fortifications were razed, and only by paying an enormous ransom was the city spared sacking.

*   *   *

The rout at Frankenhausen and the surrender of Mühlhausen would prove a turning point in the revolt. As the news circulated that thousands of peasants had been slaughtered, it spread fear among the rebels and raised hopes among the princes. As disruptive and destructive as the peasants had been, the princes—eager to ensure their utter submission—would now pursue them with unrestrained savagery.

In the forefront was Truchsess George von Waldburg. With his force augmented by troops returning from the fighting in Italy, he unleashed a vengeful pacification campaign in Franconia, burning villages, hanging rebels, massacring civilians. On May 12, at Böblingen (sixty miles northwest of Ulm), the sight of the approaching Swabian force sent the twelve-thousand-man peasant army into flight. Giving pursuit, Waldburg's horsemen stabbed, slashed, and cut to pieces every man they could catch, and for seven or eight miles the way was strewn with bodies. In Ochsenfurt, another five thousand peasants were slaughtered. Neighboring villages were set on fire, and all inhabitants who were not consumed by it were put to the sword. It was a decisive blow to the rebellion in Franconia.

By June 5, the Swabian League army was on the outskirts of Würzburg. An earlier rebel assault on the Marienberg fortress had been repelled at a cost of many lives, but five thousand to six thousand peasants and burghers remained under arms and determined to defend the town. Now, however, the burgomaster and members of the old council entered into secret negotiations with Waldburg's representatives, and Waldburg and hundreds of horsemen and mercenaries with halberds were let in. They met little resistance. All local citizens and peasants who had helped lead the revolt were ordered to assemble at three separate sites. Each site was then surrounded by armed men. Waldburg appeared on horseback in the market square, accompanied by several executioners with swords. After denouncing the men for their crimes and declaring their lives forfeit, he retired with the princes into the Rathaus to deliberate. A little more than an hour later he reappeared, and the reading of names began. According to a report by the city secretary, three executioners stepped forward "like roaming wolves" and at once beheaded a peasant captain, a pewterer, a painter, a coppersmith, and a barber. Twenty-four people were beheaded at one of the other sites and thirty more at the third. All together, eighty-one people were executed, "guilty or innocent, as the whim took them." The rank and file then had staves placed in their hands as a sign of surrender and were driven from the town. As they marched out, however, they were set upon by the mercenaries who were prowling about, and many more were slain.

While this bloodletting was going on in Würzburg, Margrave Kasimir of Brandenburg-Ansbach was carrying out a similarly sadistic campaign in the surrounding countryside. In Kitzingen, eighty were beheaded and sixty-nine had their eyes put out; twelve died from the pain and others were left to lie in the street. It was forbidden on severe penalty to shelter or guide them or give any medical assistance. After Rothenburg was taken on June 20, 1525, twenty-five rebels, including the town's most prominent preacher, were beheaded in two days.

For sheer butchery, however, Alsace would stand out. Responding to the pleas of its nobles and burghers, Duke Antoine of Lorraine assembled a large force that included German, Italian, and East European mercenaries. In mid-May, they appeared before Saverne, where the main Alsatian force was encamped. On May 17, a body of peasants that had come to relieve the force at the town was defeated and driven back to an outlying village, which was surrounded and burned. After fierce fighting, the duke's army was able to penetrate the peasant stockade and enter the village. The defenders took refuge in the church, but fires broke out on all sides, and when the flames reached the church itself and they begged for mercy, it was too late. Rushing from the building, they were mercilessly cut down. In all, between two thousand and six thousand were slain. The East European mercenaries added an element of cold-blooded cruelty. Children as young as eight, ten, and twelve were killed; women and girls were dragged through the cornfields, raped, and murdered.

When news of these atrocities reached Saverne, the town surrendered, and the next morning the peasants opened the gates. Promised mercy by the duke, they streamed out without their arms and bearing white staves; the duke's freelances accompanied them. "Long live Luther!" some peasants shouted, taunting the soldiers. A quarrel broke out between a mercenary and a peasant who feared being robbed, and suddenly a cry went up among the soldiers: "Strike! It is allowed us!" Skirmishing quickly escalated into slaying, with the freelances pursuing and striking down the defenseless peasants as they desperately tried to reenter the town. There the killing continued, with not only peasants but also many town dwellers cut down. The princes finally intervened to stop the bloodshed, but not before sixteen thousand to twenty thousand lay dead. So many bodies were heaped at the town's gates that it was barely possible to pass through. The rotting flesh gave off such a stench that many women would eventually flee the area, some of them abandoning their children, who perished of hunger.

In the Black Forest, a Swiss chronicler noted, the lords stripped the peasants "of their honor and weapons, especially their firearms and armor, their fine clothing, berets, and leather shoes" and prohibited them from visiting inns "on pain of life and property." They were prohibited from banding together and sounding the alarm and "had to undertake an oath to seize, stab, and execute any refugees." Even those peasants who had resisted the rebels and been useful to the lords and were therefore "hardly or not guilty at all" were "shorn and butchered." Finally, not only were all the demands that the peasants had put forward rejected, but the rejection was "enforced with strict prohibitions and relentless punishments. In sum, what the peasants and their supporters undertook, namely, to free the Gospel and themselves through rebellion, was itself overthrown by rebellion, so that evangelical teaching and preaching were accused under the names of Luther, Zwingli, and the Anabaptists of being 'evan-hellical' and rebellious." The gospel in many places was "rooted out with severe destruction of life and property. And so it was that the burdened peasantry had slipped their cart traces, but were now bound to the wagon with chains."

Here and there, pockets of rebels held out. Near Basel, fighting would continue into the summer, and in Austria, where many miners had joined the peasants, resistance persisted well into 1526. In most of Germany, however, the revolt was quashed by midsummer 1525. The death toll was estimated at between 100,000 and 130,000; another 50,000 became fugitives. The peasants were certainly guilty of many crimes. Coercion and threats were used to force many to join the rebel cause, and those who refused faced social ostracism and economic hardship. The drunken sprees and wanton behavior spread much terror. But it was property that bore the brunt of the peasants' fury. Most of the carnage was inflicted by the armies of the princes. For years afterward, the maimed and blinded could be seen stumbling pitifully about, a chilling reminder of the price of protest.

No one fared worse than Thomas Müntzer. Held in the dungeon of the castle at Heldrungen, he was subjected to various tortures. Thus brutalized, he admitted to a long list of offenses—that he had believed that the nobility with their many castles were "grievously oppressive" and had imposed compulsory dues and other forms of exploitation; that the purpose of the rebellion had been to make all Christians equal; that he wanted the holy sacrament to be adored not in an external way "but only in the spirit," with each individual allowed to decide for himself. Müntzer also stated that he wished to die "a true and reconciled member" of the Catholic Church. The agony he suffered cast doubt on the sincerity of these statements. Nonetheless, his "confession" was quickly circulated, first in handwritten copies and then in print, in an effort to discredit him.

On May 25, 1525, Müntzer along with Pfeiffer was brought to Duke George's camp at Görmar. Two days later the sentence was handed down. Müntzer was so physically and mentally shattered that he could barely say the Apostles' Creed. He stammered that he had attempted matters beyond his power, and he urged the nobles to deal mercifully with their subjects. He then fell silent, awaiting the executioner's stroke. It quickly came. Pfeiffer, who scorned confession and the taking of the sacrament, was similarly dispatched. The heads and bodies of both men were struck on pikestaffs and displayed outside the city of Mühlhausen. Twenty-six others were also executed.

Luther received a copy of Müntzer's confession from John Rühel, the Mansfeld counselor. Rühel added an account of the princes' vengeful campaign in Thuringia, including the incident in Frankenhausen in which the prisoners' wives had cudgeled two priests to death. Many of Luther's supporters, Rühel noted, believed that Luther had allowed the peasants "to be slain without pity by the tyrants." In Leipzig it was being said that because of Frederick's death, "you are afraid for your skin and play the hypocrite to Duke George by approving of his deeds."

Luther was hearing similar charges on all sides. His *Against the Robbing and Murdering Hordes*, with its exhortation to smite and slay the peasants, had appeared as the mass killing was under way, making it seem as if the princes were following his advice, although in fact the bloodletting had begun before its publication. Whatever the timing, Luther's full-throated support for slaughtering the peasants was causing widespread revulsion. The title of a tract issued by a Catholic polemicist summed up the case against him: *Luther Speaks with Forked Tongue, or How Luther, on the One Hand, Led the Peasants Astray, While, on the Other, He Condemned Them.* From Magdeburg, his old friend Nikolaus von Amsdorf wrote that Luther was being called a toady of the princes.

Luther did not care. The peasants, he believed, were getting exactly what they deserved. "They have gone mad and will not hear the Word, and so they must bear the rod, that is, the guns," he wrote to Rühel. "It serves them right. We ought to pray for them that they may be obedient; if not, let the shot whistle, or they will make things a thousandfold worse." As for Müntzer, Luther was greatly displeased by his confession—not because of the savage means used to extract it, but because of its content. Upset that Müntzer had maintained to the end that he had done no wrong, Luther observed, "I should have asked very different questions." He took satisfaction, however, in his execution: "Anyone who has seen Müntzer can say that he has seen the very devil, and at his worst. O God! If this is the spirit that is in the peasants it is high time that they were killed like mad dogs." To Amsdorf he wrote that "it is better that all the peasants be killed than that the magistrates and princes perish, because the peasants took the sword without divine authority." Under the princes "it is possible for both kingdoms to exist. Therefore no pity, no patience is due the peasants."

With so much blood being shed across Germany, Luther was under intense pressure to explain or even retract his strong language, and with great reluctance he agreed to draft *An Open Letter on the Harsh Book Against the Peasants.* As was so often the case when he felt on the defensive, he restated his position in even starker terms. He was proud that his tract against the peasants had been so severely criticized, he wrote, and all who condemned it were themselves "rebels at heart." To those who said that he was being unmerciful, Luther (relying as always on Romans 13) wrote that "this is not a question of mercy; we are talking of God's word. It is God's will that the king be honored and the rebels destroyed." The "Scripture passages that speak of mercy apply only to the kingdom of God" and "not to the kingdom of the world," for "it is a Christian's duty not only to be merciful, but also to endure every kind of suffering—robbery, arson, murder, devil, and hell." The tool of that kingdom "is not a wreath of roses or a flower of love, but a naked sword; and a sword is a symbol of wrath, severity, and punishment." Those who are advocates of the peasants "say that we are flattering the furious princes and lords when we teach that they are to punish the wicked. And yet they are themselves ten times worse flatterers of the murderous scoundrels and wicked peasants." Therefore, he went on, "as I wrote then so I write now: Let no one have mercy on the obstinate, hardened, blinded peasants who refuse to listen to reason; but let everyone, as he is able, strike, hew, stab, and slay, as though among mad dogs."

Interestingly, Luther conceded the point—made by some of his critics—that the peasants had slain no one in the way they themselves were being slain. The reason for this, he insisted, was that they had forced people to do what they wanted. To those who argued that the princes were wielding their sword cruelly, Luther said that when he had the time, he would attack them, too, "for in my office of teacher, a prince is the same to me as a peasant." For now, he wrote, "the donkey needs to feel the whip, and a people need to be ruled with force." As for the complaint that it was innocents who were suffering the most, Luther maintained that it is ever thus in wartime. "These are plagues that God sends; and they are always well deserved." It is time "to stop complaining and murmuring and thank God that, by his grace and mercy, we have not experienced the greater misfortune that the devil intended to bring us through the peasants." The work of the head of government is so essential to society that when he comes under attack, everyone must help rescue him "by stabbing, hewing, and killing" and risking his own life and goods. Even though he himself was a clergyman, if he saw his own lord in danger, "I would forget my spiritual office and stab and hew as long as my heart beat," for rebellion "is a crime that deserves neither a court trial nor mercy."

With such statements, disillusionment was setting in even among his staunchest backers. Hermann Mühlpfort, the mayor of Zwickau, to whom Luther had dedicated *The Freedom of a Christian*, wrote to a correspondent in Wittenberg, "Doctor Martin has fallen into great disfavor with the common people, also with both learned and unlearned." The preachers in Zwickau "have been greatly disconcerted and amazed by the tracts recently issued." The nobility would rely on Luther's statements to convince themselves that the blood they had spilled would "gain them eternal salvation." Whoever now spoke out on behalf of the common man would be accused of being a rebel.

A nobleman named Heinrich von Einsiedel, feeling pangs of conscience at the corvées (forced labor) and other obligations being reimposed on the peasants, wrote to Luther to ask his opinion. He need not feel troubled, Luther replied. In fact, it would not be a good thing if the corvées were eliminated, for without such burdens, the common man would become overbearing. However harsh such treatment might seem, it actually pleased God. Melanchthon thought that even serfdom was too soft for the obstinate Germans and held that the lord's right of punishment and the servant's duty of obedience should be absolute.

Writing to John Rühel and other Mansfeld officials, Luther acknowledged how radically his image had changed: "What an outcry of Harrow, my dear sirs, has been caused by my pamphlet against the peasants! All is now forgotten that God has done for the world through me. Now lords, parsons and peasants are all against me and threaten my death."

Until 1525, the reform movement had been national in scope and Luther its undisputed standard-bearer. The hopes of the German people had rested with him, and his every word and pronouncement had been eagerly followed and analyzed. Now he seemed the leader of a faction. Far from being the Joshua who would lead the people into the promised land, he seemed the Judas who had betrayed them. Luther was so loathed by ordinary Germans that it became dangerous for him to travel outside Wittenberg. Among peasants, he was reviled as Dr. Liar and a lapdog of the princes. According to Friedrich Engels, Luther extracted from the

Bible "a veritable hymn to the authorities ordained by God—a feat hardly exceeded by any lackey of absolute monarchy."

As acidly as he mocked Luther, Engels extolled Müntzer, calling him a "magnificent figure" whose political program represented "a genius' anticipation of the conditions for the emancipation of the proletarian element that had just begun to develop among the plebeians." Ironically, Engels, in attributing such importance to Müntzer, was following Luther's own lead. He was not alone. From the time of the Enlightenment on, this rabid apostle of religious violence would become a symbol of revolutionary struggle. The German Democratic Republic would place an image of Müntzer on its five-mark note, and Mühlhausen would be renamed Thomas-Müntzer-Stadt.

Over time, Luther would come to recognize his own contribution to the peasant calamity. "I, Martin Luther, slew all the peasants in the uprising," he would say in his Table Talk, "for I ordered that they be put to death; all their blood is on my neck. But I refer it all to our Lord God, who commanded me to speak as I did."

The peasants themselves turned irrevocably away not only from Luther but from the Reformation as a whole. In their view, the new gospel, which had stirred them to action, had deserted them at the decisive moment. Some would become atheists in all but name. Others would glumly return to the Catholic fold. Quite a few heeded the radicals whom Luther had scorned and became Anabaptists. Everywhere cynicism toward organized religion took hold. Though social and economic protests would still periodically break out, the awakening of the lower classes stalled, and the masses in general became sullen and apathetic. Though the nobles could not afford to wipe out the tillers of the soil as a class, serfdom was strengthened, and it would persist in parts of Germany into the nineteenth century.

Intellectual progress faltered as well. Priceless archival and manuscript collections were lost, and learning as a whole—already under assault from the radicals—became even more suspect. Censorship increased, support for scholarship receded, and the Renaissance love of books and ideas was replaced by a grim emphasis on piety, doctrine, and orthodoxy. Luther's own frequency of publication would fall off after 1525, and the great flood of popular pamphlets that had eulogized the evangelical peasant would suddenly dry up.

The populist preachers vanished. Every day, Erasmus observed, "priests are arrested, tortured, hanged, decapitated, or burnt at the stake." In many regions, strict measures were taken to ensure that the Bible was taught according to traditional interpretations. In August 1525, the margraves Kasimir and George of Brandenburg issued an edict ordering all pastors to teach that Scripture makes clear that "Christian freedom does not consist in the removal of rents, interest, dues, tithes, taxes, services, or other similar external burdens" but "is only an inward and spiritual thing" and that "all subjects are obliged to obey their authorities" in all temporal affairs. In Austria, Archduke Ferdinand, in the course of suppressing the revolt, would seek to eradicate Lutheran influences and reinforce the power of the Catholic Church. Of seventy-one people accused of heresy who were brought before the Austrian court at Ensisheim, only one was acquitted; the rest were burned, drowned, or broken on the wheel. The current Catholic character of both Austria and Bavaria can be traced not only to the vigorous policies of the Counter-Reformation but also to the fierce suppression of the new gospel in the aftermath of the Peasants' War.

The war's impact would extend much deeper than that, however. The emphasis on resistance and individual conscience that Luther had embraced in his early years receded. He would instead relentlessly stress the need for acquiescence and suffering. In his preaching, he would proclaim with monotonous regularity the importance of obedience to the government and submission to the state. With his stress on conformity, respect for authority, and acceptance of injustice, Luther would imprint German Lutheranism with the idea that Christians must at all times accommodate themselves to political and social conditions and that organized resistance to authority was not only futile but unjustified.

In this landscape of retreat and ruin, Luther was determined to move ahead with his plans to marry Katharina von Bora. His friends were unanimously opposed to his choice, thinking her unsuitable, but Luther did not care, and the ceremony took place at the Black Cloister on June 13, 1525, with little fanfare and only five people present, including Lucas Cranach and his wife, who stood in for his parents; Bugenhagen officiated. After the ceremony, the forty-one-year-old Martin and the twenty-six-year-old Katharina went to the nuptial bed and lay down on it in front of Justus Jonas, who served as the customary witness (and who then left them). The next day the same circle gathered for a celebratory breakfast. In a letter to Nikolaus von Amsdorf, Luther admitted, "I neither love my wife nor burn for her, but esteem her." He had married her, he explained, "to silence the mouths which are accustomed to bicker at me"; that is, which had spread rumors about his relations with Katharina. He also wanted to please his father, who had asked him to marry and leave descendants, and to set an example for the many who are "as yet afraid even in the present great light of the Gospel."

Luther's decision to marry was thus as much a political as a personal act, putting the final seal on his break with the Catholic Church. His timing, however, caused an uproar. As a pamphlet by a student put it, "Everywhere the smoke still rises from the ravaged villages, thousands of peasants are led away in chains, the rivers are red with the blood that has been shed," yet Luther had chosen that very moment to carry out this celebratory act.

Even Melanchthon was taken aback. To his great annoyance, he was not invited to—nor even informed of—the wedding. Writing to his friend Joachim Camerarius three days after the ceremony, he observed, "You might be amazed that at this unfortunate time, when good and excellent men everywhere are in distress, he not only does not sympathize with them, but, as it seems, waxes wanton and diminishes his reputation, just when Germany has especial need of his judgment and authority." Melanchthon hoped that Luther's new situation might "sober him down, so that he will discard the low buffoonery which we have often censored." Melanchthon denied the rumors racing across Germany that Luther and Katharina had had sexual relations prior to their marriage. (Well aware of the sensitivity of his letter, Melanchthon wrote it entirely in Greek, and its contents did not become generally known until the late nineteenth century.)

The criticism of Luther's decision to marry simply reinforced his belief that it was the right thing to do. To spite his enemies, he decided to hold a very public feast, scheduled for June 27, 1525, and invitations were sent to many friends and relatives. Luther wrote to Leonhard Koppe, the man who had helped free Katharina and her fellow nuns, to ask him to bring not herring but a keg of "the best Torgau beer." In a letter to John Rühel and other Mansfeld officials, Luther took note of the continuing violence in Thuringia: "The land is in such a state that I hardly dare ask you to undertake the journey; however, if you can do so, pray come, along with my dear father and mother." His parents did come. After a special service at the town church, a banquet was held at the Black Cloister, followed by an *Ehrentanz* (a kind of square dance) at the Rathaus. The couple then set up house in the newly renovated friary.

Remarkably, around the same time as their celebration, there appeared on their doorstep a most unexpected visitor: Karlstadt. Threatened, hunted, and terrified that he would suffer the same fate as Müntzer, Karlstadt on June 12 had written to Luther from Frankfurt, asking for his forgiveness and help in returning to Saxony. Karlstadt had then made his way to Wittenberg, and he now threw himself on Luther's mercy. Having just gotten married, Luther was furious at the prospect of this heavenly prophet who had called him a "bloody sow" and a "mad sophist" living under his roof. But Karlstadt had nowhere else to go. As the price for giving him shelter, Luther demanded that he prepare and publish a full recantation of his doctrine of the Eucharist and that he promise never to write, preach, or teach again. Karlstadt felt (as he would later recall) that he would have been better off if he had been among the Turks, but he had little choice. The retraction did appear, and for the next two to three months he would live in secret in the Black Cloister, keeping the newlyweds company.

FATAL DISSENSION

In the years before his marriage, Luther had led a spartan and solitary life. Working himself to exhaustion, he would fall into bed "oblivious of everything," as he later put it. For a full year before his wedding day, his bed had not been made, and the straw was rotting from his sweat. Now he suddenly found his life joined to that of another. In the first year of marriage, he observed in his Table Talk, a man "has strange thoughts." When sitting at the table, he thinks, "Before I was alone; now there are two." When waking up in bed, "he sees a pair of pigtails lying beside him which he hadn't seen there before."

At first, Katharina's loquacity annoyed him. Having spent so much of her life in enforced silence, she now seemed determined to make up for it. Sitting next to Luther at her spinning wheel while he was engrossed in study, she would suddenly interject questions and observations. "Doctor, is the grandmaster [of Prussia] the margrave's brother?" she once asked. Luther informed her with exasperation that the grand master *was* the margrave. "I must be patient with the pope," he observed, "I must be patient with the *Schwärmer*, I must be patient with the Junkers, I must be patient with my family, I must be patient with Katharina von Bora. . . . My whole life is nothing but patience."

But the advantages of wedlock quickly asserted themselves. Despite her lack of experience in domestic affairs, Katharina proved an astute household manager. The Black Cloister, with its large rectory, drafty corridors, and cramped cells, seemed an unpromising home—because of Frederick's stinginess, it had never been finished—but John, his successor, would prove far more generous. At one point, he essentially deeded over the structure to the Luthers. He also provided one hundred guldens as a wedding gift and doubled Luther's salary to two hundred guldens. To Luther's surprise, the couple also received twenty guldens from Luther's old adversary, Albrecht of Mainz. Clearly, the archbishop was hoping to stay on Luther's good side in case he decided to go over to the Reformation. Luther saw the money as tainted and wanted to return it, but Katharina, seeing the many uses to which it could be put, insisted on keeping it. It was their first serious marital quarrel, and Katharina prevailed. Measurements were taken for a new mattress and sent to Gabriel Zwilling, the former fire-breathing friar, who was now a considerably more sedate pastor in Torgau and who would help the Luthers with their household needs.

Katharina quickly took stock of the many improvements that needed doing, including refurbishing the second-floor room that would become their main living space. Just west of the cloister stood the *Brauhaus*, or brewery, and Katharina, assuming control, prepared the family beer from the barley sent annually by the elector. She also took over the barnyard, with its pigs, cows, hens, and ducks, as well as an orchard outside town that produced apples, pears, grapes, and nuts. "It is a good thing that God came to my aid and gave me a wife," Luther later observed. "She takes care of domestic matters, so that I don't have to be responsible for [them]."

That was fortunate, for in such matters he proved inept. At one point Luther acquired a lathe with the idea of doing some carpentry, but he never got the hang of it. He was no more skilled at bookkeeping. One thing Katharina felt comfortable entrusting to him was the garden, and Luther quickly discovered its pleasures. He wrote to Wenceslas Link in Nuremberg to ask for seeds and tools for boring and turning. Soon, lettuces, cabbages, peas, beans, and cucumbers were sprouting, and Luther expressed wonder at the "immense amount of space" taken up by the melons and gourds.

Luther's tending to his garden suggests his newly reduced horizons. In the autumn of 1525, he received an invitation to Spalatin's wedding. After Frederick's death, Spalatin had resigned his post at the electoral court and taken a position as a pastor in Altenburg, seventy-five miles away. Luther wrote back to say that he would not be able to attend, because Katharina feared for his safety. A few weeks later, he sent Spalatin a racy message about his new wife, who was also named Katharina: "When you have your Katharina in bed, sweetly embracing and kissing her, think: Lo, this being, the best little creation of God, has been given me by Christ." On the same night that Spalatin received the letter, Luther continued, "I will love my wife in memory of you with the same act."

In short, the former friar was learning the joys of sex. As he would later remark, people sin more when they are alone; man is meant to be part of a couple. Having railed in print against the Church's embrace of celibacy and virginity, Luther was now putting his own personal stamp on his rebellion. In doing so, he was making concrete the revolution in sexual attitudes that Erasmus had helped set in motion with his praise of matrimony and questions about the sacramental status of marriage.

But the thought of the unfrocked monk and runaway nun having physical relations set off a flood of salacious rumors and sneers. "Death to Whoring!" was Duke George's succinct greeting to the new couple. One disaffected student would later write a raunchy satire, titled *Monachopornomachia*—"The Battle Between the Monks and the Whores." An early exercise in pornography, it alleged wild liaisons between the pious men of Wittenberg and the nymphs brought by Katharina from the convent.

Even Erasmus fed the mill, writing to a colleague in October 1525 that "a few days after the singing of the wedding hymn the new bride gave birth to a child!" Erasmus also surmised that Luther's marriage was the reason that he had failed to respond to *The Freedom of the Will*. "Luther is now becoming more moderate," he wrote in September. "There is nothing so wild that it cannot be tamed by a wife."

He was wrong on both counts. Katharina did not show the first signs of pregnancy until three months after the wedding, and it was not until June 7, 1526—nearly a year after their union—that she gave birth to a son, whom they named Hans, after Luther's father.

Nor was marriage mellowing Luther. As he settled into his new domestic life, he simply could not bear the thought of responding to Erasmus's vainglorious text. Physically exhausted and emotionally drained, he longed for a break from the punishing routine of writing and lecturing, preaching and contending. But there was growing talk about his failure to respond. *De Libero Arbitrio* had appeared in twelve editions in 1524 and was the subject of vigorous debate among German scholars. Seven Strasbourg theologians, led by Wolfgang Capito, sent Luther a letter describing the confusion Erasmus's work was causing in the Netherlands and Cologne. "What is he up to?" they wondered.

> Does he not everywhere brush aside the authority of Scripture and prefer the calm of the Antichrist to the revolutionary character of the kingdom of Christ? . . . We therefore implore you for Christ's sake: Don't let yourself be appeased by flesh and blood! Give priority to what you once wrote Erasmus—for the sake of Christ one must be able to hate one's parents. . . . You know how much the Lord has sought to lay on you, how many thousands hang on to your lips.

Joachim Camerarius, whose visit to Erasmus in the spring of 1524 had left him with a reservoir of esteem for the Dutchman but who remained devoted to Luther and Melanchthon, was deeply troubled by *The Freedom of the Will*. Could Erasmus be correct? On a visit to Wittenberg in August 1525, he pressed Katharina to convince her husband of the importance of replying, and at her prodding Luther gave in. "I am altogether taken up with my reply to Erasmus," he wrote to Nicholas Hausmann on September 27. Having broken so spectacularly with the peasants, he now prepared for a decisive reckoning with the humanists.

Given the fury that Luther had provoked with his tracts against both the peasants and the sacramentarians, and given the civil tone of Erasmus's own book, he could have been expected to moderate his language. But Luther remained temperamentally incapable of such restraint, and the loathing and resentment he felt for Erasmus ensured a fierce response.

Still, more than personal pique was involved. With the challenge from Erasmus, Luther felt that his entire gospel was at stake. *The Bondage of the Will* (*De Servo Arbitrio*), as he gravely titled his response, would be one of his last important theological tracts; of all his books, he would later say, only it, together with his catechisms, was worth preserving. The central tenet of Luther's theology—that the sinner is justified by faith and grace alone, without the works of the law—rested on the idea that humans are incapable of finding salvation through their own acts. If an individual could choose to perform deeds that merited God's favor, Luther's whole system would collapse. What for Erasmus was a lively clash of ideas was for Luther a matter of life and death, and he brought to the task an intensity to match.

Working in his cramped study, he adopted the mocking tone he favored when seeking to bring low the lofty. As his point of entry, he slyly used his long delay in responding. "That I have taken so long to reply to your *Diatribe Concerning Free Will*, venerable Erasmus, has been contrary to everyone's expectation and to my own custom," he wrote. There perhaps had been some surprise "at this new and unwonted forbearance—or fear!—in Luther," with many congratulating Erasmus on his victory and triumphantly chanting, "Ho, ho! Has that Maccabee, that most obstinate Assertor, at last met his match, and dares not open his mouth against him?" And he had to confess that Erasmus, being far superior to him in eloquence and native genius, had dampened his spirit and eagerness and left him exhausted "before I could strike a blow."

That, however, was not due to any anxiety at being vanquished. Rather, it was because Erasmus had treated the subject at hand with such reasonableness that it was impossible for Luther to be angry with him. Erasmus had moreover failed to say anything important that had not already been said. It was sad to see him convey such unworthy material with such rich elegance, like "refuse or ordure being carried in gold and silver vases." If there remained anyone who had absorbed so little of the new gospel that he could be moved by Erasmus's arguments, Luther had thought, he did not deserve to be rescued by him. It was thus neither the pressure of work, nor the difficulty of the task, nor Erasmus's great eloquence, that had sapped his desire to reply, "but sheer disgust, anger, and contempt."

That he had finally decided to respond was due to the urgings of many faithful Christians, who, pointing to Erasmus's great authority, said that the truth of Christian doctrine was in peril. He actually owed Erasmus thanks, for in stating the case for free will with such vigor, he had helped show more clearly than ever that the idea "is a pure fiction." Having at last decided to write, Luther hoped that, just as he had put up with Erasmus's ignorance, Erasmus would bear with his lack of eloquence.

Turning his attention to the preface of *De Libero Arbitrio*, Luther focused on what he considered Erasmus's greatest offense: his reluctance to make assertions. This, he wrote, was not the mark of a true Christian mind. Asserting meant adhering, affirming, maintaining, persevering. "Take away assertions and you take away Christianity"—indeed, all religion and piety. Erasmus's language was that of the skeptic—of one who does not care what anyone believes as long as the peace of the world is maintained and who thinks it is silly to contend over Christian dogma. Erasmus thus showed that he was at heart "a Lucian or some other pig from Epicurus' sty, who, having no belief in God himself, secretly ridicules all who have a belief and confess it." A "pig from Epicurus' sty" (an image from Horace's *Epistles*) referred to the Epicurean school of philosophy, which considered self-contented equanimity the greatest good. In applying the phrase to Erasmus, Luther was accusing him not just of misapprehending key Christian doctrines but of lacking faith altogether.

Luther took similar offense at Erasmus's position that the Bible is not always clear. If some scriptural passages seem difficult, it is due to human ignorance of their vocabulary and grammar. On all essential matters, the meaning of the Bible is consistent and unambiguous. Luther was further riled by Erasmus's placing of free will among those subjects not suitable for general discussion. If it was superfluous to ask whether God foreknows and foreordains everything and whether our will can accomplish anything pertaining to salvation, then what was relevant or useful to know? "*Das ist zu viel*"—"That is too much"—Luther exclaimed, using German for the first and only time in his tract.

Finally arriving at the substance of the matter, Luther stated his position with unshakable certainty: It is fundamentally necessary and salutary for a Christian to know that God foresees and does all things "by his immutable, eternal, and infallible will. Here is a thunderbolt by which free will is completely prostrated and shattered." If there were any doubts about whether God foreknows all things, then one could not place full trust in his promises, and Christian faith would be entirely extinguished. Amid all the adversities Christians face, their one supreme consolation is "to know that God does not lie, but does all things immutably, and that his will can neither be resisted nor changed nor hindered."

In refusing to acknowledge this, Erasmus's book was so impious and blasphemous as to be without equal. The book treated free will as if it were simply a matter between the two of them of recovering a sum of money, the loss of which should not cause much stir. For Erasmus, outward peace and tranquility were "far more important than faith, conscience, salvation, the Word of God, the glory of Christ, and God himself." What Luther was after in this dispute was so serious and necessary that "it ought to be asserted and defended to the death," even if the whole world had to be thrown into "strife and confusion" and returned to "total chaos." As he had in the period before Worms and while he was at the Wartburg, Luther cited Christ's declaration that he came with a sword and Paul's statement that he sought to turn the world upside down. "Truth and doctrine must be preached always, openly, and constantly, and never accommodated or concealed." "Tumults, commotions, disturbances, seditions, sects, discords, wars"—all these were ways in which the world "is shaken and shattered on account of the Word of God."

Luther did not deny freedom of choice to man in all realms. Where purely earthly matters are concerned, such as what to eat, whether to marry, and which vocation to pursue, he wrote, man is free to choose how to use his faculties and possessions. But when it comes to man's relation to God and to matters pertaining to salvation and damnation, he "has no free choice, but is a captive, subject and slave either of the will of God or the will of Satan." The human will is placed between these two "like a beast of burden." If ridden by God, it goes where God wills; if ridden by Satan, it goes where Satan wills. The beast itself is incapable of choosing its rider.

This image (which would become famous) captures Luther's brute concept of human nature. Man is but a donkey to be ridden by forces beyond his control or understanding. The contrast with Erasmus's gentle image of the fumbling child guided by his loving father could not be sharper.

To prove the truth of his assertions, Luther of course relied on Scripture. Taking on Erasmus's citations one by one, he produced a dense thicket of exegesis. On God's hardening of the pharaoh's heart, for instance, he went on for many pages trying to show (on the basis of passages from the Old Testament) that God imposed his will on the Egyptian ruler in the face of human intention. Judas, he maintained, was not forced to betray Christ, but his act was necessary in the eternal unfolding of the divine plan of redemption; God in his foreknowledge had seen what Judas would do. Luther was especially dismissive of Erasmus's argument that the many commandments in the Bible imply man's ability to carry them out, and he derided the Dutchman for his failure to understand verbs of the imperative mood—"something that even grammarians and street urchins know."

More generally, Luther taunted Erasmus for the poor quality of his scholarship. "I am amazed and astounded that a man can be so utterly ignorant of Holy Writ who has worked so long and hard at it." Where, he wondered, was "that sharp Greek mind of yours, which used to invent lies with at least some semblance of charm, but is here uttering falsehoods naked and unadorned?" Luther gleefully mocked Erasmus's title, calling it "our Diatribe," "Madam Diatribe," and "that dilettante Diatribe." "See how the invincible and all-powerful truth has cornered witless Diatribe and turned wisdom into folly."

Of all the charges Luther leveled at Erasmus, the most serious was Pelagianism. Nearly ten years earlier, in his first approach to Erasmus (through Spalatin), Luther had sought to warn him about his bias in favor of free will and human perfectibility. It was now clear that Erasmus had learned nothing. "No one since the Pelagians has written more correctly about free choice than Erasmus!" he wisecracked. Luther, meanwhile, remained committed to the same notions about divine omnipotence and human depravity that he had arrived at in his initial lectures on the Psalms and Romans. The description at Romans 9:20–21 of man being in God's hands like clay in the potter's, he wrote, "stands unshaken as a most effective demonstration that freedom of choice is as nothing in the sight of God." By this one simile, Diatribe "is baffled and beaten" and shown to be nothing but "rubbish."

"If we believe it to be true," Luther wrote in his conclusion, "that God foreknows and predestines all things, that he can neither be mistaken in his foreknowledge nor hindered in his predestination, and that nothing takes place but as he wills it," then by "reason itself there cannot be any free choice in man or angel or any creature." In a patronizing farewell, he returned to the contrast between his own certainty and Erasmus's lack thereof. Unless Erasmus could do better than he had done in his Diatribe, he should remain content with his own "special gift" and promote languages and literature as he had hitherto done with such "profit and distinction." Luther acknowledged his own debt to Erasmus in this area. On the matter at hand, however, God had not willed that he should be equal to it. That Erasmus did not yet properly understand Scripture was shown by his preference for discourse over assertion. "I for my part in this book *have not discoursed, but have asserted and do assert*, and I am unwilling to submit the matter to anyone's judgment, but advise everyone to yield assent." (The italics are Luther's.)

The deities described in Erasmus's and Luther's dueling tracts could hardly be more dissimilar. Erasmus's God is an even-tempered rationalist who sagely judges men and women by how they behave in the world. Luther's God is an inscrutable being who acts according to his own unfathomable logic, apart from human understanding and expectation. Erasmus's God requires the existence of free will to ensure that his rule is just; Luther's God has to reject free will to make sure his power is unbounded. Whereas Erasmus wanted to protect the freedom of man to choose, Luther wanted to safeguard the freedom of God to act.

In the end, though, Erasmus and Luther were separated as much by their approaches to interpreting Scripture as by their visions of the Almighty. Erasmus believed that while some passages in the Bible (mostly having to do with the precepts for a good life) are clear, many others remain obscure, and that on such passages pious Christians can differ. Christians should thus respect dissenting viewpoints and not press their own opinions too insistently lest violence and upheaval result. To Luther, such a stance was abhorrent. For him, the meaning of the Bible was utterly clear, and anyone disagreeing with his own particular interpretation deserved to be condemned as a skeptic and nonbeliever. For Erasmus, the ideal setting is a dinner party at which scholars amicably discuss Bible passages over capon and wine. For Luther, it is the pulpit, from which God's unassailable Word is ardently proclaimed. (Erasmus's tolerant attitude, however, did not extend to the Jews.)

The debate between Erasmus and Luther marked an important bifurcation in Western thought. Prior to the appearance of Erasmus's tract, Luther, while subscribing to the doctrine of predestination, had never given it his full attention. Now, goaded by Erasmus, he was fatefully placing it at the heart of his theology. The idea of predestination as outlined in *The Bondage of the Will* would later be taken up and amplified by John Calvin. Promoted by him, predestination would become a pillar of the Reformed faith and through it a theological fixture of English and American Puritanism.

Erasmus's belief in free will and human autonomy, meanwhile, pointed toward the Enlightenment. The argument described in *The Freedom of the Will* in many ways anticipated the moral philosophy of Immanuel Kant. In *Religion Within the Limits of Reason Alone*, written in 1793, Kant (who was raised a pious Lutheran) stressed the importance of human capacity and the freedom of the individual to choose to act, and he embraced the individual's moral responsibility in a way that strongly recalled Erasmus's philosophy of Christ. "Man *himself*," Kant wrote, must make himself "into whatever, in a moral sense, whether good or evil, he is or is to become." Either way, the outcome "must be an effect of his free choice," since "otherwise he could not be held responsible for it and could therefore be *morally* neither good nor evil."

Luther finished his book in mid-November 1525. The printing, by Hans Luftt in Wittenberg, was completed on the last day of the year. The volume came to 383 octavo pages—nearly four times the length of *The Freedom of the Will*. Over the next year, it would be reprinted in Mainz, Strasbourg, Cologne, Nuremberg, Tübingen, and Wittenberg itself—a dozen editions in all.

With *The Bondage of the Will*, Luther was finalizing his break from not only Erasmus but also Christian humanism in general, with its emphasis on autonomy, pluralism, and rationalism. With it, one can see the Reformation parting ways with the Renaissance. Viewed more broadly, Luther was creating a new religious model in Western Christendom—that of the Bible-quoting militant who considers Scripture the unchallengeable Word of God and who in asserting it is ready to cause tumult, strife, and bloodshed.

*   *   *

Word of Luther's tract and its harsh tone quickly reached Erasmus. Try as he might, though, he could not obtain a copy. He began to suspect that the Lutherans were deliberately withholding it from him so that he could not respond in time for the spring fair in Frankfurt, thus leaving the field to Luther. In fact, there was no such effort—the Wittenbergers had simply neglected to send him a copy. Erasmus was further distressed to hear that the book was already being translated into German "so as to prejudice every laborer and peasant against me."

With the publication of his diatribe on free will, Erasmus was now an outcast among the Lutherans. Yet he remained a pariah among conservative Catholics as well. "No matter what I do," he complained, "I am still considered a Lutheran and continue to be the target of vicious and defamatory pamphlets." Roman loyalists—determined to extinguish the possibility of moderate reform—now stepped up their campaign against him.

In Louvain, a group of Dominicans collaborated on an anonymous work that condemned Erasmus for both supporting the eating of meat (on fast days) and questioning the sacramental nature of penance. His longtime adversary Jacobus Latomus published three works that, though not mentioning him, were clearly aimed at him, especially at the questions he had raised about whether confession had been instituted by Christ.

On top of it all, a group of "rabble-rousers" were "moving heaven and earth to destroy the Collegium Trilingue," as Erasmus put it. By that point, the college had gained a Continent-wide reputation for humanistic scholarship, but the Louvain theologians continued to see it as an enemy agent that, under the cover of promoting Greek and Hebrew, was seeking to weaken the authority of the Vulgate and by extension the Church. Exasperated, Erasmus sent a trusted agent to Rome to ask Clement VII to silence the Louvain faculty. The pope agreed, and an emissary was dispatched to Louvain with such an order. But the Louvain theologians refused to heed it. The need to suppress heresy outweighed any obligation to obey the pope, they maintained, and in the end they won over the emissary himself.

By then, however, Louvain as a center of anti-Erasmian agitation was being eclipsed by Paris. In May 1526, a committee appointed by the Sorbonne denounced a long list of passages in the *Colloquies* as objectionable and called for the work "to be forbidden to all, especially the young, because under the pretext of eloquence a youth might be more corrupted than instructed by such reading." Pierre Cousturier, who had earlier condemned vernacular translations of the Bible, now accused Erasmus of committing blasphemy against the Virgin Mary for having written in his paraphrases that a kind of coitus had taken place between God and the Virgin and that Gabriel was the "groomsman" for their marriage. (Erasmus had indeed used such suggestive language.) Noël Béda published a collection of annotations on Erasmus's paraphrases that listed passages he considered erroneous, impious, schismatic, contrary to good morals, and—most damning of all—Lutheran. And Louis de Berquin, Erasmus's French translator, who in 1523 had been imprisoned after being condemned by the Paris faculty, was arrested and imprisoned a second time as a relapsed heretic for his continuing efforts to promote Erasmus's books and the reform cause.

With the most powerful theology faculty in Europe thus seeking to crush him, Erasmus turned to his most influential French supporter: the king. In January 1526, Francis I, after nearly eleven months as Charles's prisoner, had finally signed a peace treaty in which he made huge territorial concessions (and which he guaranteed by handing over his two young sons as surety). He arrived back in France in March. In June, Erasmus sent him an urgent plea to muzzle Béda, Cousturier, and other "godforsaken souls" in France "who were born to hate good literature and the public peace." If "the outrageous behavior of these Pharisees goes unpunished, no good man will feel safe in the future." Moved by his appeal, Francis in early August ordered the removal of Béda's tract from all bookstores, and agents were sent around to ensure compliance. By then, however, only 50 or so of the 650 copies in print remained, and a new edition was quickly produced in Cologne.

Amid all this opprobrium, Erasmus found some diversion in the presence of an urbane houseguest. Jan Łaski was a Polish nobleman and humanist in his midtwenties, and Erasmus was taken with both his quick mind and his youthful male charm. Łaski further endeared himself to Erasmus by picking up his household expenses during his six-month stay. Erasmus, in turn, tutored Łaski in his vision of ethics-based Christianity. When he left, in October 1525, Erasmus was disconsolate. Upon his return to Poland, however, Łaski would help stimulate interest in Erasmus's works among the Polish elite, and Cracow would become a lonely outpost of Erasmian humanism in Eastern Europe. (Yet, like so many young disciples of Erasmus, Łaski would eventually join the evangelical camp, becoming an influential early promoter of Calvinism.)

While spreading to the east, Erasmianism was also traveling westward. Erasmus had long had a loyal following among the educated elite of Spain. At the University of Alcalá, where the Complutensian Bible had been produced, he was widely admired for his contribution to scriptural studies, and the court of Charles V included many Burgundians who considered themselves Erasmians, among them Mercurino Gattinara, the powerful chancellor, and Guy Morillon, the imperial secretary. Even Alonso Manrique de Lara, the archbishop of Seville who in September 1523 was named Spain's inquisitor-general, was an admirer.

Then, in 1526, the *Enchiridion* was translated into Spanish, and all of Spain was smitten. Juan Maldonado, a priest in Burgos, reported to Erasmus that not only were Latin-speakers "falling in love with your brilliant books" but also "the ordinary masses" were "clamoring to hear about you and want to become acquainted with your ideas." Even "weak and ignorant women burn with desire to find out about the teachings of this Erasmus whose fame is blazoned abroad throughout the learned world." To satisfy them, "a bevy of scholars are busy translating your works into our language." Of the *Enchiridion*, he added, "the printers cannot meet the demand, although they have run off thousands of copies." Overall, the excitement stirred by the translation of this primer of piety (as well as of some of the *Colloquies*) would help make Spain Europe's most vibrant center of Erasmian humanism—at least for the time being.

In Basel, meanwhile, the furor set off by Karlstadt's tracts on the Eucharist was spreading. In September 1525, Oecolampadius issued a commentary on "This is my body" in which he emphatically denied that any physical change takes place in the communal bread and wine. In Zurich, Zwingli published two tracts that similarly rejected the doctrine of transubstantiation, emphasizing instead the spiritual aspects of Communion. Bucer, Bugenhagen, Pirckheimer, and half a dozen others all weighed in as well. The sacramentarian "heresy," Erasmus observed, had "caught on everywhere with the speed of fire running towards naphtha."

The matter held a special risk for him. Both Zwingli and Oecolampadius, in proposing a spiritual interpretation of the Eucharist, claimed to have drawn on Erasmus's own writings and his embrace of the spirit over the flesh. Erasmus himself admitted that Oecolampadius's book was "so carefully written and so buttressed with argument and supporting evidence that even the elect could be led astray." But transubstantiation was a core Catholic belief, and Erasmus emphatically rejected any questioning of it. When he heard that Conradus Pellicanus, a well-known Basel Hebraist and longtime admirer who was now close to Oecolampadius, was spreading rumors that Erasmus had privately expressed skepticism about the doctrine, Erasmus angrily admonished him: "You can imagine what an uproar there would be if I were rash enough to declare there is nothing in the Eucharist except bread and wine." Erasmus made it unequivocally clear where his allegiance lay: "When I find a better church than the one I belong to, I shall stop calling this one 'Catholic.' But I have not found such a church." Amid the growing sectarian fury, Erasmus was increasingly ready to defer to Rome's authority.

In early February 1526, he finally saw a copy of *The Bondage of the Will*. He was shocked by its virulence. "Who can believe that the spirit of Christ dwells in a heart from which flow words of such arrogance, bitterness, savagery, malice, and abuse?" he complained to Duke John of Saxony. Erasmus was especially unsettled by Luther's dismissal of him as a pig from Epicurus's sty. Rather than treat him as a fellow Christian who sincerely disagreed with him on several theological points, Luther had essentially called him an atheist—a charge even graver than that of heretic.

At the time, Erasmus was working on a book about matrimony at the request of Catherine of Aragon, but he immediately put it aside so that he could respond to Luther. He wanted to have his reply ready for the spring fair in Frankfurt, and this left him no more than ten or twelve days in which to complete it. He decided to leave the discussion of scriptural passages for a follow-up volume and instead concentrate on Luther's discussion of his methods and beliefs. He called his work *Hyperaspistes*—an obscure term from the Septuagint for a warrior's shield against an enemy's attack. No longer feeling the need to exercise restraint, Erasmus decided at last to say what he really thought about the man who had so upended his life.

"How much there is in your book that is completely off target, how much that is superfluous, how many commonplaces dwelled on at length, how many insults, how much that is manifestly inane, how many ruses, how many sly digs, how much that is shamelessly twisted and distorted, and how many tragical conclusions drawn from the distortions, and how much undeserved vociferation inspired by the conclusions!"—all, he wrote, in response to his own moderate discussion. Many monarchs and princes of the Church had begged him to use all his eloquence "to thunder and fulminate" against Luther, but he had long resisted, worried that if he had complied, he would have unwittingly injured a cause that had at first enjoyed near-universal support. In his own work on free will, he had deliberately used a temperate style so as to deny Luther any pretext for offering outrageous insults. Yet Luther in his response had directed at him more "enmity and bitterness" than he had at anyone else.

Erasmus fastened on Luther's claim that Scripture is nowhere obscure. If that were so, why was there so much disagreement among his own evangelical brothers? Karlstadt had raged against Luther and Luther against Karlstadt, while Zwingli and Oecolampadius had opposed Luther's opinion in multiple volumes. Even in that "tiny little town" of Wittenberg, he wrote, not everyone seemed to agree. Every day new dogmas appeared among the reformers, and every day new quarrels arose over them, yet Luther bristled if anyone dared disagree with him. As for the supposedly simple story of the Gospels, talented people had for centuries sweated to harmonize the many inconsistencies among them. Erasmus expressed special exasperation with Luther's passing off his own interpretation of the Bible as God's Word: "And so, away with this 'word of God, word of God.' I am not waging war against the word of God but against your assertion."

While Luther derided the Scholastics, Erasmus observed, he proposed arguments and distinctions no less sophistical and outlandish than theirs. Erasmus offered example after example of the inconsistencies, contradictions, and absurdities that he felt riddled Luther's texts and which for years had so maddened him. At the end, he issued an anguished cry at the destruction that he felt the "seditious wantonness" of Luther's pen had wrought:

> The people are stirred up against bishops and princes; magistrates are hard pressed to put down mobs eager to revolt; cities which once were joined by very close ties now quarrel among themselves with fierce hatred; now you can hardly find any man you can safely trust; all freedom has been taken away.

The slavery that Luther had set out to overthrow "has been redoubled; the yoke is heavier; the chains are not shaken off but tightened"—a reference to the Peasants' War. "Liberal studies, together with languages and good writing, are everywhere disregarded because you have loaded them down with ill will." The outstanding monuments of the ancients "are rejected, and in their place the world is filled with quarrelsome and defamatory books which infect the reader with poison and disease."

Luther had drawn countless people away from their bishops, "and now they wander around like scattered sheep, having no shepherd, especially when they see that your church is shaken by so many quarrels and thrown into tumult by internal warfare." Reaffirming his own enduring faith in Christ, Erasmus expressed his wish that the Lord would "renew a good spirit" in Luther so as to help restore harmony to the Christian world and so that the two of them might "pray with one voice to him whose teachings we now assert with discordant voices."

After nearly two weeks of feverish writing, Erasmus had eighty thousand words. To get them ready for the spring fair, Froben devoted five or six presses to them. When completed, the volumes were at once sent off to Frankfurt, 240 miles away. At the fair, customers who bought *The Bondage of the Will* could now also pick up the *Hyperaspistes* and read two of Europe's top thinkers squaring off on the most pressing issues of the day.

In the early spring of 1525, Erasmus received a letter from Luther. It has not survived, but it is clear from Erasmus's response that Luther was even more condescending than he had been in the *Bondage*, taking pity on Erasmus as an unbelieving soul who should be grateful that he had not written against him even more harshly.

"So you restrained your pen!" Erasmus fumed. What, he asked, "is the point of all those scurrilous insults and the false charges that I am an atheist, an Epicurean, a skeptic in matters belonging to the Christian faith, a blasphemer, and whatever else comes into your head—to say nothing of the many other accusations you claim to pass over in silence?" Had he made his case with the usual intensity but without the raging insults, he would have stirred fewer people against him. "What distresses me, as it distresses all decent people, is the fact that because of your arrogant, insolent, and turbulent personality you cause a fatal dissension that unsettles the whole world, you expose good men and lovers of the humanities to the fury of the Pharisees, and you arm wicked and rebellious men for revolution." The calamity and universal confusion afflicting the world "we owe to no one but you with your headstrong nature."

This would be the last letter between the two men. The hatred between them now flared too brightly to allow for any further exchanges.

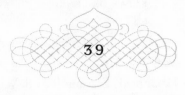
INVASION BY SCRIPTURE

Erasmus's broadside landed in Wittenberg with the intended impact. "Have you ever read anything more bitterly written than Erasmus' *Hyper-aspistes*?" Melanchthon wrote to Joachim Camerarius on April 11, 1526. "He is certainly a viper." (Melanchthon used the term *aspis*, a play on Erasmus's title.) Though he had expected a stern reply to Luther's attack on *The Freedom of the Will*, he observed, he was surprised at its vulgarity. And he was sure Luther would respond in kind. While he had hoped that Luther over time "would grow used to these things and be somewhat milder" when confronted with them, he was instead "becoming more and more vehement."

Luther was in fact furious. "That enraged viper, Erasmus of Rotterdam, is again writing against me," he reported to Spalatin. "How much eloquence this vainglorious beast uses up this time in trying to knock Luther down!" In another letter, he called Erasmus "an instrument of Satan" who did not properly appreciate the moderation of his own book against him.

The dismay that Luther and Melanchthon felt over the *Hyperaspistes* suggests the air of unreality that had settled over Wittenberg. They were somehow unable to grasp how abusive Luther's tract had been. Such obliviousness, in turn, reflected their own growing sense of beleaguerment. In July 1525, several princes, led by Duke George, met in the town of Dessau to discuss forming a league to wipe out the "cursed Lutheran sect." In response, several pro-Lutheran princes met to discuss organizing a defensive alliance, and soon afterward work began on new fortifications in Wittenberg "so that it may be impregnable," as Luther put it.

Luther's growing isolation helps explain an episode that would prove among the most embarrassing of his career. In the spring of 1525, King

Christian II of Denmark informed the Saxon court that Henry VIII was becoming more favorably inclined toward the evangelical cause, and he suggested that Luther send the king a conciliatory note. Spalatin reported this to Luther and urged him to follow through. Luther, though skeptical, agreed. In his letter to the king, dated September 1, 1525, he apologized for his earlier harsh response to the booklet on the seven sacraments and said that he had learned that the work had actually been written not by Henry but by "crafty men" who had abused his name, foremost among them that "pest of your kingdom," the cardinal of York (Wolsey).

He went on: "I cast myself with the utmost possible humility at your Majesty's feet, and pray and beseech you, by the love and cross and glory of Christ, to deign leave off your anger and forgive me for what I have done to injure your Majesty, as Christ commands us in His prayer to forgive each other." If the king wished him to recant publicly, he had only to say so and he would immediately oblige. In the meantime, he should not let his royal ears be filled "with the pestilent songs of those sirens who do nothing but call Luther a heretic," for what harm could there be in his teaching that salvation comes through faith in Christ alone? With so many princes and wise men in Germany embracing the new gospel, Luther expressed his hope that Henry would soon join them.

The abject tone of Luther's letter reflected his craving for support in the aftermath of the revolt by the peasants, the war over the Eucharist, and his break with Erasmus. Unfortunately, the information about Henry turned out to be false: the king despised him as much as ever. And Luther's assertion that Henry had not actually written his book further inflamed him. In the summer of 1526, the king—still relishing his status as a defender of the faith—prepared a mocking response in Latin in which he detailed Luther's many offenses, including undermining the Mass, denying free will, inciting the peasants, and marrying a nun.

Henry sent a copy to Duke George, who quickly arranged for a German translation. Its title—*Luther's Offer to Recant in a Letter to the King of England*—angered Luther even more than the document itself, and he informed Spalatin that he would answer the king, who, he wrote, was "merely a mask for Erasmus." In *Against the Title of the English King's Slan-*

derous Writing, Luther wrote that he had tried to keep the peace with both Henry and Erasmus, "but I am a sheep and must remain a sheep to think that I can pacify such men."

At the same time that Henry and Luther were trading blows, however, the way was being prepared for one of history's most astonishing about-faces: Henry's break with the Catholic Church. In just a few years, this faithful follower of Rome would become one of its fiercest detractors. The cause (as every student of history knows) was Henry's infatuation with Anne Boleyn, which bloomed in the early months of 1526. Unlike her sister Mary, with whom Henry had had an affair, Anne refused to become his mistress. This, however, only fanned his desire, and Henry began thinking of ending his marriage to Catherine and making Anne his queen.

For the moment, he kept his intentions secret. Not until the spring of 1527 would Henry ask Wolsey to begin secret proceedings to annul his marriage, and not until June of that year would he inform Catherine of his plans. Her refusal to go along and his insistence on proceeding would precipitate a profound political and religious crisis, leading to a showdown with the pope, the disestablishment of the Catholic Church in England, and the start of the English Reformation.

That reformation would take a course very different from the one unfolding on the Continent. It would follow a more flexible, less dogmatic (though very violent) "third way" between the two great warring faiths. It would, to a degree, reflect the ideas of Erasmus. The Christian humanist ideals that Erasmus had been disseminating since his first visit to England in 1499 would help shape many aspects of Tudor religious and political policies.

Erasmus's influence in England had spread through a variety of channels: the curriculum he had developed for John Colet and St. Paul's School; his personal ties and correspondence with leading clergymen and scholars in England, through which he had tirelessly pressed his reform ideas; and, of course, his writings. The log of an Oxford bookseller for the first ten months of 1520 shows that, of the 2,114 books he sold, 175 were by Erasmus, including 15 copies of the *Enchiridion*, 17 of *De Copia*, and 48 of the *Colloquies*. The English elite adorned their letters with

Erasmus's adages; wrote Latin according to his style manuals; read the New Testament with his annotations at their side; heeded the admonitions in the *Enchiridion* to nurture the inner spirit; took note of his denunciations of war and despotism; studied his explanations of Jesus's parables in the paraphrases; laughed at his gibes against monasticism; and shared in his disdain for pious superstition. The 1526 edition of the *Colloquies* included "A Pilgrimage for Religion's Sake," which drew on visits that Erasmus had made years earlier to two of England's most famous shrines—Our Lady of Walsingham (which featured a vial of the Virgin's milk) and the crypt of Thomas à Becket at Canterbury (a collection of bones, jewels, and gilt artifacts). In Erasmus's account, the shrines were aimed more at gulling pilgrims than promoting faith. In the 1530s, both would be destroyed as part of Henry's headlong assault on monasteries, shrines, and relics.

In mounting that assault, of course, Henry did not need Erasmus's encouragement, and he carried out his policies with a brutality that was decidedly un-Erasmian. But Erasmus's writings played a key part in discrediting the old order in England and fostering a preference for doctrinal flexibility over dogmatic assertion. Erasmus's influence would be most evident during the reign of Henry's daughter Elizabeth I (1558 to 1603). At a time of bloody competition between Catholics and Protestants, Elizabeth would pursue a flexible course that came to be known as the *via media* ("middle way"), seeking to avoid both the excessive ceremonialism of Catholicism and the creedal certitudes of Protestantism. On such key matters as original sin, the Trinity, and the Eucharist, Elizabeth would support a deliberate ambiguity similar to that advocated by Erasmus, and her policies showed a pragmatic centrism that seemed to draw on his spirit (though, again, they were carried out with a ruthlessness that would no doubt have appalled him). Overall, England would become the sole European showcase of Erasmus's reform ideas.

Remarkably, at the very moment that Henry was beginning to consider dissolving his marriage to Catherine, Erasmus was completing the treatise on matrimony that she had requested. The *Institutio Christiani Matrimonii* ("Institution of Christian Matrimony") would add to the large and influential body of Erasmus's work on this subject. As always, he worked on two fronts, promoting the superiority of marriage over celibacy while also arguing for a way out of failing unions. "Death," he wrote, "may be a lighter affliction than an unhappy marriage, where the living suffer the torments of hell and utter the wails of the damned on earth." For this state of affairs, he largely blamed the Church. The many impediments to marriage stipulated in canon law allowed clergymen to meddle endlessly in conjugal matters, leading to great heartache. "If one looks at social life today, if one considers the many thousands throughout Christendom who are enmeshed in the toils of marriage," then one could only wish that "an indulgent Mother Church, always attentive to the edification and not the destruction of her children," would allow some relaxation, much as a learned physician varies his prescription to suit the age and condition of his patient.

Erasmus dedicated the *Institutio* to Catherine. In the "saintliness of your character," he wrote, "one can find the perfect model of a most holy and blessed marriage." After he sent the tract to the queen (in mid-1526), months went by without any word of thanks or acknowledgment, and Erasmus wondered if he had somehow offended her. Not until the following year would he learn of the troubled state of Catherine's own marriage. Eventually, Mountjoy wrote to assure Erasmus that the queen was in fact pleased with the work. Whether in fact that was true—the *Institutio* was exasperatingly prolix and maddeningly digressive—the treatise would further Erasmus's campaign to loosen the Church's grip on matrimony (though not fast enough for Henry).

In the end, Erasmus's greatest impact on England would come through his work on the Bible. He had initially conceived his program to revive Greek and restore Scripture in England, and its fullest fruit would be realized there. The key figure would be neither More nor Colet nor any other member of the humanist fraternity, however, but an obscure linguist from the provinces named William Tyndale.

Tyndale's work as a Bible translator would have a decisive impact on the course of the English Reformation—indeed, on the formation of the English people. The fifty or so scholars whom King James I convened in 1604 to produce a new translation of the Bible relied heavily on Tyndale's Old and New Testaments. An estimated 90 percent of the King James Version—the cornerstone of the Church of England—came from Tyndale. Other than Shakespeare, no individual would do more to shape the English language. Even today, the Bible read by most Englishmen is substantially the work of William Tyndale. And, though he would eventually become an ardent Lutheran, Tyndale got his initial inspiration from Erasmus.

After earning bachelor's and master's degrees at Oxford and (it's believed) studying at Cambridge, Tyndale in around 1521 took a job as a tutor to the two young sons of Sir John Walsh in the village of Little Sodbury in Gloucestershire. In his spare time, he translated Erasmus's *Enchiridion* into English. With its embrace of piety over pomp and its praise for Scripture as a guide to an ethical life, this moral manual would influence Tyndale more than any other book save the Bible.

The *Paraclesis* also left a deep impression. Struck by Erasmus's call for the production of vernacular Bibles so that ordinary Christians could read them, Tyndale decided to produce such a text in English. At the time, the English Church regarded all English-language editions as subversive, and it zealously sought to suppress them. Under Henry, translating the Bible into English remained a criminal offense, and England was the last major country in Europe without a vernacular Bible in print.

None of this would deter Tyndale. He was austere, contentious, self-righteous, humorless, and uncompromising. He also had a great gift for languages—he would master Latin, Greek, Hebrew, and German—as well as a knack for creating phrases that catch the ear and register on the mind. He was, in effect, a modern-day Jerome. Like that Church Doctor, Tyndale came to see translating the Bible as his life's calling, for which he was willing to endure cold, hunger, loneliness, exile—even death.

Seeking support for his project, he decided in 1523 to travel to London to see Cuthbert Tunstall, the bishop of London, whom Tyndale had learned of from a favorable mention in Erasmus's New Testament annotations. Though not unfriendly, Tunstall informed Tyndale that he already had four chaplains and did not need another, and he advised him to instead seek work in London. Following his counsel, Tyndale found a room in west London and took up preaching.

By then, Tyndale had discovered Luther. Like so many other reform-minded young men, he found Luther's teachings about salvation by faith and grace more emotionally satisfying than Erasmus's appeal to free will and moral rectitude. Tyndale's Lutheran views gained him entrée to London's cloth merchants. These men—objecting to the Church's prohibition of usury and other restrictions—identified with Luther and his challenge to Rome. Tyndale's idea of translating the Scriptures into English appealed to them, and one of them provided him with lodging. Eventually, several merchants—aware of the danger of embarking on such a project in England—offered to pay his way to the Continent. Tyndale accepted, and in the spring of 1524 he left England, never to set foot there again.

He went to Hamburg. He may have also spent some months in Wittenberg (the record is inconclusive). Wherever he was, Tyndale devoted himself to translating, assisted by a former friar named William Roye. He worked from the Vulgate, Luther's German New Testament, and Erasmus's revised New Testament (including its Greek text and Latin translation). In addition to borrowing some phraseology from Luther, Tyndale added a number of marginal comments that mirrored Luther's own notes, plus a prologue that relied heavily on Luther's introduction to the New Testament. Overall, though, Tyndale went his own way. Drawing on his vast vocabulary, he was able to freshen familiar expressions. Taking everyday speech, he found ways to intensify and surpass it, creating a new type of prose that was at once simple and dignified. Among his coinages: "my brother's keeper," "the salt of the earth," "the powers that be," "the signs of the times," "our father which art in heaven," "lead us not into temptation but deliver us from evil," "seek and you shall find," "judge not that you not be judged," "the spirit is willing but the flesh is weak," and "eat, drink, and be merry."

In addition to his linguistic innovations, Tyndale showed theological audacity. Like both Erasmus and Luther, he sought to strip away the Scholastic accretions that had obscured the true spirit of the text. Whereas the Greek *agape* was traditionally translated as "charity," Tyndale gave "love." He replaced "grace" with "favor" and "confession" with "knowledgement." He translated *presbyter* not as "priest" but as "senior" and, following Erasmus, gave *metanoia* as "repent" rather than "do penance." Most boldly, Tyndale, following Luther, gave *ekklesia* not as "church" but as "congregation." The word "church," signifying an organized body of clergy, barely appeared.

Tyndale went with Roye to Cologne, where, despite its Catholic leanings, they quickly found a printer. While the printing was under way, though, word of the project leaked out, and the municipal authorities, wanting to avoid trouble, ordered it to stop. Worried that they might be arrested, Tyndale and Roye grabbed as many printed sheets as they could and found a boat to take them up the Rhine to Worms. In the four years since Luther's appearance at the diet in that city, it had turned decisively in his favor, and they found another printer. To both hasten the process and keep down costs, the edition was to be a compact octavo offering only the bare text. Six thousand copies were run off; Tyndale's name nowhere appeared.

Word quickly spread. In December 1525 Wolsey was warned that a dangerous new translation of the Bible would soon be heading to England. The royal government immediately sprang into action. The bloody spectacle of the Peasants' War in Germany showed the violence and anarchy that could result from making the Scriptures available to the common man. With Lutheranism spreading into Flanders, Holland, and Scandinavia, royal officials worried that England would be next. A watch was ordered on all ports, and customs officials boarded and searched merchant ships. Nonetheless, many volumes—concealed in bales of merchandise and cases of dry goods—got through. Arriving at landing stages in London and elsewhere, they were carried by colporteurs and sold in churchyards, inns, and taverns; copies were also read clandestinely by Lollard followers of Wyclif. For the first time, the English people could read the Bible in a printed edition in their own language.

Church officials were dismayed. Through this translation, wrote Robert Ridley, a chaplain to Cuthbert Tunstall, "we shall lose all these Christian words, penance, charity, confession, grace, priest, church, which he always calleth a congregation." In the note on Matthew 16:18, Tyndale (following Erasmus and Luther) maintained that the rock on which

Christ's congregation was to be built was not Peter but the confession he had made—a clear challenge to papal authority. The fact that the English New Testament came from a German press made it doubly suspect.

On October 24, 1526, Tunstall issued a solemn admonition to all archdeacons in his diocese, ordering all copies to be handed over within thirty days. A bonfire was scheduled for December at St. Paul's church-yard. In a sermon delivered on that occasion, Tunstall railed against the translation as being both seditious and full of errors, of which he claimed to have found two thousand. When he finished, all the volumes that had been collected were fed to the flames. In early 1527, Archbishop William Warham, in a more novel expedient, ordered the buying up of all copies of the translation. That served only to stimulate sales, however, and a new edition was soon being prepared in Antwerp.

Clearly, sterner measures were needed, and to devise them, Tunstall turned to Thomas More. Now serving as both counselor to the king and chancellor of the duchy of Lancaster, More was growing increasingly im-patient with any theological straying from official teachings. In 1524, Jo-hannes Bugenhagen had come out with an *Appeal to the English*, in which he hailed the many Englishmen who were embracing the new gospel and called on others to do the same. With the Lutherans thus directly tar-geting England, More believed more than ever that the carriers of the new doctrines had to be destroyed. In this period he would emerge as England's most determined hunter of heretics, putting in place a system of surveillance, intimidation, and entrapment aimed at stamping out all expressions of sedition and dissent.

On a Friday evening in early 1526, More led a raid on Hanseatic mer-chants in the Steelyard, a district of docks and warehouses on the Thames near London Bridge that served as the base for the Hanseatic League in England and which was a stronghold of Lutheran thinking. Accompanied by several noblemen and their armed guards, he burst in on the men as they were about to sit down to dinner and announced that he had received reports that many of them had books by Luther. More had three of the merchants arrested and demanded that the names of the rest be submit-ted the following morning. Returning then, he ordered the handing over of all Lutheran books; the rooms of the merchants were then searched. Eight of them were taken to Westminster and brought before Wolsey, who forbade them and all other Steelyard residents to leave England over the next twenty days. In February, four German merchants and a doctor of divinity named Robert Barnes were brought to St. Paul's on suspicion of heresy and forced to kneel in the aisle with faggots tied to their backs—a warning of what would happen to them if they persisted.

Determined to move every lever against the new threat, More decided to approach Erasmus. He had been very pleased with the acerbity of the first part of the *Hyperaspistes* and was eager for the promised second part. In mid-December 1526, at the king's palace in Greenwich, More drafted an urgent appeal to his old friend, its hectoring tone reflecting his grow-ing ardor. "I pray God you will be able to bring" to "a happy conclusion" the "brilliant series of works by which you are nurturing the Christian faith," More wrote. He noted "the eager anticipation" with which so many awaited the remaining volume of the *Hyperaspistes*; the wicked, by contrast, were "puffed up and exultant at the tardiness of your reply." If Erasmus's hesitation was due to a lack of courage brought on by fear of the consequences of proceeding, More continued, "I cannot tell you how surprised and disappointed I am. God forbid, my dearest Erasmus, that you, who have faced such hardships, run such risks, taken upon yourself such Herculean tasks, and spent the best years of your life in unremitting toil and sleepless vigils for the benefit of all mankind," should now be ready "to desert the work of God rather than face the possibility of defeat." It was not the time to be crushed by fear. By issuing a thousand copies of the first part "like so many affidavits, you have bound yourself before the world to do all in your power to finish the work."

Concluding on a friendlier note, More wrote that the "painter friend" whom Erasmus had sent his way had arrived in England. Though the man was a "wonderful artist," he observed, he feared that he would "not find English soil as rich and fertile as he hoped." More would be proved wrong. Before traveling to England, Hans Holbein the Younger had painted two portraits of Erasmus; Erasmus had been so impressed that he agreed to write letters of introduction for him to friends in Antwerp and London. Holbein would remain in England until the summer of 1528, then return to Basel. He would return to England a few years later and remain there until his death in 1543. During that time, he would become the leading painter of the English court, producing the most memorable images of Henry VIII and the Tudor world.

Soon after writing to Erasmus, More sat for Holbein. The portrait (now hanging in the Frick Collection in New York) shows More as a self-assured man of state, the gold chain of Tudor service draped over a black velvet cloak, his short brown hair tucked firmly inside a black cap. Aside from the few days' stubble on his chin, More seems all authority and self-control. Beneath the regalia, however, he was wearing his hair shirt, its painful chafing providing a test—and confirmation—of the constancy of his faith.

When More's letter arrived, in the first part of 1527, Erasmus was annoyed. A full year had passed since the publication of the first part of the *Hyperaspistes*, and he had begun to think that he could get away without producing the second. His scholarly projects were fully absorbing him. With the world seeming about to descend into barbarian darkness, he was intent on recovering as much ancient knowledge as possible. Thrilling as ever to the hunt for manuscripts, he dispatched messengers to scriptoria and libraries across Europe in search of them.

The previous spring, for instance, he had sent Hieronymus Froben, the eldest son of Johann, to Italy with letters of introduction explaining that the young man was "prepared to purchase, beg, borrow, or steal" to get old manuscripts. Froben's initial efforts bore no fruit; at Padua, the monks proved impregnable. But his persistence eventually paid off. Among his finds were several rare manuscripts by John Chrysostom, a prominent Eastern Father whose homilies and other writings offered revealing glimpses into the state of fourth-century Christianity. On receiving them, Erasmus felt he had acquired the riches of Croesus. He translated the homilies from Greek to Latin, weeding out the many corruptions that had crept into the text. They would become part of a five-volume edition of Chrysostom that, published in 1530, would help restore his place in Western Christendom.

To Ferry de Carondelet, an aristocratic friend and a canon at the cathedral of Besançon in eastern France (and the brother of Jean), Erasmus wrote to see if its library had any old manuscripts of the Gospels and Epistles. While he was at it, he requested a cask of Burgundy wine, "a light ruby in color, not too fiery, but of good quality, though it should be well aged." Ancient manuscripts and dry wine—two of the things Erasmus most prized in life.

Erasmus needed those manuscripts for the fourth edition of his New Testament. In the decade since the appearance of the first edition, this work had ballooned into an immense exegetical apparatus, with multiple prefaces and methodological guides and a multitude of annotations, some so long that they were reprinted as mini treatises. As much as Erasmus longed to escape the tedium of collation, correction, and explanation, he again found himself on the treadmill. His New Testament had become a mainstay of biblical scholarship across Europe—by his own estimate, more than 100,000 copies of the various editions had been printed—and, despite the drudgery, he needed to make it as accurate as possible. Though one other edition would appear, in 1535, it would offer only minor changes from the fourth, so upon its publication, in March 1527, the fourth edition would stand in some ways as Erasmus's own final testament.

A week after it appeared, on March 30, Erasmus answered More's letter. Explaining why he had not yet completed the *Hyperaspistes*, he exploded in exasperation: "What a fate is mine! I am feared by the highest prelates in the world, but am spat upon, shit upon, and pissed upon by the dregs of mankind!" He offered a roll call of all those who were hounding him: former friends like Oecolampadius, Pellicanus, and Capito; "Parisian Furies" like Béda and Cousturier; a new group of critics in Spain and Poland; Dominicans and Benedictines; Latomus and his fellow hotheads in Louvain; libeling pamphleteers in Strasbourg; his many detractors in Rome; and, finally, Luther.

Any further assault on the German reformer, Erasmus wrote, would be pointless. "With what weapons will you throw a person to the ground if he accepts nothing but the Sacred Scriptures and interprets them according to his own rules?" If Erasmus proceeded with the *Hyperaspistes*, he would "only stir up the hornet's nest" (a phrase from the *Adages*). "In a short time this smoldering fire will break out into a worldwide conflagration. That is where the insolence of the monks and the intransigence of the theologians are leading us." Despite his many misgivings, though, he wrote, he would comply with More's request and complete the *Hyperaspistes*.

And so with weary resignation the aging humanist prepared yet again to do battle with the raging prophet of Wittenberg.

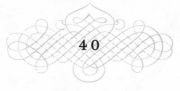

VANDALS

The conflagration that Erasmus predicted in his letter to Thomas More was more imminent than he could have imagined. On the same day that he wrote it, the imperial army—a ragged, raving, half-starved force of more than twenty thousand men—broke camp in San Giovanni, Italy, not far from Bologna, and began marching south. They included some fourteen thousand *Landsknechts*, German mercenaries who had passed through the Alps the previous November; five thousand Spaniards in the service of Charles V; and three thousand Italians, French, and assorted hangers-on. For months they had bivouacked in northern Italy, enduring rain and snow, mud and cold, hunger and vermin, while the emperor, a thousand miles away in Granada, Spain, mulled his next move. Charles's decisive victory over the French at Pavia two years earlier had left him in a position to gain control of the entire Italian peninsula, but rather than exploit his advantage, he had devoted his time to finding a wife—eventually settling on Isabella of Portugal—and planning the wedding.

Isabella brought a dowry of a million ducats—money Charles desperately needed. Despite the stores of gold and silver being shipped from the New World, he was deeply indebted to the Fuggers and other bankers, and his troops in Italy had gone eight months without pay. Promises that the money was on its way had been repeatedly broken, and the troops—hungry, shivering in the constant downpours, sleeping in swamp-like conditions—had turned mutinous. The only thing restraining them was the prospect of plunder. Seventy-five miles away was Florence, with its Medician riches, and 170 miles farther south was Rome, with its lavish palaces and bejeweled churches. For the *Landsknechts*, many of whom were Lutheran, the prospect of pillaging the Eternal City offered the added allure of paying the pope back for all the crimes and abuses that had been charged to him. "To Rome! To Rome!" the cry went up throughout the camp, and on March 30, 1527, the horde set off.

Two things stood in their way. One was the Apennines, still covered with snow at that time of year. The other was the army of the Holy League of Cognac. This inaptly named anti-imperial alliance had been formed in May 1526 by Pope Clement VII. While Clement was far more solemn than his cousin Leo X, forgoing frivolous pastimes for sober management, he, too, suffered from that grave defect of the Renaissance papacy—a passion for geopolitical meddling. Both indecisive and unscrupulous, he kept switching his allegiance between Charles and Francis, alienating both in the process. With Charles now the main threat, Clement joined with France, together with Venice and the duchy of Milan, to form the new league. Through it, the pope hoped not only to regain lost papal lands but also to restore Italy to the position it had held prior to the French invasion of 1494. In thus provoking the emperor, Clement seemed oblivious to the weakness of the league, the depleted state of his treasury, and the physical vulnerability of Rome.

With the imperial army expected to attack Florence, the Holy League sent troops to protect it, but the imperial commander—Charles, the duke of Bourbon, who was a cousin of Francis I and a charismatic veteran of many campaigns—decided to bypass the city and instead head southeast along the ancient Via Emilia into the upper Arno valley. Braving torrential rains, the ravenous infantrymen crossed the mountains well south of Florence, pillaging and burning as they went. On April 20, they were in the upper Tiber valley. Six days later, they struck the road to Rome, and by early May they were in Viterbo, just fifty miles from the city.

As word of the advancing army reached Rome, its residents braced for yet another calamity. In the previous year they had had to endure flooding, an outbreak of the plague, and a brutal spree of looting and rapine carried out by a band of adventurers under the command of Cardinal Pompeo Colonna, still fuming over having been bypassed for pope. Fanatical preachers were foretelling a catastrophe that would strike the city as punishment for its sinful ways. The citizenry, meanwhile, was irate over a new war tax the pope had levied. Now that war loomed.

To this point, Rome had been largely untouched by the religious storm north of the Alps. Despite Luther's outbursts against Rome and the multiplying grievances against the Vatican, the Holy See had continued its extravagant and dissipated ways. Now bearing down on it, however, was a raging mass of German Lutherans, Spanish adventurers, and French and Italian freebooters intent on grabbing the spoils they had dreamed of through the long months of sodden encampment.

With typical equivocation, Clement had not prepared for the onslaught. Not until May 4, 1527, when the imperial army had reached Monte Mario, a hill in the northwestern suburbs that overlooked the city, did he finally summon the great council of Rome. Even then, he assumed that the crisis would quickly pass, and he managed to raise no more than eight thousand armed men, including two thousand Swiss Guards. The city did not even take the obvious precaution of raising its bridges; residents insisted that they remain open so as not to interfere with business. When it became clear that the imperial force was approaching the city's walls, panic broke out. Nobles, cardinals, and merchants retreated into the dozens of palaces clustered in the heart of the city, desperately seeking hiding places for their valuables; foreigners frantically boarded boats to carry them down the Tiber to Ostia and the sea.

The imperial army took up positions along the city's western perimeter from the Vatican south to the Janiculum Hill and Trastevere. The main body was encamped in the vineyards behind St. Peter's. The duke of Bourbon set up his headquarters in a Hieronymite cloister in Trastevere, and at a war council held there on May 5, it was decided to storm the Vatican the following morning. The duke rode among his troops, rallying them with the cry "Victory or death." Throughout the night of May 5 and the early hours of May 6, the bell on the Capitoline tolled, summoning Rome's defenders to their posts along the walls. At four in the morning the attack began, with Germans and Spaniards storming the city from the north and west. Meeting strong resistance, they were forced to withdraw with heavy losses.

But then a thick mist rose from the Tiber, and under its cover the attackers were able to advance to the foot of the walls. There they propped up ladders fashioned from trellises they had uprooted in the vineyards. The defenders—their guns virtually useless in the fog—could do little more than throw rocks and direct shouts of "Jews," "infidels," and "Lutherans" at the unseen enemy while getting off an occasional volley. One shot found the duke of Bourbon, who was carried off to a nearby chapel, where he died. The news of his death caused despair in the imperial ranks, but the soldiers quickly regrouped and were soon clambering over and slipping through breaches in the wall. By six in the morning, both the Spaniards and the *Landsknechts* were laying siege to the Vatican. All around St. Peter's there was fierce fighting, with the Swiss Guard putting up strong resistance, but it was nearly wiped out. In a blind fury, soldiers invaded the hospital of Santo Spirito and killed almost all inside; the residents of the neighboring orphanage were similarly slaughtered.

Praying in his private chapel in the Vatican, Clement could hear the cries of battle. With mournful sobs he was led along the covered stone corridor linking the Vatican to the Castel Sant'Angelo. Over the years, successive popes had turned this hulking brown mausoleum of Hadrian's into a fortified retreat that, provisioned with enormous jars of grain, oil, and wine, could hold out for up to three years. Thirteen cardinals along with several thousand men, women, and children were able to push their way in; when the portcullis suddenly dropped, some of those trying to enter were crushed to death.

With the castle's powerful guns lobbing shells, the imperial troops were forced to withdraw from the Vatican, and the attackers decided to deploy their forces farther to the south. At about seven in the evening, the first columns arrived at the Ponte Sisto, one of three bridges leading from Trastevere into the city proper. About two hundred Roman horsemen appeared at the bridge to try to turn back the invaders, but they were quickly overwhelmed. The imperial troops raced into the heart of the city, slashing and stabbing to death all they encountered, including old women and young children, priests and monks. Everywhere the cry rang out, "Empire! Spain! Victory!" By nightfall, the Germans had occupied the Campo de' Fiori and the Spaniards the Piazza Navona.

When the soldiers saw that all resistance had ended and that no force was on its way to fight them, their leaders could no longer restrain them. Thousands of tattered, unwashed, and lustful soldiers surged through the streets of Rome, determined at last to get their due. Carrying lighted wax candles, they passed in bands from house to house in the darkness, seizing gold, silver, jewels, and finery and killing all who resisted. The Sack of Rome had begun.

On the morning of May 7, 1527, there were everywhere scenes of appalling destruction. The air echoed with the wails of women, the shrieks of children, the report of weapons, the crash of burning roofs. Using battering rams, soldiers broke into the great palaces in search of spoils. Noblemen who refused to divulge the hiding places of their treasures were subjected to savage torture. One merchant was tied to a tree and had a fingernail pulled out for each day that he could not pay the required ransom. Some were forced to eat their own ears or noses; others had their teeth pulled out or were branded with red-hot irons.

Once done with the palaces, the troops headed for the convents. Thousands of women who had taken refuge in them found themselves cruelly trapped. Delicately raised girls were stripped and brutalized by filthy, fantastically attired mercenaries. Hospitals were invaded and their patients murdered. The streets filled with corpses, severed limbs, and heads that had been lopped off.

Special fury was aimed at the clergy, particularly by Lutheran *Landsknechts*. Some priests were eviscerated; others were stripped naked and forced on pain of death to utter blasphemies or to take part in profane travesties of the Mass. Nuns were savagely violated. Some soldiers draped an ass in bishop's vestments, led it into a church, and demanded that a priest incense the beast and offer it the sacred host; when the priest refused, he was slashed to pieces. A Bavarian captain who dressed up as the pope bade his comrades, gotten up as cardinals, to kiss his hands and feet. The whole gang made their way to the Vatican, where, to the sound of trumpets and fifes, they shouted, "Luther for pope!"

Cardinal Cajetan, who in 1518 had interrogated Luther in Augsburg and who now at fifty-eight was an adviser to Clement, was dragged through the streets in chains, insulted, and tortured. Every church was plundered. Costly vestments, vessels, and works of art were carried off by the rampaging troops, flung away on dice or wine, or sold to Jews. The precious settings of relics were torn off and destroyed. Supplies of the host were spat on, trampled, and desecrated in every way imaginable.

Not even St. Peter's was spared. For the German soldiers, the half-built basilica was the supreme symbol of Roman oppression, and they surged in, seeking blood and retribution. "Even on the high altar of St. Peter's," went one report, "five hundred men were massacred, as holy relics were burned or destroyed." Emperor Constantine's golden cross, which for more than twelve hundred years had rested in St. Peter's, was stolen and never recovered. The tombs of Julius II and other popes were opened and pillaged for valuables, and the leaden seals of papal bulls were melted down and made into bullets.

In the *stanze* of the Vatican, a German soldier scrawled the name of Martin Luther on one of Raphael's frescoes—a symbolic act of desecration. Generally, though, neither the *stanze* nor Michelangelo's Sistine ceiling suffered much damage. Frescoes had no value for the rampaging troops; it was precious metals and jewels they were after. Like the rebellious peasants in Germany, the soldiers became enraged at the sight of artifacts of learning. Many monastic libraries were gutted and the manuscript collections of scholars scattered or burned.

For at least eight days this initial wave of looting and killing continued unchecked. Throughout, the pope and his court remained sequestered in the Sant'Angelo castle, living in the *maschio*, the central tower that sat on the structure's massive circular drum, protected by a papal garrison of about five hundred. Clement kept awaiting the arrival of the troops of the Holy League, but they remained encamped ten miles to the north. With no prospect of relief, the pope on June 5, 1527, signed a treaty with the imperial force, agreeing to pay the fantastic sum of 400,000 ducats and to cede huge swaths of papal territory.

For Rome itself, the agreement provided no respite. Days after it was signed, a Spaniard described the scene: "In Rome, the chief city of Christendom, no bells ring, no churches are open, no Masses are said, Sundays and feast-days have ceased. Many houses are burned to the ground; in others the doors and windows are broken and carried away; the streets are changed into dunghills. The stench of dead bodies is terrible; men and beasts have a common grave, and in the churches I have seen corpses that dogs have gnawed." In the piazzas "tables are set close together at which piles of ducats are gambled for. The air rings with blasphemies fit to make good men—if such there be—wish that they were deaf. I know nothing wherewith I can compare it, except it be the destruction of Jerusalem."

By May 17, the first signs of plague had appeared, and over the next two months several thousand Germans would be carried off. Yet even the pestilence could not stop the marauding. Having picked Rome bare, the mercenaries moved out into the countryside, preying on towns like Narni. "We took the town and castle without firing a shot, by God's grace," a German soldier wrote, "and then put to death about 1,000 men and women."

In all, *il Sacco di Roma* left as many as thirty thousand houses destroyed and reduced the city's population by half. It also delivered a crushing blow to Rome's literary and artistic communities. The painters, poets, scholars, and philosophers who had come to the city over the decades fled. Sapienza, the university, was ruined. Paolo Bombace, the great Italian humanist and friend of Erasmus, was murdered in the first days of the sack. Johann Küritz, a major patron of arts and letters, fled at the earliest opportunity and never returned. The grammarian Julianus Camers committed suicide, and the poet Marcantonio Casanova, forced to beg for bread in the streets, died of hunger and disease. The humanist scholar Angelo Colocci was twice captured and twice tortured; he managed to escape further abuse only by paying an immense bribe, and even then he was forced to watch dolefully as his manuscript collection was burned.

For humanists, the sack marked the end of the golden era ushered in by the crowning of Petrarch as poet laureate in 1341. His vision of restoring Rome's position as *caput mundi*, head of the world, which had seemed so fanciful at the time, had to a remarkable degree been realized as aspiring men of letters from around Europe came seeking inspiration, patrons, and fame. Now that world had been brutally shattered, and the city's cultural life would take decades to recover.

"We have seen Rome sacked more cruelly than it was in ancient times by the Gauls or by the Goths," Erasmus lamented. Not even the Vandals or the Huns had in their fury burned books, "a sacred possession." The catastrophe befalling Rome, he wrote, was one affecting all nations, since the city was not only the citadel of Christianity and the domicile of the Muses but also "the common mother of all peoples." Assuredly, the sack "was more truly the destruction of the world than of a city."

Nine years later, when Michelangelo resumed work on the Sistine Chapel, he covered the wall behind the altar with *The Last Judgment*, its wrathful Christ and huddled figures begging for mercy offering a grim contrast to the classically inspired images of grace and power he had earlier applied to the ceiling.

For Luther, the irony of the sack was unmistakable. The emperor Charles, who had persecuted Luther on the pope's behalf, was now destroying the pope on Luther's behalf. Like many others, Luther believed that Rome was receiving divine punishment for its iniquitous ways. Yet the event gave him little satisfaction, for it seemed another sign of the final days. In addition to various natural oddities and fires appearing in the skies, the Ottomans were again threatening Christian Europe. On August 29, 1526, at the town of Mohács on the Danube, the 100,000-man force of Sultan Suleiman had wiped out virtually the entire 20,000-man Hungarian army. Among the fallen was King Louis II, who drowned in a marsh while trying to retreat. The Turks marched triumphantly into Buda, putting to the torch every major building except the royal palace. They occupied half of Hungary, pillaging and leveling as they went. Vienna—two hundred miles to the northwest—seemed next. The Turks, Luther felt sure, were agents of Satan working to overthrow Christ.

During this period, Satan was paying visits to Luther himself. He usually slipped into his room at night, planting disturbing thoughts in his head. Lying in bed next to Katharina, Luther thought of all the chaos he had caused, all the hatred he had stirred. Tens of thousands of peasants invoking his name had been butchered, and pastors preaching his doctrines were being tortured and beheaded. Luther was especially troubled by the case of Leonhard Kaiser, a middle-aged vicar who had returned to his hometown of Schärding, in Bavaria (today Austria), to tend to his ailing father. Kaiser had recently studied in Wittenberg and gotten to know Luther well. While in Schärding, he had continued to preach, infuriating the Catholic authorities. After an investigation found his views to be Lutheran, he was condemned to death. Luther sent him a letter of comfort while he awaited execution. He was tormented by the spectacle of such pious men shedding their blood for the gospel while he slept safely in his bed. And what if his teachings were false? "How many people must you have led astray!" the Devil frequently challenged him. A doctor must be sure that he is "called by God," Luther said; otherwise he "is lost."

In short, the *Anfechtungen*—the spells of spiritual anguish that had so darkened Luther's early years in the monastery—were again striking. An especially serious attack occurred on the evening of July 6, 1527. Luther had invited Justus Jonas and his wife for supper, but when they arrived they found Luther complaining of a troublesome roaring in his left ear, and he retired to his bedroom to rest. Jonas followed, and Luther, feeling faint, said that if he did not get some water at once, he would die. Jonas poured cold water on his face and his back. "O Lord," Luther wailed, "if it be Thy will, if this is the hour Thou hast set for me, Thy will be done." Katharina came in and, seeing her husband lying on his bed almost lifeless, called for the servants. As Luther prayed, a professor of medicine at the university arrived and applied some hot bags; Bugenhagen, to whom he had confessed that morning, also showed up. Imagining the great joy his enemies would feel at his death, Luther began sobbing uncontrollably. He asked after his son, Hans, who was brought in, and Luther praised him. He then regained some strength and was left to rest. The doctor told Jonas that Luther's spiritual distress was "twice as great" as any bodily illness he was suffering.

For more than a week, Luther felt a sickness unto death. After the worst had passed, he wrote to Melanchthon that he had "almost lost Christ in the waves and blasts of despair and blasphemy against God," but God had taken pity on him and rescued his soul "from the lowest hell."

Adding to his misery was his growing conflict with the sacramentarians. In April 1527, Luther came out with a blistering attack on the Swiss. Titled *That These Words of Christ, "This Is My Body, etc.," Still Stand Firm Against the Ranting Spirits*, the tract insisted that those words be taken literally. Zwingli quickly countered with *That These Words of Jesus Christ, "This Is My Body Which Is Given for You," Will Forever Retain Their Ancient, Single Meaning, and Martin Luther with His Latest Book Has by No Means Proved or Established His Own and the Pope's Views*, in which he made the case for regarding the communal bread and wine as spiritual symbols of Christ's sacrifice. Reading the work, Luther erupted, denouncing Zwingli as "worthy of holy hatred, so insolently and unworthily does he deal with the holy Word of God." In contending with Zwingli, Oecolampadius, and the other sacramentarians, Luther wrote to Nicholas Gerbel, he felt as if he were amid "wild beasts, vipers, lionesses, and leopards, in almost greater peril than Daniel himself in the den of lions."

Because the sacramentarians often appealed to Erasmus's writings, Luther lumped them all together as "Judases" who he felt had abandoned him. "Would that Erasmus and the sacramentarians might feel the anguish of my heart for a quarter of an hour," he wrote, "I can safely say that they would be converted and saved thereby, but now my enemies are strong and live and add grief to my grief, and whom the Lord hath smitten they persecute."

On top of it all, Wittenberg in August 1527 was hit by the plague. Striking first in the fishermen's quarter outside town, it quickly reached the center. By the middle of the month, the contagion had carried off eighteen people, including the young son of Justus Jonas; the daughter of the printer Johann Rhau-Grunenberg; and the burgomaster's wife, who died almost in Luther's arms. Many fled. The entire university moved to Jena, where it would remain until the following spring. (Luther lectured to the few students who stayed behind.) Many of the stricken showed up at the Black Cloister, which became an impromptu infirmary. Luther's son, Hans, became so ill that Luther feared for his life. When Luther himself grew weak. Elector John urged him to leave, but he considered it his duty to remain to minister to the people.

Hans ultimately pulled through, but Luther's exposure to so much suffering deepened his despair. Terrified of being alone, he asked Bugenhagen to come live with him. For his insomnia, Luther found another remedy: alcohol. He began drinking heavily in this period—a problem that would intensify with time.

Luther's spirits were further dampened by what he saw as a rapid decline of morality in Wittenberg. Sexual license, lewdness, cursing, cheating, and intoxication were all rampant. One day Luther passed someone who was defecating in public and reproached him; in a sermon, he mentioned the incident as an example of the shamelessness and lack of respect that were spreading in the town. Christian worship was also suffering.

Attendance at Sunday services was down. Many of the women who did come were dressed as if for a dance. A German Mass had been introduced at Christmas 1525, but the congregants, unhappy with the changes, sat through it like blocks.

Luther was especially troubled by the stinginess of his congregation. "This week we are asking for an offering," he said in a sermon. "I hear that people will not give the collectors anything and turn them away. . . . I am amazed, and I do not know if I will preach any more, you uncouth rascals."

The decline in morality was in part a by-product of Luther's own theology. His doctrine of justification by faith alone was breeding contempt for the law. Since attending church, going to confession, and providing charity were no longer seen as meritorious acts leading to salvation, many simply gave them up. In the countryside, meanwhile, all was chaos. With the disappearance of the Church, there was a profusion of doctrines, customs, and worship practices; with the abolition of tithes, villagers were refusing to support pastors. Many actually considered pastors superfluous since they could now read the Gospels on their own. With no endowed Masses for the dead, churches were going into debt.

To try to restore some order, Luther proposed to Elector John that teams of wise men be sent into the countryside to assess the situation on the ground. John agreed. The electorate was divided into five regions, each of which was to receive a delegation from Wittenberg. The visitors were to inspect schools and churches, assess the quality and conduct of pastors, mediate disputes, and recommend improvements.

In early July 1527, a six-member team led by Melanchthon left for Weida, south of Leipzig. The six spent the next month visiting communities in and around the Saale valley. They were shocked by what they found. The pastors included many misfits and oddballs with only a rudimentary knowledge of evangelical doctrines. Some could barely recite the Apostles' Creed or the Lord's Prayer. Of the two hundred clergymen in the region, all but a handful were openly fornicating; many frequented taverns and gambling dens.

"Everything is in confusion, partly through ignorance, and partly through the immorality of the teachers," Melanchthon wrote, adding:

"My heart bleeds when I regard this misery. Often when we have completed the visitation of a place, I go to one side and pour forth my distress in tears." Interestingly, this was the same region where three years earlier Karlstadt had preached and Luther been challenged by plowmen quoting Scripture. That so few now knew or cared about matters of faith suggested the pall of apathy and cynicism that had settled over the countryside following the peasants' defeat.

After completing the tour, Melanchthon drew up a set of articles to guide future visitations. After weeks of discussion, including comments from Luther, these appeared in March 1528 as a handbook, *Instructions for the Visitors of Parish Pastors in Electoral Saxony*. Predictably, it called on pastors to preach the importance of faith. Surprisingly, it also urged them to stress the need to do good works, including upholding the Ten Commandments. They were also to teach that man has free will. The emphasis placed on good works and free will seemed a clear departure from Lutheran orthodoxy, and Catholic commentators gleefully pounced on it, but it was considered necessary to combat the breakdown of morality in the countryside. Strong stress was also placed on obedience to, and respect for, the government, and schools were to instruct students in the essentials of both Christian living and grammar. (Remarkably, the curriculum was to include Erasmus's *Colloquies*.) To ensure compliance, each region was to be overseen by a superintendent, who was to make sure that pastors were fit for office, that they led pious lives, and that they properly preached the Word of God.

The *Instructions* did not address what was perhaps the most critical question of all: who rules? Without a pope or bishop, who was to have the ultimate say over church matters? The answer soon became clear: the sovereign. The final arbiter of religious matters in Saxony was to be not the congregation, or the theologians, or a body of elders, but the elector. During the seven years of his rule, John, who supported the Reformation far more vigorously than had his brother Frederick, would meet frequently with Luther to discuss everything from the selection of pastors and the order of services to the financing of churches and the establishment of schools. This development reflected the need for a strong hand to keep the peace. It also mirrored the ongoing change in Luther's own thinking, away from his early populism and belief in congregational control toward an emphasis on order and authority. The visitation instructions of 1528 thus marked an important step in the creation of the so-called territorial church, in which the prince, acting as the bishop, oversaw all ministerial activities. Over time, the supervisory tasks of the visitations would be assumed by consistories—ecclesiastical bodies formed to address marriage matters, uphold moral discipline among the peasants, and monitor the performance of pastors. In addition, a superintendent would be appointed to carry out the duties previously assigned to bishops. The final say, though, remained with the ruler. This model, in which the church became an arm of the state, would be adopted by other territories as they embraced Luther's gospel.

And there would be many such territories, for the Reformation was about to enter a period of rapid growth, due in part to a critical measure adopted at the 1526 Diet of Speyer. Because the Edict of Worms had proved unenforceable, the delegates decided to suspend it. In its place, each prince was urged to conduct himself in a way answerable to both God and the emperor. In effect, this gave princes the right to determine the religious practices in their territories.

Princes sympathetic to Luther moved at once to capitalize. In 1526, the landgrave Philip of Hesse formally declared for the Reformation and quickly began seizing the Catholic monasteries in his territory. (Expropriating Church property was a common motive for joining the Reformation.) Ambitious, restless, and strategically savvy, Philip would become the political leader of the Lutheran cause, directing negotiations, forming alliances, and rallying his more phlegmatic colleagues. In 1527, in Marburg, the landgrave founded a university, which in the coming years would inspire the creation of scores of similar institutions throughout the Protestant world.

In cities, it was town councils that took the lead. When in 1528 the north-central city of Brunswick decided to become Lutheran, its council asked Wittenberg to send a theologian to help oversee the transition. Luther reluctantly agreed to part with Bugenhagen. For more than a year, Bugenhagen lived in Brunswick, helping to implant Lutheran institutions. Soon afterward, he would travel north to Hamburg to do the same. In the coming years, Bugenhagen's work would be instrumental in establishing the Reformation in the Hanseatic cities of Magdeburg, Bremen, Lübeck, Rostock, Danzig, and Riga. In northeastern Germany, Albert of Brandenburg-Ansbach, who had converted to the evangelical cause in 1525, continued the process of converting his duchy, Prussia, into a Lutheran state.

In the south, the new faith prevailed in several important cities, including Nuremberg, Augsburg, Strasbourg, and Ulm. Here, images were removed from churches, meat was eaten on fast days, preaching was based exclusively on Scripture, and private Masses were abolished. The money formerly spent on such Masses was redirected to schools, hospitals, and poor relief. In 1526, Nuremberg, responding to Luther's call for towns to establish schools, opened a Latin school in a former convent. Melanchthon spent much of the month of May there, shaping its curriculum and giving its inaugural address. (The school, known as the Melanchthon-Gymnasium, is still in operation.) In the years to come, three thousand such schools would be established in territories aligned with the Reformation. The stress on schooling, literacy, libraries, and printing would become a hallmark of Protestantism, which looked to the Book rather than the pope for direction.

Large parts of southern Germany, however, continued to look to the pope. Bavaria, along with the powerful archbishoprics of Mainz, Trier, and Cologne, remained loyal to Rome. In these years, the religious map of modern Germany was beginning to take shape, with a largely Lutheran north and east and a generally Catholic south. Ten years after the posting of Luther's lonely protest against indulgences, his ideas had become the reigning creed in nearly half the land.

The growing division of Christendom left Erasmus deeply demoralized. His reform program was based on the idea of a united Europe rooted in a common Christian culture, but with that community now splintering, the space for Erasmus's vision was shrinking. It suffered a major blow on December 16, 1527, when the Paris faculty of theology voted formally to condemn his writings. The faculty cited 112 propositions from his paraphrases and his rebuttals of Béda, plus twenty-two instances in which he was said to have misread or disagreed with the Vulgate. In Louvain, there arose a dogged new critic, the Franciscan Frans Titelmans. A tenacious defender of the Vulgate, Titelmans in public lectures denounced Erasmus for rashly modifying that text and thereby diminishing its authority. Echoing Dorp, he claimed that the Vulgate had been prepared under divine guidance and that it was thus insolent to offer a new translation, as Erasmus had done.

The strongest strike against Erasmus, however, came in Spain. The Spanish translation of the *Enchiridion*, which had set off such a frenzy of interest in Erasmus, had also produced a furious backlash among the monks. That work's statement that monasticism is not piety, along with other perceived insults to that institution, had inflamed the Dominicans and Franciscans, who now set out to blacken Erasmus's image and isolate his admirers. "Men speak ill of me everywhere simply because I am a supporter of Erasmus," Alonso Ruiz de Virués, a Benedictine monk in Burgos, complained to a fellow Spaniard. Such vilification was not confined to private conversations or to out-of-the-way places, he noted: "In courts, theaters, and crowded gatherings I am reviled, snubbed, and hissed at." The charge "is heresy, and it is made in sermons and delivered from the pulpit." The monks were secretly stationing agents in bookstores, where, pretending to be occupied with something else, they tried to warn off those interested in buying Erasmus's works by citing their offensive content.

With Erasmus facing such opprobrium, Alonso Manrique de Lara, the Spanish inquisitor-general, directed his critics to submit their objections in writing, to be taken up at an ecclesiastical assembly scheduled for the summer of 1527 in Valladolid. The charges included defaming Jerome, undermining the Trinity, placing too much faith in ancient manuscripts, and impugning the authority of the Vulgate. Because of an outbreak of the plague, the conference was adjourned before a final judgment could be reached. Erasmus's Spanish friends advised him to let the matter rest. Refusing, he produced a searing *Defense Against Some Spanish Monks*. This inflamed the monks further, and after Charles left Spain in 1529, taking the Erasmian-inflected court with him, Erasmus's enemies declared war on his supporters. They were investigated, fined, forced to issue public recantations, and in some cases imprisoned. By the mid-1530s, reading Erasmus had become a virtual crime in Spain.

Amid all these clashes, Erasmus managed to find the time to make good on his promise to Thomas More to complete the second part of the *Hyperaspistes*. Twice the length of the first, it was one of Erasmus's longest—and most vitriolic—works. He scorned Luther's "supersophistical trash," his "prolix and pretentious palaver," his smoke screens and hairsplitting. "It is worthwhile to hear how he shakes and sifts this passage," he wrote of one Lutheran gloss, "for he does so not like a person examining something carefully but like a wild horse shaking its rider off the saddle and into the mud." Whether discussing the pharaoh's heart, Judas's betrayal, or the potter's clay, Luther had done nothing but "cockadoodled"—a term Erasmus repeatedly flung like a school-yard taunt.

Here and there, he took a break from the name-calling to offer a heartfelt summary of the main differences between him and Luther and, in effect, between the Renaissance and the Reformation. Within man, he wrote, there is a faculty of reason that enables him to distinguish good from evil and turn from the one to the other. The tears that grown men shed at the sight of extraordinary acts of virtue show that the seeds of such behavior lie deep within us. Even the most dissolute individuals retain some faculty of moral awareness. But Luther had so exaggerated man's depravity and his need for grace as to make him seem almost a Satan. Even when performing the noblest deeds, Luther claimed, man does nothing but sin. But even if one grants that virtuous acts alone are not sufficient to achieve justification, people do not do wicked deeds when they honor their parents, love their children and wives, support the poor and sick. Many perform such acts for no other reason than that they think them worthy of a good person and would want the same done to them if they found themselves in similar circumstances.

At the end of his tract, Erasmus offered a simple statement that, perhaps more than any other in his vast oeuvre, summed up his philosophy of Christ: Rather than make finespun distinctions over how God's grace works in us, we should devote our efforts to obtaining that grace. Scripture does not say that all human endeavor is in vain—that God will save or damn you as he pleases. Rather, it says: Turn to me and I will turn to you. Struggle to enter by the narrow gate. Transgressors, return to your senses. Forgive and you will be forgiven. Help the poor and show favor to the orphan. "Let brother say to brother, 'Let us love one another'; let us change for the better if we have sinned through ignorance; let us strive for God's grace by pious works."

Thus far, Basel had managed to escape the strife and recrimination engulfing Europe, remaining a haven of openness and pluralism, and in the afternoon Erasmus liked to retreat to Froben's garden to read and edit the ancients. In 1527 and 1528, he brought out new editions of Chrysostom, Athanasius, Irenaeus, Origen, Ambrose, Seneca, and—towering over them all—Augustine. The collected edition of the great Doctor that he had been working on since 1521 was so massive (ten thick volumes) that it would take two full years to print.

But the advocates of reform in Basel were growing in both number and fervor. They were concentrated in the Steinenvorstadt, a working-class district in the center of town that was home to many weavers and other laborers who felt marginalized by the oligarchs—both secular and ecclesiastical—who ruled the town. For them, religious and political reform went hand in hand, and they were noisily demanding both. Leading the way was Oecolampadius. In a measure of the fury being generated by the dispute over the Eucharist, Oecolampadius in early 1527 came out with a pamphlet declaring that the blasphemous conduct of the servants of the Mass was worse than robbery, whoring, adultery, treason, manslaughter, and murder. In October, four hundred evangelicals held a rally to demand that the town council abolish the Catholic Mass in Basel's churches. The councilors refused, maintaining that all citizens should be free to follow their conscience and worship as they saw fit.

The agitation continued, however, and on April 15, 1528 (Good Friday), a group of iconoclasts barged into two of the city's churches and removed pictures from them. The next day, town councilors had the activists arrested and placed in chains, but two hundred citizens protested so loudly that they were quickly released. Hoping to restore calm, the council issued an order stating that "no man should call another papist or Lutheran, heretic or adherent of the new faith or of the old, but that each should be left unembarrassed and unscorned in the exercise of his own belief."

This only incited the reformers further, however. Shortly before Christmas, a group of guild members sent the council a petition demanding that the evangelical faith be declared the only acceptable one. As discontent spread, mediators were summoned from Strasbourg and other Swiss cantons. With their help, the council on January 5, 1529, decreed that from then on all preaching was to be based solely on the Bible—a concession to the reformers—while, in a nod to the Catholics, Mass was to be celebrated once a day in three churches. This pleased no one. Catholic priests refused to accept the quota on Masses, while evangelicals issued defamatory leaflets demanding that the Mass be abolished altogether.

Before dawn on February 8, some eight hundred mostly poor citizens gathered in the Franciscan church in the center of Basel and elected a committee to press the council to abolish the Mass, dismiss its Catholic members, and adopt democratic reforms. The council convened in the town hall on the marketplace to deliberate. When by nightfall no decision had been reached, a thousand demonstrators gathered in the square, built a huge bonfire, put brass crossbows in place, and planted a cannon in front of the hall. Catholics organized a counterdemonstration.

After noon the next day, forty armed men, unwilling to wait any longer, marched up the hill to the Münster and surged in. A clumsy guild member tipped over an altarpiece with a halberd, causing it to shatter. When the men left to get reinforcements, the chaplains locked the church. A loud and raucous crowd of about two hundred reappeared and, forcing their way in, began smashing and hacking crucifixes, altars, and images of the Virgin Mary and the saints. The iconoclasts then fanned out to other churches and carried out similar sprees. The next morning, Basel looked out on shards of statues, shreds of canvases, stumps of candelabra, and other remnants of centuries of Catholic devotion.

Terrified, the Catholic members of the council resigned. Nearly all of the professors at the university relinquished their posts and left town. The burgomaster escaped at night by boat; had he remained, he would probably have been hanged. With angry crowds still occupying the marketplace, the new pro-reform council oversaw a more thorough, and orderly, cleansing of the churches. As Erasmus described the scene to Willibald Pirckheimer,

> The dissidents, with the assistance of workmen and artisans, removed from the churches whatever they pleased. . . . No statues were left in the churches, or in vestibules, or cloisters, or monasteries. All painted images were covered over with whitewash. Anything that would burn was thrown on the fire; what would not burn was torn into shreds. Neither value nor artistic merit ensured that an object would be spared. Soon the Mass was totally prohibited; it was not even permissible to celebrate the sacred rite at home or attend it in a neighboring village.

Erasmus was relieved that no houses had been broken into and no blood shed, but, as he laconically summed up the transfer of power, "Oecolampadius is taking over all the churches." On April 1, 1529, the approval of a Reform Ordinance made it official: Basel had joined the Reformation. From then on, people could attend only reformed services, and all monks and nuns had to abandon their habits. Those who missed Sunday sermons without good cause had to pay a substantial fine.

By that point, Erasmus had had enough. The sense of openness that had attracted him to Basel was gone. Without a sympathetic town council to protect him, he felt that he would be at the mercy of the mob. And if he stayed, he would be seen as having endorsed the change. So, despite his advancing age and declining health, he decided to leave the city that had been his home for the last eight years.

But where to go? Erasmus had many options. From Henry VIII he had received an effusive letter asking him to settle in England. ("Our love for you . . . has reached such magnitude as to exceed all bounds," the king gushed.) But Erasmus dreaded the thought of making another Channel crossing and, once in England, of becoming entangled in Henry's messy divorce. Charles V had repeatedly invited him to Spain, but that land was too distant, hot, and teeming with hostile monks. Ferdinand had offered a salary of four hundred florins a year if he moved to Vienna; King

Sigismund was trying to lure him to Poland; and Margaret, the regent of the Netherlands, was urging him to return to his native land. While reveling in such royal regard, Erasmus recoiled at the thought of becoming a courtier.

In the end, he decided on Freiburg. Just forty miles to the north, it was a quiet university town within a day's journey of the Froben presses. Located in territory ruled by Ferdinand and the Hapsburgs, it was solidly Catholic. From Ferdinand, Erasmus obtained a letter of recommendation and a guarantee of safe passage through Hapsburg lands. He quietly sent ahead his money and furniture.

When his intention to leave Basel became known, there was an outcry. Erasmus's presence in the city had been a source of great pride, and to lose him would dim its reputation as a seat of letters and learning. Oecolampadius was especially upset. Since 1515, when he had helped Erasmus with his landmark New Testament, he had looked up to him, and he continued to do so despite their theological differences. When Erasmus heard of his distress, he invited him for a conversation. It took place in Froben's garden on or about the afternoon of April 10, 1529. Oecolampadius pressed him to change his mind, but Erasmus noted that he had already sent ahead his possessions. They parted with a friendly handshake.

Erasmus wanted to leave from a secluded dock so as to avoid "a public spectacle," but the council insisted that he use the customary embarkation point at the Rhine Bridge in the center of town. On April 13, Erasmus arrived with a few friends who were to accompany him on his journey. At the last moment, he composed a quatrain expressing his gratitude for all the hospitality that the city had shown him:

> Basel, farewell. No other city made
> Me half so welcome now for many a year.
> I wish you well, and may no future guest
> More dreadful than Erasmus settle here.

He and his friends then boarded the boat, and a small crowd watched in melancholy silence as Europe's most famous scholar disappeared around the great bend of the Rhine on his way north to Catholic Germany.

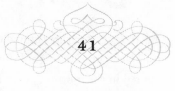

THE CRACK-UP

In Wittenberg, Luther was becoming something of a homebody. Exhausted by the raging battles over doctrine and authority, he was devoting more and more time to his responsibilities as a husband and a father. Even in that capacity, though, he could not avoid attracting attention. With monasteries emptying, celibacy declining, and monks and nuns marrying, the new evangelical clergy looked to him for guidance.

The Black Cloister, where dark-robed monks once shuffled in silence, was now a place of bustle and commotion as the Luther family rapidly expanded. On December 10, 1527, Katharina gave birth to a daughter, Elizabeth. Sadly, she would die the following August, but in May 1529 another daughter, Magdalena, arrived. (The Luthers would have six children in all, four of whom would survive into adulthood.) When Luther's sister Margarete died that same year, her four children came to live in the cloister. They were later joined by Katharina's aunt, Magdalene von Bora, as well as two nephews and a grandniece of Katharina's. At one point, sixteen Luther children were living in the cloister. Young Hans, now walking and talking, often barged into his father's study and began singing. "If it gets too loud I scold him some," Martin affectionately observed. "He goes on singing just the same, but he does it more furtively, becoming rather anxious and shy."

Luther also put up many runaway monks and nuns until they could find permanent lodging. Because Wittenberg had few inns, dignitaries visiting the town often stayed at the Black Cloister, hoping to meet him. One prince preparing to visit was, however, warned that "an odd assortment of young people, students, young girls, widows, old women and children lives in the Doctor's home; this makes for great disquiet in the house, and there are many who pity Luther because of it."

A number of the cloister's forty cells were now occupied by students, who, in return for lodging and meals, either tutored the children or paid a modest fee—a welcome supplement to the tight Luther budget. The main meal was usually served at ten in the morning, with a light supper offered at five in the afternoon. Luther was always the center of attention, speaking in a mix of Latin (on theological topics) and German (on everyday ones). Some of the young men at the table began taking notes. After Luther's death, a thick folio of this Table Talk would appear. (The Weimar edition has about seven thousand entries in six volumes.) Sometimes rude, often coarse, always frank, the *Tischreden* would embarrass generations of Protestants, but the unexpurgated version offers a bracing look into the mind of one of history's titans as he held forth on everything from Scripture and doctrine to local customs and national characteristics.

The German people, Luther remarked on one occasion, are "simpler and more attached to the truth than Frenchmen, Italians, Spaniards, and Englishmen." The German tongue was the best of all, though there were so many dialects that the Germans often did not understand one another. Their greatest vice was drinking—"a disgraceful nuisance" that "injures body, soul, and goods." Whoever invented the brewing of beer had set a curse on the German people. Luther disliked German tailors, who seemed careless and used too much cloth without giving the proper shape; Italian tailors were far superior. He disliked lawyers of every nationality, believing that most were greedy and robbed their clients blind. "If I had a hundred sons," he said, "I wouldn't bring up one of them to be a lawyer."

A frequent presence in the Table Talk is Tölpel, Luther's beloved dog. "Oh, if I could only pray the way this dog watches meat!" he observed. "All his thoughts are concentrated on the piece of meat." On the subject of heretics and opponents, Luther said that he found them useful. Johann Eck, for one, "made me wide awake." He "gave me my first ideas, and without him I would never have got this far." For Jerome, by contrast, Luther felt only disgust: "I know no doctor whom I hate so much, although I once loved him ardently and read him voraciously. . . . Surely there's more learning in Aesop than in all of Jerome."

Luther despised Erasmus most of all. No other contemporary appears in the Table Talk as often or in as negative a light. "Erasmus is an eel. Nobody can grasp him except Christ alone. He is a double-dealing man."

He had "corrupted the youth with the wicked opinions he expressed in his colloquies. God keep him in check!" Erasmus did not think that God is in any way superior to man and would not acknowledge that the Holy Scriptures are confirmed by such miracles as the raising of the dead and the expulsion of demons. "I hate Erasmus from the bottom of my heart because he calls into question what ought to be our joy." After breakfast one morning, Luther took a piece of chalk and wrote on the table: "Substance and words—Philipp [Melanchthon]. Words without substance—Erasmus. Substance without words—Luther. Neither substance nor words—Karlstadt."

(After leaving the Luther household, Karlstadt had tried to make a living as a farmer in Kemberg, a village not far from Wittenberg. Constantly harassed by Luther, though, he left Saxony in early 1529. After serving as a deacon for four years in Zurich, he settled in Basel, where he became a professor of the Old Testament and taught Hebrew until his death in December 1541.)

Once, while Luther was responding to students' questions, Katharina suddenly interjected, "Doctor, why don't you stop talking and eat?" "I wish," Luther snapped, "that women would repeat the Lord's Prayer before opening their mouths." On another occasion, he said that his wife was an eloquent speaker but that "eloquence in women shouldn't be praised; it's more fitting for them to lisp and stammer," whereas for men eloquence "is a great and divine gift." Luther's Table Talk is full of such patronizing remarks. "Men have broad shoulders and narrow hips, and accordingly they possess intelligence," he said. "Women have narrow shoulders and broad hips" and "a wide rump to sit on," showing that they were created to stay at home and raise children. Punning on his wife's name, Luther sometimes called her *Kette*, German for "chain." At the cloister, Katharina was the subject of many jokes and endless gossip, and the students frequently treated her like a servant.

She no doubt often felt like one. She had to rise at four every morning to get her work done. She drove the wagon, did the shopping, cultivated the fields, fed the animals, slaughtered the cattle, made butter and cheese, did the shopping, brewed the beer, and regularly hosted meals for up to forty people. Katharina was always modernizing and remodeling the cloister; at one point, she had installed a new bathroom made of sandstone. Katharina often complained about her husband's lack of interest in earning money. Thanks to her savvy, however, the family prospered, and a 1542 inventory showed it in possession of five cows, nine calves, one goat with two kids, eight swine, two sows, and three piglets.

"The lady of the pig market" is how Martin sometimes affectionately addressed her in letters. He also called her "my dearest" and signed off as "your loved one." If prior to his marriage Luther had frankly acknowledged he did not love Katharina, over time he came to, saying that "I wouldn't give up my Katy for France or for Venice." (Katharina, however, usually addressed her husband as "Mr. Doctor.") In the coming years, as Luther suffered from a series of ailments, including gout, constipation, hemorrhoids, the stone, dizziness, insomnia, and ringing in the ears, Katharina would be forever at his side, offering comfort and balm. She was a master of the *Dreckapotheke*, or excrement pharmacy, preparing concoctions of pig's dung to calm the blood, horse manure in wine for coughs, and human excrement for bodily wounds.

Though skeptical about such remedies, Luther appreciated his wife's good sense and quiet tenderness—qualities that shaped his attitudes toward domestic life in general. It "is the pleasantest kind of life," he observed, "to have a moderate household, to live with an obedient wife, and to be content with little." "Imagine what it would be like without this sex. The home, cities, economic life, and government would virtually disappear. Men can't do without women." Admiring a portrait of his wife, Martin called marriage "the divine institution from which everything proceeds and without which the whole world would have remained empty."

During the Middle Ages, the iconic woman had always been the nun—virginal, silent, devout. Now Katharina was providing an alternative: the caring and competent clerical spouse. And the Luther household—busy, convivial, energetic—was giving rise to a new institution: the evangelical parsonage. Equipped more with books and ideals than money or property, it would come to occupy a prominent place in Protestant culture in both Europe and America. (The vicars and preachers in the novels of Trollope, Eliot, and Gaskell come to mind.) The new clerical household, in turn, would elevate the status of family life. With the monastery fading, the family would gradually take its place as the main locus of piety in Protestant life.

The influence of the evangelical household would be reinforced by an important instructional work that Luther prepared in 1529. The idea for it came from a series of visitations he made in 1528 to villages around Wittenberg. Like Melanchthon, he was shocked at local conditions. "The peasants learn nothing, know nothing, pray nothing, do nothing except abuse their liberty," he wrote to Spalatin. "They go neither to confession nor to communion, as though they had been liberated from all the duties of religion." Luther blamed "papistical bishops" who had failed to carry out their duties, but his comments offered further evidence of the lethargy and indifference that had pervaded the countryside after the peasant debacle.

To combat such ignorance, Luther decided to produce a catechism—a summary of religious teachings for use in instruction. The Catholic Church had for centuries offered these summaries, and in the 1520s a flood of such instructional books issued from reformers; none, though, would have the impact of Luther's catechism. Actually, he produced two catechisms—a large one, for preachers and advanced adults, and a small one, for children and beginners. The latter would become very popular. Barely more than a dozen pages long, it offered concise explanations of the Ten Commandments, the Apostles' Creed, the sacraments, the Lord's Prayer, and other key prayers, framed in question-and-answer form. A central theme was obedience. Concerning civil government, the booklet stated, "Let everyone be subject to the governing authority. For whoever the governing authority is, it is ordained by God. But whoever resists the governing authority, resists God's order." Wives were to submit to their husbands, children were to obey their parents, and servants, day laborers, and workers were to be obedient to their earthly masters "with fear and trembling." And everyone was to love his neighbor as himself.

According to Luther, it was every father's duty to question and examine his children and servants at least once a week on the contents of the catechism and to ascertain what they knew, and "if they do not know it, to keep them faithfully at it." Luther himself would recite parts of the catechism every morning and more if time allowed, and he required the same of his wife and children. Under his influence, the home would become a center of religious study for Protestants in a way it would not for Catholics, for whom the church and clergy remained the main agents of instruction. This stress on study would not, however, encourage independent thinking. Luther's catechisms provided a fixed set of beliefs, with little room for deviation or questioning, and in his rules for their use, he insisted on rote memorization of the text.

Martin and Katharina together would create a model for German households for centuries to come, establishing it as a place of learning, industry, and comfort on the one hand, and patriarchy, discipline, and conformity on the other.

While Luther and Katharina in Wittenberg were helping to mold German domestic life, the shape of the Reformation as a whole was being determined at three historic conclaves held over a span of seventeen months. The first, the 1529 Diet of Speyer, would produce one of history's most famous religious labels. The Catholic delegates—dismayed at the rapid gains made by the Lutherans since the 1526 diet—set out to reverse them. Henceforth, they declared, Catholic services were to be tolerated in all Lutheran lands while Lutheran services were to be prohibited in all Catholic ones. The Edict of Worms was to be reinstated, priests were to teach the Bible according to standards set by the Church, and the confiscation of ecclesiastical properties was to cease. In effect, the Catholic delegates were trying to freeze the Reformation in place.

The reformers loudly objected. On April 19, 1529, six princes, including John of Saxony and Philip of Hesse, along with fourteen imperial cities, submitted a *protestatio*, or protestation, summarizing their beliefs. In it, they objected to all measures they saw as incompatible with the Word of God, with their conscience, and with the guarantees of religious freedom made at the 1526 diet. Reworked and expanded, their protestation was rushed into print. On this basis, they would be called "Protestants." By a quirk of history, the new faith would become known by this impromptu term. (Luther, however, would continue to refer to his movement as *evangelische*, or evangelical.)

Worried that the Catholics would strike back, the Protestant princes in Speyer on April 22 made a secret agreement to defend one another if that happened. This effort was led by Philip of Hesse. Given the great manpower and resources of the Catholics, he believed that the Protestants could survive only by uniting. The main obstacle to that was the bitter division between German and Swiss reformers over the Lord's Supper. Intent on overcoming it, Philip sent Zwingli a letter inviting him to meet with Luther and other reformers to try to reach an agreement.

After Zwingli affirmed his willingness to participate, Philip approached Luther. He was adamantly opposed to such a meeting, certain that nothing good would come of it. Only after being subjected to the "shameless insistence" of the "restless and hotheaded" landgrave, as he put it, did he give in. In mid-September 1529, Luther, Melanchthon, Justus Jonas, and several other Wittenbergers set off on the two-hundred-mile journey to Marburg, home to Philip's family castle. Arriving on the morning of September 30, Luther found himself in the same room as colleagues and rivals he had known mostly through tracts, letters, and gossip. Oecolampadius had come from Basel, Bucer from Strasbourg, and Zwingli from Zurich. Zwingli, who wore a black tunic with a short sword at his side and who had a large retinue, held back from the Wittenbergers, with whom he had so furiously clashed. Also present were leading reformers from Nuremberg, Augsburg, Frankfurt, and Cologne. The Marburg Colloquy would be the only time that all the fathers of the Reformation were gathered in one spot. Many accounts and reconstructions of the meeting have survived, offering a dramatic inside look at this historic encounter.

The principals stayed at Philip's castle, an impressive fortress perched on a hill overlooking the town. Luther, though dazzled by the regal trappings and sumptuous meals, was put off by Melanchthon's ease at making small talk, and he found Bucer a *Klappermaul*, or chatterbox. On October 1, a series of private discussions was held among the leaders, with Luther pairing off with Oecolampadius and Melanchthon with Zwingli. (It was thought best to keep Luther and Zwingli—the two strongest personalities of the Reformation—apart.)

When these exchanges failed to produce any progress, a more general discussion was held among the leaders the next day in the landgrave's large bedchamber (which had the advantage of being heated). Philip and his counselors listened as Luther and Melanchthon (representing the Germans) engaged Zwingli and Oecolampadius (representing the Swiss). Luther had trouble following what he called the "tangled, matted" dialect of the Swiss, and he was annoyed at Zwingli's flaunting of his Greek. Whereas Oecolampadius seemed kind and gentle, Zwingli seemed boorish and superior. Nonetheless, the two sides were able to reach agreement on fourteen points, including the Trinity, original sin, redemption, baptism, good works, and, finally, justification by faith, which all acknowledged to be the core of their creed.

A fifteenth—the Lord's Supper—proved more intractable. Over two days the disputants sparred over Matthew 26 and other key passages in a bid to determine what exactly happens to the bread and wine during Communion. Zwingli argued that because we know Christ to be in heaven, sitting at the right hand of the Father, he could not at the same time be present in the bread and wine. Luther replied that since Christ was omnipresent, why could he not be in both places at once? Hours were spent parsing the meaning of "is" and "signifies," "body" and "blood," "flesh" and "eating." While the Swiss argued with cool humanist logic, Luther frequently grew emotional. "If God commanded me to eat dung," he insisted at one point, "I should eat it." God, Zwingli stiffly replied, "does not give commands of that type." "Pray that God will open your eyes!" Luther cried. At one point during the discussion, Luther scribbled something in chalk on the table in front of him and then covered it with a velvet cloth. At a key moment of Swiss resistance, he removed the cloth to reveal what he had written: *Hoc est corpus meum*—"This is my body." "Here," he declared, "is our Scriptural passage." From this position, he would not budge. Zwingli in his exasperation was moved nearly to tears.

As the meeting was breaking up, Zwingli and his party asked the Wittenbergers to recognize them as brothers in Christ and to take Holy Communion with them as a goodwill gesture. Luther refused. "They were humble beyond measure in asking for peace," he reported to his friend Agricola while on his way back to Wittenberg, but they were "clumsy and inexperienced in argument. Even though they perceived that their arguments proved nothing, they were not willing to yield on the point of the presence of the body of Christ." In the end, "they asked that we at least acknowledge them as brethren, and the prince was very urgent about it, but that could not be granted. Nevertheless we gave them the right hand of peace and charity, agreeing that for the present harsh words and writings should cease, and each teach his own opinion without invective, but not without defense and refutation."

Luther's obduracy reflected the zeal and intolerance of the times, when even small differences over doctrine could produce bitter conflict; even so, his refusal to acknowledge the Swiss reformers as brothers in Christ was an act of extreme intransigence. And the consequences would be profound. With the failure at Marburg, the gulf that Karlstadt had helped open up with his Eucharistic tracts of 1524 would become fixed in place. Largely because of their differences over the interpretation of these four words, the Lutheran and Swiss reformers would remain divided, and the competition between them would prove as debilitating as Philip of Hesse had feared.

Back in Wittenberg, Luther's congregants felt the lash of his growing distemper. In the pulpit, he repeatedly scolded them for their brazen misconduct. Couples were sneaking off into the woods to have sex. Prostitution flourished. Drunkenness was such a problem that Luther wanted the taverns closed during Sunday services. People remained unwilling to support pastors or aid the poor. And no amount of sermonic admonition seemed to make any difference.

His frustration finally boiling over, Luther announced on January 1, 1530, that because of the congregation's ingratitude and flouting of God's Word, he was going to stop preaching. In the ensuing uproar, the congregants, promising to do better, begged him to stay. Elector John also implored him, saying that if he followed through, it would have "grievous consequences." In the end, Luther gave in and resumed preaching. But the moral laxness would persist. Since salvation depended on faith alone, why bother to do good works? That question would vex Luther, and Protestant pastors in general, for many years to come.

But a much more immediate challenge loomed. In early March 1530, Elector John received from Charles V a summons to attend the next Imperial Diet, due to begin in April in Augsburg. The emperor himself planned to attend, in what would be his first appearance on German soil since the Diet of Worms. In his summons, he explained that he had decided to participate in the hope of overcoming the divisions among Christians and restoring "one single Christian truth." Because theological matters were to be high on the agenda, John asked Luther, along with Melanchthon, Jonas, and Bugenhagen, to travel to Torgau, where they were to prepare a summary of Lutheran beliefs for submission to the diet. From there they were to accompany the elector to Coburg—the southernmost princely residency in Electoral Saxony—while safe-conducts were arranged for the trip to Augsburg. Quickly finding others to fill in for them, the Wittenbergers on April 3 set off with great anticipation.

Charles's presence at the diet ensured that it would be the most important such gathering since Worms. It represented a last-gasp effort to repair the fissure that at that diet had opened up within Western Christendom. In Torgau, Luther, Melanchthon, and Jonas drafted a statement of Lutheran principles that would become known as the Torgau Articles. They then traveled with the elector and his retinue to Coburg. Along the way the group heard that the emperor's journey was taking longer than expected, causing the diet's opening to be delayed. After resting for several days in Weimar, the Saxons traveled on to Coburg, arriving on April 15, 1530. While they were there, safe-conducts were arranged for all the Wittenbergers except Luther. Because he remained an outlaw under the Edict of Worms, he would have to stay behind in Coburg. The Saxons promised to send regular reports. (A mounted courier could cover the 150 miles between Augsburg and Coburg in three or four days.) To keep Luther company and to serve as his secretary, Veit Dietrich, a Wittenberg student who had accompanied the group to Coburg, would also remain behind.

The two men stayed in the Coburg castle, which, sitting on a hill above the town, was one of the largest strongholds in Germany. As at the Wartburg, Luther again found himself in "the wilderness," as he called it. As then, he needed to remain incognito and so let his beard grow. Though frustrated at not being able to attend the diet, he at first enjoyed the break from the commotion at the Black Cloister. "This place is extremely pleasant and most suited for studying," he wrote to Melanchthon. Luther was impressed by the large flocks of birds that struck up a chorus beginning at four in the morning and continuing without letup into the late afternoon. In the cawing and maneuvering of the jackdaws (black-plumed members of the crow family), he saw a metaphor for the deliberations at the diet. Among them were "magnanimous kings, dukes, and other noblemen of the kingdom," who "with untiring voice proclaim their decisions and dogmas through the air." Luther planned to use his time to write and to continue his translation of the Old Testament. He also hoped to translate some of Aesop's fables and prepare a commentary on the Psalter.

In Luther's absence, it would fall to Melanchthon to represent the Wittenberg theologians in Augsburg, and as he approached the city he was overcome by anxiety. He had to produce a statement of Protestant faith that could serve as a basis for negotiations with the Catholics in an eleventh-hour bid to avert a rupture in the Western Church. On his arrival, he got a sobering look at what lay ahead. To help control the expected crowds, hundreds of mercenaries had been hired, and preparations had been made to close off the streets with chains. Around 1,200 nobles were due to attend, along with 20 prominent Catholic theologians, among them Luther's old adversary, Johann Eck. In anticipation of the diet, Eck had drafted 404 articles in which he caustically chronicled the record of heretical deviations from Roman doctrine. Luther was called the greatest of blasphemers, the father of lies, the fountain from which the many streams of contemporary heresy flowed. The work was on sale in Augsburg's bookstores, and Melanchthon, examining a copy, could feel the malice and scorn surging through the Catholic camp.

He could, though, count on much goodwill as well. Back in 1518, when Luther traveled to Augsburg to be interrogated by Cardinal Cajetan, the Church's hold on the city seemed unshakable. Now Catholic preachers were outnumbered by Lutherans and Zwinglians, who from their pulpits inveighed loudly against penance and the Mass, papal despotism and clerical overreach.

Working away in his room, Melanchthon, using the Torgau Articles as his foundation, sought to produce a measured document acceptable to both the radicals in his own camp and the moderates among the Catholics. Like Luther, he was beset by doubts as to whether their defiance of Rome had been justified. Feeling panic over how much rested on his every word, he frequently burst into tears at his desk. Drawing on his mastery of doctrine and command of Scripture, however, he was able to produce a comprehensive statement divided into two sets of articles—those of faith, which expounded the core Lutheran beliefs, and those of abuse, which described the proliferation and superfluity of Roman rites and doctrines.

By May 11, 1530, Melanchthon had a good working draft of his *Apologia*, or confession, as he called it. On that same day, Elector John sent a copy to Luther at the Coburg, along with a letter asking him to read it at once and send his comments back with the same courier. Reading it through, Luther was impressed. Melanchthon's *Apologia* "pleases me very much," he wrote; "I know nothing to improve or change in it, nor would this be appropriate, since I cannot step so softly and quietly." Letter in hand, the messenger returned at once to Augsburg.

Soon, however, the letters dried up. Days and then weeks passed without any word from Augsburg. As the silence grew, Luther's mood darkened. The chatter of the jackdaws lost its charm. He began to suffer from a terrible ringing in his head. He developed a toothache and a sore throat, and an abscess on his shin opened. An eagerly awaited pair of eyeglasses sent by a Wittenberg goldsmith was so poorly made that he could barely see a thing through it. Though he was supposed to be in hiding, word of his whereabouts spread, and so many visitors began showing up that the castle became "a place for pilgrimage," as he joked. The most frequent visitor, unfortunately, was the Devil, who at night preyed on his fears and doubts. To cope, Luther drank heavily, and Katharina in her letters warned him about it.

By May 10, he was near collapse, and for several days he could not work. Pining for his family, he pinned on the wall a drawing of his daughter Magdalena, and to his son Hans he wrote a touching letter about a beautiful garden where children pick fine apples and pears and sing and jump and ride nice ponies with golden reins and silver saddles. He urged Hans "to pray and study diligently" so that he might be able to enter the garden and get whistles and drums and dance and shoot with little crossbows.

On June 5, 1530, word arrived that his father had died. Though Martin had seen Hans only sporadically since his entry into the monastery, his father had remained a dominant presence in his life. Their bitter falling-out over his decision to become a friar had gradually given way to mutual respect, and Martin had belatedly come to feel his father's love. The news of his death left him crushed, and he withdrew into his room with a Psalter and wept for two whole days. The storm then passed. While at the Coburg, Veit Dietrich later observed, he frequently overhead Luther praying. Not a day went by without Luther's "devoting at least three hours, and sometimes more, to prayer, hours which would otherwise be most suitable for work." Dietrich was struck by the intimate tone Luther used in addressing God—how he beseeched God to intervene on behalf of not only him but also his colleagues in Augsburg.

The long stretches of solitude made the silence from Augsburg all the more galling. Working himself into a rage, Luther dashed off angry letters to the Saxon delegation, complaining in one to Melanchthon that he had crucified him by his silence. He began to fear that something terrible had happened. In fact, the Saxons had been sending him letters, but for some reason they had not gotten through.

It was also true that there was not much to report, for the opening of the diet continued to be delayed by Charles's tardiness. Before traveling to Germany, the emperor had decided to go to see his newly conquered lands in Italy. Though he refused to accept responsibility for the Sack of Rome, pinning the blame instead on mutinous troops, the event had unnerved the pope, and on June 29, 1529, Charles and Clement VII signed an "eternal alliance" confirming Spanish dominance of Italy. After sailing from Barcelona to Genoa, the emperor set off on a long, triumphal tour of his new dominions before arriving in Bologna. There, in November, he met Clement for the first time. Over the next four months, the two men, staying in adjoining houses connected by a door, held a series of private conversations in which they drew close. On February 24, 1530—Charles's thirtieth birthday—Clement, in a pomp-filled ceremony in the Bologna cathedral, placed Charlemagne's crown on his head, finally confirming his position as Holy Roman Emperor. (He would be the last emperor so crowned.)

Thus anointed, Charles could now address the two obstacles standing in the way of his long-sought goal of world domination. One was the

Turks. In 1529, Suleiman had followed up his occupation of Hungary by laying siege to Vienna. The city resisted, however, and the Ottomans had been forced to retreat. Their westward push nonetheless dramatized the threat they posed to Christian Europe. Backed by a huge army, Suleiman exercised more absolute power than any Western sovereign, and reports were circulating that he had vowed to force all of Europe to practice Islam. Those reports were highly exaggerated, but with Turkish troops having appeared before the ramparts of Vienna, Charles saw subduing Suleiman as his top priority. The great rivalry between the Hapsburgs and the Ottomans that would disrupt Europe until the early twentieth century had begun.

To prevail, the emperor needed a united Christendom, and that meant reaching a settlement with the Protestants. In a remarkable turn, Charles, who for so long had regarded Luther and his followers as apostates deserving death, was now eager for an accord. With the arrival of spring, the emperor left Bologna for the journey across the Alps. He headed not for Augsburg, however, but for Innsbruck, to visit his brother Ferdinand. From there he proceeded in leisurely stages through southern Germany, finally reaching Augsburg on June 15, 1530. Charles's entry into the city was an occasion for one of the most sumptuous pageants of the era—a swirling extravaganza of silk and damask, gold and purple, caparisoned horses and phalanxes of foot soldiers, joined by a parade of Germany's most prominent archbishops, bishops, electors, dukes, and landgraves. Charles stayed with the Fuggers, on whose financial support he continued to rely.

The following day, Charles and Ferdinand met with some of the leading delegates. Filing into the emperor's chamber, the delegates were immediately struck by the change in his demeanor. The callow, boyish-looking prince they had seen nine years earlier now looked closer to fifty than thirty. He was already suffering from gout, brought on by his prodigious eating and drinking. Whereas earlier he had been hesitant and in need of constant advice from his counselors, he now projected the stately confidence of an absolute monarch, and his black Spanish garb made him seem grave and unapproachable. As the discussion got under way, Ferdinand demanded an end to all evangelical preaching in the city. This drew sharp protests from several Lutheran princes, one of whom declared that he would rather kneel down and be beheaded on the spot than give in to such a demand; taken aback, Charles eventually withdrew it.

More generally, the emperor was far more open to hearing out the evangelicals than he had been at Worms. His inner circle included several moderates who had been strongly influenced by the Erasmian surge in Spain, among them the emperor's Spanish secretary, Alfonso de Valdés, a frequent correspondent of Erasmus's. Erasmus himself—unable to attend the diet because of a succession of serious ailments—sent a series of letters from Freiburg to Valdés as well as to Melanchthon and Lorenzo Campeggio, the papal nuncio, urging compromise and the granting of concessions to the Lutherans. As hard as it would be to tolerate such sects, Erasmus warned, war would be far worse. How France had been ravaged! How Italy had been stricken! Soon, it seemed, much of the world "will be bathed in blood." Such appeals went unheeded, however. For all of the emperor's new reasonableness, his commitment to Rome remained undiminished, and Campeggio, like Jerome Aleander before him, would work hard to prevent any accord with the Lutherans.

Melanchthon, however, shared Erasmus's preference for reconciliation over violence. In his twenty-one articles of faith, he sought to refute the charge that the reformers were heretics by downplaying their differences with Rome. In his article on justification through faith, for instance, he omitted the word "alone," and he took special pains to dispel the impression that the Lutherans rejected good works, even while making clear that these had merit only as a by-product of faith and could not bring about grace or a remission of sins, for which only faith was efficacious. Melanchthon was more expansive in the seven articles describing Rome's abuses and the steps the Protestants had taken to correct them. Allowing priests to marry, he argued, was necessary because of the infirmity of human nature; private Masses had to be eliminated because they had become instruments of profit. He steered clear of one key issue—papal authority.

By June 15, 1530, the document was nearly done. Over the next few days, several Lutheran princes and theologians met to revise it, and Gregory Brück, a Saxon chancellor, contributed a preface expressing hope for a harmonic outcome. Five princes and two cities endorsed the text, and versions were prepared in both German and Latin.

The *Confessio Augustana*—the Augsburg Confession—was to be presented to the *Kaiser* and the estates on the afternoon of June 24. The imperial secretaries had intentionally placed several items of business on the agenda so as to leave little time for the Confession, and by the time Brück was finally recognized, it was too late for the document to be read. The secretaries asked that a copy be submitted. The Protestants, however, were determined to have the statement read aloud, and the Saxon chancellor won the right for a hearing the next afternoon.

That session was to be held not in the usual gathering place—the town hall—but at the episcopal palace, in the chapter room, which could accommodate no more than two hundred people. By three o'clock, when the proceedings began, the room was packed, and a crowd had excitedly gathered in the courtyard outside to listen through the windows. Brück, bearing a copy of the Confession in Latin, and his colleague Christian Beyer, with a German version, stepped to the center of the room while the Lutheran representatives rose to their feet. The emperor, whose German remained rudimentary and who no doubt wanted to deny the Protestants a full hearing, demanded that the Latin copy be read. But Elector John said that since they were on German soil, the document should be read in German, and Charles reluctantly agreed. Beyer read the Confession loudly and slowly so that those outside could hear it; he took two hours. Both texts were then presented to the imperial secretaries.

In many ways, the reading of the Augsburg Confession was as significant as its contents. Nine years earlier, at Worms, Luther had been denied the right to explain his position. Now his doctrines had been distilled into a grand statement and publicly proclaimed before the Holy Roman Emperor and the German ruling class. With the reading of the Augsburg Confession, the Lutheran creed for the first time had received an official hearing.

On the day after the submission of the Confession, Melanchthon sent a copy to Luther. By then, several letters from Augsburg had reached him, showing that his colleagues had in fact been trying to keep him informed. In one of his recurrent displays of petulance, however, he remained convinced that he was being ignored. Luther was further annoyed at Melanchthon's complaints about being under intense pressure. Curt toward his junior colleague even in normal circumstances, Luther now pitilessly derided him: "Those great cares by which you say you are consumed I vehemently hate; they rule your heart not on account of the greatness of the cause but by reason of the greatness of your unbelief." The obstacles faced by Jan Hus and others like him were much greater than anything Melanchthon had to endure. Luther had regularly prayed for Melanchthon but now felt that his worrywart ways had canceled out his prayers. Luther's own scrutiny of Scripture had made him feel more certain than ever that their cause was just.

Melanchthon's concerns were not unfounded, however, for his handiwork came under immediate fire. Zwingli, unhappy with the document's statement on the Lord's Supper, submitted a fierce confession of his own, making clear his readiness to use force to defend it. Strasbourg and three other south German cities submitted a statement objecting to both the Zwinglians and the Lutherans. Most unhappy of all were the Catholics, who, intent on discrediting Melanchthon's manifesto, appointed a group of theologians to prepare a rebuttal, with the irrepressible Eck in charge. Working at a prodigious clip, he quickly turned out a 351-page counterattack, which after a round of edits was sent to the emperor. Charles was unhappy with its harsh tone. The Catholic delegates, too, found it unnecessarily bellicose, and it was sent back to the theologians for revision. By the start of August 1530, they had a more temperate document that acknowledged the existence of many possible points of agreement between the Catholics and the Lutherans and expressed the hope that a common platform could be reached. On August 3, in the same room in which the Augsburg Confession had been presented, the *Confutatio Pontificia*—the Papal Confutation—was read aloud to the estates.

In mid-August, after much discussion, a committee was formed, with equal numbers of Catholics and Lutherans, to see if a compromise could be achieved. The negotiations dragged on without resolution, so a smaller group was appointed, including Eck and Melanchthon. The soft-spoken classicist—outnumbered, worn down, and craving an accord—agreed to a number of concessions, including the recognition of auricular confession, fasts, episcopal jurisdiction, and even (with some qualifications) papal authority. To him, these were secondary matters; for many Protestants, though, they were vital, and Melanchthon was denounced as a greater enemy of the faith than any Romanist. Appeals were made over his head to Luther, who characteristically opposed all compromise. "If we yield a single one of their conditions," he wrote to Melanchthon on September 20, "be it that on the Canon or on private masses, we deny our whole doctrine and confirm theirs." Saying that he "would not yield an inch to those proud men, seeing how they play upon our weakness," Luther instructed him to "break off all transactions at once and return hither."

Melanchthon remained in Augsburg, however, and he set to work preparing a refutation of the Papal Confutation. With the negotiations deadlocked, however, and the delegates desperate to leave Augsburg after five months of being confined there, Charles on September 22, 1530, declared a recess. The recess document gave the Lutherans until April 15 of the following year to accept the articles that remained unsettled. Until then, all religious innovations were to cease. The implicit threat to the Lutherans was clear: either accept these terms or face war. The next day, after the document was read, the Lutherans immediately withdrew to consult; they then returned and protested. Brück offered to present the refutation that Melanchthon had drafted, but the emperor refused to receive it. Concluding that nothing more could be accomplished, Elector John left Augsburg on September 23.

With that, the crack that had opened in the Church at Worms became permanent. In 1054, the Eastern Church had formally split from the Western; now the Western Church itself had irrevocably split. The Augsburg Confession—reworked by Melanchthon after his return to Wittenberg and published the following spring—would become the central creed of the Lutheran church (which it remains to this day). It would also influence the writing of many other Protestant confessions, including the Thirty-Nine Articles of the Church of England and John Wesley's Methodist Articles of Reform.

On October 4, 1530, after nearly 170 days of confinement, Luther finally left Coburg. On his arrival back in Wittenberg, the town council showed its appreciation by giving him a small barrel of Rhine wine and a keg of Einbeck beer. Whatever relief he felt, though, was tempered by the escalating threats from the Catholics. In November, the rump of the diet, in its final statement, condemned all forms of Protestantism, demanded enforcement of the Edict of Worms, and called for the initiation of legal actions against all who had expropriated Church property.

Seeking to rally the Protestants, Philip of Hesse invited a number of princes and representatives of cities to meet in the small town of Schmalkalden, on the southwestern slope of the Thuringian Forest. There, they formed the Schmalkaldic League, which would soon become the most powerful Protestant force in Europe. Dominated by princes, it would further solidify the hold of sovereigns over the reform movement.

The Diet of Augsburg had been called to bridge the chasm in Christendom. Instead, it had widened it. Western Europe now had two great confessional blocs, each convinced that it embodied the will of God, and each prepared to use force to impose that will on the other.

MADNESS

Freiburg turned out to be far more pleasant than Erasmus had expected. Scenically set on the Dreisem River at the edge of the Black Forest, it had a temperate climate, and his health quickly improved. His house, the White Lily, was the most handsome in town. Though Erasmus had several friends in Freiburg, it was well off the literary circuit, and there were far fewer visitors than in Basel. Dinner parties were more infrequent as well, and while Erasmus missed the sparkle of wine-flecked conversation, the quiet was conducive to his work. "I like this well-mannered city," he wrote to Bonifacius Amerbach. "I hear no one speaking ill of one another."

Now in his early sixties, Erasmus kept up the work pace of a man half his age. Incapable as always of ignoring criticism, he drafted a series of polemical attacks, including a "Letter Against False Evangelicals" that assailed the pastors of Strasbourg for promoting discord and destroying everything good in the Church. Erasmus also continued his campaign to recover lost knowledge. Among his quarries was a Greek codex of Josephus's *Jewish History of the Sack* (of Jerusalem). Hearing that it was in the possession of the bishop of Rieux in Brittany, Erasmus sent him a request to borrow it. Through a roundabout route, the manuscript had ended up in the hands of a proofreader working for a publisher in Lyon, who was instructed to forward it to Erasmus when a messenger became available. The proofreader was François Rabelais. Then completely unknown, the Franciscan friar turned scholar revered Erasmus, and, when a courier did materialize, he sent along with the codex a note full of humanist adulation. Just as pregnant women nourish and protect offspring they have never seen, so had Erasmus nourished him "with the most chaste breasts" of his divine learning. If he did not ascribe to Erasmus his "whole worth and being," he would be "the most ungrateful of all men." Erasmus's influence would be apparent in Rabelais's *Gargantua and Pantagruel*, with its jests at sophists, sayings lifted from the *Adages*, and send-ups of the abundant style.

Even in sleepy Freiburg, Erasmus was able through his network of correspondents to stay abreast of the news around Europe. It was not good. As the great schism opened up in Christendom, a sort of religious lunacy had set in, with apostles and zealots of every stripe declaring theirs to be the only true creed and ready to slash and flay anybody who followed a different one. "There is peace nowhere, no road is safe," Erasmus lamented; "people are suffering everywhere from the high cost of living, and from poverty, hunger, and plague; the whole world is torn apart by sects." Soon, he predicted, "the long war of words and pamphlets" would be waged "with halberds and cannons."

After arriving in Freiburg, Erasmus learned the fate of Louis de Berquin, his French translator. In 1526, Berquin, after having been imprisoned a second time for his heretical activities, had been freed as a result of an appeal from Erasmus to Francis I. But Berquin had continued to issue provocative statements, and in 1528 he was subjected to another trial. In early April 1529, the verdict came down: Berquin's books were to be burned, he was to abjure certain articles, his tongue was to be pierced with iron, and he was to remain in prison for the rest of his life. Shocked at the severity of the sentence, Berquin appealed to the king and pope for clemency. Indignant, the judges—intent on preventing any more such appeals—sentenced him to death. On April 17, Berquin was transported by cart to the Place de Grève (now the Place de l'Hôtel de Ville), the traditional site for executions in Paris. To prevent disturbances, hundreds of armed guards were stationed in the square. Berquin gave no sign of agitation as he was escorted to the stake and tied to it. In an act of mercy, he was first strangled, then burned.

Erasmus was deeply shaken. Berquin, he wrote, was a pious and modest man, "completely free from any kind of pretense" and with "little sympathy for the teachings of Luther"; he had simply been led astray by the arguments of others. "It sets a strange precedent to send a man to the stake for a mistake in judgment." To "condemn, quarter, crucify, burn, behead, these are the actions of good judges as well as of pirates and tyrants."

No group could more attest to that than the Anabaptists. This radical sect was spreading with a rapidity that surprised and unsettled many. "I feel sorry for the Anabaptists," Erasmus observed; "they could be helped if baptism were the only issue, but they introduce confusion into everything. They are possessed of a kind of madness; yet I am told that some members of this sect are not at all evil people."

The Anabaptists represented a sort of third way emerging in Europe in the aftermath of the Peasants' War. With that effort at social transformation having so spectacularly failed, the Anabaptists sought to withdraw from society. Most were ordinary workingpeople—farmers, tailors, bakers, shoemakers—seeking to live in strict conformity with the Bible. Their pacifism, simple piety, and moral striving echoed Erasmus's philosophy of Christ. Some historians, in fact, consider Erasmus their spiritual father. But their literal interpretation of the Bible, and their rigidity in seeking to apply it, were utterly foreign to Erasmus.

Their true forebear was Karlstadt. In the same way that he had sought to create in Orlamünde a community living in strict adherence to the Word of God, so did the Anabaptists try to live biblically wherever they alighted. Because Jesus in the New Testament said not to swear, they refused to take oaths. Because he said not to kill, they rejected military service. Embracing the apostolic idea of sharing all things in common, they cut the locks to their homes and cellars; shunning costly fabrics, they wore coarse clothes and broad felt hats. Above all, they rejected infant baptism. This was mentioned nowhere in the Bible and so seemed to lack scriptural sanction. Moreover, since newborns could not declare their faith, it seemed wrong to initiate them into the Church through this rite. Baptism should be reserved for adults who were able to recognize and admit their sins and willingly repent. Hence the name Anabaptist (*ana* meaning "again" in Greek).

Years earlier, Luther, when dealing with the Zwickau Prophets, had feared that the subject of infant baptism would create turmoil, and this was now coming to pass. The Anabaptists first appeared in and around Zurich in 1525. Drawn to Zwingli's brand of sweeping reform but frustrated by his go-slow approach, they began holding private services at which they baptized one another. From Zurich the movement quickly spread to communities around Lake Zurich and Lake Constance. On hillsides, in fields, and on riverbanks, humble Christians gathered for simple services and readings from the New Testament, followed by an anointing with water. In their effort to create a sanctified society, the Anabaptists stopped attending sermons lest they be corrupted by them; to show their separation from the world, they refused to greet outsiders. In Zurich, they grew increasingly vehement and disruptive, parading about town with ropes around their waists and willow rods in hand, crying, "Woe to Zurich" and calling Zwingli the Antichrist.

In their refusal to take oaths and to serve in the military, the Swiss Brethren (as these early Anabaptists were called) posed a direct challenge to the authority of both the town council and Zwingli himself—a situation neither could tolerate. In an attempt to address it, a disputation was held in Zurich from November 6 to 8, 1525; it attracted such a crowd that it was moved from the town hall to Zurich's largest church. The meeting quickly descended into name-calling, however, and several of the movement's early leaders were arrested and jailed. On March 7, 1526, in a mandate that would become notorious, the Zurich council declared that anyone caught rebaptizing another could be subject to the death penalty.

On December 3, 1526, one Anabaptist leader, Felix Mantz, was seized in Zurich for violating the mandate. Refusing to recant, he was sentenced to death. On January 5, 1527, he was walked from the fish market to the Limmat River. Waiting along the way were his mother and brother, who encouraged him to remain true to his beliefs. He did so, praising God as he went. Mantz was trussed, with a stick thrust between his bound-together legs and arms, and lowered by rope from a boat into the icy water. "Into thy hands, O Lord, I commend my spirit," he sang. He thus became the first evangelical executed by other evangelicals.

Though traumatized by Mantz's execution, the Anabaptists were determined to carry on. Scattering from Zurich, they traveled up the Rhine to Strasbourg and the Low Countries; north to Augsburg, Thuringia, and beyond; and east into the Tirol and Moravia. Seeking hope in hard times, peasants and craftsmen came out to be baptized anew and commit themselves to a life of repentance and renewal. Most of those converting were pious, peace-loving men and women seeking to imitate the lives of the early Christians, but their insistent detachment and aggressive proselytizing inflamed the authorities. At all times, the Anabaptists faced the threat of execution, but their stoic acceptance of it, along with the irreproachability of their lives, won them many followers.

The campaign against them intensified after the 1529 Diet of Speyer. There, the death penalty was mandated for all adult baptizers. In the following years, both Ferdinand and his brother Charles V would seek zealously to enforce it, and with so many Anabaptists going willingly to the stake, it was decreed that their tongues should be cut out to keep them from confessing their faith. Protestant leaders were no less ruthless. In January 1530, six relapsed Anabaptists were executed at Reinhardsbrunn in Saxony. When Elector John requested an opinion from the Wittenberg theologians, Melanchthon prepared an enthusiastic endorsement of the death penalty for Anabaptists. Luther, who saw them as the offspring of Karlstadt and Müntzer, concurred. Earlier, he had opposed the use of capital punishment in the case of such "false prophets," considering banishment more appropriate, but the Anabaptists were causing him to reconsider. "Although it seems cruel to punish them with the sword," he wrote, "it is crueler that they condemn the ministry of the Word and have no well-grounded doctrine and suppress the true and in this way seek to subvert the civil order." Between 1527 and 1533, an estimated eight hundred Anabaptists would be executed in Europe.

When the Anabaptists themselves gained power, however, they could be just as brutal as their persecutors, as the infamous case of Münster in northwestern Germany showed. In 1534, a group of apocalyptically minded Anabaptists gained control of that town and, seeking to transform it into a New Jerusalem, they imposed a reign of revolutionary terror. Catholic and Lutheran unbelievers were driven out, all books but the Bible were burned, the practice of polygamy was introduced, and grisly executions were held. After sixteen months of such grotesque carnival, the town was starved into submission by the prince-bishop of Münster. Three of the Anabaptist ringleaders were taken to the marketplace. For a full hour, their skin was torn away by red-hot pincers. Their tongues were then pulled out, and a burning dagger was plunged into their hearts.

Their bodies were placed in cages, hung from the steeple of St. Lambert's church, and there left to rot.

After the Münster debacle, practicing Anabaptism became even more dangerous. Most of the remaining adherents preached nonviolence and brotherhood, but their opponents did not. Menno Simons, a Dutch reformer who accepted the faith in 1536, offered a grim catalog of their persecution:

> Some they have hanged, some they have tortured with inhuman tyranny and afterward choked with cords on the stake. Some they have roasted and burned alive. Some they have killed with the sword and given to the fowls of the air to devour. Some they have cast to the fishes; some have had their houses destroyed; some have been cast into slimy bogs. Some had their feet cut off, one of whom I have seen and conversed with. Others wander about here and there, in want, homelessness and affliction, in mountains and deserts, in holes and caves of the earth, as Paul says. They must flee with their wives and little children from one country to another, from one city to another. They are hated, abused, slandered, and belied by all men. By the theologians and magistrates they are denounced. They are deprived of their food, are driven forth in the cold of winter and pointed at with the finger of scorn.

Menno Simons himself was hunted throughout his life. He managed to survive by staying constantly on the move, eventually ending up in Lübeck on the shores of the Baltic. The Mennonites are named after him. They, along with another group of Anabaptist offspring, the Amish, would ultimately find refuge in America. Today, in Lancaster County, Pennsylvania, and Holmes County, Ohio, one can see modern-day versions of the type of biblical community that Karlstadt had sought to set up in Orlamünde.

Zwingli, who so violently sought to suppress the Anabaptists, would himself fall prey to religious violence. With his mix of evangelical fervor and

Erasmian concern for moral improvement, he became increasingly auto-cratic, and in the late 1520s he began a push to turn Zurich into Europe's first truly puritanical city. Church attendance was made compulsory. Organ playing was forbidden as a distraction from the solemn devotion demanded by God. A marriage court was set up, and it quickly became a morals tribunal that monitored residents through a network of informers. Courting couples were spied on, and husbands returning home late were reported to the court. According to one city council member, "There is fear and suspicion everywhere, among families and officials alike, every-one is afraid to go near the pulpit."

Not content with purifying Zurich, Zwingli wanted to evangelize all of Switzerland, with himself as its supreme leader. In 1529, he created a Christian Civic Union, in which Zurich was joined by Bern, Basel, the German city of Constance, and other territories that had adopted the Reformation. Through this league, Zwingli immediately began working to subdue and suppress Switzerland's "forest" cantons, which remained Catholic. Feeling threatened and encircled, these cantons formed their own Christian Alliance. Mobilizing, Zwingli raised a large army while issuing broadsides against the Catholics. The Catholics countered by forming an army of their own. Zwingli doggedly sought to provoke them, and in the first week of June 1529 the two forces clashed near the town of Kappel, twelve miles south of Zurich. After sixteen days during which few shots were fired, a peace was concluded in which each side agreed to let the other worship as it saw fit.

It would not hold. To Zwingli, the peace constituted a betrayal of the Gospel, and he imposed an economic and food blockade on the Catholics. On October 9, 1531, the Catholic cantons, in a surprise move, declared war on Zurich. Because of internal divisions, Zurich was slow to mobi-lize, but on October 11 a disorganized force of 3,500 Zurichers set off once more toward Kappel. They included many pastors, Zwingli among them. The Catholic army was twice as large, and when the two forces met, on the mountain slope above the former Cistercian abbey at Kappel, the Zurichers were quickly routed. Zwingli, discovered wounded on the battlefield, was run through with a sword. His body was quartered and burned and his ashes were mixed with dung and thrown to the wind—a gruesome end for the onetime pacifistic Erasmian.

When word of Zwingli's fate reached Basel, Johannes Oecolampadius—already gravely ill—became heartbroken, and six weeks later he, too, was dead. Erasmus could not hide his relief at the passing of these two former disciples turned evangelists. With their deaths, the first generation of leaders of the Swiss Reformation was gone. It would take another decade for a new one to appear, led by an even more resolute reformer who would complete in Geneva what Zwingli had begun in Zurich.

For Erasmus—as for much of Europe—it was the dramatic turn of events in England that was most shocking. In September 1529, he had sent a servant to England with letters to various friends and patrons as well as copies of the recently published edition of Augustine. When the servant returned (sometime before the end of the year), he delivered two sensational bits of news: Henry—desperate for a papal dispensation to invalidate his marriage to Catherine—had dismissed Thomas Wolsey as his lord chancellor. And as Wolsey's replacement, he had named Thomas More. Erasmus, together with humanists across Europe, marveled at the elevation of one of their own to England's highest appointed post. More himself, however, was less sanguine, for he was a supporter of Catherine and wary of getting drawn into the king's "great matter," as the divorce was called. As chancellor, though, he would be able to draw on the full powers of the state to pursue his main preoccupation: fighting heresy.

Just a few months before his appointment, More had issued his *Dialogue Concerning Heresies*, a long and furious tirade against "the pestilent sect of Luther and Tyndale." By that point, as many as twenty thousand copies of Tyndale's New Testament were in circulation, many of them in England. With weavers and shepherds now able to read the Gospels in their own tongue, More worried about the seditious ideas they might develop. In his *Dialogue*, he offered a fierce defense not only of Rome and the pope but also of pilgrimages, relics, saints, and other forms of traditional piety. On miracles alone he spent fourteen chapters, fiercely seeking to defend their validity. Because the Church can never err, More insisted, all

Christians must obey it. Heretics were evil men whose notions, if adopted, would lead to the end of religious belief and the destruction of civilization. Tyndale's translation was not a true rendering of the Christian Scriptures but rather a clever fabrication created in the interests of heresy, and More expressed dismay that any good Christian could oppose its being burned. Yet it was not just books that in his view deserved the flames; More devoted an entire chapter to explaining why the burning of heretics "is lawful, necessary, and well done."

As chancellor, More would now be in a position to act on such convictions. On December 24, 1529, he issued a decree in the king's name that called on the civil authorities to assist the Church with their "whole power and diligence" to root out heresy. The measure prohibited the sale, import, and possession of heretical books and demanded that every officeholder in the land seek out such texts. It offered a list of 118 banned titles, with Tyndale's New Testament at the top. A follow-up decree banned all vernacular translations of the Bible, citing "the malignity of this present time, with the inclination of people to erroneous opinions."

It had been many years since the last burning of a heretic in England, but that would soon change. Thomas Hitton was a Catholic priest who, embracing both Luther and Zwingli, had become an evangelical "runner," carrying messages and books between England and the Low Countries. On a brief visit to England in 1529 to contact supporters, he was seized near the mouth of the Thames and found to possess letters from English exiles. Arrested on the grounds of heresy, he was interrogated, probably tortured, and condemned to death. In early 1530, Hitton was burned at the stake—the first English Protestant to be executed. More was not directly involved in the case, but he would later express satisfaction at its outcome, calling Hitton "the devil's stinking martyr."

In 1530, More gained an important new ally. Cuthbert Tunstall, the longtime bishop of London, was replaced by John Stokesley. A former chaplain and almoner to Henry, Stokesley would become known as the hammer of heretics for his unrelenting efforts to suppress them. Together, he and More would introduce a sort of English inquisition, with church and state joining forces to combat religious radicalism in a bid to avert the type of catastrophe that had befallen Germany.

In his writings, More candidly described how he went about intercepting letters and interrogating suspects. Some of the examinations took place in the Star Chamber, the secret court that met at Westminster Palace. Others were carried out at More's Chelsea home; suspects were placed in stocks while he probed, harassed, and threatened them, seeking information about Tyndale and his accomplices. Royal agents were sent to the Continent to try to find Tyndale. Somehow he managed to elude them. Though his whereabouts in this period are not clear, Tyndale was probably in Antwerp, moving from house to house, living hand to mouth. When he saw a copy of More's *Dialogue*, he prepared the equally venomous *Answer unto Sir Thomas More's Dialogue*, accusing More of having started out on the road to reform, only to turn back after being bribed by the clergy. (This was but one of many polemical works turned out by Tyndale, whose lexicon of invective was no less extensive than More's.)

Throughout, Tyndale continued to translate, moving on from the New Testament to the Old. When he left England, he knew little or no Hebrew. (England had expelled its Jews in 1290, so there were no instructors.) On the Continent, Tyndale was able to gain a working knowledge of the language, and with it he made his way through the Five Books of Moses. Given Antwerp's proximity to England, Tyndale felt that printing the translation there would be too dangerous, so he sailed for Hamburg. Off the coast of Holland, however, his ship was driven off course in a storm and smashed to pieces on some rocks. With other passengers and crew members he managed to make it ashore, but he lost his entire manuscript along with his reference books. Some weeks later, he reached Hamburg by another ship. Tyndale worked around the clock to reconstruct his translation. By the end of the year he had a full text. He quickly found a printer, and by the early summer of 1530 copies of his Moses were entering England.

It would prove no less pathbreaking than his Gospels. For יהוה (YHWH), the unpronounceable tetragrammaton of God's name, Tyndale came up with "Jehovah"; for פסה ("Pesach"), he gave "Passover." Where the Wyclif Bible at Genesis 1:3 had "light be made," he gave "let there be light." He also introduced "flowing with milk and honey," "the fat of the land," "the apple of his eye," and "a stranger in a strange land."

Replicating the classic Hebrew pattern of noun plus noun, he created phrases like "gate of heaven" (instead of "heaven's gate") and "children of Israel" (rather than "Israel's children"). There was something in this pattern that pleased the English ear, and it would become a fixture of the English language. Where the Hebrew seemed ungainly, Tyndale found ways to lighten it. Moses's appeal to the pharaoh at Exodus 5:1, for instance, translated literally as "Send free my people"; Tyndale instead came up with "Let my people go."

Unwilling to let his translation speak for itself, however, he included marginal glosses, many of them highly tendentious. For instance, at Exodus 32:28, which describes the slaughter of three thousand Israelites for worshipping the golden calf, Tyndale observed, "The pope's bull slayeth more than Aaron's calf." To Catholics, Tyndale's Moses, like his Gospels, seemed a cleverly camouflaged device for spreading Lutheran views, and so the dragnet against him and his allies was tightened. When a book smuggler named George Constantine was arrested, More had him placed in the stocks at his home. After days of interrogation, Constantine revealed the names of collaborators and described smuggling methods, including the identity of a shipment and the secret marks placed on packets to indicate contraband books. Acting on this information, More was able to seize and burn many volumes as well as round up more suspects, several of whom were condemned to the stake. Of one victim, More would later gloat that he had relapsed into heresy "like a dog returning to his vomit." In all, at least four and perhaps six people went to the stake for their religious views during More's chancellorship. The degree of his personal responsibility is unclear; the wholeheartedness of his approval is not. Between twenty and forty others were condemned to prison, many for long periods.

Paradoxically, while More was hunting down these opponents of Rome, Henry was turning toward them. At one point, Anne Boleyn gave him a copy of a recently published tract by Tyndale, *The Obedience of a Christian Man*. Drawing heavily on Luther, Tyndale argued that kings rule by divine right and that whoever resists the sovereign—even if he is a tyrant—"resists God." The book also attacked the pope for not seeing that Scripture is the fountainhead of Christianity, and it maintained that the king should have authority over ecclesiastical affairs. "This is the book for me and all kings to read," Henry is reported to have said on sampling it.

Infuriated by Rome's intransigence, Henry began an aggressive campaign against ecclesiastical authority in England, criticizing clerical pomp and privilege with an asperity that sounded almost Lutheran. Beginning on November 3, 1529, and continuing for more than six years, Parliament met in a series of sessions that would mount a broad assault on the Church's wealth and power. This "Reformation Parliament," as it came to be known, moved cautiously at first. It checked the clergy's control over probate wills and curtailed its right to collect taxes. It prohibited the holding of plural benefices and stipulated that clerics charged with felonies should thenceforth be tried in civil courts. The revenues from annates and other fees for ecclesiastical offices were to remain in England rather than go to Rome. In 1531, Henry was acknowledged as the protector and supreme head of the Church in England "as far as the law of Christ allows." The king floated the idea of producing a Bible in English so as to give Christians clear springs from which to drink.

By July 1531, Henry had abandoned his effort to win Catherine's approval for the divorce. She was banished to a castle in Hertfordshire and denied permission to see her daughter, Mary. Seeking support for his position, Henry solicited the opinions of major universities, both in England and on the Continent; with few exceptions, they endorsed it. He also sought the views of several leading theologians—Luther included. By now, Henry had become so embarrassed by the book he had written against Luther that he sought to disown it, claiming that it had been urged on him by Wolsey and others. Gaining Luther's approval of his divorce would be a great coup. To solicit it, Robert Barnes, a friend of Bugenhagen's who had left England to avoid persecution, went to Wittenberg and provided Luther with copies of the briefs issued by the universities. (It is unclear if Barnes was acting on royal authority.) Reading the argument in support of the king's right to divorce the queen, Luther categorically rejected it. Since matrimony was a matter of divine law, he was unalterably opposed to divorce; if the king divorced the queen, he would "most gravely sin" against that law. As an alternative, Luther proposed that Henry take two wives.

Henry, however, wanted only one, and relations between the English king and the German reformer took another step backward.

With Catherine rudely pushed aside, More—one of her few overt supporters—felt increasingly isolated. The precariousness of his situation grew as the royal push against clerical privilege advanced. On May 15, a church assembly, through a measure known as the Submission of the Clergy, ceded the power of the clergy to make church laws without royal assent. With that, the anticlerical program had clearly triumphed, and the next day More (claiming ill health) resigned.

Shortly afterward, he sent a letter to Erasmus that offered a revealing look into his state of mind. He described a visit he had received while chancellor from Simon Grynaeus, a professor of Greek at Basel. A prominent humanist, Grynaeus was known for his skill at locating rare manuscripts. Because the university in Basel was barely functioning, he decided to visit England to search the libraries of Oxford. Though he had Zwinglian leanings, Erasmus considered him a serious scholar and so agreed to provide him with letters of introduction to More and others. Arriving in England in the spring of 1531, Grynaeus was pleasantly surprised at the amount of time the chancellor was able to spare for him. When More himself was unavailable, he assigned others to guide him. Grynaeus later thanked More for his hospitality.

More explained his reasons for it in his letter to Erasmus. His friends had warned him to be on guard against Grynaeus because of his suspect views. Thanks to the vigilance of bishops and the influence of the king, the new radical sects had until then been kept in check, but it was remarkable "what tricks" heretics used to sneak into a place and then with pertinacity to "crash their way through." He referred to Englishmen who, through a steady stream of books written in the vernacular and containing mistranslations of Scripture, had been sending into the country "every brand of heresy" from the Low Countries. In short, More had been keeping Grynaeus under surveillance.

Even now, as a private citizen, More remained vigilant. No longer able to enlist sheriffs and executioners, he turned to invective and polemic. In the months before his resignation, he had begun work on his rebuttal of Tyndale's response to his *Dialogue Concerning Heresies*. Now, in the library of his Chelsea home, he finished it. The *Confutation of Tyndale's Answer* would weigh in at half a million words, making it the longest—and perhaps most vitriolic—religious tract in the English language. Celebrating the burning of the "Judases" who had been exposed by his surveillance methods, More wrote that if such men had been allowed to operate without restraint, England would suffer the same destruction that the Hussites had visited on Bohemia, the Lutherans on Germany, and the Zwinglians on Switzerland. Expressing regret that the campaign against them had been too soft, More stated that "there should have been more burned by a great many than there have been within this seven years past." As for Tyndale, he was a "hellhound" fit for "the hogs of hell to feed upon," a "shameful, shameless, unreasonable, railing ribald," a "beast" who discharged a "filthy foam of blasphemies out of his brutish beastly mouth"— just a few of the insults More heaped on him.

With More gone, Thomas Cromwell now became Henry's top man. Theologically, Cromwell was an Erasmian. As a young man, he had reportedly memorized Erasmus's Latin translation of the New Testament, and he subscribed to the broad outlines of Erasmus's creed. The same was true of Thomas Cranmer, who in 1533 became archbishop of Canterbury (succeeding William Warham, who had died in August 1532). Under their joint leadership, England would gradually adopt many elements of the Erasmian reform program. In carrying them out, however, Cromwell would prove more of a Machiavellian, enlarging More's spy network and creating an atmosphere of distrust and terror throughout the land.

First, though, there remained the king's great matter. Sometime in December 1532, Anne Boleyn became pregnant, and on January 25, 1533, she married Henry in a secret ceremony. On June 1, Cranmer crowned her queen, and on September 7 she gave birth—to a daughter. Deeply disappointed, Henry did not even attend her christening. (She was named Elizabeth, after both of her grandmothers.)

Acting on the king's wishes, Cromwell in 1534 helped push Parliament to adopt a series of historic acts that further curbed the power of the Church; they included the end of all payments to Rome for benefices. The Act of Succession declared Catherine's daughter illegitimate, thus making Elizabeth heir to the throne; it further required all subjects of the king to take an oath to uphold the contents of the act. Later in the year, Parliament passed the Act of Supremacy, unconditionally declaring Henry the head of the English Church. Cromwell also began preparing a series of visitations to the country's monasteries and abbeys intended to produce a record of their wealth—a prelude to the abrupt and dramatic dissolution of those institutions that would unfold between 1536 and 1541.

Given More's still considerable prestige, Henry was eager for his approval of the succession; any sign of opposition from him could encourage popular resistance. On April 13, 1534, More was called before a panel of royal commissioners to take the oath. He said that he was willing to swear to the succession but not to the supremacy of the Crown over the Church; in his mind, papal authority remained the foundation of Christianity and hence of the social order. Four days later, More was arrested and sent by river to the Tower. Also imprisoned was John Fisher, the bishop of Rochester, who likewise supported Catherine (and who was a close friend of Erasmus).

While in the Tower, More was forced to undergo a series of interrogations and examinations—many led by Cromwell—designed to break him. Throughout, More maintained that he was a faithful subject of the king, but he nonetheless refused to take the oath. Though he would not say why, the reason was clear: if he so swore, he would be sanctioning the demise of the Church's authority in England—the very aim of the heretics he had so tirelessly battled. He would also be endorsing what he saw as Henry's growing absolutism.

On June 22, 1535, Fisher was beheaded. On July 1, More received a final trial, held in Westminster Hall before a panel of judges, including Cromwell and Thomas Boleyn, Anne's father. More was so weak that he had to sit, and he was no doubt dirty and pale from having been imprisoned for so long. The proceedings were a show trial with but one acceptable outcome. More was sentenced to be hanged, drawn, and quartered. In recognition of his long years of service, Henry commuted his sentence to beheading. On July 6, 1535, More mounted the scaffold. It was old and unsteady, and he needed help climbing up. After asking the people to pray for him, More declared that he died the king's good servant but God's first. He was killed with a single stroke of the ax. The executioner picked up his head from the straw and, showing it to the crowd, shouted, "Behold the head of a traitor." The head was boiled, placed on a pike, and raised above London Bridge.

More's defiance of Henry recalls Luther's performance at Worms. Both men refused to yield before the highest authority in the land on a matter of personal conscience. Both showed supreme courage and conviction. There were, however, important differences. Standing before the emperor, Luther had pleaded without success for an opportunity to explain why he refused to recant his views. More was urged to explain his position but refused to do so until after judgment was handed down. By remaining silent, he no doubt hoped to be spared. He wasn't, of course. Unlike Luther, More had no prince to protect him, no castle in which to hide. More suffered the end Luther had expected.

Remarkably, in December 1534, while More was still in the Tower, the English bishops, in a dramatic about-face, asked the king to authorize a new English translation of the Bible. Thomas Cromwell, who subscribed to the Erasmian principle of making Scripture available to all, took charge of the matter. Seeking the right man for the task, he enlisted Miles Coverdale, who (it's believed) had worked with Tyndale on his Pentateuch. Coverdale drew heavily on Tyndale's translations (as well as the Vulgate and two German translations, one of them by Luther). In 1537, two revised editions of Coverdale's Bible appeared with the king's full blessing. At long last, England had a Bible in English—one deeply indebted to Tyndale.

Tyndale himself, though, would not be around to see it. After More's death and Henry's change of heart, the English pursuit of him was called off, but he remained wanted by Charles V for his support of justification by faith and other Lutheran doctrines. After years of furtive living, diligent translating, and working with the poor, Tyndale was betrayed by Henry Phillips, an Englishman working for the emperor. Seized by imperial agents in Antwerp, he was confined in the castle of Vilvorde outside Brussels. During his five hundred days of imprisonment, Tyndale was interrogated by a panel led by Jacobus Latomus—the same Louvain theologian who had hounded both Erasmus and Luther. He was found guilty of heresy and condemned to the stake. On October 6, 1536, he was led to the place of execution in Vilvorde. In an act of mercy, he was strangled before being burned. Tyndale thus fell victim to the same surge of fanaticism and intolerance that had consumed his own persecutor, More.

When Erasmus heard of More's execution, he—like most of Europe—was aghast. "In the death of More, I feel as if I had died myself, but such are the tides of human things," he wrote. "We had but one soul between us." Beyond that clipped statement, however, Erasmus would not go. He offered no eulogy, issued no protest. Damião de Goes, a Portuguese humanist and friend of Erasmus, wrote to him from Padua about the surprise that he and others felt at his failure to comment more fully on the death of such close friends as More and Fisher. Any such expressions, however, would have displeased Henry. Since their first meeting, in 1499, when Erasmus had hurriedly drafted a poem at the request of the then-eight-year-old prince, he had worked hard to stay in Henry's good graces, and even now, after the king had ordered the deaths of two of his oldest friends, he shrank from offending him. Erasmus's reaction was further blunted by his disappointment at More's campaign against heretics. "Would that he had never mixed in this perilous business, but had left theology to the theologians!" he tersely observed.

Erasmus had spent much of his life opposing such zeal. With Europe dividing into rival confessional camps and his dream of a united Christendom fading, Erasmus decided to make one last bid to salvage it. In 1533, he was at work on a commentary on Psalm 83 (Psalm 84 in modern editions). The psalm describes how, in the altars of the Lord, "The sparrow has found a home for herself, and the turtle dove a nest where she may lay her young: your altars, O Lord of hosts, my King and my God." Moved, Erasmus turned his essay into a call for Christian unity. Where doctrine is concerned, he wrote, there are many who, putting the worst possible cast on statements of religious belief, furiously shout, "Heresy, heresy! To the fire, to the fire!" In so doing, they actually stir sympathy for the accused. Christians should put aside their private hatreds and insane quarrels and instead nurture a spirit of accommodation in which each side makes concessions to the other so that peace can reign.

Erasmus went on to offer a series of propositions on which he felt all

Christians could agree: Believers are justified by faith, but works of charity are necessary as well. Confession can be beneficial, as long as one does not dwell excessively on one's sins and resolves to do better. On fast days, those who eat should not insult those who abstain, and those who abstain should not condemn those who eat. More generally, Erasmus urged Christians to "do nothing by violent or disorderly means, nor inflict on anyone anything for which, if done to us, we should call on heaven and earth and sea; nor force on anyone a new form of religion which he finds abhorrent." Surely it was right for those who do not wish to suffer violence for religious reasons to refrain from inflicting it on others.

> If then we temper our counsels and calm our emotions, and devote ourselves to mending the concord of the church, the prophecy of Isaiah will be fulfilled: "And my people shall dwell in the beauty of peace, and in the tabernacles of faith, and in abundant resting places." And with one voice, rejoicing with each other, we shall all together say, "How lovely are your tabernacles, O Lord of hosts."

On Mending the Peace of the Church (as Erasmus titled his essay) was a resonant call for religious tolerance (at least among Christians)—a formative document, in fact, in the development of that tradition. Within a year, nine editions appeared. Both Catholics and Protestants, however, would rush to condemn it.

Luther would be among them. After reading *On Mending the Peace*, his friend Nikolaus von Amsdorf urged him to write against it. Luther needed little coaxing. In a long letter to Amsdorf that would quickly appear in print, he scornfully rejected Erasmus's call for concord. Where matters of doctrine are concerned, there could be no compromise. Referring to Erasmus's fear of being labeled a Lutheran, Luther sardonically observed that he could reliably attest he was not one. Rather, he was an evil enemy sowing tares among the wheat.

On April 1, 1533, Luther, forced by a bout of illness to remain idle, decided to read Erasmus's prefaces to the New Testament. He was reminded of everything he detested about the Dutch humanist. Erasmus saw Christ as little more than a Solon, a lawgiver. He belittled the authority of Paul and treated his Epistle to the Romans as if it "had no relevance for our time." Erasmus's famous edition of the Greek New Testament with its annotations had become outdated and should be suppressed, especially in light of how Zwingli and others had been led astray by it.

Luther's main activity in this period was completing his own translation of the Old Testament. His work on it had been repeatedly interrupted—by the peasant uprising, his recurring ailments, and his theological disputes. The text itself posed profound difficulties. The account of the building of Solomon's temple was so full of obscure terms that Luther visited crafts-men in their workshops to inquire about their tools. The prophets were especially elusive. "How hard it is to make these Hebrew writers talk German!" he complained to his friend Wenceslas Link. "They resist us, and do not want to leave their Hebrew and imitate our German barbarisms. It is like making a nightingale leave her own sweet song and imitate the monotonous voice of the cuckoo, which she detests." No less than with the New Testament, Luther wanted to Germanize the Old.

To help him, he convened in his home a *collegium biblicum*—a linguis-tic think tank that included Melanchthon, Justus Jonas, and the Hebrew scholar Aurogallus. Over sixteen sessions they worked hard to eliminate Hebraisms so as to produce a seamless German text. In taking such liber-ties, Luther knew that some would object, but, he wrote, the translator, in seeking the sense of a passage, should ask himself, " 'Pray tell, what do the Germans say in such a situation?' Once he has the German words to serve the purpose, let him drop the Hebrew words and express the meaning freely in the best German he knows." In contrast to Tyndale, who coined "Jehovah" for the unpronounceable name of God, Luther used *HERR* (in caps)—German for "master," "lord," or "sovereign." This reinforced the idea that German rulers were instruments of God and so deserving of unqualified obedience.

Luther wanted the Hebrew patriarchs not only to speak German but also to sound Christian. "The Jews think we should learn the Bible from them," he observed. "Indeed! Should we learn the Bible from those who are the greatest enemies of the Bible? . . . When Moses speaks to me of Christ I will accept him, otherwise he shall be nothing to me." As he bluntly put it, he tried to get rid of the Hebraisms in the text "so that no one can say that Moses was a Hebrew." From start to finish, Luther read the Old Testament as a record of Christ and salvation and saw its people and places as prefigurements of the New, and his translation reflected this.

In September 1534—more than twelve years after he had begun translating the Scriptures—the complete Bible was done. The printing, carried out by Hans Lufft, was a mammoth undertaking, including not only the text but also multiple prefaces and many marginal comments, plus 117 color woodcuts prepared by the Cranach workshop. These illustrations—showing biblical figures dressed like Saxon lords and buildings resembling ducal palaces—further cast the Bible as a story about Germany. By now, it was safe to place Luther's name on the title page. Finding its way into pulpits, schoolrooms, and households, the Luther Bible would become the cornerstone of Lutheran culture in Germany.

Erasmus, in seeking to restore the text of the New Testament, had hoped to provide a purified version around which Christians could rally and unite. In calling for the Scriptures to be translated into all the languages, he had similarly hoped to forge a common Christian culture. Instead, the Bible was appearing in vernacular editions tailored to national customs and expectations. As the Scriptures became more accessible, they were growing more particular and insular and in the process feeding the polarization and fragmentation of Europe.

In Freiburg, Erasmus was putting the finishing touches on the fifth and final edition of his own New Testament. The work that had been inspired by Colet's lectures at Oxford and the discovery of Valla's annotations in the monastery outside Louvain had swelled into a 783-page folio. The annotations, with their layers of corrections, emendations, and elaborations, offered a sort of palimpsest of Erasmus's theological views as they had evolved over two decades of controversy and dispute.

Erasmus was also rushing to complete the tenth and final edition of the *Adages*. The 818 entries that had appeared in the first slender volume published in Paris had ballooned into a thick compendium of 4,151. No other work had done more to revive and popularize classical culture. From "Pandora's box" to "make haste slowly" to "leave no stone unturned," the

Adages would leave an imprint on Western language long after the Latin in which it was so lovingly written had died out.

While preparing these and other texts (including a bulky tract on the art of preaching), Erasmus had grown increasingly disenchanted with Freiburg. It was expensive and dirty, and its small-town charm had long since faded. Even here, the friars had started up against him. In a wrenching personal misfortune, many of his valuables were stolen. With his body battered by gout and the stone, his doctors recommended a change of scenery, and Erasmus at once thought of Basel. Since the death of Oecolampadius, the storms there had subsided. The manuscripts he had in hand were to be published by the house of Froben, and while in Basel he could see them through the presses. So, despite his frailty, Erasmus decided to move one last time. In mid-May 1535, his old friend Bonifacius Amerbach came to get him. He was so feeble that he had to be carried on a litter.

Basel was now under the spiritual direction of Oswald Myconius, a former Zurich schoolteacher of Zwinglian views. The walls of its churches remained bare, and its pulpits still rang with proclamations on the primacy of faith and grace, but the university had reopened, and Erasmus was warmly greeted by a delegation of professors. "I still have ill-wishers here," he wrote, "but at my age, and with my experience, I am in no more danger at Basel than elsewhere." Because of his ailments, Erasmus was confined to his bed much of the time, but every day he rose for three hours around lunchtime and another three after dinner. He also received many visitors, though not always happily. One kept him sitting by the fire for three hours, arguing about dogmas and creeds, and he would have gone on all night if Erasmus had not cut him off and shooed him away. His correspondence was as extensive as ever, but now he could keep up with it only by dictating to his *famulus*.

One of Erasmus's last letters was to Christoph Eschenfelder, the customs inspector he had met in 1518 in the tiny town of Boppard while returning to Louvain from Basel after preparing the second edition of his New Testament. The memory of that moment, when Luther was still barely known and the glow of the New Learning seemed about to light up the world, was no doubt bittersweet. "Christ called Matthew from the customs-house to the Gospel, but you, Christoph, have taken Christ and the Gospel inside the customs-house," he wrote. Some think that Christ "is to be found nowhere but in monasteries, but in fact he is present wherever there is a pious soul, be it in the courts of princes, the camps of soldiers, or the triremes of sailors." This was another way of saying *Monachatus non est pietas*—"Monasticism is not piety"—the remark that, more than thirty years earlier, Erasmus had innocuously included in the *Enchiridion* and which had kicked up such a storm.

By now, most of his close friends—Colet, Reuchlin, Mountjoy, Warham, More, Fisher, Gilles, Froben, Pirckheimer—were gone. By the start of the summer of 1536, Erasmus felt his own life draining away. Lonely and listless, he came down with a sudden bout of dysentery, and three weeks later, on the night of July 11–12, 1536, his body finally gave out. He was buried in the Münster, the stately (and now Protestant) church that overlooked the Rhine—the grand waterway at whose mouth Erasmus had been born nearly seventy years earlier and whose course through many different countries and cultures paralleled Erasmus's own search for a united and peaceful Christendom.

ENEMIES OF CHRIST

"He lived and died as Epicurus, without minister and consolation," Luther remarked on hearing of Erasmus's death. "He went to hell." One day at supper, Luther trenchantly summed up his differences with Erasmus without actually naming him. "Doctrine and life must be distinguished," he said, adding, "I don't scold myself into becoming good, but I fight over the Word and whether our adversaries teach it in its purity." This was his calling. "Others have censured only life, but to treat doctrine is to strike at the most sensitive point." Erasmus wanted to improve lives; Luther, to purify doctrine.

Purifying doctrine would consume Luther over the remaining fifteen years of his life. Many biographers pass quickly over this period, preferring to focus on Luther's dynamic early years. As he aged, his less attractive qualities—his obstinacy and petulance, crudeness and intolerance—came increasingly to the fore, and even his friends began to avoid him to escape a public scouring.

Luther's growing grumpiness was in part a by-product of his ongoing physical decline. He was almost always ill. In 1537, for instance, he suffered a near-fatal bout of kidney stones. An enema administered by a physician not only failed to provide relief but caused severe diarrhea that further weakened him, and for eight days he was unable to urinate. Luther was given broth made from almonds, and a concoction of garlic and raw manure was applied. But his condition worsened, resulting in indigestion, vomiting, and insomnia. Finally, Luther passed six stones, one as large as a bean. His physicians urged him to follow a strict diet, but he continued to prefer fatty pork to dry venison and stringy game. Eventually, the pain in his legs brought on by gout forced him to walk with a cane. He also continued to drink heavily, causing his body to bloat, and he was assailed by constant headaches.

Such bodily ailments were only the start of his difficulties, though. A ceaseless stream of visitors came to Wittenberg demanding his time. Unhappy couples continued to seek him out to help resolve their differences. Congregations petitioned him for pastors and pastors pestered him for pulpits. His wife was the subject of endless vilification, and ugly rumors spread about his own private life. Luther was held responsible for the schism that had opened up in Christendom and blamed for the rivers of blood that had been spilled. He continued to be terrified of being alone and to suffer incapacitating bouts of doubt and angst.

Most debilitating of all, though, were the bitter divisions opening up among his closest colleagues. In 1532, the Diet of Nuremberg agreed to allow Protestants to continue the innovations they had introduced and to suspend all proceedings against them until the religious question could be settled in a great council. This "Nuremberg truce" would allow Luther to live in relative peace to the end of his days. With the external pressure from Catholics thus abating, however, the need for Protestant unity diminished as well, and as it did, internal conflicts grew. These disputes would take on critical importance as Luther prepared to pass from the scene.

One controversy centered on Melanchthon. Over the years, no one had worked harder to clarify Luther's ideas and promote his gospel. Melanchthon's reward had been constant criticism and belittlement. Such treatment added to his unhappiness at having to live in provincial Wittenberg. In 1536, Elector John had a new house built to replace his run-down cabin, but Melanchthon continued to pine for the more cosmopolitan Rhineland. He also retained his humanist leanings, and certain features of Luther's theology continued to trouble him. The doctrine of predestination, for instance, seemed both to absolve man of responsibility for his actions and to imply that God was the author of evil in the world. In both his lectures and his writings, Melanchthon was placing so much stress on free will and good works as to sound positively Erasmian.

Among those who noticed was Conrad Cordatus, a pastor in the nearby town of Niemegk. In the summer of 1536, Cordatus, while attending a class in Wittenberg, was surprised to hear the instructor—working from notes by Melanchthon—emphasize the importance of repentance in becoming justified before God. Since repentance is a human work, this seemed to diminish the place of faith. Concerned that students might be infected with Erasmian ideas, Cordatus asked the instructor to explain himself. When he refused, Cordatus demanded a public correction of this "papistic" teaching. He also proposed that the second edition of Melanchthon's *Loci Communes* (published in 1535) be recalled because its views too strongly echoed those of Erasmus.

Taken aback, Melanchthon declared that he had no intention of diverging from Luther's teachings; he would rather leave Wittenberg than face such accusations. Unyielding, Cordatus demanded that Melanchthon acknowledge that faith offers the only true path to salvation. Eventually both Justus Jonas (the rector of the university) and Elector John were drawn in, and Luther felt compelled to state publicly that "the article of justification is the master and sovereign, lord, leader, and judge" of all doctrine. The dispute grew so heated that people began identifying themselves as either "genuine Lutherans" or "Melanchthonians," and relations between the two men grew even more strained.

While Melanchthon was accused of placing too much stress on works, Johann Agricola wanted to do away with them altogether. One of Luther's oldest associates, Agricola had for several years been in Eisleben, preaching and heading a grammar school. He was not popular, however, owing to his heavy drinking and proclivity for fights. Longing to return to Wittenberg, he finally did so, in late 1536. Because he had neglected to arrange housing, he and his family took up temporary residence in the Black Cloister. Not long afterward, Luther had to attend a meeting in Schmalkalden, and he asked Agricola to look after his house and preach in his place. While he was gone, some anonymous theses appeared that attacked both Melanchthon and Luther for abandoning the core teachings about faith and allowing too great a place for works. On his return, Luther at once saw that Agricola was behind them.

When confronted, Agricola showed no contrition. On the contrary, he stepped up his campaign to make clear that the law has no part to play in salvation. The matter held great peril for Luther. For years, he had been accused of encouraging people to believe that, since salvation depends on faith alone, their conduct does not matter—an outlook known as antinomianism. Agricola, by arguing that true Lutheranism does not in fact require works, was providing fodder for Luther's critics. In his defense, Luther in January 1539 issued *Against the Antinomians*, attacking Agricola with such force that, he hoped, no one would ever pin that label on him again. Denouncing the book as libelous, Agricola filed a formal complaint against Luther with both the university and the town church, demanding a public hearing. An investigation into Agricola's conduct was launched. Before it could get too far, Agricola left Wittenberg, accepting a position as court preacher to Joachim II in Berlin, and the great antinomian controversy subsided.

Among the residents of Wittenberg, however, good works seemed in short supply. Drunkenness was rife and greed rampant. Routine hoarding drove up the price of bread. Weddings and baptisms were celebrated with unseemly extravagance. Prostitutes brazenly plied their trade, leading Luther to declare that those who infected the youth should be executed. Annoyed by the constant coughing in the town church, he told those suffering from colds to stay home. "I have been preaching this gospel for nearly twenty-five years," he complained in a 1537 sermon, "and we see how we have improved. The older we get, the stingier; the longer we live, the more wicked." Germany, he declared in another, "is a land of pigs and filthy people who are destroying their body and life."

Luther's frustration with his congregation was no doubt reciprocated. In the pulpit and at the lectern, he harped incessantly on a few well-worn themes. In June 1535, he began a series of lectures on Genesis, and he would keep at it for more than ten years (with some interruptions), moving at a glacial pace as he sought to wring every drop of meaning from each word and phrase. (When preparing to lecture on Noah's drunkenness, he felt that he should get inebriated the night before so that he could discuss the matter with authority.) One can imagine the waves of weariness that washed over both students and parishioners as Luther declaimed yet again on the saving power of faith and the central place of grace, offering expositions and admonitions that they had heard a hundred times before.

Whatever the level of popular disaffection, however, the Reformation remained unshakable in Electoral Saxony, thanks in part to Luther's close relationship with its sovereign. John, who died in August 1532, was succeeded by his son, John Frederick. A man of prodigious girth and a bottomless capacity for alcohol, he was known as "the Magnanimous," and he was certainly that toward Luther. On matters ranging from military preparedness to pastoral compensation, the two regularly collaborated, helping create a tight bond between the state and the church.

The cost of such cooperation was high, however. With the sovereign so heavily involved in religious affairs, the church in Electoral Saxony became an increasingly top-down and regimented institution, with limited input from pastors or parishioners. And the problem was not unique to that territory. In the late 1530s, the Reformation was about to enter a period of rapid growth, especially in northern and central Germany, but the expansion was due less to demands made from below than to decisions made from on high.

The most dramatic case occurred in Ducal Saxony. On April 17, 1539, Duke George, Luther's longtime adversary, died. As strenuously as George had opposed the Reformation, his brother Henry, who succeeded him, embraced it. On May 22, Luther and Melanchthon led a team to Leipzig. Luther preached in the same hall where, in 1519, he had debated Eck and made his fateful remark about Jan Hus. Now, in meetings with theologians, professors, and town officials, he and his colleagues helped prepare a new order of worship for the duchy. In a single stroke, a territory that had been steadfastly Catholic turned Lutheran, and its inhabitants had no choice but to go along. Similar changes were taking place in many other northern territories, including the duchy of Holstein, the electorate of Brandenburg (which included Berlin), the principality of Brunswick-Wolfenbüttel, and the region of Pomerania on the Baltic Sea. (Catholic rulers were no less insistent on imposing their faith on their subjects.)

Scandinavia was turning Protestant as well. In Denmark, King Christian III, needing resources to rebuild his country after a devastating civil war, hungrily eyed the property of the Church, which included 30 to 40 percent of all land. He began expropriating it. After officially declaring for the Reformation, in 1537, Christian brought Bugenhagen from Wittenberg to help oversee the transformation. Over the next two years, the "Reformer of the North" would lay the foundation for a Lutheran-style church in Denmark. Norway and Iceland, which were united with Denmark, followed suit. In Sweden, King Gustavus Vasa—the founder of modern Sweden—gradually seized ecclesiastical power and property, culminating in a 1538 directive that placed the church under direct royal control. From that point on, Lutheranism would be the dominant religion of Scandinavia.

As the Scandinavian experience shows, princes enlisting in the Reformation often acted less out of belief or conviction than from a desire to confiscate property, consolidate power, and create a national identity. With princes rather than theologians directing the movement, political considerations often took priority over religious ones. With little space for innovation or experimentation, spirituality grew cold. The angry disputes over doctrine in Wittenberg added to the disaffection.

On top of it all, Luther in 1539 made one of his most serious missteps. Landgrave Philip of Hesse—syphilitic, trapped in a loveless marriage, and conscience-ridden over his many affairs—became taken with a seventeen-year-old Saxon noblewoman and wanted to marry her. As a Lutheran, he had no recourse to the Catholic expedient of an annulment, and because his wife had been faithful to him, divorce was not an option. He solicited Luther's and Melanchthon's opinion. Influenced by the example of the Old Testament patriarchs, who practiced polygamy, they advised him to secretly marry the young woman. The ceremony took place on March 4, 1540, and in his delight Philip sent Luther a cartload of wine. But word of the union—and of Luther's part in it—quickly leaked out, and when the full facts came to light, he was widely denounced as unscrupulous.

Disillusionment with the reformer grew. With great longing, people recalled the young Luther—the defiant firebrand who had roused Europe with his bold denunciations of Roman tyranny and soaring appeals to Christian freedom. Without a new source of vigor, it was feared, the Reformation would founder.

In October 1539, the name of such a source appeared in Luther's correspondence. Writing to Martin Bucer in Strasbourg to explain why he had not written more often (too much work, advancing age), Luther asked him to "please greet reverently Mr. John Sturm [a leading Protestant educator] and John Calvin; I have read their books with special pleasure."

Then living in Strasbourg, Calvin had recently come out with a vigorous defense of Protestant principles—the book to which Luther referred. It is not clear if Luther had read another volume by Calvin—the *Institutes of the Christian Religion*—which had appeared three years earlier. The *Institutes* would prove the single most influential work of the Reformation, and Calvin was to become the leader of a new generation of reformers (excluding Lutherans) who would shape Protestantism for centuries to come.

John Calvin was not an original thinker. Most of his core ideas came from Luther (and Augustine). But he was able to express those ideas far more lucidly than Luther himself ever could—a reflection of their very different temperaments. Whereas Luther was tempestuous, florid, poetic, and wild, Calvin was orderly, precise, logical, and intensely disciplined. In writing, Luther would pour out his thoughts in a red heat, then send off the manuscript to the printer without even rereading it. Calvin would compulsively revise his *Institutes*, making sure every modifier, antecedent, and punctuation mark was in its place. Luther's scriptural exegesis flowed on for page after unruly page; Calvin's struck with piquant force. Luther provided the combustion, Calvin the engine to harness it.

Like so many other evangelical leaders, Calvin (who was born in 1509) began as a humanist. His first work in print was a commentary on Seneca's *De clementia*, for which he used an edition by Erasmus. In his preface, he called the Dutchman the "second glory and the darling of literature." Even then, however, Calvin was showing signs of his future rigor. In 1523, when he was fourteen, he went to Paris to study at the university. Soon after arriving, he entered the Collège de Montaigu—the same institution where Erasmus had suffered as a young man. Calvin felt none of Erasmus's revulsion; on the contrary, the college's austerity suited his exacting, no-nonsense mind. (Among students, he became known as the "accusative case.") In 1528, at the urging of his father, Calvin began to study law at Orléans, but in 1531 he returned to Paris to pursue his scholarly interests. Intent on improving his Greek, he entered the Collège Royal, a newly created institute of higher learning modeled on the College of Three Tongues in Louvain.

At the time, Luther's ideas were circulating in Paris, and sometime between the summer of 1532 and the spring of 1534, Calvin underwent a "sudden conversion," as he would later put it, accepting the central place of faith in attaining God's grace. (Modern scholars, examining his writings, have had trouble detecting the change.) In the autumn of 1533, Nicholas Cop, a friend from Calvin's days at Montaigu, was named rector of the University of Paris. In his inaugural address, delivered on November 1, 1533, Cop, with a vehemence that seemed almost Lutheran, denounced the Scholastic doctors of Paris and called for ecclesiastical reform. The university erupted, and the Parlement (the highest court in Paris) initiated proceedings against him for heresy. Calvin—warned that he faced arrest as a suspected coconspirator—fled Paris, and he began preparing a comprehensive summary of his theological views. He returned clandestinely to Paris, but early in the morning on October 18, 1534, it, along with several other cities, was plastered with inflammatory placards that denounced the Mass as idolatry and the pope and Catholic clergy as "apostates" and "murderers of souls." One poster appeared on the door of the bedchamber of Francis I himself—a serious breach of security that enraged the king and resulted in a wave of arrests. Fleeing, Calvin traveled around France under an assumed name. He ended up in Basel, where he continued work on his tract. (His stay there overlapped with that of Erasmus by several months, but there is no evidence that the two men met.)

While thus occupied, Calvin learned of the horrible outcome of the affair of the placards in Paris. Hundreds of suspected Protestants were arrested and about two dozen were burned; some were attached to chains and repeatedly lowered into and raised from the flames. The king himself watched with pleasure as the men slowly roasted to death. Once a great patron of humanists, Francis would from that point on seek to stamp out all traces of dissent and reformism. In his book, Calvin hoped to convince the king that not all French evangelicals were irresponsible radicals, and in his preface he urged Francis to distinguish between the reasonable reformers who were loyal to him and the seditious hooligans who had posted the placards.

The first edition of the *Institutes of the Christian Religion*, written in Latin and appearing in Basel in March 1536, was only six chapters long. Over the next quarter century of revision and elaboration, it would swell into a massive tome longer than the Old Testament. It would be the grand Reformation summa that Luther himself never produced; indeed, Calvin is often compared to Thomas Aquinas for his ability to synthesize and systematize. In meticulous detail Calvin described the depravity of man and the majesty of God; the false promise of works and the justifying power of faith; the inherent fallibility of human law and the unimpeachable authority of God's Word. In expounding these doctrines, Calvin intensified and distilled them. As frail and powerless as man is in Luther's world, he is utterly bereft in Calvin's. For him, the Fall was the defining event in history, and with elegiac sorrow he described the state of bliss that man would have enjoyed had Adam not violated the divine command.

As for God, his power is even more absolute in Calvin's universe than in Luther's. From both Luther and Augustine he took the idea of predestination and expanded it. According to Calvin, God foreordained not only those who will be saved, as Luther held, but also those who will be condemned—a doctrine that came to be known as double predestination. "All are not created in equal condition," Calvin declared; "rather, eternal life is foreshadowed for some, eternal damnation for others." God makes this determination with complete foreknowledge, for all things "always were, and perpetually remain, under his eyes." Calvin expressed contempt for those who, insisting on man's free will, "bitterly loathe" the doctrine of predestination "as dangerous, not to say superfluous"—a clear reference to Erasmus.

As Calvin himself acknowledged, this decree was *horribile*—terrifying. To make it more palatable, he joined the doctrine of predestination to the idea of the "elect"—the small sliver of humanity preselected by God for salvation. Calvin usually put the ratio of those saved at one in a hundred, though in more charitable moments he increased it to one in twenty or even one in five. Whatever the number, those elected could expect great blessings. Once the "light of divine providence" shines on a man, Calvin wrote, "he is then relieved and set free not only from the extreme anxiety and fear that were pressing him before, but from every care." The elect individual takes comfort in knowing "that he has been received into God's safekeeping and entrusted to the care of his angels, and that neither water, nor fire, nor iron can harm him, except insofar as it pleases God as governor to permit." The clearest sign that one is among the elect is the undertaking of tireless work to build the kingdom of Christ on earth.

These ideas about predestination and election were not fully formed when Calvin prepared the first edition of the *Institutes*; only over subsequent editions would they take shape as he worked to apply his theology to the real world—a process that would soon get under way. After a brief return to France to settle some family affairs, Calvin in the summer of 1536 prepared to travel to Strasbourg and devote himself to his studies. Because of imperial troop movements, however, he had to make a detour through Geneva. He planned to stay just for the night, but Guillaume Farel—a fiery evangelical who years earlier had clashed with Erasmus— now headed the reform party in the city, and he browbeat the reluctant Calvin into staying and helping. At the time, Geneva was known for its lax behavior, with high rates of gambling, drinking, and prostitution. In addition to introducing Protestant practices, Farel and Calvin sought to reform personal morals. A stern code of conduct was enacted; under it, repeat offenders were subject to excommunication or exile. With resistance rising, the city council directed both men to stay clear of politics. When they refused, they were ordered to leave, and their departure, in April 1538, set off public celebrations.

Calvin's expulsion, however, would prove a stroke of fortune. He went to Strasbourg, where he found a wife (the widow of an Anabaptist), developed his skills as a teacher and pastor, and produced a commentary on the Epistle to the Romans. He also completed a greatly expanded edition of the *Institutes*, including a French version that would become a model of French style. Most important, Calvin saw how Martin Bucer was able to use the local clergy to govern the city without producing the type of backlash that had developed in Geneva. As he revised the *Institutes*, Calvin added sections on the structure and governance of a reformed church, providing a sort of handbook for establishing a church based on biblical principles.

The chance to establish such a church would soon arise. Since his departure from Geneva, moral probity had declined while religious strife had increased, and the city council sent Calvin several messages urging him to return. Calvin refused, saying that he would rather die a hundred times than take up that cross again. But the entreaties kept coming, and Calvin eventually gave in. On his return to Geneva, on September 13, 1541, he was greeted with honors and apologies. He was provided with a large house and appointed pastor at St. Peter's cathedral. Once installed, he set out to cleanse the city. He drafted a set of Ecclesiastical Ordinances—a detailed blueprint for governance that would prove one of the Reformation's most significant documents. It established four orders of officers: pastors to preach and indoctrinate; teachers to instruct the faithful and safeguard doctrinal purity; deacons to distribute alms to the poor and help the sick; and, most important, elders to oversee discipline and guide souls. These elders were to "watch over the lives of everyone," "admonish in love" those who erred, and report malefactors for "fraternal correction."

Among the many activities proscribed were drunkenness, gambling, card playing, profanity, dancing (said to incite lust), indecent songs, immodest dress, promiscuous bathing, extravagant living, the introduction of unapproved doctrines, and the neglect of Scripture. Attendance at Sunday sermons was made compulsory, even for those who subscribed to another creed. Penalties were imposed for making loud sounds or laughing during services and for inappropriate behavior on the Sabbath. Enforcement and discipline were entrusted to a Consistory, which, made up of pastors and elders, became the city's most powerful agency. Once a year every household received a visit from an elder who questioned the occupants on all phases of their lives. Any person charged with an infraction could be summoned before the Consistory, and a network of informers was set up to report cases of moral turpitude.

Calvin himself had little trouble living up to this code. Strict, methodical, and single-minded, he worked up to eighteen hours a day, lived sparingly, fasted frequently. He preached prodigiously, taught theology, supervised churches and schools, and maintained a correspondence that in volume and breadth rivaled that of Erasmus. And he worked hard to make sure the city's moral code was strictly enforced. A woman was detained for piling her hair to an immoderate height. Gamblers were put in the stocks and adulterers punished by jail terms of up to nine days on bread and water. Calvin also banned the naming of children after Catholic saints, and many parents erupted in anger at the baptismal font when informed that the name they had chosen was unacceptable.

One thing Calvin could not control while in Geneva was his temper. His self-effacement before God was matched by his high-handedness toward men, and he raged at those who dared challenge him. And there were many, including not only Catholics who resented having to worship a Protestant God but also citizens who detested his stringent moral controls and demands for theological conformity. Calvin's doctrine of predestination in particular rankled many citizens, who rejected the assertion that man has no control over his destiny. Calvin called his opponents "libertines," implying moral laxity.

Dissenters paid a heavy price. Jacques Gruet, a young freethinking patrician, was accused of putting up a placard on Calvin's pulpit that denounced him as a "puffed-up hypocrite." A search of his room turned up papers mocking the authority of Scripture and dismissing the immortality of the soul as a fairy tale. Gruet was also accused of having appealed to France to intervene in Geneva. He was tortured twice daily for thirty days until he confessed to having put up the placard and conspiring with French agents. As punishment, he was beheaded, with Calvin's consent.

Far more damaging to Calvin's reputation was the case of Michael Servetus. An accomplished physician, skilled cartographer, and eclectic theologian from Spain, Servetus held maverick (and sometimes unbalanced) views on many points of Christian doctrine. In 1531, he published *Seven Books on the Errors of the Trinity*, enraging both Catholics and Protestants, Calvin among them. At one point, Servetus took up residence in Vienne, a suburb of Lyon about ninety miles from Geneva, where, under an assumed name, he began turning out heterodox books while also practicing medicine. His magnum opus, *The Restitution of Christianity*—a rebuttal of Calvin's *Institutes*—rejected predestination, denied original sin, called infant baptism diabolical, and further deprecated the Trinity. Servetus imprudently sent Calvin a copy. Calvin sent back a copy of his *Institutes*. Servetus filled its margins with insulting comments, then returned it. A bitter exchange of letters followed, in which Servetus announced that the Archangel Michael was girding himself for Armageddon and that he, Servetus, would serve as his armor-bearer. Calvin sent Servetus's letters to a contact in Vienne, who passed them on to Catholic inquisitors in Lyon. Servetus was promptly arrested and sent to prison, but after a few days he escaped by jumping over a prison wall.

After spending three months wandering around France, he decided to seek refuge in Naples. En route, he inexplicably stopped in Geneva. Arriving on a Saturday, he attended Calvin's lecture the next day. Though disguised, Servetus was recognized by some refugees from Lyon and immediately arrested. Calvin instructed one of his disciples to file capital charges against him with the magistrates for his various blasphemies. After a lengthy trial and multiple examinations, Servetus was condemned for writing against the Trinity and infant baptism and sentenced to death. He asked to be beheaded rather than burned, but the council refused, and on October 27, 1553, Servetus, with a copy of the *Restitution* tied to his arm, was sent to the stake. Shrieking in agony, he took half an hour to die.

Calvin approved. "God makes clear that the false prophet is to be stoned without mercy," he explained in *Defense of the Orthodox Trinity Against the Errors of Michael Servetus.* "We are to crush beneath our heel all affections of nature when his honor is involved. The father should not spare the child, nor the brother his brother, nor the husband his own wife or the friend who is dearer to him than life."

Among humanists, however, Servetus's execution caused a storm. Sebastian Castellio, a professor of Greek at the University of Basel, felt compelled to speak out. Though Basel was no longer the humanist mecca it had once been, Erasmus's spirit lingered, and Castellio was inspired by his writings. A protest attributed to him, titled *Concerning Heretics, Whether They Should Be Persecuted*, is widely considered the first modern defense of religious tolerance. Among Christians, Castellio wrote, contention had become so fierce that scarcely anyone could "endure another who differs at all from him." They fought over the Trinity, predestination, free will, and a host of other issues that were ultimately irresolvable and that in any case were not critical to salvation. The result was "banishments, chains, imprisonments, stakes, and gallows" and a "miserable rage to visit daily penalties" upon those holding contrary views. Satan himself "could not devise anything more repugnant to the nature and will of Christ!" Given the many faults all men have, the best course for each would be to look within and correct his own life rather than to condemn that of others.

Castellio's most famous pronouncement came in a subsequent work aimed directly at Calvin. "To kill a man," he wrote, "is not to defend a doctrine, but to kill a man. When the Genevans killed Servetus, they did not defend a doctrine; they killed a man." This captured with epigrammatic power the horror many humanists felt at the willingness of Calvin and his supporters to burn Christians for their beliefs. Such views were so controversial that Castellio dared not attach his name to them; his books were published anonymously or pseudonymously. Calvin had little trouble identifying him, however, and for years he led a campaign to silence and defame him.

Ironically, Calvin's attacks on Servetus's ideas would help spread them, and they would become one of two key sources of Unitarianism. (The other was Erasmus's rejection of the Trinitarian passage at 1 John 5:7.) At the time, however, Servetus's execution strengthened Calvin's position in not only Geneva but also Europe as a whole, for it showed how far he was willing to go to defend the faith. From that moment on, he was seen as not just one reformer among many but as the outstanding voice of Protestantism. In Geneva, the apparatus of discipline and control was tightened. In the mid-1550s, four of Calvin's chief opponents in Geneva were beheaded—an act seen by evangelicals as a triumph for both Calvin and God. From 1541 to 1564, when Calvin was in control of Geneva, an estimated fifty-eight people were executed and seventy-six banished.

With opposition largely suppressed within the city, Calvin looked to spread his ideas beyond it. Geneva had steadily filled with Protestants who, fleeing persecution in France and other Catholic lands, came to participate in this exciting endeavor to build a heavenly community. To help train them, Calvin in 1559 set up an institute of higher learning. Offering instruction in Latin, Greek, rhetoric, and the Bible, the Geneva Academy turned out pastors and missionaries who, after graduating, returned to their homelands to preach the gospel according to Calvin. To further promote his views, Calvin supported a vibrant publishing industry that flooded France with theological texts.

With its rigorous schools, vigilant morals squads, and attentive congregations, Geneva became a beacon to evangelicals across Europe. Just as Calvin's theology gave Protestantism a clear statement of beliefs, so did his governing structure provide a model by which a truly Christian society could be organized. That model would prove especially effective at spreading the Reformation in regions with hostile governments. Whereas Lutherans often collaborated with princes, Calvinists would encourage the formation of disciplined, tight-knit groups expert at winning converts in unwelcoming settings. Working clandestinely, these cells were difficult to detect and uproot. Through them, Calvinism would make major inroads in France, Hungary, Poland, and Germany itself. It would gain control of the northern Netherlands after the 1550s and Scotland after 1560. In the seventeenth century, Calvinism would inspire the Puritan revolution in England and, across the ocean, become the dominant faith in colonial New England. Calvinism thus restored to the Reformation a dynamism and an expansionist energy that had largely disappeared from Lutheranism.

In the process, however, something critical got lost: the individual. In Luther's theology, the central focus was on the Christian standing alone before God, provisioned with nothing but his faith. Even with Luther's growing stress on order and obedience, his respect for the individual conscience was not extinguished. With Calvin, it largely was. The idea of justification by faith, so central to Luther, was less important to Calvin and his followers; for them, it was the community of believers working to establish God's kingdom that was key. In addition to being more activist than Lutheranism, then, the Reformed tradition (as Calvinism came to be known) was more collectivist. And more controlling. The Consistory— the elite body at the core of Calvinist governance—provided a means by which the clergy and their lay abettors could organize and direct the population. It was in effect a new priesthood, taking the place of the Catholic clergy and in some ways exceeding it in power and authority.

Luther's friendly feelings toward Calvin would evaporate in 1541, when he saw a pamphlet by him on the Eucharist. Calvin strongly criticized Luther's view that Christ's flesh and blood are physically present in the bread and the wine, calling it a "diabolical reverie." He also rejected the sacramentarian view that these elements are mere symbols. Taking a middle course, Calvin held that the elements are instruments of God's grace, which unite the believer to Christ. Seeing this, Luther wanted nothing more to do with him. As a result, any chance of a reconciliation between the Lutheran movement based in Germany and the Reformed movement based in Switzerland vanished, and the bitter competition between them in the decades to come would weaken the Reformation as a whole, allowing the Catholic Church to stage a vigorous comeback.

Given a choice, most reformers would probably have preferred spending a night drinking beer with the lenient Luther than discussing the Psalms with the unbending Calvin. They might have also chosen to live in permissive Wittenberg rather than regimented Geneva. Reflecting his own unruly temperament, Luther had little interest in imposing the type of repressive regime that Calvin would establish in Geneva.

His intolerance instead took a different form: a virulent hatred for members of different faiths. In the past, of course, Luther had expressed rage at many adversaries, from popes and peasants to Erasmus and the sacramentarians. Now, however, his fury would be directed at three groups whom he considered enemies of Christ, with grave consequences that would persist for centuries.

One was the Muslims. Back in 1529, as the Turks prepared to attack Vienna and all of Europe braced in terror, Luther had come out with a blistering polemic, *On War Against the Turk*. The Turk, he wrote, was "the servant of the devil, who not only devastates land and people with the sword" but "also lays waste the Christian faith and our dear Lord Jesus Christ." Yet Luther's animosity toward the Turks was tempered by his awareness that the threat they posed had been critical to the survival of the Reformation. Had Charles V not been preoccupied with defeating them, he would have been free to level his guns at the Protestants. Luther moreover viewed Turkish aggression as a form of divine punishment for Christians' sins and held that the best way to resist it was with "repentance, tears, and prayer." In his tract, Luther was much tougher on the pope than on the Turks, decrying his constant calls for a crusade against the Ottomans and his unending demands for German money to pay for it. The pope's decretals are, like the Koran, "a new law" that "he enforces with the ban just as the Turk enforces his Koran with the sword."

At that point, Luther actually had little familiarity with the Koran. Though the book had been translated into Latin in the twelfth century, no edition had appeared in print. In 1542, however, the Zurich theologian Theodore Bibliander produced a Latin version that met scholarly standards, and the Basel printer Johannes Oporin agreed to bring it out. When the Basel city council learned of this, it barred publication and ordered Oporin's arrest. Hearing of the council's decision, Luther sent it a message urging it to lift the ban. It did, and Luther agreed to contribute a preface explaining why he supported publication.

It was not to promote interfaith understanding. Though in the past he had sought to refute "the pernicious beliefs of Muhammed," he wrote, he knew that doing so more effectively would require close study of Muhammed's writings, and so he wanted the complete text of the Koran made available. Just as the "madness" of the Jews was more easily observed once "their hidden secrets" were exposed, so would pious persons more readily grasp "the insanity and wiles" of the Islamists once the book of Muhammed became widely known. "We must fight on all fronts against the ranks of the devil," Luther wrote. The learned must "read the writings of the enemy in order to refute them more keenly, to cut them to pieces and to overturn them," so that "they might be able to bring some to safety" or at least "fortify our people with more sturdy arguments."

In Luther's preface, the Jews came in for nearly as much abuse as the Muslims—further evidence of the dramatic shift taking place in his attitudes toward that people. In 1523, in *That Jesus Was Born a Jew*, he had called for the Jews to be treated cordially, according to the law of Christian love. That position reflected his belief that, with the true gospel having at last been revealed, the Jews would finally convert. As the years passed and no such change occurred, however, Luther's wrath grew.

In August 1536, Elector John Frederick issued a mandate prohibiting Jews from staying in Electoral Saxony, engaging in business there, or even passing through. The following year, Josel of Rosheim in Alsace, who served as a spokesman for German Jewry, asked Luther (through Wolfgang Capito) to intercede with John Frederick to rescind the mandate. Luther refused. "You should reflect," he wrote to Josel, "on whether God will release you from the present misery, which by now has lasted more than 1,500 years. This will not happen, unless you accept with us Gentiles your cousin and Lord, the dear crucified Christ." Dismissing Luther's objections, the elector granted Josel's request and modified the decree to allow Jews to travel through Electoral Saxony. Other lords, too, seemed to be softening toward them. Incensed, Luther set out to dissuade them. He wanted to convince the princes (as he put it in his Table Talk in 1542) "to chase all the Jews out of their land." If he were a lord, he would "take them by the throat. . . . They're wretched people."

Luther's brief to the princes, appearing in 1543, was titled *On the Jews and Their Lies*. In it, he returned to the savage rhetoric of his first lectures on the Psalms. The Jews, he wrote, were "boastful, arrogant rascals," "real liars and bloodhounds," the "vilest whores and rogues under the sun," who, steeped in greed, "steal and murder where they can" and "teach their children to do likewise." A Jew "is such a noble, precious jewel that God and all the angels dance when he farts." Luther credulously repeated the popular libels of the day, writing that the Jews "have been accused of poisoning water and wells, of kidnapping children, of piercing them through with an awl, of hacking them in pieces, and in that way secretly cooling their wrath with the blood of Christians, for all of which they have often been condemned to death by fire." In light of all this, "we are even at fault in not slaying them. Rather, we allow them to live freely in our midst despite all their murdering, cursing, blaspheming, lying, and defaming; we protect and shield their synagogues, houses, life, and property."

To give the Jews their due, Luther proposed a seven-point program. First, the princes should "set fire to their synagogues or schools" and "bury and cover with dirt whatever will not burn." This was to be done "in honor of our Lord and of Christendom, so that God might see that we are Christians, and do not condone or knowingly tolerate such public lying, cursing, and blaspheming of his Son and of his Christians." Second, the houses of the Jews should similarly "be razed and destroyed, and they should be forced to lodge under a roof or in a barn, like the gypsies." Their prayer books and Talmudic writings should be taken from them and their rabbis forbidden to teach "on pain of loss of life and limb," for these "villains" infuse the people with their "poison, cursing, and blaspheming." All safe-conducts on highways should be abolished for the Jews, "for they have no business in the countryside. . . . Let them stay at home." In addition, they should be prohibited from practicing usury, and all their cash, silver, and gold should be taken and placed in safekeeping. Finally, young Jews and Jewesses should be given flails, axes, spades, or spindles and forced to "earn their bread in the sweat of their brow, as was imposed on the children of Adam." If these measures did not succeed in subjugating the Jews, "we must drive them out like mad dogs, so that we do not become partakers of their abominable blasphemy and all their other vices and thus merit God's wrath and be damned with them."

The frenzied language and persecutory proposals of *On the Jews and Their Lies* strongly echoed the literature produced three decades earlier by Johannes Pfefferkorn, Jacob van Hoogstraten, and other anti-Jewish polemicists during the battle over Hebrew books. Clearly, Luther was drawing on that literature in preparing his own indictment. And he would work hard to get his program adopted. On May 6, 1543, Electoral Saxony issued a stern new mandate that barred the Jews from settling in or passing through the territory and that ordered the seizure of their property. The mandate referred specifically to *On the Jews and Their Lies*, and the elector hosted Luther on the day it was issued. The tract also helped convince Margrave Hans of Brandenburg-Küstrin to banish the Jews, and when Prince George expelled the Jews from Anhalt in June 1543, Luther thanked him. When, by contrast, counts Philip and Hans George of Mansfeld showed favor toward the Jews, Luther became so enraged that he said he wanted to kill a blaspheming Jew.

In his hatred of the Jews, Luther was very much a product of medieval Christianity. As Erasmus had put it, "If it is Christian to detest the Jews, on this count we are all good Christians, and to spare." Yet, in its fury and violence, *On the Jews and Their Lies* stood out. "Never before," Josel of Rosheim wrote of the treatise, "has a *Gelehrter*, a scholar, advocated such tyrannical and outrageous treatment of our poor people." And it was just one of several virulently anti-Jewish works Luther produced in this period.

His savage Judaeophobia would inject a toxic strain into German Protestant culture, with calamitous results.

As hard as it is to imagine a tract any viler than *On the Jews and Their Lies*, Luther came close with *Against the Roman Papacy, an Institution of the Devil*. He wrote it in 1545 after Pope Paul III, the successor to Clement VII (who had died in 1534), announced his intention of convening a council to address the pressing issues facing the Catholic Church. Luther was one of many who had long called for such a council, and now it was finally going to happen, in Trent, Italy. From the pope's statements, however, Luther had concluded that the council's main business would be not rectifying Catholic abuses but reversing Protestant gains—and destroying him personally.

No one, he declared in his tract, would attend the council but "the miserable devil" and his "whoring children"—the pope, the cardinals, "and the rest of his devilish scum in Rome." The pope was "a true werewolf," a "farting ass," "a brothel-keeper over all brothel-keepers and all vermin," with "long donkey ears and accursed liar's mouth!" Claiming the power of the keys, "the most hellish father" felt entitled to create whatever binding laws he liked, such as, "Whoever does not kiss my feet" and "lick my behind" is "guilty of a deadly sin and deep hell." The papal court was made up of "Sodomists" and "hermaphrodites" who deserved being "struck down by lightning and thunder, burned by hellish fire," and attacked by the plague, syphilis, epilepsy, leprosy, and carbuncles. "We should take" the pope, the cardinals, and the rest of the blasphemous "riffraff" in Rome and "tear out their tongues from the back, and nail them on the gallows."

Even more unhinged than the text of *Against the Roman Papacy* were its illustrations, which were designed by Luther and executed by Cranach. One showed the pope riding a sow while holding in his hand a pile of dung at which the animal eagerly sniffs. In another, the pope and cardinals hang from a crossbeam, their hands bound and heads in nooses. In the most notorious, a she-devil gives birth to the pope and cardinals through her anus. In the great flood of antipapal literature during the Reformation, the pope had never been so vilified. *Against the Roman Papacy* would add to the rancor that for decades had been mounting between Protestants and Catholics and that would continue to rage for centuries.

Luther's own congregants would feel his scourge. With no vice police as in Geneva, Wittenberg was prone to the usual misdemeanors, and Luther regularly denounced its residents for their stinginess, selfishness, and moral delinquency. On June 14, 1545, his exasperation boiled over. Since the people seemed incapable of change, he declared, it would be better for all if he gave up. On July 25, he left on an extended visit to Zeitz, thirty miles south of Leipzig, to settle a dispute between some pastors. From there he wrote to Katharina that his heart had grown cold. Tired of Wittenberg, he did not wish to return, and he raised the possibility of deeding the Black Cloister back to the elector. Luther referred to a type of lewd dance that had become popular in Wittenberg, in which a man spun his partner around, causing her skirt to flare open. In 1540 the University of Wittenberg had prohibited the dance, and Luther had frequently preached against it, but to his dismay it had persisted. "Away from this Sodom!" he wrote. He would rather "eat the bread of a beggar" than torture his old age "with the filth at Wittenberg, which destroys my hard and faithful work."

Luther's statement caused an uproar in Wittenberg. Melanchthon and others at once traveled to Torgau to inform the electoral court of the gravity of the situation. The elector John Frederick sent his personal physician to find Luther and deliver a letter to him. The news of Luther's departure from Wittenberg, he wrote, would only bring joy to his Catholic enemies. Had the elector been notified of his dissatisfaction, he could have taken steps to address it. After receiving the letter, Luther on August 16 traveled to Torgau to meet with the elector. The next day he returned to Wittenberg, and soon afterward he resumed preaching. At the end of 1545, the elector issued an ordinance against extravagant weddings, suggestive dances, and shouting in the streets. Luther doubted that these measures would be properly enforced, and he once again threatened to leave if no improvement occurred.

For all of Luther's disgruntlement, Wittenberg was now flourishing. When he had settled there nearly thirty-five years earlier, the town was a run-down huddle of weather-beaten shacks, rutted streets, and roaming pigs. Now the market square was bordered by stately stone mansions, including Lucas Cranach's huge workshop-home complex. Enrollment at the university, which had fallen to around two hundred during the 1520s, now exceeded five hundred. Every year, more than one hundred pastors were ordained and sent out into the field to spread the gospel of justification by faith alone, and Wittenberg now had its own Latin school. Its main economic motor was the printing industry. Wittenberg was now Germany's top publishing center, and Luther's German Bible was a perennial bestseller. During his lifetime, ninety-one printings of the whole or parts of it would come off Wittenberg's presses (with another 253 partial or complete editions printed elsewhere).

In 1545, those presses issued a collection of Luther's writings in Latin. In the preface he prepared for it, he reflected back over the early milestones of his career, including his attack on indulgences, his colloquy with Cajetan, the Leipzig disputation, the Miltitz interlude, and the actions of Albrecht of Mainz. Luther placed the entire blame for the upheaval on the archbishop, who, he maintained, "wanted to suppress my doctrine and have his money, acquired by the indulgences, saved." Luther also described his discovery of the new gospel and the exultation it had brought: "Here I felt that I was altogether born again and had entered paradise itself through open gates." With this account, Luther left to the world a stirring narrative of personal rebirth and transformation that would serve as a template for Christians for generations to come.

The Black Cloister itself was now famous, with Katharina the celebrated wife, cook, brewer, and household manager and Luther the giant of history holding forth at the dinner table before teachers, ministers, students, and visiting dignitaries. The one jarring note was the racket produced by the new bastions being built around the city—part of an effort by John Frederick to turn Wittenberg into a "mighty fortress" in the face of the growing threat from Charles V. As the sound of picks and shovels drew near, Luther had a sense of foreboding about the fate of the humble Hippo on the Elbe.

In early 1546, the counts of Mansfeld asked Luther for help in arbitrating a bitter dispute that had broken out among them about their inheritance. Luther was reluctant to go. His health had continued to decline, and his sixty-two-year-old frame had grown abnormally heavy. "I'm like a ripe stool, and the world's like a giant anus, and so we're about to let go of each other," he remarked. But the dispute touched on his family's interest in the smelting business, whose operations the counts had taken over, and so he agreed to intervene. On January 23, 1546, Luther, accompanied by his sons, Hans, Martin, and Paul, set off for Eisleben, where he planned to stay. As his clumsy carriage rumbled along the dreadful Thuringian roads, the shaking no doubt caused him great pain.

The conditions were severe. Reaching the Saale River at Halle, the party could not cross because of flooding and floating ice. Three days later, sixty Mansfeld horsemen arrived and succeeded in getting Luther across. He suffered a dizzy spell. The cause was probably a circulatory problem brought on by the cold, but in a letter to Katharina he speculated that the true source of the problem was the Jews living in the nearby village of Rissdorf. Once the matter of the mines was settled, he wrote, "I have to start expelling the Jews. Count Albrecht is hostile to them and has already outlawed them. But no one harms them as yet. If God grants it, I shall aid Count Albrecht from the pulpit, and outlaw them, too."

The appearance in the distance of the slate-colored rock heaps signaled the approach of Eisleben, and on January 28 Luther and his party arrived. The negotiations proved difficult, involving many lawyers wrangling over the tangled affairs of the princes, and the days turned into weeks. During his stay, Luther gave four sermons at St. Andrew's church, and at several points in them he lashed out at the Jews. At the time, about fifty of them were living in Eisleben, and Luther denounced them as blasphemers, leeches, and potential murderers. To his next-to-last sermon he appended *An Admonition Against the Jews*. Should the Jews convert and receive Christ, he declared, "then we will gladly regard them as our brothers," but if they continued to refuse, "we should not tolerate it." Every day he prayed to the Son of God; "to Him I must run and flee if the devil, sin, or other misfortune assails me." For this reason, he could have "neither fellowship nor patience with the stubborn blasphemers and slanderers of this dear Savior." Forty years after Luther's entry into the monastery in search of certainty about his fate, he continued to experience doubt—the true wellspring of his hate.

While in Eisleben, he ate and drank with abandon, and his condition worsened. By mid-February, a settlement seemed within reach, with only a few technical points to be resolved. During his last sermon, Luther was so overcome by dizziness that he had to stop. On February 17, 1546, after the evening meal, he retired to his room and later complained of a sharp pain in his chest. Doctors were summoned and hot baths and a massage were administered to improve his circulation. Luther fell asleep but the pains returned, and in the early morning hours of February 18, in the city of his birth, he died.

On February 19, a funeral service was held at St. Andrew's. The next morning, a message arrived from John Frederick requesting the return of the body to Wittenberg so that it could be buried there, and in the early afternoon a funeral procession left Eisleben. Just as a quarter century earlier townsmen and villagers had lined the road to show their support for Luther on his journey to Worms, so now did crowds of mourners appear to pay him their final respects, and bells tolled as the casket passed. On the morning of February 22, the party reached Wittenberg, passing through the Elster Gate near the university. Faculty members, city officials, and citizens joined the procession as it made its way down the long avenue leading to the Castle Church. Near the town square they were joined by the student body, led by Melanchthon, Jonas, and Bugenhagen, among others. Heading the march was a mounted knight, followed by sixty horsemen, the hearse, and, immediately behind it, a carriage bearing Katharina and her sons.

By the time the procession reached the Castle Church, the crowd had grown to several thousand. In his oration, Melanchthon praised Luther's vigor of mind; his unshakable courage; the integrity of his character; and his many achievements, including his elucidation of Paul's doctrine of justification by faith and his waging of "incessant war with the adversaries of evangelical truth." Some said that Luther had displayed "too much asperity," and this, Melanchthon said, he could not deny; ardent spirits are sometimes "betrayed into undue impetuosity." In Luther's defense, he recalled a remark from Erasmus: "God has sent in this latter age a violent physician on account of the magnitude of the existing disorders." Surely neither Luther nor Erasmus would have approved.

After the service, Luther's body was lowered into a grave that had been dug beneath the floor in front of the pulpit of the Castle Church, not far from where nearly thirty years earlier he had posted the defiant propositions that had set off such an explosion, and whose reverberations have continued to resound.

AFTERMATH: ERASMUS

Erasmus and Luther passed from the scene, but their ideas did not. What afterlife did those ideas have? What follows is a proposed trajectory of influence. The account is not meant to be comprehensive; rather, it seeks to suggest a pathway by which the ideas of these two men entered into and shaped the Western tradition, with end points that are entirely unpredictable.

That is especially so in the case of Erasmus, for after his death his ideas all but disappeared. The Catholics worked particularly hard to extinguish them. Shocked by the great gains made by the Protestants, Rome mounted a fierce counteroffensive that came to be known as the Counter-Reformation. (Some historians, finding that term too negative, prefer "Catholic Reformation," with an emphasis placed on Catholic efforts at renewal.) The contours of this offensive were determined at the Council of Trent. Meeting in twenty-five sessions between 1545 and 1563, this conclave would define the doctrines and style of piety that were to characterize Catholicism for the next four centuries. With its very first substantive decree, adopted on April 8, 1546, the council showed that it would tolerate no Erasmian middle. The Vulgate, it declared, was the only acceptable edition of the Holy Scriptures; no one "under any pretext whatever" was to dare reject it. With this article, the Catholic Church was repudiating the new methods of biblical criticism that Erasmus had helped pioneer. (The Vulgate would remain the official Bible of the Catholic Church until the mid-twentieth century.)

In other sessions, the delegates endorsed the invocation of saints, the veneration of relics, the value of shrines, the sacred use of images, and other forms of popular devotion derided by Erasmus. They also reaffirmed the traditional interpretation of original sin. Anyone who asserted that Adam by his act of disobedience injured only himself and not all of his progeny, and who held that through such defilement he had transmitted only death and not sin to the whole human race, was to be "anathema" (the most solemn ecclesiastical curse). This decree sought to dispel the questions that Erasmus had raised about original sin through his grammatical deconstruction of Romans 5:12. At Trent, this doctrine would be inscribed in Catholic thinking.

The council was especially emphatic in rejecting Erasmus's calls for the Church to show greater flexibility on matters concerning marriage. It reasserted the "perpetual and indissoluble bond of matrimony," thus ruling out any possibility of divorce or the easing of the requirements for annulment. The council also condemned all who maintain that "the married state excels the state of virginity or celibacy," and it strictly forbade concubinage among priests. In a categorical rejection of Protestant leniency, the Catholic clergy would remain resolutely celibate.

The Council of Trent did affirm Erasmus's teachings on one key point: free will. Anyone who denied that man has free will was to be anathema. The main target of this decree, of course, was Luther and his insistence that man cannot will to do good. The council similarly rejected the doctrine of justification by faith alone. Faith without works, it declared, is dead, and no one should consider himself exempt from observing the commandments. This measure—adopted after six months of fierce debate—put the final seal on the Catholics' break with Protestantism.

Overall, the delegates at Trent adopted a strict and highly orthodox body of Catholic doctrine. At the same time, they recognized the decline in discipline and morality that had set in among the clergy, and they approved a series of remedial measures. To fight profligacy, they admonished cardinals to live modestly; to reduce absenteeism, they directed bishops to reside in their dioceses. Benefices were to be limited to one per person, parishes were to receive regular visitations to ensure effective pastoral care, and seminaries were to be created to serve as "perpetual nurseries of ministers for the worship of God."

The task of implementing these decrees—and of leading the fight against Protestantism—was to fall to the pope. During the Counter-Reformation, the papacy would be reinvigorated and ecclesiastical power newly concentrated in Rome. The tone was set by Paul IV. Elected in 1555 at the age of seventy-nine, he was known for his austerity, fanaticism, temper, and hatred of heresy. In 1542, as a cardinal, he had been instrumental in setting up the Roman Inquisition with the charge to identify, interrogate, imprison, and, when necessary, execute dissenters. As pope, Paul oversaw the creation of the first Index of Prohibited Books. It proposed three classes, the first of which included authors whose whole body of work, even when containing nothing about faith, was to be absolutely forbidden. (The second class consisted of the names of authors of whom only certain books were condemned, while the third listed individual books that contained pernicious doctrines and that had for the most part been written anonymously.) About 550 authors were placed in the first category, Erasmus among them. To punctuate the point, Paul wrote next to Erasmus's name the works of his that were to be prohibited: "all his commentaries, annotations, *scholia*, dialogues, letters, opinions, translations, books and writings, even if these include nothing against or about religion."

Paul's index stirred much protest, especially among booksellers concerned about their sales, and after his death a scaled-down version was issued. Now only a handful of works by Erasmus were banned, including the *Praise of Folly*, the *Colloquies*, the *Institution of Christian Matrimony*, and the Italian translation of the paraphrase of Matthew. All of his other works on religion were to be proscribed until purged of offensive passages by the faculties of Paris or Louvain—a stipulation that effectively kept them off-limits to Catholic readers. The index also sought to keep vernacular Bibles out of the hands of the laity; anyone who wanted to read such a Bible had to get permission from the local bishop. From 1567 to 1773, no Italian-language edition of the Bible would be printed in Italy. By the end of the sixteenth century, the Italian peninsula would be virtually free of all traces of Erasmianism (not to mention Protestantism).

While thus enforcing conformity to its doctrines, the Church sought to make the faith more appealing by encouraging new, more emotional forms of piety. The confessional was introduced as a piece of furniture, reflecting the renewed stress on the sacrament of penance. Bones from the Roman catacombs were sent to churches around Europe to augment their collections of relics. A new emphasis was placed on miracles; worship of the Virgin Mary was encouraged; a special body was set up to handle the canonization of saints; and a highly theatrical artistic and architectural style—the baroque—was introduced. There was also a proliferation of new monastic orders and religious associations, including the Capuchins, Theatines, and Lazarists (for men) and the Ursulines, Visitandines, and Angelic Sisters of St. Paul (for women)—part of a monastic revival that stood as a rebuke to Erasmus's declaration that "monasticism is not piety" and to the more general Protestant revolt against the cloister.

The most famous of the new orders was the Society of Jesus—the Jesuits—founded by Ignatius Loyola. A Basque adventurer with dreams of military glory, Loyola in 1521 was wounded in battle at Pamplona; while convalescing, he underwent a spiritual transformation and decided to become a priest. Making his way to Paris, he, like Erasmus, studied at the Collège de Montaigu. When he read Erasmus, however, he was repelled; the *Enchiridion*, he said, chilled his spirit and made his ardor grow cold. His favorite book was Thomas à Kempis's *Imitation of Christ*, with its call to suppress the self and surrender to God. To help ordinary Christians achieve such a state, Loyola prepared his *Spiritual Exercises*, a spiritual handbook that taught austerity, self-discipline, an absolute commitment to Christ, and unconditional obedience to the pope. The one aspect of Erasmus's work that Loyola did admire was his humanist curriculum, and he made it the basis for the Jesuit schools that would soon begin appearing across Europe. In addition to teaching, the Jesuits served as preachers, polemicists, confessors to the powerful, and missionaries to the heathens in lands stretching from the New World to the Far East. For all this, the Jesuits became known as the shock troops of the Counter-Reformation. Erasmus was a perennial target. He was denounced for promoting Pelagianism, undermining the Trinity, weakening the authority of the Church, and planting his "filthy feet" in the Vulgate and other sacred books, as one Jesuit controversialist put it.

The Protestants were no less condemnatory. After Luther's death, Melanchthon—still drawn to Erasmus's teachings—tried to retain a place for free will and good works in Lutheran theology, but orthodox Lutherans (called Gnesio-Lutherans, after the Greek word for "authentic"), angrily denouncing him, demanded unwavering adherence to the enslaved will and justification by faith alone. The rancor became so great that, as Melanchthon's final days approached, he expressed a willingness to die so as to escape "the rage of the theologians." After his passing, on April 19, 1560, he was buried in the Castle Church next to Luther—a recognition of all that he had done for the Reformation—but the Gnesio-Lutherans now had the edge in their campaign to snuff out all flickers of Erasmian laxity. Among Protestants in general, Erasmus was reviled as a man who had seen the light of the new gospel but refused to embrace it out of a mixture of fear, fecklessness, and opportunism.

Over the next century, Erasmianism went underground as men of faith zealously sought to enforce worship of their own particular God. In France, Francis I's early success in squashing dissent after the affair of the placards proved fleeting amid the Calvinist invasion from Geneva. Beginning with a handful of clandestine groups, the Huguenots (as French Calvinists were called) had nearly two million adherents by the early 1560s. As their numbers grew, so did their militancy. Religious meetings became occasions for mass demonstrations; bands of worshippers invaded churches and smashed icons. Catholics, viewing the Huguenots as interlopers tainting the purity of French society, started organizing into local leagues. This began a cycle of retaliation and revenge that resulted in eight religious wars, which, extending over a quarter century, would constitute one of the most savage periods in French history.

The worst outbreak occurred on August 24, 1572—St. Bartholomew's Day. During a wedding ceremony to which the royal government, in a gesture of reconciliation, had invited both Protestants and Catholics, royal troops assassinated several members of the Protestant party. Taking this as a signal, Catholic mobs fell on Paris's Huguenots, leaving hundreds or even thousands dead. Several times that number died as the violence spread to provincial cities. The French state nearly disintegrated in the bloodletting that followed. It ended only in 1598, when Henry IV signed the Edict of Nantes, granting Protestants a degree of freedom of conscience and private worship.

By then, the Low Countries were well into their own Eighty Years' War, driven by a revolt against the rule of Philip II of Spain. Even more than his father, Charles V, Philip saw himself as God's appointed champion of the Catholic cause; under him, Spain would surpass even Italy as the driving force behind the Counter-Reformation. Despite residing in distant Madrid, Philip insisted on exercising total control over the Low Countries, and to suppress the rampant heresy there he greatly expanded the inquisitorial apparatus set up by his father. Thousands were dragged from their homes to face horrific torture and gruesome execution. As in France, however, the Calvinist surge proved unstoppable, and in 1566 Protestant preachers provoked an Iconoclast Fury, during which hundreds of churches were looted and wrecked. Enraged, Philip in 1567 sent a nine-thousand-man force to occupy the country. It was commanded by the duke of Alva, a fanatical Catholic, who, in addition to levying punitive taxes, set up a Council of Troubles that sent so many people to the stake that among local residents it became known as the Council of Blood.

Leading the resistance to these abuses was William the Silent, Prince of Orange. Despite his name, William made clear his support for political autonomy and religious liberty, and he raised an army that, spearheaded by Calvinists, mounted a series of attacks on Spanish garrisons. In January 1579, the seven northern provinces of the Netherlands, through the Union of Utrecht, effectively declared their independence. In 1584, William was assassinated by a Burgundian Catholic, but the fighting wound on. It would eventually result in the division of the Low Countries into a Protestant north (the Dutch Republic) and a Catholic south (which would much later become Belgium). In 1609, a twelve-year truce was signed, but when it expired the fighting resumed, and the region was sucked into the great continental conflagration that had broken out in 1618.

The Thirty Years' War—the most destructive conflict in Europe prior to World War I—was an Armageddon-like contest for control of the Continent between the forces of the Reformation and those of the Counter-Reformation. Raging from the Baltic to the Alps, the Rhine to the Oder, it drew in all the great Western powers as they sought to feed on the bloated body of the Holy Roman Empire. Set off by a series of local provocations, including the "Second Defenestration of Prague" (in which two Hapsburg officials and a secretary were hurled from a window), the conflict had many causes: geopolitical aspirations, military ambitions, a fight between German princes and the emperor for control of the empire, and the prevailing belief that only a uniform society was acceptable and that all who refused to conform deserved silence, expulsion, or death. The war featured prolonged sieges, torched villages, mass rapes, the widespread use of waterboarding and other tortures, and frenzied witch hunts. The armies consisted mostly of mercenaries, who, expected to live off the land, plundered and stripped it. Famine and contagions spread, winnowing the population. In the course of the war, the German population was reduced by as much as a third, and the roads of Central Europe were filled with columns of wretched refugees. The great territorial gains that Protestantism had made over the previous century were reversed and its southern borders eventually pushed back by hundreds of miles.

The loathing between Catholics and Protestants (and between nations) was so great that when the antagonists finally agreed to negotiate, it took five years to bring the carnage to an end. The Peace of Westphalia, signed on October 24, 1648, ended more than a century of religion-stoked violence, dating back to the first executions of Luther's followers in the Netherlands in the early 1520s. The fanaticism and savagery set off by the Reformation had led to the dispossession, maiming, execution, and slaughter of millions of people. German commerce and manufacturing lay in ruins, and intellectual life stagnated as many scholars fled and those who remained withdrew into an arid conservatism. While Catholics and Protestants continued to detest one another, they grudgingly agreed not to kill one another, and a tenuous pluralism took hold.

The main victors of the Thirty Years' War were the states. The Peace of Westphalia marked the emergence of the modern nation-state. Newly strengthened sovereigns exercised strict control over the churches in their lands. While individuals were granted freedom of worship and dissidents guaranteed civil rights, ecclesiastical affairs would be even more tightly regulated than they had been before the Reformation. The confessional divisions in Europe fossilized into patterns that would shape life on the Continent for centuries to come. With churches closely associated with princes, clergy with the state, and faith with orthodoxy, Erasmian humanism seemed all but dead.

*   *   *

Yet the calamity of the Thirty Years' War opened up a new space in Europe. With Christianity in retreat and religion as a whole discredited, the search was on for a new design for living, and interest in Erasmus revived—especially in his homeland. At the start of the seventeenth century, the Dutch Republic was entering its Golden Age—a century-long period of growing trade, spreading literacy, expanding cities, and soaring prosperity. In addition to being the wealthiest corner of Europe, Holland was the most open, welcoming Huguenots from France, Jews from Portugal, Socinians (anti-Trinitarians) from Poland, Quakers from England, and Mennonites from Germany. The country thus became a hothouse of innovation, protest, and dissent. Among Dutch burghers, the memory of Erasmus and his creed of modest piety was venerated, and in 1622 a large bronze statue of him was installed on one of Rotterdam's main squares (the same one that is on display in the city today). The University of Leiden, founded in 1575, quickly established itself as one of Europe's top learning centers, and its faculty included many admirers of Erasmus.

Yet the same Erasmian moderation and flexibility that so appealed to the urban elite riled the ruling Calvinists. As the leaders of the revolt against Spain, they enjoyed great prestige. The Dutch Reformed Church was the only religious body allowed to perform its rites in public, and acceptance of its doctrines was a condition for holding public office. As the country flourished and diversified, the resistance to Calvinist domination and dogmatism grew.

Among the dissenters was Jacobus Arminius. Studying in Geneva with Theodore Beza, Calvin's famous successor, Arminius absorbed Calvinism in its most concentrated form, and after being ordained a minister, he took a position in 1588 in Amsterdam. While preaching on the Epistle to the Romans, however, he began to develop doubts about the doctrine of predestination. Its insistence that God had decided the fate of all men from the beginning of time seemed to Arminius a truly horrible decree, for it held that God had created people knowing that they would sin and that he would duly condemn them. He instead supported the idea of conditional election, by which the conferring of grace is conditioned on whether one accepts or rejects Christ—a decision God can foresee. Arminius was thus restoring to man a modicum of free will. Like Erasmus, he was accused of being a Pelagian, and in his defense he cited his Dutch forebear, along with the Church Fathers. In 1603, Arminius accepted a position as a professor of theology at Leiden, but the attacks on him increased. His attempts to carve out a place for human initiative in Calvinist theology nonetheless proved popular with educated Dutchmen, and there took root an Arminian movement supporting some human autonomy. It represented a crack in the rampart of Calvinist orthodoxy—and offered an early sign of Erasmus's renewed influence.

The most important heir to the Erasmian tradition, however, would, remarkably, be a Jew. Baruch (later Benedict) Spinoza was the product of a well-to-do Portuguese Jewish family that had come to the Netherlands at the start of the seventeenth century to escape the Iberian Inquisition. Raised in the heterodox environment of Amsterdam, Spinoza had a uniquely rich education. In addition to learning Hebrew and reading the Old Testament, he studied with a radical former Jesuit who taught him Latin and exposed him to the great works of the classical tradition. Along the way, Spinoza developed doubts about the authority of the Bible and key Judaic tenets, and on July 27, 1656, the Jewish elders of Amsterdam—citing his "abominable heresies" and "monstrous deeds"—excommunicated him.

Intent on pursuing his studies, Spinoza left the bustle of Amsterdam for, first, Rijnsburg, a town outside Leiden, and then the village of Voorburg near The Hague. Supporting himself as a lens grinder, Spinoza fell in with the many Collegiants in the area—freethinkers who, shunning membership in any organized church, met instead in informal "colleges" and who, like Erasmus, rejected dogmatic sectarianism, opposed religious persecution, and considered moral action more important than confessional purity. Spinoza—having borne the wrath of the rabbis and felt the suffocating control of the Calvinist clergy—conceived of a project to challenge clerical authority in general. The result was his first great treatise, the *Tractatus Theologico-Politicus*. Though Erasmus's name appears nowhere in it, his spirit is palpable throughout. In the same way that the Dutch scholar had used his command of Greek and the Fathers to deconstruct the New Testament, Spinoza now applied his knowledge of Hebrew and the prophets to the Old, seeking in the process to undermine its claims to divine revelation.

"I have often wondered," Spinoza observed Erasmically in his preface, "that persons who make a boast of professing the Christian religion . . . should quarrel with such rancorous animosity, and daily display towards one another such bitter hatred." Religion had been largely reduced to its outward forms, while faith had become "a mere compound of credulity and prejudices," a "tissue of ridiculous mysteries" that held men in thrall. As a result, he had decided "to examine the Bible afresh in a careful, impartial, and unfettered spirit." Spinoza proceeded to offer a piercing analysis of both the authority of the Hebrew Bible and the superstition he felt pervaded it. He questioned not only Moses's authorship of the five books attributed to him (a question others had asked before him) but the very idea that those books represented God's word. To Spinoza, the Hebrew prophets were not oracles of divine wisdom but rather men of vivid imagination. To demonstrate this, he compared the writing styles of the various books of the Bible, suggested the different eras in which they had been written, pointed out inconsistencies in the text, and cited errors likely to have been introduced by scribes.

Many passages in the *Tractatus* echo Erasmus. "The true meaning of Scripture," Spinoza wrote, "is in many places inexplicable, or at best mere subject for guesswork," but "the precepts of true piety are expressed in very ordinary language, and are equally simple and easily understood." (In his diatribe on free will, Erasmus had observed that "there are numerous places in the Holy Scriptures whose meaning many have guessed at but whose ambiguity no one has clearly resolved," while God intended certain other things "to be absolutely clear to us: such are the precepts for a good life.") Like Erasmus, Spinoza argued that, apart from a small number of core doctrines, including the existence of God and his supreme dominion over all things, "everyone should be free to choose for himself the foundation of his creed." The true enemies of Christ are those who persecute honorable and justice-loving men because they do not subscribe to the same religious beliefs; as the Bible makes clear, whoever loves justice and charity is a true man of faith. If such a course were followed, "there would be no further occasion for controversies in the Church."

Erasmus—writing at a time when the authority of sovereigns seemed incontestable—accepted princely rule as more or less a given. Spinoza, writing in an era of far greater openness, held out democracy as the system of government "most consonant with individual liberty." Theocracy, by contrast, could only breed instability and rebellion. Most tyrannical of all are those governments that make crimes of opinions, "for everyone has an inalienable right over his thoughts." Spinoza lamented the many schisms that had arisen in the Church "from the attempt of the authorities to decide by law the intricacies of theological controversy!" Everyone "should think what he likes and say what he thinks."

In issuing a general call for freedom of belief in a democratic system, Spinoza was recasting Erasmus's views for a new secular age. He was, in effect, stripping the "Christian" from the Christian humanism that Erasmus had expounded. That Spinoza nowhere acknowledged his debt to Erasmus shows how Erasmus's ideas and methods helped shape the Western liberal tradition even when his contribution was not explicitly recognized.

Even during the Enlightenment, when such Erasmian values as rationalism, skepticism, and toleration were widely embraced, Erasmus himself was not. As one scholar has noted, the *philosophes* "cited Erasmus, but scarcely read him." In Diderot's *Encyclopédie*, Erasmus was mentioned occasionally, but almost always fleetingly. Even Voltaire, whose irony, concern for justice, and attacks on superstition placed him squarely in the Erasmian tradition, produced only a few fragments about him. One was a dialogue among Lucian, Erasmus, and Rabelais in the Champs Élysées. In it, Lucian expresses delight at finding that Erasmus, though living in a barbarous land, had excelled in the same enterprise Lucian had—making fun of all. Yes, Erasmus says, but he had had a much harder time of it, for whereas the Greek gods of Lucian's day were considered little more than actors on a stage, Erasmus was surrounded by religious fanatics ready to send anyone who disagreed with them to the stake, and as a result he had

had to show far more caution. As a monk, moreover, he was subject to various vows and other institutional constraints. Asked by Lucian to explain what a monk is, Erasmus says that it is someone "useless to the human race" and living "in dependency on others." At one point Rabelais enters, and Erasmus notes that, as a priest rather than a monk, he was able to go much further in expressing his scorn. "You were perhaps too reserved in your raillery," Rabelais says, "and I was perhaps too bold in mine, but at present we both think the same." Soon Jonathan Swift shows up, and all four head off to dinner.

The dialogue captures the aspect of Erasmus's work that Voltaire most valued—his mocking of the clergy. Erasmus's program to correct the Bible and revitalize Christendom held little appeal for a man whose attitude toward organized religion was summed up in his celebrated cry, *Écrasez l'infâme* ("Crush the infamous thing"). For Enlightenment thinkers as a whole, Erasmus's efforts to blend classical harmony and Christian piety into a philosophy of Christ seemed stuffy and passé. In the century preceding the French Revolution, the *Praise of Folly* appeared in more than sixty editions, many of them in French; reform tracts like the *Enchiridion* and *A Complaint of Peace*, by contrast, were seldom reprinted.

As the rationalism and classicism of the Enlightenment gave way to the passion and drama of romanticism, the neglect of Erasmus turned to contempt. Poets and artists valued the heroic and authentic, the sensual and spontaneous—qualities Erasmus was deemed to lack. To German thinkers in particular, the Dutchman stood for cowardly vacillation, especially when measured against the boldness and vigor of Luther. Johann Gottfried von Herder, the chief theorist of German romanticism, celebrated the expressiveness of national languages in contrast to the sterility of Latin, and he praised Luther for waking the German language, previously "a sleeping giant." Seeking to encourage a sense of German national identity, Herder wrote an essay hailing Ulrich von Hutten for his fearless actions on behalf of the German people. Erasmus, by contrast, he dismissed as a self-regarding intellectual who disgracefully refused to receive his desperate, ailing friend.

Throughout the nineteenth century, this image of Erasmus as an effete equivocator prevailed. "A great scholar but a weak character" was the judgment of Ludwig Pastor, the renowned (Catholic) author of a forty-volume history of the popes that began appearing in the 1890s; Pastor's formulation was repeated over and over by Catholic and Protestant scholars alike. Amid the enthusiasm for the mother tongue and the fatherland, soil and blood, folklore and mythology, Erasmus's calls for concord and brotherhood seemed the musty artifacts of an obsolete cosmopolitanism.

Even after Europe's nationalist rivalries helped precipitate the cataclysm of World War I, Erasmian-style humanism remained out of favor, as was apparent in a biography by Johan Huizinga. A professor of history at Leiden from 1915 to 1942, Huizinga won international acclaim for *The Waning of the Middle Ages*, an elegiac study of cultural and intellectual life in France and the Low Countries in the fourteenth and fifteenth centuries. His *Erasmus of Rotterdam*, published in 1924, was erudite, informed—and laced with condescension. Huizinga made light of Erasmus's physical frailties, his obsession with hygiene, his "maidenly coyness." "Let us try ever to see of that great Erasmus as much as the petty one permits," he wrote. Huizinga did credit Erasmus with being "the enlightener of an age from whom a broad stream of culture emanated" and "the fervently sincere preacher of that general kindliness which the world so urgently needs," but, he flatly declared, "his influence has ceased. He has done his work and will speak to the world no more." After the book appeared, Huizinga acknowledged that he felt little admiration for Erasmus and tried to put him out of his mind.

Huizinga's study did, however, inspire another writer, the Austrian Stefan Zweig. Reading the book against the backdrop of Hitler's rise to power, Zweig identified with Erasmus's struggles, and in 1934 he came out with a biographical study. Although Erasmus was "the greatest and most brilliant star" of his century, Zweig wrote, he had become "hardly more than a name." In fact, he was "the first conscious European, the first to fight on behalf of peace, the ablest champion of the humanities and of a spiritual ideal." Under his leadership, there had taken hold the unheard-of ideal of "a United States of Europe under the aegis of a common culture and a common civilization."

But, Zweig wrote, that ideal was never realized, and the reason was clear. Erasmus and his fellow humanists, in overestimating the effects of civilization, had "overlooked the terrible and well-nigh insoluble problem of mass-hatred and the vast and passionate psychoses of mankind." They had mistakenly sought to teach the masses "from the heights of their idealism" rather than go down among them and try to understand and learn from them. Meanwhile, there arrived on the scene someone who did understand those masses: Luther. Just as the Germanic hordes of old had descended on the world of classical Rome, so did this "fanatical man of action, backed by the irresistible force of a mass movement," sally forth "to swamp and destroy" the dream of a united Europe. Zweig called Luther "a swaggering, brimming, almost bursting piece of living matter, the embodiment of the momentum and fierceness of a whole nation assembled in one exuberant personality." Summoning the world to arms, this "werewolf raging with uncouth and unjustifiable scorn" split Christian Europe in two. Though Erasmus tried with his pen to defend European unity and the "world-citizenship of humanity," he proved unequal to the task.

The rivalry between Erasmus and Luther thus became for Zweig an allegory for the crisis afflicting Nazi Germany and Europe as a whole. And he remained gloomy about the prospects for the Erasmian ideal. Erasmus's thought, he wrote, had never taken sufficient shape and substance "to exercise a tangible influence" on the molding of European destinies. The "great humanistic dream" of resolving disputes in a spirit of justice and of achieving the unification of nations under the banner of a common culture had remained a Utopia, never yet established and perhaps unattainable.

For Zweig himself, the humanistic dream would, sadly, prove insufficient to sustain him. In 1942, while living in exile in Brazil, he committed suicide. And the inferno consuming Europe seemed to bear out his judgment that that dream could not become reality. Yet, remarkably, just the opposite occurred. The spectacle of mass graves, razed cities, displaced populations, and death camps that confronted Europe in 1945 drove home the urgent need to make the utopian real—to set aside narrow national loyalties and historical enmities in favor of a new internationalist order designed to make future wars unthinkable. In 1946, Winston Churchill, speaking at the University of Zurich, called for a "United States of Europe," and three years later Robert Schuman, the French foreign minister, delivered an address in Strasbourg that would in many ways mark the birth of a united Europe. "Our century," he declared, "which has witnessed the catastrophes resulting in the unending clash of nationalities and nationalisms, must attempt and succeed in reconciling nations in a supranational association," with the goal of putting an end to war and guaranteeing an eternal peace. He cited the "audacious minds" that over the centuries had conceived the framework for such an association: Dante, Erasmus, Abbé de Saint Pierre, Rousseau, Kant, and Proudhon.

Making that abstraction a reality began with the formation of the European Coal and Steel Community in 1952, designed to coordinate policies among six nations in two industries considered essential to any war effort. It was followed by the creation in 1957 of the European Economic Community, forming a common market, and the direct election of a European Parliament in 1979. In 1993, after the signing of the Maastricht Treaty, the European Union (EU) came into being, and in 1999 the euro became its common currency. In 2000 the EU Charter of Fundamental Rights was proclaimed, guaranteeing freedom of thought, religion, conscience, expression, and assembly; the right to an education; equality before the law; social security; and much else. (The charter did not become legally binding until 2009.)

While the principles underlying the European Union clearly have many sources, they closely reflect the reform program that Erasmus had spent so many years preparing and promoting. His call for a pan-European identity transcending borders and nationalities as spelled out in *A Complaint of Peace*; his appeals for tolerance and mutual understanding as expressed in such works as *On Mending the Peace of the Church* and his preface to the Hilary edition; his admonitions to Christian princes to avoid wars and foreign adventures and instead devote themselves to enhancing the welfare of their people; his stress on keeping doctrinal differences to a minimum and emphasizing all that binds humankind together; his statement that he would like to be "a citizen of the world, to be a fellow-citizen to all men"—all are ideals on which the EU is built. Erasmus would no doubt have taken special pleasure in the EU's matrix of regulatory agencies aimed at ensuring food safety, protecting the workplace, preventing disease, and safeguarding the environment—fulfillments of his repeated calls for improved hygiene and cleanliness. And one can only imagine the wonder he would have felt at seeing a train whisk passengers between London and Paris in just over two hours, gliding beneath the perilous channel that had caused him such dread and discomfort.

Erasmus's contribution to the EU has been explicitly recognized in one of its most popular initiatives. Through the Erasmus Program, students in one member country can spend up to a year at a university in another, with grants to help defray the cost. Since it began, in 1987, more than three million students have participated, taking the opportunity to learn new languages, experience other cultures, make friends in foreign lands, and have romances. The program inspired the 2002 film *L'Auberge Espagnole* ("The Spanish Inn"), about an economics graduate student who, seeking a government job in Paris, is told that spending a year in Spain would boost his chances. Through the Erasmus Program, he arranges to study in Barcelona. There he shares a flat with students from around Europe, learns Spanish, lingers in bars, meets a girl. On his return to Paris, he decides to give up economics and become a writer, with his Erasmus experience the subject of his first book.

The Erasmus Program (now called Erasmus+) is a fitting tribute to a nomadic scholar who traveled from city to city in search of libraries, printers, good wine, bright conversation, and the freedom to think and write, and who placed education at the core of his program to form a new type of citizen committed to a new Europe. Umberto Eco, in a 2012 interview with *La Stampa*, credited the Erasmus Program with helping to create "the first generation of young Europeans. I call it a sexual revolution: a young Catalan man meets a Flemish girl—they fall in love and get married and they become European, as do their children." A 2014 study by the European Commission calculated (based on fertility rates) that the Erasmus Program had been responsible for producing one million babies since 1987.

Yet questions have been raised about how widely the benefits of that program have been shared. Only about 5 percent of all European graduates participate in it, and they tend to come from better-off families. An Erasmus sojourn has become a marker of distinction and privilege, and the improved job prospects it brings reinforce the advantages of those participating. In short, the program has taken on an elitist air.

That, of course, is a concern for the European project as a whole. The vote by Britain in June 2016 to leave the EU exposed the gulf between the well-to-do urbanites of London and Oxbridge and the less mobile residents of smaller communities who have felt left behind in the great global gold rush. The flood of migrants and succession of terrorist acts have produced a backlash against open borders, while economic stagnation has raised questions about the viability of the euro. More generally, the control that unelected policy makers and bureaucrats in Brussels and Frankfurt have over the lives of the EU's 500 million people has fed charges of unaccountability and high-handedness, further exposing the union's fragility. At a Conservative Party conference in October 2016, the British prime minister Theresa May declared, "If you believe you are a citizen of the world, you are a citizen of nowhere"—an *Adages*-like statement that seemed aimed directly at Erasmus.

These developments would no doubt have seemed familiar to Erasmus. His rationalist, ethics-based, pluralistic, and internationalist creed came under constant assault. As Stefan Zweig observed, Erasmus failed to find a way to communicate his ideals to the masses. He wrote in Latin for a highly educated slice of society. He and his fellow humanists rarely mingled with ordinary people and had only limited knowledge of their attitudes, needs, and appetites. So, when it came to defending his ideals in the face of rising nationalism, disruptive technology, and deepening social and economic rifts, he lacked both the tools and vocabulary. European humanists today often seem similarly at a loss. If humanists think that their own values represent those of all humanity and offer the best design for living, they should be able to do a better job of making that case.

AFTERMATH: LUTHER

If tracing Erasmus's influence is difficult because his fingerprints are so faint, tracing Luther's is difficult because his offspring are so plentiful. Today, the Protestant faith that he helped found has an estimated 800 million adherents (second only to Roman Catholicism, with 1.1 billion). Worldwide, there are eleven thousand Protestant denominations. The varieties of Protestant experience include Southern Baptists praying in suburban megachurches, Methodists worshipping in Main Street sanctuaries, Quakers gathering in Spartan meeting houses, Jehovah's Witnesses ringing doorbells, Mennonites refusing to bear arms, Seventh-day Adventists observing the Sabbath on Saturday, premillennialists awaiting the rapture, and televangelists proclaiming the prosperity gospel. In one form or another, all of these groups can trace their origins back to the moment in late October 1517 when Luther posted his Ninety-Five Theses in Wittenberg.

Yet, in many of them, Luther's presence is hard to detect. A large and growing number of Protestants belong to the Pentecostal and Charismatic movements. Both movements believe in the blessings conferred by the Holy Spirit and feature faith healing, speaking in tongues, and other "spiritual gifts" that recall the practices of the Zwickau Prophets whom Luther so excoriated. The Anglican Communion, with about eighty-five million adherents, features a Catholic-like hierarchy and an Erasmian aversion to doctrinal certitude that Luther would no doubt condemn. In Scotland, the Netherlands, Switzerland, and France, the dominant form of Protestantism is a version of the Reformed faith that goes back not to Luther but to Zwingli and Calvin.

In Europe, Luther's most direct descendants are, naturally, in Germany, and it is there that one would most expect to find his imprint. In 2003, German public television conducted a call-in poll to determine *Un-*

sere Besten—"Our Best," i.e., the greatest Germans. Luther placed second, ahead of Marx, Bach, Goethe, Bismarck, and Einstein and behind only Konrad Adenauer—a showing all the more impressive in that Adenauer is a figure of the twentieth century and Luther is one of the sixteenth. This obstinate, forceful, audacious, and fervent patriarch remains a towering presence in his homeland, as can be seen in the undiminished popularity of the Luther Bible (150,000 copies published annually), the continued use of his catechisms, and the prominent place in German society of the Lutheran pastor (Angela Merkel is the daughter of one). Nearly 30 percent of all Germans belong to churches affiliated with the Evangelische Kirche in Deutschland, Germany's main Protestant federation and the heir to Luther's movement.

Yet these measures of influence are to a degree misleading. As esteemed as Luther is among the German people, his ideas have gradually lost their hold on them—a result of a series of struggles, setbacks, and fatal missteps, as well as of more general social and political developments in Germany as in Europe as a whole.

In 1555, when the Peace of Augsburg was signed, Lutheranism seemed an unstoppable force in Germany. That pact—ending eight years of warfare between the forces of Charles V and those of the Schmalkaldic League—granted each ruler in the Holy Roman Empire the right to determine the faith of his subjects, and many of those rulers were Lutheran. Most of northern Germany was Lutheran, as were half of Franconia and about fifty of the empire's sixty-five imperial free cities. The Catholic Church had disappeared from much of the country; hundreds of parishes had no priest, and many monasteries were empty. Around 1560, however, the Counter-Reformation got underway in earnest. The Roman Church—reinvigorated by Trent, urged on by prince-bishops, propelled by Jesuit educators and propagandists—set out to re-Catholicize Europe. From Geneva, meanwhile, militant Calvinists were infiltrating Germany, where they clashed with the Lutherans over the Eucharist and where a number of princes went over to the Reformed faith.

The Lutherans themselves continued to assail one another. In an effort at peacekeeping, a group of theologians met to produce a new confession. The Formula of Concord, as it was called, offered a codifi-

cation of Lutheran positions on such key matters as original sin, justification, and works. While helping to reduce strife, however, the Formula
was so detailed, dense, and convoluted as to be intelligible only to those
who had drafted it. Lutheran theologians proceeded to turn out arcane,
long-winded commentaries, capped by the *Loci Theologi* of Johann Gerhard—a nine-volume Scholastic thicket. Aristotelian logic was used to
defend Lutheran propositions, and Aristotle's *Metaphysics* was smug-
gled back into university curricula. Lutheranism thus entered its "age of
orthodoxy."

Thus consumed with doctrine and dialectic, the Lutherans were unprepared when war broke out in 1618. Over the next thirty years, the
armies of Catholic states reclaimed huge swaths of the Holy Roman Empire. The Peace of Westphalia compounded the problem. The control
that princes gained over the churches in their territories was even more
complete in Protestant than in Catholic territories. Attendance at church
and knowledge of the catechism were firmly enforced, and the Lutheran
clergy often seemed agents of the state—a legacy of Luther's own history
of collaboration with the princes.

Amid such rigidity and control, there was a growing desire for more
heartfelt forms of devotion, and a new reformer stepped forth to provide
it. Philipp Jakob Spener, while studying Luther's theology at Strasbourg,
was struck by his teaching that all Christians are priests. Clearly, this
principle had gotten lost. In 1670, while serving as a pastor in Frankfurt,
Spener began hosting small groups in his home to pray, read the Bible, and
discuss how to apply it to their lives. These *collegia pietatis*, as he called
them, stressed the spiritual regeneration of individuals over the memorization of creeds and the performance of rites.

Spener summed up this new approach in a book titled *Pia Desideria* ("Pious Desires"). After caustically cataloguing the "corrupt conditions" in the Lutheran church—the fruitless meddling by the princes,
the sterile exercises of the theologians, the "sins and debaucheries" of the
Lutheran authorities—he proposed a series of concrete ideas for renewal,
based on the same type of groups he had introduced in Frankfurt. In these
"churches within the church," Scripture was to be restored as the chief
source of authority and instrument of salvation. Preachers were encour-

aged to edify their congregations rather than show off their learning, and princes were admonished to stick to the temporal realm. More generally, Spener urged Christians to practice the "diligent exercise of the spiritual priesthood."

Soon, *collegia pietatis* were appearing across Germany, in a movement that came to be known as Pietism. From the start, however, it faced fierce opposition. Spener was charged with heresy for ignoring doctrine, and his groups were accused of "separatism" for operating outside official channels. The rulers of Prussia were more sympathetic, however, and Spener accepted an invitation to continue his work in Berlin. In 1694, the Prussian government established a university at Halle, and August Hermann Francke, a disciple of Spener's, became a professor there. Like Spener, Francke wanted to show how faith could be made active in the world, and he established a school for poor children, a home for orphans, a Bible institute, a pharmacy, and a printing house to spread the word. Halle became Pietism's "New Jerusalem," attracting earnest students from around Germany. To that point, Lutheranism had not shown much interest in proselytizing, but Francke started a missionary training school, and soon graduates were heading off to the Americas, South African, even India—the start of Protestantism's global expansion.

The most eye-catching—and peculiar—Pietist experiment occurred on the estate of Nikolaus Ludwig Zinzendorf, an engaging but eccentric Saxon count. Inheriting some land near Dresden, Zinzendorf in 1722 opened it up to religious refugees, including the Moravian Brethren. Heirs to the Hussite movement, the Moravians had suffered intense persecution during the Church's brutal recovery of Czech lands. Under Zinzendorf's protection, they established a village, called Herrnhut ("the Lord's watch"), in which they sought to build a new Christian order. It developed into a sort of commune, with families replaced by "choirs" organized by age, sex, and marital status and responsible for providing education and child care. From around Europe, mystics and seekers came to see this center of evangelistic renewal. Its very success, however, made it suspect to the authorities, and Zinzendorf was banished from his estate.

The Moravians themselves developed cult-like features, including chiliastic outbursts, continuous prayer watches, and an almost erotic preoccupation with Christ's wounds. The Pietists as a whole seemed to delight in alienating others. Their leaders demanded strict austerity in personal conduct, including rigid observance of the Sabbath and a ban on card-playing and theater-going. The emphasis placed on conversion bred disdain for those who failed to measure up; with Scripture held up as the sole authority, scholarship and learning were often neglected. In the end, though, what stirred the most opposition was the Pietists' offer of a form of devotion outside official institutions . Had they been allowed to form a new denomination, they might have become an established presence, but this was prohibited by law, and by the time of Francke's death, in 1727, the movement had lost much of its vitality. In Germany, there was little room for the priesthood of all believers.

Pietism would not disappear, however. Its warm spirituality and sense of fellowship appealed to the lowly and learned alike. Many of the leading figures of the German Enlightenment, in fact, had religious roots, in contrast to the more skeptical *philosophes* of France. The result, however, would be to undo religion from within.

The pioneer of the German Enlightenment, Gottfried Wilhelm Leibniz, was born (in 1646) into a pious Lutheran family in Leipzig. As a young prodigy, however, he became interested in mathematics and jurisprudence, and by the age of forty he had developed calculus independently of Newton. Reflecting his scientific bent, Leibniz saw the universe as an orderly place whose harmonic operations could be described by the laws of logic. His God was not an angry, inscrutable figure but a rational and benevolent father who rewarded men and women according to their deeds. Human sinfulness was not an innate and ineradicable condition but a relative weakness that could be overcome by making the right choices. For Leibniz, in short, the relationship between God and man more closely resembled Erasmus's father leading his son to the apple than Luther's hapless rider of a donkey, and the reformer would no doubt have condemned his ideas as gross blasphemies.

Leibniz's claim that the universe is the best of all possible worlds would be satirized by Voltaire in the figure of Doctor Pangloss. But his belief in a just God and man's ability to do good would become a fixture of the

German Enlightenment, as was apparent in the work of its supreme representative, Immanuel Kant. Born in 1724, Kant was raised in a family of devout Pietists in Königsberg, the capital of East Prussia; at the university there, he came under the influence of a Pietist professor of logic and metaphysics. But he also studied Newtonian science, and in his writings on religion he would ruthlessly suppress all traces of the supernatural, as was apparent in the title of his main work on the subject: *Religion Within the Limits of Reason Alone* (published in 1793). No Pangloss, Kant believed in the existence of "*radical* innate *evil*" in humankind—a concept akin to original sin. But he also believed that man has a "seed of goodness" within and that he must work continually to overcome the evil and strive for the good. Human freedom and choice were at the heart of Kant's vision. "It is not essential, and hence not necessary, for everyone to know what God does or has done for his salvation," he wrote. It is essential, however, "to know *what man himself must do* in order to become worthy of this assistance." Kant dismissed prayer, churchgoing, and other practices aimed at pleasing God as elements of a "fetish-faith," and he mocked those who seek through the means of grace to become "favorites" of God rather than strive to fulfill the human duty to behave ethically.

For such put-downs of conventional religion, Kant was denounced by the Prussian authorities, but the damage was done. His ideas would provide a foundation for a new school: liberal Protestantism. It equated religion with morality, saw Christ primarily as an ethical guide, and considered man capable of constant self-betterment. By the end of the eighteenth century, Luther's doctrine of justification by faith was all but dead among German intellectuals; though raised Lutheran, they were all turning Erasmian.

Luther's influence would further recede as a result of the radical advances taking place in biblical studies. Building on the innovations of the Renaissance, German scholars set out to determine the identity and intent of the authors of the books of the Bible. Whereas Valla and Erasmus had used grammar and philology to arrive at the most reliable version of the text, the higher criticism (as it was called) raised questions about the accuracy and authenticity of that text. The most sensational work to emerge from this school was the *Life of Jesus, Critically Examined*, by David Friedrich Strauss. Published in 1835, when Strauss was just twenty-seven, it subjected the four Gospels to an exhaustive critical analysis. The miraculous deeds described in the New Testament, Strauss argued, were best understood as myths created by the followers of Jesus to fulfill the Judaic prophecies about the coming of the Messiah. Such events as the virgin birth and the resurrection were nothing more than inventions designed to establish Christ's divinity. Loudly attacked for undermining the articles of the faith, Strauss was banned from future theological employment, but his *Life* ushered in a new era of scholarship in which Scripture was ruthlessly deconstructed and demystified. Paradoxically, then, it was in Germany, where Luther had proclaimed the Bible the lone authority, that its sacral quality was most unceremoniously stripped away.

Outside the intelligentsia, however, Luther was far from interred. Among traditional groups like the nobility, the peasantry, and the lower middle class in the towns, the enthronement of reason and the overthrow of the Bible caused a backlash. The French Revolution, with its efforts to engineer an ideal society, seemed an exercise in hubris, while the ensuing violence and chaos seemed a form of divine punishment. In 1792, France declared war on Prussia and Austria, initiating a period of French domination of Central Europe. In early October 1806, Napoleon smashed the Prussian army at Jena and Auerstädt, and later that month he marched triumphantly into Berlin, consolidating French control from the Rhine to the Elbe. Spurred by its defeat, Prussia rebuilt its armed forces, and after the rout of Napoleon's army in Russia in 1812, it mobilized. In October 1813, in a series of battles known as the wars of liberation, the Prussians drove the French from German territory.

During the French occupation, German nationalism had surged. At the same time, the political and social reforms introduced by France had stirred interest in representative government. University students formed patriotic unions committed to personal renovation and political liberalization. With the approach of the three-hundredth anniversary of the posting of the Ninety-Five Theses, there was new interest in Luther's efforts on behalf of German emancipation. On October 18, 1817—the fourth anniversary of the wars of liberation—several hundred students met at the Wartburg, chosen for its association with Luther. Luther was hailed as the "internal liberator" of Germany paralleling the external liberation by the generals. A victory fire was lit, and, in a reenactment of Luther's burning of the papal bull, printed paper bearing the names of despised reactionary authors was cast into it.

But the old regime, led by Count Metternich, was unbowed. After a deranged student stabbed a conservative playwright to death, Metternich ordered the unions disbanded and enacted a series of repressive measures aimed at crushing all dissent. The Protestant church remained a pillar of that regime. In these years, there arose a neo-Lutheran movement that took "back to Luther" as its slogan and held throne and altar to be inseparable.

From this milieu of renewed piety emerged Otto von Bismarck. While living as a country squire in Prussia, he met the daughter of a conservative aristocratic family known for its Pietism. While courting her, he had a religious conversion that gave him both a sense of inner strength and a renewed commitment to the old order. Bismarck came to see the state as a Christian entity that got its ultimate sanction from God, and he felt only contempt for the elite liberals who held up England as a model for Prussia. His successful campaign to consolidate the German states into the Second Reich (Empire)—proclaimed on January 18, 1871—seemed to many Protestants to complete what Luther had begun. The Lutheran church became a strong backer of the new *Kaiser*, Wilhelm I, and of monarchism in general.

But new social forces were gathering. Spurred by the great capitalist boom of the late nineteenth century, Germany became a land of giant companies, big agriculture, powerful banks, swelling cities, and an expanding proletariat whose radicalism grew as its misery deepened. The Protestants, attached to the ruling class, were incapable of developing a program to attract the working class. In the cities, workers turned dramatically away from religion. Berlin, which in the first decade of the twentieth century had a population of more than 2 million, had only about a hundred places of worship, earning it a reputation as a "spiritual cemetery."

Instead, those workers turned to a new faith—socialism. The Social Democratic Party grew so fast that by 1890 it was outpolling all other parties. Marxist historians showed new interest in the Peasants' War.

In 1897, Karl Kautsky, a leading party theorist, came out with *Commu-nism in Central Europe at the Time of the Reformation*. Echoing Friedrich Engels, he hailed Thomas Müntzer as a hero of the working class and reviled Luther for having backed the princes. Among liberal Protestant theologians, meanwhile, Luther was scorned as a medieval figure whose attachment to faith and rejection of human agency held little relevance for the modern age. In 1906, Ernst Troeltsch, a prominent theologian at the University of Berlin, gave a lecture on the significance of Protestantism for the beginning of the modern world. He dismissed the "old Protestantism" of Luther's time as backward-looking and uninspired and censured it for its withdrawal from the world and glorification of the state. The true start of the modern age, Troeltsch asserted, was not the German Reformation but the Enlightenments in England and France, and he urged Germany to follow the democratic and pluralistic course being pursued in England and America.

Among those in the audience for Troeltsch's lecture was a church histo-rian named Karl Holl. Though a liberal Protestant, Holl was troubled by Troeltsch's attempt to consign Luther to history's dustbin. No less unsettling were the new attacks from the Catholics. In 1904, Heinrich Denifle, a Dominican historian working as an archivist at the Vatican, published a scathing indictment of Luther's scholarship, conduct, and character. Denifle had seen a copy of Luther's recently discovered lecture notes on the Epistle to the Romans, and, drawing on it, he dismissed his doctrine of justification by faith as unsupported by both Scripture and the Fathers. He also called attention to Luther's frank admissions about his carnal desires. He was, Denifle wrote, "a fallen-away monk with un-bridled lust, a theological ignoramus, an evil man" who "used immorality to begin the Reformation." Luther was charged with apostasy, buffoon-ery, hypocrisy, mendacity, and drunkenness. Praised in Rome, the book caused an outcry in Germany, and even liberal Protestants rushed to the reformer's defense.

Prodded by Denifle, Holl got hold of a copy of Luther's lecture notes. Far from being disappointed, he was dazzled. In commenting on Paul's passages about justification, Luther seemed to arrive at a completely original understanding of the relationship between man and God. His insights seemed all the more significant as the First World War approached. Like many Protestants, Holl was caught up by in the patriotic surge in Germany. Luther seemed to embody the vigor and creativity of the German people, in contrast to the pallid pluralism and sterile rationalism of the West. When the far-right German Fatherland Party was formed in September 1917, Holl—showing how far he was moving from his liberal roots—joined it.

On October 31, 1917—the four-hundredth anniversary of the posting of the Ninety-Five Theses—Holl gave a memorial lecture at the University of Berlin. In it, he described Luther's religion as a religion of conscience that represented a decisive breakthrough for the modern era. Holl's recovery of the theology of the young Luther from the mire of confessions and commentaries that had swallowed it caused great excitement, and he spent the next several years expanding his lecture. He worked against the backdrop of the many upheavals shaking Germany: its defeat in the war, the fall of the monarchy, the socialist revolution of the winter of 1918–1919, the humiliation of Versailles. The new Weimar Republic brought democracy, night clubs, Expressionism, jazz, Josephine Baker, the disestablishment of the church, and other developments that seemed a betrayal of traditional German values.

In 1921, Holl came out with a collection of essays, including his expanded lecture. "What Did Luther Understand by Religion?", the essay was titled. Luther, Holl declared, was "the great awakener of the conscience in his day." In emphasizing that religion addresses itself to "personal freedom" and "personal decision," Luther provided the foundation for an autonomy that was "more than merely an imperfect preliminary form of the autonomy espoused by the Enlightenment." In a jab at Troeltsch, Holl claimed that Luther stood out "so sharply from the Middle Ages" and appeared "so much as the transformer of the whole life of the mind that it is impossible to associate him with the Middle Ages." But, he hastened to add, Luther was not a proponent of unbridled individualism. On the contrary, he was "the principal advocate of the community concept in religion." Only when a community's members are united with God, he taught, does it deserve to be called a church of Christ. During the Peasants' War, Luther had courageously protected the gospel by making sure it was not recruited for use in the social struggle. (Holl made no mention of Luther's statements about stabbing and slaying the peasants or of his close ties to the princes.)

While many aspects of Luther's religion were distinctively German, Holl concluded, it would be arrogant of the German people to lay claim to him for themselves alone, for Luther showed how the "profound genius" of the German people had within it a "universally human element." Luther "belongs not only to us Germans, he belongs to humanity. This is why we are confident that his attainments will continue to be cherished."

Holl's resurrection of the young Luther and his veneration of him as a symbol of German greatness caused a sensation, and the accompanying flood of essays and studies would become known as the Luther Renaissance. Conservatives in particular rallied to Holl's portrayal of Luther as an outstanding German with much to teach the rest of the world. Holl's vision of the church as a national community, meanwhile, became the basis for the idea of a *Volkskirche* (people's church) that embodied the unique values of German Christians—an idea that resonated with the many young Protestants flocking to the standard of militant Christian nationalism.

In the 1920s, Protestants voted overwhelmingly for the right-wing German National People's Party and then for its successor, the National Socialists. In the election of July 1932, the Nazis won 37 percent of the overall vote but 56 percent in Protestant-dominated regions (compared to 23 percent in Catholic ones). Hitler skillfully appealed to the Protestants' resentment of Weimar, and many Protestant theologians and ministers saw his rise as offering a last chance to establish a true people's church. The German Christians, as his Protestant supporters became known, sought to take over church bodies from within and turn them into the spiritual home for the "true Christians" of the Third Reich. "Stormtroopers for Christ," they called themselves.

Many Protestants objected, however, and in May 1934 a group of them met in Barmen to form a competing body, the Confessing Church. Rejecting the totalitarian claims of the state over society and religion, they sought to protect the independence of the Protestant church. More ministers affiliated with this body than with the German Christians. Even they, however, were motivated more by a desire to maintain clerical autonomy against Nazi encroachments than to resist Hitler's war aims and his murderous attacks on the Jews and other groups.

This lack of opposition reflected, in part, the menacing repression that all dissidents faced; many who did resist, like Dietrich Bonhoeffer, paid with their lives. But it also reflected the longstanding Lutheran tradition of deference to the state. One of the few open dissenters, the great Swiss theologian Karl Barth, wrote in 1939 that Luther's idea of "two kingdoms," with its insistence on keeping the secular and spiritual apart, "lies like a cloud over the ecclesiastical thinking and action of more or less every course taken by the German Church." During the war, as word began arriving of the atrocities committed on the eastern front and against the Jews, all but a handful of Confessing church members remained silent.

In October 1945, some surviving leaders of that church issued a "Declaration of Guilt," expressing "great anguish" over the "inestimable suffering" inflicted "on many peoples and lands." "We accuse ourselves for not witnessing more courageously, for not praying more faithfully, for not believing more joyously, and for not loving more ardently." Though the declaration was tepid—it made no mention of the Jews, for instance—it marked the start of a painful (and ongoing) effort by German Protestants to atone for their performance during the war. In an effort to serve society, the Protestant church mounted an ambitious social-welfare program, establishing a network of schools, hospitals, homes for the elderly, and youth programs. While helping offset the perception of Protestant indifference, however, these efforts gave rise to a vast bureaucracy that sapped spiritual spontaneity and stymied innovation.

In 1967, Karl Kupisch, a German church historian, offered an assessment of the Luther Renaissance fifty years after it had begun, and it was harsh. Led by theologians, he wrote, the movement had "created a theologically mummified Luther who was a stranger to the mass of evangelical churchgoers." Luther had as a result remained "one of the great unknown figures in German history. Like Snow White, he lies asleep in his (theological) glass coffin, and the time of his awakening cannot be foreseen."

Reexamining his life and work, Kupisch went on, remained "a vital task" for the German people, for "he is as much a part of their confused history as Goethe and Bismarck. He cannot be swept under a theological carpet: for that he was too great a man."

Yet Luther largely remains in his coffin. With the steady advance of Erasmian-style humanism in Germany, the country's churches have experienced a precipitous fall-off in attendance. Between 1990 and 2010, the Protestant federation closed 340 churches; 46 were demolished and others were turned into restaurants or converted into mosques. The retreat from faith has been especially marked in eastern Germany. A 2012 global survey found that 52 percent of the population in that region said that they do not believe in God—a higher proportion than in any other part of the world, earning the region the label "the most godless place on earth." "Where have all the Protestants gone?" the pastor of St. Mary's, the Wittenberg town church, has lamented. On an ordinary Sunday, no more than fifty to a hundred of the town's residents show up for services.

They are greatly outnumbered by tourists. In addition to St. Mary's, tourists visit the Luther House, a modernized version of the old Black Cloister that now houses the world's largest museum about the Reformation; the (rebuilt) Castle Church, whose north portal features bronze doors bearing the text of the Ninety-Five Theses; the homes of Melanchthon and Cranach; and shops selling Reformation beer, wine, and socks embroidered with the statement, "Here I Stand." Cruise ships regularly put in on the Elbe, and for overnight visitors there's a Best Western steps from the cloister. Lutherstadt-Wittenberg (as it is now officially known) has become a Reformation theme park.

The flow of visitors greatly increased in the period leading up to October 31, 2017—the five-hundredth anniversary of the posting of the Ninety-Five Theses. For a full decade beforehand, the Lutheran church sponsored a series of commemorative conferences, exhibitions, concerts, and tours, thus hoping to spark another back-to-Luther movement. It is an uphill battle, given the ongoing de-Christianization of Germany (as of Europe as a whole). Luther's own writings pose an additional obstacle. Today, no conference on the reformer is complete without a discussion of his anti-Jewish writings and of how much responsibility he bears for the Holocaust. *On the Jews and Their Lies* remains an indelible stain on Luther's reputation and a major stumbling block to any new Luther Renaissance.

To find the modern-day impact of Luther's ideas, one must look beyond Germany. Thanks in part to the missionary work begun by the Pietists, Protestantism today commands a worldwide empire stretching from Nigeria (60 million adherents) and South Africa (37 million) to China (58 million) and Brazil (40 million). In sub-Saharan Africa alone there are 295 million Protestants, dwarfing the 100 million in Europe. The single largest Protestant congregation is the Yoido Full Gospel Church, in Seoul, South Korea; its average weekly attendance is 200,000.

The largest concentration of Protestants, however, is in the United States, where just under half of the population identifies as such. For more than two centuries, America has been the capital of world Protestantism, and it is there that one must look for Luther's current influence.

The natural place to begin is with America's Lutherans. There are about seven million of them, concentrated in the Upper Midwest. Most are descendants of German and Scandinavian immigrants who came to America in the eighteenth and nineteenth centuries. Their most well-known community is Lake Wobegon, which, though fictitious, embodies the traits for which American Lutherans are best known: modesty, reticence, stoicism, insularity. As Lutherans themselves like to joke, their prototypical figure is a shy Norwegian bachelor farmer. Proportionately many fewer Lutherans have served in Congress or the Cabinet than have Episcopalians, Presbyterians, or Methodists; the highest office attained has been that of chief justice of the Supreme Court (William Rehnquist). This record reflects Luther's own rejection of political engagement. All in all, the Lutherans are an inconspicuous presence in America.

To find Luther's influence, one must look beyond the denominations that bear his name. Consider, for instance, the Southern Baptists. With more than fifteen million members and 46,000 churches, the Southern Baptist Convention is the largest denomination in America; through its seminaries, publications, office in Washington, and network of missionaries, it has profoundly affected American political, social, and cultural life. The Baptists' various statements of belief bear Luther's stamp throughout, beginning with the prime place assigned to Scripture. The Bible, they maintain, is the "supreme standard" by which all human conduct and religious opinion should be measured. It is "a perfect treasure of divine instruction," having "God for its author, salvation for its end, and truth, without any mixture of error, for its matter." This is essentially a restatement of Luther's principle of Scripture alone (except on the matter of biblical inerrancy, which he never endorsed).

For Southern Baptists, the "starting point" of everything related to their churches is each individual's "personal faith in Jesus Christ as Savior and Lord of their lives." Under the related doctrine of "soul competency," the Baptists affirm "the accountability of each person before God." "Your family cannot save you. Neither can your church. It comes down to you and God." This is a plainspoken version of Luther's doctrine of justification by faith alone.

Finally, the Southern Baptists explicitly embrace "the priesthood of all believers," asserting that "laypersons have the same right as ordained ministers to communicate with God, interpret Scripture, and minister in God's name." This, of course, goes back directly to Luther.

Needless to say, there are some significant differences between the beliefs of the Baptists and those of Luther. The former, for instance, practice adult baptism, and they consider the Lord's Supper a symbolic rite—positions that Luther vehemently rejected. On many key points, however, the Baptists' statements of belief parallel those of Luther, despite the fact that his name nowhere appears in them.

Billy Graham offers another example. From the fall of 1949, when he led a crusade in Los Angeles that first brought him to national attention, until the 1980s, Graham was the face of evangelical Christianity in America. Invoking the Bible as his sole authority, he offered a simple message centered on Christ's atoning death on the cross for mankind's sins and his resurrection from the dead for its salvation. "No matter who we are or what we have done," Graham observed in *Just As I Am*, his autobiography, "we are saved only because of what Christ has done for us. I will not go to Heaven because I have preached to great crowds. I will go to heaven for one reason: Jesus Christ died for me, and I am trusting Him alone for my salvation."

This intense focus on the Bible and on salvation through faith in Christ apart from works reflects the impact Luther had on Graham. In his autobiography, Graham describes a visit he made to Wittenberg in 1982, during which he preached from the pulpit at the town church, using as his text Romans 1:17 ("the just shall live by faith"), which was so central for Luther. Afterward, Graham went to the Castle Church to see Luther's grave. The next day, in Dresden, he told a Saxon synod about his trip to Wittenberg and about how much Luther's life and thought had influenced him. The leading evangelical figure in America in the postwar era, then, preached a message drawn largely from Luther.

Luther's impact on American life is most apparent in the place of the Bible in it. According to surveys, nearly nine of ten American households own a Bible, with each owning an average of three Bibles. Nearly half of all adult Americans say that the Bible is the inspired Word of God. The American Bible Association distributes up to five million Bibles a year and (together with the international United Bible Societies) has sponsored the translation of the Bible into 1,800 languages. Bible study groups have become fixtures in schools, workplaces, locker rooms, and halls of government, including the White House under Democratic and Republican presidents. In late 2017, a massive $500 million Museum of the Bible opened in Washington just south of the Mall; offering thousands of biblical artifacts, it is the creation of Steven Green, the chief executive of the Hobby Lobby craft-store chain and a member of a prominent evangelical family. All of this can be traced back to Luther's doctrine of *sola scriptura*.

Such connections are seldom made, however. Even in history books about American religion, Luther is rarely mentioned. Calvin instead gets all the attention. Most historians are wed to a "Puritan" interpretation of America's religious origins, stressing the dominant influence of Calvinist New England and its enduring impact on American society. New England Calvinism certainly did leave a lasting mark; it can be seen, for instance, in the belief in American exceptionalism and the periodic campaigns to purify society morally. But Luther's ideas have been no less influential. They were especially critical in inspiring the Second Great Awakening of the late eighteenth and early nineteenth centuries, when American evangelicalism was born.

In a book on the Reformation, it's not possible to offer a detailed account of how that happened. It is possible, though, to suggest a new path of inquiry. Its starting point would be the career of the man who served as the main conduit of Luther's ideas from Europe to America: John Wesley. Like so many other inspirational Christian figures, this Anglican priest was tormented by his inability to make his behavior conform to his will. In 1735, when he was in his early thirties, Wesley accepted an invitation to serve as a minister in the colony of Georgia. On the voyage over, he became close to a group of Moravian Brethren—the same enthusiasts who had gathered on Count Zinzendorf's estate in Saxony. Wesley was impressed by their humble piety and by the unshakable calm they showed in the face of a terrible storm at sea. During his two years in America, however, he was unable to measure up. His efforts to convert Native Americans foundered, and he fell in love with a woman who—tired of waiting for him to declare himself—married someone else. Incensed, Wesley refused to administer Communion to her, touching off a scandal that eventually forced him to return to England.

On May 24, 1738, a despondent Wesley reluctantly accepted an invitation from some Moravians to attend a religious meeting on Aldersgate Street in London. It featured a reading of Luther's preface to the Epistle to the Romans. "About a quarter before nine," Wesley later recalled, while the reader "was describing the change which God works in the heart through faith in Christ, I felt my heart strangely warmed. I felt I did trust in Christ, Christ alone, for salvation, and an assurance was given me that He had taken away my sins, even mine, and saved me from the law of sin and death." Wesley thus had a conversion experience similar to the one described by Luther in his 1545 preface, and Luther's teachings about salvation by faith and grace would become the foundation for Wesley's own theology. In August of 1738, he went to Herrnhut and for two weeks absorbed the intimate spirituality of German Pietism, with its roots in Luther's ideas of *sola scriptura* and the priesthood of all believers.

There was one aspect of Luther's teachings that Wesley could not accept, however: predestination. A restless man of action, he rejected the idea that God had foreordained all who would be saved and that no one could do anything about it. Wesley was instead drawn to the writings of Arminius—the Dutch theologian who had challenged the Calvinists in Holland by asserting a place for human agency. While Wesley continued to accept the Lutheran (and Calvinist) belief in human depravity and the need for divine grace, he rejected the idea that salvation is available only to a predetermined few. Instead, he stressed the cooperative part that an individual, drawing on his free will, can play in seeking God's favor. Going further, he maintained that a Christian, after being born again, can through an exercise of will move toward a state of "sanctification," in which the heart is filled with love for both God and one's neighbor and in which the individual achieves victory over sin. Wesley was thus modifying—and modernizing—Luther's theology, stripping it of the fatalism that had repelled so many.

Eager to spread his new vision, Wesley began traveling around England, preaching in churches when they opened their doors to him and in public squares and fields when they did not. The response was electric. The doctrine of justification by faith, modified to accommodate free will, proved popular with weavers, miners, and other working people, especially in economically struggling regions neglected by the Church of England. Wesley organized them into small Pietist-like groups that met for Bible study and prayer. Their systematic approach to devotion gave the movement its name: Methodism. Like the Lutheran Church in Germany, the Church of England disapproved of the fervor of these upstarts, and Wesley himself was frequently attacked in sermons and in print, but Methodism quickly spread, introducing into England an evangelical enthusiasm it had previously lacked.

Wesley was no revolutionary, however; in his sermons, he supported the existing order, and he made sure that the emotions unleashed by his movement were kept in check. Not until 1795, four years after his death, did the Methodists formally separate from the Church of England, and even then they continued to show submission to authority and respect for tradition.

Not so in America. With its open spaces, contending denominations, and restless population, the New World would prove far more open than the Old to Luther's doctrines as amended by Wesley. In 1769, the first Methodist preachers commissioned by him arrived from England. They were quickly organized into a system of circuit riders, each of whom was assigned to a particular territory. Mostly single, poor, and self-educated, these itinerant preachers had to endure loneliness, bad weather, and poor roads; half would die before the age of thirty. They were sustained, however, by the outbursts of emotion they inspired. Preaching in cabins, courthouses, and clearings, they rallied crowds of farmers and laborers with the cry "No creed but the Bible" and a simple message of salvation through faith and sanctification through the performance of good works.

That message was especially suited to people on the frontier. Living in isolated cabins, enduring the hardships of daily life, these backwoodsmen were an independent and bellicose lot, given to profanity, drinking, gambling, and fighting. On August 6, 1801, in one of the most extraordinary spectacles in American religious history, twenty thousand men and women gathered in a clearing around a meetinghouse in Cane Ridge, Kentucky, to pray and hear sermons. They were urged to take their salvation into their own hands through acts of faith and repentance. Some, overwhelmed and transported, fell to the ground and lay there motionless for hours; others burst out in spasms of jerking and barking, dancing and singing, in what were taken as signs of the Holy Spirit. For six or seven days such displays continued, with thousands declaring themselves for Christ. Such camp meetings quickly became a fixture of the frontier. With their egalitarian spirit, they fitted the temper of the new republic by inviting individuals to change themselves.

Toward the end of the eighteenth century, as the new American republic was taking shape, these impassioned bouts suddenly erupted, setting off the four-decade convulsion that would become known as the Second Great Awakening. (The First Great Awakening, flaring in the mid-1730s, had died out within a decade.) It was a popular uprising against the religious establishment, inviting ordinary people to take charge of their spiritual lives and make a personal commitment to Christ.

Lasting into the 1840s, the Second Great Awakening represented the greatest surge in religious fervor in the West since the early days of the Reformation and was in a sense a continuation of it. At a time when European churches were losing touch with the people, American churches were attracting them with a version of Luther's radically individualist creed. Unlike Europe, America had no popes, princes, or established churches to crack down on them. In a union where "we the people" ruled, the popular priesthood took root and spread. These new believers called themselves *evangelicals*, reviving the term Luther himself had used. Wesley's experience of being born again—inspired by Luther—became the spiritual model.

The Second Great Awakening would leave a permanent mark on American society. Rejecting all authority but that of the individual, it accelerated the advent of a social order characterized by competition and self-expression, entrepreneurship and free enterprise. Evangelical leaders proudly insisted on their lay orientation, creating an environment in which the non-credentialed and unaccredited could thrive. The Awakening, in short, gave rise to the expansive Christian populism that would become such a prominent feature of American society—a populism rooted in the Lutheran-Wesleyan creed that everyone can read the Bible on his or her own and that each individual is personally accountable before God.

Over time, that populism would undergo many mutations and assume many different forms, from the revival meetings of Dwight Moody and the fundamentalist testimonies of William Jennings Bryan to the motivational sermons of Joel Osteen and the purpose-driven appeals of Rick Warren. While there is much in this populism that Luther would surely find objectionable—the universal American presumption that one can attain salvation through one's own actions runs directly counter to Luther's rejection of works as a pathway to heaven—America's evangelical population seems animated by the same type of faith-based individualism he championed. The message from the pulpits in evangelical America is overwhelmingly one of self-reliance, personal responsibility, and getting one's relationship right with God and Christ. Change is to be sought not without, in one's circumstances, but within, in the heart. Underlying all is the principle that a layperson has the same right as a minister or theologian to read the Bible and interpret God's Word. America, in short, is the true home of the priesthood of all believers.

In deciding to undertake this project, I was motivated in part by my sense of the pervasive impact that Luther's ideas have had on America (and of the impact that Erasmus's ideas have had on Europe). As I reach the end, I remain struck by how alive the Reformation seems in America and by how the pathway that Luther forged out of his own spiritual crisis on the borderland of civilization in sixteenth-century Saxony continues to provide a lifeline to many millions of Americans.

ORIGINS AND ACKNOWLEDGMENTS

This book arose out of periodic visits I began making to Rome in the 1990s. Like so many before me, I was overwhelmed by the city's beauty, vitality, and layers of history. A key moment came one afternoon when, while walking along the Via dei Fori Imperiali near the Colosseum, I saw a set of marble maps that, hanging on the wall of an ancient basilica, showed the Roman Empire at four different points. In the first, keyed to the eighth century B.C.E., Rome was a dot. In the second, at the end of the Punic Wars, in 146 B.C.E., it included the entire Italian peninsula, half of Iberia, the eastern Adriatic coast, and most of the Balkan Peninsula. In the third, at the time of Augustus's death, in 14 C.E., the empire encompassed most of Europe west of the Rhine and south of the Danube, plus much of Asia Minor, the Levant, and northern Africa. In the fourth, during the reign of Trajan in the early second century, it stretched unbroken from Britain to Mesopotamia. This last map, showing the Roman Empire at its height, was all the more striking in light of the imperial ruins that lay around me. How Rome went from that dot to ruler of the Western world to today's tourist magnet eluded me.

I was no less struck by the city's churches—especially St. Peter's. As I walked around the basilica's vast interior, with its giant marble pilasters, grandiose papal tombs, and splendid works of art, I felt I was in one of the great strongholds of Western culture, yet I had no idea how the Catholic Church had gained such wealth and power. Raised in a middle-class Jewish neighborhood in Baltimore, I had dutifully attended Hebrew school, read the Torah, and learned the history of the Jewish people. About Christianity, I had learned nothing. Most American Jews resist exposing their children to the Christian tradition for fear that they will be sucked up into it. As a result, I had never read the New Testament, could not distinguish Peter from Paul, knew little about the birth of Christianity. On my visits to Rome, the question nagged: How did a small underground sect that had splintered off from Judaism and been so fiercely persecuted by Rome manage, in the course of four centuries, to conquer the empire and replace it as Europe's organizing force?

Seeking the answer, I began my own personal tutorial. At Labyrinth Books (now Book Culture) near Columbia University, I sought out volumes on Rome and early Christianity. The story of Rome's fall and the Church's rise proved so absorbing that, on reaching 476, when the empire collapsed and the Church set out to absorb the heathen masses, I decided to keep reading. Guided by such texts as Norman Cantor's *The Civilization of the Middle Ages*, I worked my way through the next millennium. Reaching the Renaissance, I felt on more familiar ground; everyone knows about Leonardo, Michelangelo, and Raphael and the artistic and cultural renewal they helped spark.

But then I discovered the Northern Renaissance and the great intellectual, moral, and religious debates taking place north of the Alps. In the center of it all was Erasmus. Reading of his long and lonely effort to learn Greek so that he could revise the Latin Vulgate as part of a broad campaign to reform Christian Europe, I was captivated. Discovering how celebrated Erasmus was in his own day, I became curious as to why he is so little known today. As I read on, the source of his obscurity became clear: Martin Luther. In the three-plus years between his posting of the Ninety-Five Theses and his appearance at the Diet of Worms, Luther became Europe's most famous citizen, and the more support he gained for his platform of radical reform, the more Erasmus's moderate program faded. As I read about their rivalry, I felt that I had stumbled upon a remarkable story that foreshadowed many of the conflicts and tensions gripping our world today.

Thinking that that story had the makings of a book, I was fortunate to have the opportunity to think through my ideas at the Medway Plantation in South Carolina, generously hosted by Bokara Legendre. Early on, Tim Duggan at HarperCollins saw the potential in my project, and as I struggled to make the transition from practicing journalism to writing history, he offered many valuable pointers, such as don't start so many sections with a date and avoid quoting too much from other books. Feeling my way through the unfamiliar terrain of the Reformation, I benefited from conversations with three experts whose books had influenced me: Steven Ozment of Harvard (*The Age of Reform, 1250–1550*), Euan Cameron of the Union Theological Seminary (*The European Reformation*), and Anthony Grafton of Princeton (*The Foundations of Early Modern Europe, 1460–1559*, with Eugene F. Rice, Jr.).

As the book began to take shape, I had the support of three extraordinarily perceptive readers. Ann Peters was in many ways an ideal reader, combining a wonderful ear for language with an informed curiosity about the subject matter. Ann read draft after draft of chapter after chapter, showing heroic patience while offering suggestions and criticism with a supportive spirit that reflects her own fundamental kindness and decency. At an early stage, when my writing seemed to sit flat on the page, she suggested that I write out my chapters longhand—an inspired stroke. She was also instrumental in helping me integrate the back stories on Petrarch, Jerome, and others into the main narrative. When Ann's energy finally flagged, Larry Zuckerman stepped in. Larry's excitement for the stories I was unearthing helped boost my morale during the long stretches when I wondered what I had gotten into. With his signature analytical acuity, he urged me to make the opaque clear, spell out the implicit, and cut the extraneous. "What's this section on the Anabaptists doing here?" he demanded at one point. (I moved it.) When I felt I could no longer impose on him, Judith Gurewich took over. Drawing on her own hard-won experience as a publisher, Judith read all the chapters of the book—many of them multiple times—and her periodic flights of wonder at the material helped rekindle my own enthusiasm. Seeing layers of meaning that I had somehow missed, she constantly pushed me to dig deeper and think harder. Our ongoing conversation about Luther's impact on America proved invaluable when it came to writing my aftermath on him, and she firmly admonished me when she felt I was being too hard on Erasmus. Without the generous contributions of Ann, Larry, and Judith, I'm not sure I would have ever made it to the finish line.

Many others offered valuable help along the way. Honor Moore was an early and enthusiastic booster of the project, offering insights gleaned from her own rich personal history. Brenda Wineapple provided encouragement as, first, the director of the Leon Levy Center for Biography, and then as a friend who, in reading chapters, drew on her own acclaimed work as a biographer and historian. For their friendship, encouragement, and (in some cases) cooking, I'd like to thank Patti Cohen and Eddie Sutton, Peter Maass and Alissa Quart (and Cleo Maass), Phil Weiss, Ruti Teitel and Rob Howse, Anya Schiffrin, Alex Stille, Diane Cole, and Rachel Cobb. I greatly appreciate the help that Ellen Thomas provided with translations and the insightful comments on chapters offered by Jon Swan, Amy Davidson, and Todd Gitlin (who urged me to expand on the "chamberpot" aspects of life in that period). I owe a special debt to two departed editors. When I was a neophyte editor at the *Columbia Journalism Review*, Spencer Klaw, with gentle patience and good humor, helped guide my work as a writer. And, over the course of three decades of writing for *The New York Review of Books*, I had the privilege of being edited, encouraged, cajoled, and challenged by Robert Silvers; I greatly regret that Bob (a great admirer of Erasmus) is not here to see the finished product. Thanks, too, to Eric Banks for inviting me to present my ideas to the fellows of the New York Institute for the Humanities, and to the MacDowell Colony for providing me a comfortable cabin in which to work in the middle of a New Hampshire winter. (How Erasmus would have loved having his lunch deposited on his doorstep every day.)

Christine Helmer deserves a special citation. As a professor of religious studies at Northwestern University, she sought me out when she heard I was working on the Reformation. In addition to opening up the great storehouse of her knowledge about Luther and commenting keenly on chapter drafts, Christine became a friend whose encouragement meant a great deal as I stepped through the minefield of Reformation studies. Her insights into Lutheranism past and present and her impassioned efforts to understand the living legacy of the Reformation have left a deep imprint on this book. Christine also invited me to present my ideas at two conferences at Northwestern, where I benefited from the comments of numerous scholars. One of them, Paul Hinlicky, provided important guidance as I struggled to understand the ideas of the Apostle Paul and make narrative sense of his life. Christine also introduced me to Aaron Moldenhauer, a doctoral candidate in theology and a Lutheran pastor, who closely read the manuscript and offered many helpful suggestions and clarifications. I also appreciate the insights I gained from conversations with Heinrich Assel, Richard Cimino, Seth Dowland, Mark Granquist, Mary Jane Haemig, Jan van Herwaarden, Robert Kolb, Volker Leppin, Charles Marsh, Martin Marty, Mark Noll, Hans Trapman, and Martin Treu. Special help was offered by Henk Jan de Jonge, who, in addition to showing me around Leiden, carefully read two chapters about Erasmus and brought to bear on them the knowledge gained from his lifelong immersion in the work of his fellow Dutchman. On a visit to Luther sites in Germany, I had several guides who kindly showed me around. I would also like to express my appreciation for the marvelous libraries of Columbia University and the Union Theological Seminary, on whose shelves I found many of the worn volumes I needed for my research.

I would be remiss if I did not also acknowledge my undergraduate studies in History and Literature at Harvard College. Not until I was well into this project did I realize the extent to which the training I had received back then in reading and thinking about texts (fictional and factual) was helping me to unlock the meaning of the texts (sacred and profane) at the heart of this book. I fondly recall the many invigorating conversations I had with Professor John Clive about how to write history. My special concentration was English and French history and literature from 1750 on. At the time, I felt that nothing before that year really mattered. My visits to Rome made me aware of how short-sighted that notion was, and helped set me off on this journey into the more distant past.

In making that journey, I received tremendous support from the team at HarperCollins. I came greatly to value the wise judgment of my editor, Jonathan Jao. His keen sense of what to keep and what to cut helped prevent this book from being even longer than it is; his reflections were especially helpful in shaping my aftermaths. The highly versatile Sofia Groopman helped with everything from illustrations to emendations, and her sunny disposition proved especially welcome in the face of recurrent deadlines. I would also like to thank the copyeditors and proofreaders for their many catches; Rachel Elinsky, for her energetic efforts to get the book a hearing; and Jonathan Burnham, for his patience and forbearance. And I hardly know where to begin in thanking my agent, Kathy

Robbins—for her sage editorial advice, her negotiating aplomb, her fierce protectiveness, and, most important, her steadfast moral support during many difficult passages. Through times both lean and fat, Kathy has been there for me, leaving me deeply in her debt.

Finally, I would like to acknowledge the memory of my father, the support of my sister, and the unflagging backing of my mother, who not only proved a bulwark during some rough stretches but also learned to show restraint in asking when the book would be done.

NOTES

FREQUENTLY CITED WORKS

Collected Works of Erasmus. Toronto and Buffalo: University of Toronto Press, 1974–.

Contemporaries of Erasmus: A Biographical Register of the Renaissance and Reformation. Toronto and Buffalo: University of Toronto Press, 1985–1987.

Luther's Correspondence and Other Contemporary Letters, trans. and ed. Preserved Smith and Charles M. Jacobs. Philadelphia: The Lutheran Publication Society, 1913–1918.

Luthers Werke: D. Martin Luthers Werke Kritische Gesamtausgabe. Weimar: 1883–1983.

Luther's Works. St. Louis: Concordia Publishing House; Philadelphia: Fortress Press, 1955–1986.

Opera Omnia Desiderii Erasmi. Leiden, Amsterdam: Brill, 1969–.

Many of the Bible citations in the text are from *The New Oxford Annotated Bible*, augmented third edition. Oxford: Oxford University Press, 2007.

Publication information for most of the works cited below can be found in the Bibliography.

INTRODUCTION

x received a bundle of letters: *Collected Works of Erasmus*, vol. 4, December 11, 1516, 165–169.

xii and Hebrew: Parts of the Old Testament Vulgate were translated from the Greek Septuagint.

CHAPTER 1: THE NEW EUROPE

4 a renowned Latin school: James D. Tracy, *Erasmus, The Growth of a Mind*, 26.

4 most widely read devotional work: Robert S. Miola, *Early Modern Catholicism: An Anthology of Primary Sources* (Oxford: Oxford University Press, 2007), 285.

4 the *Devotio Moderna* spread: Jonathan I. Israel, *The Dutch Republic: Its Rise, Greatness, and Fall, 1477–1806*, 41–42; Steven Ozment, *The Age of Reform, 1250–1550*, 96–98; Albert Hyma, *The Youth of Erasmus*, 125.

4 left a deep mark: Hyma, *Youth of Erasmus*, 125.

4 barbarous: *Collected Works of Erasmus*, vol. 4, 404.

4 there was a small house: Preserved Smith, *Erasmus: A Study of His Life, Ideals, and Place in History*, 7; Israel, *The Dutch Republic*. A photo of a house

built on the site appears in Hyma, *Youth of Erasmus*, opposite p. 52.

5 "between the banks": Smith, *Erasmus*, 4.

5 a tall bronze statue: Nicolaas van der Blom, "The Erasmus Statues in Rotterdam," *Erasmus in English*, 6: 5–9, June 1973. I am obliged to Jan van Herwaarden of the Erasmus Center for Early Modern Studies in Rotterdam for showing me, and explaining the history of, the statue.

5 The confusion: A. C. F. Koch, *The Year of Erasmus' Birth*. On the circumstances of Erasmus's birth and early childhood, see his autobiographical sketch, *Compendium Vitae Erasmi Roterodami*, in *Collected Works of Erasmus*, vol. 4, 400–410; Hyma, *Youth of Erasmus*, 51–58; Cornelis Augustijn, *Erasmus: His Life, Works, and Influence*, 21; Léon-E. Halkin, *Erasmus: A Critical Biography*, 1; Johan Huizinga, *Erasmus and the Age of the Reformation*, 5–6; Smith, *Erasmus*, 5–7; Jan van Herwaarden, *Between Saint James and Erasmus*, 511–515.

5 "longed for" in Latin: Huizinga (*Erasmus*, 6) notes that he first used the full form of his name, Desiderius Erasmus Roterodamus, in 1506.

6 his first few years: *Collected Works of Erasmus*, vol. 4, 404; Hyma, *Youth of Erasmus*, 63. On Gouda, see Israel, *Dutch Republic*, 114, 119.

6 was less distinguished: Hyma, *Youth of Erasmus*, 62–63; P. S. Allen, *The Age of Erasmus*, 34. As these accounts note, Erasmus during these years apparently spent some time as a choirboy in Utrecht.

6 "Greasy of mouth and palate": Quoted in R. J. Schoeck, *Erasmus of Europe: The Making of a Humanist, 1467–1500*, 31.

6 remained a medieval town: Hyma, *Youth of Erasmus*, 67–69. For general information on life in medieval towns, see Morris Bishop, *The Middle Ages*, 191–196; Joseph Gies and Frances Gies,

Life in a Medieval City, 30–31. Deventer's population is given in Israel, *Dutch Republic*, 114.

7 high rates of crime and violence: J. R. Hale, *Renaissance Europe, 1480–1520*, 26–27.

7 most rudimentary sanitation: Hyma, *Youth of Erasmus*, 69; Bishop, *Middle Ages*, 194–195.

7 once a fortnight: Hyma, *Youth of Erasmus*, 69.

7 most highly urbanized region: Israel, *Dutch Republic*, 14–16, 113–118; James D. Tracy, *Erasmus of the Low Countries*, 10–11. Erasmus's remark about "many towns" appears in "Auris Batava," in William Barker, ed., *The Adages of Erasmus*, 371–374.

8 Fernand Braudel: Fernand Braudel, *The Structures of Everyday Life*, 479.

8 was at or below sea level: Israel, *Dutch Republic*, 9–18, 106, 111.

8 established commercial ties abroad: Ibid., 16.

8 most articulate spokesman: Paul Johnson, *A History of Christianity*, 272–273.

8 its first printing press: Jozef Ijsewijn, "The Coming of Humanism to the Low Countries," in *Itinerarium Italicum*, 238; Israel, *Dutch Republic*, 44.

9 ships were constantly putting in: Hyma, *Youth of Erasmus*, 67.

9 there was St. Lebwin's: Tracy, *Growth of a Mind*, 26; Allen, *Age of Erasmus*, 35.

9 passport to a better life: Kristian Jensen, "The Humanist Reform of Latin and Latin Teaching," in Jill Kraye, ed., *The Cambridge Companion to Renaissance Humanism*, 63–64.

9 curriculum in the lower grades: Hyma, *Youth of Erasmus*, 85; Tracy, *Growth of a Mind*, 21–29; Allen, *Age of Erasmus*, 36; *Collected Works of Erasmus*, vol. 4, 404; "the most barbarous book": *Collected Works of Erasmus*, vol. 26, 592–593.

9 "horrific shrieks of pain": *Collected Works of Erasmus*, vol. 26, 341 (Erasmus is

here writing of classrooms in general);
uncouth manners: vol. 26, 324, 325.

9 The torments inflicted: Ibid., 325.

10 The students themselves: Ibid., 331.
Erasmus's opposition to corporal
punishment appears at 293.

10 the language had constantly evolved:
Ijsewijn, "Coming of Humanism," 195;
Jensen, "Humanist Reform of Latin,"
in Kraye, *Cambridge Companion to
Renaissance Humanism*, 75–76.

10 "secret natural force": *Collected Works of
Erasmus*, vol. 9, 294.

11 easy to spot: Albert Hyma, *The Brethren
of the Common Life*, 66, 109–111.

11 dominant institution in northern
Europe: Norman Cantor, *The
Civilization of the Middle Ages*, 163, 178,
185; Hyma, *Youth of Erasmus*, 5–6;
Diarmaid MacCulloch, *The Reformation*,
30; Hale, *Renaissance Europe*, 218ff;
Johan Huizinga, *The Waning of the
Middle Ages*, 151ff.

11 what one could eat: Eamon Duffy, *The
Stripping of the Altars*, 41–42.

11 were all rampant: Bishop, *Middle Ages*,
232.

11 one of every three women: Clifford R.
Backman, *The Worlds of Medieval Europe*,
348.

12 an array of customs: For an overview
of medieval piety, see Francis Rapp,
"Religious Belief and Practice," in *The
New Cambridge Medieval History*,
vol. 7, 203–219.

12 Veneration of the saints: Duffy, *Stripping
of the Altars*, 155ff, 178, 191.

12 shrines to the saints: Ibid., 191ff;
"The Pilgrim's Guide to St. James
of Compostella," in Mary-Ann
Stouck, ed., *Medieval Saints: A Reader*
(Peterborough, Ont.: Broadview Press,
1999), 313–314; Bishop, *Middle Ages*,
149. Hale, in *Renaissance Europe* (40),
observes that probably more pilgrims
were on the move in this period than
ever before or since.

12 quality of its relics: Jonathan Sumption,

*Pilgrimage: An Image of Medieval
Religion*, 22–53; MacCulloch,
Reformation, 18–19; Huizinga, *Waning of
the Middle Ages*, 167.

13 the most venerated figure: MacCulloch,
Reformation, 18–21; Bishop, *Middle Ages*,
145.

13 the Mass: MacCulloch, *Reformation*,
10–14.

13 monasteries grew wealthy: Hyma, *Youth
of Erasmus*, 5–6.

13 large packs of hounds: See *Collected
Works of Erasmus*, vol. 39, 509.

14 one of the most famous tales: The tenth
story of the third day.

15 Peter Waldus: Williston Walker et
al., *A History of the Christian Church*,
305–307.

15 John Wyclif: Ibid., 377–381.

15 Jan Hus: Ibid., 381–385. For more on
Hus, see my chapter 20.

15 Girolamo Savonarola: MacCulloch,
Reformation, 90–92; Ludwig Pastor, *The
History of the Popes, from the Close of the
Middle Ages*, vol. 6, 17–54.

16 Geert Groote: Hyma, *Brethren*, 15–46;
Israel, *Dutch Republic*, 41; introduction
to *The Imitation of Christ*, xxxix–xliii.

16 some of his followers: Hyma, *Brethren*,
21–28.

17 Thomas à Kempis: Ibid., 32–34.

17 "The Kingdom of God": *Imitation of
Christ*, 53; Habit and tonsure, 24; run off
to distant shrines, 215; Judgment Day,
4–6; one path to salvation, 76–77.

18 nearly fifty more editions: Ibid., liii;
Thomas More . . . Ignatius Loyola:
www.christianitytoday.com/history
/people/innertravelers/thomas-kempis
.html.

18 "Do not desire": *Imitation of Christ*, 8–9.

18 was being imprinted: Hyma, *Youth of
Erasmus*, 125–127.

18 Rodolphus Agricola: *Collected Works of
Erasmus*, vol. 9, 294; Hyma, *Youth of
Erasmus*, 113–116; Israel, *Dutch Republic*,
42–43; "Agricola, Rodolphus," in
Contemporaries of Erasmus.

19 "was one of the first": Quoted in Hyma, *Youth of Erasmus*, 48. See also *Collected Works of Erasmus*, vol. 1, 38.

19 Alexander Hegius: *Collected Works of Erasmus*, vol. 1, 38; "Hegius, Alexander," in *Contemporaries of Erasmus*.

19 Erasmus had been exposed: Hyma, *Youth of Erasmus*, 12, 36; Israel, *Dutch Republic*, 45.

19 hit by the plague: Hyma, *Youth of Erasmus*, 132; Koch, *Year of Erasmus' Birth*, 30–31; *Collected Works of Erasmus*, vol. 4, 405, and vol. 1, 2.

CHAPTER 2: MINER'S SON

20 his lowly origins: See Martin Brecht, *Martin Luther: His Road to Reformation*, (hereafter cited as Brecht, *Martin Luther*), 2, 9–10, 3.

21 one of Europe's top producers: Lyndal Roper, *Martin Luther: Renegade and Prophet*, 4.

21 the town of Mansfeld: Heiko Oberman, *Luther: Man Between God and the Devil*, 83; Brecht, *Martin Luther*, 10; Roper, *Martin Luther*, 5.

21 "they finally forced me": *Luther's Works*, vol. 54, "Table Talk," 235, 157.

21 one of the most famous studies: Erik H. Erikson, *Young Man Luther: A Study in Psychoanalysis and History*; "jealously ambitious" father, 255; "excessive harshness," 28; "angry, and often alcoholic, impulsiveness," 66; "suppressed rage," 38; "he rebelled," 74.

22 curtly dismissive: See, for instance, Brecht, *Martin Luther*, 6–7; Richard Marius, *Martin Luther: The Christian Between God and Death*, 23; Richard Friedenthal, *Luther: His Life and Times*, 224–226; Ozment, *Age of Reform*, 223–231. Ozment (227) writes that "Erikson's portrait of Luther's father" is "demonstrably fabricated, and the weight of reliable historical evidence strongly indicates that Luther's childhood was unhappy neither at home nor in school."

22 Erikson himself acknowledged: Erikson, *Young Man Luther*, 50.

22 "use of repudiative": Ibid., 247; "demonological preoccupation," 232.

22 quickly worked his way up: Brecht, *Martin Luther*, 2–3; Oberman, *Luther*, 91; Roper, *Martin Luther*, 5; Friedenthal, *Luther*, 9. The smelting process is described at the Mansfeld Museum in nearby Hettstedt.

22 need to scrimp: Brecht, *Martin Luther*, 5; Oberman, *Luther*, 85.

22 ferocity of the mining world: Georgius Agricola, *De Re Metallica*, 6, 101ff.

23 outpost of early capitalism: Gerhard Brendler, *Martin Luther: Theology and Revolution*, 23.

23 the entrepreneur: Oberman, *Luther*, 87.

23 "pernicious pests": Agricola, *De Re Metallica*, 217.

23 Luther's world abounded: Friedenthal, *Luther*, 10; Roland Bainton, *Here I Stand*, 19; Robert Herndon Fife, *The Revolt of Martin Luther*, 10; Marius, *Martin Luther*, 26–28.

24 "We may not doubt": Cited in Fife, *Revolt of Martin Luther*, 11.

24 presence of the Devil: Brecht, *Martin Luther*, 11–12. Heiko Oberman considered the Devil central to Luther's thinking, as the title of his biography indicates (*Luther: Man Between God and the Devil*); see especially 102–107.

24 Hell, meanwhile: Bainton, *Here I Stand*, 20.

24 the judging Christ: Brecht, *Martin Luther*, 76–78; Fife, *Revolt of Martin Luther*, 13.

25 Nearly every church: Barbara Tuchman, *A Distant Mirror*, 135.

25 The violence in these depictions: Roper, *Martin Luther*, 10–11; Hale, *Renaissance Europe*, 26–28; Friedenthal, *Luther*, 340–341.

25 Salzburg municipal ordinance: Cited in Will Durant, *The Reformation*, 758.

25 a general obsession with death: Huizinga, *Waning of the Middle Ages*, 138ff. "No

other epoch," Huizinga writes, "has laid so much stress as the expiring Middle Ages on the thought of death." See also Marius, *Martin Luther*, 28–30; Duffy, *Stripping of the Altars*, 310ff.

26 Anne, the mother of Mary: Duffy, *Stripping of the Altars*, 181–182; Hale, *Renaissance Europe*, 238; Brecht, *Martin Luther*, 11.

26 an altarpiece honors: Accessible at www .neurorepair-2008.de/files/lutherstadt _en.pdf.

26 "in the pants": *Luthers Werke, Tischreden*, vol. 5, no. 5537, 222.

CHAPTER 3: CANDLELIGHT STUDIES

28 Pieter Winckel: *Collected Works of Erasmus*, vol. 4, no. 447, to Lambertus Grunnius [August 1516], 6–32. This letter to a fictitious addressee describes Erasmus's dealings with Winckel and his entry into the monastery; though the names are changed, it is considered a more or less reliable guide to this period of his life. Other details are provided by Hyma, *Youth of Erasmus*, 128ff; Schoeck, *Erasmus of Europe*, 55–57.

28 "Time flies": *Collected Works of Erasmus*, vol. 1, 2.

28 "This incident": Ibid., vol. 26, 326, 325.

28 fit for monastic life: R. R. Post, in his exhaustive *The Modern Devotion: Confrontation with Reformation and Humanism*, notes (660) that Erasmus's comments accurately describe the situation at 's Hertogenbosch.

29 "garden of the Muses": *Collected Works of Erasmus*, vol. 4, 17.

29 the conflict then raging: Hyma, *Youth of Erasmus*, 15–17, 153; Israel, *Dutch Republic*, 27–30; Roland H. Bainton, *Erasmus of Christendom*, 24. Erasmus's own description can be found in Barker, *Adages of Erasmus*, 186.

29 burned down in 1549: *Collected Works of Erasmus*, vol. 4, 407.

29 basic plan of the medieval cloister: www .medieval-life-and-times.info/medieval -religion/medieval-monastery.htm.

30 "so much decayed": *Collected Works of Erasmus*, vol. 4, 18.

30 followed a less severe regimen: Schoeck, *Erasmus of Europe*, 90.

30 the day was built around: See ibid., 93–94, for a typical day at the monastery.

31 nine have survived: None of the letters from Servatius has.

31 "If we cannot be together": *Collected Works of Erasmus*, vol. 1, no. 4 [c. 1487], 6.

31 "You surely know": Ibid., no. 5 [c. 1487], 7.

31 "What is it that": Ibid., no. 7 [c. 1487], 9, 11.

31 The few days: Ibid., no. 8 [c. 1487], 11.

31 When a letter finally arrived: Ibid., no. 9 [c. 1487], 14–15.

32 "Do not be ashamed": Ibid., no. 15 [c. 1488], 19–22.

32 Some have dismissed them: Ibid., introductory note to letter no. 4. See also the introduction to vol. 85, xv.

32 A. L. Rowse: A. L. Rowse, *Homosexuals in History: A Study of Ambivalence in Society, Literature and the Arts*, 6–10.

32 "to accept the halter": *Collected Works of Erasmus*, vol. 4, 21.

32 The joys of ancient literature: Ibid., vol. 1, no. 20, to Cornelis Gerard [May 1489?], 31, and vol. 4, no. 447, 18 (where Erasmus writes that he read these works "in furtive and nocturnal sessions"); Erika Rummel, *Erasmus as a Translator of the Classics*, 6; Halkin, *Erasmus*, 6; Hyma, *Youth of Erasmus*, 155.

33 abound in references: *Collected Works of Erasmus*, vol. 1, 28, 50; "bond of affection," 27.

33 *Carmen Buccolicum: Collected Works of Erasmus*, vol. 85, xvii, 287ff.

33 a play by Terence: *Collected Works of Erasmus*, vol. 1, no. 31 [1489?], 57–60.

34 the Italian Renaissance meant: Margaret Mann Phillips, *Erasmus and the Northern Renaissance*, 16–17; Paul Oskar Kristeller, *Renaissance Thought*, 19–23.

34 *ad fontes*—to the sources: According to van Herwaarden (*Between Saint James and Erasmus*, 560–561), Erasmus used this phrase sparingly, but it aptly summed up his program: "The quest for pure sources was an absolute necessity" for him "in order to show others the path to true Christian godliness."

34 Petrarch is best known: Nicholas Mann, "The Origins of Humanism," in *The Cambridge Companion to Renaissance Humanism*, 6, 9–10.

35 a "Dark Age": As Charles G. Nauert Jr. notes in *Humanism and the Culture of Renaissance Europe* (3), the idea that for a thousand years prior to the Renaissance Europe was sunk in barbarism and superstition is now considered greatly exaggerated, but, he adds, Renaissance humanism did represent the emergence of a new culture.

35 father of Renaissance humanism: Mann, "Origins of Humanism," in Kraye, *The Cambridge Companion to Renaissance Humanism*, 6; Nauert, *Humanism and the Culture of Renaissance Europe*, 21.

35 born in Arezzo, Tuscany: For details of Petrarch's life, see Morris Bishop, *Petrarch and His World*.

35 The papal court became: For details about the deplorable conditions in Avignon under the popes, see Pastor, *History of the Popes*, vol. 1, 59–83.

35 "the most dismal": Quoted in Bishop, *Petrarch and His World*, 48.

36 the courtly conventions: "Petrarch," in *The Columbia Encyclopedia*, 5th ed.

36 enamored of Cicero: *Letters from Petrarch*, trans. Morris Bishop, 292–293.

36 When foreign visitors appeared: Bishop, *Petrarch and His World*, 91.

36 creating a network: On Petrarch's book-hunting zeal, see James Westfall

Thompson, *The Medieval Library*, 524–527.

36 "No one can doubt": Quoted in Bishop, *Petrarch and His World*, 91. See also *Cambridge Modern History*, vol. 1, *The Renaissance*, 549.

36 a paradox of history: L. D. Reynolds and N. G. Wilson, *Scribes and Scholars*, 70–72; Cantor, *Civilization of the Middle Ages*, 146.

37 notoriously hard to penetrate: Stephen Greenblatt, *The Swerve*, 29–30.

37 got under way in earnest: Ibid., 23.

37 first modern tourist: Bishop, *Petrarch and His World*, 92.

37 "Who knows": *Letters from Petrarch*, 295.

37 His first great find: Bishop, *Petrarch and His World*, 91–97.

37 the ecclesiastical library in that city: *Letters from Petrarch*, 295–296.

37 These gifted men: "The Speech on Behalf of Archias the Poet," in Loeb Classical Library, vol. 158, 39.

38 "ambition is a universal factor": Ibid., 35.

38 One phrase in Cicero's speech: Ibid., 8. See also Nauert, *Humanism and the Culture of Renaissance Europe*, 12–15.

38 tempered by his sorrow: *Letters from Petrarch*, 154.

38 had an early success: Mann, "Origins of Humanism," in Kraye, *The Cambridge Companion to Renaissance Humanism*, 9–10; Bishop, *Petrarch and His World*, 91. Petrarch's manuscript of Livy's history as edited by him is currently in the British Library.

38 he was in Rome: Bishop, *Petrarch and His World*, 113–125.

39 wandered amid the ruins: *Letters from Petrarch*, 63–66. See also Christopher Hibbert, *Rome: The Biography of a City*, 97–99.

39 so he moved: Bishop, *Petrarch and His World*, 125, 129–130, 144.

39 came up with the idea: Ibid., 160–171.

40 would prove even more consequential: Nauert, *Humanism and the Culture of*

Renaissance Europe, 22; Bishop, *Petrarch and His World*, 229–231. On the library at Verona, see Thompson, *Medieval Library*, 145–146.

40 he was shocked: *Letters from Petrarch*, 205–210; Cicero, "Selections from His Correspondence," *Selected Works*, 58–100.

40 Cicero's letters showed Petrarch: See the introduction to *Letters from Petrarch*, v–vi.

40 early expression of the individualism: Jacob Burckhardt, *The Civilization of the Renaissance in Italy*, 98ff. As Burckhardt writes (319), the Italian humanists were "the advance guard of an unbridled individualism."

41 "Just as the horse": *De finibus*, II:13 (Loeb Classical Library, vol. 17, 127). See also Eugene F. Rice Jr. and Anthony Grafton, *The Foundations of Early Modern Europe, 1460–1559*, 87–89.

41 "O great man": *Letters from Petrarch*, 153.

41 "on the Gospel alone": Quoted in Pastor, *History of the Popes*, vol. 1, 2.

41 Augustine's *Confessions*: Bishop, *Petrarch and His World*, 110–111.

42 Giovanni Boccaccio: Ibid., 281; Reynolds and Wilson, *Scribes and Scholars*, 117–119.

42 Florence became the center: Nauert, *Humanism and the Culture of Renaissance Europe*, 24–28; Reynolds and Wilson, *Scribes and Scholars*, 119; Glenn N. Andres et al., *The Art of Florence*, vol. 1, 321–324.

43 the Vatican Library: Anthony Grafton, "The Vatican and Its Library," in Anthony Grafton, ed., *Rome Reborn: The Vatican Library and Renaissance Culture*, 4ff.

43 humanists congratulated themselves: John F. D'Amico, *Renaissance Humanism in Papal Rome*, 3–4; James Hankins, "The Popes and Humanism," in Grafton, *Rome Reborn*, 48–50.

43 became enslaved to it: James Hankins, "Humanism and the Origins of Modern

Political Thought," in Kraye, *The Cambridge Companion to Humanism*, 119–124; D'Amico, *Renaissance Humanism in Papal Rome*, 111–112.

43 a compelling alternative: As Burckhardt observes, many humanist orators sought "not only to flatter the vanity of distinguished hearers, but to load their speeches with an enormous mass of antiquarian rubbish" (*Civilization of the Renaissance in Italy*, 157).

43 Lorenzo Valla: See D'Amico, *Renaissance Humanism in Papal Rome*, 146; Nauert, *Humanism and the Culture of Renaissance Europe*, 37ff; Jerry H. Bentley, *Humanists and Holy Writ: New Testament Scholarship in the Renaissance*, 32–69; E. Harris Harbison, *The Christian Scholar in the Age of the Reformation*, 44–49; Anthony Grafton and Lisa Jardine, *From Humanism to the Humanities: Education and the Liberal Arts in Fifteenth- and Sixteenth-Century Europe*, 66–82.

43 Donation of Constantine: Valla, *The Treatise of Lorenzo Valla on the Donation of Constantine*; comment on "satrap," 85.

44 the plausibility of the Trinity: Grafton and Jardine, *From Humanism to the Humanities*, 75.

44 secure an appointment: Pastor, *History of the Popes*, vol. 2, 198.

44 most daring work: Bentley, *Humanists and Holy Writ*, 35; Alaistair Hamilton, "Humanists and the Bible," in Kraye, *The Cambridge Companion to Renaissance Humanism*, 104–105; Harbison, *Christian Scholar*, 45–46.

45 *De Elegantiae*: Nauert, *Humanism and the Culture of Renaissance Europe*, 38; Jensen, "Humanist Reform of Latin," in Kraye, *The Cambridge Compendium to Renaissance Humanism*, 64.

45 fifty-nine editions: Michael D. Reeve, "Classical Scholarship," in Kraye, *The Cambridge Companion to Renaissance Humanism*, 40.

45 became his intellectual compass: Erasmus had actually first encountered

this work while at St. Lebwin's in
Deventer.

46 "you have hurt": *Collected Works of
Erasmus*, vol. 1, 54.

46 *Antibarbari*: Ibid., vol. 23, 1–122.

46 becoming unbearable: Phillips, *Erasmus
and the Northern Renaissance*, 21–22.

47 left to wait: *Collected Works of Erasmus*,
vol. 1, no. 33, from Willem Hermans
[1493?], 62–64.

47 he had a rough draft: Hyma, *Youth of
Erasmus*, 183.

CHAPTER 4: PENANCE AND DREAD

48 It was in his youth: Brecht, *Martin
Luther*, 47. (See *Luthers Werke,
Briefwechsel*, vol. 4, 319.)

48 its curriculum was similar: Brecht,
Martin Luther, 12–14; Bainton, *Here I
Stand*, 18; Fife, *Revolt of Martin Luther*,
15; Brendler, *Martin Luther*, 25–26.

48 beaten fifteen times: *Luther's Works*,
vol. 54, "Table Talk," 457; "a hell and
purgatory," vol. 45, 369.

49 envisioning for him a legal career: Roper,
Martin Luther, 33.

49 he got an early glimpse: Brecht, *Martin
Luther*, 16–17.

50 Her family members: Ian D. Kingston
Siggins, *Luther and His Mother*, 46–50;
Michael A. Mullett, *Martin Luther*, 22;
Roper, *Martin Luther*, 23–24.

50 "My beloved city": Brendler, *Martin
Luther*, 28.

50 This one modest church: See Neil
MacGregor, *Germany: Memories of a
Nation*, 111.

50 An estimated one-tenth: E. G.
Schwiebert, *Luther and His Times: The
Reformation from a New Perspective*, 124.

50 "nest of priests": Fife, *Revolt of Martin
Luther*, 25.

51 doctrines surrounding penance: Ozment,
Age of Reform, 216; Siggins, *Luther
and His Mother*, 52ff; MacCulloch,
Reformation, 14.

51 Medieval sermons: Emile V. Telle, "Ways
and Fashions in the Art of Preaching
on the Eve of the *Religious Upheaval* in
the Sixteenth Century," in *Erasmus of
Rotterdam Society Yearbook*, 2: 21–22,
1982; Edwin Charles Dargan, *A History
of Preaching*, vol. 1 (New York: Hodder
and Stoughton, 1905), 191–193,
300–310; Pierre Riché, *Daily Life in the
World of Charlemagne*, trans. Jo Ann
McNamara (Philadelphia: University
of Pennsylvania Press, 1978), 202;
MacCulloch, *Reformation*, 30.

51 As Erasmus would observe: *Collected
Works of Erasmus*, vol. 27, 118.

52 This sacrament had three parts: Ozment,
Age of Reform, 216–222.

52 The obligation of Christians to confess:
Ibid., 217–219; Jacques Le Goff, *The
Birth of Purgatory*, 213–216; Thomas N.
Tentler, *Sin and Confession on the Eve of
the Reformation*, 57, 78.

52 One manual: Tentler, *Sin and Confession*,
140–142.

52 prepared an entire volume: Ibid., 91.

52 "aggravating circumstances": Ibid., 116.

53 not mentioned in the Bible: Le Goff,
Birth of Purgatory, 133–134.

53 The main motif: Le Goff, *Birth of
Purgatory*, 7–11.

53 "The least pain": *Summa Theologica*,
Supplement Appendix I, Q2. See also
"Purgatory," in *The Oxford Dictionary of
the Christian Church*.

53 In Dante's *Purgatorio*: For an analysis
of the theological aspects of this
work, see Le Goff, *Birth of Purgatory*,
334–348.

53 conjured up the torments: H. Maynard
Smith, *Pre-Reformation England*,
200–201.

54 never-ending anxiety: Tentler, *Sin and
Confession*, 156, 347.

54 main agent was the priest: Ibid., 22–27,
57–68, 344–345.

55 the Church's penitential system:
Ozment, *Age of Reform*, 227.

CHAPTER 5: BREAKTHROUGH

56 Erasmus was moving: Schoeck, *Erasmus of Europe*, 132; Bainton, *Erasmus of Christendom*, 31–2.

56 The diocese of Cambrai: See Schoeck, *Erasmus of Europe*, 134–142, on the diocese and the bishop.

56 helped Hendrik: Ibid., 137–138; Huizinga, *Erasmus*, 17.

56 Hendrik's campaign: Schoeck, *Erasmus of Europe*, 139; Huizinga, *Erasmus*, 17.

56 consoled himself with books: The monk's quote is in Schoeck, *Erasmus of Europe*, 138.

57 remained in many ways medieval: Schoeck, *Erasmus of Europe*, 162–163; Phillips, *Erasmus and the Northern Renaissance*, 25; Smith, *Erasmus*, 20; Cantor, *Civilization of the Middle Ages*, 319; "Paris," in *Encyclopedia of the Middle Ages*; Barbara Tuchman, *A Distant Mirror*, 22ff, 158–160.

57 Europe's leading book center: Andrew Pettegree, *The Book in the Renaissance*, 44; Lucien Febvre and Henri-Jean Martin, *The Coming of the Book*, 173–175; Schoeck, *Erasmus of Europe*, 168.

57 Collège de Montaigu: Schoeck, *Erasmus of Europe*, 165–166. Erasmus described the conditions at the college in a 1526 Colloquy, "A Fish Diet," *Collected Works of Erasmus*, vol. 40, 715; see also the note at 756–757.

58 the cold was debilitating: On the problem of the cold at medieval universities, see Hastings Rashdall, *The Universities of Europe in the Middle Ages*, vol. 3, *English Universities: Student Life*, 415.

58 reinforce his aversion: Huizinga, *Erasmus*, 21.

58 the University of Paris: Schoeck, *Erasmus of Europe*, 163–166; Cantor, *Civilization of the Middle Ages*, 441, 531; Friedrich Heer, *The Medieval World*, 245–252.

58 movement known as Scholasticism: Walker, *History of the Christian Church*, 322–325; Cantor, *Civilization of the Middle Ages*, 320; Schoeck, *Erasmus of Europe*, 178–179; "Scholasticism," in *Encyclopedia of the Middle Ages*.

59 seemed pointless: *Collected Works of Erasmus*, vol. 1, no. 64, to Thomas Grey [August 1497], 135–138. See also Bainton, *Erasmus of Christendom*, 37–39.

59 The questions posed: Erasmus provided some of these examples in the *Praise of Folly*, in *Collected Works of Erasmus*, vol. 27, 126–127.

59 the dominant figure: Cantor, *Civilization of the Middle Ages*, 357–360; Richard E. Rubenstein, *Aristotle's Children: How Christians, Muslims, and Jews Rediscovered Ancient Wisdom and Illuminated the Middle Ages*, 4–9.

60 undergoing a mini-renaissance: Backman, *Worlds of Medieval Europe*, 231–232.

60 Peter Abelard: Cantor, *Civilization of the Middle Ages*, 330–331; Walker, *History of the Christian Church*, 327–330; Harbison, *Christian Scholar*, 20–25; Heer, *Medieval World*, 110–116; Backman, *Worlds of Medieval Europe*, 234–236.

61 "took cruel vengeance": James Bruge, *Heloise & Abelard*, 133.

61 about the Trinity: Rubenstein, *Aristotle's Children*, 116–118.

61 Peter Lombard: Walker, *History of the Christian Church*, 331; Backman, *Worlds of Medieval Europe*, 236.

62 a sensational scholarly discovery: Walker, *History of the Christian Church*, 332–334; Rubenstein, *Aristotle's Children*, 4–9; Cantor, *Civilization of the Middle Ages*, 357–361.

62 they at once decided: Rubenstein, *Aristotle's Children*, 15–22.

63 offered a rational: Ibid., 8.

63 The concept of sin: Ibid., 179–180.

63 proposed a mechanistic God: Cantor, *Civilization of the Middle Ages*, 360.

63 stand up to the challenge: Ibid., 357; Rubenstein, *Aristotle's Children*, 199.

63 made him required reading: Rubenstein, *Aristotle's Children*, 199.

63 Thomas Aquinas: Harbison, *Christian Scholar*, 25–28; Walker, *History of the Christian Church*, 340–348; Cantor, *Civilization of the Middle Ages*, 443–444; "Thomas Aquinas and Thomism," in *The New Encyclopaedia Britannica*, 15th ed., vol. 28, 645–649.

64 an encyclical letter: *Aeterni Patris* is available at https://w2.vatican.va /content/leo-xiii/en/encyclicals /documents/hf_1-xiii_enc_04081879 _aeterni-patris.html.

64 the *Summa Theologica*: Backman, *Worlds of Medieval Europe*, 308–309; Cantor, *Civilization of The Middle Ages*, 443.

64 most modern-day editions: See, for instance, "Treatise on the Angels" in The Great Books of the Western World edition of the *Summa Theologica* (Chicago: Encyclopaedia Britannica, 1952, 1990), vol. 1, 269–333.

65 comments about man: Rubenstein, *Aristotle's Children*, 221; Walker, *History of the Christian Church*, 343–344; Ozment, *Age of Reform*, 233.

65 man has free will: Question LXXXIII, Article I of the First Part, *Summa Theologica*, vol. 1, 436–438; "Otherwise, counsels": 437.

65 in a state of grace: Question CXI, Part I of the Second Part, ibid., vol. 2, 351–356.

65 "I cannot": Robert Barron, *Thomas Aquinas: Spiritual Master*, 24.

65 Eager to suppress it: Rubenstein, *Aristotle's Children*, 234; Walker, *History of the Christian Church*, 349.

66 John Duns Scotus: Walker, *History of the Christian Church*, 348–352; "Duns Scotus," in *New Catholic Encyclopedia*; "Duns Scotus," in *Encyclopedia of the Middle Ages*.

66 "The quiddity or definition": Eugene R. Fairweather, ed., *A Scholastic Miscellany: Anselm to Ockham*, 430.

66 doctrine of the Immaculate Conception: Walker, *History of the Christian Church*, 351; Jaroslav Pelikan, *Reformation of Church and Dogma (1300–1700)*, 46–50.

66 was still raging: Smith, *Erasmus*, 21. Its establishment as dogma is noted at Pelikan, *Reformation of Church and Dogma*, 50.

67 "If only you could see": *Collected Works of Erasmus*, vol. 1, no. 64, to Thomas Grey [August 1497], 137–138. See also Bainton, *Erasmus of Christendom*, 37–38.

67 "baptized wherever they went": Erasmus wrote this in the *Praise of Folly*, in *Collected Works of Erasmus*, vol. 27, 128.

67 Josse Bade's famous printing house: Schoeck, *Erasmus of Europe*, 168.

67 sent him a letter: Erasmus's letter has not survived, but Gaguin's response has: *Collected Works of Erasmus*, vol. 1, no. 43 [September 1495?], 83–85.

67 developed a genuine bond: Ibid., no. 44, from Robert Gaguin, September 24 [1495?], 85–87.

67 he relapsed: Ibid., no. 45, to Robert Gaguin [beginning of October 1495], 87–91.

68 would attract little notice: Ironically, Gaguin is remembered today mainly for his connection to Erasmus.

68 rained without stop: *Collected Works of Erasmus*, vol. 1, 106.

68 not to waste his time: Ibid., 98.

68 took on two brothers: Ibid., 110.

68 They were soon joined: Ibid., 116.

68 "sweetest Thomas": Ibid., no. 58, to Thomas Grey [July 1497], 116–123.

68 "lovers' letters": Ibid., no. 63, to Thomas Grey [August 1497], 134.

68 turn it to his advantage: Huizinga, *Erasmus of Christendom*, 27; Tracy, *Erasmus of the Low Countries*, 28; Schoeck, *Erasmus of Europe*, 206–208.

69 traveled to Holland: *Collected Works of Erasmus*, vol. 1, 152–154.

69 "I greatly fear": Ibid., no. 83, to Willem Hermans, December 14 [1498], 167–171.

69 William Blount: Ibid., 156. Then about nineteen, Blount would remain Erasmus's friend and patron for more than thirty years. See also "Blount, William," in *Contemporaries of Erasmus.*

69 how perilous the trip was: Smith, *Erasmus,* 59. Erasmus would later write of his wish that there were a bridge joining England to the Continent: *Collected Works of Erasmus,* vol. 5, 269.

70 "nymphs of divine appearance": *Collected Works of Erasmus,* vol. 1, 193.

70 fruits of early Tudor rule: *The New Encyclopaedia Britannica,* 15th ed., vol. 29, 47–48.

70 circle of influential humanists: Frederic Seebohm, *The Oxford Reformers,* 2–8.

70 More's "sweetness": *Collected Works of Erasmus,* vol. 7, 18.

71 fretted about his appearance: Ibid., vol. 4, 409.

71 walk there with him: Erasmus described this visit years later in a letter to Johann von Botzheim, *Collected Works of Erasmus,* vol. 9, no. 1341A, January 30, 1523, 299–300.

71 poem in Latin: "An Ode by Erasmus of Rotterdam in Praise of Britain and of King Henry VII and the Royal Children," *Collected Works of Erasmus,* vol. 85, 31–41.

71 dedicatory letter: Ibid., vol. 1, no. 104, to Prince Henry [Autumn 1499], 195–197.

71 had forbidden anyone: Ibid., 197.

71 named John Colet: Ibid., 198. See also "Colet, John," in *Contemporaries of Erasmus;* Seebohm, *Oxford Reformers,* 8–13. Erasmus provides much information about Colet in a long sketch, in *Collected Works of Erasmus,* vol. 8, no. 1211, 232–244.

72 he had been drawn: Seebohm, *Oxford Reformer,* 1–2; Harbison, *Christian Scholar,* 55–67.

72 his lectures treated Paul: *John Colet's Commentary on First Corinthians,* 30–31, 36.

72 Like dogs returning to vomit: Ibid., 123.

72 were a landmark: Harbison, *Christian Scholar,* 58; Seebohm, *Oxford Reformers,* 2, 17–24, 46–53.

73 walks in the Oxford gardens: Allen, *Age of Erasmus,* 128.

73 Colet could be very severe: *Collected Works of Erasmus,* vol. 8, 236.

73 best way to understand Scripture: *John Colet's Commentary on First Corinthians,* 218–219.

73 got into an argument: The translation of Mark 14:36 is from *Collected Works of Erasmus,* vol. 1, 202.

73 he wrote to Colet: *Collected Works of Erasmus,* vol. 1, no. 108, to John Colet [October 1499], 202–206; no. 109, to John Colet [October 1499], 206–211; Surely at that moment, 208; "to set us an example," 210. See also Seebohm, *Oxford Reformers,* 76–78.

73 "here is a man": *Collected Works of Erasmus,* vol. 1, no. 111, to John Colet [October 1499], 215, 214.

74 "How could I ever": Ibid., no. 108, to John Colet [October 1499], 205.

74 he at one point said: *John Colet's Commentary on First Corinthians,* 273, 333.

74 "I have never": *Collected Works of Erasmus,* vol. 1, no. 118, to Robert Fisher, December 5 [1499], 235.

CHAPTER 6: THE VOW IN THE STORM

76 Known as "Little Rome": Brecht, *Martin Luther,* 23–27; Fife, *Revolt of Martin Luther,* 34; Friedenthal, *Luther,* 21–22; Schwiebert, *Luther,* 129–130.

77 the day was as regimented: Brecht, *Martin Luther,* 31–32; Fife, *Luther,* 32–39.

77 "to refrain from plots": Fife, *Luther,* 38.

77 the city was no better than: *Luthers Werke, Tischreden,* vol. 2, no. 2719b.

77 On the Erfurt faculty: Brecht, *Martin Luther,* 27–29; Marius, *Martin Luther,* 33; Friedenthal, *Luther,* 18, 20; Roper, *Martin Luther,* 31–32.

77 completed the program: Brecht, *Martin Luther*, 33.

77 drilled in dialectic: Ibid., 38; Marius, *Martin Luther*, 35; Fife, *Luther*, 43–44.

77 participated in fifteen disputations: Fife, *Luther*, 66.

78 "the new Scholastics": Erika Rummel, *The Humanist-Scholastic Debate in the Renaissance & Reformation*, 40.

78 "the most ingenious": *Luthers Werke, Tischreden*, vol. 3, no. 3722.

78 Ockham, who was born: On Ockham, see Walker, *History of the Christian Church*, 353–357; Cantor, *Civilization of the Middle Ages*, 532–535; Backman, *Worlds of Medieval Europe*, 395–398; "William of Ockham," in *The New Encyclopaedia Britannica*, 15th ed., vol. 8, 867.

78 "Whatever can be done": Quoted in Walker, *History of the Christian Church*, 355.

78 the radical empiricism: Cantor, *Civilization of the Middle Ages*, 533; Walker, *History of the Christian Church*, 356.

79 bitter conflict with the pope: Arthur Stephen McGrade, *The Political Thought of William of Ockham*, 7–14; Walker, *History of the Christian Church*, 319–321, 353; Cantor, *Civilization of the Middle Ages*, 533–534.

80 "Munich academy": McGrade, *Political Thought of William of Ockham*, 26.

80 His followers took this step further: Ozment, *Age of Reform*, 233–235; Walker, *History of the Christian Church*, 354; Schwiebert, *Luther*, 168–169; Philip S. Watson, *Let God Be God! An Interpretation of the Theology of Martin Luther*, 15–16.

81 an inescapable presence: Brecht, *Martin Luther*, 33–36; Schwiebert, *Luther*, 134–136; Fife, *Luther*, 49–50.

81 "Without Aristotle": Quoted in Brecht, *Martin Luther*, 34.

81 The "whole Aristotle": *Luther's Works*, vol. 31, 12.

81 "this damned, conceited": Ibid., vol. 44, 201.

81 "nothing can be learned": Ibid., 200, 201. See also Ozment, *Age of Reform*, 235.

82 virtue is not a natural attribute: Aristotle's views on virtue are described in Book II of the *Nicomachean Ethics*, Great Books of the Western World (Chicago: Encyclopaedia Britannica, 1952, 1990), vol. 8, 348–355.

82 his *Anfechtungen* intensified: Brecht, *Martin Luther*, 49.

82 the rattle of death: Ibid., 45–47; Fife, *Luther*, 73.

83 "What majesty": Quoted in Fife, *Revolt of Martin Luther*, 47.

83 Luther was returning: Brecht, *Martin Luther*, 48; Bainton, *Here I Stand*, 15, 25.

83 "gate of Paradise": Heer, *Medieval World*, 62.

84 he held a farewell dinner: Brecht, *Martin Luther*, 50.

CHAPTER 7: BACK TO THE FATHERS

87 The troubles that Erasmus encountered: *Collected Works of Erasmus*, vol. 1, no. 119, to Jacob Batt [February 1500], 236–246.

87 "very tired from traveling": Ibid., 245.

88 "My readings in Greek": Ibid., no. 123 [March 1500], 249.

88 "to buy some Greek authors": Ibid., no. 124, to Jacob Batt, April 12 [1500], 252.

88 "only consolation": Ibid., no. 131, to Augustin Vincent [September 1500], 277.

88 caused Erasmus to grow weak: Ibid., 250.

88 got the idea of gathering adages: Ibid., no. 126, to William Blount [June 1500], 255–266.

89 "gardens of the classics": Ibid., 257.

89 he had 818 proverbs: Ibid., 255. See also Barker, *Adages of Erasmus*, xii; Margaret Mann Phillips, *The "Adages" of Erasmus*:

A Study with Translations, 41–45, 54; Huizinga, *Erasmus*, 39.

89 "Twice-cooked cabbage is death": Barker, *Adages of Erasmus*, xv–xvi.

89 "the one-eyed man is king": Ibid., 276–277.

89 "Pandora's box" and "to call a spade a spade": Ibid., xxxix, 32–34, 170.

89 to give public lectures: *Collected Works of Erasmus*, vol. 1, 269.

89 a hundred copies disappeared: Ibid., vol. 1, 281–284.

90 meager and formulaic: Ibid., vol. 2, 139, and vol. 4, 236; see also Schoeck, *Erasmus of Europe*, 214.

90 occupy him for the rest of his life: Phillips, *"Erasmus and the Northern Renaissance*, 1.

90 "If anyone had taken me": Quoted in ibid., 1.

90 "ferreting his way": *Collected Works of Erasmus*, vol. 1, 287.

90 documented in his letters: Ibid., vol. 1, nos. 128, 129, 130, 138, 139.

90 Lady Anna van Borssele: Ibid., vol. 1, 157.

91 sent back detailed instructions: Ibid., vol. 1, no. 139, to Jacob Batt [c. December 12] 1500, 300–306; quote, 301–302.

91 wrote to Lady Anna directly: Ibid., vol. 2, no. 145, January 27, 1501, 12–18; quote, 15. Huizinga (*Erasmus*, 38) calls Erasmus's instructions to Batt "shameless." By contrast, Harbison (*Christian Scholar*, 80) finds a "kernel of integrity" in his actions; while "others had had to sacrifice comfort, family, and pleasure to finish a work of scholarship," Erasmus "had to sacrifice his self-respect."

91 his "good fortune": *Collected Works of Erasmus*, vol. 2, no. 149 [March 16, 1501], 24–27.

92 the underlying Greek: Since the original language of the Psalms is Hebrew, the Greek itself was a translation.

92 served as the scriptural foundation:

Bruce M. Metzger, *The Early Versions of the New Testament: Their Origin, Transmission, and Limitations*, 285; G. Henslow, *The Vulgate: The Source of the False Doctrines*, vi.

93 full of spelling mistakes: Bruce M. Metzger, *The Text of the New Testament: Its Transmission, Corruption, and Restoration*, 76 and chap. 7, "The Causes of Error in the Transmission of the Text of the New Testament," 186–206.

93 the name of the pool: Bentley, *Humanists and Holy Writ*, 83.

93 introduced another level of distortion: Metzger, *Early Versions of the New Testament*, 365ff; Arthur Vööbus, "Early Versions of the New Testament," Papers of the Estonian Theological Society in Exile (Stockholm, 1954), 59; Henslow, *Vulgate*, vi, 2, 72ff.

93 so unnerved conservative churchmen: Rummel, *Humanist-Scholastic Debate*, 108.

93 considered schismatic: Bentley, *Humanists and Holy Writ*, 15.

94 have a profound impact: Simon Goldhill, *Who Needs Greek? Contests in the Cultural History of Hellenism*, especially chap. 1, "Learning Greek Is Heresy! Resisting Erasmus," 14–59.

94 "we are perfectly satisfied": *Collected Works of Erasmus*, vol. 2, 26.

94 second only to Scripture itself: Cantor, *Civilization of the Middle Ages*, 66.

94 the most elegant stylist: *The Cambridge History of the Bible*, vol. 1, 517.

94 During his lifetime: The year of Jerome's birth is a subject of debate. The standard biography, J. N. D. Kelly, *Jerome: His Life, Writings, and Controversies* (1), gives it as 331, but most historians believe it occurred sometime in the middle to late 340s.

95 the center of an ardent cult: Eugene F. Rice Jr., *Saint Jerome in the Renaissance*, 49–83.

95 began reviving Jerome's image: Ibid., 84, 102ff, 113.

95 one of the four richest caches: F. A. Wright, introduction to *Select Letters of St. Jerome* (Loeb Classical Library, vol. 282), xiii.

96 showed how scholarship and devotion: Rice, *Jerome in the Renaissance*, 91–95.

96 copied out all of Jerome's letters: *Collected Works of Erasmus*, vol. 61, xiii; Rice, *Jerome in the Renaissance*, 116.

96 "filled with mistakes": *Collected Works of Erasmus*, vol. 2, 26–27.

96 critical to his own career: Ibid., vol. 61, xxxiii–xxxv.

96 would have to refashion him: See Lisa Jardine, *Erasmus, Man of Letters: The Construction of Charisma in Print*, especially chap. 2, "The In(de)scribable Aura of the Scholar-Saint in His Study: Erasmus' *Life* and *Letters* of Saint Jerome," 55–82.

97 Jerome got his charge: Kelly, *Jerome*, 80–87. See also "Jerome as Biblical Scholar," in *The Cambridge History of the Bible*, vol. 1, 513.

97 was in disarray: *The Cambridge History of the Bible*, vol. 1, 527; Metzger, *Early Versions of the New Testament*, 285–330.

97 scribal errors were introduced: Metzger, *Early Versions of the New Testament*, 322–330; Bart D. Ehrman, *The Orthodox Corruption of Scripture: The Early Christological Controversies on the Text of the New Testament*, xi–xii, 3–4, 24–29.

97 a "living text": Kurt Aland and Barbara Aland, *The Text of the New Testament: An Introduction to the Critical Editions and to the Theory and Practice of Modern Textual Criticism*, 69–71.

98 "almost from the very cradle": Quoted in *The Cambridge History of the Bible*, vol. 1, 510.

98 sampled the city's pleasures: Kelly, *Jerome*, 21.

98 "half-barbarous banks of the Rhine": Quoted in ibid., 25.

98 a violent blowup that blackened his reputation: Ibid., 33–35.

99 had a dream: Jerome, Letter 22, written in 384, at www.newadvent.org /fathers/3001022.htm, section no. 30. See also Kelly, *Jerome*, 41–44.

100 citing as justification: Letter 70, written in 397, at www.newadvent .org/fathers/3001070.htm. See also Rice, *Jerome in the Renaissance*, 5–6; Kelly, *Jerome*, 43. The reference is to Deuteronomy 21:10–13.

100 ferry his requests: See Letter 5, written about 374, at www.newadvent.org /fathers/3001005.htm.

100 would describe his torment: Letter 22, section 7.

101 Like many early Christians: Peter Brown, *The Body and Society: Men, Women, and Sexual Renunciation in Early Christianity*, 428–446.

101 "frenzy" of the Arians: Letter 16, written in 377 or 378, at www.newadvent.org /fathers/3001016.htm.

101 Eusebius's famous *Chronicle*: Kelly, *Jerome*, 72–75.

101 In his reply: Letter 18, written in 381, at www.newadvent.org/fathers/3001018 .htm. See also *The Cambridge History of the Bible*, vol. 1, 513.

102 largely unknown in the West: *The Cambridge History of the Bible*, vol. 1, 513.

102 "Is there a man": "Prefaces to the Vulgate Version of the New Testament—The Four Gospels," at www.newadvent.org /fathers/3002.htm.

102 "there are almost": Ibid.

103 proceeded with caution: Rice, *Jerome in the Renaissance*, 11–12.

103 in some 3,500 places: Metzger, *Early Versions of the New Testament*, 353.

103 Jerome was often inconsistent: Ibid., 353–354; *The Cambridge History of the Bible*, vol. 1, 523–6; Vööbus, "Early Versions of the New Testament," 59; Kelly, *Jerome*, 87.

103 craved female company: Kelly, *Jerome*, 91ff.

103 a sixteen-thousand-word letter: Letter 22,

at www.newadvent.org/fathers/3001022
.htm; "Assuredly no gold," section 23;
"may be lost," section 5; "women pale
and thin," section 17; "I praise wedlock,"
section 20.

104 part of an ardent campaign: Kelly,
Jerome, 106, 335; Rice, *Jerome in the
Renaissance*, 139–140.

104 Ambrose and Augustine: Kelly, *Jerome*,
102; Cantor, *Civilization of the Middle
Ages*, 68–69.

104 Mary's perpetual virginity: Rice, *Jerome
in the Renaissance*, 46.

104 first protests were raised: Kelly, *Jerome*,
110.

104 "two-legged asses": Letter 27, written
in 384, at www.newadvent.org
/fathers/3001027.htm.

104 "the detestable tribe of monks": Quoted
in Kelly, *Jerome*, 108.

105 "Let Rome keep her bustle": Letter 43,
written in 385, in Wright, *Select Letters of
St. Jerome*, 175, 177; "I thank my God,"
Letter 45, written in 285, 187.

105 set up a monastic community: Kelly,
Jerome, 129.

105 these pilgrims helped spread: Ibid.,
139–40.

105 visited only at night: Metzger, *Early
Versions of the New Testament*, 332.

105 the Septuagint: "Scripture, Privileged
Translations of," in *The Encyclopedia
of Judaism*. As this entry notes, the
Septuagint is actually older than the
standard Hebrew Masoretic text of the
Hebrew Bible and so in some passages
may offer a more reliable reading.

106 discussed it with Jews: Jerome, Letter 57,
written in 395, at www.newadvent.org
/fathers/3001057.htm, section 11.

106 the *Hebraica veritas*: *The Cambridge
History of the Bible*, vol. 1, 515; Kelly,
Jerome, 158.

106 "filthy swine": Quoted in Kelly, *Jerome*,
157.

106 a correspondence that offers: Peter
Brown, *Augustine of Hippo*, 274. Brown
calls their long correspondence "a unique

document in the Early Church," showing
"two highly-civilized men conducting
with studied courtesy a singularly
rancorous correspondence."

106 Augustine wrote to Jerome: Augustine,
Letter 71, written in 403, at www.new
advent.org/fathers/1102071.htm. See also
Kelly, *Jerome*, 263–272.

107 Jerome testily replied: Jerome, Letter
112, written in 404, at www.newadvent
.org/fathers/1102075.htm; "for I have
not followed," section 20; Jerome guessed
that it was his translation, section 22.

107 two models of Christian scholarship:
Harbison, *Christian Scholar*, 18–19.

107 Jerome's translation of the Old
Testament: Kelly, *Jerome*, 162–163.

107 had serious defects: *The Cambridge
History of the Bible*, vol. 1, 525–526,
states that "what is most remarkable is
the variety of Jerome's renderings. Time
and again he gives the impression that
the last thing he would think of doing
is to use a word or phrase twice in the
same context if he could possibly avoid
it." In practice, he "translated very much
as he happened himself to feel at any
particular moment." See also Metzger,
Early Versions of the New Testament,
353–355.

108 most famous example: Kelly, *Jerome*, 301.

108 would spend his remaining years: Ibid.,
225.

108 a mob, inflamed: Ibid., 322.

109 was working on a commentary: *The
Cambridge History of the Bible*, vol. 1,
516.

109 much that Erasmus had to overlook:
Rice, *Jerome in the Renaissance*, 133.

109 responsible for only part of the Vulgate:
Collected Works of Erasmus, vol. 15, 278,
notes that Erasmus always distinguished
between the text of the Vulgate and the
version of Jerome, which, he believed,
had been lost.

109 This assessment is shared: *The Cambridge
History of the Bible*, vol. 1, 519; Metzger,
Text of the New Testament, 76.

109 many faults that had crept into the text: Metzger, *Text of the New Testament*, 76.

109 asked his court scholar Alcuin: Christoph de Hamel, *The Book: A History of the Bible*, 34–38; Frederic Kenyon, *Our Bible and the Ancient Manuscripts*, 257–261.

110 led to the undoing: Metzger, *Early Versions of the New Testament*, 346; "Vulgate," in *Dictionary of the Bible*.

110 another layer of corruption: H. H. Glunz, *History of the Vulgate in England from Alenin to Roger Bacon*, 253–254.

110 the trade in Bibles: *The Cambridge History of the Bible*, vol. 2, 145–154; Kenyon, *Our Bible*, 161–162; de Hamel, *The Book*, 130–139.

110 Roger Bacon: Beryl Smalley, *The Study of the Bible in the Middle Ages*, 329–333; Glunz, *History of the Vulgate in England*, 259ff, 284.

110 he used a Paris version: Laura Light, "The Bible and the Individual: The Thirteenth-Century Paris Bible," in Susan Boynton and Diane J. Reilly, eds., *The Practice of the Bible in the Middle Ages: Production, Reception, and Performance in Western Christianity*, 228–246; de Hamel, *The Book*, 201.

111 "I am not unaware": *Collected Works of Erasmus*, vol. 2, no. 161, to Antonius of Luxembourg, July 18 [1501], 46–48.

111 drafted it at the request: Ibid., 51.

111 rereading Plato: Erasmus in this period was strongly affected by the Neoplatonist revival that was taking place in Italy and spreading to humanist circles in northern Europe; he was especially drawn to its stress on the divide between the body and the spirit. See Bainton, *Erasmus of Christendom*, 59–61; Carlos Eire, *Reformations: The Early Modern World, 1450–1650*, 108.

111 Jean Vitrier: *Collected Works of Erasmus*, vol. 2, 50. See also Erasmus's lengthy sketch of Vitrier, vol. 8, 226–232; "you would be," 230. (The quotation has been slightly edited for clarity.)

112 unable to carry around: *Collected Works of Erasmus*, vol. 66, 9.

112 "There is really no attack": John P. Dolan, trans., *The Essential Erasmus*, 36; "seek the invisible," 61; "The entire spiritual life," 62–63; "their greatest legacy," 66; "if you live as if," 65; "is in profiting," 80. On the importance of the fifth rule, see Augustijn, *Erasmus*, 46.

113 "Monasticism is not piety": Dolan, *Essential Erasmus*, 92. Dolan gives *pietas* as "holiness," but other accounts use "piety."

113 "Just as Christ": Ibid., 68.

113 lacks the snap: Heiko Oberman, in *The Reformation: Roots and Ramifications* (Grand Rapids: Eerdmans, 1994), 72, calls the *Enchiridion* "the most boring book in the history of piety," adding that "at least that was the judgment of his contemporaries, because it was a publishing failure."

113 "no beast so ferocious": Dolan, *Essential Erasmus*, 47.

113 "I would prefer": Ibid., 71.

113 more than fifteen printings: See the Universal Short Title Catalogue (ustc.ac.uk/index.php); *Collected Works of Erasmus*, vol. 66, 4–7; Smith, *Erasmus*, 57–58.

114 the tribune of liberal religious reform in Europe: Bainton, in *Erasmus of Christendom* (65), says that the *Enchiridion* made Erasmus "the mouthpiece of liberal Catholic reform." Phillips, in *Erasmus and the Northern Renaissance* (44), writes that with the *Enchiridion*, Erasmus began "his work of liberation." See also the discussion by Augustijn, who writes (*Erasmus*, 55) of the spirit of individualism that permeates this work.

114 to offer Erasmus a lectureship: *Collected Works of Erasmus*, vol. 2, 58–59.

114 "The study of Greek": Ibid., 59–60.

114 "a Delian prophet": Ibid., 108.

114 "The shortness of life and the limitations": Ibid., 87.

114 "The most enjoyable sport": Ibid., 89.

114 found a codex by Lorenzo Valla: Ibid., no. 182 [about March] 1505, 89–97.

115 Of particular consequence: Bentley, *Humanists and Holy Writ*, 186. See also Lorenzo Valla, *De Collatione Novi Testamenti*, Matthew 3:2, and 2 Corinthians 7:10.

115 gave Erasmus the idea: *The Cambridge History of the Bible*, vol. 2, 495.

115 "I do not really believe": *Collected Works of Erasmus*, vol. 2, 94.

116 we can see a line extending: See Harbison, *Christian Scholar*, 84; *The Cambridge History of the Bible*, vol. 2, 494–496.

116 a letter he sent in late 1504: *Collected Works of Erasmus*, vol. 2, no. 181 [about December] 1504, 85–89.

116 back in his beloved England: Ibid., 98–99.

CHAPTER 8: ANGRY WITH GOD

117 "dead to the world": *Luthers Werke, Tischreden*, vol. 4, no. 4707, 440.

117 the Augustinian Hermits: Brecht, *Martin Luther*, 52–53; "Hermits of St. Augustine," in *The Catholic Encyclopedia* at www.newadvent.org /cathen/07281a.htm.

117 not a monk but a friar: Kenneth Hagen, "So You Think Luther Was a Monk? Stop It!" *Logia: A Journal of Lutheran Theology*, 19(2): 35–37, Eastertide 2010; Diarmaid MacCulloch, "The World Took Sides," *London Review of Books*, 38(16): 25–27, August 11, 2016.

118 he "went crazy": Quoted in Brecht, *Martin Luther*, 58.

118 was led to his cell: It is today possible to see Luther's cell (and to stay at the guesthouse) in the former monastery in Erfurt, now a pilgrimage site for tourists.

118 the Rule of Augustine: George Lawless, *Augustine of Hippo and His Monastic Rule*, 75–109; Friedenthal, *Luther*, 42–43; Brecht, *Martin Luther*, 60.

119 "unchaste hearts": Lawless, *Augustine of Hippo and His Monastic Rule*, 89.

119 the canonical hours: Bainton, *Here I Stand*, 27–28; Friedenthal, *Luther*, 43; Brecht, *Martin Luther*, 63–64.

119 four to five hours a day in church: John M. Todd, *Luther: A Life*, 31.

119 alive in the heart: Lawless, *Augustine of Hippo and His Monastic Rule*, 85; Brecht, *Martin Luther*, 64–65.

120 "horrible temptations to pollution": *Luther's Works*, vol. 54, "Table Talk," no. 3921, 295.

120 pride, impatience, and anger: Friedenthal, *Luther*, 35.

121 cleaning the latrines: Brecht, *Martin Luther*, 91.

121 "among the choir of angels": Quoted in Fife, *Revolt of Martin Luther*, 96.

122 the yoke of obedience: Brecht, *Martin Luther*, 61.

122 the habit of the order: Ibid., 63; Friedenthal, *Luther*, 39.

122 "how peaceful and quiet Satan": *Luther's Works*, vol. 44, 387.

122 Gabriel Biel: Brecht, *Martin Luther*, 71; Friedenthal, *Luther*, 60.

123 such emissions were so frequent: *Luther's Works*, vol. 54, "Table Talk," no. 3921, 295.

123 the best of books: Ibid., no. 3722, 264; Bainton, *Here I Stand*, 30; Ozment, *Age of Reform*, 231–232.

123 said to have committed a great crime: *Luther's Works*, vol. 14, 294–295.

123 made a grand entrance: Ibid., vol. 54, "Table Talk," no. 1558, 156; Friedenthal, *Luther*, 47.

124 Taking his place: *Luther's Works*, vol. 54, "Table Talk," no. 1558, 156; no. 3556a, 234; no. 4574, 354; Bainton, *Here I Stand*, 30–33.

124 "With what tongue": Quoted in Bainton, *Here I Stand*, 30.

124 "Don't you know": *Luther's Works*, vol. 54, "Table Talk," no. 623, 109; no. 4574, 354. Luther also later recalled this exchange in a letter to his father,

vol. 48, no. 104, November 21, 1521, 332. See also Friedenthal, *Luther*, 47.

125 was especially troubled: See Luther's 1545 preface to his Latin writings, in John Dillenberger, ed., *Martin Luther: Selections from His Writings*, 11; *Luther's Works*, vol. 54, "Table Talk," no. 3232c, 193–194.

125 was becoming a burden: Brecht, *Martin Luther*, 61, 67–69; Bainton, *Here I Stand*, 40–42.

125 Though he constantly confessed: *Luther's Works*, vol. 27, 73.

126 "You are a fool!": Ibid., vol. 54, "Table Talk," no. 122, 15.

126 though abbreviated in length: Ibid., vol. 31, 129.

126 "the cause of all sedition": Ibid., vol. 54, "Table Talk," no. 1240, 127–128.

126 The main text was the *Sentences*: Friedenthal, *Luther*, 56–57.

127 "I am well, thank God": Preserved Smith, ed., *Luther's Correspondence and Other Contemporary Letters*, vol. 1, no. 2, to Johan Braun, March 17, 1509, 24.

127 A copy of the volume he used: Fife, *Revolt of Martin Luther*, 149.

127 Luther cited the bishop of Hippo: Ibid., 154; Oberman, *Luther*, 159; Brecht, *Martin Luther*, 94.

128 none would have a more galvanizing effect: MacCulloch, *Reformation*, 108.

128 a volume of Augustine's writings: Oberman, *Luther*, 158–159.

128 "devoured" him: *Luther's Works*, vol. 54, "Table Talk," 49.

128 was the *Confessions*: The volume of Augustine that Luther annotated contained *The Trinity* and the *City of God*. It is clear, though, that Luther also closely read the *Confessions*, for he cited the work many times in his *First Lectures on the Psalms*, which he began in August 1513; see, for instance, *Luther's Works*, vol. 10, 27, 43, 57, 64, 86, 142.

128 grew up in a small inland town: For the essentials of Augustine's life and writings, see Brown, *Augustine of Hippo*; Walker, *History of the Christian Church*, 197–206.

129 read the comedies of Terence: *Confessions*, trans. R. S. Pine-Coffin, 37, 33, 35.

129 seized by an impulse: Ibid., 43, 49, 45.

129 Augustine lied to his tutor: Ibid., 47, 49, 52.

129 The second city in the Western Empire: Brown, *Augustine of Hippo*, 65.

129 "hissing cauldron of lust": *Confessions*, 55.

130 "swollen with conceit": Ibid., 58.

130 "began to throb": Ibid., 58–59.

131 to feel himself held fast: Ibid., 164.

131 "unclean whispers": Ibid., 176.

132 "How long shall I go on saying": Ibid., 177.

132 "Take it and read": Ibid., 177; "it was as though," 178.

132 he began writing the *Confessions*: Brown, *Augustine of Hippo*, 161–181.

133 notorious swearers of oaths: Ibid., 149.

133 gives the *Confessions* its modern feel: See James J. O'Donnell, *Augustine: A New Biography*, 83–84; Joseph Havens, "Notes on Augustine's 'Confession,'" *Journal for the Scientific Study of Religion*, 5(1): 141–143, Autumn 1965. William James, in *The Varieties of Religious Experience* (147), refers to Augustine's "psychological genius" in recounting the travails of his "divided self" (New York: Collier, 1961).

133 "My sin was this": *Confessions*, 40–41; "There can be no hope": 233.

133 the one with Pelagius: On Pelagius, see B. R. Rees, introduction, *The Letters of Pelagius and His Followers*; Walker, *History of the Christian Church*, 206–209; Brown, *Augustine of Hippo*, 341–355, 365–375; MacCulloch, *Reformation*, 104–107; O'Donnell, *Augustine*, 261–264, 271–278.

134 Pelagius bristled at Augustine's stress: Brown, *Augustine of Hippo*, 343; O'Donnell, *Augustine*, 262.

134 Arriving in Hippo in 410: Brown, *Augustine of Hippo*, 340–344; Walker, *History of the Christian Church*, 207.

134 "It is possible to do": Letter to Demetrias, in Rees, *Letters of Pelagius and His Followers*, 37, 54. As Rees notes, this letter—addressed to the fourteen-year-old daughter of an aristocratic Roman widow—offers the most complete account of Pelagius's views. With its praise for chastity and instructions for virgins, it touches on many of the same themes as Jerome's letter to Eustochium.

134 set out to discredit: Walker, *History of the Christian Church*, 208; Rees, *Letters of Pelagius and His Followers*, 21.

135 "a dolt of dolts": Quoted in *The Cambridge History of the Bible*, vol. 1, 516.

135 masterwork, the *City of God*: See the discussion in Brown, *Augustine of Hippo*, 302–329; Walker, *History of the Christian Church*, 204–206.

135 into the medieval world: Cantor, in *Civilization of the Middle Ages* (75), calls Augustine the first medieval thinker.

135 in most modern editions: The Penguin edition of *City of God* cited here (trans. Henry Bettenson) is 1,091 pages long.

135 had been powerless to prevent: Ibid., 8–9, 50ff, 69, 131ff, 143ff.

135 the Fall: Ibid., 524, 538–541, 541, 547, 580. See also Brown, *Augustine of Hippo*, 238–239; Ozment, *Age of Reform*, 22–28; MacCulloch, *Reformation*, 104.

136 "Death has passed": *City of God*, 511.

136 to give it such prominence: Justo L. González, *A History of Christian Thought*, vol. 2 (Nashville: Abington Press, 1971), 42–44; Charles Freeman, *The Closing of the Western Mind*, 288–293. Norman Powell Williams, in *The Idea of the Fall of Original Sin* (London: Longmans, Green, 1927), notes (xix) that it was Augustine who elaborated Paul's inchoate references on the subject into a theory.

136 man's warped nature: *City of God*, 1065.

136 "undeserved": Ibid., 547.

136 knows all things before they happen: Ibid., 192.

136 "why should he not have": Ibid., 976.

137 The one is a community: Ibid., 573.

137 one of the most damning epithets: MacCulloch, *Reformation*, 110.

137 its proponents were branded as heretics: Brown, in *Augustine of Hippo* (367), observes that the victory of Augustine's ideas over those of Pelagius is "one of the most important symptoms of that profound change that we call 'The End of the Ancient World and the Beginning of the Middle Ages.'"

137 the Vandals: Ibid., 424.

137 Pelagianism would not die: Walker, *History of the Christian Church*, 210–211; Cantor, *Civilization of the Middle Ages*, 84–85.

138 came to be known as semi-Pelagian: Rees, *Letters of Pelagius and His Followers*, 5–6; Bernhard Lohse, *A Short History of Christian Doctrine*, 122–131.

138 endorsed such an approach: Walker, *History of the Christian Church*, 212–217; Cantor, *Civilization of the Middle Ages*, 85.

138 Augustine offered the framework: Brown, *Augustine of Hippo*, 206–208, 214; Cantor, *Civilization of the Middle Ages*, 78.

138 further diluted by the late Scholastics: Ozment, *Age of Reform*, 233–234.

CHAPTER 9: RENAISSANCE TOUR

140 "I believe": *Collected Works of Erasmus*, vol. 2, no. 191, to Richard Whitford, May 1, 1506, 113.

140 "are generally spread": Ibid., vol. 10, 471.

141 He wore simple clothes: These details are taken from a long portrait written by Erasmus years later, *Collected Works of Erasmus*, vol. 7, no. 999, to Ulrich Hutten, July 23, 1519, 15–25.

141 "Remedies for Ending": Clarence H. Miller et al., eds., *The Complete Works of St. Thomas More* (New Haven: Yale University Press, 1984), vol. 3, part 2, 267.

141 Fascinated by excrement: Peter Ackroyd, *The Life of Thomas More*, 230–231.

141 lived in the Charterhouse: Ibid., 97–98; Derek Wilson, *In the Lion's Court: Power, Ambition, and Sudden Death in the Court of Henry VIII*, 23–24.

141 jointly set out to translate them: Rummel, *Erasmus as a Translator of the Classics*, 49ff.

142 most popular author of the Renaissance: Smith, *Erasmus*, 193.

142 An irreverent misanthrope: Christopher Robinson, "Lucian," in T. James Luce, ed., *Ancient Writers: Greece and Rome*, vol. 2 (New York: Charles Scribner's Sons, 1982), 1081–1095.

142 "satirizes everything": *Collected Works of Erasmus*, vol. 2, 116.

142 would show up in many of Erasmus's works: Christopher Robinson, *Lucian and His Influence in Europe*, 165–197; Robert P. Adams, *The Better Part of Valor: More, Erasmus, Colet, and Vives on Humanism, War, and Peace*, 33–34.

142 to meet William Warham: *Collected Works of Erasmus*, vol. 9, 297–298.

143 to send his two sons: Ibid., vol. 2, 118.

143 "at the mercy of wind and wave": Ibid., 115, 117, 120.

143 "On the Troubles of Old Age": *Collected Works of Erasmus*, vol. 85, 12–25.

143 early version of a diploma mill: Paul F. Grendler, "How to Get a Degree in Fifteen Days: Erasmus' Doctorate of Theology from the University of Turin," *Erasmus of Rotterdam Society Yearbook* 18: 40–64, 1998.

144 The Italian wars: Charles Oman, *A History of the Art of War in the Sixteenth Century*, 3–13, 30–39. Max Boot, in his introduction to *War Made New: Technology, Warfare, and the Course of History, 1500 to Today* (New York: Gotham Books, 2006), writes that the French invasion of Italy in 1494 marked the start of the modern age "in which warfare, which had remained relatively static for a thousand years, would change with bewildering and accelerating rapidity."

144 slipped from its control: Peter Partner, *The Lands of St. Peter: The Papal State in the Middle Ages and Early Renaissance*, 437.

144 the pope decided on military action: E. Rodocanachi, *Histoire de Rome: Le Pontificat de Jules II*, 61ff.

144 were all at work: Phillips, *Erasmus and the Northern Renaissance*, 46.

144 triumphantly entered it: Pastor, *History of the Popes*, vol. 6, 281; Rodocanachi, *Histoire de Rome*, 73–76.

145 a "mighty groan": Quoted in Bainton, *Erasmus of Christendom*, 81; "waging war," *Collected Works of Erasmus*, vol. 2, 128.

145 could see the effects: Barker, *Adages of Erasmus*, 121.

145 The ducat was an international coin: R. A. Scotti, *Basilica: The Splendor and the Scandal: Building St. Peter's*, 80.

145 sent a letter to Aldus Manutius: *Collected Works of Erasmus*, vol. 2, no. 207, October 28 [1507], 129–33; see also 139–40 for details about his approach to Aldus.

145 Europe's richest, grandest, most cosmopolitan city: Deno John Geanakoplos, *Byzantium: Church, Society, and Civilization Seen Through Contemporary Eyes*, 69–70; David Chambers and Brian Pullan, eds., *Venice: A Documentary History, 1450–1630* (Toronto: University of Toronto Press, 2001), 5–20.

146 Europe's leading book center: Martin Lowry, *The World of Aldus Manutius: Business and Scholarship in Renaissance Venice*, 7ff.

146 the Aldine Press was king: Lowry, ibid., 149, notes, however, that the house had reached its peak in 1502–1503.

146 Aldus became so fed up: Ibid., 165–166. "Whoever you are": Chambers and Pullan, *Venice*, 360.

146 a sort of international house: Elizabeth L.

Eisenstein, *The Printing Revolution in Early Modern Europe*, second edition, 112.

146 The Aldine house: Febvre and Martin, *Coming of the Book*, 145–146; Lowry, *World of Aldus Manutius*, 130–131.

146 a dolphin wrapped around an anchor: An illustration appears in Barker, *Adages of Erasmus*, 133.

147 a much larger cascade: Febvre and Martin, *Coming of the Book*, 248–255, 264–266.

147 to produce octavo editions: Lowry, *World of Aldus Manutius*, 142–143, 147–148.

148 invited him to join his academy: *Collected Works of Erasmus*, vol. 2, 139–140. See Erasmus's own description of his relations with Aldus in his adage "Make Haste Slowly," in Barker, *Adages of Erasmus*, 144–145.

148 "I'm learning": Quoted in Phillips, *"Adages" of Erasmus*, 68. See also Huizinga, *Erasmus*, 64.

148 on *Herculei labores*: Barker, *Adages of Erasmus*, 219–238; "to restoring the monuments," 223; "a few snorts of contempt," 224; "immense labors," 225; carried off the prize, 236.

149 giving birth to the modern personal essay: Peter Mack, "Humanist Rhetoric and Dialectic," in Kraye, *The Cambridge Companion to Renaissance Humanism* (95), observes that the essay was the most important new genre of the sixteenth century.

149 *Adagorium chiliades*: See Phillips, *"Adages" of Erasmus*, 69–86.

150 a reeking, overgrown wasteland: On Rome's appearance in this period, see Rodocanachi, *Histoire de Rome*, 40–44; Ingrid D. Rowland, *The Culture of the High Renaissance: Ancients and Moderns in Sixteenth-Century Rome*, 8–9; Charles L. Stinger, *The Renaissance in Rome*, 61; Peter Partner, *Renaissance Rome*, 81, 95–96.

150 "Rome is not Rome": *Collected Works of Erasmus*, vol. 28, 431.

150 Its economy: Partner, *Renaissance Rome*,

47–73; information about Rome's courier service, 52.

151 humanists dominated the Curia: D'Amico, *Renaissance Humanism in Papal Rome*, xvi, 3–4, 12.

151 While in Rome: Erasmus was actually in Rome three times, with side trips taken to Siena and Naples.

151 fell in with this group: D'Amico, *Renaissance Humanism in Papal Rome*, 138–139; Halkin, *Erasmus*, 69.

151 exclusive world of the cardinals: D'Amico, *Renaissance Humanism in Papal Rome*, 46–56; Rodocanachi, *Histoire de Rome*, 83–86; Stinger, *Renaissance in Rome*, 30.

152 Raffaele Riario: See "Riario, Raffaele," in *Contemporaries of Erasmus*.

152 "In Rome": *Collected Works of Erasmus*, vol. 2, 297.

152 "I myself never enjoyed": Quoted in Halkin, *Erasmus*, 70.

153 "raving against Christ": *Collected Works of Erasmus*, vol. 17, 331.

153 "For seven whole years now": Ibid., vol. 28, 346, 384–387; see also D'Amico, *Renaissance Humanism in Papal Rome*, 123–142; Smith, *Erasmus*, 114.

153 Julius had established himself: Hibbert, *Rome*, 139–141; Rodocanachi, *Histoire de Rome*, 78, 81–83, 85; Pastor, *History of the Popes*, vol. 6, 212–217.

154 asked Erasmus to compose: *Collected Works of Erasmus*, vol. 9, 351.

154 wanted to restore the city: Pastor, *History of the Popes*, vol. 6, 229, 493–496; Partner, *Renaissance Rome*, 180–181.

154 one giant construction site: Julian Klaczko, *Rome and the Renaissance: The Pontificate of Julius II*, 24.

154 became a sort of minister: Pastor, *History of the Popes*, vol. 6, 461.

154 the Vatican: Ibid., 484–487; Rowland, *Culture of the High Renaissance*, 171–174; Hibbert, *Rome*, 142; Partner, *Renaissance Rome*, 118–119; Rodocanachi, *Histoire de Rome*, 54–58; Stinger, *Renaissance Humanism in Papal Rome*, 267–272.

155 Julius brought Raphael: Pastor, *History of the Popes*, vol. 6, 540ff.

155 a grand monument to himself: Scotti, *Basilica*, 33; Hibbert: *Rome*, 143.

156 one real possibility: James Lees-Milne, *Saint Peter's: The Story of Saint Peter's Basilica in Rome*, 89ff; Pastor, *History of the Popes*, vol. 6, 461ff; Scotti, *Basilica*, 37–39.

156 in urgent need of repair: Lees-Milne, *Saint Peter's*, 124, 135–136; Scotti, *Basilica*, 35–40.

156 produced a design: Pastor, *History of the Popes*, vol. 6, 464–468.

156 At dawn on April 18, 1506: Ibid., 473–474; Scotti, *Basilica*, 7–10; Rodocanachi, *Histoire de Rome*, 54–55.

157 The wrecking crews: Pastor, *History of the Popes*, vol. 6, 476–480; Lees-Milne, *Saint Peter's*, 142; Klaczko, *Rome and the Renaissance*, 20.

157 an enormous strain on papal finances: Scotti, *Basilica*, 80, 104.

157 Europe's wealthiest institution: On the sources of the Church's wealth, see Scotti, *Basilica*, 68–72; "Papacy," in *Encyclopedia of the Renaissance*.

157 found the coffers nearly empty: Rodocanachi, *Histoire de Rome*, 33; Scotti, *Basilica*, 67.

158 the Roman Curia: Stinger, *Renaissance in Rome*, 123–140; Partner, *Renaissance Rome*, 56–64; D'Amico, *Renaissance Humanism in Papal Rome*, 21ff; "Papacy," in *Encyclopedia of the Renaissance*.

158 The hub of all this: Stinger, *Renaissance in Rome*, 124–128.

158 Agostino Chigi: Pastor, *History of the Popes*, vol. 8, 116–120; Scotti, *Basilica*, 81–83.

159 in the final days of his papacy: Scotti, *Basilica*, 104.

159 "the bright lights": *Collected Works of Erasmus*, vol. 3, 94.

159 "the swill of men": Ibid., vol. 28, 431.

159 an urgent letter: Ibid., vol. 2, no. 215, May 27 [1509], 147–151.

160 Erasmus left: Ibid., 151.

161 He mused on how closely More's name: Ibid., 161.

CHAPTER 10: SELF-RIGHTEOUS JEWS

162 a grave disturbance in his order: Schwiebert, *Luther*, 181; Brecht, *Martin Luther*, 53, 99–100; Marius, *Martin Luther*, 79–80; David Gutierrez, *The Augustinians in the Middle Ages, 1357–1517*, vol. 1, part 2, *History of the Order of St. Augustine* (Villanova: Augustinian Historical Institute, 1983), 11–13, 43–46.

162 on foot: Schwiebert, in *Luther* (181), estimates that on a good day it was possible to cover twenty-five miles on foot.

162 walked one behind the other: Friedenthal, *Luther*, 70; Fife, *Revolt of Martin Luther*, 165–168; Heinrich Bochmer, *Road to Reformation*, 72–77.

163 Luther was impressed: *Luther's Works*, vol. 54, "Table Talk," no. 3930, 296, and no. 3956, 298; Friedenthal, *Luther*, 78.

163 "Hail, sacred Rome": Quoted in Fife, *Revolt of Martin Luther*, 168; original is in *Luthers Werke, Tischreden*, vol. 5, no. 6059, 467.

163 to make a one-day tour: Brecht, *Martin Luther*, 102–103; Friedenthal, *Luther*, 82–83; Boehmer, *Road to Reformation*, 63.

164 "Who knows whether it is true?": Brecht, *Martin Luther*, 103.

164 several unsettling moments: *Luther's Works*, vol. 14, 6; *Luthers Werke, Tischreden*, vol. 3, no. 3428, 313. See also Brecht, *Martin Luther*, 102; Boehmer, *Road to Reformation*, 67; Bainton, *Here I Stand*, 37; Friedenthal, *Luther*, 86; Oberman, *Luther*, 149.

164 also saw St. Peter's: Friedenthal, *Luther*, 83.

165 "madman full of religious zeal": Quoted in Schwiebert, *Luther*, 188; Luther's Works, vol. 14, 6.

165 "Like a fool": *Luthers Werke*, vol. 47, 392.

See also Boehmer, *Road to Reformation*, 80.

165 Wittenberg seemed more a village: Schwiebert, *Luther*, 199–220; Brecht, *Martin Luther*, 107–111.

165 Luther would later remark: Cited in Fife, *Revolt of Martin Luther*, 130.

166 smaller than the one in Erfurt: Brecht, *Martin Luther*, 107, 121.

166 had the right to brew beer: Ibid., 110.

166 "very borderland of civilization": Quoted in Schwiebert, *Luther*, 205.

166 all vied for supremacy: Ibid., 268ff; Maria Grossmann, *Humanism in Wittenberg*, 54, 85; Brecht, *Martin Luther*, 120.

167 remained a stalwart Catholic: Grossmann, *Humanism in Wittenberg*, 25–26; Brecht, *Martin Luther*, 111, 117.

167 forward-looking on cultural ones: Grossmann, *Humanism in Wittenberg*, 116ff; Friedenthal, *Luther*, 69–70.

167 Albrecht Dürer: Grossmann, *Humanism in Wittenberg*, 123.

168 main sources of revenue: Ibid., 34.

168 created a library: Ibid., 100, 109; Schwiebert, *Luther*, 244–253.

168 George Spalatin: See the biographical note in *Luther's Works*, vol. 48, 8. On Spalatin and the library, see Grossmann, *Humanism in Wittenberg*, 105–112; Andrew Pettegree, *Brand Luther*, 44–46.

169 Johann Rhau-Grunenberg: Grossmann, *Humanism in Wittenberg*, 94–98; Pettegree, *Brand Luther*, 42–44.

169 Lucas Cranach the Elder: Grossmann, *Humanism in Wittenberg*, 125–129; Pettegree, *Brand Luther*, 148–163. For a full biographical treatment, see Steven Ozment, *The Serpent and the Lamb: Cranach, Luther, and the Making of the Reformation*.

169 described its citizens as drunken: Grossmann, *Humanism in Wittenberg*, 64.

170 welcomed the numbness: Brecht, *Martin Luther*, 64.

170 confessions steadily lengthened: Ibid., 68.

170 "My conscience": *Luther's Works*, vol. 27, 13, 73.

170 "a damned ungrateful papal ass": Quoted in Fife, *Revolt of Martin Luther*, 145.

171 *Humpelwerk* and *Puppensünde*: Cited in Brecht, *Martin Luther*, 69; "If Christ is to help you": quoted in Friedenthal, *Luther*, 45.

171 tried to expose him: Luther described the impact of Staupitz's instruction in a letter of May 30, 1518, to him, in *Luther's Works*, vol. 48, no. 21, 64–70.

171 Staupitz came up with a plan: *Luthers Werke, Tischreden*, vol. 5, no. 5371, 98; no. 6422, 654. See also Bainton, *Here I Stand*, 45; Boehmer, *Road to Reformation*, 83.

171 from this "poor little room": Quoted in Friedenthal, *Luther*, 94; original is in *Luthers Werke, Tischreden*, vol. 2, nos. 2540a and 2540b, 509–510.

172 became a doctor of theology: Brecht, *Martin Luther*, 127.

172 the first two: As Brecht notes (ibid., 129), it is unclear if Luther gave an earlier set of lectures.

172 the central place these hymns had: "Psalms," in *Encyclopedia of Christianity*.

172 "A precious and beloved book": *Luther's Works*, vol. 35, "Preface to the Psalter," 253–257.

173 "is properly a garden of nuts": *Luther's Works*, vol. 10, "First Lectures on the Psalms I," 257.

173 they were probably composed: Robert Alter, introduction to *The Book of Psalms* (New York: W. W. Norton, 2007), xvi. See also the introduction to the Psalms in *The New Oxford Annotated Bible* (Oxford: Oxford University Press, 2007, augmented third edition), 775–777.

173 Nicholas of Lyra: Jeremy Cohen, *The Friars and the Jews: The Evolution of Medieval Anti-Judaism*, 170–195; Deanna Copeland Klepper, *The Insight of Believers: Nicholas Lyra and Christian*

Readings of Jewish Texts in the Later Middle Ages (Philadelphia: University of Pennsylvania Press, 2007), 1–6, 31.

174 the *Quincuplex Psalterium*: Charles M. Cooper, "Jerome's 'Hebrew Psalter' and the New Latin Version," *Journal of Biblical Literature*, 69(3): 233–244, September 1950.

174 burgeoning new field of Hebraic studies: As both Smalley in *Study of the Bible* (365) and Cohen in *Friars and the Jews* (171–172) point out, there was an earlier flourishing of Hebrew studies among Christians in the thirteenth century.

174 was even more difficult: W. Schwarz, *Principles and Problems of Biblical Translation*, 63–68.

174 hard to come by: Ibid., 67.

174 So were instructors: Ibid., 65.

175 often reluctant to teach Hebrew: Salo Wittmayer Baron, *A Social and Religious History of the Jews*, vol. 13, 165.

175 was thus considered contaminated: Ibid., 164. "Those who study the language become Jews," was how a Freiburg monk put it (as quoted in *The Cambridge History of the Bible*, vol. 3, 43).

175 he had obtained a copy: Grossmann, *Humanism in Wittenberg*, 79. According to David H. Price in *Johannes Reuchlin and the Campaign to Destroy Jewish Books* (213), Luther was one of the most diligent students of Reuchlin's book during the 1510s.

176 present from a very early point: Baron, in *Social and Religious History of the Jews*, vol. 13 (220–221), observes that of his thirty-two years of teaching at Wittenberg, Luther devoted only three or four to the New Testament and the rest to the Hebrew Bible: his lifetime preoccupation with the Old Testament, Baron adds, made him less rather than more friendly to contemporary Jews. Mullett, in *Martin Luther* (52), notes of his lectures on the Psalms that "in this his first major work that has come down to us, Luther initiated the anti-Judaism

that would characterise many of his writings throughout his career."

176 far from occupying: Heiko Oberman, in *The Roots of Anti-Semitism in the Age of Renaissance and Reformation* (94), writes that it is time "we faced the fact that the Jewish question does not occupy a dark corner in Luther's work, but a central place in his theology."

176 Almost single-handedly, Johannes Reuchlin: For biographical information, see Price, *Johannes Reuchlin*; Lewis W. Spitz, *The Religious Renaissance of the German Humanists*, 61–80; "Reuchlin, Johann," in *Contemporaries of Erasmus*.

176 Hebrew, he declared, is simple: Price, *Johannes Reuchlin*, 59.

176 he seemed to see God himself: Cited in Schwarz, *Principles and Problems of Biblical Translation*, 82–83.

177 a learned Jew named Calman: Spitz, *Religious Renaissance of the German Humanists*, 62.

177 A turning point came in 1490: Price, *Johannes Reuchlin*, 64. On Pico and the Kabbalah, see Baron, *Social and Religious History of the Jews*, vol. 13, 174–176.

177 *The Miracle-Working Word*: Spitz, *Religious Renaissance of the German Humanists*, 68–69.

178 Obadiah Sforno: Price, *Johannes Reuchlin*, 67.

178 Reuchlin prepared a rudimentary guide: Ibid., 14, 23, 68–69. Schwarz, in *Principles and Problems of Biblical Translation* (66–67), notes that although a Hebrew grammar had been published a few years earlier by Conradus Pellicanus, it was of poor quality; *De Rudimentis*, he adds, marked the true beginning of Hebrew studies in Europe.

179 Johannes Pfefferkorn: Price, *Johannes Reuchlin*, 95–112.

179 "criminal dogs": Ibid., 106.

179 deprived of their books: Erika Rummel, *The Case Against Johannes Reuchlin*, 9–10.

179 led the anti-Jewish agitation: Price, *Johannes Reuchlin*, 109–110.

180 Pfefferkorn chose Frankfurt: Ibid., 111–112.

180 The Frankfurt city council: H. Graetz, *History of the Jews*, vol. 4, 429–431.

180 supported the confiscations: Price, *Johannes Reuchlin*, 126–127.

181 In a forty-plus page analysis: Johannes Reuchlin, *Recommendation Whether to Confiscate, Destroy, and Burn All Jewish Books*, trans. Peter Wortsman; "I have no doubt," 86.

181 represented an extraordinary moment: Price, *Johannes Reuchlin*, 137, 227ff; Heiko Oberman, "Reuchlin and the Jews: Obstacles on the Path to Emancipation," in *The Impact of the Reformation*, 169–170; Oberman, "Three Sixteenth-Century Attitudes Toward Judaism: Reuchlin, Erasmus, and Luther," in B. D. Cooperman, ed., *Jewish Thought in the Sixteenth Century* (Cambridge, MA: Harvard University Press, 1983), 93; Graetz, *History of the Jews*, vol. 4, 448–449.

181 a distinction they hold to this day: Spitz, *Religious Renaissance of the German Humanists*, 77.

182 another noxious pamphlet: Price, *Johannes Reuchlin*, 141–143.

182 Titled *Augenspiegel*: Graetz, *History of the Jews*, vol. 4, 446–449; Valerie Hotchkiss and David Price, *Miracle Within a Miracle: Johannes Reuchlin and the Jewish Book Controversy*, 15–17.

182 lodged charges of heresy: Price, *Johannes Reuchlin*, 145–146; Hotchkiss and Price, *Miracle Within a Miracle*, 14–15.

182 In his fierce *Defense*: Price, *Johannes Reuchlin*, 148–150.

183 condemned *Augenspiegel*: Ibid., 150–152.

183 issued its judgment: Hotchkiss and Price, *Miracle Within a Miracle*, 18.

183 a letter to the Dutch scholar: *Collected Works of Erasmus*, vol. 2, no. 290, April 1514, 284–285.

184 a deeper reason for Erasmus's reticence: See James H. Overfield, *Humanism and Scholasticism in Late Medieval Germany*, 287–289.

184 "see the entire Old Testament": *Collected Works of Erasmus*, vol. 5, 181.

184 "I see them as a nation": Ibid., 347–348.

184 "I wish he were an entire Jew": Ibid., 179.

185 "This half-Jew Christian": Ibid., no. 713, November 15 [1517], 204.

185 "If it is Christian to detest": Ibid., vol. 7, 49.

185 Erasmus's rancor toward the Jews: There is an extensive literature on this subject. See, for instance, Oberman, *Roots of Anti-Semitism* (38–40), who writes that "the entire body of Erasmus's thought is permeated by a virulent theological anti-Judaism." Hilmar M. Pabel, in "Erasmus of Rotterdam and Judaism: A Reexamination in the Light of New Evidence," *Archiv für Reformationsgeschichte*, 87: 1996, notes (16, 36) that Erasmus in his paraphrases poured "scorn upon Jews and their religion" and showed "an unmistakable hostility towards Judaism." By contrast, Shimon Markish, in *Erasmus and the Jews* (142–143), argues that it is "unfounded to speak of Erasmus' hatred for Jews"; rather, he was indifferent to them. Erasmus's "judeophobic 'eruptions,'" he adds, were few and "incidental" to his work and reflected "not Erasmus' worldview but rather common 'folk' anti-Semitism, a mass psychology alien to and despised by Erasmism." In an extraordinary afterword to Markish's book, Arthur A. Cohen, a Jewish philosopher who helped arrange for it to be translated from Russian into English, argues (146, 154) that Markish unwittingly succeeded "in showing that Erasmus is thoroughly anti-Jewish." Erasmus's anti-Judaism, he added, "was frequently gratuitous, crude, malicious, intemperate, lacking in all that grace and charity with which he otherwise pursued his return to the sources of Christian civilization in the ancient world." Erasmus, Cohen concludes, "is surely

within a grand tradition of contempt and supersession that leads, if not to the crude fulminations of Julius Streicher, then surely through the permutations of secular diabolism straight to the death camps." In seeking to put Markish right, Cohen may be erring in the opposite direction.

185 "the most pernicious plague": *Collected Works of Erasmus*, vol. 4, 267.

185 among its leading purveyors: See Oberman, "Reuchlin and the Jews," 166; Price, *Johannes Reuchlin* 217, 229.

185 the Jews themselves were being purged: "Germany," in *Encyclopaedia Judaica*. Price, in *Johannes Reuchlin* (225), notes that during Reuchlin's lifetime, Jewish communities probably reached the lowest point of their historical decline prior to the Holocaust, with only about one-eighth of the urban Jewish communities of the year 1400 still existing in 1520. As Arthur A. Cohen notes in Markish, *Erasmus and the Jews* (148), "every thinker of the northern Renaissance was to a more or less significant degree anti-Semitic."

186 the one Christian country: Jeremy Cohen, *Friars and the Jews*, 159.

186 He knew few actual Jews: Marius, *Luther*, 372; E. Gordon Rupp, *Martin Luther and the Jews* (London: Council of Christians and Jews, 1972), 10; Ronny Kabus, *Juden der Lutherstadt Wittenberg im III. Reich* (Elbe-Druckerei Wittenberg GMbH, 2003), 8.

186 a popular motif in German-speaking lands: Frederick M. Schweitzer, "Medieval Perceptions of Jews and Judaism," in Marvin Perry, ed., *Jewish-Christian Encounters over the Centuries: Symbiosis, Prejudice, Holocaust, Dialogue* (New York: Peter Lang, 1994), 155–156.

186 Spalatin sought Luther's opinion: Brecht, *Martin Luther*, 162.

186 In his letter: *Luther's Works*, vol. 48, no. 3, to George Spalatin, August 5, 1514, 8–11.

187 "The first psalm speaks": Ibid., vol. 10, "First Lectures on the Psalms," I, 11.

187 fundamentally about Christ: In his preface to his notes on the Psalms, Luther wrote that "every prophecy and every prophet must be understood as referring to Christ the Lord, except where it is clear from plain words that someone else is spoken of." Ibid., 7.

187 The "man," Luther wrote: Ibid., 11.

187 "This is what the Jews": Ibid., 12.

187 "that death-dealing doctrine": Ibid., 13.

187 mediate on vanities: Ibid., 17, 19, 18.

188 set up their own righteousness: Ibid., 28.

188 "did not set up his own righteousness": Ibid., 26–27.

188 an arresting paradox: Ibid., 31, 34.

189 only a handful of them: As calculated by David Nirenberg in *Anti-Judaism: The Western Tradition*, 254.

189 "look for an exclusively human deliverance": *Luther's Works*, vol. 10, 227–228, 394.

190 audience consisted mostly: Ibid., 8.

190 "a man of middle stature": Quoted in Wilhelm Pauck, introduction to *Luther: Lectures on Romans*, lxi–lxii.

190 "Earrings": *Luther's Works*, vol. 10, 189; "goats," 320; "frog," vol. 11, "First Lectures on the Psalms," II, 75; "curdled mountains," vol. 10, 336.

190 that he was righteous: Ibid., vol. 11, 172–174.

191 he suggested that the faithful: Ibid., vol. 11, 534.

CHAPTER 11: A BLUEPRINT FOR EUROPE

192 stayed with Thomas More: *Collected Works of Erasmus*, vol. 2, 161. Erasmus described the More household in a sketch of his friend, vol. 7, 16–25.

192 the excitement sweeping England: Jasper Ridley, *Henry VIII*, 35–36, 41; Alison Weir, *Henry VIII: King and Court*, 1–3.

192 a "golden age": Miller, *Complete Works of St. Thomas More*, vol. 3, part 2, 113–115.

193 Henry was widely read: Ridley, *Henry VIII*, 39; Weir, *Henry VIII*, 128; J. J. Scarisbrick, *Henry VIII*, 12–17 ("a pretty woman," 13).

193 forced to remain indoors: *Collected Works of Erasmus*, vol. 2, 161.

193 The *Praise of Folly*: Dolan, *Essential Erasmus*, 98–173; "The fellow who kisses," 112, Old women, "so like corpses," 121–122; "What divorces," 113; "because they have gold rings," 137; "what could be more enjoyable," 128; "a lock of goat's wool," 142; the British take pride, 132; "Why should I go on," 132; Thomists, Nominalists, 144, 152; Did divine generation, 143–144; "magnificent creatures," 148–151; reproaches bishops, 156; "a great many copyists," 157; buffoons who calculate, 129, 147, 165, 144; Jesus could have mounted a lion, 168; "whom the ardor of religion," 169; "suffer from something akin to madness," 172; "that is not quite coherent," 172.

197 first bestselling work: *Collected Works of Erasmus*, vol. 27, 78–82; Smith, *Erasmus*, 123–125.

197 disappears from the historical record: Allen, *Age of Erasmus*, 143.

197 "two lost years": See J. K. Sowards, "The Two Lost Years of Erasmus: Summary, Review, and Speculation," *Studies in the Renaissance* 9 (1962): 161–186.

198 in the City: Roy Porter, *London: A Social History*, 26ff, 42.

198 the impact of the new economic system: Philip Hughes, *The Reformation in England*, vol. 1, 7–19, 28–29; E. Lipson, *The Economic History of England*, vol. 2, *The Age of Mercantilism*, 3rd ed., 1–93; Eleanora Carus-Wilson, "The Woolen Industry," in *The Cambridge Economic History of Europe*, vol. 2, *Trade and Industry in the Middle Ages*, 413–416, 420–428.

198 "so rich and full of silver vessels": Quoted in R. W. Chambers, *Thomas More*, 105.

199 The binding agent: On its influence, see Stephen Inwood, *A History of London* (London: Macmillan, 1998), 138–144; Maynard Smith, *Pre-Reformation England*, chap. 2, "The State of the Church," 11–90.

199 "the ringing isle": Maynard Smith, *Pre-Reformation England*, 105; "abbey lubbers," 205.

199 Old St. Paul's: William Bonham and Charles Welch, *Medieval London* (The Portfolio, London, no. 42, November 1901), 16; Inwood, *History of London*, 142; Ann Saunders, *St. Paul's: The Story of the Cathedral* (London: Collins and Brown, 2001), 16.

200 ecclesiastical power seem greater: Maynard Smith, *Pre-Reformation England*, 11.

200 chipping away at it: The case for Erasmus's influence on the English Reformation is most fully laid out by James Kelsey McConica in *English Humanists and Reformation Politics Under Henry VIII and Edward VI*, (2–4, 12, 42–43, 280). Erasmianism, he argues, won the allegiance of "the whole English humanist community in the years before the crisis of the royal divorce" and through it had a strong impact on English thinking as a whole. J. J. Scarisbrick, in *The Reformation and the English People* (47), observes that while "Erasmianism did not necessarily radicalize," it "undoubtedly helped to undermine the old order nonetheless." See also A. G. Dickens and Whitney R. D. Jones, *Erasmus the Reformer*, chap. 9, "The English Erasmians," 193–216.

200 London's most outspoken prelate: Seebohm, *Oxford Reformers*, 83–86; Maynard Smith, *Pre-Reformation England*, 454–456.

200 two early manuscripts: *Collected Works of Erasmus*, vol. 3, 198. On the New Testament manuscripts that Erasmus used in England, see Andrew J. Brown, "The Manuscript Sources and Textual

Character of Erasmus' 1516 Greek New Testament," in *Basel 1516: Erasmus' Edition of the New Testament*, Martin Wallraff, Silvana Seidel Menchi, Kaspar von Greyerz, eds., 130–137.

200 a more systematic collation: Erika Rummel describes the process in *Erasmus' Annotations on the New Testament*, 109–111.

200 Colet had decided: John Gleason, *John Colet*, 220–223, 228–230; J. H. Lupton, *The Life of John Colet, D.D.: Dean of St. Paul's and Founder of St. Paul's School*, 154–177.

201 *De Copia: Collected Works of Erasmus*, vol. 24, 296–659; "an ugly and offensive fault," 302; "Your letter pleased me mightily," 348ff; "Always, as long as I live," 354ff.

201 would in fact lampoon Erasmus: See Mack, "Humanist Rhetoric and Dialectic," in Kraye, *The Cambridge Companion to Renaissance Humanism*, 93.

201 eighty-five editions: *Collected Works of Erasmus*, vol. 2, 225, and vol. 24, 283.

202 *De Ratione Studii*: Ibid., vol. 24, 665–691; "almost everything worth learning," 667.

202 proposed an alternative: Ibid., 669; "the extremely elegant arbiter," 670.

202 history was to be learned: See Smith, *Erasmus*, 305–307.

202 would become the basis: William Harrison Woodward, *Studies in Education During the Age of the Renaissance*, vol. 2, 104–126; T. W. Baldwin, *William Shakspere's Small Latine & Lesse Greeke*, vol. 1, 94, 99, 130, 179. ("Shakspere" is his spelling.) J. K. Sowards, "Erasmus and the Apologetic Textbook," *Studies in Philology* 55: 122–135, 1958.

203 "Without Erasmus": Baldwin, *William Shakspere's Small Latine*, vol. 1, 116.

203 "we teach nothing but the classics": Quoted in Jonathan Gathorne-Hardy, *The Public School Phenomenon*, 31.

203 Leonard Woolf: Leonard Woolf, *Sowing: An Autobiography of the Years 1880–1904*, 79, 213–214, 80–81, 84, 96–97.

203 prove so stultifying: Baldwin, in *William Shakspere's Small Latine*, vol. 1, 163, writes that the Erasmian system was "simple but inhumanly thorough—at least on paper. No wonder the master had to flog the boys throughout. One wonders how a human being, either teacher or boy, endured it. . . . Education! Education! What crimes are committed in thy name!"

203 Latin would become entombed: Gathorne-Hardy, *Public School Phenomenon*, 30–31.

204 education of the common man: Commenting on the many "barbarous languages" in use, Erasmus (*Collected Works of Erasmus*, vol. 26, 390) wrote that "it is important for scholars to confine themselves to those languages that have almost exclusively been used in learned writing. The reason is that they do not depend for their guarantee on ordinary people. The people are poor custodians of quality."

204 failed to develop a broad social base: Louise Holborn, in "Printing and the Growth of a Protestant Movement in Germany from 1517 to 1524," *Church History*, 11(2): June 1942, observes (125–26) that "none of the writings of the humanist groups had a decisive or even kindling effect on the people in general. The chief reason was that these writers wrote only for scholars and thus used the Latin language almost exclusively. Some of their writings were translated into German and in this form were read by larger groups," but "their dignified skepticism and constantly critical tone did not kindle enthusiasm, while their rough satire awoke only a temporary exhilaration." See also Smith, *Erasmus* (305), on Erasmus's preoccupation with the training of an elite.

204 a letter sent from Dover: *Collected Works of Erasmus*, vol. 2, no. 218, to Andrea Ammonio, April 10 [1511], 155–157.

204 always received cordially: *Collected Works of Erasmus*, vol. 2, 298.

205 Erasmus lived in a room: For an overview of Erasmus's time in Cambridge, see D. F. S. Thomson and H. C. Porter, *Erasmus and Cambridge: the Cambridge Letters of Erasmus*.

205 "nods and gestures": *Collected Works of Erasmus*, vol. 2, 187.

205 the everyday Erasmus: Or, as one writer put it, the letters show Erasmus "in slippers" (quoted in Thomson and Porter, *Erasmus and Cambridge*, 65).

205 "If you are in a position": *Collected Works of Erasmus*, vol. 2, no. 226, August 25, 1511, 169.

205 "everyone is running away": Ibid., no. 278, October 31 [1513], 260.

206 "is a lonely place for me": Ibid., no. 282, to Andrea Ammonio, November 28 [1513], 266.

206 "I cannot without anguish": Ibid., no. 253, 214.

206 faring little better with his lectures: Ibid., no. 233, to Andrea Ammonio, October 16, 1511, 176–177; Thomson and Porter, *Erasmus and Cambridge*, 38–39.

206 "the most unbeatable": *Collected Works of Erasmus*, vol. 2, no. 237, to John Colet, October 29 [1511], 183.

206 "I often curse": Ibid., no. 241, to Roger Wentford [November 1511?], 196.

206 several important manuscripts: Thomson and Porter, *Erasmus and Cambridge*, 47–48; *Collected Works of Erasmus*, vol. 3, 217; Bentley, *Humanists and Holy Writ*, 125–126; A. J. Brown, "The Manuscript Sources," in Wallraff, *Basel 1516*, 130–131.

206 "inspired by some god": *Collected Works of Erasmus*, vol. 2, 253.

206 "half eaten away and mutilated": These observations are from a dedicatory letter to the Jerome edition in *Collected Works of Erasmus*, vol. 3, no. 396, April 1, 1516, 260–261.

207 Erasmus had some reservations: Ibid., vol. 3, 63–68. This letter is the preface to Erasmus's edition of Seneca's *Lucubrationes*, published in August 1515.

207 the great gulf: See Mary Beard, "How Stoical Was Seneca?" in *New York Review of Books*, October 9, 2014 (available at www.nybooks.com/articles/2014/10/09 /how-stoical-was-seneca/); Robin Campbell, introduction to Seneca's *Letters from a Stoic*, 7–26.

207 Gaining access to two ancient manuscripts: *Collected Works of Erasmus*, vol. 3, 65.

208 "brought philosophy down from heaven to earth": Ibid., vol. 11, 104–105.

208 "How to Distinguish a Flatterer": Ibid., vol. 2, 249–250.

208 dedicated the translation to Henry VIII: Ibid., no. 272 [July 1513], 250–252.

209 "how things are in Italy": Ibid., no. 233 [October 16, 1511], 177.

209 Ammonio informed him: Ibid., no. 236, October 27, 1511, 179–182; no. 239, November 8, 1511, 188–190.

209 "What you tell me": Ibid., no. 240, November 11 [1511], 192.

209 "in the ascendant": Ibid., no. 247, November 28 [1511], 206–207.

209 liked to linger at his palace: Weir, *Henry VIII*, 11; Ridley, *Henry VIII*, 46.

210 The price of everything: *Collected Works of Erasmus*, vol. 2, no. 288, to Antoon van Bergen, March 14, 1514, 279.

210 "I cannot tell you": Ibid., no. 265 [Autumn 1512], 235.

210 Colet chastised the English clergy: Seebohm, *Oxford Reformers*, 142–157; Adams, *Better Part of Valor*, 65–66.

211 Colet boldly denounced: See Erasmus's account in *Collected Works of Erasmus*, vol. 8, 242–243.

211 English army departed: Scarisbrick, *Henry VIII*, 33–39; Weir, *Henry VIII*, 162.

212 "We are shut in": *Collected Works of Erasmus*, vol. 2, no. 283, December 2 [1513], 272.

212 a long, impassioned letter: Ibid., no. 288, March 14, 1514, 278–283.

213 to arouse the public: Adams, *Better Part of Valor*, 90.

213 War, he maintained: "War," in *Augustine Through the Ages*, Allan D. Fitzgerald (Grand Rapids, MI: William B. Eerdmans Pub., 1991); Roland Bainton, *Christian Attitudes Toward War and Peace: A Historical Survey and Critical Reevaluation*, 96–97.

213 "on account of some fault": *Summa Theologica*, Second Part of the Second Part, Question 40, Article 1.

213 "Two armies advance": Barker, *Adages of Erasmus*, 328–329; "forbad anyone," 334; "why should you prefer," 345; "the sure marks of Christians," 346; "if they attack us," 349; if "you have left nothing untried," 352.

215 ran through the revised *Adages*: See Phillips, *"Adages" of Erasmus*, 35.

215 *A mortuo tributum exigere*: Barker, *Adages of Erasmus*, 119–124; *Spartam nactus es, hanc orna*, 183–191; *Scarabaeus aquilam quaerit*, 281–315.

215 *Sileni Alcibiadis*: Ibid., 241–268; "a divine being," 244; "what a treasure," 245.

216 had made enough progress: *Collected Works of Erasmus*, vol. 2, 292.

216 William Warham had arranged: Ibid., 216; Smith, *Erasmus*, 69–70.

216 As he boarded his boat: *Collected Works of Erasmus*, vol. 2, 292–293.

CHAPTER 12: THE GATE TO PARADISE

217 elected district vicar: *Luther's Works*, vol. 48, no. 5, May 29, 1516, 14–16; like being the prior of eleven monasteries, no. 10, to John Lang, October 26, 1516, 28.

217 "This made my head split": Ibid., vol. 54, "Table Talk," no. 495, 85.

218 lectures were due to start: See Pauck,

introduction to *Luther: Lectures on Romans*, xix–xx.

218 famous autobiographical fragment: Dillenberger, *Martin Luther: Selections*, 10–12.

219 led Reformation scholars to search: For a summary of the debate, see Alister McGrath, *Luther's Theology of the Cross*, 141–147. The encyclopedia *Religion Past and Present*, in its entry on Luther, notes that the conjectured dates of Luther's breakthrough fall into two groups—those favoring an early dating (between 1512 and 1515/1516) and a later group centered on 1518, with a consensus eventually forming that places his discovery in 1515/1516, with its consequences becoming clear between 1517 and 1520.

219 a remarkable scholarly find: Described in Pauck, *Luther: Lectures on Romans*, xxi–xxiv; Friedenthal, *Luther*, 103.

221 considered indisputably his: *Dictionary of Paul and His Letters*, 838.

221 most reliable sources of information: Günther Bornkamm, *Paul, Paulus*, xiv.

221 "The most profound work in existence": T. Ashe, ed., *The Table Talk and Omniana of Samuel Taylor Coleridge* (London: G. Bell and Sons, 1888), 228.

222 Paul, though, had a very different background: On the life of Paul, see Bornkamm, *Paul*; Michael Grant, *Saint Paul*; A. N. Wilson, *Paul: The Mind of the Apostle*; "Paul," in *The Anchor Bible Dictionary*.

222 "zealous" for the faith: Galatians 1:14.

224 three such journeys: See *The Harper Atlas of the Bible* (New York: Harper and Row, 1987), 172–175; "Paul," in *Anchor Bible Dictionary*, 188–189. For an evocative account of Paul's journeys, see H. V. Morton, *In the Steps of St. Paul*.

224 he covered nearly ten thousand miles: Wayne A. Meeks, *The First Urban Christians: The Social World of the Apostle Paul* (New Haven: Yale University Press, 1983), 16–18.

224 "Five times I have received": 2 Corinthians 11:24–27; For the sake of Christ, Philippians 3:8.

224 thorn in the flesh: 2 Corinthians 12:7; "Wretched man that I am!" Romans 7:24; "I do not do," Romans 7:19.

225 went to Jerusalem: Some, including Bornkamm (*Paul*, 31ff), believe that this visit occurred before the first missionary journey. The principal account of the meeting is Galatians 2:1–10.

225 By lifting the requirement of circumcision: Baron, *Social and Religious History of the Jews*, vol. 2, 86.

227 arrived in Ephesus: The well-preserved ruins of this town give modern-day visitors a good sense of the world in which Paul moved.

228 "I am astonished": Galatians 1:6; "let that one be accursed!" 1:9; "We ourselves are Jews," 2:15–16; "under a curse," 3:10; "for in Christ Jesus," 3:26; "a yoke of slavery," 5:1; "would castrate themselves!" 5:12; "For the whole law," 5:14.

229 the Magna Carta of Christian liberty: See, for instance, Grant, *Saint Paul*, 96, 99; Bornkamm, *Paul*, 115.

229 "Do not be deceived!": 1 Corinthians 6:9; "it is better to marry," 7:9; condemned divorce, 7:12; "shameful" for women, 14:35; "If there is anything," 14:35; "If I speak in the tongues," 13:1–2.

230 The Epistle to the Romans: For an overview of its main points, see *Dictionary of Paul and His Letters*, 838–850.

230 denounce the ungodly: Romans 1:26–32; "by patiently doing good," 2: 6–8; "the hearers of the law," 2:13; since all have sinned, 3:23–28.

231 has perplexed scholars: *Dictionary of Paul and His Letters*, 844.

232 "do not persist in unbelief": Romans 11:23.

232 should love one another: Romans 12:9–12; "Bless those who persecute you," 12:14–16; If your enemies are hungry, 12:20; "Owe no one anything," 13:8; "let every person be subject," 13:1.

232 a follower writing in his name: *The Anchor Bible Dictionary*, vol. 3, 622–623.

232 "but fails in one point": James 2:10; "is justified by works and not by faith alone," 2:24; "What good is it," 2:14–17; "Religion that is pure and undefiled," 1:27.

233 the difference between the Pauline and Jamesian approaches: Grant, *Saint Paul*, 92.

233 Before leaving for Rome: The main source for the remainder of Paul's life is Acts 20 to 28.

234 in the resulting vacuum: Grant, *Saint Paul*, 168–171, 186, 192; Jeffrey J. Bütz, *The Brother of Jesus and the Lost Teachings of Christianity*, 100, 171, 178; Baron, *Social and Religious History of the Jews*, vol. 2, 82–83.

235 was eventually included: According to *The Anchor Bible Dictionary* (vol. 3, 621), the epistle became part of the New Testament canon in the latter part of the fourth century.

235 Erasmus in the *Enchiridion*: Dolan, *Essential Erasmus*, 93.

235 Jacques Lefèvre d'Étaples: MacCulloch, *Reformation*, 108.

235 Luther had a copy of Lefèvre's translation: Mullett, *Martin Luther*, 58; Pauck, introduction to *Luther: Lectures on Romans*, xxx. Preserved Smith, in "Luther's Development of the Doctrine of Justification by Faith Only," *Harvard Theological Review*, 6(4): 413–414, October 1913, writes that it is "certain that Luther took his most famous doctrine bodily from Lefèvre."

236 "The sum and substance": Pauck, *Luther: Lectures on Romans*, 3–5; "praise themselves in their hearts," 3; the four stages of perdition, 25–26; the threefold way, 31; "separated unto the gospel," 10.

236 Luther observes that Paul: Ibid., 101.

236 to offer a parable: Ibid.

237 it is either a "whole faith": Ibid., 102–103; "So it has been determined," 109.

237 always retain some inclination toward evil: Ibid., 114, 118–119.

237 the "thousand tricks": Ibid, 121.

238 "to the foolish enterprise": Ibid.

238 Man, Luther observed: Ibid.

238 finally found the idea: Mullett, in *Martin Luther* (60–61), points specifically to these verses in Romans as the place of Luther's breakthrough. Alister McGrath in *The Intellectual Origins of the European Reformation* (162) and Smith in "Luther's Development of the Doctrine of Justification" (420), though less specific, similarly date Luther's breakthrough to 1515 or early 1516.

238 they had taught that original sin: Pauck, *Luther: Lectures on Romans*, 128.

239 "O you fools": Ibid., 129.

239 "I have been in the grind": Ibid., 236.

239 foolish perverters: Ibid., 131, 129; *iustitiarii*, 266.

239 "every teaching that prescribes": Ibid., 197; "who have turned the gospel," 199.

239 "bitter and hard": Ibid., 247.

240 seems to have omitted: See Pauck, introduction, *Luther: Lectures on Romans*, xviii, lxii.

CHAPTER 13: ANNUS MIRABILIS

241 causing Erasmus to wrench his back: *Collected Works of Erasmus*, vol. 3, 9–11.

241 Erasmus was astonished: Ibid., 12–15; Smith, *Erasmus*, 129–130, 136–137.

241 appended a prefatory address: *Collected Works of Erasmus*, vol. 3, 12.

242 this tidy town: On Basel, see Hans R. Guggisberg, *Basel in the Sixteenth Century: Aspects of the City Republic Before, During, and After the Reformation*, 3–11; Earle Hilgert, "Johann Froben and the Basel University Scholars, 1513–1523," *Library Quarterly*, 41(2): 141–161, April 1971; Smith, *Erasmus*, 138; *Collected Works of Erasmus*, vol. 40,

1122–1123; Phillips, *Erasmus and the Northern Renaissance*, 56; Wallraff, *Basel 1516*, preface, x–xi.

242 start of a partnership: *Collected Works of Erasmus*, vol. 61, xix.

242 "I seem to myself": Ibid., vol. 3, 243–244.

243 took charge of the first four: Ibid., vol. 61, xxii; Rice, *Jerome in the Renaissance*, 118–130.

243 "I believe that the writing": *Collected Works of Erasmus*, vol. 3, no. 396, to William Warham, April 1, 1516, 252–266; quote, 262.

243 a "Life of Jerome": Ibid., vol. 61, 19–62. See also Harbison, *Christian Scholar*, 94; Rice, *Jerome in the Renaissance*, 130–136.

243 "Who ever drew Sacred Scripture": *Collected Works of Erasmus*, vol. 61, 52–53.

244 preparing his material on the New Testament: For a description of Erasmus's work on the New Testament in Basel, see the long note in *Collected Works of Erasmus*, vol. 3, 216–221; Rummel, *Erasmus' Annotations*, 18–26, 121; J. K. Elliott, " 'Novum Testamentum editum est': The Five-Hundredth Anniversary of Erasmus's New Testament," *Bible Translator*, 67(1): 9–28, 2016. It is not exactly clear when Erasmus decided to undertake a new translation of the New Testament. Some argue that he began it while in England, prior to his trip to Basel; others believe that he embarked on it only after his arrival there. See Andrew J. Brown, "The Date of Erasmus' Latin Translation of the New Testament," *Transactions of the Cambridge Bibliographical Society*, 8(4): 351–380, 1984; H. J. de Jonge, "The Date and Purpose of Erasmus's *Castigato Novi Testamenti*: A Note on the Origins of the *Novum Instrumentum*," in *The Uses of Greek and Latin: Historical Essays*, A. C. Dionisotti, Anthony Grafton, and Jill Kraye, eds., 97–110; H. J. de Jonge, "Erasmus's Translation of the

New Testament: Aim and Method,"
Bible Translator, 67(1): 29–41, 2016;
Mark Vessey, "Basel 1514: Erasmus'
Critical Turn," in Wallraff, *Basel 1516*,
16–25. Erasmus himself would later
write (*Collected Works of Erasmus*, vol. 9,
311) that the idea for the new translation
originated with members of the house
of Froben, who pressed it on him; in so
maintaining, however, he may have been
trying to deflect responsibility for the
controversial project.

244 the Complutensian Polyglot: Bentley,
Humanists and Holy Writ, 70–111;
Metzger, *Text of the New Testament*,
96–98.

244 had a half-dozen codices: See Patrick
Andrist, "Structure and History of the
Biblical Manuscripts Used by Erasmus
for His 1516 Edition," 81–124, and
Andrew J. Brown, "The Manuscript
Sources," 125–144, in Wallraff, *Basel
1516*.

245 Erasmus wrote to him: *Collected Works of
Erasmus*, vol. 3, no. 300 [August 1514],
5–8; the note on 7–8 offers information
about the codices in question.

245 in a letter to Jacob Wimpfeling: Ibid., no.
305, 32.

245 a sudden trip to England: Ibid., vol. 3,
77.

245 "Froben is asking": Ibid., vol. 3, no. 328,
April 17, 1515, 79–82.

246 an ominous letter: Ibid., vol. 3, no. 304
[September 1514], 17–23.

247 a strongly worded (and long-winded)
reply: Ibid., vol. 3, no. 337 [end of May]
1515, 111–139; "peevish pedantry," 116;
to offer "guidance," 115; "poke fun at
Greek," 122; "abandon Christ," 136.

248 annus mirabilis: Ibid., vol. 4, xi.

248 the revised New Testament: For an
overview of Erasmus's work on this project,
see ibid., vol. 3, no. 373, "To the Reader,"
195–205 (the preface to his annotations),
along with the introductory note.

248 Among the manuscripts: On the
manuscripts of the New Testament used

by Erasmus, see ibid., vol. 3, no. 384,
"To Leo X" (the preface to his New
Testament), including the introductory
note, 216–224. See also the introduction
by Andrew J. Brown to *Opera Omnia
Desiderii Erasmi*, 6(2): 1–9.

249 Far more important: See Henk Jan de
Jonge, "Novum Testamentum a Nobis
Versum: The Essence of Erasmus'
Edition of the New Testament," *Journal
of Theological Studies*, n.s., 35, part 2:
394–412, October 1984.

249 Where there were textual corruptions:
Bentley, *Humanists and Holy Writ*, 148–
152; de Jonge, "Erasmus's Translation of
the New Testament," *Bible Translator*,
37–40.

249 "they had learned Greek": Quoted in
Rummel, *Erasmus' Annotations*, 140.

249 were his annotations: For an extended
analysis, see ibid., 89–121.

249 lack of consistency in translation: Ibid.,
96.

249 in the first chapter of John: *Opera Omnia
Desiderii Erasmi*, 6(6): 46.

249 Erasmus salted his annotations: See
Rummel, *Erasmus' Annotations*, 31–33;
Bentley, *Humanists and Holy Writ*,
187–188; Smith, *Erasmus*, 172–173.

250 Ephesians 5:32: *Opera Omnia Desiderii
Erasmi*, 6(9): 254. See also John B.
Payne, *Erasmus: His Theology of the
Sacraments*, 112–113.

250 Romans 5:12: *Collected Works of
Erasmus*, vol. 56, "Annotations on
Romans," 139ff. For the Latin, see *Opera
Omnia Desiderii Erasmi*, 6(7): 136–139.
See also Bentley, *Humanists and Holy
Writ*, 170–172; Robert Coogan, *Erasmus,
Lee, and the Correction of the Vulgate: The
Shaking of the Foundations*, 35; *Collected
Works of Erasmus*, vol. 76, xxvii.

250 this passage had become the foundation:
Lohse, *Short History of Christian
Doctrine*, 113.

250 struck at the cult of the Virgin Mary:
Opera Omnia Desiderii Erasmi, 6(5):
458. See also Bentley, *Humanists and*

Holy Writ, 169–170; Rummel, *Erasmus'*
Annotations, 167–168.

251 his handling of 1 John 5:7: *Opera
Omnia Desiderii Erasmi*, 6(10): 540.
See also Bentley, *Humanists and
Holy Writ*, 152–153; H. J. de Jonge,
"Erasmus and the *Comma Johanneum*,"
*Extrait des Ephemerides Theologicae
Lovanienses*, 56(4): 381–389, 1980;
Grantley McDonald, "Erasmus and the
Johannine Comma (1 John 5.7–8)," *Bible
Translator*, 67(1): 42–55, 2016.

251 It came at Matthew 3:2: *Opera Omnia
Desiderii Erasmi*, 6(5): 110. See also
Bentley *Humanists and Holy Writ*, 169;
C. A. L. Jarrott, "Erasmus' Biblical
Humanism," *Studies in the Renaissance*,
17:125–126, 1970; Smith, *Erasmus*, 167–
168; Rummel, *Erasmus'* Annotations,
152–153.

252 "Christ's words": *Opera Omnia Desiderii
Erasmi*, 6(5): 516. See also Rummel,
Erasmus' Annotations, 143.

252 In a note to 1 Timothy 1:6: Rummel,
Erasmus' Annotations, 143.

252 "was undeniably a saint": *Opera Omnia
Desiderii Erasmi*, 6(6): 170–174. See also
Rummel, *Erasmus'* Annotations, 59.

252 even sharper toward Aquinas: Rummel,
Erasmus' Annotations, 77–80; Bentley,
Humanists and Holy Writ, 175.

253 faced a delicate problem: *Collected Works
of Erasmus*, vol. 3, 219; Metzger, *Text
of the New Testament*, 99; A. J. Brown,
introduction to *Opera Omnia Desiderii
Erasmi*, 6(4): 3–21.

253 two presses were devoted full-time:
Collected Works of Erasmus, vol. 3, 216.
Erasmus describes the haste in which
the process was carried out in a letter
to Guillaume Budé, vol. 3, no. 421
[June 19, 1516], 305–306.

253 "among the clanging of the presses":
Quoted in Rummel, *Erasmus'*
Annotations, 25.

253 was "rushed into print": *Collected Works
of Erasmus*, vol. 3, 273.

254 a messenger from Duke Ernst: Ibid., 295.

254 a *Paraclesis*: The text is in John C.
Olin, ed., *Christian Humanism and
the Reformation: Selected Writings
of Erasmus*, 97–108; Platonists,
Pythagoreans, 99; "which offer the
most certain," 99; "as if the strength"
and "published as openly as possible,"
101; "I would that even the lowliest,"
101; "since it is nothing" and "is indeed
truly a theologian," 102.

255 At bottom, the *Paraclesis*: For an analysis
of its importance, see Phillips, *Erasmus
and the Northern Renaissance*, 62–65.

255 the New Testament was done: *Collected
Works of Erasmus*, vol. 3, 216.

255 dedication to Pope Leo X: Ibid.,
221–224.

255 a milestone in biblical scholarship:
Bentley, in *Humanists and Holy Writ*
(193), writes that "in Erasmus' work,
modern New Testament scholarship
and scholarly methods took their first
great leap forward, and this was perhaps
the most enduring of all the legacies
Erasmus bequeathed to his cultural
heirs." Coogan, in *Erasmus, Lee, and
the Correction of the Vulgate* (15), calls
Erasmus's New Testament "the greatest
achievement of Christian humanism
in the Renaissance." *The Cambridge
History of the Bible* (vol. 2, 493) says that
Erasmus "represents that first flowering
of New Testament exegesis, based on
criticism and philology, through which
the Renaissance . . . was to prepare
the way for modern exegesis." And
Smith, in *Erasmus* (159), calls his New
Testament "the effective beginning of
that philological criticism of the Bible
that, after so hard a battle, has at last
done so much to free Christendom from
the bondage of superstition and of the
letter." See also Marijke H. de Lang,
"'Fidelius, apertius, significantius': The
New Testament Translated and Edited
by Erasmus of Rotterdam, 1516," *Bible
Translator*, 67(1): 5–8, 2016.

256 "You have protected your name":

Collected Works of Erasmus, vol. 3, no. 409, May 20, 1516, 287–288.

256 "all scholars and true Christians": Ibid., vol. 4, no. 495 [end November 1516], 156–158, and no. 500 [about December 1516], 165.

256 the tribute he received from John Colet: Ibid., vol. 3, no. 423, June 20 [1516], 311–313.

256 still in the presses: Ibid., vol. 3, 288; vol. 27, introductory note to *The Education of a Christian Prince*, 200.

257 "The number of horses": Ibid., vol. 3, no. 412 [c. June 3, 1516], 290–293.

257 found the Jerome on sale there: Ibid., vol. 4, 94.

257 obtain a papal dispensation: Ibid., vol. 4, 188–190.

257 received from Thomas More: Ibid., vol. 4, no. 461, September 3 [1516], 66–68.

257 had completed *The Prince*: This work was completed by December 1513 but not published until 1532.

258 "Only those who dedicate themselves": *Collected Works of Erasmus*, vo. 27, 222; the quality of its schools, 259; Taxation should be kept low, 260–261; "to prevent the wealth," 261; The penalties for crimes, 266; establish public institutions, 267; boost the economy, 280–281; Rather than undertake costly tours, 260; enlarging his retinue, 261; "this long-standing and terrible mania," 287.

258 Machiavelli had witnessed: Miles J. Unger, *Machiavelli: A Biography*, 137, 182.

258 "A man who strives": Daniel Donno, trans., *The Prince*, 62; Ideally, a prince would be both, 66; "a prince must have no other objective," 59; "characteristic fierceness and haste," 93; "It is better to be impetuous," 94. (The translation of the last quotation has been slightly altered for clarity.)

259 Everyone lives in one: Paul Turner, trans., *Utopia*, 70; Everyone farms, 75–76; no wine taverns, 84; no private property, 73; everyone is watched, 84;

disapprove of cosmetics, 105; see no value in gems, 87–89; use silver and gold, 86; have no tailors, 75; also have slaves, 101–102.

260 had no actual political experience: See Unger, *Machiavelli*, 221–223.

260 would appear in fifteen editions: See Universal Short Title Catalogue (ustc .ac.uk/index.php). Alister E. McGrath, in *A Life of John Calvin: A Study in the Shaping of Western Culture* (55), notes that in 1515 the *Enchiridion* suddenly became a cult work.

261 A new era of enlightenment: Harbison, in *Christian Scholar* (88), observes that the years immediately following the appearance of Erasmus's New Testament "marked the moment of most enraptured hope among a few in Europe that the deep-rooted evils of the day were about to yield before the onslaught of a little company of devoted and enlightened Christian scholars." Huizinga, in *Erasmus* (99), writes that Erasmus "had become the international pivot on which the civilization of his age hinged."

261 "Everywhere in all Christendom": *Collected Works of Erasmus*, vol. 4, no. 450 [c. August 13, 1516], 36.

261 "The devotees of literature": Ibid., vol. 3, no. 399, April 11, 1516, 269.

261 Thomas More wrote to warn: Ibid., vol. 4, no. 481, October 31 [1516], 114–117.

261 Wolfgang Capito: Ibid., vol. 4, no. 459, September 2, 1516, 58–65.

262 was even more flawed: A. J. Brown, in the introduction to *Opera Omnia, Desiderii Erasmi*, 6(4) (page 7), writes that in the Apocalypse (Revelation), "many readings which had little or no attestation from Greek manuscripts became established in the *Textus Receptus*, and forms of wording which Erasmus himself had originated were mistakenly accepted as authentic and given the status of divinely inspired scripture." Many of Erasmus's textual changes in the Apocalypse, he adds (11), "were of poor quality." Nonetheless, "it

remains true that many other of Erasmus' textual choices were successful." He goes on to cite (20–21) fifty passages in Erasmus's Greek New Testament that seem to have "originated in the mind of Erasmus and did not belong to the text of the original author."

262 the codices on which Erasmus relied: Bentley, *Humanists and Holy Writ*, 127, 137; Metzger, *Text of the New Testament*, 102–103; Smith, *Erasmus*, 163–164.

262 hundreds of printer's errors: H. J. de Jonge, "Novum Testamentum a Nobis Versum," 409. This article discusses the many deficiencies in Erasmus's Greek New Testament while arguing that they resulted in part from the fact that Erasmus considered the Greek version of only secondary importance; the Latin version was his priority.

262 seems unfair to hold Erasmus: Bentley, *Humanists and Holy Writ*, 138; Jan Krans, "Deconstructing the Vulgate: Erasmus' Philological Work in the *Capita* and the *Soloecismi*," in Wallraff, *Basel 1516*, 204–205. William M. Combs, in "Erasmus and the Textus Receptus" (*Detroit Baptist Seminary Journal*, 1: 35–53, Spring 1996), notes that some modern-day fundamentalists contend that the *Textus Receptus* contains God's original words; their insistence, in part, derives from the fact that the *Textus Receptus* was the basis for the King James Version, which many fundamentalists regard as the truest version of the Scriptures.

262 came to be known as the *Textus Receptus*: For the history of this development, see Metzger, *Text of the New Testament*, 103–106; *The Cambridge History of the Bible*, vol. 2, 499.

263 "the most faulty book I know": Quoted in Metzger, *Text of the New Testament*, 99. The scholar is F. H. A. Scrivener.

263 a letter from George Spalatin: *Collected Works of Erasmus*, vol. 4, no. 501, December 11, 1516, 165–169.

263 Erasmus never replied: It is also possible that Erasmus never received the letter.

CHAPTER 14: A FRIAR'S CRY

264 "Some, like Laurentius Valla": *Luther: Lectures on Romans*, 271–272.

264 Luther lamented: Ibid., 337; into a "market place," 339; singled out the All Saints' Foundation, 350.

265 denunciation of "spiritual rulers": Ibid., 360–361.

265 "I must perform my duty": Ibid., 364.

265 Christian law does not set aside: Ibid., 381, 384, 387.

266 In his letter to Spalatin: *Luther's Works*, vol. 48, no. 9, 23–26.

266 wrote to its director, Johann Lang: Ibid., no. 5, May 29, 1516, 14–16. See also Brecht, *Martin Luther*, 157–160.

267 "I have enough useless friars": *Luther's Works*, vol. 48, no. 10, 27–32.

267 "My place is here": Ibid., 31.

267 "My life daily approaches": Quoted in Brecht, *Martin Luther*, 160.

268 say anything about the relics: Hans J. Hillerbrand, ed., *The Reformation: A Narrative History Related by Contemporary Observers and Participants*, 47–49.

268 could bring about a reduction: Bainton, *Here I Stand*, 53.

268 a key source of income: Brecht, *Martin Luther*, 178; Todd, *Luther*, 98; Bainton, *Here I Stand*, 54; Friedenthal, *Luther*, 140.

268 indulgences did not actually: MacCulloch, *Reformation*, 117–119; Schwiebert, *Luther*, 303–306.

269 Indulgences also gave believers: Boehmer, *Road to Reformation*, 178–179.

269 Luther decided to speak out: Ibid., 176; Bainton, *Here I Stand*, 54; Schwiebert, *Luther*, 312–313, 796. It is not clear if Luther gave the sermon at the Castle Church.

269 his promise to send Luther: *Luther's Works*, vol. 48, 33.

269 a new indulgence being offered: For a good description of the indulgence trade, see Friedenthal, *Luther*, 132–141.

270 perfected the art of marketing them: Hillerbrand, *Reformation*, 43–45; Boehmer, *Road to Reformation*, 181.

270 Don't you hear: Hillerbrand, *Reformation*, 42.

270 "As soon as the coin": See Pastor, *History of the Popes*, vol. 7, 349–350.

270 Luther was hearing: Hillerbrand, *Reformation*, 45–46.

271 offered one of the first statements: *Luther's Works*, vol. 51, "Sermon on St. Matthew's Day, Matt. 11: 25–30," 26–31; "Oh, the dangers of our time!", 31.

271 Tetzel appeared in the towns: Hillerbrand, *Reformation*, 45–47; Brecht, *Martin Luther*, 183.

272 construction of the new St. Peter's: Scotti, *Basilica*, 113–116.

272 the man chosen to head the Church: Pastor writes in *History of the Popes* (vol. 7, 7) that "at this, the most severe crisis which had met her [the Church] in her fifteen hundred years of history, the right ruler was wanting." Expanding on this (vol. 8, 459), he observes of Leo that "while the tempest was ready to break in which a third part of Europe was to be torn from the chair of St. Peter, he gave himself up with a light and joyous mind and without anxiety to the enjoyments and preoccupations of the world."

272 brought his family's priceless library: Hibbert, *Rome*, 151; William Roscoe: *The Life and Pontificate of Leo X*, vol. 2, 145, 134, 177, 391; Pastor, *History of the Popes*, vol. 8, chap. 5, "The Renaissance in the Field of Literature," 183–280.

273 a reputation for self-indulgence: Hibbert, *Rome*, 147; Scotti, *Basilica*, 116–118; Pastor, *History of the Popes*, vol. 8, chap. 3, "Personality and Manner of Life of Leo X," 71–125.

273 Carcasses of exotic animals: Hibbert, *Rome*, 149–150; Roscoe, *Life and*

273 Entertainment was provided: Pastor, *History of the Popes*, vol. 8, 151–154.

274 Leo had suffered through: Scotti, *Basilica*, 118.

274 During the nine years: Ibid., 123–124; Lees-Milne, *Saint Peter's*, 146–150.

274 his favorite artist, Raphael: Pastor, *History of the Popes*, vol. 8, 359–367; Scotti, *Basilica*, 126–136; Lees-Milne, *Saint Peter's*, 149–150.

275 that cost was skyrocketing: Pastor, *History of the Popes*, vol. 8, 367–368; Scotti, *Basilica*, 134.

275 Leo had frittered it all away: Pastor, *History of the Popes*, vol. 8, 90–91, 96ff; Scotti, *Basilica*, 144; Lees-Milne, *Saint Peter's*, 153.

275 derived from an inventive doctrine: Boehmer, *Road to Reformation*, 167–179; Friedenthal, *Luther*, 133ff; Pastor, *History of the Popes*, vol. 7, 333–343.

276 began issuing indulgence letters: For a sample letter, see Hillerbrand, *Reformation*, 44. See also Boehmer, *Road to Reformation*, 178–179, 174; Schwiebert, *Luther*, 305.

276 converted their office: Boehmer, *Road to Reformation*, 174.

276 announced the revocation: Pastor, *History of the Popes*, vol. 7, 329.

276 in the authorizing bull: Brecht, *Martin Luther*, 178–180; Pastor, *History of the Popes*, vol. 7, 344–345.

276 the resentment that was building: For an overview of Rome's financial exactions and the dissatisfaction they were causing in Germany, see Pastor, *History of the Popes*, vol. 7, 291–328.

277 had one feature: Ibid., 331–332, 343–345.

277 Albrecht was not a model candidate: Friedenthal, *Luther*, 146–147; Brecht, *Martin Luther*, 179; "Albert of Brandenburg," in *Contemporaries of Erasmus*.

277 a creative arrangement: Brecht, *Martin*

Luther, 179; Pastor, *History of the Popes*, vol. 7, 331–332.

278 Without Christ's resurrection: *Luther's Works*, vol. 27, 168, 170. See also Fife, *Revolt of Martin Luther*, 230–231.

278 "I follow Erasmus": *Luther's Works*, vol. 27, 402, 212, 315.

278 "I am reading our Erasmus": Ibid., vol. 48, no. 13, March 1, 1517, 40.

279 "Our theology and St. Augustine": Ibid., no. 14, May 18, 1517, 42.

279 won over Andreas von Karlstadt: Ronald J. Sider, *Andreas Bodenstein von Karlstadt: The Development of His Thought*, 8, 17–18.

279 prepared ninety-seven theses: *Luther's Works*, vol. 31, "Disputation Against Scholastic Theology," 9–16.

280 a copy of a booklet: Brecht, *Martin Luther*, 180–182; Hillerbrand, *Reformation*, 37–41.

280 even had a fee schedule: Hillerbrand, *Reformation*, 39.

280 an important discovery: Luther later described this new awareness in a letter to Johann von Staupitz, in *Luther's Works*, vol. 48, no. 21, May 30, 1518, 64–70. See also Brecht, *Martin Luther*, 184–185; Friedenthal, *Luther*, 105–106. "With what avidity," *The Cambridge History of the Bible* observes (vol. 3, 11), "Luther laid hold of this translation to bolster his critique of the penitential system of the Church!" See also David M. Whitford, "Erasmus Openeth the Way Before Luther," *Church History and Religious Culture*, 96: 535–540, 2016.

281 his most famous document: *Luther's Works*, vol. 31, "Ninety-Five Theses, or Disputation on the Power and Efficacy of Indulgences," 25–33.

281 "*Poenitentiam agite, &c*": This is how this phrase reads in the Latin in which Luther wrote it; see *Luthers Werke*, vol. 1, 233.

282 does not have the power to remit any penalties: Thesis no. 5; this power could be applied, no. 8; Nor was there divine authority, no. 27; "When money clinks,"

no. 28; it was not consistent, no. 35; Any Christian who is truly repentant, no. 36; Christians should be taught, no. 45; They should also be taught, no. 50; If the need arose, no. 51; Whereas in the past, nos. 65 and 66; If the pope could indeed, no. 82; Since the pope's income, no. 86; to suppress them by force, no. 90; his final four theses, nos. 92–95.

283 to be printed as a folio sheet: *Luther's Works*, vol. 31, 22; the page declared at the top, 25.

283 Around noon on October 31, 1517: See, for instance, Schwiebert, *Luther*, 314–315; Boehmer, *Road to Reformation*, 184.

284 scholars have raised questions: The doubts arise from the fact that Luther himself never spoke about posting the theses on the door. Marius sums up the debate in *Martin Luther*, 137–139; he concludes that Luther never did post the theses on the door. Among the many others who maintain that he did are Brecht, in *Martin Luther* (200–202), and Pettegree, in *Brand Luther* (71–72).

284 a letter explaining his actions: *Luther's Works*, vol. 48, October 31, 1517, 45–49.

284 his own relics collection: Brecht, *Martin Luther*, 179; Marius, *Martin Luther*, 129.

284 they were printed: Pettegree, *Brand Luther*, 74–75.

285 "as if the angels themselves": Quoted in Hillerbrand, *Reformation*, 47.

285 "It is a mystery to me": Ibid., 54.

CHAPTER 15: FOR THE WANT OF GREEK TYPE

289 decided to settle in Louvain: Leuven in Flemish. *Collected Works of Erasmus*, vol. 5, xi; Grant Allen, *Cities of Belgium* (London: Grant Richards, 1912), 157–159; "Louvain" and "Louvain, Catholic University of," in *The New Encyclopaedia Britannica*, 15th ed.

289 the Louvain theology faculty: *Collected Works of Erasmus*, vol. 71, introduction,

"Erasmus and the Louvain Circle,"
ix–li.

290 allotted a spacious room: Halkin,
Erasmus, 119.

290 few scholars could pass through:
Huizinga, *Erasmus*, 96.

290 "It ravished my heart": *Collected Works
of Erasmus*, vol. 5, no. 674, September 17
[1517], 133–134.

290 "We are daily expecting": Ibid., vol. 4,
no. 581, May 10, 1517, 348.

290 a new form of intimate portraiture: See
Willibald Sauerländer, "Germany: When
Faces Defied Death," *New York Review
of Books*, November 24, 2011, 61. The
portrait of Erasmus was paired with one of
his friend Pieter Gillis—part of a diptych
the two men commissioned to send as a
gift to their friend Thomas More.

291 "one infallible oracle of Christ": *Collected
Works of Erasmus*, vol. 5, no. 710,
November 13, 1517, 195–199. This letter
is the preface to the paraphrase.

291 *Querela Pacis*: See the dedicatory preface,
ibid., vol. 5 [July? 1517], 21–25. The
tract itself is in vol. 27, 292–322; "What
land has not been soaked," 305; "What
has a miter to do," 307: "The English are
hostile," 315.

292 in more than twenty editions: Ibid.,
vol. 27, 291. José Chapiro brought out
an edition of *Querela Pacis* with the
title *Erasmus and Our Struggle for Peace*
(Boston: Beacon Press, 1950), dedicated
to "The United Nations—Embodiment
of the Ideals of Erasmus and Source of
the Highest Hopes of Our Time."

292 *Julius Exclusus e Coelis*: *Collected Works of
Erasmus*, vol. 27, 168–197; "I suppose,"
169; not to those carrying, 174; "You
won't open up," 197.

293 "How I have enjoyed": Ibid., vol. 4,
no. 532, February 18 [1517], 245.

293 An "egregious absurdity": Ibid., vol. 5,
66.

293 he did not have a mind: Ibid., vol. 5, 84.

293 Thomas More sent him: Ibid., vol. 4,
no. 502, December 15, [1516], 169–172.

294 Erasmus had embarked on a project:
Ibid., vol. 71, xix–xxii; Henry de Vocht,
*History of the Foundation and the Rise
of the Collegium Trilingue Lovaniense,
1517–1550*, part 1, 1ff, 46ff; Augustijn,
Erasmus, 115–116.

294 Matthaeus Adrianus: De Vocht, *History
of the Foundation*, 60, 241–256.

294 several old manuscripts: *Collected Works
of Erasmus*, vol. 4, 173. See also Bentley,
Humanists and Holy Writ, 132–133.

294 the first attack: *Collected Works of
Erasmus*, vol. 5, no. 597, to Thomas More
[July 10, 1517], 11; Augustijn, *Erasmus*,
113–15; Huizinga, *Erasmus*, 132–133;
Bainton, *Erasmus of Christendom*, 138;
Erika Rummel, *Erasmus and His Catholic
Critics*, vol. 1, 49–59.

295 "impious and most unworthy": Rummel,
Erasmus and His Catholic Critics, vol. 1,
50.

295 "If only you had refrained": Quoted in
Augustijn, *Erasmus*, 115.

296 Many were troubled: See, for instance,
the letter from Symphorien Champier, a
French physician and admirer of Lefèvre,
in *Collected Works of Erasmus*, vol. 5, no.
680A [September 1517], 142–145.

296 sent Erasmus a barbed letter: Ibid., vol. 5,
no. 769, February 2, 1518, 287–293.

296 In a caustic reply: Ibid., vol. 6, no. 844,
May 15, 1518, 27–36.

297 Edward Lee: Ibid., vol. 5, no. 765
[January 1518] 281–282;
vol. 7, no. 106, February 1, 1520,
171–195; vol. 72, xi–xxv, 7–9. See also
Coogan, *Erasmus, Lee, and the Correction
of the Vulgate*, 20; Bainton, *Erasmus of
Christendom*, 136–137.

298 He was deeply troubled: *Collected Works
of Erasmus*, vol. 72, 408, 412; Coogan,
*Erasmus, Lee, and the Correction of the
Vulgate*, 53ff.

298 Lee (like Luther) feared: *Collected
Works of Erasmus*, vol. 72, 269; Coogan,
*Erasmus, Lee, and the Correction of the
Vulgate*, 35–36.

299 "How I wish": *Collected Works of*

Erasmus, vol. 5, no. 815, April 17 [1518], 388.

299 "They thank me openly": Ibid., vol. 5, no. 794, to Pierre Barbier, March 6, 1518, 339.

299 sent a courier with letters: Ibid., vol. 5, 297.

299 went to Thomas More: Ibid., vol. 5, no. 785, March 5, 1518, 325–329.

CHAPTER 16: A DRUNKEN GERMAN

300 "My poor worn body": Luther's Works, vol. 48, no. 21, May 30, 1518, 69. On his cowl, see vol. 48, 50.

300 There wasn't any: As Brecht notes in Martin Luther (202), Luther's letters until January make no mention of the indulgence issue.

300 he began to provide it: Luther's Works, vol. 31, introduction to "Explanations of the Ninety-Five Theses," 79; "Test everything," 83.

301 Luther recommended to his friend: Luther's Correspondence, vol. 1, no. 49, February 19 [1518], 71–72.

301 "that such a conflict": Luther's Works, vol. 48, no. 18, to George Spalatin, January 18, 1518, 55.

301 "is so merry": Luther's Correspondence, vol. 1, no. 42 [early November 1517], 63.

301 he thought of translating the work: Ibid., vol. 1, no. 130, 165.

301 In a message to Spalatin: Ibid., vol. 1, no. 46, December 31, 1517, 67.

302 Whenever he addressed opponents: Luther's Works, vol. 48, no. 18, to George Spalatin, January 18, 1518, 53–54.

302 heard the first rumbles: Brecht, Martin Luther, 203, 207; Schwiebert, Luther, 323; Fife, Revolt of Martin Luther, 261.

302 One of those peddlers: Luther's Correspondence, vol. 1, 76.

302 "overwhelmed with abuse": Ibid., vol. 1, to George Spalatin, February 15, 1518, 70–71.

303 tirade directed at him: Brecht, Martin Luther, 211.

303 "is nothing less than": Luther's Correspondence, vol. 1, 76.

303 Titled Asterisks: Fife, Revolt of Martin Luther, 335–336.

304 Sermon on Indulgences and Grace: Ibid., 263; Friedenthal, Luther, 159–160; Brecht, Martin Luther, 208; Pettegree, Brand Luther, 80–81. As noted in The Annotated Luther, vol. 1, The Roots of Reform, ed. Timothy J. Wengert (3–4), it was this work, even more than the Ninety-Five Theses, that made Luther widely known.

304 "I know perfectly well": Luther's Correspondence, vol. 1, no. 54, to Johann Staupitz, March 31, 1518, 78.

304 to be held in Heidelberg: On the Heidelberg disputation, see Brecht, Martin Luther, 213–215; Bainton, Here I Stand, 65–66; Todd, Luther, 120–123; Mullett, Martin Luther, 79; Luther's Works, vol. 31, 37–38.

305 "Everybody advises me": Luther's Correspondence, vol. 1, no. 51, March 21, 1518, 74–75.

305 left Wittenberg on foot: Ibid., vol. 1, no. 55, to George Spalatin, April 15, 1518, 79.

305 "terribly fatigued": Ibid., vol. 1, no. 56, April 19, 1518, 79–80.

306 Luther had prepared: Luther's Works, vol. 31, "Heidelberg Disputation," 39–70; "that he can obtain grace," 50.

306 Luther made a strong impression: Friedenthal, Luther, 165.

306 "If the peasants would hear this": Luther's Works, vol. 48, 61.

306 The count palatine wrote to Frederick: Luther's Correspondence, vol. 1, no. 58, May 1, 1518, 83.

306 "Although our chief men": Ibid., vol. 1, no. 57, May 1, 1518, 81–83.

307 were largely immune: Luther's Works, vol. 48, no. 20, to George Spalatin, May 18, 1518, 60–63.

307 "twice-deadly cabbage": Ibid, 62.

308 the Church's use of excommunication:

Friedenthal, *Luther*, 166–167; Schwiebert, *Luther*, 331.

308 Luther inveighed against these practices: Schwiebert, *Luther*, 332–333; Bainton, *Here I Stand*, 67–68; Todd, *Luther*, 125.

309 the Dominicans had spies: Schwiebert, *Luther*, 340–341.

309 "The more they threaten": *Luther's Correspondence*, vol. 1, to Wenzel (Wenceslas) Link, July 10, 1518, 97.

309 *Explanations of the Ninety-Five Theses: Luther's Works*, vol. 31, 79–252; "a very good pope," 155; "he is a human being," 171; the "horrible murders," 171; a "veritable Babylon," 156; "infernal abyss," 237–238; "extortion," 249; "future reformation," 250.

310 the accompanying letter: Ibid., vol. 48, no. 21, May 30, 1518, 64–70.

310 In that letter: Preserved Smith, *The Life and Letters of Martin Luther*, 44–46.

310 was close to realizing his goal: See Roscoe, *Life and Pontificate of Leo X*, vol. 2, 113; Pastor, *History of the Popes*, vol. 8, 184ff; "Leo X," in *The Catholic Encyclopedia*.

310 "All men who have any gifts": *Collected Works of Erasmus*, vol. 3, no. 340, July 18, 1515, 144–145.

311 eighty-eight lecturers: Burckhardt, *Civilization of the Renaissance in Italy*, 141.

311 Fifth Lateran Council: Pastor, *History of the Popes*, vol. 7, 5–6, and vol. 8, 384ff.

311 named thirty-one new cardinals: Ibid., vol. 7, 196–208.

312 800,000 ducats: Ibid., 211.

312 a crusade against the Turks: Ibid., 213–235.

313 projected cost of such an expedition: Ibid., 224–225.

313 Raphael remained in charge: Scotti, *Basilica*, 134–136.

313 Luther recalled having heard: Fife, *Revolt of Martin Luther*, 257.

313 Volta had relayed that demand: *Luther's Correspondence*, vol. 1, 106.

313 their annual chapter meeting: Schwiebert, *Luther*, 338–339.

314 asked Sylvester Prierias: Ibid.; Bainton, *Here I Stand*, 68; Todd, *Luther*, 132–133; Fife, *Revolt of Martin Luther*, 276–277.

314 *Dialogue Against the Presumptuous Conclusions*: Brecht, *Martin Luther*, 242–243.

314 Count Albrecht of Mansfeld wrote: *Luther's Correspondence*, vol. 1, no. 69, Luther to Wenzel (Wenceslas) Link, July 10, 1518, 97.

314 the treacherous act Luther experienced: Ibid., vol. 1, no. 117, Luther to George Spalatin, January 14 [1519], 149–152; Todd, *Luther*, 134–135.

315 a "wild, entangled jungle": *Luther's Works*, vol. 48, 72, 79.

315 a blistering response: Brecht, *Martin Luther*, 243–245.

315 "I now need your help": *Luther's Works*, vol. 48, no. 22, August 8, 1518, 70–73.

316 Maximilian was writing to Leo: *Luther's Correspondence*, vol. 1, no. 70, August 5, 1518, 98–100.

316 hurriedly drew up a *breve*: Ibid., vol. 1, no. 73, August 23, 1518, 101–104; Pastor, *History of the Popes*, vol. 7, 368–370.

316 Leo drafted a stern note: *Luther's Correspondence*, vol. 1, no. 74, August 23, 1518, 105–106.

316 Luther anxiously implored Spalatin: Ibid., vol. 1, no. 76, August 28, 1518, 108–109.

CHAPTER 17: UNBRIDLED

318 able to find a horse: *Collected Works of Erasmus*, vol. 5, 329.

318 sent a gift of sixty angel-nobles: Ibid., vol. 5, 410–411.

318 prepared a fierce attack: Ibid., vol. 6, no. 843, May 7, 1518, 3–26. The location that the editors give for this letter—"On the Rhine?"—suggests some uncertainty about exactly where Erasmus wrote it; "The business in hand," 15.

318 Arriving in Basel: Ibid., vol. 6, 39.

319 "put a bridle of self-restraint": Ibid., vol. 4, September 2, 1516, 62.

319 would be the most provocative: Ibid., vol. 6, introductory note to letter no. 864, 107.

319 Erasmus offered a lengthy catalog: Smith, *Erasmus*, 172; Coogan, *Erasmus, Lee, and the Correction of the Vulgate*, 30; Jarrott, "Erasmus' Biblical Humanism," 140–143; *Opera Omnia Desiderii Erasmi*, 6(5): 204–211.

319 even bolder at Matthew 16:18: Bentley, *Humanists and Holy Writ*, 185; *Opera Omnia Desiderii Erasmi*, 6(5): 247–248.

319 Erasmus condemned the proliferating shrines: *Opera Omnia Desiderii Erasmi*, 6(5): 298–300; J. A. Froude, *Life and Letters of Erasmus*, 129–130.

320 note on 1 Corinthians 7:36–39: *Opera Omnia Desiderii Erasmi*, 6(8): 142–190; Payne, *Erasmus*, 121–125.

320 some fifty highly obscure questions: Rummel, *Erasmus' Annotations*, 144–145.

321 a letter to his friend Paul Volz: *Collected Works of Erasmus*, vol. 6, no. 858, August 14, 1518, 72–91; "the whole philosophy of Christ," 77; "that some of them think," 86; "a refuge from the world," 89.

322 "tend not to Christ's glory": Ibid., vol. 6, 79.

323 "Here you have the theological works": *Luther's Correspondence*, vol. 1, no. 94, Wolfgang Capito to Candid Theologians (October 1518), 129–130.

323 the anthology appeared in October 1518: *Collected Works of Erasmus*, vol. 6, 190–193; Smith, *Erasmus*, 218.

323 the typesetters mischievously changed: *Luther's Works*, vol. 48, 110.

323 arranged for his *famulus*: *Collected Works of Erasmus*, vol. 6, 107.

324 his detailed account of his journey: Ibid., vol. 6, no. 867, [first half of October] 1518, 112–126; "dirty pease porridge," 114.

324 "a customs officer devoted to the Muses": Ibid., vol. 6, no. 879, October 19, 1518, 150.

324 "countrified and simple style": Ibid., vol. 6, 12.

324 A good example came at Matthew 6:12: *Opera Omnia Desiderii Erasmi*, (6)5: 157–158.

325 At Matthew 3:2: Jarrott, "Erasmus' Biblical Humanism," 125–126; *Opera Omnia Desiderii Erasmi*, 6(5): 110–112.

325 one-word alteration he made: Bentley, *Humanists and Holy Writ*, 170; Rummel, *Erasmus and His Catholic Critics*, vol. 1, 123–125; *Opera Omnia Desiderii Erasmi*, 6(2): 13.

325 *Ratio Verae Theologiae*: See Marjorie O'Rourke Boyle, *Erasmus on Language and Method in Theology*, 59–127; Bainton, *Erasmus of Christendom*, 156; Halkin, *Erasmus*, 128; de Vocht, *History of the Foundation*, part I, 303–306; Bentley, *Humanists and Holy Writ*, 180; Seebohm, *Oxford Reformers*, 278.

326 "Summary Arguments Against": See Rummel, *Erasmus and His Catholic Critics*, vol. 1, 21–22; Jan Krans, "Deconstructing the Vulgate," in Wallraff, *Basel 1516*, 191–194.

326 he complained that ten secretaries: *Collected Works of Erasmus*, vol. 6, no. 873, to Heinrich Beyming, October 17 [1518], 141.

326 Two young humanists: Ibid., vol. 6, no. 870, to Conradus Mutianus Rufus, October 17, 1518, 131–132.

327 "Eleutherius, I hear": Ibid., vol. 6, no. 872, October 17 [1518], 137, 139.

327 sent Wolfgang Capito an update: Ibid., vol. 6, no. 877, October 19 [1518], 147–149.

CHAPTER 18: ONTO THE WORLD STAGE

328 "It seems to me that the world": *Luther's Correspondence*, vol. 1, no. 80, September 14, 1518, 113.

328 he recommended his relative: Brecht, *Martin Luther*, 277–278. Schwartzerd is often described as Reuchlin's grandnephew, but the exact nature of

their kinship is unclear. What is clear is that Philip was Reuchlin's protégé. See Timothy J. Wengert, *Human Freedom, Christian Righteousness: Philip Melanchthon's Exegetical Dispute with Erasmus of Rotterdam*, 6; Price, *Johannes Reuchlin*, 19.

329 a paean to Erasmus: *Collected Works of Erasmus*, vol. 4, no. 454, August 20, 1516, 40–42.

329 he arrived in Wittenberg: Brecht, *Martin Luther*, 277–278; Friedenthal, *Luther*, 200–201, 223; Fife, *Revolt of Martin Luther*, 303.

329 gave his inaugural address: Hillerbrand, *Reformation*, 58–60.

329 "extremely learned and absolutely faultless": *Luther's Works*, vol. 48, no. 24, August 31, 1518, 78.

330 "Never was there a greater man": Quoted in Schwiebert, *Luther*, 299.

330 the Imperial Diet in Augsburg: On Luther's appearance at Augsburg, see Brecht, *Martin Luther*, 246–261; Fife, *Revolt of Martin Luther*, 286–297; Bainton, *Here I Stand*, 70–76; Schwiebert, *Luther*, 350–353; Mullett, *Martin Luther*, 82–89; Todd, *Luther*, 138–142; Friedenthal, *Luther*, 171–187; Roper, *Martin Luther*, 99–107. Luther's own account is in *Luther's Works*, vol. 31, "Proceedings at Augsburg," 255–292.

331 no happy encounters: Todd, *Luther*, 137.

331 "Now I must die": *Luthers Werke, Tischreden*, vol. 2, no. 2668a; Bainton, *Here I Stand*, 70.

331 a population of 50,000: Hajo Holborn, *A History of Modern Germany*, vol. 1, *The Reformation*, 72–76; Greg Steinmetz, *Jacob Fugger: The Richest Man Who Ever Lived*, 1; "Augsburg," in *Encyclopedia of the Renaissance*.

332 visited by one of Cajetan's Italian courtiers: *Luther's Correspondence*, vol. 1, no. 83, October 10, 1518, 116–118.

332 sent a letter to Melanchthon: Ibid., vol. 1, no. 84, October 11, 1518, 118.

332 the Fugger Palace: Friedenthal, *Luther*, 171; Steinmetz, *Jacob Fugger*, 94.

332 the extraordinary wealth of the Fuggers: Steinmetz, *Jacob Fugger*, xiii–xv, 22, 111; Holborn, *History of Modern Germany*, vol. 1., 73–74.

333 Cajetan could not wait to leave it: On the cardinal, see Todd, *Luther*, 129, 131; Friedenthal, *Luther*, 172–175; Fife, *Revolt of Martin Luther*, 292; Brecht, *Martin Luther*, 246–247; Mullet, *Martin Luther*, 85; "Cajetan," in *The Oxford Encyclopedia of the Reformation*.

334 "hound of hell": Pastor, *History of the Popes*, vol. 7, 247.

334 "sons of Nimrod": Quoted in Todd, *Luther*, 130.

334 Ulrich von Hutten: Friedenthal, *Luther*, 174.

334 Maximilian's physical decline: Todd, *Luther*, 130.

335 A *fratellino*: Friedenthal, *Luther*, 175.

335 the cardinal told Luther: Luther's account of his meetings with Cajetan appears in *Luther's Works*, vol. 31, "Proceedings at Augsburg," 259–292.

336 completely unsupported by Scripture: Ibid., 264–265.

337 wrote to his colleague Andreas von Karlstadt: *Luther's Correspondence*, vol. 1, no. 85, October 14, 1518, 120.

337 he wrote out his statement: *Luther's Works*, vol. 31, 264–275; "I did not possess," 266–267; "As long as these Scripture passages," 274–275.

337 presented his statement to the cardinal: These events are recounted in Luther's letter to Spalatin, ibid., vol. 48, no. 26, October 14, 1518, 83–87.

338 "Go, and do not return": Ibid., vol. 48, 86.

339 imparted a valedictory word: Ibid., vol. 48, no. 69, to Johann von Staupitz, January 14, 1521, 191.

339 wrote a farewell note: Ibid., vol. 48, no. 27, October 18, 1518, 87–89.

339 On the night of October 20, 1518: Schwiebert, *Luther*, 353–354;

Friedenthal, *Luther*, 185; Brecht, *Martin Luther*, 260.

339 "I have come to-day": *Luther's Correspondence*, vol. 1, no. 93, October 31, 1518, 128–129.

340 "You are not a bad Christian": *Luther's Works*, vol. 31, 278–279; "I do not care," 282; "the clever tricks they used," 285.

340 "setting things in order": Ibid., vol. 48, no. 29, November 25, 1518, 93–94.

340 prepared his parishioners: Schwiebert, *Luther*, 367.

341 there arrived another letter: Brecht, *Martin Luther*, 263.

341 Frederick sent Cajetan his response: Ibid., 264.

341 they were snapped up by townspeople: Todd, *Luther*, 143.

CHAPTER 19: UNCOMMITTED

342 Karl von Miltitz: On Miltitz, see Schwiebert, *Luther*, 370–379; Brecht, *Martin Luther*, 265–273; Friedenthal *Luther*, 188–195; Fife, *Revolt of Martin Luther*, 307–326; Mullett, *Martin Luther*, 92–95; Pastor, *History of the Popes*, vol. 7, 380–384.

342 "the more they rage": *Luther's Correspondence*, vol. 1, no. 103, December 9, 1518, 137.

343 even if Miltitz had 25,000 Swiss soldiers: *Luthers Werke, Tischreden*, vol. 3, no. 3418, 308.

343 he agreed to remain silent: See Luther's two letters to Frederick, in *Luther's Works*, vol. 48, no. 31, January 5 or 6, 1519, 96–100; no. 33, between January 13 and 19, 1519, 103–106.

344 a "a kiss of Judas": Brecht, *Martin Luther*, 269.

344 In his letter to Leo: *Luther's Works*, vol. 48, no. 32, January 5 or 6, 1519, 100–102.

344 "With paternal love": *Luther's Correspondence*, vol. 1, no. 137, March 29, 1519, 172–173.

344 "We have sent six hundred copies": Ibid., vol. 1, no. 125, February 14, 1519, 161–162.

345 "Switzerland and the Rhine country": Ibid., vol. 1, no. 127, February 18, 1519, 163–164.

345 he had scoured the whole city: Ibid., vol. 1, no. 153, May 23, 1519, 191.

345 Huldrych Zwingli: Bainton, *Here I Stand*, 93.

345 concealed in bales of cotton: Schwiebert, *Luther*, 427.

345 couriers arrived: Fife, *Revolt of Martin Luther*, 463.

345 "Our town can hardly hold them": *Luther's Works*, vol. 48, no. 39, to George Spalatin, May 22, 1519, 122–124.

345 "In this way": Ibid., vol. 48, no. 30, December 9, 1519, 95–96.

345 "The best studies": *Luther's Correspondence*, vol. 1, no. 103a, to Guy Bild, December 10, 1518, 137–138.

345 on Paul's Epistle to the Galatians: Brecht, *Martin Luther*, 286–289. The lectures are in *Luther's Works*, vol. 27, 153–410. "Now that the whole Christian world," 163.

346 "that theologian too great": *Luther's Correspondence*, vol. 1, no. 123, to Peter Lupinus and Andreas Karlstadt [January 1519], 159.

346 "Free will collapses": *Luther's Works*, vol. 27, 328.

346 Wolfgang Capito had written to him: *Luther's Correspondence*, vol. 1, no. 78, September 4, 1518, 110.

346 jab at those who profit: *Collected Works of Erasmus*, vol. 6, 79.

346 decided to write to him directly: *Luther's Works*, vol. 48, no. 37, March 28, 1519, 116–119.

347 With the arrival of the Froben collection: De Vocht, *History of the Foundation*, part 1, 424–425; Schwiebert, *Luther*, 427–430. Schwiebert notes that it was probably the second edition of the Froben collection that was used in both Louvain and Cologne.

348 *Letters of Obscure Men: Epistolae Obscurorum Virorum*, Francis Griffin Stokes, xliv–lxviii. See also Price, *Johannes Reuchlin*, 176; Joseph Lortz, *The Reformation in Germany*, vol. 1, 75–77; Smith, *Erasmus*, 134.

348 Erasmus strongly disapproved: *Collected Works of Erasmus*, vol. 5, no. 622, to Johannes Caesarius, August 16, 1517, 66.

348 support for Reuchlin: Price, *Johannes Reuchlin*, 196.

348 The first volley against Erasmus: *Collected Works of Erasmus*, vol. 6, no. 946 [April 1519], 306–308, and vol. 71, introduction to "Defense of the Declamation of Marriage," 86–87; Augustijn, *Erasmus*, 116; Halkin, *Erasmus*, 123–124; de Vocht, *History of the Foundation*, part 1, 313–314.

348 "a barren way of life": Erika Rummel, ed., *Erasmus on Women*, 58.

348 all the anger and resentment: *Collected Works of Erasmus*, vol. 6, no. 948, to Petrus Mosellanus, April 22, 1519, 310–318.

348 progress being made by the College of Three Tongues: De Vocht, *History of the Foundation*, part 1, 360–363.

349 Jacobus Latomus: Ibid., 324ff; Augustijn, *Erasmus*, 116; *Collected Works of Erasmus*, vol. 6, 283–285, and vol. 71, xxix–xxxiii.

349 Edward Lee: *Collected Works of Erasmus*, vol. 72, 8–9, 15; Rummel, *Erasmus and His Catholic Critics*, vol. 1, 96–98.

349 "the peaceful home of literary studies": *Collected Works of Erasmus*, vol. 6, no. 948, to Petrus Mosellanus, April 22, 1519, 311.

350 "Do not, I beg you": Ibid., vol. 6, no. 938, April 8, 1519, 294–295.

350 The threat worked: Ibid., vol. 6, 191–193, note.

350 dominated by large folios: Pettegree, *Brand Luther*, 144; Louise Holborn, "Printing and the Growth of a Protestant Movement in Germany," 126.

350 "almost superhuman art": *Collected Works of Erasmus*, vol. 6, no. 919, February 23, 1519, 253–256.

351 here Luther would lead the way: Holborn, "Printing and the Growth of a Protestant Movement in Germany," 126–127; Pettegree, *Brand Luther*, 105, 115–116; Fife, *Revolt of Martin Luther*, 445–446.

351 *Meditation on Christ's Passion: Luther's Works*, vol. 42, 5–14; on the number of editions, see Universal Short Title Catalogue (ustc.ac.uk).

351 "I have a swift hand": Quoted in Boehmer, *Road to Reformation*, 299.

352 the sound and cadence: Friedenthal, *Luther*, 213.

352 "Here is the beast": Ibid., 213.

352 eight or sixteen pages long: Pettegree, *Brand Luther*, 106, 147.

352 one of Europe's top book producers: Ibid., xii–xiii; Holborn, "Printing and the Growth of a Protestant Movement in Germany," 133.

352 Overall, in the first decade: Pettegree, *Book in the Renaissance*, 102.

353 instrumental in spreading dissident ideas: John L. Flood, "The Book in Reformation Germany," in Jean-François Gilmont, ed., *The Reformation and the Book*, 96.

353 "an unquenchable flame": Quoted in Holborn, "Printing and the Growth of a Protestant Movement in Germany," 137.

353 decided to write to the elector again: *Collected Works of Erasmus*, vol. 6, no. 939, April 14, 1519, 295–299.

354 "The letter of Erasmus pleases me": *Luther's Works*, vol. 48, to George Spalatin, May 22, 1519, 122.

354 the arrival in Louvain: *Collected Works of Erasmus*, vol. 6, 332. The letter from Leo X is in vol. 6, no. 864, September 10, 1518, 106–108; the editor's note offers the details about the volume.

355 "No words of mine": Ibid., vol. 6, no. 980, May 30, 1519, 391–393.

CHAPTER 20: THE GREAT DEBATE

357 The Leipzig disputation: For general information, see Brecht, *Martin Luther*, 299–348; Friedenthal, *Luther*, 196–211; Marius, *Martin Luther*, 168–189; Schwiebert, *Luther*, 384–437; Fife, *Revolt of Martin Luther*, 327–394; Bainton, *Here I Stand*, 86–92; Boehmer, *Road to Reformation*, 271–297. See also *Luther's Works*, vol. 31, "The Leipzig Debate," 309–325, which includes Luther's own account.

357 Leipzig's theologians: See *Luther's Correspondence*, vol. 1, no. 105, December 16, 1518, 139–140, and no. 109, December 30, 1518, 143–144.

357 Luther was the real prize: Schwiebert, *Luther*, 384–385; Fife, *Revolt of Martin Luther*, 331–334; Boehmer, *Road to Reformation*, 283–284.

357 arid and didactic style: Friedenthal, *Luther*, 161–162.

358 arguing that the claims: *Luther's Works*, vol. 31, 318.

358 "glory-hungry beast": Ibid., vol. 48, no. 34, to George Spalatin, February 7, 1519, 107.

358 in the weeks leading up to the event: Ibid., vol. 48, no. 36, to George Spalatin, March 13, 1519, 114; Todd, *Luther*, 157; Mullett, *Martin Luther*, 96; Schwiebert, *Luther*, 389–391.

358 massive tract on papal power: Brecht, *Martin Luther*, 307–309; W. H. T. Dau, *The Leipzig Debate of 1519: Leaves from the Story of Luther's Life*, 106.

358 might be the "Antichrist himself": *Luther's Works*, vol. 48, no. 36, 114.

359 like an intramural championship match: Schwiebert, *Luther*, 391; Friedenthal, *Luther*, 202; Boehmer, *Road to Reformation*, 277; Dau, *Leipzig Debate of 1519*, 116.

359 produced reports: See, for instance, *Luther's Correspondence*, vol. 1, no. 204, Peter Mosellanus to Julius Pflug,

December 7, 1519, 257–262; Hillerbrand, *Reformation*, 67–76.

359 When the procession reached Grimma: Boehmer, *Road to Reformation*, 277–278.

360 delivered an address: Fife, *Revolt of Martin Luther*, 353.

360 Eck, tall and solidly built: *Luther's Correspondence*, vol. 1, 261–262.

360 Karlstadt was short: Ibid., 261.

361 station thirty-four armed guards: Schwiebert, *Luther*, 399.

361 "with nine or ten arguments": *Luther's Correspondence*, vol. 1, no. 169, Nikolaus von Amsdorf to Spalatin, August 1, 1519, 211.

361 he vociferously argued: Ibid., vol. 1, 260.

362 "almost count his bones": Ibid., 261.

362 carried a bouquet of pink flowers: Fife, *Revolt of Martin Luther*, 359; Boehmer, *Road to Reformation*, 285.

362 began right in on: Brecht, *Martin Luther*, 319–322.

362 "I impugn these decretals": Quoted in Bainton, *Here I Stand*, 88.

362 argued that the true head: See Melanchthon's report, *Luther's Correspondence*, vol. 1, no. 163, July 21, 1519, 200–202.

363 on the morning of the second day: Hillerbrand, *Reformation*, 67–70.

363 Luther (apparently) took the opportunity: According to Bainton, *Here I Stand* (89), Luther during lunch went to the university library and read the acts of the Council of Constance.

363 "certain that many of the articles": Hillerbrand, *Reformation*, 67.

364 Duke George bellowed: Schwiebert, *Luther*, 408; Brecht, *Martin Luther*, 320; Dau, *Leipzig Debate of 1519*, 165.

364 Jan Hus was named: For general information on Hus, see David S. Schaff, *John Huss: His Life, Teaching and Death, After Five Hundred Years*; Schaff's Introduction to Hus's *The Church (De Ecclesia)*, vii–xlii; Matthew Spinka, *John Hus: A Biography*; "Jan Hus" and

"Hussites," in *The Oxford Encyclopedia of the Reformation*; "Jan Hus," in *The Encyclopedia of Christianity*; Diarmaid MacCulloch, *Christianity: The First Three Thousand Years*, 571–574; Walker, *History of the Christian Church*, 381–384.

365 some 1,500 German students: Schaff, *John Huss*, 81–83; Spinka, *John Hus*, 97–99.

365 *De Ecclesia*: See Spinka, *John Hus*, 184–186, and Schaff, Introduction to *The Church*, xii–xxxi.

366 thrown into a dungeon: On the treatment of Hus during the early part of his stay in Constance, see Schaff, *John Huss*, 179ff.

367 Hus over the next month: Ibid., 229ff.

367 Hus was led to a meadow: Ibid., 255–259.

367 protests erupted: Walker, *History of the Christian Church*, 384.

367 the Eucharistic chalice: Francis Lutzow, *The Hussite Wars*, 5.

367 an inflamed mob: Ibid., 9; MacCulloch, *Christianity*, 572.

368 "Four Articles of Prague": Walker, *History of the Christian Church*, 384–385.

368 declared a crusade: Lutzow, *Hussite Wars*, 37ff.

368 Marching through Bohemia and Moravia: Walker, *History of the Christian Church*, 384–385; MacCulloch, *Christianity*, 572; Friedenthal, *Luther*, 164; "Hussites," in *The Oxford Encyclopedia of the Reformation*.

368 up to the very walls of Leipzig: Lutzow, *Hussite Wars*, 239.

369 pressing his advantage: Hillerbrand, *Reformation*, 68–71; Brecht, *Martin Luther*, 320–321; Dau, *Leipzig Debate in 1519*, 166–167.

369 swelling up like an adder: *Luther's Works*, vol. 31, 322.

369 "I will tell you": Quoted in Fife, *Revolt of Martin Luther*, 363.

370 would afterward praise: *Luther's Correspondence*, vol. 1, 261.

370 moved on to the subject of indulgences: *Luther's Works*, vol. 31, 322.

370 "the impatient monk": Quoted in Schwiebert, *Luther*, 412.

371 For eleven days he remained: Ibid., 419.

371 "I have experienced hatred before": *Luther's Works*, vol. 31, 325.

371 made it in fact seem the case: Ibid., vol. 31, 311.

371 smooth his rough edges: Schwiebert, *Luther*, 423; Roper, *Martin Luther*, 127–128.

371 Word also spread: *Luther's Correspondence*, vol. 1, no. 178, October 3, 1519, 220.

372 turned out sixteen works: *Luther's Works*, vol. 44, 117.

372 *Tesseradecas Consolatoria*: *Luther's Works*, vol. 42, 119–166.

372 Wittenberg would surpass: Roper, *Martin Luther*, 130.

372 In one chilling episode: Smith, *Life and Letters of Martin Luther*, 68.

372 a sorrowful letter he sent: *Luther's Correspondence*, vol. 1, no. 178, October 3, 1519, 219–221.

373 on the long journey to Rome: Pastor, *History of the Popes*, vol. 7, 386; Brecht, *Martin Luther*, 348. Some accounts conjecture that Eck was summoned by Rome.

CHAPTER 21: THE VIPER STRIKES

374 "What justice": The preface is in *Collected Works of Erasmus*, vol. 7, no. 1013, September 10, 1519, 71–73.

374 such "apostolic energy": Ibid., vol. 7, no. 1000, July 31, 1519, 25–31.

374 suggested a principle: Ibid., vol. 7, no. 1039, November 1, 1519, 119–128.

374 Erasmus was charged: Ibid., vol. 7, 195–201; Rummel, *Erasmus and His Catholic Critics*, vol. 1, 137ff; Augustijn, *Erasmus*, 92.

375 "have got it into their heads": *Collected Works of Erasmus*, vol. 7, no. 993, July 1, 1519, 3.

375 the faculty began an investigation: Augustijn, *Erasmus*, 121.

375 an accord was reached: *Collected Works of Erasmus*, vol. 7, no. 1022, 96.

375 Hoogstraten arrived: Ibid., vol. 71, xxxvii.

375 "purveyor of cabalistic perfidy": Ibid., vol. 7, no. 1006, to Jacob of Hoogstraten, August 11, 1519, 47.

375 "How I wish you had spent that effort": Ibid., 48, 53.

375 brought it with him to Louvain: Ibid., vol. 7, 128; de Vocht, *History of the Foundation*, part 1, 424–428.

375 the Cologne faculty: Brecht, *Martin Luther*, 338–339.

376 pact with Erasmus broke down: *Collected Works of Erasmus*, vol. 7, no. 1033, to Albrecht of Brandenburg, October 19, 1519, 108–116.

376 Erasmus decided to appeal: Ibid.

376 a devotee of good letters: Friedenthal, *Luther*, 147.

377 Ulrich von Hutten: On Hutten, see Spitz, *Religious Renaissance of the German Humanists*, 110–129; Bainton, *Here I Stand*, 100–104; Friedenthal, *Luther*, 230–239; "Hutten, Ulrich von," in *Contemporaries of Erasmus*.

378 suspected Hutten of treachery: *Collected Works of Erasmus*, vol. 7, 108; Smith, *Erasmus*, 225–227.

378 the Louvain theology faculty met: H. J. de Jonge, *L'ancienne faculté de théologie de Louvain au premier siècle de son existence, 1432–1540: Ses Débuts, son organisation, son enseignement, sa lutte contre Érasme et Luther*, 213; Schwiebert, *Luther*, 427–430.

378 "Gangs of conspirators": *Collected Works of Erasmus*, vol. 7, no. 1053, to Thomas Lupset, December 13, 1519, 159.

379 "The battle grows more barbarous": Ibid., vol. 7, no. 1007, to Pope Leo X, August 13, 1519, 55–59.

379 prepared to use every available means: The relations between Erasmus and Lee are described in a long letter from Lee to Erasmus, *Collected Works of Erasmus*, vol. 7, no. 1061, February 1, 1520, 171–195, and in Erasmus's "An Apologia in Response to the Two Invectives of Edward Lee," vol. 72, 3–65. See also Rummel, *Erasmus and His Catholic Critics*, vol. 1, 95–120; Huizinga, *Erasmus*, 135.

380 "The English viper": *Collected Works of Erasmus*, vol. 7, no. 1074, to Wolfgang Faber Capito [end of February 1520], 215–219.

380 listed Erasmus's alleged offenses: Ibid., vol. 72, 70–71.

380 for giving a lascivious cast: Rummel, *Erasmus and His Catholic Critics*, vol. 1, 101.

381 "is an invention of the theologians": *Collected Works of Erasmus*, vol. 72, 269–270.

381 Erasmus's greatest offense: Ibid., 403–419; Rummel, *Erasmus and His Catholic Critics*, vol. 1, 104–105 ("Such great negligence," 105); Bentley, *Humanists and Holy Writ*, 152–153; Coogan, *Erasmus, Lee, and the Correction of the Vulgate*, 53, 101–13; "we will fall once again," *Collected Works of Erasmus*, vol. 72, 412; "Let the church," vol. 72, 417.

381 "My friends": *Collected Works of Erasmus*, vol. 7, no. 1088, 254–255.

382 "I pray he may enjoy": Ibid., vol. 7, no. 1095, April 30 [1520], 270.

382 "out of his native darkness": Ibid., vol. 7, no. 1084, March 19, 1520, 235.

382 "Go hang yourself!": Quoted in Rummel, *Erasmus and His Catholic Critics*, vol. 1, 112.

382 Two schoolmasters: Ibid., 113.

382 posted in more than ten places: *Collected Works of Erasmus*, vol. 7, 222, 403.

382 "If a clandestine attack": Ibid., vol. 7, 186, 185, 181, 183, 184.

382 "Good God!": Quoted in Rummel, *Erasmus and His Catholic Critics*, vol. 1, 102.

383 "I did the only thing possible": *Collected Works of Erasmus*, vol. 72, 404, 408. See also de Jonge, "Erasmus and the *Comma Johanneum*," 381–389.

383 "I beseech you": *Collected Works of Erasmus*, vol. 72, 413.

383 Lee's notes: De Jonge, in "Erasmus and the *Comma Johanneum*" (385), calls Lee "a truly quarrelsome individual" and a "myopically conservative theologian" who "troubled and pestered Erasmus for several years with his criticisms, which were unusually mediocre, of the *Novum Instrumentum*."

383 Henry Standish: Erasmus describes this episode in a letter to Hermannus Buschius, *Collected Works of Erasmus*, vol. 8, July 31, 1520, 7–17. See also Rummel, *Erasmus and His Catholic Critics*, vol. 1, 122–127.

383 "a little Greek somebody": Quoted in Boyle, *Erasmus on Language and Method in Theology*, 6.

384 a hastily written defense: Erasmus actually wrote two apologias, one published in February 1520 and an expanded version published in August. They are in *Collected Works of Erasmus*, vol. 73, 1–40; the relevant passages are on page 18. The preface to the first defense is in vol. 7, 211–212. See also Boyle, *Erasmus on Language and Method in Theology*, 8.

384 "I am greatly surprised": *Luther's Correspondence*, vol. 1, no. 202, December 4, 1519, 256–257.

384 *Condemnation of Luther by Cologne and Louvain*: Brecht, *Martin Luther*, 339; Fife, *Revolt of Martin Luther*, 473–474.

384 "The university here": *Collected Works of Erasmus*, vol. 7, no. 1088, April 9, 1520, 255.

384 were the first steps: Coogan, in *Erasmus, Lee, and the Correction of the Vulgate* (19),

observes that "Lee ought to be recognized as the vanguard of the Catholic opposition to Erasmus' *Annotationes* as well as the one who forecast the theological revolution then beginning."

CHAPTER 22: THUNDERCLAPS

385 Alsatians and Walloons: Boehmer, *Road to Reformation*, 268–269.

385 "I left Italy": *Luther's Correspondence*, vol. 1, no. 197, to John Lang, November 19, 1519, 251.

385 "all ages will remember": Ibid., vol. 1, no. 259, May 15, 1520, 323.

385 "If God help me": Ibid., vol. 1, no. 221 [February 1520], 280–281.

385 undergone a deep emotional crisis: Erwin Panofsky, *The Life and Art of Albrecht Dürer* (Princeton: Princeton University Press, 1943), 198–199.

386 "Everything is very expensive": *Luther's Works*, vol. 48, no. 57, May 31, 1520, 165.

386 Matthaeus Adrianus: See Luther's letter to Spalatin, ibid., vol. 48, no. 45, November 7, 1519, 132–133.

386 "this little Greek": Ibid., vol. 48, no. 58, to George Spalatin, June 25, 1520, 165–167; *Luther's Correspondence*, vol. 1, no. 207, to John Lang, December 18, 1519, 264.

386 a Wittenberg widow: *Luther's Works*, vol. 48, no. 49, to George Spalatin, December 31, 1519, 142.

386 city council of Kemberg: Ibid.

387 "wicked lust of the flesh": Ibid., vol. 44, "A Sermon on the State of Marriage," 10.

387 taking place in Luther's mind: Todd, *Luther*, 167.

387 a treatise on the Eucharist: *Luther's Works*, vol. 35, "The Blessed Sacrament of the Holy and True Body of Christ, and the Brotherhoods," 47–73; the recommendation on giving the laity the cup as well as the bread is on page 50.

387 To Duke George: Brecht, *Martin Luther*, 361–365.

388 "Was [Christ] scurrilous": *Luther's Correspondence*, vol. 1, no. 228, to George Spalatin, [between February 12 and 18] 1520, 286–289.

388 "God so carries me on": Ibid.

389 to send Spalatin a formal denial: *Luther's Works*, vol. 48, January 14, 1520, 143–148.

389 A copy of *De Ecclesia* arrived: *Luther's Correspondence*, vol. 1, 219–220.

389 "In short we are all Hussites": *Luther's Works*, vol. 48, no. 52, February 14, 1520, 151–153.

389 "I have at hand": *Luther's Correspondence*, vol. 1, no. 230, February 24, 1520, 290–291.

390 the same "doctrinal asses": Ibid., vol. 1, 315.

390 In a blistering counterattack: Fife, *Revolt of Martin Luther*, 474–475.

390 *Treatise on Good Works: Luther's Works*, vol. 44, 17–114; "Apart from faith," 113; a heathen, 25; Just as a husband, 26–27; a great jumble of opinions, 55, 76, 89.

391 a new emperor: See Friedenthal, *Luther*, 194–195; Rice and Grafton, *The Foundations of Early Modern Europe*, 124–132; *Luther's Works*, vol. 48, introduction to no. 63, 175–176.

391 an astonishing 543,000 florins: Hajo Holborn, *History of Modern Germany*, vol. 1, 74–75.

391 such royal bloodlines: Rice and Grafton, *Foundations of Modern Europe*, 125.

392 "Sire," his chancellor Mercurino Gattinara wrote: Quoted in Karl Brandi, *The Emperor Charles V: The Growth and Destiny of a Man and of a World-Empire*, 112.

392 Hutten in his *Roman Trinity*: Quoted in Bainton, *Here I Stand*, 101.

392 "I have the intention": *Luther's Correspondence*, vol. 1, no. 266 [before June 8, 1520], 329.

392 He had no army: Friedenthal, *Luther*, 214.

393 *To the Christian Nobility: Luther's Works*, vol. 44, 123–217. "The time for silence," 123; building three walls, 126–127; The first wall, 127; "all Christians are truly of the spiritual estate," 127; "Because we are all," 129; "yet they are all alike," 130; It was "intolerable," 132.

394 world-altering concept: Brecht, in *Martin Luther* (371), writes that Luther "was demolishing the stratification of the society of the medieval church, an action of enormous emancipatory significance."

394 The second wall: *Luther's Works*, vol. 44, 133; "Since these Romanists," 133–134; "that only the pope," 134; "why should we not," 135; Balaam's ass, 136.

394 The final wall: Ibid., 136; If a fire breaks out, 137; "Let us awake," 139.

394 "worldly and ostentatious style": Ibid., 139; "almost a wilderness," 141; "drunken Germans," 141; "How is it," 142; "Today, however," 143.

395 the many insidious devices: Ibid., 143–153.

395 the Datary: Ibid., 153–154.

395 twenty-seven-point reform program: Ibid., 156ff; "think that eating butter," 184; "must be leveled," 185; must admit that Jan Hus, 195; Heretics should be overcome, 196; Priests should not be compelled, 178.

396 "It grieves me to the quick": Ibid., 201; the Bible should be taught, 204ff; "a bad reputation," 214.

397 "We have paid": Ibid., 209; "from his intolerable taxing," 211.

397 the most devastating attack: Friedenthal, *Luther*, 214–215.

397 "I would rather have the wrath": *Luther's Works*, vol. 44, 217.

397 a print run of four thousand copies: Ibid., vol. 44, 119. See also Pettegree, *Brand Luther*, 127.

397 "Good heavens!": *Luther's*

Correspondence, vol. 1, no. 299, September 19, 1520, 358.

397 "I have never read": Ibid., vol. 1, no. 317, to Boniface (Bonifacius) Amerbach [October 22, 1520], 378–379.

398 Then Johann Eck arrived: See his letter, ibid., vol. 1, no. 253, May 3, 1520, 315–316; Boehmer, *Road to Reformation*, 350; Friedenthal, *Luther*, 240.

398 "Let them lick": *Luther's Correspondence*, vol. 1, no. 365, to Spalatin, June 7, 1520, 328.

398 The Italians found Eck's boasting: Fife, *Revolt of Martin Luther*, 495–497.

398 this body drew up a bull: On the drafting of the bull, its presentation to the pope, and the subsequent discussion at the Vatican, see Pastor, *History of the Popes*, vol. 7, 394–403; Brecht, *Martin Luther*, 390–395; Friedenthal, *Luther*, 241–248; Bainton, *Here I Stand*, 111–114; Boehmer, *Road to Reformation*, 350–353; Todd, *Luther*, 177–178. For the contents of the bull, see Hillerbrand, *Reformation*, 80–84.

398 draft to Magliana: On this retreat, see Pastor, *History of the Popes*, vol. 8, 164–166.

400 were burned in the Piazza Navona: Bainton, *Here I Stand*, 121; Fife, *Revolt of Martin Luther*, 497.

400 designated Jerome Aleander: Brecht, *Martin Luther*, 395; Friedenthal, *Luther*, 254–257. Aleander's name in Italian is Girolamo Aleandro.

CHAPTER 23: BONFIRES

402 Charles had grown up: On his background, see Brandi, *Emperor Charles V*; Royall Tyler, *The Emperor Charles the Fifth*; W. L. McElwee, *The Reign of Charles V, 1516 to 1558*; Wim Blockmans, *Emperor Charles V, 1500–1558*; Friedenthal, *Luther*, 262–266; Rice and Grafton, *Foundations of Early Modern Europe*, 124–132.

402 Erasmus in 1516 had dedicated: *Collected Works of Erasmus*, vol. 3, no. 393 [about March 1516], 247–250.

402 Charles's court included: Tyler, *Emperor Charles the Fifth*, 84–85.

402 had been seen as a foreign occupier: Ibid., 43–47; *The New Encyclopaedia Britannica*, 15th ed., vol. 3, "Charles," and vol. 28, "Spain," 41–42.

403 went with his court to La Coruña: Scarisbrick, *Henry VIII*, 76.

403 received an invitation: Ibid., 74–75; *Collected Works of Erasmus*, vol. 7, introductory note to no. 1106, 288–290.

403 From Wolsey's standpoint: Scarisbrick, *Henry VIII*, 71–75; Brandi, *Emperor Charles V*, 117–118.

403 signed a peace treaty: J. J. Scarisbrick, *Henry VIII*, 71–74.

404 Charles and his fleet: Brandi, *Emperor Charles V*, 117–118; Scarisbrick, *Henry VIII*, 76.

404 Erasmus had received a note: *Collected Works of Erasmus*, vol. 7, 289–290.

404 Field of Cloth of Gold: Scarisbrick, *Henry VIII*, 76–78. For a fuller treatment, see Joycelyne G. Russell, *The Field of Cloth of Gold: Men and Manners in 1520*.

405 Erasmus *was* present: *Collected Works of Erasmus*, vol. 7, 288–290. Erasmus describes his meeting with Henry in a letter to Luther, vol. 8, no. 1127A, August 1 [1520], 21.

405 Erasmus (it is believed) accompanied: Ibid., vol. 7, 290.

405 Charles still seemed: Friedenthal, *Luther*, 262–266.

406 the most powerful man in the world: Rice and Grafton, *Foundations of Early Modern Europe*, 124–132.

406 hobbled by gout: MacCulloch, *Reformation*, 265–266; McElwee, *Reign of Charles V*, 211–214.

407 "The potbellies": *Collected Works of Erasmus*, vol. 8, 135.

407 "a second Lee": *Collected Works of*

Erasmus, vol. 8, 23, and endnote on page 360; Rummel, *Erasmus and His Catholic Critics*, vol. 1, 145–177; "Diego López Zúñiga," in *Contemporaries of Erasmus*.

408 Wearily acknowledging the Spaniard's: For Erasmus's early impressions of Diego López Zúñiga (Stunica), see *Collected Works of Erasmus*, vol. 8, no. 1216, to Pierre Barbier, June 26, 1521, 250–252.

408 to send the Augustinian friar another letter: Ibid., vol. 8, no. 1127A, August 1 [1520], 19–23.

408 he described its gist: *Luther's Correspondence*, vol. 1, no. 337, November 17, 1520, 395–396.

409 The two were well acquainted: "Aleandro, Girolamo," in *Contemporaries of Erasmus*; *Collected Works of Erasmus*, vol. 71, xxxix–xl; Fife, *Revolt of Martin Luther*, 566–568.

409 arrived in Cologne: On his movements at this time, see Smith, *Life and Letters of Martin Luther*, 98.

410 he had an audience: Todd, *Luther*, 188; Fife, *Revolt of Martin Luther*, 568; *Luther's Correspondence*, vol. 1, no. 318, Jerome Aleander to Pope Leo X (October 23, 1520), 379.

410 Aleander accompanied him: *Collected Works of Erasmus*, vol. 8, 83, 376; Bainton, *Here I Stand*, 122–123.

411 Louvain thus became the site: *Collected Works of Erasmus*, vol. 8, 83, and vol. 71, xl–xli; Fife, *Revolt of Martin Luther*, 568; Brecht, *Martin Luther*, 416; Bainton, *Here I Stand*, 122–123.

411 immediately felt the impact: This episode is described in *Collected Works of Erasmus*, vol. 8, no. 1153, to Godschalk Rosemondt, October 18, 1520, 68–74.

411 protested Baechem's remarks: Ibid., vol. 8, no. 1162, to Thomas More [November] 1520, 91–98.

411 *Acts of the University of Louvain Against Luther*: The document is in *Collected Works of Erasmus*, vol. 71, 101–105; the introduction on pages 98–100 contains

useful background information, as does the endnote on page 385 in vol. 8.

412 this bit of scurrility: Pastor, in *History of the Popes* (vol. 7, 423), writes that "every method, even the most reprehensible, seemed permissible to Erasmus, if only it would enable him to sweep from the face of the earth this Bull, which was so dangerous to his plans."

412 Charles entered the town: Brandi, *Emperor Charles V*, 122.

412 Erasmus was in Cologne: Erasmus's activities in Cologne are described in *Collected Works of Erasmus*, vol. 8, note at 77–78.

413 *Consilium*: See ibid., vol. 71, 108–112, for this document.

413 "neither overwhelmed": Ibid., vol. 8, 82.

413 He, too, was in Cologne: Smith, *Life and Letters of Martin Luther*, 100; Schwiebert, *Luther*, 494. As Brecht notes in *Martin Luther* (416), we know of Charles's comment to Frederick about Luther and the diet only from Erasmus.

413 Aleander, too, wanted to meet: Smith, *Erasmus*, 235; Smith, *Life and Letters of Martin Luther*, 100; Brandi, *Emperor Charles V*, 127; Brecht, *Martin Luther*, 416–417.

413 invited him to his quarters: *Collected Works of Erasmus*, vol. 8, 78; Smith, *Erasmus*, 235–236; Brecht, *Martin Luther*, 417–418; Augustijn, *Erasmus*, 124.

414 twenty-two axioms: *Collected Works of Erasmus*, vol. 71, 106–107. See also Friedenthal, *Luther*, 260–261.

415 Frederick rejected the nuncios' request: Brecht, *Martin Luther*, 418.

415 agreed to meet: *Collected Works of Erasmus*, vol. 8, 387.

415 "In short": *Luther's Correspondence*, vol. 1, no. 384, to Cardinal de' Medici [February 8], 1521, 458.

415 They were set ablaze: Fife, *Revolt of Martin Luther*, 572–573.

416 "Even in the hills": *Collected Works of Erasmus*, vol. 8, no. 1169, to

Agostino Scarpinelli, December 13, 1520, 123.

416 his books were piled high: *Luther's Correspondence*, vol. 1, no. 374, Beatus Rhenanus to Boniface (Bonifacius) Amerbach, January 7, 1521, 438–449; Fife, *Revolt of Martin Luther*, 573; Bainton, *Here I Stand*, 123.

416 "Lament over the Lutheran Conflagration": Quoted in Bainton, *Here I Stand*, 123–124.

417 as Erasmus discovered: *Collected Works of Erasmus*, vol. 8, no. 1164, to Godschalk Rosemondt [December 1520], 99–101; no. 1165, to Wolfgang Faber Capito, December 6, 1520, 101–105.

417 prepared a long, emotional defense: Ibid., vol. 8, no. 1167, December 6, 1520, 108–121.

CHAPTER 24: FAITH AND FURY

420 began protesting: Brecht, *Martin Luther*, 295–296; Fife, *Revolt of Martin Luther*, 520.

420 Luther was furious: *Luther's Correspondence*, vol. 1, no. 277, to Spalatin, July 14, 1520, 339; no. 278, to Spalatin, July 17, 1520, 339–341.

420 "I almost wish": Quoted in Brecht, *Martin Luther*, 348.

421 "You can if you will": Quoted in Bainton, *Here I Stand*, 111.

421 "great and silent grief": *Luther's Correspondence*, vol. 1, no. 275, to George Spalatin, July 9, 1520, 336.

421 "The world presses me down": Ibid., vol. 1, no. 325, to Jerome Dungersheim [June 1520], 327.

421 "Almost all condemn": *Luther's Works*, vol. 48, no. 60, to Wenceslas Link, August 19, 1520, 170.

421 "another little song": Ibid., vol. 44, 217.

421 *The Babylonian Captivity of the Church*: Ibid., vol. 36, 11–126; "into mere merchandise," 35–36; "a good work and a sacrifice," 35; divine promise of forgiveness, 38; only if it was performed,

52; "as if they were too sacred," 41; "in a loud clear voice," 54; "Rise up then," 24; "to set up a seed bed," 112; "does not belong to the priests," 27; "We are all equally priests," 116.

424 Luther similarly dismissed: Ibid., vol. 36, confirmation, 91; extreme unction, 117; marriage, 92–106; Erasmus's observation, 93–94; "filthy lucre," 96; "The Romanists of our day," 97.

424 "Vulvas and penises": *Vulvas et veretra* in Latin. The translation in *Luther's Works* gives this as "vulvas and genitals," but *The Annotated Luther*, vol. 3, *Church and Sacraments*, translates it more precisely (101).

424 the only circumstances: *Luther's Works*, vol. 36, 102–104.

424 He considered it so repellent: Ibid., 105; to warn parents, 80.

425 its true value: Ibid., 59–61; "unmask the tyranny," 81; a workshop "of greed and power," 85; "torture poor consciences," 89–90.

425 "Neither pope nor bishop": Ibid., 70, 72.

426 all had gone smoothly: Brecht, *Martin Luther*, 400–401.

426 Eck reached Leipzig: Ibid., 401; *Luther's Correspondence*, vol. 1, 360–363.

426 headed for Erfurt: *Luther's Correspondence*, vol. 1, 381, 387–388.

427 "At last that Roman bull": *Luther's Correspondence*, vol. 1, no. 304, October [11], 1520, 365–366.

427 Luther had drafted an appeal: *Luther's Works*, vol. 48, no. 63, to Emperor Charles V, August 30, 1520, 175–179.

428 In their meeting: *Luther's Correspondence*, vol. 1, 366–367; Brecht, *Martin Luther*, 404–405.

428 Matthaeus Adrianus: *Luther's Correspondence*, vol. 1, 387.

428 *The Freedom of a Christian*: *Luther's Works*, vol. 31, 343–377; "A Christian is a perfectly," 344; The one thing on which a Christian life, 345; "Every Christian is by faith," 354; "unbearable

bondage," 356; "I answer," 358; took an image from Aristotle, 361; the obligations a faithful Christian, 364; The truly Christian life, 365; A Christian should not distinguish, 367; By that standard, 370.

430 his letter to Leo X: Ibid., vol. 31, 334–343.

432 "No one's books": *Luther's Correspondence*, vol. 1, no. 324, November 1, 1520, 383.

432 "I care nothing": Ibid., vol. 1, no. 315, to Michael Mäurer, October 20, 1520, 376–377.

432 "to preach, lecture": *Luther's Works*, vol. 48, no. 65, to Duke John Frederick, October 30, 1520, 181–182.

433 to abandon the canonical hours: Roper, *Martin Luther*, 134.

433 "pious and zealous youth": Smith, *Life and Letters of Martin Luther*, 100–101. On the events of this day, see Friedenthal, *Luther*, 251–253; Brecht, *Martin Luther*, 423–426; Schwiebert, *Luther and His Times*, 490–492; Hillerbrand, *Reformation*, 85–86.

433 Luther wrote a note: *Luther's Correspondence*, vol. 1, no. 355, December 10, 1520, 414–415.

433 was even more daring: Brecht, *Martin Luther*, 424.

434 he admonished the students: Hillerbrand, *Reformation*, 86.

434 "Everything is tending": *Luther's Correspondence*, vol. 1, no. 349, December 4, 1520, 405–408.

434 *Why the Books of the Pope: Luther's Works*, vol. 31, 383–395; "If they are allowed," 394. See also Friedenthal, *Luther*, 252–253; Brecht, *Martin Luther*, 425–426.

435 *Decet Romanum Pontificem*: Brecht, *Martin Luther*, 427.

CHAPTER 25: WILL HE COME?

436 In the weeks prior to its start: Fife, *Revolt of Martin Luther*, 614–615; Thomas M.

Lindsay, *A History of the Reformation*, vol. 1, *The Reformation in Germany from Its Beginning to the Religious Peace of Augsburg*, 3rd ed., 267–270.

436 had to share a room: Friedenthal, *Luther*, 272.

436 simmered with discontent: Lindsay, *History of the Reformation*, vol. 1, 268–269.

437 "The people buy these pictures": *Luther's Correspondence*, vol. 1, no. 363, Aleander to Cardinal de' Medici [December 18, 1520], 429.

437 the papal nuncio was struck: Ibid., vol. 1, no. 359, to Cardinal de' Medici [middle of December] 1520, 420–423; "I feel less safe": 423.

437 the Ebernburg: Todd, *Luther*, 195.

437 "Do you think": Quoted in Bainton, *Here I Stand*, 130.

437 the nuncio had reserved rooms: *Luther's Correspondence*, vol. 1, no. 359, Aleander to Cardinal de' Medici [middle of December] 1520, 423.

438 "The Emperor is a man": Ibid., 420.

438 had sent a friendly letter: Ibid., vol. 1, no. 342, November 28, 1520, 398–399.

438 only one of his many preoccupations: Friedenthal, *Luther*, 269–271.

438 Suleiman I the Magnificent: Blockmans, *Emperor Charles V*, 40–41.

438 wanted their own concerns addressed: Brecht, *Martin Luther*, 433; McElwee, *Reign of Charles V*, 59–60; Brandi, *Emperor Charles V*, 128–129.

439 The delegates were divided: Lindsay, *History of the Reformation*, vol. 1, 270.

439 a "heretic a thousand times worse": *Luther's Correspondence*, vol. 1, 417, 423.

439 In his speech: Aleander's speech is summarized at ibid., vol. 1, no. 362, Aleander to Cardinal Pucci [December 17], 1520, 425–428.

439 sent Frederick a letter: Ibid., vol. 1, no. 361, December 17, 1520, 424–425.

440 Frederick and his advisers arrived: Brecht, *Martin Luther*, 434; Lindsay, *History of the Reformation*, vol. 1, 274.

440 The streets swarmed: Lindsay, *History of the Reformation*, vol. 1, 269.

440 The major items: Brandi, *Emperor Charles V*, 128.

440 latest list of German grievances: Hans J. Hillerbrand, ed., *The Protestant Reformation*, rev. ed., 3–13.

440 The Reichstag consisted of three estates: Thomas A. Brady, *German Histories in the Age of Reformations, 1400–1650*, 153.

441 "has twenty thousand comrades": *Luther's Correspondence*, vol. 1, no. 369, Andrew Rosso to a friend, December 30, 1520, 434.

441 Luther as the German Hercules: Brecht, *Martin Luther*, 431.

441 found his position undermined: *Luther's Correspondence*, vol. 1, no. 363, Aleander to Cardinal de' Medici [December 18, 1520], 429; no. 394 [February 8], 1521, 457–459.

441 "the greatest corner-stone": Ibid., vol. 1, 459.

441 Aleander circulated an epigram: Friedenthal, *Luther*, 257.

441 "Luther is pestilential": *Collected Works of Erasmus*, vol. 8, 190.

441 *Die göttliche Mühle*: Ibid., vol. 8, 208, which shows the drawing.

442 "His *De captivitate Babylonica*": Ibid., vol. 8, no. 1186, to Nicolaas Everaerts, February 25, 1521, 157.

442 "a maniac": Ibid., vol. 8, no. 1188, to Nicolaas Everaerts [March 1521], 160.

442 "Never was the time": Ibid., vol. 8, no. 1180, from Leo X, January 15, 1521, 145.

443 "I would rather be": Ibid., vol. 8, no. 1155, November 8, 1520, 78.

443 He instead wrote a series of letters: Ibid., vol. 8, note, 194–195; Smith, *Erasmus*, 245–246.

443 "have no ideas": *Collected Works of Erasmus*, vol. 8, no. 1195, to Luigi Marliano, March 25 [1521], 171.

443 left for Antwerp: Ibid., vol. 8, 198. Also see "Antwerp," in *Encyclopedia of the Renaissance*; "Antwerp," in *Europe: 1450–1789: Encyclopedia of the Early Modern World*.

443 the commotion over Luther: *Collected Works of Erasmus*, vol. 8, 402.

444 Luther's teachings: See Friedenthal, *Luther*, 259.

444 "No one's danger": *Luther's Works*, vol. 48, no. 68, December 29, 1520, 188–191.

444 "Rumor constantly tells us": *Luther's Correspondence*, vol. 1, no. 350, December 5, 1520, 408–411.

444 Luther quickly drafted a pamphlet: Ibid., vol. 44, "An Instruction to Penitents Concerning the Forbidden Books of Dr. M. Luther," 223–229; "Let nothing on earth," 227. See also *Luther's Correspondence*, vol. 1, 472.

445 Johann von Staupitz: *Luther's Correspondence*, vol. 1, no. 372, January 4, 1521, 437.

445 "If Christ loves you": Smith, *Life and Letters of Martin Luther*, 108–109.

445 he kept four presses busy: *Luther's Correspondence*, vol. 1, no. 405, Matthew Philip to Stephan Roth, February 26, 1521, 472.

445 The latter: *Luther's Works*, vol. 32, "Defense and Explanation of All the Articles," 7–99; "God did not choose": 9.

446 *Answer to the Hyperchristian*: Ibid., vol. 39, 143–224; "must and should cause quarreling," 133.

446 Joachim I: *Luther's Correspondence*, vol. 1, 442; Duke Bogislav: 451–452.

447 felt disgust at their "verbosity": Ibid., vol. 1, no. 408, to Conrad Pelican [end of February], 1521, 477–478.

447 "There is racing and jousting": Quoted in Friedenthal, *Luther*, 270.

447 intently studied Charles V: Ibid., 263.

447 "The court is so utterly parlous": Ibid., 270.

447 Charles's top priority: Ibid., 270–271.

447 the *Flugschriften* pouring into Worms: Fife, *Revolt of Martin Luther*, 618–619;

Lindsay, *History of the Reformation*, vol. 1, 300–305.

448 "To the Champions": See *Luther's Correspondence*, vol. 1, 460.

448 "The whole of Germany": Ibid., vol. 1, no. 394, to Cardinal de' Medici [February 8], 1521, 454–461.

448 "Heretics," he wrote: Ibid., vol. 1, no. 401, to Johann Eck, February 17, 1421, 466–468.

448 Lasting three hours: For Aleander's own description of his talk, see ibid., vol. 1, no. 397, to Cardinal de' Medici [February 14], 1521, 462–464. See also Brecht, *Martin Luther*, 440.

449 It caused a storm: *Luther's Correspondence*, vol. 1, no. 407, Aleander to Cardinal de' Medici, February 27, 1521, 473–477. See also Brecht, *Martin Luther*, 442.

449 "to obtain information": *Luther's Correspondence*, vol. 1, no. 412, Emperor Charles V to Luther, March 6, 1521, 482–483; no. 413, "Safe-Conduct of Charles V. for Luther," March 6, 1521, 483–484.

449 the horrified Aleander thought: Ibid., vol. 1, no. 424, Aleander to Cardinal de' Medici [March 15 and 16], 1521, 496.

449 the document was not signed: Boehmer, *Road to Reformation*, 390.

449 On March 16: Ibid.

CHAPTER 26: JUDGMENT AT WORMS

450 another furious broadside: Marius, *Martin Luther*, 283.

450 "Good heavens!": *Luther's Correspondence*, vol. 1, no. 414, March 7, 1521, 485.

450 The *Answer to the Book*: Marius, *Martin Luther*, 283–285; Boehmer, *Road to Reformation*, 395–397.

450 a series of woodcuts: Brecht, *Martin Luther*, 432; Hillerbrand, *Reformation*, 96–97.

451 The town fathers: Brecht, *Martin Luther*,

448; Boehmer, *Road to Reformation*, 400.

451 "My dear brother": Quoted in Lindsay, *History of the Reformation*, vol. 1, 273.

451 crossed the Elbe and headed south: On Luther's journey to Worms, see Schwiebert, *Luther*, 496–501; Todd, *Luther*, 196–197; Fife, *Revolt of Martin Luther*, 650–653; Brecht, *Martin Luther*, 448–451.

451 ordinary people came out: Marius, *Martin Luther*, 288.

452 As the party approached Weimar: Brecht, *Martin Luther*, 448; Fife, *Revolt of Martin Luther*, 650–651.

452 As Erfurt neared: Brecht, *Martin Luther*, 448–449; Boehmer, *Road to Reformation*, 401–402.

452 Luther was asked to preach: *Luther's Works*, vol. 51, "Sermon Preached at Erfurt on the Journey to Worms," 60–66; "I will tell the truth," 65–66.

453 "I am coming, my Spalatin": Ibid., vol. 48, no. 71, 198.

453 a great crowd: *Luther's Correspondence*, vol. 1, no. 447, Aleander to the Vice-Chancellor de' Medici, April 16, 1521, 521–522; no. 449, Guy Warbeck to Duke John of Saxony, April 16, 1521, 523.

453 Philip of Hesse: Boehmer, *Road to Reformation*, 405–406.

454 Ulrich von Pappenheim: The following account draws in part on *Luther's Works*, vol. 32, "Luther at the Diet of Worms," 105–131, which contains reports by Luther and his supporters as well as by Aleander.

454 led out through the garden: Friedenthal, *Luther*, 274; Lindsay, *History of the Reformation*, vol. 1, 278–279.

455 one of the great moments: Bainton, *Here I Stand*, 141.

455 Their first impression: Friedenthal, *Luther*, 275.

455 "That fellow": Quoted in Bainton, *Here I Stand*, 141.

455 had summoned him for two reasons: *Luther's Works*, vol. 32, 106.

456 he had written all of the books: Ibid., vol. 32, 107.

456 "I thought His Imperial Majesty": Ibid., vol. 48, no. 73, to Lucas Cranach, April 28, 1521, 201–203.

456 Eck again addressed him: Ibid., vol. 32, 107.

457 "I shall not in all eternity": Ibid., vol. 48, no. 72, April 17, 1521, 200.

457 "Do you wish to defend": Luther's speech, ibid., vol. 32, 108–112.

459 Eck stepped forward: His response to Luther, ibid., vol. 32, 126–130.

460 "horned": In Latin, *cornutum*; on its meaning, see Smith, *Life and Letters of Martin Luther*, 117–118.

460 "Since then": *Luther's Works*, vol. 32, 112.

460 those words do not appear: Ibid., vol. 32, 113; Fife, *Revolt of Martin Luther*, 666; Friedenthal, *Luther*, 269. Bainton, seeking to justify the title of his biography (*Here I Stand*), writes (144) that "the words, though not recorded on the spot, may nevertheless be genuine, because the listeners at the moment may have been too moved to write."

460 As he passed out of the hall: Friedenthal, *Luther*, 278–279; Lindsay, *History of the Reformation*, vol. 1, 292; *Luther's Correspondence*, vol. 1, no. 453, Aleander to Cardinal de' Medici [April 18 and 19], 1521, 529–530.

461 Just as the birth of modern France: See Fife, *Revolt of Martin Luther*, 655.

461 wrote Thomas Carlyle: *On Heroes, Hero Worship, and the Heroic in History* (Oxford: Oxford University Press, 1845, 1965), 176–177.

461 drawn entirely from Werner's imagination: See Schwiebert, *Luther*, 501.

462 As one historian has noted: MacCulloch, *Reformation*, 127.

462 This differed fundamentally: Hajo Holborn, in *History of Modern Germany*, vol. 1 (130–131) writes that Luther's religion "was more than the culmination of the historical trend toward a more personalistic piety, and remained separated by a deep gulf from Renaissance individualism." It was "a tremendous step to find the essence of religion entirely in the personal conscience, to admit, at least in principle, no other authority than personal faith, and to expect the individual to apply this faith in a creative manner to the solution of all the problems of life." But Luther "was a world apart from any modern conception under which man has within himself the capacity to reach for the stars." He was "absolutely convinced that the Word of God was clear. He was, therefore, not prepared to tolerate unorthodox people."

463 "I did wrong": Quoted in Friedenthal, *Luther*, 279.

463 "The movement is now": *Luther's Correspondence*, vol. 1, no. 437, to Vice-Chancellor de' Medici, April 5, 1521, 509.

464 he had it read: Ibid., vol. 1, no. 453, Aleander to Vice-Chancellor Cardinal de' Medici [April 18 and 19], 1521, 528–531; *Luther's Works*, vol. 32, 114–115; Brandi, *Emperor Charles V*, 131.

464 they turned "pale as death": *Luther's Correspondence*, vol. 1, no. 453, 530.

464 hit by a new wave of fly sheets: Ibid., vol. 1, no. 463, Gaspar Contarini to Matthew Dandolo, April 26, 1521, 539; no. 464, Marino Caracciolo and Jerome Aleander to Vice-Chancellor Cardinal de' Medici [April 27], 1521, 540. See also Fife, *Revolt of Martin Luther*, 670–671; Brecht, *Martin Luther*, 463–464; Lindsay, *History of the Reformation*, vol. 1, 293.

464 The *Bundschuh*, the sturdy leather shoe: Lindsay, *History of the Reformation*, vol. 1, 103–106; Bainton, *Here I Stand*, 146; Friedenthal, *Luther*, 282.

465 Adding to the alarm: Todd, *Luther*, 195; Brecht, *Martin Luther*, 447.

465 "The Emperor has not": *Luther's Correspondence*, vol. 1, no. 444, Aleander to Vice-Chancellor de' Medici, April [15], 1521, 516.

465 Albrecht of Mainz: Ibid., vol. 1, 540.

465 a commission was appointed: Ibid., vol. 1, no. 464, Caracciolo and Aleander to Vice-Chancellor Cardinal de' Medici [April 27], 1521, 539–547; Bainton, *Here I Stand*, 146; Fife, *Revolt of Martin Luther*, 673–688.

466 "He declined all that": *Luther's Correspondence*, vol. 1, no. 464, 545, 546.

466 As he would put it: Ibid., vol. 1, no. 471, Luther to Count Albert of Mansfeld, May 3, 1521, 558.

466 "Thus we parted": Ibid., 558.

467 he was informed: Fife, *Revolt of Martin Luther*, 689; Brecht, *Martin Luther*, 470–471.

467 toasted some slices of bread: The papal nuncios took note of this detail in their dispatch, *Luther's Correspondence*, vol. 1, no. 464, 547.

467 Luther wrote to Lucas Cranach: *Luther's Works*, vol. 48, no. 73, April 28, 1521, 201–203.

467 completed the draft of a letter: *Luther's Correspondence*, vol. 1, no. 465, to Emperor Charles V, April 28, 1521, 547–551.

468 "This letter was never given": Ibid., 547.

468 Luther and his party: Luther describes these events in a letter he wrote to Spalatin some ten days after the event, *Luther's Works*, vol. 48, no. 80, May 14, 1521, 222–228. See also Smith, *Life and Letters of Martin Luther*, 119–120; Todd, *Luther*, 208–209; Brecht, *Martin Luther*, 472.

468 two of his most precious possessions: Brecht, *Martin Luther*, 472.

469 at about eleven in the evening: *Luther's Works*, vol. 48, 219, 227.

CHAPTER 27: THE MARTYR'S CROWN

473 The news of Luther's disappearance: Friedenthal, *Luther*, 287; Lindsay, *History of the Reformation*, vol. 1, 295–296.

473 "raise a rebellion": *Luther's Correspondence*, vol. 1, no. 475, Aleander to Vice-Chancellor Cardinal de' Medici [May 8], 1521, 564.

473 "I know not whether": Smith, *Life and Letters of Martin Luther*, 120; Panofsky, *Life and Art of Albrecht Dürer*, 151; Lindsay, *History of the Reformation*, vol. 1, 188.

474 "perhaps is in safe keeping": *Collected Works of Erasmus*, vol. 8, no. 1203, May 14, 1521, 211–212.

474 *The Lamentations of Peter*: Bainton, *Erasmus of Christendom*, 168.

474 "There is not a drinking-party": *Collected Works of Erasmus*, vol. 8, no. 1225, to Pierre Barbier, August 13, 1521, 280.

474 open letter of admonishment: Ibid., vol. 8, no. 1196 [middle of March 1521], 175–194; "Ever since you moved," 176.

474 wrote a long appeal to Jonas: Ibid., vol. 8, no. 1202, May 10, 1521, 201–211; "I wonder very much," 202; "in a savage torrent," 203; follow the example of Christ, 204; Skilled physicians, 205; "my own work," 210; "be disastrous to every man," 210.

475 what to do about the *comma Johanneum*: Andrew J. Brown, introduction, part 2, "Excursus: Codex 61 (Montfortianus) and 1 John 5, 7–8," *Opera Omnia Desiderii Erasmi*, 6(4): 27–111. See also Grantley McDonald, "Erasmus and the Johannine Comma," *Bible Translator*, 67(1): 42–55, 2016; J. K. Elliott, "'Novum Testamentum editum est': The Five-Hundredth Anniversary of Erasmus's New Testament," *Bible Translator*, 67(1): 24–26, 2016.

476 "no cause for making malicious accusations": *Opera Omnia Desiderii Erasmi*, 9(2): 258–259, translated at

Opera Omnia Desiderii Erasmi, 6(4): 32–33.

476 a steady flow of gifts: Jean Hoyoux, "Les moyens d'existence d'Érasme," *Bibliothèque d'humanisme et Renaissance*, Travaux & Documents, vol. 5 (Paris: Librarie E. Droz, 1944), 7–59.

476 "a regular grandee": *Collected Works of Erasmus*, vol. 8, no. 1205, to William Warham, May 24, 1521, 215; see also notes 4 and 9 on page 417.

477 "pills and enemas": Ibid., vol. 8, 269.

477 Pieter Wichmans: Ibid., 223.

477 "to grow young again": Ibid., 269.

477 works of Augustine: Erasmus describes this project in a letter ("To the Reader") accompanying Vives's edition of *City of God*, ibid., vol. 9 [August 1522], 168–173.

477 a letter to his friend Richard Pace: Ibid., vol. 8, no. 1218, July 5, 1521, 257–259.

478 centuries, in fact: See Bainton, *Erasmus of Christendom*, 167.

478 the delegates in fetid Worms: Friedenthal, *Luther*, 288–289.

478 A priest from the imperial court: *Luther's Correspondence*, vol. 1, 560.

479 the Edict of Worms would: An abridged version is in Hillerbrand, *Reformation*, 95–100. The full version is available at crivoice.org/creededictworms.html.

480 a declaration of war: Friedenthal, in *Luther* (291), calls the edict "the first and most thorough restrictive edict and censorship measure of the dawning age of modern times."

480 inaugurated a period: Writing in 2005, Eisenstein (*Printing Revolution in Early Modern Europe*, 178) refers to "the long war between the Roman church and the printing press," which lasted for four centuries after it began "and has not completely ended."

480 quoted from Ovid's *Art of Love*: Friedenthal, *Luther*, 290.

480 "Here you have": Quoted in Lindsay, *History of the Reformation*, vol. 1, 298–299.

481 The great confrontation: *Collected Works of Erasmus*, vol. 8, 438–439; Friedenthal, *Luther*, 287; Blockmans, *Emperor Charles V*, 51–52; Marius, *Martin Luther*, 337.

481 frequently rode into Brussels: *Collected Works of Erasmus*, vol. 9, 368, and vol. 8, 268–269.

481 catch "many hares in one field": Ibid., vol. 8, 294.

482 Erasmus was present: Ibid.

482 a bonfire had been scheduled: *Luther's Correspondence*, vol. 2, 29–30.

482 Wolsey had sent the king: Smith, *Life and Letters of Martin Luther*, 192–193.

482 *Assertio Septem Sacramentorum*: See Scarisbrick, *Henry VIII*, 110–113.

482 Erasmus was also suspected: *Collected Works of Erasmus*, vol. 9, 181–182, 394–395.

482 the *Assertio* set out: Henry VIII, *Assertio Septem Sacramentorum or Defence of the Seven Sacraments*; "brags so clearly," 276; Henry also condemned, 298–300; "first of all sacraments," 364–366; "indissolvable bond," 368; "impertinent calumnies," 368; venomous serpent, a "detestable trumpeter," 188; "hellish wolf," 456; "this one little monk," 462; "more harmful than," 462.

483 as soon as it was printed: Scarisbrick, *Henry VIII*, 111–117; *Collected Works of Erasmus*, vol. 8, 327.

484 "I greatly long": *Collected Works of Erasmus*, vol. 8, no. 1227, August 23, 1521, 282.

484 similarly pressed by Jean Glapion: Ibid., vol. 9, 50.

484 "All the other labors": Ibid., vol. 8, no. 1213, June 18, 1521, 247.

484 "Luther's party are crazier": Ibid., vol. 8, no. 1241, October 14, 1521, 317.

485 Writing to Pierre Barbier: Ibid., vol. 8, no. 1225, August 13, 1521, 271–281.

485 signed a secret treaty: Scarisbrick, *Henry VIII*, 88–89; Tyler, *Emperor Charles the Fifth*, 52–53.

485 "The whole Christian world": *Collected*

Works of Erasmus, vol. 8, no. 1238, to Nicolaas Everaerts, [October] 1521, 312.

486 a letter to Guillaume Budé: Ibid., vol. 8, no. 1233, [September] 1521, 294–299.

486 moving beyond the suffocating paternalism: See J. K. Sowards, "Erasmus and the Education of Women," *Sixteenth Century Journal*, 13(4): 77–89, Winter 1982.

487 a man for all hours: Erasmus had first applied this phrase to More in 1511 in his preface to the *Praise of Folly*; see *Collected Works of Erasmus*, vol. 2, 163. Robert Whittington, in his play *Vulgarius*, called More "a man for all seasons"—a phrase made famous by the 1960 play and the 1966 movie titled *A Man for All Seasons*. See Richard S. Sylvester, "The 'Man for All Seasons' Again: Robert Whittington's Verses to Sir Thomas More," *Huntington Library Quarterly*, 26(2): 147, February 1963; Whittington's phrase, Sylvester notes, "probably echoes Erasmus' phrasing in the preface to the *Praise of Folly*."

487 Erasmus returned from serene Anderlecht: Ibid., vol. 8, 443.

487 "He seemed to be": Ibid., vol. 9, no. 1342, to Marcus Laurinus, February 1, 1523, 370.

487 Departing on October 28, 1521: Ibid., vol. 8, 319.

CHAPTER 28: OUTLAW

488 At the Wartburg: On Luther's stay there, see Martin Brecht, *Martin Luther: Shaping and Defining the Reformation*, 1–25; Friedenthal, *Luther*, 280–286; Heinrich Bornkamm, *Luther in Mid-Career*, 1–50; Bainton, *Here I Stand*, 149–152; Schwiebert, *Luther*, 513–531; Marius, *Martin Luther*, 299–316; Mullett, *Martin Luther*, 131–135; Todd, *Luther*, 209–227; Roper, *Martin Luther*, 183–205.

488 Its centerpiece: Günter Schachardt, "The Wartburg—World's Heritage"
(Regensburg: Schnell und Stein, 2001), 4. The Wartburg today is a popular tourist attraction, visited by fans of Wagner, Catholic admirers of Elizabeth, Lutherans eager to see the reformer's hideout, and sightseers drawn by the dramatic setting.

489 "a strange prisoner": *Luther's Works*, vol. 48, no. 79, to John Agricola, May 12, 1521, 221.

489 "many evil and astute demons": Ibid., vol. 48, no. 101, to George Spalatin, November 1, 1521, 324.

489 sent a note to Melanchthon: Ibid., vol. 48, no. 77, May 12, 1521, 215–217.

490 To his friend Nikolaus von Amsdorf: Ibid., vol. 48, no. 78, May 12, 1521, 218–220; the German is at *Luthers Werke, Briefwechsel*, vol. 2, 334.

490 "in the land of the birds": *Luther's Works*, vol. 48, 236.

490 "I am sitting here": Ibid., vol. 48, no. 80, May 14, 1521, 222–228.

490 "I cannot believe": Ibid., vol. 48, no. 81, May 26, 1521, 228–236.

491 Luther brooded obsessively: These thoughts are recorded in *The Misuse of the Mass*, which Luther wrote that fall. Ibid., vol. 36, 134.

491 Dedicating his commentary: Ibid., vol. 48, no. 83, June 1521, 248–252.

491 Samuel Taylor Coleridge: *The Friend: A Series of Essays*, 3rd ed. (London: William Pickering, 1837), vol. 1, 184. "I can scarcely conceive a more delightful volume than might be made from Luther's letters, especially from those that were written from the Warteburg [*sic*]," Coleridge wrote.

492 able to borrow books: Friedenthal, *Luther*, 297.

492 to switch from Latin to German: *Luther's Works*, vol. 48, 229, 237ff.

492 Christians should not "treat the Jews": Brooks Schramm and Kirsi I. Stjerna, eds., *Martin Luther, the Bible, and the Jewish People: A Reader*, 74–75.

492 Responding with a profane blast: This appears in *Judgment of Martin Luther on Monastic Vows, Luther's Works*, vol. 44, 276.

492 "He thinks that everything": *Luther's Correspondence*, vol. 2, no. 506, September 19, 1521, 56–59.

493 "It is impossible that I endure": *Luther's Works*, vol. 48, no. 85, July 13, 1521, 256–263.

493 Some scholars, however: See, for instance, Friedenthal, *Luther* (299), who writes that Luther's self-accusations "have very misguidedly been used to draw conclusions about 'sensual excesses' and sins, and indeed they lend themselves to this interpretation if they are taken out of their context." On the other hand, Brecht, in *Shaping and Defining* (2), writes that "sexual desires bothered him," and Todd, in *Luther: A Life* (213), similarly observes that "sexual tension had begun to be a threat."

494 "Be a sinner and sin boldly": *Luther's Works*, vol. 48, no. 91, August 1, 1521, 282.

494 "You are now well supplied": Ibid., vol. 48, no. 85, July 13, 1521, 262.

494 some powerful new laxatives: Ibid., vol. 48, no. 90, to George Spalatin, July 31, 1521, 276.

494 to go on a hunting expedition: *Luther's Correspondence*, vol. 2, no. 503, to George Spalatin, August 15, 1521, 53–54.

494 *On Confession*: Brecht, *Shaping and Defining*, 18–21.

495 the arrival of two sets of theses: *Luther's Correspondence*, vol. 2, no. 501, to Philipp Melanchthon, August 1, 1521, 47–51.

495 The second set of theses: Ibid., vol. 2, no. 503, to Spalatin, 52–54; *Luther's Works*, vol. 48, no. 92, to Philipp Melanchthon, August 3, 1521, 283–289.

496 "Since he is rich in the Word": *Luther's Correspondence*, vol. 2, no. 506, to Spalatin, September 19, 1521, 56–59.

496 the Reformation was indeed moving ahead: On events in Wittenberg, see Gordon Rupp, *Patterns of Reformation*, 79–110; Roper, *Martin Luther*, 206–228; Brecht, *Shaping and Defining*, 25–45; Friedenthal, *Luther*, 314–327; Marius, *Martin Luther*, 317–330; Bainton, *Here I Stand*, 152–156; Lindsay, *History of the Reformation*, vol. 1, 311–316.

496 "brothers at one in Christ": Lindsay, *History of the Reformation*, vol. 1, 311–312.

497 Karlstadt had been away: Rupp, *Patterns of Reformation*, 87; Marius, *Martin Luther*, 318–319; Brecht, *Shaping and Defining*, 26–27.

497 Three priests: Brecht, *Shaping and Defining*, 21–22.

497 Bartholomew Bernhardi: "Bernhardi, Bartholomeus von Feldkirchen," in *The Oxford Encyclopedia of the Reformation*.

497 Melanchthon wrote a defense: Clyde Leonard Manschreck, *Melanchthon: The Quiet Reformer*, 72.

498 The clergy at the Castle Church: Bainton, *Here I Stand*, 157.

498 Gabriel Zwilling: Marius, *Martin Luther*, 319–320; Bornkamm, *Luther in Mid-Career*, 24–25: "a second prophet," 24.

499 a group of mendicants: Bornkamm, *Luther in Mid-Career*, 25.

499 the Masses on October 13: *Luther's Correspondence*, vol. 2, no. 511, Albert Burer to Beatus Rhenanus, October 19, 1521, 62–63.

500 the elector's position: Bainton, *Here I Stand*, 158; Marius, *Martin Luther*, 320.

501 Justus Jonas was assigned to preach: *Luther's Correspondence*, vol. 2, no. 516, "anonymous letter" [December 4, 1521], 75–78.

501 One Sunday he was so ill: Ibid., 77.

501 half of the Wittenberg Augustinians: *Luther's Works*, vol. 48, 337.

501 "What a mess we are in": Quoted in Bainton, *Here I Stand*, 157.

501 "at last my behind": *Luther's Works*, vol. 48, no. 99, October 7, 1521, 316.

502 *The Misuse of the Mass*: Ibid., vol. 36, 133–230; "that is, on the most abominable," 178; "are used for nothing," 178; "an unbelieving people," 154; "a new sea-monster," 159; "be eradicated," 158; "by so much as a single letter," 140; "an addition of the devil," 142; the "Scriptures cannot err," 137; "is a spiritual priesthood," 138; "willed the awakening," 229.

503 "I have decided to attack": Ibid., vol. 48, no. 103, November 11, 1521, 328.

503 *Judgment of Martin Luther on Monastic Vows*: Ibid., vol. 44, 251–400; sounding like "pipe organs," 324–325; attracted by the granaries, 358; turned men into "idlers," 335; If a monk sees someone, 329; love only their own kind, 333; "Almost everything about it," 369; "how many uncleannesses," 343; "inward and intrinsic tyrant," 339; A man under the influence, 340; yet it was precisely here, 345.

504 held one person responsible: Ibid., vol. 44, 306–307; letter to Eustochium, 346; celibacy should be regarded, 262.

505 "I want the whole idea": Ibid., vol. 44, 328.

505 emotional prefatory letter: Ibid., vol. 48, no. 104, November 21, 1521, 329–336.

505 The collection's nearly nine thousand items: Friedenthal, *Luther*, 300; Bornkamm, *Luther in Mid-Career*, 21.

506 prepared a stinging protest: See *Luther's Works*, vol. 48, no. 99, to George Spalatin, October 7, 1521, 315–317.

506 "I have hardly ever read": Ibid., vol. 48, no. 103, to George Spalatin, November 11, 1521, 325–328.

506 decided to write to Albrecht directly: Ibid., vol. 48, no. 106, December 1, 1521, 339–343.

507 rode down from the Wartburg: Brecht, *Shaping and Defining*, 29; Bornkamm, *Luther in Mid-Career*, 36.

CHAPTER 29: WAS NOWHERE SAFE?

508 Erasmus had a stroke of luck: *Collected Works of Erasmus*, vol. 9, 371–374.

508 "pestilent rheum": Ibid., vol. 9, 46.

508 "thumbed everywhere": Ibid., vol. 8, 331.

508 he took up Matthew: The preface, dedicated to Charles V, ibid., vol. 9, no. 1255, January 13, 1522, 6–11; the paraphrase itself is in vol. 45, 84–139.

509 "Since the evangelists wrote down": Ibid., vol. 9, 11.

509 to press "his slanderous views": Ibid., vol. 9, no. 1260, from Jakob Ziegler, February 16, 1522, 23–36.

509 Stunica was intent on exposing: Ibid., vol. 9, no. 1277, from Juan de Vergara, April 24, 1522, 69–73.

509 to "burn in a coat of pitch": Ibid., vol. 8, no. 2 (in the Vergara-López Zuñiga correspondence), January 9, 1522, 341; see also the endnote to that passage, 457.

509 found an egregious example: Ibid., vol. 9, 398–399.

509 "Luther's party": Ibid., vol. 9, no. 1259, February 12 [1522], 22–23.

510 "All Luther's party": Ibid., vol. 9, no. 1276, April 23, 1522, 68–69.

510 preparing a new volume: The *Colloquies*, ibid., vols. 39 and 40. For background on them, see the introduction by Craig R. Thompson in vol. 39, xvii–xlix; Smith, *Erasmus*, 286–319; Phillips, *Erasmus and the Northern Renaissance*, 76–89; Halkin, *Erasmus*, 182–206; Augustijn, *Erasmus*, 161–171.

510 with at least thirty reprints: *Collected Works of Erasmus*, vol. 39, xxiv.

511 declaring in his Table Talk: *Luthers Werke, Tischreden*, vol. 1, no. 817, 397; *Tischreden*, vol. 4, no. 4899, 573.

511 In "Inns": *Collected Works of Erasmus*, vol. 39, 370–375.

512 proposes various preventive measures: Ibid., vol. 40, 852–854.

512 deal with marriage, courtship, and women: Ibid., vol. 39, 256.

512 it is up to the wives: Ibid., vol. 39, 318.

512 "A Marriage in Name Only": Ibid., vol. 40, 842–854.

512 "The Abbott and the Learned Lady": Ibid., vol. 39, 501–505.

512 true and false piety: Ibid., vol. 39, xxix.

512 "The Shipwreck": Ibid., vol. 39, 352–360.

513 "The Godly Feast": Ibid., vol. 39, 175–207; "St Socrates," 194.

514 as a butcher in the colloquy "A Fish Diet" remarks: Ibid., vol. 40, 707–708, 687.

514 On Ash Wednesday: Hillerbrand, Reformation, 127; MacCulloch, Reformation, 135; G. R. Potter, Zwingli, 74–75; Ulrich Gäbler, Huldrych Zwingli: His Life and Work, 53–54.

514 Froschauer maintained: Hillerbrand, Reformation, 128.

515 "How dare a man": Ibid., 130.

515 Zwingli would be its father: On Zwingli's life and thinking, see Potter, Zwingli; Gäbler, Huldrych Zwingli; Hillerbrand, Reformation, 104–169; Walker, History of the Christian Church, 441–447; Ozment, Age of Reform, 318–328; MacCulloch, Reformation, 133–135, 141–147; Carter Lindberg, The European Reformations, 169–181.

515 began as an Erasmian: Gottfried W. Locher, "Zwingli and Erasmus," Erasmus in English, 10: 2–11, 1979–1980; "Zwingli, Huldrych," in Contemporaries of Erasmus; Potter, Zwingli, 64–65, 71; Gäbler, Huldrych Zwingli, 39–40; Smith, Erasmus, 372–373.

516 an Erasmian-style pacifist: Gäbler, Huldrych Zwingli, 40.

516 an effusive thank-you note: Collected Works of Erasmus, vol. 3, no. 401, April 29 [1516], 271–272.

516 "This is the best way": Ibid., vol. 3, no. 404 [May 8, 1516], 281.

516 Zwingli was among the first: Potter, Zwingli, 39.

516 In a letter of self-defense: Hillerbrand, Reformation, 115–117; Ozment, Age of Reform, 321–322.

517 decided to start at the beginning:

517 would undergo a dramatic change: Potter, Zwingli, 69–70; Lindberg, European Reformations, 177.

517 "The Song of Pestilence": Hillerbrand, Reformation, 120–123.

518 Zwingli began reading Luther: Hillerbrand, Reformation, 123–127; Potter, Zwingli, 62–64, 71; Gäbler, Huldrych Zwingli, 45–47; Lindberg, European Reformations, 175.

518 invite skepticism about that claim: See, for instance, Euan Cameron, The European Reformation, 181–182. Cameron writes that "if Zwingli really did develop the distinctively 'Reformation' message of salvation by free forgiveness, apprehended through faith, simultaneously but entirely independently of Luther, it was the most breathtaking coincidence of the sixteenth century." MacCulloch (Reformation, 134) concurs. On the other hand, Ozment (Age of Reform, 322–323) observes that prior to 1520 Zwingli identified more with Erasmus than with Luther and that he "seems not even to have read Luther seriously" before that year. And Lindberg (European Reformations, 175) writes that "there is little evidence of deep theological influence from Luther."

518 the maid admitted: Hillerbrand, Reformation, 127.

518 On the Choice and Freedom of Food: An excerpt is in Hillerbrand, Reformation, 129–131; "In a word": Lindberg, European Reformations, 169. See also Potter, Zwingli, 76–77.

519 the town council admonished: Hillerbrand, Reformation, 131.

519 "astonishing uproar": Collected Works of Erasmus, vol. 9, no. 1293, to Bonifacius Amerbach, June 24, 1522, 110–111; the dinner is described in note 8.

519 Wilhelm Reublin: Ibid.

520 De Esu Carnium: Ibid., vol. 73, 64–101; Christ taught, 66; Paul said, 93; Why,

then, 76; As for the holy days, 70–72; priestly celibacy, 73–74; Long ago, 74. See also Augustijn, *Erasmus*, 147–150; Rummel, *Erasmus and His Catholic Critics*, vol. 1, 181–184.

521 a great success: See Universal Short Title Catalogue (ustc.ac.uk).

521 one of his three most disliked works: *Collected Works of Erasmus*, vol. 39, xlviii.

CHAPTER 30: SATAN FALLS
UPON THE FLOCK

522 a gang of students: *Luther's Works*, vol. 45, 55; Roper, *Martin Luther*, 202–203; Brecht, *Shaping and Defining*, 30–31.

522 "Everything . . . pleases me very much": *Luther's Works*, vol. 48, no. 107, 350–352.

523 pressed him to take on a project: Brecht, *Shaping and Defining*, 46.

523 some eighteen editions: M. Reu, *Luther's German Bible*, 73; Eric W. Gritsch, "Luther as Bible Translator," in Donald K. McKim, ed., *The Cambridge Companion to Martin Luther*, 62; Friedenthal, *Luther*, 305.

523 strongly discouraged the production of vernacular Bibles: In 1485, for instance, Archbishop Berthold of Mainz prohibited the publication of German Bibles; see Gritsch, "Luther as Bible Translator," in McKim, *The Cambridge Companion to Martin Luther*, 62.

523 "I wish every town": *Luther's Works*, vol. 48, no. 109, to John Lang, 356.

524 one titled *Karsthans*: Ibid., vol. 45, 57–58. See also Friedenthal, *Luther*, 315; Todd, *Luther*, 226.

524 the homes of some clergymen: Brecht, *Shaping and Defining*, 2.

524 *A Sincere Admonition*: *Luther's Works*, vol. 45, 57–74; "no insurrection," 63; "Have I not," 67; "all the swarming vermin," 68; "let them call," 70.

525 "My dear doctor": *Luther's Correspondence*, vol. 2, no. 519, December 21, 1521, 80–81.

525 "I shall translate": *Luther's Works*, vol. 48, no. 111, January 13, 1522, 363.

526 the German language was highly fragmented: Ruth H. Sanders, *German: Biography of a Language*, 137–138, 147.

526 "people thirty miles apart": Quoted in Reu, *Luther's German Bible*, 138.

526 the type of *Volksbuch*: Mullett, *Martin Luther*, 149.

526 had a number of reference works at hand: Reu, *Luther's German Bible*, 149–151, 158; Marius, *Martin Luther*, 348–353; Bornkamm, *Luther in Mid-Career*, 45; Friedenthal, *Luther*, 304.

527 developed a procedure: Bainton, *Here I Stand*, 255.

527 At Matthew 5:16: For these examples and others, see Stephan Füssel, *The Book of Books: The Luther Bible of 1534*, 54–55; Brecht, *Shaping and Defining*, 49–50. (The forms and spellings of some of these terms changed over the various editions of Luther's Bible.)

527 Luther instead used *Gemeinde*: Mullett, *Martin Luther*, 150; Bornkamm, *Luther in Mid-Career*, 48.

527 Matthew 3:2: The passage appears in *Luthers Werke, Die Deutsche Bibel*, vol. 7, 20; Luther refers to Erasmus's annotation on this passage in his note on page 624. See also Smith, *Life and Letters of Martin Luther*, 267. In later editions, Luther would revert back to the traditional *tut Busse*.

528 at Luke 1:28: Luther discusses this passage in "On Translating: An Open Letter," published in 1530, at *Luther's Works*, vol. 35, 191–192. See also Mullett, *Martin Luther*, 150.

528 he sharpened the sense: Brecht, *Shaping and Defining*, 50.

528 prepare a defense: "On Translating: An Open Letter" (1530), *Luther's Works*, vol. 35, 181–202; "papal asses," 187; "tremendous fuss," 182; "even less than," 183; He knew very well, 188; "We do not have," 189; "with the main point," 195;

"this raging and raving," 197; *allein* "will stay," 198.

530 Karlstadt moved to take charge: On the events in Wittenberg, see Rupp, *Patterns of Reformation*, 97–100; Lindsay, *History of the Reformation*, vol. 1, 311–313; Sider, *Andreas Bodenstein von Karlstadt*, 153–173; Brecht, *Shaping and Defining*, 34; Marius, *Martin Luther*, 322; Bainton, *Here I Stand*, 159–161; Roper, *Martin Luther*, 206–214; Todd, *Luther*, 231–233.

530 the "whole town": Bainton, *Here I Stand*, 159–160. Karlstadt's sermon is in Ronald J. Sider, ed. *Karlstadt's Battle with Luther: Documents in a Liberal-Radical Debate*, 5–15.

531 a wave of jubilation: Brecht, *Shaping and Defining*, 38.

531 "that many poor": Sider, *Andreas Bodenstein von Karlstadt*, 160–161.

531 three wild-eyed men: On the Zwickau Prophets, see *Luther's Correspondence*, vol. 2, no. 520, Melanchthon to Frederick, December 27, 1521, 81–82; Friedenthal, *Martin Luther*, 318–320; Brecht, *Shaping and Defining*, 34–36; Marius, *Martin Luther*, 323–324; Smith, *Life and Letters of Martin Luther*, 137–138.

532 "Melanchthon continually clings": *Luther's Correspondence*, vol. 2, no. 522, Felix Ulscenius to Wolfgang Capito, January 1, 1522, 82–83.

532 "They preach strange things": Ibid., vol. 2, no. 520, December 27, 1522, 81–82.

532 "I do not approve": *Luther's Works*, vol. 48, no. 112, January 13, 1522, 364–372.

533 Zwickau was a cradle: On events in this town, see Tom Scott, *Thomas Müntzer: Theology and Revolution in the German Reformation*, 17–18; Norman Cohn, *The Pursuit of the Millennium*, 234–237; Brecht, *Shaping and Defining*, 34–35; Marius, *Martin Luther*, 323; Bornkamm, *Luther in Mid-Career*, 52–58.

533 Thomas Müntzer: On Müntzer's early life, see Scott, *Thomas Müntzer*, 1–28; Rupp, *Patterns of Reformation*, 157–168.

533 would describe Müntzer: Friedrich Engels, *The Peasant War in Germany*, 56, 66.

534 senior Augustinian friars: Bornkamm, *Luther in Mid-Career*, 59.

535 led a group of friars in destroying: Roper, *Martin Luther*, 214.

535 moved to solidify his control: Sider, *Andreas Bodenstein von Karlstadt*, 160; Friedenthal, *Luther*, 320; Brecht, *Shaping and Defining*, 38.

535 In his sermons: Bornkamm, *Luther in Mid-Career*, 61; Manschreck, *Melanchthon*, 76; Rupp, *Patterns of Reformation*, 103–104. Karlstadt's 1522 tract, "On the Removal of Images and That There Should Be No Beggars Among Christians," is in E. J. Furcha, ed. and trans., *The Essential Carlstadt*, 100–128; passages like Exodus, 102; "God hates," 103; "churches in which images," 116.

535 "Better one heart-felt prayer": Quoted in Bainton, *Here I Stand*, 161.

536 The *Praiseworthy Order*: Ibid., 160; Brecht, *Shaping and Defining*, 38–39; Marius, *Martin Luther*, 326; Lindsay, *History of the Reformation*, vol. 1, 314–315; Rupp, *Patterns of Reformation*, 101–102; Bornkamm, *Luther in Mid-Career*, 60–61.

536 George sent a fierce directive: *Luther's Correspondence*, vol. 2, no. 525, February 10, 1522, 86–89.

537 issued an order: Bainton, *Here I Stand*, 162; Sider, *Andreas Bodenstein von Karlstadt*, 171.

537 sent Luther an urgent message: Smith, *Life and Letters of Martin Luther*, 140.

538 sent Frederick a brief note, *Luther's Works*, vol. 48, no. 116, February 22, 1522, 386–388.

538 the elector rushed a letter: *Luther's Correspondence*, vol. 2, no. 528 [end of February 1522], 90–93.

538 would later write an account: An excerpt is in Smith, *Life and Letters of Martin*

Luther, 141–143. See also Mullett, Martin Luther, 139–140.

539 "I have received the gospel": *Luther's Works*, vol. 48, no. 117, March 5, 1522, 388–393.

540 Luther drafted a statement: Ibid., vol. 48, no. 118, March 7 or 8, 1522, 393–399.

540 all that had occurred: See Friedenthal, *Luther*, 324–325; Todd, *Luther*, 231. According to Schwiebert, *Luther* (604), enrollment at the university dropped from 552 in 1520 to around 200 in 1522.

CHAPTER 31: THE POPE OF WITTENBERG

541 He needed to find the right words: On Luther's sermons, see Todd, *Luther*, 236–341; Friedenthal, *Luther*, 325–327; Brecht, *Shaping and Defining*, 57–61; Bornkamm, *Luther in Mid-Career*, 69–78; Mullett, *Martin Luther*, 141–143; Marius, *Martin Luther*, 330–335. The sermons themselves are in *Luther's Works*, vol. 51, 69–100.

541 "The summons of death": *Luther's Works*, vol. 51, 70; "And here, dear friends," 71; People should not insist, 71–72; "I would not have gone," 72; he could have been consulted, 74.

542 A student who was present reported: *Luther's Correspondence*, vol. 2, no. 541, Albert Burer to Beatus Rhenanus, March 27, 1522, 115.

542 "a mere mockery": *Luther's Works*, vol. 51, 76; "Had I desired," 77; "I simply taught," 77; If a monk wanted to leave, 79–81; people had grown so angry, 91; "I will go without urging," 89.

543 "There is great gladness": *Luther's Correspondence*, vol. 2, no. 534, March 15, 1522, 102–103.

543 "Gabriel" was: Ibid., vol. 2, no. 539, Luther to Wenzel (Wenceslas) Link, March 19, 1522, 112.

543 Not so with Karlstadt: Ibid., vol. 2, no. 547, Luther to Spalatin, April 21, 1522, 121; Marius, *Martin Luther*, 334;

Brecht, *Shaping and Defining*, 65; Rupp, *Patterns of Reformation*, 107.

543 made a scapegoat: Marius writes in *Martin Luther* (334) that Karlstadt, "became a scapegoat for what was in fact a large and fervent popular movement, led not only by Karlstadt but by the city council."

543 Luther had sent him a letter: *Luther's Works*, vol. 48, no. 113, January 27, 1522, 372–379.

544 his close friendship with Erasmus: "Capito, Wolfgang Faber," in *Contemporaries of Erasmus*.

544 was even more captivated: *Luther's Correspondence*, vol. 2, no. 534, Jerome Schurff to Elector Frederick, March 15, 103.

544 Luther's putting a brake: *Luther's Works*, vol. 49, 46, note 5; Marius, *Martin Luther*, 333; Bornkamm, *Luther in Mid-Career*, 78–79; Mullett, *Martin Luther*, 142–143; Roper, *Martin Luther*, 225–228. By "siding with the authorities," Roper writes, Luther "cut himself off from what was going on in the rest of the empire." The ideals of brotherhood and compromise "were alien to him"; the result was a dangerous narrowing of vision. The notion of "communal Reformation" would surface elsewhere.

545 there was much indignation: *Luther's Correspondence*, vol. 2, no. 538, Hans von der Planitz to Elector Frederick, March 18, 1522, 111–112. Planitz, Frederick's representative at the diet, wrote that "it would not be a bad plan" for Luther "to keep himself quiet and hidden a little while longer, either at Wittenberg or elsewhere, until things take another turn."

545 "I must warn your Grace": Ibid., vol. 2, no. 540, Duke George to Elector Frederick [March 21, 1522], 114–115.

545 Jacob Probst: Brecht, *Shaping and Defining*, 102.

545 "The whole Rhine is bloody": *Luther's Correspondence*, vol. 2, no. 536, Luther

to Hartmuth von Cronberg [mid-March 1522], 109.

546 "They are planning to burn me": Ibid., vol. 2, no. 551, Luther to Johann von Staupitz, June 27, 1522, 130.

546 He mocked Duke George: Ibid., vol. 2, no. 536, 106–107.

546 If the princes continued to listen: Ibid., vol. 2, no. 539, Luther to Wenzel (Wenceslas) Link, March 19, 1522, 113.

546 "so that people may see": *Luther's Works*, vol. 49, no. 123, Luther to George Spalatin, June 7, 1522, 9.

546 "for the sake of the belly": *Luther's Correspondence*, vol. 2, no. 542, Luther to Johann Lang, March 28, 1522, 116.

547 "How I dread preaching": *Luther's Works*, vol. 45, "The Estate of Marriage," 17; "Away with this foolishness," 24.

547 was Johannes Bugenhagen: Walter M. Ruccius, *John Bugenhagen Pomeranus* (Philadelphia: United Lutheran Publication House, n.d.), available at https://archive.org/details/ johnbugenhagenpo00rucc; his experience with *The Babylonian Captivity* is at 20–21. See also Friedenthal, *Luther*, 330.

547 this man "alone sees the truth": Quoted in Pettegree, *Brand Luther*, 177.

547 "Next to Philipp": *Luther's Correspondence*, vol. 2, no. 556 [September 20, 1522], 141.

548 "to give us simple terms": Ibid., vol. 2, no. 544, March 30, 1522, 118–119.

548 hoped to have the translation ready: Pettegree, *Brand Luther*, 185–188.

548 "Everywhere people are thirsting": *Luthers Werke, Briefwechsel*, vol. 2, no. 580, 5–6; Bornkamm, *Luther in Mid-Career*, 91.

549 decided to go on a preaching tour: Brecht, *Shaping and Defining*, 68–70; Marius, *Martin Luther*, 344–345; Todd, *Luther*, 242–243; Bornkamm, *Luther in Mid-Career*, 90.

549 In a letter informing the former firebrand: *Luther's Correspondence*, vol. 2, no. 546, April 17, 1522, 120–121.

550 *Epistolae ad Diversos*: The preface is in *Collected Works of Erasmus*, vol. 8, no. 1206, May 27 [1521], 215–221. See also Marius, *Martin Luther*, 336.

550 "Christ I recognize": *Collected Works of Erasmus*, vol. 8, to Luigi Marliano, March 25 [1521], 171.

550 In a letter to William Warham: Ibid., vol. 8, no. 1228, August 23, 1521, 286.

550 To Spalatin, Luther complained: *Luthers Werke, Briefwechsel*, vol. 2, no. 490, May 15, 1522, 527.

550 a letter to an anonymous addressee: *Luther's Works*, vol. 49, no. 122, May 28, 1522, 6–8.

550 the appearance that summer: Erwin Doernberg, *Henry VIII and Luther: An Account of Their Personal Relations*, 26ff; Brecht, *Shaping and Defining*, 85–87; Marius, *Luther*, 339; Smith, *Life and Letters of Martin Luther*, 192–193.

551 "Since with malice aforethought": Smith, *Life and Letters of Martin Luther*, 193; Doernberg, *Henry VIII and Luther*, 28; *Luther in England* (London: E. Palmer and Son, 1841), 57.

552 set off a furor: Marius, *Martin Luther*, 340–341.

552 Seeking to justify his harsh language: *Luther's Correspondence*, vol. 2, no. 533, "to an unnamed correspondent," August 28, 1522, 132–134.

552 Henry turned to his own court: Smith, *Life and Letters of Martin Luther*, 193.

552 three presses: Pettegree, *Brand Luther*, 188.

552 one introducing the volume: Dillenberger, *Martin Luther: Selections*, 14–19.

553 audacious statements: See Mullett, *Martin Luther*, 146.

553 had his own scriptural preferences: On the contrast between Erasmus and Luther with regard to the New Testament, see Marius, *Martin Luther*, 358–359.

554 a preface to the Epistle to the Romans: Dillenberger, *Martin Luther: Selections*, 19–34.

554 A folio of 222: Reu, *Luther's German Bible*, 162.

554 two months' salary: Füssel, *Book of Books*, 56.

554 Lotther printed some three thousand copies: Pettegree, *Brand Luther*, 186–187.

555 helped forge a common basis: MacGregor, *Germany*, 107–111. "By the end of the sixteenth century," MacGregor writes, "written German throughout the Holy Roman Empire was the German of the Luther bible." Luther "didn't just catch the way ordinary German people spoke, he also shaped the way they would speak." See also Sanders, *German*, 118; Friedenthal, *Luther*, 310; Gritsch, "Luther as Bible Translator," in McKim, *The Cambridge Companion to Luther*, 71.

555 "created the German language": For the comments by Heine, Goethe, and Herder, see Jonathan Sheehan, *The Enlightenment Bible: Translation, Scholarship, Culture* (Princeton: Princeton University Press, 2005), 175.

555 Nietzsche: Friedrich Nietzsche, *Beyond Good and Evil*, trans. Walter Kaufmann (New York: Vintage Books, 1966), 184.

555 Even Johannes Cochlaeus: Quoted in Philip Schaff, *History of the Christian Church*, vol. 6, *Modern Christianity: The German Reformation* (New York: Charles Scribner's Sons, 1895), 350.

CHAPTER 32: THE NEW GOSPEL SPREADS

556 Adam Petri: Guggisberg, *Basel in the Sixteenth Century*, 21; Pettegree, *Brand Luther*, 188–189; Peter G. Bietenholz, "Printing and the Basle Reformation, 1517–1565," in Jean-François Gilmont, ed., *The Reformation and the Book*, 244–249.

556 came to be dominated by him: James Westfall Thompson, ed., *The Frankfort Book Fair*, 34.

556 publishing history of the *Enchiridion*: See Universal Short Title Catalogue (http://ustc.ac.uk).

556 absorbed in editing Augustine: *Collected Works of Erasmus*, vol. 9, no. 1309 [August 1522], 168–173.

557 a letter from Duke George: Ibid., vol. 9, no. 1298, July 9, 1522, 119–120.

557 Erasmus in his reply: Ibid., vol. 9, no. 1313, September 3, 1522, 178–183.

557 Erasmus remained wary: Ibid., vol. 9, no. 1259, to Willibald Pirckheimer, February 12 [1522], 22–23.

557 Erasmus sent back a friendly demurral: Ibid., vol. 9, no. 1314, September [3], 1522, 183–186. Zwingli's letter has not survived.

558 to that of clerical celibacy: Potter, *Zwingli*, 78–79; Lindberg, *European Reformations*, 172–173.

558 *Apologeticus Archeteles*: Potter, *Zwingli*, 81–86; *Collected Works of Erasmus*, vol. 9, 183–185.

558 "there was much": *Collected Works of Erasmus*, vol. 9, no. 1315, September 8, 1522, 186–187.

558 Johannes Oecolampadius: Rupp, *Patterns of Reformation*, 3–22; "Oecolampadius, Johannes," in *Contemporaries of Erasmus*; "Oecolampadius, Johannes," in *The Oxford Encyclopedia of the Reformation*.

559 Erasmus was struck: Erasmus would later make an unflattering (though veiled) reference to Oecolampadius's appearance in a colloquy; see *Collected Works of Erasmus*, vol. 40, 872.

559 began corresponding with Zwingli: Rupp, *Patterns of Reformation*, 21.

559 began lecturing at the university: Guggisberg, *Basel in the Sixteenth Century*, 23.

560 The election of Adrian: Pastor, *History of the Popes*, vol. 9, 45–47.

560 Erasmus's ties to Adrian: See the introductory note, *Collected Works of Erasmus*, vol. 9, no. 1304, to Adrian VI, August 1, 1522, 144.

560 In his cover letter: Ibid., vol. 9, no. 1310, [September] 1522, 173–175.

561 Erasmus heard rumors: See the

introductory note, ibid., vol. 9, no. 1324, December 1, 1522, 203.

561 decided to send Adrian another appeal: Ibid., vol. 9, no. 1329, December 22, 1522, 218–220.

561 In fact, Adrian had gotten: On Adrian VI, see Friedenthal, *Luther*, 348–358; Pastor, *History of the Popes*, vol. 9, 34–126.

561 a fifty-ship flotilla: Pastor, *History of the Popes*, vol. 9, 59–62.

561 with great trepidation: Friedenthal, *Luther*, 351–352.

561 radiated monkish self-denial: Ibid., 354; Pastor, *History of the Popes*, vol. 9, 65.

562 urged to hold his coronation: Pastor, *History of the Popes*, 65–68.

562 In his inaugural speech: Ibid., 92–100.

562 dispensed with the swollen staffs: Ibid., 71–77; Friedenthal, *Luther*, 354.

563 "Everyone trembles": Quoted in Pastor, *History of the Popes*, vol. 9, 94.

563 the plague was claiming: Ibid., 100–106.

563 an even graver threat: Ibid., 155–156.

563 he burst into tears: Ibid., 170.

564 new Imperial Diet: Ibid., 127–128.

564 The final version: *Collected Works of Erasmus*, vol. 9, no. 1324, December 1, 1522, 203–209. Another draft is in vol. 9, 1324A, 209–212.

565 Nuremberg was one: See Gerald Strauss, *Nuremberg in the Sixteenth Century*; "Nuremberg," in *The Oxford Encyclopedia of the Reformation*; "Nuremberg," in *Europe 1450 to 1789: Encyclopedia of the Early Modern World*; Harold J. Grimm, *Lazarus Spengler: A Lay Leader of the Reformation*, 7–14; Fedja Anzelewsky, *Dürer: His Art and Life* (New York: Alpine Fine Arts Collection, 1980), 9–14.

565 held three times a year: Strauss, *Nuremberg*, 141. On the city's crafts, see 134–142.

565 its effective governance: Ibid., 57ff. On Nuremberg's many regulations and inspections, see 99ff, 144–145; on its policy toward pigs, 192.

566 the Sodalitas Staupitziana: Grimm, *Lazarus Spengler*, 32–34; "Staupitz, Johann von," in *The Oxford Encyclopedia of the Reformation*; Strauss, *Nuremberg*, 160–161; Steven Ozment, *The Reformation in the Cities: The Appeal of Protestantism to Sixteenth-Century Germany and Switzerland*, 74–79.

566 Andreas Osiander: "Osiander, Andreas," in *The Oxford Encyclopedia of the Reformation*; Strauss, *Nuremberg*, 164.

566 The Meistersinger: Strauss, *Nuremberg*, 264–269; Grimm, *Lazarus Spengler*, 23–24.

567 Hans Sachs: Strauss, *Nuremberg*, 267–269; Friedenthal, *Luther*, 333–334; "Sachs, Hans," in *The Oxford Encyclopedia of the Reformation*.

567 when the nuncio Chieregati arrived: Friedenthal, *Luther*, 357.

567 During the initial weeks: Pastor, *History of the Popes*, vol. 9, 128–129; Grimm, *Lazarus Spengler*, 60–63.

567 received from Adrian a brief: *Luther's Correspondence*, vol. 2, no. 558, November 25, 1522, 141–148; Pastor, *History of the Popes*, vol. 9, 129–138.

568 "many abominations": *Luther's Correspondence*, vol. 2, 146; "to actors and stable-boys," 148.

568 he added several warnings: Grimm, *Lazarus Spengler*, 62.

569 protesters filled its streets: Strauss, *Nuremberg*, 166.

569 a letter from Willibald Pirckheimer: *Collected Works of Erasmus*, vol. 9, no. 1344, February 17, 1523, 402–408.

569 rejected Chieregati's demands: *Luther's Correspondence*, vol. 2, no. 574, Estates of the Empire to Chieregati, February 5, 1523, 168–171; Grimm, *Lazarus Spengler*, 62.

569 summoned to the Rathaus: Strauss, *Nuremberg*, 165.

569 Chieregati wrote: *Luther's Correspondence*, vol. 2, no. 566, Chieregati to the Marquis of Mantua, January 10, 1523, 159–160.

569 especially its cities: Strauss, *Nuremberg*, 164–165; Bernd Moeller, *Imperial Cities and the Reformation*, 41–74; Cameron, *European Reformation*, 210–263; Ozment, *Age of Reform*, 192; Ozment, *Reformation in the Cities*, 13, 165.

569 literacy rates were higher: Cameron, *European Reformation*, 227; C. Scott Dixon, *The Reformation in Germany*, 100.

570 In Strasbourg: Cameron, *European Reformation*, 216–218, 231; "Zell, Matthias," in *The Oxford Encyclopedia of the Reformation*; Miriam Usher Chrisman, *Strasbourg and the Reform: A Study in the Process of Change*, 98–107.

570 preachers fanned out: Lindsay, *History of the Reformation*, vol. 1, 305–310; Friedenthal, *Luther*, 329; R. W. Scribner and C. Scott Dixon, *The German Reformation*, 20–22, 39.

570 working a dramatic change: See Todd, *Luther*, 249–250.

570 his *Breve aureum: Collected Works of Erasmus*, vol. 9, 203.

570 In his reply: Ibid., vol. 9, no. 1352 [March 22, 1523], 434–441.

571 "my own executioner": Ibid, vol. 9, 418.

CHAPTER 33: TRUE CHRISTIAN WARFARE

572 the man at the center of it all: Friedenthal, *Luther*, 374; Marius, *Martin Luther*, 393.

572 three other printers: Pettegree, *Book in the Renaissance*, 191.

572 he complained to Spalatin: *Luther's Correspondence*, vol. 2, no. 586, May 27, 1523, 183.

572 Henry VIII: Ibid., vol. 2, no 568, January 20, 1523, 160–163.

572 sent Luther an angry note: Ibid., vol. 2, no. 562, December 30, 1522, 153–154. Luther's reply is at no. 565, January 3, 1523, 158–159.

573 took aim at his books: Marius, *Martin Luther*, 364; *Luther's Works*, vol. 45, 84.

573 *Temporal Authority: Luther's Works*, vol.

45, 81–129; "The soul is not," 111; As for the "tyrants," 112; Heresy "can never be," 114; "has been or will be," 115; "Men will not," 116; "and not in God's name!" 117.

574 a dispute in Leisnig: Ibid., vol. 39, *That a Christian Assembly or Congregation Has the Right and Power to Judge All Teaching and to Call, Appoint, and Dismiss Teachers, Established and Proven by Scripture*, 305–314; "Spiritual tyrants," 308; "they still could not," 311–312.

575 A revealing snapshot: See Bornkamm, *Luther in Mid-Career*, 291–292.

577 In his preface: *Luther's Works*, vol. 35, "Preface to the Old Testament," 235–251; "for he is the man," 247; "that even the Jews," 249.

577 "to make Moses speak": *Luthers Werke, Tischreden*, vol. 2, no. 2771a, 648; Roland H. Bainton, *The Reformation of the Sixteenth Century*, 62.

577 *That Jesus Christ Was Born a Jew: Luther's Works*, vol. 45, 199–229; He denounced the popes, 200; By forbidding the Jews to labor, 229; "dolts and blockheads," 200; "We must receive them," 229; "many of them will become," 200. See also Mullett, *Martin Luther*, 154–157.

578 a letter to Bernard: *Luther's Correspondence*, vol. 2, no. 588 [May 1523], 185–187.

578 a group of nuns: On the Nimbschen nuns, see Schwiebert, *Luther*, 583–586; Friedenthal, *Luther*, 375–376, 435–436; Brecht, *Shaping and Defining*, 100–101.

579 "Nine fugitive nuns": *Luther's Correspondence*, vol. 2, no. 583, April 10, 1523, 179–181. See also no. 584, Nikolaus Amsdorf to Spalatin, April 11, 1523, 181–182.

579 She had been born: Friedenthal, *Luther*, 435.

579 "The monks and nuns": *Luther's Correspondence*, vol. 2, no. 591, June 20, 1523, 190–191.

580 Oecolampadius's lectures on Isaiah: Magne Saebo, ed., *Hebrew Bible/*

Old Testament: The History of Its Interpretation, vol. 2, *From the Renaissance to the Enlightenment* (Göttingen: Vandenhoeck & Ruprecht, 2008), 408–412.

581 "Another piece of nonsense": *Collected Works of Erasmus*, vol. 9, December 9, 1522, 214.

581 the brutal treatment of Sigismund Steinschneider: Ibid., vol. 73, "Notes on the Letter About Abstinence," 104–134; "it was thought," 105.

581 in his preface: Ibid., vol. 9, no. 1334, to Jean de Carondelet, January 5, 1523, 245–274; "Once," he wrote, 257; all kinds of abstract propositions, 258; "What arrogance," 252. See also John C. Olin, "Erasmus and His Edition of St. Hilary," *Erasmus in English*, 9: 8–11, 1978.

582 the Sorbonne would censure it: *Collected Works of Erasmus*, vol. 9, 245.

582 More was undergoing a dramatic change: Richard Marius, *Thomas More: A Biography*, 280–290; Ackroyd, *Life of Thomas More*, 227–231.

583 "free to practice": Thomas More, *Utopia*, 119.

583 to respond to Luther: *Response to Luther*, in *The Complete Works of St. Thomas More*, ed. John M. Headley, vol. 5, part 1, 1–711; a "mad friarlet," 683. See also Ackroyd, *Life of Thomas More*, 230.

584 Erasmus sent a servant to England: *Collected Works of Erasmus*, vol. 10, 79–80.

584 a letter from his friend Cuthbert Tunstall: Ibid., vol. 10, no. 1367, June 5, 1523, 24–28.

584 he felt that he had to proceed: Ibid., vol. 10, no. 1369 [end of June 1523], 30–34.

584 "the princes all urge me": Ibid., vol. 10, no. 1383, August 29 [1523], 78–80.

584 with his old acquaintance Ulrich von Hutten: See the introduction to Randolph J. Klawiter, ed., *The Polemics of Erasmus of Rotterdam and Ulrich von Hutten*, 3–34. This work contains Hutten's *Expostulatio* against Erasmus. See also Bainton, *Erasmus of Christendom*, 174–178; Smith, *Erasmus*, 332–335; Augustijn, *Erasmus*, 128–129.

585 a long letter that Erasmus had sent: *Collected Works of Erasmus*, vol. 9, February 1, 1523, 364–401.

586 "Would you have us believe": Klawiter, *Polemics of Erasmus*, 60; "as a cesspool," 66; "a certain cowardice," 68–69; Erasmus in his anxiety, 69; "This sacrilegious utterance," 104; Did Christ not predict, 102; Erasmus faced two choices, 100; If he refused to commit, 112; "we must fight this out," 126.

587 Erasmus heard of it: Ibid., 14–21.

587 *Spongia Adversus Aspergines Hutteni: Collected Works of Erasmus*, vol. 78, 30–145; "false accusations," 145; "the muck he threw," 38; that he had in fact been informed, 39–40; He rejected Hutten's claim, 127–28; "Had Hutten received," 128; He charged the German reformer, 98; "that the Spirit of Christ," 112.

588 a letter he sent to Henry VIII: Ibid., vol. 10, no. 1385, September 4, 1523, 85.

588 "a perfect fury": Ibid., vol. 10, no. 1386, to Theodore Hezius [?], September 16, 1523, 85–88.

589 a letter to Conradus Pellicanus: *Luther's Correspondence*, vol. 2, no. 600, October 1, 1523, 204–206.

589 "Luther passionately abuses": *Collected Works of Erasmus*, vol. 10, no. 1397, November 21, 1523, 109–111.

590 thirty-sixth article: Ibid., vol. 76, 301–310.

CHAPTER 34: A SHOWER OF STONES

592 "on account of the grandeur": *Luther's Correspondence*, vol. 2, no. 613, February 23, 1524, 221–222.

592 Jerome Baumgärtner: Ibid., vol. 2, no. 642, Luther to Jerome Baumgärtner, October 12, 1524, 257–258.

592 began introducing changes: Brecht, *Shaping and Defining*, 121–126; Marius, *Martin Luther*, 382–383; Todd, *Luther*, 251–252; Bainton, *Here I Stand*, 272.

593 the introduction of hymns: Christopher Boyd Brown, *Singing the Gospel: Lutheran Hymns and the Success of the Reformation* (Cambridge, MA: Harvard University Press, 2005), 1–25.

593 wrote to Spalatin of his intention: *Luther's Correspondence*, vol. 2, no. 608 [before January 14, 1524], 211–212.

593 the first Reformation hymnal: Brecht, *Shaping and Defining*, 130–131.

593 congregational singing: Bainton, *Here I Stand*, 266–271.

593 leading two centuries later: MacGregor, *Germany*, 111.

593 had resurfaced with a radical program: Sider, *Andreas Bodenstein von Karlstadt*, 174–181; Furcha, *Essential Carlstadt*, "The Meaning of the Term *Gelassen* and Where in Holy Scripture It Is Found," 133–168; "Bodenstein von Karlstadt, Andreas," in *The Oxford Encyclopedia of the Reformation.*

594 put aside his academic dress: Sider, *Andreas Bodenstein von Karlstadt*, 177; Rupp, *Patterns of Reformation*, 112–113, 118–121; Friedenthal, *Luther*, 328.

594 His authority to fill the post: Sider, *Andreas Bodenstein von Karlstadt*, 182–184.

594 the vicarage was in serious decline: Ibid., 184–185; Rupp, *Patterns of Reformation*, 113–114.

594 to "become angry, howl, and curse": Ronald J. Sider, ed., *Karlstadt's Battle with Luther: Documents in a Liberal-Radical Debate*, 65. The passage comes from an essay, "Whether One Should Proceed Slowly and Avoid Offending the Weak in Matters That Concern God's Will" (50–71), which describes Karlstadt's position on this matter.

594 conceived of a parish: Sider, *Andreas Bodenstein von Karlstadt*, 188–189.

595 *Reasons Why Andreas Karlstadt Remained Silent*: Furcha, *Essential Carlstadt*, 169–184.

595 "I have read Karlstadt's monstrosities": *Luther's Correspondence*, vol. 2, no. 614, March 14, 1524, 222–223.

595 Luther complained: Sider, *Andreas Bodenstein von Karlstadt*, 190–191.

595 Müntzer had gone to Bohemia: Scott, *Thomas Müntzer*, 28ff.

595 "The Prague Manifesto": Michael G. Baylor, ed., *The Radical Reformation*, 1–10.

596 the first worship service: Bornkamm, *Luther in Mid-Career*, 152–153.

596 "honey-sweet Christ": Scott, *Thomas Müntzer*, 61–62.

596 an agitated crowd: Ibid., 65; Bornkamm, *Luther in Mid-Career*, 154–155.

597 "The murderous spirit of Allstedt": *Luther's Correspondence*, vol. 2, no. 652, to the Christians of Strassburg, [December 17, 1524], 278.

597 Eoban Hess: See Luther's reply to Hess, ibid., vol. 2, no. 580, March 29, 1523, 175–177. For the drop-off in enrollment at Erfurt and Wittenberg, see *Luther's Works*, vol. 45, 343.

597 *To the Councilmen of All Cities: Luther's Works*, vol. 45, 347–378; "schools are everywhere," 348; "despicable trick," 350; A city's greatest strength, 356; Both boys and girls, 370; The revival of ancient tongues, 360–361; the reputation of being beasts, 377; "O my beloved Germans," 352.

598 new schools would be established: Schwiebert, *Luther*, 676; Pettegree, *Brand Luther*, 262–266, 323.

599 "I have now been silent": *Collected Works of Erasmus*, vol. 10, no. 1443 [April 15], 1524, 243–247.

600 the two men left: Ibid., vol. 10, note 2, 251–252; *Luther's Works*, vol. 49, note 3, 77.

600 "You have dragged": *Collected Works of Erasmus*, vol. 10, no. 1405 [December 1523], 135–137; no. 1406 [December 1523], 137–146.

600 "new gospellers": Ibid., vol. 10, 320.

600 "I no longer judge": Ibid., vol. 10, no. 1400, to Francis I, December 1, 1523, 113–126.

601 *Tusculanae quaestiones*: Erasmus's preface, ibid., vol. 10, no. 1390 [October] 1523, 95–101. For a description of the influence of this work on Erasmus's thinking, see Marjorie O'Rourke Boyle, *Rhetoric and Reform: Erasmus's Civil Dispute with Luther*, 8–20.

601 *The Freedom of the Will*: Ibid., vol. 76, 5–89. (The editors of this volume use an alternative translation of the title, "A Discussion of Free Will.") For an analysis, see the introduction to this volume by Charles Trinkaus, xvi–cvi; Bainton, *Erasmus of Christendom*, 187–196; A. N. Marlow and B. Drewery, in *Luther and Erasmus: Free Will and Salvation*, E. Gordon Rupp and Philip S. Watson, eds., introduction, 1–32; Boyle, *Rhetoric and Reform*, 5–142.

601 "far from a crime": *Collected Works of Erasmus*, vol. 76, 6; "without abuse," 7; a "slight bias," 8; "absolutely clear," 10; "God created man," 21; story of Cain and Abel, 33–34; "I have placed," 34; At 7:20, for instance, 41; God acted in this way, 46–49; Even the verses in the Pauline Epistles, 41–42; "just as many proofs," 73–74; man should claim no credit, 75; A God who foreordained, 76; had vastly exaggerated, 84; the potter and his clay, 75, 80–82; to allow the ungodly, 87; Luther's godly and Christian assertions, 88; "with evangelical mildness," 88.

604 The God whom Erasmus conjures up: Phillips, in *Erasmus and the Northern Renaissance* (138–139), observes that Erasmus's view of free will was in many respects the traditional one of the Church.

604 "I send you the first draft": *Collected Works of Erasmus*, vol. 10, no. 1419 [February 1524], 179–180.

604 "If your Majesty": Ibid., vol. 10, no. 1430 [March] 1524, 200–201.

604 Erasmus would dedicate this work: Preface, ibid., vol. 10, no. 1414, January 31, 1514, 163–166.

605 had little time to spare for him: Ibid., vol. 10, 386.

605 drafted a reply to Luther: Ibid., vol. 10, no. 1445, May 8, 1524, 253–356.

606 he wrote to Pirckheimer: Ibid., vol. 10, no. 1466, July 21, 1524, 302–305.

606 He had initially planned to dedicate the book: Ibid., vol. 10, 353.

606 "The die is cast": Ibid., vol. 10, no. 1493, September 6, 1524, 373–374.

CHAPTER 35: THE GOSPEL OF DISCONTENT

609 Gian Matteo Giberti wrote: *Collected Works of Erasmus*, vol. 10, no. 1509, October 19, 1524, 407–408.

609 Duke George of Saxony wrote: Ibid., vol. 10, no. 1503 [October] 1524, 399–400.

609 Juan Luis Vives reported: Ibid., vol. 10, November 13, 1524, no. 1513, 417–419.

609 "My book on the freedom of the will": Ibid., vol. 10, no. 1506, to Gian Matteo Giberti, October 13, 1524, 404–405.

609 a letter from Melanchthon: Ibid., vol. 10, no. 1500, September 30, 1524, 390–392.

610 he felt absolute loathing: These initial impressions of Erasmus's tract are taken from the opening pages of Luther's eventual reply, *The Bondage of the Will*, in *Luther's Works*, vol. 33, 15–19.

610 "It is annoying": *Luthers Werke, Briefwechsel*, vol. 3, no. 789, 368.

610 informed his friend Nicholas Hausmann: *Luther's Correspondence*, vol. 2, no. 645, 259.

610 largest popular uprising: MacCulloch, *Reformation*, 154.

610 actually invited Müntzer to preach: Scott, *Thomas Müntzer*, 69–76; Eric W. Gritsch, *Thomas Muntzer: A Tragedy of Errors*, 65–71; George Huntston Williams, *The Radical Reformation*, 54–56; Brecht, *Shaping and Defining*, 153–154.

610 took as his portion: "Sermon to the Princes," in Baylor, *Radical Reformation*, 11–32; to take up the sword, 30; "Brother Fattened-swine" and "Brother Soft-life," 23; "strangled without any mercy," 30.

611 members of his congregation marched: Scott, *Thomas Müntzer*, 83ff.

611 *Letter to the Princes: Luther's Works*, vol. 40, 49–59; "lords of the world," 51. See also Brecht, *Shaping and Defining*, 151–152.

611 the reply he helped draft: "Letter from the Community of Orlamünde to the People of Allstedt," in Baylor, *Radical Reformation*, 33–35.

612 finally summoned Müntzer: Scott, *Thomas Müntzer*, 89–92.

612 sent Luther a message: *Luthers Werke: Briefwechsel*, vol. 3, no. 754, June 24, 1524, 309–310.

612 he set off into the aroused countryside: Brecht, *Shaping and Defining*, 159–162; Schwiebert, *Luther*, 549.

612 met at the Black Bear Inn: "Confrontation at the Black Bear," in Sider, *Karlstadt's Battle with Luther*, 36–48. See also Roper, *Martin Luther*, 230–247.

613 Luther received a letter: Brecht, *Shaping and Defining*, 160–161; *Luther's Works*, vol. 40, *Letter to the Christians at Strassburg in Opposition to the Fanatic Spirit*, 69, and *Against the Heavenly Prophets in the Matter of Images and Sacraments*, 100–101.

614 "unheard and unconvicted": See Mark U. Edwards Jr., *Luther and the False Brethren*, 47.

614 Müntzer had resurfaced in Mühlhausen: Scott, *Thomas Muntzer*, 108–114; Gritsch, *Thomas Muntzer*, 83–85; G. H. Williams, *Radical Reformation*, 75–76.

615 *A Highly Provoked Defense*: The document is in Baylor, *Radical Reformation*, 74–94; "Sleep softly, dear flesh!," 93. This quote has been edited for the sake of clarity, with help from the version in Scott, *Thomas Müntzer*, 108.

615 the Upper Rhine valley: See Cameron, *European Reformation*, 202–204; Michael G. Baylor, *The German Reformation and the Peasants' War: A Brief History with Documents*, 7–8; Tom Scott and Bob Scribner, trans. and eds., *The German Peasants' War: A History in Documents*, 6–14; G. R. Elton, *Reformation Europe, 1517–1559*, 9–10.

616 usurped many of the traditional rights: Marius, *Martin Luther*, 416–417; Peter Blickle, *The Revolution of 1525: The German Peasants' War from a New Perspective*, xii–xiv, 31; Baylor, *German Reformation*, 3–8.

616 Taxes and fees: Friedenthal, *Luther*, 406; Blickle, *Revolution of 1525*, 46.

617 In a word, serfdom: "Serfdom," in *Europe 1450 to 1789: An Encyclopedia of the Early Modern World*.

617 the itinerant preachers: E. Belfort Bax, *The Peasants War in Germany, 1525–1526*, 31–32; Dixon, *Reformation in Germany*, 59–62.

617 cited Luther's own pronouncements: Ozment, *The Age of Reform*, 277.

617 Luther's personal example: Blickle, *Revolution of 1525*, xxiii.

618 for monasteries and abbeys: Friedenthal, *Martin Luther*, 407; Blickle, *Revolution of 1525*, 57.

618 The notorious abbey at Kempten: Scott and Scribner, *German Peasants' War*, 73–78.

618 the pamphlets and broadsheets: R. W. Scribner, "Images of the Peasant, 1514–1525," in Janos Bak, ed., *The German Peasant War of 1525*, 29–48.

618 "Peasants and pigs": See Marius, *Martin Luther*, 417.

618 "The Wittenberg Nightingale": Strauss, *Nuremberg in the Sixteenth Century*, 166–168.

619 events in neighboring Switzerland: Scott and Scribner, *German Peasants' War*, 96–100.

619 In his *Sixty-Seven Articles*: Baylor, *German Reformation*, 61–65.

619 closely followed in Waldshut: Christof
Windhorst, "Balthasar Hubmaier:
Professor, Preacher, Politician," in
Hans-Jürgen Goertz, ed., *Profiles of
Radical Reformers: Biographical Sketches
from Thomas Müntzer to Paracelsus*,
144–157; Tom Scott, "Reformation and
Peasants' War in Waldshut and Environs:
A Structural Analysis," *Archiv für
Reformationsgeschichte*, 69: 82–102, 1978,
and 70: 140–168, 1979; Schwiebert,
Luther, 562.

620 One of the first major peasant outbreaks:
Scott and Scribner, *German Peasants'
War*, 20. As Baylor notes (*German
Reformation*, 15–16), the outbreak at
Lupfen was one of a series of defiant and
rebellious acts, both rural and urban,
that marked the onset of the storm.

620 Hans Müller: Scott and Scribner,
German Peasants' War, 24, 233.

620 Müller led a contingent: Baylor, *German
Reformation*, 16; Bax, *Peasants War in
Germany*, 37–38.

620 thirty thousand peasants were under
arms: *The Cambridge Modern History*,
vol. 2, *The Reformation*, 179.

621 letter to Heinrich Stromer: *Collected
Works of Erasmus*, vol. 10, no. 1522,
December 10, 1524, 437–441.

621 two Basel printers: Ibid., vol. 10, 445. See
also *Luther's Works*, vol. 40, 76.

621 The reigning interpretation: See Amy
Nelson Burnett, introduction, *That These
Words of Christ, "This Is My Body," etc.,
Still Stand Firm Against the Fanatics*, in
The Annotated Luther, vol. 3, *Church
and Sacraments*, ed. Paul W. Robinson,
163–170.

622 he argued that the Eucharist: "Dialogue
or Discussion Booklet on the Infamous
and Idolatrous Abuse of the Most Blessed
Sacrament of Jesus Christ," in Furcha,
The Essential Carlstadt, 269–316.

622 "He who partakes": "Concerning the
Anti-Christian Misuse of the Lord's
Bread and Cup," in Sider, *Karlstadt's
Battle with Luther*, 83.

622 The city was alive: Chrisman, *Strasbourg
and the Reform*, 81–83; "Strasbourg,"
in *The Oxford Encyclopedia of the
Reformation*.

623 Wolfgang Capito: Chrisman, *Strasbourg
and the Reform*, 88–90, 108–112;
James M. Kittelson, *Wolfgang Capito:
From Humanist to Reformer*, 100–108.

623 Martin Bucer: Chrisman, *Strasbourg and
the Reform*, 83–88.

623 as usual caused an uproar: Brecht,
Shaping and Defining 162–163.

624 In a November 23, 1524, letter: *Luthers
Werke, Briefwechsel*, vol. 3, no. 797,
381–387.

CHAPTER 36: UPRISING

625 referred to them as his wives: *Luther's
Correspondence*, vol. 2, no. 672, to
Spalatin, April 16, 1525, 305. On the von
Schönfeld sisters, see 180.

625 Katharina was heartbroken: Ibid., vol. 2,
no. 642, Luther to Jerome Baumgärtner,
October 12, 1524, 257–258.

625 unable to send a wedding gift: Brecht,
Shaping and Defining, 201.

625 "If it should happen": *Luther's
Correspondence*, vol. 2, no. 649,
December 2, 1524, 264–265.

626 "Not that I lack": Ibid., vol. 2, no. 648,
November 30, 1524, 263–264.

626 Luther was following the persecution:
Ibid., vol. 2, no. 645, Luther to Nicholas
Hausmann, November 17, 1524,
258–260.

626 informed him of the malicious things:
Ibid., vol. 2, no. 651, Luther to Nicholas
Gerbel, December 17, 1524, 272–274.

626 *To the Christians at Strassburg*: *Luther's
Works*, vol. 40, 65–71; "loose, lame,"
68; "glad that he," 69; Christ "finds not
only," 66; "fanaticism," "new prophets,"
66–67. (Strassburg is the German version
of the city's name.)

627 *Against the Heavenly Prophets*: Ibid., vol.
40, 79–223; "Karlstadt has deserted
us," 79; "that he has a perverted spirit,"

82; a "murderous weapon," 106; Luther mocked Karlstadt, 117; It was not necessary, 131–132; "in a Karlstadtian manner," 89; For page after page, 154–186; "The ass's head," 162; Karlstadt latched on to, 186–187.

628 "displeases almost everyone": *Luther's Correspondence*, vol. 2, no. 669, to John Schwebel, March 30, 1525, 302–303.

628 Gerbel rued the fact: Ibid., vol. 2, 345, introductory note.

628 "I owe a book": Ibid., vol. 2, no. 666, March 26, 1528, 298–299.

628 the agitation in the German southwest: Blickle, *Revolution of 1525*, 97–99.

629 the Baltringen *Haufen*: Scott and Scribner, *German Peasants' War*, 25–27, 122–126; Bax, *Peasants War in Germany*, 55–56.

629 Sebastian Lotzer: Barbara Bettina Gerber, "Sebastian Lotzer: An Educated Layman in the Struggle for Divine Justice," in Goertz, *Profiles of Radical Reformers*; "Whoever has two coats," 75. On Memmingen, see Blickle, *Revolution of 1525*, 105ff.

630 The Twelve Articles: The document is in Scott and Scribner, *German Peasants' War*, 252–257. See also Friedenthal, *Luther*, 414–415; Brecht, *Shaping and Defining*, 174.

631 the Twelve Articles were reprinted: Pettegree, *Brand Luther*, 238–239; Blickle, *Revolution of 1525*, 18.

632 When the Twelve Articles arrived: Bax, *Peasants War in Germany*, 77; Bak, *German Peasant War of 1525*, 10–13.

632 the abbey of Ottobeuren: Govind P. Sreenivasan, "The Social Origins of the Peasants' War in Upper Swabia," *Past and Present*, 171: 30–65, May 2001.

632 the lords were like "old women": Quoted in Scott and Scribner, *German Peasants' War*, 151–152.

633 George von Waldburg: Ibid., 57–58.

633 The first major encounter: Ibid.

634 Hans Müller led a campaign: Ibid., 135–136.

634 Müller's sights were set on Freiburg: Ibid., 187–189.

634 "Everything here": Quoted in Johannes Janssen, *History of the German People at the Close of the Middle Ages*, vol. 4, 244–245.

634 spilling westward across the Rhine: Bax, *Peasants War in Germany*, 222–227; Francis Rapp, "The Social and Economic Prehistory of the Peasant War in Lower Alsace," in Bob Scribner and Gerhard Benecke, eds., *The German Peasant War of 1525—New Viewpoints*, 52–62; Scott and Scribner, *German Peasant War*, 44–49; Baylor, *German Reformation*, 44–45; Chrisman, *Strasbourg and the Reform*, 145–151.

635 into Franconia: Rudolf Endres, "The Peasant War in Franconia," in Scribner and Benecke, *German Peasant War of 1525*, 63–83; Bax, *Peasants War in Germany*, 154–186; Scott and Scribner, *German Peasants' War*, 28–36.

635 In Nuremberg: Strauss, *Nuremberg in the Sixteenth Century*, 174–177.

635 Rothenburg, became: G. H. Williams, *Radical Reformation*, 68–73; Scott and Scribner, *German Peasants' War*, 28–29; Janssen, *History of the German People*, vol. 4, 252–257; Roy L. Vice, "Ehrenfried Kumpf, Karlstadt's Patron and Peasants' War Rebel," *Archiv für Reformationsgeschichte*, 86: 153–174, 1995; Bax, *Peasants War in Germany*, 155–158.

636 the nearby Tauber valley: Roy L. Vice, "The Leadership Structure of the Tauber Band During the Peasants' War in Franconia," *Central European History*, 21(2): 175–195, June 1988; Scott and Scribner, *German Peasants' War*, 29.

636 George Metzler: Scott and Scribner, *German Peasants' War*, 243–244.

636 A notorious exception occurred at Weinsberg: Ibid., 29, 32, 158, 236–237; Bax, *Peasants War in Germany*, 113–133.

637 rampage through the bishopric of

Bamberg: Janssen, *History of the German People*, vol. 4, 257–260; Endres, "Peasant War in Franconia," in Scribner and Benecke, *German Peasant War of 1525*, 77.

637 The one major holdout was Würzburg: Scott and Scribner, *German Peasants' War*, 35; Bax, *Peasants War in Germany*, 163–175; Endres, "Peasant War in Franconia," in Scribner and Benecke, *German Peasant War of 1525*, 76.

638 swept northward into Hesse and Thuringia: Scott and Scribner, *German Peasants' War*, 36–44.

638 Müntzer arrived: Scott, *Thomas Müntzer*, 141–146.

638 Müntzer sent sympathetic preachers: Ibid., 152–153.

638 "The time has come": Scott and Scribner, *German Peasants' War*, 238; Cohn, *Pursuit of the Millennium*, 248.

639 a request from Count Albrecht: See *Luther's Correspondence*, vol. 2, no. 672, Luther to Spalatin, April 16, 1525, 305.

639 The *Admonition to Peace: Luther's Works*, vol. 46, 17–43; "We have no one," 19; Luther endorsed the peasants' demands, 22–25; As Paul taught at Romans 13, 25–26; all teach that Christians should suffer, 29; "even a child," 29; "As long as there is a heartbeat," 32; a "lying preacher," 38; the peasants should first humbly ask, 38; "Did not Abraham," 39; "to obey and respect," 20.

642 "It is not the case": Quoted in Scott and Scribner, *German Peasants' War*, 238.

642 continued on through northern and central Thuringia: Bornkamm, *Luther in Mid-Career*, 376–377; Brecht, *Shaping and Defining*, 178–179.

643 The peasants "are forming bands": Quoted in Scott and Scribner, *German Peasants' War*, 159.

643 estimated that there were 35,000 troops: Bornkamm, *Luther in Mid-Career*, 375–376.

643 Almost alone among the princes: Hajo Holborn, *History of Modern Germany*, vol. 1, *The Reformation*, 174.

643 "In many ways": Quoted in Bornkamm, *Luther in Mid-Career*, 375.

643 Luther sent Rühel a letter: *Luther's Works*, vol. 49, no. 154, May 4, 1525, 106–112.

CHAPTER 37: THE MURDERING HORDES

645 "It is not safe for me": *Collected Works of Erasmus*, vol. 11, no. 1554, February 24, 1525, 54–56.

645 Capito was now sending: Ibid., vol. 10, no. 1374, July 6, 1523, 44–49.

645 "My neighbors": Ibid., vol. 11, no. 1607, September 5, 1525, 262–264.

645 Basel itself was untouched: Ibid., vol. 11, xi–xiii.

646 The center of complaint: Ibid., vol. 11, xvi–xvii.

646 Pierre Cousturier: Ibid., vol. 11, 99, note 10; Rummel, *Erasmus and His Catholic Critics*, vol. 2, 61–73.

646 "Mere rhetoricians": Quoted in James K. Farge, *Orthodoxy and Reform in Early Reformation France: The Faculty of Theology of Paris, 1500–1543*, 187.

646 Béda had served as the head: *Collected Works of Erasmus*, vol. 11, no. 1571, introductory note, 95–96; Rummel, *Erasmus and His Catholic Critics*, vol. 2, 29–59.

647 Béda sent him a long and menacing letter: *Collected Works of Erasmus*, vol. 11, no. 1579, May 21, 1525, 117–128.

647 In a lengthy rejoinder to Béda: Ibid., vol. 11, no. 1581, June 15, 1525, 130–162; "labyrinthine intricacies," 151; "clinging to them," 153; "A few radical preachers," 159.

648 in a letter to Willibald Pirckheimer: Ibid., vol. 11, no. 1603, August 28, 1525, 249–257.

648 the peasants had overrun Salzburg: Scott and Scribner, *German Peasants' War*, 51–52; *The Cambridge Modern History*, vol. 2, *The Reformation*, 182; Bax, *Peasants War in Germany*, 187–213.

648 "not a few pious men": Bax, *Peasants War in Germany*, 205.

649 In Alsace: Chrisman, *Reformation in Strasbourg*, 150–153; Janssen, *History of the German People*, vol. 4, 242–243.

649 In the Black Forest: Scott and Scribner, *German Peasants' War*, 27, 189.

649 Wine in particular: Bax, *Peasants War in Germany*, 164–165. "It must . . . be admitted by the best friends of the peasants and their cause," Bax writes, "that gluttony and wine-bibbing contributed as potently as any other influence to the politically unproductive character of the peasant successes and to that lack of cohesion and discipline which led the way to the final catastrophe and soaked the German soil with the blood of its tillers."

649 The peasants' occupation of Würzburg: Scott and Scribner, *German Peasants' War*, 166–169.

650 a wine war: Bax, *Peasants War in Germany*, 164.

650 Karlstadt included: G. H. Williams, *Radical Reformation*, 71–73; Bax, *Peasants War in Germany*, 180–181; Vice, "Ehrenfried Kumpf, Karlstadt's Patron and Peasants' War Rebel," *Archiv für Reformationsgeschichte*, 86: 153–174, 1995. For Karlstadt's own (somewhat self-exculpatory) account of his experiences during the peasant uprising, see "Apology by Dr. Andreas Carlstadt Regarding the False Charge of Insurrection Which Has Unjustly Been Made Against Him," in Furcha, *Essential Carlstadt*, 378–386.

651 "I was among the peasants": Quoted in Furcha, *Essential Carlstadt*, 383.

651 his pleas grew more urgent: Edwards, *Luther and the False Brethren*, 73ff.

651 *Against the Robbing and Murdering Hordes: Luther's Works*, vol. 46, 49–55; "are robbing and raging," 49; "a great fire," 50; "Therefore," 50; If a ruler is a Christian, 52; he himself "becomes guilty," 53; "may be a true martyr," 53; A "pious Christian," 54; "Let whoever can stab," 54.

652 Philip of Hesse: Scott and Scribner, *German Peasants' War*, 39, 159–160.

652 major center of resistance: Scott, *Thomas Müntzer*, 161.

653 the prospect of plunder intervened: Scott and Scribner, *German Peasants' War*, 145–147; Scott, *Thomas Müntzer*, 156.

653 When Müntzer finally did set out: On the battle of Frankenhausen, see Friedenthal, *Luther*, 421–424; Scott and Scribner, *German Peasants' War*, 289–291; Cohn, *Pursuit of the Millennium*, 248–251; Scott, *Thomas Müntzer*, 161–166; Gritsch, *Thomas Müntzer*, 101–105.

653 "In your Lutheran gruel": Quoted in Bornkamm, *Luther in Mid-Career*, 382–383.

654 another count, Ernst: Scott and Scribner, *German Peasants' War*, 239.

654 seeking to rouse the camp: Bax, *Peasants War in Germany*, 264; Cohn, *Pursuit of the Millennium*, 250.

654 the peasants broke ranks: Scott and Scribner, *German Peasants' War*, 289–291; Friedenthal, *Luther*, 423; Bax, *Peasants War in Germany*, 263–266.

655 "their heads were like": Quoted in Bax, *Peasants War in Germany*, 266.

655 Müntzer, on whose head: Scott and Scribner, *German Peasants' War*, 292; Scott, *Thomas Müntzer*, 166; Gritsch, *Thomas Müntzer*, 105.

655 the princes marched their armies: Gritsch, *Thomas Müntzer*, 109; Bax, *Peasants War in Germany*, 270; Scott and Scribner, *German Peasants' War*, 241, 292–294.

656 unleashed a vengeful pacification campaign: Scott and Scribner, *German Peasants' War*, 149–153; Bax, *Peasants War in Germany*, 284–291.

656 on the outskirts of Würzburg: Scott and Scribner, *German Peasants' War*, 163–169, 296–298; "like roaming wolves," 297; "guilty or innocent," 298.

657 Margrave Kasimir: Ibid., 299–301; Bax, *Peasants War in Germany*, 283–284.

657 Alsace would stand out: Bax, *Peasants War in Germany*, 312–317; Scott and Scribner, *German Peasants' War*, 48, 308.

658 In the Black Forest: Scott and Scribner, *German Peasants' War*, 302–303.

658 The death toll: Bax, *Peasants War in Germany*, 353.

659 No one fared worse: Gritsch, *Thomas Müntzer*, 105–109; Scott, *Thomas Müntzer*, 167–169; Scott and Scribner, *German Peasants' War*, 239–240; Bax, *Peasants War in Germany*, 269–270.

659 On May 25, 1525, Müntzer: Scott, *Thomas Müntzer*, 169.

659 Luther received a copy: Scott and Scribner, *German Peasants' War*, 291–292.

660 *Luther Speaks with Forked Tongue*: Quoted in Ozment, *Age of Reform*, 286.

660 Nikolaus von Amsdorf wrote: See *Luther's Correspondence*, vol. 2, no. 686, Luther to Nikolaus von Amsdorf, May 30, 1525, 319.

660 "They have gone mad": Ibid., vol. 2, no. 687, May 30, 1525, 320–322.

660 To Amsdorf he wrote: Ibid., vol. 2, no. 686, May 30, 1525, 320.

660 *An Open Letter on the Harsh Book*: *Luther's Works*, vol. 46, 63–85; "rebels at heart," 65; "this is not a question," 66; The "Scripture passages," 70; Those who are advocates, 71; "as I wrote then," 73; Luther conceded the point, 74; when he had the time, 75; "the donkey needs," 76; "These are plagues," 78; is time "to stop complaining," 79; everyone must help rescue him "by stabbing," 80; "I would forget my spiritual office," 81.

662 Herman Mühlpfort: Quoted in Scott and Scribner, *German Peasants' War*, 322–324.

662 Heinrich von Einsiedel: Bax, *Peasants War in Germany*, 351–352.

662 Melanchthon thought that even serfdom: *The Cambridge Modern History*, vol. 2, 193; Bax, *Peasants War in Germany*, 352; Robert Kolb, "The Theologians and

the Peasants: Conservative Evangelical Reactions to the German Peasants' Revolt," *Archiv für Reformationsgeschichte*, 69: 103–131, 1978.

662 "What an outcry of Harrow": *Luther's Correspondence*, vol. 2, no. 690, June 15, 1525, 323.

662 Now he seemed the leader: *The Cambridge Modern History*, vol. 2, 194; Marius, *Martin Luther*, 425; MacCulloch, *Reformation*, 156; Eire, *Reformations*, 210.

662 According to Friedrich Engels: Engels, *The Peasant War in Germany*; "a veritable hymn," 62; a "magnificent figure," 47; "a genius' anticipation," 66.

663 The German Democratic Republic: For an image of the note, see Eire, *Reformations*, 198.

663 "slew all the peasants": *Luther's Works*, "Table Talk," vol. 54, 180.

663 The peasants themselves: Rice and Grafton, *Foundations of Early Modern Europe*, 183; Hajo Holborn, *History of Modern Germany*, vol. 1, 176–177.

663 great flood of popular pamphlets: Holborn, *History of Modern Germany*, vol. 1, 177.

664 "priests are arrested": *Collected Works of Erasmus*, vol. 11, no. 1653, December 24, 1525, to Nicolaas Everaerts, 393.

664 the margraves Kasimir and George of Brandenburg: Scott and Scribner, *German Peasants' War*, 330–331.

664 Archduke Ferdinand: Bax, *Peasants War in Germany*, 359.

664 The current Catholic character: Bainton, *Here I Stand*, 221.

664 Luther would imprint German Lutheranism: Marius, *Martin Luther*, 424, 427–428.

665 went to the nuptial bed: *Luther's Correspondence*, vol. 2, no. 689, Justus Jonas to George Spalatin, June 14, 1525, 322; Martin Marty, *Martin Luther*, 106.

665 In a letter to Nikolaus von Amsdorf: *Luther's Correspondence*, vol. 2, no. 695,

June 21, 1525, 329. See also Brecht, *Shaping and Defining*, 197.

665 "Everywhere the smoke": Quoted in Friedenthal, *Luther*, 432.

665 Writing to his friend Joachim Camerarius: *Luther's Correspondence*, vol. 2, no. 692, June 16, 1525, 324–327.

666 decided to hold a very public feast: Friedenthal, *Luther*, 438–439.

666 to Leonhard Koppe: *Luther's Correspondence*, vol. 2, no. 694, June 21, 1525, 328–329.

666 In a letter to John Rühel: Ibid., vol. 2, no. 690, June 15, 1525, 323.

666 Karlstadt on June 12 had written: Ibid., vol. 2, no. 703, Luther to Elector John, September 12, 1525, 336–337; *Luthers Werke, Briefwechsel*, vol. 3, no. 889, 429–430. Karlstadt's epithets against Luther are cited in *Against the Heavenly Prophets, Luther's Works*, vol. 40, 186.

666 he would live in secret: See *Luther's Works*, vol. 49, no. 158, to John Briessmann [after August 15] 1525, 120–125, in which Luther reports that "that miserable man found a secret refuge in my house." See also Edwards, *Luther and the False Brethren*, 79–80.

CHAPTER 38: FATAL DISSENSION

667 "oblivious of everything": Quoted in Friedenthal, *Luther*, 439; For a full year: Bainton, *Here I Stand*, 226.

667 "has strange thoughts": *Luther's Works*, vol. 54, "Table Talk," 191.

667 "Doctor, is the grandmaster": Ibid.

667 "I must be patient": *Luthers Werke, Tischreden*, vol. 2, no. 2173A, 347; Friedenthal, *Luther*, 446.

667 proved an astute household manager: On Katharina's life with Luther, see Kirsi Stjerna, *Women and the Reformation*, 51–70; Roland H. Bainton, *Women of the Reformation in Germany and Italy*, 29–43; Bainton, *Here I Stand*, 226–228; Friedenthal, *Luther*, 434–444; Bornkamm, *Luther in Mid-Career*,

411–415; Brecht, *Shaping and Defining*, 201–204.

667 also received twenty guldens: Friedenthal, *Luther*, 439.

668 sent to Gabriel Zwilling: *Luther's Works*, vol. 49, no. 163, January 2, 1526, 142.

668 "It is a good thing that God": Ibid., vol. 54, "Table Talk," 23.

668 Luther acquired a lathe: *Luther's Correspondence*, vol. 2, no. 758, Luther to Wenzel (Wenceslas) Link, May 19, 1527, 399.

668 to Wenceslas Link: *Luther's Works*, vol. 49, no. 173, July 5, 1527, 166–167.

668 he would not be able to attend: *Luther's Correspondence*, vol. 2, no. 715, November 11, 1525, 352–353.

668 he sent Spalatin a racy message: Ibid., vol. 2, no. 719, December 6, 1525, 355–356.

669 Duke George's succinct greeting: Quoted in Ozment, *Serpent and the Lamb*, 178.

669 *Monachopornomachia*: Friedenthal, *Luther*, 432; Roper, *Martin Luther*, 364–366.

669 "a few days after the singing": *Collected Works of Erasmus*, vol. 11, no. 1633, to Daniel Mauch, October 10, 1525, 323–326.

669 "Luther is now becoming more moderate": Ibid., vol. 11, no. 1653, to Nicolaas Everaerts, December 24, 1525, 392–393.

669 appeared in twelve editions: See Universal Short Title Catalogue (ustc .ac.uk); Pettegree, *Brand Luther*, 233.

669 Seven Strasbourg theologians: *Luthers Werke, Briefwechsel*, vol. 3, no. 797, November 23, 1524, 381–387; Bornkamm, *Luther in Mid-Career*, 417.

670 Joachim Camerarius: Brecht, *Shaping and Defining*, 225.

670 "I am altogether": *Luther's Correspondence*, vol. 2, no. 704, September 27, 1525, 337–338.

670 *The Bondage of the Will*: *Luther's Works*, vol. 33, 15–295.

670 he would later say: Ibid., vol. 50, no.

282, to Wolfgang Capito, July 9, 1537, 171–174.

671 What for Erasmus was a lively clash: See Smith, *Erasmus*, 351.

671 "That I have taken so long": *Luther's Works*, vol. 33, 15–16; Erasmus had treated the subject, 16; "refuse or ordure," 16; "but sheer disgust," 17; "is a pure fiction," 18; Luther hoped that, 19; "Take away assertions," 21; "a Lucian or some other pig," 24; Luther took similar offense, 24–28; *Das ist zu viel*, 29; "by his immutable," 37; "to know that God," 43; "far more important than faith," 50; "it ought to be asserted," 50; "Truth and doctrine," 56; "Tumults, commotions," 53; "has no free choice," 70; "like a beast of burden," 65; On God's hardening of the pharaoh's heart, 164–175; Judas, he maintained, 185, 195; "something that even," 127; "I am amazed," 151; "that sharp Greek mind," 83; gleefully mocked Erasmus's title, 125, 128; "See how the invincible," 115; "No one since the Pelagians," 107; "stands unshaken," 205; Diatribe "is baffled and beaten," 210–211; "if we believe," 293; his own "special gift," 294; "I for my part," 295.

675 The deities described: For a discussion of this contrast, see Ozment, *Age of Reform*, 290–302; Smith, *Erasmus*, 352–354; Marty, *Martin Luther*, 130–133.

676 taken up and amplified by John Calvin: Smith, *Erasmus*, 354.

676 "Man *himself*": Immanuel Kant, *Religion Within the Limits of Reason Alone*, trans. Theodore M. Greene and Hoyt H. Hudson, 40. On the similarities between the ideas of Erasmus and Kant, see E. C. Galbraith, "Kant and Erasmus," *Scottish Journal of Theology*, 46(2): 191–212, January 1993. "We may conclude," Galbraith writes (210), "that there are good grounds not only for considering Erasmus to be the forerunner of Kant, but also for placing Kant's thought, especially with regard to evil and

salvation, closer to Catholic doctrine than to Luther."

676 Luther finished his book: *Luther's Works*, vol. 49, note 3, 140.

676 it would be reprinted: See Universal Short Title Catalogue (ustc.ac.uk).

676 was creating a new religious model: Volker Leppin, in the introduction to *The Bondage of the Will* in *The Annotated Luther*, vol. 2, *Word and Faith*, ed. Kirsi I. Stjerna, observes (156) that Luther in this work "laid the grounds for the fundamentalist Lutheran understanding of the infallibility of Scripture and its centrality in Lutheran theology, especially prominent in so-called Lutheran orthodoxy." Marius (*Martin Luther*, 468) writes that "for those who admire Luther and his treatise, it stands as an unequivocal assertion of God's sovereignty, stirring as some declaration of war or a brave defiance that comes with a refusal to surrender to overwhelming forces. To us in the late twentieth century, who have lived through declarations of war, defiant refusals to surrender, and the willingness of zealots of all sorts both to be martyrs to their causes and to kill others in the name of their righteousness, Luther's uncompromising rhetoric reeks of sadness and futility and of bloodshed to come in rivers of anguish throughout Europe and the Americas."

677 he could not obtain a copy: *Collected Works of Erasmus*, vol. 12, xiii–xiv.

677 "so as to prejudice": Ibid., vol. 12, no. 1678, to Michel Boudet, March 13, 1526, 81.

677 "No matter what I do": Ibid., vol. 11, no. 1624, to Thomas Lupset [October 4] 1525, 307.

677 a group of Dominicans collaborated: Ibid., vol. 11, no. 1571, to Noël Béda, April 28, 1525, 101, note 14.

677 Jacobus Latomus: Ibid., vol. 11, 146, note 58; vol. 12, xvi.

677 a group of "rabble-rousers": Ibid.,

vol. 11, no. 1554, to Jean Lalemand, February 24, 1525, 56; vol. 12, 165, note 6.

678 a committee appointed by the Sorbonne: Farge, *Orthodoxy and Reform in Early Reformation France*, 191.

678 Pierre Cousturier: *Collected Works of Erasmus*, vol. 12, no. 1687, to Willem Bibaut, April 7, 1526, 133.

678 Noël Béda published a collection: Ibid., vol. 12, no. 1721, to the Parlement of Paris, June 14, 1526, introductory note, 237. See also Rummel, *Erasmus and His Catholic Critics*, vol. 2, 33–37.

678 Louis de Berquin: "Berquin, Louis de," in *Contemporaries of Erasmus*.

678 sent him an urgent plea: *Collected Works of Erasmus*, vol. 12, to Francis I, June 16, 1526, 243–247. See also Rummel, *Erasmus and His Catholic Critics*, vol. 2, 36–37.

678 Jan Łaski: See "Łaski, Jan," in *Contemporaries of Erasmus*; *Collected Works of Erasmus*, vol. 11, no. 1593, to Krzysztof Szydłowiecki, August 14, 1525, 214–222, especially 221, note 18. On Erasmus's growing reputation in Poland, see his letter to Thomas Wolsey, vol. 12, no. 1697, April 25, 1526, 172–173; MacCulloch, *Reformation*, 246–247.

679 among the educated elite of Spain: Dickens and Jones, *Erasmus the Reformer*, 225–230.

679 the *Enchiridion* was translated into Spanish: See *Collected Works of Erasmus*, vol. 12, no. 1742, from Juan Maldonado, September 1, 1526, 314–324. Erasmus's influence in Spain is minutely chronicled in Marcel Bataillon's monumental *Érasme et l'Espagne*. Originally published in two volumes in 1937, it was reissued by Librarie Droz in 1991 in three volumes. Bataillon makes large claims on behalf of Erasmus's influence in Spain, maintaining, for instance (vol. 1, 844), that Cervantes's literary tendencies were shaped by Erasmian humanism—a

position that cannot be easily proved or disproved.

679 the furor set off by Karlstadt's tracts: See Burnett, introduction, *That These Words of Christ, "This Is My Body," etc., Still Stand Firm Against the Fanatics*, in *The Annotated Luther*, vol. 3, 163–170.

680 The sacramentarian "heresy": *Collected Works of Erasmus*, vol. 11, no. 1624, to Thomas Lupset [October 4] 1525, 305–308. On Zwingli, see vol. 11, 298, note 14; on Oecolampadius, see vol. 11, 288, notes 2 and 4.

680 "so carefully written": Ibid., vol. 11, no. 1621, to Pierre Barbier, October 3, 1525, 300.

680 "You can imagine what an uproar": Ibid., vol. 11, no. 1637, to Conradus Pellicanus [October 15, 1525], 344–350; no. 1640, to Conradus Pellicanus [October 1525], 364–366.

680 "Who can believe": Ibid., vol. 12, no. 1670, March 2, 1526, 51.

680 *Hyperaspistes*: Ibid., vol. 76, 93–297; "How much there is," 97; more "enmity and bitterness," 101; why was there so much disagreement, 143; "And so, away with," 181; "seditious wantonness," 293; "has been redoubled," 294; "and now they wander," 295; "renew a good spirit," 296.

682 five or six presses: Ibid., vol. 12, no. 1683, to Hieronymus Emser [March 19, 1526], 108.

683 "So you restrained your pen!": Ibid., vol. 12, no. 1688, to Martin Luther, April 11, 1526, 135–138.

683 "fatal dissension": Ibid., 137. The phrase in Latin is *exitiabili dissidio*, which can also be translated as "fatal discord"; see, for instance, Marius, *Martin Luther*, 467.

CHAPTER 39: INVASION BY SCRIPTURE

684 "Have you ever read anything": *Luther's Correspondence*, vol. 2, no. 730, April 11, 1526, 370–371.

684 "That enraged viper": *Luther's Works*,

vol. 49, no. 164, March 27, 1526, 143–147.

684 "an instrument of Satan": *Luther's Correspondence*, vol. 2, no. 724, to Nicholas Hausmann, January 20, 1526, 363.

684 "cursed Lutheran sect": *Luther's Works*, vol. 49, 119–120, note 24.

684 "so that it may be impregnable": *Luther's Correspondence*, vol. 2, no. 747, to John Agricola, January 1, 1527, 388–389.

685 In his letter to the king: Ibid., vol. 2, no. 700, September 1, 1525, 333–335.

685 "merely a mask for Erasmus": Ibid., vol. 2, no. 754, to Spalatin, February 1, 1527, 396.

686 "but I am a sheep": Quoted in Smith, *Life and Letters of Martin Luther*, 195.

686 The log of an Oxford bookseller: McConica, *English Humanists and Reformation Politics Under Henry VIII and Edward VI*, 89.

687 heeded the admonitions in the *Enchiridion*: Seven English editions of this work would appear between 1533 and 1550; see Dickens and Jones, *Erasmus the Reformer*, 211.

687 "A Pilgrimage for Religion's Sake": *Collected Works of Erasmus*, vol. 40, 621–650.

687 the sole European showcase of Erasmus's reform ideas: Scarisbrick, *Henry VIII* (398), observes that "the years following the breach with Rome saw the implementation of what might be loosely described as an Erasmian reform programme—the attack on 'superstitions' like relics, shrines, pilgrimages, as well as on monasticism; the printing of the Bible and primers in English; the outpouring of Erasmian writings, many of them translations of Erasmus's own works, others original pieces of lay pietism, devotional literature and prayer manuals, alongside the innumerable treatises on education, social and economic justice, service to the prince and the commonwealth, medicine,

etc. produced by the humanist circles which formed first around Thomas Cromwell and then Queen Catherine Parr." McConica, in *English Humanists and Reformation Politics Under Henry VIII and Edward VI*, devotes a chapter to "Erasmianism"—a creed that he calls (42–43) a "blend of humanism and reform that was the joint manufacture of More and Erasmus, swayed undoubtedly by the fervent genius of John Colet"; its influence "played an active role in shaping a religious settlement unique in the annals of the Reformation." In *Erasmus the Reformer*, Dickens and Jones spend a chapter ("The English Erasmians") describing Erasmus's influence in England, concluding (216) that "perhaps it was indeed on English soil that his propagation of the *philosophia Christi* found its most fertile seed-bed and put down its deepest roots." And Bainton, in *Erasmus of Christendom* (279), observes that "England was the land where the influence of Erasmus was paramount at his death. The entire English Reformation has been characterized as Erasmian, and with justice, if it be remembered that the vogue of his ideas is not necessarily to be attributed solely to his personal impact, since other men of influence in England, like Colet and More, were of like mind. No one can deny the immense popularity of Erasmian works during the latter years of Henry VIII and well into the period of Elizabeth."

687 *Institutio Christiani Matrimonii: Collected Works of Erasmus*, vol. 69, 214–438; "Death," he wrote, 275; "If one looks at social life today," 278.

688 the "saintliness of your character": Ibid., vol. 12, no. 1727, July 15, 1526, 257–259.

688 Erasmus's greatest impact on England: See John N. King, *English Reformation Literature: The Tudor Origins of the Protestant Tradition*, 44–46, 54–55.

688 Tyndale's work as a Bible translator:

On Tyndale and his influence, see David Daniell, *William Tyndale: A Biography*; Brian Edwards, *William Tyndale: The Father of the English Bible*; David Teems, *Tyndale: The Man Who Gave God an English Voice*; Benson Bobrick, *Wide as the Waters: The Story of the English Bible and the Revolution It Inspired*, 79–81, 89–91, 96–124; H. Maynard Smith, *Henry VIII and the Reformation*, 280–321.

688 relied heavily on Tyndale's Old and New Testaments: See Adam Nicolson, *God's Secretaries: The Making of the King James Bible*, xii–xiii, 221–225.

689 this moral manual would influence Tyndale: Daniell, *William Tyndale*, 64–74; Marius, *Thomas More*, 318.

689 remained a criminal offense: Daniell, *William Tyndale*, 92–100.

689 to see Cuthbert Tunstall: Ibid., 83–87.

690 entrée to London's cloth merchants: Ibid., 102–107; Maynard Smith, *Henry VIII and the Reformation*, 286–287.

690 devoted himself to translating: Daniell, *William Tyndale*, 111–116, 134–142; Maynard Smith, *Henry VIII and the Reformation*, 288–289, 293–298; Bobrick, *Wide as the Waters*, 98, 103–106.

690 Tyndale showed theological audacity: Daniell, *William Tyndale*, 122, 148–149; Bobrick, *Wide as the Waters*, 112–116; Marius, *Thomas More*, 319–323.

691 quickly found a printer: Daniell, *William Tyndale*, 108–111, 134; Edwards, *William Tyndale*, 84–91.

691 Wolsey was warned: Maynard Smith, *Henry VIII and the Reformation*, 291–292.

691 "we shall lose": Quoted ibid., 297.

692 made it doubly suspect: Ibid., 294–295.

692 issued a solemn admonition: Ibid., 299; Daniell, *William Tyndale*, 174–176.

692 growing increasingly impatient: Ackroyd, *Life of Thomas More*, 247–248; Marius, *Thomas More*, 289–291; G. R. Elton, "Sir Thomas More and the Opposition to

Henry VIII," in R. S. Sylvester and C. P. Marc'hadour, eds., *Essential Articles for the Study of Thomas More*, 81.

692 More led a raid: Ackroyd, *Life of Thomas More*, 246; Marius, *Thomas More*, 323.

693 were brought to St. Paul's: Marius, *Thomas More*, 337.

693 "I pray God you will be able": *Collected Works of Erasmus*, vol. 12, no. 1770, December 18 [1526], 414–419.

693 Hans Holbein the Younger: Ibid., vol. 12, 417, note 11.

694 "prepared to purchase": Ibid., vol. 12, no. 1705, to Leonard Casembroot, May 1, 1526, 190–191; vol. 12, no. 1720, from Leonard Casembroot, June 6, 1526, 234–237.

694 several rare manuscripts by John Chrysostom: Ibid., vol. 12, no. 1661, to John Claymond, January 30, 1526, 16–18, especially note 2, which mentions Erasmus's five-volume edition.

695 wrote to see if its library: Ibid., vol. 12, no. 1749, September 7, 1526, 353–354.

695 100,000 copies of the various editions: Ibid., vol. 12, 249.

695 upon its publication: Ibid., vol. 12, 336, note 27.

695 Erasmus answered More's letter: Ibid., vol. 13, no. 1804, March 30, 1527, 9–28.

CHAPTER 40: VANDALS

697 The conflagration: On the Sack of Rome, see E. R. Chamberlin, *The Sack of Rome*; Hibbert, *Rome*, 153–162; Pastor, *History of the Popes*, vol. 9, 373–423; Friedenthal, *Luther*, 465–479; "Rome, Sack of," in *Encyclopedia of the Renaissance*.

697 On the same day: Pastor, *History of the Popes*, vol. 9, 376.

697 money Charles desperately needed: Friedenthal, *Luther*, 466–467.

698 "To Rome!": Ibid., 469.

698 Clement was far more solemn: Pastor, *History of the Popes*, vol. 9, 248–253.

699 Now bearing down on it: Chamberlin, *Sack of Rome*, 9–10.

699 Not until May 4, 1527: Hibbert, *Rome*, 157.

699 raising its bridges: Ibid., 156.

699 The imperial army took up positions: Chamberlin, *Sack of Rome*, 154–157; Pastor, *History of the Popes*, vol. 9, 387.

699 a thick mist rose from the Tiber: Chamberlin, *Sack of Rome*, 157–159; Pastor, *History of the Popes*, vol. 9, 388–393; Hibbert, *Rome*, 157–158.

700 Clement could hear the cries: Chamberlin, *Sack of Rome*, 159–180; Pastor, *History of the Popes*, vol. 9, 393–396; Hibbert, *Rome*, 158.

700 "Empire! Spain! Victory!": Pastor, *History of the Popes*, vol. 9, 398.

701 scenes of appalling destruction: Ibid., vol. 9, 399ff; Hibbert, *Rome*, 158–160; Chamberlin, *Sack of Rome*, 167ff.

701 Special fury was aimed at the clergy: Pastor, *History of the Popes*, vol. 9, 403ff; Hibbert, *Rome*, 159.

701 "Luther for pope!": Quoted in Friedenthal, *Luther*, 471.

702 "Even on the high altar": Quoted in Hibbert, *Rome*, 158.

702 scrawled the name of Martin Luther: James Hankins, "The Popes and Humanism," in Anthony Grafton, ed., *Rome Reborn: The Vatican Library and Renaissance Culture*, 85.

702 enraged at the sight of artifacts: Hibbert, *Rome*, 160.

702 signed a treaty: Pastor, *History of the Popes*, vol. 9, 421–422.

702 "In Rome, the chief city": Quoted in Hibbert, *Rome*, 160.

703 "We took the town": Quoted in Chamberlin, *Sack of Rome*, 190.

703 thirty thousand houses destroyed: Ibid., 207; Hibbert, *Rome*, 161.

703 "We have seen Rome": *Collected Works of Erasmus*, vol. 14, no. 2059, to Jacopo Sadoleto [October 1] 1528, 366–371.

704 when Michelangelo resumed work: *The Vatican: Spirit and Art of Christian Rome* (New York: Metropolitan Museum of Art and H. N. Abrams, 1982), 126–130.

704 The emperor Charles: *Luther's Correspondence*, vol. 2, no. 767, to Nicholas Hausmann, July 13, 1527, 408.

704 the case of Leonhard Kaiser: Ibid., vol. 2, no. 797, to Wenzel (Wenceslas) Link, May 12, 1528, 444; Brecht, *Shaping and Defining*, 349–350; Roper, *Martin Luther*, 305–307.

705 "How many people": *Luther's Works*, vol. 54, "Table Talk," 95.

705 An especially serious attack: *Luther's Correspondence*, vol. 2, no. 764, Justus Jonas to John Bugenhagen, July 7, 1527, 403–404; no. 765, "Justus Jonas's Account of Luther's Illness," July 7, 1527, 404–407.

705 "almost lost Christ": Ibid., vol. 2, no. 768, to Melanchthon, August 2, 1527, 409.

705 growing conflict with the sacramentarians: Ibid., vol. 2, no. 778, to Melanchthon, October 27, 1527, 419; Brecht, *Shaping and Defining*, 310–314.

705 *That These Words of Christ*: See Burnett, introduction, *That These Words of Christ, "This Is My Body," etc., Still Stand Firm Against the Fanatics*, in *Annotated Luther*, vol. 3, 163–170.

706 amid "wild beasts": *Luther's Correspondence*, vol. 2, no. 801, to Nicholas Gerbel, July 28, 1528, 450–451.

706 "Judases": Ibid., vol. 2, no. 780, to Justus Jonas [November 11, 1527], 420–422.

706 was hit by the plague: Ibid., vol. 2, no. 768, Luther to Melanchthon, August 2, 1527, 409; no. 769, Elector John to Luther, August 10, 1527, 409–410; no. 770, Luther to Spalatin, August 19, 1527, 410–411; no. 779, Luther to Nicholas Hausmann, November 7, 1527, 420.

706 he asked Bugenhagen: Ibid., vol. 2, no. 779, Luther to Nicholas Hausmann, November 7, 1527, 420.

706 Luther's spirits were further dampened: Brecht, *Shaping and Defining*, 257, 287–292.

707 "This week we are asking": Quoted ibid., 289.

707 Luther proposed to Elector John: *Luther's Works*, vol. 40, 265–267. On the visitations, see Brecht, *Shaping and Defining*, 259–273; Bornkamm, *Luther in Mid-Career*, 489–500; Mullett, *Martin Luther*, 182–188; Manschreck, *Melanchthon*, 136–143.

707 "Everything is in confusion": Quoted in Manschreck, *Melanchthon*, 137.

708 *Instructions for the Visitors: Luther's Works*, vol. 40, 269–320.

708 to include Erasmus's *Colloquies*: Ibid., vol. 40, 316–317.

708 John, who supported the Reformation: Brecht, *Shaping and Defining*, 239.

709 the so-called territorial church: Ibid., 267; Holborn, *History of Modern Germany*, vol. 1, 187; Bainton *Here I Stand*, 244–245.

709 the 1526 Diet of Speyer: MacCulloch, *Reformation*, 159–160; Holborn, *History of Modern Germany*, vol. 1, 205–206; Bainton, *Reformation of the Sixteenth Century*, 148.

709 Philip of Hesse: MacCulloch, *Reformation*, 159; Friedenthal, *Luther*, 482–483; Elton, *Reformation Europe*, 37–38.

709 agreed to part with Bugenhagen: "Lutheranism," in *The Encyclopedia of the Lutheran Church*; Cameron, *European Reformation*, 216–217.

710 prevailed in several important cities: Cameron, *European Reformation*, 216–219.

710 Melanchthon spent much of the month: Manschreck, *Melanchthon*, 133–134.

710 the religious map of modern Germany: Holborn, *History of Modern Germany*, 219–221; Rice and Grafton, *Foundations of Early Modern Europe*, 193–195; Cameron, *European Reformation*, 268–272.

710 when the Paris faculty of theology voted: Farge, *Orthodoxy and Reform in Early Reformation France*, 195.

711 Frans Titelmans: *Collected Works of Erasmus*, vol. 13, no. 1823, to Frans Titelmans, May 18, 1527, 136–138; no. 1857A, from Frans Titelmans [1527], 172–177. See also Rummel, *Erasmus and His Catholic Critics*, vol. 2, 14–22.

711 "Men speak ill of me": *Collected Works of Erasmus*, vol. 12, appendix, no. 4, Alonso Ruiz de Virués to Juan de Vergara, October 9, 1526, 529–533.

711 The monks were secretly stationing agents: Ibid., vol. 13, no. 1814, from Juan de Vergara, April 24, 1527, 91.

711 facing such opprobrium: Ibid., vol. 12, no. 1742, introductory note, 314–316; vol. 12, no. 1786, 458, note 5; vol. 13, no. 1814, from Juan de Vergara, April 24, 1527, 81–103; Rummel, *Erasmus and His Catholic Critics*; vol. 2, 89ff; Augustijn, *Erasmus*, 155–157.

711 declared war on his supporters: *Collected Works of Erasmus*, vol. 14, xiv; Elton, *Reformation Europe*, 69–71.

712 the second part of the *Hyperaspistes*: *Collected Works of Erasmus*, vol. 77, 335–749; "supersophistical trash," 591; "prolix and pretentious palaver," 515; smoke screens and hairsplitting, 519–520; "It is worthwhile," 345; "cockadoodled," 373, 397, 401, 419, 443; there is a faculty of reason, 592; make him seem almost a Satan, 595; even if one grants, 648; Rather than make finespun distinctions, 747–749.

713 he brought out new editions: Ibid., vol. 13, xvi.

713 collected edition of the great Doctor: Ibid., vol. 15, no. 2157, to Alonso de Fonseca [May] 1529, 219–241. (This letter is the edition's preface.)

713 in the Steinenvorstadt: Guggisberg, *Basel in the Sixteenth Century*, 28–30.

713 came out with a pamphlet: Smith, *Erasmus*, 388.

713 The agitation continued: Ibid., 386–392. On these events, see also Huizinga, *Erasmus*, 173–175; Bainton, *Erasmus of Christendom*, 219–223.

713 "no man should call": Quoted in Smith, *Erasmus*, 389.

714 Shortly before Christmas: *Collected Works of Erasmus*, vol. 15, 82, note 1.

714 mostly poor citizens gathered: For Erasmus's firsthand account, ibid., vol. 15, no. 2158, to Willibald Pirckheimer, May 9, 1529, 241–247.

714 Basel looked out: Bainton, *Erasmus of Christendom*, 220.

715 "the dissidents": *Collected Works of Erasmus*, vol. 15, no. 2158, May 9, 1529, 242.

715 "Oecolampadius is taking over": Ibid., vol. 15, no. 2134, to Alonso de Fonseca, March 25, 1529, 175.

715 the approval of a Reform Ordinance: Ibid., vol. 16, no. 2248, from Bonifacius Amerbach, January 9, 1530, 116–118, especially note 5.

715 Erasmus had many options: He lists them at ibid., vol. 14, no. 2029, to Christoph von Stadion, August 28, 1528, 273.

715 "Our love for you": Ibid., vol. 13, no. 1878, from Henry VIII, September 18 [1527], 339.

715 Ferdinand had offered: Ibid., vol. 14, no. 2028, to Willibald Pirckheimer, August 25, 1528, 267–268.

716 he decided on Freiburg: Ibid., vol. 15, no. 2145, to Anton Fugger, April 5, 1529, 200–204.

716 there was an outcry: Ibid., vol. 15, no. 2196, to Willibald Pirckheimer, July 15, 1529, 351–360.

716 he invited him for a conversation: Ibid., vol. 15, no. 2147, to Johannes Oecolampadius [April 10, 1529], 205–207; the meeting is described in vol. 15, no. 2158, to Willibald Pirckheimer, May 9, 1529, 243.

716 to avoid "a public spectacle": Ibid., 245.

716 Erasmus arrived with a few friends: Ibid., vol. 15, no. 2196, to Willibald Pirckheimer, July 15, 1529, 351–356.

CHAPTER 41: THE CRACK-UP

717 was now a place of bustle: Stjerna, *Women and the Reformation*, 51–70;

Brecht, *Shaping and Defining*, 201–211, 429–433; Friedenthal, *Luther*, 441.

717 "If it gets too loud": *Luthers Werke, Tischreden*, vol. 1, no. 148, 70.

717 "an odd assortment": Quoted in Friedenthal, *Luther*, 443.

718 this Table Talk: *Luther's Works*, vol. 54; "simpler and more attached," 309; "a disgraceful nuisance," 371; "If I had a hundred sons," 236; "Oh, if I could only pray," 38; "made me wide awake," 445; "I know no doctor," 72; "Erasmus is an eel," 19; "I hate Erasmus," 84; "Substance and words," 245. Marius (*Martin Luther*, 442) observes of Luther that Erasmus was "the man whom he probably hated as much as any enemy he encountered in his lifetime."

719 Karlstadt had tried to make a living: See *Luther's Correspondence*, vol. 2, no. 805, Andreas Karlstadt to Elector John of Saxony, August 12, 1528, 453–454; "Bodenstein von Karlstadt, Andreas," in *The Oxford Encyclopedia of the Reformation*.

719 "Doctor, why don't you": Quoted in Bainton, *Here I Stand*, 235.

719 "eloquence in women": *Luther's Works*, vol. 54, "Table Talk," 317. "Men have broad shoulders," 8.

719 sometimes called her *Kette*: Bainton, *Here I Stand*, 227.

719 She had to rise at four: Friedenthal, *Luther*, 440; Martin Brecht, *Martin Luther: The Preservation of the Church*, 240–243.

720 "The lady of the pig market": See, for instance, *Luther's Works*, vol. 50, no. 290, July 2, 1540, 208.

720 "I wouldn't give up: Ibid., vol. 54, "Table Talk," 7.

720 usually addressed her husband as "Mr. Doctor": Roper, *Martin Luther*, 271.

720 master of the *Dreckapotheke*: Brecht, *Shaping and Defining*, 429–430; Friedenthal, *Luther*, 447–448.

720 It "is the pleasantest": *Luther's Works*, vol. 54, 218; "Imagine," 161; "the divine institution," 223.

720 was providing an alternative: Stjerna, *Women and the Reformation*, 69.

720 giving rise to a new institution: MacCulloch, *Reformation*, 631; Roper, *Martin Luther*, 286. Luther, Roper observes, "is often credited with having created the modern, companionate marriage after centuries in which monastic writings had presented married life as the spiritually lesser option, though "what he understood by marriage is often very surprising and very alien."

721 "The peasants learn nothing": *Luther's Correspondence*, vol. 2, no. 816, to Spalatin [January 15] 1529, 464.

721 to produce a catechism: Kirsi I. Stjerna, introduction, *The Large Catechism of Dr. Martin Luther, 1529*, in *The Annotated Luther*, vol. 2, *Word and Faith*, 279–288; Timothy J. Wengert, introduction, *The Small Catechism, 1529*, in *The Annotated Luther*, vol. 4, *Pastoral Writings*, ed. Mary Jane Haemig, 201–211; Bainton, *Here I Stand*, 263–264; Brecht, *Shaping and Defining*, 275–280; "Catechism," in *The Encyclopedia of the Lutheran Church*; "Catechisms," in *New Catholic Encyclopedia*.

721 "Let everyone be subject": *Small Catechism*, in *Annotated Luther*, vol. 4, 239–241.

721 it was every father's duty: *Large Catechism*, in *Annotated Luther*, vol. 2, 294–295.

721 Luther himself would recite parts: *Large Catechism*, in *Annotated Luther*, vol. 2, 290.

722 create a model for German households: Luther, Bainton writes in *Here I Stand* (233), "did more than any other person to determine the tone of German domestic relations for the next four centuries."

722 the 1529 Diet of Speyer: Ibid., 248; Holborn, *History of Modern Germany*, vol. 1, 208–209; Hillerbrand, *Reformation*, 376.

723 sent Zwingli a letter: *Luther's Correspondence*, vol. 2, no. 826, April 22, 1529, 473–474.

723 "shameless insistence": Ibid., vol. 2, no. 841, to John Brismann, July 31, 1529, 488–489.

723 The Marburg Colloquy: For reports on this event, see *Luther's Works*, vol. 38, "The Marburg Colloquy and the Marburg Articles," 5–89. See also Edwards, *Luther and the False Brethren*, 104–111; Bornkamm, *Luther in Mid-Career*, 635–661; Bainton, *Here I Stand*, 248–251; Friedenthal, *Luther*, 503–506; Brecht, *Shaping and Defining*, 325–334; Schwiebert, *Luther*, 695–714. For firsthand reports by Luther and his colleagues, see *Luther's Correspondence*, vol. 2, no. 850, Luther to Nicholas Gerbel, October 4, 1529, 495–496; no. 851, Luther to Katharina Luther, October 4, 1529, 496–497; no. 852, Justus Jonas to William Reifenstein [October 4, 1529], 497–499; no. 853, Melanchthon to Elector John [October 4, 1529], 500; no. 855, Luther to John Agricola, October 12, 1529, 500–501; no. 858, Luther to Wenzel (Wenceslas) Link, October 28, 1529, 503–504.

724 "tangled, matted" dialect: Quoted in Friedenthal, *Luther*, 505. See also *Luther's Works*, vol. 54, "Table Talk," 376.

724 proved more intractable: Friedenthal, *Luther*, 505; Brecht, *Shaping and Defining*, 329–333; *Luther's Works*, vol. 38, 15ff.

724 Luther scribbled something in chalk: *Luther's Works*, vol. 38, 67. See also Edwards, *Luther and the False Brethren*, 108; Friedenthal, *Luther*, 505.

724 "They were humble": *Luther's Correspondence*, vol. 2, no. 855, October 12, 1529, 501.

725 would become fixed in place: Potter, in *Zwingli* (341–342), observes that "the story of the relations between Luther and Zwingli is one of the saddest in the history of religion." The repercussions

of their differences at Marburg "are felt in the twentieth century, for such is the power of history."

725 his growing distemper: Brecht, *Shaping and Defining*, 288–290, 433–439.

725 "grievous consequences": *Luther's Correspondence*, vol. 2, no. 866, Elector John to Luther, January 18, 1530, 512–513.

726 "one single Christian truth": Ibid., vol. 2, no 871, Elector John to Luther, Jonas, Bugenhagen, and Melanchthon, March 14, 1530, 522–524. See also *Luther's Works*, vol. 49, no. 205, Luther to Nicholas Hausmann, April 18, 1530, 280–287, including the introductory note, 280–283, which describes the preparations for the diet; Brecht, *Shaping and Defining*, 369–372.

726 stayed in the Coburg castle: On Luther's time there, see Brecht, *Shaping and Defining*, 372–379; Bornkamm, *Luther in Mid-Career*, 667–669; Smith, *Life and Letters of Martin Luther*, 247–262.

726 in "the wilderness": See, for instance, *Luther's Works*, vol. 49, 304.

726 "This place is extremely pleasant": Ibid., vol. 49, no. 206, to Melanchthon [April 24] 1530, 287–291.

727 "magnanimous kings": *Luther's Works*, vol. 49, no. 207, to Spalatin [April 24] 1530, 292–295.

727 overcome by anxiety: On Melanchthon's time in Augsburg, see Manschreck, *Melanchthon*, 177–209.

727 hundreds of mercenaries: *Luther's Works*, vol. 49, 317.

727 Eck had drafted: Manschreck, *Melanchthon*, 178–180; M. Reu, *The Augsburg Confession: A Collection of Sources with an Historical Introduction*, 56–64.

728 "pleases me very much": *Luther's Works*, vol. 49, no. 208, to Elector John, May 15, 1530, 295–299.

728 the letters dried up: Ibid., vol. 49, no. 212, to Melanchthon, June 5, 1530,

316–319. See also Brecht, *Shaping and Defining*, 374–376.

728 "a place for pilgrimage": *Luther's Works*, vol. 49, no. 211, June 5, 1530, 314.

728 he wrote a touching letter: Ibid., vol. 49, no. 214 [around June 19, 1530], 321–324.

728 word arrived that his father had died: Ibid., vol. 49, no. 212, to Melanchthon, June 5, 1530, 318–319. See also Brecht, *Shaping and Defining*, 378.

729 Veit Dietrich later observed: Bornkamm, *Luther in Mid-Career*, 679.

729 complaining in one to Melanchthon: *Luther's Works*, vol. 49, no. 215, June 29, 1530, 324–333.

729 Charles's tardiness: Holborn, *History of Modern Germany*, vol. 1, 211; Elton, *Reformation Europe*, 96–98.

729 the Turks: Elton, *Reformation Europe*, 98–101.

730 one of the most sumptuous pageants: Friedenthal, *Luther*, 486.

730 met with some of the leading delegates: Ibid., 487; *Luther's Works*, vol. 49, 339.

731 sent a series of letters: See, for instance, *Collected Works of Erasmus*, vol. 16, nos. 2341 and 2343; vol. 17, no. 2366. See also Froude, *Life and Letters of Erasmus*, 379ff; Smith, *Erasmus*, 360–363; Augustijn, *Erasmus*, 179–180; Bainton, *Erasmus of Christendom*, 262–264.

731 How France had been ravaged!: *Collected Works of Erasmus*, vol. 17, no. 2366, to Lorenzo Campeggi, August 18, 1530, 27.

731 his twenty-one articles of faith: Philip Schaff, ed., *The Creeds of Christendom*, vol. 3, *The Evangelical Protestant Creeds* (Grand Rapids, MI: Baker Books, 1931, 1993), 3–73.

731 theologians met to revise it: Manschreck, *Melanchthon*, 191–192.

732 The *Confessio Augustana*: Reu, *Augsburg Confession*, 109–113; Manschreck, *Melanchthon*, 193–194; "Augsburg Confession," in *The Oxford Encyclopedia of the Reformation*.

733 "Those great cares": Smith, *Life and Letters of Martin Luther*, to Melanchthon, June 27, 1530, 257–258; *Luther's Works*, vol. 49, no. 215, to Melanchthon, June 29, 1530, 324–332.

733 submitted a fierce confession of his own: Roper, *Martin Luther*, 334–335; Bainton, *Here I Stand*, 253; Manschreck, *Melanchthon*, 198–199.

733 appointed a group of theologians: Reu, *Augsburg Confession*, 120–127; Manschreck, *Melanchthon*, 199.

733 a committee was formed: *Luther's Works*, vol. 49, no. 229, introductory note, 403–406; Manschreck, *Melanchthon*, 201ff; Brecht, *Shaping and Defining*, 402–405.

734 "If we yield a single one": Smith, *Life and Letters of Martin Luther*, 261–262.

734 he set to work preparing: Manschreck, *Melanchthon*, 206.

734 declared a recess: Holborn, *History of Modern Germany*, vol. 1, 214; Reu, *Augsburg Confession*, 133; Brecht, *Shaping and Defining*, 405–407.

734 the central creed of the Lutheran church: "Augsburg Confession," in *The Encyclopedia of the Lutheran Church*. The Confession is such a "clear and courageous testimony of evangelical faith," this entry states, "that after more than four centuries it is still the principal 'symbol' of the Lutheran Church, holding a position second only to the Scriptures themselves."

734 It would also influence: "Augsburg Confession," in *New Catholic Encyclopedia*.

735 Luther finally left Coburg: *Luther's Works*, vol. 49, 422; Brecht, *Shaping and Defining*, 407.

735 the rump of the diet: Elton, *Reformation Europe*, 102.

735 Philip of Hesse invited: Friedenthal, *Luther*, 492–493; Brecht, *Shaping and Defining*, 414–415; Elton, *Reformation Europe*, 104.

CHAPTER 42: MADNESS

736 "I like this well-mannered city": *Collected Works of Erasmus*, vol. 15, no. 2151, April 25, 1529, 211–212.

736 "Letter Against False Evangelicals": Ibid., vol. 16, xviii; vol. 17, xv.

736 sent along with the codex a note: Quoted in Smith, *Erasmus*, 411–414. See also "Rabelais, François," in *Contemporaries of Erasmus*.

737 "There is peace nowhere": *Collected Works of Erasmus*, vol. 16, no. 2249, to Giambattista Egnazio [January] 1530, 120; no. 2263, to Cuthbert Tunstall, January 31, 1530, 165.

737 learned the fate of Louis de Berquin: Ibid., vol. 15, no. 2188, to Karel Uutenhove, July 1, 1529, 320–331. See also "Berquin, Louis de," in *Contemporaries of Erasmus*.

737 "completely free": *Collected Works of Erasmus*, vol. 15, no. 2188, 323; "It sets a strange precedent," 330; To "condemn," 331.

738 "I feel sorry for the Anabaptists": Ibid., vol. 16, no. 2341, to [Lorenzo Campeggi], July 7, 1530, 367–368.

738 The Anabaptists represented: On the Anabaptists, see Bainton, *Reformation of the Sixteenth Century*, 95–109; "Anabaptists," in *The Oxford Encyclopedia of the Reformation*; Elton, *Reformation Europe*, 60–67; G. H. Williams, *Radical Reformation*, 118–148; Ozment, *Age of Reform*, 328–332.

738 consider Erasmus their spiritual father: See, for instance, G. H. Williams, *Radical Reformation*, 8–14, 34–35.

738 Their true forebear was Karlstadt: See "Karlstadt," in *Global Anabaptist Mennonite Encyclopedia Online*, at http://gameo.org/index.php?title=Karlstadt,_Andreas_Rudolff-Bodenstein_von_(1486–1541). Karlstadt, this entry notes, "became the first Reformer to develop a Baptist theology. He wielded

a seminal influence, especially among nonresistant Anabaptists."

738 first appeared in and around Zurich: See Potter, *Zwingli*, 167–188; Holborn, *History of Modern Germany*, vol. 1, 178–181.

739 Felix Mantz: Potter, *Zwingli*, 187; G. H. Williams, *Radical Reformation*, 142–146.

739 the Anabaptists were determined to carry on: Elton, *Reformation Europe*, 61.

740 after the 1529 Diet of Speyer: Holborn, *History of Modern Germany*, vol. 1, 179.

740 six relapsed Anabaptists: Brecht, *Shaping and Defining*, 338–339.

740 Melanchthon prepared an enthusiastic endorsement: Bainton, *Here I Stand*, 294–296; "Although it seems cruel," 295. See also Brecht, *Preservation*, 34–39; Walker, *History of the Christian Church*, 455; "Martin Luther," in *Global Anabaptist Mennonite Encyclopedia Online*, at http://gameo.org/index.php?title=Luther,_Martin_(1483–1546).

740 an estimated eight hundred Anabaptists: MacCulloch, *Reformation*, 163.

740 the infamous case of Münster: Ibid., 199–206.

741 "Some they have hanged": At www .mennosimons.net/horsch06.html.

741 The Mennonites: Holborn, *History of Modern Germany*, vol. 1, 180–181.

742 he became increasingly autocratic: Friedenthal, *Luther*, 500–501, 505; "There is fear," 506. See also Bainton, *Reformation of the Sixteenth Century*, 86–90.

742 Zwingli wanted to evangelize all of Switzerland: Friedenthal, *Luther*, 506–507; Bainton, *Reformation of the Sixteenth Century*, 90–94.

742 declared war on Zurich: Potter, *Zwingli*, 390–415; Ozment, *Age of Reform*, 338; MacCulloch, *Reformation*, 171–172.

743 he, too, was dead: "Oecolampadius, Johannes," in *Contemporaries of Erasmus*.

743 sent a servant to England: *Collected Works of Erasmus*, vol. 16, 64, note 16; no. 2253, to Juan de Vergara [January 13, 1530], 125.

743 his *Dialogue Concerning Heresies*: See Ackroyd, *Life of Thomas More*, 279–283. See also Marius, *Thomas More*, 338–350; "is lawful, necessary, and well done," 347.

744 issued a decree in the king's name: Bobrick, *Wide as the Waters*, 128.

744 A follow-up decree: Ackroyd, *Life of Thomas More*, 300; Marius, *Thomas More*, 387.

744 Thomas Hitton: Ackroyd, *Life of Thomas More*, 299; Marius, *Thomas More*, 395–396; Daniell, *William Tyndale*, 182.

744 Stokesley would become known: Ackroyd, *Life of Thomas More*, 300; Daniell, *William Tyndale*, 183.

745 how he went about intercepting letters: Ackroyd, *Life of Thomas More*, 300; Marius, *Thomas More*, 395.

745 *Answer unto Sir Thomas More's Dialogue*: Daniell, *William Tyndale*, 269–274.

745 Tyndale continued to translate: Edwards, *William Tyndale*, 111–114; Bobrick, *Wide as the Waters*, 117; Daniell, *William Tyndale*, 283–315.

745 no less pathbreaking: Bobrick, *Wide as the Waters*, 118–121; Daniell, *William Tyndale*, 288–291. Tyndale's Pentateuch is available at http://archive.org/details /williamtyndalesf00tynd.

746 included marginal glosses: Edwards, *William Tyndale*, 116.

746 a book smuggler named George Constantine: Ackroyd, *Life of Thomas More*, 304–305; Marius, *Thomas More*, 402–404.

746 "like a dog returning to his vomit": Quoted in Marius, *Thomas More*, 403.

746 at least four and perhaps six people: Elton, "Sir Thomas More and the Opposition to Henry VIII," in Sylvester and Marc'hadour, *Essential Articles for the Study of Thomas More*, 81ff; Leland Miles, "Persecution and the *Dialogue of*

Comfort: A Fresh Look at the Charges Against Thomas More," *Journal of British Studies*, 5(1): 19–30, November 1965; Ackroyd, *Life of Thomas More*, 306.

746 *The Obedience of a Christian Man*: Daniell, *William Tyndale*, 209, 223ff. "This is the book for me": Ackroyd, *Life of Thomas More*, 284.

747 Henry began an aggressive campaign: Scarisbrick, *Henry VIII*, 236–237, 245, 287ff; Maynard Smith, *Henry VIII and the Reformation*, 47ff.

747 Henry had abandoned: Neville Williams, *Henry VIII and His Court*, 117–118.

747 Gaining Luther's approval: Scarisbrick, *Henry VIII*, 400–401; Brecht, *Shaping and Defining*, 422; *Luther's Works*, vol. 50, no. 245, to Robert Barnes [September 3, 1531], 27–40.

748 More (claiming ill health) resigned: Marius, *Thomas More*, 415.

748 Simon Grynaeus: "Grynaeus, Simon," in *Contemporaries of Erasmus*.

748 More explained his reasons: *Thomas More: Selected Letters*, ed. Elizabeth Frances Rogers (New Haven: Yale University Press, 1961), no. 44, June 14, 1532, 172–177.

749 The *Confutation of Tyndale's Answer*: Ackroyd, *Life of Thomas More*, 307–311; Marius, *Thomas More*, 424–428; Bobrick, *Wide as the Waters*, 113; Edwards, *William Tyndale*, 125–129; Teems, *Tyndale*, 192–195. Teems notes that More and Tyndale between them introduced more than five hundred words into the English language.

749 Cromwell was an Erasmian: Scarisbrick, *Henry VIII*, 303. As Bainton observes in *Erasmus of Christendom* (279), Cromwell "initiated an extensive program of translation" of Erasmian works "in order to bolster the Henrician reform." See also "Cromwell, Thomas," in *Contemporaries of Erasmus*.

749 England would gradually adopt: Scarisbrick, *Henry VIII*, 398–399; King, *English Reformation Literature*, 48.

749 enlarging More's spy network: Bobrick, *Wide as the Waters*, 141–142.

749 did not even attend her christening: Scarisbrick, *Henry VIII*, 323–324.

749 Cromwell in 1534 helped push Parliament: Ibid., 392ff; Ackroyd, *Life of Thomas More*, 356–357.

750 was arrested and sent by river to the Tower: Ackroyd, *Life of Thomas More*, 359ff.

750 a series of interrogations: Ibid., 384ff.

750 More received a final trial: Ibid., 399ff.; Marius, *Thomas More*, 504–514.

751 asked the king to authorize: Bobrick, *Wide as the Waters*, 142–149; "Cromwell, Thomas," in *The Oxford Encyclopedia of the Reformation*.

751 would not be around to see it: Bobrick, *Wide as the Waters*, 131–135.

752 "In the death of More": Froude, *Life and Letters of Erasmus*, 419; Smith, *Erasmus*, 418–419.

752 Damião de Goes: *Opus epistolarum Des Erasmi Roterodami*, ed. P.S. Allen, vol. 11, no. 3085, January 26, 1536, 270.

752 "Would that he had never mixed": Ibid., vol. 11, no. 3048, to Bartholomew Latomus, August 24, 1535, 216; Smith, *Erasmus*, 417.

752 a commentary on Psalm 83: *Collected Works of Erasmus*, vol. 65, "On Mending the Peace of the Church," 134–216; "Heresy, heresy!" 199; "do nothing by violent or disorderly means," 213; "If then we temper," 216. The psalm itself is translated at 132–133. See also Halkin, *Erasmus*, 249–251.

753 nine editions appeared: Universal Short Title Catalogue (http://ustc.ac.uk/index .php).

753 Amsdorf urged him to write against it: Brecht, *Preservation*, 80–82.

753 decided to read Erasmus's prefaces: Ibid., 79, 84; *Luther's Works*, vol. 54, "Table Talk," 189.

754 "How hard it is": *Luther's Correspondence*, vol. 2, no. 798, to Wenzel (Wenceslas) Link, June 14, 1528, 445.

754 a *collegium biblicum: Luther's Works*, vol. 35, "Defense of the Translation of the Psalms," 206; "'Pray tell,'" 213–214.

754 Luther used *HERR*: Ibid., vol. 35, "Preface to the Old Testament," 248–249.

754 "The Jews think": *Luthers Werke, Tischreden*, vol. 5, no. 5535, 220; Reu, *Luther's German Bible*, 265.

755 tried to get rid of the Hebraisms: *Luthers Werke, Tischreden*, vol. 2, no. 2771a, 648; Reu, *Luther's German Bible*, 269.

755 read the Old Testament as a record of Christ: Baron, in *A Social and Religious History of the Jews*, vol. 13 (221–222), observes, "By thus strengthening the forces of German nationalism, Luther's Bible version, as well as his newly introduced German prayers, indirectly helped further to undermine the position of German Jewry."

755 the complete Bible was done: Brecht, *Preservation*, 98–100; Füssel, *Book of Books*, 59–66; Pettegree, *Brand Luther*, 191.

755 more particular and insular: As Eisenstein notes (*Printing Revolution in Early Modern Europe*, 189), "Vernacular Bible translation took advantage of humanist scholarship only in order to undermine it by fostering patriotic and populist tendencies."

755 the fifth and final edition of his own New Testament: Elliott, "'Novum Testamentum editum est,'" *Bible Translator*, 67.1: 19, 2016; Bentley, *Humanists and Holy Writ*, 123.

755 tenth and final edition of the *Adages*: Barker, *Adages of Erasmus*, x–xviii.

756 grown increasingly disenchanted with Freiburg: Smith, *Erasmus*, 419; Halkin, *Erasmus*, 258.

756 Bonifacius Amerbach came to get him:

Froude, *Life and Letters of Erasmus*, 413.

756 "I still have ill-wishers here": Ibid., 418.

756 One kept him sitting: *Opus epistolarum Des Erasmi Roterodami*, vol. 11, no. 3095, to Gilbert Cognatus, February 12, 1536, 282.

756 only by dictating: Halkin, *Erasmus*, 258.

756 was to Christoph Eschenfelder: *Opus epistolarum Des Erasmi Roterodami*, vol. 11, no. 3086, January 27, 1536, 272.

757 most of his close friends: Huizinga, *Erasmus*, 184.

CHAPTER 43: ENEMIES OF CHRIST

758 "He lived and died as Epicurus": *Luthers Werke, Tischreden*, vol. 4, no. 3963, 37.

758 "Doctrine and life": *Luther's Works*, vol. 54, "Table Talk," 110.

758 Many biographers pass quickly: Ibid., vol. 50, xiv.

758 began to avoid him: Friedenthal, *Luther*, 520.

758 suffered a near-fatal bout: Ibid., 448; Brecht, *Preservation*, 185–188, 229; Roper, *Martin Luther*, 367–368.

759 the Diet of Nuremberg adopted: *Luther's Works*, vol. 50, xiii–xiv; Holborn, *History of Modern Germany*, vol. 1, 217–218.

759 had a new house built: "Wittenberg," in *The Oxford Encyclopedia of the Reformation*.

759 Among those who noticed: Brecht, *Preservation*, 148–152.

760 Johann Agricola wanted: Ibid., 156–168; "Agricola, Johann," in *The Oxford Encyclopedia of the Reformation*.

761 good works seemed in short supply: Brecht, *Preservation*, 250–256.

761 began a series of lectures on Genesis: Ibid., 136–141; *Luther's Works*, vol. 1, ix. The Genesis lectures take up the first eight volumes of the English edition of Luther's collected works.

762 John Frederick: Friedenthal, *Luther*, 509.

762 the church in Electoral Saxony: Ibid., 512–513; Brecht, *Preservation*, 287ff.

762 about to enter a period of rapid growth: "Lutheranism," in *The Oxford Encyclopedia of the Reformation*; Holborn, *History of Modern Germany*, vol. 1, 219–221.

762 The most dramatic case: Brecht, *Preservation*, 73–74, 287–288; "Lutheranism," in *The Oxford Encyclopedia of the Reformation*.

762 Similar changes were taking place: Holborn, *History of Modern Germany*, 219–221; Cameron, *European Reformation*, 268–269.

762 Scandinavia was turning Protestant as well: Elton, *Reformation Europe*, 84–88; "Lutheranism," "Sweden, Lutheranism in," and "Denmark, Lutheran Church of," in *The Encyclopedia of the Lutheran Church*.

762 brought Bugenhagen: Elton, *Reformation Europe*, 86; "Bugenhagen, Johann," in *The Encyclopedia of the Lutheran Church*.

763 one of his most serious missteps: Brecht, *Preservation*, 205–209; Roper, *Martin Luther*, 349–352; Bainton, *Here I Stand*, 293.

763 Disillusionment with the reformer grew: Friedenthal, *Luther*, 520; Brecht, *Preservation*, 147; Roper, *Martin Luther*, 359–360, 366–367.

763 Writing to Martin Bucer: *Luther's Works*, vol. 50, no. 287, October 14, 1539, 190–191.

764 was not an original thinker: Ozment (*Age of Reform*, 372) calls Calvin "the least original of the major reformers." *The Oxford Encyclopedia of the Reformation*, under "Calvinism," observes that "Calvinist (and Reformed) teachings were in most respects close to those of Luther, as Calvin himself repeatedly emphasized in his attempts to promote Protestant unity."

764 began as a humanist: On Calvin, see McGrath, *Life of John Calvin*; John T. McNeill, *The History and Character of Calvinism*; Elton, *Reformation Europe*, 147–168; Ozment, *Age of Reform*, 352–380; MacCulloch, *Reformation*, 189–192, 230–240; Hillerbrand, *The Reformation*, 170–217; Walker, *History of the Christian Church*, 471–480; Eire, *Reformations*, 286–317.

764 His first work in print: McNeill, *History and Character of Calvinism*, 104–105; McGrath, *Life of John Calvin*, 60–61. The reference to Erasmus is at http://media.sabda.org/alkitab-7/library/calvin/cal_sene.pdf, 5.

764 became known as the "accusative case": Ozment, *Age of Reform*, 354.

765 underwent a "sudden conversion": Calvin's firsthand account is in Hillerbrand, *Reformation*, 175–176. See also McNeill, *History and Character of Calvinism*, 107–118; Ozment, *Age of Reform*, 354–356; Elton, *Reformation Europe*, 148–149; McGrath, *Life of John Calvin*, 69–78.

765 plastered with inflammatory placards: McGrath, *Life of John Calvin*, 74–75.

765 the *Institutes*: *Institutes of the Christian Religion*, 2 vols., ed. John T. McNeill, trans. Ford Lewis Battles. On the work's origins and structure as well as its general contents, see McNeill's introduction, xxix–lxxi. See also his *History and Character of Calvinism*, 119–128; Elton, *Reformation Europe*, 150–156; Eire, *Reformations*, 292–296; McGrath, *Life of John Calvin*, 136–174; Rice and Grafton, *Foundations of Early Modern Europe*, 162–163.

766 often compared to Thomas Aquinas: See, for instance, Harbison, *Christian Scholar*, 139.

766 From both Luther and Augustine, he took the idea of predestination: *The New Encyclopaedia Britannica*, 15th ed., vol. 15, 437.

766 "All are not created": *Institutes*, vol. 2, 926 (Book III, chap. 21, sec. 5).

766 "bitterly loathe": Ibid., vol. 1, 256 (II.2.1).

766 this decree was *horribile*: Ibid., vol. 2, 955 (III.23.7). See also McGrath, *Life of John Calvin*, 167.

766 the idea of the "elect": Calvin describes the nature of the "eternal elect" in *Institutes*, vol. 2, 920–932 (III.21). See also Eire, *Reformations*, 295–296; McGrath, *Life of John Calvin*, 258. (The last quotation has been edited for clarity.)

766 usually put the ratio: MacCulloch, *Reformation*, 237.

766 "light of divine providence": *Institutes*, vol. 1, 224 (I.17.11).

766 "that he has been received" Ibid., vol. 1, 224 (I.17.11).

767 These ideas about predestination: See McGrath, *Life of John Calvin*, 166–169.

767 prepared to travel to Strasbourg: For firsthand accounts and contemporary documents on this phase in Calvin's life, see Hillerbrand, *Reformation*, 179–183. See also Ozment, *Age of Reform*, 361–362; Elton, *Reformation Europe*, 156–158.

767 He went to Strasbourg: McGrath, *Life of John Calvin*, 100–102; Ozment, *Age of Reform*, 363–365; MacCulloch, *Reformation*, 191–192; Eire, *Reformations*, 298–299.

767 sent Calvin several messages: Hillerbrand, *Reformation*, 185–187.

768 set out to cleanse the city: MacCulloch, *Reformation*, 230–240; Elton, *Reformation Europe*, 159–161; Eire, *Reformations*, 299–303; Ozment, *Age of Reform*, 366–368; McNeill, *History and Character of Calvinism*, 184–196.

768 Ecclesiastical Ordinances: An abridged version is in Hillerbrand, *Reformation*, 188–194.

769 many parents erupted in anger: MacCulloch, *Reformation*, 233.

769 his temper: Even his close colleague Theodore Beza acknowledged that Calvin was "naturally of a keen temper"; see Hillerbrand, *Reformation*, 209–210.

769 Jacques Gruet: Ibid., 199–200; McNeill,

History and Character of Calvinism, 170–171; Ozment, *Age of Reform*, 368.

769 the case of Michael Servetus: On Servetus, see Roland H. Bainton, *Hunted Heretic: The Life and Death of Michael Servetus, 1511–1553*; Ozment, *Age of Reform*, 369–371; MacCulloch, *Reformation*, 237–238; Lindberg, *European Reformations*, 267–270.

769 *The Restitution of Christianity*: McNeill, *History and Character of Calvinism*, 173–174; Bainton, *Hunted Heretic*, 128–147.

770 took half an hour to die: Bainton, *Hunted Heretic*, 212.

770 "God makes clear": Quoted in Roland H. Bainton, *The Travail of Religious Liberty* (Philadelphia: Westminster Press, 1951), 70.

770 Sebastian Castellio: See Roland H. Bainton, "Sebastian Castellio, Champion of Religious Liberty," in *Castellioniana: Quatre Études sur Sébastian Castellion et l'Idée de la Tolérance*, 25–77; McNeill, *History and Character of Calvinism*, 168–169, 176; "Castellion, Sébastien," in *The Oxford Encyclopedia of the Reformation*.

770 Erasmus's spirit lingered: Bainton ("Sebastian Castellio," 48) takes note of this spirit but says Basel's tolerance impact should not be exaggerated; he does, however, cite Erasmus's writings as a key inspiration for Castellio (53–56). Castellio in fact cited excerpts from those writings (as well as some of Luther's) in his own work.

770 *Concerning Heretics: Concerning Heretics, Whether They Are to Be Persecuted and How They Are to Be Treated* (an anonymous work attributed to Sebastian Castellio), ed. Roland H. Bainton; could "endure another," 122; "banishments, chains," 122; "could not devise," 123.

771 "To kill a man": Ibid., 271.

771 one of two key sources of Unitarianism: Peter W. Williams, *America's Religions: From Their Origins to the Twenty-First Century*, 150.

771 strengthened Calvin's position: McNeill, *History and Character of Calvinism*, 176–77; MacCulloch, *Reformation*, 238.

771 four of Calvin's chief opponents: MacCulloch, *Reformation*, 239.

771 an estimated fifty-eight people: Eire, *Reformations*, 300–301.

771 Calvin looked to spread his ideas: Ibid., 303–309; Elton, *Reformation Europe*, 163–168; Ozment, *Age of Reform*, 372; Hillerbrand, *Reformation*, 205–206.

772 restored to the Reformation a dynamism: Elton, *Reformation Europe*, 168.

773 a "diabolical reverie": Quoted in ibid., 154. See also MacCulloch, *Reformation*, 240–245.

773 *On War Against the Turk: Luther's Works*, vol. 46, 161–205; "the servant of the devil," 174–175; "repentance, tears," 184; "a new law," 197.

774 little familiarity with the Koran: Sarah Henrich and James L. Boyce, "Martin Luther—Translations of Two Prefaces on Islam," *Word and World*, 16(2): 250–266, Spring 1996. See also Brecht, *Preservation*, 354–357.

774 the dramatic shift taking place in his attitudes: A good resource on Luther's views of the Jews is Schramm and Stjerna, *Martin Luther, the Bible, and the Jewish People*. See also Brecht, *Preservation*, 334–351; Roper, *Martin Luther*, 378–385; Oberman, *Luther*, 292–297; Marius, *Martin Luther*, 372–380; Mullett, *Martin Luther*, 241–250.

774 issued a mandate: Schramm and Stjerna, *Martin Luther, the Bible, and the Jewish People*, "Letter to Josel of Rosheim," 126–128. (In 1432, the Jews had already been forbidden to take up permanent residence in Electoral Saxony.)

775 "to chase all the Jews out": *Luther's Works*, vol. 54, "Table Talk," 426.

775 *On the Jews and Their Lies: Luther's Works*, vol. 47, 137–306; "boastful, arrogant rascals," 156; "real liars and bloodhounds," 156; "vilest whores,"

167; "steal and murder," 227; "is such a noble," 261; "have been accused," 264–265; "we are even at fault," 267; "set fire to their synagogues," 268; the houses of the Jews, 269; "on pain of loss of life," 269; "for they have no business," 270; to "earn their bread," 272; "we must drive them out," 292.

776 strongly echoed: David Price notes this link (*Johannes Reuchlin*, 218).

776 issued a harsh new mandate: Brecht, *Preservation*, 349–350.

776 "If it is Christian": *Collected Works of Erasmus*, vol. 7, 49.

776 "Never before": *Luther's Works*, vol. 47, 135.

776 one of several virulently anti-Jewish works: Another was *On the Ineffable Name and on the Lineage of Christ*, an assault on the supposed claim by some Jews that Jesus had performed his miracles through sorcery. The tract was filled with references to excrement and the Devil; Luther also referred favorably to the image of the *Judensau* that was engraved on the exterior wall of the town church in Wittenberg. (See my chapter 10.) See also Schramm and Stjerna, *Martin Luther, the Bible, and the Jewish People*, 177–180.

777 savage Judaeophobia: See Mullett, *Martin Luther*, 246–247. The editors of the American edition of *On the Jews and Their Lies* (*Luther's Works*, vol. 47, 268) observe that "it is impossible to publish Luther's treatise today . . . without noting how similar to his proposals were the actions of the National Socialist regime in Germany in the 1930's and 1940's." The editors referred specifically to Kristallnacht—the night of November 9, 1938, when rioters destroyed hundreds of synagogues and damaged thousands of Jewish businesses and homes—and directed readers to *The Rise and Fall of the Third Reich*, William Shirer's firsthand account of Germany from 1934 to 1940.

"It is difficult to understand the behavior of most German Protestants in the first Nazi years," Shirer writes (236), "unless one is aware of two things: their history and the influence of Martin Luther. The great founder of Protestantism was both a passionate anti-Semite and a ferocious believer in absolute obedience to political authority." Luther's call to Germany to rid itself of its Jews, deprive them of their money, set fire to their synagogues and schools, and destroy their houses "was literally followed four centuries later by Hitler, Goering and Himmler."

This may go too far. As much as Kristallnacht seemed a fulfillment of Luther's proposals, there is no evidence that the Nazis were following them; Hitler did not need Luther to come up with his program of annihilation. What Luther did do, however, was give his sanction as the founder of Protestantism to a worldview that, by dehumanizing the Jews and demonizing them as the "other," made them seem deserving of murderous hatred. Along with his insistent demands for total obedience toward the state, such feverish rhetoric created an environment in which the Nazis' exterminationist program would find broad support and Protestant ministers would stand silently by.

On November 11, 2015, a synod of the Evangelical Church in Germany, as part of the commemoration of the five-hundredth anniversary of the birth of the Reformation, unanimously adopted a declaration on "Martin Luther and the Jews," expressing "shame," "sorrow," and a "history of guilt" at Luther's "undisguised hatred of Jews" and its consequences. "The fact that Luther's anti-Judaic recommendations in later life were a source for Nazi anti-Semitism" constitutes "a burden weighing on the Protestant churches in Germany."

777 *Against the Roman Papacy*: *Luther's Works*, vol. 41, 263–376; "the miserable devil," 264; "a true werewolf," 358; a "farting ass," 281; "a brothel-keeper," 357; "long donkey ears," 376; "the most hellish father," 336; "Whoever does not kiss," 337; "Sodomists," 287; deserved being "struck down," 288–289; "We should take," 308. See also Brecht, *Preservation*, 357–367.

778 continue to rage for centuries: See Roper, *Martin Luther*, 372.

778 his exasperation boiled over: Brecht, *Preservation*, 262–264.

778 he wrote to Katharina: *Luther's Works*, vol. 50, no. 312, July 28, 1545, 273–281.

778 caused an uproar in Wittenberg: Brecht, *Preservation*, 263–264; *Luther's Works*, vol. 50, no. 312, introductory note, 273–277.

779 Enrollment at the university: Schwiebert, *Luther*, 607; more than one hundred pastors, 622–623.

779 the printing industry: Pettegree, *Brand Luther*, 280.

779 ninety-one printings: Brecht, *Preservation*, 101.

779 the preface he prepared for it: "Preface to the Complete Edition of Luther's Latin Writings," in Dillenberger, *Martin Luther: Selections*, 3–12.

779 the new bastions being built: Friedenthal, *Luther*, 526.

779 asked Luther for help: *Luther's Works*, vol. 50, no. 313, to Count Albrecht of Mansfeld, December 6, 1545, 281–284; Brecht, *Preservation*, 369–374.

780 "I'm like a ripe stool": *Luther's Works*, vol. 54, "Table Talk," 448.

780 in a letter to Katharina: Ibid., vol. 50, no. 316, February 1, 1546, 290–292.

780 gave four sermons: Ibid., vol. 50, 317.

780 about fifty of them were living in Eisleben: Luther gives this figure in his February 1 letter to Katharina, ibid., vol. 50, 291.

780 *An Admonition Against the Jews*:

Schramm and Stjerna, *Martin Luther, the Bible, and the Jewish People,* 200–202.

781 was so overcome by dizziness: *Luther's Works,* vol. 50, 318; Brecht, *Preservation,* 375–376.

781 On February 19: *Luther's Works,* vol. 50, 318; Brecht, *Preservation,* 378–379.

781 Melanchthon praised: His oration is at http://www.bartleby.com/268/7/9.html. See also James Michael Weiss, "Erasmus at Luther's Funeral: Melanchthon's Commemorations of Luther in 1546," *Sixteenth Century Journal,* 16(1): 91–114, Spring 1985; Brecht, *Preservation,* 380–382.

AFTERMATH: ERASMUS

783 the Counter-Reformation: H. Outram Evennett, *The Spirit of the Counter-Reformation,* 1–22; Rice and Grafton, *Foundations of Early Modern Europe,* 169–177; Elton, *Reformation Europe,* 129–137.

783 prefer "Catholic Reformation": See, for instance, Michael A. Mullett, *The Catholic Reformation,* 1–28.

783 the Council of Trent: See H. J. Schroeder, trans., *The Canons and Decrees of the Council of Trent;* Pastor, *History of the Popes,* vol. 15, 366–378; MacCulloch, *Reformation,* 227–229, 294–296; Ozment, *Age of Reform,* 406–408; Eire, *Reformations,* 378–384; Holborn, *History of Modern Germany,* vol. 1, 270–274; H. R. Trevor-Roper, "Desiderius Erasmus," in *Historical Essays,* 51–52.

783 very first substantive decree: Schroeder, *Canons and Decrees,* 17–20; Pastor, *History of the Popes,* vol. 12, 259–260.

783 would remain the official Bible: See "Bible (Versions)" in *An Introductory Dictionary of Theology and Religious Studies,* eds. Orlando O. Espín and James B. Nickoloff.

783 Anyone who asserted: Schroeder, *Canons and Decrees,* 21–23.

784 the "perpetual and indissoluble": Ibid., 180–190, 246–248; MacCulloch, *Reformation,* 588.

784 one key point: Schroeder, *Canons and Decrees,* 29–46; Pastor, *History of the Popes,* vol. 12, 341; Elton, *Reformation Europe,* 137.

784 a series of remedial measures: Schroeder, *Canons and Decrees,* 46–50, 56, 105–114, 175–179, 190–196; Pastor, *History of the Popes,* vol. 15, 371–376.

784 Paul IV: Pastor, *History of the Popes,* vol. 14, 65–70, 259–288; Elton, *Reformation Europe,* 133–134, 145–146; MacCulloch, *Reformation,* 269–272.

785 Index of Prohibited Books: Pastor, *History of the Popes,* vol. 14, 277–281; Eire, *Reformations,* 384–388.

785 "all his commentaries": Bruce Mansfield, *Phoenix of His Age: Interpretations of Erasmus c. 1550–1750,* 26; Smith, *Erasmus,* 422.

785 Now only a handful of works: Smith, *Erasmus,* 422.

785 to keep vernacular Bibles: MacCulloch, *Reformation,* 394, 271–272.

785 to make the faith more appealing: Ibid., 318–319, 440–441; Pastor, *History of the Popes,* vol. 14, 177ff; Eire, *Reformations,* 393–413; Rice and Grafton, *Foundations of Early Modern Europe,* 175–177.

786 proliferation of new monastic orders: Eire, *Reformations,* 414–441; Elton, *Reformation Europe,* 126–128.

786 Society of Jesus: MacCulloch, *Reformation,* 212–219, 313–315; Elton, *Reformation Europe,* 137–146; Rice and Grafton, *Foundations of Early Modern Europe,* 171–172; Ozment, *Age of Reform,* 409–417; Eire, *Reformations,* 442–465; Pastor, *History of the Popes,* vol. 12, 58–123.

786 When he read Erasmus: Mansfield, *Phoenix of His Age,* 48; Huizinga, *Erasmus,* 189.

786 Erasmus was a perennial target: Mansfield, *Phoenix of His Age,* 41, 48, 51, 56, 297.

786 After Luther's death, Melanchthon: Holborn, *History of Modern Germany*, vol. 1, 235, 255–256; MacCulloch, *Reformation*, 337–341; Walker, *History of the Christian Church*, 526–529.

787 "the rage of the theologians": Quoted in Smith, *Erasmus*, 424.

787 Erasmus was reviled as a man: Mansfield, *Phoenix of His Age*, 97–99, 228.

787 Erasmianism went underground: Paul Johnson, in *A History of Christianity* (318 ff), makes the case that after Erasmus's death, a "third force" of Erasmianism was at work underground in Europe.

787 In France: MacCulloch, *Reformation*, 327–329; Walker, *History of the Christian Church*, 516–518, 520–521, 525–526; *The New Encyclopaedia Britannica*, 15th ed., vol. 19, 479–481; Eire, *Reformations*, 533–542.

787 the Low Countries: Israel, *Dutch Republic*, 85, 96, 96–105, 139, 155ff; Walker, *History of the Christian Church*, 518–520, 521–522; Eire, *Reformations*, 542–548; *The New Encyclopaedia Britannica*, 15th ed., vol. 24, 883–889; "Dutch Revolt" and "Dutch Republic" in *Europe, 1450–1789: Encyclopedia of the Early Modern World*; "Netherlands" in *The Oxford Encyclopedia of the Reformation*.

788 The Thirty Years' War: MacCulloch, *Reformation*, 469–483; Holborn, *History of Modern Germany*, vol. 1, 305–360; Eire, *Reformations*, 548–553; Matthew Stewart, *The Courtier and the Heretic: Leibniz, Spinoza, and the Fate of God in the Modern World*, 39–40.

789 pushed back by hundreds of miles: MacCulloch, *Reformation*, 647.

789 ended more than a century: Ibid., 646–650; Eire, *Reformations*, 561.

789 The main victors: MacCulloch, *Reformation*, 468; Holborn, *History of Modern Germany*, vol. 1, 368–374.

790 opened up a new space in Europe: Alister McGrath, *Christianity's Dangerous Idea*, 143–144.

790 entering its Golden Age: Israel, *Dutch Republic*, 328ff, 392; "Dutch Republic" in *Europe, 1450–1789*; Mansfield, *Phoenix of His Age*, 147–148.

790 Jacobus Arminius: Israel, *Dutch Republic*, 393; Walker, *History of the Christian Church*, 538–542. On Arminius's career, see A. W. Harrison, *Arminianism*, 9–42.

791 Baruch (later Benedict) Spinoza: Steven Nadler, *Spinoza: A Life*, 100–111, 120; Lewis Samuel Feuer, *Spinoza and the Rise of Liberalism*, 17–22; Israel, *Dutch Republic*, 395, 913, 916–921; Stewart, *The Courtier and the Heretic*, 18–38; *The New Encyclopaedia Britannica*, 15th ed., vol. 11, 99–101.

791 Spinoza left the bustle of Amsterdam: Nadler, *Spinoza*, 138–141, 180–182, 203, 279–285; Feuer, *Spinoza*, 38–47, 58ff.

791 the *Tractatus Theologico-Politicus*: Israel, *Dutch Republic*, 787–789; Feuer, *Spinoza*, 58–75.

792 "I have often wondered": Benedict de Spinoza, *A Theologico-Political Treatise and a Political Treatise*, trans. R. H. M. Elwes, 6–7; "to examine the Bible afresh," 8; "The true meaning of Scripture," 112–113; apart from a small number, 186; "everyone should be free," 10; The true enemies of Christ, 185–186; "most consonant with individual liberty," 207; "for everyone has an inalienable right," 241; "from the attempt of the authorities," 262; "should think," 265. The Erasmus quote is at *Collected Works of Erasmus*, vol. 76, 10.

793 the *philosophes* "cited Erasmus": Bruce Mansfield, *Man on His Own: Interpretations of Erasmus c. 1750–1920*, 15.

793 In Diderot's *Encyclopédie*: Mansfield, *Phoenix of His Age*, 15–16. Citations of Erasmus in this work can be found at ARTFL *Encyclopédie* Project: http://artfl srv02.uchicago.edu/cgi-bin/philologic /search3t?dbname=encyclopedie0416

&word=erasme&CONJUNCT=
PHRASE&dgdivhead=&dg
divocauthor=&ExcludeDiderot3
=on&dgdivocsalutation=&OUT
PUT=conc&POLESPAN=5.

793 Even Voltaire: Mansfield, *Man on His Own*, 18–25; Smith, *Erasmus*, 435; *The New Encyclopaedia Britannica*, 15th ed., vol. 29, 524–527.

793 a dialogue among Lucian: "Lucien, Érasme, et Rabelais dans les Champs Élysées," in *Oeuvres Complètes de Voltaire*, vol. 6, part 2 (Paris: L'Imprimerie de Fain, 1817), 1410–1413.

794 held little appeal for a man: See Peter Gay, *The Enlightenment: An Interpretation—The Rise of Modern Paganism*, 274–275, 373. Erasmus, Gay observes, "was not a Voltaire before his time." While the Renaissance "had come a long way from Petrarch," even Erasmus was "not a modern secularist." It is ironic, Gay adds, that "the Enlightenment should have used Erasmus's writings to separate what he had worked so diligently to keep united, and to pit, with his own words, philosophy against Christ. Voltaire's Erasmus was the supple man of letters perpetually threatened by fanatics, the pitiless adversary of monasticism."

794 appeared in more than sixty editions: See Ferdinand van der Haeghen, *Bibliotheca Erasmiana: Repertoire des Oeuvres des Érasme*, 1er sér.

794 turned to contempt: Mansfield, *Man on His Own*, 118, 121–122.

794 Herder wrote an essay: Ibid., 58–61.

794 "A great scholar but a weak character": Pastor, *History of the Popes*, vol. 7, 315.

795 Huizinga made light: Huizinga, *Erasmus and the Age of Reformation* (as the English translation is titled), 123, 129, 190, 194.

795 Huizinga acknowledged: Mansfield, *Man on His Own*, 371.

795 inspire another writer: Mansfield, *Erasmus in the Twentieth Century: Interpretations c. 1920–2000*, 8, 236.

795 "the greatest and most brilliant star": Stefan Zweig, *Erasmus of Rotterdam*, trans. Eden and Cedar Paul, 3; "the first conscious European," 4; "a United States of Europe," 108–109; "overlooked the terrible," 119; "from the heights of their idealism," 123; "fanatical man of action," 129; "a swaggering, brimming," 133; "werewolf raging," 141; "world-citizenship of humanity," 159; "to exercise a tangible influence," 242–243.

796 became for Zweig an allegory: See George Prochnik, *The Impossible Exile: Stefan Zweig at the End of the World*, 127–129.

796 Winston Churchill: His statement is available at https://europa.eu/european -union/sites/europaeu/files/docs/body /winston_churchill_en.pdf.

797 "Our century": This statement is available at http://www.schuman.info /Strasbourg549.htm.

798 the Erasmus Program: The official site is at https://ec.europa.eu/programmes /erasmus-plus/node_en. See also "Erasmus Program" in *Europe Since 1914: Encyclopedia of the Age of War and Reconstruction*.

798 Umberto Eco: Gianni Riotta, "Umberto Eco: It's Culture, not War, that Cements European Identity," *La Stampa*, January 26, 2012.

798 one million babies: European Commission, press release, September 22, 2014, available at http://europa.eu /rapid/press-release_IP-14-1025_en .htm.

798 questions have been raised: See "Erasmus Students" in *Dictionary of European Actors*; Magali Ballatore and Martha K. Ferede, "The Erasmus Programme in France, Italy and the United Kingdom: Student Mobility as a Signal of Distinction and Prestige," *European Educational Research Journal*, 12(4): 525–533, 2013 (available at journals .sagepub.com/doi/pdf/10.2304/eerj .2013.12.4.525). On the popularity of

the Erasmus Program and the social
status of its participants, see Aurelien
Breeden, "For Europe's Young, Unifying
Identity Is Shaken," *New York Times*,
July 3, 2016. The article describes the
four "E's" associated with the younger
generation in Europe: Erasmus, easyJet,
the euro, and elite.

799 "If you believe": Quoted in *Washington
Post*, October 5, 2016, available at
https://www.washingtonpost.com
/news/worldviews/wp/2016/10/05
/theresa-may-criticized-the-term-citizen
-of-the-world-but-half-the-world-identifies
-that-way/.

AFTERMATH: LUTHER

801 800 million adherents: "Global
Christianity: A Report on the Size and
Distribution of the World's Christian
Population," Pew Research Center,
December 19, 2011, available at http://
www.pewforum.org/2011/12/19/
global-christianity-exec/. Somewhat
different estimates are offered by Todd
M. Johnson, Gina A. Zurlo, Albert
W. Hickman, and Peter F. Crossing,
"Christianity 2017: Five Hundred Years
of Protestant Christianity," *International
Bulletin of Mission Research*, available at
http://www.gordonconwell.edu/ockenga/
research/documents/IBMR2017.pdf

801 *Unsere Besten*: See http://www.zdf-
jahrbuch.de/2003/programmarbeit/
arens.htm

802 150,000 copies: Deutsche Welle,
"German Protestants to Revise
Landmark Luther Bible," available
at http://www.dw.com/en/german
-protestants-to-revise-landmark-luther
-bible/a-18171554

802 Nearly 30 percent: See https://www.ekd
.de/ekd_en/ds_doc/EKD_facts_and
_figures_2016.pdf (The EKD includes
both Lutheran and Reformed churches.)

802 Lutheranism seemed an unstoppable
force in Germany: Walker, *History*

of the Christian Church, 529; Elton,
Reformation Europe, 189; Holborn,
History of Modern Germany, vol. 1,
242–246, 252–255, 266–268;
278–294.

802 Counter-Reformation got underway in
earnest: Rice and Grafton, *Foundations of
Early Modern Europe*, 171; MacCulloch,
Reformation, 312ff.

802 clashed with the Lutherans over the
Eucharist: MacCulloch, *Reformation*,
341.

802 Formula of Concord: Walker, *History of
the Christian Church*, 526–529; "Formula
of Concord," in *The Oxford Encyclopedia
of the Reformation*; "Germany,
Lutheranism," in *The Encyclopedia of the
Lutheran Church*; "Protestantism," in
The New Encyclopaedia Britannica, 15th
edition, vol. 26, 238.

803 Johann Gerhard: "Gerhard, Johann," in
The Encyclopedia of the Lutheran Church;
Walker, *History of the Christian Church*,
529; "Protestantism," in *The New
Encyclopaedia Britannica*, 15th edition,
vol. 26, 238.

803 Age of Orthodoxy: Holborn, *History of
Modern Germany*, vol. 2, *1648–1840*,
129–135; "Germany, Lutheranism in,"
in *The Encyclopedia of the Lutheran
Church*; "Protestantism," in *The New
Encyclopaedia Britannica*, 15th edition,
vol. 26, 238.

803 the control that princes gained: Holborn,
History of Modern Germany, vol. 2, 4–9,
39, 125, 128–129, 373–375.

803 Philipp Jakob Spener: On Spener and
Pietism, see "Pietism," in *The New
Schaff-Herzog Encyclopedia of Religious
Knowledge*; Walker, *History of the
Christian Church*, 587–592; Holborn,
History of Modern Germany, vol. 2,
137–144; Alex Ryrie, *Protestants: The
Faith That Made the Modern World*,
159–168; David A. Rausch and Carl
Hermann Voss, *Protestantism—Its
Modern Meaning*, 49–53.

803 *Pia Desideria*: Rausch, *Protestantism*, 50;

Walker, *History of the Christian Church*, 588.

804 "diligent exercise of the spiritual priesthood": Quoted in Ryrie, *Protestants*, 162.

804 August Hermann Francke: "Pietism," in *The New Schaff-Herzog Encyclopedia of Religious Knowledge*.

804 a missionary training school: Ibid; Walker, *History of the Christian Church*, 590–591.

804 Nikolaus Ludwig Zinzendorf: Holborn, *History of Modern Germany*, vol. 2, 141; Ryrie, *Protestants*, 168–169; Walker, *History of the Christian Church*, 592–596; "Nikolaus Ludwig, count von Zinzendorf," at Britannica.com.

805 to delight in alienating others: "Pietism," in *The New Schaff-Herzog Encyclopedia of Religious Knowledge*; Ryrie, *Protestants*, 163–168.

805 this was prohibited by law: Holborn, *History of Modern Germany*, vol. 2, 140. According to the editors of *The New Schaff-Herzog Encyclopedia of Religious Knowledge* (vol. 9, 64), "If conditions in Germany in the seventeenth and the eighteenth centuries had made possible the rise of denominations, as in England, the religious life of the nation might have attained to and maintained a higher standard, and the triumph of rationalism in the Enlightenment might have been averted."

805 the movement had lost much of its vitality: Walker, *History of the Christian Church*, 591.

805 Pietism would not disappear: Holborn, *History of Modern Germany*, vol. 2, 141–142; "Pietism," in *The New Schaff-Herzog Encyclopedia of Religious Knowledge*.

805 the German Enlightenment: "Enlightenment," in *The New Schaff-Herzog Encyclopedia of Religious Knowledge*; Walker, *History of the Christian Church*, 567–572; "Germany," in *Religion Past and Present*, 395.

805 Gottfried Wilhelm Leibniz: Holborn,

History of Modern Germany, vol. 2, 158–159; "Leibniz, Gottfried Wilhelm," in *Encyclopedia of the Enlightenment*; "Leibniz, Gottfried Wilhelm," in *The New Encyclopaedia Britannica*, 15th edition; Stewart, *The Courtier and the Heretic*, 235–241; Rausch, *Protestantism* 59–61.

806 Immanuel Kant: See the introduction by Theodore M. Greene to Immanuel Kant, *Religion Within the Limits of Reason Alone*, ix–lxxviii; Holborn, *History of Modern Germany*, vol. 2, 334–340, 486; Walker, *History of the Christian Church*, 628–629; "Kant, Immanuel," in *The Encyclopedia of Protestantism*; "Immanuel Kant: Philosophy of Religion," in *Internet Encyclopedia of Philosophy*.

806 *radical* innate *evil*: Kant, *Religion Within the Limits of Reason Alone*, trans. Theodore M. Greene and Hoyt H. Hudson, 28; "seed of goodness," 41; "It is not essential," 47; a "fetish-faith," 181; to become a "favorite": 188–190.

806 liberal Protestantism: Holborn, *History of Modern Germany*, vol. 2, 310–314, 485; "Liberal Protestantism," in *The Encyclopedia of Protestantism*; Gordon A. Craig, *Germany: 1866–1945*, 182–183.

806 radical advances taking place in biblical studies: Holborn, *History of Modern Germany*, vol. 2, 491; *The New Encyclopaedia Britannica*, 15th edition, vol. 26, 238.

806 David Friedrich Strauss: "Strauss, David Friedrich," in *The Encyclopedia of Protestantism*; Walker, *History of the Christian Church*, 636; Rausch, *Protestantism*, 86.

807 Among traditional groups: Holborn, *History of Modern Germany*, vol. 2, 486–487, 494–495; "Germany," in *The New Encyclopaedia Britannica*, 15th edition., vol. 20, 101–105.

807 During the French occupation: Holborn, *History of Modern Germany*, vol. 2, 386ff, 424ff.

807 formed patriotic unions: Ibid., 464–466.

807 On October 18, 1817: Ibid., 464; "Protestantism," *The New Encyclopaedia Britannica*, 15th edition, vol. 26, 238.

808 the old regime: "Germany," in *The New Encyclopaedia Britannica*, 15th edition, vol. 20, 105–106; Holborn, *History of Modern Germany*, vol. 2, 424ff, 457ff.

808 pillar of that regime: Holborn, *History of Modern Germany*, vol. 3, *1840–1945*, 109–110.

808 a neo-Lutheran movement: "Neo-Lutheranism," in *The Encyclopedia of the Lutheran Church*; "Protestantism," in *The New Encyclopaedia Britannica*, 15th edition, vol. 26, 238.

808 Otto von Bismarck: "Bismarck," in *The New Encyclopaedia Britannica*, 15th edition., vol. 15, 121–124.

808 to complete what Luther had begun: Rausch, *Protestantism*, 118.

808 great capitalist boom: Holborn, *A History of Modern Germany*, vol. 3, 122–123; "Germany," in *The New Encyclopaedia Britannica*, 15th edition, vol. 20, 106, 113–115.

808 incapable of developing a program: Craig, *Germany*, 183–185.

808 had only about a hundred places of worship: Andrew Landale Drummond, *German Protestantism Since Luther*, 220–222. See also Craig, *Germany*, 180–181.

808 The Social Democratic Party grew so fast: "Germany," in *The New Encyclopaedia Britannica*, 15th edition, vol. 20, 114–115.

808 Marxist historians: James M. Stayer, *Martin Luther, German Saviour: German Evangelical Theological Factions and the Interpretation of Luther, 1917–1933*, 27.

809 *Communism in Central Europe*: The text is available at https://www.marxists .org/archive/kautsky/1897/europe /index.htm

809 Ernst Troeltsch: Stayer, *Martin Luther*, 13–26; "Luther Renaissance," in *The Oxford Encyclopedia of the Reformation*; "Troeltsch, Ernst," in *The New*

Encyclopaedia Britannica, 15th edition, vol. 11, 937.

809 a church historian named Karl Holl: Stayer, *Martin Luther*, 18–47, 118–124; "Luther Renaissance," in *The Oxford Encyclopedia of the Reformation*; Karl Holl, *What Did Luther Understand by Religion?*, eds. James Luther Adams and Walter F. Bense, trans. Fred W. Meuser and Walter R. Wietzke, introduction by Walter F. Bense, 1–14.

809 Heinrich Denifle: "Denifle, Heinrich Seuse," in *New Catholic Encyclopedia*. A translation of the volume (*Luther and Lutherdom, from original sources*) is available at https://babel.hathitrust.org /cgi/pt?id=cool.ark:/13960/t50g47q19.

810 patriotic surge in Germany: Stayer, *Martin Luther*, 17.

810 gave a memorial lecture: Holl, *What Did Luther Understand by Religion?*, 1.

810 The new Weimar Republic: Holborn, *History of Modern Germany*, vol. 3, 532ff, 661–662; Rausch, *Protestantism*, 119; "Germany," in *The New Encyclopaedia Britannica*, 15th edition, vol. 20, 116–118; "Luther Renaissance," in *The Oxford Encyclopedia of the Reformation*.

810 "great awakener of the conscience of his day": Holl, *What Did Luther Understand by Religion?*, 109; "personal freedom," 50; "more than merely," 110; stood out "so sharply," 110; "the principal advocate," 97; had courageously protected the gospel, 102; "profound genius," 110; "belongs not only to us Germans," 110. See also "Luther Renaissance," in *The Oxford Encyclopedia of the Reformation*; Stayer, *Martin Luther*, 39–47.

811 the Luther Renaissance: Karl Kupisch, "The 'Luther Renaissance,' " *Journal of Contemporary History*, 2(4): 39–49, October 1967; Holl, *What Did Luther Understand by Religion?*, 2. "Luther Renaissance," in *The Oxford Encyclopedia of the Reformation*.

811 Conservatives in particular rallied:

"Luther Renaissance," in *The Oxford Encyclopedia of the Reformation*.

811 militant Christian nationalism: Ibid.

811 Protestants voted overwhelmingly: Rausch, *Protestantism*, 119–120; Holborn, *History of Modern Germany*, vol. 3, 739–741.

811 In the election of July 1932: Friedrich Weber and Charlotte Methuen, "The Architecture of Faith under National Socialism: Lutheran Church Building(s) in Braunschweig, 1933–1945," *Journal of Ecclesiastical History* 66(2): 343 (April 2015).

811 The German Christians: Holborn, *History of Modern Germany*, vol. 3, 740–741; Stayer, *Martin Luther*, 126–127; "German Christians," in *The Encyclopedia of Protestantism*.

811 The Confessing Church: "Confessing Church," in *The Encyclopedia of Protestantism*.

812 "lies like a cloud": Quoted in Ryrie, *Protestants*, 270.

812 Declaration of Guilt: "Confessing Church," in *The Encyclopedia of Protestantism*. The text is available at http://www.history.ucsb.edu /faculty/marcuse/projects/niem/Stutt gartDeclaration.htm.

812 atone for their performance: "Holocaust," in *The Encyclopedia of Protestantism*; "Germany," in *The Encyclopedia of Christianity*, vol. 2, 402–403.

812 an ambitious social-welfare program: "Germany," in *The Encyclopedia of Christianity*, vol. 2, 402.

813 closed 340 churches: "Germany's Great Church Sell-Off," *Spiegel Online*, available at http://www.spiegel.de /international/zeitgeist/german-catholic -and-protestant-churches-sell-off-church -buildings-a-883054.html.

813 A 2012 global survey: See http://www .norc.org/PDFs/Beliefs_about_God _Report.pdf.

813 "the most godless place on earth": See https://www.welt.de/politik

/deutschland/article106205333/Warum -so-wenige-Ostdeutsche-an-einen-Gott -glauben.html; https://www.theguardian .com/commentisfree/belief/2012/sep/22 /atheism-east-germany-godless-place.

813 "Where have all the Protestants gone?": See Elisabeth Braw, "In Martin Luther's Church the Pastor Asks: Where Have All the Protestants Gone?" *Newsweek*, February 24, 2014, available at http://www.newsweek.com /2014/02/28/martin-luthers-church -pastor-asks-where-have-all-protestants -gone-245572.html.

813 Lutherstadt-Wittenberg: "Lutherstadt Wittenberg," a pamphlet published by Wittenberg-Information.

813 For a full decade beforehand: See https:// www.luther2017.de/en/2017/luther -decade/.

813 ongoing de-Christianization of Germany: See "Germany," in *The Encyclopedia of Christianity*; Noll, *Protestantism: A Very Short Introduction*, 120–121; "Secularization," in *The Encyclopedia of Protestantism*; T. R. Reid, "Hollow Halls in Europe's Churches," *The Washington Post*, May 6, 2001.

814 an indelible stain: See Christopher J. Probst, *Demonizing the Jews: Luther and the Protestant Church in Nazi Germany*, 2–15, 172–175.

814 a worldwide empire: "Global Christianity: A Report on the Size and Distribution of the World's Christian Population," Pew Research Center, December 19, 2011.

814 single largest Protestant congregation: Mark A. Noll, *Protestantism: A Very Short Introduction*, 2.

814 just under half of the population: See "America's Changing Religious Landscape," Pew Research Center, May 12, 2015, available at http://www .pewforum.org/2015/05/12/americas -changing-religious-landscape/.

814 America has been the capital of world Protestantism: MacCulloch, *Reformation*,

527. "The American varieties of English Protestantism," MacCulloch writes, are "the most characteristic forms of Protestant Christianity today, and indeed they are probably the most dynamic forms of Christianity worldwide." See also Noll, *Protestantism: A Very Short Introduction*, 122–123.

814 America's Lutherans: Williams, *America's Religions*, 358–362. Mark Noll, a prominent chronicler of the American Protestant experience, has lamented the marginal presence of American Lutherans in American life: "The surprising thing for those who are acquainted with the penetrating vision of Luther, the scholarly aplomb of Melanchthon, the irenic efficiency of the Concord formulators, the surging brilliance of Bach, the passionate wisdom of Kierkegaard, or the heroic integrity of Bonhoeffer is how inconspicuous the Lutherans have been in America. Beyond their instructive experience as immigrants, it is hard to isolate identifiably Lutheran contributions to the larger history of Christianity in America." ("The Lutheran Difference," *First Things*, February 1992, available at https://www.firstthings .com/article/1992/02/004-the-lutheran -difference.) For more on the current state of American Lutheranism, see Richard Cimino, ed., *Lutherans Today: American Lutheran Identity in the Twenty-First Century*.

814 the Southern Baptist Convention: See Mark A. Noll, *American Evangelical Christianity: An Introduction*, 58; Harold Bloom, *The American Religion: The Emergence of the Post-Christian Nation*, 191–199.

815 The Baptists' various statements of belief: See http://www.sbc.net/aboutus/ basicbeliefs.asp and http://www.sbc.net/ aboutus/positionstatements.asp.

815 explicitly embrace "the priesthood of all believers": In *The American Religion* (202), Bloom observes that "like so many American denominations (the Mormons included), the Southern Baptists affirm the priesthood of all believers, leaving to the preachers only the prime function of exhortation."

815 Billy Graham offers another example: Mark A. Noll, *American Evangelical Christianity*, 44–55; Frances Fitzgerald, *The Evangelicals: The Struggle to Shape America*, 169–207.

815 "No matter who we are": Billy Graham, *Just As I Am: The Autobiography of Billy Graham*, 728.

816 a visit he made to Wittenberg: Ibid., 513–514.

816 the place of the Bible in it: Noll, *American Evangelical Christianity*, 59–60; Randall Balmer, *Mine Eyes Have Seen the Glory: A Journey into the Evangelical Subculture in America*, 155–170. "American evangelicals," Ballmer writes (156–157), have "an almost mystical attachment to the Bible." Detractors "have accused evangelicals of bibliolatry: elevating the Bible to the status of an idol that is itself worshipped."

816 According to surveys: See the data gathered by the Pew Research Center, available at http://www.pewforum.org /religious-landscape-study/frequency-of -reading-scripture/.

816 Nearly half of all adult Americans: According to a May 2017 Gallup poll, available at http://www.gallup.com /poll/210704/record-few-americans -believe-bible-literal-word-god.aspx.

816 Museum of the Bible: See Candida Moss and Joel S. Baden, "Just What is the Museum of the Bible Trying to Do?," *Politico*, October 15, 2017. The authors, professors at the University of Birmingham and the Yale Divinity School respectively, write that though the museum presents itself as nonsectarian, "the idea that a museum can be devoted just to the Bible's words, without presenting the history of its interpretation and the cultural contexts

in which that interpretation has taken place, is a distinctly Protestant one." Available at http://www.politico.com /magazine/story/2017/10/15/just-what -is-the-museum-of-the-bible-trying -to-do-215711.

816 Most historians are wed: See Jon Butler, *Awash in a Sea of Faith: Christianizing the American People*. He writes (1–5) that the tendency of historical accounts to concentrate on the familiar themes of New England Calvinism, evangelicalism, voluntarism, and declining religious adherence "slights America's rich religious complexity and is ultimately unable to explain Christianity's extraordinary power and its highly variable expressions in nineteenth-and twentieth-century America." He proposes that "we attach less importance to Puritanism as the major force in shaping religion in America and more importance to the religious eclecticism" that took root in the eighteenth century. It is also important, he notes, to restore a sense of the European roots of early American religion. The "close connections between early modern Europe and America, the conscious resort to European models by American colonists, and the overwhelmingly derivative nature of early American society make it impossible to understand America's religious origins apart from Europe." See also Roger Finke and Rodney Stark, *The Churching of America, 1776–2005: Winners and Losers in Our Religious Economy*, second edition (1–24, 57–60), on the need for a new approach to American religious history.

817 John Wesley: Walker, *History of the Christian Church*, 596–606; MacCulloch, *Reformation*, 675–676; Williams, *America's Religions*, 135–139; For a full biographical treatment, see Roy Hattersley, *John Wesley: A Brand from the Burning*.

817 a despondent Wesley reluctantly accepted: Walker, *History of the Christian Church*, 601.

817 become the foundation for Wesley's own theology: See Philip S. Watson, *Let God Be God! An Interpretation of the Theology of Martin Luther*, 3.

817 that Wesley could not accept: Mark A. Noll, *The Work We Have to Do: A History of Protestants in America*, 53–54; Balmer, *Mine Eyes Have Seen the Glory*, 202–203.

818 a state of "sanctification": George M. Marsden, *Fundamentalism and American Culture: The Shaping of Twentieth-Century Evangelicalism, 1870–1925*, 72–74.

818 stripping it of the fatalism: Wesley, in short, was a Pelagian. It is surprising how few accounts of American religious history take full note of the important part Wesley played in it. Among the exceptions are Mark A. Noll, *The Rise of Evangelicalism*; Bloom, *American Religion* (49); and Balmer, *Mine Eyes Have Seen the Glory* (x). "Wesley's evangelical experience," Balmer writes, "has served as a model for many American evangelicals. They, like him, point to some sudden, instantaneous, datable experience of grace, and they aspire to the kind of warm-hearted piety so characteristic of Wesley's spiritual life."

818 Wesley began traveling around England: Noll, *The Rise of Evangelicalism*, 116–118; Alister E. McGrath, *Christianity's Dangerous Idea: The Protestant Revolution—A History from the Sixteenth Century to the Twenty-First*, 147–148; E. P. Thompson, *The Making of the English Working Class*, 37ff, 350ff. The excitement that Methodist preachers stirred among English workers is captured by George Eliot in *Adam Bede*.

818 The Church of England disapproved: Finke, *Churching of America*, 67–68.

819 the first Methodist preachers commissioned by him: Noll, *Work We Have to Do*, 41.

819 "no creed but the Bible": Quoted in Nathan O. Hatch, *The Democratization of American Christianity*, 166.

819 suited to people on the frontier: Sydney E. Ahlstrom, *A Religious History of the American People*, 429–436; P. Williams, *America's Religions*, 184–186.

819 in Cane Ridge, Kentucky: Ahlstrom, *Religious History*, 432–436; Williams, *America's Religions*, 185–186; Finke, *Churching of America*, 92–96, 108; Harold Bloom, *American Religion*, 59–64. "The American Jesus," Bloom writes (64), "was born at Cane Ridge, and is with us still."

819 became a fixture of the frontier: Hatch, *Democratization*, 49–56; Ahlstrom, *Religious History*, 435–436; Noll, *Work We Have to Do*, 55–56.

819 the Second Great Awakening: Williams, *America's Religions*, 182–189; Finke, *Churching of America*, 76, 85–86; Fitzgerald, *Evangelicals*, 25–32; Garry Wills, *Head and Heart: American Christianities*, 287–299; Grant S. Wood, *The Radicalism of the American Revolution*, 331–335.

819 a continuation of it: Jonathan Edwards called the United States "the principal nation of the Reformation" (quoted in Martin Marty, *Righteous Empire: The Protestant Experience in America*, 49). On American Protestantism's building on the Reformation, see MacCulloch, *Reformation*, 676.

820 took root and spread: As Gordon Wood puts it in *The Radicalism of the American Revolution* (331), "as the Republic became democratized, it became evangelized."

820 would leave a permanent mark: Hatch, *Democratization*, 3–16, 40–46, 58; Wood, *Radicalism of the American Revolution*, 329–334. "By the second quarter of the nineteenth century," Wood writes (333), "the evangelical Protestantism of ordinary people had come to dominate American culture to an extent the founding fathers had never anticipated."

820 The message from the pulpits: Arlie Russell Hochschild, in *Strangers in Their Own Land: Anger and Mourning on the American Right*, writes (124) of her time attending church services in Lake Charles, Louisiana, that the word from the pulpits "seemed to focus more on a person's *moral strength to endure* than on the will to change the circumstances that called on that strength." At the same time, she adds, "the service offered a collective, supportive arena" that gave strength to the individual "to endure what had to be endured."

BIBLIOGRAPHY

Ackroyd, Peter. *The Life of Thomas More.* New York: Doubleday, 1998.

Adams, Robert P. *The Better Part of Valor: More, Erasmus, Colet, and Vives on Humanism, War, and Peace, 1496–1535.* Seattle: University of Washington Press, 1962.

Agricola, Georgius. *De Re Metallica.* Translated by Herbert Clark Hoover and Lou Henry Hoover. New York: Dover Publications, 1950.

Ahlstrom, Sydney E. *A Religious History of the American People.* New Haven: Yale University Press, 1972.

Aland, Kurt, and Barbara Aland. *The Text of the New Testament: An Introduction to the Critical Editions and to the Theory and Practice of Modern Textual Criticism.* Translated by Erroll F. Rhodes. Grand Rapids, Mich.: W. B. Eerdmanns, 1987.

Allen, P. S. *The Age of Erasmus.* New York: Russell & Russell, 1963.

Amiot, François. *History of the Mass.* Translated by Lancelot C. Sheppard. New York: Hawthorn Books, 1959.

Andres, Glenn M., John M. Hunisak, and A. Richard Turner. *The Art of Florence.* 2 vols. New York: Artabras, 1988.

Aquinas, Thomas. *Nature and Grace: Selections from the Summa Theologica of Thomas Aquinas.* Edited by A. M. Fairweather. Philadelphia: Westminster Press, 1954.

———. *The Summa Theologica of Saint Thomas Aquinas.* Translated by Father Laurence Shapcote. Chicago: Encyclopaedia Britannica, 1952, 1990.

Aristotle. *The Works of Aristotle.* Translated by W. D. Ross. Chicago: Encyclopaedia Britannica, 1952.

Augustijn, Cornelis. *Erasmus: His Life, Works, and Influence.* Toronto: University of Toronto Press, 1986, 1991.

Augustine. *City of God.* Translated by Henry Bettenson. London: Penguin, 1972.

———. *Confessions.* Translated by R. S. Pine-Coffin. London: Penguin, 1961.

Backman, Clifford R. *The Worlds of Medieval Europe.* New York: Oxford University Press, 2003.

Bainton, Roland H. *Christian Attitudes Toward War and Peace: A Historical Survey and Critical Re-evaluation.* New York: Abingdon Press, 1960.

———. *Erasmus of Christendom.* New York: Charles Scribner's Sons, 1969.

———. *Here I Stand: A Life of Martin Luther.* New York: Meridian, 1950.

——. *Hunted Heretic: The Life and Death of Michael Servetus, 1511–1553*. Boston: Beacon Press, 1953.

——. *The Reformation of the Sixteenth Century*. Enlarged edition. Boston: Beacon Press, 1952, 1985.

——. "Sebastian Castellio, Champion of Religious Liberty." In *Castellioniana: Quatre études sur Sébastien Castellion et l'idée de la tolérance*, 25–79. Leiden: E. J. Brill, 1951.

——. *Women of the Reformation in Germany and Italy*. Minneapolis: Augsburg, 1971.

Bak, Janos, ed. *The German Peasant War of 1525*. London: F. Cass, 1976.

Baldwin, T. W. *William Shakspere's Small Latine & Lesse Greeke*. 2 vols. Urbana: University of Illinois Press, 1944.

Balmer, Randall Herbert, ed. *The Encyclopedia of Evangelicalism*. Waco, TX: Baylor University Press, 2004.

——. *Mine Eyes Have Seen the Glory: A Journey into the Evangelical Subculture in America*. New York: Oxford University Press, 1989.

Baron, Salo Wittmayer. *A Social and Religious History of the Jews*. Second edition. Vols. 2, 13. New York: Columbia University Press, 1952–1983.

Barron, Robert. *Thomas Aquinas: Spiritual Master*. New York: Crossroad, 1996.

Bataillon, Marcel. *Érasme et L'Espagne*. Edited by Charles Amiel. 3 vols. Geneva: Librarie Droz, 1991.

Baylor, Michael G. *The German Reformation and the Peasants' War: A Brief History with Documents*. Boston: Bedford/St. Martin's, 2012.

——. ed. and trans. *The Radical Reformation*. Cambridge: Cambridge University Press, 1991.

Bax, E. Belfort. *The Peasants War in Germany, 1525–1526*. New York: Russell & Russell, 1899, 1968.

Bentley, Jerry H. "Biblical Philology and Christian Humanism: Lorenzo Valla and Erasmus as Scholars of the Gospels." *Sixteenth Century Journal* 8 (July 1977): 8–28.

——. *Humanists and Holy Writ: New Testament Scholarship in the Renaissance*. Princeton: Princeton University Press, 1983.

Bishop, Morris. *The Middle Ages*. Boston: Houghton Mifflin, 1968, 1996.

——. trans. *Letters from Petrarch*. Bloomington: Indiana University Press, 1966.

——. *Petrarch and His World*. Bloomington: Indiana University Press, 1963.

Blickle, Peter. *The Revolution of 1525: The German Peasants' War from a New Perspective*. Translated by Thomas A Brady Jr. and H. C. Erik Midelfort. Baltimore: The Johns Hopkins University Press, 1977, 1981.

Blockmans, Wim. *Emperor Charles V: 1500–1558*. London: Arnold, 2002.

Bloom, Harold. *The American Religion: The Emergence of the Post-Christian Nation*. New York: Simon & Schuster, 1992.

Bobrick, Benson. *Wide as the Waters: The Story of the English Bible and the Revolution It Inspired*. New York: Simon & Schuster, 2001.

Boehmer, Heinrich. *Road to Reformation: Martin Luther to the Year 1521.*
Translated by John W. Doberstein and Theodore G. Tappert. Philadelphia:
Muhlenberg Press, 1946.

Bolgar, R. R. *The Classical Heritage and Its Beneficiaries.* Cambridge:
Cambridge University Press, 1958.

Boot, Max. *War Made New: Technology, Warfare, and the Course of History,
1500 to Today.* New York: Gotham Books, 2006.

Bornkamm, Günther. *Paul, Paulus.* Translated by D. M. G. Stalker. New York:
Harper & Row, 1969, 1971.

Bornkamm, Heinrich. *Luther in Mid-Career, 1521–1530.* Edited by Karin
Bornkamm. Translated by E. Theodore Bachmann. Philadelphia: Fortress
Press, 1983.

Boyle, Marjorie O'Rourke. *Erasmus on Language and Method in Theology.*
Toronto: University of Toronto Press, 1977.

———. *Rhetoric and Reform: Erasmus' Civil Dispute with Luther.* Cambridge,
Mass.: Harvard University Press, 1983.

Brady, Thomas A. *German Histories in the Age of Reformations, 1400–1650.*
Cambridge: Cambridge University Press, 2009.

Brandi, Karl. *The Emperor Charles V: The Growth and Destiny of a Man and of a
World-Empire.* New York: A. A. Knopf, 1939.

Braudel, Fernand. *The Structures of Everyday Life: The Limits of the Possible.*
Translated from the French and revised by Siân Reynolds. Berkeley:
University of California Press, 1992.

Brecht, Martin. *Martin Luther: His Road to Reformation, 1483–1521.* Translated
by James L. Schaaf. Minneapolis: Fortress Press, 1981, 1985.

———. *Martin Luther: Shaping and Defining the Reformation, 1521–1532.*
Translated by James L. Schaaf. Minneapolis: Fortress Press, 1986, 1990.

———. *Martin Luther: The Preservation of the Church, 1532–1546.* Translated
by James L. Schaaf. Minneapolis: Fortress Press, 1987, 1993.

Brendler, Gerhard. *Martin Luther: Theology and Revolution.* Translated by
Claude R. Foster Jr. New York: Oxford University Press, 1991.

Brown, Andrew J., "The Date of Erasmus' Latin Translation of the New
Testament," *Transactions of the Cambridge Bibliographical Society* 8, no. 4
(1984): 351–380.

Brown, Christopher Boyd. *Singing the Gospel: Lutheran Hymns and the Success of
the Reformation.* Cambridge, Mass.: Harvard University Press, 2005.

Brown, Peter. *Augustine of Hippo: A Biography.* Berkeley: University of
California Press, 1967.

———. *The Body and Society: Men, Women, and Sexual Renunciation in Early
Christianity.* New York: Columbia University Press, 1988.

Burckhardt, Jacob. *The Civilization of the Renaissance in Italy.* Translated
by S. G. C. Middlemore. London: Penguin, 1990.

Burge, James. *Heloise and Abelard: A New Biography.* New York:
HarperSanFrancisco, 2003.

Butler, Jon. *Awash in a Sea of Faith: Christianizing the American People.* Cambridge, Mass.: Harvard University Press, 1990.

Bütz, Jeffrey J. *The Brother of Jesus and the Lost Teachings of Christianity.* Rochester, Vt.: Inner Traditions, 2005.

Calvin, Jean. *Institutes of the Christian Religion.* Edited by John T. McNeill. Translated by Ford Lewis Battles. 2 vols. Philadelphia: Westminster Press, 1960.

Cambridge History of the Bible, The. 3 vols. Cambridge: Cambridge University Press, 1963–1970.

Cambridge Medieval History, The New. Vol. 7. Edited by Christopher Allmand. Cambridge: Cambridge University Press, 1998.

Cambridge Modern History, The. Vol. 2. Edited by A. W. Ward, G. W. Prothero, and Stanley Leathers. New York: Macmillan, 1934.

Cameron, Euan. *The European Reformation.* Oxford: Clarendon Press, 1991.

Cantor, Norman F. *The Civilization of the Middle Ages.* New York: HarperPerennial, 1993.

Carlstadt, Andreas Bodenstein von. *The Essential Carlstadt.* Edited and translated by E. J. Furcha. Waterloo, Ontario: Herald Press, 1995.

Castellion, Sébastian. *Concerning Heretics: Whether They Are To Be Persecuted and How They Are To Be Treated; A Collection of the Opinions of Learned Men, Both Ancient and Modern; an anonymous work attributed to Sebastian Castellio.* Edited by Roland H. Bainton. New York: Columbia University Press, 1935.

Chamberlin, E. R. *The Sack of Rome.* London: B. T. Batsford, 1979.

Chambers, David, and Brian Pullan, eds. *Venice: A Documentary History, 1450–1630.* Toronto: University of Toronto Press, 2001.

Chambers, R. W. *Thomas More.* London: J. Cape, 1935.

Chrisman, Miriam Usher. *Strasbourg and the Reform: A Study in the Process of Change.* New Haven: Yale University Press, 1967.

Cicero. *Selected Works.* Translated by Michael Grant. London: Penguin, 1971.

Cimino, Richard, ed. *Lutherans Today: American Lutheran Identity in the Twenty-First Century.* Grand Rapids, Mich.: Wm. B. Eerdmans, 2003.

Cohen, Jeremy. *The Friars and the Jews: The Evolution of Medieval Anti-Judaism.* Ithaca: Cornell University Press, 1982.

Cohn, Norman. *The Pursuit of the Millennium: Revolutionary Millenarians and Mystical Anarchists of the Middle Ages.* Revised and expanded edition. New York: Oxford University Press, 1961, 1970.

Colet, John. *John Colet's Commentary on First Corinthians: A New Edition of the Latin Text, with Translation, Annotations, and Introduction.* Translated by Bernard O'Kelly and Catherine A.L. Jarrott. Binghamton, N.Y.: Medieval & Renaissance Texts & Studies, 1985.

Combs, William W. "Erasmus and the Textus Receptus," *Detroit Baptist Seminary Journal* 1 (Spring 1996): 35–53.

Coogan, Robert. *Erasmus, Lee and the Correction of the Vulgate: The Shaking of the Foundations.* Geneva: Librairie Droz, 1992.

D'Amico, John F. *Renaissance Humanism in Papal Rome: Humanists and Churchmen on the Eve of the Reformation.* Baltimore: The Johns Hopkins University Press, 1983.

Daniell, David. *William Tyndale: A Biography.* New Haven: Yale University Press, 1994.

Dau, W. H. T. *The Leipzig Debate of 1519: Leaves from the Story of Luther's Life.* St. Louis: Concordia, 1919.

Dickens, A.G. *The English Reformation.* Second edition. London: B.T. Batsford, 1964, 1989.

———, and Whitney R. D. Jones. *Erasmus the Reformer.* London: Methuen, 1994.

Dillenberger, John, ed. *Martin Luther: Selections from His Writings.* New York: Anchor, 1962.

Dixon, C. Scott. *The Reformation in Germany.* Oxford: Blackwell, 2002.

Doernberg, Erwin. *Henry VIII and Luther: An Account of Their Personal Relations.* Stanford, Calif.: Stanford University Press, 1961.

Duffy, Eamon. *The Stripping of the Altars: Traditional Religion in England, c. 1400–c. 1580.* New Haven: Yale University Press, 1992.

Durant, Will. *The Reformation: A History of European Civilization from Wyclif to Calvin, 1300–1564.* New York: Simon & Schuster, 1957.

Edwards, Brian. *William Tyndale: The Father of the English Bible.* Farmington Hills, Mich.: William Tyndale College, 1976.

Edwards, Mark U., Jr. *Luther and the False Brethren.* Stanford, Calif.: Stanford University Press, 1975.

Ehrman, Bart D. *Misquoting Jesus: The Story Behind Who Changed the Bible and Why.* New York: HarperSanFrancisco, 2005.

Eire, Carlos M. N. *Reformations: The Early Modern World, 1450–1650.* New Haven: Yale University Press, 2016.

Eisenstein, Elizabeth L. *The Printing Revolution in Early Modern Europe.* Second edition. Cambridge: Cambridge University Press, 1983, 2005.

Elliott, J. K. " 'Novum Testamentum editum est': The Five-Hundredth Anniversary of Erasmus's New Testament." *The Bible Translator* 67, no. 1 (2016): 9–28.

Elton, G.R. *England Under the Tutors.* London: Metheun, 1955, 1962.

———. *Reformation Europe, 1517–1559.* Second edition. Oxford: Blackwell, 1963.

Engels, Friedrich. *The Peasant War in Germany.* New York: International Publishers, 1926.

Epistolae Obscurorum Virorum. Translated and introduced by Francis Griffin Stokes. London: Chatto & Windus, 1909.

Erasmus, Desiderius. *The Adages of Erasmus.* Edited by William Barker. Toronto: University of Toronto Press, 2001.

————. *The Essential Erasmus*. Translated by John P. Dolan. New York: Meridian, 1964.

————. *The Julius Exclusus of Erasmus*. Translated by Paul Pascal. Bloomington: Indiana University Press, 1968.

————. *Opus Epistolarum Des. Erasmi Roterodami*. Edited by P. S. Allen. Oxford: Clarendon, 1906–1958.

————. *The Polemics of Erasmus of Rotterdam and Ulrich von Hutten*. Translated by Randolph J. Klawiter. Notre Dame: University of Notre Dame Press, 1977.

————. *Christian Humanism and the Reformation: Selected Writings of Erasmus*. Edited John C. Olin. Third edition. New York: Fordham University Press, 1987.

Erikson, Erik H. *Young Man Luther: A Study in Psychoanalysis and History*. New York: Norton, 1958, 1962.

Evennett, H. O. *The Spirit of the Counter-Reformation*. Notre Dame: University of Notre Dame Press, 1968.

Fairweather, Eugene R., ed. *A Scholastic Miscellany: Anselm to Ockham*. Philadelphia: Westminster Press, 1956.

Farge, James K. *Orthodoxy and Reform in Early Reformation France: The Faculty of Theology of Paris, 1500–1543*. Leiden: E. J. Brill, 1985.

Febvre, Lucien, and Henri-Jean Martin. *The Coming of the Book: The Impact of Printing 1450–1800*. Verso: London, 1976.

Feuer, Lewis Samuel. *Spinoza and the Rise of Liberalism*. Boston: Beacon Press, 1958.

Fife, Robert Herndon. *The Revolt of Martin Luther*. New York: Columbia University Press, 1957.

Finke, Roger, and Rodney Stark. *The Churching of America, 1776–2005: Winners and Losers in Our Religious Economy*. New Brunswick, N.J.: Rutgers University Press, 2005.

Fitzgerald, Frances. *The Evangelicals: The Struggle to Shape America*. New York: Simon & Schuster, 2017.

Flood, John L. "The Book in Reformation Germany." In *The Reformation and the Book*. Edited by Jean-François Gilmont. Translated by Karen Magg. Aldershot, Hants, England: Ashgate, 1998.

Freeman, Charles. *The Closing of the Western Mind: The Rise of Faith and the Fall of Reason*. New York: Vintage, 2002.

Friedenthal, Richard. *Luther*. Translated by John Nowell. London: Weidenfeld and Nicolson, 1967.

Froude, J.A. *Life and Letters of Erasmus*. New York: Charles Scribner's Sons, 1895, 1971.

Füssel, Stephan. *The Book of Books: The Luther Bible of 1534*. Cologne: Taschen, 2003.

Gäbler, Ulrich. *Huldrych Zwingli: His Life and Work*. Translated by Ruth C. L. Gritsch. Philadelphia: Fortress, 1986.

Gathorne-Hardy, Jonathan. *The Public School Phenomenon, 597–1977.* London: Hodder and Stoughton, 1977.

Gay, Peter. *The Enlightenment: An Interpretation—The Rise of Modern Paganism.* New York: Knopf, 1966.

Geanakoplos, Deno John, ed. *Byzantium: Church, Society, and Civilization Seen Through Contemporary Eyes.* Chicago: University of Chicago Press, 1984.

Gies, Joseph, and Frances Gies. *Life in a Medieval City.* New York: Thomas W. Crowell, 1969.

Giese, Rachel. "Erasmus' Greek Studies." *The Classical Journal* 29, no. 7 (1934): 517–526.

Gleason, John B. *John Colet.* Berkeley: University of California Press, 1989.

Goertz, Hans-Jürgen, ed. *Profiles of Radical Reformers: Biographical Sketches from Thomas Müntzer to Paracelsus.* Kitchener, Ontario: Herald Press, 1982.

Goldhill, Simon. *Who Needs Greek? Contests in the Cultural History of Hellenism.* Cambridge: Cambridge University Press, 2002.

Graetz, H. *History of the Jews.* Vol. 4. Philadelphia: The Jewish Publication Society of America, 1891–1898.

Grafton, Anthony, and Lisa Jardine. *From Humanism to the Humanities: Education and the Liberal Arts in Fifteenth-and Sixteenth-Century Europe.* London: Duckworth, 1986.

Grafton, Anthony, ed. *Rome Reborn: The Vatican Library and Renaissance Culture.* New Haven: Yale University Press, 1993.

Graham, Billy. *Just As I Am: The Autobiography of Billy Graham.* San Francisco: HarperSanFrancisco, 1997.

Grant, Michael. *Saint Paul.* London: Phoenix Press, 1976.

Greenblatt, Stephen. *The Swerve: How the World Became Modern.* New York: W. W. Norton, 2011.

Grimm, Harold J. *Lazarus Spengler: A Lay Leader of the Reformation.* Columbus: Ohio State University Press, 1978.

Gritsch, Eric W. *Thomas Müntzer: A Tragedy of Errors.* Minneapolis: Fortress Press, 1989.

Grossmann, Maria. *Humanism in Wittenberg: 1485–1517.* Nieuwkoop: De Graaf, 1975.

Guggisberg, Hans R. *Basel in the Sixteenth Century: Aspects of the City Republic before, during, and after the Reformation.* St. Louis: Center for Reformation Research, 1982.

Haeghen, Ferdinand van der. *Bibliotheca Erasmiana: Répertoire des Oeuvres d'Érasme,* 1er sér. Nieuwkoop: B. de Graaf, 1961.

Hale, J.R. *Machiavelli and Renaissance Italy.* New York: Macmillan, 1960.

———. *Renaissance Europe, 1480–1520.* London: Fontana Press, 1971.

Halkin, Léon-E. *Erasmus: A Critical Biography.* Oxford: Blackwell, 1987, 1993.

Hamel, Christopher de. *The Book. A History of the Bible*. London: Phaedon Press, 2001.

Harbison, E. Harris. *The Christian Scholar in the Age of the Reformation*. New York: Charles Scribner's Sons, 1956.

Harrison, A. W. *Arminianism*. London: Duckworth, 1937.

Hatch, Nathan O. *The Democratization of American Christianity*. New Haven: Yale University Press, 1989.

Hattersley, Roy. *John Wesley: A Brand from the Burning*. London: Little Brown, 2002, 2003.

Hawthorne, Gerald F., and Ralph P. Martin, eds. *Dictionary of Paul and His Letters: A Compendium of Contemporary Biblical Scholarship*. Downers Grove, Ill.: InterVarsity Press, 1993.

Heer, Friedrich. *The Medieval World: Europe 1100–1350*. New York: New American Library, 1961.

Helmer, Christine, ed. *The Global Luther: A Theologian for Modern Times*. Minneapolis: Fortress Press, 2009.

Hendrix, Scott H. *Martin Luther: Visionary Reformer*. New Haven: Yale University Press, 2015.

Henry VIII. *Asssertio Septem Sacramentorum* or *Defence of the Seven Sacraments*. Edited by Rev. Louis O'Donovan. New York: Benzinger Brothers, 1908.

Henslow, G. *The Vulgate: The Source of the False Doctrines*. London: Williams & Norgate, 1909.

Herwaarden, Jan van. *Between Saint James and Erasmus: Studies in Late-Medieval Religious Life: Devotion and Pilgrimage in the Netherlands*. Translated by Wendie Shaffer and Donald Gardner. Leiden: Brill, 2003.

Hibbert, Christopher. *Rome: The Biography of a City*. New York: Norton, 1985.

Hilgert, Earle. "Johann Froben and the Basel University Scholars, 1513–1523." *The Library Quarterly* 41, no. 2 (April 1971): 141–169.

Hillerbrand, Hans. J., ed. *The Protestant Reformation*. Revised edition. New York: Harper Perennial, 2009.

———, ed. *The Reformation: A Narrative History Related by Contemporary Observers and Participants*. New York: Harper & Row, 1964.

Hochschild, Arlie Russell. *Strangers in Their Own Land: Anger and Mourning on the American Right*. New York: The New Press, 2016.

Holborn, Hajo. *A History of Modern Germany*. 3 vols. New York: A. A. Knopf, 1959–1969.

———. *Ulrich von Hutten and the German Reformation*. Translated by Roland H. Bainton. New Haven: Yale University Press, 1937.

Holborn, Louise. "Printing and the Growth of a Protestant Movement in Germany from 1517 to 1524." *Church History* 11, no. 2 (June 1942): 123–137.

Holl, Karl. *What Did Luther Understand by Religion?* Edited by James Luther Adams and Walter F. Bense. Translated by Fred W. Meuser and Walter R. Wietzke. Philadelphia: Fortress Press, 1977.

Hotchkiss, Valerie, and David Price. *Miracle Within a Miracle: Johannes Reuchlin and the Jewish Book Controversy.* Urbana-Champaign: University of Illinois Press, 2011

Hughes, Philip. *The Reformation in England.* New York: Macmillan, 1956.

Huizinga, Johan. *Erasmus and the Age of the Reformation.* Translated by F. Hopman. Mineola, N.Y.: Dover Publications, 2001.

———. *The Waning of the Middle Ages.* New York: Anchor Books, 1954, 1989.

Hus, Jan. *De ecclesia.* Translated by David S. Schaff. New York: C. Scriber's Sons, 1915.

Hyma, Albert. *The Brethren of the Common Life.* Grand Rapids: Eerdmans, 1950.

———. *The Youth of Erasmus.* New York: Russell & Russell, 1931, 1959.

IJsewijn, Jozef. "The Coming of Humanism to the Low Countries." In *Itinerarium Italicum: The Profile of the Italian Renaissance in the Mirror of Its European Transformations,* edited by Heiko A. Oberman with Thomas A. Brady Jr., 193–301. Leiden: E. J. Brill, 1975.

Israel, Jonathan I. *The Dutch Republic: Its Rise, Greatness, and Fall, 1477–1806.* Oxford: Clarendon Press. 1995.

Janssen, Johannes. *A History of the German People at the Close of the Middle Ages.* Vol. 4. Translated by A. M. Christie. St. Louis: B. Herder, 1900.

Jardine, Lisa. *Erasmus, Man of Letters: The Construction of Charisma in Print.* Princeton: Princeton University Press, 1993.

Jarrott, C. A. L. "Erasmus' Biblical Humanism." *Studies in the Renaissance* 17 (1970): 119–152.

Jerome. *Select Letters of St. Jerome.* Translated by F. A. Wright. London: W. Heinemann, 1933.

Johnson, Paul. *A History of Christianity.* New York: Simon & Schuster, 1976.

Jonge, Henk Jan de. "The Date and Purpose of Erasmus's *Castigatio Novi Testamenti:* A Note on the Origins of the *Novum Instrumentum.*" In *The Uses of Greek and Latin: Historical Essays,* edited by A. C. Dionisotti, Anthony Grafton, and Jill Kraye, 97–110. London: Warburg Institute, 1988.

———. "Erasmus and the *Comma Johanneum.*" *Extrait des Ephemerides Theologicae Lovanienses,* t. 56, fasc. 4 (1980): 381–389.

———. "Erasmus's Translation of the New Testament: Aim and Method." *The Bible Translator* 67, no. 1 (2016): 29–41.

———. "Novum Testamentum a Nobis Versum: The Essence of Erasmus' Edition of the New Testament." *Journal of Theological Studies* 35, no. 2 (October 1984): 394–413.

Jongh, H. De. L'ancienne faculté de théologie de Louvain au premier siècle de son existence, 1432–1540: ses débuts, son organisation, son enseignement, sa lutte contre Érasme et Luther. Utrecht: HES, 1980.

Kant, Immanuel. *Religion Within the Limits of Reason Alone.* Translated by Theodore M. Greene and Hoyt H. Hudson. New York: Harper, 1960.

Kelly, J.N.D. *Jerome: His Life, Writings, and Controversies.* New York: Harper & Row, 1975.

Kenyon, Frederic. *Our Bible and the Ancient Manuscripts*. London: Eyre & Spottiswoode, 1958.

King, John N. *English Reform Literature: The Tudor Origins of the Protestant Tradition*. Princeton: Princeton University Press, 1982.

Kittelson, James M. *Wolfgang Capito: From Humanist to Reformer*. Leiden: E. J. Brill, 1975.

Klaczko, Julian. *Rome and the Renaissance: The Pontificate of Julius II*. Translated by John Dennie. New York: G. P. Putnam's Sons, 1903.

Klepper, Deeana Copeland. *The Insight of Unbelievers: Nicholas Lyra and Christian Readings of Jewish Text in the Later Middle Ages*. Philadelphia: University of Pennsylvania, 2007.

Kling, David W. *The Bible in History: How the Texts Have Shaped the Times*. Oxford: Oxford University Press, 2004.

Knowles, David. *The Religious Orders in England*. Vol. 3, *The Tudor Age*. Cambridge: Cambridge University Press, 1948–1959.

Koch, A. C. F. *The Year of Erasmus' Birth*. Utrecht: Haentjens Dekker & Gumbert, 1969.

Kraye, Jill, ed. *The Cambridge Companion to Renaissance Humanism*. Cambridge: Cambridge University Press, 1996.

Kristeller, Paul Oskar. *Renaissance Thought: The Classic, Scholastic, and Humanistic Strains*. New York: Harper & Row, 1961.

Kupisch, Karl. "The 'Luther Renaissance.' " *Journal of Contemporary History* 2, no. 4 (October 1967): 39–49.

Le Goff, Jacques. *The Birth of Purgatory*. Translated by Arthur Goldhammer. Chicago: University of Chicago Press, 1984.

Lawless, George. *Augustine of Hippo and His Monastic Rule*. Oxford: Clarendon Press, 1987.

Lees-Milne, James. *Saint Peter's: The Story of Saint Peter's Basilica in Rome*. London: Hamish Hamilton, 1967.

Lindberg, Carter. *The European Reformations*. Oxford: Blackwell, 1996.

Lindsay, Thomas M. *A History of the Reformation*. Vol. 1, *The Reformation in Germany from Its Beginning to the Religious Peace of Augsburg*. Third Edition. New York: Charles Scribner's Sons, 1914.

Lohse, Bernhard. *A Short History of Christian Doctrine*. Translated by F. Ernest Stoeffler. Philadelphia: Fortress Press, 1966.

Lortz, Joseph. *The Reformation in Germany*. Vol. 1. Translated by Ronald Walls. London: Darton, Longman & Todd, 1968.

Lowry, Martin. *The World of Aldus Manutius: Business and Scholarship in Renaissance Venice*. Ithaca, N.Y.: Cornell University Press, 1979.

Luce, T. James, ed. *Ancient Writers: Greece and Rome*. Vol. 1, *Homer to Caesar*. New York: Scribner, 1982.

Lupton, J.H. *The Life of John Colet, D.D., Dean of St. Paul's and Founder of St. Paul's School*. Hamden, Conn.: Shoe String Press, 1961.

Luther, Martin. *The Annotated Luther*. Edited by Hans J. Hillerbrand, Kirsi I.

Stjerna, and Timothy J. Wengert. 5 vols. Minneapolis, Minn.: Fortress Press: 2015–.

———. *Luther: Lectures on Romans,* edited and translated by Wilhelm Pauck. Philadelphia: Westminster Press, 1961.

Lutzow, Francis. *The Hussite Wars.* London: J. M. Dent, 1914.

MacCulloch, Diarmaid. *Christianity: The First Three Thousand Years.* New York: Viking, 2010.

———. *The Reformation.* New York: Viking, 2003.

MacGregor, Neil. *Germany: Memories of a Nation.* New York: Alfred A. Knopf, 2015.

Machiavelli, Niccolò. *The Prince.* Translated by Daniel Donno. New York: Bantam, 1966.

Manschreck, Clyde Leonard. *Melanchthon: The Quiet Reformer.* New York: Abingdon, 1968.

Mansfield, Bruce. *Erasmus in the Twentieth Century: Interpretations c 1920–2000.* Toronto: University of Toronto Press, 2003.

———. *Man on His Own: Interpretations of Erasmus c 1750–1920.* Toronto: University of Toronto Press, 1992.

———. *Phoenix of His Age: Interpretations of Erasmus c 1550–1750.* Toronto: University of Toronto Press, 1979.

Marius, Richard. *Martin Luther: The Christian Between God and Death.* Cambridge, Mass.: Belknap Press of Harvard University Press, 1999.

———. *Thomas More: A Biography.* New York: Alfred A. Knopf, 1985.

Markish, Shimon. *Erasmus and the Jews.* Translated by Anthony Olcott. Chicago: University of Chicago Press, 1986.

Marsden, George M. *Fundamentalism and American Culture: The Shaping of Twentieth-Century Evangelicalism, 1870–1925.* Oxford: Oxford University Press, 1980.

Marty, Martin. *Martin Luther.* New York: Viking, 2004.

———. *Righteous Empire: The Protestant Experience in America.* New York: Harper & Row, 1970.

McConica, James. *Erasmus.* Oxford: Oxford University Press, 1991.

———. *English Humanists and Reformation Politics under Henry VIII and Edward VI.* Oxford: Clarendon Press, 1965.

McDonald, Grantley. "Erasmus and the Johannine Comma." *The Bible Translator* 67, no. 1 (2016): 42–55.

McElwee, William. *The Reign of Charles V, 1516–1558.* London: Macmillan, 1936.

McGrade, Arthur Stephen. *The Political Thought of William of Ockham: Personal and Institutional Principles.* London: Cambridge University Press, 1974.

McGrath, Alister E. *Christianity's Dangerous Idea: The Protestant Revolution— A History from the Sixteenth Century to the Twenty-first.* New York: HarperOne, 2007.

———. *The Intellectual Origins of the European Reformation*. Second edition. Malden, MA.: Blackwell, 1987.

———. *A Life of John Calvin: A Study in the Shaping of Western Culture*. Oxford: Basil Blackwell, 1990.

McKim, Donald K., ed. *The Cambridge Companion to Martin Luther*. Cambridge: Cambridge University Press, 2003.

McNeill, John T. *The History and Character of Calvinism*. New York: Oxford University Press, 1954.

Metzger, Bruce M. *The Early Versions of the New Testament: Their Origin, Transmission, and Limitations*. Oxford: Clarendon Press, 1977.

———. *The Text of the New Testament: Its Transmission, Corruption, and Restoration*. New York: Oxford University Press, 1992.

Moeller, Bernd. *Imperial Cities and the Reformation: Three Essays*. Durham, N.C.: Labyrinth Press, 1982.

More, Thomas. *The Complete Works of St. Thomas More*. 15 vols. New Haven: Yale University Press, 1963–1997.

———. *Utopia*. Translated by Paul Turner. London: Penguin, 1965.

Morton, H. V. *In the Steps of St. Paul*. New York: Dodd, Mead, 1936.

Mullett, Michael A. *The Catholic Reformation*. London: Routledge, 1999.

———. *Martin Luther*. London: Routledge, 2004.

Nadler, Steven. *Spinoza: A Life*. Cambridge: Cambridge University Press, 1999.

Nauert, Charles G., Jr. *Humanism and the Culture of Renaissance Europe*. Cambridge: Cambridge University Press, 2006.

Nicholas, David. *Urban Europe, 1100–1700*. Houndsmills, Basingstoke, Hampshire: Palgrave MacMillan, 2003.

Nicolson, Adam. *God's Secretaries: The Making of the King James Bible*. New York: HarperCollins, 2003.

Nirenberg, David. *Anti-Judaism: The Western Tradition*. New York: W. W. Norton, 2013.

Noll, Mark A. *American Evangelical Christianity: An Introduction*. Oxford: Blackwell, 2001.

———. "The Lutheran Difference." *First Things*. February 1992: 31–40.

———. *Protestantism: A Very Short Introduction*. Oxford: Oxford University Press, 2011.

———. *The Rise of Evangelicalism: The Age of Edwards, Whitefield and the Wesleys*. Leicester, England: Inter-Varsity Press, 2004.

———. *The Work We Have To Do: A History of Protestants in America*. Oxford: Oxford University Press, 2000, 2002.

Oberman, Heiko A. "Discovery of Hebrew and Discrimination against the Jews: the *Veritas Hebraica* as Double-Edged Sword in Renaissance and Reformation." In *Germania Illustrata*, edited by Andrew C. Fix and Susan C. Karant-Nunn, 19–34. Kirksville, Mo: Sixteenth Century Journal Publishers, 1992.

———. *The Impact of the Reformation*. Edinburgh: T & T Clark, 1994.

————. *Luther: Man Between God and the Devil*. Translated by Eileen Walliser-Schwarzbart. New Haven: Yale University Press, 1982, 1989.

————. *The Roots of Antisemitism in the Age of Renaissance and Reformation*. Translated by James I. Porter. Philadelphia: Fortress Press, 1984.

O'Day, Rosemary. *The Debate on the English Reformation*. London: Methuen, 1986.

O'Donnell, James J. *Augustine: A New Biography*. New York: Harper Perennial, 2005.

O'Malley, John W. *Trent: What Happened at the Council*. Cambridge, Mass.: Belknap Press of Harvard University Press, 2013.

Oman, Charles. *A History of the Art of War in the Sixteenth Century*. Elstree, Hertfordshire: Greenhill Books, 1987.

Orme, Nicholas. *Medieval Schools: From Roman Britain to Renaissance England*. New Haven: Yale University Press, 2006.

Overfield, James H. *Humanism and Scholasticism in Late Medieval Germany*. Princeton: Princeton University Press, 1984.

Oxford Encyclopedia of the Reformation, The. Edited by Hans J. Hillerbrand. New York: Oxford University Press, 1996.

Ozment, Steven. *The Age of Reform 1250–1550: An Intellectual and Religious History of Late Medieval and Reformation Europe*. New Haven: Yale University Press, 1980.

————. *The Reformation in the Cities: The Appeal of Protestantism to Sixteenth-Century Germany and Switzerland*. New Haven: Yale University Press, 1975.

————. *The Serpent & the Lamb: Cranach, Luther, and the Making of the Reformation*. New Haven: Yale University Press, 2011.

Pabel, Hilmar M. "Erasmus of Rotterdam and Judaism: A Reexamination in the Light of New Evidence." *Archiv für Reformationsgeschichte* 87 (1996): 9–37.

Partner, Peter. *The Lands of St. Peter: The Papal State in the Middle Ages and the Early Renaissance*. Berkeley: University of California Press, 1972.

————. *Renaissance Rome, 1500–1559: A Portrait of a Society*. Berkeley: University of California Press, 1976.

Pastor, Ludwig, Freiherr von. *The History of the Popes: from the Close of the Middle Ages*. 40 vols. St. Louis: Herder, 1949–.

Payne, John B. *Erasmus: His Theology of the Sacraments*. Richmond, Va.: John Knox Press, 1970.

Pelagius. *The Letters of Pelagius and His Followers*. Edited by B. R. Rees. Woodbridge, Suffolk: The Boydell Press, 1991.

Pelikan, Jaroslav. *The Christian Tradition: A History of the Development of Doctrine*. Volume 4: *Reformation of Church and Dogma (1300–1700)*. Chicago: University of Chicago Press, 1971–1989.

Pettegree, Andrew. *The Book in the Renaissance*. New Haven: Yale University Press, 2010.

————. *Brand Luther: 1517, Printing, and the Making of the Reformation*. New York: Penguin, 2015.

Phillips, Margaret Mann. *The "Adages" of Erasmus: A Study with Translations*. Cambridge: Cambridge University Press, 1964.

————. *Erasmus and the Northern Renaissance*. Woodbridge, Suffolk: The Boydell Press, 1949, 1981.

Post, R. R. *The Modern Devotion: Confrontation with Reformation and Humanism*. Leiden: E. J. Brill, 1968.

Potter, G. R. *Zwingli*. Cambridge: Cambridge University Press, 1976.

Price, David. *Johannes Reuchlin and the Campaign to Destroy Jewish Books*. Oxford: Oxford University Press, 2011.

Probst, Christopher. *Demonizing the Jews: Luther and the Protestant Church in Nazi Germany*. Bloomington: Indiana University Press, 2012.

Prochnik, George. *The Impossible Exile: Stefan Zweig at the End of the World*. New York: Other Press, 2014.

Rashdall, Hastings. *Universities of Europe in the Middle Ages*. New edition. Vol. 3. Oxford: Clarendon Press, 1987–.

Rausch, David A., and Carl Hermann Voss. *Protestantism—Its Modern Meaning*. Philadelphia: Fortress Press, 1987.

Renaudet, Augustin. *Érasme et l'Italie*. Geneva: Librarie Droz, 1998.

Reu, M. *The Augsburg Confession: A Collection of Sources with An Historical Introduction*. Chicago: Wartburg Publishing House, 1930.

————. *Luther's German Bible: An Historical Presentation*. Columbus, Ohio: The Lutheran Book Concern, 1934.

Reuchlin, Johannes. *Recommendation Whether to Confiscate, Destroy and Burn All Jewish Books*. Translated by Peter Worstman. New York: Paulist Press, 2000.

Reynolds, L.D., and N.G. Wilson. Scribes and *Scholars: A Guide to the Transmission of Greek and Latin Literature*. Oxford: Clarendon Press, 1974.

Rice, Eugene F., Jr. *Saint Jerome in the Renaissance*. Baltimore: The Johns Hopkins Press, 1985.

————, with Anthony Grafton. *The Foundations of Early Modern Europe, 1460–1559*. Second edition. New York: Norton, 1994.

Ridley, Jasper Godwin. *Henry VIII*. London: Constable, 1984.

Robinson, Christopher. *Lucian and His Influence in Europe*. London: Duckworth, 1979.

Rodocanachi, E. *Histoire de Rome: Le Pontificat de Jules II, 1503–1513*. Paris: Hachette, 1928.

Roper, Lyndal. *Martin Luther: Renegade and Prophet*. New York: Random House, 2017.

Roscoe, William. *The Life and Pontificate of Leo the Tenth*. Vol. 2. London: Henry G. Bohn, 1853.

Rowland, Ingrid D. *The Culture of the High Renaissance: Ancients and Moderns in Sixteenth-Century Rome*. Cambridge: Cambridge University Press, 1998.

Rowse, A.L. *Homosexuals in History: A Study of Ambivalence in Society, Literature and the Arts.* New York: Macmillan, 1977.

Rubenstein, Richard E. *Aristotle's Children: How Christians, Muslims, and Jews Rediscovered Ancient Wisdom and Illuminated the Middle Ages.* Orlando: Harcourt, 2003.

Rummel, Erika. *The Case Against Johann Reuchlin: Religious and Social Controversy in Sixteenth-Century Germany.* Toronto: University of Toronto Press, 2002.

———. *Erasmus and His Catholic Critics.* 2 vols. Nieuwkoop: De Graaf Publishers, 1989.

———. *Erasmus as a Translator of the Classics.* Toronto: University of Toronto Press, 1985.

———, ed. *Erasmus on Women.* Toronto: University of Toronto Press, 1996.

———. *The Humanist-Scholastic Debate in the Renaissance & Reformation.* Cambridge, Mass.: Harvard University Press, 1995.

Rupp, E. Gordon. *Martin Luther and the Jews.* London: The Council of Christians and Jews, 1972.

———. *Patterns of Reformation.* Philadelphia: Fortress Press, 1969.

———, and Philip S. Watson, eds. and trans. *Luther and Erasmus: Free Will and Salvation.* Philadelphia: Westminster Press, 1969.

Russell, Jocelyne G. *The Field of Cloth of Gold: Men and Manners in 1520.* New York: Barnes & Noble, 1969.

Ryrie, Alec. *Protestants: The Faith that Made the Modern World.* New York: Viking, 2017.

Sanders, Ruth H. *German: Biography of a Language.* Oxford: Oxford University Press, 2010.

Scarisbrick, J.J. *Henry VIII.* Berkeley: University of California, 1968.

Schaff, David S. *John Huss: His Life, Teachings, and Death, After Five Hundred Years.* New York: Scribner's, 1915.

Schoeck, R.J. *Erasmus of Europe: The Making of a Humanist, 1467–1500.* Savage, Maryland: Barnes & Noble Books, 1990.

Schramm, Brooks, and Kirsi I. Stjerna, eds. *Martin Luther, the Bible, and the Jewish People: A Reader.* Minneapolis: Fortress Press, 2012.

Schroeder, H.J, trans. *Canons and Decrees of the Council of Trent.* Rockford, IL: Tan Books, 1941, 1978.

Schwarz, Werner. *Principles and Problems of Biblical Translation.* Cambridge: Cambridge University Press, 1955.

E. G. Schwiebert. *Luther and His Times: The Reformation from a New Perspective.* St. Louis: Concordia, 1950.

Scott, Tom. *Thomas Müntzer: Theology and Revolution in the German Reformation.* Basingstoke, Hampshire: Macmillan, 1989.

———, and Bob Scribner, eds. *The German Peasants' War: A History in Documents.* New Jersey: Humanities Press International, 1991.

Scotti, R.A. *Basilica: The Splendor and the Scandal: Building St. Peter's*. New York: Viking, 2006.

Scribner, Bob, and Gerhard Benecke, eds. *The German Peasant War of 1525—New Viewpoints*. London: Allen & Unwin, 1979.

Scribner, R. W., and C. Scott Dixon. *The German Reformation*. Second edition. Houndsmills, Basingstoke, Hampshire: Palgrave Macmillan, 2003.

Seebohm, Frederic. *The Oxford Reformers: Colet, Erasmus, and More*. London: J. M. Dent & Sons, 1929.

Seneca. *Letters from a Stoic*. Translated by Robin Campbell. London: Penguin, 1969, 2004.

Shirer, William. *The Rise and Fall of the Third Reich: A History of Nazi Germany*. New York: Simon & Schuster, 1960.

Sider, Ronald J. *Andreas Bodenstein von Karlstadt: The Development of His Thought, 1517–1525*. Leiden: E. J. Brill, 1974.

———, ed. *Karlstadt's Battle with Luther: Documents in a Liberal-Radical Debate*. Philadelphia: Fortress Press, 1978.

Siggins, Ian D. Kingston. *Luther and His Mother*. Philadelphia: Fortress Press, 1981.

Smalley, Beryl. *The Study of the Bible in the Middle Ages*. Oxford: B. Blackwell, 1983.

Smith, H. Maynard. *Henry VIII and the Reformation*. London: MacMillan, 1948.

———. *Pre-Reformation England*. London: Macmillan, 1938.

Smith, Preserved. *The Age of the Reformation*. New York: Henry Holt, 1920.

———. *Erasmus: A Study of His Life, Ideals and Place in History*. New York: Harper & Brothers, 1923.

———. *The Life and Letters of Martin Luther*. USA: Frank Cass & Co., 1911, reprinted 1968.

———. "Luther's Development of the Doctrine of Justification by Faith Only." *The Harvard Theological Review* 6, no. 4 (October 1913): 407–425.

Sowards, J.K. "The Two Lost Years of Erasmus: Summary, Review, and Speculation," *Studies in the Renaissance* 9 (1962): 161–186.

Spinka, Matthew. *John Hus: A Biography*. Princeton: Princeton University Press, 1968.

Spinoza, Benedict de. *A Theologico-Political Treatise and a Political Treatise*. Translated by R. H. M. Elwes. New York: Dover Publications, 1951.

Spitz, Lewis W. *The Religious Renaissance of the German Humanists*. Cambridge, Mass.: Harvard University Press, 1963.

Stayer, James M. *Martin Luther, German Saviour: German Evangelical Theological Factions and the Interpretation of Luther, 1917–1933*. Montreal: McGill-Queens University Press, 2000.

Steinmetz, Greg. *The Richest Man Who Ever Lived: The Life and Times of Jacob Fugger*. New York: Simon & Schuster, 2015.

Stewart, Matthew. *The Courtier and the Heretic: Leibniz, Spinoza, and the Fate of God in the Modern World.* New York: W. W. Norton: 2006.

Stinger, Charles. L. *The Renaissance in Rome.* Bloomington: Indiana University Press, 1985.

Stjerna, Kirsi Irmeli. *Women and the Reformation.* Malden, Mass.: Blackwell, 2009.

Stow, John. *A Survey of London: Written in the Year 1598.* Phoenix Mill, UK: A Sutton Publishing, 1994.

Strauss, Gerald. *Nuremberg in the Sixteenth Century.* New York: John Wiley & Sons, 1966.

Sumption, Jonathan. *Pilgrimage: An Image of Medieval Religion.* Tutowa, New Jersey: Rowman and Littlefield, 1975.

Sylvester, R. S., and C. P. Marc'hadour, eds. *Essential Articles for the Study of Thomas More.* Hamden, Conn: Archon Books, 1977.

Tarelli, C.C., "Erasmus's Manuscripts of the Gospels." *Journal of Theological Studies* 44, nos. 175–176 (July 1943): 155–62.

Teems, David. *Tyndale: The Man Who Gave God an English Voice.* Nashville, Tenn.: Thomas Nelson, 2012.

Tentler, Thomas N. *Sin and Confession on the Eve of the Reformation.* Princeton: Princeton University Press, 1977.

Thomas à Kempis. *The Imitation of Christ.* Milwaukee: Bruce Publishing Company, 1940.

Thompson, James Westfall. *The Medieval Library.* Chicago: University of Chicago Press, 1939.

———, ed. *The Frankfort Book Fair.* Chicago: Caxton Club, 1911.

Thomson, D. F. S., trans., and H. C. Porter, ed. *Erasmus and Cambridge: The Cambridge Letters of Erasmus.* Toronto: University of Toronto Press, 1963.

Todd, John M. *Luther: A Life.* London: Hamish Hamilton, 1982.

Tracy, James D. *Erasmus of the Low Countries.* Berkeley: University of California Press, 1996.

———. *Erasmus: The Growth of a Mind.* Geneva: Librarie Droz, 1972.

Trevor-Roper, H. R. *Historical Essays.* London: Macmillan, 1957.

Tuchman, Barbara W. *A Distant Mirror: The Calamitous 14th Century.* New York: Ballantine, 1978.

Tyler, Royall. *The Emperor Charles the Fifth.* Fair Lawn, New Jersey: Essential Books, 1956

Unger, Miles. *Machiavelli: A Biography.* New York: Simon & Schuster, 2012.

Valla, Lorenzo. *The Treatise of Lorenzo Valla on the Donation of Constantine.* Translated by Christopher B. Coleman. Toronto: University of Toronto Press, 1993.

Vocht, Henry de. *History of the Foundation and the Rise of the Collegium Trilingue Lovaniense, 1517–1550. Part the First: The Foundation.* Louvain: Bibliothèque de l'Université, Bureau du Recueil, 1951.

———. *Monumenta Humanistica Lovaniensia: Texts and Studies about Louvain*

Humanists in the First Half of the XVI Century: Erasmus, Vives, Dorpius, Clenardus, Goes, Maringus. Louvain: Uystpruyst, 1934.

Vööbus, Arthur. *Early Versions of the New Testament: Manuscript Studies.* Stockholm: Papers of the Estonian Theological Society in Exile, 1954.

Vries, Jan de. *The Dutch Rural Economy in the Golden Age, 1500–1700.* New Haven: Yale University Press, 1974.

Wacker, Grant. *America's Pastor: Billy Graham and the Shaping of a Nation.* Cambridge, Mass.: Belknap Press of Harvard University Press, 2014.

Walker, Williston, Richard A. Norris, David W. Lotz, and Robert T. Handy. *A History of the Christian Church.* Fourth Edition. New York: Charles Scribner's Sons, 1985.

Wallraff, Martin, Silvana Seidel Menchi, and Kaspar Von Greyerz, eds. *Basel 1516: Erasmus' Edition of the New Testament.* Tübingen: Mohr Siebeck, 2016.

Watson, Philip S. *Let God Be God! An Interpretation of the Theology of Martin Luther.* Philadelphia: Muhlenberg Press, 1949.

Weber, Max. *The Protestant Ethic and the Spirit of Capitalism.* Translated by Talcott Parsons. London: Routledge Classics, 2001.

Weir, Alison. *Henry VIII: King and Court.* London: J. Cape, 2001.

Whitford, David M. "Erasmus Openeth the Way Before Luther: Revisiting Humanism's Influence on *The Ninety-Five Theses* and the Early Luther." *Church History and Religious Culture* 96, no. 4 (2016): 516–540.

Williams, George Huntston. *The Radical Reformation.* Philadelphia: Westminster Press, 1962.

Williams, Neville. *Henry VIII and His Court.* New York: Macmillan, 1971.

Williams, Peter W. *America's Religions: From Their Origins to the Twenty-First Century.* Urbana, Ill.: University of Illinois Press, 2002.

Wills, Garry. *Head and Heart: American Christianities.* New York: Penguin Press, 2007.

Wilson, A. N. *Jesus: A Life.* New York: Fawcett Columbine, 1992.

———. *Paul: The Mind of the Apostle.* New York: W. W. Norton, 1997.

Wilson, Derek. *In the Lion's Court: Power, Ambition and Sudden Death in the Court of Henry VIII.* London: Hutchinson, 2001.

Wood, Gordon S. *The Radicalism of the American Revolution.* New York: Alfred A. Knopf, 1992.

Woodward, William Harrison. *Studies in Education During the Age of the Renaissance, 1400–1600.* New York: Teachers College Press, 1967.

Woolf, Leonard. *Sowing: An Autobiography of the Years 1880 to 1904.* New York: Harcourt, Brace, 1960.

Zweig, Stefan. *Erasmus of Rotterdam.* Translated by Eden Paul and Cedar Paul. New York: Viking, 1934, 1962.

INDEX

ABOUT THE AUTHOR

Michael Massing is a former executive editor of the *Columbia Journalism Review* and a frequent contributor to the *New York Review of Books*. He is the author of *The Fix*, a critical study of the US war on drugs, and *Now They Tell Us: The American Press and Iraq*. He is a cofounder of the Committee to Protect Journalists and sits on its board. He received a bachelor's degree from Harvard College and a master's degree from the London School of Economics and Political Science. In 1992, he was named a MacArthur Fellow, and from 2010 to 2011, he was fellow at the Leon Levy Center for Biography at CUNY. A native of Baltimore, he lives in New York City.